Lecture Notes in Artificial Intelligence 3789

Edited by J. G. Carbonell and J. Siekmann

Subseries of Lecture Notes in Computer Science

Alexander Gelbukh   Álvaro de Albornoz
Hugo Terashima-Marín (Eds.)

MICAI 2005: Advances in Artificial Intelligence

4th Mexican International Conference
on Artificial Intelligence
Monterrey, Mexico, November 14-18, 2005
Proceedings

 Springer

Series Editors

Jaime G. Carbonell, Carnegie Mellon University, Pittsburgh, PA, USA
Jörg Siekmann, University of Saarland, Saarbrücken, Germany

Volume Editors

Alexander Gelbukh
National Polytechnic Institute (IPN)
Center for Computing Research (CIC)
Av. Juan Dios Bátiz, Col. Zacatenco
07738 DF, Mexico
E-mail: gelbukh@gelbukh.com

Álvaro de Albornoz
Technológico de Monterrey (ITESM)
Campus Ciudad de México (CCM)
Calle del Puente 222, Col. Ejudos de Huipulco
Tlalpan, 14360 DF, Mexico
E-mail: albornoz@itesm.mx

Hugo Terashima-Marín
Technológico de Monterrey (ITESM)
Campus Monterrey (MTY)
Eugenio Garza Sada 2501, Col. Technológico
64849, Monterrey, NL, Mexico
E-mail: terashima@itesm.mx

Library of Congress Control Number: 2005935947

CR Subject Classification (1998): I.2, F.1, I.4, F.4.1

ISSN   0302-9743
ISBN-10   3-540-29896-7 Springer Berlin Heidelberg New York
ISBN-13   978-3-540-29896-0 Springer Berlin Heidelberg New York

This work is subject to copyright. All rights are reserved, whether the whole or part of the material is concerned, specifically the rights of translation, reprinting, re-use of illustrations, recitation, broadcasting, reproduction on microfilms or in any other way, and storage in data banks. Duplication of this publication or parts thereof is permitted only under the provisions of the German Copyright Law of September 9, 1965, in its current version, and permission for use must always be obtained from Springer. Violations are liable to prosecution under the German Copyright Law.

Springer is a part of Springer Science+Business Media

springeronline.com

© Springer-Verlag Berlin Heidelberg 2005
Printed in Germany

Typesetting: Camera-ready by author, data conversion by Scientific Publishing Services, Chennai, India
Printed on acid-free paper   SPIN: 11579427   06/3142   5 4 3 2 1 0

Preface

The Mexican International Conference on Artificial Intelligence (MICAI) is aimed at promoting research in artificial intelligence (AI) and cooperation among Mexican researchers and their peers worldwide. MICAI is organized by the Mexican Society for Artificial Intelligence (SMIA) in collaboration with the American Association for Artificial Intelligence (AAAI).

After the success of the three previous biannual conferences, we are pleased to announce that MICAI conferences are now annual, and we present the proceedings of the 4th Mexican International Conference on Artificial Intelligence, MICAI 2005, held on November 14–18, 2005, in Monterrey, Mexico. This volume contains the papers included in the main conference program, which was complemented by tutorials, workshops, and poster sessions, published in supplementary proceedings. The proceedings of past MICAI conferences were also published in Springer's Lecture Notes in Artificial Intelligence (LNAI) series, vols. 1793, 2313, and 2972.

Table 1. Statistics of submissions and accepted papers by country/region

Country/Region	Authors Subm	Authors Accp	Papers[1] Subm	Papers[1] Accp	Country/Region	Authors Subm	Authors Accp	Papers[1] Subm	Papers[1] Accp
Algeria	2	–	0.66	–	Lithuania	3	1	1.5	0.50
Argentina	27	4	8.66	1.5	Malaysia	2	–	1	–
Australia	7	–	2.66	–	Mexico	383	139	131.91	47.44
Brazil	48	14	15.16	3.66	Netherlands	3	2	1.2	1
Bulgaria	1	1	0.5	0.5	New Zealand	4	4	1	1
Canada	13	4	4.75	2	Norway	4	1	2.33	1
Chile	14	10	6	4	Poland	8	2	3	1
China	288	65	107.33	23.66	Portugal	2	–	0.5	–
Colombia	1	–	1	–	Romania	2	2	0.5	0.5
Cuba	6	–	1.66	–	Russia	10	3	7	1.5
Czech Republic	1	–	1	–	Singapore	3	–	2	–
Denmark	3	3	0.75	0.75	Slovakia	1	–	1	–
France	24	10	10.33	4.66	Spain	71	25	20.81	7.6
Germany	2	1	2	1	Sweden	4	–	1	–
Hong Kong	3	1	1.16	0.33	Taiwan	8	–	3	–
India	6	–	4	–	Thailand	1	–	0.25	–
Iran	6	–	4	–	Tunisia	5	–	2	–
Ireland	3	3	1	1	Turkey	11	8	3.5	2.5
Italy	8	–	3.5	–	UK	23	17	9.50	7.16
Japan	13	2	5	1	USA	29	8	11.33	3.37
Korea, South	71	7	33	2	Uruguay	4	–	1.00	–
Lebanon	2	–	1	–	Total:	1130	341	423	120

[1] Counted by authors: e.g., for a paper by 3 authors: 2 from Mexico and 1 from USA, we added $\frac{2}{3}$ to Mexico and $\frac{1}{3}$ to USA.

The number of submissions to MICAI 2005 was significantly higher than that of the previous conferences: 423 full papers by 1130 authors from 43 different countries were submitted for evaluation, see Tables 1 and 2.

Each submission was reviewed by three independent Program Committee members. This book contains revised versions of 120 papers by 341 authors

Table 2. Statistics of submissions and accepted papers by topic[2]

Topic	Submitted	Accepted
Assembly	7	2
Automated Theorem Proving	3	1
Belief Revision	7	4
Bioinformatics	17	2
Case-Based Reasoning	10	3
Common Sense Reasoning	6	3
Computer Vision	37	12
Constraint Programming	12	2
Data Mining	50	10
Expert Systems/Knowledge-Based Systems	25	6
Fuzzy Logic	33	11
Genetic Algorithms	50	14
Hybrid Intelligent Systems	46	12
Intelligent Interfaces: Multimedia; Virtual Reality	15	1
Intelligent Organizations	13	3
Intelligent Tutoring Systems	18	3
Knowledge Acquisition	24	5
Knowledge Management	24	7
Knowledge Representation	44	13
Knowledge Verification; Sharing and Reuse	7	3
Logic Programming	6	2
Machine Learning	91	28
Model-Based Reasoning	9	2
Multiagent Systems and Distributed AI	54	11
Natural Language Processing/Understanding	33	13
Navigation	11	4
Neural Networks	64	21
Nonmonotonic Reasoning	6	2
Ontologies	22	4
Philosophical and Methodological Issues of AI	19	4
Planning and Scheduling	24	8
Qualitative Reasoning	4	1
Robotics	45	21
Sharing and Reuse	7	3
Spatial and Temporal Reasoning	7	2
Uncertainty/Probabilistic Reasoning	29	12
Other	62	20

[2] According to the topics indicated by the authors. A paper may be assigned to more than one topic.

selected after thorough evaluation for inclusion in the conference program. Thus the acceptance rate was 28.3%. The book is structured into 14 thematic fields representative of the main current areas of interest within the AI community:

- Knowledge Representation and Management,
- Logic and Constraint Programming,
- Uncertainty Reasoning,
- Multiagent Systems and Distributed AI,
- Computer Vision and Pattern Recognition,
- Machine Learning and Data Mining,
- Evolutionary Computation and Genetic Algorithms,
- Neural Networks,
- Natural Language Processing,
- Intelligent Interfaces and Speech Processing,
- Bioinformatics and Medical Applications,
- Robotics,
- Modeling and Intelligent Control,
- Intelligent Tutoring Systems.

The conference featured excellent keynote lectures presented by Erick Cantú-Paz of CASC, John McCarthy of Stanford University, Katsushi Ikeuchi of the University of Tokyo, Tom Mitchell of Carnegie Mellon University, Jaime Simão Sichman of Universidade de São Paulo, and Piero P. Bonissone of General Electric.

The following papers received the Best Paper Award and the Best Student Paper Award, correspondingly (the Best Student Paper was selected from papers for which the first author was a full-time student):

1st Place: A Framework for Reactive Motion and Sensing Planning: a Critical Events-Based Approach, by *Rafael Murrieta Cid, Alejandro Sarmiento, Teja Muppirala, Seth Hutchinson, Raul Monroy, Moises Alencastre Miranda, Lourdes Muñoz Gómez, Ricardo Swain*;

2nd Place: A Noise-Driven Paradigm for Solving the Stereo Correspondence Problem, by *Patrice Delmas, Georgy Gimel'farb, Jiang Liu, John Morris*;

3rd Place: Proximity Searching in High Dimensional Spaces with a Proximity Preserving Order, by *Edgar Chavez, Karina Figueroa, Gonzalo Navarro*;

Student: A Similarity-Based Approach to Data Sparseness Problem of the Chinese Language Modeling, by *Jinghui Xiao, Bingquan Liu, Xiaolong Wang, Bing Li*.

We want to thank all people involved in the organization of this conference. In the first place these are the authors of the papers constituting this book: it is the excellence of their research work that gives value to the book and sense to the work of all other people involved.

Our *very special* thanks goes to Ángel Kuri and Raúl Monroy, who carried out a huge part of the effort of preparation of the conference in general and reviewing process in particular with professionalism and enthusiasm without which this conference would not have been possible and this book would not have appeared.

We thank the members of the Program Committee and the conference staff. We are deeply grateful to the Tecnológico de Monterrey at Monterrey for their warm hospitality to MICAI 2005. We would like to express our gratitude to Francisco J. Cantú-Ortiz, Dean of Research and Graduate Studies of Tecnológico de Monterrey at Monterrey, and to all members of this office, with special thanks to Leticia Rodríguez for coordinating activities on the local arrangements. We are also deeply grateful to Fernando J. Jaimes, Dean of the Division of Information Technology and Electronics, and Rogelio Soto-Rodríguez, Director of the Center for Intelligent Systems, and all members of this center. We thank Hiram Calvo of CIC-IPN and Manuel Vilares of University of Vigo for their significant contribution to the reviewing process.

The entire submission, reviewing, and selection process, as well as putting together the proceedings, was supported for free by the EasyChair system (www.EasyChair.org); we express our gratitude to its author Andrei Voronkov for his constant support and help. Last but not least, we deeply appreciate the Springer staff's patience and help in editing this volume—it is always a great pleasure to work with them.

September 2005

Alexander Gelbukh
Álvaro de Albornoz
Hugo Terashima

Organization

MICAI 2005 was organized by the Mexican Society for Artificial Intelligence (SMIA), in collaboration with the Tecnológico de Monterrey at Monterrey and at Mexico City, the Centro de Investigación en Computación del Instituto Politécnico Nacional, the Instituto Tecnológico Autónomo de México, and the Instituto Nacional de Astrofísica, Óptica y Electrónica. The contribution of the following sponsors is acknowledged and greatly appreciated: Company PHAR, S. A. de C. V., TCA Group, and the Government of the State of Nuevo Leon, Mexico.

Conference Committee

Conference Chairs:	Álvaro de Albornoz (ITESM-CCM)
	Angel Kuri Morales (ITAM)
Program Chairs:	Alexander Gelbukh (CIC-IPN)
	Raúl Monroy (ITESM-CEM)
Tutorial Chairs:	Manuel Valenzuela (ITESM-MTY)
	Horacio Martínez (ITESM-MTY)
Workshop Chairs:	Ramón Brena (ITESM-MTY)
	José Luis Aguirre (ITESM-MTY)
Keynote Speaker Chair:	Carlos Alberto Reyes (INAOE)
Award Committee:	Alvaro de Albornoz (ITESM-CCM)
	Angel Kuri Morales (ITAM)
	Alexander Gelbukh (CIC-IPN)
Local Chairs:	Hugo Terashima (ITESM-MTY)
	Rogelio Soto (ITESM-MTY)
	Ricardo Swain (ITESM-MTY)
Local Arrangements Chair:	Leticia Rodríguez (ITESM-MTY)
Finance Chair:	Carlos Cantú (ITESM-MTY)
Publicity Chair:	Patricia Mora (ITESM-MTY)

Program Committee

Ajith Abraham
José Luis Aguirre
Juan Manuel Ahuactzin
Inés Arana
Gustavo Arroyo Figueroa
Víctor Ayala Ramírez
Ruth Aylett

Antonio Bahamonde
Soumya Banerjee
Olivia Barrón Cano
Ildar Batyrshin
Ricardo Beausoleil Delgado
Bedrich Benes
Ramón F. Brena

Carlos A. Brizuela
Paul Brna
Wolfram Burgard
Osvaldo Cairó
Nicoletta Calzolari
Francisco Cantú Ortíz
Maria Carolina Monard
Oscar Castillo López
Edgar Chávez
Yuehui Chen
Carlos A. Coello Coello
Simon Colton
Santiago E. Conant Pablos
Ulises Cortés
Carlos Cotta-Porras
Nareli Cruz Cortés
Nicandro Cruz Ramírez
Victor de la Cueva
Antonio D'Angelo
Louise Dennis
Alexandre Dikovsky
Juergen Dix
Marco Dorigo
Armin Fiedler
Bob Fisher
Juan J. Flores
Olac Fuentes
Alexander Gelbukh (Co-chair)
Eduardo Gómez Ramírez
Andrés Gómez de Silva
Jose A. Gamez Martin
Matjaz Gams
Leonardo Garrido Luna
Luis Eduardo Garza Castañón
José Luis Gordillo
Crina Grosan
Neil Hernández Gress
Arturo Hernández
Brahim Hnich
Jesse Hoey
Johan van Horebeek
Dieter Hutter
Pablo H. Ibarguengoytia G.
Bruno Jammes
Leo Joskowicz

Mario Köppen
Ingrid Kirschning
Zeynep Kiziltan
Ryszard Klempous
Angel Kuri Morales
Ramón López de Mantaras
Pedro Larrañaga
Christian Lemaître León
Eugene Levner
Jim Little
Vladimír Mařík
Jacek Malec
Toni Mancini
Pierre Marquis
Carlos Martín Vide
José Francisco Martínez Trinidad
Horacio Martinez Alfaro
Oscar Mayora
René Mayorga
Efrén Mezura Montes
Chilukuri K. Mohan
Raúl Monroy (Co-chair)
Guillermo Morales Luna
Eduardo Morales Manzanares
Rafael Morales
Rafael Murrieta Cid
Juan Arturo Nolazco Flores
Gabriela Ochoa Meier
Mauricio Osorio Galindo
Andrés Pérez Uribe
Manuel Palomar
Luis Alberto Pineda
Andre Ponce de Leon F. de Carvalho
David Poole
Bhanu Prasad
Jorge Adolfo Ramírez Uresti
Fernando Ramos
Carlos Alberto Reyes García
Abdennour El Rhalibi
Maria Cristina Riff
Roger Z. Rios
Dave Robertson
Horacio Rodríguez
Riccardo Rosati
Isaac Rudomín

Alessandro Saffiotti
Gildardo Sánchez
Alberto Sanfeliú Cortés
Andrea Schaerf
Thomas Schiex
Leonid Sheremetov
Grigori Sidorov
Carles Sierra
Alexander V. Smirnov
Maarten van Someren
Juan Humberto Sossa Azuela
Rogelio Soto
Thomas Stuetzle
Luis Enrique Sucar Succar

Ricardo Swain Oropeza
Hugo Terashima
Demetri Terzopoulos
Manuel Valenzuela
Juan Vargas
Felisa Verdejo
Manuel Vilares Ferro
Toby Walsh
Alfredo Weitzenfeld
Nirmalie Wiratunga
Franz Wotawa
Kaori Yoshida
Claus Zinn
Berend Jan van der Zwaag

Additional Referees

Juan C. Acosta Guadarrama
Héctor Gabriel Acosta Mesa
Teddy Alfaro
Miguel A. Alonso
José Ramón Arrazola
Stella Asiimwe
Séverine Bérard
Fco. Mario Barcala Rodríguez
Axel Arturo Barcelo Aspeitia
Adam D. Barker
Alejandra Barrera
Gustavo E. A. P. A. Batista
Abderrahim Benslimane
Arturo Berrones
Bastian Blankenburg
Pascal Brisset
Andreas Bruening
Mark Buckley
Olivier Buffet
Diego Calvanese
Hiram Calvo
Niccolo Capanni
Carlos Castillo
Sutanu Chakraborti
Carlos Chesñevar
Federico Chesani
Wu Feng Chung

Murilo Coelho Naldi
Mark Collins
Jean-François Condotta
Miguel Contreras
Sylvie Coste-Marquis
Anne Cregan
Ronaldo Cristiano Prati
Juan A. Díaz
Víctor Manuel Darriba Bilbao
Michael Dekhtyar
Deepak Devicharan
Luca Di Gaspero
Marissa Diaz
Luigi Dragone
Edgar Duéñez
Mehmet Önder Efe
Arturo Espinosa Romero
Katti Faceli
Antonio Fernandez Caballero
Antonio Ferrández
Armin Fiedler
Alfredo Gabaldón
Arturo Galván Rodríguez
Ariel García
Cormac Gebruers
Karina Gibert
Andrea Giovannucci

Fernando Godínez
Giorgi Goguadze
Miguel González
Jorge Graña
Federico Guedea
Alejandro Guerra-Hernández
Daniel Gunn
Everardo Gutiérrez
Christian Hahn
Emmanuel Hebrard
Benjamín Hernández
Martin Homik
Rodolfo Ibarra
Boyko Iliev
Bartosz Jablonski
Jean-Yves Jaffray
Sylvain Jasson
Daniel Jolly
Narendra Jussien
Lars Karsson
Ryszard Klempous
Jerzy Kotowski
A. Krizhanovsky
Juan Carlos López Pimentel
David Lambert
Darío Landa Silva
Jérme Lang
Huei Diana Lee
Domenico Lembo
Paul Libbrecht
Ana Carolina Lorena
Robert Lothian
Henryk Maciejewski
Fernando Magan Muñoz
Michael Maher
Donato Malerba
Salvador Mandujano
Ana Isabel Martinez Garcia
Patricio Martinez-Barco
Jarred McGinnis
Andreas Meier
Manuel Mejia Lavalle
Corrado Mencar
Thomas Meyer
Erik Millan

Monica Monachini
Rebecca Montanari
Andrés Montoyo
Jaime Mora Várgas
José Andrés Moreno Pérez
Rafael Muñoz
Martin Muehlenbrock
Rahman Mukras
Amedeo Napoli
Gonzalo Navarro
Adeline Nazarenko
Juan Carlos Nieves
Peter Novak
Slawomir Nowaczyk
Oscar Olmedo Aguirre
Magdalena Ortiz de la Fuente
María Osorio
Joaquín Pacheco
Marco Patella
Jesús Peral
Mats Petter Pettersson
Steven Prestwich
Bernard Prum
José Miguel Puerta Callejón
Alonso Ramírez Manzanárez
Fernando Ramos
Orión Fausto Reyes Galaviz
Francisco Ribadas Peña
Fabrizio Riguzzi
Leandro Rodríguez Liñares
Juan A. Rodríguez-Aguilar
Raquel Ros
Maximiliano Saiz Noeda
S. Sandeep
P. Sanongoon
Cipriano Santos
Vitaly Schetinin
Marvin Schiller
Przemyslaw Sliwinski
Jasper Snoek
Thamar Solorio
Claudia Soria
Eduardo J. Spinosa
Cyrill Stachniss
Ewa Szlachcic

Armagan Tarim
Choh Man Teng
Paolo Torroni
Elio Tuci
Carsten Ullrich
L. Alfonso Ureña López
Diego Uribe
Mars Valiev
Maria Vargas-Vera

Wamberto Vasconcelos
José Luis Vega
José Luis Vicedo
Jesús Vilares Ferro
Mario Villalobos-Arias
Nic Wilson
Sean Wilson
Claudia Zepeda
Juergen Zimmer

Table of Contents

Knowledge Representation and Management

Modelling Human Intelligence: A Learning Mechanism
    Enrique Carlos Segura, Robin Whitty 1

Compilation of Symbolic Knowledge and Integration with Numeric Knowledge Using Hybrid Systems
    Vianey Guadalupe Cruz Sánchez, Gerardo Reyes Salgado, Osslan Osiris Vergara Villegas, Joaquín Perez Ortega, Azucena Montes Rendón 11

The Topological Effect of Improving Knowledge Acquisition
    Bernhard Heinemann 21

Belief Revision Revisited
    Ewa Madalińska-Bugaj, Witold Lukaszewicz 31

Knowledge and Reasoning Supported by Cognitive Maps
    Alejandro Peña, Humberto Sossa, Agustin Gutiérrez 41

Temporal Reasoning on Chronological Annotation
    Tiphaine Accary-Barbier, Sylvie Calabretto 51

EventNet: Inferring Temporal Relations Between Commonsense Events
    Jose Espinosa, Henry Lieberman 61

Multi Agent Ontology Mapping Framework in the AQUA Question Answering System
    Miklos Nagy, Maria Vargas-Vera, Enrico Motta 70

A Three-Level Approach to Ontology Merging
    Agustina Buccella, Alejandra Cechich, Nieves Brisaboa 80

Domain and Competences Ontologies and Their Maintenance for an Intelligent Dissemination of Documents
    Yassine Gargouri, Bernard Lefebvre, Jean-Guy Meunier 90

Modelling Power and Trust for Knowledge Distribution: An Argumentative Approach
    Carlos Iván Chesñevar, Ramón F. Brena, José Luis Aguirre 98

Application of ASP for Agent Modelling in CSCL Environments 109
Gerardo Ayala, Magdalena Ortiz, Mauricio Osorio

Logic and Constraint Programming

Deductive Systems' Representation and an Incompleteness Result in the Situation Calculus 119
Pablo Sáez

Geometric Aspects Related to Solutions of #kSAT 132
Guillermo Morales-Luna

A Syntactical Approach to Belief Update 142
Jerusa Marchi, Guilherme Bittencourt, Laurent Perrussel

A Fuzzy Extension of Description Logic ALCH 152
Yanhui Li, Jianjiang Lu, Baowen Xu, Dazhou Kang, Jixiang Jiang

An Approach for Dynamic Split Strategies in Constraint Solving 162
Carlos Castro, Eric Monfroy, Christian Figueroa, Rafael Meneses

Applying Constraint Logic Programming to Predicate Abstraction of RTL Verilog Descriptions 175
Tun Li, Yang Guo, SiKun Li, Dan Zhu

Scheduling Transportation Events with Grouping Genetic Algorithms and the Heuristic DJD 185
Hugo Terashima-Marín, Juan Manuel Tavernier-Deloya, Manuel Valenzuela-Rendón

Radial Search: A Simple Solution Approach to Hard Combinatorial Problems 195
José Antonio Vázquez Rodríguez, Abdellah Salhi

Uncertainty Reasoning

Rough Sets and Decision Rules in Fuzzy Set-Valued Information Systems 204
Danjun Zhu, Boqin Feng, Tao Guan

Directed Cycles in Bayesian Belief Networks: Probabilistic Semantics and Consistency Checking Complexity 214
Alexander L. Tulupyev, Sergey I. Nikolenko

Fuzzeval: A Fuzzy Controller-Based Approach in Adaptive Learning for
Backgammon Game
    Mikael Heinze, Daniel Ortiz-Arroyo, Henrik Legind Larsen,
    Francisco Rodriguez-Henriquez 224

Analysis of Performance of Fuzzy Logic-Based Production Scheduling
by Simulation
    Alejandra Duenas, Dobrila Petrovic, Sanja Petrovic 234

Multiagent Systems and Distributed AI

Agent-Based Simulation Replication: A Model Driven Architecture
Approach
    Candelaria Sansores, Juan Pavón 244

Effects of Inter-agent Communication in Ant-Based Clustering
Algorithms: A Case Study on Communication Policies in Swarm
Systems
    Marco Antonio Montes de Oca, Leonardo Garrido,
    José Luis Aguirre 254

Coordination Through Plan Repair
    Roman van der Krogt, Mathijs de Weerdt 264

Enabling Intelligent Organizations: An Electronic Institutions Approach
for Controlling and Executing Problem Solving Methods
    Armando Robles P., B.V. Pablo Noriega, Francisco Cantú,
    Rubén Morales-Menéndez 275

An Extended Behavior Network for a Game Agent: An Investigation of
Action Selection Quality and Agent Performance in Unreal Tournament
    Hugo da Silva Corrêa Pinto, Luis Otávio Alvares 287

Air Pollution Assessment Through a Multiagent-Based Traffic
Simulation
    Jesús Héctor Domínguez, Luis Marcelo Fernández,
    José Luis Aguirre, Leonardo Garrido, Ramón Brena 297

Computer Vision and Pattern Recognition

A Noise-Driven Paradigm for Solving the Stereo Correspondence
Problem
    Patrice Delmas, Georgy Gimel'farb, Jiang Liu, John Morris 307

Invariant Descriptions and Associative Processing Applied to Object
Recognition Under Occlusions
  Roberto Antonio Vázquez, Humberto Sossa, Ricardo Barrón 318

Real Time Facial Expression Recognition Using Local Binary Patterns
and Linear Programming
  Xiaoyi Feng, Jie Cui, Matti Pietikäinen, Abdenour Hadid 328

People Detection and Tracking Through Stereo Vision for Human-Robot
Interaction
  *Rafael Muñoz-Salinas, Eugenio Aguirre, Miguel García-Silvente,
  Antonio Gonzalez* 337

Mapping Visual Behavior to Robotic Assembly Tasks
  *Mario Peña-Cabrera, Ismael López-Juárez, Reyes Rios-Cabrera,
  Jorge Corona-Castuera, Roman Osorio* 347

Multilevel Seed Region Growth Segmentation
  Raziel Álvarez, Erik Millán, Ricardo Swain-Oropeza 359

A CLS Hierarchy for the Classification of Images
  Antonio Sanchez, Raul Diaz, Peter Bock 369

Performance Evaluation of a Segmentation Algorithm for Synthetic
Texture Images
  *Dora Luz Almanza-Ojeda, Victor Ayala-Ramirez,
  Raul E. Sanchez-Yanez, Gabriel Avina-Cervantes* 379

Image Retrieval Based on Salient Points from DCT Domain
  Wenyin Zhang, Zhenli Nie, Zhenbing Zeng 386

Machine Learning and Data Mining

Selection of the Optimal Parameter Value for the ISOMAP
Algorithm
  Chao Shao, Houkuan Huang 396

Proximity Searching in High Dimensional Spaces with a Proximity
Preserving Order
  Edgar Chávez, Karina Figueroa, Gonzalo Navarro 405

A Neurobiologically Motivated Model for Self-organized Learning
  Frank Emmert-Streib 415

Using Boolean Differences for Discovering Ill-Defined Attributes in
Propositional Machine Learning
  Sylvain Hallé 425

Simplify Decision Function of Reduced Support Vector Machines
  Yuangui Li, Weidong Zhang, Guoli Wang, Yunze Cai 435

On-Line Learning of Decision Trees in Problems with Unknown
Dynamics
  Marlon Núñez, Raúl Fidalgo, Rafael Morales 443

Improved Pairwise Coupling Support Vector Machines with Correcting
Classifiers
  Huaqing Li, Feihu Qi, Shaoyu Wang 454

Least Squares Littlewood-Paley Wavelet Support Vector Machine
  Fangfang Wu, Yinliang Zhao 462

Minimizing State Transition Model for Multiclassification by
Mixed-Integer Programming
  Nobuo Inui, Yuuji Shinano 473

Overview of Metaheuristics Methods in Compilation
  Fernanda Kri, Carlos Gómez, Paz Caro 483

Comparison of SVM-Fuzzy Modelling Techniques for System
Identification
  *Ariel García-Gamboa, Miguel González-Mendoza,
  Rodolfo Ibarra-Orozco, Neil Hernández-Gress,
  Jaime Mora-Vargas* 494

Time-Series Forecasting by Means of Linear and Nonlinear Models
  Janset Kuvulmaz, Serkan Usanmaz, Seref Naci Engin 504

Perception Based Time Series Data Mining with MAP Transform
  Ildar Batyrshin, Leonid Sheremetov 514

A Graph Theoretic Approach to Key Equivalence
  J. Horacio Camacho, Abdellah Salhi, Qingfu Zhang 524

Improvement of Data Visualization Based on ISOMAP
  Chao Shao, Houkuan Huang 534

Supporting Generalized Cases in Conversational CBR
  Mingyang Gu 544

Organizing Large Case Library by Linear Programming
   Caihong Sun, Simon Chi Keung Shiu, Xizhao Wang 554

Classifying Faces with Discriminant Isometric Feature Mapping
   Ruifan Li, Cong Wang, Hongwei Hao, Xuyan Tu 565

A Grey-Markov Forecasting Model for the Electric Power Requirement in China
   Yong He, Min Huang 574

A Fault Detection Approach Based on Machine Learning Models
   *Luis E. Garza Castañon, Francisco J. Cantú Ortiz,
   Rubén Morales-Menéndez, Ricardo Ramírez* 583

Evolutionary Computation and Genetic Algorithms

A Mixed Mutation Strategy Evolutionary Programming Combined with Species Conservation Technique
   Hongbin Dong, Jun He, Houkuan Huang, Wei Hou 593

Coevolutionary Multi-objective Optimization Using Clustering Techniques
   Margarita Reyes Sierra, Carlos A. Coello Coello 603

A Comparison of Memetic Recombination Operators for the MinLA Problem
   Eduardo Rodriguez-Tello, Jin-Kao Hao, Jose Torres-Jimenez 613

Hybrid Particle Swarm – Evolutionary Algorithm for Search and Optimization
   *Crina Grosan, Ajith Abraham, Sangyong Han,
   Alexander Gelbukh* 623

Particle Swarm Optimization with Opposite Particles
   Rujing Wang, Xiaoming Zhang 633

Particle Evolutionary Swarm Optimization with Linearly Decreasing ϵ-Tolerance
   *Angel E. Muñoz Zavala, Arturo Hernández Aguirre,
   Enrique R. Villa Diharce* 641

Useful Infeasible Solutions in Engineering Optimization with Evolutionary Algorithms
   Efrén Mezura-Montes, Carlos A. Coello Coello 652

A Hybrid Self-adjusted Memetic Algorithm for Multi-objective
Optimization
  Xiuping Guo, Genke Yang, Zhiming Wu 663

Evolutionary Multiobjective Optimization Approach for Evolving
Ensemble of Intelligent Paradigms for Stock Market Modeling
  *Ajith Abraham, Crina Grosan, Sang Yong Han,
  Alexander Gelbukh* 673

Genetic Algorithms for Feature Weighting: Evolution vs. Coevolution
and Darwin vs. Lamarck
  Alexandre Blansché, Pierre Gançarski, Jerzy J. Korczak 682

A Deterministic Alternative to *Competent* Genetic Algorithms That
Solves to Optimality Linearly Decomposable Non-overlapping Problems
in Polynomial Time
  *Manuel Valenzuela-Rendón, Horacio Martínez-Alfaro,
  Hugo Terashima-Marín* 692

Neural Networks

K-Dynamical Self Organizing Maps
  *Carolina Saavedra, Héctor Allende, Sebastián Moreno,
  Rodrigo Salas* 702

Study of Application Model on BP Neural Network Optimized by
Fuzzy Clustering
  Yong He, Yun Zhang, Liguo Xiang 712

Application of Modified Neural Network Weights' Matrices Explaining
Determinants of Foreign Investment Patterns in the Emerging Markets
  Darius Plikynas, Yusaf H. Akbar 721

Neural Network and Trend Prediction for Technological Processes
Monitoring
  *Luis Paster Sanchez Fernandez, Oleksiy Pogrebnyak,
  Cornelio Yanez Marquez* 731

Natural Language Processing

Underspecified Semantics for Dependency Grammars
  Alexander Dikovsky 741

Distributed English Text Chunking Using Multi-agent Based Architecture
  Ying-Hong Liang, Tie-Jun Zhao 752

A Similarity-Based Approach to Data Sparseness Problem of Chinese Language Modeling
  Jinghui Xiao, Bingquan Liu, Xiaolong Wang, Bing Li 761

Self-training and Co-training Applied to Spanish Named Entity Recognition
  Zornitsa Kozareva, Boyan Bonev, Andres Montoyo 770

Towards the Automatic Learning of Idiomatic Prepositional Phrases
  Sofía N. Galicia-Haro, Alexander Gelbukh 780

Measurements of Lexico-Syntactic Cohesion by Means of Internet
  Igor A. Bolshakov, Elena I. Bolshakova 790

Inferring Rules for Finding Syllables in Spanish
  René MacKinney-Romero, John Goddard 800

A Multilingual SVM-Based Question Classification System
  Empar Bisbal, David Tomás, Lidia Moreno, José Vicedo, Armando Suárez 806

Language Independent Passage Retrieval for Question Answering
  José Manuel Gómez-Soriano, Manuel Montes-y-Gómez, Emilio Sanchis-Arnal, Luis Villaseñor-Pineda, Paolo Rosso 816

A New PU Learning Algorithm for Text Classification
  Hailong Yu, Wanli Zuo, Tao Peng 824

A Domain Independent Natural Language Interface to Databases Capable of Processing Complex Queries
  Rodolfo A. Pazos Rangel, Joaquín Pérez O., Juan Javier González B., Alexander Gelbukh, Grigori Sidorov, Myriam J. Rodríguez M. 833

Intelligent Interfaces and Speech Processing

An Efficient Hybrid Approach for Online Recognition of Handwritten Symbols
  John A. Fitzgerald, Bing Quan Huang, Tahar Kechadi 843

Environment Compensation Based on Maximum a Posteriori
Estimation for Improved Speech Recognition
   Haifeng Shen, Jun Guo, Gang Liu, Pingmu Huang, Qunxia Li 854

ASR Based on the Analasys of the Short-MelFrequencyCepstra Time
Transform
   Juan Arturo Nolazco-Flores 863

Building and Training of a New Mexican Spanish Voice for Festival
   Humberto Pérez Espinosa, Carlos Alberto Reyes García 870

Bioinformatics and Medical Applications

A New Approach to Sequence Representation of Proteins in
Bioinformatics
   Angel F. Kuri-Morales, Martha R. Ortiz-Posadas 880

Computing Confidence Measures in Stochastic Logic Programs
   Huma Lodhi, Stephen Muggleton 890

Using Inductive Rules in Medical Case-Based Reasoning System
   Wenqi Shi, John A. Barnden 900

Prostate Segmentation Using Pixel Classification and Genetic
Algorithms
   Fernando Arámbula Cosío 910

A Novel Approach for Adaptive Unsupervised Segmentation of MRI
Brain Images
   *Jun Kong, Jingdan Zhang, Yinghua Lu, Jianzhong Wang,
   Yanjun Zhou* 918

Towards Formalising Agent Argumentation over the Viability of
Human Organs for Transplantation
   Sanjay Modgil, Pancho Tolchinsky, Ulises Cortés 928

A Comparative Study on Machine Learning Techniques for Prediction
of Success of Dental Implants
   *Adriano Lorena Inácio de Oliveira, Carolina Baldisserotto,
   Julio Baldisserotto* 939

Infant Cry Classification to Identify Hypo Acoustics and Asphyxia
Comparing an Evolutionary-Neural System with a Neural Network
System
   Orion Fausto Reyes Galaviz, Carlos Alberto Reyes García 949

Robotics

Applying the GFM Prospective Paradigm to the Autonomous and
Adaptive Control of a Virtual Robot
Jérôme Leboeuf Pasquier 959

Maximizing Future Options: An On-Line Real-Time Planning Method
Ramon F. Brena, Emmanuel Martinez 970

On the Use of Randomized Low-Discrepancy Sequences in
Sampling-Based Motion Planning
Abraham Sánchez, Maria A. Osorio 980

A Framework for Reactive Motion and Sensing Planning: A Critical
Events-Based Approach
*Rafael Murrieta-Cid, Alejandro Sarmiento, Teja Muppirala,
Seth Hutchinson, Raul Monroy, Moises Alencastre-Miranda,
Lourdes Muñoz-Gómez, Ricardo Swain* 990

Visual Planning for Autonomous Mobile Robot Navigation
Antonio Marin-Hernandez, Michel Devy, Victor Ayala-Ramirez 1001

Gait Synthesis Based on FWN and PD Controller for a Five-Link
Biped Robot
Pengfei Liu, Jiuqiang Han 1012

Hybrid Fuzzy/Expert System to Control Grasping with Deformation
Detection
Jorge Axel Domínguez-López, Gilberto Marrufo 1022

Adaptive Neuro-Fuzzy-Expert Controller of a Robotic Gripper
Jorge Axel Domínguez-López 1032

A Semantically-Based Software Component Selection Mechanism for
Intelligent Service Robots
Hwayoun Lee, Ho-Jin Choi, In-Young Ko 1042

An Approach for Intelligent Fixtureless Assembly: Issues and
Experiments
*Jorge Corona-Castuera, Reyes Rios-Cabrera, Ismael Lopez-Juarez,
Mario Peña-Cabrera* 1052

On the Design of a Multimodal Cognitive Architecture for Perceptual
Learning in Industrial Robots
*Ismael Lopez-Juarez, Keny Ordaz-Hernández, Mario Peña-Cabrera,
Jorge Corona-Castuera, Reyes Rios-Cabrera* 1062

CORBA Distributed Robotic System: A Case Study Using a Motoman
6-DOF Arm Manipulator
  *Federico Guedea-Elizalde, Josafat M. Mata-Hernández,
  Rubén Morales-Menéndez* 1073

Modeling and Intelligent Control

An Integration of FDI and DX Techniques for Determining the Minimal
Diagnosis in an Automatic Way
  *Rafael Ceballos, Sergio Pozo, Carmelo Del Valle,
  Rafael M. Gasca* 1082

Evolutionary Dynamic Optimization of a Continuously Variable
Transmission for Mechanical Efficiency Maximization
  *Jaime Alvarez-Gallegos, Carlos Alberto Cruz Villar,
  Edgar Alfredo Portilla Flores* 1093

Performance Improvement of Ad-Hoc Networks by Using a
Behavior-Based Architecture
  Horacio Martínez-Alfaro, Griselda P. Cervantes-Casillas 1103

Analysis of the Performance of Different Fuzzy System Controllers
  *Patrick B. Moratori, Adriano J.O. Cruz, Laci Mary B. Manhães,
  Emília B. Ferreira, Márcia V. Pedro, Cabral Lima,
  Leila C.V. Andrade* 1113

Discrete-Time Quasi-Sliding Mode Feedback-Error-Learning
Neurocontrol of a Class of Uncertain Systems
  Andon Venelinov Topalov, Okyay Kaynak 1124

Stable Task Space Neuro Controller for Robot Manipulators Without
Velocity Measurements
  Gerardo Loreto, Rubén Garrido 1134

Input-Output Data Modelling Using Fully Tuned RBF Networks for a
Four Degree-of-Freedom Tilt Rotor Aircraft Platform
  Changjie Yu, Jihong Zhu, Jianguo Che, Zengqi Sun 1145

A Frugal Fuzzy Logic Based Approach for Autonomous Flight Control
of Unmanned Aerial Vehicles
  Sefer Kurnaz, Emre Eroglu, Okyay Kaynak, Umit Malkoc 1155

Sensor-Fusion System for Monitoring a CNC-Milling Center
  *Rubén Morales-Menéndez, Sheyla Aguilar M, Ciro A. Rodríguez,
  Federico Guedea Elizalde, Luis E. Garza Castañon* 1164

Intelligent Tutoring Systems

A Probabilistic Model of Affective Behavior for Intelligent Tutoring Systems
Yasmín Hernández, Julieta Noguez, Enrique Sucar, Gustavo Arroyo-Figueroa 1175

A Semi-open Learning Environment for Virtual Laboratories
Julieta Noguez, L. Enrique Sucar 1185

Author Index 1195

Modelling Human Intelligence: A Learning Mechanism

Enrique Carlos Segura[1] and Robin Whitty[2]

[1] Departamento de Computacion,
Facultad de Ciencias Exactas y Naturales,
Universidad de Buenos Aires,
Ciudad Universitaria, Pabellon I, (1428) Buenos Aires, Argentina
[2] School of Business, Computing and Information Management,
London South Bank University,
London SE1A 0AA, UK

Abstract. We propose a novel, high-level model of human learning and cognition, based on association forming. The model configures any input data stream featuring a high incidence of repetition into an association network whose node clusters represent data 'concepts'. It relies on the hypothesis that, irrespective of the high parallelism of the neural structures involved in cognitive processes taking place in the brain cortex, the channel through which the information is conveyed from the real world environment to its final location (in whatever form of neural structure) can transmit only one data item per time unit. Several experiments are performed on the ability of the resulting system to reconstruct a given underlying 'world graph' of concepts and to form and eventually maintain a stable, long term core of memory that we call 'semantic' memory. The existence of discontinuous, first order phase transitions in the dynamics of the system is supported with experiments. Results on clustering and association are shown as well.

Keywords: Association network, memory, learning, graph, stability.

1 Introduction

The problem of building a model of human intelligence requires the distinction between two aspects: 1) storing information (learning) and 2) thinking about this information (cognition). However, it is not plausible a separation between these two functions in the model itself, neither physically (implementation) nor temporally (a learning phase followed by a cognition phase). Associative or distributed memory models [5],[6] remove this separation but at a low level of individual 'concepts'. We propose a model at a higher level: a collection of networks continuously stores incoming data from the outside world.

Suppose we provide a tourist with a list of the London bus routes, but without information on the topology of the town (e.g. a map). He or she can only pick different buses and concatenate pieces of routes so as to make up a continuous tour. Although the process of constructing a mental representation of that topology is a complex, high-dimensional one, we can assume that he will ultimately be able to do it from the temporal sequence of inputs (bus stops, say).

In this paper we present a system, the Association Network (AN) that is able to model this and other situations involving some learning process from a certain real environment, and confirms the ability to infer complex topological relations from a single input stream, as would be expected from an intelligent agent.

The example above illustrates the philosophical basis for our model:

learning = the reconstruction of some network on the basis of random walks on that network.

The network is a hypothesised worldview or 'world graph'; its reconstruction, incorporating approximations, abstractions and lacunae, may be thought of as long-term memory. How do we learn our way around a new neighbourhood? By making random walks in it. How do we learn natural language? By random walks on some hypothesised language network. How do we learn a game of chess or football? By random walks in the network of possible sequences of play. Of course, these walks are not Markovian (although our London bus routes were traversed in this way) but rather are generated by some stochastic process. The human brain is thereby presented with a sequence of random inputs and must configure these to reconstruct a worldview. This is done by making associations via repetitions in the random walk: it is striking how much structure can be imparted to AN's, merely by local identifications based on such repetitions.

We structure the paper as follows: in section 2 we present the basic mechanism for storing an incoming data stream into a network. In section 3 we present experiments upon randomly generated worldview graphs and upon a worldview graph of London bus routes. These experiments are used to confirm that interesting and stable structure may be stored in the network model. Finally, in section 4 we discuss our model in the context of AI and interactive computing.

2 Association Networks: The Learning Algorithm

Our network will be built according to four principles:

1. input data is stored in the nodes of the network;
2. at any point in time, in a non-empty network, there is a **current node** with which any new input will be associated;
3. there is a notion of distance in the net; and
4. there is a **threshold distance**, such that two nodes with the same data and being at most this distance apart, are to be identified with each other.

We may take the distance between two nodes to be the smallest number of edges in some directed path from one to the other. In our example we will set the threshold distance to be two edges. Assume the network is initially empty and suppose that the following input stream is presented to the network:

$$a\ b\ c\ a\ d\ c\ e\ a\ c\ e\ c\ e\ a\ f\ c\ a\ c\ b\ a\ c\ d\ a$$

The network starts off as a single node, which we draw with a square to indicate that it is the current node. When a new input arrives, it becomes the data for a new node which is then linked back by a new directed edge to the current node. The new node then becomes the current node. In this way, the first four inputs would generate the structure shown in fig. 1(a), the second 'a' being added when 'c' is the current node. However, with a threshold distance of 2, this second 'a' will be discovered to be a repetition, by searching up to the threshold distance from 'c'. So rather than adding 'a' as a new node, instead a link is created forward from the first 'a', as shown in fig. 1(b), as though the second 'a' node in fig. 1(a) had been picked up and placed on the first. Now with the first 'a' as current node, we add 'd' as shown in fig. 1(c) and then input 'c' causes another identification to take place, resulting in fig. 1(d).

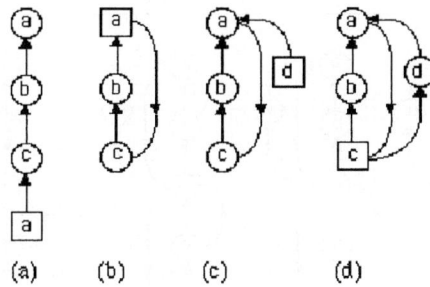

Fig. 1. Network built from input sequence *a b c a d c* , with threshold distance 2

By continuing the example we encounter some more idiosyncracies of net building. In fig. 2(a), 'e' and 'a' have been added. Once again there are two copies of 'a', but this time they are too far apart for identification to have taken place. After a further input of 'c', the second 'a' gets a link forward from 'c' (fig. 2(b)) and the effect is to bring the two copies of 'a' within distance 2 of each other. However, no identification takes place because searching and identification must involve the current node and is only triggered by the addition of data at the current node. In fig. 2(c), the next input, 'e', has been recognised as a repetition and the current node has accordingly moved to the 'e' node; but no extra edge is added since the identification merely duplicates an existing edge. However, when 'c' is now added, the identification, taking place in the opposite direction to this existing edge, does generate a new link (fig. 2(d)).

Now consider sending *e a* to the network that we have built so far. The input 'e' will move the current node to node 'e' without adding a new edge. A search from this node for 'a' will locate only the bottommost copy since the top 'a' is beyond the threshold distance. Again, the current node moves but no edge is added. In fig. 3(a) the result is shown when a further two inputs, 'f' and 'c', have arrived. The next two inputs are 'a' and 'c'. On 'a', a link is formed from the bottommost existing 'a' (fig. 3(b)). There are now two copies of 'c' within the

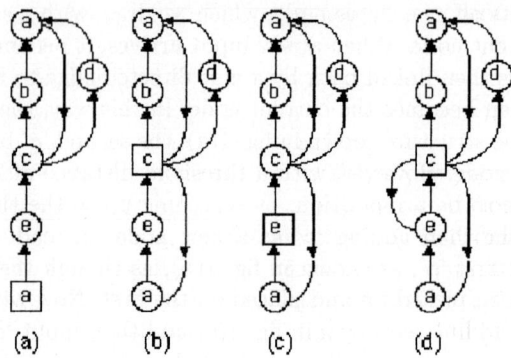

Fig. 2. Effect of presenting inputs *e a c e c* to the network in fig. 1(d)

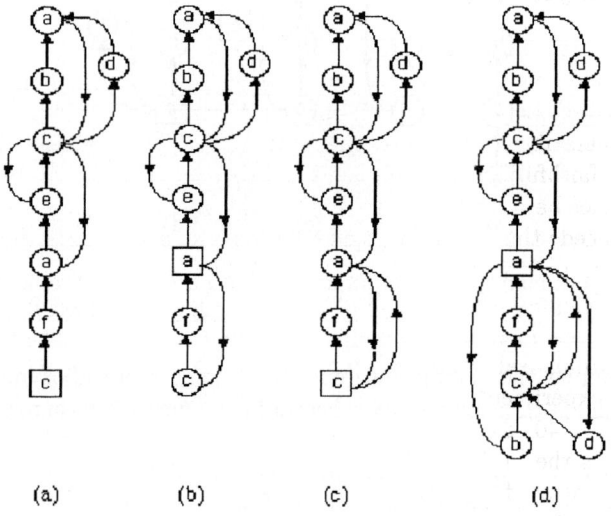

Fig. 3. Effect of presenting inputs *e a c e c* to the network in fig. 2(d)

threshold distance of the current node. We will suppose that searching is carried out in a breadth-first manner, fanning out from the current node and terminating as soon as a repetition is found or the threshold distance is reached. According to this, input 'c' will produce the network in fig. 3(c): only an identification with the bottommost 'c' has occurred, since it is found earlier than the topmost 'c'. Finally, inputs *b a c d a* produce the network in fig. 3(d).

We note that, given an input stream which is sufficiently repetitive, the simple principles with which we started can lead to quite intricate structures, with multiple copies of data within the threshold distance, nodes of arbitrary degree, cycles of any length, and so on.

We would contend that, given an evolutionary pressure to store inputs selectively, the forming of associative links to eliminate repetition is a plausible response[1]. There are two parameters: **network capacity** C (maximum number of nodes allowed in the network) and **node capacity** c (maximum number of edges which may be incident with a node). These constraints are crucial, since learning, to us, means reconstructing a worldview graph *incompletely*. What is left out of the reconstruction is as important as what goes in: including everything encountered during random walk would place an intolerable burden on the processes of cognition[2]. We must decide what to do when C or c are exceeded — for the former we ignore inputs requiring new nodes to be added; for the latter we delete the oldest link. These policies could also be selected by evolution.

3 Experiments: Learning in Association Networks

3.1 First Experiment: The "World Graph"

With our main assumption stated and the basic model described, we can wonder what its learning ability might be. Learning is seen as reading a training set presented as a stream of elements in temporal sequence, drawn from the original graph by generating a random walk along it. The AN is expected to replicate the graph as faithfully as possible, and its learning capacity will be scored from the resemblance between the constructed graph and the original one. We are not bound to concede the actual existence of such a structure according to which a particular aspect of the "natural world" would be organised, except from a rather speculative viewpoint. Our definition assumes that every learning process may be seen as that of inferring a highly dimensional tissue of concepts from a one-dimensional, temporal sample random walk of arbitrary, though finite length.

The first experiment was to generate a random graph with 500 nodes and a maximum, Δ, of 40 edges per node, up to a total of 10000 edges (half the number of nodes times the number of edges per node). Random walks were produced with a total length of 30,000 steps (nodes) and the parameters of the AN were C, c (see section 2) and the semantic threshold, defined as the minimum number of consecutive time units that a node has to be **accessible** (i.e. connected to the graph) in order to be deemed as a **semantic** (i.e. stable) item of memory.

Fig. 4 shows the performance of the AN as a function of time, for c at 5, 10, 20 and 30, with C=500 (same size as in the original graph) and semantic threshold at 3000. We can describe the dynamics as a cyclic, quite regular, alternation between periods of rapid growth of the accessible memory and simultaneous and slower growth of the semantic one, and sudden collapses leading to dramatic loss of memory. Two phenomena are easily observable: first, the evolution of semantic memory replicates that of accessible memory, but with a smaller amplitude; this

---

[1] A similar algorithm has been independently proposed for data compression by Mojdeh [8].

[2] We are reminded of the story "Funes, the Memorious" by Borges, in which Funes, who remembers everything, is completely unable to operate intelligently.

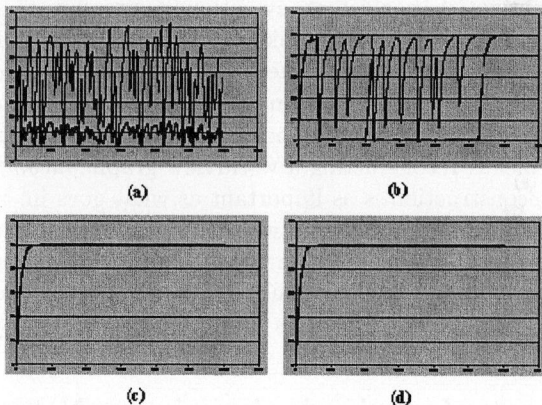

Fig. 4. Reconstructed graph from random walk on near-regular graph. Upper (light): accessible memory, lower (dark): semantic memory. Number of Nodes in graph: 500. Node Capacities: (a) 5, (b) 10, (c) 20, (d) 30.

is particularly apparent for low values of c. Second, the frequency of collapse decreases with increasing c, as one would expect, until some critical value beyond which the system acquires a core of stable memory: no matter whether any collapses occurred in the past, the system can be deemed to have reached an equilibrium point and the probability of a new collapse becomes negligible.

3.2 Second Experiment: A Case of "Real Life"

Our second experiment aimed at testing the ability of the AN to infer complex topological relations from a single input stream, and the practical problem chosen was that of the tourist having to construct a mental representation of the topology of a town (see the Introduction) from a set of bus routes presented as a temporal sequence of relevant bus stops drawn from those routes.

An input file was produced by concatenating all the public bus routes (red buses) serving London and Greater London. After appropriate filtering and standardising, the file was in condition to be processed so as to generate the "world graph", whose nodes are the stops and that has an edge connecting a pair of nodes if both are consecutively included in at least one route. This graph contained 430 nodes with degrees ranging from 2 to 10. Again, a random walk was generated from this graph, with a total length of 30,000 steps, as in the previous experiment; the parameters were also the same.

Fig. 5 shows the performance of the memory as a function of time, for c at 6, 7, 8, 9 and 10, with $C=430$ and semantic threshold at 3000. We can roughly observe the same general behaviour as in the previous case (randomly generated regular graph). However, whilst in the previous case a c of at most 50% of the maximum degree of the original graph ($c/\Delta = 20/40$) was enough for the system to eventually overcome the cyclic phase of alternating "memory growth - collapse", in this "real case" only by raising the node capacity to 80% of

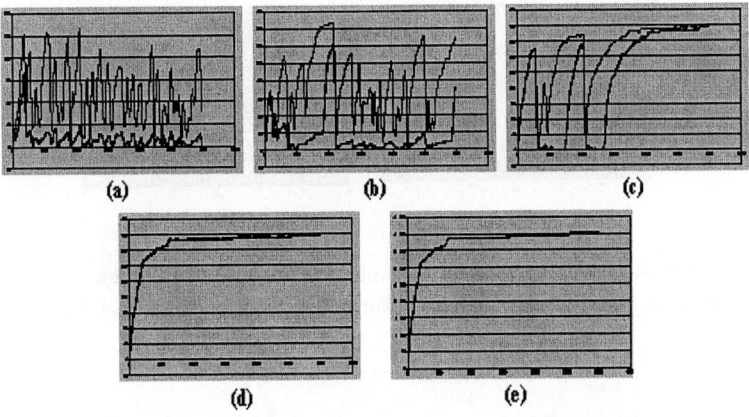

Fig. 5. Reconstructed graph from random walk on Bus Routes. Upper (light): accessible memory, lower (dark): semantic memory. Number of nodes in graph: 430. Node capacities: (a) 6, (b) 7, (c) 8, (d) 9, (e) 10.

the maximum degree (8/10) does the system succeed in reaching a stable regime. We explain this difference: in the random graph the variance of node degrees was small, the graphs being close to regular. Conversely, the variance for the "world graph" of London is so large that, given a certain ratio c/Δ, the probability of becoming disconnected and collapsing in a few steps is, on average, much higher.

We can conclude that no fixed dependence can be stated between the critical value for c (to ensure assymptotic stability) and the size and maximum degree of the original graph, but also the variance of degrees has to be considered.

3.3 Phase Transition Diagrams

On the basis of the previous results (and similar ones), we can distinguish qualitative phase states for the dynamics of the learning system, i.e. different landscapes for the temporal evolution of the process of memory formation. For c/Δ below some r (that basically depends on the structure of the original world graph), a state of rather regular alternation between memory growth and memory collapse takes place. For $c/\Delta > r$, an equilibrium is suddenly reached and the system rapidly evolves to complete reconstruction of the node structure, within the limitations of connectivity imposed by the ratio c/Δ at which the AN is set.

We can properly speak of *phase transition*, moreover a first order phase transition, since no smooth change takes place between the cyclic, unstable phase and the stable one in terms of frequency of collapses, but rather when a certain critical period is reached, the system enters the equilibrium phase. For the bus routes case, for example, this critical value is typically around 7000 steps.

Fig. 6 shows the diagrams. In the regular graph, the border line is more definite since we had more values of c/Δ. As for the London graph, the line is straight: the dynamics changes abruptly from transition point at $t \sim 13000$ for $c/\Delta = 0.8$ to no transition (process stable from the beginning) for $c/\Delta = 0.9$.

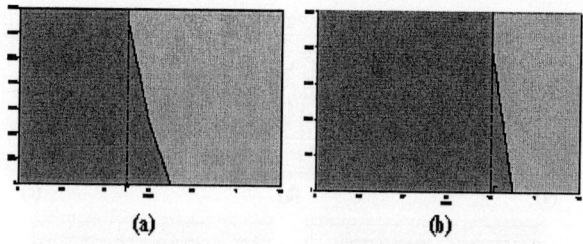

Fig. 6. Transition diagrams for the dynamics of memory formation: (a) Randomly generated regular graph (500 nodes) (b) "World Graph" for Central London (430 nodes)

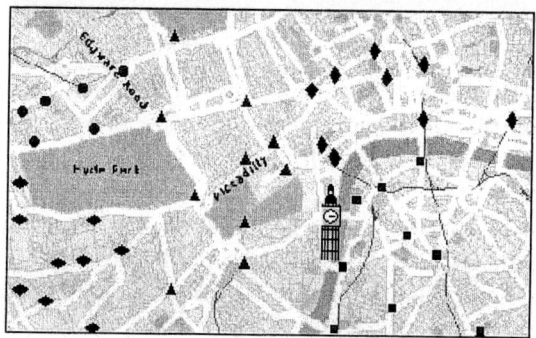

Fig. 7. Organisation of main places of London, according to neighbourhood relations, in five clusters, represented by: circles (top left), triangles (middle), vertical diamonds (top right), horizontal diamonds (bottom left), squares (bottom right)

3.4 Clustering and Classification

The AN can be used for clustering and classification. By virtue of the topological way in which it organises the information, the AN can extract relationships between concepts that are implicit in the temporal order of the input stream.

Two types of experiments were carried out: *clustering* and *association*. The first consisted of presenting an input sequence to the system and causing it to construct the corresponding AN. Then, standard clustering was applied, using as distance between two nodes the length of the shortest path between them. Fig. 7 shows the organisation of the main places of London in clusters, according to their neighbourhood relations, as derived from the bus routes network.

The second experiment, association or stimulus-response, was undertaken on the same network and consisted of entering a new input and searching for its immediate neighbours in the graph. A new parameter, called **semantic relevance** (SR), is used for rating the significance of an item of information: it is set initially to zero for every new item, and is decreased by 1 each time the same information appears in the input stream. If the SR has fallen below a fixed threshold, the replicated data is no longer added to the network. The effect of SR can be understood by using the AN in the stimulus-response (association) mode. With a threshold of SR of -10, the answer to *Westminster* was the set {LambethPalace, CabinetWarRooms, DowningSt, Archway, HorseGuards, VauxhallBridge, Victoria, HydeParkCorner}, while for a threshold of -5, the response was {BuckinghamPal, HydeParkCorner, LambethPalace, CabinetWarRooms, DowningSt}. Finally, for a threshold of 0 (only the first occurrence of each word is considered for constructing the net), the response was just {BuckinhamPal, HydeParkCorner}. Hence the SR prevents node degrees from growing too large, much like c: if the threshold is set to a value giving little or no restriction, e.g. -10, roughly the same three groups of answers shown for the question *Westminster* can be obtained with c at 10, 5/6 and 2, respectively.

Many fields are suitable for this model, e.g. in extracting relations between terms in a text. We took successive editions of the *Times* online to produce an input stream. After eliminating punctuation signs and changing capital to lower case, the input size was 7771 words. We used it to produce chains of associated concepts. For example, starting with the word "children" and ending in "judge", the sequence { *children - people - rights - laws - judge* } was obtained.

4 Discussion

We have introduced a system, the Association Network, that is able to model situations of learning from real environments, and to infer complex relations from a single input stream, as expected from an intelligent (human) agent. Our hypothesis is that, irrespective of the high parallelism of the neural structures involved in cognitive processes at the brain cortex, the channels through which information is conveyed from the environment to its final location (in whatever form of neural structure) can transmit only one data item per time unit.

Experiments showed the abilities of the AN: learning of complex topological structures; clustering and association; existence of a phase transition regime. This work is preliminary; behaviour in the limit could be analysed, given certain parameter settings. The WWW and other very-large-scale systems have given rise to new techniques in the field of random structures, ideal for this work [4][2].

Some comment is necessary on the somewhat metaphysical concept of "world graph", i.e. the implicit hypothesis that any domain of the natural world is isomorphic to some "mental model" and this is, in its turn, representable as a graph or a network of concepts. Maybe this concept is justifiable case by case; e.g., in the process of learning a language, some semantic network might be deemed as implicitly present in a dictionary and could be constructed from it.

We distinguish this model from that provided by associative or distributed memories, as being at a higher semantic level than these, or than reinforcement learning or evolutionary computation. Our approach is closer to schemata or frame models of memory, going back to Bartlett's work [1] and our dependence on association forming owes more to James [3] than to the PDP group [6].

That said, we must respond to the standard GOFAI (Good Old-Fashioned Artificial Intelligence) criticism that our model relies on the pre-existence of data concepts ('bus stop', 'football', 'chess piece') which themselves represent the core challenge for AI. In some cases, it might be appropriate to declare that the nodes of a certain AN were individual associative memories; the job of the AN being to provide a higher level interconnecting structure for these memories. Ultimately, the co-evolution of many communicating networks, at many levels of abstraction, performing different tasks might implement something like Minsky's Society of Mind [7], a (still) very persuasive view of how the human mind operates.

As for the emergence of different levels in an intercommunicating structure of AN's, we explored how semantic relevance (see subsection 3.4), rather than merely rejecting repeated items, might provide a filter, whereby such items are transferred as input to a higher level network (and from that network to one yet higher, etc). This might operate in processing language, where recurring words (e.g. articles or connectives) might be stored elsewhere both to avoid false associations between verbs and nouns and to capture their structural significance.

Our model is interactive: learning and application (cognition) are simultaneous, unlike the classical machine learning approach in which these two processes are consecutive. From the computational perspective, we propose a general way of structuring repetition rich sequential data. More important, but more speculative, is the possibility that we have invented a credible model of learning, i.e. concept formation in humans or, at least, given a major step in that direction.

References

[1] Bartlett, F.C.: Remembering: a Study in Experimental and Social Psychology. Cambridge University Press (1932)
[2] Bollobas, B. and Riordan, O., Coupling scale-free and classical random graphs. Submitted to Internet Mathematics (2003)
[3] James, W.: The Principles of Psychology, vol. 1. New York (1890), reprinted by Dover Publications (1950)
[4] Kleinberg, J.M, Kumar, R., Raghavan, R., Rajagopalan, S. and Tomkins, A.S.: The web as a graph: measurements, models, and methods. In Proc. 5th Int. Conf. on Computing and Combinatorics, Tokyo, Japan, 1999, Springer Verlag (1999), 1-17
[5] McClelland, J. L. and Rumelhart, D. E.: Distributed memory and the representation of general and specific information. J. Exp. Psych.: General, 114(2) (1985) 159-188
[6] McClelland, J. L., Rumelhart, D. E. and the PDP Res. Group: Parallel Distributed Processing: Explorations in the Microstructure of Cognition (2 vols). MIT Press (1986)
[7] Minsky, M.: The Society of Mind. Simon and Schuster, New York (1986)
[8] Mojdeh, D.: Codes and Graphs. 2nd European Workshop on Algebraic Graph Theory, Univ. Edinburgh (July 2001), (preprint, Univ. Mazandaran, Iran)

Compilation of Symbolic Knowledge and Integration with Numeric Knowledge Using Hybrid Systems

Vianey Guadalupe Cruz Sánchez, Gerardo Reyes Salgado,
Osslan Osiris Vergara Villegas, Joaquín Perez Ortega, and Azucena Montes Rendón

Centro Nacional de Investigación y Desarrollo Tecnológico (cenidet),
Computer Science Department, Av. Palmira S/n,
Col. Palmira. C. P. 62490. Cuernavaca Morelos México
{vianey, greyes, osslan, jperez, amr}@cenidet.edu.mx

Abstract. The development of Artificial Intelligence (AI) research has followed mainly two directions: the use of symbolic and connectionist (artificial neural networks) methods. These two approaches have been applied separately in the solution of problems that require tasks of knowledge acquisition and learning. We present the results of implementing a Neuro-Symbolic Hybrid System (NSHS) that allows unifying these two types of knowledge representation. For this, we have developed a compiler or translator of symbolic rules which takes as an input a group of rules of the type IF ... THEN..., converting them into a connectionist representation. Obtained the compiled artificial neural network this is used as an initial neural network in a learning process that will allow the "refinement" of the knowledge. To prove the refinement of the hybrid approach, we carried out a group of tests that show that it is possible to improve in a connectionist way the symbolic knowledge.

1 Introduction

During the last years a series of works have been carried out which tend to diminish the distance between the symbolic paradigms and connectionist: the neuro–symbolic hybrid systems (NSHS). Wertmer [1] proposes a definition: "the NSHS are systems based mainly on artificial neural network that allows a symbolic interpretation or an interaction with symbolic components". These systems make the transfer of the knowledge represented by a group of symbolic rules toward a module connectionist. This way, the obtained neural network allows a supervised learning starting from a group of examples.

For their study, the symbolic knowledge (obtained from rules) has been treated as the "theory" that we have on a problem and the numeric knowledge (obtained from examples) as the "practice" around this problem. This way, the objective of implementing a neuro-symbolic hybrid system is to combine " theory " as well as the " practice " in the solution of a problem, because many of the times neither one source of knowledge nor the other are enough to solve it.

From the works developed by Towell [2] and Osorio [3] we have implemented a symbolic compiler that allows transforming a set of symbolic rules into an ANN. This ANN would be "refined" later on thanks to a training process in a neural simulator using a base of examples. To prove the NSHS we use the benchmark Monk's Problem [4], which has a base of examples as well as a base of rules.

2 Symbolic and Numeric Knowledge

The symbolic knowledge is the set of theoretical knowledge that we have in a particular domain. For example, we can recognize an object among others by means of the set of characteristics of that object. This description can be considered a symbolic representation. A disadvantage of this kind of representation is that the theory in occasions cannot describe all the characteristics of the object. The above-mentioned is due to the fact that it cannot make an exhaustive description of the object in all its modalities or contexts.

For example, the description of a Golden apple says that "the fruit is big and of golden colour, longer than wide, with white and yellowish meat, fixed, juicy, perfumed and very tasty. The peduncle is long or very long and the skin is thin" [5]. If a person uses only the theory to be able to recognize this fruit in a supermarket, it is possible that this person may have difficulty to recognize an apple that is blended or next to another kind of fruits (for example, pears) or another kind of apples. These fruits have a very similar symbolic description. Here, we realize that the symbolic knowledge can be insufficient for a recognition task.

On the other hand, so that this knowledge can be used in a computer system, a formal representation should be used. For this, we have different knowledge representations: propositional logic, predicates logic, semantic networks, etc. The representation mostly used is the symbolic rules.

Another source of knowledge, is that called "practical", integrated by a group of examples about an object or problem in different environments or contexts.

For the case of the Golden apple, we need to describe it presenting an image base of the fruit in different environments, contexts, positions and with different degrees of external quality. We will use for it a numeric description (colour in RGB, high, wide, etc.). As it happened to the symbolic representation, it is impossible to create a base of images sufficiently big so as to cover all the situations previously mentioned. For the above-mentioned, a base of examples is also sometimes insufficient to describe all and each one of the situations of an object. We believe that a hybrid approach can be the solution to problems of objects recognition.

3 Characteristic of Neuro-symbolic Hybrid Systems

A hybrid system is formed by the integration of several intelligent subsystems, where each one maintains its own representation language and a different mechanism of inferring solutions. The goal of the implementation of the hybrid systems is to improve the efficiency and the reasoning power as well as the expression power of the intelligent systems.

The hybrid systems have potential to solve some problems that are very difficult to confront using only one reasoning method. Particularly, the neuro-symbolic hybrid systems can treat numeric and symbolic information with more effectiveness than systems that act separately. Some of the advantages of the hybrid systems are: they exploit the whole available knowledge of a problem; they mix different kinds of information (symbolic, numeric, inexact and imprecise); they improve the total execution and they eliminate the weaknesses of the methods applied individually creating robust reasoning systems.

4 Compilation of Symbolic Knowledge into an ANN

The neuro-symbolic hybrid system that we proposed has a compiler in charge of mapping the symbolic rules into a neural network. This compiler generates the topology and the weights of an ANN (we will call this ANN "compiled"). The topology of the neural network represents the set of rules that describes the problem and the weights represent the dependences that exist between the antecedents and the consequents of these rules. The compilation is carried out by means of a process that maps the components of the rules towards the architecture of an ANN (see Table 1).

Table 1. Correspondence between the symbolic knowledge and the ANN

Symbolic knowledge	ANN
Final conclusions	Output units
Input data	Input units
Intermediate conclusions	Hide units
Dependences	Weights and connections

4.1 Compilation Algorithm

For the compilation module we implemented the algorithm proposed by Towell [2] which consists of the following steps:

1. Rewrite the rules.
2. Map the rules into an ANN.
3. Determine the level between the hidden and output units and the input units.
4. Add links between the units.
5. Map the attributes not used in the rules.

1. Rewrite the rules. The first step of the algorithm consists of translating the set of rules to a format that clarifies their hierarchical structure and that makes it possible to translate the rules directly to an artificial neural network.

In this step, we verify if a consequent is the same for one or more antecedents. If it exists more than an antecedent to a consequent, then each consequent with more than one antecedent it will be rewritten. For example, in Figure 1 the rewriting of two rules, with the same consequent is observed.

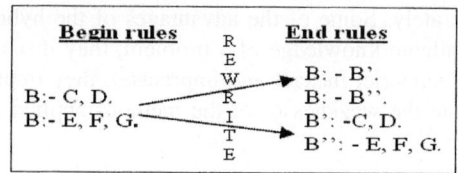

Fig. 1. Rewrite two rules with the same consequent

Where :
:- it means "IF ... THEN";
, it means the conjunction of antecedents.

In Figure 1, the rule B: - C, D has as antecedent C and D and as consequent B. It is interpreted as: If C and D are true, Then B is true. The rule B: - E, F, G is read in the following way: If E and F and D are true, Then B is true. Because these two rules have the same consequent, these should be rewrite as to be able to be translated to the ANN. The rules at the end of this step can be observed in the Figure 1.

2. Mapping the rules to an ANN. The following step of the algorithm consists of mapping a transformed group of rules to an artificial neural network.

If we map the rules of the Figure 1, these would be like it is shown in the Figure 2a. In the Figure 2.b the weight and the assigned bias are shown. The assigned weight will be –w or w if the antecedent is denied or not, respectively. Towell proposes a value of the weight of w = 4, [2]. On the other hand, it will be assigned to B' and B'' a bias of $(-2P-1/2)*w$, since they are conjunctive rules, while we will assign a bias of $-w/2$ to B because it is a disjunction.

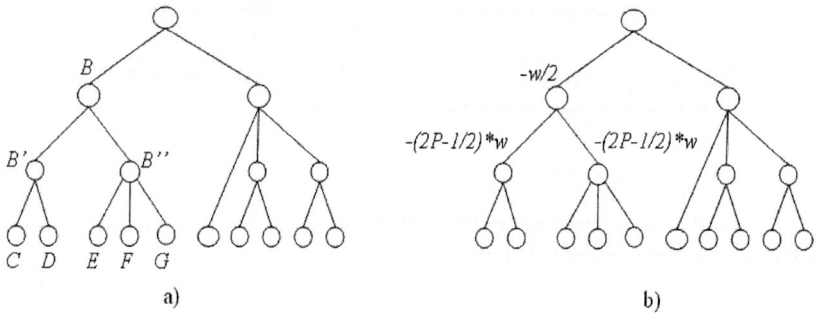

Fig. 2. a) Mapping of rules to an ANN b) Weights and bias assigned

3. Determine the level between the hidden and output units and the input units. The level can be defined by means of some of the following ways: Minimum or maximum length that exists among a hidden or output unit to an input unit (see Figure 3).

4. Add links among the units. In this step the links are added between the units that represent the non existent attributes in the rules and the output units.

5. Mapping the attributes not used in the rules. In this stage an input is added to the neural network by each one of the attributes of the antecedents not present in the initial rules. These inputs will be necessary for the later learning stage.

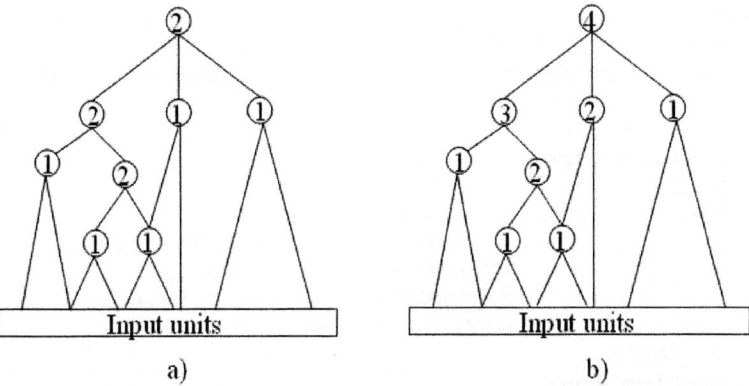

Fig. 3. a) Determination of the level using the minimum distance toward an input unit. b) Determination of the level using the maximum distance toward an input unit.

5 Implementation of the Symbolic Compiler

In our research we implement a symbolic compiler (we call this SymbComp). This compiler uses the method proposed by Towell (see section 4.1). For the implementation of SymbComp we use the software AntLr Terence [6] that allows carrying out the lexical, syntactic and semantic analysis of a file type text. This file will be the input to SymbComp. The system is made of four sections (see program bellow):

- Head. It contains the variables and constant definition, as well as the name of the file and comments.
- Attributes. It contains the definition of each one of the attributes that appear in the antecedents and consequent of the rules. The attributes are made of Labels; Type; Value. CompSymb implements four types of attributes:
  a) Nominal: it has discrete values such as small, medium, big.
  b) Continuous: it has values in a continuous space.
  c) Range: it has continuous values with a maximum and minimum value.
  d) Binary: it has two possible values, true / false.
- Rules. It contains the symbol
- ic rules that will be compiled and which are written in language Prolog.
- Attributes added by the user. It contains attributes that are not used in the antecedents of the previous rules but that are present in the base of examples.

SymbComp carries out the lexical, syntactic and semantic analysis and the compilation (together with Builder C++ 5.0 Charte [7]) of the previously defined file. The result of this process is two files: one of topology and another one of weight of an artificial neural network that we will call "compiled network".

```
//section one
//Simbolic file example.symb
#BEGIN
//section two
```

```
#ATTRIBUTES
   stalk: BINARY:T/F;
   size: CONTINUOS:small[3,5], medium[6,8], big[9,11];
   shape: NOMINAL: heart, circle;
#END_ ATTRIBUTES
//section three
#RULES
   Red_Delicius:-shape(heart),
               IN_RANGE(Colour_Red,108,184),
               IN_RANGE(Colour_Green,100,150),
               IN_RANGE(Colour_Blue,50,65);
   Quality:- stalk(T),size(big),Red_Delicius.
#END_RULES
//section four
#ATTRIB_ADDED_USER
   Colour_Red:    RANGE: [0,255];
   Colour_Green:  RANGE: [0,255];
   Colour_Blue:   RANGE: [0,255];
#END
```

6 Integration of Symbolic and Numeric Knowledge

The integration of numeric and symbolic knowledge will be carried out once we have compiled the rules. For it, we will use the compiled neural network and the base of examples of the problem. For the integration the Neusim system Osorio[3] was used, which uses the CasCor Fahlman [8] paradigm. Neusim was selected because it allows loading a compiled neural network and from this to begin the learning. Also, with Neusim it is possible to carry out the learning directly from the base of examples or to use the neural network as classifier. On the other hand, the advantage of using CasCor as a learning paradigm is that we can see the number of hidden units added during the learning and thus, follow the process of incremental learning. We have also planned for a near future to carry out a detailed analysis of the added units with the purpose of explaining knowledge.

By means of this integration stage we seek that the numeric and symbolic knowledge are integrated in a single system and at the end we have a much more complete knowledge set.

7 Test Using the NSHS for the Integration and the Refinement of Knowledge

To prove the integration and refinement capacity of knowledge of the NSHS we made use of examples and rules base known as Monk's Problem Thrun [4]. This benchmark is madeof a numeric base of examples and of a set of symbolic rules. Monk's problem is presented with three variants: Monk's 1, Monk's 2 and Monk's 3. For our experimentation we use the first case. The characteristics of Monk's 1 are as follows:

- Numeric base of examples.

 Input attributes: 6 (a1, a2, ... a6).
 Output: 1 (class).
 Total of examples of the base: 432.

 Description of attributes:
 a1:   1, 2, 3
 a2:   1, 2, 3
 a3:   1, 2
 a4:   1, 2, 3
 a5:   1, 2, 3, 4
 a6:   1, 2.
 class: 0, 1

- Symbolic Rules.

 IF (a1 = a2) OR (a5 = 1), THEN class = 1.
 This rule can be translated into two disjunctive rules:

 R1 : IF (a1 = a2),THEN class = 1;
 R2 : IF (a5 = 1), THEN class = 1;

As it can be observed in these two rules, the used attributes are a1, a2 and a5, while the attributes a3, a4 and a6 are not considered in these rules. This observation is important because in the base of examples the six attributes are present and they will be used during the learning step. To compile these rules it was necessary to create a text file that will serve as input to SymbComp. Once compiled the rules carry out three types of tests using NeuSim:

Case a) Connectionist approach: Learning and generalization from the base of examples.
Case b) Symbolic approach: Generalization from the compiled ANN.
Case c) Hybrid approach: Learning and generalization using the compiled ANN and the base of examples.

For the three cases we vary the number of used rules (two rules, one rule) and the percentage of the examples used during the learning (100%, 75%, 50%, 25%). The results are shown in the Table 2. In the Table the percentage of obtained learning and the time when it was reached, the generalization percentage on the total of the base of examples and the hidden units added are indicated.

From the results obtained we can observe that in the some cases where the numeric and the symbolic knowledge are integrated, the percentage in the generalization is, in most of cases, higher than those tests where only the numeric knowledge is used.

For example, for the *connectionist* approach (case a) using 50% of the base of examples we achieve a generalization of 59.95%, while if we use the hybrid approach (case c) with the rule 1 and 50% of the base of examples we obtain a generalization of 94.21%. Another interesting result is when we use the rule 2 and 50% of the base of examples, obtaining a generalization of 63.42% (also better than the connectionist approach). For the same hybrid approach, if we use the rule 1 and 25% of the base of examples we arrive at a generalization percentage of 77.03%, much better than 55.09% of the connectionist approach. For all these cases we reduce the number of learning periods and the number of hidden units added.

Table 2. Results obtained for the study of Monk's problem

Case (approach)	Compiled rules	Examples used %	Knowledge %	Generalization	Hidden units added	Learning epochs
a) Connectionist	-	100	100	99.07	2	484
	-	75	100	87.03	7	1614
	-	50	100	59.95	5	983
	-	25	55.09	55.09	2	320
b) Symbolic	R1, R2	-	-	100	0	0
	R1	-	-	93.05	0	0
	R2	-	-	81.94	0	0
c) Hybrid	R1, R2	100	100	98.61	1	84
	R1, R2	75	100	98.61	1	95
	R1, R2	50	100	98.61	1	92
	R1, R2	25	100	95.13	1	82
	R1	100	100	99.53	1	82
	R1	75	100	99.30	1	78
	R1	50	100	94.21	1	69
	R1	25	100	77.03	1	67
	R2	100	100	95.83	3	628
	R2	75	100	73.14	6	1226
	R2	50	100	63.42	4	872
	R2	25	100	51.85	1	58

On the other hand, if we compare the symbolic approach (case b) where we use only the rule 2 against the hybrid approach using the same rule and 100% of the base of examples, we realize that the generalization is better in the second case (81.94% against 95.83%, respectively). The same thing would happen if we use the rule 1 instead of the rule 2.

A result at the side of the objectives of this work is the discovery that rule 1 is "more representative" that rule 2. This can be observed on table 2: with the compilation of the rule 1 a generalization of 93.05% is reached against 81.94% for the rule 2.

8 Conclusions

In this paper we present a method of knowledge refinement using a neuro-symbolic hybrid system. For this, a compiler that converts a set of symbolic rules into an artificial neural network was implemented. Using this last one, we could "complete" the knowledge represented in the rules by means of a process of numeric incremental learning. Thanks to the tests carried out on Monk's Problem we could demonstrate that when we use the numeric or symbolic knowledge separately it is unfavourable with regards to the use of a hybrid system.

The results obtained from tests as: the increase in the generalization percentage, the reduction of the number of hidden neurons added and the reduction of the number of learning epochs, demonstrate that the hybrid systems theory is applicable when a lack of knowledge exists and this can be covered with the integration of two types of knowledge. At the moment, we are working to apply this principle to problems of visual classification of objects in which descriptive rules and numeric examples (visual characteristic) are known. Our objective in this case is to create tools that help the supervision and control processes of the visual quality. We are also intending to enlarge SymbComp to be able to compile other kind of rules (for example fuzzy rules), as well as to study the problem of the knowledge explicitation from the refined neural networks.

We consider that this theory (compilation mechanism) it is applicable to simple rules of the type IF...THEN... and it cannot be generalized to all type of rules. For the group of rules that was proven, the accepted attributes were of type: nominal, binary and in range. For the compilation of another rule types, for example rules that accept diffuse values, the application of this theory would imply modifications to the algorithm. Some works that actually are developed addressed this problem.

Acknowledgement

Authors would like to thank: *Centro Nacional de Investigación y Desarrollo Tecnológico (cenidet)* the facilities offered for the execution of this research.

References

1. Wermter, Stefan and Sun, Ron. (Eds.): Hybrid neural systems. Springer Heidelberg. (2000).
2. Towell, G.: Symbolic Knowledge and Neural Networks: Insertion, Refinement and Extraction. Ph.D. Thesis. Univ. of Wisconsin - Madison. USA. (1991).
3. Osório, F. S.: INSS - Un Système Hybride Neuro-Symbolique pour l'Apprentissage Automatique Constructif. PhD Thesis, LEIBNIZ-IMAG, Grenoble – France (February 1998).
4. Thrun Sebastian.: The Monk's Problems. School of Computer Science, Carnegie Mellon University. Pittsburgh, PA 15213, USA. (1992).
5. The apple. Copyright infoagro.com (2003).
6. Terence Parr.: An Introduction To ANTLR. Another tool for language recognition. (2003).
7. Charte, Francisco: Programation in C++Builder 5. Anaya Multimedia Editions. (2000)
8. Fahlman, S.E., Lebiere, C.: The Cascade-Correlation Learning Architecture. Carnegie Mellon University. Technical Report. CMU-CS-90-100. (1990).
9. Arevian G., Wermter S., Panchev C.: Symbolic state transducers and recurrent neural preference machines for text mining. International Journal on Approximate Reasoning, Vol. 32, No. 2/3, pp. 237-258. (2003).
10. McGarry K., MacIntyre J.: Knowledge transfer between neural networks, proceedings of the sixteenth european meeting on cybernetics and systems research. Vienna, Austria, pp. 555-560. (April 2002).

11. Osorio, F. S., AMY, Bernard.: Aprendizado de máquinas: métodos para inserção de regras simbólicas em redes neurais artificiais aplicados ao controle em robótiva autônoma. Revista SCIENTIA, Vol. 12, Nro. 1, p.1-20. Editora da Unisinos, Out. (2001).
12. Rashad U., Arullendran P., Hawthorne M., Kendal S.: A hybrid medical information system for the diagnosis of dizziness. Proceedings 4th International Conference Neural Networks and Expert Systems in Medicine and Healthcare. Greece. (June 2001).
13. Wermter S., Panchev C.: Hybrid preference machines based on inspiration from neuroscience. Cognitive Systems Research. Vol. 3, No. 2, pp. 255-270. (2002).

The Topological Effect of Improving Knowledge Acquisition

Bernhard Heinemann

Fachbereich Informatik, FernUniversität in Hagen,
58084 Hagen, Germany
Phone: +49 2331 987 2714, Fax: +49 2331 987 319
Bernhard.Heinemann@fernuni-hagen.de

Abstract. In this paper, we extend Moss and Parikh's bi-modal language for knowledge and effort by an additional modality describing improvement. Like the source language, the new one too has a natural interpretaion in spatial contexts. The result of this is that concepts like the comparison of topologies can be captured within the framework of modal logic now. The main technical issue of the paper is a completeness theorem for the tri-modal system arising from the new language.

Keywords: Reasoning about knowledge, modal logic and topology, spatial reasoning, completeness.

1 Introduction

The idea of *knowledge* has undoubtedly proven useful for several areas of computer science and AI, eg, designing and analysing multi-agent systems. Knowledge is then *ascribed externally* to the agents (by the designer or analyst), and the multi-modal system $S5_m$ provides the basic language for and logic of knowledge, respectively, in case m agents are involved (where $m \in \mathbb{N}$); cf the standard textbooks [1] or [2].

For a more dynamic setting enabling one to reason about the change of knowledge in the course of *time*, the latter notion has to be added to the basic system. This is done for the usual logic of knowledge in an explicit way, i.e., by means of temporal operators ranging over certain mappings from the domain of time into the set of all states of the world, so-called *runs;* cf [1], Ch. 4.

The fact that a *spatial* component too inheres in the temporal knowledge structures arising from that, has hardly received attention in the relevant literature. Actually, knowledge can be viewed as *closeness* and, respectively, knowledge acquisition as *approximation to points* in suitable *spaces of sets* (consisting of a domain of states, X, and a system $\mathcal{O}$ of subsets of X, the *knowledge states* of the agents). This view constitutes, essentially, the 'generic' example showing how concepts from *topology* enter the formal framework of evolving knowledge.

The topological content of knowledge was discovered and basically investigated in the paper [3] first. The details concerning this were drawn up in [4]. The fundamental outcome of these papers is a general bi-modal system called, interestingly enough, TOPOLOGIC. In the single-agent case, one of the operators of TOPOLOGIC corresponds with *knowledge* and the other with computational *effort*. Thus the latter models some knowledge acquisition procedure, by means of which *time* is (implicitly) encoded.

Focussing on these characteristics of knowledge leads one to a new area of application. As the title of the paper [3] (and [4], respectively) already suggests, one could take TOPOLOGIC as the starting point for a system supporting spatial reasoning to such an extent that those properties being part of topology can be captured. However, pursuing this idea causes new expressiveness requirements very soon.

In order to meet some of these requirements, the ground language has to be extended. This can be done in various ways, depending on the applications one has in mind. A recent example featuring the language of *hybrid logic* is contained in the paper [5].[1] Unlike that paper, we follow strictly the purely modal approach given by TOPOLOGIC here. In fact, the subject of this paper is an additional modal operator representing *improvement*.

Suppose that two knowledge acquisition procedures, P_1 and P_2, are available to an agent A. How to compare P_1 with P_2? Or, more specifically, under what circumstances would P_2 be regarded no worse than P_1, thus possibly preferred to P_1? Intuitively, this should be the case if A using P_1 could achieve at least the same knowledge by appealing to P_2. That is to say, every knowledge state of A with respect to P_1 should also be a knowledge state of A with respect to P_2. Or, in mathematical terms, the set $\mathcal{O}_1$ of all P_1-knowledge states is a subset of the set $\mathcal{O}_2$ of all P_2-knowledge states.

This consideration shows that our modelling of improvement goes beyond TOPOLOGIC to the extent that *systems* of sets of knowledge states have to be taken into account now, instead of mere sets of knowledge states. Thus the semantics of the new language will be built on *set system spaces,* replacing the set spaces fundamental to the semantics of TOPOLOGIC. And, from a spatial point of view, the modality describing improvement turns out to be a *refinement operator* on such set system spaces, actually. This means to the context of topology that we are now able to get to grips with a modal treatment of, eg, the *comparison of topologies* (cf [8], I, 2, 2).

The following technical part of the paper is organized as follows. In the next section, we define precisely the language for knowledge, effort and improvement. We also state a couple of properties that can be expressed with it. Afterwards, in Section 3, the logic arising from the new language is investigated. We prove the soundness and completeness of a corresponding axiomatization with respect to the class of all intended structures. This is the main result of the present paper. It turns out that a certain Church-Rosser property for effort and improvement, which is not quite easily seen at first glance, is crucial to its proof. The paper is then finished with some concluding remarks.

Concluding this introduction, we would like to mention the papers [9], [10] and [11] on special systems of TOPOLOGIC. It would be interesting to revisit these systems regarding improvement.

---

[1] As to the basics of hybrid logic cf [6], Sec. 7.3, or [7].

2 Extending the Language

In this section, we add to the language of TOPOLOGIC a unary operator modelling *improvement*. First, the new language, $\mathcal{L}$, will be defined precisely, and second, some of its features will be discussed.

Let PROP $= \{A, \ldots\}$ be a denumerable set of symbols called *proposition letters*. We define the set WFF of *well-formed formulas* of $\mathcal{L}$ over PROP by the rule $\alpha ::= A \mid \neg \alpha \mid \alpha \wedge \beta \mid K\alpha \mid \Box \alpha \mid \boxplus \alpha$. The operators K and $\Box$ represent *knowledge* and *effort*, respectively, as it is common for TOPOLOGIC. $\boxplus$ is called the *improvement operator*. The missing boolean connectives $\top, \bot, \vee, \rightarrow, \leftrightarrow$ are treated as abbreviations, as needed. The duals of K, $\Box$ and $\boxplus$ are denoted L, $\Diamond$ and $\oplus$, respectively.

We now give meaning to formulas. For a start, we define the domains where $\mathcal{L}$-formulas will be interpreted in. We let $\mathcal{P}(S)$ designate the powerset of a given set S.

Definition 1 (Set system frames and models).

1. Let $X \neq \emptyset$ be a set and $\mathfrak{S} \subseteq \mathcal{P}(\mathcal{P}(X))$ a system of subsets of $\mathcal{P}(X)$. Then $\mathfrak{F} := (X, \mathfrak{S})$ is called a set system frame.
2. Let $\mathfrak{F} = (X, \mathfrak{S})$ be a set system frame. The set of situations of $\mathfrak{F}$ is defined by $\mathcal{S}_{\mathfrak{F}} := \{(x, U, \mathcal{Q}) \mid x \in U, U \in \mathcal{Q} \text{ and } \mathcal{Q} \in \mathfrak{S}\}$.[2]
3. Let $\mathfrak{F}$ be as above. An $\mathfrak{F}$-valuation is a mapping $V : \text{PROP} \longrightarrow \mathcal{P}(X)$.
4. A set system space or model (or, in short, an SSM) is a triple $\mathfrak{M} := (X, \mathfrak{S}, V)$, where $\mathfrak{F} := (X, \mathfrak{S})$ is a set system frame and V an $\mathfrak{F}$-valuation; $\mathfrak{M}$ is then called based on $\mathfrak{F}$.

By generalizing the semantics of *topologic*, cf [4], the relation of satisfaction between situations and formulas, is now defined with regard to SSMs.

Definition 2 (Satisfaction and validity). Let $\mathfrak{M} = (X, \mathfrak{S}, V)$ be an SSM and $x, U, \mathcal{Q}$ a situation of $\mathfrak{F} = (X, \mathfrak{S})$. Then

$$x, U, \mathcal{Q} \models_{\mathfrak{M}} A \quad :\Longleftrightarrow\quad x \in V(A)$$
$$x, U, \mathcal{Q} \models_{\mathfrak{M}} \neg \alpha \quad :\Longleftrightarrow\quad x, U, \mathcal{Q} \not\models_{\mathfrak{M}} \alpha$$
$$x, U, \mathcal{Q} \models_{\mathfrak{M}} \alpha \wedge \beta \quad :\Longleftrightarrow\quad x, U, \mathcal{Q} \models_{\mathfrak{M}} \alpha \text{ and } x, U, \mathcal{Q} \models_{\mathfrak{M}} \beta$$
$$x, U, \mathcal{Q} \models_{\mathfrak{M}} K\alpha \quad :\Longleftrightarrow\quad y, U, \mathcal{Q} \models_{\mathfrak{M}} \alpha \text{ for all } y \in U$$
$$x, U, \mathcal{Q} \models_{\mathfrak{M}} \Box \alpha \quad :\Longleftrightarrow\quad \forall U' \in \mathcal{Q} : (x \in U' \subseteq U \Rightarrow x, U', \mathcal{Q} \models_{\mathfrak{M}} \alpha)$$
$$x, U, \mathcal{Q} \models_{\mathfrak{M}} \boxplus \alpha \quad :\Longleftrightarrow\quad \forall \mathcal{Q}' \in \mathfrak{S} : (\mathcal{Q} \subseteq \mathcal{Q}' \Rightarrow x, U, \mathcal{Q}' \models_{\mathfrak{M}} \alpha),$$

where $A \in \text{PROP}$ and $\alpha, \beta \in \text{WFF}$. In case $x, U, \mathcal{Q} \models_{\mathfrak{M}} \alpha$ is true we say that α holds in $\mathcal{M}$ at the situation $x, U, \mathcal{Q}$. A formula α is called valid in $\mathfrak{M}$ (written '$\mathfrak{M} \models \alpha$'), iff it holds in $\mathfrak{M}$ at every situation of $\mathfrak{F}$.

---

[2] Situations are often written without brackets later on.

Some remarks on this definition seem to be opportune here.

Remark 1. 1. The meaning of proposition letters is independent of subsets and systems of subsets of the domain by definition, thus 'stable' with respect to $\Box$ and $\boxplus$. This fact will be reflected in two special axioms later on (Axioms 6 and 11 from Sec. 3).
2. Note that each modal operator concerns one component of a 'semantic atom' of our language, i.e., a situation $x, U, \mathcal{Q} : K$ quantifies across *points* (the elements of U), $\Box$ quantifies 'downward' across *sets* (within $\mathcal{Q}$), and $\boxplus$ quantifies across certain *systems of sets* (the 'refinements' of $\mathcal{Q}$ contained in $\mathfrak{S}$).
3. The above semantics appears to make a three-dimensional language out of $\mathcal{L}$; cf [12]. But, appearances are deceptive here since the components of situations are not independent of each other.
4. According to Definition 2, every set system frame $\mathfrak{F} = (X, \mathfrak{S})$ gives rise to a usual tri-modal Kripke frame $\mathcal{F} = (W, R_1, R_2, R_3)$ in the following way:
   - $W := \mathcal{S}_{\mathfrak{F}}$,
   - $(x, U, \mathcal{Q}) R_1 (x', U', \mathcal{Q}') : \iff U = U'$ and $\mathcal{Q} = \mathcal{Q}'$,
   - $(x, U, \mathcal{Q}) R_2 (x', U', \mathcal{Q}') : \iff x = x'$, $U \supseteq U'$ and $\mathcal{Q} = \mathcal{Q}'$, and
   - $(x, U, \mathcal{Q}) R_3 (x', U', \mathcal{Q}') : \iff x = x'$, $U = U'$ and $\mathcal{Q} \subseteq \mathcal{Q}'$.

The accessibility relation R_1 of this frame corresponds to the operator K, R_2 to $\Box$, and R_3 to $\boxplus$.

Furthermore, a Kripke model $\mathcal{M} = (\mathcal{F}, \sigma)$ corresponding to an SSM $\mathfrak{M} = (\mathfrak{F}, V)$ can be defined by

$$(x, U, \mathcal{Q}) \in \sigma(A) : \iff x \in V(A),$$

for all proposition letters A. Then we have that both

$$(x, U, \mathcal{Q}) R_2 (x', U', \mathcal{Q}') \Rightarrow ((x, U, \mathcal{Q}) \in \sigma(p) \iff (x', U', \mathcal{Q}') \in \sigma(p))$$

and

$$(x, U, \mathcal{Q}) R_3 (x', U', \mathcal{Q}') \Rightarrow ((x, U, \mathcal{Q}) \in \sigma(p) \iff (x', U', \mathcal{Q}') \in \sigma(p))$$

are satisfied for $\mathcal{M}$, due to the first clause of Definition 2; cf item 1 of this remark. Moreover, we have that

$$x, U, \mathcal{Q} \models_{\mathfrak{M}} \alpha \iff \mathcal{M}, (x, U, \mathcal{Q}) \models \alpha$$

holds for all $\alpha \in \text{WFF}$ and $(x, U, \mathcal{Q}) \in \mathcal{S}_{\mathfrak{F}}$.

We now turn to valid formulas. The general validity of the formula schema $K\Box\alpha \to \Box K\alpha$ is typical of TOPOLOGIC. This schema was called the *Cross Axiom* in the paper [4]. It can easily be seen that the Cross Axiom remains valid in every SSM, too. The same is true for *all* the axioms of TOPOLOGIC (see Axioms 1 – 10 below). Now, the question comes up naturally whether this list can be supplied in such a way that an axiomatization of the set of all $\mathcal{L}$-validities results. The following candidates suggest themselves: $\boxplus\Box\alpha \to \Box\boxplus\alpha$ and $\boxplus K\alpha \leftrightarrow K\boxplus\alpha$, where $\alpha \in \text{WFF}$. For a start, we get that these schemata are in fact valid in every SSM.

Proposition 1. *Let $\mathfrak{M}$ be any SSM and $\alpha \in$ WFF a formula. Then,*

$$\mathfrak{M} \models \boxplus\Box\alpha \to \Box\boxplus\alpha \quad \text{and} \quad \mathfrak{M} \models \boxplus K\alpha \leftrightarrow K\boxplus\alpha.$$

Thus, we have that the operators K and $\boxplus$ are fully interchangeable, whereas K and $\Box$ as well as $\boxplus$ and $\Box$ can be interchanged 'only in one direction'. Actually, the interaction between $\boxplus$ and $\Box$ turns out to be a bit more intricate than displayed by the first schema from Proposition 1, as we shall see below.

3 The New Logic

Our starting point to this section is the system of axioms for TOPOLOGIC from [4]. For convenience of the reader, some comments on the meaning of these axioms are given. We then add the schemata which the new modality is involved in. The resulting list proves to be sound with respect to the class of all SSMs. Later on in this section, we show that our proposal of axioms is even sufficient for completeness. – The just mentioned axiomatization of TOPOLOGIC reads as follows:

1. All instances of propositional tautologies
2. $K(\alpha \to \beta) \to (K\alpha \to K\beta)$
3. $K\alpha \to \alpha$
4. $K\alpha \to KK\alpha$
5. $L\alpha \to KL\alpha$
6. $(A \to \Box A) \wedge (\Diamond A \to A)$
7. $\Box(\alpha \to \beta) \to (\Box\alpha \to \Box\beta)$
8. $\Box\alpha \to \alpha$
9. $\Box\alpha \to \Box\Box\alpha$
10. $K\Box\alpha \to \Box K\alpha$,

where $A \in$ PROP and $\alpha, \beta \in$ WFF. In this way, it is expressed that for every Kripke model validating these axioms

- the accessibility relation $\xrightarrow{K}$ belonging to the knowledge operator is an equivalence,
- the accessibility relation $\xrightarrow{\Box}$ belonging to the effort operator is reflexive and transitive,
- proposition letters are stable with respect to $\xrightarrow{\Box}$ (see Remark 1.1 above), and
- the relations for knowledge and effort commute as described by Axiom 10.

One can see from items 11 – 14, and 17, of the following second group of axioms that the improvement operator shares, in particular, all the stability, S4, and commutativity properties, respectively, with the effort operator $\Box$.

11. $(A \to \boxplus A) \wedge (\oplus A \to A)$
12. $\boxplus(\alpha \to \beta) \to (\boxplus\alpha \to \boxplus\beta)$

13. $\boxplus \alpha \to \alpha$
14. $\boxplus \alpha \to \boxplus \boxplus \alpha$
15. $\boxplus \Box \alpha \to \Box \boxplus \alpha$
16. $\oplus \Box \alpha \to \Box \oplus \alpha$
17. $\boxplus K \alpha \leftrightarrow K \boxplus \alpha$,

where $A \in \mathrm{PROP}$ and $\alpha, \beta \in \mathrm{WFF}$. – Note that we encountered Axioms 15 and 17 already in Proposition 1. Axiom 16, corresponding to a certain confluence property of the relations $\xrightarrow{\Box}$ and $\xrightarrow{\boxplus}$, was implicitly announced at the end of Section 2. The way all these axioms work will become apparent in the course of the proof of completeness below.

A logical system called T^+, indicating *extended* TOPOLOGIC, is obtainable from the above list by adding the standard proof rules from modal logic, viz *modus ponens* and *necessitation with respect to each modality*.

Definition 3 (The logic). *Let T^+ be the smallest set of formulas containing the axiom schemata 1 – 17 and closed under application of the following rules:*

$$(\text{MODUS PONENS}) \quad \frac{\alpha \to \beta, \alpha}{\beta} \qquad (\Delta\text{-NECESSITATION}) \quad \frac{\alpha}{\Delta \alpha},$$

where $\alpha, \beta \in \mathrm{WFF}$ and $\Delta \in \{K, \Box, \boxplus\}$.

The following result is one of the main issues of this paper.

Theorem 1 (Soundness and completeness). *A formula $\alpha \in \mathrm{WFF}$ is valid in all SSMs, iff it is T^+-derivable.*

The soundness part of Theorem 1 is easy to prove. Thus we need not go into that in more detail.

For the remainder of this section, we outline the proof of completeness. Let $\alpha \in \mathrm{WFF}$ be not T^+-derivable. We can get to an SSM falsifying α by an infinite 'three-dimensional' step-by-step construction. In each step, an approximation to the final model is defined. In order to ensure that this 'limit structure' behaves as desired, several requirements on the intermediate models have to be kept under control.

Let us now turn to some details of the construction. Let $\mathcal{C}$ be the set of all maximal T^+-consistent sets of formulas, and

$$\xrightarrow{K}, \xrightarrow{\Box}, \text{ and } \xrightarrow{\boxplus},$$

the distinguished accessibility relations on $\mathcal{C}$ induced by the modalities $K, \Box$ and $\boxplus$, respectively. Suppose that $\Gamma_0 \in \mathcal{C}$ is to be realized (i.e., Γ_0 contains $\neg \alpha$). We choose a denumerably infinite set of points, Y, fix an element $x_0 \in Y$, and construct inductively a sequence of quintuples $(X_n, \Sigma_n, \sigma_n, \delta_n, s_n)$ such that, for every $n \in \mathbb{N}$,

- $X_n \subseteq Y$ is a finite set containing x_0;
- Σ_n is a finite set of finite trees, which is itself a finite tree with respect to the 'is isomorphically embeddable'-relation, denoted $\preccurlyeq$;
- σ_n is a function selecting exactly one element, designated P_n, from Σ_n;
- δ_n is a finite set of mappings, $\delta_n = \{d_P \mid P \in \Sigma_n\}$, such that, for all $P, Q \in \Sigma_n$:
  - $d_P : P \longrightarrow \mathcal{P}(X_n)$,
  - $d_P(p_P) = X_n$, where p_P denotes the root of P,
  - $p \leq q \iff d_P(p) \supseteq d_P(q)$,[3] for all $p, q \in P$, and
  - $P \preccurlyeq Q \iff \operatorname{Im}(d_P) \subseteq \operatorname{Im}(d_Q)$;
- $s_n : X_n \times P_n \times \Sigma_n \longrightarrow \mathcal{C}$ is a partial function such that, whenever $x, y \in X_n$, $p, q \in P_n$ and $P, Q \in \Sigma_n$, then
  - $s_n(x, p, P)$ is defined, iff $x \in d_{P_n}(p)$ and $P_n \preccurlyeq P$; in this case it holds that
    * if $y \in d_{P_n}(p)$, then $s_n(x, p, P) \xrightarrow{K} s_n(y, p, P)$,
    * if $p \leq q$, then $s_n(x, p, P) \xrightarrow{\square} s_n(x, q, P)$, and
    * if $P \preccurlyeq Q$, then $s_n(x, p, P) \xrightarrow{\boxplus} s_n(x, p, Q)$;
  - $s_n(x_0, p_{P_0}, P_0) = \Gamma_0$.

We explain next to what extent the intermediate structures $(X_n, \Sigma_n, \sigma_n, \delta_n, s_n)$ approximate the desired model. Actually, it can be guaranteed that, for all $n \in \mathbb{N}$,

- $X_n \subseteq X_{n+1}$;
- Σ_{n+1} differs from Σ_n in at most one element P', which is
  - either an *end extension* of $(P_n, \leq)$ (i.e., a super-structure of $(P_n, \leq)$ such that no element of $P' \setminus P_n$ is strictly smaller than some element of P_n)
  - or an isomorphic copy of P_n that is disjoint from P_l for all $l \leq n$;
  in the first case we have that $\Sigma_{n+1} = (\Sigma_n \setminus \{P_n\}) \cup \{P'\}$, and in the second case $\Sigma_{n+1} = \Sigma_n \cup \{P'\}$;
- $d_{P'}(p) \cap X_n = d_{P_n}(p)$, for every $p \in P_n$ (where we have identified p and its copy in the second case of the previous item);
- $s_{n+1} \mid_{X_n \times P_n \times \Sigma_n} = s_n$, and $s_{n+1}(x, p, P') = s_n(x, p, P_n)$ in the first case of the last but one item ($x \in X_n$ and $p \in P_n$).

Furthermore, the construction complies with the following 'existential obligations':

- if $L\beta \in s_n(x, p, P)$, then there are $n < k \in \mathbb{N}$ and $y \in d_P(p)$ (where $d_P \in \delta_k$) such that $\beta \in s_k(y, p, P)$,
- if $\lozenge\beta \in s_n(x, p, P)$, then there are $n < k \in \mathbb{N}$ and $q \in P_k$ such that $p \leq q$ and $\beta \in s_k(x, q, P)$, and
- if $\oplus\beta \in s_n(x, p, P)$, then there are $n < k \in \mathbb{N}$ and $Q \in \Sigma_k$ such that $P \preccurlyeq Q$ and $\beta \in s_k(x, p, Q)$.

Let us assume for the moment that the construction has been carried out successfully, meeting all these requirements. Let $(X, \Sigma, \sigma, \delta, s)$ be the *limit* of the structures $(X_n, \Sigma_n, \sigma_n, \delta_n, s_n)$, i.e.,

---

[3] To facilitate readability, we suppress some indices, eg, the index 'P' to $\leq$.

- $X = \bigcup_{n \in \mathbb{N}} X_n$;
- Σ consists of all elements of the form $\bigcup \mathcal{I}$, where $\mathcal{I}$ is a maximal chain of elements of the intermediate sets Σ_n (with respect to the substructure relation);
- σ is a function selecting exactly one element from Σ;[4]
- δ is a set of mappings, $\delta = \{d_P \mid P \in \Sigma\}$, such that, for all $P \in \Sigma$,
  - $d_P : P \longrightarrow \mathcal{P}(X)$ and, for all $p \in P$,
  - $d_P(p) = \bigcup_{m \geq n} d_{P_m}(p)$, where n is the smallest number l such that $d_l(p)$ is defined and P is an end extension of P_l;
- s is given by $s(x, p, P) := s_n(x, p, P_n)$, where n is the smallest number l such that $s_l(x, p, P_l)$ is defined and P an end extension of P_l ($x \in X$ and $p \in P$).

Let $\mathfrak{S} := \{\operatorname{Im}(d_P) \mid d_P \in \delta\}$ and $\mathfrak{F} := (X, \mathfrak{S})$. We define an $\mathfrak{F}$-valuation V by

$$V(A) := \{x \in X \mid A \in s(x, p_{P_0}, P_0)\},$$

for all $A \in \text{PROP}$. Then, $\mathfrak{M} := (X, \mathfrak{S}, V)$ is an SSM. Moreover, as the mappings d_P and s, respectively, satisfy 'global' counterparts of the above 'local' conditions, the following *Truth Lemma* can be proved just as Lemma 2.5 of the paper [4], i.e., by induction on the structure of formulas.

Lemma 1 (Truth Lemma). *For every formula $\beta \in \text{WFF}$ and situation*

$$x, d_P(p), \operatorname{Im}(d_P), \text{ where } p \in P,$$

of the frame $\mathfrak{F}$, we have that

$$x, d_P(p), \operatorname{Im}(d_P) \models_\mathfrak{M} \beta \text{ iff } \beta \in s(x, p, P).$$

Letting x_0 and Γ_0 be as above, $P_0 := \{p_{P_0}\}$, $s_0(x_0, p_{P_0}, P_0) := \Gamma_0$, $\beta := \neg\alpha$, $x := x_0$, and $P \in \Sigma$ any extension of P_0, then Theorem 1 follows immediately from that.

It remains to define $(X_n, \Sigma_n, \sigma_n, \delta_n, s_n)$, for all $n \in \mathbb{N}$. The case $n = 0$ has, essentially, just been given. If $n \geq 1$, then some existential formula contained in some maximal T^+-consistent set $s_m(x, p, P)$, where $m < n$, is to be realized in a way meeting all the above requirements. In order to ensure that all possible cases are eventually exhausted, processing has to be suitably scheduled with regard to the modalities involved. This can be done by means of appropriate enumerations.

Apart from the difficulties in book-keeping arising from that, the concrete implementation of the separate steps is rather lengthy and not carried out here thus. However, we discuss some of the principles being fundamental to this part of the proof in the following. Actually, we confine ourselves to those arising from Axioms 15 – 17. Let $\mathcal{C}$ be the set of all maximal T^+-consistent sets of formulas, as above.

---

[4] This component is not really needed, but quoted here in order to have the limit structured like the approximations.

Proposition 2. *Let $\Gamma_1, \Gamma_2, \Gamma_3 \in \mathcal{C}$ satisfy $\Gamma_1 \xrightarrow{\square} \Gamma_2 \xrightarrow{\boxplus} \Gamma_3$. Then, there exists $\Gamma \in \mathcal{C}$ such that $\Gamma_1 \xrightarrow{\boxplus} \Gamma \xrightarrow{\square} \Gamma_3$.*

Proposition 2 is a consequence of Axiom 15.[5]

The statement from Proposition 2 can easily be visualized as a certain diagram property. In fact, the proposition says that drawing $\xrightarrow{\square}$-arrows horizontally and $\xrightarrow{\boxplus}$-arrows vertically, a 'rectangle' with correspondingly annotated vertices can be completed out of its 'right upper triangle'

$$\Gamma_1 \xrightarrow{\square} \Gamma_2$$
$$\downarrow \boxplus$$
$$\Gamma_3$$

by 'going round to the left'. A similar diagram property is associated with Axiom 16, but the starting point is now some 'left upper triangle' (i.e., we have a certain *Church-Rosser property*). This is the content of the next proposition.

Proposition 3. *Let $\Gamma_1, \Gamma_2, \Gamma_3 \in \mathcal{C}$ satisfy $\Gamma_1 \xrightarrow{\square} \Gamma_2$ and $\Gamma_1 \xrightarrow{\boxplus} \Gamma_3$. Then, there exists $\Gamma \in \mathcal{C}$ such that $\Gamma_2 \xrightarrow{\boxplus} \Gamma$ and $\Gamma_3 \xrightarrow{\square} \Gamma$.*

Turning to Axiom 17, we find the same situation as in the last but one case. However, the double-arrow has to be taken into account now. Consequently, the assertion of the next proposition splits up into two parts.

Proposition 4. *1. Let $\Gamma_1, \Gamma_2, \Gamma_3 \in \mathcal{C}$ satisfy $\Gamma_1 \xrightarrow{K} \Gamma_2 \xrightarrow{\boxplus} \Gamma_3$. Then, there exists $\Gamma \in \mathcal{C}$ such that $\Gamma_1 \xrightarrow{\boxplus} \Gamma \xrightarrow{K} \Gamma_3$.*

2. Let $\Gamma_1, \Gamma_2, \Gamma_3 \in \mathcal{C}$ satisfy $\Gamma_1 \xrightarrow{\boxplus} \Gamma_2 \xrightarrow{K} \Gamma_3$. Then, there exists $\Gamma \in \mathcal{C}$ such that $\Gamma_1 \xrightarrow{K} \Gamma \xrightarrow{\boxplus} \Gamma_3$.

Propositions 2 – 4 are, in fact, applied at decisive points of the inductive definition of $(X_n, \Sigma_n, \sigma_n, \delta_n, s_n)$. These guarantee that every time the new objects can be inserted coherently in the model constructed so far.

All in all, the completeness part of Theorem 1 is finally yielded in this way.

4 Concluding Remarks

It remains to summarize the outcome of this paper, point to some open problems, and finish off the discussion on the comparison of topologies started in the introduction.

Just to sum up, we added an operator modelling *improvement* to the language of TOPOLOGIC. This operator was interpreted in spaces of set systems,

---

[5] The detailed proof of Proposition 2 is omitted here, and the same is the case with the subsequent propositions.

representing sets of knowledge states of an agent. We determined the logic of such structures by providing a sound and complete axiomatization of the set of all validities.

Actually, the present paper marks only the very beginning of the study of *extended* TOPOLOGIC, T^+. Though our results are quite promising, a lot of basic work has still to be done. The next question to tackle is the *decidability problem* for T^+.

To round off the paper, we have to say a few words more about the comparison of topologies. As we pointed out in Sec. 1, the modality ⊞, viewed topologically, acts as a *refinement operator*. Now, for a real comparison we must also have a 'coarsening operator' at our disposal. And we would have to study the interplay between refinement and coarsening. Maybe the picture here turns out to look similar to that of TOPOLOGIC where the basic nature of *shrinking* and *extending* the knowledge state, respectively, proved to be different; cf [13].

References

1. Fagin, R., Halpern, J.Y., Moses, Y., Vardi, M.Y.: Reasoning about Knowledge. MIT Press, Cambridge, MA (1995)
2. Meyer, J.J.C., van der Hoek, W.: Epistemic Logic for AI and Computer Science. Volume 41 of Cambridge Tracts in Theoretical Computer Science. Cambridge University Press, Cambridge (1995)
3. Moss, L.S., Parikh, R.: Topological reasoning and the logic of knowledge. In Moses, Y., ed.: Theoretical Aspects of Reasoning about Knowledge (TARK 1992), San Francisco, CA, Morgan Kaufmann (1992) 95–105
4. Dabrowski, A., Moss, L.S., Parikh, R.: Topological reasoning and the logic of knowledge. Annals of Pure and Applied Logic **78** (1996) 73–110
5. Heinemann, B.: A spatio-temporal view of knowledge. In Russell, I., Markov, Z., eds.: Proceedings 18th International Florida Artificial Intelligence Research Society Conference (FLAIRS 2005). Recent Advances in Artificial Intelligence, Menlo Park, CA, AAAI Press (2005) 703–708
6. Blackburn, P., de Rijke, M., Venema, Y.: Modal Logic. Volume 53 of Cambridge Tracts in Theoretical Computer Science. Cambridge University Press, Cambridge (2001)
7. Blackburn, P.: Representation, reasoning, and relational structures: a hybrid logic manifesto. Logic Journal of the IGPL **8** (2000) 339–365
8. Bourbaki, N.: General Topology, Part 1. Hermann, Paris (1966)
9. Georgatos, K.: Knowledge theoretic properties of topological spaces. In Masuch, M., Pólos, L., eds.: Knowledge Representation and Uncertainty, Logic at Work. Volume 808 of Lecture Notes in Artificial Intelligence., Springer (1994) 147–159
10. Georgatos, K.: Knowledge on treelike spaces. Studia Logica **59** (1997) 271–301
11. Weiss, M.A., Parikh, R.: Completeness of certain bimodal logics for subset spaces. Studia Logica **71** (2002) 1–30
12. Gabbay, D.M., Kurucz, A., Wolter, F., Zakharyaschev, M.: Many-dimensional Modal Logics: Theory and Applications. Volume 148 of Studies in Logic and the Foundation of Mathematics. Elsevier (2003)
13. Heinemann, B.: Linear tense logics of increasing sets. Journal of Logic and Computation **12** (2002) 583–606

Belief Revision Revisited

Ewa Madalińska-Bugaj[1] and Witold Łukaszewicz[2]

[1] Institute of Informatics, Warsaw University, Warsaw, Poland
[2] Dept. of Computer Science, Linköping University, Sweden and
College of Economics and Computer Science TWP, Olsztyn, Poland

Abstract. In this paper, we propose a new belief revision operator, together with a method of its calculation. Our formalization differs from most of the traditional approaches in two respects. Firstly, we formally distinguish between defeasible observations and indefeasible knowledge about the considered world. In particular, our operator is differently specified depending on whether an input formula is an observation or a piece of knowledge. Secondly, we assume that a new observation, but not a new piece of knowledge, describes exactly what a reasoning agent knows at the moment about the aspect of the world the observation concerns.

1 Introduction

Belief revision [1] is the task of modifying a reasoner's knowledge base when new information becomes available. More formally, given a knowledge base KB, representing the reasoner's belief set, and a piece of new information α, the task is to specify the new reasoner's knowledge base $KB * \alpha$. There are three important assumptions underlying belief revision. Firstly, it is supposed that the reasoner's knowledge base is incomplete and possibly incorrect. Secondly, the reasoner's environment is assumed to be static.[1] Thirdly, whenever a new piece of information is inconsistent with the current knowledge base, new information is considered more reliable than the knowledge base.[2]

The classical specification of belief revision has been proposed in [1] in the form of eight *rationality postulates*, known in the AI literature as AGM postulates. Two of them are of special interest in this paper.

(R1) If $KB \not\models \neg\alpha$, then $KB + \alpha \subseteq KB * \alpha$, where $KB + \alpha$ is the deductive closure of $KB \cup \{\alpha\}$.
(R2) If $KB_1 \equiv KB_2$, then $KB_1 * \alpha \equiv KB_2 * \alpha$.

The next example shows that the postulate (R1) is sometimes very problematic from the intuitive point of view.

Example 1. Watching TV yesterday, I learned that on the next Sunday there would be rain in Paris. So my knowledge base KB is $\{r\}$. Watching TV today, I have learned that on the next Sunday there will be rain or snow in Paris, i.e. $\alpha = r \vee s$. According

---

[1] There is another important form of belief change, called *belief update* [2]. In contrast to belief revision, it deals with dynamic settings, where a piece of new information is the result of a performed action.
[2] A comprehensive literature on the subject of belief revision can be found in [3].

to (R1), the resulting knowledge base, $KB * \alpha$, should contain r. However, intuition dictates that $KB * \alpha = Cn(r \vee s)$.[3] ∎

Note that when we say that the resulting knowledge base in Example 1 should be $Cn(r \vee s)$, we make an implicit assumption that a new observation is exactly what an agent knows at the moment about the aspect of the world the observation is concerned with. Thus, if a new observation is weaker than KB, KB should be weakened.[4]

Consider now the postulate (R2). At the first glance, it seems to be indisputable. However, as the following example illustrates, the situation is more subtle.

Example 2. Let $KB_1 = \{p, p \Rightarrow s\}$ and $\alpha = \neg p$, where p and s stand for "Tweety is a penguin" and "Tweety is a bird", respectively. Since the truth of s directly depends on the truth of p, intuition dictates that the resulting knowledge base is $KB*\alpha = Cn(\neg p)$.[5]

Consider now the knowledge base $KB_2 = \{p, s\}$ and $\alpha = \neg p$, where p and s stand for "Mr Smith is rich" and "Mr Jones is rich", respectively. In this case, $KB * \alpha$ should be $Cn(\neg p \wedge s)$. On the other hand, KB_1 and KB_2 are logically equivalent. ∎

Although KB_1 and KB_2 from Example 2 are logically equivalent, they differ significantly as regards the type of information they contain. Whereas facts like "Tweety is a bird" or "Mr Jones is rich" represent an agent's observations about the considered world, the sentence "If Tweety is a penguin, Tweety is a bird" represents rather the agent's knowledge about the world that can be used to draw conclusions from observations.[6]

Example 2 shows that we should distinguish between observations and a general knowledge about the world under consideration. And we should treat this knowledge as more reliable than an ordinary observation.

In this paper, we propose a new formalization of belief revision. It differs from the traditional approaches in two respects. Firstly, it is always assumed that new information describes exactly what a reasoning agent knows at the moment about the aspect of the world the observation concerns. Secondly, we formally distinguish between observations and knowledge about the considered world. More specifically, a knowledge base is not a set of formulae, but a pair of sets of formulae, $\langle OB, A \rangle$, where OB and A represent observations of an agent and its knowledge (i.e. domain axioms) about the world, respectively. Whereas observations have status of beliefs, i.e. they can be invalidated by a piece of new information, formulae representing the agent's knowledge about the world are assumed to be always true.

Domain axioms correspond closely to integrity constraints considered in the theory of data (knowledge) bases. However, there is a subtle difference between these notions.

---

[3] Here Cn stands for the consequence operator of classical propositional logic.

[4] In [4], we are presented with a new form of belief revision, called *conservative belief change*, where a similar assumption is made. The relationship between this approach and our proposal presented in the rest of this paper will be discussed in section 6.

[5] One can also argue that the resulting knowledge base should be represented in an equivalent form, namely $Cn(\neg p \wedge (p \Rightarrow s))$. This will make it possible to retrieve s, if the next piece of new information is p again.

[6] The term "observation" here means either an observation made directly by an agent or communicated to the agent by other sources.

Integrity constrains are usually assumed to be fixed and external with respect to a data base. Domain axioms, on the other hand, are considered as a part of a knowledge base and a new domain axiom can be learned by a reasoning agent. As we shall see later, $KB * \alpha$ should be differently specified depending on whether α is an observation or a new domain axiom.

The paper is structured as follows. In section 2, we provide preliminary definitions. In section 3, we formally describe our belief revision operator under the assumption that an input formula is a new observation. We also illustrate our proposal by considering a number of examples. In section 4, we specify our belief revision operator under the assumption that an input formula is a new domain axiom. In section 5, we shortly discuss our proposal in the context of AGM postulates. Section 6 is devoted to related work. Finally, section 7 contains concluding remarks and future work.

2 Preliminaries and Terminology

We deal with a propositional language with a finite set of propositional symbols, called atoms. We assume that each language under consideration contains two special atoms $\top$ and $\bot$, standing for truth and falsity, respectively. Formulae are built in the usual way using standard connectives $\wedge, \vee, \Rightarrow, \neg$ and $\Leftrightarrow$.

A formula of the form of p or $\neg p$, where p is an atom, is called a *literal*. Interpretations are identified with maximal consistent sets of literals. For any formula α, we write $\mid \alpha \mid$ to denote the set of all *models* of α. We use the symbol Cn to denote the consequence relation of classical propositional logic.

Let α be a formula. By $ATM(\alpha)$ we denote a set of all non-redundant atoms occurring in α. An atom p occurring in α is said to be redundant iff $\alpha[p \leftarrow \top] \equiv \alpha[p \leftarrow \bot] \equiv \alpha$[7].

Let p be an atom and suppose that α is a formula. We write $\exists p.\alpha$ to denote the formula $\alpha[p \leftarrow \top] \vee \alpha[p \leftarrow \bot]$. If $P = \{p_1, \ldots, p_n\}$ is a set of atoms and α is a formula, then $\exists P.\alpha$ stands for $\exists p_1 \cdots \exists p_n.\alpha$.

A formula of the form $\exists P.\alpha$, where $P = \{p_1, \ldots, p_n\}$, is called an *eliminant of* $\{p_1, \ldots, p_n\}$ *in* α. Intuitively, such an eliminant can be viewed as a formula representing the same knowledge as α about all atoms from $ATM(\alpha) - P$ and providing no information about the atoms in P. Formally, this property is stated by the following theorem [5].

Theorem 1. Let α and β be formulae such that

$$ATM(\beta) \subseteq (ATM(\alpha) - P), \text{ where } P = \{p_1, \ldots, p_n\}.$$

Then $\alpha \models \beta$ iff $(\exists P.\alpha) \models \beta$. ∎

A *clause* is a formula of the form $l_1 \vee \ldots \vee l_n$, $n \geq 1$, where l_i, $1 \leq i \leq n$, is a literal.

We say that a clause c' *absorbs* a clause c if c' is a subclause[8] of c. For instance, the clause a absorbs the clause $a \vee l$. Let α be a formula in conjunctive normal form (*CNF*).

---

[7] $\alpha[p \leftarrow \top]$ (resp. $\alpha[p \leftarrow \bot]$) is the formula obtained from α by replacing all occurrences of p by $\top$ (resp. $\bot$).

[8] A clause c' is a subclause of c iff c' entails c, but not vice versa.

We write $ABS(\alpha)$ to denote the formula obtained from α by deleting all absorbed clauses. Clearly, α and $ABS(\alpha)$ are equivalent.

Two clauses are said to have an *opposition* if one of them contains a literal l and the other the literal $\neg l$.

Suppose that two clauses, c_1 and c_2, have exactly one opposition. Then the *resolvent* of c_1 and c_2, written $res(c_1, c_2)$, is the clause obtained from the disjunction $c_1 \vee c_2$ by deleting the opposed literals as well as any repeated literals. For example, $res(\neg a \vee l, a \vee d)$ is $l \vee d$.

Definition 1. Let α be a formula. We say that a clause c is a prime implicate of α iff

(i) $\alpha \Rightarrow c$ is a tautology;
(ii) there is no clause c' which is a subclause of c and $\alpha \Rightarrow c'$ is a tautology. ∎

Algorithm 2. Let α be a formula. The *prime implicates form of* α, written $PIF(\alpha)$, is the formula obtained from α by the following construction.

1. Let β be the conjunctive normal form of α.
2. Repeat as long as possible:
   if β contains a pair c and c' of clauses whose resolvent exists and no clause of β is a subclause of $res(c, c')$, then $\beta := \beta \wedge res(c, c')$.
3. Take $ABS(\beta)$. This is $PIF(\alpha)$. ∎

The following result holds ([6]).

Theorem 2. Let α be a formula.

(i) $PIF(\alpha)$ is a conjunction of all prime implicates of α.
(ii) $PIF(\alpha)$ and α are equivalent.
(iii) All atoms occurring in $PIF(\alpha)$ are non-redundant. ∎

Let α and β be formulae. A *tail of* α and β, written $TL(\alpha, \beta)$, is the conjunction of those prime implicates of $\alpha \wedge \beta$ that are neither prime implicates of α nor prime implicates of β. Intuitively, $TL(\alpha, \beta)$ can be viewed as those additional conclusions which can be derived by combining α and β. The formula $TL(\alpha, \beta)$ can be constructed using the following algorithm.

Algorithm 3.

1. $\gamma := PIF(\alpha) \wedge PIF(\beta);\ TL(\alpha, \beta) := \top$.
2. Repeat as long as possible:
   if γ contains a pair c and c' of clauses whose resolvent exists and no clause of γ is a subclause of $res(c, c')$, then
   $\gamma := \gamma \wedge res(c, c')$;
   $TL(\alpha, \beta) := TL(\alpha, \beta) \wedge res(c, c')$.
3. $TL(\alpha, \beta) := ABS(TL(\alpha, \beta))$. ∎

3 Defining Belief Revision Operator

Definition 4. A knowledge base is a pair $KB = \langle OB, A \rangle$, where OB is a finite set of formulae, called observations, and A is a finite set of formulae, called domain axioms. In the sequel, we will never distinguish between finite sets of formulae and their conjunctions. In particular, both OB and A will be often considered as single formulae. Any knowledge base KB uniquely determines a belief set. This set, denoted by $Cn(KB)$, is the set $Cn(OB \wedge A)$. KB is said to be consistent iff $Cn(KB)$ is consistent. ∎

Now we define our revision operator $*$. There are two cases to consider.

1. New information is an ordinary observation.
2. New information is a new piece of knowledge.

In this section we consider the former of the above cases. The latter will be discussed in section 4.

We start with some intuitions underlying our approach. Suppose that $KB = \langle OB, A \rangle$ is a consistent knowledge base and α is a new observation. Recall that we make an implicit assumption that a new observation is exactly what is known at the moment about the aspect of the world it concerns. In particular, if a new observation is weaker than KB, KB should be suitably weakened. A natural way to achieve this goal is to delete all information concerning atoms occurring in α. This can be technically done using eliminants [9]. Denote the weakened observation formula by OB'. The formula $OB' \wedge \alpha$ is a natural candidate for the observation formula in the revised knowledge base $KB*\alpha$. It is easily seen that $OB' \wedge \alpha$ and $OB' \wedge A$ are both consistent. The problem, however, is that $OB' \wedge \alpha \wedge A$ may be not. If this is the case, OB' should be further weakened. Observe that the source of inconsistency can be new conclusions which can be derived from $A \wedge \alpha$. Note that these new conclusions are represented by $TL(A, \alpha)$. Therefore, we must delete information concerning atoms occurring in those conjuncts of $TL(A, \alpha)$ which are inconsistent with OB'. The resulting formula, strengthened by α, is the observation formula in the revised knowledge base $KB * \alpha$.

The above intuitions are formalized below.

Definition 5. Let $KB = \langle OB, A \rangle$ be a knowledge base and α be a new observation. The new knowledge base, $KB * \alpha$, is $\langle OB_1, A \rangle$, where OB_1 obtains from OB by the following construction.
Let $TL(A, \alpha) = c_1 \wedge \ldots \wedge c_n$.

(1) $P := ATM(\alpha)$;
(2) $OB' := \exists P.OB$;
(3) $R := \{\}$;
(4) for i:=1 to n do
 if $OB' \wedge c_i \equiv \bot$ then $R := R \cup ATM(c_i)$;
(5) $OB_1 := \alpha \wedge \exists R.OB'$. ∎

---

[9] Note that we cannot weaken KB by weakening A, because domain axioms represent knowledge about the world and hence cannot be invalidated.

3.1 Examples

The following examples illustrate an application of Definition 5 to compute $KB * \alpha$.

Example 3. Let $KB = \langle OB, A \rangle$ be a knowledge base, where $OB = p$ and $A = (p \Rightarrow s)$. Suppose further that a new observation is $\alpha = \neg p$. The new knowledge base is $KB_1 = \langle OB_1, A \rangle$, where OB_1 is computed in the following steps:[10]

- $ATM(\alpha) = \{p\}$.
- $OB' = \exists p.p \equiv \top$.
- $PIF(A) = \neg p \vee s$; $PIF(\alpha) = \neg p$.
- $TL(A, \alpha) = \top$.
- Since, after performing step (4), $R = \{\}$,
  $OB_1 = \alpha \wedge \top \equiv \neg p$.

Thus $Cn(KB * \alpha) = Cn(\neg p \wedge (p \Rightarrow s))$. Note that $Cn(KB * \alpha)$ does not contain s. ∎

Example 4. Let $KB = \langle OB, A \rangle$ be a knowledge base, where $OB = p \wedge s$ and $A = \{\}$. A new observation is $\alpha = \neg p$. The resulting knowledge base is $KB_1 = \langle OB_1, A \rangle$ where OB_1 is computed as follows.

- $ATM(\alpha) = \{p\}$.
- $OB' = \exists p.p \wedge s \equiv s$.
- $PIF(A) = \top$; $PIF(\alpha) = \neg p$.
- $TL(A, \alpha) = \top$.
- $OB_1 = \alpha \wedge OB' = \neg p \wedge s$.

Therefore $Cn(KB * \alpha) = Cn(\neg p \wedge s)$. Observe that according to our intuitions, s is a member of $Cn(KB * \alpha)$. ∎

Example 5. Let $KB = \langle OB, A \rangle$ be a knowledge base, where $OB = p$ and $A = (p \Rightarrow s)$ and let a new information α be $\neg s$. We compute OB_1.

- $ATM(\alpha) = \{s\}$.
- $OB' = \exists s.p \equiv p$.
- $PIF(\alpha) = \neg s$; $PIF(A) = \neg p \vee s$.
- $TL(A, \alpha) = \neg p$.
- After performing step (4), we get $R = \{p\}$.
- $OB_1 = \neg s \wedge \exists p.p \equiv \neg s$.

Thus, $Cn(KB * \alpha) = Cn(\neg s \wedge (p \Rightarrow s))$. Note that according to our intuitions p does not belong to $Cn(KB * \alpha)$. ∎

Example 6. Let $KB = \langle OB, A \rangle$ be a knowledge base, where $OB = p \wedge s$ and $A = (p \Rightarrow q) \wedge (q \Rightarrow r)$ and let a new observation α be $\neg q$. The computation of OB_1 is the following.

- $ATM(\alpha) = \{q\}$.
- $OB' = \exists q.p \wedge s \equiv p \wedge s$.

---
[10] We use the symbol '$\equiv$' as the meta symbol denoting that two formulae are equivalent.

- $PIF(\alpha) = \neg q;\ PIF(A) = (\neg p \vee q) \wedge (\neg q \vee r) \wedge (\neg p \vee r)$.
- $TL(A, \alpha) = \neg p$.
- After performing step (4), we get $R = \{p\}$.
- $OB_1 = ((\exists p.OB') \wedge \alpha) \equiv s \wedge \neg q$

$Cn(KB * \alpha) = Cn(s \wedge \neg q \wedge (p \Rightarrow q) \wedge (q \Rightarrow r))$. Observe that $\neg p$ is a member of $Cn(KB * \alpha)$. ∎

4 Absorbing New Knowledge

In this section we define revision operator under the assumption that an input formula α is a new piece of knowledge. To fix some intuitions, consider the following example.

Example 7. Let $KB = \langle \{b\}, \{\} \rangle$, where b stands for "Tweety is a black penguin". Suppose that I learned that penguins are always black or grey. This allows me to conclude that Tweety is black or grey, so a new piece of knowledge is $b \vee g$, where g stands for "Tweety is a grey penguin". Clearly, the resulting knowledge base should be $\langle \{b\}, \{b \vee g\} \rangle$ because learning that all penguins are black or grey I should not assume that my earlier observation that Tweety is black should be weakened. ∎

The above example illustrates that our definition of belief operator given in section 3 should be modified in the case when new information is a piece of knowledge. Even, as in this paper, if we assume that a new observation always gives us exact information about the aspect of the world it concerns, this assumption makes little sense in the context of a new domain axiom. The role of domain axioms is to put some constraints on the world under consideration, so the only observations that should be invalidated by domain axioms are those that are inconsistent with them.

Suppose that $KB = \langle OB, A \rangle$ is a consistent knowledge base and α is a new domain axiom. Denote the resulting knowledge base KB_1 by $\langle OB_1, A_1 \rangle$. Obviously, A_1 should be $A \wedge \alpha$. Now we would like to put $OB_1 := OB$. The problem, however, is that $OB \wedge A_1$ can be inconsistent. Since the original knowledge base KB is consistent, the source of inconsistency can be only α, i.e. conjuncts from $PIF(\alpha)$, and these new conclusions which can be derived from A and α, i.e. conjuncts from $TL(A, \alpha)$. Combining them together we receive $ABS(TL(A, \alpha) \wedge PIF(\alpha))$. Therefore, we must delete information concerning atoms occurring in those conjuncts of $ABS(TL(A, \alpha) \wedge PIF(\alpha))$ which are inconsistent with OB.

A formalization of above idea is given below.

Definition 6. Let $KB = \langle OB, A \rangle$ be a knowledge base and α be a new piece of knowledge. $KB * \alpha = \langle OB_1, A_1 \rangle$, where $A_1 = A \wedge \alpha$ and OB_1 is obtained from OB by the following construction.
Let $ABS(TL(A, \alpha) \wedge PIF(\alpha)) = c_1 \wedge \ldots \wedge c_n$.

(1) $P := \{\}$;
(2) for i:=1 to n do
    if $OB \wedge c_i \equiv \bot$ then $P := P \cup ATM(c_i)$;
(3) $OB_1 := \exists P.OB$. ∎

Notice that the above algorithm is a slight modification of steps (3)-(5) of algorithm presented in Definition 5. Note also that the resulting knowledge base $KB * \alpha$ is inconsistent if and only if the formula $A \wedge \alpha$ is inconsistent.

4.1 Examples

We now present a number of examples illustrating the construction from Definition 6.

Example 8. Let $KB = \langle OB, A \rangle$, where $OB = p \wedge q \wedge s$ and $A = (p \Rightarrow r)$. Suppose that $\alpha = (q \Rightarrow \neg s)$. The new knowledge base $KB * \alpha$ is $\langle OB_1, A_1 \rangle$, where $A_1 = (p \Rightarrow r) \wedge (q \Rightarrow \neg s)$ and OB_1 is computed as follows.

- $ABS(TL(A, \alpha) \wedge PIF(\alpha)) = (\neg q \vee \neg s)$.
- $OB \wedge (\neg q \vee \neg s) \equiv \bot$, so $OB_1 := \exists q, s.OB \equiv p$.

Thus, $Cn(KB * \alpha) = Cn(p \wedge (p \Rightarrow r) \wedge (q \Rightarrow \neg s))$. ∎

Example 9. Let $KB = \langle OB, A \rangle$, where OB is $(p \vee q) \wedge (s \vee r)$ and A is $p \Rightarrow r$. Assume that $\alpha = (q \Rightarrow \neg s)$. The new knowledge base $KB * \alpha$ is $\langle OB_1, A_1 \rangle$, where $A_1 = (p \Rightarrow r) \wedge (q \Rightarrow \neg s)$ and OB_1 is computed as follows.

- $ABS(TL(A, \alpha) \wedge PIF(\alpha)) = (\neg q \vee \neg s)$.
- $OB \wedge (\neg q \vee \neg s) \not\equiv \bot$, so $OB_1 := OB$.

Thus, $Cn(KB_1) = Cn((p \vee q) \wedge (s \vee r) \wedge (p \Rightarrow r) \wedge (q \Rightarrow \neg s)) \equiv Cn((p \vee q) \wedge r \wedge (\neg q \vee \neg s))$. ∎

Example 10. Let $KB = \langle OB, A \rangle$, where OB is $p \wedge s \wedge (q \vee r)$ and A is $p \Rightarrow r$. Let $\alpha = (r \Rightarrow \neg s)$. The new knowledge base $KB * \alpha$ is $\langle OB_1, A_1 \rangle$, where $A_1 = (p \Rightarrow r) \wedge (r \Rightarrow \neg s)$ and OB_1 is computed as follows.

- $ABS(TL(A, \alpha) \wedge PIF(\alpha)) = (\neg r \vee \neg s) \wedge (\neg p \vee \neg s)$.
- $OB \wedge (\neg r \vee \neg s) \not\equiv \bot$; $OB \wedge (\neg p \vee \neg s) \equiv \bot$. So, $OB_1 = \exists p, s.OB \equiv (q \vee r)$.

Thus, $Cn(KB_1) = Cn((q \vee r) \wedge (p \Rightarrow r) \wedge (r \Rightarrow \neg s))$. ∎

5 Postulates

In this section, we specify postulates for our revision operator. We start with some terminology and notation.

Definition 7. Let $KB_1 = \langle OB_1, A_1 \rangle$ and $KB_2 = \langle OB_2, A_2 \rangle$ be knowledge bases. We say that KB_1 and KB_2 are equivalent, denoted by $KB_1 \equiv KB_2$, iff $OB_1 \equiv OB_2$ and $A_1 \equiv A_2$. ∎

If X and α are formulae, then $X + \alpha$ stands for $Cn(X \wedge \alpha)$. If $KB = \langle OB, A \rangle$ is a knowledge base and α is a formula, then $KB + \alpha$ stands for $Cn(OB \wedge A \wedge \alpha)$. We write $KB \models \alpha$ iff $(OB \wedge A) \models \alpha$. KB_{OB} and KB_A denote the sets OB and A, respectively.

The following postulates, corresponding loosely to AGM postulates, hold for our revision operator.

(R1) $KB * \alpha$ is a belief set, i.e. $Cn(KB * \alpha) = KB * \alpha$.
(R2) $\alpha \in KB * \alpha$.
(R3) $KB * \alpha \subseteq KB + \alpha$.
(R4) If $KB \not\models \neg\alpha$ and $KB + \alpha \subseteq Cn((\exists ATM(\alpha).KB_{OB}) \wedge \alpha)$, then $KB + \alpha \subseteq KB * \alpha$.
(R5) $KB * \alpha$ is inconsistent iff $\{\alpha\} \cup KB_A$ is inconsistent.
(R6) If $KB_1 \equiv KB_2$, then $KB_1 * \alpha \equiv KB_2 * \alpha$.
(R7) If $ATM(\alpha) \subseteq ATM(\alpha \wedge \beta)$ and $KB \not\models \neg\alpha \vee \neg\beta$ then $KB * (\alpha \wedge \beta) \subseteq (KB * \alpha) + \beta$.
(R8) If $KB \not\models \neg\alpha \vee \neg\beta$ and $(KB * \alpha) + \beta \subseteq (\exists ATM(\alpha \wedge \beta).KB_{OB}) + (\alpha \wedge \beta)$, then $(KB * \alpha) + \beta \subseteq KB * (\alpha \wedge \beta)$.

The postulates (R1)-(R3) and (R6) are exactly the AGM postulates, whereas the remaining postulates are weaker forms of the AGM postulates.

6 Related Work

An important property of our formalization of belief revision is the assumption that a new observation is exactly what an agent knows at the moment about the aspect of the world the observation is concerned with. As we remarked earlier, this assumption is also made in [4], where an interesting formalization of belief revision, called *conservative belief revision* (CBR, for short), is presented. However there are two important differences between CBR and our formalization.

(i) The semantics for CBR is based on Grove's system of spheres ([7]), originally developed for AGM-revision. What typifies Grove's semantics is that the revision operator it defines depends on an ordering over all interpretations (of the considered language) signifying their level of plausibility. In consequence, CBR is not a single belief revision operator, but rather a class of such operators. The problem, of course, is that it is not clear which of them should be chosen in practical applications. Our formalization, on the other hand, provides a unique belief revision operator.

(ii) In contrast to our approach, CBR does not distinguishes between defeasible observations and knowledge about the considered world. As we argued earlier, such distinction is important, because observations are subject to invalidation, whereas knowledge is not.

In [8], a belief update operator, called MPMA, has been defined. As the belief revision operator specified here, MPMA is heavily influenced by the notion of an eliminant. However, there is a crucial difference between these formalisms due to the general difference between belief revision and belief update. As we stated earlier, belief revision is based on the assumptions that a world being modelled is static and beliefs describing a reasoner's environment may be incorrect. In belief update, on the other hand, we assume that a piece of new information represents an effect of a performed action and the current set of the reasoner's beliefs is correct (see [2]). This distinction manifests clearly in the presence of domain axioms (called integrity constraints in MPMA). The next example illustrate this.

Example 11. Let $KB = \langle OB, A \rangle$, where $OB = w$ and $A = (w \Rightarrow a)$ (here a and w stand for "a turkey is alive" and " a turkey is walking"). Thus, $Cn(KB)$ contains $w \wedge a$. Assume that a piece of new information α is $\neg w$. If KB is considered from the belief revision perspective, the resulting knowledge base should be $\neg w$, because there is no reason to believe a when w has turned out to be false. On the other hand, if KB is considered from the update perspective, the resulting knowledge base should be $\neg w \wedge a$, because there is no reason to conclude that an action that have made the turkey non-walking made it dead. ∎

7 Conclusions and Future Work

We have presented a new belief revision operator. Our approach assumes that a new observation provides exact information about the aspect of the considered world it concerns. Also, we formally distinguish between defeasible observations and indefeasible knowledge about the considered world.

There are three topics that we left for further research.

(1) Our belief revision operator has been specified syntactically. It would be interesting to provide its semantical characterization.
(2) A dual notion to belief revision is belief contraction. This is a task of specifying a new knowledge base under the assumption that some beliefs are retracted but no new beliefs are added. It seems that the notion of an eliminant provides a very natural basis to solve this task.
(3) AGM postulates do not address the issue of iterated belief revision [9]. On the other hand, in practical applications we are interested in a sequence of belief revisions rather, than in a single one. It would be interesting to investigate our belief operator in this context.

References

1. Alchourrón, C.E., Gärdenfors, P., Makinson, D.: On the logic theory change: Partial meet contraction and revision functions. Journal of Symbolic Logic **50** (1985) 510–530
2. Katsuno, H., Mendelzon, A.O.: On the difference between updating a knowledge base and revising it. In: Proceedings of the 2nd International Conference on Principles of Knowledge Representation and Reasoning. (1991) 387–394
3. Delgrande, J.P., Schaub, T.: A consistency-based approach for belief change. Artificial Intelligence Journal **151** (2003) 1–41
4. Delgrande, J.P., Nayak, A.C., Pagnucco, M.: Gricean belief change. Studia Logica (2004) To appear. Electronic version can be found at http://www.cs.sfu.ca/ jim/publications.html.
5. Brown, F.M.: Boolean Reasoning. Kluwer Academic Publishers (1990)
6. Quine, W.: A way to simplify truth functions. American Mathematical Monthly **62** (1955) 627–631
7. Grove, A.: Two modellings for theory change. Journal of Philosophical Logic **17** (1988) 157–170
8. Doherty, P., Łukaszewicz, W., Madalinska-Bugaj, E.: The PMA and relativizing minimal change for action update. Fundamenta Informaticae **44** (2000) 95–131
9. Darwiche, A., Pearl, J.: On the logic of iterated revision. Artificial Intelligence Journal **89** (1997) 1–29

Knowledge and Reasoning Supported by Cognitive Maps

Alejandro Peña[1,2,3], Humberto Sossa[3], and Agustin Gutiérrez[3]

[1] WOLNM, [2] UPIICSA & [3] CIC – [2,3] National Polytechnic Institute,
31 Julio 1859, # 1099-B, Leyes Reforma, DF, 09310, México
apenaa@ipn.mx, {hsossa, atornes}@cic.ipn.mx

Abstract. A powerful and useful approach for modeling knowledge and qualitative reasoning is the *Cognitive Map*. The background of Cognitive Maps is the research about learning environments carried out by Cognitive Psychology since the nineteenth century. Along the last thirty years, these underlying findings inspired the development of computational models to deal with causal phenomena. So, a Cognitive Map is a structure of concepts of a specific domain that are related through cause-effect relations with the aim to simulate behavior of dynamic systems. In spite of the short life of the causal Cognitive Maps, nowadays there are several branches of development that focus on qualitative, fuzzy and uncertain issues. With this platform wide spectra of applications have been developing in fields like game theory, information analysis and management sciences. Wherefore, with the purpose to promote the use of this kind of tool, in this work is surveyed three branches of Cognitive Maps; and it is outlined one application of the Cognitive Maps for the student modeling that shows a conceptual design of a project in progress.

1 Introduction

Causal knowledge and reasoning involves many interacting concepts that make them difficult to face, and for which analytical techniques are inadequate [1]. In this case, techniques stemmed from qualitative reasoning, can be used to cope with this kind of knowledge. Thus, a Cognitive Map (CM) is a tool suitable for dealing with interacting concepts. Generally, the underlying elements of the CM are simple. The entities, factors and events of the domain model are outlined as concepts. The causal influences between these concepts are considered as cause-effects relations. So, a CM is graphically depicted as a digraph, where the nodes represent the concepts, the arcs correspond to the causal relations and the direction pictured by the arrow of the arc shows the causation of the target by the source.

In general, there are three basic types of causal influences: positive, negative and neutral. The positive means that the source concept stimulates in a direct way the state of the target concept, so when the intensity of the cause concept grows a positive stimulus is trigged to enhance the state of the effect concept, but if the active level of the source concept diminishes then a negative influence is produced on the target concept to decrease its state.

The negative causal influence operates in an inversely way to the positive. So a promotion in the values of the source concept leads to a decrease in the target concept state; and a decrease in the cause concept produces a raise in the effect concept.

Finally, the neutral causal influence means that no matter the changes of state that happen in the source concept, they are not going to influence in any way to the target concept; or that there is no a causal relation between this couple of concepts.

As regards the kind of CM adopted, the causal influences are outlined by: a set of symbols, a set of crisp values, real values in a continuous range, linguistic variables, probabilistic estimations, or bipolar values. Thus, the basic form to depict the values is by means of the set of symbols {+, -, 0}, which corresponds to positive, negative and neutral causal influences respectively. This set of values is acknowledged by the acronym NPN (negative-positive-neutral). Wherefore, in order to storage and manipulate the causal influence values of a CM it is used an adjacency matrix (w), of size n (the number of concepts), whose entries show the value of the causal relation between the concepts. So, the entry w_{ij} contains the value of the causal influence depicted by the arc that comes from the source concept i to the target concept j.

Regarding the arcs and its arrows of a CM, two nodes i and j can be linked by a path in three kinds of causal relations: null, direct and indirect. The null causal relation means that there is no a possible path to join the nodes i and j. The direct causal relation corresponds to paths of length equal to one arc. A path with more than one arc, which includes at least one intermediate node different to i and j, depicts an indirect causal relation. So, a propagation of the causal effect is done by the syllogism hypothetic principle. In resume, in a CM two nodes i and j are linked by a null causal relation; or by one direct causal relation and/or at least one indirect causal relation.

With this baseline, three versions of a CM are depicted and two applications are outlined next. Thus, the organization of the paper is as follows: in the second section the causal, fuzzy and probabilistic models of a CM are sketched through the underlying formal model of the approach. In the third section it is described the use of two versions of a CM to depict the student modeling process stemmed by the learning experiences in a Web-based Education System. In these cases, the Student Model is the application responsible to fulfill an individual profile of the student in order to provide an adaptive student-centered service. In the conclusions section are presented some comments about the properties of a CM and the CM-based application, besides of identify further work regarding to the automatic generation of a CM.

2 Profile of Cognitive Maps

The research on spatial learning begins in the nineteenth century focus on orientation task in animals and human beings. However, was Tolman [2] in 1948, who called CM to the mental structure that storages and recalls the spatial knowledge. Next in 1955, Kelly introduces the Personal Construct Theory to depict an individual's multiple perspectives [3]. Afterwards, in 1976 Axelroad [3] states the computational version of a CM. Nowadays new work has been doing to face imprecise knowledge, uncertainty and fuzzy views of domain. So, along this section it is resumed the underlying concepts of three versions of a CM: causal, fuzzy and probabilistic.

2.1 Causal Cognitive Maps

The baseline of the Causal Cognitive Map (CCM) rests in the relational theory outlined by Axelroad [4] and Nakamura et al. [5], who work out in the fields of the international relations and the decisions support respectively. Thus, a CCM is a directed graph that represents an individual's beliefs with respect to the model domain that is defined as: *CM:= (C, A)*. Where *C* is the set of concepts pictured like vertices, and *A* is the set of causal relations, depicted like arcs, between the concepts.

The arrows are labeled by elements of the set $\delta:=\{+, -, 0, \oplus, \Theta, \pm, a, ?\}$ that means respectively: positive, negative, neutral, positive or neutral, negative or neutral, positive or negative, conflict, and positive, negative or neutral causal effect.

Four operators are defined on the set δ of causal relations. They are union (U), intersection (∩), sum (|) and multiplication (*). The laws of union and intersection are derived from: +, -, 0, ⊕, Θ, ±, a, ?; when they are considered as shorthands for: {+}, {-}, {0}, {0, +}, {0, -}, {+, -}, {}, {+, 0, -} respectively. The guidelines of these operators are outlined in the Table 1, where *C* is the set of concepts.

Table 1. Laws for the causal operators. Union (U), intersection (∩), sum (|) and multiplication (*), with *do* meaning *distributes over*.

U (union) and ∩ (intersection)			(sum)	* (multiplication)
	For any $x, y \in C$	For any $x, y \in C$
(1a) ⊕ = 0 U +	(2a) 0	y = y	(3a) + * y = y
(1b) Θ = 0 U -	(2b) a	y = a	(3b) 0 * y = 0, if y ≠ a
(1c) ± = + U -	(2c) y	y = y	(3c) a * y = a
(1d) ? = 0 U + U -	(2d) +	- = ?	(3d) - * - = +
(1e) a = + ∩ 0 = + ∩ - = 0 ∩ -	(2e)	do U	(3e) * do U
	(2f) x	y = y	x	(3f) x * y = y * x

The multiplication (*) operator estimates indirect causal effects, e.g., if a path from node *i* to node *j* has an intermediate node k, with the effects (i) -→ (k)-→(j); so it produces a positive indirect effect according to (3d). Whereas the sum (|) operator computes direct causal effects from different paths that link two nodes *i* and *j*; e.g., there is one path from *i* to *j* with negative total indirect effect and other path with positive total indirect effect, then the total direct effect is ?, according to law (2d).

The operators * and | can be lifted to matrices, as follows. Consider *A* and *B* as square valency matrices of size *n*. The addition and multiplication operators are defined by equations (1) and (2). The *nth* power of a square matrix *A*, for *n > 0* is defined in (3). Thus, the total effect of one concept on another is estimated by the total effect matrix A_t whose entry A_{ij} owns the total effect of *i* on *j*, according as (4). Due to the sum (|) operator is monotonic, there is a *k* such that represents the total causal effect from one concept on another, depicted by (5). This model for a CCM is based on an intuitive perspective with *ad hoc* rules, and lacks of a formal treatment of relations. Wherefore, it is advisable to review the proposal stated by Chaib-draa [6] to deal with this issues; his model has a precise semantics based on relation algebra and it has been used for qualitative decision-making and agent reasoning.

$$(A \mid B)_{ij} = A_{ij} \mid B_{ij}. \tag{1}$$

$$(A * B)_{ij} = (A_{i1} * B_{1j}) \mid ... \mid (A_{in} * B_{nj}). \tag{2}$$

$$A^1 := A; \text{ and } A^n := A * A^{n-1}.\tag{3}$$

$$A_t = A^1 \mid A^2 \mid A^3 \mid A^4 \mid \ldots.\tag{4}$$

$$A_t = A^1 \mid A^2 \mid A^3 \mid A^4 \mid \ldots \mid A^k.\tag{5}$$

2.2 Fuzzy Cognitive Maps

Kosko [7] in 1986 proposes the Fuzzy Cognitive Map (FCM) as a CM whose causal relations and concept values are defined by fuzzy knowledge. The arcs and nodes values are depicted by fuzzy membership functions that are associated to fuzzy sets. These functions translate real world values to qualitative measures of the concepts presence in a conceptual domain, by mean of crisp values of a set, as {0, 1} or {-1, 0, 1}, or a real values in a range, as [-1, 1]. Concepts with positive values indicate that the concept is strongly present. Values around zero mean the concept is practically inactive in the conceptual domain. Negative values outline negative states of presence of the concept. Whereas, positive, zero and negative arc values depict different gray levels of the causal influence from the source concept on the target concept. Thus, besides of the adjacency matrix for the fuzzy values of the causal relations, there is a vector concept used to describe along the time the values state of the concepts.

Once the FCM is depicted, a simulation process is activated to predict causal behavior. This process is carried out along discrete steps, where the values of the concept vector change, according to the fuzzy causal influences; whereas the values of the valency matrix remain fixed, unless the FCM has an adaptive behavior. So, with the aims to produce the initial values of the concept vector, real world domain values are estimated for feeding the fuzzy membership functions. Once it is depicted the initial concept vector, an iterative process begins at step time $t = 0$. In each cycle a new state for the concepts is computed by taking the normalize result of the sum of the inputs. At step t, the inputs to the concept i are estimated by the state values, at step $t = t-1$, of the nodes j with edges coming into i, multiplied by the corresponding weights w_{ij}. Due to a FCM is a qualitative model; a threshold function is applied to the result of the sum of the product of the inputs by the weights to normalize the concept values according to the set or range associated to the concept.

The formal representation of the state of a FCM is defined in formula (6), where C is the state concept vector, t is the iteration, u is the threshold function, s is the result of the sum of the inputs, and w_{ij} is the entry with the fuzzy value of the arc from concept j to concept i. Also, the equations (7) to (9) picture the threshold functions used to achieve respectively the sets {0, 1} and {-1, 0, 1}, and the range [-1, 1].

$$C_i(t) = u(s); \quad \text{where}: s = (\sum_{j=1}^{n} w_{ij} * C_j(t-1)).\tag{6}$$

$$u(s) = 0, \, s \leq 0; \quad u(s) = 1, \, s > 0.\tag{7}$$

$$u(s) = -1, s \leq -0.5; u(s) = 0, s > -0.5 \wedge s < 0.5; u(s) = 1, s \geq 0.5. \quad (8)$$

$$u = 1/(1+e^{-cs}). \quad (9)$$

where, according to Mohr [8], c is critical in determining the degree of fuzzification of the function, due to at large values, the logistic signal function approaches discrete threshold functions, so a $c=5$ value is advisable.

Stability in dynamic systems, as a FCM, is typically analyzed through the use of Lyapunov functions. Thus, a FCM with discrete threshold functions, as (7) or (8), will either converge to a limit cycle or reach an equilibrium state, due to these functions force fuzzy state vectors to non-fuzzy values. Whereas, a FCM using the logistic signal threshold function, as (9), may become nonlinear under some conditions of feedback. Since the state vector of the map at time t is determined by its values at time $t-1$, the equilibrium state of a FCM may be easily detected by comparing two successive patterns of states concepts, composed by one or more state vectors. If they are identical, then the map has reached an equilibrium state and the execution ends.

In despite of the single inference mechanism of a FCM, the outcomes achieved by the FCM can be non-linear, and the problem of finding whether a state is reachable in the FCM simulation is nondeterministic polynomial (NP) hard. Wherefore, it is advisable to review the study carried out by Miao and Liu [9], that focuses on the causal inference mechanism of a FCM with crisp binary concept states {0, 1}. They stated that given initial conditions, a FCM is able to reach only certain states in its state space. So, they show that splitting the whole FCM in several basic FCM modules, it is possible to study their inference patterns in a hierarchical fashion.

2.3 Probabilistic Cognitive Maps

Wellman, in 1994 [10], carries out a Probabilistic version of a Cognitive Map (PCM) focuses on the assurance of the soundness of the inference for the sign relations of a CCM. This sign relation is depicted by (1) and (2), but now they are integrated by equation (10), where $P_{a,b}$ is the set of paths in the PCM from a to b, and δ is the causal sign of the arc between the nodes c, and c'. In this version, it is considered that: if the signs denote a causal correlation and the concepts random variables, then the path tracing is not sound. So, for instance, if i is negatively correlated with j, and j negatively correlated with k, it is still possible that i and k be negatively correlated, instead of positively supported by the law (3d). Thus, correlation is not a good interpretation for the sign of causal relations. Other issues that Wellman addressed were: the effect of blocking the path by instantiated evidence and the evidential reasoning produced by the effect concept on the cause concept.

In any of those cases, it would be possible to conditionalize the conclusion on partial information about the concepts, assuming that the values of some of them may have been observed or revealed.

With the aim to determine the validity of inference rules, such the depicted in (10), the definition of the rule should be local as far as possible. Thus, in assessing the validity of a signed edge *(c, c', δ)*, where δ is a causal sign, the attention is limited to the neighborhood of concepts c and c'. The rule should be unambiguously determined by the *precise causal relation* among the concepts, so that the sign relation, depicted by (10), is an abstraction of the precise relation. Thus, if the precise relation were a functional dependency, the sign would be an abstraction of the function relating the concepts. So, if the causal relation were probabilistic, the sign would be an abstraction of the probabilistic dependence, defined in terms of conditional probability (*Pr*).

With this baseline, the PCM is depicted as follows: The PCM is an *acyclic digraph*, with nodes (*a*, *b*) regarding to concepts and signed edges picturing abstract causal relations. The concepts are interpreted as random variables, although the variables domains need not be explicitly specified, what matters is: *the relative ordering among values*. The edges denote the sign of probabilistic dependence. So an edge (*c*, *c'*, +) means that for all values $c_1 > c_2$ of *c*, c'_0 of *c'*, and all assignments *x* to other predecessors of *c'* in the PCM, applies the correlation stated by equation (11).

$$\underset{p \in Pa,b}{*} \left(\underset{(c,c',\delta) \in p}{|} \delta \right). \tag{10}$$

$$\Pr(c' \geq c'_0 \mid c_1 x) \geq \Pr(c' \geq c'_0 \mid c_2 x). \tag{11}$$

where symbols *, | correspond to sum and multiplication operators, *P* depicts a path and *Pr* a conditional probability.

An edge (*c*, *c'*, -) is defined analogously with ≤ to substitute the central inequality in (11). If there is no edge from *c* to *c'* and no path from *c'* to *c*, then the left and right hand sides of (11) are equal; so, *c* and *c'* are conditionally independent given the predecessors of *c'*. If none of these cases hold, and there is no path from *c'* to *c*, then there is an ambiguous edge (*c*, *c'*, ?). The path analysis formula (10) applies to direct paths from *a* to *b* that corresponds to pure causal inference, but in a CM there may be undirected pathways between two variables that not all of them are purely causal paths. Wherefore, sometimes appear situations where the values of the variables have been observed, so that these variables have the effect of blocking the path where they are. Thus, if *e* is observed evidence, and *e* is in some of the paths between the concepts *a* to *b*, then all the paths that includes *e* have to be removed from $P_{a,b}$.

Other type of inference is the evidential reasoning produced by the effect concept on the cause concept. The sign of the probabilistic dependence from *c'* to *c* is the same as that from *c* to *c'*, as a result of applying the Baye's rule to (11). Other issues considered in the PCM are: the intuitive relations among target concepts of the same source concept, the causes of the same effect, and the relation between two causes given their common effect depend on how they interact in producing the effect.

3 A Case of Use of Cognitive Maps

This section shows an example of the use of a CM to support the student modeling in Web-Based Education Systems (WBES) stemmed from the currently work done by the authors [11, 12]. Thus, among the trends of the WBES is the provision of student-centered education with the support of the artificial intelligence. The aim is that the WBES carries out an adaptive behavior to depict the plans, the content and the learning experiences according to the dynamic student needs. So, the student model depicts a belief-based student profile, with regard to his/her cognitive skills, learning preferences, behavior, outcomes and knowledge domain acquired.

Due to the WBES works out a teaching-learning process, the CM was selected as the underlying approach to achieve the student model. Wherefore, the teaching task can be see as the cause concept, and the learning activity as the effect concept. So a logical analogy arises between the teaching-learning application domain and the CM-based student model. Thus in this section are introduced a couple of student models depicted by causal and fuzzy Cognitive Map versions.

3.1 Causal Cognitive Map-Based Student Model

Before delivering a teaching-learning experience, it is necessary to consider the causal effects that the subjects of the knowledge domain, produce on the student's cognitive performance. So, a small version of CCM is sketched in the Figure 1, is able to depict with them and to simulate the causal impact along the further iterations, as follows:

The CCM pictures four concepts regarding to the development of reusable computer programs. These concepts are sketched as the nodes (a) to (d), whereas their causal relations are show as labeled arcs, with positive (+) or negative (-) values. As regards the arrows, it is possible to identify and to follow the causal flow among the concepts. Thus, several paths are appreciated; some of them are direct paths as (a) + →(b); others are indirect paths as (a)+ →(b)- →(d). The CCM is a cyclic map due there are two paths, (a)+ →(b)- →(d) and (a)+ →(c)+ →(d), that arrive to concept (d); and one link, (d) + →(a), that points to the concept (a) in order to trigger a new cycle.

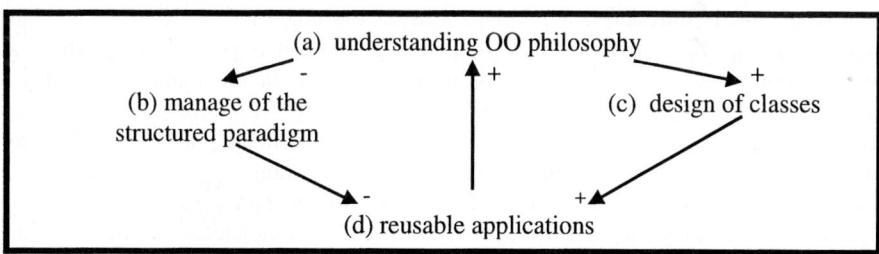

Fig. 1. Student Model depicted by a Causal Cognitive Map

The behavior of the CCM is computed through the use of the equations (1) to (5) along several iterations. As a consequence of the activation, the adjacency matrix of the CCM is transformed to depict the causal effects in the way showed in the Table 2.

Table 2. Evolution of the Adjacency Matrix of the Causal Cognitive Map through 4 states

A^1 Initial State, i=1	a	b	c	D	A^2 After 1 iteration, i=2	a	B	c	d
a		-	+		a				+
b				-	b	-			
c				+	c	+			
d	+				d		-	+	

Table 2. (*Continued*)

A^3 After 2 iterations, i=1	a	b	c	D	A^4 After 3 iteration, i=4	a	b	c	d
a	+				a				+
b		+	-		b	-			
c		-	+		c	+			
d				+	d			-	+

where A^1 corresponds to the initial state, before begin the simulation process. For this reason, the values in the matrix are the *direct* causal relations among each couple of concepts linked by only one arc. A^2 shows the *indirect* causal effects among couples of concepts linked by a path with two arcs. For instance, in the relation between *a* and *d* there are two paths, the first path is (a)- →(b)- →(d) with the indirect causal value of + (positive); and the second path is (a)+ →(c)+ →(d) with the indirect causal value of +, as a result of apply the laws of * (multiplication) and the laws of | (sum). Thus, in the entry $A^2_{a,d}$ appears + as the indirect causal value between *a* and *d*. Matrix A^3 corresponds to the values achieved by paths with lengths of 3 arcs (e.g., (a)- →(b)- →(d) + →(a) the result produced is – (negative). Finally, in matrix A^4 it is possible to identify that it has been reached a matrix with *equilibrium states*, due to the resulting values are the same that those in matrix A^2, therefore the process ends.

3.2 Fuzzy Cognitive Map-Based Student Model

In this section is introduced a FCM to analyze the cognitive skills of the student model. Through the activation of a simulation process, it is possible to predict the fuzzy evolution of the states of the concepts involved in the model. So, a brief example of this approach is sketched in the Figure 2 with four concepts. They represent cognitive skills elicited by the tutor of the student. According to the fuzzy causal relations, which are labeled by real values in the range [-1, 1], is appreciated that: the *concentration* enhances *abstraction; abstraction* promotes *logic* reasoning; *logic* contributes *problems solution*; *problems solution* stimulates *concentration*; but *concentration* feedbacks negatively to *problems solution* as a result of the work done.

The fuzzy causal values for the concepts and their relations are represented in the Table 3, where the entries of the 2nd to the 6th rows correspond to the values of the relations between cause concepts, stated as rows, and effect concepts, identified in the column headers; whereas, in the last row appears initial concept vector.

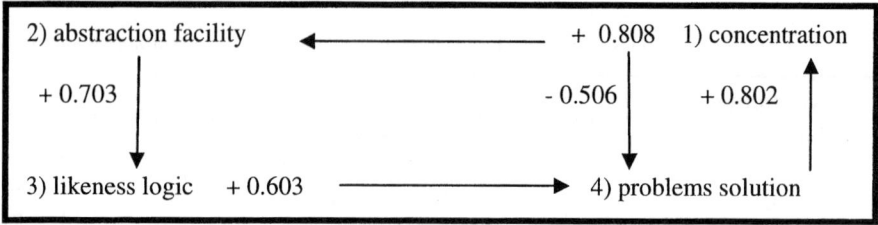

Fig. 2. Fuzzy Cognitive Map. Depicts some cognitive skills for student modeling.

Table 3. Valency Matrix and State Vector of the Fuzzy Cognitive Map

Adjacency Matrix	(1) concentration	(2) abstraction	(3) logic	(4) solution
1) concentration		+0.808		-0.506
2) abstraction facility			+0.703	
3) likeness logic				+0.603
4) problems solution	+0.802			
Initial State Vector	+0.5	+0.6	-0.2	0

The causal simulation of the FCM is sketched in the Table 4. So, in this table appear the results estimated for the four concepts along several iterations, according to the equations (6) and (9). In the entries of a specific column, it is possible to appreciate the behavior of a particular cognitive skill; e.g., the right column, shows the state evolution of the concept *solution*, which begins with 0, grows to 0.80, and drops to 0.63, where achieves an equilibrium state. In the same way, the behavior of the whole FCM is represented by the state vector depicted in each row. Thus, the simulation begins with the initial state, evolves through successively iterations until arrive to a stable situation produced in the eighteen cycle. So that, the interpretation is that the skills *concentration, abstraction* and *logic* reasoning achieve a high active state, but the *solution* skill develops a lightly positive increase in its state. This interpretation is stemmed from the sigmoid threshold function (9), where values close to 1.0 mean high positive activation, values around 0.5 represent lightly activation, and values close to 0.0, outline high negative activation of presence in the model.

Table 4. Evolution of the State Vector. As a result of the activation of the fuzzy Cognitive Map.

Iteration	(1) concentration	(2) abstraction	(3) logic	(4) solution
1	0.5	0.6	-0.2	0
2	0.5	0.883013	0.891978	0.133612
3	0.630904	0.883013	0.957176	0.806615
4	0.962182	0.927605	0.957176	0.784781
10	0.928551	0.977212	0.968884	0.639364
16	0.92876	0.977124	0.968872	0.639974
18	0.928759	0.977125	0.968872	0.639971

4 Conclusions

In this work it has been presented the baseline of Cognitive Maps and three versions oriented to deal with causality, fuzziness and non-deterministic situations. All of them are related to qualitative knowledge representation and causal reasoning. The CM is suitable to deal with dynamic systems modeling, where there are significant feedback and a nonlinear behavior along the simulation of the problem domain. Wherefore, the CM represents a qualitative approach for modeling a wide range of situations in fields as the political, social, economical, education, and engineering.

As an instance of a CM application, in this paper were outlined two student models by causal and fuzzy versions of a CM. In these cases, the preferences and the mental skills of the student were depicted and two simulations of behavior were achieved.

As a further work is the development of an approach oriented to automatically generate CM through the use of evolutionary strategies and ontologies of the domain, with the aim to generate a student model in an adaptive fashion.

Acknowledgments

The first author states that: this work was inspired in a special way for my Father, my brother Jesus and my Helper as part of the research projects of World Outreach Light to the Nations Ministries (WOLNM). Also this work was partially supported by the IPN, CONACYT under project 46805, and Microsoft México.

References

1. Park, K.S.: Fuzzy Cognitive Maps Considering Time Relationships. Int. J. of Man and Machine Studies. 42 (1995) 157-168
2. Tolman, E.C.: Cognitive Maps in Rats and Men. Psychological Review, July (1948) 198
3. Axelrod, R.: Structure of Decision the Cognitive Maps. Princeton University Press (1976)
4. Kelly, G.A.: The Psychology of Personal Constructs. Norton. (1955)
5. K. Nakumara, S. Iwai, & T. Sawaragi, Decision support using causation knowledge base. IEEE Tran. on Systems, Man and Cybernetics, 1982, 765.
6. Chaib-draa, B.: Causal Maps: Theory, Implementation and Practical Applications in Multi-Agent Environments. IEEE Transactions on Knowledge and Data Engineering (2002) 6
7. Kosko, B.: Fuzzy Cognitive Maps. International Journal of Man-Machine Studies (1986)
8. Mohr, S.T.: The Use and Interpretation of Fuzzy Cognitive Maps, Rensselaer P.I. (2003)
9. Miao, Y., and Liu, Z.:. On Causal Inference in Fuzzy Cognitive Maps. IEEE Transactions on Fuzzy Systems, vol. 8, No. 1, January, (2000)
10. Wellman, M.: Inference in Cognitive Maps. Mathematics and Computers in Simulation, vol.36 (1994) 137-148
11. Peña, DFMA'2005, Collaborative Student Modeling by Cognitive Maps, Proceedings of the First International Conference on Distributed Frameworks for Multimedia Applications (IEEE), February 6-9, 2005, Besançon, France (2005)
12. Peña and H. Sossa, Negotiated Learning by Fuzzy Cognitive Maps, In: Proc. 4th IASTED Int. Conf. on Web-Based Education, February 21-23, Grindelwald, Switzerland (2005)

Temporal Reasoning on Chronological Annotation

Tiphaine Accary-Barbier and Sylvie Calabretto

LIRIS CNRS UMR 5205, INSA de Lyon,
Bat. Blaise Pascal 7, avenue Jean Capelle, 69621 Villeurbanne cedex, France
tiphaine.accary@liris.cnrs.fr
http://liris.cnrs.fr/~taccary

Abstract. Interval algebra of Allen [4] propose a set of relations which is particularly interesting on historical annotating tasks [1]. However, finding the feasible relations and consistent scenario has been shown to be NP-complete tasks for interval algebra networks [11, 10]. For point algebra networks and a restricted class of interval algebra networks, some works propose efficient algorithms to resolve it. Nevertheless, these sets of relations (made of basic relation disjunctions) are not intuitive for describing historical scenarios. In this paper we propose a set of concrete relations for the annotator, and we formalize it in terms of temporal algebras. We then describe how our model can be matched with other ones to merge calculation efficiency and information suitability.

1 Introduction

When a reader annotates temporal informations while reading documents, he builds his own implicit temporal model. This task is done thanks to the reader's reasoning capacities and to the integration of several documents (which can have many forms). Moreover human commentators can be satisfied by expressing partially the relations between events. Thus, when they note that an event e_1 takes place during another event e_2, and that e_2 occurs before e_3, the fact that e_1 also occurs before e_3 is implicit. Temporal informations issued from historical annotations are such as "Lyon's forum construction took place during the roman period". No quantitative information such as date or duration information is specified here. It only expresses the qualitative information that the interval of time associated with one event occurred during the interval of time of another event. Allen [4] first gives an Algebra for representing such temporal relations between pairs of intervals. This algebra is actually useful in many application areas as natural language processing [3], planning, knowledge representation and others [5, 6].

Meanwhile, besides some complexity problems, this type of representation involves some drawbacks when they are used to annotate historical events. First, the proposed relations are too simple and the expression of uncertainty require to practice relations disjunction which is not a natural process. Next, with this representation we can not express point-events. In order to join event network with temporal points, it would be useful to work with an intermediate model using point algebra [11].

The outline of this paper is the following. In section 2, we recall the main temporal algebras frameworks on incomplete qualitative informations (intervals and points). We then briefly show the principles of reasoning tasks which are feasible on these models. In section 3, we develop our new set of relations dedicated to temporal annotation. We show how our relations are translatable into end-point relations, and give exemples of use of such relations in different domains. Finally, in section 4, we will describe how our model can be matched with other ones to merge calculation efficiency and information suitability. We will conclude with a brief description of our actual research plans.

2 Representing Temporal Information

Representing and reasoning about incomplete and indefinite qualitative temporal information is an essential part of many artificial intelligence tasks [3, 5]. In this section, we first recall temporal algebra frameworks [4, 11] for representing such qualitative information. We then recall the reasoning tasks allowed on networks using these models.

2.1 Temporal Algebras

Allen's Framework. The interval algebra IA [4] presents the thirteen basic relations that can hold between two intervals (Table 1).

Table 1. Allen's basic relations between intervals

IA Relation	Notations	Meaning
before | after	$A\{b\}B \mid B\{bi\}A$	
meets | met by	$A\{m\}B \mid B\{mi\}A$	
equals	$A\{eq\}B$	
during | contains	$A\{d\}B \mid B\{di\}A$	
start | started by	$A\{s\}B \mid B\{si\}A$	
finish | finished by	$A\{f\}B \mid B\{fi\}A$	
overlaps | overlaped by	$A\{o\}B \mid B\{oi\}A$	

To represent indefinite information, a relation between two intervals may be a disjunction of basic relations. To list disjunctions, we use subsets of $I = \{b, bi, m, mi, o, oi, d, di, s, si, f, fi, eq\}$ which is the one of all basic relations. Then, the relation $\{m, o, s\}$ between events A and B represents the disjunction: (A m B) ∨ (A o B) ∨ (A s B). On the representation network, vertices represent events and directed edges are labelled with sets of relations. Any edge without explicit knowledge is labeled with I.

Vilain and Kautz's Framework. The point algebra PA formalized by Vilain and Kautz's [11, 10] defines the three basic relations that can hold between two points $\{<, >, =\}$. In order to represent indefinite information, the relation between two points can be a basic disjunction of relations which are list in subsets of PA relations. As the possible disjonctions are very few, we can directly use disjonctive relations taken into $\{\emptyset, <, \leq, =, >, \geq, \neq, ?\}$ to express possible relations between two points. As an exemple, we can use $\leq$, instead of $\{<, =\}$.

Other Algebras. Vilain and Kautz [11] also show that there exists a restricted class of interval algebra, denoted SA networks, which can be translated into point algebra networks without losses of information. The SA set of relations is the IA subset which can be translated in terms of PA relations between intervals end-points. A description of this set can be found in [9, 7]. As an example, the relation: *roman period* $\{di, fi, si, eq\}$ *champdolian time* can be translated into the PA network shown on Figure 1 (where *roman period*$^-$ and *roman period*$^+$ are the end-points of interval *roman period*).

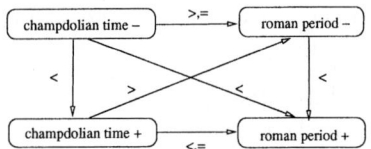

Fig. 1. Translation between SA and PA networks

Van Beek and Cohen [9] define a new point algebra and a new corresponding subset of the interval algebra. PA_c is the algebra with the same operators and underlying set as PA without $\neq$. The subscript 'c' indicates that the sets of tuples defining the relations in PA_c are convex. SA_c is the subset of SA that can be translated into relations between the end-points of intervals using only the relations in PA_c. An enumeration of the SA_c relations is shown in [9].

2.2 Reasoning Tasks

Using interval or sub-classes of interval algebra networks for temporal annotation is particularly fit for many reasons. First, the proposed relations have a very plain semantic. Moreover, many works has been done on constraint inference. At least, finding feasible relations between all events is a useful mean to avoid hazardous human annotation. Automatically determining feasible relations between events on the network can be viewed as determinating the deductive consequences of temporal knowledge. Using some algorithms which saturate the constraint network, it is possible to derive and complete information on some edges labeled with I. These methods also permit both to refine ambiguous relations and to detect disjunction into annotations.

Path Consistency. The idea behind the path consistency problem is the following: If we choose any three vertices i, j and k in the network, the labels on the edges (i,j) and (j,k) potentially constrain the label on the edge (i,k) that completes the triangle. For example, consider the three vertices *beuvreysian time (BT), wabenian time (WT)* and *roman period (RP)* on the Figure 2:

$$(BT\{<\}WT) \wedge (WT\{mi\}RP) \rightarrow (BT\{<,o,m,d,s\}RP)$$

We can then change the label on the edge (*beuvreysian time,roman period*) from I to the set $\{<,o,m,d,s\}$ (see Figure 2). To perform this deduction, the path

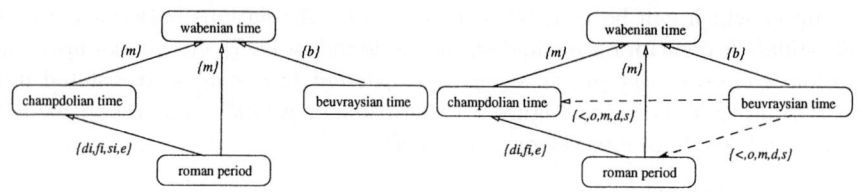

Fig. 2. Constraint propagation and adding of new relations

consistency algorithm [2, 8] uses the operations of set intersection ($\cap$) and composition ($\cdot$) of labels and checks whether $C_{ik} = C_{ik} \cap C_{ij} \cdot C_{jk}$, where C_{ik} is the label on edge (i,k). If C_{ik} is updated, it may further constrain other labels, so (i,k) is added to a list to be processed in turn, provided that the edge is not already on the list. The algorithm iterates until any changes are possible. As the inverse of a label is the inverse of each of its elements, a unary operation, "inverse", is also used to speed up the algorithm.

Finding Feasible Relations. The labeled graph is stored in a $n \times n$ table C where entry C_{ij} is the label on edge (i,j). A relation $R_k \in C_{ij}$ is feasible with respect to a network if and only if there exists a consistent instantiation of the network where R_k is satisfied. The minimal label between two events (or points) in the network is the set consisting of *all and only* the $R_k \in C_{ij}$ that are feasible. The reasoning task is to determine the minimal labels of the network. As an example, on Figure 2, the relation between *roman period (RP)* and *champdolian time (CT)* is the disjunctive set $\{di, fi, eq\}$. So, there exists a consistent instanciation where $RP\{di\}CT$, an other where $RP\{fi\}CT$ and a last one where $RP\{eq\}CT$ (see Figure 3). Finding a consistent scenario and

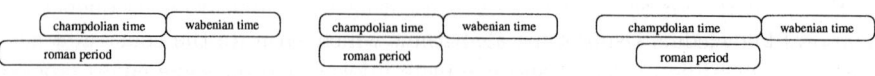

Fig. 3. Possible arrangements for *champdolian time, wabenian time* and *roman period*

finding the feasible relations have been shown to be NP-complete for interval algebra networks [11, 10]. So we will work on restricted class of interval algebra networks and use Van Beek [8] algorithms.

3 A New Model of Relations for Temporal Annotation

It is unimaginable to leave human (expert or not) annotate documents only with basic interval relations. These are too much precise and it requires to use disjunctive notations which is an unusual practice. However, we want relations with precise semantics. We also need relations which will be connected with a well-known temporal algebra, in order to take advantage of efficient works already done on temporal constraint propagation.

3.1 Disjunctive Relations Proposed for Annotation Task

Finding useful relations in annotating tasks requires to parse what can be expressed or not with the existing relations. Allen's relations, presented in section 2.1, allow to describe some temporal scenarios. The relation *no_ info*, which is the global disjunction is automatically used to specify that any information is known between events. If events end-points position are known, Allen's relations can then perfectly describe situations. However, when we have fuzzy knowledges to express, the use of disjunction of relations is necessary. To handle disjunction is not an intuitive phenomenon during an annotating stage: It is hardly to do very constricting for the commentator. A solution is then to propose a choice of pre-disjunctive or "fuzzy" relations[1] to the annotator. The choice of these relations have to be done in association with usual annotation tasks. In the chronology annotating framework, we have thus defined a restricted set of relations describing current scenarios. Consider the case of chronological annotation

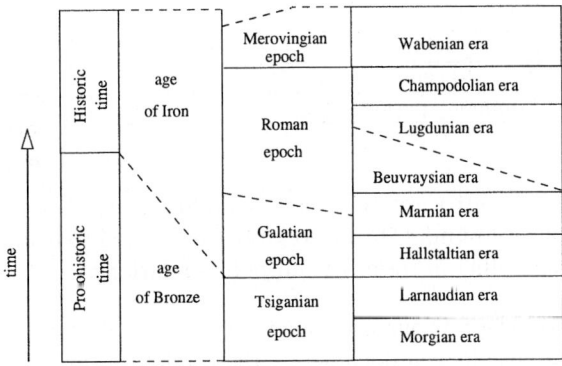

Fig. 4. Fuzzy prehistoric chronology

in archaeology. Figure 4, which presents a prehistoric chronology, is a typical case of scenarios we need to express. On this representation, some end-points are fuzzy defined. For more legibility, we will call each event by his first letter (AI = Age of Iron).

---
[1] Our fuzzy relations are not Zadeh's ones [12].

To build this chronology, we can use Allen's basic relations. For example, we can express that *Halstaltian era meets Marnian era*. But a large part of these information are more fuzzy. Let us consider the *age of Iron* and the *Protohistoric time*. The only information which we can lay out there is that the start point of *AI* is during *PT*. We will annotate this scenario with *AI begin_in PT*. If you look at the relation between the *Galatian epoch* and the *Marnian era*, all we can say is that *GE* ends into *MaE* (*GE end_in MaE*). An other interesting scenario that can be noticed is the relation between the *Tsiganian epoch* and the *age of Bronze*. We know that *TE* is fully inserted into *AB* but without information on *AB* end-points positions. *TE* can be equal, during, starting or finishing *AB*: we will note this relation *TE fuzzy_during AB*. At least, the table shows us that there is an uncertainty about the existence of the Beuvraysian era. It implies than the *Marnian era* can have met the *Lugdunian era* or being before. We will express this situation with *MaE fuzzy_before LE*. These statements led us to

Table 2. Disjunctive relations proposed for events temporal ordering and corresponding end-points relations

Annotation relation	end-point positions			
	A^-B^-	A^-B^+	A^+B^-	A^+B^+
fuzzy_before	<	<	≤	<
fuzzy_during	≥	<	>	≤
common_begin	=	<	>	?
common_end	?	<	>	=
begin_in	≥	≤	>	?
end_in	?	<	≥	≤
begin_before	<	<	?	?
first_to_end	?	<	?	≤
common_period	?	≤	≥	?

define a set of disjunctive relations corresponding to these temporal scenarios. Table 2 shows our set of nine "fuzzy" relations dedicated to historical annotation and their corresponding in terms of end-points relations.

An Example of Use: If our previous works leed us to develop this model for annotation of archaeological documents, these relations are not "dedicated" to this task. We can show an example of uses in others domains. Let us consider the exemple of events description shown on Figure 5. Temporal relations between events are not unambiguously given in the description. The first sentence only tells us that the time over which Fred reads the paper had a common part with the one over which he ates his breakfast. We can represent this sentence by *Paper common_period Breakfast*. This relation can afford a "wrong" possibility because it allows the *m* relation (telling that common period can be just on end-point) but such uncertainty does not penalize the system and the propagation will fastly compensates it. The second sentence gives the relationship between

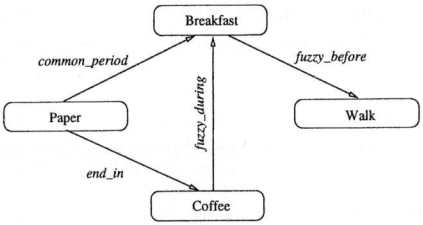

Fig. 5. Text description: *Fred was reading the paper while eating his breakfast. He put the paper down and drank the last of his coffee. After breakfast he went for a walk.*

the end-points of the interval where Fred reads his paper and those where he drinks his coffee. The sentence is indefinite about other points. We can represent it as *Paper end_in Coffee*. If it does not appear in the text, we also know that drinking coffee is part of breakfast and occurs then during breakfast. Meanwhile, we can not know if Fred only takes a coffee as breakfast or if he drinks coffee at the beginning, at the end or during a part of his breakfast. We then represent it as *Coffee fuzzy_during Breakfast*. Finally, the third sentence tells us that Fred had a walk after breakfast. This walk can have been done immediately or a long time after. We then represent it as *Breakfast fuzzy_before Walk*. The resulting network is shown on Figure 5. The system can then convert the network into end-points relations and accomplishes constraint propagation.

3.2 Coding the Network of Fuzzy Relations

As a convention, we will note interval of events I and relations R. The network of events i, j, and k will be represented as

$$I_i \stackrel{R_{i,j}}{\to} I_j \stackrel{R_{j,k}}{\to} I_k$$

To store a network of n events, we use a $n \times n$ table. Each table cell contains the matrix of end-points relation beetween I_i and I_j. The calculation of missing relations on the network is done by matrix product. The matrix $M_{i,k}$ is the result of $M_{i,j} \times M_{j,k}$. We can then use some efficient algorithms for PA networks (see section 2.2) to spread constraint and thus complete knowledge. Let $\overline{M_{i,k}}$ be the matrix which symbols are the opposite of $M_{i,k}$ ones. $M_{k,i}$ is fastly obtained as the transposed matrix of $\overline{M i}_{i,k}$.

Consider the network issued from the temporal description example shown on Figure 5. Let $M_{C,W}$ denote the matrix of end-points between events *Coffee (C)* and *Walk (W)*. This network is stored in the matrix table shown on Table 3. $M_{C,W}$ is computed as the product of $M_{C,B}$ and $M_{B,W}$

$$M_{C,B} \times M_{B,W} \iff \begin{pmatrix} \geq & < \\ > & \leq \end{pmatrix} \times \begin{pmatrix} < & < \\ \leq & < \end{pmatrix} \stackrel{results}{\to} \begin{pmatrix} < & < \\ \leq & < \end{pmatrix} \iff M_{C,W}$$

This result can then be compared with the one already stored in the table. If the two relations are the same or if the new one can refine the other, it will

Table 3. Storage of end-points relations matrix for the network of Figure 5. Cells in grey represents matrix issued from the translation of the given relations. Other matrix are issued from computation.

	$B^- B^+$	$W^- W^+$	$P^- P^+$	$C^- C^+$
B^-	$=\ <$	$<\ <$	$?\ \leq$	$\leq\ <$
B^+	$>\ =$	$\leq\ <$	$\geq\ ?$	$>\ \geq$
W^-	$>\ \geq$	$=\ <$	$\geq\ ?$	$>\ \geq$
W^+	$>\ >$	$>\ =$	$>\ ?$	$>\ >$
P^-	$?\ \leq$	$\leq\ <$	$=\ <$	$?\ <$
P^+	$\geq\ ?$	$?\ ?$	$>\ =$	$\geq\ \leq$
C^-	$\geq\ <$	$<\ <$	$?\ \leq$	$=\ <$
C^+	$>\ <$	$\leq\ <$	$>\ ?$	$>\ =$

replace it. Else, an inconsistency will be point out to the user. Finally, we can then translate back the resulting end-points matrix in terms of fuzzy relations. Here, $M_{C,W}$ will be translated into *Coffee fuzzy_before Walk*.

4 Knowledge Reconstruction

It is relevant to discern computational knowledge which is expressed in terms of end-points (and is too fuzzy to be understood humanly), and knowledge contained at annotation level. Our system is really more interesting if the results of propagation process can be returned to the user in a comprehensible language. A return expressed in terms of events end-points relations is incomprehensible. What is pertinent, is to return an interval network labeled whith relations taken into our fuzzy set. For the sake of clarity, this set will be denoted as F.

We notice that F is a subset of the SA_c relations (see section 2.1). End-points matrix computed by the propagation use PA_c relations. All these matrix can then be translated in terms of SA_c relations but not necessarily in terms of F relations. To return to the annotator a network solely labeled with F relations, we have to pass cross a "simplification" stage in which each relation of $SA_c - (SA_c \cap F)$ must be akin to an F relation.

These classifications can lead to a punctual loss of precision on the information returned. However, just the result at t time can suffer these loss and the under layer network is not modified. Thus, information contained in the network still remain complete and the ones returned to the user are nevertheless meaningfull[2]. These "losses" can then be considered as an avdantage for user's relation perception.

Let us consider the matrix table issued from the description of Fred's breakfast (Table 3). We have previously seen that the computed matrix $M_{C,W}$ can be translated in terms of F relation without any loss of information. Now, it is different when we will compute $M_{P,W}$ which is the product of $M_{P,B}$ and $M_{B,W}$

---

[2] They can be understanding by users.

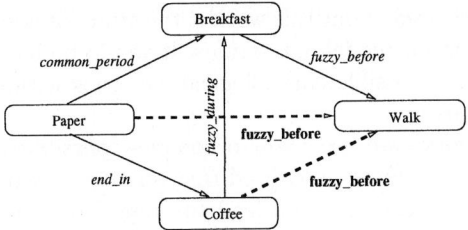

Fig. 6. Fully informed network for Fred's breakfast example after reconstruction stage

$$M_{P,B} \times M_{B,W} \iff \begin{pmatrix} ? & \leq \\ \geq & ? \end{pmatrix} \times \begin{pmatrix} < & < \\ \leq & < \end{pmatrix} \xrightarrow{results} \begin{pmatrix} \leq & < \\ ? & ? \end{pmatrix} \iff M_{P,W}$$

This resulting matrix is not the end-points expression of one of our fuzzy relations. In terms of SA_c relation, it matches with the relation $I - \{bi, d, oi, mi, f\}$. When we project this relation in the F set, the corresponding relation is no_info. In this case we can lose a few informations about constraint on events end-points. Meanwhile, this loss is not very significant for two reasons. First, the missing end-points information could not have been represented in terms of temporal scenarios. Next, during the propagation, the matrix $M_{P,W}$ is also compute with the product of $M_{P,C}$ and $M_{C,W}$.

$$M_{P,C} \times M_{C,W} \iff \begin{pmatrix} ? & < \\ \geq & \leq \end{pmatrix} \times \begin{pmatrix} < & < \\ \leq & < \end{pmatrix} \xrightarrow{results} \begin{pmatrix} < & < \\ \leq & < \end{pmatrix} \iff M_{P,W}$$

This resulting matrix can be automatically translated into F relation: *Paper fuzzy_before Walk*. Now the network is fully informed (see Figure 6).

5 Perspectives

In this paper we have presented a new model of temporal relations adapted to the description of chronology in Archaeology.

The prospects of our works are the following. First of all, we notice that the detection of inconsistencies is interesting only when it can be accompanied by a correction, or at least, by a support for correction. For the moment, when an edge is already labelled, the system is allowed to refine the already known relation if it is consistent or to provide an error if there is a conflict. In the case of refinement, two situations have to be considered. If the previous relation is the result of a calculation, the substitution is rightful. But if the "fuzzier" relation has been given by the user, it would be preferable to inform the user that a refinement was calculated and to let it decides of its implementation. This differenciation then requires the use of a flag system on relations to store their source. In the case of detection of inconsistency the error is provided but it will be useful to propose to the user both the "false" relation and the calculated solution with the list of human arcs which produce this result.

Another research area about this work is the study of possible consistent scenarios algorithms on our model of relations. It would be indeed very interesting to be able to propose possible chronological scenarios within the framework of temporal annotations.

In our future work, we also plan to compare possible visualization means for the results. We are indeed convinced that an adequate mode, in addition to facilitate the data processing, could lead the researcher to the construction of new assumptions.

References

[1] T. Accary, A. Bénel, S. Calabretto, A. Iacovella: Confrontation de points de vue sur des corpus documentaires : Le cas de la modélisation du temps archéologique. In: Actes du 14ème Congrès Francophone AFRIF-AFIA de Reconnaissance des Formes et Intelligence Artificielle [RFIA], (2004), 197–205.
[2] James F. Allen: Time and Time Again: The Many Ways to Represent Time. In: International Journal of Intelligent Systems, vol. 6, nř4, (1991), 341–355.
[3] J. F. Allen: Towards a general theory of action and time. Artificial Intelligence, 23, (1982), 123–154.
[4] J. F. Allen: Maintaining Knowledge About Temporal Intervals. Communications of the ACM, 26(11), (1983), 832–843.
[5] J. Euzenat, C. Bessière, et al.: Dossier Raisonnement Temporel et spatial. In: Bulletin de l'Association Française pour l'Intelligence Artificielle, volume 29, (Avril 1997), 2–13.
[6] J.P. Haton, N. Bouzid, F. Charpillet, et al.: Le Raisonnement en Intelligence Artificielle : Modèles, techniques et architectures pour les systèmes à bases de connaissances. Inter Edition (ed), (1991), 183–229.
[7] P. B. Ladkin, R. Maddux: On Binary Constraint Networks. Technical Report, Kestrel Institute, Palo Alto, Calif., (1988)
[8] P. Van Beek: Reasoning about qualitative temporal information. In: Artificial Intelligence, 58, (1992), 297–326.
[9] P. Van Beek, R. Cohen: Exact and approximate reasoning about temporal relation. in: Computational Intelligence, 6, (1990), 132–144.
[10] M. Vilain, H. Kautz, P. van Beek: Constraint propagation algorithms for temporal reasoning: A revised report. In D.S. Weld and J. de Kleer editors, Readings in Qualitative Reasoning about Physical Systems, Morgan-Kaufman, (1989), 373–381.
[11] M. Vilain, H. Kautz: Constraint propagation algorithms for temporal reasoning. In: Proceedings of the National Conference of the American Association for Artificial Intelligence (AAAI-86), Philadelphia, Pa., (1986), 377–382.
[12] L.A. Zadeh: Fuzzy sets. Information and Control, Vol. 8, (1965), 338–353.

EventNet: Inferring Temporal Relations Between Commonsense Events

Jose Espinosa and Henry Lieberman

MIT Media Lab, Software Agents Group, 20 Ames St.,
Cambridge, Massachusetts, 02139, USA
{jhe, lieber}@media.mit.edu
http://agents.media.mit.edu

Abstract. In this paper, we describe EventNet, a toolkit for inferring temporal relations between Commonsense events. It comprises 10,000 nodes and 30,000 temporal links mined from the Openmind Commonsense Knowledge Base. It enables applications to deduce "obvious" (to people) temporal relations between commonly occurring events, for example: First, you wake up, then you can leave the house in the morning. The temporal relation might be one of cause and effect, of action/goal or prerequisite relations, or simply that they tend to follow each other in a commonly occurring "script". In addition, the algorithm has some built-in heuristics to infer when its information is not enough. It then finds semantically similar nodes to dynamically search the knowledge base. EventNet has been used in projects such as an intelligent kitchen, and in intelligent interfaces for consumer electronics devices.

1 Introduction

Building applications that successfully interact with humans in everyday life requires considerable knowledge about the world, people, and everyday life. These applications need to know about people's goals, motivations and desires. We'd like to infer that if a person is filling a carafe with water just after waking up, it's likely that the person is making coffee; and the effect of drinking coffee is to become more awake. This allows building systems that provide more proactive interaction with users.

This paper focuses on one particular aspect of Commonsense knowledge – understanding temporal relations between events. Temporal reasoning allows an interface to *predict* what might happen next, enabling proactive interfaces that automatically make suggestions that the user might find pertinent to upcoming situations. It allows a system to *infer antecedents* – infer from the present state what has likely led up to that state. Antecedent events allow the system to fill in gaps in incomplete explicit information supplied by the user. It also permits the system to understand events that might take place concurrently with the current event.

We extract temporal information from a more general knowledge base concerning Commonsense knowledge in general, Open Mind Common Sense [1], described in the next section. We then turn specifically to EventNet, where we show how we extract temporal event information and provide a simple spreading-activation inference algorithm to propagate temporal relations. We then describe application-oriented tools, including a plan recognizer. Finally, we describe some specific application projects, such as improved interfaces to networks of consumer electronics devices, and an intelligent kitchen.

1.1 Openmind Commonsense Project

Giving computers commonsense has been one of the biggest goals of Artificial Intelligence since the beginning. A program should know that in order to use your car it should be in the same place you are (or at least at reasonable distance) [2]. To accomplish this goal it is necessary to solve two main problems: a) collecting and storing all the knowledge, and b) building reasoning algorithms. The largest and longest-standing effort in this direction is Lenat's CYC [3]. CYC is produced by a team of knowledge engineers who have worked for two decades to carefully encode Common Sense in a formal language, CYCL.

In contrast, our Openmind Commonsense Project collects common sense knowledge from volunteers over the web. It is a website where the users are asked to fill templates like *"Something that might happened when you go to ____ is that you might ____"* using plain English [1]. By the spring of 2005, the site has collected around 750,000 sentences from 16,000 contributors. An example of the knowledge find in this project is *"Something that might happen when you go to the zoo is that you might see exotic animals"* and *"The effect of walking in the rain is getting wet."*

By mining the templates in OpenMind and parsing techniques, a semantic network, called ConceptNet, was created [4]. This network has 300,000 nodes and 1.6 millions links, like *[Subevent "go to the zoo" "see exotic animals"]* or *[EffectOf "walk in the rain" "get wet"]*. ConceptNet has operations like getting the context of a given topic, analogy making, topic spotting, and classification [4]. ConceptNet has been used to embed commonsense reasoning into interactive applications [5].

Using the temporal links from ConceptNet a dynamic Bayesian network called LifeNet is created by "egocentric" nodes of the form *"I go to the zoo"* and a set of probabilities linking the nodes. This network uses belief propagation [6] to perform a variety of temporal operations like predicting what else might be true now, in the near future or in the near past, explaining why some event happened, or filtering nodes that are not likely to be true. Due to its semantic imprecision, we introduce probabilistic reasoning into LifeNet [7].

2 EventNet

EventNet uses the temporal nodes in LifeNet to create an association network. It can make predictions of the more likely preceding or subsequent events associated with a certain set of events, in contrast to LifeNet's single-event predictions. Also, it can compute paths between two events. It is able to infer that, in order to watch a movie, it is necessary to buy a ticket, and that a person is likely to buy popcorn. EventNet is a suitable inference engine for applications that have to watch users' actions and give them advice or suggestions. (See section 3 for current examples).

The EventNet links are expressed as triplets of the form *(0.504 "I go to a zoo" "I see exotic animals")*. The first element is the weight of the link, the second the parent (preceding) node and the third, the son (subsequent) node. In this network all the nodes are expressed in an egocentric way with no distinctions between the subject executing or receiving the action. Examples of EventNet nodes are "I run," "I eat breakfast," or "I am sick."

2.1 EventNet Inference Algorithm

EventNet uses a spreading activation algorithm to do its inferences. At each step, every energized node spreads a fraction of its energy to its adjacent nodes. The value of the spread energy is directly proportional to the weight between the nodes.

The energy of any node after a spreading step is calculated using the formula,

$$n_i = \sum_{j=links(n_i)} energy(n_j) * weight(n_i, n_j) \qquad (1)$$

This causes the nodes with high connectivity to increase their likelihood, filtering out the irrelevant or noise links. Spreading energy from the node "I rain" will reach the concepts "I paint someone's house," "I get wet," "I go to baseball game," "I walk in rain," "I go to zoo" in the first iteration. In the second iteration the top-ten concepts are "I walk in rain," "I catch a cold," "I get wet," "I am cold," "I wash someone's

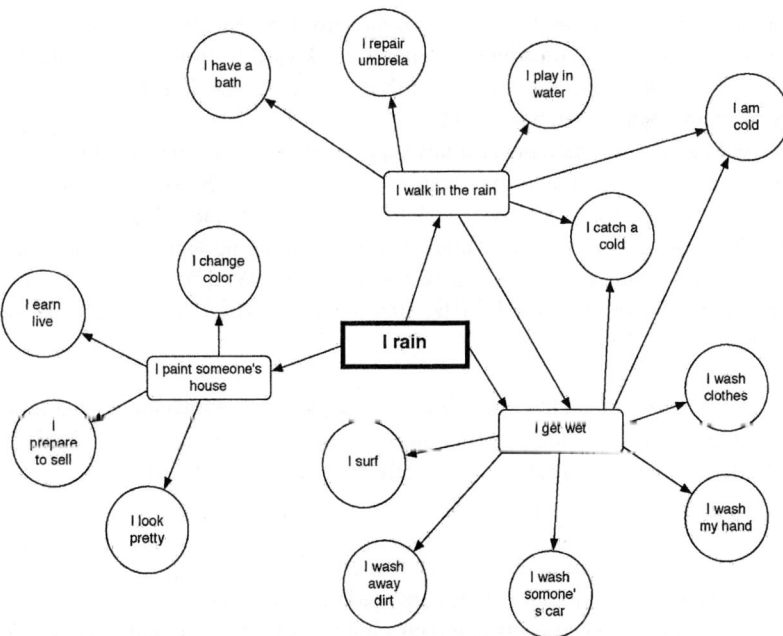

Fig. 1. Spreading activation over one node. The bold square node is the query node, the rounded-rectangle nodes are the nodes reached on the first iteration. The circular nodes are reached in the second iteration. The unlikely node "I paint someone's house" is de-empasized, in contrast to the more plausible "I get wet" and "I walk in the rain"

car," "I wash away dirt," "I have clothes to clean," "I repair my umbrella," "I play in water," "I have a bath." Note that the unlikely nodes ("I paint someone's house" and "I go to a baseball game") are filtered out in the second iteration (Fig. 1).

Despite EventNet's origin in a Bayesian network, it uses spreading activation instead of a Bayes-rule inference algorithm. The latter method does not allow changing the topology of the network during the inference; this is needed to add the semantic links. Also, spreading activation *emphasizes* highly connected nodes by adding multiple paths while Bayes networks *subtracts* the extra overlap.

2.2 EventNet Temporal Toolkit

EventNet is designed to be a temporal reasoning toolkit. It provides two basic operations: plan recognition and paths between events. EventNet is implemented in Common Lisp; in addition the main API has been packaged as an XML-RPC server to be easily accessed by external applications. It provide two basic operations:

Plan Recognizer. This operation is able to infer what are the user's next actions or goals based on a set of observed events. This operation works by applying a certain amount of energy φ_{node} to one or more observed events, then applying the spreading activation algorithm described in the previous section. This operation infers a set of possible next events, previous events or temporal related events. The future events are calculated by spreading the energy forward from the parents to its sons. The past events are calculated by spreading the energy backward from the sons to its parents. The temporally related events treat EventNet as a undirected graph, giving you the composition of the next and past events.

The API for the plan recognizer allows specifying the times the spreading step will be applied before giving the answer and the desired size of the answer. For example: calling the function (find-next-state "wake up" :size 100 :ntimes 2) gives you the top-100 ranked nodes associated with future events of "wake up" after speeding the node two times. EventNet returns the top 100 temporally related nodes in 0.001 seconds average using a PowerPC G4 500 MHz, 1024MB Ram, Mac OS X 10.2.8 and Macintosh Common Lisp 5.0.

Paths Between Events. This operation finds a plausible explanation of a temporal relation, as a sequence of temporally related events between the two. This algorithm is inspired on a planning algorithm originally proposed by Maes [8].

The algorithm works as follows:

1. Each of the source and goal nodes is excited with energy φ_{source} and φ_{goal} respectively. In addition, the source nodes are marked as activated.
2. The source nodes spread energy to their children and the goal nodes spread energy to their parents. The amount of energy injected is directly proportional to the current energy of the node and the weight of the link, as expressed in function 1.
3. All the nodes that have received energy from at least one of their parents keep spreading the energy to their sons. In the same way, all the nodes that have received energy from at least one of their sons keep spreading the energy to their parents.

4. After each spreading step, the energy of the nodes is averaged to a certain value φ. This step keeps the total energy within the network constant.
5. All the nodes that have at least one of their parents marked as activated and their energy above a threshold θ are marked as active. If no nodes are marked as activated the threshold θ is decreased by 10%.
6. If in a single iteration no new nodes are excited, there are no paths between the source and goal nodes. In this case the network uses the semantic information within the nodes to generate a new link and connect the two otherwise unconnected nodes. See the explanation about the semantic link calculus below.
7. Repeat steps 2, 3, 4, 5, and 6 until there is at least one path of activated nodes between the source node and the goal node.

This operation provides an explanation of plausible events, without committing to whether the events are necessary or just stereotypical. A path between the event "I wake up" and "I go to work" can be "I wake up," "I take a bath," "I put my clothes on," "I eat breakfast," "I drive my car," and "I go to work." In this path just the node "I put my clothes on" is *necessary* to accomplish the goal, but it is safe to assume that the other nodes are also true.

Create Semantic Links. EventNet is formed by 10,000 nodes and 30,000 links. It is not a fully connected graph; there is not always a path between two nodes. To bridge this gap, the system can dynamically create new links between two nodes that are semantically similar. This similarity is calculated using synonyms from WordNet [9] and analogies from ConceptNet [4]. This operation is an extension of Cohen's WHIRL [10] using WordNet's and ConceptNet's semantic information.

For example, we try to find a path between the nodes "I get money" and "I eat lunch", but the nodes are not directly connected. The algorithm generates new links based on the semantic similarity of the nodes. In this case the nodes "I buy pizza" is semantically linked with the nodes "I have hamburger" and "I have hot dog". This semantic expansion also is used to match existing nodes to process text queries, getting a close match by semantic similarity rather than plain keyword matching.

3 Using EventNet in Interactive Applications

The plan recognizer function of EventNet is used to infer a set of actions, goals and events based on the user's actions. Some current applications include: reducing complexity of consumer electronic interfaces, a kitchen scheduler, and an integrated calendar/to-do list.

3.1 Reducing Complexity of Consumer Electronics Interfaces

Current consumer electronic interfaces are difficult to use because the designers try to map an increasing number of functions of the device to a limited set of buttons. So, when the designers try to map to many functions to a handful of buttons they have to create menus, modes, push-and-hold buttons; these are the kind of interactions that frustrate the user.

We are exploring a new approach to interaction, where the devices are continually watching the users actions and proactively proposing actions that might satisfy the user's goals. We use EventNet's plan recognizer as an inference engine for this application. Furthermore, the devices are able to propose actions necessary to reach the users goals, execute them automatically, or self-debug when things go wrong.

For example: when the user plugs a guitar into the amplifier, the system asks EventNet for the next actions after the event "I plug my guitar". The answer to the query contains the nodes "I play music" and "I record a song," among others. These nodes trigger the device's functions for playing and recording music. Since EventNet doesn't make a distinction between goals and events, the device's functions are considered actions. This heuristic will filter out the nodes that cannot de executed by the system. For example, the node "I dance" is retrieved but it is ignored since there is no device function capable of dancing.

In addition, the system can suggest device functions according to the user's expressed goals; if the user says, "I want to watch the news," the system is able to recognize this as a goal and ask EventNet for the events preceding by the node "I watch the news." The answer that comes out from EventNet makes the system suggest the device actions *watch-television* and *hear-radio*. Later, the user can complain "Why I am not hearing anything?" The system uses the path-finding algorithm of EventNet between the current goal ("I hear the radio") and the user's desired action "I hear." The EventNet answer is compared to the state of the system devices, looking for the cause of the user's complaints.

The system can adapt to the user by updating the weights of the links. If an option is continually picked after performing one action, the probability of the link is increased, promoting the action. On the other hand, if the user critiques an action, like changing the sound setting when a DVD is inserted, the relative weight of the event will decrease, decreasing the likelihood that the behavior will happen again.

3.2 Kitchen Scheduler

One of the most stressful and error prone moments in holding dinner parties is assuring that all dishes are prepared on time. A dinner party may involve preparing more than one dish, with limited resources, in a timely manner. To help chefs to plan complex meals, we are building a scheduler for a context aware kitchen [11], using EventNet.

The scheduler first asks EventNet for actions that might not be explicitly expressed in the recipe, and allocates time for their execution. For example, it will recommend taking the meat out of the freezer two hours before starting to cook it, or soaking the vegetables for fifty minutes to defrost them.

Second, the system use ConceptNet [4] 'UsedFor' link to determine what kitchen utensils can be used to perform steps stated in the recipe; "heat water" can be performed by the microwave or the stove. Third, with this information, and the help of a planner, a schedule is shown to the user. In addition, the recipes are loaded on the device, the microwave displays a function names "bake cake" with the cooking time stated in the recipe.

Finally, while cooking, the kitchen watches the chef and uses EventNet plan recognizer to infer the current step of the recipe, and adjusts the plan to the current step.

This makes the schedule flexible enough so it will be useful even if the chef does not follow the scheduler's advice.

3.3 Calendar and To-Do List Integration

When planning an event or meeting, there is often a series of prerequisites that are needed. When the user adds a new event in her calendar, a calendar system implemented by Alex Faaborg and Christopher Tsai, using EventNet, asks for the temporal implications. For example: the user wants to schedule a day at the beach, so she sets a new calendar item with the text "go to the beach." The answer that EventNet returns contains "I run at the beach" and "I bring towel." Then, the system looks for specific verbs to identify which portion of the answer is a suitable for a To-Do list and suggests them to the user.

4 Evaluation

To evaluate the inference quality, the top ten answers to five random nodes were sent to a group of human judges. In addition, a person unrelated to the project was asked to write ten temporally related events to the same five nodes and the answer was sent to a different group of judges. The difference between the two groups is shown in the next table.

Table 1. EventNet evaluation

	Mean	Standard deviation
EventNet inference	62%	21
Human	69%	19

We found that participants did not always agree on what should be considered *temporally related*. One of the nodes evaluated was "I study": the answer given by one participant contained the node action "I sleep"; some of the judges had, however, a different line of thought. They thought that, for investing time studding it is necessary give up some sleep.

We also evaluated the coverage of the knowledge by asking five people to write down ten events related to the nodes. We compared their answers to the first hundred EventNet answers. The inference algorithm matched on an average 3.68 out of 10 answers.

The tools described in this paper was conceived to enable interactive applications to integrate better to everyday life. The authors think that the use of EventNet to create successful applications is the best way to test the algorithm.

5 Related Work

We are most interested in *Commonsense* temporal reasoning, as opposed to formal temporal reasoning. There has been considerable work in Artificial Intelligence in applying formal methods such as first-order logic to temporal reasoning (see, for example [12]), by explicitly introducing variables representing time, time intervals, causality, probability of occurrence, etc.

One example of more formal work in Commonsense theory of time is Allen [13]. His main thesis defines a basic temporal operation – *meet(:)* – which says that one period of time meets another period without time between them and without sharing – and use it to infer other temporal relations. This allows him to deduce many properties of temporal events which are not guaranteed by the less stringent representations we use. This work differs from the one proposed here since our approach is more concerned with making predictions about likely future or past events, rather than conceptualizing all possible temporal relations. Similarly, work based on networks of known causal relations or quantified known probabilities of events following other events can make much stronger statements than we do about inferred temporal relations. This is a limitation of our approach. As the other, more formal approaches gain traction, we can certainly incorporate some of their techniques to refine our approach.

It is not our goal here to perform this kind of formal reasoning. We are simply interested in representing what an average person might be able to quickly infer (however inaccurately or incompletely) about temporal relations between everyday events, regardless of whether they arise because of causal relations, prerequisites, consequences, shared influences, or contingent probability of occurrence. In the applications we are considering, it is not important to accurately predict the causality or quantify the probabilities of occurrence of the event, though that would certainly be helpful. We believe we have shown that merely by generating a set of plausible possibilities for event occurrence, and using Commonsense reasoning, application context and user interaction to choose from those possibilities, we can significantly improve the behavior of many interactive applications.

6 Future Work

Other methods of temporal representation are being explored to provide better structure of temporal events. We plan to diversify the semantic sources to improve the expansion. Particularly we are going to use VerbOcean [14] to have a richer semantics to control the creating of the links.

EventNet is part of a more comprehensive effort of create an inference architecture composed by multiple layers of inference each one capable to infer, reflect and correct the knowledge in the layer below [15].

References

1. Singh, Push Lin, T., Mueller, E, Lim, G, Perkins, T., and Zhu, W.: Open Mind Common Sense: Knowledge acquisition from the general public. First International Conference on Ontologies, Databases, and Applications of Semantics for Large Scale Information Systems. Irvine, CA. (2002)
2. McCarthy, John: Programs with Common Sense. In Mechanization of Thought Process, Proceedings of the Symposium of National Physics Laboratory, London, HMOS (1959) 77-84

3. Lenat, Douglas: CYC: A Large-Scale Investment in Knowledge Infrastructure. Communications of the AMC, 38, No. 11, (1995) 33-38
4. Liu, Hugo, Singh, Push: ConceptNet – a practical commonsense reasoning toolkit. BT Technology Journal, (2004) 22(4): 211-226
5. Lieberman, Henry, Liu, Hugo, Singh, Push, and Barry, Barbara. Beating Common Sense into Interactive Applications. AI Magazine 25(4): Winter 2005, 63-76.
6. Pearl, Judea.: Probabilistic Reasoning in Intelligent Systems: Networks of Plausible Inference. San Mateo, CA: Morgan Kaufman. (1988)
7. Singh, Push, Williams, William.: LifeNet: A Propositional Model of Ordinary Human Activity. Proc. Workshop on Distributed and Collaborative Knowledge Capture. Sanibel Island, FL. (2003)
8. Maes Pattie.: How to Do the Right Thing. Connection Science Journal, Vol. 1, No. 3., also MIT AI-Memo #1180. (1989)
9. Fellbaum, Christiane (Ed.): WordNet: An electronic lexical database, 1998. MIT Press.
10. Cohen, William.: WHIRL: A word-based information representation language. Journal of Artificial Intelligence, (2000) 163-196
11. Bonanni, Leonardo, Lee, Chia-Husun, Selker, Ted.: CounterOntelligence: Augmented Reality Kitchen, 2005. Proc. Computer-Human Interaction, ACM. April 2-7, Portland, Oregon, USA. 2005
12. Lluis Vila: A survey on temporal reasoning in artificial intelligence. AI Communications, 7(1), (March 1994)
13. Allen J., Hayes, P.: A common-sense theory of time. In Proc. Of the 9th International Joint Conference on Artificial Intelligence, Morgan Kaufmannm (1985) 528-531.
14. Chklovski, Timothy and Pantel, Patrick, VerbOcean: Mining the Web for Fine-Grained Semantic Verb Relations, 2004. In Proceedings of Conference on Empirical Methods in Natural Language Processing (EMNLP-04). Barcelona, Spain.
15. Singh, Push, Minsky, Minsky, Eslick, Ian: An architecture for computing common sense. BT Technology Journal. (2004) 22(4): 201-210.

Multi Agent Ontology Mapping Framework in the AQUA Question Answering System

Miklos Nagy, Maria Vargas-Vera, and Enrico Motta

Knowledge Media Institute (KMi), The Open University,
Walton Hall, Milton Keynes, MK7 6AA, United Kingdom
miklos.nagy@jrc.nl, {m.vargas-vera, e.motta}@open.ac.uk

Abstract. This paper describes an ontology-mapping framework in the context of query answering (QA). In order to incorporate uncertainty inherent to the mapping process, the system uses the Dempster-Shafer model for dealing with incomplete and uncertain information produced during the mapping. A novel approach is presented how specialized agents with partial local knowledge of the particular domain achieve ontology mapping without creating global or reference ontology. Our approach is particularly fit for a query-answering scenario, where an answer needs to be created in real time that satisfies the query posed by the user.

1 Introduction

An important aspect of ontology mapping is how the incomplete and uncertain results of the different similarity algorithms can be interpreted during the mapping process started to become a well-acknowledged research direction. As the latest research started moving towards a more automated mapping process it has been recognized that current approaches do not fully investigate the nature of the produced similarity information and mainly rely on a human domain expert to make a judgment about the correctness of the established mapping. However in the context of question answering like the AQUA [1,2] system the dynamic nature of the source information (e.g. web enabled databases) would require domain expert knowledge every time the source changes to follow up the modifications in the existing mapping. However in practice this is clearly not feasible. Our novel approach to address this problem utilizes a multi agent framework where the different mapping agents possess local sub-domain specific knowledge about particular entities (e.g. material, specimen, etc.). From the end user perspective our system addresses the problem of data integration of scientific databases containing vast number of experimental Semantic Web enabled data in order to facilitate better knowledge sharing and reuse between the scientific communities. Although these databases are accessible, the seamless data exchange between different databases is still an unsolved problem in spite of the fact that different XML based languages were defined by the different scientific communities e.g. MatML(Materials Markup Language) on the field of material science to facilitate a standardized XML based data exchange. This solution solved a number of interoperability issues but makes the assumption that both parties agreed the syntax of the data exchange. This assumption fails when one would search for existing experimental data available on the WWW since neither the syntax nor the semantics of the requested data is known before the submission of the query. The problem is that different research institutions, companies use different standards and naming conventions in their logical data model for the same data, additionally these data model is not always even accessible on the WWW. Hence a vast number of experimental data are remaining inaccessible, or unanalyzed that probably hides undiscovered correlations of science disciplines. The mapping agents use the Dempster-Shafer theory of evidence [3] to assess and combine the belief in the correctness of the different similarity algorithms. Our approach also does not assume the existence of global or reference ontology that is the superset of the different source ontologies and contains the existing mappings a priory. This approach makes it possible to perform query answering effectively with multiple source ontologies. In our first experimental system we consider query answering over Web enabled S&T (Scientific and Technical) or engineering databases those are described with their own domain specific ontologies.

The paper is organized as follows:

Section 2 introduces the similarity algorithm used by the framework to assess syntactic and semantic similarities between the posed query and the local ontologies. Section 3 describes how the problem of uncertain information created by the similarity mapping process is resolved and handled by the mapping framework. Section 4 presents the architecture of the mapping framework and describes how mapping agents on the different levels are carrying out the mapping. Section 5 presents a working example. Section 6 discusses the related work and section 7 gives conclusions as well as the future research directions.

2 Similarity

The similarity-mapping algorithm takes one entity from O1 and tries to find similar entity in O2. The similarity mapping process has different levels as follows:

- Concept-name similarity with Character-based Jaccard measure [4].
- Property set similarity with token based Jaccard distance: As first approach the property names are flattened into a bag of words per each node so similarity algorithms from the information retrieval field can be considered when two graph like structure are compared.
- Instance values similarity based on string similarity.
- Concept-property similarity graph assessment.

In order to increase the correctness of our similarity measures the obtained similarity coefficients need to be combined. Establishing this combination method is the primary objective that needs to be delivered with our outlined system. Further once the combined similarity has been calculated we need to develop a methodology to derive a belief mass function that is the fundamental property of Dempster-Shafer evidence theory.

In our prototype it is necessary to assess not only the syntactic but also the semantic similarity between concept, relations and the properties. The main reason why semantic heterogeneity occurs in the different ontology structures is the fact that different institutions developed their own meta-data that contains overlapping concepts from the same domain. Assessing the above-mentioned similarities in our multi agent framework we adapted and extended the SimilarityBase and SimilarityTop algorithms [5,6] used in the current AQUA system for multiple ontologies. The goal of our approach is that the specialized agents simulate the way in which a human designer would describe its own domain based on a well-established dictionary. What also needs to be considered when the two graph structures obtained from both the user query fragment and the representation of the subset of the source ontology is that there can be a generalization or specialization of a specific concepts present in the graph which was obtained from the local source and this needs to be handled correctly. In our multi agent framework the extended and combined SimilarityBase and SimilarityTop algorithms can be described as follows:

1. Based on the WordNet a directed graph is constructed for the concepts and properties that has similar meaning to the FOL query fragment where there are bi-directional edges between the nodes representing the concepts and there are directed edges from the concepts to the property nodes. In this step the specialized agents try determine all possible alternatives for the meaning of the query fragment that it can be aware of. Figure 1 depicts the graph representation of the hasName(material, 10 CrMo 9 10) FOL query fragment.

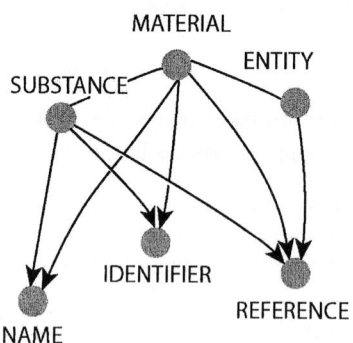

Fig. 1. G0 query fragment graph

2. Based on the before mentioned character and token based Jaccard distance similarity measure the specialized agent builds up a directed graphs from the local ontology structures that supposedly answers the query fragment. Figure 2 depicts two graphs obtained from two different sources.

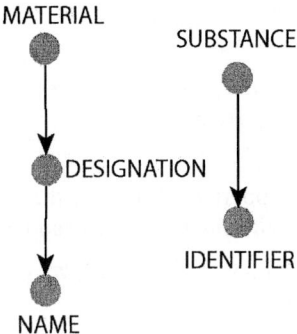

Fig. 2. G1 and G2 graph representation of the local ontology fragment

3. Top-down sub-graph (isomorphism) similarity assessment (for details see section 5) is applied on the graph G0 in order to find the subgraph G1 and G2 respectively. The aim is to find identical subgraphs to G1 and G2 in order to assess the similarity of the concepts and properties that can answer the query fragment. We call this method a top-down assessment because the search for the sub-graphs starts from the concept nodes towards property nodes through the directed edges. Once we reached the property node the search stops. If along the path we walked through the graph we found a sub graph identical (isomorph) to G1 and G2 that agent can deduce that the query fragment can be answered from the sources that belong to the particular ontology and the concepts or properties identified in the different sources are similar to both each other and to the query fragment and a basic mass function can be calculated that express the extent of belief in the existence of the similarity mapping between them. In case G1 or G2 contains nodes that could not be found in the G0, because of the nature of the top down assessment the agent can deduce that the particular concept node is a specialization of the concept that was identified by the algorithm.

3 Uncertainty

In our framework we use the Dempster Shafer [3] theory of evidence, which provides a mechanism for modeling and reasoning with uncertain information in a numerical way especially when it is not possible to assign a belief to a single element of a set of values. The main advantage of the Dempster-Shafer theory over the classical probabilistic theories that the evidence of different levels of abstraction can be represented in a way that clear discrimination can be made between uncertainty and ignorance. Further advantage is that the theory provides a method for combining the effect of different learned evidences to a new belief by the means of the Dempster's combination rule. Basic concepts of the theory are as follows:

Belief mass function (m): is a finite amount of support assigned to the subset of Θ. It represents a strength of some evidence and

$$\sum_{A \subseteq \Theta} m(A) = 1 \tag{1}$$

where m(A) is our exact belief in a proposition represented by A. The similarity algorithms itself produce these assignment based on the before mentioned (for details see section 2) similarities.

Belief: amount of justified support to A that is the lower probability function of Dempster, which accounts for all evidence E_k that supports the given proposition A.

$$belief_i(A) = \sum_{E_k \subseteq A} m_i(E_k) \tag{2}$$

Once all the necessary variables have been assigned to a qualitative value we need to combine the belief mass functions that was created by the different agents for the particular query fragment.

Dempster's rule of combination: Suppose we have two mass functions $m_i(E_k)$ and $m_j(E_k')$ and we want to combine them into a global $m_{ij}(A)$. Following Dempster's combination rule

$$m_{ij}(A) = m_i \oplus m_j = \sum_{E_k \cap E_{k'}} m_i(E_k) * m_j(E_{k'}) \tag{3}$$

However when $E_k \cap E_{k'} = \emptyset$ the mass $m_i(E_k) * m_j(E_{k'})$ would go to $\emptyset$, it is necessary to normalize the mass function with the lost mass so

$$m_{ij}(A) = \frac{\sum_{E_k \cap E_{k'}} m_i(E_k) * m_j(E_{k'})}{1 - \sum_{E_k \cap E_{k'} = \emptyset} m_i(E_k) * m_j(E_{k'})} \tag{4}$$

An important part of the system is how the similarity measures are applied in the concrete scenario and how the particular agent assesses the belief mass functions and belief functions. In our experimental system we consider basic probability assessment over the following entities:

1. **Class:** The most basic concepts in the domain that correspond to classes that are the root of the various taxonomies.
2. **Object properties:** Relation between the instances of two classes.
3. **Data type properties:** Relation between instances of classes and RDF literals and XML Schema data types therefore it describes that the particular class e.g. material has a data type property called name that which is a string.

The combination rule is applied in each agent thus the problem space is distributed, which makes Dempsters's rule of combination feasible in large and complex domains.

4 System Architecture

The high-level system architecture figure 3 shows how the functional parts of the system are related with each other. In the mediator layer the agents are organized in different levels. Agents on the broker level responsible for decomposing the query into sub queries, based on the global descriptor. The decomposed query parts are sent into the mapping agents located in the mapping layer. Mapping agents obtain the relevant information from the sources through the source agents. When only one source corresponds to the query the scenario is pretty straightforward and there is no need for any mapping between the sources, the query can be answered from the source. In a real case scenario this possibility is not so likely and this is why the mapping between local ontologies is a justified scenario in our case.

The idea that has been investigated in our research is that mapping agents can build up mappings simultaneously, utilizing different similarity measures based on their belief agents need to harmonize their beliefs based on trust that is formed during the mapping process.

This is a two-step process:
1. Mapping agent based on evidences that is available to them built up belief about the mapping.
2. Group of mapping agents need to harmonize their beliefs over the solution space.

The key components of the prototype are grouped by the different functional levels and from bottom to up as follows.

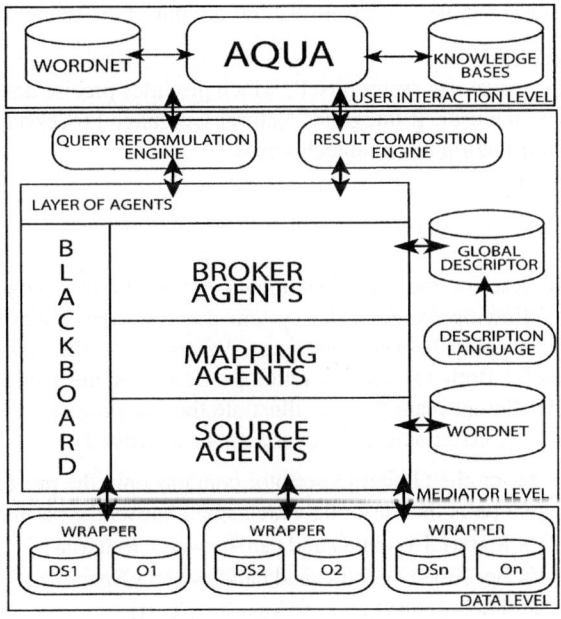

Fig. 3. Architecture of the Multi-ontology mapping framework

Data Level
On the data level the heterogeneous data sources are represented by their ontologies. The format of these sources varies from relational databases to simple files.
- Data source (DS): actual data represented in the database, file etc.
- Ontology (O) Semantic metadata that describes the particular data source.

- Wrapper creates a unified XML representation of the source that is queried by the particular resource agents.

Mediator Level
Layer of agents: Typically three kind of agents: broker that receives a FOL (First Order Logic) query and decomposes it into sub queries based on the global descriptor, mapping that has knowledge of a particular domain specific area and cooperatively map up the source concept with the concepts contained by the query string, source that access a particular data source and it's ontology and passes it to the mapping agents on a request basis.

Global descriptor and description language: Key component of the system that describes what kind of information can be found in the different sources, and which agent is able to answer the query posed by the user based on the entities in the query. Practically FOL knowledge base that contains information about the agents and entities as well as the resources.

Query reformulation and result composition engine: Query that is raised by the user needs to be reformulated and decomposed before entered into the system, which is the purpose of the query reformulation engine. Information flow stems from the mapping process needs to be composed into a single coherent answer, which is done by result composition engine. These subsystems are out of the scope of our research.

User Interaction Level
The AQUA query answering system itself, which provides precise answers to specific questions raised by the user. It integrates Natural Language Processing (NLP), Logic, Ontologies and Information retrieval techniques.

5 Test Bed

In this section we describe the main functionality of our system with a rather simple example. In the following example the system uses two ontologies O_1 and O_2 and creates similarity mapping between the query fragment and the concepts in the ontologies respectively. Both O_1 and O_2 ontology describes mechanical material test information from different institutes. To illustrate the mapping process in our system the following steps are taken before the query can be answered:

1. At system startup the Global Descriptor contains only the pre-defined concept-mapping agent pairs that describe which agent knows the particular concept:
    $\forall x$ MaterialAgent(x) and canAnswer(x,Material)
    $\forall x$ SpecimenAgent(x) and canAnswer(x,Specimen)
    $\forall x$ TestAgent(x) and canAnswer(x,Test)
    $\forall x$ SourceAgent(x) and canAnswer(x,Source)
    $\forall x$ TestConditionAgent(x) and canAnswer(x, TestCondition)
2. FOL Query passed to the broker agent:
    Which test has been carried out on a bar shaped specimen?
    $(\forall x, \exists y)$ (Test(x) and Specimen(y) and form(y,bar) and carriedOutOn(x,y))
3. Broker agent decomposes the query based on the information present in the Global Descriptor and forwards it to the particular agents:

- TestAgent receives Test(x) and carriedOutOn(x,y)
- SpecimenAgent receives Specimen(y) and form(y,bar) and carriedOutOn(x,y)

Both agent received part of the query that corresponds to multiple entities. Since this is a relation between the two concepts, agents need to share the meaning of this expression. Agents place this into a blackboard, which is visible for all agents.
- carriedOutOn(x,y) added to the Blackboard

4. Test and Specimen agents retrieve fragments of two ontologies. Test Agent identifies two similar concepts:
- O_1 contains TestResult and O_2 contains Test

Specimen Agent identifies two similar properties:
- O_1 contains Form and O_2 contains SpecimenForm
   a) Dempster-Shafer belief mass function is evaluated based on the node name similarities
   b) Dempster-Shafer belief mass function is evaluated based on the node structure similarities Test(Control,Temperature,Standard)-TestResult(TestControl, TestTemperature, TestStandard)= 0.5 Specimen(Name,Form,Characterization) and Geometry(SpecimenForm,SpecimenName, SpecimenChar)=0.6
   c) Combined similarity, belief function can be calculated cooperatively by the two agents. TestResult in O_1 is similar concept to Test in O_2 with belief function 0.8 Geometry in O_1 is similar concept to Specimen in O_2 and Form in O_1 is similar property in SpecimenForm in O_2

5. New findings can be added to the global descriptor:

$\forall$x TestAgent(x) and canAnswer(x,TestResult)

$\forall$x SpecimenAgent(x) and canAnswer(x,Geometry)

6 Related Work

Ontology mapping is widely investigated area and a numerous approaches led to different solutions. Derived from the data engineering community several solutions have been proposed that based on a mediator architecture where logical database schemas are used as shared mediated views over the queried schemas. A number of systems have been proposed e.g. TSIMMIS[7], Information Manifold [8], InfoSleuth [9], MOMIS [10] that shows the flexibility and the scalability of these approaches. Derived from the knowledge engineering community solutions the use of ontologies (conceptual domain knowledge schemas) is the main approach for resolving semantic differences in heterogeneous data sources. To date uncertainty handling during the mapping process was not in the focus of the research community since initially only different logic (FOL, Description Logics) based approaches have been utilized. As practical application of ontologies emerged on the web it has been acknowledged that considering the dynamic nature of the Web the problem of inconsistencies, controversies and lack of information needs to be handled. First systems that used probabilistic information like LSD, GLUE [11] proved that combining different similarity measures based on their probability could significantly improve the accuracy of the mapping process. It is worth to note that the Bayesian networks and different variants dominate current research addressing the qualitative reasoning and decision-making problem under uncertainty. Although these approaches successfully lead to numerous real world applications there are several situations where the problem cannot be represented properly within the classical probability framework. The most related research for ontology mapping framework under uncertainty using Bayesian networks [12] to tackle this problem.

7 Conclusions and Future Work

In our prototype we successfully addressed the problem of a system that is limited by its knowledge, perspective, and its computational resources. It is clear that if we try to move towards a fully automated ontology mapping in order to provide a better integration of the heterogeneous sources we need to investigate the limitations of multi agent systems such as our prototype. In this complex environment different scientific disciplines need to be utilized together to achieve better results comparing to a single application if we want to provide answer for the users' query within an acceptable time frame. We think that in our implementation we have made encouraging step towards a theoretical solution but the different key system components such as similarity measure or the uncertainty handling part needs to be investigated further. In our future research we are planning to establish a qualitative comparison of the similarity algorithms that fulfill all the requirements of our examined domain and our tasks. We believe that probability theory and distribution does not have enough expressive power to tackle certain aspects of the uncertainty e.g. total ignorance. As a consequence we expect that evidence (Dempster-Shafer) theory is the most suitable approach and needs to be investigated in ontology mapping context thought this has not been done so far. The reason is that Dempster-Shafer combination rule can easily be unfeasible in case of domains with large number of variables. Different optimizations methods have been developed but to date we could not find approaches that considered distributed environment. Local computation and valuation networks uses joint tree structure to narrow down the number of focal elements and different architectures has been proposed based on message passing schemes to carry our inference and resolve the problem of the Dempster's rule of combination. In our scenario we assume a dynamic multi agent environment where different agents has partial knowledge of the domain.

References

1. Vargas-Vera M. and Motta E. (2004) AQUA - Ontology-based Question Answering System. Third International Mexican Conference on Artificial Intelligence (MICAI-2004), Lecture Notes in Computer Science 2972 Springer Verlag, (eds R. Monroy et al.), April 26-30, 2004.
2. Vargas-Vera M., Motta E. and Domingue J. (2003) AQUA: An Ontology-Driven Question Answering System. AAAI Spring Symposium, New Directions in Question Answering, Stanford University, March 24-26, 2003.

3. Shafer Glenn,(1976) A Mathematical Theory of Evidence. Princeton University Press.
4. Haveliwala T, Gionis A., Klein D., and Indyk P (2002). Evaluating strategies for similarity search on the web. Proceedings of WWW, Hawai, USA, May 2002.
5. Vargas-Vera M. and Motta E. (2004) A Knowledge-Based Approach to Ontologies Data Integration. KMi-TR-152, The Open University, July 2004.
6. Vargas-Vera M. and Motta E. (2004) An Ontology-driven Similarity Algorithm. KMI-TR-151, Knowledge Media Institute, The Open University, July 2004.
7. Garcia-Molina, H.; Papakonstantinou, Y.; Quass, D.; Rajararnan, A.; Sagiv, Y.; Ullman, J.;Vassalos, V.; Widom, J (1997) The TSIMMIS Approach to Mediation: Data Models and Languages, Journal of Intelligent Information Systems, 8(2):117-132.
8. A. Halevy (1998) The Information manifold approach to data integration. IEEE Intelligent Systems, vol. 13, pp.12-16, 1998
9. Bayardo, R.; et al. (1997) Infosleuth Agent-based Semantic Integration of Information in Open and Dynamic Environments. In Proceedings of ACM SIGMOD Conference on Management of Data, 195-206. Tucson, Arizona.
10. Beneventano, D.; Bergamaschi, S.; Guerra, F.; Vincini, M..(2001) The MOMIS Approach to Information Integration. In ICEIS(1), 194-198.
11. Doan, A. H.; Madhavan, J.; Domingos, P.; Halevy (2002) A. Learning to Map between Ontologies on the Semantic Web. In WWW 2002.
12. Zhongli Ding, Yun Peng, Rong Pan. A Bayesian Approach to Uncertainty Modeling in OWL Ontology. In Proceedings of 2004 International Conference on Advances in Intelligent Systems - Theory and Applications (AISTA2004). November 15-18, 2004, Luxembourg-Kirchberg, Luxembourg.

A Three-Level Approach to Ontology Merging

Agustina Buccella[1], Alejandra Cechich[1], and Nieves Brisaboa[2]

[1] Departamento de Ciencias de la Computación, Universidad Nacional del Comahue,
Buenos Aires 1400, Neuquén, Argentina
{abuccel, acechich}@uncoma.edu.ar
[2] Departamento de Computación, Universidade de A Coruña,
La Coruña, España
brisaboa@udc.es

Abstract. Ontology merging is the process of creating a new ontology from two or more existing ontologies with overlapping parts. Currently, there are many domain areas in Computer Science interested in this topic. Federated Databases and Semantic Web are some of them. In this paper we introduce a three level approach that provides a semi-automatic method to ontology merging. It performs some tasks automatically and guides the user in performing other tasks for which his intervention is required.

1 Introduction

More and more enterprises are currently undertaking projects to integrate their information sources. Organizations realize that one of the more difficult tasks to be faced is determining how data from one source match semantically with data from other sources. This fact involves the concept of *Data integration,* which is concerned with unifying data by sharing some common semantics, but originated from different sources. Although data integration comes in a variety of forms, they share a common task – the *matching of semantically heterogeneous data*. Here is where ontologies take place [6]. In this context, the problem of integrating different sources of information is shifted to integrate different ontologies corresponding to these sources or domains. In this way, the semantic heterogeneity problems will be on ontology terms. There is *ontological heterogeneity* [21] if two systems make different ontological assumptions about their knowledge of the domain. The ontological heterogeneity has a series of inherent problems because each ontology, corresponding only to one information source, can be created independently.

In previous works [1,2,3] we have proposed a three level approach (Figure 1) that allows us to build similarities expressed as mappings. We mainly focus on two concepts: *ontology merging* [11] and *ontology mapping*. *Ontology merging* generates the creation of a new ontology from two or more existing ontologies with overlapping parts, which can be either virtual or physical. *Ontology mapping* relates similar (according to some metric) concepts or relations from different sources to each other by an equivalence relation. A mapping results in a virtual integration.

This paper is organized as follows: Section 2 presents related works in the literature together with relations to our approach. Section 3 contains a detailed explanation of each level of our approach. Then, a case study illustrating how the method works is presented in Section 4. Finally, future work and conclusions are addressed afterwards.

2 Related Works

Several similarity methods to ontology merging and alignment are found in the literature [10]. Among them, the method described in [7] defines several heuristics to identify corresponding concepts in different ontologies. e.g. comparing the names and the natural language definitions of two concepts, and checking the closeness of two concepts in the concept hierarchy. Only super and subclasses relations, and the names of the classes and the definitions are considered.

In [5], the PROMPT tool is described. It is also an interactive ontology-merging tool that guides the user through the merging process. PROMPT starts with the identification of matching class names. Based on this initial step, an iterative approach is carried out to performing automatic updates, finding resulting conflicts, and making suggestions to remove these conflicts. We applied PROMPT to our case study to analyse the set of suggestions that this system produces. The main problem with the PROMPT tool is that when two ontologies contain similar classes (matched syntactically) with datatype properties represented by different names, this tool does not suggest if these properties are the same or not because there is no analysis of similarities between concepts named differently, unless they have the same relations. Therefore, this method is highly dependent on the names of the concepts in the ontology.

Chimarea is presented in [15], an interactive merging tool based on Ontolingua ontology editor [16]. It provides support for merging of ontological terms from different sources, checking the coverage and correctness of ontologies and maintaining ontologies over time. Chimarea is closest to the PROMPT tool due to the type of suggestions made during the interactive process. But in several situations referring to structural aspect of the ontologies, Chimarea does not make any suggestion to the user. The only taxonomic relation that Chimarea considers is the subclass/superclass relation.

Another approach is FCA-MERGE [20]. It is a different method because the comparisons of ontologies are made up using a set of shared instances or a shared set of documents annotated with concepts from source ontologies.

Finally, the work in [14] is similar to our method – a lexical and a conceptual layer are used to find similarities – but thesaurus or other sources of semantic information are not used. At the lexical level, the method uses a lexical function called lexical similarity measure (SM). At the conceptual level, concepts (classes and properties) are compared taking into account the taxonomies in which they appear. Besides, the concept of Semantic Cotopy (SC) is used to define all the super/subconcepts of a specific concept within a taxonomy. A different function is used when the properties or relations must be compared. To do so, authors compare domains and ranges of the properties by using another concept called Upwards Cotopy (UC), which defines all the superconcepts of a specific concept. Datatype properties are not considered by this method. As an improvement, our method compares these properties by analyzing datatype compatibility and syntactic similarity. Special properties are compared in a similar way to our method because domain and range are analyzed separately. However, we also take into account their syntaxes, look for thesauruses and consider property's restrictions. All of these factors have influences when searching similarities because two ontologies may have two properties with the same domain and range, but with different meanings. Besides, there is no supporting tool to implement this approach, and apparently there are no suggestions presented to the user.

3 Our Three-Level Approach

Finding similarities between concepts of different ontologies is a very complex activity. In general, it is not possible to determine fully automatically all mappings between them – primarily because of ontological heterogeneity problems (synonyms, different classifications, etc.). Therefore, the similarity functions we introduce in this paper only determine mapping candidates that users should accept, reject or change.

In our approach, the concepts of an ontology are compared by using three comparison levels: *syntactic*, *semantic* and *user*. Figure 1 presents our three level approach for searching similarities.

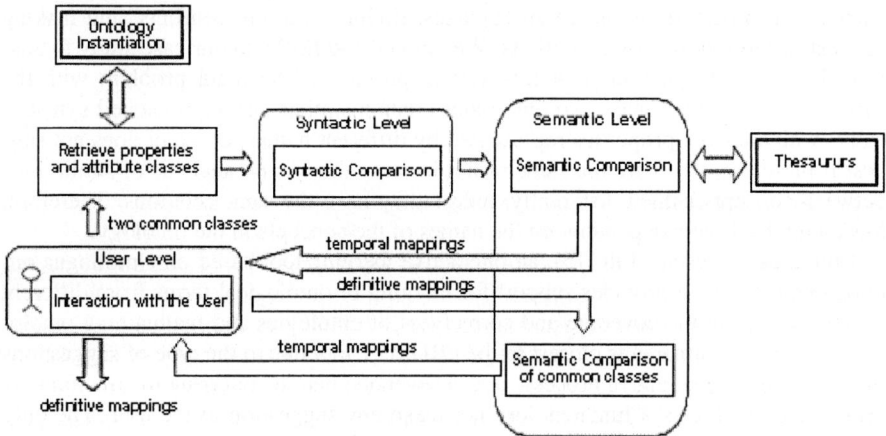

Fig. 1. Approach for searching similarities

Ontology Instantiation and *Thesaurus* are the two external modules in our approach. The former, obtains the object structure from ontologies described in some ontology language. The ontology is divided into classes and properties. Classes are subdivided into *common classes* and *attribute classes*. The common classes have the role of representing things about the domain, and the attribute classes have the role of representing information about a common class (attribute). Properties are also divided into *datatype properties* and *special properties*. Datatype properties are properties relating a class or a set of classes (intersection of classes) with a data type; meanwhile special properties are properties relating classes to each other. The latter, the *Thesaurus* module, uses thesauruses to search for synonyms, which are detected by the module through the use of a similarity function.

In Figure 1, two common classes (of different ontologies) are indicated by the user. These two classes are inputs of the *Retrieve Properties and Attribute Classes* module, which retrieves the attribute classes and special and datatype properties of each class by using the object structure of each ontology.

This retrieved information enters of the *Syntactic Comparison* module, which analyses syntactically classes and properties relating with the concepts. Four similarity functions are used in this level: the *edit distance* function [12,14], the *trigram* function [13], the *data type* function, and the *check restriction* function. The edit function (1) returns a degree of similarity between 0 and 1, where 1 stands for perfect match and 0 for bad match. Given two strings, it considers the number of changes that must be done to turn one string into the other, and weights the number of these changes with respect to the length of the shortest string.

$$sim_{ed}(x,y) = \max\left(0, \frac{\min(|x|,|y|) - ed(x,y)}{\min(|x|,|y|)}\right) \in [0,1] \quad (1)$$

For example, $ed(animal, animals) = 1$, because one insert operation changes the string "animal" into "animals", $\min(|animal|,|animals|) = \min(6,7) = 6$, therefore $sim_{ed}(animal, animals) = \max(0, 5/6) = 5/6$.

The *trigram function* (2) is based on the number of different trigrams in two concepts or strings:

$$sim_{tri}(x,y) = \frac{1}{1 + |tri(x)| + |tri(y)| - 2 \times |tri(x) \cap tri(y)|} \quad (2)$$

where $tri(x)$ is the set of trigrams in x. For example, $tri(animal) = \{ani, nim, ima, mal\}$. If we compare the *animal* word with the *animals* word, we have: $|tri(animal)| = 4$, $|tri(animals)| = 5$ and $(|tri(animal)| \cap |tri(animals)|) = 4$, therefore $sim_{tri}(animal, animals) = 1/2$.

The *data type function* or *datatype compatibility* is a straightforward function because it only compares the data types of two concepts (datatype properties). For example string to string, or string to integer. If there is a logical conversion of a data type into another this function returns 1, and returns 0 otherwise.

Finally, the *check restriction* function compares the restrictions applied to the properties, for example functional, transitive, symmetric, etc. Only when both properties have the same restrictions the function returns 1, otherwise it returns a percentage according to the number of restrictions that are the same.

When properties are special properties, ranges are recursively compared, and the process will stop when the ranges are attribute classes (because they do not have properties to be compared).

The *Semantic Comparison* module compares the classes and properties semantically. To do so, we extract semantic information from the *Thesaurus* module in order to find synonym relationships. Using the results of the syntactic level functions, we construct functions that combine these values together with the thesaurus information.

In the *Interaction with the User* module all the mappings that exceed a threshold[1] are shown to the user, and he decides if the mappings are correct. The accepted mappings are classified as definitive mappings.

The *Semantic Comparison for Common Classes* module receives the definitive mappings and compares the common classes of the two ontologies. It uses the mappings added by the comparison of properties in order to denote the set of similar attributes (properties) of both classes. The similarity function described in [1,19] is used in this level:

---

[1] By a series of proofs with real ontologies extracted from Internet, we have determined that 0.45 is the minimum value of the threshold.

$$sim_{att}(x,y) = \frac{|X \cap Y|}{|X \cap Y| + a(x,y)|X/Y| + (1 - a(x,y))|Y/X|} \quad for \ 0 \leq a \leq 1 \quad (3)$$

where the functions x and y are concepts and X and Y correspond to description sets of x and y respectively. The α function indicates the depth of the concepts within a taxonomy. It calculates the most common superclass between two concepts and then it counts the depth of these concepts in the hierarchy. If the depth of two concepts is the same, the α function is equal to 0.5; (see [2] for more details). For example, if the *animal* concept is described by three attributes (*color, weight* and *age*), and the *animals* concept is also described by three attributes (*color, age* and *mammal*), the parts of the function are:

|X ∩ Y|=|{color,weigth,age}∩{color,age,mammal}| = 2,
|X/Y|=|{color,weigth,age}/{color,age,mammal}| = 1 and
|Y/X|=|{color,age,mammal}/{color,weigth,age}| = 1; and in this case
α(*animal,animals*) = 0.5. Therefore sim_{att}(*animal,animals*) = 2/3.

One more time, in the *Interaction with the User* module, all mappings are displayed to the user and he decides if these mappings must be added permanently.

3.1 A Supporting Tool

In order to implement our approach for searching similarities, we have developed an interactive software tool. It was developed using the Java Platform [8], and Eclipse [4] as the working environment. The interfaces were created in the Web browser. Connections between users and the server are made by using the technology of Java Servlet [9]. The server uses the Linux operating system and the PostgreSQL [17] database. Currently, the system is off-line and only works locally because it is still under testing. For a detailed description of the structure of software components used to implement the supporting tool we refer the reader to [3].

4 A Case Study

Firstly, we have extracted two ontologies named *Air_Reservation* and *Car_Rental*[2] from repositories on the Web. In this paper, we represent the ontologies by using a diagrammatic notation instead of ontology code to facilitate reading. In the Figures, arrows represent special properties of the common classes. The datatype properties are represented as attributes within the class definition as name_of_property → datatype. The first element is the property's name and the second is the data type. Therefore, a datatype property maps the class in which it is in (domain) to its datatype element (range).

Figure 2 shows the *Air_Reservation* ontology. As we can see, this ontology has twelve classes together with their properties representing an air reservation domain. For example, the *Record* class has two subclasses (*Reservation_record* and *Payment_record*). The *Reservation_record* class represents information about a reservation

---

[2] http://protege.stanford.edu/plugins/prompt/prompt.html

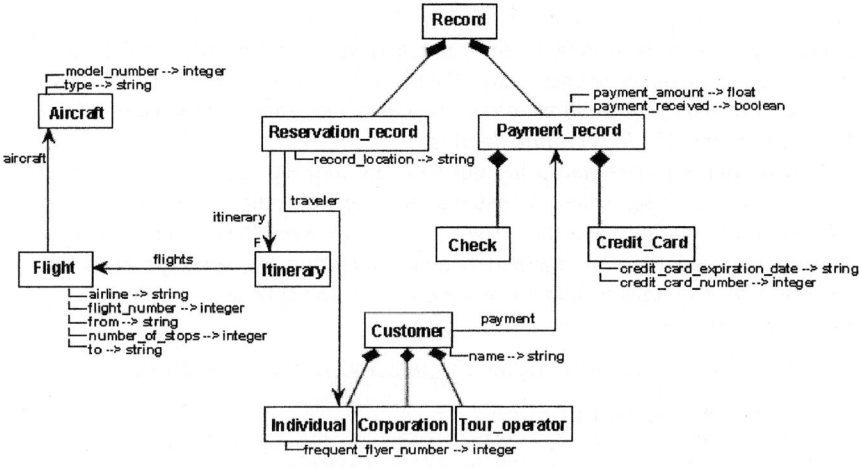

Fig. 2. *Air_Reservation* Ontology

containing one datatype property, *record_location,* related to the String type; and two special properties, *traveller* and *itinerary*. The *traveller* special property relates one reservation to the *Individual* class, and the *itinerary* special property relates one reservation to the *Itinerary* class. The *Payment_record* class is also important because it represents information about the payment. It contains two subclasses, *Check* and *Credit_Card*. Two datatype properties describe the *Credit_Card* class, with information about the number and the expiration date. Finally, the *Customer* class contains one special property, *payment*, relating this class to the *Payment_record* class.

Figure 3 shows the *Car_Rental* Ontology. This ontology has nine classes together with their properties representing a car rental domain. Again, the *Record* class has two subclasses (*Reservation_record* and *Payment_record*). The *Reservation* class represents information about a car reservation containing four datatype properties that denote information about the customer type, the reservation number, etc.; and four special properties, that are related to other classes in the ontology. For example, the

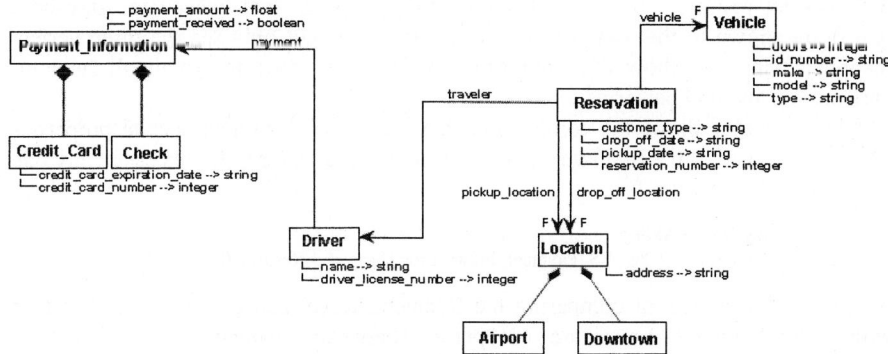

Fig. 3. *Car_Rental* Ontology

traveller special property contains the *Driver* class as range. The *Driver* class contains two datatype properties to indicate the name and the driver license number; and one special property *payment* (Functional) related to the *Payment_Information* class. Finally the *Payment_Information* class contains the same information as *Payment_record* in the *Air_Reservation* ontology.

Following our approach and using our software tool we begin the similarity process. Suppose that a user enters a first mapping between the *Customer* class of the *Air_Reservation* ontology and the *Driver* class of the *Car_Rental* ontology. In order to dertermine similarity, our method begins comparing the datatype properties of these classes to other classes that are related to (by using special properties).

In this case, the tool shows:

> COMPARING TWO ONTOLOGIES: AIR_RESERVATION - CAR_RENTAL
> Select bad matches
> DATATYPE PROPERTIES
> Customer Class, name Property VS. Driver Class, name Property ==> Result = 1.0
> Customer Class, name Property VS. Driver Class, driver_license_number Property ==> Result = 0.26136363
> Payment_record Class, payment_amount Property VS. Payment_Information Class, payment_amount Property ==> Result = 1.0
> Payment_record Class, payment_amount Property VS. Payment_Information Class, payment_received Property ==> Result = 0.31130952
> Payment_record Class, payment_received Property VS. Payment_Information Class, payment_amount Property ==> Result = 0.31130952
> Payment_record Class, payment_received Property VS. Payment_Information Class, payment_received Property ==> Result = 1.0

Note that the datatype properties of the *Payment_record* and *Payment_Information* classes have been compared together with the datatype properties of the two first classes (*Customer* and *Driver*). This is because these two classes contain a special property, *payment*, which relates them to *Payment_record* and *Payment_Information* respectively. All these properties have been compared using the first three modules of our approach (Figure 1), that is, they were compared using the syntactic functions within the Syntactic Level and the thesaurus function within the Semantic Level. Now at the Interaction with the User module within the User Level, the user has to decide which of these mappings must be stored as definitive and which ones must be rejected. As we can see, there are three mappings with low results and three mappings with perfect results. Remember that only the mappings that exceed the threshold (0.45) are shown to the user, so in this case the user will only see the three perfect mappings. Here, we show all mappings (with low values too) to explain all the comparisons our method performs.

Then, our tool shows the comparisons between classes without special properties which are related to the first two classes (*Customer* and *Driver*). In this case, only one comparison is shown:

> COMMON CLASSES
> Payment_record Class VS. Payment_Information Class ==> Result = 0.7312411

In spite of the results of comparing the Syntactic Level and the thesaurus function within the Semantic Level are not perfect between *Payment_record* and *Payment_Information* classes, the Semantic Comparison of the Common Classes module returns a perfect result because these classes are similar structurally. That is, they contain two datatype properties that were selected as definitive mappings and they do not have special properties. Therefore, the result of all comparisons is 0.7312411.

Now, our tool shows the result of comparing the special property by relating *Customer* and *Driver* to *Payment_record* and *Payment_Information* respectively.

> SPECIAL PROPERTIES
> Customer Class, payment Property VS. Driver Class, payment Property ==> Result = 1.0

This mapping generates a perfect value because the comparison was perfect in all the modules. The payment property is similar syntactic and semantically and it contains the same class range (*Payment_record* and *Payment_Information*) compared in previous steps.

Finally, as the tool have compared all the special and datatype properties and classes without properties related to the two first classes, it only shows the last comparison, between *Customer* and *Driver*:

> COMMON CLASSES
> Customer Class VS. Driver Class ==> Result = 0.5650808

The mapping generates the value of 0.5650808 because both classes are different syntactic and semantically, but they contain the same special properties and some datatype properties. Then, the Semantic Comparison of the Common Classes module returns a high value.

Now, our tool shows the definitive mappings generated by our method:

```
COMPARING TWO ONTOLOGIES: AIR_RESERVATION - CAR_RENTAL
Generated Mappings
DATATYPE PROPERTIES
Customer Class, name Property <--> Driver Class, name Property
-------------------o-------------------o-------------------o-------------------o-------------------
Payment_record Class, payment_amount Property <--> Payment_Information Class, payment_amount Property
-------------------o-------------------o-------------------o-------------------o-------------------
Payment_record Class, payment_received Property <--> Payment_Information Class, payment_received Property
-------------------o-------------------o-------------------o-------------------o-------------------
Customer Class, payment Property <--> Driver Class, payment Property
-------------------o-------------------o-------------------o-------------------o-------------------
ATTRIBUTE CLASSES
COMMON CLASSES
Payment_record Class <--> Payment_Information Class
-------------------o-------------------o-------------------u-------------------o-------------------
Customer Class <--> Driver Class
-------------------o-------------------o-------------------o-------------------o-------------------
```

Following, we will perform two modifications to the *Car_Rental* ontology in order to show how our method might find more mappings based on the user's decisions. The first modification renames the *Payment_Information* class as *Fee* and the second modification deletes the two datatype properties contained in this class (*payment_amount* and *payment_received*).

With these two changes in mind, we execute our method again. In this case, the comparison of the *Payment_Record* class (of the *Air_Reservation* ontology) to the *Fee* class (of the *Car_Rental* ontology) returns a very low value (0.34). Therefore this mapping is not showed to the user because it does not exceed the threshold. As in the aforementioned example, our method continues comparing the properties of the classes. *Payment* is the only special property to compare because the *Fee* class has not datatype properties. This comparison generates a high value (0.8) because both are similar syntactic and semantically – only the comparison between the range classes (*Payment_Record* and *Fee*) failed. Following, this mapping is shown to the user and when they determine that this mapping is correct, our method shows the mapping between *Payment_record* and *Fee* classes. This happens because our method is based on the user's choices. If the *payment* special property was selected as the same, we can assume that the range classes are also the same. If these classes are selected as the same, the method adds the same definitive mappings as in the previous example. Similarly, if the user rejects this last mapping, the method automatically deletes the mapping generated between the *payment* special properties.

The same happens when we have similar classes but the properties relating them are represented by using very different names, so it is impossible to find a synonym relationship in the thesaurus. In spite of our method returns a very low value (less than 0.45), the tool will show these properties when the classes are selected as the same by the user.

5 Conclusion and Future Work

Our method allows a user to find several correct mappings, taking into account the structure of the ontologies and their syntactic and semantic relationships. One problem with our approach is that mappings are dependent on the structure, that is, when two ontologies represent information in a very different fashion, the mappings are very difficult to find.

As a future work, we are developing techniques to find mappings when the structure of the ontologies are different, for example when one property in one ontology is represented by two properties in the other. Additionally, another implementation of our method is being implemented in order to integrate it to Protégé [18].

References

1. Buccella A., Cechich A. and Brisaboa N.R. An Ontology Approach to Data Integration. JCS&T, Vol.3(2). Available at http://journal.info.unlp.edu.ar/default.html, pp. 62-68, 2003.
2. Buccella A., Cechich A., and Brisaboa N. A Federated Layer to Integrate Heterogeneous Knowledge, VODCA 2004: First International Workshop on Views on Designing Complex Architectures, Bertinoro, Italy, 11-12 Sept. 2004. Electronic Notes in Theoretical Computer Science, Elsevier Science B.V.
3. Buccella A., Cechich A. and Brisaboa N.R. An Ontology-based Environment to Data Integration. IDEAS 2004, pp. 79-90, 3-7 May, 2004.
4. Eclipse Home Page. http://www.eclipse.org.
5. Fridman Noy, N. and Musen, M. PROMPT: algorithm and tool for automated ontology merging and alignment. Proc. AAAI '00, 450–455.
6. Gruber, T. A translation approach to portable ontology specifications. Knowledge Acquisition 1993 –Vol.5(2): pp. 199–220, 2003.

7. Hovy, E. Combining and standardizing large-scale, practical ontologies for machine translation and other uses. Proc. 1st Intl. Conf. on Language Resources and Evaluation, Granada, Spain, 1998.
8. Java SE Platform. http://java.sun.com.
9. Java Servlet. http://java.sun.com/products/servlet/.
10. Kalfoglou, Y. and Schorlemmer, M. Ontology mapping: the state of the art. The Knowledge Engineering Review, 18(1), pp. 1–31, 2003.
11. Klein, M. Combining and relating ontologies: an analysis of problems and solutions. IJCAI-2001 Workshop on Ontologies and Information Sharing, Seattle, WA, 2001.
12. Levenshtein, I. V., Binary codes capable of correcting deletions, insertions, and reversals. Cybernetics and Control Theory, Vol.10(8), pp. 707-710, 1996.
13. Lin, D. An Information-Theoretic Definition of Similarity. Proceedings of the Fifteenth International Conference on Machine Learning, pp.296-304, July 24-27, 1998.
14. Maedche, A., Staab, S. Measuring Similarity between Ontologies. EKAW 2002: 251-263.
15. McGuinness, D., Fikes, R., Rice, J. and Wilder, S. An environment for merging and testing large Oontologies.Proc. KR '00, 483–493.
16. Ontolingua Editor. http://ontolingua.stanford.edu/index.html.
17. PostgreSQL Home Page. http://www.postgresql.org/.
18. Protégé Editor. http://protege.stanford.edu/
19. Rodriguez, A., Egenhofer, M. Determining Semantic Similarity among Entity Classes from Different Ontologies. IEEE Transactions on Knowledge and Data Engineering, Vol.15(2), pp. 442-456, March/April 2003..
20. Stumme, G. and Madche, A. FCA-Merge: Bottom-up merging of ontologies. In 7th Intl. Conf. on Artificial Intelligence (IJCAI '01), pages 225–230, Seattle, WA, 2001.
21. Visser, P., Jones, D., Bench-Capon, T., Shave, M. An Analysis of Ontology Mismatches; Heterogeneity versus Interoperability. AAAI Spring Symposium on Ontological Engineering, 1997.

Domain and Competences Ontologies and Their Maintenance for an Intelligent Dissemination of Documents

Yassine Gargouri[1], Bernard Lefebvre[2], and Jean-Guy Meunier[1]

[1] Laboratory of Cognitive Information Analysis
[2] Laboratory of Knowledge Management, Diffusion and Acquisition,
University of Quebec at Montreal, Montreal (Quebec) H3C 3P8, Canada
{gargouri.yassine, lefebvre.bernard,
meunier.jean-guy}@uqam.ca

Abstract. One of the big challenges of the knowledge management is the active and intelligent dissemination of the know-how to users while executing their tasks, without bothering them with information that is too far from their competences or out of their interest fields. Delivering a new document to the concerned users consists basically on appreciating the semantic relevance of the content of this document (domain ontology) in relation with users' competences (competences ontology). In this paper, we illustrate the importance, within a documentary dissemination service, of the integration of an ontologies system, essentially based on the domain and the competences, but also on the users, the documents, the processes and the enterprise. The maintenance of these ontologies and basically those related to documents, to domain and to competences is a crucial aspect for the system survival. So, we describe what role the texts analysis can play for the maintenance of these ontologies.

1 Introduction

Inside an organisational environment, the information can only become knowledge if it is listed, structured and available to access to the concerned persons, and at the right moment. The implementation of computer solutions for knowledge management, as an answer to these objectives, is rather a recent phenomenon [16]. This implies in fact, the difficult integration of concepts and techniques coming from various domains such as the artificial intelligence, the information systems engineering, the processes reengineering or the behaviour of the organisations and their human resources [11].

The project MDKT (Management and Dissemination of Knowledge in Telecommunication) deals with this topic [10]. It aims basically to facilitate the competences development of human resources for the enterprise needs. It consists of a computer environment which aims to offer a concrete and precious help to users accomplishing their activities, and consequently, to increase their productivity. This should help them to enrich their professional knowledge and contribute as a result, to their permanent training.

Within an environment, where knowledge related to professional activities grows up very quickly and where it is not correctly structured, the users (experts, technicians ...)

are not always conscious about the existence of useful information for their activities. And even when they are, they don't know necessarily how to access them. Having an active dissemination service in order to forward useful and relevant information to the concerned persons is consequently an obvious need.

One of the big challenges of the active and intelligent dissemination of documents to users is to not bothering them with information that is too far from their competences or out of their interest fields. Beyond information management, we deal with knowledge management, and more specifically to the semantics that can be associated to information or its context. We propose in this paper a response to this challenge, fundamentally based on a dissemination service driven by domain and competences ontologies, but also by documents, processes, users and enterprise ontologies.

After a brief review of the MDKT project structure, we describe the contents of the domain and the competences ontologies and show their importance to construct a documents dissemination service to the concerned users. Then, we present the maintenance process for updating the domain ontology and as a consequence, the one of competences. This process is essential for the long term survival of the system.

2 The MDKT Project

Among works having similar objectives as the ones of the MDKT project, we can mention the works of Abecker et al. [1] based on the "KnowMore" platform which is developed on the basis of an architecture of the organisational memory to meet the querying requirements within a task context. While this project is principally based on the domain knowledge to describe the documents, the MDKT project integrates an additional dimension, the one of the competences for a better users characterisation.

Like the « Ontologging » project [15], the MDKT is also based on agents contributing for a better personalization of the knowledge dissemination.

In artificial intelligence, ontologies have been developed as a response to the problems of knowledge representation and manipulation inside data processing systems. The Web researchers have adopted the term "ontology" to refer to a document (or file) defining, in a formal way, the relations between terms [3]. Inside the semantic Web, ontologies are used as a system core to access structured information as well as inference rules supporting the automatic reasoning [3]. These ontologies also offer the capability for a program to find the various terms referring to a same concept. In this specific case, we are dealing with domain ontologies.

The knowledge model structure of the MDKT project is thus principally based on ontologies [10], which are the ontologies of domain, competences, documents, business processes, users (or employees) and enterprise.

- *The domain ontology* describes the general elements and properties of the domain knowledge organisation (which is, in this project, wireless telecommunication).
- *The document ontology* (or *the information ontology*) describes the different documentary information resources related to the domain. Its links to the others ontologies (competences, enterprise and business processes) can also be useful

for filtering the information within the dissemination service to avoid documents that don't match the users selection criteria.
- *The competences ontology* represents the knowledge model core and is described further. This is a key element in the filtering process.
- *The business process ontology* describes components of the professional activity for an enterprise.
- *The employee ontology* is used to describe the profile of the system users (the enterprise employees).
- *The enterprise ontology* presents the concept of roles which can be played by the employees.

The knowledge creation, control and maintenance of the MDKT system is a complex and crucial task. In order to facilitate these tasks, various services were used or developed inside this project. Among them, we mention an ontologies editor (Protege-2000 [13]), a documents analysis system (SATIM [4]), a system for the domain ontology maintenance (ONTOLOGICO [7,8]), a system helping for the documents annotation (AnnoCitaTool) and various services allowing ontologies exploration (NORD), dissemination and querying of documents.

3 The Competences Ontology

A competence is a know-how, a knowledge or a behaviour that appears inside a professional situation for a purpose or a result. It necessitates a certain level of expertise. It's important, within the context of the MDKT project, to measure the employee's competences level. However, the competence is hardly measurable, but can be represented by action fields and elements that can be treated on a hierarchical basis.

The competence is defined in relation to other concepts describing the capacity, the ability and the expertise of the employee when executing a professional activity. Inside the MDKT project, these elements and their relations constitute the competences model, as detailed in [10]. In particular, the relation between the employees and the competences is, not only specified in a direct manner, but also, in an indirect way through the roles executed by these employees. This relation represents the requirements they have to respect when executing an activity for the enterprise. Other relations exist also between the competences themselves. They are relations of analogy, generalisation and aggregation [12]:

- Analogy relation: the competences can be similar from the point of view of their functionality, their result or their definition.
- Generalisation relation: describe the relation between two competences; one of them is more general than the other according to the classic meaning adopted within the context of the object oriented programming paradigm.
- Aggregation relation: this relation is used when a competence is a component of an other one.

In the context of the MDKT project, the competences are classified in two groups: the specific competences and the transversal ones. The first group refers to competences directly needed for the execution of work processes, whereas the second refers to competences useful for the achievement of many work processes and are generally related to the domain knowledge. A competence is characterized by an expertise level. The level 1 refers to a beginner and the level 5 to an expert. Moreover, the competences can be identified by capability verbs that are organized in different levels of complexity [14].

4 Documents Dissemination

An active and efficient dissemination consists on semantically filtering the potential employees, for whom, a document can be useful. After a semantic content analysis of a new document, the filtering process considers the competences, the abilities, the expertise levels, the employees roles and tasks, in order to deliver this document to the persons able to understand it and interested to consult it.

The documents dissemination to the appropriate employees is a big challenge. In fact, it aims to offer a precious and realistic help for the achievement of the professional activities of the employees, without bothering them by information that does not belong to their interest fields or that does not match their competences. The dissemination also aims to enrich their professional knowledge, ameliorate their productivity, produce a saving time and improve their efficiency by allowing accessing the relevant information, at the time of the tasks execution and according to a user-friendly form.

Carrying out such objectives should, as a consequence, respect a set of rules, defined inside a knowledge base. For example, the documents must be filtered according to the key concepts of these documents, compared to the task the employee has to accomplish. The documents filtering must also consider the expertise level of the user which is related to a transversal competence associated to a concept that is present in the document. This judgment is based on the concept of *proximal zone of development* [17] which is " the distance between the level of the current development determined by the way a person resolves a problem by himself and the level of the potential development, as the way it resolves problems when it is assisted by an external element". This concept has practical consequences on learning. It helps characterizing the development direction and determining the objectives of the learner on the basis of the mediator intervention. This interaction must be situated inside the proximal zone of development of the learner in order to help him exceeding his current competences.

The identification of this zone needs the definition of relations between the competences and their classification according to hierarchical levels.

The dissemination service architecture, as described in (fig.1) consists basically of two parts, the *filtering engine* and the *diffusion service*. The first one is in charge of selecting users whether the corresponding document belongs or not to their proximal zone of development. The filtering engine provides an appropriate users list which is sent to the dissemination service for the proper delivering of the documents.

The semantic reasoning associated to filtering is executed thanks to implicit or explicit relations between entities represented in the ontologies. It is based on inference processes such as subsumption as well as heuristics in order to give to this semantic reasoning, naturals and intelligent behaviours.

For example : the set of persons having the expertise "*InstallNetwork_3*" consists, not only of persons having exactly this characteristic, but also of the ones having the expertises "*InstallNetwork_4*" and "*InstallNetwork_5*" which are of a higher level.

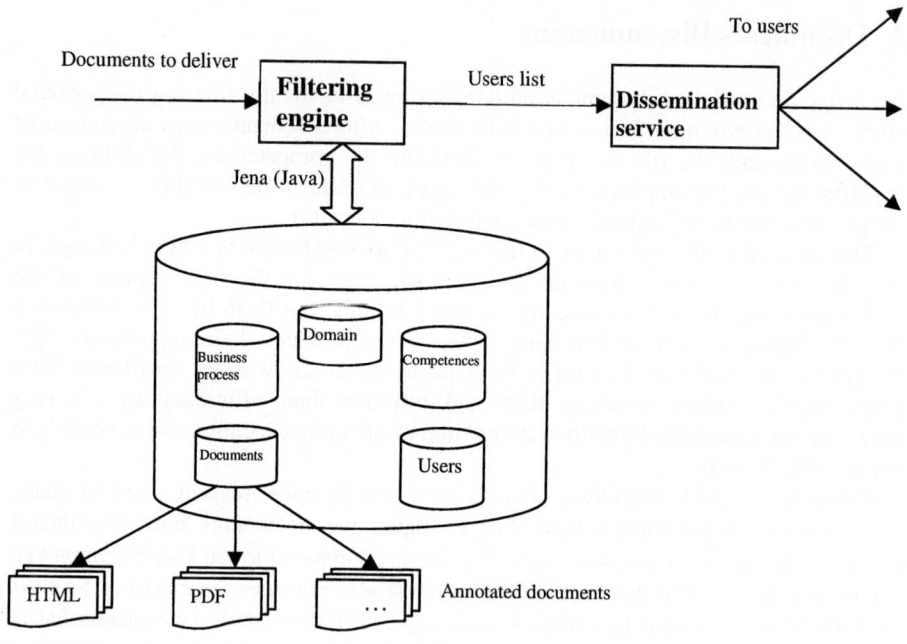

Fig. 1. Dissemination service architecture

Some other heuristic arguments, implemented inside the system, concern the aggregation relation ("*isDecomposeIn*") and the analogy relation ("*sameAs*") between the competences.

The characteristics of the competences, relative to capability verbs are also considered within the reasoning depending on the nature, more or less general of these verbs [14].

A documentary querying service also uses the functionalities of the filtering engine to provide to users, documents they look for, not only according to specific criteria, like a task or a concept of the domain but also, with respect to the users expertises and those required by a candidate document.

5 Maintenance System of the Domain Ontology

The technical terms specific to a particular domain change and evolve in a perpetual way. As a consequence, the domain ontologies have to be maintained to face incompleteness and errors, or to be adapted to the innovations in the domain. The completeness and accuracy of terms of a specific domain inside the ontology are considered as an important pre-processing, to assure the usefulness and the efficiency of the ontology, and as a consequence, the effectiveness of the dissemination service.

Initially, the conception of the domain ontology has been achieved by the mean of a set of tools integrated inside a platform named SATIM. The role of these tools and principally the GRAMEXCO module is to assist for the detection of terms and concepts from documents. These tools are also used to facilitate the annotation of new documents and their association to the domain ontology.

In addition, the maintenance of the domain ontology follows a structured process [7] implemented as a chain of processes of the platform SATIM, named ONTOLOGICO [8]. Since it is difficult and tedious to detect new relations between terms by reading textual data and to evaluate their pertinence compared to the current ontology, the use of a technique, at least semi-automatic, is considered to be essential.

ONTOLOGICO aims as a consequence to assist the domain experts in their maintenance task of the domain ontology. This later is here viewed as the incremental upgrade of the ontology as new concepts are extracted from domain texts. The processing sequence ONTOLOGICO is made of the following modules: a simple terms extractor, a complex terms extractor, a classifier, a lemmatisation module, a segmentation module, a domain thesaurus, a semantic refinement module (based on the Latent Semantic Indexing) and an identifier of related terms (based on the computation of semantic similarity between couples of conceptual vectors).

The process begins with the application of the documents classification technique (using GRAMEXCO) to identify, at the first step, groups of terms that appear together in a same class of documents and which are potentially semantically related.

Then, from these groups of terms, we intend to extract couples of highly related concepts. This task is accomplished using the *Latent semantic Indexing* technique (LSI) [5], associated with the *Singular Values Decomposition* (SVD) [9]. The complementary aspects between the documents classification technique, which is in our case based on the neural networks (ART1), and the Latent semantic Indexing approach, constitutes an extremely powerful refinement process [8]. This process allows detecting, from the terms groups issued from the classification, the most representative of the information located in the documents of a same class.

The next objective is to identify pairs of concepts represented by terms having a certain semantic similarity. For this purpose, we propose a method based on the representation of concepts by vectors. These vectors are built from lexical items associated to the corresponding concept, according to relations of synonymy, antonymy, hyponymy or meronymy. These relations can be extracted from a thesaurus or from the current ontology.

Using a measure of semantic similarity between conceptual vectors, that is the thematic distance, we identify the couples presenting a high probability to be semantically related. This method is based on the semantic hypothesis of Firth [6], according to which, words having a same lexical surrounding are supposed having associated semantics and their conceptual vectors are therefore, similar. This hypothesis allows an interesting preliminary analysis of the domain, which is after that, refined by the manual identification of pertinent relations (synonymy …).

These relations between terms have finally to be checked and analysed by an expert to confirm their pertinence, compared to the current ontology. A set of rules insuring the coherence of the entire model has to be respected. The expert has also to associate labels to these relations. Finally, terms and relations between terms (resulting from the previous process) are integrated into the current ontology.

In this way, the maintenance of the domain ontology allows to have a better representation of the documentary base using up-to-date domain knowledge. Indeed, the semantic content of new documents (as well as the former ones) is better structured thanks to the practically total integration of key terms of the domain in the ontology.

6 The Maintenance of the Competence Ontology

Since the competence acquisition is a continuous process, the competences ontology has also to be up-to-date. During their professional life, the employees maintain and improve their experiences by trainings or by practical experiences. So, new competences can appear, associated for example to new concepts integrated in the domain ontology. For a user for whom, a document introducing new concepts has been delivered, one can infer the existence of new competences that can be characterised at the beginning, by a very low expertise level and by a verb of capability, like "know".

Finally, we support the idea of an integration of the dissemination service with the querying system, so that the first one can consider the habits of use of the second one. The behaviours and reactions of a user, when he processes queries of documents can be considered, by a learning process, to adjust the depth of the proximal zone of development for each user and consequently, to improve the personalization of the dissemination.

7 Conclusion and Future Work

Delivering a new document to the appropriate users means to basically judging the relevance of the semantic content of the document in relation to the users competences. We had shown in this paper the importance, in this documentary dissemination service, of the integration of an architecture of ontologies.

However, the existence of new documents, having new key terms of the domain, implies the emergence of gaps inside the domain ontology, in the absence of a progressive evolution process of the ontology. In fact, this one has to integrate the new concepts to assure a robust annotation of documents, i.e a form of semantic representation that is sensibly complete.

In regard to the complexity and the cost of this maintenance process of the domain ontology, the usefulness of such assistance tools for maintenance such as the ones described in this paper is more and more confirmed. For this purpose, our future works will go deeper in the process of maintenance by the support of ONTOLOGICO chain of processes and will present more contributions of this chain.

References

1. Abecker, Andreas; Bernardi, Ansgar; Hinkelmann, Knut; Kuhn, Otto, and Sintek, Michael, 1998. Toward a Technology for Organizational Memories. IEEE Intelligent Systems. 1998; 1340-48.
2. Achaba, Hicham : Système de diffusion documentaire basé sur des ontologies. Mémoire de maîtrise en informatique, Université du Québec à Montréal, 2004.
3. Berners-Lee, Tim; Hendler, James, and Lassila, Ora. The semantic Web. Scientific American. 2001 May; 284(5):35; ISSN: 00368733.
4. Biskri, I. and Meunier, J.G. (2002) "SATIM : Système d'Analyse et de Traitement de l'Information Multidimensionnelle", Proceedings of JADT 2002, St-Malo, France, 185-196.
5. Deerwester, S., Dumais, S. T., Furnas, G. W., Landauer, T. K., Harshman, R. (1990) "Indexing by latent semantic analysis". JASIS, 41(6), 391-407.
6. Firth, J. R. 1957. A synopsis of linguistic theory 1930–1955. In Studies in Linguistic Analysis,Philological Society, Oxford, England, 1–32. (Reprinted in F. R. Palmer (ed.), Selected Papers of J. R. Firth 1952–1959, Longman, London, England, 1968).
7. Gargouri, Y., Lefebvre, B. et Meunier, J.G. « ONTOLOGICO : vers un outil d'assistance au développement itératif des ontologies ». Journées d'études sur Terminologie, Ontologie, et Représentation des connaissances (TERMINO'2004). Lyon, France, janvier 2004.
8. Gargouri, Y., Lefebvre, B. et Meunier, J.G. « Ontology Maintenance using Textual Analysis », SCI'2003 : The 7th World Multiconference Systems, Cybernetics and Informatics, p. 248 - 253, Orlando, Florida, July 2003 - Systems, Cybernetics and Informatics Journal.
9. Golub, G. H., Reinsch, C. (1969) "Singular value decomposition and least squares solutions". Handbook for Automatic Computation, Springer-Verlag, New York, 134-151.
10. Lefebvre, B., Tadié, S. Gauthier, G. , Duc, T.H., Achaba, H. « Competence ontology for domain knowledge dissemination and retrieval », Workshop on Grid Learning Services, GLS'2004, Maceio, Brazil, August 30, 2004, pp. 94-104.
11. Liebowitz J. : Knowledge management handbook, Boca Raton, Fla, CRC Press, 1999.
12. Nkambou, R. : Modélisation des connaissances de la matière dans un système tutoriel intelligent : modèles, outils et applications. 1996.
13. Noy N. F., Sintek M., Decker S., Crubezy M. and others, "Creating semantic Web contents with protege-2000", IEEE Intelligent Systems, vol. 16, no 2, March 2001-April 2001, p. 60.
14. Paquette Gilbert 02. Modélisation des connaissances et des compétences : un langage graphique pour concevoir et apprendre. Sainte-Foy: Presses de l'Université du Québec; 2002;
15. Razmerita, L.; Angehrn, A., and Maedche, A. Ontology based user modeling for Knowledge Management Systems. Proceedings of the User Modeling Conference; Pittsburgh, USA. Springer-Verlag; 2003: 213-217.
16. Rubenstein-Montano B., Liebowitz J., Buchwalter J., Mccaw D., Newman B. and others, "A systems thinking framework for knowledge management", Decision Support Systems, vol. 31, no 1, May 2001, p. 5.
17. Vygotski, L. S., 1934, Traduction française : Pensée et langage, Paris, Messidor, 1985. Réédition: Editions La Dispute, 1997.

Modelling Power and Trust for Knowledge Distribution: An Argumentative Approach

Carlos Iván Chesñevar[1], Ramón F. Brena[2], and José Luis Aguirre[2]

[1] Artificial Intelligence Research Group, Department of Computer Science,
Universitat de Lleida, Campus Cappont,
C/Jaume II, 69, E-25001 Lleida, Spain
cic@eps.udl.es
[2] Centro de Sistemas Inteligentes, Tecnológico de Monterrey,
64849 Monterrey, N.L., México
{ramon.brena, jlaguirre}@itesm.mx

Abstract. Knowledge and Information distribution, which is one of the main processes in Knowledge Management, is greatly affected by *power* explicit relations, as well as by implicit relations like *trust*. Making decisions about whether to deliver or not a specific piece of information to users on the basis of a rationally justified procedure under potentially conflicting policies for power and trust relations is indeed a challenging problem. In this paper we model power relations, as well as delegation and trust, in terms of an argumentation formalism, in such a way that a dialectical process works as a decision core, which is used in combination with the existing knowledge and an information distribution system. A detailed example is presented and an implementation reported.

Keywords: Argumentation, reputation, knowledge distribution, multi-agent systems, trust.

1 Introduction and Motivations

Power relations inside organizations have been the subject of many studies in Knowledge Management (KM) [1,2]. Even though modern organization theories emphasize flexibility and learning over rigid hierarchical structures [3,4], formal power relations have remained as a key component in any large organization. A counterpart of formal relations are informal relations in organizations, notably *trust* relations [5], which are normally not represented in the organization's formal structure, but are nonetheless extremely important. Trust and reputation relations have been formalized for computational purposes [6,7] with the goal of defining what is believed to be reliable in the context of such informal relations.

Disseminating pieces of information and knowledge (IK) among the members of large organizations is a well known problem in KM [8], involving several decision-making processes. Indeed, a central concern in KM is to facilitate *knowledge flow* within relevant actors within an organization. Organizations typically have different criteria establishing their information distribution *policies*, and in many real situations these policies conflict with each other.

In previous research work [9,10] we have shown how a multiagent framework can been used for delivering highly customized notifications just-in-time to the adequate users in large distributed organizations. This paper extends that framework by incorporating the possibility of representing power and trust capabilities associated with the agents involved, thus encompassing both formal and informal relations in organizations. Conflicts emerging from potentially contradictory policies as well as from trust and empowerment issues are solved on the basis of a dialectical analysis whose outcome determines whether a particular information item should be delivered or not to a specific user.

2 Basic Concepts

We have developed [10,11] a multiagent-based system for disseminating pieces of IK among the members of a large or distributed organization. It is aimed to deliver the right IK to the adequate people just-in-time. IK is characterized by *metadata* (such as a content classification in terms of technical disciplines, intended audience, etc.) and users are characterized by *profiles*, which give the user function or position in the organization, rights and duties, interests, etc.

Our agent model [10,11] includes a collections of *Personal Agents* (PA) which work on behalf of the members of the organization. They filter and deliver useful content according to user preferences. The *Site Agent* (SA) provides IK to the PAs, acting as a *broker* between them and *Service agents*, which collect and detect IK pieces that are supposed to be relevant for someone in the organization. Examples of service agents are the Web Service agents, which receive and process external requests, as well as monitor agents which are continuously monitoring sources of IK (web pages, databases, etc.). That knowledge is hierarchically described in the form of taxonomies, usually one for interest areas and one describing the organization structure. For example, in an academic institution, the interest areas could be the science domains in which the institution is specialized, and the organizational chart of the institution gives the organization structure. SAs are the heart of a "cluster" composed by one SA and several PAs served by the former. In an organization, clusters would be associated with departments, divisions, etc., depending on the size of them. Networks can be made up connecting several SAs. Distributed organizations like multinational companies would have a web of many connected SAs.

Defeasible logic programming (DeLP) [12] is a general-purpose defeasible argumentation formalism based on logic programming, intended to model inconsistent and potentially contradictory knowledge. A defeasible logic program (in what follows just "program") is a set $\mathcal{P} = (\Pi, \Delta)$, where Π and Δ stand for sets of strict and defeasible knowledge, respectively. The set Π of strict knowledge involves *strict rules* of the form $p \leftarrow q_1, \ldots, q_k$ and *facts* (strict rules with empty body), and it is assumed to be *non-contradictory*.[1] The set Δ of defeasible knowledge involves *defeasible rules* of the form $p \prec q_1, \ldots, q_k$, which

---

[1] Contradiction stands for entailing two complementary literals p and $\sim p$ (or p and not p) in extended logic programming [12].

stands for "$q_1, \ldots q_k$ provide a *tentative reason* to believe p." The underlying logical language is that of extended logic programming, enriched with a special symbol "$\prec$" to denote defeasible rules. Both default and explicit negation are allowed (denoted not and $\sim$, resp.). Syntactically, the symbol "$\prec$" is all that distinguishes a *defeasible* rule $p \prec q_1, \ldots q_k$ from a *strict* rule $p \leftarrow q_1, \ldots, q_k$. Deriving literals in DeLP results in the construction of *arguments*.

Definition 1 (Argument). *Given a program $\mathcal{P}$, an* argument $\mathcal{A}$ *for a query q, denoted $\langle \mathcal{A}, q \rangle$, is a subset of ground instances of defeasible rules in $\mathcal{P}$ and a (possibly empty) set of default ground literals "not L", such that: a) there exists a defeasible derivation for q from $\Pi \cup \mathcal{A}$; b) $\Pi \cup \mathcal{A}$ is non-contradictory, and c) $\mathcal{A}$ is minimal wrt set inclusion. An argument $\langle \mathcal{A}_1, Q_1 \rangle$ is a* sub-argument *of another argument $\langle \mathcal{A}_2, Q_2 \rangle$ if $\mathcal{A}_1 \subseteq \mathcal{A}_2$.*

The notion of defeasible derivation corresponds to the usual query-driven SLD derivation used in logic programming, performed by backward chaining on both strict and defeasible rules. Given a program $\mathcal{P}$, an argument $\langle \mathcal{A}, q \rangle$ can be *attacked* by counterarguments. Formally:

Definition 2 (Counterargument–Defeat). *An argument $\langle \mathcal{A}_1, q_1 \rangle$ is a* counterargument *for an argument $\langle \mathcal{A}_2, q_2 \rangle$ iff (a) There is an subargument $\langle \mathcal{A}, q \rangle$ of $\langle \mathcal{A}_2, q_2 \rangle$ such that the set $\Pi \cup \{q_1, q\}$ is contradictory. (b) A literal not q_1 is present in some rule in $\mathcal{A}_1$. A partial order $\preceq$ will be used as a* preference criterion *among conflicting arguments. An argument $\langle \mathcal{A}_1, q_1 \rangle$ is a* defeater *for an argument $\langle \mathcal{A}_2, q_2 \rangle$ if $\langle \mathcal{A}_1, q_1 \rangle$ counterargues $\langle \mathcal{A}_2, q_2 \rangle$, and $\langle \mathcal{A}_1, q_1 \rangle$ is preferred over $\langle \mathcal{A}_2, q_2 \rangle$ wrt $\preceq$.*

Specificity is used in DeLP as a syntax-based criterion among conflicting arguments, preferring those arguments which are *more informed* or *more direct* [13].[2] An *argumentation line* starting in an argument $\langle \mathcal{A}_0, Q_0 \rangle$ (denoted $\lambda^{\langle \mathcal{A}_0, q_0 \rangle}$) is a sequence $[\langle \mathcal{A}_0, Q_0 \rangle, \langle \mathcal{A}_1, Q_1 \rangle, \langle \mathcal{A}_2, Q_2 \rangle, \ldots, \langle \mathcal{A}_n, Q_n \rangle \ldots]$ that can be thought of as an exchange of arguments between two parties, a *proponent* (evenly-indexed arguments) and an *opponent* (oddly-indexed arguments). Each $\langle \mathcal{A}_i, Q_i \rangle$ is a defeater for the previous argument $\langle \mathcal{A}_{i-1}, Q_{i-1} \rangle$ in the sequence, $i > 0$. In order to avoid *fallacious* reasoning, dialectics imposes additional constraints (e.g. disallowing circular argumentation[3]) on such an argument exchange to be considered rationally valid. An argumentation line satisfying the above restrictions is called *acceptable*, and can be proven to be finite [12]. Given a program $\mathcal{P}$ and an initial argument $\langle \mathcal{A}_0, Q_0 \rangle$, the set of *all acceptable argumentation* lines starting in $\langle \mathcal{A}_0, Q_0 \rangle$ accounts for a whole dialectical analysis for $\langle \mathcal{A}_0, Q_0 \rangle$ (ie., all possible dialogues rooted in $\langle \mathcal{A}_0, Q_0 \rangle$), formalized as a *dialectical tree*.

Nodes in a dialectical tree $\mathcal{T}_{\langle \mathcal{A}_0, Q_0 \rangle}$ can be marked as *undefeated* and *defeated* nodes (U-nodes and D-nodes, resp.). A tree $\mathcal{T}_{\langle \mathcal{A}_0, Q_0 \rangle}$ will be marked as an AND-OR tree: all leaves in $\mathcal{T}_{\langle \mathcal{A}_0, Q_0 \rangle}$ will be marked U-nodes (as they have no defeaters), and every inner node is to be marked as *D-node* iff it has at least one U-node as a child, and as *U-node* otherwise. An argument $\langle \mathcal{A}_0, Q_0 \rangle$ is ultimately accepted as valid (or *warranted*) wrt a program $\mathcal{P}$ iff the root of its

---

[2] It must be noted that other alternative partial orders could also be used.
[3] For an in-depth treatment of DeLP and its features the reader is referred to [12].

associated dialectical tree $\mathcal{T}_{\langle \mathcal{A}_0, \mathcal{Q}_0 \rangle}$ is labeled as *U-node*. Solving a query q wrt a given program $\mathcal{P}$ accounts for determining whether q is supported by a warranted argument. Different answers for a query q are possible according to the associated status of warrant, in particular: (a) Believe q (resp. $\sim q$) when there is a warranted argument for q (resp. $\sim q$) that follows from $\mathcal{P}$; (b) Believe q is *undecided* whenever neither q nor $\sim q$ are supported by warranted arguments.[4]

3 Modelling Knowledge Distribution, Power and Trust

Consider a set $I = \{i_1, i_2, \ldots, i_k\}$ of information items to be distributed among a set $U = \{u_1, \ldots, u_s\}$ of users. Every item $i \in I$ could be delivered to some users in U. A distribution policy p can be formally defined as a mapping $p : I \to \wp(U)$. Distributing an item i to a user u is *compliant* with a policy p when $(i, \{\ldots, u, \ldots\}) \in p$. Clearly policies are not usually formulated in this way, but instead they are specified by restrictions enforced by the organization (e.g. access rights). If P is a set of possible policies in the organization, given two policies $p_1, p_2 \in P$, we say they are in *conflict* whenever $(i, \{\ldots, u, \ldots\}) \in p_1$ but $(i, \{\ldots, u, \ldots\}) \notin p_2$, or viceversa. A conflict means that an information item i cannot be compliant with two policies p_1 and p_2 at the same time. We can define a *dominance* partial order $\prec$ among possible policies in P, writing $p_1 \prec p_2$ to indicate that a policy p_2 is preferred over policy p_1 in case they are in conflict. In this setting, the "information distribution problem" could then be recast as follows: *Send every information item $i \in I$ to a user $u \in U$ following a distribution p iff p is compliant with every non-dominated policy $p' \in P$.*[5]

Our previous work on integrating defeasible argumentation with IK distribution was restricted to aspects like corporate hierarchies, domain classifications and individual preferences [10], leaving out some relevant aspects of modeling large organizations, namely the presence of different levels of *trust* and *empowerment*, which are the novel aspects considered in this paper. In our current proposal we consider some distinguished sets: a set U of *users* (user identifiers), a set I (implemented actually as a list) of specific *information items* to be delivered, a set S of *information sources* (usually other agents in the organization), a set P of *permission levels* (like "everybody", "ceo", etc.), and a set F of *fields or areas*. Every information item $i \in I$ will have attributes, like a $f \in F$ (which is related to i by the $isAbout(i, f)$ relation) and the *source* of that information item (related to i by the $source(i, s)$ relation, with $s \in S$). A subset $M \subseteq I$ corresponds to *mandatory* items; non-mandatory items are said to be *optional*. We assume that fields in the organization are organized in hierarchies by means of the $subField(f_1, f_2)$ relation, with $f_1, f_2 \in F$. In particular, the $isAbout$ relation is based on computing the transitive closure of $subField$.

---

[4] Computing warrant is non-contradictory [12]: if there is a warranted argument $\langle A, h \rangle$ based on a program $\mathcal{P}$, then there is no warranted argument $\langle B, \sim h \rangle$ based on $\mathcal{P}$.
[5] Note that characterizing p depends on the specific sets U, I and P under consideration. Here we do not discuss the problem of finding out whether such a mapping actually exists, but rather focus on enforcing dominance on conflicting policies.

```
ALGORITHM DistributeItems
{Executed by Site Agent Ag_S to decide distribution of items in I
according to power & trust information available}
INPUT: List I = [item_1,...,item_k] of incoming items, DeLP programs P_S, P_1,..., P_n
OUTPUT: Item distribution to Personal Agents
BEGIN
    P'_S := P_S ∪ {info(item_1),...,info(item_k)}
    {Encode incoming items as new facts for Site Agent}
    FOR every item item ∈ I
        FOR every Personal Agent Ag_i supervised by Ag_S
            Let P = P'_S ∪ P_{Ag_i}
            Let s = source of item
            IF reputation_{Ag_i}(S) > Threshold THEN
                Using program P, solve query deliver(item, Ag_i)
                IF deliver(Item, Ag_i) is warranted
                    THEN
                        Send message item to agent Ag_i
                        reputation_{Ag_i}(S) ← reputation_{Ag_i}(S) + EvalMsg(item, Ag_i)
END
```

Fig. 1. Algorithm for Knowledge Distribution using DeLP in a Site Agent

Users have attributes too, like $permissions(u,p)$ with $u \in U, p \in P$. The organizational hierarchy is established through the $subordinate(l_1, l_2)$ relation, for permission levels l_i, and its transitive closure $depends(l_1, l_2)$. In order to be able to delegate power from an user u_1 to another user u_2 it is required that the user u_2 *depends on* user u_1. This is captured by the $can\_delegate$ relation. Trust is modeled using the $relies(u, s, f)$ relation, with $u \in U$, $s \in S$ and $f \in F$, meaning that user u is confident about information items coming from source s when those items are about field f. We consider a low-level *reputation* management mechanism (see algorithm in Fig. 1) for numerically adjusting a reputation level; this is reflected in the knowledge represented at the logical level through the $conf$ predicate. Finally, at the top level of our model we define the $deliver(i, u)$ relation, which indicates that an item i is to be distributed to user u according to the knowledge available for the SA and the particular user profile associated with the user u. Other details can be found in the DeLP code given in Fig.3.

As explained in Section 2, a Site Agent Ag_S is responsible for distributing IK among different PAs $Ag_1, \ldots Ag_n$. We will use DeLP programs $P_{Ag_1}, \ldots, P_{Ag_n}$ to represent user preferences associated with these agents, possibly based on trust relationships wrt other agents or parts of the organization. Knowledge in the Site Agent Ag_S will be represented by another program P_S. In contrast with the knowledge available to PAs, P_S will contain organizational *corporate rules* defining power and trust relationships (hierarchies, declarative power, etc.) as well as (possibly conflicting) policies for IK distribution among personal agents.

Given a list $I = [Item_1, \ldots, Item_i]$ of IK items to be distributed by the SA Ag_S among different PAs $Ag_1, \ldots, Ag_n$, a distinguished predicate $deliver(I, U)$ will be used to determine which items in I are intended to be delivered to a specific user $u \in U$. This will be solved on the basis of a program P taking into account the SA's knowledge, the metadata corresponding to the incoming items to be distributed and the personal preferences of the PAs involved. This is made explicit in the algorithm shown in Fig. 1. Note that every time a new item i is delivered to a PA Ag_i, the source $s \in S$ where this item i comes from (probably another PA) is identified. Every PA has a built-in *reputation* function to assess the reliability of every possible source s. The reputation of s wrt Ag_i will be increased (resp. decreased) if the items delivered by s to Ag_i are satisfactory (resp. non-satisfactory) according to some acceptance criterion. Should the reputation of s be lower than a given threshold for Ag_i, then s is no longer considered to be a reliable source. [6] Solving queries based on the *deliver* predicate wrt the DeLP inference engine will automate the decision making process for SAs, providing a rationally justified decision even for very complex cases, as we will see in Section 4. The complexity of the algorithm in Fig. 1 is clearly polynomial, but of course there is a hidden cost in solving the query $deliver(item, Ag_i)$, which could depend on the number of items and agents involved.

4 A Worked Example

Next we present an illustrative example of the our approach. We assume a typical corporate environment where members (users) could have different rights within the organization (e.g. CEO, managers, supervisors, etc.), belonging to different organization areas (e.g. production, marketing, etc.).

Case Study: Let us suppose that there are memos (items) which have to be delivered by a Site Agent to different users in the organization. The SA is required to take hierarchies into account, performing inheritance reasoning to make inferences: the manager can give orders to programmers, but programmers cannot give orders to the manager. Note that there could be *exceptions* to such hierarchies, e.g. if the CEO empowers a programmer to decide about software purchase. In our example, IK items made available from the organization to the SA will correspond to different memos, which will be encoded with a predicate $info(Id, A, L, M, S)$, meaning that the memo with identifier Id is about area A and it can be accessed by users of at least level L. Other attributes associated with the memo are whether it is mandatory ($M = 1$) or optional ($M = 0$), and the source of origin S. Thus, the fact $info(id_3, computers, manager, 0, peter)$ $\leftarrow$ indicates that the memo id_3 is about *computers*, it is intended at least for managers, it is not mandatory, and it has been produced by *peter*.

Fig. 3 shows a sample DeLP code associated with a Site and a particular Personal agent. [7] Strict rules s_1 to s_{10} characterize permissions and extract information from memos. Rule s_1 defines that a user P is *allowed* access to item I if he/she has the required *permissions*, which are given as facts (f_7, f_8 and f_9). Permissions are also propagated using the strict rules s_4, s_5 and s_6, where the binary predicate *depends* establishes the organization hierarchy, stating that the first argument person is (transitively) subordinated to the second one. This predicate is calculated as the transitive closure of a basic predicate *subordinate* (defined by facts f_{10} and f_{11}), which establishes subordinate relationships pairwise. Thus, having e.g. granted permissions as CEO allows the CEO to have

---

[6] For space reasons the computation of $reputation_{Ag_i}(S)$ is not analyzed in this paper.
[7] Note that we distinguish strict rules, defeasible rules, and facts by using s_i, d_i and f_i as clause identifiers, respectively.

access to every memo corresponding to lower level permissions. Rule s_7 indicates when an organization member can delegate power on some other member. Delegation of power is also based on subordination relationships. Rule s_2 and s_3 define the predicate $isAbout(I, A)$ as an information hierarchy among subfields. The basic case corresponds to a subfield for which specific information is available (rule s_2), otherwise relationships in this hierarchy (facts f_{12}-f_{17}) are used). Finally, rules s_8, s_9 and s_{10} define auxiliary predicates *source*, *mandatory* and *field* (yes/no) which allow to extract these particular attributes from *info* facts, simplifying the subsequent analysis.

Let us now consider the defeasible rules for our Site Agent. Rules d_1-d_3 define when an item I should be delivered to a specific user U: either because it is interesting for U, or because it is mandatory for U, or because it comes from an authorized source. Rule d_4 defines when something is interesting for a given user. Rule d_5-d_7 define when a user relies on a source (another user) wrt some field F. Note that rule d_7 establishes that unreliability is defined as *"not ultimately provable as reliable"* via default negation. Rules d_8-d_{11} define criteria for authorizing a source for delivering information on a field F: either because the source works on F (d_9), or because the source got explicit power delegation from a superior (d_{11}). Rule d_{10} establishes an exception to d_9 (users who falsified reports are not authorized). Facts f_1-f_3 characterize trust relationships (e.g. *joe* trusts *mike* about *computers*, but not about *politics*) stored by the SA.[8] Similarly, facts f_4-f_6 characterize explicit authorizations and delegations. Finally, let us consider the DeLP program associated with a particular PA (e.g. Joe). A number of facts represent Joe's preferences (interest fields), and a defeasible rule d'_1 associated with his preferences indicates that he is not interested in memos from unreliable sources.

Solving Power and Trust Conflicts Using Argumentation

Let us assume that there is a list of information items $[Memo_1, Memo_2, Memo_3]$ corresponding to memos to be distributed by our Site Agent, which encodes organization policies as a DeLP program $\mathcal{P}_S$. By applying the algorithm given in Fig. 1, these items will be encoded temporarily as a set $\mathcal{P}_{items} = \{info(Memo_1), info(Memo_2), info(Memo_3)\}$ (facts f_a-f_c in Fig. 3). For the sake of simplicity, we will assume that there is only one single Personal Agent involved, associated with a specific user *joe*, whose role is *manager*. Joe's Personal Agent mirrors his preferences in terms of a DeLP program $\mathcal{P}_{joe} = \{d'_1, f'_1, f'_2, f'_3\}$, which together with $\mathcal{P}_S$ and $\mathcal{P}_{items}$ will provide the knowledge necessary to decide which IK items should be delivered to this specific user. Following the algorithm in Fig. 1, the Site Agent will have to solve the queries $deliver(id_1, joe)$, $deliver(id_2, joe)$ and $deliver(id_5, joe)$ wrt the DeLP program $\mathcal{P}_S \cup \mathcal{P}_{items} \cup \mathcal{P}_{joe}$. We will show next how every one of these queries is solved in different examples that show how DeLP deals with conflicts among organization policies and user preferences.

---

[8] Such trust relationships among Personal Agents can be established on the basis of the reputation function mentioned in Section 3, computed by the Site Agent.

Example 1. Consider the query $deliver(id_3, joe)$. In this case joe is *allowed* to receive this item (s_1), but it is neither of interest for him (d_1) nor coming from an authorized person (d_3). However, id_3 is mandatory (f_c), and hence the Site Agent can compute an argument $\langle \mathcal{A}_1, deliver(id_3, joe)\rangle = \{\ deliver(id_3, joe) \prec allowed(id_3, joe), mandatory(id_3)\ \}$. This argument has no defeaters, and hence it is warranted. Thus id_3 will be delivered to joe. The corresponding dialectical tree has one node (Fig 2(i)).

Example 2. Consider the query $deliver(id_1, joe)$. For this query the DeLP inference engine will find the argument $\langle \mathcal{B}_1, deliver(id_1, joe)\rangle$ with $\mathcal{B}_1 = \{\ deliver(id_1, joe) \prec allowed(id_1, joe), interest(id_1, joe);\ interest(id_1, joe) \prec isAbout(id_1, politics), interestField(politics, joe)\}$. However, $\langle \mathcal{B}_1, deliver(id_1, joe)\rangle$ has as defeater the argument $\langle \mathcal{B}_2, \sim interest(id_1, joe)\rangle$, with $\mathcal{B}_2 = \{\sim interest(id_1, joe) \prec isAbout(id_1, politics), interestField(politics, joe), source(id_1, mike), \sim relies(joe, mike, politics); \sim relies(joe, mike, politics) \prec \text{not } relies(joe, mike, politics)^9\ \}$ (according to joe's confidence criteria, joe has no confidence on $mike$ when he talks about politics, so the source is unreliable.) In this case, $\mathcal{T}_{\langle \mathcal{B}_1, distribute(id_1, joe)\rangle}$ has two nodes in a single branch (see Fig. 2(ii)). There are no other arguments to consider. Therefore the answer to the query is No, and hence the Site Agent will not deliver id_1 to joe.

Example 3. Consider the query $deliver(id_2, joe)$. Although joe is *allowed* to receive this item (s_1), note that it is neither of interest for joe (d_1) nor mandatory (d_2). However, in this case there is an argument $\langle \mathcal{C}_1, deliver(id_2, joe)\rangle$ with

$\mathcal{C}_1 = \{\ deliver(id_2, joe) \prec allowed(id_2, joe), authorized\_deliver(id_2, joe);$
$authorized\_deliver(id_2, joe) \prec source(id_2, peter), field(id_2, hardware),$
$isauthorized(peter, hardware)\ ;$
$isauthorized(peter, hardware) \prec worksOn(peter, hardware)\ \}.$

But $\langle \mathcal{C}_1, deliver(id_2, joe)\rangle$ has as a defeater $\langle \mathcal{C}_2, \sim isauthorized(peter, hardware)\rangle$, with

$\mathcal{C}_2 = \{\sim isauthorized(peter, hardware) \prec worksOn(peter, hardware),$
$falsified\_reports(peter)\ \}.$

($peter$ falsified reports, hence he should not be authorized). However this is superseded by $dana$'s delegation, with an argument $\langle \mathcal{C}_3, isauthorized(peter, hardware)\rangle$, where

$\mathcal{C}_3 = \{isauthorized(peter, hardware) \prec authorized(dana, hardware),$
$delegates(dana, peter), can\_delegate(dana, peter)\ \}.$

In this case, the dialectical tree $\mathcal{T}_{\langle \mathcal{C}_1, distribute(id_2, joe)\rangle}$ has three nodes (see Fig. 2(iii)). Therefore the answer to the query is Yes, and the Site Agent will deliver id_2 to joe.

$\langle \mathcal{A}_1, deliver(id_3, joe)\rangle^U$	$\langle \mathcal{B}_1, deliver(id_1, joe)\rangle^D$	$\langle \mathcal{C}_1, deliver(id_2, joe)\rangle^U$
	|	|
	$\langle \mathcal{B}_2, \sim interest(id_1, joe)\rangle^U$	$\langle \mathcal{C}_2, \sim isauthorized(peter, hardware)\rangle^D$
		|
		$\langle \mathcal{C}_3, isauthorized(peter, hardware)\rangle^U$
(i)	(ii)	(iii)

Fig. 2. Dialectical trees for queries $deliver(id_1, joe)$, $deliver(id_2, joe)$ and $deliver(id_3, joe)$ (examples 1, 2 and 3)

---

[9] The literal "not $relies(joe, mike, politics)$" holds as "$relies(joe, mike, politics)$" is not supported by a (warranted) argument.

	Site Agent Knowledge
s_1)	$allowed(I, U) \leftarrow info(I, A, L, M, S), permissions(U, L).$
s_2)	$isAbout(I, A) \leftarrow info(I, A, L, M, T, S)$
s_3)	$isAbout(I, A) \leftarrow subField(SuperA, A), isAbout(I, SuperA).$
s_4)	$permissions(U, X) \leftarrow depends(X, Y), permissions(U, Y).$
s_5)	$depends(X, Y) \leftarrow subordinate(X, Y).$
s_6)	$depends(X, Z) \leftarrow subordinate(Y, Z), depends(X, Y).$
s_7)	$can\_delegate(U1, U2) \leftarrow depends(U2, U1).$
s_8)	$source(I, S) \leftarrow info(I, \_, \_, \_, \_, S).$
s_9)	$mandatory(I) \leftarrow info(I, \_, \_, 1, \_).$
s_{10})	$field(I, F) \leftarrow info(I, F, \_, \_, \_).$
d_1)	$deliver(I, U) \prec allowed(I, U), interest(I, U).$
d_2)	$deliver(I, U) \prec allowed(I, U), mandatory(I).$
d_3)	$deliver(I, U) \prec allowed(I, U), authorized\_deliver(I, U).$
d_4)	$interest(I, U) \prec isAbout(I, A), interestField(A, U).$
d_5)	$relies(U, S, F) \prec conf(U, S, F).$
d_6)	$relies(U, S, F) \prec conf(U, S1, F), relies(S1, S, F).$
d_7)	$\sim relies(U, S, F) \prec not\ relies(U, S, F).$
d_8)	$authorized\_deliver(I) \prec source(I, S), field(I, F), isauthorized(S, F).$
d_9)	$isauthorized(S, F) \prec worksOn(S, F).$
d_{10})	$\sim isauthorized(S, F) \prec worksOn(S, F), falsified\_reports(S).$
d_{11})	$isauthorized(S, F) \prec authorized(S1, F), delegates(S1, S), can\_delegate(S1, S).$

Facts about Confidence, Authorizations, and Power delegation

f_1)	$conf(joe, mike, computers).$	f_4)	$\sim authorized(peter, software).$
f_2)	$\sim conf(joe, mike, politics)$	f_5)	$authorized(dana, hardware).$
f_3)	$conf(mike, bill, computers).$	f_6)	$delegates(dana, peter).$
		f_x)	$falsified\_reports(peter).$

Facts about Permissions, Roles and Hierarchies

f_7)	$permissions(joe, manager) \leftarrow$	f_{13})	$subField(processors, hardware) \leftarrow$
f_8)	$permissions(peter, everybody) \leftarrow$	f_{14})	$subField(software, computers) \leftarrow$
f_9)	$permissions(dana, ceo) \leftarrow$	f_{15})	$subField(programing, software) \leftarrow$
f_{10})	$subordinate(everybody, manager) \leftarrow$	f_{16})	$subField(computers, infotopics) \leftarrow$
f_{11})	$subordinate(manager, ceo) \leftarrow$	f_{17})	$subField(politics, infotopics) \leftarrow$
f_{12})	$subField(hardware, computers) \leftarrow$	f_{18})	$worksOn(peter, software) \leftarrow$

Information Items as facts	PA Knowledge – user preferences
f_a) $info(id_1, politics, everybody, 0, mike) \leftarrow$	d'_1) $\sim interest(I, joe) \prec isAbout(I, A),$
f_b) $info(id_2, hardware, manager, 0, peter) \leftarrow$	$\quad interestField(A, joe), source(I, S),$
f_c) $info(id_3, processors, manager, 1, mary) \leftarrow$	$\quad \sim relies(joe, S, A).$
	f'_1) $interestField(computers, joe) \leftarrow$
	f'_2) $\sim interestField(hardware, joe) \leftarrow$
	f'_3) $interestField(politics, joe) \leftarrow$

Fig. 3. DeLP code for a Site Agent and a Personal Agent in JITIK

5 Related Work and Conclusions

In this paper we have extended the previous proposal in [10] for knowledge distribution in large organizations by incorporating the representation of power and trust capabilities explicitly by means of defeasible logic programming. As we have shown, the main advantage obtained is an increased flexibility in modelling different normative situations in organizations and trust relationships. Potentially contradictory knowledge involved in such aspects is suitably handled by the DeLP inference engine. To the best of our knowledge there are no similar approaches as the one presented in this paper. In other approaches related to Virtual Organizations [14,15] a central concern is also to monitor information flow among members wishing to cooperate on a shared project.

An implementation of the IK distribution system that contains the Site Agent, the Personal Agents, an Ontology Agent and various Service Agents (web monitoring and others) has been reported elsewhere [9], using the JADE agent platform [16]. Our experiments regarding this integration of IK distribution with defeasible argumentation for modelling power and trust relationships only account as a "proof of concept" prototype, as we have not been able yet to carry out thorough evaluations in the context of a real-world application. In particular, the sample problem presented in Section 4 was encoded and solved successfully using a Java-based DeLP environment.[10]

Part of our current work is focused on adapting the approach proposed in this paper into a truly distributed algorithm, which could improve both the multiagent nature of the procedure as well as its performance and scalability.

Acknowledgments

The authors would like to thank anonymous reviewers for their suggestions. This work was supported by the Monterrey Tech CAT-011 research chair, by Projects TIC2003-00950, TIN 2004-07933-C03-03, by Ramón y Cajal Program (MCyT, Spain) and by CONICET (Argentina).

References

1. Liebowitz, J., Wilcox, L.: Knowledge Management. CRC Press (1997)
2. Horibe, F.: Managing Knowledge Workers. John Wiley and Sons (1999)
3. Liebowitz, J., Beckman, T.: Knowledge Organizations. St. Lucie Press (1998)
4. Atkinson, R., Court, R., Ward, J.: The knowledge economy: Knowledge producers and knowledge users. The New Economic Index (1998) http://www.neweconomyindex.org/
5. Gelati, J., Governatori, G., Rotolo, A., Sartor, G.: Declarative power, representation and mandate: A formal analysis. In: Proceedings of 15th Conf. on Legal Knowledge and Inf. Systems, IOS Press (2002) 41–52
6. Sabater, J., Sierra, C.: REGRET: reputation in gregarious societies. In Müller, J.P., Andre, E., Sen, S., Frasson, C., eds.: Proceedings of the Fifth International Conference on Autonomous Agents, Montreal, Canada, ACM Press (2001) 194–195
7. Mui, L.: Computational Models of Trust and Reputation: Agents, Evolutionary Games, and Social Networks. PhD thesis, MIT (2003)
8. Borghoff, U., Pareschi, R.: Information Technology for Knowledge Management. Springer (1998)
9. Brena, R., Aguirre, J.L., Trevino, A.C.: Just-in-time information and knowledge: Agent technology for km bussiness process. In: Proc. of the 2001 IEEE Conference on Systems, Man and Cybernetics, Tucson, Arizona, IEEE Press (2001)
10. Chesñevar, C., Brena, R., Aguirre, J.: Knowledge distribution in large organizations using defeasible logic programming. In: Proc. 18th Canadian Conf. on AI (in LNCS 3501, Springer). (2005) 244–256

---

[10] See http://cs.uns.edu.ar/~ags/DLP/ for details.

11. Aguirre, J., Brena, R., Cantu, F.: Multiagent-based knowledge networks. Expert Systems with Applications **20** (2001) 65–75
12. García, A., Simari, G.: Defeasible Logic Programming: An Argumentative Approach. Theory and Practice of Logic Programming **4** (2004) 95–138
13. Simari, G., Loui, R.: A Mathematical Treatment of Defeasible Reasoning and its Implementation. Art. Intelligence **53** (1992) 125–157
14. Wasson, G., Humphrey, M.: Toward explicit policy management for virtual organizations. In: IEEE Workshop on Policies for Distributed Systems and Network (POLICY '03). (2003) 173–182
15. Norman, T., Preece, A., Chalmers, S., Jennings, N., Luck, M., Dang, V., Nguyen, T., Deora, V., Shao, J., Gray, W., Fiddian, N.: Conoise: Agent-based formation of virtual organisations. In: Proc. of the 23rd Intl. Conf. on Innovative Techniques and Applications of AI. (2003) 353–366
16. Bellifemine, F., Poggi, A., Rimassa, G.: Jade - a fipa-compliant agent framework. In: Proceedings of PAAM99, London. (1999)

Application of ASP for Agent Modelling in CSCL Environments

Gerardo Ayala, Magdalena Ortiz, and Mauricio Osorio

Centro de Investigación en Tecnologías de Información, y Automatización, CENTIA,
Universidad de las Américas, Puebla, México
ayalasan@mail.udlap.mx

Abstract. This paper presents the pertinence of the use of the Answer Set Programming (ASP) formalism for developing a computational model of a software agent for Computer Supported Collaborative Learning (CSCL) environments. This analytic model is based on a representation of for agent's beliefs about the learner and the domain, together with the corresponding inference system with the appropriate rules to derive new beliefs about the capabilities of the learner, and its use in order to support effective collaboration and maintain learning possibilities for the group members. The model provides a representation of the structural knowledge frontier and the social knowledge frontier of the learner, which are the components for the definition of the learner's zone of proximal development (zpd). Based on the zpd of its learner the agent can propose her a learning task and maintain the zpd for the learner in the group. The complete code of the model is presented in the declarative language of DLV, a logic programming language for implementing ASP models.

1 Analytic Models and CSCL

Analytic models are considered a way to model group activities in Computer Supported Collaborative Learning (CSCL) environments. According to Hoppe & Ploetzner [1] an analytic model, in the context of collaborative learning environments, is a *"...formally represented computational artifact that can be used to simulate, reconstruct, or analyze aspects of actions or inter-actions occurring in groups".*

Logical propositions have been useful to represent computational models, like the proposal for student modelling by Self [2] that integrates computational and theoretical aspects for modelling the domain, reasoning, monitoring and reflection levels of an agent. Self [3] also proposed some computational models to represent a viewpoint as a set of beliefs held by the agent. In this approach, the domain model is considered as a viewpoint, and the student model as an incremental viewpoint based on the domain. Logic programming was used in the GRACILE project [4] implementing intelligent agents for a CSCL environment in PROLOG.

Declarative logic programming is widely accepted for the representation and manipulation of knowledge and belief systems. Beliefs systems for software agents deal naturally with incomplete information and non-monotonicity in the reasoning process. Nowadays, Answer Set Programming (ASP) is a well logic programming formalism known and accepted for non-monotonic reasoning and reasoning with incomplete information [5]. However, there are few real applications based on ASP an none concerning learning environments.

In the context of agent based Computer Supported Collaborative Learning (CSCL) environments, logic programming allow us a more human-like heuristic approach for learner modelling and reasoning on learning opportunities and intelligent task proposals for the learners in a group. From the logic and formalization approaches, we have been working on the application of the answer sets programming framework for supporting collaboration in agent-based CSCL environments [6, 7] because its convenience for the representation and manipulation of the beliefs of the agent about the capabilities of the learners.

This paper presents the analytical model of an agent for CSCL environments, based on the ASP formalism. The model is presented in DLV, a system for implementing ASP models. We propose a representation schema for the agent's beliefs about the learner and the domain, together with the corresponding inference system with the appropriate rules to derive new beliefs about the capabilities of the learner and its use in order to support effective collaboration and maintain learning possibilities for the group members.

2 Modelling with ASP

Answer Set Programming (ASP) has been recognized as an important contribution in the areas of Logic Programming and Artificial Intelligence [5]. Nowadays, there is a significant amount of research work inspired on this formalism, well known and accepted for non-monotonic reasoning. ASP is more expressive than normal (disjunction free) logic programming and allow us to deal with uncertainty.

ASP has two types of negation: weak negation (*not x*) and strong negation (~x). Using weak negation, *not x* in interpreted as "there is no evidence of x", while using strong negation, ~x means "there is evidence that x is false".

Because beliefs can not be treated correctly in classical logic (PROLOG), ASP is useful as a logical framework for agent modelling. ASP allows us to have a direct and clear representation of the beliefs of an agent, especially in dynamic situations, incomplete information and uncertainty.

2.1 DLV

DLV is a system for answer set programming [8]. The computational model of our agent is implemented in DLV, based on the ASP formalism. The result of a computation is a *set of models,* each one as a consistent explanation of the world, as far as the system can derive it. DLV tries to find all the models of the world which correctly and consistently explain the facts and rules of the program. A model assigns a truth value to each atom appearing in the program, and is represented as a set of atoms that are true in a certain model. If a program is inconsistent there will be no model. A model is considered an *epistemic state of the agent*, as a closed theory under the logic defined by a program [6]. Each model is interpreted as the implicit (derivable) and explicit beliefs of the agent.

2.2 Agent Modelling Using DLV

We are applying DLV as a logical framework for agent modelling in CSCL environments. DLV allows us to have a direct and clear representation of the structure of the domain, and the beliefs of the agent about the learner's capabilities and learning possibilities in a group. The advantages of using DLV as a methodology of agent modelling for CSCL environments are:

a) have a specification of the model as a set of rules and testing them with facts, in order to obtain correct and consistent models that ensure the coherence of the agent model;
b) use double negation for derivation of beliefs under uncertainty and incomplete information. This is useful for representing the beliefs of the agent about the capabilities of its learner;
c) use integrity constraints to represent conditions that can make the model inconsistent;
d) have a formalization of the model.

In the following sections we present in DLV the formalization of our agent model for CSCL environments. The results of several simulations of the model show that it keeps the zones of proximal development of the learners by determining an appropriate task proposal to the members of a learning group.

3 Pedagogical Organization of the Domain Knowledge

Our model is valid for structured knowledge domains, where we have knowledge elements (i.e. grammar rules for a second language collaborative learning environment) that can be defined and pedagogically or epistemologically organized. A knowledge element has an identification, which is represented by the predicate:

knowledgeElement(*knowledgeElementId*).

For the pedagogical and epistemological organization of the knowledge elements, we adopt a *genetic graph* approach [9]. The genetic graph is a very powerful structure for determining the learner's a knowledge frontier and learning opportunities. We have the following predicates and rules for its definition:

generalization(*knowledgeElementId, generalKnowledgeElementId*).

specialization(*KnowledgeElementId, SpecializedKnowledgeElementId*):-
　　generalization(*SpecializedKnowledgeElementId, KnowledgeElementId*).

refinement(*knowledgeElementId, refinedKnowledgeElementId*).

simplification(*KnowledgeElementId, SimpleKnowledgeElementId*) :-
　　refinement(*SimpleKnowledgeElementId, KnowledgeElementId*).

analogy(*knowledgeElementId, analogKnowledgeElementId*).

analogy(*KnowledgeElementId, analogKnowledgeElementId*) :-
　　analogy(*analogKnowledgeElementId, KnowledgeElementId*).

3.1 Knowledge Application: Situations and Tasks

A knowledge element is applicable in a given situation. For example, a grammar rule, as a knowledge element, is applied in a situation like a speech act, like "ask somebody to do something" or "apologize". We have the following predicates to represent it:

situation(*situationId*).
applicable(*knowledgeElementId, situationId*).

We use *integrity constraints* in DVL in order to represent that if there is no information of a knowledge element applicable in a given situation, then the model is inconsistent:

:- **applicable**(*KnowledgeElementId,_*),
   not **knowledgeElement**(*KnowledgeElementId*).

In the same way, if there is no information of a situation where a given knowledge element is applied, then the model is also inconsistent:

:- **applicable**(_,*SituationId*), not **situation**(*SituationId*).

A task is a collaborative learning activity and implies one or more situations. This is represented by the predicates:

task(*taskId*)
implies(*taskId, situationId*).

In a similar way, if there is no information of a situation which corresponds to a task, then the model is inconsistent. Also, it will be inconsistent if there is no information of a task for a situation:

:-**implies**(_, SituationId), not **situation**(SituationId).
:-**implies**(TaskId, _), not **task**(TaskId).

4 Modelling the Learner and Her Learning Opportunities

The agent identifies a learner with the predicate **learner**(*learnerId*). The set of beliefs concerning the learner capabilities corresponds to the beliefs of the agent about its learner's *actual development level* [10]. The belief that the learner is capable of apply a knowledge element of the domain is represented by:

capability(*learnerId, knowledgeElementId*).

With the model we can derive new beliefs using derivation rules. In these rules the use of *double negation* allows the derivation with incomplete information. The agent believes that the learner is capable of applying a knowledge element if it believes that she is able to apply a knowledge element considered its generalization, and *there is no evidence that the learner is not able to apply it:*

capability(*LearnerId, KnowledgeElementId*) :-
    capability(*LearnerId, GeneralKnowledgeElementId*),
    specialization(*GeneralKnowledgeElementId, KnowledgeElementId*),
    not ~capability(*LearnerId, KnowledgeElementId*).

Also, the agent will believe that the learner is capable of applying a knowledge element if she is able to apply a knowledge element considered its simplification, and *there is no evidence that the learner is not able to apply it:*

capability(*LearnerId, SimpleKnowledgeElementId*) :-
  capability(*LearnerId, KnowledgeElementId*),
  simplification(*KnowledgeElementId,SimpleKnowledgeElementId*),
  not ~capability(*LearnerId, SimpleKnowledgeElementId*).

When considered appropriate, the predicate ~**capability**(*learnerId, knowledgeElementId*) can be included when there is evidence that the learner is not able to apply the corresponding knowledge element.

4.1 Structural Knowledge Frontier

The *structural knowledge frontier* is based on the concept of "knowledge frontier" of the genetic graph [9] and was used successfully in the GRACILE project [11] We call it structural knowledge frontier since it depends only in the genetic graph structure, and also in order to make the difference with the social knowledge frontier. A knowledge element is part of the learner's structural knowledge frontier when there is no evidence that the learner is able to apply it, and the agent believes that she is able to apply another knowledge element, which is genetically related to the one in question. In the case of the generalization relation the rule is:

structuralKnowledgeFrontier(*LearnerId, KnowledgeElementId*) :-
  capability(*LearnerId, RelatedKnowledgeElementId*) ,
  generalization(*RelatedKnowledgeElementId, KnowledgeElementId*),
  not capability(*LearnerId, KnowledgeElementId*).

The rest of the rules are similar, making reference to the refinement, analogy, simplification and specialization genetic relations. Also, a knowledge element will be part of the learner's structural knowledge frontier if there is no evidence that the learner is able to apply it, and is considered an element of the basic knowledge set. We consider members of the basic knowledge set those knowledge elements which are not generalizations or refinements:

structuralKnowledgeFrontier(*LearnerId, KnowledgeElementId*):-
  basicKnowledge(*KnowledgeElementId*),
  not capability(*LearnerId, KnowledgeElementId*),
  knowledgeElement(*KnowledgeElementId*),
  learner(*LearnerId*).

4.2 Social Knowledge Frontier

The concept of *social knowledge frontier* is based on the assumption that there are social issues that make the learners of a group to learn some knowledge elements first and more easily than others. Those issues may be the situations of their application, the relevance of it (be capable to apply the knowledge element in order to be a productive member in the group) or the nature and characteristics of it. For the agent, a knowledge element is part of the social knowledge frontier of the learner if there is no evidence that the learner is able to apply it, but the agent believes that other learner in her group does. The rule is the following:

socialKnowledgeFrontier(*LearnerId, KnowledgeElementId*):-
  not capability(*LearnerId, KnowledgeElementId*),
  capability(*OtherLearnerId, KnowledgeElementId*),
  knowledgeElement(*KnowledgeElementId*),
  learner(*LearnerId*),
  learner(*OtherLearnerId*),
  LearnerId <> *OtherLearnerId*.

The social knowledge frontier implies the *cooperation among agents*, sharing their beliefs in their learner models.

4.3 Collaborative Learning Opportunities

In our model, the learning plan, and therefore the tasks proposals to the learner by her agent, is based on the representation of her zone of proximal development [10] or zpd. The actual development level of the learner is the set of beliefs concerning her capabilities in the domain. The *potential development level* corresponds to the structural knowledge frontier. A knowledge element is part of the zpd of the learner if is member of both, her structural knowledge frontier and her social knowledge frontier. The rule is:

zpd(*LearnerId, KnowledgeElementId*) :-
  structuralKnowledgeFrontier(*LearnerId, KnowledgeElementId*),
  socialKnowledgeFrontier(*LearnerId, KnowledgeElementId*).

4.4 Planning Individual and Collaborative Learning Activities

The learning plan of a learner is used in order to generate appropriate tasks proposals, and consists of the knowledge elements considered in her zpd:

learningPlan(*LearnerId, KnowledgeElementId*):-
  zpd(*LearnerId, KnowledgeElementId*).

However, in the case when the learner does not have a zpd, her learning plan will be her structural knowledge frontier (potential development level):

learningPlan (*LearnerId, KnowledgeElementId*):-
  not hasZpd(*LearnerId*),
  structuralKnowledgeFrontier(*LearnerId, KnowledgeElementId*).

The learning plan is individual. In order to keep a zpd for the members of the learning group, it is necessary to have an individual learning plan which also *supports the maintenance of a zpd for the other learners* in the group. This provides more learning possibilities to the group and therefore maintenance of the motivation to participate. We defined the *group supportive learning plan* as the set of knowledge elements considered part of the learning plan of the learner and part of the structural knowledge frontier of another learner, who has no zpd.

groupSupportiveLearningPlan(*LearnerId, KnowledgeElementId*):-
  not hasZpd(*OtherLearnerId*),
  learningPlan (*LearnerId, KnowledgeElementId*),
  structuralKnowledgeFrontier(*OtherLearnerId, KnowledgeElementId*),
  LearnerId <> *OtherLearnerId*.

5 Learning Task Proposals from the Agent

A learning task is defined as the cooperation of two learners, each one applying a knowledge element in a corresponding situation that occurs in the task. Once the agent has a representation of the learning plan of its learner, the next step is to propose her a task, based on that. First, the agent must determine if there is possible to assign a task based on the learner's group supportive learning plan. These tasks are called group supportive tasks. Working in a group supportive task, the learner cooperates with other learner trying to apply a knowledge element of her group supportive learning plan, in the corresponding situation, while the other learner cooperates by applying a knowledge element in his learning plan:

    groupSupportiveTask(*LearnerId, KnowledgeElementId, SituationId,*
        OtherLearnerId,OtherKnowledgeElementId,
        OtherSituationId, Task):-
        groupSupportiveLearningProposal(*LearnerId, KnowledgeElementId*),
        learningPlan (*OtherLearnerId, OtherKnowledgeElementId*),
        KnowledgeElementId <> *OtherKnowledgeElementId*,
        LearnerId <> *OtherLearnerId*,
        applicable(*KnowledgeElementId, SituationId*),
        applicable(*OtherKnowledgeElementId, OtherSituationId*),
        implies(*SituationId, Task*),
        implies(*OtherSituationId, Task*).

    hasGroupSupportiveTask(*LearnerId*):-
        groupSupportiveTask(*LearnerId,_,_,_,_,_,_*).

In order to present an *intelligent task proposal* to the learner, the agent generates a set of task candidates. First, the agent will consider a group supportive task as a task candidate for its learner:

    taskCandidate(*LearnerId, KnowledgeElementId, SituationId,*
        OtherLearnerId, OtherKnowledgeElementId,OtherSituationId,
        Task):-
        groupSupportiveTask(*LearnerId, KnowledgeElementId, SituationId,*
            OtherLearnerId, OtherKnowledgeElementId,
            OtherSituationId, Task).

However, if there is not a group supportive task for the learner, the task candidate will consist of the cooperation of the learner trying to apply a knowledge element of her learning plan, in the corresponding situation, while the other learner cooperates by applying a knowledge element in his learning plan.

    taskCandidate(*LearnerId, KnowledgeElementId, SituationId,*
        OtherLearnerId, OtherKnowledgeElementId,
        OtherSituationId, Task):-
        not hasGroupSupportiveTask(*LearnerId*),
        learningPlan (*LearnerId, KnowledgeElementId*),
        learningPlan (*OtherLearnerId, OtherKnowledgeElementId*),
        KnowledgeElementId <> *OtherKnowledgeElementId*,
        LearnerId <> *OtherLearnerId*,
        applicable(*KnowledgeElementId, SituationId*),
        applicable(*OtherKnowledgeElementId, OtherSituationId*),
        implies(*SituationId, Task*),
        implies(*OtherSituationId, Task*).

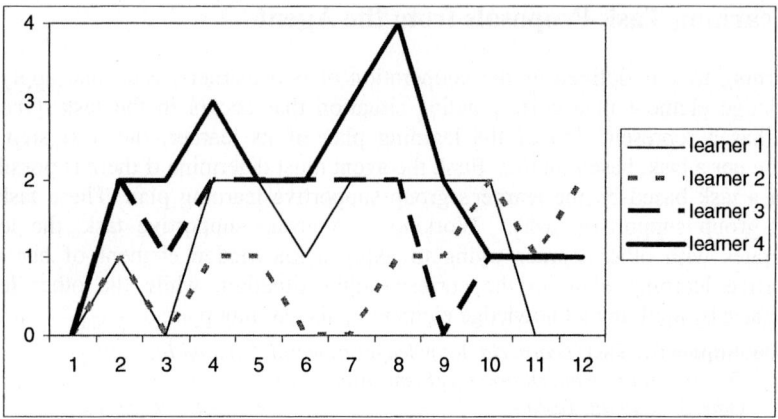

Fig.1. The agents maintain the zpd in a homogeneous group. (The x axis represents the number of session (time) and the y axis the number of knowledge elements in the learner's ZPD).

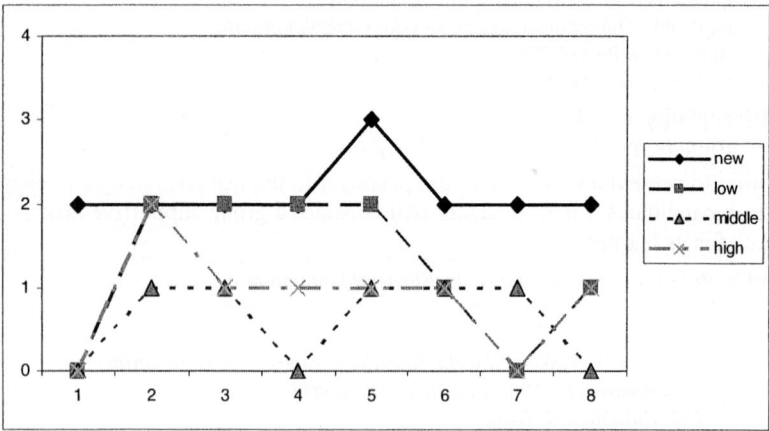

Fig. 2. The agents maintain the zpd in a heterogeneous group. (The x axis represents the number of session (time) and the y axis the number of knowledge elements in the learner´s ZPD).

The agent must propose its learner a set of learning tasks, and then the learner decides which one to commit to perform. The agent must present to the learner a list of tasks candidates. Among the set of task candidates, the agent determines some tasks as an *intelligent proposal*. A task proposal for a learner is a task candidate which implies that the knowledge element to be applied in the situation of the task is believed to be a capability of the other learner participating in the task.

    TaskProposal(*LearnerId, KnowledgeElementId, SituationId,*
       OtherLearnerId, OtherKnowledgeElementId, OtherSituationId,
       Task):-
          taskCandidate(*LearnerId, KnowledgeElementId, SituationId,*

OtherLearnerId, OtherKnowledgeElementId,
OtherSituationId, Task),
capability(*OtherLearnerId, KnowledgeElementId*),
KnowledgeElementId <> OtherKnowledgeElementId,
LearnerId <> OtherLearnerId.

6 Simulations and Results

The computational model presented here is implemented in DLV. We performed several simulations, running the system in order to obtain a set of consistent and complete models for zones of proximal development and task proposals. At every time, we selected some changes in the capabilities of the virtual learners performing a task from those proposed by the agent. We ran the simulations with a domain of knowledge elements representing the grammar rules of Japanese Language, and we consider a small group of 4 learners. We ran all the simulations for the case of an homogeneous group as well as the case of an heterogeneous group.

6.1 Homogeneous Group

These simulations considered a group of four learners, all new in the domain (none was believed to be able to apply a knowledge element in the beginning). After running the model with its corresponding actualizations on the learners capabilities with respect to the tasks proposed, the average of zpd for a member of the group was of 1.31 knowledge elements. Due to the group supportive task, few times the zpd was an empty set, and there was always a recovery in the following task (see figure 1). Concerning the tasks proposed, the 68.57% of the task proposals implied the zpd of a learner. The 50% of them implied the zpd of both learners involved, while 33% only the zpd of one learner and 16.66% tasks did not imply the zpd of any of the learners.

6.2 Heterogeneous Group

In this case we considered a heterogeneous group of four learners with the initial state as follows: one new learner (0 knowledge elements learned), one low level learner (2 elements learned), other middle level (4 elements learned) and a high level learner (6 elements learned). We ran the model with the corresponding actualizations on the learners capabilities with respect to the tasks proposed. The average of zpd for a member of the group was of 1.21 knowledge elements. For the new learner the average zpd was 2.125 knowledge elements; for the low level 1.25, for the middle level it was 0.625 and for the high level learner 0.875 (see figure 2). The 72.08% of the task proposals implied the zpd of a learner. The 62.5% implied the zpd of both learners, while 25% only the zpd of one learner and there was a 12.5% of tasks which do not imply the zpd of the learners.

7 Conclusions

ASP is a pertinent application of Artificial Intelligence to CSCL environments. The analytic model presented allows a formalization of notions of knowledge synergies in a learning group, which is a foundational issue for CSCL, from a computational point of view. DLV resulted in an appropriate system to elaborate a logically correct and consistent computational model of an agent for structured domain CSCL environments. The model proposed provides a representation of the structural knowledge frontier and the social knowledge frontier of the learner, which are the components for the definition of the learner's zone of proximal development. Based on the zpd of its learner the agent can propose her an intelligent learning task. Thanks to the concept of group supportive task the agents are able to maintain the zpd for the learners in the group. The analytical model, as it is presented in the paper, runs using the DLV system that can be easily downloaded from the internet [12].

References

1. Hoppe, U. H. & Ploetzner, R. Can Analytic models Support Learning in Groups (1998)
2. http://www.collide.info/Lehre/GestaltungInteraktiverLehrLernsysteme/downloads/esf98f.pdf
3. Self, J. Dormobile: a Vehicle for Metacognition, in Invited Talks, International Conference on Computers in Education ICCE'93, Taipei, Taiwan (1993).
4. Self, J. Computational Viewpoints, in Knowledge Negotiation, Moyse, R. & Elsom-Cook, M. (Eds.), Academic Press, (1992) 21-40
5. Ayala, G. & Yano, Y. GRACILE: A Framework for Collaborative Intelligent Learning Environments, Journal of the Japanese Society of Artificial Intelligence, Vol.10. 6. (1995) 156-170
6. Baral, C. Knowledge Representation, Reasoning and Declarative Problem Solving, Cambridge University Press, (2003).
7. Ortiz, M., Ayala, G. & Osorio, M. Formalizing the Learner Model for CSCL Environments, proceedings of the Fourth Mexican International Conference on Computer Science ENC 03, IEEE Computer Society and Mexican Society for Computer Science, (2003) 151-158.
8. Ortiz, M. An Application of Answer Sets Programming for Supporting Collaboration in Agent-based CSCL Enviroments, European Summer School of Logic, Language and Information ESSLLI03, Student Session, (Balder Cate, Ed.) Vienna, Austria, (2003) .
9. Bihlmeyer, R., Faber,W., Ielpa, G. & Pfeifer, G. DLV- User Manual, (2004)
10. http://www.dbai.tuwien.ac.at/proj/dlv/man/
11. Goldstein, I. P. The Genetic Graph: a representation for the evolution of procedural knowledge, *Intelligent Tutoring Systems*, D. Sleeman and J. S. Brown (Eds.) Academic Press, (1982) 51-77
12. Vygotsky, L. S. *Mind in Society; the development of higher psychological processes*, Harvard University Press, London, (1978).
13. Ayala, G. & Yano, Y. Learner Models for Supporting Awareness and Collaboration in a CSCL Environment. *Intelligent Tutoring Systems*, Lecture Notes in Computer Science 1086, Claude Frasson, Gilles Gauthier and Alan Lesgold (Eds.), Springer Verlag, (1996) 158-167.
14. Koch, C. The DLV Tutorial, (2004)
15. http://chkoch.home.cern.ch/chkoch/dlv/dlv_tutorial.html

Deductive Systems' Representation and an Incompleteness Result in the Situation Calculus*

Pablo Sáez

Departamento de Ingeniería Informática y Ciencia de la Computación,
Facultad de Ingeniería, University of Concepción, Chile
psaez@inf.udec.cl

Abstract. It is shown in this paper a way of representing deductive systems using the situation calculus. The situation calculus is a family of first order languages with induction that allows the specification of evolving worlds and reasoning about them and has found a number of applications in AI. A method for the representation of formulae and of proofs is presented in which the induction axiom on states is used to represent structural induction on formulae and proofs. This paper's formalizations are relevant for the purpose of meta reasoning and of automated or manual deduction in the context of situation calculus specifications. An example proof is given for the fact that no deductive system is complete for arbitrary situation calculus specifications (an expectable result).

1 Introduction

The situation calculus, as conceived in 1969 by Mc Carthy and Hayes in [6], is a family of first order languages that allows the specification of evolving worlds and reasoning about them. An important obstacle for the popularization of the situation calculus since 1969 was the *frame problem* [6], that is, the problem of efficiently specifying not only what changes in a particular domain but also what does *not* change. Reiter solved in 1991 in [8] the frame problem, based on previous works by Pednault [7] and Schubert [12]. Since then a number of interesting applications of the situation calculus have been found in areas such as databases [9,11], robotics [1], planning [2] and others.

The situation calculus has been used as a modeling tool for the representation of the behaviour of databases [11], logic programs [5], and robots [3] among others. We provide in this paper a sound representation of deductive systems in the situation calculus. We show a general framework for that purpose, and study the example of Hilbert's deductive system. A representation of formulae and of proofs is given in which the situation calculus induction axiom on states [10] is used to represent structural induction on formulae and on proofs. The situation calculus, being a first order language, has a formal semantics, and the solution

---

* This research was supported by project 201.093.0041-1.0 of the Dirección de Investigación, University of Concepción.

to the frame problem has made it possible to develop a number of reasoning formalisms and applications based on it, for example [13,14]. Therefore a formal representation of deductive systems such as the one proposed in this paper can be used for the purpose of meta-reasoning, that is, reasoning about proofs, taking advantage of the above mentioned features of the situation calculus as a modelling and reasoning tool.

We give an example of such an application, namely a situation calculus version of Gödel's incompleteness proof. The result is namely the fact that no deductive system is sound and complete for situation calculus specifications. This result is not surprising, given the presence of the induction axiom on states, and moreover can be derived from previous results [4,5] (for instance in [5], Lin and Reiter show that logic programs can be encoded in the situation calculus, and since transitive closure can be easily encoded by a logic program and cannot be captured by first order logic, we have that the situation calculus is incomplete).

The interest of this example proof, besides being a new, alternative one, is that it is more understandable than the original proof by Gödel for natural numbers, due to the tree-like structure of situations in the situation calculus, which is closer to the structure of a deductive system than that of natural numbers. Therefore it can be of pedagogical interest as well.

The ideas contained in this paper can be easily applied to other deductive systems, such as resolution, term rewriting and so on. With a (practical) formalization of those deductive systems, such as the one proposed here, one could imagine mechanically proving theorems about mechanical theorem proving itself.

In section 2 an overview of the situation calculus is given. In section 3 a method for representing first-order formulae in the situation calculus is shown. In section 4 a way of representing deductive systems in the situation calculus is described. In section 5 a proof is given for the fact that no deductive system is complete for the situation calculus. Finally, in section 6 some conclusions are given.

2   The Situation Calculus

We will consider throughout this paper as "situation calculus" essentially what is presented in [11] in terms of language, formulae and specifications. We make in this section a brief review of the concepts involved.

The situation calculus is a family of second order languages in which the only second order formula is (1) below (all other formulae are first order). Its purpose is to allow the specification of evolving worlds and reasoning about them. Its ontological assumptions are that the world has an initial state named S_0 (S_0 is a constant of the language), that the world goes discretely from state to state and that the world can change its state only as an effect of *actions* performed by some agent.

Let us describe a generic language $\mathcal{L}$ of the situation calculus family. $\mathcal{L}$ is a sorted second order language with equality with three disjoint sorts: sort *action*, sort *situation* and sort *item*. It includes a finite set of functions symbols of sort *action* that take arguments of sort *item*. For example term $drop(box)$ may represent the action of dropping item box. $\mathcal{L}$ also includes infinitely many function symbols of sort *item* for each arity, none of which take an argument of sort *situation*.

States of the world are called *situations*. The situation that results from the performance of action a at situation s is called $do(a, s)$. Symbol do is a function symbol of sort *situation* that takes two arguments: one of sort *action* and another of sort *situation*. For example, if $drop(box)$ is the action of dropping item box then $do(drop(box), s_1)$ is the situation that results from situation s_1 after dropping item box. Functions do and S_0 are the only functions of sort *situation* in $\mathcal{L}$. Therefore situations are first order terms that are either S_0 or $do(a, s)$, where a is an action and s is another situation. Axiom (1) below states precisely this fact, namely that the only situations are those obtained from situation S_0 by a finite number of applications of the do function. Axiom (1) is a part of every situation calculus specification.

Besides the above described functions and constants, $\mathcal{L}$ includes a finite set of predicates that take among their arguments exactly one of sort *situation*, which is normally the last one. Those predicates are called *fluents*. For example, fluent $on(x, y, s)$ may mean that item x is on item y at situation s, that is, $on(x, y, s)$ represents a predicate that varies with time, from situation to situation.

Also, $\mathcal{L}$ includes two distinguished predicate symbols: $Poss(.,.)$ and $<$. $Poss$ takes an argument of sort *action* and another argument of sort *situation*. The meaning of $Poss(a, s)$ is that action a's performance is possible at situation s. That is, $Poss(a, s)$ is an atom that is defined to be logically equivalent to the precondition of action a in situation s. Predicate $<$ takes two arguments of sort *situation*. The meaning of $s_1 < s_2$ is that situation s_2 is equal to situation obtained from situation s_1 by a finite number of applications of the do symbol with actions that are possible at each intermediary situation. Atom $s_1 \leq s_2$ is an abbreviation for $s_1 < s_2 \vee s_1 = s_2$.

Finally, $\mathcal{L}$ includes infinitely many predicate symbols of each arity, none of which take arguments of sort *situation* or *action*. These predicates, called simply *predicates*, are such that its truth values do not depend on the state of the world (situation).

With respect to formulae, in [11]'s setting a situation calculus specification $\mathcal{D}$ is the union of six sets of formulae: $\Sigma, \mathcal{D}_{ss}, \mathcal{D}_{tp}, \mathcal{D}_{uns}, \mathcal{D}_{unt}$ and $\mathcal{D}_{S_0}$. Σ consists of the induction axiom

$$(\forall p)([p(S_0) \wedge (\forall a, s)(p(s) \supset p(do(a, s)))] \supset (\forall s)p(s)) \qquad (1)$$

and of the following two axioms:

$$(\forall s)\neg s < S_0$$
$$(\forall a, s, s')s < do(a, s') \equiv Poss(a, s') \wedge s \leq s'$$

that axiomatize relation $<$. Set $\mathcal{D}_{uns}$ contains the following two axioms

$$(\forall a, s)S_0 \neq do(a, s)$$
$$(\forall a, s, a', s')do(a, s) = do(a', s') \supset (a = a' \wedge s = s')$$

that axiomatize symbol do. They say basically that S_0 and do are free constructors of type *state*.

$\mathcal{D}_{unt}$ contains, for each pair of different action function symbols A and A' an axiom of the form

$$(\forall x_1, ..., x_m, y_1, ..., y_n) A(x_1, ..., x_m) \neq A'(y_1, ..., y_n)$$

and for each action function symbol A an axiom of the form

$$(\forall x_1..x_n, y_1..y_n) A(x_1, ..., x_n) = A(y_1, ..., y_n) \supset (x_1 = y_1 \wedge ... \wedge x_n = y_n).$$

These axioms say that action function symbols are free constructors of type *action*. $\mathcal{D}_{tp}$ contains, for each action function symbol A an axiom of the form

$$(\forall x_1..x_n) Poss(A(x_1, ..., x_n), s) \equiv \Pi_A$$

where Π_A is a simple formula whose free variables are among $x_1...x_n, s$. Simple formulae, following [11], are those first order formulae which do not mention the predicate symbols $Poss$ or $<$, whose fluents do not mention the function symbol do and which do not quantify over variables of sort *situation*. $\mathcal{D}_{tp}$ is therefore a formal specification of the action preconditions.

Assuming two action function symbols, $drop(x)$ above and $move(y, z)$ meaning moving object y onto object z, the following is an example of $\mathcal{D}_{tp}$:

$(\forall o, s) Poss(drop(o), s) \equiv \neg on(o, Floor, s) \wedge o \neq Floor \wedge \neg(\exists o') on(o', o, s)$
$(\forall o_1, o_2, s) Poss(move(o_1, o_2), s) \equiv o_1 \neq Floor \wedge o_1 \neq o_2 \wedge$
  $\neg(\exists o') on(o', o_1, s) \wedge \neg(\exists o') on(o', o_2, s).$

$\mathcal{D}_{ss}$ consists, for each fluent F, of a *successor state axiom* of the form

$$(\forall a, s) Poss(a, s) \supset (\forall x_1, ..., x_n)(F(x_1, ..., x_n, do(a, s)) \equiv \Phi_F)$$

where Φ_F is a simple formula whose free variables are among $a, s, x_1, ..., x_n$. In [8], successor state axioms are derived from *effect axioms* that specify the effect of actions on fluents. This derivation constitutes a solution to the frame problem. For example, the following axioms specify the effect of actions $drop$ and $move$:

$(\forall o_1, o_2, s) Poss(drop(o_1), s) \wedge on(o_1, o_2, s) \supset \neg on(o_1, o_2, do(drop(o_1), s))$
$(\forall o, s) Poss(drop(o), s) \supset on(o, Floor, do(drop(o), s))$
$(\forall o_1, o_2, o_3, s) Poss(move(o_1, o_3), s) \wedge on(o_1, o_2, s) \wedge o_2 \neq o_3 \supset$
  $\neg on(o_1, o_2, do(move(o_1, o_3), s))$
$(\forall o_1, o_2, s) Poss(move(o_1, o_2), s) \supset on(o_1, o_2, do(move(o_1, o_2), s)).$

Following [8], effect axioms are gathered into two logically equivalent general effect axioms, a positive and a negative one for each fluent. In the example:

$(\forall o_1, o_2, a, s) Poss(a, s) \wedge (a = drop(o_1) \wedge on(o_1, o_2, s) \vee$
  $(\exists o_3)(a = move(o_1, o_3) \wedge o_2 \neq o_3) \wedge on(o_1, o_2, s)) \supset$
  $\neg on(o_1, o_2, do(a, s))$ \hfill (2)
$(\forall o_1, o_2, a, s) Poss(a, s) \wedge (a = drop(o_1) \wedge o_2 = Floor \vee$
  $a = move(o_1, o_2)) \supset on(o_1, o_2, do(a, s)).$ \hfill (3)

Assuming that (2) are the only conditions under which fluent *on* becomes false and that (3) are the only conditions under which fluent *on* becomes true, the following successor state axiom is derived:

$$(\forall a, s) Poss(a, s) \supset (\forall o_1, o_2)(on(o_1, o_2, do(a, s)) \equiv on(o_1, o_2, s) \wedge \\ \neg(a = drop(o_1) \wedge on(o_1, o_2, s) \vee (\exists o_3)(a = move(o_1, o_3) \wedge o_2 \neq o_3) \wedge \\ on(o_1, o_2, s)) \vee a = drop(o_1) \wedge o_2 = Floor \vee a = move(o_1, o_2))$$

and corresponds to $\mathcal{D}_{ss}$ in the example.

Finally, $\mathcal{D}_{S_0}$ is a set of formulae such that S_0 is the only term of sort *situation* mentioned by the fluents in $\mathcal{D}_{S_0}$ (therefore, no variable of sort *situation* is mentioned in $\mathcal{D}_{S_0}$ and the symbol *do* does not appear either). We will assume in this paper that $\mathcal{D}_{S_0}$ has a unique model for the initial situation S_0. This is not an unusual assumption, and means that a perfect knowledge of the initial state of the world is available. The following is an example of $\mathcal{D}_{S_0}$:

$$\{(\forall o_1, o_2) on(o_1, o_2, S_0) \equiv (o_1 = O_1 \wedge o_2 = Floor \vee o_1 = O_2 \wedge o_2 = O_1), \\ O_1 \neq O_2, O_1 \neq Floor, O_2 \neq Floor\}.$$

It is possible to prove that situation calculus of the form presented here are categorical, that is, they have a unique model, up to isomorphisms, for situations s such that $s \geq S_0$, since they have a unique model for the initial situation S_0 and successor state axioms are based on logical equivalences. The proof is by induction on situations.

3 Formulae Representation in the Situation Calculus

We represent in the situation calculus formulae of a first-order language $\mathcal{L}$ by elements of sort *item* in the following way. Functions are defined between elements of sort *item* that represent relationships between formulae. For instance:

$$implies : item \times item \rightarrow item$$
$$not : item \rightarrow item$$
$$all : item \times item \rightarrow item$$
$$p_1 : item \times ... \times item \rightarrow item$$
$$...$$
$$p_k : item \times ... \times item \rightarrow item$$
$$f_1 : item \times ... \times item \rightarrow item$$
$$...$$
$$f_l : item \times ... \times item \rightarrow item$$

(assuming that $\mathcal{L}$ has k predicate letters and l function symbols)

The intended meaning of the above functions is that item $not(i_1)$ is a representation of formula $\neg \varphi$ if item i_1 is a representation of formula φ; that

$implies(i_1, i_2)$ is a representation of formula $\varphi \supset \psi$ if items i_1 and i_2 are representations of formulae φ and ψ respectively; that item $all(i_1, i_2)$ is a representation of formula $(\forall x)\varphi$ if items i_1 and i_2 are representations of variable x and formula φ respectively; that if items $i_1...i_n$ are representations of terms $t_1...t_n$ then item $p_1(i_1, ..., i_n)$ is a representation of atom $p(t_1, ..., t_n)$ (assuming that predicate p of language $\mathcal{L}$, represented by function p_1, is n-ary); and so on, for all other predicate symbols in $\mathcal{L}$; and finally that if items $i_1...i_m$ and function f_1 are representations of terms $t_1...t_m$ and of function symbol f respectively then $f_1(i_1, ..., i_m)$ is a representation of term $f(t_1, ..., t_m)$ (assuming that function symbol f of language $\mathcal{L}$ is m-ary); and so on for all other function symbols in $\mathcal{L}$.

One problem to be solved in formula and term representation is the closure of the set of formulae and of terms, i.e. the problem of how to express the fact that the only formulae and terms are those obtained by a finite number of applications of the above mentioned functions. Clearly some kind of second order axiom is necessary for that purpose, but in the situation calculus the only second order axiom is the induction axiom on situations. It is therefore necessary to somehow use that axiom to specify the closure of the set of formulae. One way to do this is as follows:

Assuming that predicate $variable(.)$ represents the variables of language $\mathcal{L}$ and that predicate $constant(.)$ represents the constants of language $\mathcal{L}$, define the set of terms constructed at situation S_0 as follows:

$$(\forall i) term(i, S_0) \equiv (variable(i) \lor constant(i)) \qquad (4)$$

and the set of terms constructed at successor situations by the following effect axioms:

$$(\forall i_1...i_m, s) Poss(c_{f_1}(i_1, ..., i_m), s) \supset$$
$$term(f_1(i_1, ..., i_m), do(c_{f_1}(i_1, ..., i_m), s)) \qquad (5)$$

$$...$$

$$(\forall i_1...i_{m'}, s) Poss(c_{f_l}(i_1, ..., i_{m'}), s) \supset$$
$$term(f_l(i_1, ..., i_{m'}), do(c_{f_l}(i_1, ..., i_{m'}), s)), \qquad (6)$$

one axiom for each function f in $\mathcal{L}$ where an action c_{f_j} is defined for the function f_j that represents function f. Action c_{f_j} "constructs" the representation of term $f(t_1, ..., t_n)$ from the representations of terms $t_1...t_n$.

Next define the set of constructed formula at situation S_0 as empty:

$$(\forall i) \neg formula(i, S_0) \qquad (7)$$

and the set of constructed formulae at successor situations by axioms similar to those used above for term definitions:

$$(\forall i_1...i_n, s) Poss(c_{p_1}(i_1, ..., i_n), s) \supset$$
$$formula(p_1(i_1, ..., i_n), do(c_{p_1}(i_1, ..., i_n), s)) \qquad (8)$$

$$...$$

$$(\forall i_1...i_{n'}, s) Poss(c_{p_k}(i_1, ..., i_{n'}), s) \supset$$
$$formula(p_k(i_1, ..., i_{n'}), do(c_{p_k}(i_1, ..., i_{n'}), s)) \qquad (9)$$

one axiom for each p in $\mathcal{L}$ where an action c_{p_j} is defined for the function p_j that represents predicate p. Next, define three actions that "construct" formulae with the following set of effect axioms:

$$(\forall i_1, i_2, s) Poss(c_{implies}(i_1, i_2), s) \supset$$
$$formula(implies(i_1, i_2), do(c_{implies}(i_1, i_2), s)) \tag{10}$$
$$(\forall i, s) Poss(c_{not}(i), s) \supset formula(not(i), do(c_{not}(i), s)) \tag{11}$$
$$(\forall i_1, i_2, s) Poss(c_{all}(i_1, i_2), s) \supset$$
$$formula(all(i_1, i_2), do(c_{all}(i_1, i_2), s)). \tag{12}$$

Finally, define $\mathcal{D}_{tp}$ to be the following set of precondition axioms

$$(\forall i_1, ..., i_m, s) Poss(c_{f_1}(i_1, ..., i_m), s) \equiv$$
$$term(i_1, s) \wedge ... \wedge term(i_m, s) \tag{13}$$
$$...$$
$$(\forall i_1, ..., i_n, s) Poss(c_{p_1}(i_1, ..., i_n), s) \equiv term(i_1, s) \wedge ... \wedge term(i_n, s)$$
$$...$$
$$(\forall i_1, i_2, s) Poss(c_{implies}(i_1, i_2), s) \equiv formula(i_1, s) \wedge formula(i_2, s)$$
$$(\forall i, s) Poss(c_{not}(i), s) \equiv formula(i, s)$$
$$(\forall i_1, i_2, s) Poss(c_{all}(i_1, i_2), s) \equiv variable(i_1) \wedge formula(i_2, s). \tag{14}$$

Define the sets Σ, $\mathcal{D}_{uns}$ and $\mathcal{D}_{unt}$ as usual, define $\mathcal{D}_{S_0}$ to be the set of two formulae (4) and (7), and define the set $\mathcal{D}_{ss}$ to be the set of two successor state axioms that correspond to effect axioms (5) through (6), (8) through (9), (10), (11) and (12). It is possible to prove from those axioms that every formula of the language is constructed at some situation, i.e. for every formula φ of the language there exists a $s \geq S_0$ such that $formula(i, s)$, where i is the representation of formula φ; and on the opposite, every constructed formula is the representation of a formula in the language. The proof of those facts is by induction on situations.

4 Deductive Systems' Representation in the Situation Calculus

In this section we propose a way of representing deductive systems in the situation calculus. As an example, Hilbert's deductive system for first order logic consists of the axioms

$$\varphi \supset (\psi \supset \varphi) \tag{15}$$
$$(\varphi \supset (\psi \supset \chi)) \supset ((\varphi \supset \psi) \supset (\varphi \supset \chi)) \tag{16}$$
$$(\neg \psi \supset \neg \varphi) \supset (\varphi \supset \psi) \tag{17}$$
$$(\forall x)\varphi(x) \supset \varphi(t) \tag{18}$$

where t is a term and of the rules

$$\frac{\vdash \varphi \quad \vdash \varphi \supset \psi}{\vdash \psi}$$

(modus ponens) and

$$\frac{\vdash \varphi \supset \psi(x)}{\vdash \varphi \supset (\forall x)\psi(x)}$$

(quantifier rule) where x does no appear free in φ.

Axioms (15) through (18) of Hilbert's deductive system can be represented by the following effect axioms:

$$(\forall i_1, i_2, s) Poss(c_{ax1}(i_1, i_2), s) \wedge formula(i_1, s) \wedge formula(i_2, s) \supset$$
$$deduc(implies(i_1, implies(i_2, i_1)), do(c_{ax1}(i_1, i_2), s)) \quad (19)$$

$$(\forall i_1, i_2, i_3, s) Poss(c_{ax2}(i_1, i_2, i_3), s) \wedge formula(i_1, s) \wedge formula(i_2, s) \wedge$$
$$formula(i_3, s) \supset deduc(implies(implies(i_1, implies(i_2, i_3)),$$
$$implies(implies(i_1, i_2), implies(i_1, i_3))), do(c_{ax2}(i_1, i_2, i_3), s)) \quad (20)$$

$$(\forall i_1, i_2, s) Poss(c_{ax3}(i_1, i_2), s) \wedge formula(i_1, s) \wedge formula(i_2, s) \supset$$
$$deduc(implies(implies(not(i_2), not(i_1)),$$
$$implies(i_1, i_2)), do(c_{ax3}(i_1, i_2), s)) \quad (21)$$

$$(\forall i_1, i_2, i_3, i_4, s) Poss(c_{ax4}(i_1, i_2, i_3), s) \wedge formula(i_1, s) \wedge variable(i_2) \wedge$$
$$term(i_3, s) \wedge sub(i_1, i_2, i_3, i_4, s) \supset$$
$$deduc(implies(all(i_2, i_1), i_4), do(c_{ax4}(i_1, i_2, i_3), s)) \quad (22)$$

where $deduc(i, s)$ means that the formula represented by item i has been deduced at situation s. Actions c_{ax1}, c_{ax2}, c_{ax3} and c_{ax4} represent applications of axioms (15), (16), (17) and (18) respectively. Fluent $sub(i_1, i_2, i_3, i_4, s)$ means that the formula represented by i_4 is the result of replacing variable represented by item i_2 by the term represented by i_3 within the formula represented by i_1. Considering the same generic language $\mathcal{L}$ as in section 3, fluent sub can be axiomatized by the following initial situation axiom:

$$(\forall i_1, i_2, i_3, i_4) sub(i_1, i_2, i_3, i_4, S_0) \equiv (variable(i_1) \wedge (i_1 = i_2 \wedge i_4 = i_3 \vee$$
$$i_1 \neq i_2 \wedge i_4 = i_1) \vee constant(i_1) \wedge i_4 = i_1) \quad (23)$$

and by the successor state axiom corresponding to the following effect axioms:

$$(\forall i_1..i_m, i, i', i'_1..i'_m, s) Poss(c_{f_1}(i_1, ..., i_m), s) \wedge$$
$$sub(i_1, i, i', i'_1, s) \wedge ... \wedge sub(i_m, i, i', i'_m, s) \supset$$
$$sub(f_1(i_1, ..., i_m), i, i', f_1(i'_1, ..., i'_m), do(c_{f_1}(i_1, ..., i_m), s)) \quad (24)$$

...

$$(\forall i_1..i_n, i, i', i'_1..i'_n, s) Poss(c_{p_1}(i_1, ..., i_n), s) \wedge$$
$$sub(i_1, i, i', i'_1, s) \wedge ... \wedge sub(i_n, i, i', i'_n, s) \supset$$

$$sub(p_1(i_1,...,i_n),i,i',p_1(i'_1,...,i'_n),do(c_{p_1}(i_1,...,i_n),s)) \qquad (25)$$

...

(one axiom for each action symbol c_{f_j} and c_{p_j}) and to the following effect axioms:

$$(\forall i_1,i_2,i_3,i_4,i_5,i_6,s)Poss(c_{implies}(i_1,i_5),s) \wedge$$
$$sub(i_1,i_2,i_3,i_4,s) \wedge sub(i_5,i_2,i_3,i_6,s) \supset$$
$$sub(implies(i_1,i_5),i_2,i_3,implies(i_4,i_6),do(c_{implies}(i_1,i_5),s))$$
$$(\forall i_1,i_2,i_3,i_4,s)Poss(c_{not}(i_1),s) \wedge sub(i_1,i_2,i_3,i_4,s) \supset$$
$$sub(not(i_1),i_2,i_3,not(i_4),do(c_{not}(i_1),s))$$
$$(\forall i_1,i_2,i_3,i_4,i_5,s)Poss(c_{all}(i_5,i_1),s) \wedge (sub(i_1,i_2,i_3,i_4,s) \wedge i_2 \neq i_5 \vee$$
$$formula(i_1,s) \wedge variable(i_5) \wedge term(i_3,s) \wedge i_1 = i_4 \wedge i_2 = i_5) \supset$$
$$sub(all(i_5,i_1),i_2,i_3,all(i_5,i_4),do(c_{all}(i_5,i_1),s)). \qquad (26)$$

The rules in Hilbert's deductive system can be represented by the following effect axioms:

$$(\forall i_1,i_2,s)Poss(modusPonens(i_1,i_2),s) \wedge deduc(implies(i_1,i_2),s) \wedge$$
$$deduc(i_1,s) \supset deduc(i_2,do(modusPonens(i_1,i_2),s)) \qquad (27)$$
$$(\forall i_1,i_2,i_3,s)Poss(ruleQ(i_1,i_2,i_3),s) \wedge$$
$$deduc(implies(i_1,i_2),s) \wedge \neg free(i_3,i_1,s) \supset$$
$$deduc(implies(i_1,all(i_3,i_2)),do(ruleQ(i_1,i_2,i_3),s)) \qquad (28)$$

where actions $modusPonens$ and $ruleQ$ represent applications of the modus ponens and of the quantifier rule respectively. Fluent $free(i_1,i_2,s)$ means that the variable represented by item i_1 appears free in the formula represented by item i_2. Considering the same generic language $\mathcal{L}$ as in section 3, fluent $free$ can be axiomatized by the following initial situation axiom:

$$(\forall i_1,i_2)free(i_1,i_2,S_0) \equiv variable(i_1) \wedge i_1 = i_2 \qquad (29)$$

and by the successor state axiom corresponding to the following effect axioms:

$$(\forall i',i_1..i_m,s)Poss(c_{f_1}(i_1,...,i_m),s) \wedge (free(i',i_1,s) \vee ... \vee free(i',i_m,s)) \supset$$
$$free(i',f_1(i_1,...,i_m),do(c_{f_1}(i_1,...,i_m),s)) \qquad (30)$$

...

$$(\forall i',i_1..i_n)Poss(c_{p_1}(i_1,...,i_n),s) \wedge (free(i',i_1,s) \vee ... \vee free(i',i_n,s)) \supset$$
$$free(i',p_1(i_1,...,i_n),do(c_{p_1}(i_1,...,i_n),s))$$

...

$$(\forall i_1,i_2,i_3,s)Poss(c_{implies}(i_2,i_3),s) \wedge (free(i_1,i_2,s) \vee free(i_1,i_3,s)) \supset$$
$$free(i_1,implies(i_2,i_3),do(c_{implies}(i_2,i_3),s))$$
$$(\forall i_1,i_2,s)Poss(c_{not}(i_2),s) \wedge free(i_1,i_2,s) \supset free(i_1,not(i_2),do(c_{not}(i_2),s))$$
$$(\forall i_1,i_2,i_3,s)Poss(c_{all}(i_3,i_2),s) \wedge free(i_1,i_2,s) \wedge i_1 \neq i_3 \supset$$
$$free(i_1,all(i_3,i_2),do(c_{all}(i_3,i_2),s)). \qquad (31)$$

To sum up, Hilbert's deductive system can be represented in the situation calculus by the following set $\mathcal{D}_{S_0}$:

$$(\forall i)\neg deduc(i, S_0)$$

along with formulae (4), (7), (23) and (29); by the set $\mathcal{D}_{ss}$ that includes the successor state axiom for fluent $deduc$, corresponding to effect axioms (19) through (22), (27) and (28), and the successor state axioms for fluents $formula$, $term$, sub and $free$, corresponding to effect axioms (5) through (6), (8) through (9), (10) through (12), effect axioms (24), (25), (26), and (30) through (31). Also, sets Σ, $\mathcal{D}_{uns}$ and $\mathcal{D}_{unt}$ are defined as usual and set $\mathcal{D}_{tp}$ contains the following set of axioms

$$\{(\forall i_1, i_2, s) Poss(c_{ax1}(i_1, i_2), s), (\forall i_1, i_2, i_3, s) Poss(c_{ax2}(i_1, i_2, i_3), s),$$
$$(\forall i_1, i_2, s) Poss(c_{ax3}(i_1, i_2), s), (\forall i_1, i_2, i_3, s) Poss(c_{ax4}(i_1, i_2, i_3), s),$$
$$(\forall i_1, i_2, s) Poss(modusPonens(i_1, i_2), s),$$
$$(\forall i_1, i_2, i_3, s) Poss(ruleQ(i_1, i_2, i_3), s)\}$$

along with axioms (13) through (14).

In a similar way other deductive systems can be represented by a situation calculus specification. Notice that one deductive step (application of a deductive rule) corresponds to one action in the above example. This might not be the case for other deductive systems, in which one deductive step may need to be represented by several actions (for example, one application of the resolution rule involves several steps, such as choosing the literals to be resolved, unifying and so on). Notice also that the above example is for a first-order deductive system. For second order deductive systems the axioms that construct formulae (in this case second order formulae) would need to be changed.

In general, any Turing machine can be represented by a situation calculus specification. It is then easy to see that any deductive system can also be represented in the situation calculus in the above explained manner, that is, by representing formulae as elements of sort $item$ and deductive steps as elements of sort $action$, since every computation performed in each deductive step is representable in the situation calculus because any Turing machine (and therefore any computation) is representable. A proof for the fact that any Turing machine can be represented by a situation calculus specification is given in [3].

5   The Incompleteness Result

It was shown in the previous section that any deductive system can be represented by a situation calculus specification. We show in this section that no deductive system exists that is complete for the situation calculus by applying an arbitrary deductive system to the specification that represents the deductive system itself. Given the arguments in the previous section, we will assume that for any deductive system $\vdash$ there exists a situation calculus specification $\mathcal{D}_{\vdash}$ that represents it. In particular, $\mathcal{D}_\vdash$ includes the definition of fluent $deduc(i, s)$, meaning that the formula represented by item i has been derived at situation s. We will assume also that a specification $\mathcal{D}_{sub}$ can be given that defines predicate sub from the previous section. For example, $\mathcal{D}_{sub}$ in the previous section's example corresponds to formula (23) and to the successor state axiom that corresponds to effect axioms (24) through (26).

Consider now the following formula[1] χ:

$$\mathcal{D}_\vdash \wedge \mathcal{D}_{sub} \supset (\forall s)(\forall x) s \geq S_0 \wedge sub(I, J, I, x, s) \supset \neg deduc(x, s),$$

where I is the item that represents formula

$$\mathcal{D}_\vdash \wedge \mathcal{D}_{sub} \supset (\forall s)(\forall x) s \geq S_0 \wedge sub(y, J, y, x, s) \supset \neg deduc(x, s), \quad (32)$$

where $\mathcal{D}_\vdash$ is the situation calculus specification of a particular deductive system $\vdash$, and where J is the item that represents variable y.

Now consider the problem of whether

$$\vdash \chi \quad (33)$$

i.e. the problem of whether χ is deductible using deductive system $\vdash$. Since $\mathcal{D}_\vdash$ is the specification of $\vdash$, (33) holds if and only if

$$\mathcal{D}_\vdash \models (\exists s)(s \geq S_0 \wedge deduc(C, s)), \quad (34)$$

where item C is the representation of formula χ. Since $\mathcal{D}_{sub}$ is a specification that *defines* predicate sub, $\mathcal{D}_{sub}$ adds no information regarding neither $deduc$ nor $\geq$ to $\mathcal{D}_\vdash$. Therefore (34) holds if and only if

$$\mathcal{D}_\vdash \cup \mathcal{D}_{sub} \models (\exists s)(s \geq S_0 \wedge deduc(C, s)),$$

which is the same as

$$\mathcal{D}_\vdash \cup \mathcal{D}_{sub} \models \neg(\forall s) s \geq S_0 \supset \neg deduc(C, s). \quad (35)$$

Now consider the following formula:

$$(\forall s)(\forall x) s > S_0 \wedge sub(I, J, I, x, s) \supset \neg deduc(x, s). \quad (36)$$

Given $\mathcal{D}_{sub}$, the definition of predicate sub, variable x in (36) can be replaced by the item that represents the formula that results from replacing, within the formula represented by item I, (32), variable y by item I. But this formula is χ. Therefore, given $\mathcal{D}_{sub}$ variable x in (36) can be replaced by C, giving:

$$(\forall s)(\forall x) s \geq S_0 \supset \neg deduc(C, s). \quad (37)$$

Both formulae, (36) and (37), are logically equivalent, given $\mathcal{D}_{sub}$. Therefore, replacing (37) by (36), (35) holds if and only if

$$\mathcal{D}_\vdash \cup \mathcal{D}_{sub} \models \neg(\forall s) s \geq S_0 \wedge sub(I, J, I, x) \supset \neg deduc(x, s). \quad (38)$$

---
[1] Abusing the notation, since $\mathcal{D}_\vdash$ and $\mathcal{D}_{sub}$ are sets of formulae.

Since $\mathcal{D}_\vdash$ is categorical for situations s such that $s \geq S_0$, according to section 2, and $\mathcal{D}_{sub}$ is also categorical (it is a set of definitions), (38) holds if and only if

$$\mathcal{D}_\vdash \cup \mathcal{D}_{sub} \not\models (\forall s)s \geq S_0 \wedge sub(I,J,I,x) \supset \neg deduc(x,s)$$

which is the same as[2]:

$$\not\models \mathcal{D}_\vdash \wedge \mathcal{D}_{sub} \supset (\forall s)s \geq S_0 \wedge sub(I,J,I,x) \supset \neg deduc(x,s)$$

that is
$$\not\models \chi.$$

We finally have that $\vdash \chi$ if and only if $\not\models \chi$: if $\models \chi$ then $\not\vdash \chi$, that is, deductive system $\vdash$ is incomplete. If $\not\models \chi$ then $\vdash \chi$, that is, deductive system $\vdash$ is not sound. Since χ includes a situation calculus specification, we have that every deductive system either is not sound or is incomplete for situation calculus specifications.

6 Conclusions

We showed in this paper that any deductive system can be represented by a situation calculus specification. An example was given, namely Hilbert's deductive system for first order logic. An axiomatization of the behaviour of deductive systems of the kind presented in this paper can be useful for the purpose of manually or automatically meta–reasoning. The formal semantics of the situation calculus and the solution to the frame problem make this formalism a practical one, suitable for mechanical (or manual) theorem proving.

As an application of the representation of deductive systems provided in this paper we proved that no deductive system is complete for the situation calculus. We believe that the incompleteness proof presented here can be easier to follow than Gödel's, due to the structure of situations, closer to that of a deductive system than the structure of natural numbers, so this paper can be of pedagogical interest as well. The ideas presented here can be easily applied to other deductive systems, such as resolution, term rewriting and so on. With a (practical) formalization of those deductive systems, such as the one proposed here, one could imagine mechanically proving theorems about mechanical theorem proving itself.

References

1. Lésperance, Y., Levesque, H., Lin, F., Marcu, D., Reiter, R., Scherl, R.: A Logical Approach to High–Level Robot Programming – A Progress Report. In *Proc. AAAI Fall Symposium of Control of the Physical World by Intelligent Systems*, New Orleans, LA, November 1994.
2. Lin, F.: An Ordering on Goals for Planning – Formalizing Control Information in the Situation Calculus, In *Proceedings of the International Joint Conference on Artificial Intelligence IJCAI'97*, 1997

---

[2] Again, abusing the notation.

3. Lin, F., Levesque, H.: What Robots Can Do: Robot Programs and Effective Achievability. *Artificial Intelligence*, 101, 1998.
4. Lin, F., Reiter, R: How to Progress a Database, *Artificial Intelligence*, 92(1-2),131–167, 1997.
5. Lin, F., Reiter, R.: Rules as Actions: A Situation Calculus Semantics for Logic Programs. *Journal of Logic Programming*. Special Issue on Reasoning about Action and Change. 31(1-3), 299–330, 1997.
6. McCarthy, J., Hayes, P.: Some Philosophical Problems from the Standpoint of Artificial Intelligence. In B. Meltzer and D. Michie, editors, *Machine Intelligence*, volume 4, pages 463–502. Edinburgh University Press, 1969.
7. Pednault, E.: ADL: Exploring the Middle Ground between STRIPS and the Situation Calculus. In R. Brachman H. Levesque and R. Reiter editors, *Proceedings of the First International Conference on Principles of Knowledge Representation and Reasoning (KR'89)*, pages 324–332, San Mateo, CA, 1989. Morgan Kaufmann Publishers, Inc.
8. Reiter, R.: The Frame Problem in the Situation Calculus: a Simple Solution (Sometimes) and a Completeness Result for Goal Regression. In V. Lifschitz, editor, *Artificial Intelligence and Mathematical Theory of Computation: Papers in Honor of John McCarthy*, pages 359–380. Academic Press, 1991.
9. Reiter, R.: Formalizing Database Evolution in the Situation Calculus, In *Proceedings of the Fifth Generation Computer Systems*, Tokyo, Japan, June 1992.
10. Reiter, R.: Proving Properties of States in the Situation Calculus, *Artificial Intelligence*, 64(2):337–351, 1993.
11. Reiter, R.: On Specifying Database Updates, *Journal of Logic Programming*, 25 (1):53–91, 1995.
12. Schubert, L.: Monotonic Solution of the Frame Problem in the Situation Calculus: an Efficient Method for Worlds with Fully Specified Actions. In H. Kyburg, R. Loui and G. Carlson editors, *Knowledge Representation and Defeasible Reasoning*, pages 23–67, Boston, MA, 1990. Kluwer Academic Press.
13. Bertossi, L., Pinto, J., Sáez, P., Kapur, D., Subramaniam, M.: Automating Proofs of Integrity Constraints in the Situation Calculus. In Z. Pawlak and Z.W. Ras editors, *Proc. Ninth International Symposium on Methodologies for Intelligent Systems, ISMIS'96*, Zakopane, Poland, May 1996, LNAI 1079, Springer Verlag.
14. Pinto, J.: Temporal Reasoning in the Situational Calculus, Ph. D. thesis, Department of Computer Science, University of Toronto, 1994,

Geometric Aspects Related to Solutions of #kSAT

Guillermo Morales-Luna

Computer Science, CINVESTAV-IPN,
Av. IPN 2508, Mexico City, Mexico
gmorales@cs.cinvestav.mx

Abstract. #kSAT is a complex problem equivalent to calculate the cardinalities of the null sets of conjunctive forms consisting of clauses with an uniform length. Each such null set is the union of linear varieties of uniform dimension in the hypercube. Here we study the class of sets in the hypercube that can be realized as such null sets. We look toward to characterize their cardinalities and the number of ways that they can be expressed as unions of linear varieties of uniform dimension. Using combinatorial and graph theory argumentations, we give such characterizations for very extremal values of k, either when it is very small or close to the hypercube dimension, and of the number of clauses appearing in an instance, either of value 2, or big enough to get a contradiction.

Keywords: SAT, Counting, Hypergraphs, Hypercube Geometry.

1 Introduction

#SAT is the counting version of SAT: Given a Boolean formula it is required to calculate the number of its satisfying assignments, it is a complete problem in #P, which is the class consisting of accepting computations of non-deterministic recursive devices running in polynomial-time. #SAT has had many applications by itself and in [1] there is an interesting account of the main approaches to solve it. Indeed, in [1], #SAT is treated with a modification of the classical Davis-Putnam procedure, and it is shown that for a conjunctive form with m clauses, n variables and an uniform probability p that a literal appearing in the CF appears in a clause of it, the average time complexity of the proposed algorithm is $O(m^d n)$, where $d = [\log_2(1-p)]^{-1}$.

Also, in [2] the cardinality of a finite union of subspaces, $A = \bigcup_{i=1}^{m} A_i$, which is the complement of the support set of a Boolean formula given as a conjunctive form, is approximated using the Inclusion-Exclusion formula

$$\text{card}(A) = \sum_{\mu=1}^{m} (-1)^{\mu-1} \sum_{\text{card } M = \mu} \left(\text{card} \left(\bigcap_{i \in M} A_i \right) \right). \quad (1)$$

Indeed, if the intersection sizes are known for families with at most k sets, $k \geq \Omega(\sqrt{m})$, then the union size can be approximated within a relative error of

$O\left(\exp\left(-\frac{2k}{\sqrt{m}}\right)\right)$. In a more concise way, in [3], it is shown that for instances in which the clauses have all exactly k-literals, then all summands in (1) are determined by the clause-sets of size up to $\lfloor \log_2 k \rfloor + 2$. On the other hand, #SAT has been used as a test-bed in propositional reasoning [4]. #SAT is indeed a difficult problem and even when restricted to conjunctive forms with uniform clause length 2 and all variables appearing negated cannot be approximated [5].

We are mainly concerned about the integer numbers that can be solutions of #SAT restricted to conjunctive forms with an uniform clause size. Equivalently, we are interested in characterizing the integers that can be realized as cardinalities of unions of linear varieties, all with the same dimension, in the hypercube. This is an entirely different problem than #SAT: Whenever we decide that an integer can be realized as the cardinality of a null set of a conjunctive form with an uniform length in its clauses, we will be able to find such conjunctive form. #SAT is a reciprocal decision. We are also interested in counting, for each such integer, in how many ways it can be realized as an union of linear varieties of the same dimension. Our results are conclusive for extremal values: either two varieties or the number of varieties necessary to include always a covering of the hypercube by varieties of a given dimension. However we estimate that our counting procedures may translate some statements of classical satisfiability problems into geometrical notions in the hypercube.

The paper is organized as follows: Section 2 contains the basic notions of satisfiability problems. In section 3 we characterize the integers that can be realized as solutions of #kSAT for instances involving just two clauses. Finally, in section 4 we define several set classes in the hypercube related to the stated characterization problem. We use some hypergraphs techniques to count the minimum number of k-clauses that are necessary to have always a contradiction, namely, an empty set of satisfying assignments.

2 Basic Concepts

We will denote by $[\![1, n]\!]$ the interval of integers from 1 to n: $[\![1, n]\!] = \{1, 2, \ldots, n\}$.

2.1 The Hypercube as a Linear Space

Let $\mathbb{F}_2 = \{0, 1\}$ be the least finite field consisting of just two elements. For each $n \in \mathbb{N}$, $\mathbb{F}_2^n$ is a finite-dimensional linear space over $\mathbb{F}_2$, its dimension is n and its cardinality is 2^n. Let $a \in \mathbb{R}$ be a real number such that $0 < a < 1$, and let $\mathbb{T} = \{0, a, 1\}$. For each $n \in \mathbb{N}$, the set inclusion $\mathbb{F}_2^n \subset \mathbb{T}^n$ holds. For a fixed $n \in \mathbb{N}$, let $I \subset [\![1, n]\!]$ be a subset of k indexes, $k \in [\![1, n]\!]$, and let $P_{i,I} = \mathbb{F}_2$ whenever $i \in I$ and $P_{i,I} = \{0\}$ otherwise. The Cartesian product $C_I = \prod_{i=1}^{n} P_{i,I}$ is a k-dimensional linear subspace in $\mathbb{F}_2^n$. In this context, the *dimension* of a subspace H in $\mathbb{F}_2^n$ is the cardinality of a maximal set of linearly independent vectors in H.

For each $\epsilon \in \mathbb{T}^n$, let $I(\epsilon) = \epsilon^{-1}(a) = \{i \in [\![1, n]\!] | \epsilon_i = a\}$ be the set of entries at ϵ with value a, and let $C_\epsilon = C_{I(\epsilon)}$ be the corresponding product subspace. Let $\epsilon' = (\epsilon'_i)_{i=1}^{n}$ be such that $\epsilon'_i = \epsilon_i$ if $\epsilon_i \neq a$ and $\epsilon'_i = 0$ if $\epsilon_i = a$: ϵ' "fixes" with the value 0 the entries with value a in ϵ. The *linear variety determined* by ϵ is $V(\epsilon) = \{\delta \in \mathbb{F}_2^n | \forall j : (\epsilon_j \neq a \Rightarrow \delta_j = \epsilon_j)\}$. Or $V(\epsilon) = C_\epsilon + \epsilon'$. The dimension of $V(\epsilon)$ coincides thus with the number of entries in ϵ whose value is a.

Given $\delta \in \mathbb{F}_2^n$ and $\epsilon \in \mathbb{T}^n$ let us say that δ *matches* ϵ, $\epsilon \preceq \delta$, if $\delta \in V(\epsilon)$:

$$\epsilon \preceq \delta \iff \forall j \in [\![1,n]\!] : (\epsilon_j \neq a \Rightarrow \delta_j = \epsilon_j).$$

The following relations are immediate:

1. If $\epsilon \in \mathbb{T}^n$ has k values a then there are 2^k vectors in $\mathbb{F}_2^n$ matching ϵ.
2. For each $\delta \in \mathbb{F}_2^n$ there are 2^n vectors $\epsilon \in \mathbb{T}^n$ such that $\epsilon \preceq \delta$.

Let us define a relation in $\mathbb{T}^n$: for any $\epsilon_1, \epsilon_2 \in \mathbb{T}^n$, $\epsilon_1 \sim \epsilon_2$ if and only if $\exists \delta \in \mathbb{F}_2^n : \epsilon_1, \epsilon_2 \preceq \delta$. For instance, the point $\epsilon_1 = (a, 0, 1, a, 0) \in \mathbb{T}^5$ is matched by $\delta = (0, 0, 1, 1, 0) \in \mathbb{F}_2^n$, which also matches $\epsilon_2 = (a, 0, a, 1, 0) \in \mathbb{T}^5$. Thus, $(a, 0, 1, a, 0) \sim (a, 0, a, 1, 0)$. The following relations are pairwise equivalent:

- $\epsilon_1 \sim \epsilon_2$.
- $V(\epsilon_1) \cap V(\epsilon_2) \neq \emptyset$.
- $\forall j \in [\![1, n]\!] : [\epsilon_{1,j} \neq \epsilon_{2,j} \Rightarrow a \in \{\epsilon_{1,j}, \epsilon_{2,j}\}]$.

Finally, let us say that the *complementary vector* of a vector $\epsilon \in \mathbb{T}^n$ is $\bar{\epsilon}$ obtained by interchanging the values 0,1: $\forall j \in [\![1, n]\!]$, $\epsilon_j \neq a \Rightarrow \bar{\epsilon}_j = 1 - \epsilon_j$.

2.2 Problem SAT

Let $\mathbf{X} = \{X_j\}_{j=1,\ldots,n}$ be a set of *Boolean variables*, and let $\mathbf{1}, \mathbf{0}$ be the respective constants acting as units of "$\wedge$": $F \wedge \mathbf{1} = \mathbf{1} \wedge F = F$, and "$\vee$": $C \vee \mathbf{0} = \mathbf{0} \vee C = C$. The *literals* are either variables or negated variables: L literal if $\exists X \in \mathbf{X} : (L = X) \vee (L = \neg X)$. The *clauses* are disjunctions of literals: $\forall \epsilon \in \mathbb{T}^n$ let $\mathrm{Claus}(\epsilon) = \bigvee_{1 \leq j \leq n} X_j^{\epsilon_j}$ where $\forall X \in \mathbf{X}$: $X^1 = X$, $X^a = \mathbf{0}$ and $X^0 = \neg X$. The *length* of a clause is the number of literals appearing in the clause. A *k-clause* is a clause of length k. A *conjunctive form* (CF) is a conjunction of clauses. If $F = \bigwedge_{1 \leq i \leq m} \bigvee_{1 \leq j \leq n} L_{ij}$ we may write $F = [L_{ij}]_{i,j}$. A *k-CF*, is a CF consisting just of k-clauses. As usual, the empty clause is identified with the *False* value $\mathbf{0}$, while the empty CF is identified with the *True* value $\mathbf{1}$. Any vector $\epsilon \in \mathbb{T}^n$ is an *assignment* and determines truth values in literals, clauses and CF's as follows:

$$\forall j \in [\![1, n]\!], \delta \in \mathbb{F}_2 : \; \epsilon_j \neq a \;\&\; \delta = \epsilon_j \Longrightarrow X_j^\delta(\epsilon) = 1$$

$$\epsilon_j \neq a \;\&\; \delta \neq \epsilon_j \Longrightarrow X_j^\delta(\epsilon) = 0$$

$$\epsilon_j = a \Longrightarrow X_j^\delta(\epsilon) = a$$

$$C = \mathrm{Claus}(\epsilon_1) : \; (\exists j : X_j^{\epsilon_{1j}}(\epsilon) = 1) \Longrightarrow C(\epsilon) = 1$$

$$(\forall j : X_j^{\epsilon_{1j}}(\epsilon) = 0) \Longrightarrow C(\epsilon) = 0$$

$$\text{(any other case)} \Longrightarrow C(\epsilon) = a$$

$$F = \bigwedge_i C_i : \; (\forall i : C_i(\epsilon) = 1) \Longrightarrow F(\epsilon) = 1$$

$$(\exists i : C_i(\epsilon) = 0) \Longrightarrow F(\epsilon) = 0$$

$$\text{(any other case)} \Longrightarrow F(\epsilon) = a$$

Each CF F determines a map $F : \mathbb{T}^n \to \mathbb{T}$ and its restriction to $\mathbb{F}_2^n$ is a Boolean map $F : \mathbb{F}_2^n \to \mathbb{F}_2$. The *support* of any map $f : \mathbb{F}_2^n \to \mathbb{F}_2$ is $Spt(f) = f^{-1}(1) = \{\delta \in \mathbb{F}_2^n | f(\delta) = 1\}$ and the *null set* is its complement, $Nul(f) = \mathbb{F}_2^n - Spt(f)$.

The following problems are prototypical:

SAT. Given a CF F decide whether $Spt(F) \neq \emptyset$.

#SAT. Given a CF F calculate the cardinality of the support of F, $card(Spt(F))$.

MaxSAT. Given a CF $F = \bigwedge_{i \in I} C_i$ find a maximal subset $J \subset I$ such that $\bigcap_{j \in J} Spt(C_j)) \neq \emptyset$.

kSAT, #kSAT and Max$k$SAT are the corresponding problems restricted to k-CF's. 3SAT and Max2SAT are typical NP-complete problems. The already classical result due to Valiant [6] states that #SAT is complete in the class #P. #2SAT is NP-hard and it is not even approximable [5].

We will analyze the possible solutions to #kSAT in terms of n and k.

3 Solutions of #kSAT for CF's with Just Two Clauses

As illustration of the proposed geometrical approach, let us consider very simple instances of #kSAT. Let n be the number of variables and let $k \leq n$ be a fixed clauses length. Let us remark the following basic facts: the support and the null set of any literal are two parallel hyperplanes in $\mathbb{F}_2^n$. Any clause Claus(ϵ), with $\epsilon \in \mathbb{T}^n$, has as null set the linear variety $V(\overline{\epsilon})$ determined by the complement of ϵ. Consequently, the null set of any conjunctive form is realized as the union of the linear varieties which are null sets of the involved clauses. Moreover, if Claus(ϵ) is a k-clause, then there are $n - k$ entries in ϵ with the value a and its null set $V(\overline{\epsilon})$ has dimension $n - k$. Hence, the null part of any k-CF is realized as the union of $(n - k)$-dimensional linear varieties.

For any two k-clauses Claus(ϵ_1), Claus(ϵ_2), with $\epsilon_1, \epsilon_2 \in \mathbb{T}^n$, we will say that they are *disjoint* if and only if $\exists j \in [\![1, n]\!] : \{\epsilon_{1j}, \epsilon_{2j}\} = \{0, 1\}$. Evidently,

$$Nul(\text{Claus}(\epsilon_1)) \cap Nul(\text{Claus}(\epsilon_1)) = \emptyset \iff \text{Claus}(\epsilon_1), \text{Claus}(\epsilon_2) \text{ are disjoint.}$$

Let $\mathcal{C}_{kn}$ be the set of k-clauses over n variables. There are $c_{nk} = \binom{n}{k} 2^k$ clauses in $\mathcal{C}_{kn}$ each having as null set an $(n - k)$-dimensional variety with cardinality $v_{1nk} = 2^{n-k}$. Hence, the support of a CF consisting of just one k-clause has cardinality $u_{1nk} = 2^{n-k} \left(2^k - 1\right)$.

Let $F = C_1 \wedge C_2$ be a k-CF consisting of two clauses. If the clauses are disjoint, then the null set of F has cardinality $v_{2nk} = 2 \cdot 2^{n-k} = 2^{n-k+1}$. For any k-clause C there are exactly $2^k - 1$ clauses disjoint to C, and the total number of disjoint k-clauses pairs is $r_{2nk} = \frac{1}{2} c_{nk}(2^k - 1) = \binom{n}{k} 2^{k-1}(2^k - 1)$. Let us assume now that the clauses are not disjoint. If C_1, C_2 share l literals, then the null set of F is the union of two $(n - k)$-dimensional varieties whose intersection has dimension $n + l - 2k$. Hence, the null set of F has cardinality $v_{2nkl} = 2^{n+l-2k} \left(2^{k-l+1} - 1\right)$ and its support has cardinality $u_{2nkl} = 2^{n+l-2k} \left(2^{k-l+1} \left(2^{k-1} - 1\right) + 1\right)$. Let us count the number of such pairs of clauses.

Proposition 1. Given $l \in [\![0, k-1]\!]$, the number p_{lkn} of non-disjoint k-clause pairs whose components share exactly l literals satisfies the following relations:

$$1 \le k < \frac{n}{2} \Longrightarrow p_{lkn} = \frac{1}{2}q_{lkn}$$

$$\frac{n}{2} \le k \le n \Longrightarrow p_{lkn} = \begin{cases} \frac{1}{2}q_{lkn} & \text{if } 2k - n \le l < k \\ 0 & \text{if } 0 \le l < 2k - n \end{cases}$$

where $q_{lkn} = \binom{n}{l}\binom{n-l}{k-l}\binom{n-k}{k-l}2^{2k-l}$.

Proof. Let us consider first the case where $1 \le k < \frac{n}{2}$. If $\{C_1, C_2\} \in (\mathcal{C}_{kn})^{(2)}$ is a pair of k-clauses sharing exactly l literals, let us denote by D the list of the common literals. Then we may write $C_1 = D \vee C_1'$, $C_2 = D \vee C_2'$ where C_1' and C_2' are $(k-l)$-clauses. Clearly,

1. there are $\binom{n}{l}2^l$ possibilities to select the common l-clause D,
2. there are $\binom{n-l}{k-l}2^{k-l}$ possibilities to select the remaining $(k-l)$-clause C_1',
3. there are $\binom{n-k}{k-l}2^{k-l}$ possibilities to select the remaining $(k-l)$-clause C_2', and
4. each pair of the remaining $(k-l)$-clauses $\{C_1', C_2'\}$ is counted exactly twice by the above counting process.

Let, according to the Counting Product Principle, $p_{lkn} = \frac{1}{2}q_{lkn}$ where

$$q_{lkn} = \binom{n}{l}2^l \cdot \binom{n-l}{k-l}2^{k-l} \cdot \binom{n-k}{k-l}2^{k-l} = \binom{n}{l}\binom{n-l}{k-l}\binom{n-k}{k-l}2^{2k-l}.$$

Now, if $\frac{n}{2} \le k \le n$ then p_{lkn} is computed as before if $n - k \ge k - l$. Thus,

$$p_{lkn} = \begin{cases} 0 & \text{if } 0 \le l < 2k - n \\ \frac{1}{2}q_{lkn} & \text{if } 2k - n \le l < k \end{cases}$$

All the remarks stated at this section are summarized in the following:

Proposition 2. The integer numbers that are realized as solutions of #kSAT restricted to CF's consisting of just two k-clauses are either of the form $u_{2nk} = 2^{n-k+1}(2^{k-1} - 1)$, and in this case there are $r_{2nk} = \binom{n}{k}2^{k-1}(2^k - 1)$ pairs of disjoint k-clauses realizing those numbers, or of the form

$$u_{2nkl} = 2^{n+l-2k}\left(2^{k-l+1}\left(2^{k-1} - 1\right) + 1\right),$$

with $l \in [\![0, k-1]\!]$. For each such l, the number of sets realized as supports of those instances is p_{lkn} as given in proposition 1.

4 k-CF's with an Arbitrary Number of Clauses

We analyze now the sets that can be expressed as unions of linear varieties of a given dimension.

4.1 k-Representability

Let $0 \leq k \leq n$. Let us denote the class of k-dimensional linear varieties by

$$\mathcal{V}_{kn} = \{V(\epsilon) | \epsilon \in \mathbb{T}^n \ \& \ \text{card}(I(\epsilon)) = k\}.$$

$\text{card}(\mathcal{V}_{kn}) = \binom{n}{k} 2^{n-k}$, and the "null set operator" $Nul : \mathcal{C}_{(n-k),n} \to \mathcal{V}_{kn}$, that maps a $(n-k)$-clause into its null set, $C \mapsto Nul(C)$, is a bijection.

Let us say that a set $A \subset \mathbb{F}_2^n$ is k-*representable* if there are k-dimensional linear varieties $S_1, \ldots, S_m \in \mathcal{V}_{kn}$ such that $A = \bigcup_{i=1}^m S_i$. We say that A is k-*thin* if no $S \in \mathcal{V}_{kn}$ is contained in A. The following relations hold:

1. $\emptyset$ is k-representable, since it is an empty union in $\mathcal{V}_{kn}$. $\emptyset$ is also k-thin.
2. $\mathbb{F}_2^n$ is k-representable as union of 2^{n-k} pairwise disjoint parallel sets in $\mathcal{V}_{kn}$.
3. If a set is k_1-representable and $k_2 \leq k_1$ then the set is also k_2-representable.
4. Any non-k-representable set is the disjoint union of a k-representable set and a non-empty k-thin set.
5. If A is k-representable then it has at least 2^k points, i.e. $\text{card}(A) \geq 2^k$.
6. The k-representability of a given set is algorithmically decidable. Namely, using the classical Quine-McCluskey optimization method one can decide, in time complexity $O(m^{\log_2 3} \log_2 m)$, $m = \text{card}(A)$, whether A can be expressed as an union of elements in $\mathcal{V}_{kn}$. As an alternative approach, using a greedy algorithm the same decision problem can be solved.
7. Since $\mathbb{F}_2^n$ can be partitioned as the union of 2^{n-k} pairwise disjoint elements $S_0^{(k)}, \ldots, S_{2^{n-k}-1}^{(k)} \in \mathcal{V}_{kn}$, any k-thin set A can be partitioned as a collection of 2^{n-k} pairwise disjoint sets, each with less than 2^k points, thus

$$\exists \{l_i\}_{i=0}^{2^{n-k}-1} : \left[0 \leq l_0 \leq l_1 \leq \cdots \leq l_{2^{n-k}-1} < 2^k\right] \ \&$$
$$\left[\text{card}(A) = \sum_{i=0}^{2^{n-k}-1} l_i\right]. \quad (2)$$

This is a necessary condition for k-thinness but it is not sufficient.

4.2 Some Set Classes

Using the notions introduced in section 4.1, we will begin to calculate the number of k-representable sets and the number of ways to express a k-representable set as an union of k-dimensional varieties. Let us define

$$\mathcal{R}_{kn} = \{A \subset \mathbb{F}_2^n | A \text{ is } k\text{-representable}\} , \ \rho_{kn} = \text{card}(\mathcal{R}_{kn}),$$
$$\mathcal{T}_{kn} = \{A \subset \mathbb{F}_2^n | A \text{ is } k\text{-thin}\} \quad\quad , \ \tau_{kn} = \text{card}(\mathcal{T}_{kn}),$$
$$\mathcal{E}_{kn} = \{A \subset \mathbb{F}_2^n | A \text{ satisfies eq. (2)}\} \quad , \ \eta_{kn} = \text{card}(\mathcal{E}_{kn}).$$

A set A belongs to the class $\mathcal{R}_{kn}$ if and only if it is the null set of a $(n-k)$-CF. The solutions of $\#(n-k)$SAT are thus the numbers which are realized as cardinalities of sets in the class co-$\mathcal{R}_{kn}$, consisting of complements of sets in $\mathcal{R}_{kn}$. Let us consider the set of numbers $R_{kn} = \{a \in \mathbb{N} | \exists A \in \mathcal{R}_{kn} : a = \text{card}(A)\}$. A main goal within this context is to characterize R_{kn} and as a remainder result to calculate, for each $a \in R_{kn}$, how many sets $A \in R_{kn}$ have cardinality a.

For $k = 0, n$ the following relations hold:

$$\begin{array}{llll} R_{0n} = \mathcal{P}(\mathbb{F}_2^n) , & \rho_{0n} = 2^{2^n} , & \mathcal{T}_{0n} = \emptyset , & \tau_{0n} = 0 \\ R_{nn} = \{\mathbb{F}_2^n\} , & \rho_{nn} = 1 , & \mathcal{T}_{nn} = \mathcal{P}(\mathbb{F}_2^n) - \{\mathbb{F}_2^n\} , & \tau_{nn} = 2^{2^n} - 1. \end{array}$$

We have, after relation (2), that $\tau_{kn} \leq \eta_{kn}$ and:

$$\eta_{kn} = \sum_{a=0}^{2^n - 1} \sum_{\substack{l_0 + \cdots + l_{2^{n-k}-1} = a \\ 0 \leq l_i < 2^k}} \binom{2^k}{l_0} \cdots \binom{2^k}{l_{2^{n-k}-1}}. \qquad (3)$$

Indeed, for any $k \in [\![1, n-1]\!]$, elementary manipulations of Newton's Binomial Formula allows to prove the equation

$$\eta_{kn} = \left[\prod_{i=0}^{k-1} \left(2^{2^i} + 1 \right) \right]^{2^{n-k}} \qquad (4)$$

This expression gives an exact counting of the sets satisfying eq. (2) but it is a rather high upper bound for the number of k-thin sets.

4.3 Hypergraph of k-Dimensional Varieties

Let us now approach our problem through the notion of hypergraphs. This technique will allow us to calculate how many linear varieties of an uniform dimension are enough to cover the whole hypercube. Thus, whenever there are less varieties than this number then their union will be a proper subset in the hypercube.

Let $\mathcal{G}_{kn} = (\mathbb{F}_2^n, \mathcal{V}_{kn})$ be the hypergraph whose nodes are the points in the hypercube $\mathbb{F}_2^n$ and whose hyperedges are exactly the k-dimensional linear varieties. Each hyperedge $H \in \mathcal{V}_{kn}$ is *incident* to its 2^k elements. For $k = 1$, $\mathcal{G}_{1n}$ is the common diagram of the n-dimensional hypercube.

Given two hyperedges $H_1, H_2 \in \mathcal{V}_{kn}$, let us say that they are *adjacent*, $H_1 \top H_2$, if $H_1 \cap H_2 \in \mathcal{V}_{k-1,n}$, i.e. $H_1 \top H_2$ if and only if $H_1 \cap H_2$ is a $(k-1)$-dimensional linear variety. Let $\mathcal{H}_{kn}$ be the graph whose nodes are the varieties $H \in \mathcal{V}_{kn}$ and the edges are the pairs $\{H_1, H_2\}$ such that $H_1 \top H_2$. $\mathcal{H}_{kn}$ is thus a graph with $\binom{n}{k} 2^{n-k}$ nodes, each node has degree $2k(n-k)$, and consequently there are $\binom{n}{k} 2^{n-k} k(n-k)$ edges. For instance, for $n = 3$ and $k = 2$, if we enumerate $\mathcal{V}_{23} = \{0aa, a0a, aa0, 1aa, a1a, aa1\}$ clockwise as the points of a regular hexagon, then $\mathcal{H}_{23}$ is a Star of David inscribed in the hexagon. Let us also say that a collection $\mathcal{H} \subset \mathcal{V}_{kn}$ is a k-*tree* if, when considered as a subgraph in $\mathcal{H}_{kn}$, it is indeed a tree. The k-tree $\mathcal{H}$ is a *spanning* k-*tree* if $\bigcup\{H | H \in \mathcal{H}\} = \mathbb{F}_2^n$.

Proposition 3. *Any spanning k-tree consists of $2^{n-k} - 1$ varieties.*

Proof. This can easily be seen by induction on $n \geq k$ and taking on account that the map $f_k : n \mapsto 2^{n-k} - 1$ satisfies the recurrence $f_k(n) = 2f_k(n-1) + 1$.

Now, clearly, any point $\delta \in \mathbb{F}_2^n$ is in exactly $\binom{n}{k}$ elements in $\mathcal{V}_{kn}$. Thus, there are exactly $\mu_{1kn} = \binom{n}{k}(2^{n-k} - 1)$ elements in $\mathcal{V}_{kn}$ which do not contain the point δ. If one variety is added to that collection of linear varieties, they will cover the whole space $\mathbb{F}_2^n$. The following results:

Proposition 4. *Any collection of $m_{kn} = \binom{n}{k}(2^{n-k} - 1) + 1$ elements in $\mathcal{V}_{kn}$ contains a spanning k-tree.*

Consequently any $(n - k)$-CF consisting of at least m_{kn} different clauses is a contradiction and the corresponding solution to $\#(n - k)$-SAT is 0.

The remark just before Proposition 4 allows us also to assert that only 2^n subsets of cardinality μ_{1kn} in $\mathcal{V}_{kn}$ have an union of cardinality $2^n - 1$ in $\mathbb{F}_2^n$, all other subsets of cardinality μ_{1kn} cover $\mathbb{F}_2^n$.

Similarly, for two points $\delta_1, \delta_2 \in \mathbb{F}_2^n$ the maximum number $\mu_{\ell 2kn}$ of sets in $\mathcal{V}_{kn}$ whose union is $\mathbb{F}_2^n - \{\delta_1, \delta_2\}$ depends on their Hamming distance $\ell = H(\delta_1, \delta_2)$. Namely, in order to count the number of k-dimensional linear varieties that do not contain neither δ_1 nor δ_2, let us consider for each variety that does not intersect $\{\delta_1, \delta_2\}$ two partitions of the index set $[\![1, n]\!]$. Let $L = \{i | \delta_{i1} \neq \delta_{i2}\}$, then $\ell = \text{card}(L)$, and let K be the set of coordinates with value a in the vector ϵ representing the linear variety. Then $\{L, L^c\}$ and $\{K, K^c\}$ are partitions of $[\![1, n]\!]$. Let us assume $\ell \leq k$. Let j denote the cardinality of $L \cap K^c$. Then, the cardinalities of $L \cap K$, $L^c \cap K$ and $L^c \cap K^c$ are respectively $\ell - j$, $k + j - \ell$ and $n - k - j$. By considering the possibilities for the representative vector ϵ we get,

$$\mu_{\ell 2kn} = \sum_{j=0}^{\ell} \left[\binom{\ell}{j} 2^j \binom{n-\ell}{k+j-\ell} (2^{n-k-j} - 1) + \kappa_{j\ell 2kn}^{(0)} \right],$$

$$j \leq 1 \Longrightarrow \kappa_{j\ell 2kn}^{(0)} = 0$$

$$j \geq 2 \Longrightarrow \kappa_{j\ell 2kn}^{(0)} = \binom{\ell}{j} 2(2^{j-1} - 1) \binom{n-\ell}{k+j-\ell}$$

In the same manner, by assuming $\ell > k$, let j denote the cardinality of $L^c \cap K$. Now, the cardinalities of $L \cap K$, $L \cap K^c$ and $L^c \cap K^c$ are respectively $k - j$, $\ell + j - k$ and $n - \ell - j$. By considering the possibilities for ϵ we get, in this case,

$$\mu_{\ell 2kn} = \sum_{j=0}^{\ell} \left[\binom{\ell}{k-j} 2^{\ell+j-k} \binom{n-\ell}{j} (2^{n-\ell-j} - 1) + \kappa_{j\ell 2kn}^{(1)} \right],$$

$$\ell + j - k \leq 1 \Longrightarrow \kappa_{j\ell 2kn}^{(1)} = 0$$

$$\ell + j - k \geq 2 \Longrightarrow \kappa_{j\ell 2kn}^{(1)} = \binom{\ell}{k-j} 2(2^{\ell+j-k-1} - 1) \binom{n-\ell}{j}$$

We can see that, for any $k \leq n$, $(\mu_{\ell 2kn})_{\ell=1}^n$ is non-increasing, and it is constant for $\ell \geq k$. As an alternative procedure for the calculation of $(\mu_{\ell 2kn})_{\ell=1}^n$, after a tedious but mechanical work it can be checked, from the above relations, that:

$$\mu_{12kn} = \binom{n}{k} 2^{n-k} - \left[\binom{n}{k} + \binom{n-1}{k} \right]$$

$$\forall \ell \in [\![2, k+1]\!]: \quad \mu_{\ell 2kn} = \mu_{\ell-1, 2kn} - m^{(k)}_{n, \ell-1}$$

where $M^{(k)} = \left(m^{(k)}_{\nu\ell}\right)_{\nu \geq k+1, \ell \leq k}$ has integer entries:

$$m^{(k)}_{1\ell} = 1$$
$$m^{(k)}_{\nu k} = 1$$
$$\forall \ell \in [\![1, k-1]\!]: \quad m^{(k)}_{\nu\ell} = m^{(k)}_{\nu, \ell+1} + m^{(k)}_{\nu-1, \ell}$$

Proposition 5. *Any collection of more than* $\mu_{12kn} = \binom{n}{k} 2^{n-k} - \left[\binom{n}{k} + \binom{n-1}{k}\right]$ *sets in* $\mathcal{V}_{kn}$ *has an union that fails to cover at most one point in the hypercube.*

4.4 Cardinalities and Unions of Linear Varieties

For any $\gamma \leq 2^n$ and any $\lambda \leq \binom{n}{k} 2^{n-k}$ let $\mathcal{Q}_{\gamma\lambda kn}$ consist of those sets $A \in \mathcal{R}_{kn}$ such that $\text{card}(A) = \gamma$ and A is the union of λ elements in $\mathcal{V}_{kn}$. Clearly, $\mathcal{R}_{kn} = \bigcup_{\gamma, \lambda} \mathcal{Q}_{\gamma\lambda kn}$. Let $q_{\gamma\lambda kn} = \text{card}(\mathcal{Q}_{\gamma\lambda kn})$. From the above remarks, we have:

$$\lambda > \mu_{1kn} \ \& \ \gamma < 2^n \implies q_{\gamma\lambda kn} = 0$$
$$\lambda > \mu_{12kn} \ \& \ \gamma = 2^n - 2 \implies q_{\gamma\lambda kn} = 0$$

Any instance of #1SAT has as support a linear variety, thus,

$$(\forall \kappa : \gamma \neq 2^n - 2^\kappa) \implies \forall \lambda : q_{\gamma, \lambda, n-1, n} = 0.$$

On the other hand, for $\gamma \in [\![2, 2^n]\!]$ we can build a set with exactly γ elements as an union of $\gamma - 1$ 1-dimensional linear varieties. Thus, $\forall \gamma : q_{\gamma, \gamma-1, 1, n} \geq 1$, and any $[\![2, 2^n]\!]$ is realized as a solution of $\#(n-1)$SAT in n variables.

4.5 Orders of Sets

For any non-empty set $A \subset \mathbb{F}_2^n$ let the *order* of A be the greatest k such that A is k-representable, i.e. $o(A) = \max\{k | A \in \mathcal{R}_{kn}\}$. Any set of order k is thus the null set of a $(n-k)$-CF but it cannot be the null set of a $(n-k-1)$-CF. Let

$$\mathcal{U}_{kn} = \{A \subset \mathbb{F}_2^n | o(A) = k\} \quad , \ w_{kn} = \text{card}(\mathcal{U}_{kn}),$$
$$\forall l \leq 2^n : \mathcal{V}_{lkn} = \{A \in \mathcal{U}_{kn} | \text{card}(A) = l\}, \ v_{lkn} = \text{card}(\mathcal{V}_{lkn}).$$

The following relations hold:

1. $\{\mathcal{U}_{\kappa n}\}_{k \leq \kappa \leq n}$ is a partition of $\mathcal{R}_{kn}$, thus $\rho_{kn} = \sum_{\kappa=k}^{n} w_{\kappa n}$.

2. $\{\mathcal{V}_{lkn}\}_{1 \leq l \leq 2^n}$ is a partition of $\mathcal{U}_{kn}$, thus $w_{kn} = \sum_{i=1}^{2^n} v_{lkn}$.

3. For $k = 0$,
   $v_{10n} = 2^n$: Any singleton has order 0.
   $v_{2^{n-1}0n} = 2$: The only way to choose 2^{n-1} points that form no an edge is by selecting opposite points along the main diagonal on 2-dimensional varieties.
   $\left(l > 2^{n-1} \Rightarrow v_{l0n} = 0\right)$: Any set with more than 2^{n-1} points has at least an edge.
4. For any k with $0 < k \leq n$,
   $\left(l < 2^k \Rightarrow v_{lkn} = 0\right)$: Any set of order k should have, at least, 2^k points.
   $v_{2^k kn} = 2^{n-k}\binom{n}{k}$: This is the number of k-dimensional linear varieties in the n-dimensional hypercube.
   $\left(l > 2^{n-k}(2^k - 1) \Rightarrow v_{lkn} = 0\right)$: Any set with more than $2^{n-k}(2^k - 1)$ points has at least a k-dimensional linear variety.
5. For any $k < n$, $v_{2^{n-k}(2^k-1),k,n} = 2^k$.

5 Conclusions

The geometrical translation of satisfiability problems poses some subproblems quite complex. For instance, the knowledge of the exact distribution of the numbers $(q_{\gamma\lambda kn})_{\gamma\lambda kn}$, as defined in section 4.4 entails the characterization of the integers that can be realized as solutions of #kSAT, and for each such number, the probability to find an instance giving that solution. The geometrical approach motivates and proves combinatorial equations as (4), and reduces to Graph Theory notions as stated in section 4.3. Finally, this geometrical approach allows to prove elementary relations for #kSAT corresponding to extremal values of the number of clauses involved or the uniform length k, as those shown in propositions 1-5.

References

1. Birnbaum, E., Lozinskii, E.L.: The good old Davis-Putnam procedure helps counting models. Journal of Artificial Intelligence **10** (1999) 457–477
2. Linial, N., Nisan, N.: Approximate inclusion-exclusion. Combinatorica **10** (1990) 349–365
3. Iwama, K., Matsuura, A.: Inclusion-exclusion for k-CNF formulas. In: Proc. of 5th International Symposium on the Theory and Applications of Satisfiability Testing (SAT2002). (2002)
4. Bacchus, F., Dalmao, S., Pitassi, T.: DPLL with caching: A new algorithm for #SAT and Bayesian inference. In: Proc. 44th Annual Symposium on Foundations of Computer Science, IEEE (2003)
5. Zuckerman, D.: On unapproximable versions of NP-complete problems. SIAM J. Computing **25** (1996) 1293–1304
6. Bürgisser, P.: Cook's versus Valiant's hypothesis. Theoret. Comp. Sci. **235** (2000) 71–88

A Syntactical Approach to Belief Update

Jerusa Marchi[1,2], Guilherme Bittencourt[1], and Laurent Perrussel[2]

[1] Departamento de Automação e Sistemas,
Universidade Federal de Santa Catarina,
88040-900, Florianópolis, SC, Brazil
{jerusa, gb}@das.ufsc.br
[2] IRIT - Université Toulouse I,
Manufacture des Tabacs, 21, allée de Brienne,
F-31042, Toulouse, France
laurent.perrussel@univ-tlse1.fr

Abstract. In the Belief Change domain, Katsuno and Mendelzon have proposed a set of postulates that should be satisfied by update operators. In 1989, Forbus semantically defined an update operator that satisfies these postulates. In order to calculate the resulting belief base all models of the relevant belief bases must be known. This paper proposes to use the *prime implicants* and *prime implicates* normal forms to represent these bases. Using this representation, a syntactical and computationally cheaper version of Forbus belief update operator is defined and a new minimal distance is proposed. We claim that this minimal distance ensures a better commitment between the minimal change criterion and the belief update definition.

1 Introduction

Belief change consists of incorporating a new piece of information to a belief base in a consistent way. The belief change methods should warrant that the original belief base has been minimally changed so that the new piece of information can be inserted without inconsistency [7]. Formally, minimal change is usually defined with respect to a closeness criterion between new information and original belief base. In both belief revision and belief update areas a usual notion of closeness is a distance between models, for instance those based on Dalal's distance [3]. According to Dalal, the distance between two models is given by the number of propositional symbols truth values on which they differ. Therefore the minimal change unit is an isolated symbol.

In the belief update area, Katsuno and Mendelzon [9] have proposed a set of postulates (the so-called KM postulates) that update operators should satisfy. By definition, the belief base resulting of an update operation is given by the sets of models of the new information that are the closest to each model of the original base. Following this definition, Forbus [6] has proposed an operator that satisfies the KM postulates where the closeness criterion is based on the Dalal distance.

The aim of this paper is to present belief update methods where the belief base and the new information are represented using prime normal forms. Using this representation a syntactical, equivalent and computationally cheaper version of the Forbus operator is defined; this update operator is an extension of the revision operator presented in [2]. Second, we use the notion of minimal change proposed by G. Bittencourt et al.[2] in order to define a new belief update operator, based on the "holographic" relation between literals in one prime form and the (dual) clauses, in the other prime form, in which they occur. The idea underlying this new minimal change notion is that one prime implicate is a better candidate for a change unit than a propositional symbol.

The paper is organized as follows: in section 2, we present logical definitions of primes forms in terms of conjunctive and disjunctive normal forms. In section 3, we formally define belief update, recalling the KM postulates and presenting the Forbus operator. In section 4, we introduce the syntactical operator that is equivalent to Forbus' one. In the next section, we introduce a new notion of minimal change and use it to define a syntactical operator that ensures the commitment between minimal change criterion and belief update definition. Section 7 concludes the paper by considering some open issues.

2 Preliminaries

Let $P = \{p_1, \ldots, p_n\}$ be a set of propositional symbols and $LIT = \{L_1, \ldots, L_{2n}\}$ the set of their associated literals, where $L_i = p_j$ or $L_i = \neg p_j$. A *clause* C is a *disjunction* of literals: $C = L_1 \vee \cdots \vee L_{k_C}$ and a *dual clause*, or *term*, is a *conjunction* of literals: $D = L_1 \wedge \cdots \wedge L_{k_D}$. Let $\overline{L}$ be the mirror of literal L s.t. $\overline{L} = p$ (respectively $\neg p$) iff $L = \neg p$ (respectively p). Let $\overline{D}$ be the mirror of a term D s.t. $\overline{D} = L_1 \wedge \cdots \wedge L_{k_D}$ iff $D = \overline{L_1} \wedge \cdots \wedge \overline{L_{k_D}}$.

Given a propositional logic language $\mathcal{L}(P)$ and an *ordinary formula* $\psi \in \mathcal{L}(P)$, there are algorithms for converting it into a *conjunctive normal form (CNF)* and into a *disjunctive normal form (DNF)* (e.g., [12]). The CNF is defined as a conjunction of clauses, $CNF_\psi = C_1 \wedge \cdots \wedge C_m$, and the DNF as a disjunction of terms, $DNF_\psi = D_1 \vee \cdots \vee D_w$, such that $\psi \Leftrightarrow CNF_\psi \Leftrightarrow DNF_\psi$. Let us formally define the notions of implicate and implicant:

Definition 1. (Implicate and Implicant) *Let C be a clause, D be a term and $\psi \in \mathcal{L}(\mathcal{P})$ a formula. C is an implicate of ψ iff $\psi \models C$ and D is an implicant of ψ iff $D \models \psi$.*

Definition 2. (Prime Implicate and Prime Implicant) *Let C be an implicate and D be an implicant of a formula ψ. C is a prime implicate iff for all implicates C' of ψ s.t. $C' \models C$ we have $C \models C'$ and D is a prime implicant iff for all implicants D' of ψ s.t. $D \models D'$, we have $D' \models D$.*

Alternatively, prime implicates and implicants can be defined [10,11], as special cases of CNF and DNF formulas, that consist of the smallest sets of clauses (or terms) closed for inference, without any subsumed clauses (or terms), and not containing a literal and its negation. We define PI_ψ as a conjunction of prime implicates of ψ and IP_ψ as a disjunction of prime implicants of ψ such that $\psi \Leftrightarrow PI_\psi \Leftrightarrow IP_\psi$. In propositional logic, conjunctive and disjunctive normal forms, as well as prime implicant and prime implicates are dual notions. In the sequel, conjunctions and disjunctions of literals, clauses and terms are seen as sets.

3 Belief Update

Given a belief base represented by ψ and a new information represented by μ, an update operator is a function $\diamond$ that transforms ψ in the updated belief base $\psi \diamond \mu$ [9]. Let $[\![\psi]\!]$ be the set of models of ψ. An update operation is defined in semantical terms as follows:

Definition 3. (Update operation) *Let w be a truth assignment to all the propositional symbols that occur in ψ. If ψ is true in w, then w is a model of ψ, i.e., $w \in [\![\psi]\!]$. Given a formula μ that contradicts ψ, the updated belief base $\psi \diamond \mu$ is obtained by selecting for each model w of ψ, the set of models of μ that are closest to w. The models of $\psi \diamond \mu$ are given by:*

$$[\![\psi \diamond \mu]\!] = \bigcup_{w \in [\![\psi]\!]} Min_{\leqslant_w}([\![\mu]\!])$$

where $Min_{\leqslant_w}$ selects the models of μ that are closest to w according to the total pre-order over interpretations $\leqslant_w$.

To select a total pre-order over interpretations, we need to use extra-logical criteria. A popular minimal change criterion has been proposed by Dalal [3], based on the intuition that an isolated symbol represents the minimal unit of knowledge. According to this criterion, the *distance* between interpretations is given by the set of propositional symbols that had different truth values in each interpretation.

Definition 4. (Distance between interpretations) *Let u and w be two interpretations. The distance between them is the set of symbols whose truth values differs [8]:*

$$DIST(w, u) = \{p \mid p \in w \text{ and } p \notin u\} \cup \{p \mid p \notin w \text{ and } p \in u\}$$

3.1 Forbus Operator

The operator proposed by Forbus [6] is, at this moment, the *strongest* update operator [8]. The concept of *strength* of an operator is related to the number of interpretations resulting from an update operation. The smaller is the number of interpretations, the greater is the certainty about the real state of the world. The closeness criterion is based on Dalal's semantical distance, as follows:

Definition 5. (Forbus operator distance) *Let w be a model of ψ and both u and u' be models of μ. The closeness from u and u' to w is given by the pre-order relation $\leqslant_w$:*

$$u \leqslant_w u' \text{ iff } |DIST(w, u)| \leq |DIST(w, u')|$$

where $|DIST|$ is the cardinality of the distance as introduced in definition 4.

The Forbus update operator, denoted by $\diamond_{Forbus}$, follows definition 3, using $\leqslant_w$ according to definition 5. Its complexity is exponential to generate models and polynomial to compare models among themselves, according to the number of models of ψ and μ [5].

Example 1. Consider theory ψ given by the following CNF:

$$(\neg p_3 \vee \neg p_2 \vee p_1) \wedge (\neg p_3 \vee p_1 \vee p_4) \wedge (\neg p_1 \vee p_2 \vee \neg p_3 \vee p_4) \wedge$$
$$(\neg p_4 \vee \neg p_3 \vee \neg p_2) \wedge (\neg p_2 \vee p_4 \vee p_3) \wedge (\neg p_2 \vee \neg p_1)$$

and new information μ, given by $PI_\mu = (\neg p_4 \vee p_1) \wedge (p_1 \vee p_3) \wedge (\neg p_4 \vee p_2) \wedge (p_2 \vee p_3)$. The first step of Forbus method is to calculate the models of ψ and μ. There are 7 models for ψ and 7 models for μ. The second step is to calculate the cardinality of the distances from all models of μ to each model of ψ, that is a total of 49 distances. The models are selected according to the pre-order relation $\leqslant_w$ (def. 5). We get the following models:

$$[\![\psi \diamond_{Forbus} \mu]\!] = \{\{p_1, p_2, \neg p_3, p_4\}, \{p_1, p_2, p_3, p_4\}, \{p_1, \neg p_2, p_3, \neg p_4\}, \{p_1, p_2, \neg p_3, \neg p_4\}, \{\neg p_1, \neg p_2, p_3, \neg p_4\}\}$$

These models are represented by the following set of prime implicants:

$$\psi \diamond_{Forbus} \mu = ((\neg p_3 \wedge p_1 \wedge p_2) \vee (p_1 \wedge p_2 \wedge p_4) \vee (\neg p_4 \wedge \neg p_2 \wedge p_3))$$

3.2 KM Postulates

To guide the construction of update operators, Katsuno and Mendelzon [9] have proposed a set of postulates that should be satisfied. Among the belief update operators proposed in the literature ([8] for a review), only the PMA (Possible Model Approach) [13] and Forbus [6] operators respect all KM postulates.

(U1) $\psi \diamond \mu$ implies μ.
(U2) If ψ implies μ then $\psi \diamond \mu$ is equivalent to ψ.
(U3) If both ψ and μ are satisfiable then $\psi \diamond \mu$ is also satisfiable.
(U4) If $\psi_1 \leftrightarrow \psi_2$ and $\mu_1 \leftrightarrow \mu_2$ then $\psi_1 \diamond \mu_1 \leftrightarrow \psi_2 \diamond \mu_2$.
(U5) $(\psi \diamond \mu) \wedge \phi$ implies $\psi \diamond (\mu \wedge \phi)$.
(U6) If $\psi \diamond \mu_1$ implies μ_2 and $\psi \diamond \mu_2$ implies μ_1 then $\psi \diamond \mu_1 \leftrightarrow \psi \diamond \mu_2$.
(U7) If ψ is complete then $(\psi \diamond \mu_1) \wedge (\psi \diamond \mu_2)$ implies $\psi \diamond (\mu_1 \vee \mu_2)$.
(U8) $(\psi_1 \vee \psi_2) \diamond \mu \leftrightarrow (\psi_1 \diamond \mu) \vee (\psi_2 \diamond \mu)$.

4 Rewriting Forbus Operator with Prime Implicants

Using the specific syntax of prime implicants, we redefine the Forbus update operator in a more efficient way. The new operator calculates the updated belief base using the distances between prime implicants, instead of between models. Because there are usually much less prime implicants than models, the proposed operator is cheaper than the Forbus' operator.

The first step of the proposed approach is to calculate the prime implicants of belief base ψ and of new information μ, noted IP_ψ and IP_μ. This step is NP-complete and it is done through the dual transformation algorithm [1].

The second step is to calculate, for each term of IP_ψ and each term of IP_μ, the literals that are contradictory. The complexity of this operation is $\Theta(|\ IP_\psi\ | \cdot |\ IP_\mu\ |)$ that is usually much smaller than the complexity of Forbus operator, given by $\Theta(|\ [\![\psi]\!]\ | \cdot |\ [\![\mu]\!]\ |)$. This is due to the fact that, in general, one prime implicant represents a set of models:

Proposition 1. $\Theta(|\ IP_\psi\ | \cdot |\ IP_\mu\ |) \leqslant \Theta(|\ [\![\psi]\!]\ | \cdot |\ [\![\mu]\!]\ |)$

In order to perform the update operation, we consider the contradictory literals between two terms D_ψ and D_μ. Let us suppose a formula μ that contradicts ψ, the updated belief base is obtained as follows. For each term D_ψ belonging to IP_ψ, we remove all the contradictory literals w.r.t. each term D_μ and we add the literals from D_μ. Let $D = D_\mu \cup (D_\psi - \overline{D_\mu})$ be the resulting term. Following [9], the *DNF* of $\psi \diamond \mu$ is obtained by choosing terms D which are minimal w.r.t. to a closeness criterion. Formally, we get the following definition.

Definition 6. (**Syntactical update operator** $DNF_{\psi \diamond \mu}$) *The updated belief base is given by:*

$$DNF_{\psi \diamond \mu} = \bigcup_{D_\psi \in IP_\psi} Min_{\leqslant_{D_\psi}}(\{D_\mu \cup (D_\psi - \overline{D_\mu}) |\ D_\mu \in IP_\mu\})$$

In order to respect the minimal change criterion, we need to choose the terms $D_\mu \cup (D_\psi - \overline{D_\mu})$ which are minimal. Following Dalal, we calculate the number of elements that have changed their truth values.

Definition 7. (**Distance between terms**) *Let D_ψ be a term of IP_ψ and D_μ, D'_μ be two terms of IP_μ. Let $D = D_\mu \cup (D_\psi - \overline{D_\mu})$ and $D' = D'_\mu \cup (D_\psi - \overline{D'_\mu})$. The distance between D and D' is based on the number of literals of D_ψ that are contradictory with D_μ (respectively D'_μ), defined as $|\ D_\psi \cap \overline{D_\mu}\ |$. It entails the following total pre-order:*

$$D \leqslant_{D_\psi} D' \text{ iff } |\ D_\psi \cap \overline{D_\mu}\ | \leq |\ D_\psi \cap \overline{D'_\mu}\ |$$

The following theorem ensures the equivalence between the new syntactical update operator and the Forbus' one.

Theorem 1. *Given a propositional belief base ψ and a new contradictory information μ, $\psi \diamond_{Forbus} \mu \Leftrightarrow DNF_{\psi \diamond \mu}$.*

Corollary 1. *The syntactical update operator $\diamond$ satisfies postulates* (**U1**)–(**U8**).

Due to space restrictions, proofs are not detailed.

Example 2. Consider the previous example. Theory ψ is now characterized as a conjunction of prime implicants:

$$IP_\psi = (\neg p_3 \wedge \neg p_2) \vee (\neg p_3 \wedge \neg p_1 \wedge p_4) \vee (\neg p_2 \wedge p_4)$$

and new information μ is $IP_\mu = (\neg p_4 \wedge p_3) \vee (p_1 \wedge p_2)$. There is a total of 6 distances to be computed (remember that there were 49 distances to calculate in example 1):

D_ψ	D_μ	$(D_\psi \cap \overline{D_\mu})$	$D_\mu \cup (D_\psi - \overline{D_\mu})$	k_D
$\{\neg p_3, \neg p_2\}$	$\{\neg p_4, p_3\}$	$\{\neg p_3\}$	$\{\neg p_4, \neg p_2, p_3\}$	1
$\{\neg p_3, \neg p_2\}$	$\{p_1, p_2\}$	$\{\neg p_2\}$	$\{\neg p_3, p_1, p_2\}$	1
$\{\neg p_2, p_4\}$	$\{\neg p_4, p_3\}$	$\{p_4\}$	$\{\neg p_4, \neg p_2, p_3\}$	1
$\{\neg p_2, p_4\}$	$\{p_1, p_2\}$	$\{\neg p_2\}$	$\{p_1, p_2, p_4\}$	1
$\{\neg p_3, \neg p_1, p_4\}$	$\{\neg p_4, p_3\}$	$\{\neg p_3, p_4\}$	$\{\neg p_4, \neg p_1, p_3\}$	2
$\{\neg p_3, \neg p_1, p_4\}$	$\{p_1, p_2\}$	$\{\neg p_1\}$	$\{\neg p_3, p_1, p_2, p_4\}$	1

The DNF of the updated theory is :

$$DNF_{\psi \diamond \mu} = (\neg p_4 \wedge \neg p_2 \wedge p_3) \vee (\neg p_3 \wedge p_1 \wedge p_2) \vee (p_1 \wedge p_2 \wedge p_4).$$

5 Another Notion of Minimal Change

In this section, we consider a different notion of minimal unit of knowledge: a clause rather than a propositional symbol. Our claim is based on the fact that a symbol may be involved in many clauses of a belief base and thus changing one symbol may have a great impact. In the following we show how to link literals and clauses in order to revisit belief change operations. Given a formula ψ, represented by CNF_ψ and by DNF_ψ, we introduce the concepts of *conjunctive* and *disjunctive quanta*. The rationale behind the choice of the name *quantum* is to emphasize that we are not interested in an isolated literal, but that the *minimal* unit of interest is the literal and its situation with respect to the theory in which it occurs.

Definition 8. (Conjunctive and Disjunctive quanta) *Let ψ be a propositional formula. A conjunctive (resp. disjunctive) quantum w.r.t. ψ is a pair (L, F_c) (resp. (L, F_d)), where L is a literal that occurs in ψ and $F_c \subseteq CNF_\psi$ (resp. $F_d \subseteq DNF_\psi$) is its set of conjunctive coordinates (resp. disjunctive coordinates) that contains the subset of clauses in CNF_ψ (resp. terms in DNF_ψ) to which literal L belongs.*

Whenever is clear, a quantum is usually denoted by L^F.

Example 3. Consider the previous theory ψ given by the following CNF (numbers represent clauses):

$$1: \neg p_3 \vee \neg p_2 \vee p_1 \quad 2: \neg p_2 \vee p_4 \vee p_3 \quad 3: \neg p_2 \vee \neg p_1$$
$$4: \neg p_3 \vee p_1 \vee p_4 \quad 5: \neg p_4 \vee \neg p_3 \vee \neg p_2 \quad 6: \neg p_1 \vee p_2 \vee \neg p_3 \vee p_4$$

The literals that occur in ψ are represented by the following set of conjunctive quanta:[1]

$$\{\neg p_1^{\{3,6\}}, p_1^{\{1,4\}}, \neg p_2^{\{1,2,3,5\}}, p_2^{\{6\}}, \neg p_3^{\{1,4,5,6\}}, p_3^{\{2\}}, \neg p_4^{\{5\}}, p_4^{\{2,4,6\}}\}$$

The quantum notation can be used to characterize implicates and implicants as well prime implicates and prime implicants of a formula ψ represented by CNF_ψ and by a DNF_ψ.

Proposition 2. (Implicant and Implicate using quantum notation) *Let $D = L_1 \wedge \ldots \wedge L_k$ be a term represented by a set of conjunctive quanta $L_1^{F_c^1} \wedge \cdots \wedge L_k^{F_c^k}$. D is an implicant of ψ if $\cup_{i=1}^{k} F_c^i = CNF_\psi$ with no pair of contradictory literals allowed. Analogously, let $C = L_1 \vee \cdots \vee L_k$ be a clause represented by a set of disjunctive quanta $L_1^{F_d^1} \wedge \cdots \wedge L_k^{F_d^k}$. C is an implicate of ψ if $\cup_{i=1}^{k} F_d^i = DNF_\psi$ with no pair of contradictory literals allowed.*

To characterize prime implicants and prime implicates, clauses C and terms D have to satisfy the *non redundancy condition* i.e., each of their literals should represent *alone* at least one term in DNF_ψ and respectively, one clause in CNF_ψ. To define the non redundancy condition, we introduce the notion of *exclusive conjunctive* and *exclusive disjunctive coordinates*.

---

[1] To simplify the notation, the sets of conjunctive coordinates contain the clause numbers instead of the clauses themselves.

Definition 9. (Exclusive conjunctive coordinates) *Let D be a term and $L_i \in D$ a literal s.t. $1 \leq i \leq k$, where k is the number of clauses in PI_ψ. $\widehat{F}_c^i$ represents the exclusive conjunctive coordinates of $L_i \in D$, defined by $\widehat{F}_c^i = F_c^i - \cup_{j=1, j \neq i}^k F_c^j$. $\widehat{F}_c^i$ are the clauses in set F_c^i to which no other literal of D belongs.*

Definition 10. (Exclusive disjunctive coordinates) *Let C be a clause and $L_i \in C$ a literal s.t. $1 \leq i \leq k$, where k is the number of terms in IP_ψ. $\widehat{F}_d^i$ represents the exclusive disjunctive coordinates of $L_i \in C$, defined by $\widehat{F}_d^i = F_d^i - \cup_{j=1, j \neq i}^k F_d^j$. $\widehat{F}_d^i$ are the terms in set F_d^i, to which no other literal of C belongs.*

Definition 11. (Non redundancy condition) *Let C be a clause represented as $L_1^{F_d^1} \vee \cdots \vee L_k^{F_d^k}$. C satisfies the non redundancy condition iff $\forall i \in \{1, \ldots, k\}$, $\widehat{F}_d^i \neq \emptyset$. Dually, let D be a term represented as $L_1^{F_c^1} \vee \cdots \vee L_k^{F_c^k}$. D satisfies the non redundancy condition iff $\forall i \in \{1, \ldots, k\}$, $\widehat{F}_c^i \neq \emptyset$.*

Proposition 3. (Prime Implicant and Prime Implicate using quantum notation) *Let D be a term. D is a prime implicant iff D is an implicant and satisfies the non redundancy condition as presented in definition 11. Analogously, a clause C is a prime implicate iff C is an implicate and satisfies the non redundancy condition.*

Given a theory ψ, it is possible to determine the sets of conjunctive and disjunctive quanta that, respectively, define IP_ψ with respect to PI_ψ and PI_ψ with respect to IP_ψ. This minimal quantum notation is an enriched representation for prime implicates and implicants sets, in the sense that it explicitly contains the "holographic" relation between literals in one form and the clauses (or terms) in which they occur in the other form. There exists dual transformation algorithms that builds such representations [1].

Example 4. Consider theory ψ introduced in example 3. Using the dual transformation algorithm, it is possible to determine the following set of prime implicants, represented as sets of quanta:

$$1 : \neg p_3^{\{1,4,5,6\}} \wedge \neg p_2^{\{1,2,3,5\}}$$
$$2 : \neg p_3^{\{1,4,5,6\}} \wedge \neg p_1^{\{3,6\}} \wedge p_4^{\{2,4,6\}}$$
$$3 : \neg p_2^{\{1,2,3,5\}} \wedge p_4^{\{2,4,6\}}$$

One more application of the dual transformation[2] determines the prime implicates. The pair (PI, IP) corresponding to the theory, in quantum notation, is given by:

PI	IP
$1: \neg p_3^{\{1,2\}} \vee \neg p_2^{\{1,3\}}$	$1: \neg p_3^{\{1,2\}} \wedge \neg p_2^{\{1,3,4\}}$
$2: \neg p_3^{\{1,2\}} \vee p_4^{\{2,3\}}$	$2: \neg p_2^{\{1,3,4\}} \wedge p_4^{\{2,4\}}$
$3: \neg p_2^{\{1,3\}} \vee \neg p_1^{\{2\}}$	$3: \neg p_3^{\{1,2\}} \wedge \neg p_1^{\{3\}} \wedge p_4^{\{2,4\}}$
$4: \neg p_2^{\{1,3\}} \vee p_4^{\{2,3\}}$	

---

[2] In fact, this second application is not necessary, because, once the prime implicants are known, there are polynomial time algorithms to calculate the prime implicates [4].

5.1 A New Distance

As previously mentioned, Dalal's notion of minimal change consists in changing in each model of the belief base the smallest number of propositional symbol truth values in order to have no contradictions with the new information.

With prime implicants/implicates representations and quantum notation, a literal that belongs to a term in IP represents a certain number of clauses in PI. This allows the identification of which clauses are "critically" affected by a given term and vice-versa. We consider that a clause in the conjunctive set of prime implicates, which is unique and not subsumed by any other, is a better notion of *knowledge unit*. Therefore, the minimal change criterion is defined as the quantity of clauses in PI_ψ that are involved in change. In order to know how many clauses are critically involved by a literal, we use the exclusive coordinates.

Semantically, the prime implicants represent the set of models of the theory and the prime implicates represent the rules of the domain represented by this theory. Our aim is to change the rules in a minimal way because we consider that one rule is a better notion of minimal element than a isolated literal. The new distance is defined as:

Definition 12. (Distance between terms based on exclusive conjunctive coordinates) Let D_ψ be a term of IP_ψ and D_μ, D'_μ be two terms of IP_μ. Let $D = D_\mu \cup (D_\psi - \overline{D_\mu})$ and $D' = D'_\mu \cup (D_\psi - \overline{D'_\mu})$. The distance between D and D' is based on the literals of D_ψ that conflicts with D_μ (respectively D'_μ) given by $D_\psi \cap \overline{D_\mu} = \{L_1^{F_c^1}, \ldots, L_k^{F_c^k}\}$, where the literals are represented in quantum notation. Let $\widehat{F}_c^i$ be the set of exclusive coordinates associated to each literal L_i and numerical value $|\cup_{i=1}^k \widehat{F}_c^i|$ represents the number of clauses associated to the contradicting literals. It entails the following total pre-order:

$$D \leqslant_{D_\psi}^{BPM} D' \text{ iff } \Big| \bigcup_{L_i^{F_c^i} \in D_\psi \cap \overline{D_\mu}} \widehat{F}_c^i \Big| \leqslant \Big| \bigcup_{L_i^{F_c^i} \in D_\psi \cap \overline{D'_\mu}} \widehat{F}_c^i \Big|$$

With this notion we get a new update operator $\diamond_{BPM}$ defined as follows:

Definition 13. (Syntactical operator $DNF_{\psi \diamond_{BPM} \mu}$) The updated belief base w.r.t. the total pre-order $\leqslant^{BPM}$ is given by:

$$DNF_{\psi \diamond_{BPM} \mu} = \bigcup_{D_\psi \in IP_\psi} Min_{\leqslant_{D_\psi}^{BPM}} (\{D_\mu \cup (D_\psi - \overline{D_\mu}) \mid D_\mu \in IP_\mu\})$$

As the Forbus operator, operator $\diamond_{BPM}$ respects all KM postulates.

Theorem 2. *The syntactical update operator $\diamond_{BPM}$ satisfies postulates (U1)–(U8).*

Example 5. Let us again consider theory ψ and new information μ presented in examples 3 and 2. Distances between terms from IP_ψ and IP_μ are detailed in the following table ($\widehat{k}_D$ stands for $| \cup_{L_i^{F_c^i} \in D_\psi \cap \overline{D_\mu}} \widehat{F}_c^i |$).

D_ψ	D_μ	$(D_\psi \cap \overline{D_\mu})$	$D_\mu \cup (D_\psi - \overline{D_\mu})$	$D_\psi \cap \overline{D_\mu}$	$\widehat{k}_D$
$\{\neg p_3, \neg p_2\}$	$\{\neg p_4, p_3\}$	$\{\neg p_3\}$	$\{\neg \mathbf{p_4}, \neg \mathbf{p_2}, \mathbf{p_3}\}$	$\{\neg p_3^{\{2\}}\}$	1
$\{\neg p_3, \neg p_2\}$	$\{p_1, p_2\}$	$\{\neg p_2\}$	$\{\neg p_3, p_1, p_2\}$	$\{\neg p_2^{\{3,4\}}\}$	2
$\{\neg p_2, p_4\}$	$\{\neg p_4, p_3\}$	$\{p_4\}$	$\{\neg \mathbf{p_4}, \neg \mathbf{p_2}, \mathbf{p_3}\}$	$\{p_4^{\{2\}}\}$	1
$\{\neg p_2, p_4\}$	$\{p_1, p_2\}$	$\{\neg p_2\}$	$\{p_1, p_2, p_4\}$	$\{\neg p_2^{\{1,3\}}\}$	2
$\{\neg p_3, \neg p_1, p_4\}$	$\{\neg p_4, p_3\}$	$\{\neg p_3, p_4\}$	$\{\neg p_4, \neg p_1, p_3\}$	$\{\neg p_3^{\{1\}}, p_4^{\{4\}}\}$	2
$\{\neg p_3, \neg p_1, p_4\}$	$\{p_1, p_2\}$	$\{\neg p_1\}$	$\{\neg \mathbf{p_3}, \mathbf{p_1}, \mathbf{p_2}, \mathbf{p_4}\}$	$\{\neg p_1^{\{3\}}\}$	1

Taking into account the size of the exclusive conjunctive coordinates sets of the literals to be deleted ($\widehat{k}_D$), only the first, the third and the last terms belong to $\psi \diamond_{BPM} \mu$: $(\neg p_4 \wedge \neg p_2 \wedge p_3) \vee (\neg p_3 \wedge p_1 \wedge p_2 \wedge p_4)$ which is already in prime implicants form. This set of prime implicants represents the following models: $\{\{p_1, p_2, \neg p_3, p_4\}, \{\neg p_1, \neg p_2, \neg p_4, p_3\}, \{p_1, \neg p_2, p_3, \neg p_4\}\}$. In this case, the proposed method eliminates two models (cf. example 1) and is stronger than the one proposed by Forbus.

6 Results

We made some experiments, using random theories ψ with 20 symbols and 91 clauses (rate 4.55) found in http://www.satlib.org, in order to test the new proposed operator $\diamond_{BPM}$. The new information μ is chosen as the the negation of the first n clauses of PI_ψ. We performed 500 update operations (100 theories ψ and n varing from 1 to 5). The following graphic presents the results for Fobus and BPM methods with $n = 4$. To compare the results, we used the number of clauses in PI_ψ that are subsumed by the updated kwonledge bases. In the horizontal axis, the theories are ordered by the number of clauses in PI_ψ.

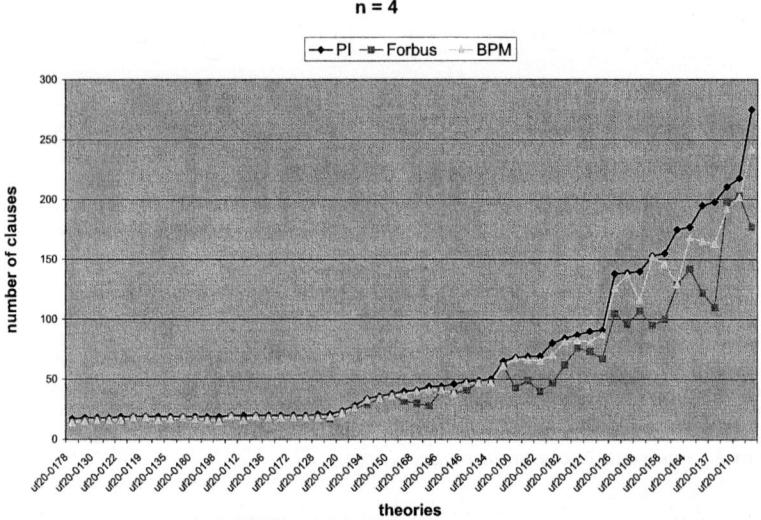

For $n = 1$ both operators give the same results. As n and the number of prime implicants increase, the BPM method subsumes more clauses than the Forbus one. In the great majority of the cases BPM is either equal or better than the Forbus operator. Only in 3 of 500 cases the Forbus operator gives a better result.

7 Conclusion

In this paper we have presented a syntactical approach of belief update based on the prime normal forms. This representation allows us to achieve a cheaper version of Forbus operator. Moreover, a new minimal change unit, based on the number of clauses in the prime implicants that are affected by a conflicting literal, has been proposed. According to this new notion of minimal change, we have shown that the update operator $\diamond_{BPM}$ is, in the great majority of the cases, more restrictive than the Forbus' one. It has also been proved that this proposed operator satisfies all KM postulates.

References

1. Bittencourt, G., Marchi, J., Padilha, R.S.: A syntactic approach to satisfaction. In Konev, B., Schimidt, R., eds.: 4th Inter. Workshop on the Implementation of Logic (LPAR03), Univ. of Liverpool and Univ. of Manchester (2003) 18–32.
2. G. Bittencourt, L. Perrussel, and J. Marchi. A syntactical approach to revision. In R. L. Mántaras and L. Saitta, editors, *Proc. of the 16th European Conf. on Artificial Intelligence (ECAI'04)*, pages 788–792, Valencia, Spain, Aug 2004. IOS Press.
3. Dalal, M.: Investigations into a theory of knowledge base revision: Preliminary report. In Proc. of AAAI'88. Volume 2., Menlo Park, CA, AAAI Press (1988) 475–479.
4. Darwiche, A., Marquis, P.: A perspective on knowledge compilation. In: IJCAI. (2001) 175–182.
5. Eiter, T., Gottlob, G.: On the complexity of propositional knowledge base revision, updates and counterfactuals. Artificial Intelligence **57** (1992) 227–270.
6. Forbus, K.: Introducing actions into qualitative simulation. In: Proceedings IJCAI-89, Detroit, MI (1989) 1273–1278.
7. Gärdenfors, P.: Knowledge in Flux: Modeling the Dynamics of Epistemic States. Bradford Books, MIT Press (1988).
8. Herzig, A., Rifi, O.: Propositional belief base update and minimal change. Artificial Intelligence **115** (1999) 107–138.
9. Katsuno, H., Mendelzon, A..: On the difference between updating a knowledge base and revising it. In Allen, J.F., Fikes, R., Sandewall, E., eds.: KR'91: Principles of Knowledge Representation and Reasoning. Morgan Kaufmann, San Mateo, California (1991) 387–394.
10. Kean, A., Tsiknis, G.: An incremental method for generating prime implicants/implicates. Journal of Symbolic Computation **9** (1990) 185–206.
11. Ramesh, A., Becker, G., Murray, N.V.: CNF and DNF considered harmful for computing prime implicants/implicates. Journal of Automated Reasoning **18** (1997) 337–356.
12. Socher, R.: Optimizing the clausal normal form transformation. Journal of Automated Reasoning **7** (1991) 325–336.
13. Winslett, M.: Reasoning about action using a possible models approach. In: Proceedings of the 7th National Conf. on Artificial Intelligence. (1988) 89–93.

A Fuzzy Extension of Description Logic $\mathcal{ALCH}$ *

Yanhui Li[1,2], Jianjiang Lu[1,2,3], Baowen Xu[1,2], Dazhou Kang[1,2], and Jixiang Jiang[1,2]

[1] Department of Computer Science and Engineering, Southeast University,
Nanjing 210096, P.R. China
[2] Jiangsu Institute of Software Quality, Nanjing 210096, P.R. China
[3] PLA University of Science and Technology, Nanjing, 210007, China
bwxu@seu.edu.cn

Abstract. Based on the idea that the cut sets of fuzzy sets are indeed crisp, but facilitate a normative theory for formalizing fuzzy set theory, this paper introduces cut sets of the fuzzy concepts and fuzzy roles as atomic concepts and atomic roles to build $\mathcal{EFALCH}$, a new fuzzy extension of $\mathcal{ALCH}$. This paper gives the definition of syntax, semantics and knowledge base of $\mathcal{EFALCH}$ and discusses the comparison among $\mathcal{EFALCH}$ and other fuzzy extensions of $\mathcal{ALCH}$. In addition, this paper defines the acyclic TBox form of $\mathcal{EFALCH}$, presents sound and complete algorithms for reasoning tasks w.r.t acyclic TBox, and proves the complexity of them is PSPACE-complete.

1 Introduction

Compared with concepts and roles in classical description logics, which describe crisp sets of individuals and their relations, fuzzy description logics [1, 2] contain fuzzy concepts and fuzzy roles that describe fuzzy sets. In fuzzy set theory [3], a fuzzy set S w.r.t a universe U is defined as a membership function $\mu_s : U \rightarrow [0,1]$, and the λ-cut set of S is defined as $S_{[\lambda]} = \{d \in U \mid \mu_s(d) \geq \lambda\}$, where $0 < \lambda \leq 1$. Based on the idea of that the cut sets are indeed crisp sets, but facilitate a normative theory for formalizing fuzzy set theory, our fuzzy extension of description logics uses cut sets instead of fuzzy concepts and fuzzy roles.

Definition 1. Consider three disjoint sets: a set N_C of fuzzy concept names (denoted A, B), a set N_R of fuzzy role names (denoted R, S), and a set N_I of individual names (denoted a, b). For any $A \in N_C$, $R \in N_R$ and $0 < \lambda \leq 1$, we call $A_{[\lambda]}$ an atomic cut concept and $R_{[\lambda]}$ an atomic cut role, where A and R is the prefix of λ, and λ is the suffix of A and R.

The semantics of fuzzy concept names and their cut sets are defined in terms of an interpretation $\mathcal{I} = <\Delta^\mathcal{I}, \cdot^\mathcal{I}>$. The domain $\Delta^\mathcal{I}$ is a nonempty set and the interpretation

---

* This work was supported in part by the NSFC (60373066, 60425206, 90412003), National Grand Fundamental Research 973 Program of China (2002CB312000), National Research Foundation for the Doctoral Program of Higher Education of China (20020286004), Excellent Ph.D. Thesis Fund of Southeast University, and Advanced Armament Research Project (51406020105JB8103).

function $\cdot^{\mathcal{I}}$ maps every individual name a to an element $a^{\mathcal{I}} \in \Delta^{\mathcal{I}}$, every fuzzy concept name $A \in N_C$ to a membership function $A^{\mathcal{I}} : \Delta^{\mathcal{I}} \to [0,1]$, and every fuzzy role name $R \in N_R$ to a membership function $R^{\mathcal{I}} : \Delta^{\mathcal{I}} \times \Delta^{\mathcal{I}} \to [0,1]$. And $\cdot^{\mathcal{I}}$ maps $A_{[\lambda]}$ and $R_{[\lambda]}$ to subsets of $\Delta^{\mathcal{I}}$ and $\Delta^{\mathcal{I}} \times \Delta^{\mathcal{I}}$:

$$(A_{[\lambda]})^{\mathcal{I}} = \{d \mid d \in \Delta^{\mathcal{I}} \wedge A^{\mathcal{I}}(d) \geq \lambda\};$$
$$(R_{[\lambda]})^{\mathcal{I}} = \{(d,d') \mid d,d' \in \Delta^{\mathcal{I}} \wedge R^{\mathcal{I}}(d,d') \geq \lambda\}. \quad (1)$$

From Equation 1, for any λ_1, λ_2 such that $0 \leq \lambda_2 \leq \lambda_1 \leq 1$, it must be true that $(A_{[\lambda_1]})^{\mathcal{I}} \subseteq (A_{[\lambda_2]})^{\mathcal{I}}$ and $(R_{[\lambda_1]})^{\mathcal{I}} \subseteq (R_{[\lambda_2]})^{\mathcal{I}}$ for any interpretation $\mathcal{I}$.

Obviously $A^{\mathcal{I}}$ and $R^{\mathcal{I}}$ are fuzzy sets w.r.t $\Delta^{\mathcal{I}}$ and $\Delta^{\mathcal{I}} \times \Delta^{\mathcal{I}}$, while their cuts $(A_{[\lambda]})^{\mathcal{I}}$ and $(R_{[\lambda]})^{\mathcal{I}}$ are actually crisp sets. Generally, a collection of $(A_{[\lambda_1]})^{\mathcal{I}}, (A_{[\lambda_2]})^{\mathcal{I}}, \cdots, (A_{[\lambda_k]})^{\mathcal{I}}$ and $(R_{[\lambda_{k+1}]})^{\mathcal{I}}, (R_{[\lambda_{k+2}]})^{\mathcal{I}}, \cdots, (R_{[\lambda_n]})^{\mathcal{I}}$ is enough to describe the semantic of $A^{\mathcal{I}}$ and $R^{\mathcal{I}}$ completely or at an acceptable degree. It facilitates a classical description logic theory for simulating the fuzzy description logic theory. Starting with atomic cut concepts and atomic cut roles, so-called cut concept descriptions (cut concepts, for short) can be inductively defined with a set of concept constructors of classical description logics. Though cut concepts describe crisp sets of individuals, they enable representation and reasoning for fuzzy information and propose more expressive power than current fuzzy description logics.

2 Extended Fuzzy Description Logic $\mathcal{EFALCH}$

2.1 Cut Concepts

We propose a fuzzy extension of the description logic $\mathcal{ALCH}$ [4], called $\mathcal{EFALCH}$, by introducing cut concepts and cut roles. $\mathcal{EFALCH}$ inherits all the concept constructors from $\mathcal{ALCH}$, including negation, conjunction, disjunction, value restriction, and existential restriction. There is no role constructor in either $\mathcal{ALCH}$ or $\mathcal{EFALCH}$.

Definition 2. The cut concepts in $\mathcal{EFALCH}$ are syntactically defined as

$$C,D ::= A_{[\lambda]} \mid \neg C \mid C \sqcap D \mid C \sqcup D \mid \forall R_{[\lambda]}.C \mid \exists R_{[\lambda]}.C \quad (2)$$

where $A \in N_C$, $R \in N_R$, and $0 < \lambda \leq 1$. The semantics of cut concepts are defined in terms of $\mathcal{I} = <\Delta^{\mathcal{I}}, \cdot^{\mathcal{I}}>$ in Definition 1 with the extension of $\cdot^{\mathcal{I}}$ for the concept constructors as follows:

$$(\neg C)^{\mathcal{I}} = \Delta^{\mathcal{I}} \setminus C^{\mathcal{I}}; (C \sqcap D)^{\mathcal{I}} = C^{\mathcal{I}} \cap D^{\mathcal{I}}; (C \sqcup D)^{\mathcal{I}} = C^{\mathcal{I}} \cup D^{\mathcal{I}};$$
$$(\exists R_{[\lambda]}.C)^{\mathcal{I}} = \{d \in \Delta^{\mathcal{I}} \mid \exists d' \in \Delta^{\mathcal{I}}, (d,d') \in (R_{[\lambda]})^{\mathcal{I}} \wedge d' \in C^{\mathcal{I}}\}; \quad (3)$$
$$(\forall R_{[\lambda]}.C)^{\mathcal{I}} = \{d \in \Delta^{\mathcal{I}} \mid \forall d' \in \Delta^{\mathcal{I}}, (d,d') \in (R_{[\lambda]})^{\mathcal{I}} \to d' \in C^{\mathcal{I}}\}.$$

The atomic cut concepts describe crisp sets, and all the concept constructors remain the same meaning as they have in $\mathcal{ALCH}$. So the cut concepts C, D also describe crisp sets. Here introduces some notions of cut concepts.

A cut concept C is in Negation Normal Form (NNF) if negation $\neg$ only occurs in front of atomic cut concepts. Every cut concept can be converted into a cut concept in NNF by exhaustively applying the following rewrite rules in linear time.

$$\neg\neg C \Rightarrow C; \quad \neg(C \sqcap D) \Rightarrow \neg C \sqcup \neg D; \quad \neg(C \sqcup D) \Rightarrow \neg C \sqcap \neg D;$$
$$\neg(\exists R_{\{\lambda\}}.C) \Rightarrow \forall R_{\{\lambda\}}.\neg C; \quad \neg(\forall R_{\{\lambda\}}.C) \Rightarrow \exists R_{\{\lambda\}}.\neg C. \qquad (4)$$

Obviously the semantics of resulting cut concept in NNF must be equivalent with that of original one from Equation 3. From now on, we assume that all cut concepts are in NNF.

2.2 Axioms and Assertions

An $\mathcal{EFALCH}$ knowledge base contains alterable terminological axioms of concepts represented in a TBox, alterable role inclusion axioms represented in a role hierarchy, as well as assertions represented in an ABox.

Definition 3. For any $A \in N_C$ and $R \in N_R$, $A_{[f(u)]}$ ($R_{[f(u)]}$) is an alterable atomic cut concept (role) decided by u, if u is a variable in a continuous domain $V \subseteq (0,1]$ and f is a function from V to $(0,1]$. Starting with alterable atomic cut concepts and roles, alterable cut concepts (denoted E, F) can be inductively defined with the concept constructors: $E, F ::= A_{[f(u)]} \mid \neg E \mid E \sqcap F \mid E \sqcup F \mid \forall R_{[f(u)]}.C \mid \exists R_{[f(u)]}.E$.

Now we make some constraints of an alterable cut concept E:

1. All alterable atomic cut concepts and atomic cut roles in E must be decided by a single variable u with same domain V, then we say E is decided by u and donated by $E_{(u)}$, and V is the domain of $E_{(u)}$. Let c be a constant in V, then $E_{(c)}$ is a cut concept by replacing any alterable suffix $f(u)$ in E with $f(c)$.

2. For $E_{(u)}$ and its domain V, $E_{(u)}$ is monotonous (either increasing or decreasing) over V. $E_{(u)}$ is increasing (decreasing) over V if for any $\lambda_1, \lambda_2 \in V$, $\lambda_1 \leq \lambda_2$ and any interpretation I, $(E_{(\lambda_1)})^I \supseteq (\subseteq)(E_{(\lambda_2)})^I$ holds. And the monotony constraints hold for any alterable atomic cut role.

Definition 4. An $\mathcal{EFALCH}$ TBox is a finite set of terminological axioms of the form $< E_{(u)} \sqsubseteq F_{(u)}, u \in V >$, where $E_{(u)}, F_{(u)}$ are alterable cut concepts and have the same domain V and monotony (both $E_{(u)}$ and $F_{(u)}$ are increasing or decreasing over V). An interpretation $\mathcal{I}$ is a model of a TBox $\mathcal{T}$ iff $\forall c \in V, (E_{(c)})^\mathcal{I} \subseteq (F_{(c)})^\mathcal{I}$ holds for all $< E \sqsubseteq F, u \in V >$ in $\mathcal{T}$. The TBox $\mathcal{T}$ is consistent iff it has a model.

Definition 5. An $\mathcal{EFALCH}$ role hierarchy is a finite set of alterable cut role inclusion axioms of the form $<R_{[f(u)]} \sqsubseteq S_{[f'(u)]}, u \in V>$, where $R_{[f(u)]}, S_{[f'(u)]}$ are alterable cut roles and have the same domain V and monotony ($R_{[f(u)]}$ and $S_{[f'(u)]}$ are both increasing or decreasing over V). An interpretation $\mathcal{I}$ is a model of a role hierarchy $\mathcal{H}$ iff $\forall c \in V, (R_{[f(c)]})^{\mathcal{I}} \subseteq (S_{[f'(c)]})^{\mathcal{I}}$ for all $<R_{[f(u)]} \sqsubseteq S_{[f'(u)]}, u \in V>$ in $\mathcal{H}$.

The assertions in $\mathcal{EFALCH}$ is similar to assertions in $\mathcal{ALCH}$ with replacing crisp concept and role with cut concept and role.

Definition 6. An $\mathcal{EFALCH}$ ABox is a finite set of assertions of the form $a:C$ (cut concept assertion) or $(a,b):R_{[\lambda]}$ (cut role assertion), where C is a cut concept, $R_{[\lambda]}$ a cut role and $a,b \in N_I$. An interpretation $\mathcal{I}$ is a model of an ABox $\mathcal{A}$ iff $a^{\mathcal{I}} \in C^{\mathcal{I}}$ holds for all $a:C$ and $(a^{\mathcal{I}}, b^{\mathcal{I}}) \in (R_{[\lambda]})^{\mathcal{I}}$ for all $(a,b):R_{[\lambda]}$ in $\mathcal{A}$. The ABox $\mathcal{A}$ is consistent iff it has a model.

An $\mathcal{EFALCH}$ knowledge base $\Sigma = (\mathcal{A}, \mathcal{T}, \mathcal{H})$ contains an ABox $\mathcal{A}$, a TBox $\mathcal{T}$, and a role hierarchy $\mathcal{H}$. An interpretation $\mathcal{I}$ is a model of $\Sigma = (\mathcal{A}, \mathcal{T}, \mathcal{H})$, iff $\mathcal{I}$ is a model of $\mathcal{T}$, $\mathcal{A}$ and $\mathcal{H}$. Σ is consistent iff it has a model.

2.3 A Quick Look to Fuzzy $\mathcal{ALCH}$

Fuzzy $\mathcal{ALCH}$ [2] is a fuzzy extension of $\mathcal{ALCH}$ by adopting fuzzy interpretation to redefine the semantics and extending the forms of axioms and assertions. Let A be an atomic fuzzy concept, R be an atomic fuzzy role, fuzzy concepts are inductively defined with the application of the concept constructors:

$$C, D ::= \top \mid \bot \mid A \mid \neg C \mid C \sqcup D \mid C \sqcap D \mid \forall R.C \mid \exists R.C \tag{5}$$

In the fuzzy interpretation $\mathcal{I} = <\Delta^{\mathcal{I}}, \cdot^{\mathcal{I}}>$ of fuzzy $\mathcal{ALCH}$, $\Delta^{\mathcal{I}}$ is a nonempty set and $\cdot^{\mathcal{I}}$ satisfies several well known restrictions: For $\forall d \in \Delta^{\mathcal{I}}$, C and D are fuzzy concepts, R is an atomic fuzzy role.

$$\begin{aligned}
&\top^{\mathcal{I}}(d) = 1; \quad \bot^{\mathcal{I}}(d) = 0; \quad (\neg C)^{\mathcal{I}}(d) = 1 - C^{\mathcal{I}}(d); \\
&(C \sqcap D)^{\mathcal{I}}(d) = \min\{C^{\mathcal{I}}(d), D^{\mathcal{I}}(d)\}; \\
&(C \sqcup D)^{\mathcal{I}}(d) = \max\{C^{\mathcal{I}}(d), D^{\mathcal{I}}(d)\}; \\
&(\exists R.C)^{\mathcal{I}}(d) = \sup_{d' \in \Delta^{\mathcal{I}}}\{\min\{R^{\mathcal{I}}(d,d'), C^{\mathcal{I}}(d')\}\}; \\
&(\forall R.C)^{\mathcal{I}}(d) = \inf_{d' \in \Delta^{\mathcal{I}}}\{\max\{1 - R^{\mathcal{I}}(d,d'), C^{\mathcal{I}}(d')\}\}.
\end{aligned} \tag{6}$$

A knowledge base of Fuzzy $\mathcal{ALCH}$ is a pair $\Sigma = (\mathcal{T}, \mathcal{A})$.

$\mathcal{T}$ is a TBox of fuzzy terminological axioms of the forms $C \sqsubseteq D$ or $R \sqsubseteq S$, where C, D are fuzzy concepts, R, S are fuzzy roles. An interpretation $\mathcal{I}$ satisfies $C \sqsubseteq D$ ($R \sqsubseteq S$) iff $\forall d, d' \in \Delta^{\mathcal{I}}$, $C^{\mathcal{I}}(d) \leq D^{\mathcal{I}}(d)$ ($R^{\mathcal{I}}(d,d') \leq S^{\mathcal{I}}(d,d')$). $\mathcal{I}$ is called a model of $\mathcal{T}$ iff $\mathcal{I}$ satisfies any axiom in $\mathcal{T}$.

$\mathcal{A}$ is an ABox of fuzzy assertions of the forms $\alpha \geq \lambda$, $\alpha > \lambda$, $\alpha \leq \lambda$ or $\alpha < \lambda$, where α is of the form $a:C$ or $(a,b):R$, a,b are individuals, C is a fuzzy concept, R is a fuzzy role and $0 \leq \lambda \leq 1$. $(a,b):R<\lambda$ and $(a,b):R\leq\lambda$ are not allowed as they relate to negative roles, which is not a part of $\mathcal{ALCH}$ [4]. Similarly for $>$, $\leq$ and $<$, $\mathcal{I}$ satisfies $a:C \geq \lambda$ ($(a,b):R \geq \lambda$) iff $C^{\mathcal{I}}(a^{\mathcal{I}}) \geq \lambda$ ($R^{\mathcal{I}}(a^{\mathcal{I}}, b^{\mathcal{I}}) \geq \lambda$). $\mathcal{I}$ is a model of ABox $\mathcal{A}$ iff I satisfies any assertion in $\mathcal{A}$.

$\mathcal{I}$ is a model of knowledge base $\Sigma(\mathcal{T},\mathcal{A})$, iff $\mathcal{I}$ satisfies both $\mathcal{T}$ and $\mathcal{A}$. Σ is consistent iff it has a model.

Fuzzy $\mathcal{ALCH}$ only supports limited and insufficient expressive power of both assertional and terminological fuzzy knowledge. For a fuzzy concept $\exists R.C$ and an individual a, fuzzy $\mathcal{ALCH}$ supports fuzzy assertion of the form $a:\exists R.C \geq \lambda$, which means $\exists b^{\mathcal{I}} \in \Delta^{\mathcal{I}}, R^{\mathcal{I}}(a^{\mathcal{I}}, b^{\mathcal{I}}) \geq \lambda$ and $C^{\mathcal{I}}(b^{\mathcal{I}}) \geq \lambda$. However, it cannot describe an individual a such that $\exists b^{\mathcal{I}} \in \Delta^{\mathcal{I}}, R^{\mathcal{I}}(a^{\mathcal{I}}, b^{\mathcal{I}}) \geq \lambda_1$ and $C^{\mathcal{I}}(b^{\mathcal{I}}) \geq \lambda_2$, where $\lambda_1 \neq \lambda_2$. Generally, fuzzy $\mathcal{ALCH}$ is not able to describe different membership degrees of concepts and roles in a single assertion. Similarly, the same problem happens in the axioms of fuzzy $\mathcal{ALCH}$. They can not express complex inclusions based on various membership degrees. For example, the fuzzy terminological axiom $C \sqsubseteq D$ only means $\forall d \in \Delta^{\mathcal{I}}$, $C^{\mathcal{I}}(d) \geq \lambda \rightarrow D^{\mathcal{I}}(d) \geq \lambda$. But sometimes, it is necessary to use $C^{\mathcal{I}}(d) \geq \lambda_1 \rightarrow D^{\mathcal{I}}(d) \geq \lambda_2$, where $\lambda_1 \neq \lambda_2$, or even more complex axioms.

2.4 Translation from Fuzzy $\mathcal{ALCH}$ to $\mathcal{EFALCH}$

A fuzzy $\mathcal{ALCH}$ knowledge base can be translated into an $\mathcal{EFALCH}$ one without losing any semantic information.

Firstly we define a function to build an $\mathcal{EFALCH}$ cut concept from a fuzzy $\mathcal{ALCH}$ concept w.r.t. the membership degree s:

$$trans(C,s) = \begin{cases} C_{[s]} & C \in N_C \\ \neg trans(D, 1-s+\varepsilon) & C = \neg D \\ trans(D,s) \sqcap trans(D',s) & C = D \sqcap D' \\ trans(D,s) \sqcup trans(D',s) & C = D \sqcup D' \\ \exists R_{[s]}.trans(D,s) & C = \exists R.D \\ \forall R_{[1-s+\varepsilon]}.trans(D,s) & C = \forall R.D \end{cases} \quad (7)$$

where ε is an infinitesimal, C, D, D' are fuzzy concepts and s be a real number in $(0,1]$ or a function with range in $(0,1]$. The $trans()$ function has some properties: the suffixes in $trans(C,s)$ can only be s or $1-s+\varepsilon$, so if $0 < s \leq 1$, then all suffixes are in $(0,1]$; let C be in NNF and $E_{(u)} = trans(C,u)$, then $E_{(u)}$ is an alterable cut concept in NNF decided by u, and obviously it satisfies the monotony restriction.

Then the translation rules from fuzzy $\mathcal{ALCH}$ to $\mathcal{EFALCH}$ are showed in Table 1.

Table 1. Translation rules from Fuzzy $\mathcal{ALCH}$ to $\mathcal{EFALCH}$

		Fuzzy $\mathcal{ALCH}$		$\mathcal{EFALCH}$
ABox		$(a,b):R \geq \lambda$	$0 < \lambda \leq 1$	$(a,b):R_{[\lambda]}$
		$a:C \geq \lambda$		$a:trans(C,\lambda)$
		$a:C < \lambda$		$a:trans(\neg C, 1-\lambda+\varepsilon)$
		$(a,b):R > \lambda$	$0 \leq \lambda < 1$	$(a,b):R_{[\lambda+\varepsilon]}$
		$a:C \leq \lambda$		$a:trans(\neg C, 1-\lambda)$
		$a:C > \lambda$		$a:trans(C,\lambda+\varepsilon)$
TBox		$C \sqsubseteq D$		$trans(C,u) \sqsubseteq trans(D,u), u \in (0,1]$
Role Hierarchy		$R \sqsubseteq S$		$R_{[u]} \sqsubseteq S_{[u]}, u \in (0,1]$

Theorem 1. There is a model of a fuzzy $\mathcal{ALCH}$ knowledge base Σ iff there is a model of the corresponding $\mathcal{EFALCH}$ knowledge base Σ', where Σ' is build from Σ by applying the transform rules in Table 1.

3 Reasoning Within $\mathcal{EFALCH}$

In classical description logic, concept satisfiability is considered as a main reasoning task, and reasoning algorithms are usually firstly developed for it and secondly extended to solve the other reasoning tasks [4, 5]. Similarly, in $\mathcal{EFALCH}$ case, we consider cut concept satisfiability as a basic reasoning task.

Cut concept satisfiability: a cut concept C is satisfiable w.r.t $\mathcal{T}$ iff there is an interpretation $\mathcal{I}$ such that $\mathcal{I}$ is a model of $\mathcal{T}$ and $C^{\mathcal{I}} \neq \emptyset$.

This section will talk about acyclic TBox form in $\mathcal{EFALCH}$, which is a restricted form of general TBox (definition 1), and design an algorithm for cut concept satisfiability w.r.t acyclic TBox.

First, we define acyclic TBox. By the comparison with the definition of acyclic TBox in $\mathcal{ALCH}$, the definition of $\mathcal{EFALCH}$ acyclic TBox is more complex.

Definition 7. An $\mathcal{EFALCH}$ acyclic TBox is an $\mathcal{EFALCH}$ TBox with three restrictions:

1. An $\mathcal{EFALCH}$ acyclic TBox $\mathcal{T}$ contains alterable concept definitions instead of alterable cut concept axioms. Alterable concept definitions are of the form $< A_{[u]} \doteq E_{(u)}, u \in V >$, where $A_{[u]}$ is an alterable atomic cut concept decided by u,

and $E_{(u)}$ is an alterable cut concept decided by u. For $A_{[u]}$ is increasing over V, $E_{(u)}$ is also increasing over V. For any interpretation $\mathcal{I}$, $\mathcal{I}$ satisfies $<A_{[u]} \doteq E, u \in V>$ iff for any $\lambda \in V$, $(A_{[\lambda]})^{\mathcal{I}} = (E_{(\lambda)})^{\mathcal{I}}$.

2. An $\mathcal{EFALCH}$ acyclic TBox $\mathcal{T}$ contains neither multiple definitions nor cyclic definitions. Multiple definitions means more than one definition of a fuzzy concept name, such as $<A_{[u]} \doteq E, u \in V>$, $<A_{[u]} \doteq F, u \in V'>$, where $V \cap V' \neq \varnothing$. Therefore, for any $<A_{[u]} \doteq E, u \in V>$, $<A_{[u]} \doteq F, u \in V'>$ in $\mathcal{T}$, it must be true that $\forall \lambda \in V, \lambda' \in V' : \lambda < \lambda'$ (written $V \prec V'$) or $V' \prec V$. Cyclic definitions means a fuzzy concept name is defined by itself, such as $<A_{1[u]} \doteq E_1, u \in V_1>$, ..., $<A_{k[u]} \doteq E_k, u \in V_k>$, where A_i occurs in E_{i-1} and A_1 occurs in E_k.

3. It ensures explicit tautology property for definitions of the same atomic fuzzy concept. For the atomic cut concepts have the property that $A_{[\lambda']} \sqsubseteq A_{[\lambda]}$ if $0 < \lambda \leq \lambda' \leq 1$, it can simulate the axiom $<E_{(u)} \sqsubseteq F_{(u)}, u \in V>$, which must be not allowed in acyclic TBox. For example, two alterable concept definitions $<A_{[u]} \doteq B_{1[u]} \sqcap B_{2[u]}, u \in [0.1, 0.2]>$ and $<A_{[u]} \doteq B_{3[u]} \sqcap B_{4[u]}, u \in [0.3, 0.4]>$ can imply the axiom $<B_{3[u+0.2]} \sqcap B_{4[u+0.2]} \sqsubseteq B_{1[u]} \sqcap B_{2[u]}, u \in [0.1, 0.2]>$. To prevent this, for any two axioms $<A_{[u]} \doteq E_{(u)}, u \in V>$ and $<A_{[u]} \doteq F_{(u)}, u \in V'>$ ($V \prec V'$) in $\mathcal{T}$, $F_{(\inf(V'))} \sqsubseteq E_{(\sup(V))}$ is satisfiable for any interpretation $\mathcal{I}$. This property guarantees any $<E_{(u)} \sqsubseteq F_{(u)}, u \in V>$ simulated by definitions in $\mathcal{T}$ is a tautology and neither considered. That is called explicit tautology property for definitions of the same atomic fuzzy concept.

Here introduces some notions of cut concepts. $A_{[\lambda]}$ is restricted by $<A_{[u]} \doteq E_{(u)}, u \in V>$ in $\mathcal{T}$ if $\inf(V) \leq \lambda$ and there is no other $<A_{[u]} \doteq F_{(u)}, u \in V'>$ in $\mathcal{T}$ such that $V \prec V'$ and $\inf(V') \leq \lambda$. By the definition, we can define unfold process to eliminate acyclic TBoxes: for a cut concept C and an acyclic TBox $\mathcal{T}$, the unfold process replaces any $A_{[\lambda]}$ in C with $A_{[\lambda]} \sqcap E_{(c)}$ to build a new cut concept C^*, where $A_{[\lambda]}$ is restricted by $<A_{[u]} \doteq E_{(u)}, u \in V>$ in $\mathcal{T}$, and $c = \min(\lambda, \sup(V))$. This process could convert reasoning tasks w.r.t acyclic TBox into ones w.r.t empty TBox, but it can cause C^* with exponential size [6]. Therefore we adopt "simple TBox" [7] to design a PSPACE algorithm for satisfiability w.r.t acyclic TBox.

For any $\mathcal{EFALCH}$ acyclic TBox $\mathcal{T}$, it can be rewritten to be a simple TBox $\mathcal{T}'$ in polynomial time by exhaustively applying the following rewrite rules (equation 8), where $\sqcup$ is analogous to $\sqcap$, $\forall$ is analogous to $\exists$, nnf($\neg E_{(u)}$) is an alterable cut concept in NNF which is equivalent to $\neg E_{(u)}$, and new generated $A_{[u]}$ is an fresh alterable atomic cut concept in $\mathcal{T}$. Let $Sim(\mathcal{T})$ be the rewritten result TBox from $\mathcal{T}$.

$$< A_{[u]} \doteq E_{(u)}, u \in V > \to < \neg A_{[u]} \doteq \text{nnf}(\neg E_{(u)}), u \in V >$$
$$< A_{[u]} \doteq E_{(u)} \sqcap F_{(u)}, u \in V > \to < A_{[u]} \doteq A'_{[u]} \sqcap F_{(u)}, u \in V >, < A'_{[u]} \doteq E_{(u)}, u \in V >$$
$$< A_{[u]} \doteq F_{(u)} \sqcap E_{(u)}, u \in V > \to < A_{[u]} \doteq F_{(u)} \sqcap A'_{[u]}, u \in V >, < A'_{[u]} \doteq E_{(u)}, u \in V > \quad (8)$$
$$< A_{[u]} \doteq \exists R_{[f(u)]}.E_{(u)}, u \in V > \to < A_{[u]} \doteq \exists R_{[f(u)]}.A'_{[u]}, u \in V >, < A'_{[u]} \doteq E_{(u)}, u \in V >$$

Theorem 2. For an $\mathcal{EFALCH}$ TBox $\mathcal{T}$ and a cut concept C_0, there is a model $\mathcal{I}$ of $\mathcal{T}$ and $C_0^\mathcal{I} \neq \emptyset$ iff there is a model $\mathcal{I}$ of $Sim(\mathcal{T} \cup \{A_{[1]}^0 \doteq C_0\})$ and $(A_{[1]}^0)^\mathcal{I} \neq \emptyset$, where $A_{[1]}^0$ is a new atomic cut concept, which is not in $\mathcal{T}$.

This theorem guarantees that satisfiability of C_0 w.r.t an acyclic TBox $\mathcal{T}$ can be equally converted to satisfiability of an atomic cut concept $A_{[1]}^0$ w.r.t the corresponding simple TBox. For $< \neg A_{[u]} \doteq E_{(u)}, u \in V >$ is allowed in a simple TBox, we additionally define $\neg A_{[\lambda]}$ is restricted by $< \neg A_{[u]} \doteq E, u \in V >$ in $\mathcal{T}$ if $\lambda \leq \sup(V)$ and there is no other $< \neg A_{[u]} \doteq F, u \in V' >$ in $\mathcal{T}$ such that $V' \prec V$ and $\lambda \leq \sup(V')$. For any $A_{[\lambda]}$ or $\neg A_{[\lambda]}$, it can only be restricted by at most one alterable axiom in $\mathcal{T}$.

And for $\mathcal{EFALCH}$ supports alterable cut role inclusion axioms, we uses "$R_{k[\lambda_k]}$-successor" to propagate the constraint of alterable cut role inclusion. $R_{k[\lambda_k]}$-successor is defined as: y is a $R_{k[\lambda_k]}$-successor of x if $\mathcal{A}$ contains $(x, y): R_{k[\lambda_k]}$ and there are a cut role sequence $R_{1[\lambda_1]}, R_{2[\lambda_2]}, \cdots, R_{k[\lambda_k]}$ such that for any $R_{i[\lambda_i]}$ and $R_{i+1[\lambda_{i+1}]}$, one of the following two condition must be satisfied:

1) $R_i = R_{i+1}$ and $\lambda_i \geq \lambda_{i+1}$ holds;

2) $< R_{i[f(u)]} \sqsubseteq R_{i+1[f'(u)]}, u \in V >$ is in $\mathcal{H}$. Let f^{-1} be the inverse function of f (for the monotony constraints, f is monotonous). $f'(f^{-1}(\lambda_i)) \geq \lambda_{i+1}$ holds.

The algorithm for satisfiability of an atomic cut concept $A_{[1]}^0$ w.r.t a simple TBox $\mathcal{T}'$ starts with an initial ABox $\mathcal{A}_0 = \{x: A_{[1]}^0\}$, and then extends $\mathcal{A}_0$ with completion rules (Figure 1) until no completion rule is applicable. If none of completion rules can applicable to current $\mathcal{A}$, we call $\mathcal{A}$ is complete. The algorithm return $A_{[1]}^0$ is satisfiable w.r.t $\mathcal{T}'$ iff in the algorithm processing, there is a complete and clash-free ABox $\mathcal{A}$.

The completeness of the algorithm is guaranteed for any completion rule is based on constraint propagation. And the soundness is proved by the monotony constraint and tautology property of acyclic TBox. The algorithm could be executed in polynomial space as a similar consequence of the algorithm for $\mathcal{ALCH}$-concept satisfiability w.r.t acyclic TBox. For Fuzzy $\mathcal{ALCH}$ concept satisfiability is PSPACE-complete[3], and Fuzzy $\mathcal{ALCH}$ can be equivalent converted into $\mathcal{EFALCH}$. Therefore $\mathcal{EFALCH}$-concept satisfiability w.r.t acyclic TBox is PSPACE-hard. We have the following theorem.

Theorem 3. Satisfiability of cut concepts w.r.t. acyclic TBoxes is PSPACE-complete.

For any ABox $\mathcal{A}$ which is clash-free, $\mathcal{T}$ is a simple TBox

$\sqcap$-rule I
Condition: $\mathcal{A}$ contains $x:A_{[\lambda]}$ restricted by $<A_{[u]} \doteq A'_{[u]} \sqcap A''_{[u]}, u \in V>$ in $\mathcal{T}$, but not both $x:A'_{[c]}$ and $x:A''_{[c]}$ such that $c = \min(\lambda, \sup(V))$.
Action: $\mathcal{A} \leftarrow \mathcal{A} \cup \{x:A'_{[c]}, x:A''_{[c]}\}$.

$\sqcap$-rule II
Condition: $\mathcal{A}$ contains $x:\neg A_{[\lambda]}$ restricted by $<\neg A_{[u]} \doteq \neg A'_{[u]} \sqcap \neg A''_{[u]}, u \in V>$ in $\mathcal{T}$, but not both $x:\neg A'_{[c]}$ and $x:\neg A''_{[c]}$ such that $c = \max(\lambda, \inf(V))$.
Action: $\mathcal{A} \leftarrow \mathcal{A} \cup \{x:\neg A'_{[c]}, x:\neg A''_{[c]}\}$

$\sqcup$-rule I
Condition: $\mathcal{A}$ contains $x:A_{[\lambda]}$ restricted by $<A_{[u]} \doteq A'_{[u]} \sqcup A''_{[u]}, u \in V>$ in $\mathcal{T}$, but either $x:A'_{[c]}$ or $x:A''_{[c]}$ such that $c = \min(\lambda, \sup(V))$.
Action: $\mathcal{A}' \leftarrow \mathcal{A} \cup \{x:A'_{[c]}\}$, $\mathcal{A}'' \leftarrow \mathcal{A} \cup \{x:A''_{[c]}\}$.

$\sqcup$-rule II
Condition: $\mathcal{A}$ contains $x:\neg A_{[\lambda]}$ restricted by $<\neg A_{[u]} \doteq \neg A'_{[u]} \sqcap \neg A''_{[u]}, u \in V>$ in $\mathcal{T}$, but either $x:\neg A'_{[c]}$ or $x:\neg A''_{[c]}$ such that $c = \max(\lambda, \inf(V))$.
Action: $\mathcal{A}' \leftarrow \mathcal{A} \cup \{x:\neg A'_{[c]}\}$, $\mathcal{A}'' \leftarrow \mathcal{A} \cup \{x:\neg A''_{[c]}\}$.

$\exists$-rule I
Condition: $\mathcal{A}$ contains $x:A_{[\lambda]}$ restricted by $<A_{[u]} \doteq \exists R_{[f(u)]}.A'_{[u]}, u \in V>$ in $\mathcal{T}$, but no $R_{[f(c)]}$-successor z of x with $z:A'_{[c]}$ such that $c = \min(\lambda, \sup(V))$.
Action: $\mathcal{A} \leftarrow \mathcal{A} \cup \{y:A'_{[c]}, (x,y):R_{[f(c)]}\}$, where y is new generated.

$\exists$-rule II
Condition: $\mathcal{A}$ contains $x:\neg A_{[\lambda]}$ restricted by $<\neg A_{[u]} \doteq \exists R_{[f(u)]}.\neg A'_{[u]}, u \in V>$ in $\mathcal{T}$, but no $R_{[f(c)]}$-successor z of x with $z:\neg A'_{[c]}$ such that $c = \max(\lambda, \inf(V))$.
Action: $\mathcal{A} \leftarrow \mathcal{A} \cup \{y:\neg A'_{[c]}, (x,y):R_{[f(c)]}\}$, where y is new generated.

$\forall$-rule I
Condition: $\mathcal{A}$ contains $x:A_{[\lambda]}$ restricted by $<A_{[u]} \doteq \forall R_{[f(u)]}.A'_{[u]}, u \in V>$ in $\mathcal{T}$, and a $R_{[f(c)]}$-successor y of x without $y:A'_{[c]}$ such that $c = \min(\lambda, \sup(V))$.
Action: $\mathcal{A} \leftarrow \mathcal{A} \cup \{y:A'_{[c]}\}$

$\forall$-rule II
Condition: $\mathcal{A}$ contains $x:\neg A_{[\lambda]}$ restricted by $<\neg A_{[u]} \doteq \forall R_{[f(u)]}.\neg A'_{[u]}, u \in V>$ in $\mathcal{T}$, and a $R_{[f(c)]}$-successor y of x without $y:\neg A'_{[c]}$ such that $c = \max(\lambda, \sup(V))$.
Action: $\mathcal{A} \leftarrow \mathcal{A} \cup \{y:\neg A'_{[c]}\}$

$\neg$-rule
Condition: $\mathcal{A}$ contains $x:A_{[\lambda]}$ and $x:\neg A_{[\lambda']}$, where $\lambda \leq \lambda'$.

Fig. 1. Completion rules for satisfiability w.r.t simple TBox

4 Related Work

Lots of endeavors have done for extension of DLs with fuzzy features. Meghini et al proposed a preliminary fuzzy DL[8]. Straccia[2] presented fuzzy $\mathcal{ALCH}$, and gave a constraint propagation calculus for reasoning. The translation from fuzzy $\mathcal{ALCH}$ to $\mathcal{EFALCH}$ has been discussed in section 2.4. In addition, $\mathcal{EFALCH}$ can overcome the insufficiencies of fuzzy $\mathcal{ALCH}$, which are discussed in section 2.3. Firstly, for an individual a satisfies $\exists b^I \in \Delta^I$ $R^I(a^I, b^I) \geq \lambda_1$ and $C^I(b^I) \geq \lambda_2$, where $\lambda_1 \neq \lambda_2$, such complex assertion can be described as $a: \exists R_{[\lambda_1]}.C_{[\lambda_2]}$; Secondly, for $\forall d \in \Delta^I$ $C^I(d) \geq \lambda_1 \rightarrow D^I(d) \geq \lambda_2$, such inclusion can be described as: $C_{[\lambda_1]} \sqsubseteq D_{[\lambda_2]}$.

5 Conclusions

This paper introduces cut sets of the fuzzy concepts and fuzzy roles as atomic concepts and atomic roles to build $\mathcal{EFALCH}$, presents sound and complete algorithms for reasoning tasks w.r.t acyclic TBox, and proves the complexity of them is PSPACE-complete. Further works includes the extension of $\mathcal{EFALCH}$ with adding more concept and role constructors.

References

[1] Straccia, U.: Reasoning within fuzzy description logics. Journal of Artificial Intelligence Research, no.14 (2001) 137-166
[2] Straccia, U.: Transforming fuzzy description logics into classical description logics. In: Proceedings of the 9th European Conference on Logics in Artificial Intelligence, Lisbon, (2004) 385-399
[3] Zadeh L A.: Fuzzy sets. Information and Control. vol.8 no.3 (1965) 338-353
[4] Baader, F., Calvanese, D., McGuinness, D.L., Nardi, D., Patel-Schneider, P.F.(Eds.): The Description Logic Handbook: Theory, Implementation, and Applications. Cambridge University Press (2003)
[5] Baader, F., Sattler, U.: An Overview of Tableau Algorithms for Description Logics. Studia Logica, Vol. 69, no. 1 (2001) 5-40
[6] Nebel, B.: Computational complexity of terminological reasoning in BACK. Artificial Intelligence, no. 34 (1988) 371-383
[7] Calvanese D. Reasoning with inclusion axioms in description logics: Algorithms and complexity. In: Proceedings of the Twelfth European Conference on Artificial Intelligence (ECAI-96), Budapest, (1996) 303-307
[8] Meghini, C., Sebastiani, F., Straccia, U.: Reasoning about the form and content for multimedia objects. In: Proceedings of AAAI 1997 Spring Symposium on Intelligent Integration and Use of Text, Image, Video and Audio, California (1997) 89-94

An Approach for Dynamic Split Strategies in Constraint Solving

Carlos Castro[1], Eric Monfroy[1,2], Christian Figueroa[1], and Rafael Meneses[1]

[1] Universidad Técnica Federico Santa María, Valparaíso, Chile
[2] LINA, Université de Nantes, France
FirstName.Name@inf.utfsm.cl

Abstract. In constraint programming, a priori choices statically determine strategies that are crucial for resolution performances. However, the effect of strategies is generally unpredictable. We propose to dynamically change strategies showing bad performances. When this is not enough to improve resolution, we introduce some meta-backtracks. Our goal is to get good performances without the know-how of experts. Some first experimental results show the effectiveness of our approach.

1 Introduction

A Constraint Satisfaction Problem (CSP) is defined by a set of variables, a set of values for each variable, and a set of constraints. The goal is to find one or all instantiations of variables that satisfy the set of constraints. One of the most common techniques for solving CSPs is a complete approach that interleaves splits (e.g., enumeration) and constraint propagations. Constraint propagation prunes the search tree by eliminating values that cannot participate in any solution of the CSP. Split consists in cutting a CSP into smaller CSPs by splitting the domain of a variable. Although all strategies of split that preserve solutions are valid, they have drastically different impacts on resolution efficiency. Moreover, no strategy is (one of) the best for all problems. The issue for efficiency w.r.t. split strategy is thus: which variable to select? how to split or enumerate its domain?

Numerous studies defined some general criteria (e.g., minimum domain) for variable selection, and for value selection (e.g., lower bound, or bisection). For some applications, such as Job-Shop Scheduling problems, specific split strategies have been proposed [7]. On the one hand, determining the best strategy can be achieved on focusing on some static criteria. In this case, the selection criteria is determined just once before resolution (see e.g., [2] for variable ordering, [9] to pre-determine the "best" heuristic, [10] to determine the best solver). However, it is well-known that an a priori decision concerning a good variable and value selection is very hard (and almost impossible in the general case) since strategy effects are rather unpredictable. On the other hand, information coming from the solving process can be used to determine the strategy (see e.g., [6] for algorithm control with low-knowledge, [17] for dynamic change of propagators, [8] for variation of strength of propagation).

In [3,4], adaptive constraint satisfaction is presented based on a chain of algorithms: bad algorithm choices are detected and dynamically changed by other candidates. In [11,12] the split strategy is fixed. However, randomisation is applied for tie-breaking when several choices are ranked equally by the strategy. Moreover, a restart policy based on a specified number of backtracks (cutoff) is also introduced: when the cutoff is reached, the algorithm is restarted at the root of the search tree to try another branch.

In this paper, we are interested in a combination of these two last types of work: we present a framework for adaptive strategies together with meta-backtracks (an adaptation of restart to save and capitalise work already achieved) to find solutions more quickly and with less variance in solution time: we try to avoid very long runs when another strategy (or sequence of strategies) can lead quickly to a solution. We are interested in dynamically detecting bad decisions concerning split strategies during resolution: instead of trying to predict the effect of a strategy, we evaluate the efficiency of running strategies, and replace the ones showing bad results. When this is not sufficient and we guess that the search is in a bad context, we also perform meta-backtracks (several levels of backtracks) to quickly undo several enumerations and restore a "better" context.

To this end, we define some measures of the solving process that are observed according to some time-based or computation-based policies. Then, this information is analysed to draw some indicators that are used to make decisions: updates of the priority of application of strategies or meta-backtracks. For priorities, we penalise strategies that have done a bad work, and we give more credits to those that we judge efficient. We select the split strategy to apply next according to these changing priorities. Meta-backtracks happen when the change of strategy cannot improve resolution: in this case, several levels of backtracks are performed at once to "erase" previous bad choices of split. This process is repeated until the CSP is solved. Some preliminary results for CSP over finite domains show the effectiveness of our framework in terms of solving efficiency.

This framework is open and flexible, thus we can consider domain specific as well as generic strategies, observations, indicators, and decisions. It could also be adapted to take into account strategies for constraint propagation, incomplete solvers, or even hybrid solvers [15]. Since our approach is orthogonal to techniques for predicting good strategies, it can be combined with such methods.

This paper is organised as follows: Section 2 gives the motivations for doing this work. Section 3 presents our framework whereas Section 4 presents an instantiation for finite domain constraints and Section 5 reports experimental results obtained with our implementation. Finally, we conclude in Section 6.

2 Motivations

Solvers based on constraint propagation alternate phases of pruning and phases of split of the search space. Although all strategies of split preserving solutions are valid, they have drastically different impacts on efficiency. But, their effect is very difficult to predict and in most cases, impossible. Moreover, no strategy

Table 1. N-queens: CPU time, number of enumerations, and backtracks

N	20			50			100			150			200		
	t	e	b	t	e	b	t	e	b	t	e	b	t	e	b
$S_{\downarrow\downarrow}$	3	76	60	32	1065	1021	14	137	41	31801	638714	638564	13955	293851	293662
$S_{\downarrow\updownarrow}$	2	41	27	4	56	11	13	110	13	49	152	7	69	207	9
$S_{\downarrow\uparrow}$	2	76	60	31	1065	1021	13	137	41	28719	638714	638564	12196	293851	293662
$S_{\updownarrow\downarrow}$	5	75	59	176	2165	2120	–	–	–	–	–	–	–	–	–
$S_{\updownarrow\updownarrow}$	105	1847	1827	–	–	–	–	–	–	622	4952	4815	–	–	–
$S_{\updownarrow\uparrow}$	6	75	59	167	2165	2120	–	–	–	–	–	–	–	–	–
$S_{\uparrow\downarrow}$	30387	650752	650717	–	–	–	–	–	–	–	–	–	–	–	–
$S_{\uparrow\updownarrow}$	12221	252979	252952	–	–	–	–	–	–	–	–	–	–	–	–
$S_{\uparrow\uparrow}$	30455	650717	650752	–	–	–	–	–	–	–	–	–	–	–	–

is (one of) the best for all problems. The issue is thus to select a variable, and then to decide how to split its domain.

To illustrate the importance of split strategies, we solved some instances of the N-Queens problem with 9 strategies[1] using the system Oz[2]. In Table 1 each cell contains 3 numbers: t, e, b. t is the CPU time in ms. Solvers that do not find a solution before the timeout of 200 s. are stopped ("-"). e is the total number of enumerations, from which many were not worth, i.e., backtracks (b). The first 3 strategies appear to be better suited for this class of problems. For a given N, and a timeout of 200 s. the ratio of time between the best and the worst solvers finding a solution can be 10^4. Considering the 20-queen problem, whereas the fastest solver achieved 41 enumerations and 27 backtracks, the worst one finding a solution required more than 6.10^5 enumerations and 6.10^5 backtracks. Again we have a ratio of more than 10^4. The time and operations ratios are even bigger when pushing up or removing the timeout.

Figure 1 shows 3 search trees for the resolution of the 10-queen problem with 3 different strategies. The first strategy ($S_{\downarrow\updownarrow}$) directly goes to a solution (6 enumerations, no backtrack). The second one ($S_{\downarrow\uparrow}$), after a bad choice for the second enumeration (generating 17 backtracks), finally goes directly to a solution. The last strategy ($S_{\uparrow\uparrow}$) performs numerous wrong choices (807 backtracks) before reaching a solution.

Obviously strategies have drastically different efficiencies, and thus it is crucial to select a good one that unfortunately cannot be predicted in the general case. We are interested in observing strategies during resolution in order to detect bad strategies and replace them by better ones. We are thus concerned with dynamic and adaptive meta-strategies: our solver uses a single strategy at a time; but when a strategy is judged to have a poor behaviour, it is replaced by another one in order to explore differently the search tree. When this is not

---

[1] The 9 enumeration strategies are the combination of 3 variable selection strategies – the variable with minimum domain (denoted $\downarrow$), with the largest domain ($\uparrow$), and with an average domain ($\updownarrow$)– and three value selection strategies – the smallest value of the domain (denoted $\downarrow$), the largest one ($\uparrow$), the middle one (denoted $\updownarrow$)–. For example, the solver which always uses the strategy that selects the variable with the largest domain and the smallest value of its domain is thus denoted $S_{\uparrow\downarrow}$.

[2] http://www.mozart-oz.org

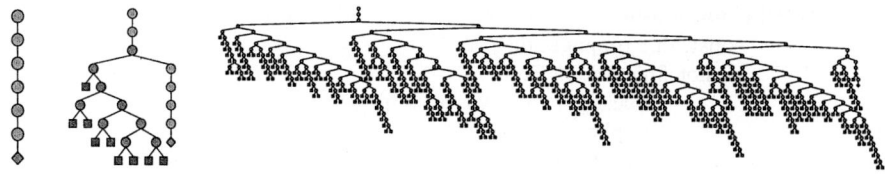

Fig. 1. 10-Queens solved with 3 strategies: $S_{\downarrow\uparrow}$, $S_{\downarrow\uparrow}$, and $S_{\uparrow\uparrow}$

sufficient anymore because of some previous bad choices, we operate some meta-backtracks (backtrack of several levels) in the search tree. Although observing resolution and storing states for meta-backtracks is an overhead, this is negligible compared to the significant differences between strategies.

3 The Dynamic Strategy Framework

Our framework for dynamic strategies is based on 4 components that communicate and exchange information. The first component runs resolution, the second one observes resolution and takes snapshots, the third one analysis snapshots and draws some indicators about strategy quality, and the fourth one makes decisions and updates strategy priorities or requests some meta-backtrack. Each component is exchangeable, and thus, for example, we can think of several components that make different decisions with the same analysis. This approach is based on two key features: change of split strategy when a strategy behaves badly and when we guess another one could do better continuing deeper in the search tree, and meta-backtracks when a change of strategies is not enough because wrong choices were made and we guess no strategy will be able to repair this.

3.1 The SOLVE Component

This component solves CSPs by running a generic solving algorithm which alternates constraint propagation with split phases. The sketch of our SOLVE algorithm (Figure 2) is simple and close to the one of [1]).

SOLVE applies a meta-strategy of splitting which consists of a sequence of several basic split strategies: only one strategy is used at a time, but it can be replaced during resolution. To this end, SOLVE has a set of split strategies, each one characterised by a priority that evolves during computation: the other components evaluate strategies and update their priorities. SOLVE is also able to perform meta-backtracks (jump back of a sequence of several splits and propagation phases) in order to repair a "desperate" state of resolution, i.e., when changing strategies is not sufficient because of several very bad prior choices.

The **constraint propagation** function carries out domain reduction applying local consistency verification (such as arc or path consistency [14]) following a given strategy (e.g., forward checking, or look ahead [13]).

A basic splitting strategy aims at splitting a CSP $\mathcal{P}$ into two or more CSPs $\mathcal{P}_i$, such that the union of solutions of the $\mathcal{P}_i$ is equal to the solutions of $\mathcal{P}$

```
WHILE not finished
        constraint propagation
        IF not finished THEN
                select a split w.r.t. the priorities
                split
                proceed by case
        END
END
```
Fig. 2. The SOLVE algorithm

(preserve solutions). Each $\mathcal{P}_i$ differs from $\mathcal{P}$ in that the split domain is replaced by a smaller domain. The two main classes of split strategies are segmentation (split a domain into two or more subdomains), and enumeration (split a domain into one value and the rest of the domain). For example, considering a CSP $\mathcal{P}$ with the variable $x \in D$, an enumeration step on variable x will produce 2 sub-CSPs: $\mathcal{P}_1$ in which $x \in D$ is replaced by $x = v$, v being a value of D; and $\mathcal{P}_2$ in which $x \in D$ is replaced by $x \in D \setminus \{v\}$.

The SOLVE component has a set Σ of basic split strategies such as bisection, enumeration, or shaving. Each strategy $\sigma_i \in \Sigma$ is given a priority p_i that evolves during computation. These priorities can be fair, but can also favour some split strategies (e.g., a higher priority can be given to a strategy known as well suited for the given problem). The **select split** function creates our meta-strategy: at each enumeration it selects the currently best split strategy of Σ with respect to the priorities p_i attached to the σ_i; our meta-strategy is thus a sequence of basic strategies. The **split** function is the application of the selected strategy.

SOLVE also manages exploration of the search space, stored as a search tree: nodes are CSPs reduced by propagation; the root node is the initial CSP; a node is split in some child nodes by split; leaves represent either a solution of the CSP or a failure. **Proceed by case** is a function that manages the choice points created by split: it may define searches such as depth first, or breadth first.

Proceed by case also manages **meta-backtracks**. A meta-backtrack jumps back to a snapshot. Each time a snapshot is taken by the OBSERVE component, the SOLVE component records the search tree and the priorities in a heap of contexts. When the UPDATE component requests one meta-backtrack (meta-bk(1)), the SOLVE component restores the state of the last snapshot: it removes the top of the heap of contexts; it replaces the search tree by the one that was recorded, and restores the priorities; finally it updates the priorities by giving to the strategy that was working at the time of the snapshot a priority smaller than the smallest current priorities (to be sure to use another strategy). A meta-backtrack of several levels (meta-bk(n)) consists in removing $n - 1$ snapshots from the heap of context, and then to perform a meta-backtrack (meta-bk(1)). In order to obtain a complete solver, the meta-backtrack feature is deactivated when the last strategy is tried at the root node of the search tree: meta-bk requests won't be executed anymore.

The Boolean **finished** indicates that resolution is completed (e.g., one, all, or optimal solution or inconsistency).

3.2 The OBSERVATION Component

This component aims at observing and recording some information of the current search tree, i.e., it spies the resolution process of the SOLVE component. These observations (called **snapshots**) are not performed continuously, and they can be seen as an abstraction of the resolution state at a time t. Taking a snapshot consists in extracting (since search trees are too large) and recording some information from a resolution state. Thus, two main issues are important: when to take snapshots, and which information to record.

Snapshots can be taken regularly, such as every n ms, or every m loops of the SOLVE algorithm. But snapshots can also be taken when some events happen, such as a variable was fixed, the search space was reduced of x %.

The recorded information aims at reflecting resolution: it will be analysed, and used to update priorities of strategies. It will thus depend on the computation domain, the split strategies, and the analysis capacities. Snapshots can mainly contain 3 types of information: characteristics of the CSP (e.g., hard variables of the problem, linear constraints, or occurrences of variables), measures of the search tree (e.g., current depth, maximal depth, fixed variables, or size of the current search space), properties of the computation (e.g., CPU time of a propagation phase or which operators were used).

3.3 The ANALYSE Component

This component analyses the snapshots taken by the OBSERVATION: it evaluates the different strategies, and provides **indicators** to the UPDATE component. Indicators can be Boolean or numeric values (δb and δn respectively). They can be extracted, computed, or deduced from one or several snapshots.

Numeric indicators are results of quantitative computations of measures recorded in snapshots. Simple indicators are the depth of the search (δn_{depth}), the number of fixed variables (δn_{fix}), or fixed by enumeration (δn_{fixen}), or the average size of domains (δn_{davg}). More complex indicators can be the difference of depth between 2 snapshots: this gives information on the evolution of the search tree (if large, a good progress was done, if small the search can be stuck at a level). The difference between the depth (δn_{depth}) of the search and the variables fixed by enumeration (δn_{fixen}) gives an indicator (δn_{yup}) of how many unsuccessful enumerations were performed on the last variable.

Boolean indicators reflect properties. Simple ones can be related to CSPs (e.g., there is a univariate constraint or a hard variable was fixed). More complex properties can be related to a quantitative analysis of the snapshots. For example, consider n consecutive snapshots such that the number of instantiated variables oscillate with a small amplitude. We can deduce that the SOLVE component alternates enumerations and backtracks on several variables, without succeeding in having a strong orientation (e.g., going deeper in the search tree or performing a significant backtracking phase): this is a thrashing type behaviour. We call this indicator δb_{osc} and set it to true in this case. We show in the next section how to interpret this information.

3.4 The UPDATE Component

The UPDATE component makes decisions using the indicators computed by ANALYSE: it makes interpretations of the indicators, and then updates the split priorities and requests some meta-backtracks in the SOLVE component. The knowledge of the UPDATE component is contained in a set of rules. The head of such a rule is a conjunction of conditions on the indicators (disjunctions can be handled by several rules). There are two types of rules: for priority update rules (⇒rules), the body is a conjunction of updates of strategies priorities:

$$\bigwedge_{i=1}^{l} (\sum_{j \in J_i} \omega_j \times \delta n_j) \; op \; c_j \; \wedge \; \bigwedge_{i=1}^{k} \delta b_i \quad \Rightarrow \quad \bigwedge_{i=1}^{l} p_i = p_i + f_i(\delta n_1, \ldots, \delta n_i)$$

where:

- the ω_j are the weights of each numeric indicator δn_j in the condition, the c_j are constants, the J_i are subsets of all the indicators, and $op \in \{\leq, \geq, =\}$;
- the δb_i are some Boolean indicators;
- the f_i are functions over the indicators that returns real numbers to increase or decrease the priority p_i of the strategy i;
- and the $\bigwedge_{i=1}^{l}$ in the body of the rule is an abuse of language that means the the l priorities can be updated.

whereas for meta-backtrack rules (→rules) the body requests n meta-backtracks:

$$\bigwedge_{i=1}^{l} (\sum_{j \in J_i} \omega_j \times \delta n_j) \; op \; c_j \; \wedge \; \bigwedge_{i=1}^{k} \delta b_i \quad \rightarrow \quad meta - bk(g(\delta n_1, \ldots, \delta n_i))$$

where g is a function over the indicators that returns an integer, i.e., the number of meta-backtrack that should be performed.

When the head of a rule is fulfilled (i.e., conditions are verified), its body is executed: for ⇒rules, the priorities of the strategies are updated in the SOLVE component. Whereas for →rules, n meta-backtracks as requested in the SOLVE component. Note that conditions of →rules must be stronger than the ones of ⇒rules to first try changing strategies before making a meta-backtrack.

We now continue with the oscillating case showed before. Consider that we have the indicators δb_{osc}, δn_{fix}, and δn_{tot} (the total number of variables). We can imagine two ⇒rules for updating the priority p of the running strategy:

$$R_1: \quad \delta n_{fixed} * 100/\delta n_{tot} \leq 5 \wedge \delta b_{osc} \quad \Rightarrow \quad p = p + 0.2$$
$$R_2: \quad 30 \leq \delta n_{fixed} * 100/\delta n_{tot} \leq 70 \wedge \delta b_{osc} \quad \Rightarrow \quad p = p - 0.5$$

For R_1, the condition means that the oscillation happens close to the root of the search tree (less than 5% of variables are fixed). This is interpreted as a phase of efficient pruning of the tree, and thus, the priority of the current strategy is increased to let it carry in the pruning. In R_2, the oscillation is close to the middle of the tree. This is judged as a bad case (i.e., a thrashing type) and the priority of the running strategy is lowered in order to replace it.

R_3 considers that performing more than m (m being 15% of the average size of domains) successive enumerations on the same variable is a problem that was caused by an earlier wrong choice. Thus, 2 meta backtracks are requested:

$$R_3: \quad \delta n_{gap} \geq 15 * \delta n_{davg}/100 \quad \rightarrow \quad meta - bk(2)$$

These 3 rules are based on some interpretations of the indicators. Other interpretations (maybe opposite) and rules could have been designed.

4 A Practical Approach

We now use a simplification and adaptation of our generic approach for finite domain CSP. Our prototype implementation in Oz uses processes for components and a mechanism of query/answer between the processes. For future extensions and modifications, we did not try to optimise performances of our system: we copy and store numerous contexts to track and trace resolution.

We fix the **constraint propagation** process: arc consistency [14] computation (with dedicated algorithms for global constraints) with a look ahead strategy [13]. The **proceed by case** is a depth first left first exploration of the search tree: this procedure selects the left hand side child node, i.e., the one that assigns a value to the enumerated variable.

For our first attempts, we consider only **9 basic enumeration strategies** that are the combination of 3 variable selection strategies –the variable with minimum domain (denoted $\downarrow$), with the largest domain ($\uparrow$), and with an average domain ($\updownarrow$)– and three value selections –the smallest value of the domain ($\downarrow$), the largest one ($\uparrow$), the middle one ($\updownarrow$)–. The strategy that selects the variable with the largest domain and the smallest value of its domain is thus denoted $\uparrow\downarrow$. The solver which always uses this strategy is denoted by $S_{\uparrow\downarrow}$. These strategies are rather common (and more especially the ones based on minimum domain selection) and are not problem specific. Strategies based on largest domain selection are usually inefficient. As expected, the experiments show that our meta-strategy quickly change these enumeration strategies. Our dynamic solvers that can change strategies and perform meta-backtracks is denoted by S_{Dyn}.

The **snapshots** are taken each n ms, n being a parameter. The snapshots focus on the search tree, and several snapshots will allow to draw some indicators on the resolution progress. Here are some of the data contained in a snapshot:

- $Maxd$: the maximum depth reached in the search tree,
- d: the depth of the current node,
- s: the size of the current search space,
- f, f': the percentage of variables fixed by enumeration (respectively by enumeration or propagation),
- v, vf, vfe: the number of variables, the number of fixed variables, the number of variables fixed by enumeration.

The **indicators** we consider reflect the resolution progress. Here are some of the indicators of our set $\mathcal{I}$ of indicators computed in the ANALYSE component. F is the last taken snapshot, and F^- the previous one:

- $\delta n_1 = Maxd_F - Maxd_{F^-}$ represents a variation of the maximum depth,
- $\delta n_2 = d_F - d_{F^-}$: if positive, the current node is deeper than the one explored at the previous snapshot,
- $\delta n_3 = 100 * (s_{F^-} - s_F)/s_{F^-}$: a percentage of reduction since F^-; if positive, the current search space is smaller than at snapshot F^-,
- $\delta n_4 = f'_F - f'_{F^-}$ (respectively $\delta n_5 = f_F - f_{F^-}$): if positive, reflects an improvement in the degree of resolution (resp. resolution made by enumeration),
- $\delta n_6 = d_{F^-} - vfe'_{F^-}$: the δn_{gap} indicator described in Section 3.3.

The schema of $\Rightarrow$**rules** and $\rightarrow$**rules** we use for updating priorities and requesting meta-backtracks is rather simple:

$$r_1 : \sum_{i \in \mathcal{I}} w_i * \delta n_i \geq c_1 \Rightarrow p = p + f_1(\mathcal{I})$$
$$r_2 : \sum_{i \in \mathcal{I}} w'_i * \delta n_i \leq c_2 \Rightarrow p = p - f_2(\mathcal{I})$$
$$r_3 : \sum_{i \in \mathcal{I}} w''_i * \delta n_i \leq g_3(\mathcal{I}) \rightarrow meta - bk(f_3(\mathcal{I}))$$

where

- p is the priority of the currently used strategy,
- w_i, w'_i and w''_i are weights used to (dis)favour some indicators,
- f_1, f_2, and f_3 are functions of the indicators that return a positive number. f_1 is the reward and f_2 is the penalty for priorities, whereas f_3 is the number of meta-backtracks,
- c_1 and c_2 are constants that present thresholds ($c_2 < c_1$).

Rule r_1 "rewards" the current strategy when it obtained a score over a given threshold, i.e., it performed well w.r.t. to our criteria. The reward is to give it a higher priority to run for more time. Rule r_2 penalises the running strategy when it is judged inefficient: the priority is decreased. A strategy obtaining a penalty may remain the one with the best priority if it worked efficiently (during several snapshots) before. Rule r_3 requests $f_3(\mathcal{I})$ meta-backtracks when the state of search is judged inadequate for quickly finding a solution: some (not all) of the previous choices will be undone.

5 Experimental Results

Here, we are interested in quickly finding the first solution. Solvers and strategies are named as above. The timeout is set to 200s. Snapshots are taken every 80 ms. We do not use all the data contained in the snapshots, but only the data described in the previous section. This also holds for the indicators.

Each strategy has a priority of 1 at the beginning. The instantiations of the rules used to draw the tables are:

$$r_1 : \sum_{i=1}^{5} \delta n_i \geq 10 \Rightarrow p = p + 1$$
$$r_2 : \sum_{i=1}^{5} \delta n_i \leq 0 \Rightarrow p = p - 3$$
$$r_3 : \delta n_6 > 4 \rightarrow meta - bk(10 * \delta n_v / 100)$$

Table 2. N-Queens: CPU time in ms, enumerations, backtracks, meta-backtracks

queens	20				50				100				200			
	t	e	b	B	t	e	b	B	t	e	b	B	t	e	b	B
$S_{\downarrow\downarrow}$	3	76	60		32	1065	1021		14	137	41		13955	293851	293662	
$S_{\downarrow\uparrow}$	2	41	27		4	56	11		13	110	13		69	207	9	
$S_{\downarrow\updownarrow}$	2	76	60		31	1065	1021		13	137	41		12196	293851	293662	
$S_{\uparrow\downarrow}$	5	75	59		176	2165	2120		−	−	−		−	−	−	
$S_{\uparrow\uparrow}$	105	1847	1827		−	−	−		−	−	−		−	−	−	
$S_{\uparrow\updownarrow}$	6	75	59		167	2165	2120		−	−	−		−	−	−	
$S_{\updownarrow\downarrow}$	30387	650752	650717		−	−	−		−	−	−		−	−	−	
$S_{\updownarrow\uparrow}$	12221	252979	252952		−	−	−		−	−	−		−	−	−	
$S_{\updownarrow\updownarrow}$	30455	650717	650752		−	−	−		−	−	−		−	−	−	
S_{**Av}	8131	172960	172946		82	1303	1259		13	128	32		8740	195969	195777	
S_{**out}	0%				44%				66%				66%			
$S_{DynAv\sim}$	120	862	819	1	534	1753	1498	4	1285	1466	1009	4	5291	1594	819	4
$S_{DynB\sim}$	5	41	27	0	21	56	11	0	126	110	13	0	859	207	9	0
$S_{DynW\sim}$	381	2631	2529	4	1203	4137	3637	9	5502	6828	5322	16	16351	5410	3579	12
$S_{Dyn\sim out}$	0%				0%				0%				6%			

r_1 and r_2 only use the first 5 indicators, with weights of 1. The reward is less than the penalty to quickly replace a bad strategy. r_3 requests n meta-backtracks, n being 10% of the number of variables. These parameters were experimentally fixed using a set of problems and they were not fine tuned especially for the n-queen problem that we treat below. However, some more studies (and/or learning) should be made to obtain a more representative set of problems.

Our solver $S_{Dyn\sim}$ uses the following dynamic meta-strategy: if the running strategy still has the best priority, do not replace it; else, choose the strategy with the best priority; if several strategies have the same priority, randomly choose one. Each time, we perform 50 runs since randomisation is used for selecting the first strategy and also for tie breaking. Tests were run on an Athlon XP 2200+ with RAM 224 MB of memory. Table 2 illustrates resolution of some N-Queen problem instances using the 9 solvers with fixed strategy, and our solver $S_{Dyn\sim}$. Each cell is composed of the CPU time in ms (t), the number of enumerations (e), the number of backtracks (b), and the number of meta-backtracks (B) (only for $S_{Dyn\sim}$ runs). The line $S_{Dyn\sim out}$ (resp. S_{**out}) represents the percentage of timeouts (200 s.) of our dynamic solver (resp. of the fixed strategy solvers). $S_{DynAv\sim}$ represents the average of the runs of $S_{Dyn\sim}$, $S_{DynW\sim}$ the worst run that do not reach the timeout, and $S_{DynB\sim}$ the best run. The line S_{**Av} is the average run of the 9 solvers with fixed strategies. Only runs that do not reached the timeout are used for S_{**Av} and $S_{DynAv\sim}$.

The first remark is that our meta-strategy significantly improves the percentage of resolution: we obtain about 0% of timeouts for 50 to 200 queens whereas about 50% of the solvers with fixed strategy could not find a solution before the timeout. Note that pushing the timeout to 600s does not change the percentage of timeouts of the solver with fixed strategy. Comparing the average solving times. For 20 queens $S_{Dyn\sim}$ is 80 times faster, but for 100-queens we cannot say anything since we do not have any timeout whereas the fixed strategies generated 66% of timeouts, and the timeouts are not considered for the average.

The best runs of $S_{Dyn\sim}$ are exactly the same as the best fixed strategies (except that the CPU time is greater): this means that our dynamic framework

Table 3. 200-Queens: sequences of strategies in various runs of S_{Dyn}

strategy	↓↓	↓↕	↓↑	↕↓	↕↕	↕↑	↑↓	↑↕	↑↑
$S_{DynAv\sim}$	212	199	291	79	83	67	94	57	75
$S_{DynB\sim}$	0	201	0	0	0	0	0	0	0
$S_{DynW\sim}$	504	627	1221	367	351	128	162	56	134

do not penalise a good strategy. We can also see the overhead of our technique on the best runs: we are a bit less than 10 times slower. However, we can significantly reduce the overhead by only recording and analysing information that we effectively use in the update. Moreover, we store a lot of contexts that are not necessary to our technique, but that we use for some further observations.

The number of meta-backtracks is very small compared to the number of backtracks: they are really used when no strategy behave well to restore a better search tree. However, the meta-backtracks are efficient: without them, we do not improve the number of timeouts in all cases.

Table 3 shows how many sequences a basic strategy was used in the meta-strategy of $S_{Dyn\sim}$ to solve the 200-Queens problem. A sequence is defined between two snapshots: thus, 1 means that the strategy was used during 80 ms, and was certainly applied several times. For the best run, only the strategy ↓↕ was applied. As seen before, this strategy is the best for 200 queens with a static strategy. Our analyse always judged it well, and thus, when starting computation with it, it is not replaced in the dynamic strategy. For the worst case, many changes of strategies happened. The computation started badly, and $S_{Dyn\sim}$ encountered problems to get a strategy that could perform well on the remaining problem. In this case, we had a slow repair of the strategy and meta-backtracks. Although the efficiency was not very good, $S_{Dyn\sim}$ could compute a solution before the timeout, whereas the solver continuing with the same "bad" fixed strategy reached the timeout without a solution.

Using the same parameters and rules, similar results were obtained for the magic square problem and the Latin square problem instances. The improvement in term of timeouts is similar (e.g., for magic squares of size 5 from 44% to 0% using $S_{Dyn\sim}$, and for Latin squares of size 25 from 66% to 28%). An interesting point is that for computing a first solution to the magic square of size 4, $S_{Dyn\sim}$ was able to find a shorter branch than the best strategy: 29 enumerations and no meta-backtrack compared to 39 enumerations for $S_{↑↓}$. However, due to the overhead, this run was not faster. It is also worth noting that for magic and Latin squares, there is not a strategy which is the best for all instances: this varies among 5 strategies ($S_{↓↓}$, $S_{↓↕}$, $S_{↓↑}$, $S_{↕↓}$, and surprisingly $S_{↑↑}$).

6 Conclusion, Discussion, and Future Work

We have presented a framework for automated selection of split strategy for constraint solving. Based on strategy performances, our dynamic approach is able to detect bad cases to replace strategies. When the context is judged very bad, meta-backtracks erase prior bad choices. The first experimental results obtained with our prototype implementation are more than encouraging and promising: they show we can get good performances without a priori choices.

Compared to [11,12] our randomisation concerns the selection of a strategy (to break tie when several strategies have the same priority) and not the choice made by a strategy. Moreover, we consider several strategies and not only one. In [3,4] the meta-strategy is a sequence (chain) of solvers: when one solver behaves badly, the next one is used. Our strategy selection is finer thanks to priorities. Moreover, a strategy that was judged badly at a given stage can be re-used later. In both [11] and [3], when the resolution process is performing badly a complete restart (jump to the root of the search tree) is done: the same algorithm is restarted with a new random seed in [11], and the next algorithm of the chain is applied on the initial problem in [3]. With our framework we try to save and capitalise the work already done: we first try to change strategies to carry on from the node that was reached; when this is not sufficient we perform a meta-backtrack to a higher node in the tree, but not necessarily to the root of the tree. In [11] the problems on which their method should work is characterised by the notion of "heavy tail" phenomena. We do not have yet such a characterisation.

The "parameters" of our framework (observations, indicators, ⇒ and →rules, snapshot frequency, ...) are crucial, thus we plan to integrate some learning in order to detect relevant "parameters" and how to tune them. Concerning solver selection some work could be done in order, for example, to fix priorities for some well-known cases where the solver sequence can be established a priori.

We plan to extend our work to constraint propagation, i.e., dynamically changing the local consistency, and the reduction strategy such as in [8,17]. We have limited our analysis to past events, but, it could be interesting to observe what remains to be solved as well. It should be interesting to integrate the notion of intelligent backtracking for our meta-backtrack [5]. Finally, we are also interested in using this framework for developing hybrid solvers based on constraint programming, local search, and genetic algorithms. Our framework seems to be well suited for hybrid solvers based on Chaotic Iterations [16].

References

1. K. R. Apt. *Principles of Constraint Programming*. Cambridge Univ. Press, 2003.
2. J. C. Beck, P. Prosser, and R. Wallace. Variable Ordering Heuristics Show Promise. In *Proceedings of the International Conference on Principles and Practice of Constraint Programming, CP'2004*, volume 3258 of *Lecture Notes in Computer Science*, pages 711–715, 2004.
3. J. Borrett, E. Tsang, and N. Walsh. Adaptive constraint satisfaction. In *15th UK Planning and Scheduling Special Interest Group Workshop*, Liverpool, 1996.
4. J. E. Borrett, E. P. K. Tsang, and N. R. Walsh. Adaptive constraint satisfaction: The quickest first principle. In *Proceedings of 12th European Conference on Artificial Intelligence, ECAI'1996*, pages 160–164. John Wiley and Sons, 1996.
5. M. Bruynooghe. Intelligent Backtracking Revisited. In J.-L. Lassez and G. Plotkin, editors, *Computational Logic, Essays in Honor of Alan Robinson*. MIT Press, 1991.

6. T. Carchrae and J. C. Beck. Low-Knowledge Algorithm Control. In *Proceedings of the National Conference on Artificial Intelligence, AAAI 2004*, pages 49–54, 2004.
7. Y. Caseau and F. Laburthe. Improved clp scheduling with task intervals. In *Proceedings of the International Conference on Logic Programming, ICLP'1994*, pages 369–383. MIT Press, 1994.
8. H. El Sakkout, M. Wallace, and B. Richards. An instance of adaptive constraint propagation. In *Proceedings of the Int. Conference on Principles and Practice of Constraint Programming, CP'96*, volume 1118 of *Lecture Notes in Computer Science*, pages 164–178. Springer, 1996.
9. P. Flener, B. Hnich, and Z. Kiziltan. A meta-heuristic for subset problems. In *Proceedings of Practical Aspects of Declarative Languages, PADL'2001*, volume 1990 of *Lecture Notes in Computer Science*, pages 274–287. Springer, 2001.
10. C. Gebruers, A. Guerri, B. Hnich, and M. Milano. Making choices using structure at the instance level within a case based reasoning framework. In *Proceedings of CPAIOR'2004*, volume 3011 of *Lecture Notes in Computer Science*, pages 380–386. Springer, 2004.
11. C. Gomes, B. Selman, and H. Kautz. Boosting combinatorial search through randomization. In *Proceedings of AAAI'98*, pages 431–437, Madison, Wisconsin, 1998.
12. H. Kautz, E. Horvitz, Y. Ruan, C. Gomes, and B. Selman. Boosting combinatorial search through randomization. In *Proceedings of AAAI'2002*, pages 674–682, 2002.
13. V. Kumar. Algorithms for Constraint-Satisfaction Problems: A Survey. *Artificial Intelligence Magazine*, 13(1):32–44, Spring 1992.
14. A. K. Mackworth. Consistency in Networks of Relations. *AI*, 8:99–118, 1977.
15. E. Monfroy and C. Castro. A Component Language for Hybrid Solver Cooperations. In *Proceedings of ADVIS*, volume 3261 of *Lecture Notes in Computer Science*, pages 192–202, 2004.
16. E. Monfroy, F. Saubion, and T. Lambert. On hybridization of local search and constraint propagation. In *Proceedings of the Int. Conference on Logic Programming, ICLP 2004*, volume 3132 of *Lecture Notes in Computer Science*, pages 299–313, 2004.
17. C. Schulte and P. J. Stuckey. Speeding up constraint propagation. In *Proceedings of International Conference on Principles and Practice of Constraint Programming, CP'2004*, volume 3258 of *Lecture Notes in Computer Science*, pages 619–633, 2004.

Applying Constraint Logic Programming to Predicate Abstraction of RTL Verilog Descriptions[*]

Tun Li, Yang Guo, SiKun Li, and Dan Zhu

National University of Defense Technology, 410073 ChangSha, HuNan, China
tunli@nudt.edu.cn

Abstract. A major technique to address state explosion problem in model checking is abstraction. Predicate abstraction has been applied successfully to large software and now to hardware descriptions, such as Verilog. This paper evaluates the state-of-the-art AI techniques—constraint logic programming (CLP)—to improve the performance of predication abstraction of hardware designs, and compared it with the SAT-based predicate abstraction techniques. With CLP based techniques, we can model various constraints, such as bit, bit-vector and integer, in a uniform framework; we can also model the word-level constraints without flatting them into bit-level constraints as SAT-based method does. With these advantages, the computation of abstraction system can be more efficient than SAT-based techniques. We have implemented this method, and the experimental results have shown the promising improvements on the performance of predicate abstraction of hardware designs.

1 Introduction

Formal verification techniques are widely applied in the hardware design industry. Among the techniques, model checking [1] is the widely used one. However, model checking suffers from state explosion problem. Therefore, abstraction techniques, which can reduce the state space, have become one of the most important techniques for successfully applying formal methods in software and hardware verification. Abstraction techniques reduce the state space by mapping the set of states of the actual, concrete system to an abstract, and smaller, set of states in a way that preserves the relevant behaviors of the system. In the software domain, the most successful abstraction technique for large systems is predicate abstraction [2]. In the hardware domain, the mostly used localization reduction is a special case of predicate abstraction.

Traditionally, predicate abstraction is computed using a theorem prover such as Simplify [3] or Zapato [4]. The typical techniques and applications can be found in [2, 5, 6, 7], and there are some typical tools such as SLAM [8], BLAST [9] and Magic [10]. In hardware domain, the SAT based abstraction method is first proposed in [11]. Then, [12] proposed SAT-based predicate abstraction techniques, and applied it to the verification of ANSI-C programs. The main idea is to form a SAT equation containing all the predicates, a basic block, and two symbolic variables for each predicate,

---

[*] This work is supported by the National Science Foundation of China (NSFC) under grant No. 60403048 and 60573173.

one variable for the state before the execution of the basic block, and one variable for the state after its execution. The SAT solver is then used to obtain all satisfiable assignments in terms of the symbolic variables. In [13], the method has been applied for word-level predicate abstraction and verifying RTL Verilog.The technique has also been applied to SpecC [14], which is a concurrent version of ANSI-C used for hardware design.

However, there are some limitations when using theorem prover and SAT for predicate abstraction. Firstly, theorem prover based method has to call the theorem prover many times during abstraction, which will make the abstraction process inefficient. Secondly, theorem provers model the variables using unbounded integer numbers. Overflow or bit-wise operators are not modeled. However, hardware description languages like Verilog provide an extensive set of bit-wise operators. Thirdly, although SAT based method can only call the SAT solver one time during abstraction, it has to flatten the word-level constraints into bit-level constraints to model word-level variables and operations, which will lose most word-level information and the runtime of this process typically grows exponentially in the number of predicates.

In this paper, following the work of [13], we focus on applying constraint logic programming (CLP) [15] to predication abstraction of RTL Verilog descriptions, especially using CLP to solving the abstraction computation constraints obtained from circuit model and predicates. First, we build the formal model of the circuit using decision diagrams (DD) models [16] extracted from Verilog descriptions. Then following the method proposed in [13], we convert the abstraction computation formula into CLP constrains and apply CLP solver to solve them.

The advantage of CLP-based method is: Firstly, it can model bit, bit-vector and bounded integer in a uniform framework, and can support various arithmetic and logic operations. Secondly, the word-level constraints are solved with word-level information and without flattening them into bit-level constraints. With these advantages, we can compute the abstraction model of concrete RTL Verilog designs very quickly. Experimental results have shown that the runtime of abstraction process grows linearly in the number of predicates. Finally, CLP combines the expressiveness of logic programming and the constraints solving techniques. Our method bridges the gap between EDA researches and the research progress in constraint satisfaction problem and artificial intelligence area.

The rest of the paper is organized as follows. In section 2, we formalize the semantics of the subset of Verilog that we handle and introduce how to model Verilog descriptions using DD models. Techniques for building formal models from DD model for Verilog descriptions are described in Section 3. In Section 4, we briefly introduce predicate abstraction method with the help of an example. Techniques for translating word-level abstraction constraints into CLP constraints are given in Section 5. We report experimental results in section 6. Finally, we conclude the paper in section 7.

2 Verilog Modeling

The Verilog subset supported in this paper is the same as that used in [13]: synthesizable Verilog with one single clock *clk*. We assume the clock is only used within either *posedge* or *negedge* event guards, but not both. We also assume that every variable is assigned values only at one place in the description.

Applying CLP to Predicate Abstraction of RTL Verilog Descriptions

```
Module main(clk);
input clk;
reg [7:0] x, y;

initial x = 1;
initial y = 0;

always @ (posedge clk) begin
   y <= x;
   if (x < 100) x <= y + x;
end

endmodule
```

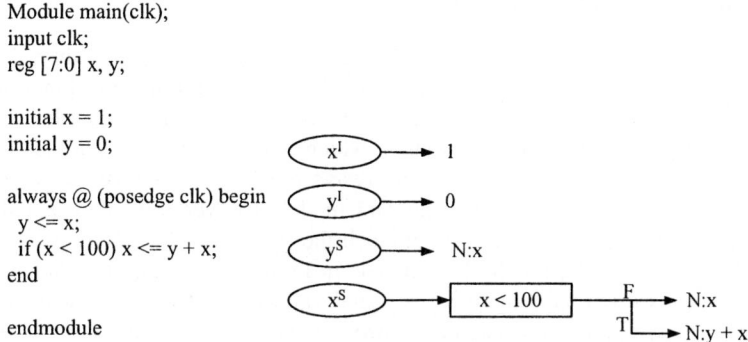

Fig. 1. Verilog example and the corresponding DD models

According to the definitions of DD model [16], we can build DD model for each variable or signal in the designs. The root node of the DD model is the variable or signal it is built for, while the terminal nodes are the expressions assigned to the variable or signal. The non-terminal nodes are the control conditions and statements that guard these assignments, which include *if*, *case* and *loop* statements, *etc*. For our convenience, we do some preprocessing before building DD model, such as translating *case* statement into a series of *if...else* statements.

Figure 1 gives a Verilog design example which was cited from [13], and the corresponding DD models for the variables used in it. The example and the DD models will be used in the follows descriptions. In the DD models shown in Figure 1, the ellipse nodes correspond to the assignment statements in the Verilog description, the rectangle nodes correspond to the condition statements, and the most-left circle node is the root of the DD model. Readers can refer to [17] for the detailed algorithm for extraction of DD model from Verilog description.

3 Formal Semantics of Verilog

We use the following formalism to model the concrete circuit: A transition system $T = (S, I, R)$ consists of a set of states S, a set of initial states $I \subseteq S$, and a transition relation R, which relates a current state $s \in S$ to a next-state $s' \in S$.

For different Verilog language constructions, we can build the formal model using different methods based on the corresponding DD models.

3.1 Continuous Assignment

The variable of *wire* type in Verilog can only be assigned by only one continuous assignment. Let w_i be the wire that is assigned by the i-th continuous assignment, and e_i the value that is assigned. If A denotes the semantics of continuous assignment, we have $A := \bigwedge_i w_i = e_i$. The formula can be obtained by traversal the DD model for w_i.

3.2 Initial and Always Statements

The statements in the *initial* blocks define the initial values of states, while the statements in the clock events guarded *always* blocks define the transition function (next state function) of the states. For the *always* blocks that do not be guarded by clock events, they define combinational circuits, which will not generate state latches. We can examine the trigger events for each always block to distinguish sequential and combinational logics. When extracting DD models for variables and signals from RTL Verilog descriptions, we can distinguish the two cases by attaching tags on the root nodes. For example, for the DD models in Figure 1, the tag "I" attached to the root node means that this assignment is initial values, while tag "S" means that this assignment is in clock event guarded *always* block. Similarly, the tag "C" not appeared in the example means assignment in combinational *always* block.

3.3 Finite State Machines Representation

The notion we used here is mainly cited from [13] with minor modification. Let V denote the set of variables, as given in the Verilog file. Let $L \subseteq R$ denote the set of state variables. The set of states S of the state machine is then defined to be: $S := \{0,1\}^{|L|}$. For a state $s \in S$, we denote the value of an expression e in that particular state by $s(e)$. The set of variables that are not state variables is denoted by C: $C := V - L$.

We define the notion of a process state to define the semantics of the statements in the *initial* and *always* blocks. A process state φ is a mapping from the variables $r \in V$ into a pair of expressions. We denote the first member of the pair by $\varphi_c(r)$ and the second member of the pair by $\varphi_f(r)$. The expression $\varphi_c(r)$ is called the current value, while $\varphi_f(r)$ is called the final value of r. The two differ in order to distinguish non-blocking assignments from blocking assignments. Non-blocking assignments only update the final value, but not the current value, while blocking assignments update both. For an expression e, $\varphi_c(e)$ denotes the evaluation of e in the current state φ_c, i.e., all variables v that are found in e are replaced by $\varphi_c(v)$.

We can also distinguish non-blocking and blocking assignments by attaching tags on the terminal nodes. For example, the tag "N:" denotes non-blocking assignments, while tag "B:" denotes blocking assignments. With these tags, we can generate FSM models by traversal DD models.

Initial States: The assignments in *initial* blocks are used to assign initial values before execution. For these initial values, we can build formal models as $I := \{s \in S \mid \bigwedge_{r \in L} s(r) = \varphi'_f(r)\}$. For the example shown in Figure 1, the model for the initial values is $x = 1 \land y = 0$.

Variable Assignments: From the root node of the DD model to the terminal nodes, when a condition node is encountered, an expression of the form "$c?t:f$", where c is the condition expression, t and f denote the expression to be assigned when the condition is evaluated to be true or false, respectively. When a terminal node is encountered, the assignment expression is used directly. The detailed DD model traversal algorithm can be found in [17]. The special case to be considered is to distinguish non-blocking and blocking assignment. For the example shown in Figure 1, the expression generated for the x' and y' (we will explain in "Next States Relations") is shown as follows:

$$y' = x$$
$$x' = ((x < 100)\,?\,(x+y) : x)$$

Next States Relations: First we can examine the tag of root node of each DD model to distinguish variables and signals belong to set L to form the states space from those used in combinational circuits. For the variables and signals used in combinational circuits, we need the new value of each one to equal to the value after assignments. Then the formal model for the combinational circuits is defined as $C := \bigwedge_{v \in C} s(v) = s(\varphi_f^C(v))$.

For the variables and signals in set L, besides generating assignments formula as discussed above, we also need the assignment formula to build the model of transition relations.

The transition relation $R(s, s')$ is defined under the constraints that for each variable $v \in L$, we require that the next state value of v—denoted v'—is the final value of v after the execution of assignments. By adding constraints for combinational circuits and continuous assignments, we can get the transition function as follows:

$$R(s, s') := \bigwedge_{v \in L} s'(v) = s(\varphi_f^S(v)) \wedge$$
$$\bigwedge_{v \in C} s(v) = s(\varphi_f^C(v)) \wedge$$
$$s(A)$$

For example, for the design shown in Figure 1, the transition relation is defined as follows:

$$R(x, y, x', y') := (x' = ((x < 100)\,?\,(x+y) : x)) \wedge (y' = x).$$

4 Predicate Abstraction

The predicate abstraction method is the same as the method proposed in [13]. We briefly introduce the method with some modification.

In predicate abstraction [2], the variables of the concrete program are replaced by Boolean variables that correspond to a predicate on the variables in the concrete program. These predicates are functions that map a concrete state $r \in S$ into a Boolean value. Let $B = \{\pi_1, \pi_2, ..., \pi_n\}$ be the set of predicates over the given program. When applying all predicates to a specific concrete state, one obtains a vector of Boolean values, which represents an abstract state $\overline{b}$. The abstract model can make a transition from an abstract state $\overline{b}$ to $\overline{b}'$ iff there is a transition from $\overline{r}$ to $\overline{r}'$ in the concrete model and $\overline{r}$ is abstracted to $\overline{b}$ and $\overline{r}'$ is abstracted to $\overline{b}'$. A symbolic variable b_i is associated with each predicate π_i. If the concrete machine makes a transition from state $\bar{r}$ to state $\bar{r}'$, then the abstract machine makes a transition from state $\bar{b}$ to $\bar{b}'$, where $b_i' = \pi_i(\bar{r}')$. Finally, let $\hat{T}$ denote the abstract machine, and $\hat{R}$ denote the abstract transition relation of $\hat{T}$, then $\hat{R}$ is defined as follows:

$$\hat{R} := \{(\bar{b},\bar{b}') \mid \exists \bar{r},\bar{r}' : \bigwedge_{i=1}^{k} b_i = \pi_i(\bar{r}) \wedge R(\bar{r},\bar{r}') \wedge \bigwedge_{i=1}^{k} b_i' = \pi_i(\bar{r}')\}$$

For the example shown in Figure 1, the transition relation is

$$R(x,y,x',y') := (x' = ((x<100)?(x+y):x)) \wedge (y' = x)$$

Suppose we want to prove that the concrete system (Verilog program) shown Figure 1 insatisfies **AG(x < 100)**. In order to perform predicate abstraction we need a set of predicates. For our example, we take {x<200, x< 100, x+y< 200} as the set of predicates. We associate symbolic variables b_1, b_2, b_3 with each predicate, respectively. Then the following equation will be generated:

$(b_1 \Leftrightarrow (x<200)) \wedge (b_2 \Leftrightarrow (x<100)) \wedge (b_3 \Leftrightarrow (x+y<200)) \wedge R(x,y,x',y') \wedge$
$(b_1' \Leftrightarrow (x'<200)) \wedge (b_2' \Leftrightarrow (x'<100)) \wedge (b_3' \Leftrightarrow (x'+y'<200))$

The equation for the initial state is :

$(b_1 \Leftrightarrow (x<200)) \wedge (b_2 \Leftrightarrow (x<100)) \wedge (b_3 \Leftrightarrow (x+y<200)) \wedge (x=1) \wedge (y=0)$

Here, we propose to use CLP to compute the abstraction of RTL Verilog descriptions and try to avoid the problem encountered in traditional theorem prover based and SAT based methods. our method can support all Verilog bounded integer and bit-vector operators. The CLP constraints generated can be very small. Finally, the bit, bit-vector and various arithmetic and logic operations can be solved under a uniform framework.

5 CLP Constraints Generation

We use GNU Prolog [18] as the constraints solver. For the abstraction formula generated in last section, we first translate them into CLP constraints, and then solve them.

To translate the Verilog expressions into constraint equations according to GNU Prolog format, it is necessary to consider separately the case of bits, bit vectors and integers, because these three types belong to different domains, and are solved in different ways.

Bit: GNU Prolog provides various operations for bit. In this case, for each expression involves bit type, a single GNU Prolog equation is produced. The domain of all constraint variables used in the equations is defined as the Boolean domain {0, 1}.

Bit-vector: If at least one variable involved in a constraint equation is a bit vector, the situation is more complex. There are two ways that the bit vectors involved in expression:

Entire: The bit vector involves in computation as an entire variables. In this case, if there are integer variables in equation, then the bit-vector will be considered as an integer variable too. Otherwise, if there are other bit-vectors in equation, then the bit-vector will be decomposed into bits and generate constraints for the decomposed bits. For example, if two 4-bit bit-vectors are involved in expression "V1==V2", then the constraint equations generated for this express is shown as following:

$$V1\_0 = V2\_0$$
$$V1\_1 = V2\_1$$
$$V1\_2 = V2\_2$$
$$V1\_3 = V2\_3$$
$$2^3 * V1\_3 + 2^2 * V1\_2 + 2 * V1\_1 + V1\_0 = V1$$
$$2^3 * V2\_3 + 2^2 * V2\_2 + 2 * V2\_1 + V2\_0 = V2$$

Vi_j represents each bit in bit-vector, where $i \in \{1,2\}$ indicating the bit-vector variable, and $j \in \{0,1,2,3\}$ indicating the bit location in each bit-vector.

Bit Selection: Bit selection means a portion of a bit-vector is involved in expression. In this case, besides generating constraints for the expression, we will also generate constraints for the selected bits. For example, the constraint equations generated for expression "V[1:0]=2'b00" are as following, where V is a 4-bit bit vector variable.

$$V\_1 = 0$$
$$V\_0 = 0$$
$$2^3 * V\_3 + 2^2 * V\_2 + 2 * V\_1 + V\_0 = V$$

Integer: GNU Prolog provides various operations for integer variables. The domain of each integer is also required to be defined.

GNU Prolog provides supports for most of the arithmetic and logical operations used in Verilog. The only thing need to be considered is the operations taken on bit-vector and bounded integer. When concern expressions with these variables or signals, we need to take care of the overflow problem. In GNU Prolog, we can solve this problem by using the *rem* operation built in GNU Prolog. Let the expression we try to translate is of the form "*a op b*", where *a* and *b* are variables of bit-vector or bounded integer type, assume the width of *a* and *b* is *n*, *op* is arithmetic operations such as addition *etc*. Then the translated results is of the form "*(a op b) rem* 2^n".

For the example formula generated in last section, the generated CLP constraints are shown as below. In general, the abstraction computation formula is a conjunction of a set of equivalent formula. For each equivalent formula in the conjunction formula, we generate a temporal variable for it and then conjunct all the generated temporal variables. Finally, we set the value of the conjunction of the temporal variables to constant 1. By solving the generated CLP constraints with the *findall* predicate of GNU Prolog, we can get all the state transitions for the abstraction system. For the example shown in Figure 1, we can get transition diagrams just the same as in [13], which is shown in Figure 2. We can also get the initial state by solving the initial state computation constraints. For the example in Figure 1, the initial state is "111".

Z #= (X + Y) rem 256,
Temp1 #<=> ((#\B1) #\/ (X #< 200)) #/\ (B1 #\/ (X #>= 200)),
Temp2 #<=> ((#\B2) #\/ (X #< 100)) #/\ (B2 #\/ (X #>= 100)),
Temp3 #<=> ((#\B3) #\/ (Z #< 200)) #/\ (B3 #\/ (Z #>= 200)),
Y_Bar #= X,
(X #< 100) #==> (X_Bar #= Z), (X #>= 100) #==> (X_Bar #= X),
Z_Bar #= (X_Bar + Y_Bar) rem 256,
Temp4 #<=> ((#\B1_Bar) #\/ (X_Bar #< 200)) #/\ (B1_Bar #\/ (X_Bar #>= 200)),
Temp5 #<=> ((#\B2_Bar) #\/ (X_Bar #< 100)) #/\ (B2_Bar #\/ (X_Bar #>= 100)),
Temp6 #<=> ((#\B3_Bar) #\/ (Z_Bar #< 200)) #/\ (B3_Bar #\/ (Z_Bar #>= 200)),

Out #<=> Temp1 #/\ Temp2 #/\ Temp3 #/\ Temp4 #/\ Temp5 #/\ Temp6,

The abstract transition relations and initial states are then converted to SMV program, and the property is verified on the abstraction system. For the above example, the property to be verified is **AG(b_2)**.

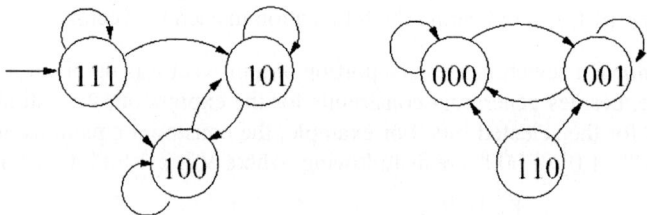

Fig. 2. State transition diagrams for the example

6 Implementation and Experimental Results

Based on the system implemented in [18], we have implemented the RTL Verilog CLP-based predicate abstraction prototype system. In order to compare our method with SAT-based method, we follow the method proposed in [12] to translate abstraction computation formula into SAT instance. First we build the circuit model for the abstraction formula, and then synthesis the circuit into BLIF format using VIS [19] system. Finally, we use the modified BLIF2CNF [20] program to convert BLIF into CNF format, which is the acceptable input format for most SAT solver. To use the SAT solver to compute all the satisfiable assignments for the generated CNF, we use zChaff [21] as the SAT solver, and modified it according to the algorithm in [22].

Table 1. Benchmark Characteristics

Benchmark	Lines of Code	Inputs	Signals
8051 Controller	350	18	59
Viper Microprocessor	400	24	57
Decoder	2092	14	94
SMU	1476	30	217
DCU	3979	43	385

Table 1 shows the characteristics of benchmarks used in our experiment. The 8051 Controller and Viper are publicly available designs. The Decoder is the instruction decoder unit of a 32-bit microprocessor implemented by ourselves. SMU and DCU is the data cache unit and stack manage unit of PicoJava microprocessor [23], respectively.

Table 2. Experimental Results

Benchmark	Predicates	CLP based method		SAT based method	
		Line of Constraints	Time (Sec.)	Literals	Time (Sec.)
8051 Controller	23	239	10.10	13972	58
Viper Microprocessor	25	247	12.34	24719	204
Decoder	25	253	15.47	17527	177
SMU	39	372	23.73	35836	361
DCU	24	255	17.49	21075	236

According to the properties to be verified, we manually extract the predicates to be used for abstraction. Then the abstraction computation formula and its corresponding CLP constraints and SAT constraints are generated automatically. We compared the performance of CLP based and SAT based method. The experimental configuration is a Windows 2000 PC with AMD Athlon XP 1.8 GHz CPU and 256MB memory.

The experimental results are shown in Table 2. In Table 2, the "Predicates" column shows the predicates used to compute the abstraction system, the "Line of Constraints" column shows the lines of generated CLP constraints, while "Literals" shows the generated SAT literals for the abstraction computation formula. The two "Time" columns under "CLP based method" and "SAT based method" shows the time used to solving the converted constraints, respectively. All times are reported in second.

We can conclude from Table 2 that CLP based abstraction computation can gain promising performance improvements than SAT based method. Although the inefficient implementation of the algorithm proposed in [22] may influencet the performance of SAT based method, we believe that the distinct characteristic such as word level modeling and constraints solving capability of CLP based method make it more efficient than SAT based method.

7 Conclusion

In this paper, we proposed to use CLP as the abstraction computation engine for predicate abstraction of RTL Verilog, and the experimental results showed the promising improvements of abstraction computation by our proposed method. In the future, we will intensively research on CLP based predicate abstraction method, such as CLP based abstraction and refinement techniques, *etc.*

References

1. E. Clarke, O. Grumberg, and D. Peled. Model Checking. MIT Press, 1999.
2. S. Graf and H. Saidi. Construction of abstract state graphs with PVS. In O. Grumberg, editor, Proc. CAV'97, LNCS 1254, pages 72–83. Springer Verlag, 1997.

3. David Detlefs, Greg Nelson, and James B. Saxe. Simplify: A theorem prover for program checking. Technical Report HPL-2003-148, HP Labs, 2003.
4. Thomas Ball, Byron Cook, Shuvendu K. Lahiri, and Lintao Zhang. Zapato: Automatic theorem proving for predicate abstraction refinement. In CAV. Springer-Verlag, 2004.
5. T. Ball and S.K. Rajamani. Boolean programs: A model and process for software analysis. Technical Report 2000-14, Microsoft Research, February 2000.
6. Cormac Flanagan and Shaz Qadeer. Predicate abstraction for software verification. POPL '02: Proceedings of the 29th ACM POPL. p 191—202, ACM Press, 2002.
7. Thomas Ball, Rupak Majumdar, Todd D. Millstein and Sriram K. Rajamani. Automatic Predicate Abstraction of C Programs. ACM PLDI, p 203-213, ACM Press, 2001.
8. T. Ball and S. K. Rajamani. Automatically validating temporal safety properties of interfaces. In SPIN 2001, LNCS 2057, pages 103–122. Springer, 2001.
9. Thomas A. Henzinger, Ranjit Jhala, Rupak Majumdar, and Gregoire Sutre. Software verification with Blast. Proceedings of SPIN 2003, LNCS 2648, Springer-Verlag, 235-239, 2003.
10. Sagar Chaki, Edmund Clarke, Alex Groce, Somesh Jha, Helmut Veith. Modular Verification of Software Components in C. IEEE Transactions on Software Engineering, Volume 30, Number 6, p 388-402, June 2004.
11. Edmund Clarke, Muralidhar Talupur, and Dong Wang. SAT based predicate abstraction for hardware verification. In Proceedings of SAT'03, 2003.
12. Edmund Clarke, Daniel Kroening, Natalia Sharygina, and Karen Yorav. Predicate abstraction of ANSI-C programs using SAT. Formal Methods in System Design (FMSD), vol. 25, no. 2-3, p 105—127, Kluwer Academic Publishers, 2004.
13. Edmund Clarke, Himanshu Jain, Daniel Kroening. Predicate Abstraction and Refinement Techniques for Verifying Verilog. Technical report, Carnegie Mellon University, CMU-CS-04-139, June, 2004.
14. Edmund Clarke, Himanshu Jain, Daniel Kroening. Verification of SpecC using Predicate Abstraction. MEMOCODE, June, 2004.
15. J. Jaffar, M. J. Maher. Constraint logic programming: A Survey. The Journal of Logic Programming, 1994, Vol. 19&20: 503~582
16. R. Ubar. Test synthesis with alternative graphs. IEEE Design & Test of Computers, 1996.13(1): 48~57.
17. Li Tun. Research on techniques of VLSI RT-Level automatic functional vectors generation [Ph.D. Thesis]. ChangSha: NUDT, 2003.
18. Tun Li, Yang Guo, SiKun Li. Functional Vectors Generation for RT-Level Verilog Descriptions Based on Path Enumeration and Constraint Logic Programming. to be appeared in Proceedings of 8th EUROMICRO CONFERENCE ON DIGITAL SYSTEM DESIGN, August, 2005, Porto, Portugal.
19. http://vlsi.colorado.edu/♡vis.
20. Joao Marques Silva. BLIF2CNF. sat.inesc-id.pt/~jpms/scripts/bin/blif2cnf.
21. M. Moskewicz, C. Madigan, Y. Zhao, L. Zhang, S. Malik. Chaff: Engineering an Efficient SAT Solver. In Proceedings of DAC 2001, Las Vegas, June 2001.
22. McMillan, K. Applying SAT Methods in Unbounded Symbolic Model Checking. In CAV 2002, Springer-Verlag, p 250-264, 2002.
23. Sun Microsystems. PicoJava technology. http://www.sun.com/microelectronics/communitysource/picojava/, 1999.

Scheduling Transportation Events with Grouping Genetic Algorithms and the Heuristic DJD

Hugo Terashima-Marín, Juan Manuel Tavernier-Deloya, and Manuel Valenzuela-Rendón

Center for Intelligent Systems, Tecnológico de Monterrey,
Ave. Eugenio Garza Sada 2501 Sur, Monterrey, Nuevo León 64849 Mexico
{terashima, valenzuela}@itesm.mx, jtavernier@amueble.com

Abstract. Grouping problems arise in many applications, and the aim is to partition a set U of items, into a collection of mutually disjoint subsets or groups. The objective of grouping is to optimize a cost function such as to minimize the number of groups. Problems in this category may come from many different domains such as graph coloring, bin packing, cutting stock, and scheduling. This investigation is related in particular to scheduling transportation events, modeled as a grouping problem, and with the objective to minimize the number of vehicles used and satisfying the customer demand. There is a set of events to be scheduled (items) into a set of vehicles (groups). Of course, there are constraints that forbid assigning all events to a single vehicle. Two different techniques are used in this work to tackle the problem: Grouping Genetic Algorithms and an algorithm based on the heuristic DJD widely used for solving bin packing problems. Both methods were adapted to the problem and compared to each other using a set of randomly generated problem instances designed to comply with real situations.

1 Introduction

Grouping problems arise in many applications, and the aim is to partition a set U of items, into a collection of mutually disjoint subsets or groups. The objective of grouping is to optimize a cost function such as to minimize the number of groups. Problems in this category may come from many different domains such as graph coloring, bin packing, cutting stock, and scheduling [1]. This investigation is related in particular to scheduling transportation events into a set of vehicles complying with various kinds of constraints. Each event contains information such as city of origin, city of destination, and its duration. Scheduling events into the vehicles is a combinatorial and NP problem [2], and in fact, it is very similar to packing problems, where events are considered as items and vehicles as bins. The idea is to minimize the number of vehicles used.

Previous studies present different approaches and heuristics to solve similar problems [3], [4], [5] and [6]. Recent work that describes and compares different approaches for the bin-packing problem can be found in the work by Ross et al. [7]. Genetic Algorithms [8] have been also used to solve the problem, in which they use special representations and genetic operators. Grouping Genetic Algorithms (GGA), developed by Falkenauer [1], are a special kind of GAs and overcome drawbacks of normal GAs when solving the problem. The GGA uses a representation which is group-oriented instead of item-oriented, that is, the chromosome has two parts: the first one encodes the solution where the item i belongs to group j, and the second one is a sequence indicating groups appearing in the first part so, serving to identify which items actually form which group. The genetic operators work very much the same as those in the regular genetic algorithm, but in the GGA they will work with the group part of the chromosome. The chromosome is variable in length. A different approach for the problem is a heuristic developed by Djang and Finch in 1998 (DJD) [9]. It works by decreasingly sorting the items, filling out the bin up to a third of its capacity, and finding combinations of one, two or three of the remaining items until the bin is completely full. If no combination is found, then the bin capacity is reduced by one and the solution process starts again.

The objective of the work presented in this paper is to adapt both the GGA and the DJD heuristic according to the specific features of the problem at hand, and show the effectiveness of each by means of a comparison.

The rest of the paper is organized as follows. Section 2 presents the methodology and solution model. Section 3 describes the experimental set up, the results and their analysis. Finally, in section 4 we include our conclusions and future work.

2 The Particular Problem and the Proposed Solution Model

A set of transportation events is given. Each event, representing a movement of goods from one city to another, is formed by the pick-up date, the delivery date, the city of origin, the city of destination and the route that the event belongs to. The route is a pre-stablished course of travel between two main cities. For example, a route between Mexico City and Monterrey can be Mexico City-Queretaro-San Luis-Saltillo-Monterrey. The duration of an event is obtained by the difference between the delivery and pick-up dates. Figure 1 shows the features of a generated event.

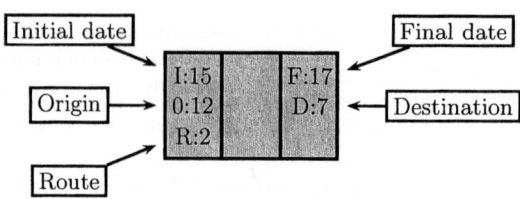

Fig. 1. Graphical description of an event

The aim is to minimize the number of vehicles needed to schedule all events in a period of 30 days. The problem was adapted from a real situation. There are several kinds of constraints involved such as avoiding overlapping events and idle vehicles, for instance. There are other soft constraints to satisfy like keeping continuity between events, that is, if an event finishes in city i, it is desirable to schedule next an event whose city of origin is i too, or at least the city of origin of the next event is not far from i. We call this concept a *link*. It is also desirable that all events in a vehicle belong to the same route. We created routes with real information according to cities and distances in Mexico. We produced events with duration from two to five days following recommendations from people we interviewed.

A problem generator was constructed in order to produce instances with several features and degrees of hardness. A probability of link was included trying to create problems closer to reality, since initial studies were performed in local transportation companies in order to have a better understanding of the problem. Instances were generated using two different probabilities of having a *link*: less restricted with 0.3, and more restricted with 0.8.

A criterion to evaluate solutions is needed. There are several constraint types in the problem divided by hard and soft constraints. The main constraint that should always be satisfied is the one stating that there is at least an available vehicle for any given event. Additionally, it is obligatory that two events assigned to the same vehicle can not overlap. These constraints are labeled R_0 and R_1, respectively. The soft constraints include: Maximize the usage of vehicle (R_2), Maximize the number of links as possible (R_3), Group events in a vehicle considering the same route as possible (R_4).

Since the problem is being tackled very similar to a packing problem, and in which we try to minimize the number of vehicles used, the objective function is given by $f(x) = \left(\frac{\sum_{i=1}^{N}(F_i/C)^k}{N}\right) + w_3 \cdot R_3 + w_4 \cdot R_4$, where N is the number of vehicles used, F_i is the sum of all event durations in vehicle i, C is the total number of days for a vehicle and k is a constant ≥ 1. In other words, the objective function tries to maximize the average usage of the vehicles, and consequently reducing the number of vehicles used. Our function is an adaptation of the function used by Falkenauer [1]. The chromosome evaluation is computed as follows: (1) Constraints R_0 and R_1 are implicitly considered and satisfied when the solution is being constructed; (2) The computation of the evaluation function considers constraint R_2, since the function tries to maximize the average usage of a vehicle; (3) Once a solution has been obtained, the number of events in each vehicle are counted and the instances of violated constraints of type R_3 are penalized accordingly in the fitness function; and, (4) Constraint R_4 is penalized in a similar way as constraint R_3.

2.1 The Grouping Genetic Algorithm

The Grouping Genetic Algorithm proposed by Falkenauer [1] was implemented for this investigation. First, it was tested for a series of bin-packing problem instances used in the literature. Secondly, it was adapted in order to tackle the specific problem in this work.

The chromosome. It is an array of integers composed of two parts, the first one encoding each item in its corresponding group, and the second one representing the group part, to identify the used groups. An example of chromosome is as follows: A_i=[2,4,3,1,2,1,2 | 1,2,3,4], where the chromosome is interpreted from left to right and placing item 1 in bin 2, item 2 in bin 4, and so on.

The genetic operators in the GGA are designed to overcome problems with the redundancy, insensitivity and schemata disruption present in straightforward representations using GAs. Redundancy is directly related to avoiding that each member of the search space be represented by more than one distinctive chromosomes. The usual representation also leads to the undesirable effect of dropping context-dependent information which may be important when crossing two chromosomes. This is called context insensitivity. In the classic crossover, once a good candidate is found, it works against its own progress by destroying the good schemata.

Crossover. The crossover operator was implemented using the steps followed by Falkenauer. We did a slight modification by using heuristic 'first fit decreasing' when reinserting items in the first parent and not replaced by items of groups in the second parent, obtaining better performance.

Mutation. Mutation operator is not applied extensively. It determines in a random way the number of groups and those which will be eliminated. After groups are eliminated, items are reinserted following a 'first fit decreasing' heuristic since it produced slightly better results than the 'first fit random' proposed by Falkenauer.

Fitness Function. The chromosome is interpreted and a matrix simulating a calendar is formed by sequentially placing events into vehicles and taking into account the given constraints. At the end, the complete calendar is evaluated returning a single value.

2.2 Modification and Implementation of Heuristic DJD

An alternative solution to the problem was based on the heuristic DJD [7]. In its original version, the heuristic is used for solving bin-packing problems. In our case, we had to adapt the heuristic in order to consider specific features of the problem and particular constraints. The implementation and adaptation consist of the following steps:

Filling a third. This heuristic assigns events to a vehicle, taking largest-duration events first, until a third of the available time on the vehicle is full. For our problem, and considering specific recommendations by the advising companies, most of the events take two days to be completed, and the rest three or four days. Given that we have a 30-day period to schedule for each vehicle, it was not practical to use a third as a value to do the initial filling. Instead we did experiments to use first a half, and then three quarters, with which the outcome was considerably better.

Number of combinations. The rest of the available time for a vehicle should be filled with combinations of one, two or three events until the vehicle time is

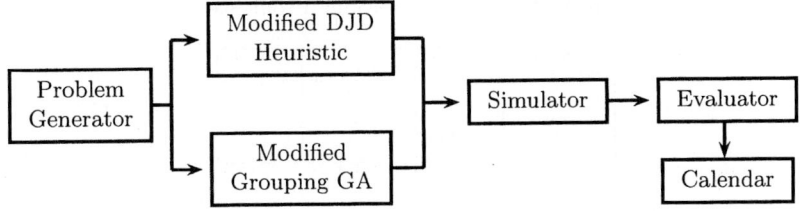

Fig. 2. Flowchart of the solution prototype

completely full. If there is no such combination, it then tries again to fill the vehicle time, but to within 1 less of its capacity. If that fails, it tries again to find such a combination but to within two of its capacity, and so on. We also tried combinations of four and five events obtaining a better performance.

Handling hard constraints. Hard constraints such as avoiding overlapping events is tested every time a combination of events is being sought. If the combination contains an event causing overlapping, it is eliminated, proceeding to generate a new combination. This step guarantees that all events in a combination are viable to be assigned.

Handling soft constraints. Once a combination has satisfied the hard constraints, the soft constraints are revised. A preset value is established by the user to determine the number of *links* a combination of events should fulfill. For instance, for each event in the combination, a counter is increased every time the event's city of origin matches the city of destination of the event already in the calendar immediately to the left. The counter is also increased if the event's city of destination is the same as the city of origin of the event to its right and already in the calendar. A similar procedure is used to handle the constraint related to schedule events in the same route. If for all possible combinations of events no one meets the preset value, events are inserted in the calendar with the first-fit decreasing type of heuristic.

Figure 2 illustrates a diagram of the prototype that was implemented and includes different modules such as the problem generator, the choice of methods, and the evaluation and graphical presentation of the solution.

3 Experiments and Results

Given that the GGA approach is rather different from the modified DJD heuristic, we ran initial experiments to measure quality of solutions and running time. We used for these experiments plain bin-packing problems used in the literature and taken from the OR-Library [10]. We selected 80 problems with 120, 250, 500, and 1000 items. We also took the 10 most difficult problems and performed the comparison. Problem features are shown in Table 1.

We had to run preliminary experiments in order to set the parameters of the GGA. Table 2 shows the parameter set depending on the problem size.

Table 1. Set of Bin Packing Problems

No. of objects (N)	container size (t)	size range	No. of problems
120	150	20-100	20
250	150	20-100	20
500	150	20-100	20
1000	150	20-100	20
200	100 000	20 000-35 000	10
		Total	90

Table 2. Parameter set for the GGA

	Small	Medium	Large
Popsize	50	50	50
No. of generations	50	100	100
Crossover Prob.	0.8	0.8	0.8
Mutation Prob.	0.01	0.01	0.01
Max. Elim. Groups	10	10	10
Min. Elim. Groups	5	5	5

Table 3. Comparison for 80 bin-packing problems plus 10 additional difficult instances with 200 objects

	120 obj		250 obj		500 obj		1000 obj		200 obj	
	GGA	DJD	GGA	DJD	GGA	DJD	GGA	DJD	GGA	DJD
Bins	49.3	50.7	102.4	104.7	202.8	203.8	404.4	403.9	57.3	56.5
Time(mins)	1.82	0.003	3.86	0.0015	7.18	0.0295	13.86	0.064	5.494	24.044
Fitness	0.9699	0.9273	0.9780	0.9435	0.9801	0.9741	0.9810	0.9857	0.92773	0.94869

Results for the first 90 bin-packing problems (including 10 difficult ones) are summarized in Table 3. For each number of objects, 20 different instances were produced. The GGA was run 10 times for each instance and the best result was taken.

Figures in Table 3 show the average of the best result for each of the 20 instances produced by the GGA. For the DJD case, figures are just the average of the single results for each of those instances. For the first 80 problems taken from the OR-library, the GGA behaves slightly better than the heuristic DJD with respect to the number of bins used, but the later algorithm takes less time. It is interesting to observe though, that DJD finds better results for problems with 1000 objects. Summarizing, and by observing Figure 3, the GGA obtains the best-known number of bins in 27.5% of the problems (DJD just 8.75), in 31.25% of the problems is within one from the optimal while DJD achieves that result in just 25% of the problems. For the difficult problems, DJD performs a bit better than the GGA, but its time to deliver the solution, in average, is around five times more than the GGA's. For these cases, DJD finds the optimal [11] in 7 out of 10 problems. We can partially conclude at this point that the behavior of both methods is very competitive, leaving the door open to perform a more complete comparison for the particular problem we are tackling in this investigation. Also results we obtained are indeed confirmed by those reported by Ross et al. [7] in their more elaborate study for bin-packing problems and hyper-heuristics.

For experimental purposes in this research, we generated a variety of problems with 50, 100, and 200 events in order to compare the performance of both

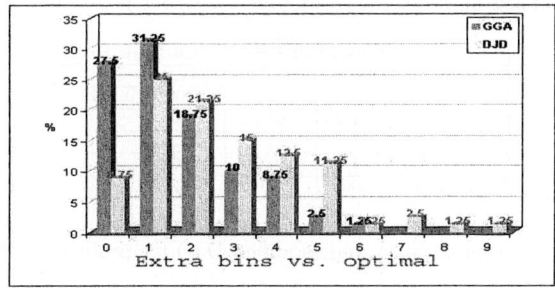

Fig. 3. Performance of GGA and DJD for 80 bin packing problems

proposed approaches. Specifically, 10 problems for each size and each link probability were produced. Our comparison includes the solution fitness, the number of vehicles used, the number of link violations, the number of route violations and the time taken by each algorithm. For the modified DJD heuristic, we ran preliminary experiments to set the minimal number of constraints that a combination should satisfy to be considered viable. This number is used in the internal process of the heuristic and was established to 4. Table 4 shows results for problems with 50 events. The results were divided according to the low and high link probabilities, and the average for the 10 problems of each type is presented. The GGA was run 10 times for each instance and the best result was used in the computation.

It can be observed that the number of vehicles used to schedule the events is slightly less in the GGA since the result reports an average of 7.2 for events with low probability of links and 7.8 for the high probability of links. A distinctive gap can be appreciated in both the number of link and route violations between the GGA and the modified DJD. On this kind of problems, however, it it clear that the DJD-based algorithm is much faster since it only takes less than one second to deliver the result.

We also ran experiments for problems with 100 and 200 events. Tables 5 and 6 show the results. The GGA produces better figures in relation to the number of link violations, even for those problems with high link probability. For instance, for problems with 100 events and low link probability, the GGA produces 43.5 while the DJD has 65.9. In average, the number of vehicles used in the GGA is around one less than the DJD for problems with 100 events, and

Table 4. Comparison of GGA and modified DJD for problems with 50 events

	Low Link Prob.		High Link Prob.	
	GGA	DJD	GGA	DJD
Fitness	0.64131	0.26935	0.64498	0.24667
Vehicles	7.2	7.8	7.8	8.4
Link Viols.	17.1	32	16.3	32.8
Route Viols.	10.1	25.2	9.1	25.7
Time(mins)	3.321	< 1 seg.	3.324	< 1 seg.

Table 5. Comparison of GGA and modified DJD for problems with 100 events

	Low Link Prob.		High Link Prob.	
	GGA	DJD	GGA	DJD
Fitness	0.87403	0.25463	0.97001	0.28175
Vehicles	14.2	15.5	13.6	15.4
Link Viols.	43.5	65.9	42.2	66.5
Route Viols.	24.4	50.2	27.5	49.2
Time(mins)	6.002	0.018	6.027	0.021

Table 6. Comparison of GGA and modified DJD for problems with 200 events

	Low Link Prob.		High Link Prob.	
	GGA	DJD	GGA	DJD
Fitness	1.19593	0.25217	1.34779	0.29308
Vehicles	24.9	26.8	22.8	24.1
Link Viols.	108.6	132.7	111.2	136.9
Route Viols.	73	101.1	74.2	100.2
Time(mins)	16.58	0.42	19.31	0.413

almost two for those instances with 200 events. The number of link violations is much less in the GGA. Contrasting the computational time, however, the DJD has definitely better performance. In average, the solution can be obtained in less than a minute, whereas the GGA can take up to 19 minutes for problems with 200 events and high link probability.

By looking at the results obtained for problems with 50, 100 and 200 events, we may conclude that the GGA approach performs better than the modified DJD. The solutions obtained satisfy all hard constraints and violate less number of soft constraints. With respect to the number of vehicles, the GGA reports a little bit less than the number produced by the DJD. With respect to performance, and specifically for problems with 100 events, convergence is reached around 3300 function evaluations.

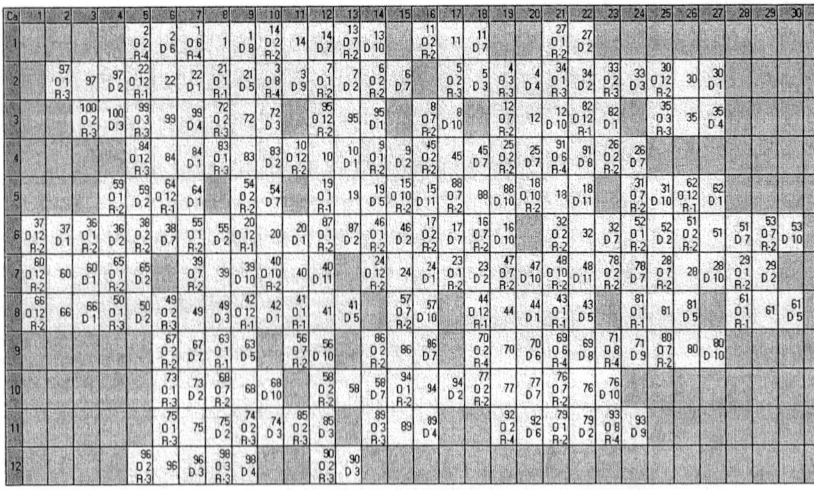

Fig. 4. Calendar produced for a problem with 100 events

Figure 4 shows an example of the outcome produced by our prototype after interpreting a given solution.

In this example, we can observe that the solution employs 12 vehicles (one for each row) to schedule 100 events in 30 days (one for each column). Vehicle 1 takes care of event number 2, with initial date on day 5 and duration of two days (final day is 6). It starts in city number 2 and its destination is city labeled 6. Immediately after, event 1 is scheduled for which the city of origin is also 6, so a link constraint is satisfied. This event has a duration of three days and its destination is city number 8. The vehicle will be idle after day 23.

4 Conclusions and Future Work

We can conclude that the problem at hand can be definitely modeled and solved as a bin packing problem and with its related solving techniques. Each transportation event can be considered as an object, and the vehicle, with a calendar of 30 available days, can be considered as a container. In addition, we have run a comparison between two specific techniques: one based on the GGA developed by Falkenauer, and the other whose core is the DJD heuristic designed by Djang and Finch. When modeling the problem and implementing its solutions, we took into consideration recommendations and suggestions coming from people in the local transportation business. They have also reviewed the results produced by our system and they are pleased. They also think that the system can be extended to handle other kinds of constraints and requirements in order to be closer to what they need. In both solution approaches, we ensure first that the hard constraints are satisfied, and then we try to violate the less number of soft constraints. We have also confirmed that the GGA-based approach is a useful tool for solving this kind of combinatorial optimization problems, and its performance is better than the DJD heuristic. We think that the DJD performance is also reasonable, and its execution time is in fact less than the GGA for all cases. We have now good options for solving the problem, whose choice may depend on the particular situation and context. There are some interesting ideas for extending this work. Other constraints can be considered in order to take this prototype closer to a commercial software for the transportation business. The application of refinement heuristics in the solution, or even in the inside procedure of the GGA, is also an alternative for improving this work.

Acknowledgments

This research was supported by ITESM under the Research Chair CAT-010.

References

1. Emanuel Falkenauer. *Genetic Algorithms and Grouping Problems.* Wiley, 1998.
2. M.R. Garey and D.S. Johnson. *Computers and Intractability.* W.H. Freeman and Company, New York, 1979.

3. Xu Hang, Chen Zhi-Long, R. Srinivas, and A. Sundar. Solving a practical pickup and delivery problem. *Transportation Science*, 37(3), 2003.
4. M. W. P. Savelsbergh and M. Sol. The general pickup and delivery problem. *Transportation Science*, 29(1), 1995.
5. Masatoshi Sakawa, Ichiro Nishizaki, and Yoshio Uemura. Interactive fuzzy programming for a decentralized two-level transportation planning and work force assignment problem. *IEEE*, 2001.
6. Jennifer L. Rich. *A Computational Study of Vehicle Routing Applications*. PhD thesis, Rice University, 1999.
7. Peter Ross, Sonia Schulenberg, Javier G. Marín-Blázquez, and Emma Hart. Hyperheuristics: learning to combine simple heuristics in bin-packing problem. *Genetic and Evolutionary Computation Conference*, 2002.
8. D. Goldberg. *Genetic Algorithms in Search, Optimization and Machine Learning*. Adison Wesley, 1989.
9. P. A. Djang and P. R. Finch. Solving one dimension bin-packing problems. *Journal of Heuristics*, 1998.
10. J E Beasley. Beasley operations research library. *Collection of problems for packing and cutting*, 2003.
11. A. Scholl and R. Klein. Bin packing library. *Collection of bin packing problems*, 2003.

Radial Search: A Simple Solution Approach to Hard Combinatorial Problems

José Antonio Vázquez Rodríguez and Abdellah Salhi

The University of Essex, Colchester CO43SQ, UK
javazq@gmail.com, as@essex.ac.uk

Abstract. We introduce a simple approach to finding approximate solutions to combinatorial problems. This approach called the Radial Search (RS) uses the concept of rings which define the location and size of search areas around current good solutions. It iteratively modifies the radii of these rings, and generates new centres, in order to cover the search space. A concentration step corresponds to choosing a solution as the centre of a new ring. An expansion step corresponds to the exploration around a given centre by increasing and reducing the radius of the ring until a better solution than the centre is found. This dynamic process of concentration and expansion of the search is repeated until a stopping condition is met.

A detailed description of RS, a discussion of its similarities and differences with current known methods, and its performance on TSP and QAP problems are given.

1 Introduction

In recent years, random search based solution methods have increased in importance. This is mainly for problems known to be inherently difficult (the so called NP-hard problems), for which deterministic methods in their variety have serious limitations. The "No free lunch theorem", [1], implies that there is not a search method efficient for all problems. This points to the necessity to develop new algorithms and improve existing ones through streamlining, hybridisation and so on, for this class of problems. Here, we present a simple method termed the Radial Search (RS) algorithm, to address these problems.

The expression "Radial Search" is used in fields such as navigation and astronomy to locate areas in the ocean or the sky. These areas are described by circles (or part of them) whose centres are determined in an appropriate system of coordinates and a radius length. In other contexts, a "Radial Search" algorithm has been employed for the analysis of biomedical images, [13], [14] and [15]. The expression can also be found in non smooth optimization [16].

RS as proposed here, makes use of the concept of "ring". The size and location of search areas are defined by rings of given radii, centred at current solutions. For a given ring, the radius measures the size of the search area and its distance to the current solution. Note, that this distance, as explained in Section 2, is not a topological measure.

At every iteration, the size of the ring is controlled by modifying its radius. In this way, if the search has converged to a local optimum, the radius is increased and so the size and the distance to the actual exploration area of the search space. If the search becomes too random so that the quality of new solutions decreases, the radius is reduced and the search concentrates on a smaller area closer to the best known solutions.

In order to show the efficiency of the RS algorithm, it was tested on two classical combinatorial problems: The Travelling Salesman Problem (TSP), [2], and the Quadratic Assignment Problem (QAP), [3]. Both are known to be NP-Hard problems in Combinatorial Optimization, ([4],[5]). They have received plenty of attention in the literature. In the TSP, the problem is that, given a set of n cities, it is required to find a tour with minimal length that passes through all the cities. In the QAP a set of n facilities is required to be located in an optimal manner in a set of n locations. Given $N = \{1, 2, ..., n\}$, $A = (a_{ij})$ and $B = (b_{kl})$ the TSP and QAP problem can be stated as:

$$\min_{\pi \in S_n} c(\pi) = \sum_{i=1}^{n-1} a_{\pi(i)\pi(i+1)} + a_{\pi(n)\pi(1)} \qquad (1)$$

and

$$\min_{\pi \in S_n} c(\pi) = \sum_{i=1}^{n} \sum_{j=1}^{n} a_{\pi(i)\pi(j)} b_{ij} \qquad (2)$$

respectively. In both equations, π is a permutation of N and S_n is the set of all possible permutations of N. A is a distance matrix that represents the distances between cities i and j or locations i and j for the TSP and QAP, respectively. B is a flow matrix. In equation(2), b_{ij} is the flow between facilities i and j.

A set of 20 problems from the TSP-LIB [6] and 20 from the QAP-LIB [7] were approached using the RS algorithm hybridized with 2-opt local search. The results were compared with those obtained by a GA hybridized with the 2-opt exchange rule. Our results show that the proposed search method is competitive on the problem instances considered.

The rest of the paper is organized as follows. Section 2 describes RS in detail. Section 3 compares RS with other known methods. Section 4 describes and reports experimental results. Section 4 is the conclusion.

2 Description of the Algorithm

2.1 Radial Search

Let S be a set of feasible solutions for a particular problem instance. Given $s \in S$, we define as its ring of radius r the set of feasible solutions that are the result of r perturbations (modifications, discussed in Section 2.2) of s. Denote as s_r the set that results from r perturbations of s. Note that $s_{a,b,...,n}$ means the set $s_a \cup s_b \cup ... \cup s_n$. For example, $s_{1,2,3,4}$ is the set of all possible solutions from 1,2,3

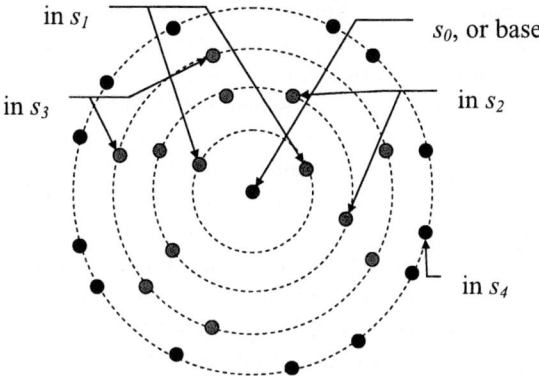

Fig. 1. Radial neighborhood or ring $s_{1,2,3,4}$

and 4 perturbations of s. $s_{1,2,3,4}$ could be represented as in Fig. 1, where the solutions belonging to s_1 are in the inner ring, s_2, s_3 and s_4 are on the outer rings.

A perturbation and the process to generate a new solution must be defined according to the problem and its representation. Both of them must be designed in such a way that the concepts of radius and rings as depicted in Fig. 1 hold. To illustrate, consider a permutation s of n elements. In this case a perturbation can be defined as the swap of a pair of elements in s. A solution in s_1 would be obtained by swapping a single pair and in s_2 by swapping two. Note that if $r > 1$ care must be taken to avoid that elements that have been changed are returned to their original positions in a posterior perturbation (e.g. swapping twice the same two elements). Because of this, the maximum number of perturbations that can be performed is limited, let us define this number as g. If we restrict the number of perturbations by element to one, even if a posterior change does not return it to its original position then the maximum number g of pairs that can be swapped without modifying twice the same element is $\lfloor n/2 \rfloor$.

Let r' be a real number in $(0, 1)$ representing the probability that a perturbation is performed. Therefore r' can be seen as a measure of the expected radius length. Returning to our example, if $n = 100$, to explore on average in s_1, the value of r' must be 0.02 given that $g = 50$ and $r = r' * g$. Note that the inclusion of r' allows the generation of solutions in rings other than s_r. However, it is expected that the solutions generated will mainly be concentrated in s_r. Bearing this in mind, for this particular example a procedure to generate a new solution around a particular centre s could be to generate a uniform random number a in $(0, 1)$. If $a < r'$ a perturbation of s is performed; this is repeated g times. In this way it is expected that the number of perturbations of the new individual with respect to the original one, to be r.

The RS algorithm works by sampling in the space s_r^i of $s^i \in S$ for $i = 1, 2, ..., f$, i.e. it samples around every solution included in set S. Elements of S are referred to as centres. The act of creating new solutions, searching in the rings of a centre, is called an expansion. At every iteration, the algorithm expands the current centres according to r'. For every centre s^i it generates a new set M^i of q new solutions (let $M = \cup_i M^i$). The objective values of the new solutions are calculated. The best f solutions in $M \cup S$ become the new set S. If the best solution in M is worse than the best solution b found so far, r' is decreased by a contraction constant $0 < c < 1$, i.e. $r' = r' * c$. This, intuitively, has the effect of reducing the size of the ring and moving it closer to the centres. If the best solution in M has the same objective value than b, the ring is increased enlarging r' by an expansion constant $e > 1$, i.e. $r' = r' * e$. This process is repeated until a satisfactory solution is found or the maximum number of iterations k is reached. To generate the first set of centres, a uniform random number $(f * q)$ of solutions is sampled; the best f solutions are the initial set S. Fig. 2 presents the general framework of the RS using r' as the radius measure.

Some additional suggestions that were observed to give positive results and improve the general framework presented in Fig. 2 (included in the algorithm used for testing in Section 3) are:

---

1. Initialise f, q, k, r', e, c.
2. $r'' = r'$.
3. Create an initial random sample M (of size $f * q$) of solutions. Let S be the set of f best solutions (centers) in M according to objective function value, and b the best solution among them.
4. $M = \emptyset$.
5. for every center s^i in S do,
    generate f new solutions (M^i) in a radius r' of the neighborhood of s^i (see examples of how to generate these new solutions in Section 2.2); $M = M \bigcup M^i$;
    (optional) apply an improving method to every element in M;
    evaluate the objective value of every element in M; m = best solution in M;
    end for.
6. if the objective value of m = objective value of b then $r' = r' * e$;
    else if the objective value of m is worse than the objective value of b then
        $r' = r' * c$;
        else $b = m$; $r' = r''$;
        end if;
    end if.
7. Let S be the set of f best solutions in $M \bigcup S$.
8. if the number of iterations so far $< k$, go to 4.
9. Return b.

Fig. 2. General framework of the Radial Search

- After a predefined number of generations without any improvement, reset r' to its initial value, generate the new set of solutions as usual, but in step 7, (Fig. 2), S will be the set of f best solutions just in M.
- r' must have a value such that $r \geq 1$ for any perturbation to take place, i.e. the number of expected perturbations to a centre is at least one, through all the search process.

2.2 Generation of New Solutions: Two Methods

The expansion of the centres, i.e. Step 5.1 of Fig. 2, are problem dependent. Figs. 3 and 4 present two methods (CRPM and RSM) for expanding a given centre s. These are suitable for permutation problems such as the TSP and QAP. Let $s = s(1), s(2), ..., s(n)$ be a permutation of n elements representing a solution for a problem instance. Let ω be an empty set representing the new permutation and g as defined previously.

---

1. $\omega = \emptyset$.
2. for $i = 0, 1, ..., n$ do
    generate a random number a in $(0,1)$;
    if $a > r'$ then $\omega(i) = s(0)$; $s = s \setminus s(0)$;
    else generate a random integer number b in $[0, |s-1|]$;
        $\omega(i) = s(b)$; $s = s \setminus s(b)$;
    end if;
    end for.
3. Return ω.

Fig. 3. Constructive Random Perturbations Method (CRPM) to generate a new solution

CRPM (Fig. 3) was observed to be more efficient for the TSP and RSM (Fig. 4) for the QAP. The TSP being a sequencing problem, the main concern is on the relative positions of the elements in relation to each other. In the case of the QAP the position in the vector is what matters. Given that in CRPM after an element is moved from its position the rest are shifted to fill the space, a single perturbation may represent the change of position of all the elements in the permutation. This is a radical change in the case of the QAP but for the TSP it may not be a change at all. For instance, if the first element is set as the last one, all the elements must be shifted one space towards the first position. This is a drastic change in the case of the QAP, but for the TSP, the relative position of all the elements remains the same. On the other hand, every perturbation in the RSM interchanges the position of two elements. For the QAP

> 1. $\omega = s$.
> 2. for $i = 1, 2, ..., n$ do
>   generate a random number a in $(0,1)$;
>   if $a < r'$ then select randomly two integer numbers b, c in $[1, n]$;
> $d = \omega(b)$, $\omega(b) = \omega(c)$, $\omega(c) = d$;
>   end if;
>   end for.
> 3. Return ω.

Fig. 4. Random Swaps Method (RSM) to generate a new solution

this is the minimum change possible to be performed. In the case of the TSP, a single perturbation in RSM introduces more relative position changes than CRPM does.

2.3   2-opt Local Search

Successful algorithms to solve both TSP and QAP problems make use of more specific information than the one provided by the objective function. For both TSP and QAP, the 2-opt local search has been widely used. Let π be a permutation representing a solution, its 2-opt neighbourhood is defined as the set of all possible solutions resulting from π by swapping two distinct elements. RS was hybridized with this local search. To do this, in Step 5.2 of the framework presented in Fig. 2, 2-opt is used as the improving method of every new solution.

In the case of the TSP, an efficient strategy is to implement 2-opt as a first-improvement principle, i.e. the 2-opt neighbourhood of a given solution is explored; when an improvement is found, the swap is accepted and the search continues. It has been observed that for the QAP the strategy of searching all the neighbourhood and accept the best among all the possible swaps that represent an improvement is more efficient, [11].

3   Comparison with Other Known Methods

RS belongs to the class of Population Based Stochastic Local Search algorithms (PB-SLS), [17], where the SLS component resembles the Variable Neighbourhood Search (VNS) algorithm, the Iterated Local Search (ILS) algorithm, and other local search strategies. In particular, it is similar to the Evolutionary Strategy (ES) algorithm, [12], when mutation is the sole search driving genetic operator.

It differs from them, however, in that it strives to implement the central idea that promising search areas described by rings are expanded, by increasing the radius of the ring through the choice of a larger k, for instance when a k-exchange perturbation rule is used, and by shrinking the nonpromising search areas through the reduction of the radius of the ring. Note, that a ring of centre x and radius k is the set of solutions that are different from x by k pairs of nodes, in the case of permutation problems. Also, while in VNS for instance, the neighbourhoods are exhaustively searched, in RS, the local search is stochastic. When RS implements a 2-opt local search, it searches exhaustively in the $k = 2$ neighbourhood of every new created solution. However, the sample of new solutions from current centres is random. With regard other global search methods such as Tabu Search and the Simulated Annealing, the main difference is in that RS maintains a population.

4 Computational Experiments

RS was tested on 40 benchmark problems, 20 of which were obtained from the TSP-LIB libray, [6], and the other 20 from the QAP-LIB library, [7]. A memetic algorithm was implemented as well. This is the combination of GA with the 2-opt rule (2optGA). The main reason for choosing this algorithm for comparison is that it is very effective on both TSP and QAP problems, (see [9] and [8] for instance).

In every problem instance both algorithms were run 10 times. Given that the local search dominates the computational time, in both algorithms the number of solution evaluations and calls to 2-opt were restricted to 10,000. The parameters for RS were as follows: the number of centres $f = 2$, solutions generated by base $q = 50$, the number of iterations $k = 500$, the radius $r' = 0.2$, the expansion constant $e = 1.1$, the contraction constant $c = 0.9$. For every 30 generations without improvement the radius was reset as described in Section 2.1. For the GA, the size of the population and maximum number of generations were set to 100. The recombination method was OX1 crossover (see [8]) with a rate of 95%. The selection method was $k = 3$ tournament selection. The mutation probability was 1%. To provide elitist pressure 4% of the best individuals were selected to become part of the new population at every generation. In both algorithms these parameters are the ones that seem to give the best results after a pre-experimental phase. In both cases, all the solutions were improved making use of 2-opt. Both algorithms were encoded in Java and run on identical PCs (Pentium IV, 3.0 Ghz, 1Gb of memory).

Table 1, shows the percentage of deviation from the best known values in every problem instance. The number in the instances name is the size of the problem. In the case of the TSP, the sizes range from 22 to 318, for the QAP, from 25 to 150. In both cases the problem types considered are symmetric. For the QAP this represents a faster performance for the 2-opt rule [11].

The one tailed t-test concluded that the mean deviation of RS in the TSP instances are smaller than the ones of 2-optGA in d198 and pr299. The conclusions are in favour of 2-optGA in eil76 and eil101. For the rest of the instances there is no evidence to support any difference. On the other hand, for the QAP the

Table 1. Percentage deviation from best known values for the TSP and QAP instances

	QAP					TSP			
	RS		2optGA			RS		2optGA	
instance	x̄	min	x̄	min	instance	x̄	min	x̄	min
chr25a	0.916	0.000	3.408	0.000	ulysses22	0.000	0.000	0.000	0.000
nug28	0.124	0.000	0.108	0.000	dantzig42	0.000	0.000	0.000	0.000
nug30	0.130	0.000	0.169	0.000	eil51	0.692	0.674	0.694	0.674
Kra30a	0.275	0.000	0.396	0.000	berlin52	0.031	0.031	0.031	0.031
ste36a	0.061	0.000	0.090	0.000	st70	0.312	0.312	0.312	0.312
Ste36b	0.000	0.000	0.000	0.000	eil76	1.240	1.184	1.184	1.184
Wil50	0.026	0.000	0.064	0.032	pr76	0.000	0.000	0.000	0.000
tai60a	1.477	1.184	2.376	2.197	rat99	0.681	0.681	0.689	0.681
esc64a	0.000	0.000	0.000	0.000	eil101	2.054	1.782	1.920	1.782
Sko64	0.088	0.000	0.111	0.000	pr124	0.001	0.001	0.001	0.001
Sko72	0.088	0.000	0.264	0.084	ch130	0.223	0.012	0.312	0.047
tai80a	1.504	1.333	2.319	2.141	pr144	0.000	0.000	0.000	0.000
Sko81	0.123	0.011	0.094	0.033	ch150	0.144	0.044	0.116	0.044
Sko90	0.192	0.000	0.179	0.066	pr152	0.058	0.002	0.059	0.002
tai100a	1.377	1.197	2.234	2.078	d198	0.307	0.198	0.398	0.316
sko100a	0.232	0.098	0.113	0.038	pr226	0.009	0.000	0.006	0.002
Sko100b	0.078	0.002	0.099	0.048	pr264	0.021	0.000	0.000	0.000
Wil100	0.0784	0.003	0.079	0.013	a280	0.461	0.341	0.559	0.346
Esc128	0.000	0.000	0.000	0.000	pr299	0.368	0.216	0.710	0.411
tho150	0.192	0.094	0.163	0.062	lin318	0.902	0.473	1.040	0.678

tests were conclusive in five instances in favour of RS (tai60a, tai80a, tai100a, Sko72, Wil50). For the rest of the instances there is no evidence to support any difference.

5 Conclusions

We introduced the general framework of RS. In its first version hybridized with 2-opt, it showed to be an effective optimization tool. Its performance is comparable with that of the 2-optGA here described, in solving well known TSP and QAP instances. Added to this is the fact that the concepts exploited by RS are easy to understand. This means that RS is worth exploring further. It was observed that RS shares some strengths with current metaheursitics: it explores different neighbourhoods as other PB-SLS algorithms, but the search is differently implemented. RS takes advantages of the competition frameworks that characterize population based methods and it dynamically controls the intensification and diversification of the search.

Current work considers elaborate implementations of the general framework to solve both of the problems here presented, and compare it with state of the art metaheuristics designed for these same problems. Moreover there seem to be interesting theoretical results regarding the search sub-spaces explored by RS to be obtained.

Acknowledgements. This research work is supported by CONACYT grant 178473.

References

1. Wolpert D. and McReady W.G. (1997). *No free lunch theorems for optimization.* IEEE Transactions on Evolutionary Computation, 1(1), 67-82.
2. Gregory G. and Abraham P. P. (2002). *The Traveling Salesman Problem and its Variations,* Kluwer Academic Publishers, 369-443.
3. Koopmans T C and Beckman M.J. (1957). *Assignment problems and the location of economics activities.* Econometrica 25:53-76.
4. Garey M. R., Graham R.L. and Johnson D. S. (1976). *Some NP-complete geometric problems,* 8th Annual ACM Symposium on Theory of computing, 10-22.
5. Shani S. and Gonzalez T. (1976). *P-complete approximation problems.* Journal of the ACM 23:555-565.
6. Reinelt G.(1991). *TSPLIB - A Traveling Salesman Problem Library.* ORSA Journal on Computing 3:376-384. It can be visited in http://www.iwr.uni-heidelberg.de/groups/comopt/soft/TSPLIB95/TSPLIB.html
7. Burkard RE, Karisch S and Rendl F(1991). *QAPLIB-A quadratic assignment problem library.* European Journal Of Operational Research 55: 115-119. It can be visited in http://www.seas.upenn.edu/qaplib/
8. Ozcan E., and Erenturk M. (2004). *A Brief Review of Memetic Algorithms for Solving Euclidean 2D Traveling Salesrep Problem,* 13th Turkish Symposium on Artificial Intelligence and Neural Networks, 99-108..
9. Fleurent C. and Ferland J. (1994). *Genetic Hybrids for the quadratic assignment problem.* DIMACS series in Discrete Mathematics and Theoretical Computer Science 16: 190-206.
10. Glover F, and Kochenberger G.(2003). *Handbook of Metaheuristics,* International Series in Operations Research & Management Science, 57, Boston Kluwer Academic Publishers, .
11. Stützle T. and Dorigo M. (2001). *Local search and metaheuristics for the quadratic assignment problem.* Technical Report AIDA-01-01, FG Intellektik, FB Informatik, TU Darmstadt, Germany.
12. Baeck, T.(1995). *Evolutionary Algorithms in Theory and Practice,* Oxford University Press, Oxford.
13. Golston, J. E., Moss, R. II. and Stoecker, W. V. (1990). *Boundary Detection in Skin Tumour Images: an Overall Approach and a Radial Search Algorithm.* Pattern Recognition, 23(11): 1235-1247.
14. Ruiz, E. E. S. and Fairhurst, M. C. (1995). *Two-Dimensional Echocardiographic Images.* IEE Proc. Vision, Image and Signal Processing 142(3): 121-127.
15. O'Gorman, L., Sanderson, A. C., Preston, K. Jnr. and Dekker, A. (1983). *Image Segmentation and Nucleus Classification for Automated Tissue Section Analysis.* IEEE Computer Vision Pattern Recognition.
16. Yuri M. E. and Andrzej R. (1995). *Convex Optimization by Radial Search.* Working paper, International Institute for Applied Systems Analysis.
17. H.H. Hoss and T. Stuttzle (2004). *Stochastic Local Search Foundations and Applications.* Elsevier.

Rough Sets and Decision Rules in Fuzzy Set-Valued Information Systems

Danjun Zhu[1], Boqin Feng[1], and Tao Guan[2]

[1] School of Electronics and Information Engineering, Xi'an Jiaotong University, Xi'an, 710049, China
[2] State Key Laboratory of Intelligent Technology and Systems(LITS), Department of Computer Science and Technology, Tsinghua University, Beijing, 100084, China

Abstract. Set-valued Information Systems(SVISs) are generalized forms of Crisp Information Systems(CISs) and common in practice. This paper defines a fuzzy inclusion relation in Fuzzy Set-valued Information Systems(FSVISs). By means of two parameters of inclusion degree λ_1 and λ_2, we define the rough sets in FSVISs, which are used to approximate fuzzy concepts in FSVISs. Furthermore, in terms of the maximum elements in the lattice derived from the universe according to decision attributes, we present the definitions and measuring methods of decision rules in FSVISs. Some examples have been given for illustration.

1 Introduction

Rough set theory(RST), proposed by Pawlak, has been used to knowledge discovery and acquirement [1], data analysis [2], feature selection [3,4], concept approximation [5], rule extraction[6,7] in inexact, uncertain or vague information in databases or information systems(ISs) and applied in such fields as data mining, web mining, medical or mechanical diagnosis during the last 20 years [2,6,8].

Rough sets concept is established on ISs denoted as (U, R) where U and R are called universe(set of objects) and equivalence relation on U, respectively. The equivalence relations, which can be constructed from some attribute set or its subset, play an important role in RSTs that partitions the universe into some classes called information granules. Capacities of RSTs for knowledge discovery include knowledge reduction, concept approximation and rule extraction. Knowledge reduction is one of most important contributions of RSTs to knowledge discovery and its aim is to search for the subsets of condition attributes which provide the same information for classification purposes as the full set of available attributes in order to refine classifiers or decision rules [9,10,11,12,13]. In these fields of information fusion and representation, concepts(or patterns) in an IS(or an approximation space) can be approximately expressed by its lower and upper approximations [5,14]. Much work on pattern construction and composition has been done by Skowron and his coauthors by using information granules. In medical diagnosis applications, RSTs based rule extraction are investigated and applied by Tsumoto.

By far, rough properties of fuzzy sets have been a focus that many investigators work on [15, 16, 17]. Fuzzy sets and rough sets are different: rough set theory [1] explains the indiscernibility between objects in the universe in terms of finite features, while fuzzy sets measure the fuzziness of boundaries between sets [18]. Two extended set theories emerge by putting fuzzy sets and rough sets together, i.e. fuzzy rough sets and rough fuzzy sets [15, 18], which have some special characteristics and applications. Recently some interesting investigation focus on rough approximations of general multisets [19] and knowledge discovery in such ISs as set-valued ISs [20], fuzzy ISs, fuzzy valued information systems. However, little attention is paid to such ISs with higher fuzziness as fuzzy set-valued ISs(FSVISs), fuzzy number ISs that are common in natural language processing, information fusion. This paper focuses on rough set based knowledge discovery and denotation of fuzzy rules in FSVISs. We present the definition and properties of rough sets in FSVISs, which use two parameters of inclusion degree λ_1, λ_2. Moreover, the common forms of fuzzy decision rules are proposed based on the lattice derived from the universe. Three measures are presented for these rules. Some examples show favorable results.

2 ISs and Rough Sets

Usually, an IS is represented as (U, A) in which U, A is the finite set of objects and the finite set of attributes, respectively. A commonly used IS is the decision table denoted as $(U, A \cup D)$ where D is the set of features, also called decision attributes [1]. Usually $D = \{d\}$. In rough set theory [1, 10], each non-empty subset $B \subset A$(or $B \subset D$) determines an indiscernibility relation

$$R_B = \{(x, y) \in U \times U : a(x) = a(y), \forall a \in B\}$$

R_B partitions U into equivalence classes(or B-granules)

$$U/R_B = \{[x]_B : x \in U\}$$

where $[x]_B$ is the equivalence class including x with respect to(wrt) B and $[x]_B = \{y \in U : (x, y) \in R_B\}$.

U/R_B consists of a crisp partition of U, i.e. $U = \bigcup\{[x]_B : x \in U\}$. The sizes(in the meaning of cardinality) of B-granules denote the degree that we know about this IS by using B. For a concept X in U(or $X \subset U$), we can approximately represent it by its lower and upper approximations as follows in U that are consist of B-granules.

$$\underline{R_B}X = \bigcup\{[x]_B \subset X : x \in U\}, \quad \overline{R_B}X = \bigcup\{[x]_B \cap X \neq \emptyset : x \in U\}$$

$\underline{R_B}X$ denotes the set of objects that belong to X with certainty while $\overline{R_B}X$ denotes the set of objects that belong possibly to X. $(\underline{R_B}X, \overline{R_B}X)$ is referenced as the rough set of X wrt B. The approximation precision of X by (U, R_B) is defined as $d_B(X) = |\underline{R_B}X|/|\overline{R_B}X|$ where $X \neq \emptyset$ and if $X = \emptyset$, then let $d_B(X) = 1$. Obviously $0 \leq d_B(X) \leq 1$.

3 Fuzzy Set-Valued ISs(FSVISs)

We firstly give the basic definition of set-valued information systems(SVISs).

Definition 1. *[20] If $U = \{x_1, x_2, \cdots, x_n\}$ is the universe, $A = \{a_1, a_2, \cdots, a_m\}$ is the attribute set, $F = \{f_l : l \leq m\}$, $f_l : U \to \mathcal{P}(V_l)$ corresponding to A, $(l \leq m)$, then (U, A, F) is called set-valued information systems, where $\mathcal{P}(V_l)$ denotes the collection of crisp subsets of V_l, V_l is the object range about a_l.*

The fuzzy version of SVISs are the FSVISs that are defined as follows.

Definition 2. *If $U = \{x_1, x_2, \cdots, x_n\}$ is the universe, $A = \{a_1, a_2, \cdots, a_m\}$ is the attribute set, $F = \{f_l : l \leq m\}$, $f_l : U \to \mathcal{F}(V_l)$, $(l \leq m)$, then (U, A, F) is called fuzzy set-valued information system, where $\mathcal{F}(V_l)$ denotes the collection of fuzzy subsets of V_l.*

In FSVISs, $a_l \times x_i$ constitutes a fuzzy subset of V_l, denoted briefly as f_{li} for $i \leq n, l \leq m$. In other words, $f_{li} : V_l \to [0,1]$. In fact, $f_l(x_i) = f_{li}$.

Example 1. If $V_1 = \{1, 2, 3\}$, $V_2 = \{1, 2\}$ for a_1, a_2, respectively, then we may have $f_1 = a_1, f_2 = a_2$ and $a_1(x_1) = f_{11} = 1/1 + 1/2 + 0/3$, $a_1(x_2) = f_{12} = 0/1 + 1/2 + 1/3$, $a_2(x_1) = f_{21} = 0/1 + 1/2$, etc.

Example 2. Especially, if f_{ij}s are fuzzy numbers, then (U, A, F) is called as fuzzy number ISs, as shown in Table 1. $'Big'$, $'Mid'$ and $'Small'$ are fuzzy numbers,

Table 1. A fuzzy number IS

U	a_1	a_2	a_3
x_1	Big	Mid	Mid
x_2	Big	Big	Mid
x_3	Small	Mid	Small

and

$$'Big'(x) = \begin{cases} 0, & 0 \leq x \leq 0.5 \\ \frac{x-0.5}{0.5}, & 0.5 \leq x \leq 1 \end{cases}; \quad 'Mid'(x) = \begin{cases} \frac{x}{0.5}, & 0 \leq x \leq 0.5 \\ \frac{1-x}{0.5}, & 0.5 \leq x \leq 1 \end{cases};$$

$$'Small'(x) = \begin{cases} \frac{0.5-x}{0.5}, & 0 \leq x \leq 0.5 \\ 0, & 0.5 \leq x \leq 1 \end{cases}.$$

When crisp decisions are included in FSVISs, we get the following definition.

Definition 3. *If $U = \{x_1, x_2, \cdots, x_n\}$ is the universe, $A = \{a_1, a_2, \cdots, a_m\}$ is the attribute set, $F = \{f_l : l \leq m\}$, $f_l : U \to \mathcal{F}(V_l)$, $(l \leq m)$, $D = \{d_1, d_2, \cdots, d_r\}$, $G = \{g_l : l \leq r\}$, $g_l : U \to V_l'$, $(l \leq r)$, then (U, A, F, D, G) is called fuzzy set-valued decision system(FSVDS), where $\mathcal{F}(V_l)$ denotes the collection of fuzzy subsets of V_l.*

Table 2. A FSVDS

U	a_1	a_2	d
x_1	f_{11}	f_{21}	1
x_2	f_{12}	f_{22}	1
x_3	f_{13}	f_{23}	2

Example 3. The following table showes a FSVDS, where $V_1 = \{1,2,3,4\}$, $V_2 = \{a,b,c,d\}$.
where f_{ij} denotes the value of x_i on a_j, which is a fuzzy set on V_j, and $f_{11} = \frac{0.8}{1} + \frac{0.9}{2} + \frac{0.1}{3} + \frac{0.1}{4}$, $f_{12} = \frac{0.1}{1} + \frac{0.9}{2} + \frac{0.8}{3} + \frac{0.1}{4}$, $f_{13} = \frac{0.9}{1} + \frac{0.2}{2} + \frac{0.1}{3} + \frac{1}{4}$; $f_{21} = \frac{0.1}{a} + \frac{0.9}{b} + \frac{1}{c} + \frac{0.1}{d}$, $f_{22} = \frac{0.1}{a} + \frac{0}{b} + \frac{0.8}{c} + \frac{0.9}{d}$, $f_{23} = \frac{0.9}{a} + \frac{0.9}{b} + \frac{0.1}{c} + \frac{0.1}{d}$.

In some situations such as ophthalmological diagnosis, significant concepts, such as myopia and hyperopia, are derived from decision attributes whose domain lie in R^+, such as eyesight of left and right eyes. The following definition presents a FSVIS whose decisions take continuous value in $[0,1]$.

Definition 4. *If $U = \{x_1, x_2, \cdots, x_n\}$ is the universe, $A = \{a_1, a_2, \cdots, a_m\}$ is the attribute set, $F = \{f_l : l \leq m\}$, $f_l : U \to \mathcal{F}(V_l)$, $(l \leq m)$, $D = \{d_1, d_2, \cdots, d_r\}$, $G = \{g_l : l \leq r\}$, $g_l : U \to [0,1]$, $(l \leq r)$, then (U, A, F, D, G) is called fuzzy set-valued fuzzy decision system(FFDS), where $\mathcal{F}(V_l)$ denotes the collection of fuzzy subsets of V_l. Moreover, if $g_l : U \to \mathcal{F}([0,1])$, $(l \leq r)$, then (U, A, F, D, G) is called fuzzy set-valued type-2 fuzzy decision system(FTDS).*

4 Approximating Concepts Via Rough Sets in FSVISs

Suppose that (U, A, F) is a FSVIS. For $\forall B \subset A$, we define the following relation.

$$R_B = \{(x_i, x_j) : f_{li} \geq f_{lj}, \forall a_l \in B\} = \{(x_i, x_j) : f_l(x_i) \supseteq f_l(x_j), \forall a_l \in B\},$$

Obviously, R_B is reflexive, transitive but not symmetric. Let $[x]_{R_B} = \{y : (x,y) \in R_B\}$, then $\{[x]_{R_B} : x \in U, B \subset A\}$ constitute a cover of U.

Definition 5. *Suppose that (U, A, F) is a FSVIS, the lower and upper approximations of crisp subset $X \subset U$ with respect to(wrt) $B \subset A$ are*

$$\underline{R_B}(X) = \{x \in U : I([x]_{R_B}, X) = 1\}, \quad \overline{R_B}(X) = \{x \in U : I([x]_{R_B}, X) > 0\} \tag{1}$$

where $I(X,Y) = \frac{|X \cap Y|}{|X|}$ denotes inclusion degree of X in Y, $|X| = \sum_{i=1}^{n} \mu(x_i)$.
If X is a fuzzy set, i.e. $X = \sum_{i=1}^{n} \frac{\mu(x_i)}{x_i}$, $\mu(\cdot)$ is the membership function of X, $\lambda_1 > \lambda_2 \geq 0$, then the lower and upper approximations are defined for $x \in U$ as

$$\underline{R_B^{\lambda_1}}(X)(x) = \inf\{\mu(x) : I([x]_{R_B}, X) \geq \lambda_1\}, \tag{2}$$

$$\overline{R_B^{\lambda_2}}(X)(x) = \sup\{\mu(x) : I([x]_{R_B}, X) \geq \lambda_2\} \tag{3}$$

$\underline{R_B^{\lambda_1}}, \overline{R_B^{\lambda_2}}$ are separately called lower approximation operator wrt λ_1 (or lower approximation operator) and upper approximation operator λ_2 (or upper approximation operator).

Additionally, $POS^{\lambda_1}(X) = \underline{R_B^{\lambda_1}}(X)$ is also called positive region of X wrt λ_1. The negative region and boundary region of X wrt λ_1, λ_2 are denoted separately as
$$NEG^{\lambda_2}(X) = U - \overline{R_B^{\lambda_2}}(X). \quad BND^{\lambda_1,\lambda_2}(X) = \overline{R_B^{\lambda_2}}(X) - \underline{R_B^{\lambda_1}}(X).$$

Property 1. In FSVIS (U, A, F), $B \subset A$, $\lambda_1 > \lambda_2 \geq 0$, the lower and upper approximation operators of fuzzy set X, Y satisfy the following properties.

(1) $\underline{R_B^1}(X) =\sim \overline{R_B^0}(\sim X)$, $\overline{R_B^0}(X) =\sim \underline{R_B^1}(\sim X)$,

(2) $\underline{R_B^{\lambda_1}}(\emptyset) = \emptyset$, $\overline{R_B^{\lambda_2}}(U) = U$,

(3) $\underline{R_B^{\lambda_1}}(X \cap Y) \subseteq \underline{R_B^{\lambda_1}}(X) \cap \underline{R_B^{\lambda_1}}(Y)$, $\overline{R_B^{\lambda_2}}(X \cup Y) \supseteq \overline{R_B^{\lambda_2}}(X) \cup \overline{R_B^{\lambda_2}}(Y)$,
$\underline{R_B^{\lambda_1}}(X \cup Y) \supseteq \underline{R_B^{\lambda_1}}(X) \cup \underline{R_B^{\lambda_1}}(Y)$, $\overline{R_B^{\lambda_2}}(X \cap Y) \subseteq \overline{R_B^{\lambda_2}}(X) \cap \overline{R_B^{\lambda_2}}(Y)$,

(4) $\underline{R_B^{\lambda_1}}(X) \subseteq X \subseteq \overline{R_B^{\lambda_2}}(X)$,

(5) $\underline{R_B^{\lambda_1}}(X) = \underline{R_B^{\lambda_1}}(\underline{R_B^{\lambda_1}}(X))$, $\overline{R_B^{\lambda_2}}(X) = \overline{R_B^{\lambda_2}}(\overline{R_B^{\lambda_2}}(X))$,

where $\hat{\alpha} \in \mathcal{F}(U), \hat{\alpha} \equiv \alpha$.

Proof. For brevity, only (3) is proved.

(3) For $\forall x \in U, B \subset A$,
$$\left.\begin{array}{l} I([x]_{R_B}, X) \geq I([x]_{R_B}, X \cap Y) \\ I([x]_{R_B}, Y) \geq I([x]_{R_B}, X \cap Y) \end{array}\right\} \Rightarrow \left\{\begin{array}{l} \underline{R_B^{\lambda_1}}(X \cap Y)(x) \leq \underline{R_B^{\lambda_1}}(X)(x) \\ \underline{R_B^{\lambda_1}}(X \cap Y)(x) \leq \underline{R_B^{\lambda_1}}(Y)(x) \end{array}\right.$$
$\Rightarrow \underline{R_B^{\lambda_1}}(X \cap Y)(x) \leq \underline{R_B^{\lambda_1}}(X)(x) \wedge \underline{R_B^{\lambda_1}}(Y)(x)$,

i.e. $\underline{R_B^{\lambda_1}}(X \cap Y) \subseteq \underline{R_B^{\lambda_1}}(X) \cap \underline{R_B^{\lambda_1}}(Y)$. For the same reason, we have
$\overline{R_B^{\lambda_2}}(X \cup Y) \supseteq \overline{R_B^{\lambda_2}}(X) \cup \overline{R_B^{\lambda_2}}(Y)$, $\underline{R_B^{\lambda_1}}(X \cup Y) \supseteq \underline{R_B^{\lambda_1}}(X) \cup \underline{R_B^{\lambda_1}}(Y)$,
$\overline{R_B^{\lambda_2}}(X \cap Y) \subseteq \overline{R_B^{\lambda_2}}(X) \cap \overline{R_B^{\lambda_2}}(Y)$ ♯

One important functionality of rough sets is to approximate concepts in the universe via conditional attributes [21], and several cases for rough approximations of $X \subset U$ are listed as follows.

(1) If $\underline{R_B^{\lambda_1}} \neq \emptyset$, and $\overline{R_B^{\lambda_2}} \neq \emptyset$, then X is rough definable.

(2) If $\underline{R_B^{\lambda_1}} = \emptyset$, and $\overline{R_B^{\lambda_2}} \neq \emptyset$, then X is internal undefinable.

(3) If $\underline{R_B^{\lambda_1}} \neq \emptyset$, and $\overline{R_B^{\lambda_2}} = \emptyset$, then X is external undefinable.

(4) If $\underline{R_B^{\lambda_1}} = \emptyset$, and $\overline{R_B^{\lambda_2}} = \emptyset$, then X is total undefinable.

In the following, the (λ_1, λ_2) approximation quality is given.

Definition 6. *Suppose (U, A, F) be a FSVIS, the approximation quality of X wrt $\lambda_1 > \lambda_2 \geq 0$ is $\alpha_{\lambda_1,\lambda_2} = |\underline{R_B^{\lambda_1}} X|/|\overline{R_B^{\lambda_2}} X|$. Obviously $0 \leq \alpha_{\lambda_1,\lambda_2} \leq 1$. The rough degree is $\rho_{\lambda_1,\lambda_2} = 1 - \alpha_{\lambda_1,\lambda_2}$.*

When $\alpha_{\lambda_1,\lambda_2} = 1$, then X is certain wrt (λ_1, λ_2); rough uncertain wrt (λ_1, λ_2) otherwise.

5 Decision Rules in FSVISs

Some authors investigate the decision rules in FSVISs [20](also called Multi-valued Decision Systems [22]). Here in order to obtain the decision rules in FSVISs, we give the denotations and definitions. Let $\mathcal{V} = \prod_{l=1}^{m} \mathcal{F}(V_l) = \{\mathbf{E} = \{E_1, E_2, \cdots, E_m\}, l \leq m\}$, $\mathbf{1} = \{V_1, V_2, \cdots, V_m\}$ and $\mathbf{0} = \{\emptyset, \emptyset, \cdots, \emptyset\}$, obviously $\mathbf{1}, \mathbf{0} \in \mathcal{V}$, then $(\mathcal{V}, \preceq)$ is a lattice in which $\preceq$ is defined by $\subseteq$.

Definition 7. *In FSVIS (U, A, F), let $\mathcal{M} = \{\mathbf{E}(x) = (f_1(x), f_2(x), \cdots, f_m(x)) : x \in U\}$, obviously $\mathcal{M} \subset \mathcal{V}$. The set of all fuzzy maximum elements derived from $\mathcal{M}$ except for $\mathbf{1}$ is defined as $H(\mathcal{M})$. The operation for elements in $\mathcal{M}$ is defined for $x \in U$ as $\overline{\mathbf{E}}(x) = \max\{\mathbf{E}(x), \mathbf{E}'(x)\} = \{f_1(x) \vee f_1'(x), f_2(x) \vee f_2'(x), \cdots, f_m(x) \vee f_m'(x)\}$, $\underline{\mathbf{E}}(x) = \min\{\mathbf{E}(x), \mathbf{E}'(x)\} = \{f_1(x) \wedge f_1'(x), f_2(x) \wedge f_2'(x), \cdots, f_m(x) \wedge f_m'(x)\}$.*

Furthermore, let $\alpha > 0.5$, if $\forall \overline{\mathbf{E}} \in H(\mathcal{M})$, $\exists \{i_1, i_2, \cdots, i_k\} \subset \{1, 2, \cdots, m\}$, $k \leq m$, $s.t. \overline{\mathbf{E}}_s(x) \geq \alpha, s \in \{i_1, i_2, \cdots, i_k\}$ and $\overline{\mathbf{E}}_t(x) < 1 - \alpha, t \notin \{i_1, i_2, \cdots, i_k\}$, then $H(\mathcal{M})$ is the collection of k-order maximum elements wrt α, denoted as $H_k^\alpha(\mathcal{M})$.

Example 4. Assume that $V_1 = \{1, 2, 3, 4\}, V_2 = \{a, b, c, d\}$, $\mathcal{M} = \{\mathbf{E}_1, \mathbf{E}_2, \mathbf{E}_3\}$, where $\mathbf{E}_1 = (f_{11}, f_{21})$, $\mathbf{E}_2 = (f_{12}, f_{22})$ and $\mathbf{E}_3 = (f_{13}, f_{23})$; $f_{11}, f_{12}, f_{13}, f_{21}, f_{22}$ and f_{23} are defined as those in Example 3.

Obviously, $\mathbf{E}_1, \mathbf{E}_2, \mathbf{E}_3$ are 2 order maximum elements wrt 0.8, i.e. $H_2^{0.8}(\mathcal{M}) = (\mathbf{E}_1, \mathbf{E}_2, \mathbf{E}_3)$.

Let $k = 3, \alpha = 0.8$, then $H_3^{0.8}(\mathcal{M}) = (\mathbf{E}_1', \mathbf{E}_2')$, where $\mathbf{E}_1' = (f_{11}', f_{21}')$; $\mathbf{E}_2' = (f_{12}', f_{22}')$, $f_{11}' = \frac{0.8}{1} + \frac{0.9}{2} + \frac{0.8}{3} + \frac{0.1}{4}$, $f_{12}' = \frac{0.9}{1} + \frac{0.9}{2} + \frac{0.1}{3} + \frac{1}{4}$, $f_{21}' = \frac{0.1}{a} + \frac{0.9}{b} + \frac{1}{c} + \frac{0.9}{d}$, $f_{22}' = \frac{0.9}{a} + \frac{0.9}{b} + \frac{1}{c} + \frac{0.1}{d}$.

In fact, α is taken as the level parameter. When $k = 3$, $H_3^{0.8}(\mathcal{M}) = (\mathbf{E}_1'', \mathbf{E}_2'')$, where $\mathbf{E}_1'' = (\{1, 2, 3\}, \{b, c, d\})$; $\mathbf{E}_2'' = (\{1, 2, 4\}, \{a, b, c\})$.

Theorem 1. *In FFDS (U, A, F, D, G), $B \subset A$, $\mathcal{M} = \{\mathcal{M}_j | j \leq m\}$. Suppose that $\{F_1, F_2, \cdots, F_r\}$ is the fuzzy partition of U derived from D as shown in Fig. 1, then*

$$H(\underline{\mathcal{M}_j}) \preceq H(\mathcal{M}_j) \preceq H(\overline{\mathcal{M}_j}),$$

where $\mathcal{M}_j = \{\mathbf{E}(y) \in \mathcal{D} : y \in F_j\}$, $\underline{\mathcal{M}_j} = \{\mathbf{E}(y) \in \mathcal{D} : y \in \underline{R_B}(F_j)\}$, $\overline{\mathcal{M}_j} = \{\mathbf{E}(y) \in \mathcal{D} : y \in \overline{R_B}(F_j)\}$, $j \leq r$. Moreover, for $0 < \alpha \leq 1, k > 0$, we have

$$H_k^\alpha(\underline{\mathcal{M}_j}) \preceq H_k^\alpha(\mathcal{M}_j) \preceq H_k^\alpha(\overline{\mathcal{M}_j}).$$

Proof. Because of $\underline{R_B}(F_j) \subseteq F_j \subseteq \overline{R_B}(F_j)$, proof is obvious. ♯

In FSVDSs, $Ind(D)$ constitutes an indiscernibility relation that partitions the universe into some equivalence classes. Let $U/Ind(D) = \{D_1, D_2, \cdots, D_p\}$, then we consider the rough approximation of $D_k, k \leq p$ by the fuzzy partition via $B \subset A$. For brevity, let $D = \{d\}$.

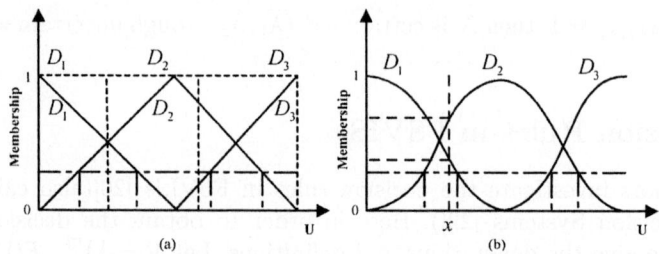

Fig. 1. Three types of the characteristic functions for decision attributes on the universe. The crisp functions as the dotted lines in (a) are constructed from symbolic decision values, the normal triangle fuzzy functions as the solid lines in (a), the normal bell functions as the solid lines in (b). Moreover, (b) shows the membership of x to D_1, D_2, D_3 in the fuzzy partition [10].

Definition 8. *In FSVIS (U, A, F), suppose $\mathcal{L} = (\mathcal{V}, \preceq)$ be a fuzzy lattice, $\mathbf{E} = (E_1, E_2, \cdots, E_m) \in \mathcal{V}, \mathbf{F} = (F_1, F_2, \cdots, F_m) \in \mathcal{V}$, we define the measure on $\mathcal{L}$ as $\mathbf{I}(\mathbf{E}, \mathbf{F}) = \frac{1}{m}\sum_{i=1}^{m} I(E_i, F_i)$, where $I(E_i, F_i) = \frac{|E_i \cap F_i|}{|E_i|}, i \leq m$.*

Theorem 2. $\mathbf{I}(\mathbf{E}, \mathbf{F})$ *is an inclusion degree on* $(\mathcal{V}, \preceq)$.

Proof. Proof is completed by verifying. ♯

Definition 9. *In FFRS (U, A, F, D, G), $0 < \beta \leq 1$, $B \subset A$, $x \in U$. Suppose that $\{F_1, F_2, \cdots, F_r\}$ is the fuzzy partition of U derived from D, we get*

(1) If $\mathbf{I}(\mathbf{E}^\alpha(x), H(\mathcal{M}_j^\beta)) = 1$, i.e. $\mathbf{E}^\alpha(x) \preceq H(\mathcal{M}_j^\beta)$, then certain fuzzy rules wrt α and β are denoted as $\mathbf{E}^\alpha(x) \to F_j^\beta$, where $\mathbf{E}^\alpha(x)$ is the α level set of $\mathbf{E}(x)$. Moreover, for $\underline{\mathbf{E}}(x) \preceq \mathbf{E}(x)$, we have $\underline{\mathbf{E}}^\alpha(x) \to F_j^\beta$,

(2) If $\forall j \leq r$, $\mathbf{I}(\mathbf{E}^\alpha(x), H(\mathcal{M}_j^\beta)) > 0$, i.e. $\forall j \leq r$, $\mathbf{E}^\alpha(x) \not\preceq H(\mathcal{M}_j^\beta)$, then decision rules having maximal inclusion degree wrt α and β are $\mathbf{E}^\alpha(x) \to F_{j_0}^\beta$, where $\mathbf{I}(\mathbf{E}^\alpha(x), H(M_{j_0}^\beta)) = max_{j \leq r}\mathbf{I}(\mathbf{E}^\alpha(x), H(M_j^\beta))$.

(3) If $\exists \mathcal{I}_s = \{j_1, j_2, \cdots, j_s\} \subset \{1, 2, \cdots, m\}, s \leq m$, s.t. $\mathbf{E}^\alpha(x) \preceq H(M_{j_t}^\beta), t \leq s$, and $\forall p, q \in \mathcal{I}_s, p \neq q, H(M_p^\beta) \neq H(M_q^\beta)$, then decision rules having maximal support degree wrt α and β are $\mathbf{E}^\alpha(x) \to F_{j_0}^\beta$, where $|\{x \in U : \mathbf{E}^\alpha(x) \preceq H(M_{j_0}^\beta)\}| \geq |\{x \in U : \mathbf{E}^\alpha(x) \preceq H(M_q^\beta)\}|, \forall q \in \mathcal{I}_s$.

Definition 10. *The Support Degree(SD), Confidence Degree(FD) and Converge Degree(VD) of $\mathbf{E}^\alpha(x) \to F_j^\beta$ are denoted separately as*
$$SD = \frac{|F_j^\beta \cap \{x|x \ \ satisfies \ \ \mathbf{E}^\alpha\}|}{|U|}, \ FD = \frac{|F_j^\beta \cap \{x|x \ \ satisfies \ \ \mathbf{E}^\alpha\}|}{|\{x|x \ \ satisfies \ \ \mathbf{E}^\alpha\}|},$$
$$VD = \frac{|F_j^\beta \cap \{x|x \ \ satisfies \ \ \mathbf{E}^\alpha\}|}{|F_j^\beta|}.$$

Example 5. By far, there are still lack of methods for rule extraction in FSVISs. This following example presents the process of producing rules in FFDSs. The

Table 3. A FFDS

U	x_1	x_2	x_3	x_4	x_5	x_6	x_7	x_8	x_9	x_0
a_1	f_{11}	f_{12}	f_{13}	f_{14}	f_{15}	f_{16}	f_{17}	f_{18}	f_{19}	f_{10}
a_2	f_{21}	f_{22}	f_{23}	f_{24}	f_{25}	f_{26}	f_{27}	f_{28}	f_{29}	f_{20}
d	0.1	0.2	0.3	0.4	0.5	0.6	0.7	0.8	0.9	1.0

obvious advantages in our method is its capacity of finding out certain rules, i.e. lower approximation rules, and uncertain rules, i.e. upper approximation rules, with different orders that is dominant over common methods on non-FSVISs. where

$$f_{11} = \frac{0.8}{1} + \frac{0.9}{2} + \frac{0.1}{3} + \frac{0.1}{4}, f_{12} = \frac{0.9}{1} + \frac{0.2}{2} + \frac{0.9}{3} + \frac{0.1}{4}, f_{13} = \frac{0.1}{1} + \frac{0.8}{2} + \frac{0.1}{3} + \frac{1.0}{4},$$
$$f_{14} = \frac{0.6}{1} + \frac{0.7}{2} + \frac{0.1}{3} + \frac{0.1}{4}, f_{15} = \frac{0.9}{1} + \frac{0}{2} + \frac{0.9}{3} + \frac{0.1}{4}, f_{16} = \frac{0.9}{1} + \frac{1.0}{2} + \frac{0.1}{3} + \frac{0.1}{4},$$
$$f_{17} = \frac{0}{1} + \frac{1.0}{2} + \frac{0.8}{3} + \frac{0.9}{4}, f_{18} = \frac{0.9}{1} + \frac{1.0}{2} + \frac{0.1}{3} + \frac{0.1}{4}, f_{19} = \frac{0.2}{1} + \frac{1.0}{2} + \frac{0.9}{3} + \frac{0.1}{4},$$
$$f_{10} = \frac{0.9}{1} + \frac{0.8}{2} + \frac{0.1}{3} + \frac{0}{4};$$

$$f_{21} = \frac{1}{a} + \frac{0.2}{b} + \frac{0.1}{c} + \frac{0.1}{d}, f_{22} = \frac{0.1}{a} + \frac{1}{b} + \frac{0.1}{c} + \frac{0.1}{d}, f_{23} = \frac{0.2}{a} + \frac{0.3}{b} + \frac{1}{c} + \frac{0}{d},$$
$$f_{24} = \frac{0}{a} + \frac{0.1}{b} + \frac{0.1}{c} + \frac{0.8}{d}, f_{25} = \frac{0}{a} + \frac{0.2}{b} + \frac{0.9}{c} + \frac{0.3}{d}, f_{26} = \frac{0}{a} + \frac{1.0}{b} + \frac{0.1}{c} + \frac{0.3}{d},$$
$$f_{27} = \frac{1.0}{a} + \frac{0.1}{b} + \frac{0.1}{c} + \frac{0.3}{d}, f_{28} = \frac{0}{a} + \frac{0.8}{b} + \frac{0.1}{c} + \frac{0.3}{d}, f_{29} = \frac{0}{a} + \frac{0.2}{b} + \frac{0.9}{c} + \frac{0.3}{d},$$
$$f_{20} = \frac{0.1}{a} + \frac{0.2}{b} + \frac{0.1}{c} + \frac{0.8}{d};$$
$$F_1(x) = d(x), F_2(x) = 1 - d(x).$$

For decision attributes, let $\beta = 0.7$, we get

$$(F_1^{0.7}, F_2^{0.7}) = (\{x_7, x_8, x_9, x_{10}\}, \{x_1, x_2, x_3\}).$$

For every object with $\alpha = 0.8$, we have
$\mathbf{E}_7^{0.8} = (\{1/2, 0.8/3, 0.9/4\}, \{1/a\})$, $\mathbf{E}_8^{0.8} = (\{0.9/1, 1.0/2\}, \{0.8/b\})$,
$\mathbf{E}_9^{0.8} = (\{1/2, 0.9/3\}, \{0.9/c\})$, $\mathbf{E}_{10}^{0.8} = (\{0.9/1, 0.8/2\}, \{0.8/d\})$,
$\mathbf{E}_1^{0.8} = (\{0.8/1, 0.9/2\}, \{1/a\})$, $\mathbf{E}_2^{0.8} = (\{0.9/1, 0.9/3\}, \{1/b\})$,
$\mathbf{E}_3^{0.8} = (\{0.8/2, 1/4\}, \{1/c\})$,

Table 4. Some examples of 3-order decision rules for $\alpha = 0.8, \beta = 0.7$

Rules	SD	FD	VD
$(\{1,2\},\{a\}) \rightarrow F_2 \geq 0.7$	0.1	1	0.33
$(\{1,3\},\{b\}) \rightarrow F_2 \geq 0.7$	0.1	1	0.33
$(\{2,4\},\{c\}) \rightarrow F_2 \geq 0.7$	0.1	1	0.33
$(\{1,3\},\{c\}) \rightarrow F_2 \geq 0.7$	0.1	1	0.33
$(\{1,2\},\{b\}) \rightarrow F_1 \geq 0.7$	0.2	1	0.5
$(\{2,3,4\},\{a\}) \rightarrow F_1 \geq 0.7$	0.1	1	0.25
$(\{2,3\},\{c\}) \rightarrow F_1 \geq 0.7$	0.1	1	0.25
$(\{1,2\},\{d\}) \rightarrow F_1 \geq 0.7$	0.1	1	0.25
$(\{1\},\{b\}) \rightarrow F_2 \geq 0.7$	0.1	1	0.5
$(\{1\},\{b\}) \rightarrow F_1 \geq 0.7$	0.2	1	0.67
$(\{4\},\{a\}) \rightarrow F_1 \geq 0.7$	0.1	1	0.25
$(\{2\},\{b\}) \rightarrow F_1 \geq 0.7$	0.2	1	0.5

$H_3^{0.8}(\mathcal{M}_1) = \{(\{1/2, 0.9/3, 1/4\}, \{1/a, 0.9/c\}), (\{0.9/1, 1/2, 0.9/3\}, \{0.9/c, 0.8/b\})\},$

$H_3^{0.8}(\mathcal{M}_2) = \{(\{0.9/1, 0.9/2, 0.9/3\}, \{1/a, 1/b\}), (\{0.8/1, 0.9/2, 1/4\}, \{1/a, 1/c\})\}$

So

$\mathbf{E}_1^{0.8} \preceq H_3^{0.8}(\mathcal{M}_2),\ \mathbf{E}_2^{0.8} \preceq H_3^{0.8}(\mathcal{M}_2),\ \mathbf{E}_3^{0.8} \preceq H_3^{0.8}(\mathcal{M}_2),$
$\mathbf{E}_4^{0.8} \npreceq H_3^{0.8}(\mathcal{M}_1) \vee H_3^{0.8}(\mathcal{M}_2),\ \mathbf{E}_7^{0.8} \preceq H_3^{0.8}(\mathcal{M}_1),$
$\mathbf{E}_8^{0.8} \preceq H_3^{0.8}(\mathcal{M}_1),\ \mathbf{E}_9^{0.8} \preceq H_3^{0.8}(\mathcal{M}_1),\ \mathbf{E}_{10}^{0.8} \preceq H_3^{0.8}(\mathcal{M}_1).$

thus, some rules can be extracted from above, for example in Table 4.

6 Conclusion

FSVISs that are the fuzzy versions of SVISs. In this paper, we present the forms of rough sets in FVISs, which are used to approximate fuzzy concepts. Moreover, we define the lattice in FSVISs to produce the decision rules in FSVISs. Some examples show the computational results.

Acknowledgement

This paper is supported by National 863 Program of China(003AA1Z2610).

References

1. Pawlak Z. Rough sets. Theoretical Aspects of Reasoning about Data. Kluwer Academic Publishers, Dortrecht, 1991.
2. Tsau Young Lin. Data Mining and Machine Oriented Modeling: A Granular Computing Approach. Applied Intelligence 13, 2000, pp.113-124
3. Ludmila Ilieva Kuncheva, Fuzzy rough sets: application to feature selection, Fuzzy Sets and Systems(1992)147-153
4. Richard Jensen and Qiang Shen. Semantics-Preserving Dimensionality Reduction: Rough and Fuzzy-Rough-Based Approaches.IEEE Transactions on Knowledge and Data Engineering, 16(12),2004, pp.1457-1471
5. Bodjanova, Slavka. Approximation of fuzzy concepts in decision making. Fuzzy Sets and Systems,85(1), 1997, pp. 23-29
6. Tsumoto, Shusaku. Automated extraction of medical expert system rules from clinical databases based on rough set theory Information Sciences 112(1-4), 1998, pp.67-84
7. Qiang Shen, Alexios Chouchoulas, A rough-fuzzy approach for generating classification rules, Pattern Recognition 35(2002)2425-2438
8. Jensen Richard and Shen Qiang. Fuzzy-rough attribute reduction with application to web categorization. Fuzzy Sets and Systems 141(3), 2004, pp.469-485
9. Swiniarski, Roman W.; Skowron, Andrzej. Rough set methods in feature selection and recognition, Pattern Recognition Letters, 24(6), March, 2003, pp.833-849
10. Guan Tao, Feng Boqin. Knowledge reduction methods in fuzzy objective information systems. Journal of Software, 15(10), pp.1470-1478.
11. Kryszkiewicz M. Comparative studies of alternative type of knowledge reduction in inconsistent systems. International Journal of Intelligent Systems, 2001,16(1): 105-120

12. Zhang WenXiu, Mi JuSheng, Wu WeiZhi, Knowledge reductions in inconsistent information systems, Chinese Journal of Computers, 26(1), pp.12-18, Jan. 2003
13. Beynon M., Reducts within the vaiable presion rough sets model: a further investigation. European Journal of Operational Research, 2001, 134: 592-605
14. Peters,J.; Skowron,A.; Stepaniuk,J. Information granules in spatial reasoning Peters. Joint 9th IFSA World Congress and 20th NAFIPS International Conference, Vol.3, 2001, pp.1355-1360
15. D. Dubois, H. Prade: Rough fuzzy sets and fuzzy rough sets. Int. J. General Systems. 17(2-3),pp.191-209,1990
16. Z. Pawlak: Rough sets and fuzzy sets. Fuzzy Sets and Systems 17(1985)99-102
17. WeiZhi Wu, Wen-Xiu Zhang. Constructive and axiomatic approaches of fuzzy approximation operators, Information Sciences 159 (2004) 233-254
18. Y.Y.Yao: A comparative study of fuzzy sets and rough sets. Journal of Information Sciences 109(1998) 227-242
19. Sadaaki Miyamoto. Generalizations of multisets and rough approximations. International Journal of Intelligent Systems, Vol.19,639-652(2004)
20. Zhang WenXiu, Liang Yi, Wu WeiZhi. Information systems and knowledge discovery. Beijing: Science Press, September, 2003(in Chinese)
21. Slavka Bodjanova. Approximation of fuzzy concepts in decision making. Fuzzy Set and Systems 85(1997)23-29
22. Wojciech Rzasa, Artur Paluch, and Zbigniew Suraj. Decision rules in multivalued decision systems. S. Tsumoto, R. Slowwinski, J. Komorowinski, J.W. Grzymala-Busse(Eds.), the 4th International Conference, RSCTC2004, Uppsala, Sweden, June 2004, pp.504-509

Directed Cycles in Bayesian Belief Networks: Probabilistic Semantics and Consistency Checking Complexity

Alexander L. Tulupyev and Sergey I. Nikolenko

St.Petersburg Institute for Informatics and Automation
of the Russian Academy of Sciences
alt@iias.spb.su
sergey@logic.pdmi.ras.ru

Abstract. Although undirected cycles in directed graphs of Bayesian belief networks have been thoroughly studied, little attention has so far been given to a systematic analysis of directed (feedback) cycles. In this paper we propose a way of looking at those cycles; namely, we suggest that a feedback cycle represents a family of probabilistic distributions rather than a single distribution (as a regular Bayesian belief network does). A non-empty family of distributions can be explicitly represented by an ideal of conjunctions with interval estimates on the probabilities of its elements. This ideal can serve as a probabilistic model of an experts uncertain knowledge pattern; such models are studied in the theory of algebraic Bayesian networks. The family of probabilistic distributions may also be empty; in this case, the probabilistic assignment over cycle nodes is inconsistent. We propose a simple way of explicating the probabilistic relationships an isolated directed cycle contains, give an algorithm (based on linear programming) of its consistency checking, and establish a lower bound of the complexity of this checking.

1 Introduction

Bayesian belief networks (BBN), originating in the works of Judea Pearl [19,20,21], have employed directed acyclic graphs (DAG) in order to describe a probabilistic distribution in a way convenient for bayesian inference (we refer to [13] for an excellent overview of the subject). Since the original works, many generalizations and similar apparata have been developed, among them being, for example, dynamic Bayesian networks (see [14] and references therein).

Many efforts went into generalizing the basic structure of the network. Always the generalizations were related to employing a more general structure to be able to build more general independency models, that is, to incorporate different statements of the kind "X is independent of Y given Z". Finally, chain graphs as described in [23] seem to solve this problem (although there is still plenty of room for improvement). They have a complex structure with three different kinds of edges and allow undirected cycles in the graph.

Returning to directed acyclic graphs, the current state of the art in the Bayesian belief networks allows to efficiently deal with undirected cycles, that is, patterns which would be cycles if the arrow directions were not taken into account. However, very little (if any) work seems to have been done in the direction of generalizing Bayesian belief networks to allow directed cycles. The article [22], despite its highly relevant title, deals with establishing Markov properties of directed cyclic graphs representing stochastically disturbed linear equations, and does not deal with semantics of a cycle in a Bayesian belief network. It is also clearly stated in [13] that there is no BBN-calculus developed to deal with directed (feedback) cycles in Bayesian belief networks.

However, this generalization seems natural and may occur in practice, since the structure of a Bayesian network is determined by the experts. In fact, the need for this generalization has already been encountered in literature: see, for example, [1]. In that article the authors simply revert an edge of the directed cycle; however, such an operation, as we shall show here, changes the semantics of the whole network and is certainly not the right thing to do.

In this paper, we consider semantics of a directed cycle in a Bayesian belief network; the network is defined over a set of atomic propositions. We show that a cycle introduces interval bounds for the joint probabilities of variables of the network, and thus requires a new formalism to deal with it. We shall need to deal with a whole family of distributions, which may be empty. Thus, we shall look for algorithms that check consistency and find the upper and lower bounds for marginal joint probabilities of the cycle's elements.

Our approach, in a certain sense, is a complement to Heckerman et al. [11,12]. They are ready to work with as many cycles as may appear in their *dependency networks* that may also be, as they say, *almost consistent* (instead of being just consistent with probability axioms). We are incorporating cycles in BBN calculi preserving consistency with probabilistic axioms and avoid using artificial constraints requiring strict positiveness of appearing probabilistic distributions, as opposed to Heckerman et al.

2 Basic Definitions

In the paper, we follow a probabilistic logic approach introduced by N. Nilsson in [18] and formalized from a logical viewpoint in [2,3,4].

Let $\mathcal{T} = \{t_1, \ldots, t_N\}$ be the set of atoms (atomic propositions, Boolean variables) that are to represent experts' elementary judgements about a certain domain. $\mathcal{S} = \{x_1, \ldots, x_n\}$ is a subset of $\mathcal{T}$: $\mathcal{S} \subseteq \mathcal{T}$. We denote the negation of x by $\bar{x}$.

An ideal of conjunctions $\mathcal{C} = \mathcal{C}(\mathcal{S})$ over $\mathcal{S}$ consists of all non-empty conjunctions of elements of $\mathcal{S}$. For example,

$$\mathcal{C}(\{x_1, x_2, x_3\}) = \{x_1, x_2, x_3, x_1x_2, x_1x_3, x_2x_3, x_1x_2x_3\}.$$

A consistent probabilistic distribution over $\mathcal{C}(\mathcal{S})$ can be uniquely extended to all propositional formulas built over $\mathcal{S}$. A consistent assignment of point-valued estimates of probabilities of the elements of $\mathcal{C}$ defines the unique probabilistic distribution over propositional formulas over $\mathcal{S}$. A consistent assignment of interval-valued estimates defines a family of probabilistic distributions. The algorithms for consistency checking for such a distribution (or a family of the distributions) have already been developed, and we shall use them to cope with a cycle in a BBN. Let us note in addition that ideal $\mathcal{C}$ can be considered as a probabilistic model for an expert's knowledge pattern with uncertainty.

A *Bayesian belief network* is traditionally defined as a directed acyclic graph (DAG) $G = (V, E)$ (where V is a finite set of nodes, and E is a set of edges, that is, $E \subseteq G \times G$) together with a joint probabilistic distribution P that satisfies the *Markov condition*, namely that each variable $x \in V$ is conditionally independent of the set of all its nondescendents given the set of all its parents (see [15] for this definition and a detailed consideration of BBNs). The probabilistic distribution in question is defined by assigning conditional probabilities to each node given its parents.

In brief, an *algebraic Bayesian network* (ABN) is a set of possibly intersecting ideals of conjunctions together with point-valued or interval-valued estimates on the joint probabilities of conjunctions appearing in these ideals. Formally, a BBN's knowledge pattern is modeled with a point-valued tensor of conditional probability. In contrast to BBN, an ABN's knowledge pattern is modeled with an ideal of conjunctions that represents marginal probabilities in a specific form. Those marginal joint probabilities may be assigned with point-valued or interval-valued estimates.

In what follows we are trying to extend the class of BBNs with directed cyclic graphs, keeping the method of defining a network. It turns out that together with the word "acyclic" we shall need to throw away the concept of having a *single* probabilistic distribution corresponding to a BBN. We should rather consider families of distributions corresponding to a cycle in a BBN.

3 Semantics of a Cycle

In this article we restrict ourselves to the simplest cyclic situation possible: a generalized Bayesian belief network consisting of a single directed cycle. We denote the nodes of the graph by $x_1, \ldots, x_n$. The cycle is presented on Fig. 1.

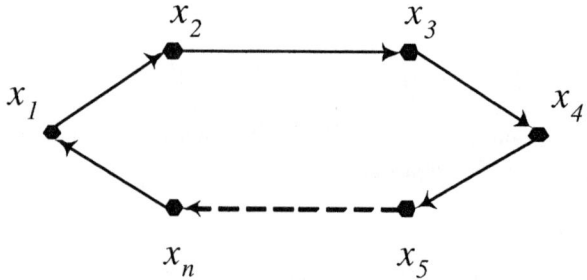

Fig. 1. An isolated cycle with n vertices

By definition, we receive as input the probabilities

$$p(x_1 \mid \tilde{x}_n), p(x_2 \mid \tilde{x}_1), \ldots, p(x_n \mid \tilde{x}_{n-1}), \quad \tilde{x}_i \in \{x_i, \bar{x}_i\}, \ i \in 1(1)n.$$

Note that there are no additional restrictions by the Markov condition in this case (because the set of nondescendents of each node in an isolated directed cycle is empty).

Let us try to deduce from the given data the marginal probabilities and the description of the probabilistic distribution this network represents. By the definition of conditional probability we can obtain the following equations:

$$\begin{cases} p(x_1) = p(x_1 \mid x_n)p(x_n) + p(x_1 \mid \bar{x}_n)(1 - p(x_n)) \\ p(x_2) = p(x_2 \mid x_1)p(x_1) + p(x_2 \mid \bar{x}_1)(1 - p(x_1)) \\ \vdots \\ p(x_n) = p(x_n \mid x_{n-1})p(x_{n-1}) + p(x_n \mid \bar{x}_{n-1})(1 - p(x_{n-1})) \end{cases} \quad (1)$$

Note that the only unknowns in this system are the probabilities $p(x_i)$. Thus, the system is a linear system (with a very simple structure) of the form

$$\begin{pmatrix} 1 & 0 & 0 & \cdots & 0 & r_{1n} \\ r_{21} & 1 & 0 & \cdots & 0 & 0 \\ 0 & r_{32} & 1 & \cdots & 0 & 0 \\ \vdots & \vdots & \vdots & \ddots & \vdots & \vdots \\ 0 & 0 & 0 & \cdots & r_{n,n-1} & 1 \end{pmatrix} \begin{pmatrix} p(x_1) \\ p(x_2) \\ p(x_3) \\ \vdots \\ p(x_n) \end{pmatrix} = \begin{pmatrix} p(x_1 \mid \tilde{x}_n) \\ p(x_2 \mid \tilde{x}_1) \\ p(x_3 \mid \tilde{x}_2) \\ \vdots \\ p(x_n \mid \tilde{x}_{n-1}) \end{pmatrix}, \quad (2)$$

where $r_{ij} = p(x_i \mid \bar{x}_j) - p(x_i \mid x_j)$. Thus, we obtain $p(x_i)$.

Remark 1. There is a special case when the system is degenerate. This may happen if the determinant of the matrix of the system is equal to zero, that is, if $1 - r_{1n}r_{21}\ldots r_{n,n-1} = 0$. This is possible only if all $r_{i,i-1} = \pm 1$. If in this case the right-hand side is non-zero, the system has no solutions, and the network is inconsistent. If the right-hand side is zero, it means that *de facto* all nodes of the network describe the same judgement x. There are no restrictions on the probability of that x, that is, all we can say is $p(x) \in [0, 1]$. In this case, of course, there is no need to draw a network, let alone a directed cycle, so we may assume that this case does not hold in practice (if it happens, the cycle may be easily reduced to one node without loss of information).

After we have calculated $p(x_i)$, we may proceed to find $p(x_i x_{i-1})$, $i = 1, \ldots, n$, by definition of conditional probability (we denote here $x_0 := x_n$ for simplicity of the formulae and freely substitute x_0 and x_n further):

$$p(x_i x_{i-1}) = p(x_{i-1})p(x_i \mid x_{i-1}) + (1 - p(x_{i-1}))p(x_i \mid \bar{x}_{i-1}). \quad (3)$$

But this is exactly where our certain knowledge about the point-valued probabilities stops.

Joint probabilities of three and more variables, and even joint probabilities of pairs of variables representing non-adjacent graph nodes may *not* in general be determined from the input. Only interval bounds may be established as a result of solving the linear programming task that will be described in Sect. 5.

4 Special Case: A Cycle with Two Vertices

The simplest (and in some ways special) case of a cyclic BBN is an isolated cycle with two vertices. This case is special because it is the only case where the input conditional probabilities determine the whole probabilistic distribution uniquely. The marginal probabilities $p(x_1)$ and $p(x_2)$ satisfy the following linear system (a special case of (2)):

$$\begin{cases} p(x_1) + (p(x_1|x_2) - p(x_1|\bar{x}_2))p(x_2) = p(x_1|\bar{x}_2) \\ (p(x_2|x_1) - p(x_2|\bar{x}_1))p(x_1) + p(x_2) = p(x_2|\bar{x}_1) \end{cases} \qquad (4)$$

After solving it we obtain explicit formulae for marginal probabilities:

$$p(x_1) = \frac{p(x_1|\bar{x}_2) - (p(x_1|x_2) - p(x_1|\bar{x}_2))p(x_2|\bar{x}_1)}{1 - (p(x_1|x_2) - p(x_1|\bar{x}_2))(p(x_2|x_1) - p(x_2|\bar{x}_1))}$$

$$p(x_2) = \frac{p(x_2|\bar{x}_1) - (p(x_2|x_1) - p(x_2|\bar{x}_1))p(x_1|\bar{x}_2)}{1 - (p(x_1|x_2) - p(x_1|\bar{x}_2))(p(x_2|x_1) - p(x_2|\bar{x}_1))}$$

It is now easy to obtain the entire distribution:

$$\begin{aligned} p(x_1 x_2) &= p(x_1)p(x_2|x_1), \\ p(x_1 \bar{x}_2) &= p(x_1)(1 - p(x_2|x_1)), \\ p(\bar{x}_1 x_2) &= (1 - p(x_1))p(x_2|\bar{x}_1), \\ p(\bar{x}_1 \bar{x}_2) &= (1 - p(x_1))(1 - p(x_2|\bar{x}_1)). \end{aligned} \qquad (5)$$

Let us note that these formulae make sense provided

$$(p(x_1|x_2) - p(x_1|\bar{x}_2))(p(x_2|x_1) - p(x_2|\bar{x}_1)) \neq 1,$$

which may happen only in the degenerate case considered in the previous section.

5 Consistency Checking

As we have seen above, a Bayesian belief network with a directed cycle may describe a whole family of probabilistic distributions rather than the only one, as a regular Bayesian belief network does. This family may, of course, be empty. Therefore, the problem of establishing the consistency of an initial probabilistic assignment arises. In this section we describe the most straightforward way to check for consistency. However, as we show further, this method is hard to improve. In this section, as in the whole article, we restrict ourselves to the case of one isolated cycle on n nodes.

To establish consistency, we must ensure that there exists a probabilistic distribution $p(\tilde{x}_1 \tilde{x}_2 \ldots \tilde{x}_n)$ over all n variables which is compatible with axioms of probability

$$\forall \tilde{x}_1 \tilde{x}_2 \ldots \tilde{x}_n \quad p(\tilde{x}_1 \tilde{x}_2 \ldots \tilde{x}_n) \geq 0; \qquad \sum_{\tilde{x}_1 \tilde{x}_2 \ldots \tilde{x}_n} p(\tilde{x}_1 \tilde{x}_2 \ldots \tilde{x}_n) = 1$$

and meets conditional probabilities given as input. To do that, we simply solve the linear programming task that may be extracted from the axioms of probability and given constraints. Its unknowns are probabilities of positive conjunctions $p(x_{i_1} x_{i_2} \ldots x_{i_k})$. The input enters the formulation of the linear programming task as $p(x_i)$ and $p(x_i x_j)$, which, as was shown above, may be deduced from the input.

Example 1. We provide the linear programming task for the case of a cycle on three nodes. In this case the problem is trivial because there is only one variable, $p(x_1 x_2 x_3)$. We should minimize and maximize it over the following set of constraints:

$$\begin{cases} p(x_1 x_2 x_3) \geq 0 \\ p(x_1 x_2) - p(x_1 x_2 x_3) \geq 0 \\ p(x_1 x_3) - p(x_1 x_2 x_3) \geq 0 \\ p(x_2 x_3) - p(x_1 x_2 x_3) \geq 0 \\ p(x_1) - p(x_1 x_2) - p(x_1 x_3) + p(x_1 x_2 x_3) \geq 0 \\ p(x_2) - p(x_1 x_2) - p(x_2 x_3) + p(x_1 x_2 x_3) \geq 0 \\ p(x_3) - p(x_1 x_3) - p(x_2 x_3) + p(x_1 x_2 x_3) \geq 0 \\ 1 - p(x_1) - p(x_2) - p(x_3) + p(x_1 x_2) + p(x_2 x_3) + p(x_1 x_3) - p(x_1 x_2 x_3) \geq 0 \end{cases}$$

By solving similar linear programming problems, we may establish interval bounds for the probabilities of unknown conjunctions in the general case. These will allow us to reconstruct the overall probability distribution (that is, the family of distributions).

Example 2. We show how conjunctions of positive literals generate the entire distribution for the case of three variables:

$$\begin{cases} p(\bar{x}_1 x_2 x_3) = p(x_2 x_3) - p(x_1 x_2 x_3) \\ p(x_1 \bar{x}_2 x_3) = p(x_1 x_3) - p(x_1 x_2 x_3) \\ p(x_1 x_2 \bar{x}_3) = p(x_1 x_2) - p(x_1 x_2 x_3) \\ p(\bar{x}_1 \bar{x}_2 x_3) = p(x_3) - p(x_2 x_3) - p(x_1 x_3) + p(x_1 x_2 x_3) \\ p(\bar{x}_1 x_2 \bar{x}_3) = p(x_2) - p(x_1 x_2) - p(x_2 x_3) + p(x_1 x_2 x_3) \\ p(x_1 \bar{x}_2 \bar{x}_3) = p(x_1) - p(x_1 x_2) - p(x_1 x_3) + p(x_1 x_2 x_3) \\ p(\bar{x}_1 \bar{x}_2 \bar{x}_3) = 1 - p(x_1) - p(x_2) - p(x_3) + \\ \qquad + p(x_1 x_2) + p(x_2 x_3) + p(x_1 x_3) - p(x_1 x_2 x_3). \end{cases}$$

However, the linear programming problem is in general very large. For a cycle of n nodes, it has 2^n constraints and $2^n - 2n - 1$ unknowns ($2n$ unknowns disappear since we can determine $p(x_i)$ and $p(x_i x_{i-1})$). Solving it for large knowledge patterns would require too much computational power. It would be extremely helpful to reduce this task to some easier ones. However, in the next section we give a negative result on this approach.

Before we proceed to complexity issues, we should remark on the nature of the result. What we had to do in order to check consistency and establish the interval bounds, is known as the *a priori inference* in the theory of algebraic Bayesian networks introduced by V. Gorodetski in [5,6,7,8,9,16] and developed in [10,24,25]. We simply immersed the cycle in question into the corresponding knowledge pattern of an algebraic Bayesian network. It is not the point of this article to compare the two formalisms, but in this case algebraic Bayesian networks turn out to be more descriptive than Bayesian belief networks, because they are able to capture this kind of relation between the boolean variables.

6 Complexity of the Consistency Checking

As we have seen in the previous section, consistency checking in general is an expensive task. Since Bayesian networks were intended to deal with decomposable distributions, a natural question arises: are we able to decompose the problem on the big knowledge pattern that includes the whole cycle to smaller problems on some subsets of the cycle?

The answer is definitely negative. Moreover, we note that, in fact, consistency of a cycle *always* has to be considered as a whole, rather than in part. The matter is that a linear chain of nodes in a Bayesian belief network is always consistent (see [13] or any other source on Bayesian belief networks); it usually comes with a number of conditional independence restrictions that allow to single one particular distribution out of the whole family, but the family is never empty anyway.

However, as soon as we engage cycles (even isolated), inconsistent cycles become possible. We give here an example of an inconsistent cycle on three vertices.

Example 3. Consider the following Bayesian belief network — a cycle on three vertices:

$$p(x_2|x_1) = 1/4,\ p(x_3|x_2) = 3/4,\ p(x_1|x_3) = 3/4,$$
$$p(x_2|\bar{x}_1) = 1/2,\ p(x_3|\bar{x}_2) = 1/6,\ p(x_1|\bar{x}_3) = 1/6.$$

By solving the linear system (2), we obtain

$$p(x_1) = p(x_2) = p(x_3) = \tfrac{2}{5},$$
$$p(x_1 x_2) = \tfrac{1}{10},$$
$$p(x_2 x_3) = p(x_1 x_3) = \tfrac{3}{10}.$$

Now restrictions on $p(x_1 x_2 x_3)$ include, on one hand, $p(x_1 x_2) - p(x_1 x_2 x_3) \geq 0$, that is, $p(x_1 x_2 x_3) \leq 1/10$, and, on the other hand, $p(x_3) - p(x_1 x_3) - p(x_2 x_3) + p(x_1 x_2 x_3) \geq 0$, that is, $p(x_1 x_2 x_3) \geq 2/10$. Thus, this cycle on three vertices is inconsistent.

Therefore, even if more efficient algorithms exist (which they may), they should take into consideration all the data at once, and consider the overall probabilistic distribution.

7 On Reverting Edges in a Cycle

A cycle, as we have shown above, forces the probabilistic semantics of a Bayesian belief network outside the realm of unique distributions that seems so natural for

Bayesian belief networks. Therefore, it is natural that the basic idea of previously suggested ways to cope with cycles has been to try and get rid of the cycle and thus reduce the problem to well-known cases. We have already mentioned in the introduction the paper [1], where the simplest way to remove a cycle is considered. The proposed technique is to revert an edge in the cycle, making it non-directed and, therefore, subject to standard Bayesian network analysis.

However, this is incorrect, because by reverting an edge (and considering the result as a regular Bayesian belief network) we would replace a whole family of distributions by a single one. In fact, the initial network might be inconsistent, but the result will always be consistent. The distribution becomes unique because reverting an edge imposes additional constraints in the form of conditional independence of certain nodes of the cycle that are now (after reverting an edge) d-separable. However, even if the initial cycle was consistent, the unique distribution appearing after reverting an edge might not even be contained in the initial family of distributions — at least, it has to be proven. There is no sound justification for this process in [1].

Such a justification might be that this unique distribution has some special properties which single it out of the family. In [17] we consider ways to look for this distribution. For example, it may be a good idea to select distributions based on the maximal entropy principle. There also exist experimental techniques for selecting a single distribution, for example, stochastic modeling. However, this problem remains open — even in the motivational phase, it is not clear what kind of a distribution to look for (since the usual decomposable ones don't work anymore).

One certainly valid way to work with a cycle is to revert all its edges at once (leaving the cycle in place, but changing its direction). This does not change the semantics of the network, because receiving as input conditional probabilities $\{p(\tilde{x}_i|\tilde{x}_{i-1})\}$, as we have shown above, to receiving joint probabilities $\{p(\tilde{x}_i), p(\tilde{x}_i\tilde{x}_{i-1})\}$, and the latter do not depend on where the edges in the cycle are directed.

For an isolated cycle this reverting is, of course, meaningless. However, it may prove useful for coping with several intersecting cycles or other Bayesian belief networks with more complex structure — for example, it may simplify this structure, remove unnecessary cycles, and so on.

8 Conclusions and Further Work

We have shown that a cycle in a BBN may represent a (possibly empty) family of probabilistic distributions over its elements and their conjunctions, rather than a single distribution a regular BBN represents. If we want to incorporate cycles into a BBN, we should therefore check the network for consistency. In this article this work is done for the case of an isolated cycle. We have also shown that to establish consistency in general it is necessary to consider the exponential-sized linear programming task, since no smaller one (none corresponding to the joint distribution of a smaller set of variables) would suffice.

All known BBN calculi deal with a single distribution defined by the network. Therefore, we should either somehow choose a single distribution out of the family of possible distributions, or generalize the calculus to deal with interval-valued estimates of probabilities of BBN nodes, as is done in the ABN approach.

One of the natural directions for further work would be to generalize the algorithms of evidence propagation to the directed cyclic case. This approach has been to some extent carried out in the theory of algebraic Bayesian networks, but there are differences between the two formalisms that make considering cyclic Bayesian belief networks a worthwhile task by itself.

However, Bayesian belief networks on directed cyclic graphs should always be treated with care, that is, one should carefully check for consistency and deal with families of distributions rather than a single one. This feature will not disappear unless too restrictive conditions are satisfied (and thus the formalism is rendered impractical). Therefore, another direction for future research is to try to establish sufficient conditions for effective consistency checking. In the current work we have shown that no effective necessary conditions exist, but some good enough sufficient conditions may cover many interesting cases.

References

1. Castillo, E., Gutierrez, J. M., Hadi, A. S. Modeling Probabilistic Networks of Discrete and Continuous Variables. *Journal of Multivariate Analysis*, **64** (1998), pp.48–65.
2. Fagin, R., Halpern, J. Y., Megiddo, N. A Logic for Reasoning about Probabilities. Report RJ 6190(60900) 4/12/88, pp. 1–41.
3. Fagin R., Halpern J. Y. Uncertainty, Belief, and Probability. Proc. of the 11th International Joint Conference on Artificial Intelligence (1989), pp. 1161–1167.
4. Fagin R., Halpern J. Y. Uncertainty, Belief, and Probability-2. Proc. of the IEEE Simposium on Logic and Computer Science, **7** (1991), pp.160–173.
5. Gorodetski, V. Adaptation Problems in Expert System. *International Journal of Adaptive Control and Signal Processing*, **6** (1992), pp.201–210.
6. Gorodetski, V. Expert Systems Adaptation. *Transactions of the Russian Academy of Sciences "Technical Cybernetics"*, **5** (1993), pp.101–110 (in Russian).
7. Gorodetski, V. Interval-valued Probabilistic Measure of Uncertainty in Knowledge Engineering. In Yusupov R.M. (ed.), *Theoretical Basis and Applied Intelligent Information Technologies*. Russian Academy of Science, SPIIRAS (1998), pp.44–58 (in Russian).
8. Gorodetski, V. I., Nesterov, V. M. Interval probabilities and knowledge engineering. In: Alefeld, G., Trejo, R. A. (eds), *Interval computations and its applications to reasoning under uncertainty, knowledge representation and control theory*, Mexico City (1998), pp.15–20.
9. Gorodetski, V., Skormin, V., Popyack, L. Data Mining Technology for Failure Prognostics of Avionics. *IEEE Transactions on Aerospace and Electronic Systems*, **38**, no. 2 (2002), pp.388–403.
10. Gorodetskii, V. I., Tulupyev [Tulup'ev], A. L. Generating Consistent Knowledge Bases with Uncertainty. *Journal of Computer and Systems Sciences International*, **5**, 1997, pp.33–42.

11. Heckerman, D., D. Chickering, D. M., Meek, C., Rounthwaite, R., Kadie, C. Dependency Networks for Density Estimation, Collaborative Filtering, and Data Visualization. *Journal of Machine Learning Research*, 1:49–75, 2000. Also appears as Technical Report MSR-TR-00-16, Microsoft Research, February, 2000.
12. Hulten, G., Chickering, D. M., Heckerman, D. Learning Bayesian Networks from Dependency Networks: A Preliminary Study. In *Proceedings of the Ninth International Workshop on Artificial Intelligence and Statistics*, Key West, FL, 2003.
13. Jensen, F. V. Bayesian networks and decision graphs. Springer-Verlag, 2002.
14. Mihajlovic, V., Petkovic, M. Dynamic Bayesian Networks: a state of the art. Technical report, 2001, no. TR-CTIT-01-34, Centre for Telematics and Information Technology, University of Twente.
15. Neapolitan, R. E. Learning Bayesian Networks. Pearson Prentice Hall, 2004.
16. Nesterov, V. M., Gorodetski, V. I. Interval algorithm for checking the consistency of the algebraic Bayesian net. In: Alefeld, G., Trejo, R. A. (eds), *Interval computations and its applications to reasoning under uncertainty, knowledge representation and control theory*. Mexico City (1998), pp.28–29.
17. Nikolenko, S. I., Tulupyev, A. L. Edge flipping as a technique for dealing with directed cycles in Bayesian networks. *MEPhI-2005 Science Session Proceedings*, vol. 3, Intellectual systems and technologies, pp. 176–178. Moscow, MEPhI, 2005 (in Russian).
18. Nilsson, N.J. Probabilistic Logic. *Artificial Intelligence*, **28** (1986), pp. 71–87.
19. Pearl, J. How to do with probabilities what people say you can't. In S. Quaglini, P. Barahona, S. Andreassen (eds.) *Artificial Intelligence in Medicine*, LNAI2101 (2001), 283–292.
20. Pearl, J. Probabilistic reasoning using graphs. In B. Bouchon, R.R. Yager (eds.) *Uncertainty in Knowledge-Based Systems*, Springer-Verlag (1987), 201–202.
21. Pearl, J. Probabilistic reasoning in intelligent systems: networks of plausible inference. San Mateo, Morgan Kauffmann, 1988.
22. Sprites, P. Directed cyclic graphical representations of feedback models. *Uncertainty in Artificial Intelligence*, **12** (1996), pp.454–461.
23. Studený, M., Bouckaert, R. On chain graph models for description of conditional independence structures. *The Annals of Statistics*, **26**, No. 4 (1998), 1434–1495.
24. Tulupyev, A.L. Algebraic Bayesian Networks: Theoretical Background and Consistency. St.-Petersburg, 1995 (in Russian).
25. Tulupyev, A. L. Algebraic Bayesian Networks: a Probabilistic Logic Approach to Modeling Knowledge Bases with Uncertainties. St.-Petersburg, 2000 (in Russian).

Fuzzeval: A Fuzzy Controller-Based Approach in Adaptive Learning for Backgammon Game

Mikael Heinze[1], Daniel Ortiz-Arroyo[2], Henrik Legind Larsen[2], and Francisco Rodriguez-Henriquez[3]

[1,2] Computer Science and Engineering Department, Aalborg University,
Esbjerg Denmark
contact@gonex.dk, {do, legind}@cs.aaue.dk
[3] Computer Science Section, CINVESTAV, Mexico DF, Mexico
francisco@cs.cinvestav.mx

Abstract. In this paper we investigate the effectiveness of applying fuzzy controllers to create strong computer player programs in the domain of backgammon. *Fuzzeval,* our proposed mechanism, consists of a fuzzy controller that dynamically evaluates the perceived strength of the board configurations it receives. Fuzzeval employs an evaluation function that adjusts the membership functions linked to the linguistic variables employed in the knowledge base. The membership functions are aligned to the average crisp input that was successfully used in the past winning games. Fuzzeval mechanisms are adaptive and have the simplicity associated with fuzzy controllers. Our experiments show that Fuzzeval improves its performance up to 42% after a match of only one hundred backgammon games played against *Pubeval,* a strong intermediate level program.

Keywords: Fuzzy controller, machine learning, artificial neural networks, computer games, reinforcement learning.

1 Introduction

Researchers in AI have applied a wide variety of techniques [1,2,3,4,5,7,10] to create effective computer programs to play board games. These techniques vary from the database and brute-force approaches, to more sophisticated mechanisms based on board pattern classification and artificial neural networks (ANNs).

Board games, such as chess and backgammon, have been the subject of intense study by the AI community. In the domain of chess, it is feasible to create a very strong chess player by applying a combination of brute-force and opening/extended book databases, as was shown by Deep Blue's approach [5]. However, this methodology does not work in the domain of backgammon. Backgammon is a game of strategy and luck [9]. The use of dice in backgammon ensures stochastic variation during the play, producing a branching factor of such a scale, that a search is impossible beyond three moves.

A backgammon game can be characterized by two main stages: the *contact* stage where players' checkers are intermixed and the *race* stage, where there is no contact between players. The strategies applied at each game stage vary. At *contact* stage *blockades* [9] may be used to delay an opponent's progress. However, at *race* stage what is important is removing most pieces as quickly as possible.

Reinforcement learning has been applied successfully in board games [1,4]. Reinforcement learning seeks to maximize a numerical reward signal in moves that turn out to be successful during a trial and error search in a game. Within this technique, each position where a mistake is made is remembered. The playing strategy changes when the mistaken position is encountered again. In reinforcement learning, evaluation functions are commonly used to estimate the performance quality of an attempted trial. A straightforward solution for learning the weights of an evaluation function is to train the program with example positions for which the exact values of the evaluation function are known. Then, the program learns to adjust the weights to minimize the error of the evaluation function for these positions. Typically this is done by a technique similar to the back-propagation training algorithm used in ANN [7].

Diverse techniques such as ANN, genetic algorithms and fuzzy logic may be used to build effective computer games. Fuzzy logic, a superset of Boolean logic, supports human type reasoning with vague and uncertain concepts. Fuzzy control, a technique derived from the application of fuzzy logic, has been used successfully in a wide variety of devices, from washing machines to industrial robots [6]. The main idea of fuzzy controllers is to build a model of an expert capable to synthesize, via interpolation, a control law. A fuzzy controller processes input signals, executes inferences, and calculates suitable control outputs. The inference mechanisms in a fuzzy controller employ a knowledge base consisting of linguistic expressions generated by a designer or expert. In spite of its conceptual simplicity, little research has explored the application of fuzzy logic-based techniques in board games [7,10].

In this paper we investigate the effectiveness of applying fuzzy controllers in creating strong players in the domain of backgammon. Fuzzeval, our proposed mechanism, is an adaptive backgammon player program that combines a fuzzy controller with simple reinforcement learning mechanisms. To evaluate the effectiveness of Fuzzeval, three types of experiments were performed. First, a fuzzy controller built with a simple knowledge base was evaluated. Afterwards, an improved version of the same knowledge base was employed. Finally, a backgammon player designed with two ANNs was implemented. The performance of Fuzzeval and the ANNs was compared when both players were set to play against *Pubeval*, a strong intermediate level player benchmarking program. Our experimental results show that Fuzzeval learns quickly, competing well with Pubeval and the ANNs. Moreover, the techniques used in Fuzzeval may be applied in a broad variety of board games.

This paper is organized as follows. In next section we briefly describe previous related work on machine learning mechanisms for board games. A detailed description of Fuzzeval is presented in Section 3. Fuzzeval's experimental performance results are discussed in Section 4. Finally, we describe future work and provide our conclusions in Section 5.

2 Related Work

The checkers program written by A. Samuel in 1956 [1], featured the first successful attempt of doing automatic evaluation function tuning by the use of reinforcement learning. Susan L. Epstein also employed reinforcement learning in *Hoyle* [4], a game system that is capable of learning a wide variety of games. In *Hoyle*, the positions encountered in a game are marked as either, *"significant"* or *"dangerous"*, depending on the result of a search for a better alternative on a loser player's positions. Positions identified as *"dangerous"* are avoided in subsequent games.

In the domain of backgammon, G. Tesauro [2] achieved a remarkable success with *TD-Gammon* [2]. The evaluation function built in TD-Gammon employs an ANN trained by the method of temporal-difference. This method, which is a variant of reinforcement learning, moves the evaluation of a played board closer to the evaluation of a subsequent played board. In the end, the evaluation of the final winning and losing boards are moved closer to one or zero, respectively. One drawback of this approach is that it requires long training times, e.g. TD-Gammon reached the master level after 1,500,000 games of self-playing. In spite of this fact, neural network-based backgammon programs are superior to any other known method to date. Tesauro also created *Pubeval*, a strong intermediate level backgammon player that is used as a benchmark to test other programs.

Chellapilla and Fogel explored the use of genetic algorithms to evolve a neural network that learned by self-play the checkers game. In the experiment described in [3], 30 neural networks were initialized in a random state and then set to play checkers against each other. In each generation, the neural nets played a series of games, and a fitness score was assigned according to their performance. The weights of the 15 best scoring neural networks were maintained as parents for the next generation. This process continued for 250 generations until a capable checkers player finally evolved.

C.T. Sun [7] used a combination of genetic algorithms and fuzzy sets in the domain of othello. In his experiments, a game was divided into several stages characterized by a fuzzy set. Afterwards, each stage was encoded into a chromosome structure.

Azaria and Sipper used genetic programming in the evolution of strategies for playing the game of backgammon. Using this technique, they report in [10] that most capable players evolved in 300 generations, after playing around 2,000,000 games.

Fuzzeval, the approach presented in this paper, differs from previous research work by including a combination of simple reinforcement learning mechanisms and a Fuzzy controller. In the next section we provide a detailed description of Fuzzeval.

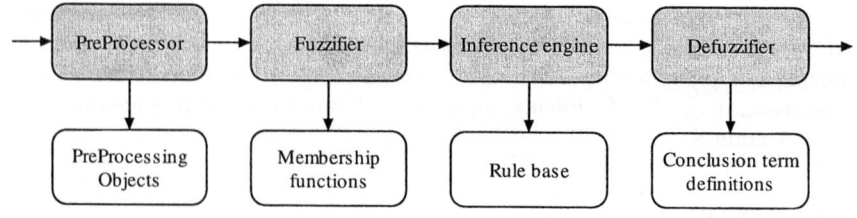

Fig. 1. Fuzzeval's fuzzy controller modules

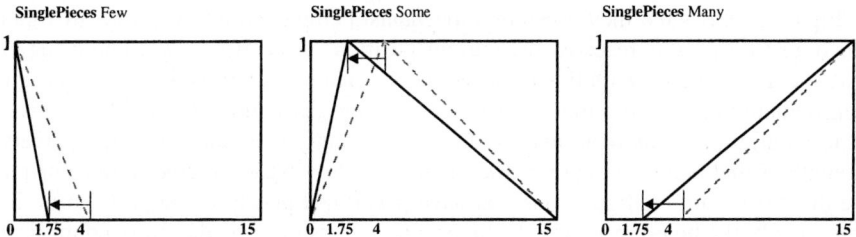

Fig. 2. Example of adjusted membership functions

3 Detailed Description of Fuzzeval

The core of Fuzzeval is a Mamdani type [7] fuzzy controller. This controller is responsible for grading the perceived strength of the board configurations it receives. The fuzzy controller consists of the four main modules illustrated in Figure 1. The *PreProcessor* module is responsible for reading the crisp linguistic input values describing a board's state. The *Fuzzifier* module employs *membership functions* to convert the crisp inputs into membership degrees for each linguistic input variable and term used. The membership degrees of all variables are then passed to the *InferenceEngine,* which calculates the fulfillment of each rule in the *rule base*. Finally, the *Defuzzifier* module generates the defuzzified output from the controller. Fuzzeval employs triangular-shaped membership functions, defined by its left, right base points, and its maximum central point. The membership functions declared as *variable* are tuned using a special function calibrator mechanism. The calibration mechanism calculates the average crisp inputs to the fuzzy controller for all the winning boards stored in a match's historic record. Subsequently, all the membership functions associated with the input values are aligned around these average values. To illustrate this process in detail, let us consider a crisp input for a typical linguistic variable such as *SinglePieces*. The range of this variable varies typically between 0 and 15. However, a player who owns more than four single checkers, is likely to be *hit* [9] by its opponent, an undesirable event that may delay his progress. A typical desirable average input value for the variable *SinglePieces* is around 1.75. The calibration procedure, applied to a membership function consists of moving the adjustment point, slightly closer to the target value matching the average crisp input. Figure 2 illustrates how Fuzzeval adjusts the membership functions, aligning them around the preferred value of 1.75. The amount of adjustment for a point in a membership function is obtained using equation 1.

$$AmountToAdjust = rate \cdot \left(\frac{\sum x_i}{n} - x_c \right) = rate \cdot \Delta x \qquad (1)$$

where Δx is the difference between the average value, obtained from the n winning boards, and the current location x_c of the adjustable point of a membership function. *Rate* is the learning rate constant, set to 0.1 in our tests.

Figure 3 shows the move selection mechanism employed in Fuzzeval. In a game, the *Board Generator* receives the current position of all pieces in a board together with the dice values. With this information, it generates all possible board configurations containing the valid moves that can be made. The *Fuzzy Controller* receives a board configuration as input and produces an output value that grades the perceived strength of that board. Using the *Match History Data Base,* the *Board Selector* module discards board configurations that have performed poorly in the past. From those that are left, the board receiving the highest score (assigned by the fuzzy controller) is selected for playing. To illustrate Fuzzeval's processing, let us consider a simple example consisting of the linguistic input/output variables and their associated terms presented in Table 1.

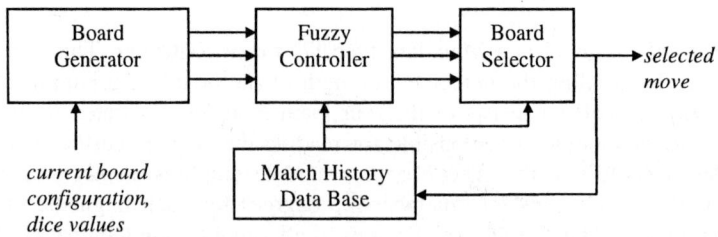

Fig. 3. Fuzzeval's move selection mechanism

Table 1. Linguistic input variables and terms used by the fuzzy controller

Linguistic variable	Linguistic terms	Base variable	Type
SinglePieces	Few, Many	0 to 15 pieces	Input
OpponentOnBar	Few, Many	0 to 15 pieces	Input
SinglePiecesInHome	Few, Many	0 to 6 pieces	Input
BoardStrength	Weak, Good	-1 and 1	Output

An example rule base defined with the previous linguistic variables is shown below:

1. If *SinglePieces* is *Many* then *BoardStrenght Weak*
2. If *SinglePieces* is *Few* then *BoardStrenght Good*
3. If *OpponentOnBar* is *Few* then *BoardStrenght Weak*
4. If *OpponentOnBar* is *Many* then *BoardStrenght Good*
5. If *SinglePiecesInHome* is *Many* then *BoardStrenght Weak*
6. If *SinglePiecesInHome* is *Few* then *BoardStrenght Good*
7. if *OpponentsOnBar* is *Many* and *SinglePiecesInHome* is *Many* then *BoardStrenght Weak.*

Finally, the membership functions associated with the input variables in Table 1 are expressed mathematically in Table 2.

Fuzzeval: A Fuzzy Controller-Based Approach in Adaptive Learning   229

Table 2. Example membership functions

SinglePieces			
$Few(x) = \begin{cases} 1 & \text{if } NumPieces(x) < 0 \\ -\dfrac{NumPieces(x)}{4} + 1 & \text{if } 0 \leq NumPieces(x) \leq 4 \\ 0 & \text{if } NumPieces(x) > 4 \end{cases}$		$Many(x) = \begin{cases} 0 & \text{if } NumPieces(x) < 1 \\ \dfrac{NumPieces(x) - 2}{13} & \text{if } 1 \leq NumPieces(x) \leq 15 \\ 1 & \text{if } NumPieces(x) > 15 \end{cases}$	
OpponentOnBar			
$Few(x) = \begin{cases} 1 & \text{if } NumPieces(x) < 0 \\ -\dfrac{NumPieces(x)}{3} + 1 & \text{if } 0 \leq NumPieces(x) \leq 3 \\ 0 & \text{if } NumPieces(x) > 3 \end{cases}$		$Many(x) = \begin{cases} 0 & \text{if } NumPieces(x) < 1 \\ \dfrac{NumPieces(x) - 1}{14} & \text{if } 1 \leq NumPieces(x) \leq 15 \\ 1 & \text{if } NumPieces(x) > 15 \end{cases}$	
SinglePiecesInHome			
$Few(x) = \begin{cases} 1 & \text{if } NumPieces(x) < 0 \\ -\dfrac{NumPieces(x)}{4} + 1 & \text{if } 0 \leq NumPieces(x) \leq 4 \\ 0 & \text{if } NumPieces(x) > 4 \end{cases}$		$Many(x) = \begin{cases} 0 & \text{if } NumPieces(x) < 1 \\ \dfrac{NumPieces(x) - 1}{5} & \text{if } 1 \leq NumPieces(x) \leq 6 \\ 1 & \text{if } NumPieces(x) > 6 \end{cases}$	

The equations in Table 2 describe the fuzzy sets *"Many"* and *"Few"* pieces at certain positions on the board. Figure 4 shows a board configuration that we will use as an example to illustrate how Fuzzeval (playing the dark pieces) calculates the perceived strength of a board in a move that will *hit* two pieces of its opponent.

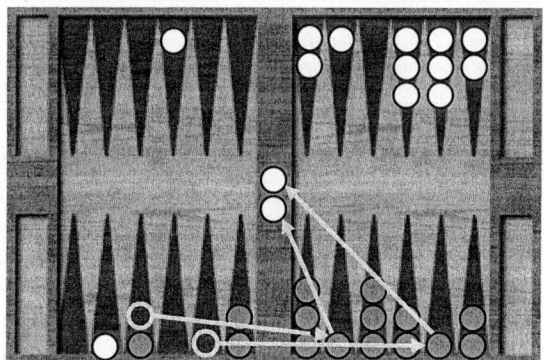

Fig. 4. Backgammon board example

Firstly the fuzzy controller's preprocessor reads the board state, consisting of the number and positions of its own pieces and those of the opponent. These values are the crisp inputs to the controller. Table 3 shows the crisp values obtained from the board shown in Figure 4.

Table 3. Crisp input for each linguistic variable

Linguistic variable	Crisp value
SinglePieces	3
OpponentOnBar	2
SinglePiecesInHome	2

After the preprocessing stage, the crisp inputs are converted into their associated fuzzy membership degrees. This step is performed for each different combination of linguistic variables and terms. The membership functions illustrated in Table 2 produce the membership degrees shown in Table 4.

Table 4. Fuzzified membership degrees for each linguistic input

Linguistic variable	Linguistic term	Membership
SinglePieces	Few	0.25
	Many	0.077
OpponentOnBar	Few	0.33
	Many	0.071
SinglePiecesInHome	Few	0.5
	Many	0.2

The degree of fulfillment is now calculated for each of the seven rules in the example. The result of this step is illustrated in Table 5.

Table 5. Fulfillment of the seven rules

Rule	Fulfillment
If *SinglePieces* is *Many* then *BoardStrenght Weak*	0.077
If *SinglePieces* is *Few* then *BoardStrenght Good*	0.25
If *OpponentOnBar* is *Few* then *BoardStrenght Weak*	0.33
If *OpponentOnBar* is *Many* then *BoardStrenght Good*	0.071
If *SinglePiecesInHome* is *Many* then *BoardStrenght Weak*	0.2
If *SinglePiecesInHome* is *Few* then *BoardStrenght Good*	0.5
If *OpponentsOnBar* is *Many* and *SinglePiecesInHome* is *Many* then *BoardStrenght Weak*	0.071

Finally, in the defuzzification step, the output of all rules in Table 5 is converted into a single value. The center of gravity is used for the purpose, as is indicated by equation 2.

$$u = \frac{\sum \mu(x_i) \, x_i}{\sum \mu(x_i)} \qquad (2)$$

where x_i is the value of the output term and $\mu(x_i)$ is the degree of fulfillment of each rule. The last rule in Table 5 uses the T-norm *min* operator for the *and* condition. Using previous equation, jointly with Table 5 and the definition of output terms in Table 1 (*Weak=-1, Good=1*), a final score of 0.095 is obtained for the example board configuration. Fuzzeval performs the evaluation procedure previously described to all boards received from the board generator module. The defuzzified values, which represent the strength of each board as perceived by the fuzzy controller, are then compared; the board receiving the highest score is selected as the best move to play.

4 Discussion of Results

To test Fuzzeval three experiments were performed. In the first test we employed a simple knowledge base similar to the one described in Section 3 but with a total of 15 rules. Using this knowledge base, Fuzzeval was able to learn effective strategies after playing only 100 games, achieving a winning rate of around 34% against Pubeval. In the second test, we extended the rule base to include a variety of situations that Fuzzeval may encounter in a game. Table 6 and Table 7, show some examples of the linguistic input variables and rules contained in the new knowledge base. Specifically, the rules shown in Table 7 are representative of the *contact* stage in backgammon.

Table 6. Some linguistic inputs used in Fuzzeval

Avoiding blots	
ToBeHitFactor	Probability of a checker being hit multiplied by a factor decided by its location on the board. Values for all single pieces are then summed together and then if result is greater than 50, rounded to 50.
SinglePiecesInHome	Amount of single pieces in one's own home board.
Maintaining blockades	
PointsOwned	Number of points occupied by two or more of one's own checkers.
PointsOwnedHome	Number of points occupied by two or more of one's own checkers within ones home board.
StrongestConsecutiveBlockade	Length of the strongest consecutive blockade.

Table 7. Some of the fuzzy rules used in Fuzzeval

Contact
If *SinglePiecesInHome* is *Few* and *Contact* is True then *BoardStrenght Good*
if *SinglePiecesInHome* is *Many* and *Contact* is True then *BoardStrenght Weak*
If *PointsOwned* is *Few* and *Contact* is True then *BoardStrenght Weak*
if *PointsOwned* is *Many* and *Contact* is True then *BoardStrenght Good*
If *PointsOwnedHome* is *Few* and *Contact* is True then *BoardStrenght Weak*
if *PointsOwnedHome* is *Many* and *Contact* is True then *BoardStrenght Good*
If *StrongestConsecutiveBlockade* is *Short* and *Contact* is True then *BoardStrenght Weak*
if *StrongestConsecutiveBlockade* is *Long* and *Contact* is True then *BoardStrenght Good*

Using the refined rule base, Fuzzeval was able to play more effectively when the conditions specified in the rule base occurred in a game. The full refined knowledge base consists of 15 linguistic variables and 30 rules. With the new knowledge base, Fuzzeval improved its performance by an additional 8%, achieving a winning rate of approximately 42% against Pubeval in a match of 100 games.

In our third experiment, a new backgammon player was created, implemented this time with ANNs. The purpose of this experiment was to determine the learning rate of the ANNs and the effect of training in their performance when the ANNs were set to play against Pubeval. The ANNs were trained by a combination of temporal difference and back-propagation algorithms, similarly as it is done in TD-Gammon [2]. Two ANN were used in this experiment: one trained for the *contact* stage, and one for the *race* stage. Both networks consist of an input layer of 196 units, a hidden layer of 80 units and an output layer of 5 units. Training was done by self-play, adjusting the network weights after the completion of each game. First, the final winning board was adjusted, then the final losing board, then the second last winning board, and the second last losing board etc., until the first played board was adjusted as the last one.

During training, the temporal difference mechanism was used to calculate the desired target output for a board pattern. The back propagation algorithm made the actual adjustment of the network weights so that the actual and desired outputs matched. In this experiment the step-size parameter in the temporal difference calculation was set to 0.1, and the networks were adjusted at training stage to get a maximum error of between 0.0035 and -0.0035 from the desired target output.

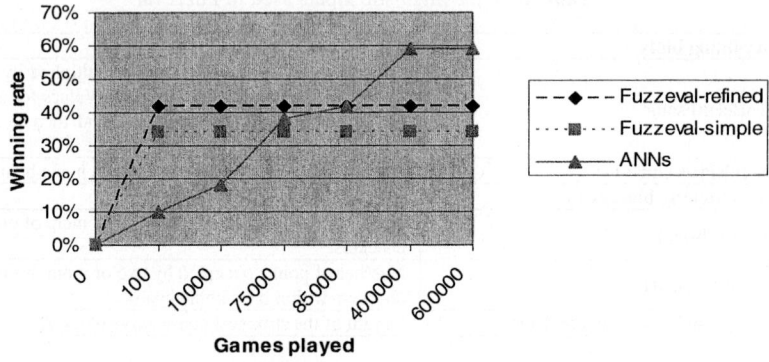

Fig. 5. Performance of Fuzzeval and ANNs

Figure 5 shows the percentage of winning games achieved by Fuzzeval, while playing against Pubeval using a simple and refined rule base. Fuzzeval was trained at same time as it was playing against Pubeval. Figure 5 also shows the performance achieved by the ANNs while playing with Pubeval. For this last case, the figure indicates how many games of self-playing training were required by the ANN to achieve a specific winning rate against Pubeval. As is shown in the figure, 75,000 and 85,000 games of training are required by the ANNs to reach the maximum playing level of Fuzzeval using a simple and a refined rule base, respectively. Figure 5 also shows that at 400,000 training games the ANNs were beating 59% of time to Pubeval and no further improvement was noted after that point.

5 Future Work and Conclusions

The experiments reported in this paper show that fuzzy controllers may be used effectively to create strong players in the domain of backgammon. Fuzzeval's approach differs from other proposed mechanisms [2,3,7] in a number of ways. Firstly, reinforcement learning and fuzzy controllers are combined in Fuzzeval to create a simple and effective backgammon player. Secondly, conversely to methods based on genetic algorithms or ANN [2,3,10], Fuzzeval approach is adaptive, i.e. Fuzzeval may be retrained after playing a few games. Thirdly, Fuzzeval mechanisms are simple comparatively with the approaches described in [7, 10], based on the application of genetic algorithms and genetic programming in the domain of othello and backgammon respectively.

In our experiments, Fuzzeval was able to adjust its playing style, to beat around 42% of the time to Pubeval. Fuzzeval reached its best performance after playing only 100 games. Comparatively, a more complex mechanism based on ANNs requires playing around 85,000 games to reach the effectiveness of Fuzzeval, and 400,000 games to exceed Fuzeval's performance by 17%. Our experiments also show that further improvement in Fuzzeval is possible with a more refined knowledge base. While the current performance of Fuzzeval is lower than the one obtained with ANNs, its combined simplicity and effectiveness makes this approach attractive. Moreover, contrary to approaches based on ANN and evolutionary techniques, Fuzzeval has the advantage of allowing humans learn why certain moves were executed.

One drawback of the fuzzy controller-based approach presented in this paper is obtaining the optimum knowledge base. As it is shown by our experiments, a few simple rules are likely to provide very good performance. However, to obtain the best performance a refined knowledge base may be more difficult to design. To overcome this problem, we are currently exploring diverse methods to generate automatically the fuzzy rules. Our preliminary experiments have shown that there are correlations between pairs of fuzzy rules. Furthermore, previous performance history of a game may be used to select, keep, or discard certain rules. Finally, for comparison purposes, we are exploring the use of approaches based on ANN and genetic algorithms to automatically learn the fuzzy rules.

References

1. A. L. Samuel, "Some studies in machine learning using the game of checkers". *IBM Journal of research and development* 44(1/2): 206-226, 2000.
2. G. Tesauro, "Temporal Difference Learning and TD-Gammon." *Communications of the ACM* 38(3): 58-68, 1995.
3. K. Chellapilla, D. B. Fogel, "Evolving neural networks to play checkers without relaying on expert knowledge." *IEEE Transactions on Neural Networks* 10(6): 1382-1391, 1999.
4. S. L. Epstein, "Learning to play expertly: A tutorial on Hoyle." *Machines that Learn to Play Games* 153-178, 2001.
5. Y. Seirawan, H. A. Simon, T. Munakata, "The implications of Kasparov vs. Deep Blue." *Communications of the ACM* 40(8): 21-25, 1997
6. L.A. Zadeh, "Making computers think like people," *IEEE. Spectrum*, 8/1984, pp. 26-32.
7. J.S. Jang, C.-T. Sun, and E. Mizutani, *Neuro-fuzzy and Soft Computing.*, Ed. Prentice Hall, New Jersey 1997
8. Backgammon Rules. http://www.bkgm.com/rules.html
9. Key Concepts in Backgammon. http://www.redtopbg.com/keyconcepts.htm
10. J.P. Azaria and M. Sipper, "GP-Gammon: Using Genetic Programming to Evolve Backgammon Players", *Proceedings of 8th European Conference, EuroGP 2005*, Lausanne, Switzerland, March 30 - April 1, 2005.

Analysis of Performance of Fuzzy Logic-Based Production Scheduling by Simulation

Alejandra Duenas[1], Dobrila Petrovic[1], and Sanja Petrovic[2]

[1] Control Theory and Applications Centre, School of Mathematical
and Information Sciences, Coventry University,
Priory Street, Coventry, CV1 5FB, UK
{A.Duenas, D.Petrovic}@coventry.ac.uk
[2] Automated Scheduling, Optimisation and Planning Research Group,
School of Computer Science and IT, University of Nottingham,
Nottingham, United Kingdom
sxp@cs.nott.ac.uk

Abstract. In this paper, a new fuzzy logic-based approach to production scheduling in the presence of uncertain disruptions is presented. The approach is applied to a real-life problem of a pottery company where the uncertain disruption considered is glaze shortage. This disruption is defined by two parameters that are specified imprecisely: number of glaze shortage occurrences and glaze delivery time. They are modelled and combined using standard fuzzy sets and level 2 fuzzy sets, respectively. A predictive schedule is generated in such a way as to absorb the impact of the fuzzy glaze shortage disruption. The schedule performance measure used is makespan. Two measures of predictability are defined: the average deviation and the standard deviation of the completion time of the last job produced on each machine. In order to analyse the performance of the predictive schedule, a new simulation tool FPSSIM is developed and implemented. Various tests carried out show that the predictive schedules have good performance in the presence of uncertain disruptions.

1 Introduction

Production scheduling concerns the allocation of machines to jobs over a period of time while optimising a predefined measure of performance [9]. In real-life scheduling unforeseen disruptions occur in the shop floor causing modification in the original schedule. Vieira et al. [11] reviewed different sources of disruptions inherent in production scheduling, including machine failure, urgent job arrival, job cancellation, due date change, delay in the arrival or shortage of materials, change in job priority, rework or quality problems, over or underestimation of process times and operator absenteeism.

Mehta and Uzsoy [7] and O'Donovan et al.[1] developed predictive scheduling approaches to single machine and job shop problems respectively, considering maximisation of the schedule predictability. They estimated the effect of machine failures on the schedule and increased the estimated job completion times accordingly. McKay et al. [6] developed an aversion dynamics heuristic that prevents scheduling of expensive jobs after a machine repair. Singer [10] solved a job shop problem with uncertain processing times caused by variability of human labour or machine breakdowns. Leon et al. [5] analysed job shop schedule delays caused by disruptions and proposed surrogate measures for delay estimation. Herrmann [4] developed a production scheduling approach where the worst-case performance is optimised. Duenas and Petrovic [3] developed a predictive-reactive scheduling approach where uncertain disruptions were modelled using possibility distributions.

In this paper, a new approach to production scheduling in the presence of uncertain disruptions is presented. It is applied to a real-life scheduling problem of a pottery company. The disruption considered is raw material shortage. Data concerning this type of disruption are not available. Therefore, they may be specified imprecisely based on managerial experience and subjective judgement. They are modelled using fuzzy sets and level 2 fuzzy sets. A predictive schedule capable of absorbing the disruptions effect is generated. Its predictability performance is analysed using a new simulation tool FPSSIM. The paper is organised as follows. The real-life problem of scheduling of parallel machines in the presence of uncertain disruptions is described in Section 2, while the new approach to predictive scheduling is presented in Section 3. FPSSIM developed for simulation of realised schedules, and the analysis of the results obtained are given in Section 4 and Section 5, respectively. Finally, conclusions are outlined in Section 6.

2 Real-Life Production Scheduling Problem

The problem under consideration is a real-life production scheduling problem defined in collaboration with Denby Pottery Ltd. in the UK. The company manufactures a wide range of ceramic tableware products. The production process comprises two main sequential phases: (1) making shapes/forms out of clay and their firing into semi-products (biscuits), (2) biscuits glazing and their firing into end products. The process analysed in this paper is the glazing process that is performed using three 'flowlines'. They are considered as identical parallel machines because they have the same speeds. At present, the glazing section leader builds the schedule by hand dealing with approximately 30 jobs on weekly basis, i.e., the scheduling time horizon is one week. A job is defined as a number of items of a specific product to be glazed. Jobs are independent and nonpreemptive, i.e., once a job begins processing, it is completed without interruptions. Due to technological requirements not all the jobs can be glazed on any of the three machines.

Investigating the present conditions of the glazing process, it is found that the parallel machine schedule is realised in the presence of uncertain disruptions that have an adverse effect on the jobs' completion times. The disruptions that have the greatest impact on the scheduling execution, occur when a machine runs out of a raw material i.e., glaze. In order to minimise the possible adverse effect of the glaze shortage on the glazing process a predictive scheduling approach is proposed.

Formally, the glazing scheduling problem is stated as an identical parallel machine scheduling problem with $N = 30$ jobs to be scheduled on $M = 3$ machines, where each job $J_j, j = 1,..., 30$, can be processed on subset M_j of the 3 machines. The jobs processing times are $p_j, j = 1,..., 30$. The objective is to generate the job's machine allocation and schedule in such a way as to minimise the makespan C_{max}, i.e. the time that takes to complete all the jobs taking into consideration uncertain glaze shortages. The makespan is defined as $C_{max} = \max\{C_j | j = 1,...,30\}$, where C_j is the completion time of job J_j.

3 Fuzzy Predictive Scheduling

A predictive schedule (*PS*) is generated in such a way as to minimise the effect of disruptions whilst achieving a good schedule performance, i.e. makespan. The predictive schedule is released to the shop floor at the beginning of the time horizon. When a disruption occurs on the shop floor, the job affected is stopped and can be continued once the required glaze arrives. Consequently, the *PS* is modified into the realised schedule (*RS*) with the same jobs allocation and machine sequences but with different job completion times (see Figure 1).

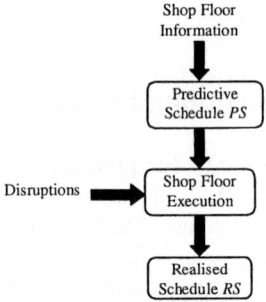

Fig. 1. Predictive scheduling (adapted from [7])

3.1 Modelling Uncertain Disruptions

Two sources of uncertainty that characterise the disruption caused by a glaze shortage are considered: (1) number of glaze shortage occurrences and (2) glaze delivery time. Since there are no records of material shortages, the associated parameters can be specified based on vague or imprecise knowledge and experience of the glazing section leader. It may be convenient to express them using linguistic terms such as 'the number of glaze shortages is *much higher* than certain value' or 'the glaze is delivered in *about* certain unit time periods'. These uncertain values are represented by fuzzy sets.

Having 8 different raw materials, m_g, $g = 1,..., 8$, as inputs to the glazing process and a discrete and finite set NOC_g that contains the possible numbers of shortage occurrences of glaze m_g, $NOC_g = \{noc_{g_1}, noc_{g_2},..., noc_{g_K}\}$, the fuzzy set O_g, which represents the number of glaze shortage occurrences per unit time period is defined as

$O_g = \sum_{k=1}^{g_K} \mu_{O_g}(noc_{g_k})/noc_{g_k}$ where $\mu_{O_g}(noc_{g_k})$ is the possibility that there is noc_{g_k} shortage occurrences per unit time period (see Figure 2(a)). The glaze m_g delivery time is represented by continuous fuzzy set R_g defined as $R_g = \int_{tr_g} \mu_{R_g}(tr_g)/tr_g$, $tr_g \in R^+$, where $\mu_{R_g}(tr_g)$ is a trapezoidal membership function specified by four parameters $(tr_{g_1}, tr_{g_2}, tr_{g_3}, tr_{g_4})$ (see Figure 2(b)).

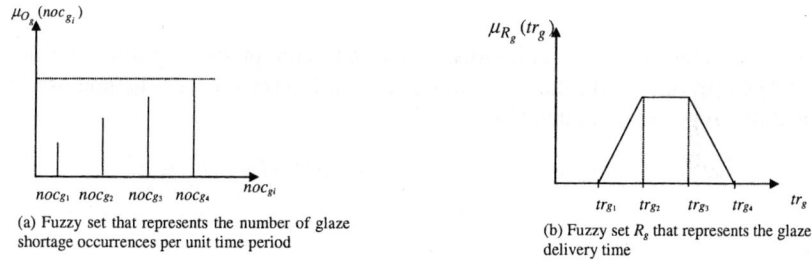

(a) Fuzzy set that represents the number of glaze shortage occurrences per unit time period

(b) Fuzzy set R_g that represents the glaze delivery time

Fig. 2. Fuzzy sets that represent uncertain disruptions caused by glaze shortage

In the new predictive scheduling approach developed, the job processing times are extended by inserting idle times, that enable the uncertain disruptions to be absorbed in the schedule. The extended processing time pd_j for job J_j, is defined as $pd_j = p_j + id_j$, $j = 1,...,30$, where id_j is the idle time equal to the total glaze delivery time during the processing time of job J_j. Time id_j is calculated as the product of the fuzzy number of glaze shortage occurrences per unit time period represented by discrete fuzzy set O_g and the fuzzy glaze delivery time represented by continuous fuzzy set R_g.

The product is calculated using an approach suggested in [8]. It is a level 2 fuzzy set, $O_g \otimes R_g$, i.e., a fuzzy set whose elements are standard fuzzy sets $noc_{g_k} \tilde{\times} R_g$, $k = 1, ..., g_K$. The standard fuzzy set is calculated as a fuzzy product $\tilde{\times}$ of scalar noc_{g_k} and fuzzy set R_g. The product $\tilde{\times}$ is determined in a standard way using the Extension principle [12]. In this case, fuzzy set $noc_{g_k} \tilde{\times} R_g$ has also a trapezoidal form determined by the following four parameters $(noc_{g_k} \times tr_{g_1}, noc_{g_k} \times tr_{g_2}, noc_{g_k} \times tr_{g_3}, noc_{g_k} \times tr_{g_4})$. The possibility of the total glaze delivery time per unit time period being $noc_{g_k} \tilde{\times} R_g$ is $\mu_{O_g}(noc_{g_k})$. Formally, the total glaze delivery time per unit time period is represented as level 2 fuzzy set, $O_g \otimes R_g = \sum_{k=1}^{g_K} \mu_{O_g}(noc_{g_k})/noc_{g_k} \tilde{\times} R_g$. An example of the level 2 fuzzy set $O_g \otimes R_g$ is given in Figure 3.

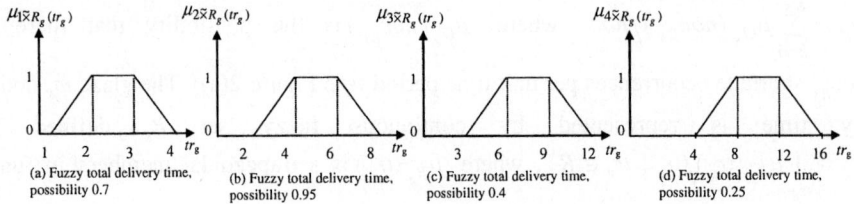

Fig. 3. Level 2 fuzzy set $O_g \otimes R_g$ where $O_g = 0.7/1 + 0.95/2 + 0.4/3 + 0.25/4$ and R_g is defined by the parameters (1, 2, 3, 4)

In order to determine a crisp idle time to add to the job processing time, it is necessary to transform this level 2 fuzzy set into a standard fuzzy set. The method used is s-fuzzification proposed by Zadeh [12] as follows:

$$s-fuzzif(O_g \otimes R_g) = \int_{tr_g} \mu_{s-fuzzif(O_g \otimes R_g)}(tr_g) \big/ tr_g, \; tr_g \in R^+ \quad (1)$$

where

$$\mu_{s-fuzzif(O_g \otimes R_g)}(tr_g) = \sup_{k=1,\ldots,g_K} \mu_{Og}(noc_{g_k}) \cdot \mu_{noc_{g_k} \tilde{\times} R_g}(tr_g) \quad (2)$$

Ordinary fuzzy set $s-fuzzif(O_g \otimes R_g)$ is then defuzzified using the centroid method [13]. Value td_g, which is used as a crisp representation of the total glaze delivery time per unit time period, is calculated as follows:

$$td_g = \frac{\int_{tr_g \in R^+} tr_g \cdot \mu_{s-fuzzif(O_g \otimes R_g)}(tr_g)}{\int_{tr_g \in R^+} \mu_{s-fuzzif(O_g \otimes R_g)}(tr_g)} \quad (3)$$

In order to calculate the idle time id_j to be added to the initial processing time p_j of job J_j, the total glaze delivery time per unit time period is multiplied by the job processing time as follows $id_j = td_g \cdot p_j$.

3.2 Dispatching Rules

Once the idle times are determined and added to the initial processing times, the *PS* schedule of the parallel machines is generated using dispatching rules. Dispatching rules are heuristics that have low computational complexity and are easy to implement [9]. The selection of the rule depends on the performance measure used and the machine environment. The two dispatching rules are combined to generate the *PS*, namely the Least Flexible Job First (LFJ) and the Longest Processing Time (LPT). Each of these dispatching rule applied individually performs well when the scheduling objective is to minimise the makespan. The LFJ rule is applied first, to allocate the job that can be processed on the smallest number of machines, to the machine that is freed. If there is more than one job that can be allocated to the machine, the LPT rule is applied which assigns the job with the longest processing time.

4 Simulation of Realised Schedule

In order to measure the *PS* performance, a new simulation tool, Fuzzy Predictive Scheduling Simulation (FPSSIM), is developed and implemented. Fuzzy sets that describe uncertain glaze shortages, including numbers of glaze shortage occurrences and glaze delivery times, are input into the simulation model that generates the *RS*. The general FPSSIM structure is presented in Figure 4.

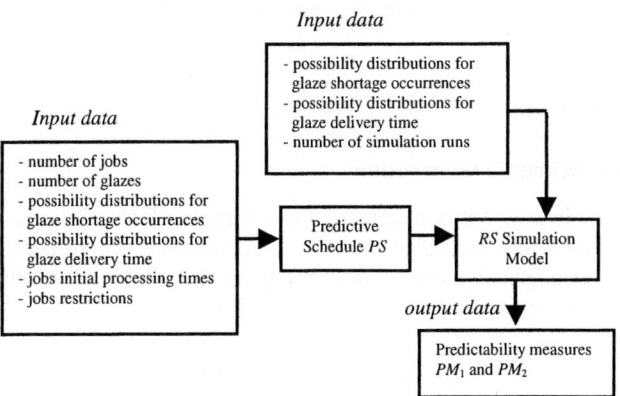

Fig. 4. The general FPSSIM structure

Firstly, the fuzzy set that represents the number of glaze shortage occurrences is used to generate the corresponding possibility distribution. It represents belief that the number of shortage will take a certain value and it is equal to the corresponding membership degree of the fuzzy set. The possibility distribution is then transformed into a probability distribution using the procedure proposed by Dubois and Prade [2]. This means that the fuzzy data is simulated in FPSSIM using the derived probability distribution. The resulting probability distribution is used to generate the random number of glaze shortage occurrences per week, for each glaze m_g, $g = 1, …, G$.

Secondly, the fuzzy set, i.e., the possibility distribution for the glaze delivery time is transformed into the corresponding probability distribution. The resulting probability distribution is used to generate the glaze delivery time for each glaze shortage occurrence.

As presented in Figure 4, the output data generated by FPSSIM are two measures defined to analyse predictability of the *PS*:

- $PM1_i$ - average deviation between the completion time $C_{\max_i}$ of the last job produced on machine i, $i = 1, …, M$ in the *PS* and RS_a, where RS_a is the realised schedule generated in simulation run a, $a = 1, …, A$:

$$PM1_i = \frac{\sum_{a=1}^{A}(C_{\max_i}(PS) - C_{\max_i}(RS_a))}{A}, i = 1,…,M \quad (4)$$

where

$$C_{max_i}(PS) = \max\{C_j | \text{job } J_j \text{ is allocated to machine } i \text{ in the } PS\}$$

$$C_{max_i}(RS_a) = \max\{C_j | \text{job } J_j \text{ is allocated to machine } i \text{ in the } RS_a\}$$

- $PM2_i$ - standard deviation of $C_{max_i}(RS)$, $i = 1, ..., M$:

$$PM2_i = \sqrt{\frac{\sum_{a=1}^{A}(C_{max_i}(PS) - C_{max_i}(RS_a))^2}{A-1}}, i = 1,...,M \qquad (5)$$

5 Results Analysis

5.1 Predictive Schedule Generation

The predictive schedule PS is generated for a sample of $N = 30$ jobs (see Table 1) where it is assumed that each glaze has 0, 1 or 2 shortage occurrences with different possibilities. These data has been obtained through collaboration with the pottery company. The makespan achieved is $C_{max} = 39.9$ hours.

Table 1. Predictive schedule PS

machine					jobs' sequence						
M_1	11	30	20	22	2	15	29	19	13	17	16	4
M_2	28	18	8	23	27	26	24	14				
M_3	21	1	10	12	25	5	9	3	7	6		
machine					completion times						
M_1	5.5	9.1	12.6	14.6	16.6	18.4	19.5	20.6	26.0	31.4	36.1	39.9
M_2	5.6	11.1	16.7	22.1	27.5	32.2	36.0	39.8				
M_3	5.5	11.0	14.6	16.6	18.4	20.2	21.3	26.7	32.0	36.8		
$C_{max} =$	39.9											

5.2 Predictability Analysis

Table 2 presents one simulated RS where the number of glaze shortages per unit time periods are $[1, 0, 1, 2, 1, 1, 2, 2]$ for the 8 glazes, respectively. Those jobs that are not affected by a glaze shortage are processed with their initial processing time p_j, the processing times of the affected jobs were extended by the corresponding glaze delivery time. It is worth noting that the PS and RS have the same job sequence on the machines but different job completion times.

Table 2. Realised schedule RS

machine					jobs' sequence						
M_1	11	30	20	22	2	15	29	19	13	17	16	4
M_2	28	18	8	23	27	26	24	14				
M_3	21	1	10	12	25	5	9	3	7	6		
machine					completion times						
M_1	3.9	8.4	11.0	12.5	14.0	15.3	16.1	17.4	21.2	27.0	32.9	35.9
M_2	4.0	8.0	15.2	23.0	27.0	30.0	34.1	37.1				
M_3	3.9	7.8	10.3	11.8	13.2	14.5	15.8	19.5	23.5	26.5		
$C_{max} =$	37.1											

Comparing the makespan of the PS (see Table 1), C_{max}= 39.9 hours, with the makespan of the RS (see Table 2), C_{max}= 37.1 hours, it can be seen that the RS is finished 2.8 hours earlier than the PS. However, the machine that processes the last job to leave the glazing holloware section in the PS is M_1 whilst in the RS is M_2. For this reason, it is appropriate to measure predictability of each machine separately. Comparing C_{max_i}, $i = 1,..., 3$, of the PS and the RS, it can be seen that the difference for machine M_1 is 4 hours, for machine M_2 is 2.7 hours and for machine M_3 is 10.3 hours. These differences are expected since in the predictive scheduling approach all jobs' processing times are increased by adding idle times whilst in the simulation, only the jobs affected by the glaze shortages have added times to their processing times.

Table 3 shows the predictability measures $PM1$ and $PM2$ for each machine and the average C_{max} achieved with different numbers of simulation runs.

Table 3. Predictability measures achieved with different number of simulation runs

number of simulation runs A	$PM1_i$			$PM2_i$			average C_{max}
	$i=1$	$i=2$	$i=3$	$i=1$	$i=2$	$i=3$	
50	5.60	5.84	8.90	1.503	1.270	1.260	35.38
100	5.54	5.75	8.83	1.653	1.870	1.386	35.45
200	5.74	5.78	8.57	1.636	1.851	1.372	35.43
300	5.72	5.71	8.47	1.561	1.777	1.379	35.53
400	5.79	5.58	8.46	1.487	1.683	1.247	35.60
500	5.90	5.58	8.43	1.472	1.665	1.235	35.52

It can be seen, that when the number of runs increases the values obtained for $PM1_i$ become more stable, in the case of 400 and 500 runs the values are very close to each other. Therefore, the results to be considered in the analysis are those generated when the number of simulation runs is 500. The predictability measures achieved are $PM1_1 = 5.90$ hours, $PM1_2 = 5.58$ hours and $PM1_3 = 8.43$ hours. In other words, the average difference between machine completion times in PS and RS_a is not bigger than 9 hours that represents 22.5 % of the 1-week time horizon. In addition, the average C_{max} obtained in 500 simulation runs is 35.52 hours. Therefore, the difference between the average C_{max} simulated 500 runs and the C_{max} in the PS (39.9 hours) is 4.38 hours, that represents the 10.95 % of the time horizon. Finally, the standard deviations $PM2_1$, $PM2_2$ and $PM2_3$ are 1.472, 1.665 and 1.235 for machines $i = 1, 2$ and 3, respectively. It can be concluded that the deviation the C_{max_i} in the PS, is small, i.e., the RSs are relatively close to the PS. This leads to the conclusion that the PS has good predictability.

It may be interesting to analyse the effect of increasing uncertainty in glaze shortage occurrences. Table 4 shows the results obtained when the number of glaze shortage occurrences is increased from 3 to 4, i.e., there are 0, 1, 2 and 3 possible shortages for each glaze.

As previously, the results obtained by running the simulation 500 times are analysed when the maximum number of glaze shortage occurrence is changed, the PS generated is also modified. The new PS has a makespan $C_{max} = 41.3$ hours. It can be

Table 4. Predictability measures achieved with different number of simulation runs when the maximum number of shortages is increased to 4

number of simulation runs A	$PM1_i$			$PM2_i$			average C_{max}
	$i=1$	$i=2$	$i=3$	$i=1$	$i=2$	$i=3$	
50	6.19	5.63	7.51	2.701	3.082	1.891	36.74
100	6.02	5.92	7.33	2.708	3.104	1.809	36.78
200	5.17	5.85	6.76	2.680	3.145	1.743	37.33
300	5.69	6.06	7.42	2.686	3.210	1.727	36.99
400	5.68	5.97	7.46	2.728	3.256	1.690	37.00
500	5.74	5.96	7.45	2.730	3.247	1.739	36.99

seen, that $PM1_1$ is 5.74 hours, $PM1_2$ is 5.96 hours and $PM1_3$ is 7.45 hours. This means that the average difference between PS and RS_a is not bigger than 7.5 hours, (18.75 % of the 1-week time horizon). Table 4 also shows that the average C_{max} is 36.99 hours. Therefore, the difference between the average C_{max} and the C_{max} in the PS (41.3 hours) is 4.33 hours (10.8 % of the time horizon). As in the previous case it can be seen, that the standard deviations $C_{max_i}(RS)$ with respect to the $C_{max_i}(PS)$ are small. Consequently, the RS generated by simulation are relatively close to the PS.

Based on the analysis carried out, it can be concluded that the PS generated using the fuzzy predictive scheduling approach has good predictive performance in terms of absorbing the negative impact of glaze shortages.

6 Conclusions

In this paper, a new fuzzy logic-based approach to production scheduling in the presences of uncertain disruptions is presented. The approach is applied to a real-life problem of a pottery company where the uncertain disruption considered is glaze shortage. The disruption modelled using standard fuzzy sets and level 2 fuzzy sets. A predictive schedule is generated in such a way as to absorb the impact of the fuzzy glaze shortage disruption where the schedule performance measure used is the makespan. In order to analyse the performance of the predictive schedule a new simulation tool that generates the realised schedule is developed and implemented. Two measure of predictability are proposed: (1) average deviation of completion times of the last job produced on each machine in the predictive schedule and the realised schedule, (2) standard deviation of completion times of the last job produced on each machine in the predictive schedule and the realised schedule.

Different test are performed showing that: (1) the realised schedules have makespans close to the predictive schedule makespan, (2) the predictive schedule has good predictability being capable of absorbing the possible glaze shortages.

Acknowledgments

This research is supported by Engineering and Physical Sciences Research Council (EPSRC), grant no. GR/R95326/01 and GR/R95319/01. This support is gratefully acknowledged. We also acknowledge the support of the industrial collaborator the Denby Pottery Company Ltd., UK.

References

1. O'Donovan, R., Uzsoy, R., McKay, K.N.: Predictable scheduling of a single machine with breakdown and sensitive jobs. International Journal of Production Research 37:18, (1999), 4217-4233
2. Dubois, D, Prade, H.: Fuzzy sets and statistical data. European Journal of Operational Research 25(1986), 345-356
3. Duenas, A., Petrovic, D.: An approach to predictive-reactive scheduling of parallel machines subject to disruptions. Reviewed and accepted to be published in the Proceedings of the 2nd Multidisciplinary International Conference on Scheduling: Theory and Applications (MISTA 2005), New York, July 18-21, (2005)
4. Herrmann, J.W.: A genetic algorithm for minimax optimization problems. Proceedings of the 1999 Congress on Evolutionary Computation, Washington DC, July 6-9, (1999)
5. Leon, V., Jorge, S., Wu, D., Robert H.S.: Robustness measures and robust scheduling for job shops. IIE Transactions 26:5, (1994), 32-43
6. McKay, K.N., Morton, T.E., Ramnath, P., Wang, J.: Aversion dynamics scheduling when the system changes. Journal of Scheduling 3:2, (2000), 71-88
7. Mehta, S.V., Uzsoy, R.: Predictable scheduling of a single machine subject to breakdowns. International Journal of Computer Integrated Manufacturing 12:1, (1999), 15-38
8. Petrovic, D., Petrovic, R., Vujosevic, M.: Fuzzy models for the newsboy problem. International Journal of Production Economics 45, (1996), 435-441
9. Pinedo, M.: Scheduling: Theory, Algorithms, and Systems, Prentice Hall (2002)
10. Singer, M.: Forecasting policies for scheduling a stochastic due date job shop. International Journal of Production Research, 38:15, (2000), 3623-3637
11. Vieira, G.E., Herrmann, J.W., Lin, E.: Rescheduling manufacturing systems: A framework of strategies, policies, and methods. Journal of Scheduling 6:1, (2003), 39-62
12. Zadeh, L.A., Fuzzy Sets. Information and Control 8, (1965), 338-353
13. Zimmermann, H–J.: Fuzzy Set Theory-and Its Applications, Third Edition. Kluwer Academic Publishers (1996).

Agent-Based Simulation Replication:
A Model Driven Architecture Approach

Candelaria Sansores and Juan Pavón[*]

Universidad Complutense de Madrid, Dep. Sistemas Informáticos y Programación,
28040 Madrid, Spain
`csansores@fdi.ucm.es, jpavon@sip.ucm.es`

Abstract. In Multi-agent based simulation (MABS) systems, computational models are built as multi-agent systems (MAS). Replication of these models can contribute to improve the reliability of the results and understanding of the system. One of the main problems for facilitating replication is the lack of a simulation integrated environment that supports the whole research process from conceptual modeling to simulation implementation and analysis. We address this issue providing a high-level conceptual modeling abstraction for simulation development, including transformation tools that facilitate the implementation of simulations on different simulation platforms. In this way, agent-based simulation development process is driven by modeling, because users focus on conceptual modeling, while implementation code is generated automatically.

1 Motivation

Multi-agent based simulation (MABS) is an important and new alternative method for studying phenomena that emerge from complex organization and non-linear interaction in an increasing number of fields including the social, economic, cognitive, behavioral and organizational sciences. A model in a simulation consists of a specification of the phenomenon we want to study. This could be a mathematical equation, a logical statement or a computer program depending of the simulation technique used. In MABS theoretical models are built like computational models using multi-agent systems (MAS), thus scientists are able to validate their theories by running the models and observing and analyzing the results that arise from agents' interaction.

Our research centers on the application of computational modeling to social sciences, more concretely, computer simulation of social phenomena. The executions of these agent-based computational models are known as Agent-Based Social Simulations (ABSS). In this technique, the ultimate modeling target is a social process and the purpose of the simulation is to help understanding that process. The construction of most published ABSS models is guided by the stages of a simulation research process that has been pointed out by [2, 6] (Conceptualization, Design, Construction,

---

[*] This work has been developed with support of the Consejo Nacional de Ciencia y Tecnología (CONACYT) from México and the project TIC2002-04516-C03-03, funded by the Spanish Council for Science and Technology.

and Evaluation). However, there is another stage of the process that is less often performed although it also needs to be considered, the replication of the execution of the models.

Replication contributes to the reliability of the model results and better understanding of the system. As [2] states, replication is one of the hallmarks of cumulative science. It needs to be confirmed whether the claimed results of a given simulation are reliable in the sense that they can be reproduced by someone starting from scratch. Without this confirmation, it is possible that some published results are simply mistaken due to programming errors, misrepresentation of what was actually simulated, or errors in analyzing or reporting the results.

In order to validate results our approach allows executing the same model on different simulation engines (there are various toolkits for developing agent-based simulation systems, such as REPAST [12], SWARM [16], MASON [9], SDML [15], etc.). The results provided by each simulation toolkit should not differ considerably between them due to particularities of each simulation platform; if they do then we have to address these particularities that affect the replication process and that are not easily identifiable without our approach. Also, our approach eases the replication of models by different modelers, since model specification with diagrams in a well-defined graphical specification language is less ambiguous then natural language descriptions.

One of the most important problems for performing replication is the lack of a simulation integrated environment that supports the whole research process from conceptual modeling to simulation implementation and analysis. Without a conceptual model specification, ambiguities in model descriptions appear. Sometimes descriptions are linked to a specific simulation platform, and the model and the implementation are not clearly identified. In these situations, the modeler who will carry out the replication faces the challenge of guessing the underlying conceptual model.

Replication and model comparison techniques are reviewed in [7]. The main of these techniques are those proposed by [2, 3]. The former implies reimplementation of the models, rewriting models that others have described on paper, so as to understand them more deeply and reproduce the stated results. The latter is known as *alignment* of computational models or *docking* for short, and is applied to determine whether two models can produce the same results.

It is important to notice that applying the reimplementation technique that involves literal reconstruction of the same simulation using the same programming infrastructure has the disadvantage that implicit assumptions built into the original version can be reproduced in the replication and are not therefore tested. A better technique may involve docking, the construction (reimplementation) of a conceptually identical simulation using different tools and even different methodology [4], that is, a mixture of both techniques.

The use of high level design and structured programming tools can assist in publishing simulation results and replication. These high level tools (for a review, see [8, 17]), can help to make writing the software easier and less prone to error. However, these tools are still implementation oriented, which implies that the way social scientists communicate their models for replication is by passing source code to each other, which demands high effort to understand and interpret the models, sometimes leading to misunderstandings.

Besides supporting replication, we also intend to satisfy the Axelrod's three main goals in the development and programming of an agent-based social model to achieve the necessary methodological rigor demanded to any scientific work: *internal validation*[1], *usability* (it must be easy to run the model and analyze the results) and *extensibility* (it must be possible to adapt and reuse the model).

Our proposal provides a framework that addresses these issues providing a high level conceptual modeling abstraction for simulation development, including transformation tools to translate simulation models to code in different simulation environments, and in this way facilitate model replication. As a result, agent-based simulation development process is driven by modeling, because users only need to concentrate on conceptual modeling, and implementation code will be generated automatically. This approach is model oriented and, as another advantage, addresses the issue of model communication misunderstandings, which usually happens when users are working with different simulation tools.

Also, this approach can facilitate the use of existing simulation tools by users who are not necessarily experts in software engineering, but in social sciences. Thus, the model driven implementation approach relies on (1) a specification language based on well established concepts of agent-oriented software engineering, in particular the INGENIAS [11] approach, which is in line and evolves with current efforts at FIPA [5] and AgentLink [1], and (2) simulation toolkits we had experience with, for which heterogeneity is an added value for replication richness.

Section 2 briefly reviews approaches for simulation modeling and presents our proposal to pass from visual modeling to simulation implementation based on the model driven architecture paradigm. Section 3 presents a case study that shows the feasibility of replicating agent-based simulation systems with our framework. Section 4 summarizes our contributions and concludes with the identification of further work.

2 Model Driven ABSS Replication

A model of a system is a description or specification of that system and its environment for certain purpose. A model is often presented as a combination of drawings and text. The text may be in a formal or natural language. Model Driven Approach (MDA) provides a means for using models to direct the course of system development [10]. That is, using modeling languages as programming languages rather than merely as design languages.

Our framework architecture is based on this paradigm. Figure 1 compares the main elements of this architecture with the *MDA* framework. On the right side of the figure we can see the *PIM*, *PSM*, *Transformation* process and *other information* in the *MDA* pattern, by which a *PIM* is transformed to a *PSM*. The *PIM* is a *Platform Independent Model* which may use a general purpose modeling language, or a language specific to the area in which the system will be used; in our case we use a visual modeling simulation language. The *PSM* is a *Platform Specific Model* which combines the

---

[1] Internal validation, also known as *verification* [6] in the simulation field, is concerned with the correctness of the transformation from the abstract representation (the conceptual model) to the program code (the simulation model). That is, with ensuring that the program code faithfully reflects the behavior that is implicit in the specification of the conceptual model [2].

specification in the *PIM* with the details that specify how that system uses a particular type of platform; in our case we use agent-based simulation platforms in which different *PSMs* will run. The model transformation is the process of converting one model into another model of the same system, as observed in Fig. 1 the platform independent model and other information (represented by the empty rectangle) are combined by the transformation to produce a platform specific model.

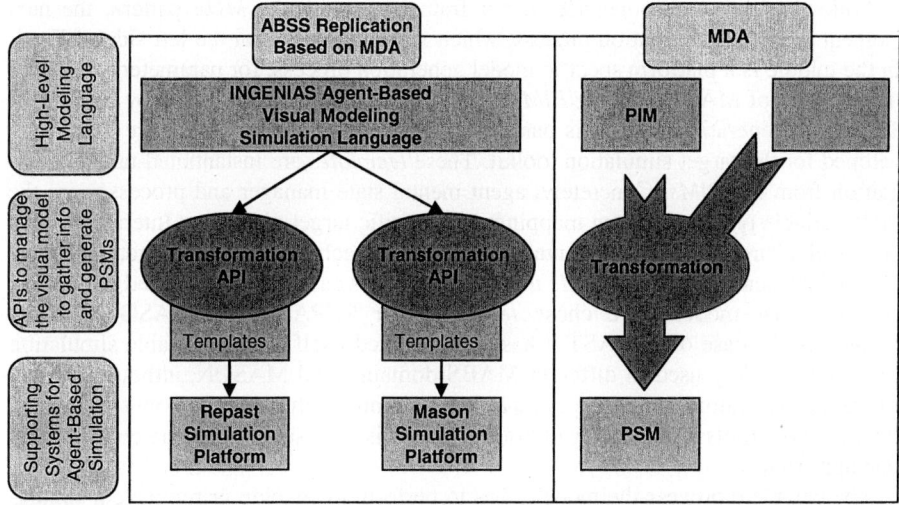

Fig. 1. The ABSS Replication framework based on the MDA pattern. On the right side we can observe the main elements of MDA and on the left side their corresponding elements in our architecture. On top the visual modeling platform-independent language, in the middle the transformation process and other information that combined generate the platform specific models on the bottom.

On the left side of Fig. 1 we can observe the corresponding elements in our framework, which is based on the agent-oriented INGENIAS Development Kit (IDK). The IDK provides a notation for modeling multi-agent systems (MAS), which is supported by tools for analysis, design, verification and code generation. These tools, as well as the notation, are based on the specification of meta-models that define the different views and concepts from which a multi-agent system can be described. By extending and refining the meta-models it is possible to adapt the notation for particular application domains, always relying on agent concepts. One example of this is the inclusion of AUML as part of the INGENIAS notation (this is referenced in www.auml.org).

This adaptability is one of the main reasons to consider INGENIAS as the basis for the visual platform-independent modeling language for our framework to generate simulation PIMs. A MAS specification with INGENIAS visual language is performed from five viewpoints, whose use is illustrated in the next section: 1) the definition, control and management of each agent mental state, 2) the agent interactions, 3) the MAS organization, 4) the environment, and 5) the tasks and objectives assigned to each agent. For simulation, we have added two new viewpoints: the Timer viewpoint and the Space viewpoint, which can be considered as extensions of the Environment viewpoint. The Timer viewpoint manages the flow of time in the model during the execution of the simulation. Because our approach assumes simulations that are going to be carried out are time driven, we need constant time steps for simulating the perception-reaction cycle of agents who act by the passage of time. The Space viewpoint describes the spatial arrangements of agents in the model. Currently, we have only defined simple spatial relationships like continuous spaces, but we plan to consider 2D, 3D, hexagonal grids, hexagonal tori, etc., spaces.

Following the correspondence of our framework with the *MDA* pattern, the next element is the transformation process, which we can observe on the left side of Fig.1. In the middle is a platform specific model generation process, for parameterization and instantiation of MAS models or *PIMs* to concrete target platforms aided by IDK APIs. The *PSMs* generation process is based on *templates*, which should be previously developed for the target simulation toolkit. These *templates* are instantiated taking information from the *PIMs*. Concretely, agent mental state manager and processor are the most variable part in different mappings for specific target platforms. Interactions can be modeled through the implementation of specific mechanisms in the target platform.

The last elements are the *PSMs* themselves, in this case, the agent-based simulation computational models. We chose *templates* for REPAST and MASON toolkits because in the case of REPAST it has demonstrated itself to be a suitable simulation framework widely used in different MABS domains, and MASON, although new, it has adequate features to create complex simulations with a huge amount of agents. Besides, both tools are open Java libraries, which is very suitable for the code generation approach.

The complete process the modeler has to perform to develop or replicate a simulation model is: 1) define an agent-based social model with the visual language, 2) generate code for the target platform, and 3) run the simulation to gather results. The task of extending the visual language (if necessary) and programming code generation modules is not normally the responsibility of the modeler, but of some ABSS platform developer, who should know INGENIAS meta-models and Java programming skills for customizing the visual language editor and the code generation tools.

3 A Replication Case Study

We have selected as case study the problem of altruism among simple and smart vampire bats, which is described and modeled in [14], because it shows the importance of modeling agents as cognitive entities and highlights the impact of intelligence, goal-based systems on the spreading of altruism, provided these systems are highly dynamic. The model considers a population of vampire bats (agents) that live in *roosts*, where they return to after hunting and perform social activities like grooming and sharing food. The entities explicitly modeled as agents are the bats. Roosts are modeled as aggregates of bats. In roosts, bats are allowed to share food and to groom one another.

The *bats population* is considered an organization, whose purpose is the goal *Survive*, as shown in Fig. 2. This organization consists of one or more *roosts* and a *credit network* (represented as groups). There is only one type of agents, Bats, which can play several roles. In a roost, a bat can play the role of *altruist* or *beneficiary* depending on whether help is given or received. In the credit network group, a bat can play the role of *reciprocity*. Bats belong to both kinds of groups and can play any of these roles. The cardinality in the associations indicates the organization can have one or more roosts and the roost one or more bats, the same applies to roles cardinality, which indicates that it is possible that the role of beneficiary, for instance, may be played by no agent.

Cardinality is an important aspect for code generation in the transformation process; it provides information for agents' instantiation.

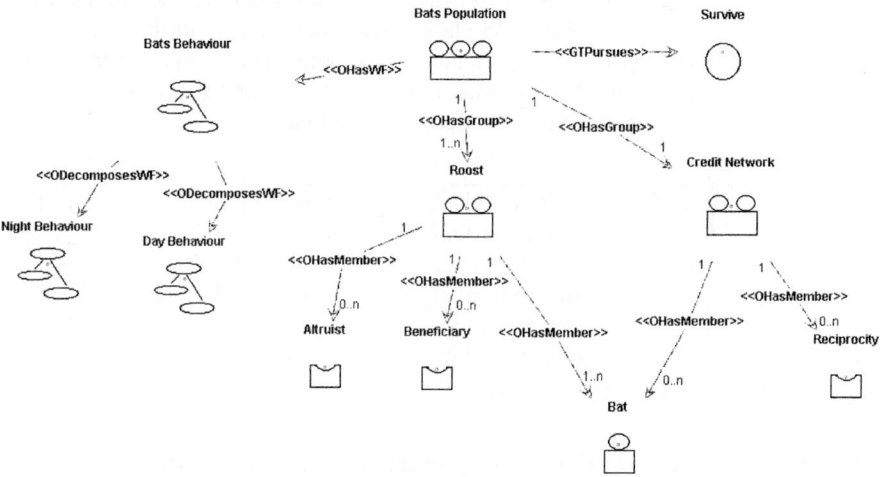

Fig. 2. The Organization model. The organization (represented as a rectangle with three circles) pursues a goal (represented as a circle), has groups (represented as rectangles with two circles) and workflows (the dynamics of the organization). Agents (a rectangle with one circle) and roles (similar to agents but without a circle) are members of one or more groups.

The behavior of the bats population is represented collectively as a workflow, *bats behavior* in Fig. 2. This workflow is broken down into *night behavior* and *day behavior*, which are further decomposed into tasks. These entities, which have been first identified in the modeling of the organization, are further detailed when looking at the system from other viewpoints, in other diagrams.

3.1 Reimplementation Issues

In this case study the goal is model reimplementation into two different simulation platforms. Fig. 2 shows a draft of the initial organization model which we generate platform specific models of. This diagram is defined with the visual modeling language of our framework; the complete set of diagrams can be seen in [14] and constitute the whole *PIM* of the case study.

Diagrams presented before are useful only to indicate what entities exist and what relationships connect them, but in the detailed implementation these entities should map to source code for different simulation toolkits. This goal is achieved by defining methods to map the specification diagrams components to source code (see Table 1).

Table 1. On the left, the table shows which specification elements will be taken into account. On the right, some indications about how they will be presented in the implementation

Model Entity	Implementation Elements
Organization	A model class that coordinates the setup and running of the model, extends the SimModelImpl and SimState classes of the simulation specific platforms tested. The simulation model sets up and controls both the representational and infrastructure parts of a simulation. Infrastructure variables will be such things as a Schedule, collection classes for agents and so forth. The largest portion of the representation variables will be initial parameters for a run of this model. For example, a numAgents variable used to set the number of agents in a simulation run.
Agent	The agent class will be largely simulation specific, in the MASON platform it will implement a Steppable interface, If the agent is to be displayed it should implement one of the Drawable interfaces on both platforms. Agents can be scheduled on a Schedule to be activated at some time step, ostensibly in order for it to change the simulation environment in some way. Agents don't have to be physically *in* the environment.
Environment Timer	The Scheduler Object responsible for altering the state of the simulation. What this means is that the schedule is told what methods to call on which objects and when. The timer sends notifications of "ticks" or time steps which are perceived by agents. This object is configurable, for instance, to set time the number of steps or the *order* of actions for each time step. An *order* is a subdivision of a single time tick, its intention is to separate the core behavior in step() from any necessary pre- or post- processing.
Environment Space	The Space Object for "spatial agents" responsible for agents location in the environment, that is, the situation of agents in a space. By now only Continuous and Network spaces are supported.
Tasks	Methods encapsulating agent actions, and which will be scheduled for execution during simulation steps.
Goals	Information within data structures of agents.
Role	Functionality associated to the role which is directly migrated to each agent playing it.
Organization Groups	Information within data structures of agents.
Interaction	Data structures associated to the agent. It incorporates state machines implementing protocols.
Protocol Specification	Several state machines distributed among different participants. Each participant only knows the state in which it collaborates.

Table 1 shows the mappings applied so far. As an example of how it works, we centred in the implementation of the case study into two target platforms, REPAST and MASON. To support the replication process, the developer performs the steps shown in Fig. 3, except step 3 which is usually performed by the modeler. The developer first describes the implementation elements of Table 1 within a prototype which is

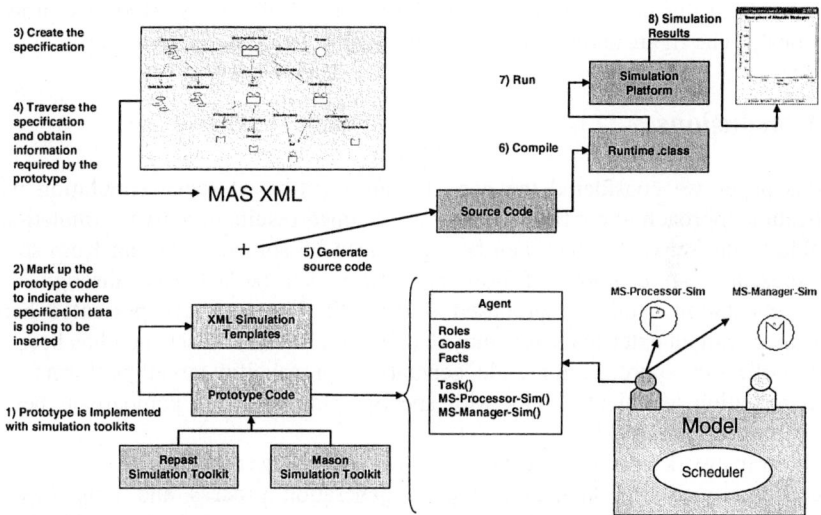

Fig. 3. Modeling and Implementation process to support replication issues. Modeler performs steps 3 creating the specification. Previously, the developer performed all other steps to create the templates which will be instantiated to specific simulation toolkits with the specification diagrams information.

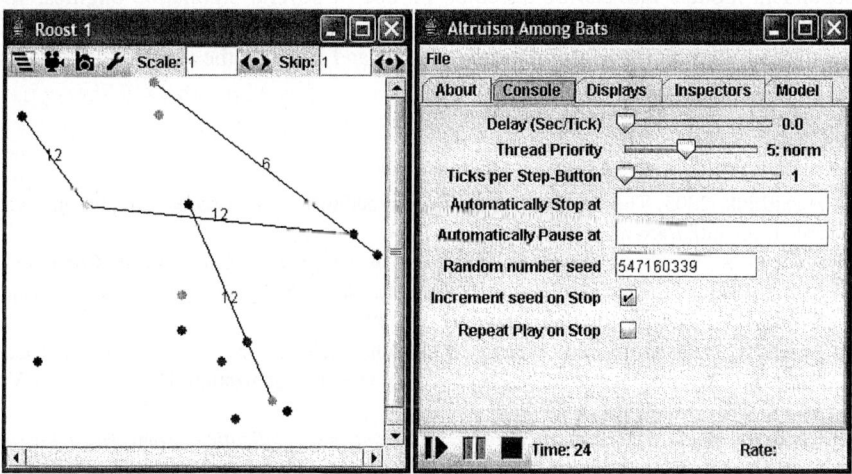

Fig. 4. A MASON simulation model generated with the ABSS replication framework

implemented with the simulation toolkits, then marks up the prototype code to indicate where specification data is going to be inserted, generating in this way the *templates*. The source code is the result of instantiating these *templates* with the specification data. The role of the IDK is to instantiate a framework made up with *templates* and conventional source code with pieces of information extracted from the specification. *Templates* are described in XML with a custom language based on a simple set of tags.

Finally, Fig. 4 illustrates a *platform specific model* generated with the replication framework, in this case, a MASON simulation model of the case study we proposed previously. The figure shows the state of bats agents in a specific time step.

4 Conclusions

In this paper we considered the need for an agent-based social simulation model replication approach to confirm whether the claimed results of a given simulation are reliable in the sense that they can be reproduced by someone starting from scratch. We presented an example of how replication can be achieved through model reimplementation using the proposed framework. The approach presented here is illustrated with an extensive case study detailed in [14]. This case study has been used to describe our approach for code generation for specific target platforms. Also, implementation technical details with specific platforms and comparison between them are described in [13].

The framework presented is based on the *MDA* pattern by means of a platform-independent modeling language, a code generation process and templates, and specific simulation platforms. The modeling language is an adaptation of INGENIAS notation and the APIs provided with the IDK allow manipulating the specification diagrams and templates for code generation for MASON and REPAST toolkits.

The interest of this original work is that we have validated the feasibility in providing modelers with a customized visual environment to specify simulation platform-independent models that can be executed on one or several simulation engines, with the ability to contrast results. As further work we intend to reinforce the replication issue including support for new simulation toolkits and improve the automation process.

References

[1] AgentLink. 2005. The european co-ordination action for agent-based computing. Available from: http://www.agentlink.org

[2] Axelrod, R. *Advancing the Art of Simulation in the Social Sciences*. In: R. Conte, et al. (Eds.): *Simulating Social Phenomena*. Lecture Notes in Economics and Mathematical Systems, Vol. 456. Berlin Springer (1997), 21-40.

[3] Axtell, R., R. Axelrod, J.M. Epstein, M.D. Cohen. *Aligning Simulation Models: A Case Study and Results*. Computational and Mathematical Organization Theory, 1996. Vol. 1(2): p. 123-141.

[4] Edmonds, B., D. Hales. *Replication, Replication and Replication: Some Hard Lessons from Model Alignment*. Journal of Artificial Societies and Social Simulation, 2003. Vol. 6(4).

[5] FIPA. 2002. Abstract Architecture Specification. Available from: http://www.fipa.org

[6] Gilbert, N., K.G. Troitzsch. *Simulation for the Social Scientist.* 1996, Buckingham, U.K.: Open University Press.
[7] Hales, D., J. Rouchier, B. Edmonds. *Model-to-Model Analysis.* Journal of Artificial Societies and Social Simulation, 2003. Vol. 6(4).
[8] Marietto, M.B., N. David, J.S. Sichman, H. Coelho. *Requirements Analysis of Agent-Based Simulation Platforms: State of the Art and New Prospects.* In: J. Sichman, et al. (Eds.): *Multi-Agent-Based Simulation II: Third International Workshop, MABS 2002.* Lecture Notes in Computer Science, Vol. 2581. Springer Bologna, Italy (2002), 125-141.
[9] Mason. 2004. Mason: Multiagent Simulation Toolkit. Available from: http://cs.gmu.edu/~eclab/projects/mason/
[10] OMG, *MDA Guide Version 1.0.1*, in *Object Management Group*, J. Miller, et al., Editors. 2003.
[11] Pavón, J., J. Gómez-Sanz. *Agent Oriented Software Engineering with INGENIAS.* In: V. Mařík, et al. (Eds.): *Multi-Agent Systems and Applications III, 3rd International Central and Eastern European Conference on Multi-Agent Systems, CEEMAS 2003.* Lecture Notes in Computer Science, Vol. 2691. Springer Prague, Czech Republic (2003), 394-403.
[12] Repast. 2004. Repast: Recursive Porus Agent Simulation Toolkit. Available from: http://repast.sourceforge.net
[13] Sansores, C., J. Pavón. *Agent Based Simulation for Social Systems: from Modeling to Implementation.* 11th Conference of the Spanish Association for Artificial Intelligence, 2005. (To appear).
[14] Sansores, C., J. Pavón, J. Gómez-Sanz. *Visual Modeling for Complex Agent-Based Simulation Systems.* Multi-Agent-Based Simulation, Sixth International Workshop on Multi-Agent-Based Simulation, MABS 2005, 2005. (To appear).
[15] SDML. 1997. SDML: a Strictly Declarative Modelling Language. Available from: http://www.cpm.mmu.ac.uk/sdml
[16] Swarm. 2004. Swarm Wiki: the agent-based modelling resource. Available from: http://wiki.swarm.org
[17] Tobias, R., C. Hofmann. *Evaluation of free Java-libraries for Social-Scientific Agent Based Simulation.* Journal of Artificial Societies and Social Simulation, 2004. Vol. 7(1).

Effects of Inter-agent Communication in Ant-Based Clustering Algorithms: A Case Study on Communication Policies in Swarm Systems

Marco Antonio Montes de Oca, Leonardo Garrido, and José Luis Aguirre

Centro de Sistemas Inteligentes Tecnológico de Monterrey,
Campus Monterrey, Eugenio Garza Sada 2501,
C.P. 64849. Monterrey, México
m.montes@exatec.itesm.mx,
{leonardo.garrido, jlaguirre}@itesm.mx

Abstract. Communication among agents in swarm intelligent systems and more generally in multiagent systems, is crucial in order to coordinate agents' activities so that a particular goal at the collective level is achieved. From an agent's perspective, the problem consists in establishing communication policies that determine *what*, *when*, and *how* to communicate with others. In general, communication policies will depend on the nature of the problem being solved. This means that the solvability of problems by swarm intelligent systems depends, among other things, on the agents' communication policies, and setting an incorrect set of policies into the agents may result in finding poor solutions or even in the unsolvability of problems. As a case study, this paper focus on the effects of letting agents use different communication policies in ant-based clustering algorithms. Our results show the effects of using different communication policies on the final outcome of these algorithms.

1 Introduction

The term *Swarm Intelligence* is used to denote the relatively new discipline that studies systems that exhibit self-organizing properties at the global level from interactions of their lower level components. These studies are often inspired by the observation of social insects and other animal societies [1]. We will refer to systems with these features as *swarm intelligent systems*.

For them to work, swarm intelligent systems need the interaction of their constituent entities. In natural settings, *stigmergy* [6] plays a key role as it provides the means for indirect communication among insects through the environment. This same phenomenon has been successfully exploited in many systems used to solve combinatorial optimization problems [4], in clustering algorithms [7], and in robotic systems [10]. In spite of these successful experiences, we need to consider the question of whether agents should/could communicate in other ways to achieve organization or better solutions to problems. There is no general answer nor general communication policy that will apply equally well to all problems. This is why we think we need to study the effects of letting agents use different communication policies. With this knowledge and considering the characteristics of a particular problem, we could either improve the performance of a swarm intelligent system or permit its application to a problem that was not possible before. This is the main motivation of our work.

2 Communication Policies Among Agents in Swarm Intelligent Systems

The collective behavior of social insects and other animal societies has inspired the design of metaheuristics that have found their first applications in the field of optimization [4, 11]. One of the first of such metaheuristics is Ant Colony Optimization, or ACO for short [3]. In ACO, a colony of artificial ants or agents cooperatively find good solutions to discrete optimization problems. The communication policy used by agents in ACO is to indirectly communicate through the environment by means of *stigmergy*. Stigmergy was first proposed by Grassé [6] to explain the construction of nests by the termites *Cubitermes* and *Macrotermes*. Grassé observed that when workers of *Macrotermes bellicosus* were placed in a container with some soil pellets, the insects carried about and put down pellets in an apparently random fashion after an exploration phase in which they moved through the container without taking any action. At this stage, a pellet just put down by a termite worker is often picked up and placed somewhere else by another worker. When a pellet is placed on top of another, the resultant structure appears to be much more attractive and termites soon start piling more pellets nearby, making the dropping spot even more attractive [17].

In ACO, we can see stigmergy in action whenever an artificial ant deposits a pheromone trail on a problem solution space. If an artificial ant come across a pheromone trail, it is attracted to it, very much like termites are attracted by clusters of soil pellets. By means of this indirect communication channel, ants share knowledge and the pheromone trail is a "blue print" to build a good solution to the problem at hand.

Another swarm intelligent system that relies on stigmergy, and that is perhaps more related to the behavior of termites, is ant-based clustering which was introduced by Deneubourg et al. [2] using a model for spatial sorting. A group of agents exhibiting the same behavior move randomly over a toroidal square grid. In the environment there are objects that were initially scattered in a random fashion. The objects can be picked up, moved or dropped in any free location on the grid. An object is picked up with high probability if it is not surrounded by other objects of the same type and is dropped by a loaded agent if its neighborhood is populated by other objects of the same type and the location of the agent has no object on it. Lumer and Faieta [12] generalized the spatial sorting algorithm to apply it to exploratory data analysis.

The implementations of the techniques described in the preceding paragraphs can be considered swarm intelligent systems. Both of them use indirect communication among agents through local modifications of the environment as their principal inter-agent communication policy. But, can we expect better results if we let agents communicate directly in ACO and ant-based clustering algorithms? Would the results obtained after doing so be problem dependent? Is it convenient to maintain the same communication policy during execution?

All these questions are related to the agents' communication policies and their effects in swarm intelligent systems. A communication policy represents the way an agent communicates with others. It must establish what information/knowledge to exchange, the way this exchange is to be done, and the appropriate moment to do so. A communication policy may be dynamic, that is, an agent may find convenient to change the way it communicates with other agents in a particular time or situation. It may also be selective, or in other words, it may apply only for a selected group of agents, etc. These and other properties may also be identified, and for all of them, there is a lack of knowledge regarding their effects on a particular problem when used in a swarm intelligent system.

By establishing well-founded guidelines for the design of communication policies among agents in swarm intelligent systems, we would be giving an important step towards the definition of a general methodology that would spread the practical use of swarm intelligence.

In this paper we focus on ant-based clustering algorithms, a particular kind of swarm intelligent system, and on the effects on the final clustering of letting agents use different communication policies.

3 Ant-Based Clustering Algorithms: A Case Study

In this section, we will describe a series of experiments that show how different inter-agent communication policies affect the performance and final outcome of a swarm intelligent system, in this case, an ant-based clustering algorithm. We will start by giving some background on ant-based clustering algorithms, then we will present our experiments setup and our results.

3.1 Background

Prior to the existence of ant-based clustering algorithms as such, Deneubourg et al. [2] proposed a computational model for spatial sorting. Deneubourg et al.'s model was later extended by Lumer and Faieta [12] to allow its application to exploratory data analysis. In their model, objects represent data items that belong to a database. These objects are randomly scattered on a periodic square grid on which randomly moving agents group them according to their similarity. In order to do that, a similarity (or dissimilarity) measure between pairs of data items is needed to compute the probabilities of picking and dropping data elements on the grid. In their model, the probability of picking a data element i is defined as $p_p(i) = \left(\frac{k_p}{k_p + f(i)}\right)^2$ where k_p is a constant and $f(i)$ is a similarity density measure with respect to element i. Likewise, the probability of dropping a data element is given by $p_d(i) = \begin{cases} 2f(i) & \text{if } f(i) < k_d \\ 1 & \text{otherwise} \end{cases}$ where k_d is a constant. The similarity density $f(i)$ for an element i, at a particular grid location τ, is defined as $f(i) = \max\left\{\dfrac{1}{s^2} \sum_{j \in Neigh(\tau)} \left(1 - \dfrac{d(i,j)}{\alpha}\right), 0\right\}$ where s^2 is the size of the perception area $Neigh(\tau)$, centered at the location of the agent and α is a scaling factor of the dissimilarity measure $d(i,j)$ between elements i and j.

After the first appearance of this algorithm, many other variations of it have been proposed to improve its output quality [13,7], its convergence speed [8], and its applicability to large databases [16]. However, no previous works are known that study the effects of different communication strategies among agents in these algorithms.

3.2 Experiments Setup

In total, four different information exchange strategies were studied: direct information exchange for updating the agents' environment representations, direct information exchange for changing the agents' dropping spot search trajectories, intentional indirect information exchange for updating the agents' environment representations, and intentional indirect information exchange for changing the agents' dropping spot search trajectories.

To design the experiments, questions such as: What information will agents exchange? When will they exchange it? How will they do it? What will they do with that information? had to be answered. Although there are no general answers to them, we tried to explore four issues when we proposed answers to them. First, what are the effects on the performance of the algorithms when agents exchange information from different levels of abstraction? Second, what is the impact on the performance of the algorithms when agents exchange information in different ways? Third, what happens when agents use the information for different purposes? And fourth, what happens when agents choose to use immediately or after some delay the exchanged information?

Let us discuss how we coped with these issues and what were our results. The information that agents exchanged in the experiments belong to two different levels of abstraction: memorized grid locations on which an agent had dropped a data object, and pointers to promising dropping locations. The first choice was needed in order to compare the performance of the algorithms with and without communicating agents. In fact, this model is just a simple extension of Lumer an Faieta's short-term memory agents model. The second choice tries to implement the idea of map exchanging agents. Maps were implemented as growing neural gas networks or GNGs [5], which are distributed in the grid and in the attribute space of data objects. GNGs provide more information than just memorized dropping spots because they can adapt to changes in the spatial distribution of objects.

GNGs were designed to overcome some of the limitations of conventional self-organizing maps; namely, the *a priori* fixed number of neurons and the problem of "dead" neurons or neurons that do not update their weight vectors due to a misplacing in the input space. The GNG training algorithm successively adds new units to an initially small network by evaluating local statistical measures gathered during previous adaptation steps. In this way, a GNG network topology is generated incrementally by using a competitive Hebbian learning rule and its dimensionality depends on the input data and varies locally.

With regard to the moment in which agents should exchange information, we decided to couple this issue with the way agents were going to exchange information. That is, agents decided when to exchange information depending on the exchange method used. When agents exchanged information directly, they did it whenever they met on the grid. When they exchanged information indirectly, they did it whenever an agent came across an information packet on the grid.

One of the most critical part in the experiments design was to decide what agents should do with the exchanged information. Our hypothesis was that agents with information about the spatial distribution of data on the grid, would be able to choose the best location on which to drop an object (if they were loaded), or the best regions of the environment to explore (if they were unloaded). With informed decisions, agents could create better clusters in a faster way. We therefore decided to explore the idea by (i) letting agents represent their environment and after every exchange, update or enrich their representations, and (ii) changing their dropping spot search trajectories, i.e., they were allowed to "change their minds" regarding their supposed best dropping spot on the grid.

To evaluate the quality of the obtained clustering, the same validity measures used by Handl et al. [7] were used: the F-Measure, which gives us some idea of how well a clustering algorithm is identifying the classes present in a database using the information of the correct classification[1]; the Rand statistic, which is a similarity measure between the known perfect classification C and the partition generated by the clustering algorithm P, considering all pairwise assignments; the Dunn index, which measures how compact and well separated are the identified clusters; and the intra-cluster variance, which measures how similar are the elements belonging to the same cluster.

We used two real data collections from the UCI Machine Learning Repository [9]. These were: the iris plant and wine recognition databases. To eliminate the bias on similarity measures provoked by different scales within data attributes, both databases were standardized. The similarity measure used in all the experiments was the cosine metric[2]. The agents' picking and dropping probabilities were computed using the same expressions as Lumer and Faieta. However, since the cosine metric is a similarity measure, the expression used to compute the similarity density is not directly applicable. Therefore, for the local similarity density $f(i)$, we used $f(i) = \frac{1}{s^2} \sum_{j \in Neigh(\tau)} \left(\frac{1}{1 + e^{-S\frac{d(i,j)}{\alpha} + D}} \right)$ where S is the steepness of the response curve and D serves as a displacement factor. In our experiments, S was fixed to 5 because it provides a similarity value close to 0 when the cosine measure is minimum, that is, when the cosine measure gives a

---

[1] Which is available for our experiments.
[2] In preliminary experiments, it proved to give better results than Euclidean distance.

value of -1, and D to 1 because this allows us to better distinguish vectors with separation angles between 0 and $\pi/2$.

To observe the effects of information exchange among agents during the clustering process, the data partition obtained every 10,000 simulation cycles was evaluated using the validity measures described above. Each simulation cycle was composed of N individual actions, where N was the number of agents in the simulation. All algorithms were tested 30 times with every database for 1,000,000 simulation cycles. We tried with populations of 10 and 30 agents within an environment of 100×100 locations in all the experiments.

4 Results

The following sections present in detail the conclusions drawn from the experimental results with each of the tested strategies. For space restrictions, we refer the interested reader to [15,14] for the complete set of results. In this paper we will only show some selected graphs to support our conclusions.

4.1 Direct Information Exchange

As we said before, direct information exchange occurs only when two or more agents meet at a location on the grid. Hence, the probability of an encounter between two agents moving randomly raises as the number of agents is increased (assuming a constant size of the grid). In these experiments, we tried to take advantage of this fact and use it to study the effect of increasing the information exchange frequency among agents. This is the reason of using two different sizes of agent populations in all the experiments.

The results obtained when the exchanged information was used for updating the agents' environment representations are somewhat discouraging. The worst performing algorithm is the one with map updating agents, and the second worst

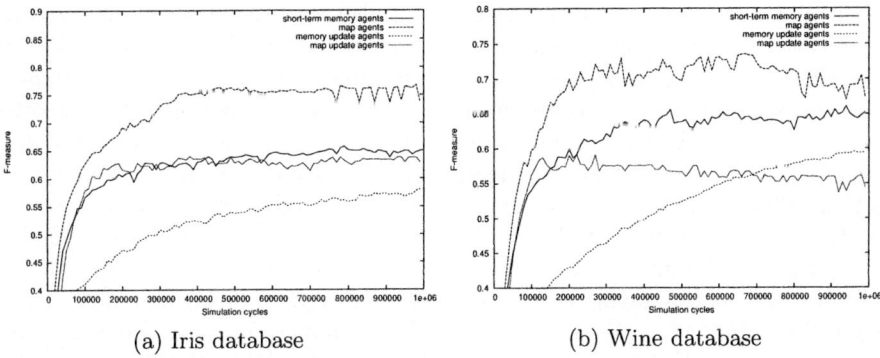

(a) Iris database (b) Wine database

Fig. 1. F-Measure scores over time for the Iris Plant and Wine databases of all tested algorithms. The results were obtained using 10 agents. Values closer to 1 are better.

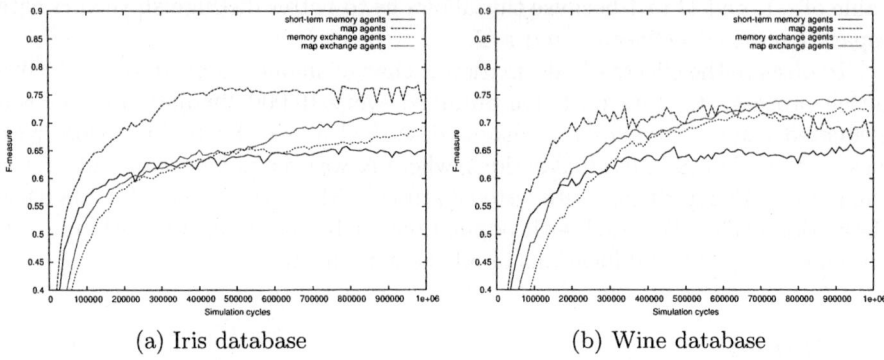

Fig. 2. F-Measure scores over time for the Iris Plant and Wine databases of all tested algorithms. The results were obtained using 10 agents. Values closer to 1 are better.

is the memory updating agents algorithm. In the case of the memory updating agents algorithm, the relatively poor performance is not as discouraging as is the obtained with map creating agents. Figure 1 shows the F-Measure scores obtained by the tested algorithms on both test databases using 10 agents.

The results obtained when the exchanged information was used for changing the agents' dropping spot search trajectory are quite different from the previous ones. In this case, the clustering quality is improved by the communicating agents algorithms. Figure 2 shows the F-Measure scores obtained by the tested algorithms on both test databases using 10 agents.

4.2 Indirect Information Exchange

In the experiments run for exploring the effects of intentional indirect information exchange among agents in ant-based clustering algorithms, agents lay packets which contain information about data distribution on the environment for others to pick and use. This strategy is inspired by the anal trophallaxis phenomenon [17] among social insects but it also has other reasons. Direct communication among agents in ant-based clustering has two disadvantages: (i) even when the number of exchanges increases, we cannot expect many of them to happen since the number of agents must be kept small (for performance reasons), and (ii) many exchanges do not have any effect since agents walk in a randomly fashion, i.e., two agents coincide many times, over and over again, before they follow different trajectories. So the idea is that if we let agents lay information on their environment, it could be possible to increase dramatically the number of exchanges without even increasing the number of agents.

Two information laying policies were studied: a periodic laying policy and an adaptive laying policy. With the periodic laying policy, an agent drops information packets every given number of simulation cycles. With the adaptive laying policy, an agent drops information after it has modified the environment and a given number of simulation cycles have passed.

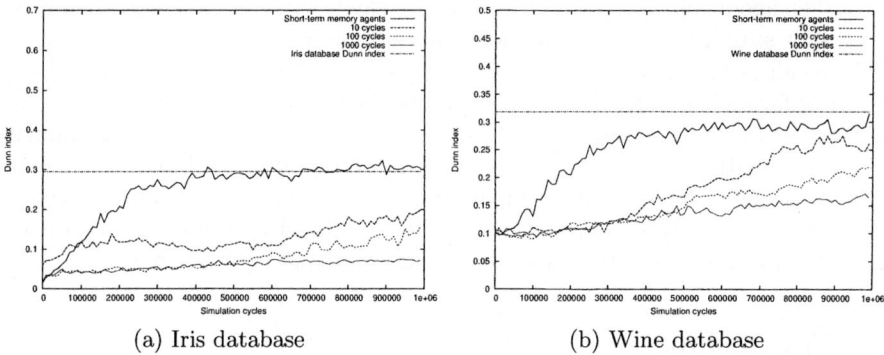

(a) Iris database (b) Wine database

Fig. 3. Dunn index scores over time for the Iris Plant and Wine databases of all tested algorithms. The results were obtained using 30 agents using a periodic laying policy. As a reference, the Dunn index of the correct clustering is shown.

The results obtained when the exchanged information was used for updating the agents' environment representations, show that the more information available to the agents, the better the performance. With a periodic laying frequency, the higher the frequency, the better. And with the adaptive laying policy, the shorter the delay, the better. This results confirm the intuition which says that to maintain an up-to-date environment representation, an agent has to acquire fresh information all the time. Figure 3 shows the Dunn index scores obtained by the tested algorithms on both test databases using 30 agents and a periodic laying policy.

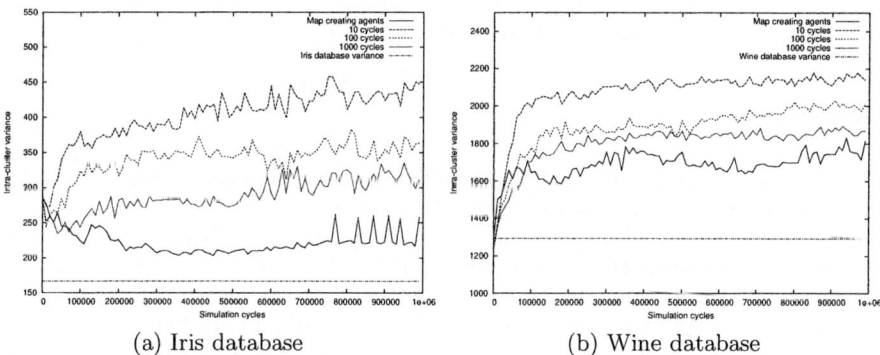

(a) Iris database (b) Wine database

Fig. 4. Total intra-cluster variance scores over time for the Iris Plant and Wine databases of all tested algorithms. The results were obtained using 10 agents using a periodic laying policy. As a reference, the total intra-cluster variance of the correct clustering is shown.

When agents use the information only to decide whether to change their dropping spot search trajectory, the more information available to them, the worse. This result is also sound if we think of agents as "changing their minds" based on the information provided by other agents. An agent may receive contradicting information or may be misleaded to a nonpromising region in the environment. Therefore, with this information exploitation strategy, high laying frequencies and short delays have negative impact on the algorithms performance. Figure 4 shows the Total intra-cluster variance scores obtained by the tested algorithms on both test databases using 10 agents and a periodic laying policy.

5 Conclusions

In this paper, the effects on clustering quality and convergence speed of direct and indirect communication among agents in ant-based clustering algorithms were studied. The results show that nonstigmergic communication among agents in these algorithms has effects on the final clustering obtained by the algorithm. The final effects depend on the type of information exchanged, its use, its availability and the number of participating agents. Our results confirm that different communication policies in swarm intelligent systems have effects on their performance. This is why we need to formalize the effects of letting agents use different communication policies. This is a first step towards that goal. With this knowledge and considering the characteristics of a particular problem, we could either improve the performance or permit the application of a swarm intelligent system to solve it. Future work should be focused on studying the effects of using different communication policies in ACO and other swarm-based approaches.

Acknowledgments

This work was supported in part by the ITESM research chair on distributed knowledge and intelligent agents technologies, CAT-011.

References

1. E. Bonabeau, M. Dorigo, and G. Theralauz. *Swarm Intelligence. From Natural to Artificial Systems*. Oxford University Press, 1999.
2. J.-L. Deneubourg, S.Goss, N Franks, A. Sendova-Franks, C. Detrain, and L. Chretien. The dynamics of collective sorting: Robot-like ants and ant-like robots. In *Proceedings of the First International Conference on Simulation of Adaptive Behavior: From Animals to Animats*, pages 356–365. MIT Press, 1991.
3. M. Dorigo, G. Di Caro, and L. M. Gambardella. Ant algorithms for discrete optimization. *Artificial Life*, 5(2):137–172, 1999.
4. M. Dorigo and T. Stützle. *Ant Colony Optimization*. MIT Press, Cambridge, MA, 2004.
5. B. Fritzke. A growing neural gas network learns topologies. In *Advances in Neural Information Processing Systems 7*. MIT Press, 1995.

6. P.-P. Grassé. La reconstruction du nid et les coordinations inter-individuelles chez bellicositermes natalensis et cubitermes sp. la theorie de la stigmergie: Essai d'interpretation des termites constructeurs. *Insectes Sociaux*, 6(1):41–83, 1959.
7. J. Handl, J. Knowles, and M. Dorigo. Ant-based clustering and topographic mapping. *Artificial Life*, 11(2), 2005. In press.
8. J. Handl and B. Meyer. Improved ant-based clustering and sorting in a document retrieval interface. In *Proceedings of the Seventh International Conference on Parallel Problem Solving from Nature (PPSN VII)*, volume LNCS 2439, pages 913–923. Springer-Verlag, 2002.
9. S. Hettich, C.L. Blake, and C.J. Merz. UCI repository of machine learning databases [http://www.ics.uci.edu/~mlearn/mlrepository.html], 1998.
10. O. Holland and C. Melhuish. Stigmergy, self-organization, and sorting in collective robotics. *Artificial Life*, 5:173–202, 1999.
11. J. Kennedy and R. C. Eberhart. Particle swarm optimization. In *Proceedings of IEEE International Conference on Neural Networks*, pages 1942–1948, 1995.
12. E. D. Lumer and B. Faieta. Diversity and adaptation in populations of clustering ants. In *Proceedings of the Third International Conference on Simulation of Adaptive Behavior: From Animals to Animats 3*, pages 501–508. MIT Press, 1994.
13. N. Monmarché, M. Slimane, and G. Venturini. On improving clustering in numerical databases with artificial ants. In D. Floreano, J.D. Nicoud, and F. Mondala, editors, *5th European Conference on Artificial Life (ECAL'99), Lecture Notes in Artificial Intelligence*, volume 1674, pages 626–635. Springer-Verlag, 1999.
14. M. A. Montes de Oca. Effects on clustering quality of direct and indirect communication among agents in ant-based clustering algorithms. Master's thesis, Instituto Tecnológico y de Estudios Superiores de Monterrey. Campus Monterrey, 2005.
15. M. A. Montes de Oca, L. Garrido, and J. L. Aguirre. Efectos de la comunicación directa entre agentes en los algoritmos de agrupación de clases basados en el comportamiento de insectos sociales. *Inteligencia Artificial*, 9(25):59–69, 2005.
16. M. A. Montes de Oca, L. Garrido, and J. L. Aguirre. An hybridization of an ant-based clustering algorithm with growing neural gas networks for classification tasks. In *Proceedings of the 2005 ACM Symposium on Applied Computing*, pages 9–13. ACM, 2005.
17. E. O. Wilson. *The Insect Societies*. The Belkap Press of Harvard University Press, 1971.

Coordination Through Plan Repair

Roman van der Krogt and Mathijs de Weerdt*

Delft University of Technology,
PO Box 5031, 2600 GA Delft, The Netherlands
{R.P.J.vanderKrogt, M.M.deWeerdt}@ewi.tudelft.nl

Abstract. In most practical situations, agents need to continuously improve or repair their plans. In a multiagent system agents also need to coordinate their plans. Consequently, we need methods such that agents in a multiagent system can construct, coordinate, and repair their plans. In this paper we focus on the problem of coordinating plans without exchanging explicit information on dependencies, or having to construct a global set of constraints. Our approach is to combine a propositional plan repair algorithm for each agent with a blackboard that auctions subgoals on behalf of the agents. Both the details of a first construction and some initial experimental results are discussed.

1 Introduction

In most application domains for distributed artificial intelligence, several autonomous agents (e.g., companies or personal assistants) each have their own goals and therefore need to plan, to coordinate their actions, to deal with uncertainty, and to interleave all this with plan execution [1, 2]. To complicate matters even more, many agents are self-interested and require some privacy concerning their plans and the dependencies of actions in their plans on other agents' actions. In fact, multiagent planning methods are often preferred above mature central planners exactly because of privacy reasons. Our goal is a system in which *self-interested* agents can *(i)* construct and *repair plans*, *(ii) coordinate* their actions, and do so while *(iii)* maintaining their *privacy*.

Our idea is to combine a dynamic planning method for each agent with an auction for delegating (sub)tasks. However, to coordinate subtasks we should deal with inter-agent dependencies [3] to prevent deadlocks. Currently, multiagent planning methods manage inter-agent dependencies at a central place [4], or by constructing and communicating a (partial) global plan [5, 6]. Besides coordinating tasks, we also have to *allocate* tasks to different agents. In contrast to existing work on task and role allocation where task allocation is seen as one static problem (such as [7, 8]), the set of subtasks that has to be allocated in our setting arises from the planning produced by the agents. Planned subtasks that agents cannot carry out themselves need to be reallocated. The planning in its turn is of course influenced by the existing task allocation.

Our approach raises a number of questions. If agents do not want to construct a set of global constraints, how can we then guarantee that there will be no deadlocks upon execution of their plans? How can agents integrate the process of auctioning or

---

* This research is supported by the Technology Foundation STW, applied science division of NWO, and the technology program of the Ministry of Economic Affairs.

bidding with the process of plan construction or adaptation? How to decompose a task into subtasks to auction to other agents? And what happens if agents discover that their assumptions about the initial state of their own actions turn out to be invalid? These questions will be addressed in this paper, resulting in a multiagent plan repair system for self-interested agents. More specifically, we let agents schedule tasks on which others depend early in their plans to prevent cyclic dependencies, we let them alternatingly plan for one goal and bid on a task, we give them some high-level information about the capabilities of others, and we allow agents to come back on their commitment of accepting a task.

Such a system can be used, for example, to plan for logistics problems. In many logistic domains, some of the transport orders are only known in the nick of time, and, as we all know, traffic is often unpredictable. Consequently, plans need to be revised all the time. Furthermore, often a significant cost reduction can arise when transportation companies coordinate their actions well. For example, a company (agent) may assign a subtask to another either because the other can do it much more efficiently (because it is already in the neighbourhood), or because the first one cannot perform the task at all. Clearly, these companies are also each other's competitor, so they simply refuse to exchange more information than just a request for or an accept of a subtask.

In the next sections, we describe the problem dealt with in this paper, and we show how a propositional plan repair method can be combined with a simple auction to solve it. We also present solutions to subproblems such as the prevention of deadlock. We illustrate our method using a logistic planning domain with one company that can transport packages by air between airports, and several other companies that can only transport packages within cities. Each of these companies has several transportation orders involving other cities, and thus other companies.

2 The Multiagent Plan Repair Problem

In this paper we propose a method that dynamically creates, coordinates, and repairs plans for agents that do not want to share crucial information. We base this work on the work of propositional planning, see e.g. [9]. We focus on problems that can be modeled as a *set of distinct propositional planning problems* $\Pi_a = \langle O_a, I_a, G_a \rangle$, one for each agent a. In such a problem the set O_a is the set of actions that the agent a can perform, I_a is the part of the initial state the agent can observe, and G_a are the goals to be achieved by the agent. The initial state is described by propositions, an action by its preconditions and effects, and goals, preconditions, and effects are all defined by conjunctions of literals [9].

The problems of all agents are mutually distinct, meaning that we require that there are no agents able to perform actions using the same resources (i.e., described by the same propositions) and each agent has complete knowledge about its own problem. At first this may seem too restrictive, but in many domains agents (companies) that are not cooperative can indeed not use each other's resources. For some resources of general use where conflicts may occur (such as cross roads) we may need to introduce an additional agent to coordinate the use of such a resource. This agent then can provide this resource on request as a service to other agents.

We model the *plan repair* problem by assuming that at some point during or after planning for each agent a its problem Π_a is replaced by a slightly different problem Π'_a. This new problem includes information about added or removed propositions in the initial state I'_a, a changed set of actions O'_a, and/or a changed set of goals G'_a.

Note that in this first approach we used a propositional plan repair method without a realistic model of the costs and duration of actions, nor of deadlines. Therefore, the length of the plan (i.e., the number of actions) is currently used as an indication of the costs.

To render the problem more manageable, we assume that all actions in the domain can be undone (are reversible), and that there are no goals that are inherently unattainable. This assumption ensures that in principle a solution can always be found. We also assume that agents do not break contracts, unless they really cannot hold to them, in which case they inform the other party immediately.

These assumptions help us to focus on the more interesting and more difficult problem of designing a system that *(i)* only communicates offers and bids, but little else, *(ii)* can dynamically add, delete, or modify goals, actions, and initial propositions, update its plan accordingly, and meanwhile *(iii)* can auction (sub)tasks to other agents, while preventing cyclic dependencies. In the following section we lay out the design of such a system and we explain how to deal with problems that may occur when building it.

3 Multiagent Plan Repair

The crux of our idea is quite simple: coordinate (single agent) plan repair systems through a task auction. To implement this idea, we suppose that we have a dynamic planner for such problems at our disposal, such as a plan repair (PR) system [10]. We require that such a system includes a heuristic function $\mathcal{U}(P, \Pi, g)$ that, given a problem Π and a plan P, estimates the costs of adding actions to achieve another goal g. Usually such a system is only able to solve *single* instances of a propositional planning problem, not a combination of them.

Goal-by-goal Planning. Our first important contribution is the idea to process the goals *one-by-one* by a plan repair system, instead of in a single batch (as is usual in planning). This has a number of advantages: firstly, failure to add a goal to the plan gives us an indication which goal we should put up for auction, while when planning for a batch of goals fails, it is not immediately obvious which of the goals cannot be achieved. Secondly, we get regular moments at which we can easily make changes in the problem. Moreover, at these moments we have a valid plan that partially achieves our goals to base our decisions on. This means that we can make a more informed decision than when we would interrupt a regular planner at certain points. There are two disadvantages, however: firstly, we cannot as easily exploit positive interactions that may exist between goals. In the section on our experimental work, we shall come back to this issue. Secondly, this goal-by-goal plan repair usually takes more time than constructing a one-shot plan for all goals. Especially when goals strongly interact, the plan repair method we use may eventually reconstruct the whole plan for all goals if necessary.

We now describe the basic steps of this goal-by-goal planning approach. The process starts by taking the original planning problem Π, and creating a goal queue Q

from it (containing all the goals that are to be solved in order to solve Π) as well as the problem Π_{PR}, initially identical to Π, but without goals. We use this problem Π_{PR} to keep track of the problem that we are trying to solve in the current iteration. To plan a single goal g from Q the system performs the following steps: *(i)* It queries the planning heuristic $\mathcal{U}$ of the plan repair system to estimate the cost of adding g to the plan, and *(ii)* the heuristic may report that it cannot incorporate the goal, or that the costs of incorporating are so large that it prefers asking other agents for help. If this is the case, the agent tries to auction this goal. Otherwise, it removes it g from Q, adds it as a goal to Π_{PR}, and updates its plan for this new planning problem.

These steps are interleaved with responding to auctions (if any), as discussed later in this section. Once the goal queue is empty, each goal of the agent is either planned for in its own plan, or has been given to another agent. From this point on, the agent continues to respond to auctions until all other agents are finished as well.

As said, an agent planning a goal first consults its planning heuristic to discover whether it is advisable to plan for this goal itself. If it turns out that the goal is unattainable, the agent will put the goal up for auction. Agents may also put subgoals up for auction, when they create a plan based on some abstract knowledge of the capabilities of other agents. We model this abstract knowledge by *external actions* in the domain of the agent. External actions are specified like regular actions and describe what (a group of) other agents can achieve. If they are included in a plan, the agent knows that it has to find other agents to carry out the task for him. The effects of the included external actions are sent to the blackboard for auction (as described below).

In the case of auctioned subgoals there is an additional issue we have to take care of: the combined plans may not contain *cyclic dependencies*. That is, it may not be that an action a is (indirectly) dependent upon an action (of another agent) that is dependent on an effect of a. In principle, agents need to know the details of the other agents' plans to ensure this property. In existing solutions to prevent cyclic dependencies either a central facility is keeping track of dependencies [4], or agent communicate to form a so-called partial global plan [5]. In our goal-by-goal approach, however, we can use the following property. When an agent plans a task for someone else, it can prevent cycles from occurring without any additional communications by placing all actions (possibly including external actions) required for this task *before* all other actions in its plan. This heuristic depends for a great deal on the fact that only one goal is auctioned by the blackboard in a single iteration. Thus, only one agent can create a new inter-agent dependency at a time. If we ensure that this new dependency is not dependent upon previously existing dependencies, we prevent cycles from occurring. Any additional external actions inserted will be auctioned only after this part of the plan has been completed.

Plan Repair. Plan repair is accomplished as follows. After every planning iteration, we observe the world to detect any differences. If the world has changed we record this in our plan by adding a special (virtual) action that reflects the change. Thus, for a changed initial condition, an action is added that transforms the new initial condition into the original initial condition that we expected. These actions are called *gap* actions, for they record the gaps that are present in the current plan.

To repair a failure, we can now remove a gap action from the plan, and hand the resulting plan over to the plan repair system. This detects that the plan has preconditions that are not met and repairs it. As a result of the repair, external actions may be removed from or added to the plan. In the latter case, they are auctioned as if they were the result of a planning step. In the former case, we notify the agent that satisfies the (now unnecessary) subgoal for us, so that it can remove the actions it had planned in order to achieve the subgoal. These actions may include external actions as well. These external actions are now no longer required, in which case the agents that have planned for these tasks are notified also. In this way, a whole chain of dependencies can be removed if necessary.

Auctions. We use a blackboard to keep track of a list of auctions, and process them one-by-one. This prevents additional difficulties that agents face when dealing with multiple simultaneous auctions (such as the "eager bidder" problem [11]). For each auction, the blackboard sends out the request for bids.

When an agent receives a request to bid on a goal, a heuristic is applied to discover whether this agent can incorporate the new goal in the current plan. If so, this also tells us what the estimated cost is of adapting the plan. This value is then sent as our bid for this goal. In the current system, we have chosen to allow the agents a single, sealed bid.

The blackboard waits for all bids, and selects the cheapest bid. The winner is awarded the goal, and receives payment equal to the second-lowest bid [12].[1] Upon being awarded a goal g, the agent adds g to the front of its goal queue. This ensures that this goal is processed immediately, and that the agent can actually attain g by repairing its plan. It also ensures that at any time there is at most one goal for another agent in the goal queue. If we allow other goals to be processed first, g might no longer be achievable. This would require decommitment of the agent, a situation that we would rather prevent. Sometimes, however, the heuristic is wrong, and the bidder discovers that it cannot actually satisfy the goal it has bid on. In this situation, the blackboard is notified which re-auctions the goal, disregarding the bids of agents that have bid on the goal and rejected it before. For now, a decommitting agent pays (as a penalty) the cost difference between its own bid and the next one. For the other type of decommitment, where an agent does not require an 'external action' by another agent any more (as described in a previous section), we currently do not issue penalties.[2]

The Complete Planning Loop. Having described the features of the algorithm in isolation, we now end this section with the complete algorithm as we use in our experiments. The algorithm (see below) starts with setting up the data structures, such as the goal queue Q, and the initial planning problem Π_{PR}. Then, in step 4, it tries to add a goal from the queue to the current plan P. At first, in step 4.2, we compute the heuristic value $\mathcal{U}(P, \Pi_{PR}, g)$ of establishing g with P. If this is estimated to cost more than acceptable (with an unsatisfiable goal returning ∞), we send the goal to the blackboard for auction. Otherwise, we update the planning problem Π_{PR}, and compute the new plan. If this plan contains any external actions, the subgoals they satisfy are sent to the blackboard for auction. Having processed a goal from the queue (if any), we check

---

[1] Note that with a repeated auction the main advantage of a Vickrey auction (that it is a dominant strategy to bid ones private value) is lost for agents that reason about future auctions. Other types of auctions are a topic for future study.

[2] We are considering leveled-commitment contracting [13] to enable strategic decommitting.

whether a goal g' is currently being auctioned. If so, we compute our cost for it (using the heuristic $\mathcal{U}$ of the PR system), and send this as a bid to the blackboard. If our bid is winning, we add the goal g' to the front of our goal queue.

Input: A problem $\Pi = \langle O, I, G \rangle$
begin
1. Setup the goal queue Q containing all goals from Π
2. Create the initial problem description $\Pi_{PR} = \langle O, I, \emptyset \rangle$
3. Create the initial (empty) plan P
4. **if** Q is not empty **then**
    4.1. **pop** goal g from Q
    4.2. Estimate cost for this goal: $c = \mathcal{U}(P, \Pi_{PR}, g)$
    4.3. **if** c is too expensive **then**
        send g to the blackboard for auction
    4.4. **else**
        4.4.1. Update problem: $\Pi_{PR} = \Pi_{PR} \cup \{g\}$
        4.4.2. Update plan: $P = PR(P, \Pi_{PR})$
        4.4.3. **if** P contains new external actions **then**
            request results (subgoals) of these actions via an auction (blackboard)
5. **elseif** P contains gap actions **then**
    5.1. Update plan: $P = PR(P, \Pi_{PR})$
    5.2. Notify the blackboard of any subgoals that are no longer required
    5.3. **if** P contains new external actions **then**
        request results (subgoals) of these actions via an auction (blackboard)
6. **if** the environment has changed **then**
    6.1. Update P with gap actions reflecting the changes
    6.2. Update Π_{PR} to reflect the new situation
7. **if** an auction is ongoing for a goal g' **then**
    7.1. **send** bid (which is $\mathcal{U}(P, \Pi_{PR}, g')$)
    7.2. **if** goal is awarded **then**
        push g' onto the front of Q
8. **if** not all agents have completed executing their plan **then**
    8.1. goto step 4
end

4 Experimental Results

As a proof-of-concept, we tested our system with multiagent versions of the logistics problems of the plan repair benchmark problems [14]. This set consists of variations on the same base problem, and the goal is to repair the plan for the base problem in order to make it a valid plan for the variation. The variations consist of additional goals, changed goals, and changed initial situations (including the removal of resources such as airplanes). These problems were converted into a multiagent problem by creating an agent for each of the cities, capable of making deliveries within that city, and an additional agent that handles the inter-city transport using airplanes.

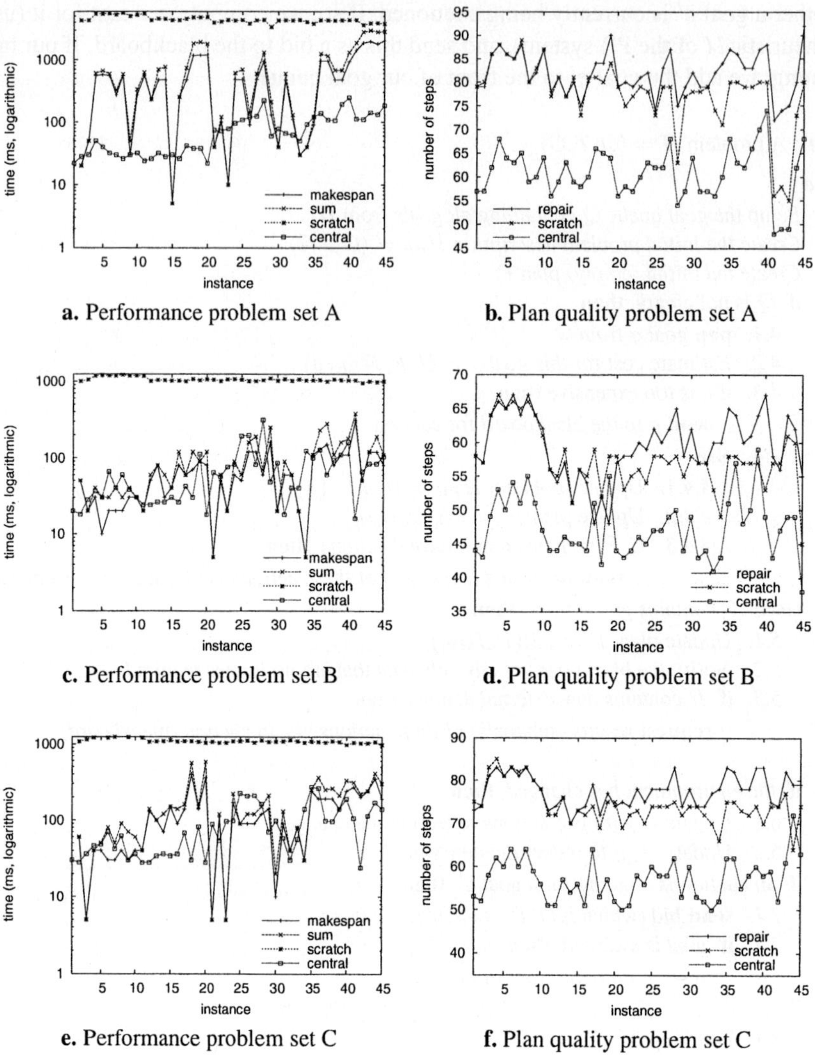

Fig. 1. Experimental results

To evaluate the run-time performance of our system, we used the benchmark set to obtain three different figures. The first is the *makespan* of our repair algorithm, i.e. the amount of time it takes the slowest of the agents to adjust its plan to the new situation. The second is the *sum* of the CPU time consumed by the agents. The third figure that we computed, is the makespan of *planning from scratch* with our system, i.e. the time it takes to distributedly compute a plan. These three figures are compared with the performance of the (central) single-agent plan repair method we have adopted [10]. Note that we report CPU times, implying that delay due to communications is not measured (waiting for incoming messages takes virtually no CPU time). However, it is reasonable to assume that for most realistic problems the CPU time involved in finding a solution is much higher than the communication delays.

The runtimes that were obtained on the multiagent variant of the Logistics benchmark set, can be seen in Figure 1. As one can observe, plan repair of a multiagent plan is quite a bit faster than planning from scratch. This can be expected because fewer goals have to be planned and fewer (sub)goals have to be auctioned: on average about 17 goals are auctioned when planning from scratch, compared to about 2 when performing plan repair. Furthermore, we can observe that the single-agent system is faster than the distributed system, although for a number of problems the difference between the makespan and the single-agent system is negligible. This increase can be attributed for a great deal to the goal-by-goal and failure-by-failure approach that we take.

Besides run-time performance, plan quality is also important. The heuristic of planning actions for others early in the plan has a negative effect on the size of the plans, compared with a centralized solution. This is because it forces an ordering on the agents' plans that is stricter than necessary. As a result, the plans that we obtain are often bigger. On average, our plans are 20% larger than plans computed by a single-agent planner (which consist of about 60-70 actions). This is the price we have to pay for not exchanging detailed information on the structure of the plans. The difference in plan size between plans distributedly produced from scratch and plans that have been repaired is significant.

The table below summarizes the results and shows the significance values obtained from a pairwise t-test.

set	issue	Multiagent plan repair	distributed, from scratch	t	p
A	performance (ms)	$\mu = 581.4, \sigma = 564.9$	$\mu = 4378.2, \sigma = 624.5$	-26.0	< 0.01
	quality (steps)	$\mu = 81.8, \sigma = 4.6$	$\mu = 77.7, \sigma = 7.4$	5.3	< 0.01
B	performance (ms)	$\mu = 68.2, \sigma = 55.0$	$\mu = 1056.9, \sigma = 67.0$	-65.3	< 0.01
	quality (steps)	$\mu = 59.6, \sigma = 4.8$	$\mu = 57.6, \sigma = 4.5$	3.0	< 0.01
C	performance (ms)	$\mu = 126.8, \sigma = 99.8$	$\mu = 1101.6, \sigma = 76.8$	-42.5	< 0.01
	quality (steps)	$\mu = 77.5, \sigma = 3.6$	$\mu = 74.2, \sigma = 4.4$	5.4	< 0.01

5 Discussion

In this paper we gave experimental evidence that, in a simplified setup, self-interested agents that have a distinct set of resources can coordinate and repair their plans while only exchanging a very small amount of information. We used an existing plan repair algorithm in a goal-by-goal setting and a simple auction, and we showed how to prevent cyclic inter-agent dependencies, and how to deal with lazy agents and decommitment.

We studied the difference in both plan size and planning time between multiagent plan repair and multiagent replanning. It turns out that although in some occasions completely replanning leads to slightly shorter plans, it usually takes much longer to reach those. Another advantage of plan repair is that inter-agent dependencies do not change that much compared to replanning from scratch, so there is much less costs for decommitting, which is especially important in real-life applications. Our distributed approach produces bigger plans than central solutions. This can be mainly attributed to our cycle-prevention heuristic, which is often too restrictive. However, it allows us to create valid multiagent plans without exchanging details about the plans, which is very important for self-interested agents. We believe that our results are also applicable to systems with more advanced market mechanisms and strategies (such as discussed below), as plan repair is just as useful in those situations. Note, however, that this system is not yet a fully continual planning system. Studying the interaction between plan repair and plan execution in a multiagent system is still a topic for future research.

This system for coordinating self-interested agents using propositional plan repair is unique in that we integrate planning and coordination without assuming that the agents are *collaborating*. Agents may even be each other's competitors. Previous work on multiagent planning, although often more advanced in modeling problems realistically (by involving time constraints, minimizing costs, and efficient use of resources), assumes that the agents are collaborative. For example, in the Cougaar system [15] cooperative agents are coordinated by exchanging more and more details of their hierarchical plans until conflicts can be resolved (similar to [6]). The General Partial Global Planning (GPGP) method [5] describes a framework for distributedly constructing a (partial) global plan to be able to discover all kinds of potential conflicts. Finally, in [16] a method using partially ordered temporal plans is proposed to solve multiagent planning problems in such a way that agents can ask others about the state of the world, who will (truthfully) answer as soon as possible. His work relaxes our assumption that agents have complete knowledge about the relevant part of the world, but in all of the above mentioned systems the agents are not self-interested.

There is, however, a substantial body of work on *task allocation* for self-interested agents. For example using market mechanisms [17], or using extensions of the contract-net protocol [18, 19]. The main difference between the work in this area and ours, is that we do not consider a set of tasks given beforehand. Instead, the set of tasks that has to be allocated arises from the results of the planning activities of the agents. In our view, task (re)allocation, cannot be disconnected from planning. Nevertheless, ideas from the work in this area may be used to improve upon our approach. For example, we might replace the simple auction by a parallel or combinatorial auction. In particular, the results presented by Hunsberger [8] are interesting. He describes how a group of autonomous agents that encounter an opportunity to collaborate on some group activity, can decide whether to commit to doing that activity, using a combinatorial auction. Although in his approach a single given set of tasks is to be performed, it might be extended to a more dynamic situation, such as we consider. Also, the work on *role (re)allocation* and *team formations* (e.g. [20]) may lead to improvements in performance and solution quality, by recognizing the different roles involved. Finally, in temporal domains, the control of the temporal network may be distributed using techniques presented in [21].

Besides looking at improvements of our goal-by-goal heuristic, we would like to test our method in other domains and study the conditions that define when this approach is feasible. Furthermore, we intend to try to relax our assumptions to be able to tackle more advanced problems. Most importantly, we would like to have a method to estimate the costs of external actions. Typically those actions are more expensive than your own actions. If all actions have costs, we can try to optimize costs instead of plan length. In most domains this may give more realistic solutions. Another important topic for future study is using a different type of auction and (de)committing mechanism [22, 13] to allow backtracking over different agents. We intend to study the applicability of such a technique in relation to the specific requirements of the problem domain of these self-interested planning agents.

References

1. DesJardins, M., Durfee, E., Ortiz, C., Wolverton, M.: A survey of research in distributed, continual planning. AI Magazine **20** (2000) 13–22
2. Pollack, M., Horty, J.: There's more to life than making plans: Plan management in dynamic, multi-agent environments. AI Magazine **20** (1999) 71–84
3. Malone, T.W., Crowston, K.: The interdisciplinary study of coordination. ACM Computing Surveys **21** (1994) 87–119
4. Wilkins, D., Myers, K.: A multiagent planning architecture. In: Proc. of the 4th Int. Conf. on AI Planning Systems. (1998) 154–162
5. Decker, K., Li, J.: Coordinating mutually exclusive resources using GPGP. Autonomous Agents and Multi-Agent Systems **3** (2000) 113–157
6. von Martial, F.: Coordinating Plans of Autonomous Agents. Volume 610 of Lecture Notes on AI. (1992)
7. Shehory, O., Kraus, S.: Methods for task allocation via agent coalition formation. Artificial Intelligence **101** (1998) 165–200
8. Hunsberger, L., Grosz, B.J.: A combinatorial auction for collaborative planning. In: Proc. Int. Conf. on Multi-Agent Systems. (2000) 151–158
9. Kambhampati, S.: Refinement planning as a unifying framework for plan synthesis. AI Magazine **18** (1997) 67–97
10. van der Krogt, R., de Weerdt, M.: Plan repair as an extension of planning. In: Proc. of the Int. Conf. on Automated Planning and Scheduling. (2005)
11. Schillo, M., Kray, C., Fischer, K.: The eager bidder problem: A fundamental problem of DAI and selected solutions. In: Proc. of the 1st Int. Conf. on Autonomous Agents and Multi-Agent Systems. (2002) 599–606
12. Vickrey, W.: Computer speculation, auctions, and competitive sealed tenders. Journal of Finance **16** (1961) 8–37
13. Sandholm, T., Lesser, V.: Leveled-commitment contracting: a backtracking instrument for multiagent systems. AI Magazine **23** (2002) 89–100
14. Gerevini, A., Serina, I.: Fast plan adaptation through planning graphs: Local and systematic search techniques. In: Proc. of the Fifth Int. Conf. on AI Planning Systems. (2000) 112–121
15. Kleinmann, K., Lazarus, R., Tomlinson, R.: An infrastructure for adaptive control of multi-agent systems. In: IEEE Int. Conf. on Integration of Knowledge Intensive Multi-Agent Systems. (2003) 230–236
16. Brenner, M.: Multiagent planning with partially ordered temporal plans. Technical Report 190, Universität Freiburg (2003)
17. Walsh, W., Wellman: A market protocol for decentralized task allocation and scheduling with hierarchical dependencies. In: Proc. of the 3rd Int. Conf. on Multi-Agent Systems. (1999) 325–332
18. Collins, J., Tsvetovatyy, M., Gini, M., Mobasher, B.: MAGNET: A multi-agent contracting system for plan execution. In: Proc. of SIGMAN. (1998)
19. Smith, R.: The contract net protocol: High-level communication and control in a distributed problem solver. IEEE Transactions on Computers **C-29** (1980) 1104–1113

20. Nair, R., Tambe, M., Marsella, S.: Role allocation and reallocation in multiagent teams: towards a practical analysis. In: Proc. of the 2nd Int. Joint Conf. on Autonomous agents and multiagent systems. (2003) 552–559
21. Hunsberger, L.: Distributing the control of a temporal network among multiple agents. In: Proc. of the 2nd Int. Conf. on Autonomous Agents and Multi-Agent Systems. (2003) 899–906
22. Hoen, P.J., t., Poutré, J.A., L.: A decommitment strategy in a competitive multi-agent transportation setting. In: Proc. of the AAMAS-03 Workshop on Agent Mediated Electronic Commerce V. Volume 3048 of Lecture Notes on Artificial Intelligence. (2003)

Enabling Intelligent Organizations: An Electronic Institutions Approach for Controlling and Executing Problem Solving Methods

Armando Robles P.[1,2], B.V. Pablo Noriega[2], Francisco Cantú[3], and Rubén Morales-Menéndez[4],

[1] TCA Research Group
[2] Institut d'Investigació en Intel.ligència Artificial,
IIIA-CSIC. Barcelona, Spain
[3] Research and Graduate Studies Office, ITESM
[4] Center for Innovation in Design and Technology, ITESM,
Monterrey, NL, México
{arobles, pablo}@iiia.csic.es,
{fcantu, rmm}@itesm.mx

Abstract. In this paper we propose a framework for controlling and executing problem solving methods in a work-flow context. The framework is founded on an extension and scaling-up of the electronic institutions theory and the use of artificial intelligence techniques in a multi agent environment. We discuss electronic institutions's theory extensions for enabling intelligent organizations using our approach. As a proof of concept of the proposal we present the prototype of a help-desk information system for assigning advisors and monitoring their performance using artificial intelligence techniques for automated reasoning.

1 Introduction

An Intelligent Organization (IO) is understood as a knowledge-based organization whose business operations and internal processes are founded on knowledge competencies and the value of its products and services is given by the knowhow, the intellectual capital and the technological advantage of the organization [5]. An IO typically operates around repositories of knowledge, information and data. Technologies like data-warehouses, multi-agent systems and data mining gather the knowledge assets and best practices within the organization and provides knowledge distribution means for applying and using that knowledge throughout business operations [6, 4].

We introduce a framework to handle the integration of Problem Solving Methods (PSM) as work-flow processes and Artificial Intelligence (AI) techniques around existing corporate information systems. The result enables IOs with multi agent system (MAS) environments that use packaged know-how to exploit the transactions of the underlying corporate systems. The framework – and the corresponding architecture– presented in this paper is a generalized electronic institution (EI) that uses Petri Net like expressible work-flow control processes [10], CommonKADS task templates [8] and distributed AI techniques as tools with which to capture and apply corporate know-how. The framework extends the current version of EIs in order to enable flexible application and on-line tuning of PSM execution and control.

As a proof of concept of our approach we have built a help-desk information system prototype that works on a real setting. Participant agents take up the functions of human users (clients, supervisors, advisors and other executives taking part in the help-desk processes). The decision-making capabilities have been modelled with standard automated reasoning techniques. Currently available EI concepts and tools were used to achieve a coherent integration of the prototype components such as message exchange conventions, work-flows and the commitment pragmatics involved in the cooperative MAS.

The paper is organized as follows. Section 2 contains some background material on EIs. Section 3 gives a description of the proposed framework. Section 4 presents the help-desk application. In section 5 we present closing remarks.

2 Electronic Institutions Fundamentals

An EI is a coordination artifact, a computational entity that facilitates effective agent coordination. An EI is a way of expressing conventions that agent interactions should follow and a way to see to it that those conventions are actually followed by participating agents. Those conventions can be thought of as constraints on the possible interactions: intuitively, for instance, as a script for a play enacted by individuals who assume certain roles, or more generally as a set of admissible dialogues, or more abstractly as a set of norms (a deontic theory) to which agents are subject to [9].

The notion of EI has been operationalized through the following concepts:

- *Dialogical Framework*. Constitutes the communication conventions that will prevail in a given institution. Agents interact with each other —always and only— by means of *illocutions*, whose object language elements and semantics are set by the institution. Consequently, the domain ontology, as far as it is ever used in an admissible institutional utterance, has to be included as part of that object language. The dialogical framework also defines the *roles* agents may play as well as the relationships and incompatibilities among these roles.
- *Performative Structure*. Specifies the interaction conventions that govern the illocutory exchanges. Or, more abstractly, the interaction flows that are admissible in the institution. That flow is expressed through the interlacing of repetitive interaction conventions called *scenes*. Connections between scenes are expressed by canonical scenes called *transitions* that establish the conditions for access or departure from a given interaction context (changes of conversation), activation of new scene enactments or even cloning of individual agents.

– *Rules of Behaviour.* Dialogical interactions —in the institution— have institutional consequences that are known to intervening agents who are bound to their satisfaction. These consequences can be thought of as *commitments* that impose constraints on actions these agents might carry out in the future.

Each of these concepts can be properly formalized in different ways. For instance scenes can be defined as finite state machines, arcs labelled by utterances, or as a declaration of prohibitions and permissions; performative structures may be predefined and static, or may evolve with use or be adapted or changed by participating agents themselves; rules of behavior maybe static or dynamic, obligatory or elective. The current formalization of those concepts (EI_0) assumes conventions are predefined and static, they are obligatory and their enforcement is strict.

There is a publicly available suit of tools (EIDE) for specification, testing and deployment of EI_0 electronic institutions.[1] It contains, among other tools, a language (ISLANDER [2]) for specification and verification of electronic institutions. The participating agents in an institution do not interact directly, they have their interactions mediated by AMELI [3] which can be seen as the social layer of the MAS, or as the execution engine for the Electronic Institution. It has four types of agents: Institution Manager, Scene Managers, Transition Managers, and Governors, the first three types manage the institutional activation and control of scenes and transitions, while the fourth type is attached to all domain (external) agents to enforce their compliance with the institutional conventions. AMELI is implemented over the JADE platform.[2] Therefore it can be distributed among different machines for scalability purposes.

3 Framework Outline

The purpose of our framework is to facilitate the packaging and use of corporate know–how in order to enable IOs to achieve extra functionality and flexibility, hence to improve their performance and adapt to the changing business environment. In order to achieve these goals, our framework allows existing —complex— corporate information systems to profit from general PSMs and AI techniques by integrating all of these into a multi-agent environment within an electronic institution. The framework proposal involves two main components: a framework architecture and a methodology. In this section we discuss the main aspects of the architecture, the methodology is outlined at the end of this section and applied in section 4.

3.1 Open MAS Approach

We intend to build a general framework that can be used on existing corporate systems of arbitrary type to provide added functionality, and we want that the resulting corporate system can then be adapted dynamically to the emerging

---

[1] see http://e-institutions.iiia.csic.es/ for details
[2] see http://jade.tilab.com/ for details

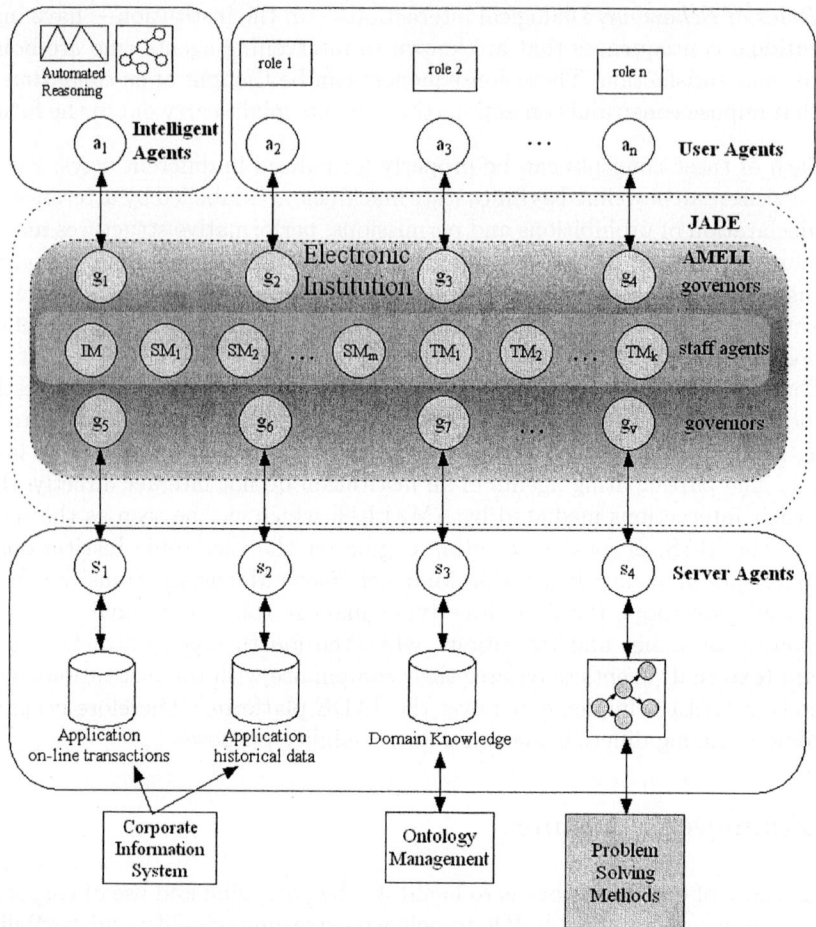

Fig. 1. Proposed Architecture, It has three main components: One electronic institution block that mediates all agent interactions using staff agents: One Institution Manager (IM), One Scene Manager (SM) per scene execution and one Transition manager (TM) per defined transition (central shaded area) and two blocks of different types of agents: server (s_i) and user (a_i) agents. Server agents handle corporate information and knowledge. User agents are involved in specific tasks and are controlled by governors (g_i). Problem Solving Methods are provided to the institution by a specialized server agent. The dashed line indicates the MAS communication layer (JADE).

needs of the organization. While agents are a convenient metaphor for decision-making components as well as active participants in a work-flow, and hence a natural technology to incorporate for this purpose, it is not easy to establish a functioning environment where agents may interact with a legacy information system without that environment being a rather *ad-hoc* device. To avoid such specificity we chose EI as our integrating technology, because its focus on interactions allows the integration of a MAS in a general and transparent way.

Technically speaking we first define an electronic institution that implements the essential *institutional* components (i.e., CIS, corporate ontology) of the intelligent organization (e.g. a hospital). On top of that institution we insert "sub–institutions" that implement organizational tasks (admissions, medical protocols, help–desk) that are performed more aptly with the intervention of human or software agents. Our contribution is that such sub–institutions, and many agents that participate in them, may be implemented, tailored or adapted on–the–fly, even automatically.

3.2 Architecture

Figure 1 outlines how an organization implements an application that accomplishes a task. The main components of the framework's architecture are:

- The *Electronic Institution* (central) block. It correspond to the organization *in toto* and grows by splicing into it new sub–institutions that correspond to the new tasks being implemented, (say the help-desk or medical protocols). As a regular EI, it contains the usual EI "staff agents" that manage scenes and transitions, and the governor agents that represent "external agents". It runs on the AMELI middleware using a JADE communication layer.
- The *User Agents* block. It contains the agents that participate in a given task. Participants in an organizational task are usually humans, but in the implementation of that task, some of these —or some of the functions of some of these— may be automated as software agents who will act as the actual participants. As in any EI, participating agents perform standard roles and all interactions are utterances, which in the case of humans are mediated through an institutional interface, and both human and software agents utterances are mediated through a *governor*.
- The *Server Agents* block. It makes available to the implemented application the corporate information and the corporate knowledge repositories, as well as the available PSM templates. The flow from the actual repositories to the EI is mediated by software "server agents" whose utterances are again filtered through their corresponding governors. Note that, in most cases, an application task draws information from the actual transactions that are taking place in real time in the organization, as well as other information that has a less transient character, hence the need for specialized server agents. Corporate knowledge may take many forms, an institutional significant one is the ontology management needs to be properly observed in (new) task implementations, particularly if these have an automatic or dynamic character, thus the corresponding specialization.
- The *Problem Solving Methods* (PSM) component holds a repository of methods that may become useful in task implementations. Templates are tailored and instantiated to a specific task. That process entails the use of corporate knowledge and adequate reference to corporate information, in order to have them properly inserted into the organizational EI. Templates may be drawn from standard repositories, e.g. CommonKADS task templates [8], as is the case in the Help-Desk exercise.

– The *Intelligent Agents* component, holds a repository of decision–making schemata and tools that may be adapted either as part of the deliberative components of a user agent (DSS tools for humans or reasoning capabilities or decision models for software agents), or may be deployed as actual agents that may become one of a given sub–institution's participants. The Intelligent Agents component, as could be the case for a PSM, capture an important type of reusable corporate know-how, hence the distinct treatment of these components in our proposal.

3.3 Tools

For the construction and deployment of our proposed architecture we have being using the EIDE suite of tools for specification, testing, monitoring and deployment of Electronic Institutions that has been developed and made publicly available by the group of multi-agent systems of the Spanish AI Research Institute (IIIA). We have profited from an *alpha* version of EIDE that allows hierarchical institutions in order to handle sub-institution splicing of a simple kind.

Most of the human agent interfaces as well as the institutional shells — communication and flow–control functionality— of participating software agents are automatically deployed. The organizational PSM have been assembled extending available CommonKADS task templates, and we have used available Bayesian and fuzzy-reasoning AI techniques. Our architecture is open enough to incorporate other standardized or *ad-hoc* elements of these sorts.

3.4 Methodology

Design. The process of implementing a new organizational task consist of rather standard steps. We indicate what we think the general process may be stating the way we have instrumented it so far:

The scope of the functionality of the system may be specified as follows:

– The domain knowledge is modelled as a *classes* diagram representing the ontology used across the application.
– The conceptual interaction for the real world application is modelled with an *UML use case* diagram.
– The design and implementation of the required PSMs starts from a template in an available template repository, like the CommonKADS task templates [8], and then the template is extended and fitted as required. In this case, the available PSM is modelled using a *UML activity diagram*. The diagram indicates the required extensions and the interactions with AI techniques if needed.
– We represent the activity diagram into the EI using ISLANDER.
– User agents and human user interfaces are built on shells generated by EIDE.

Execution. The execution of the required PSMs is controlled through the AMELI middleware. The following steps are performed:

– The PSM Server Agent provides the required protocol to the EI.
– The EI activates the corresponding scene for the PSM and starts its execution.

- The required user agents specified in the PSM enter the scene. If the user agents require information from the on-line or historical transactions, it is made available through the appropriate server agents.
 - If a specific AI technique execution is required in the PSM scene, an intelligent agent service is used.
 - The interaction between the different agents continues until the PSM terminates.

4 Case Study

4.1 Help-Desk Information System

We use a help-desk information system to illustrate our proposal. The main goal of the help-desk is to provide technical support service (through the internet) to users of an integral information system for several hotel chains which are leaders in the Latin American market. Each hotel has between 10 - 40 users whose technical support requirements are provided by the help-desk system. The process (as outlined in figure 2) is the following:

 - A user who requires technical support logs into the help-desk system and registers its needs in text form.
 - The help-desk immediately responds assigning the user a service folio that serves as a unique identification during the whole advisor service process.
 - The help-desk service supervisor receives the new folio and based on his experience, assigns each folio to an advisor. The assignment goal is to provide the customer with the best possible service.

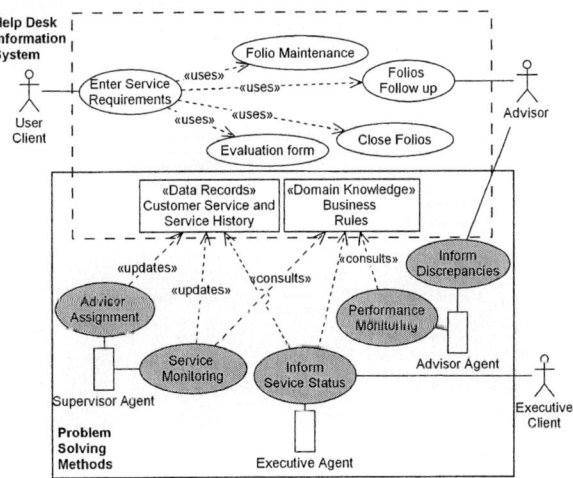

Fig. 2. UML Use Case Diagram. Dashed lines show Help Desk Information System's functionality. Shaded areas represent the Problem Solving Methods (PSM). For the case study we implemented the assignment and monitoring methods.

- The assigned advisor provides the support until the user's needs are satisfied.
- Once the user is satisfied with the solution provided by the advisor, he proceeds to close the folio, filling a form that evaluates the service received.
- As a service feedback, each month, the help-desk supervisor sends the hotel chain executives a service evaluation report including a summary of the service activities performed and the evaluation given by the users to each folio.

4.2 Applying the Framework

For the case study, we designed and implemented two PSM by extending and adjusting two available CommonKADS task templates. For choosing the best advisor to folio we use the assignment template. For monitoring the service quality provided by advisors we choose the monitoring template.

We specified the functionality of the system using the methodology described in section 3.4. The conceptual interactions diagram for the real world application using a *use case* diagram is shown in Figure 2. Shaded areas represent the PSMs.

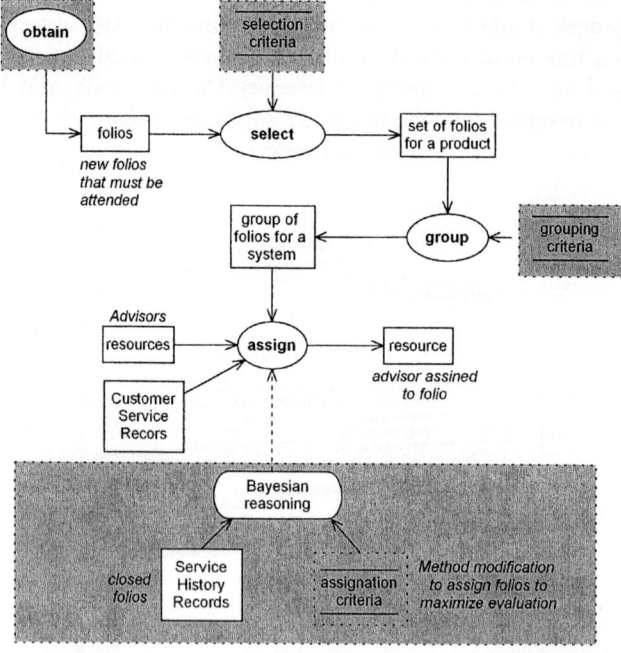

Fig. 3. UML Activity Diagram for the Assignment method. The shaded area shows the automated reasoning implemented and the extensions made to the CommonKADS task template for the assignment method. Ovals show task procedures for this method as defined in CommonKads: obtain, select, group and assign.

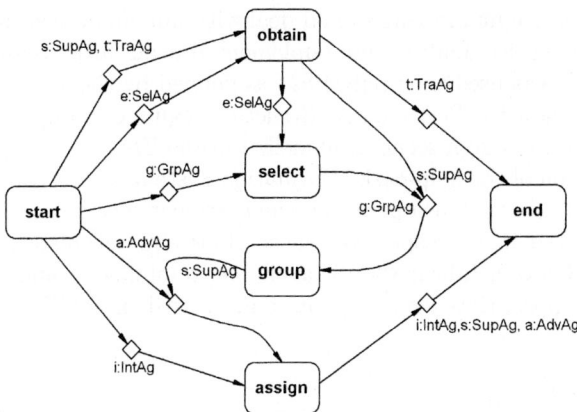

Fig. 4. Performative Structure for the Assignment method. Boxes correspond to scenes, diamonds correspond to transitions. Labels correspond to participating agents: Transaction (TraAg), Supervisor (SupAg), Advisor (AdvAg), Bayesian (BayAg), Grouping (GrpAG) and Selection (SelAg). Note the direct correspondence between task procedures in figure 3 and scenes in this figure.

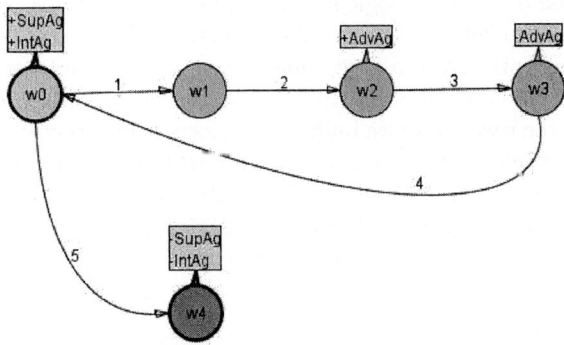

Fig. 5. Assign scene controlling the interaction between the Supervisor, Bayesian and Advisor agents. This diagram shows the details inside the assign scene shown in figure 4 as part of the Performative Structure for the Assignment method. All agent interactions are defined by illocutions expressed in LISP-like syntax:
1. (request (?s SupAg) (?b BayAg) (take ?folio))
2. (request (!b BayAg) (!s SupAg) (assign !folio ?advisor))
3. (request (!s SupAg) (!a AdvAg) (take !folio))
4. (inform (!a AdvAg) (!s SupAg) (taken !folio))
5. (inform (!s SupAg) (!i IntAg) (close))

The functionality of the supervisor role is fully implemented as a software agent. For the Supervisor agent, decision making capabilities for choosing the best advisor to folio assignment was implemented using Bayesian reasoning [7]. In Figure 3 we show the *activity* diagram for the assignment method. Due to the fact that service monitoring should deal with human perception, monitoring capabilities for service quality were implemented using fuzzy reasoning.

ISLANDER was used to specify PSM as defined by the extended templates. In Figure 4 we show the Performative Structure required to implement the PSM, Figure 5 shows the assign scene as modelled in the EI.

The execution of the help-desk Information System is carried on as usual, but as a result of its continuous operation, the customer service and service history records are stored in its respective transactions and the historical data bases are updated. Relevant information is available to intelligent and user agents by means of the appropriate server agents and is used in the EI as explained in section 3.4.

4.3 Lessons Learned

As can be seen in our case study, we are trying to "push" for a new paradigm for programming CIS using MAS technology in a work-flow context using the concept of EIs. Despite of the fact that our approach is work-flow centered, it relies mostly in the modelling of agent interactions in a normative environment.

Our example shows that the work-flow defined in each PSM is executed in a similar way as in a Petri net (PN) [10]. However, while in a PN the work-flow is controlled by business logic hardwired in the transitions, in our approach the work-flow is controlled through valid illocutions that are subject to pre and post-conditions expressed in a flow- independent normative language.

As we see in our case study, we need one performative structure to implement each PSM. For the case study we built two performative structures to implement two PSMs (assignment and monitoring). Due to the limitations of the current version of EI_0, we loaded and unloaded each PSM in a manual fashion, it seems clear that we need *splicing* of performative structures interacting in the same EI.

It should also be noted that in a more complex CIS —e.g. one where our example would be a sub-system of the whole CIS– we need to be able to handle the aggregation of several EIs.

5 Closing Remarks

We have looked into ways of going beyond current enterprise resource planning models for CIS so that the promise of intelligent organizations comes closer to feasibility. In particular our proposal addresses some of the main issues that proposals like CommonKADS have claimed to be relevant for intelligent organizations. Namely, the reusability of standard problem solving methods and the use of AI techniques for enabling intelligent functionalities. Our contributions stem from a novel use of agent technologies for capturing corporate knowledge competencies.

The help-desk example indicates that our proposal is feasible and shows the type of advantages of reusability and expressiveness intended. The example has been developed with available tools that may be improved significantly in order to exploit the potential of our proposal, specifically to allow more flexible definition of corporate processes and the possibility of automated and on-line evolution or adaptation.

We base our framework proposal on a natural separation of concerns suggested by the technologies of autonomous agents and electronic institutions we advocate. From a design standpoint, the separation between institutional conventions, on one side, and agent behavior on the other, allows for a differentiated treatment of the more stable procedures of the corporate behavior —expressible in the institutional layer— and the policy and situation-driven processes and decision-making know-how —encapsulated into staff agents. The first part is less volatile than the second and would involve the participation of high-level domain executives for the strategic definitions. The second component involves tactical considerations that should respond to the changing conditions of day to day operation and may thus require, mainly, operation experts in the specification and tuning and less specialized system designers in the implementation.

From an operational point of view, our framework allows for an automatic or semi-automatic adaptation of both layers that can be achieved off or on-line. Institutional business procedures may become more specialized, more versatile or adaptable to new requirements through the parametrization of scenes or the use of repositories of scenes and problem solving methods that may be *spliced* in a straightforward manner into the institutional layer. On the other hand, staff agents can profit from different decision-making techniques or be interchangeable with agents that embody different policies or business directives. In fact, thanks to the available agent *governors* our framework makes it possible to use all types of agents in the electronic institution (individual agents, teams, autonomous, hybrid human-software) thus enabling reactive behavior in the agents and eventually adaptation and learning of different sorts both at the agent and the institutional levels.

Our current work is geared towards the improvement of the available electronic institutions tools and theory suggested above. Two lines are worth mentioning here. One line deals with the use of problem solving environments, like NOOS [1] with learning capabilities, so that the PSM block may become a proactive element of the environment. The second line is concerned with developing the notion of electronic institutions beyond its present EI_0 version. The functionalities we are working on encompass, first the possibility of automated *splicing* of performative structures, i.e. to insert, or extract, a set of scenes in a given performative structure. With splicing, most of the PSM tailoring could be automated and new corporate flows may easily be assembled from existing ones. Second, we are pursuing the definition of hierarchical *reflexive* electronic institutions, so that we can compose a unified institution from the aggregation of two or more institutions and allow institutions to modify themselves.

References

1. Josep L. Arcos and Enric Plaza. Noos: an integrated framework for problem solving and learning. In *Proceedings of the KEML'97 Workshop on Knowledge Engineering Methods and Languages*, 1997. Also as IIIA-CSIC Technical Report 97-02.

2. Marc Esteva. *Electronic Institutions: from specification to development.* PhD thesis, Universitat Politècnica de Catalunya (UPC), Bellaterra, Catalonia, Spain, 2003. Institut d'Investigaci en Intelligncia Artificial. IIIA Monograph N. 19.
3. Marc Esteva, Juan A. Rodríguez-Aguilar, Bruno Rosell, and Josep L. Arcos. Ameli: An agent-based middleware for electronic institutions. In *Third International Joint Conference on Autonomous Agents and Multi-agent Systems (AAMAS'04)*, New York, USA, July 19-23 2004.
4. Liebowitz J. *Knowledge Management Handbook.* CRC Press, Boca raton, FL. USA, 1999.
5. Liebowitz J. and Beckman T. *Knowledge Organizations.* Saint Lucie Press, Washington, DC. USA, 1998.
6. Anandarajan M., Anandarajan A., and Srinivasan Cadambi A. *Business Intelligence Techniques.* Springer, Germany, 2004.
7. Armando Robles P., Francisco Cantú O., and Rubén Morales-Menéndez. A bayesian reasoning framework for on-line business information systems. In *Proceedings of the Eleventh Americas Conference on Information Systems*, Omaha, NE, USA, August 2005.
8. Guus Schreiber, Hans Akkermans, Anjo Anjewierden, Robert de Hoog, Niegel Shadbolt, Walter Van de Velde, and Bob Wielinga. *Knowledge Engineering and Management, The CommondKADS Methodology.* MIT Press, Boston, Massachusetts, USA, 2000.
9. Carles Sierra, Juan Antonio Rodriguez-Aguilar, Pablo Noriega, Marc Esteva, and Josep Lluis Arcos. Engineering multi-agent systems as electronic institutions. *European Journal for the Informatics Professional*, V(4):33–39, August 2004.
10. W.M.P. van der Aalst. *Making Work Flow: On the Application of Petri nets to Business Process Management.* Department of Technology Management, Eindhoven University of Technology, Eindhoven, The Netherlands, (2002).

An Extended Behavior Network for a Game Agent: An Investigation of Action Selection Quality and Agent Performance in Unreal Tournament

Hugo da Silva Corrêa Pinto and Luis Otávio Alvares

Instituto de Informática, Universidade Federal do Rio Grande do Sul (UFRGS),
Caixa Postal 15.064, 91.501-970, Porto Alegre, RS, Brazil
{hsspinto, alvares}@inf.ufrgs.br

Abstract. This work describes an application of extended behavior networks to the control of an agent in the game Unreal Tournament. Extended Behavior Networks (EBNs) are a class of action selection architectures capable of selecting a good set of actions for complex agents situated in continuous and dynamic environments. They have been successfully applied to the Robocup, but never before used in computer games. We verify the quality of the action selection mechanism and its correctness in a series of experiments. Then we asses the performance of an agent using an EBN against a plain reactive agent with identical sensory-motor apparatus and against a totally different agent built around finite-state machines. We discuss the results of our experiments, point our future work and conclude that extended behavior networks are a good control mechanism for game agents.

1 Introduction

The problem of selecting a good set of actions for a complex agent situated in a dynamic and complex environment remains a challenge. Robotics was the primary field in which this problem was deeply studied, but recently computer games have become a major motivation for revisiting it

Modern computer action games usually have the agent situated in a 3D virtual environment, interacting in varied ways with several entities in real-time. The scenarios an agent may face are varied and complex. The agent has many weapons available, each with certain properties and several items to use. It moves over different landscapes and interacts with several other agents, both opponents and teammates. The action repertory is large (run, walk, turn, crawl, shoot, change weapons, jump, strafe, pickup item and use item among others) and an agent may carry out more than one action simultaneously, such as shooting while jumping. Also, the agent has many possibly conflicting goals, such as fighting and keeping its safety.

An interesting architecture to tackle this problem is the Extended Behavior Network [1]. Behavior Networks are a class of action selection architectures for selecting good enough actions in dynamic and complex environments. They combine properties of traditional planners (chaining of actions based on preconditions and effects) and connectionist systems (activation spreading). Action selection is based in the mutual excitation and inhibition among the network nodes, via activation spreading.

Behavior Networks have been constantly evolving since their first appearance [2] as shown by [3], [4], [5] and [6]. They have been applied to animal simulation [7], interactive storytelling [4] and the Robocup [8].

Despite the good results in robotic soccer as reported in [5] and [8], extended behavior networks apparently have never been applied to computer games. Our research investigates how this technique behaves in the control of game robots, providing a novel realm of application in a needed area and contributing to the validation of Extended Behavior Networks as an action selection mechanism for autonomous agents. This last aspect is important from a theoretical AI perspective, because it was hard to tell if the good performance in the Robocup was due to the action selection mechanism employed or due to the sensory-motor system of the robots. Thus further testing of the mechanism is important for its validation.

This work is presented in the following way. We start by presenting an overview of the extended behavior network architecture followed by a presentation of the environment the agent is situated in and the agent architecture. In section 4 we investigate the quality of the action selection in a series of experiments. In sections 5 and 6 we investigate the performance of our agent compared to a totally different agent that used finite-state machines and to an agent that had identical sensors and behaviors but used a purely reactive action selection mechanism. We conclude with considerations on the suitability of behavior networks for controlling game agents and point our next research steps.

2 Extended Behavior Networks

An extended behavior network can be viewed as a set of linked modules and goals that mutually inhibit and excite each other via activation spreading, starting at the goals and flowing to the modules. The modules with higher activation and executability that do not use the same resources are selected for execution at each step. In the next subsections we examine in detail the structure of the network and the action selection algorithm.

2.1 Structure of an Extended Behavior Network

An extended behavior network (EBN) is defined by a set of behavior modules (M), a set of goals (G), a set of sensors (S), a set of resources (R) and a set of control parameters (C). Figure 1 shows the specification of a subset of the behavior network used in this work and Figure 2 the linked version of this subset.

A goal i is defined by a proposition that must be met (Gi), a strength value (Sti) and a disjunction of propositions that provide the context for that goal, called the relevance condition (Li). The strength provides the static, context-independent importance of the goal and the relevance condition the dynamic, context-dependent one. The total importance of the goal at a certain instant is obtained by multiplying the dynamic and static importances.

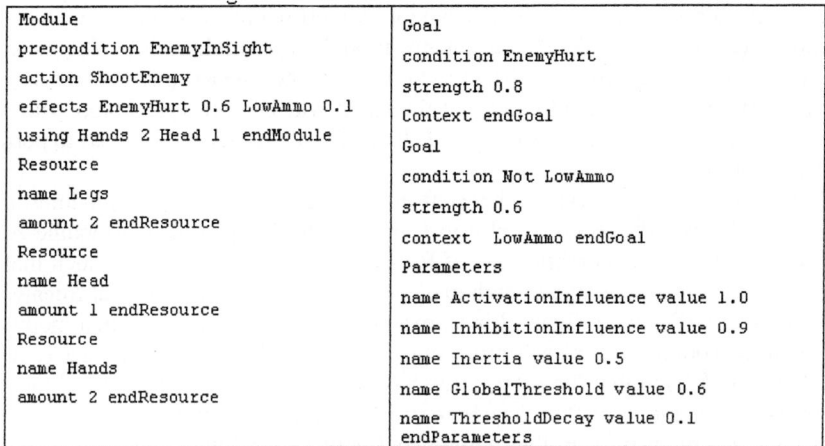

Fig. 1. Specification of a simple behavior network

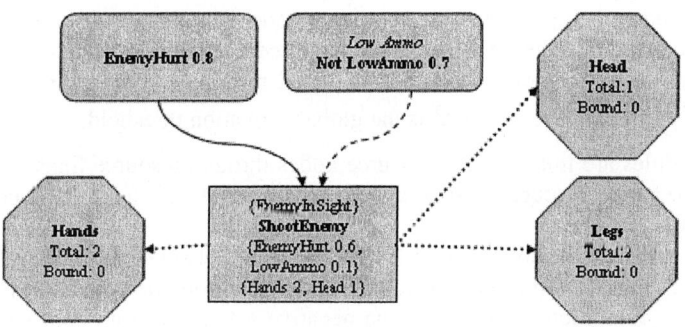

Fig. 2. Linked version of the behavior network of Figure 1. The goals are represented by round cornered rectangles, the behaviors by sharp cornered rectangles and the resource nodes by octagons. Straight lines represent predecessor links, dashed lines conflict links and pointed lines resource links.

The use of two kinds of conditions in the goals enables us to express goals that become more or less important depending on the situation the agent is in.

A context-independent goal is modeled leaving it without relevance conditions. Goal "EnemyHurt" in figure 1 is an example of such a goal. Note that a goal without relevance conditions amounts to a goal that is always relevant, i.e., its relevance is always maximal.

Each behavior module is specified by a conditions list, an effects list, an action and a resources list. The first list is a conjunction of real valued propositions that represent the needed conditions for the module to execute. The effects list is a conjunction of propositions (each possibly negated) whose values are the values that we expect them to have after the module's action execution. The resources list is made of pairs (resource, amount), each indicating the expected amount of a resource an agent uses to perform the action. Let us examine behavior "ShootEnemy" in figure 1. We see that the precondition is that there is an enemy in sight {EnemyInSight}. The expected effects are that the enemy will become hurt with 60% chance (or, conversely, that EnemyHurt verity will be 0.6) and that the agent will be with low ammo with 10% chance {EnemyHurt 0.6, LowAmmo 0.1}. It needs both hands and its head to perform the behavior {Hands 2, Head 1}.

A module receives activation energy from the goals and from other modules along two kinds of links. Predecessor links go from a module or goal B to a module A, for each proposition in the condition list of B that is in the effects list of A such that the proposition has the same sign in both ends of the link. The link from goal *EnemyHurt* to module *ShootEnemy* in figure 2 is an example. Conflict links go from a module or goal B to a module A, for each proposition in the condition list of B that is in the effects list of A such that the proposition has opposite signs at either end of the link. In figure 2, the link from *Not LowAmmo* to *ShootEnemy* is a conflict link. Conflict links take energy away from their targets and predecessor links input energy to their targets. This way a module tries to inhibit modules whose execution would undo some of its conditions and attempts to bring into execution modules whose actions would satisfy any of its conditions.

Each resource is represented by a resource node. These nodes have a function $f(s)$ that specifies the expected amount of the resource available in situation s, a variable *bound* that keeps track of the amount of bound resources and a resource activation threshold $\theta_{Res} \in (0..\theta]$, where θ is the global activation threshold.

The modules are linked to the resource nodes through resource links. For each resource type in the resources list of a module there is a link from the module to the corresponding resource node.

The control parameters are used to fine tune the network and have values in the range [0,1]. The activation influence parameter γ controls the activation from predecessor links. Inhibition influence, δ, the negative activation from conflict links. The inertia β, the global threshold θ and the threshold decay $\Delta\theta$ have their straightforward meanings. These parameters enable us to influence the degree of persistence of the agent (the higher the inertia the greater the persistence) and how reactive it is (the greater the global threshold the longer the sequence of actions considered when selecting a module for execution), amongst other properties. Default parameters that work well under various circumstances for the Robocup domain are shown in [5].

2.2 Action Selection Algorithm

The modules to be executed at each cycle are selected in the following way: 1) The activation a of the modules is calculated, first spreading from the goals and then from the modules. 2) The executability e of the module is calculated using some triangular norm operation over its condition list. 3) The execution-value $h(a,e)$ is calculated by multiplying a and e. 4) For each resource used by a module, starting by the last non-available resource, the module checks if it has exceeded the resource threshold and if there are enough resources for its execution. If so, it binds the resource. 5) If a module has bound all of its needed resources it executes and resets the resources thresholds to the value of the global threshold. 6) The module unbinds the resources used.

The thresholds of the resources linearly decay over time, ensuring that eventually a behavior will be able to bind its needed resources and that the most active behavior gets priority.

3 Agent Architecture and Environment

The game in which the agent is situated is Unreal Tournament [10], a first person shooter game. In the game mode we used, DeathMatch, the agent is an armed warrior who must kill all other warriors in an arena. The agent has many weapons available, each with certain properties and several items to use. It moves over different landscapes and interacts with several other agents, both opponents and teammates. The action repertoire is large (run, walk, turn, crawl, shoot, change weapons, jump, strafe, pickup item and use item among others) and an agent may carry out more than one action simultaneously, such as shooting while jumping. The scenarios are three- dimensional and the action happens in real-time, so the agent has to decide quickly what to do at each time step.

The primitive sensory information and actions of the agent are defined by an add-on to the game called Gamebots [11]. This package provides a socket interface to the agent and a protocol to interact with the game. Unreal Tournament server send native

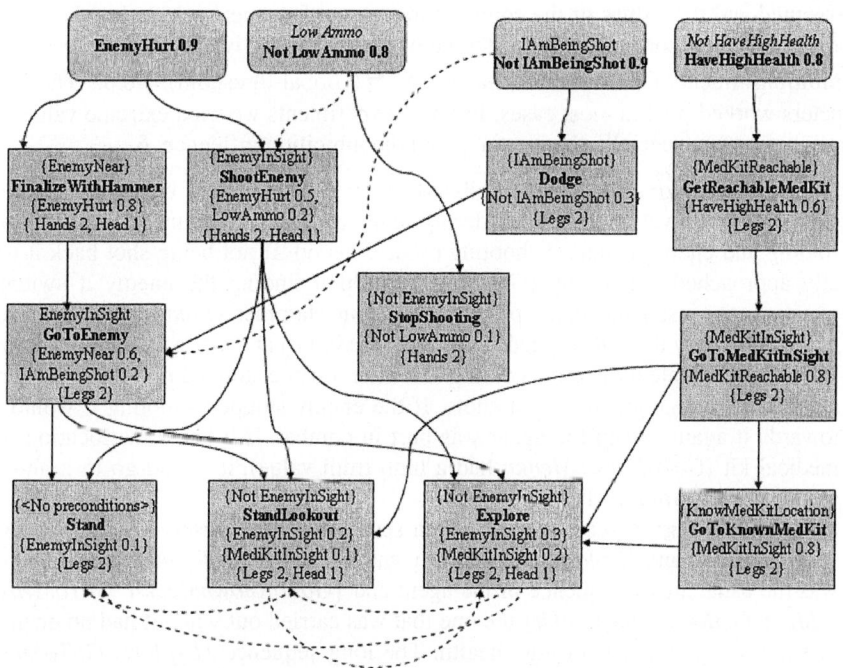

Fig. 3. Behavior Network for DeathMatch Agent. We have omitted the resource nodes and links for clarity.

game messages to Gamebots. In turn Gamebots send its own messages to our agents. Our agent's sensors process these messages and update the values of the conditions of the behavior network and the internal state of the agent. Action selection takes place and the appropriate actions are carried out by sending commands to Gamebots that in turn send low-level Unreal Tournament messages to the server.

Figure 3 gives a detailed overview of the extended behavior network of the agent.

Each proposition of the Behavior Network had a sensor associated to it. Each sensor had a proposition function P and an internal state function I. Function P took the current state of the environment and the internal state of the agent and returned a proposition with value between [0..1]. Function I updated the internal state of the agent according to its perception of the environment and the internal state

The actions of the behavior modules were implemented as augmented finite-state machines. When selected for execution each behavior action has a certain amount of time to execute. Each behavior action keeps track of its state independently and has access to the internal state of the agent. A behavior action may issue one or more primitive commands to the game when executing.

4 Assessing Action Selection Quality

Our first series of experiments were designed to asses the quality of action selection. We give a description of how the perceived state of the agent has changed, the actions it executed and the values of the control parameters of the network during the experiment. The default configuration for the network was: γ (ActivationInfluence) = 1.0, δ (InhibitionInfluence) = 0.9, β (Inertia) = 0.5, θ (Global threshold) = 0.6. These parameters worked well in most cases. In a few experiments we tried extreme values for some parameters, specially the inertia β and the inhibition influence δ.

1. **Overall Behavior:** The agent exhibited an overall intelligent behavior. It started exploring the level and kept wandering until it found an enemy (*Explore*). Upon finding and enemy it started shooting (*ShootEnemy*). If not being shot back it usually approached the enemy (*GoToEnemy*). Upon finding the enemy it switched weapons and used the more powerful weapon Hammer (*FinalizeWithHammer*). After the enemy died, it stopped shooting (*StopShoot*) and started wandering again. When shot repeatedly it kept shooting and after a while stopped going to the enemy and started dodging subsequent shots. If the enemy stopped shooting it would go towards it again. When the agent was hurt in combat, if it knew the location of a medical kit (*GoToKnownMedkit* had a high truth value), it would go to it and restore its health after a while.
2. **Action chaining:** Three common action sequences were observed. The sequence {*StopShooting* and *Explore, GoToEnemy* and *ShootEnemy, FinalizeWithHammer*} was the usual attack sequence of the agent and {*GoToKnownMedkit, GoToMedkitInSight, GetReachableMedkit*} the one that was carried out when it had no enemies in sight and was not with high health. The long sequence {*Explore, GoToEnemy* and *ShootEnemy, FinalizeWithHammer, StopShooting* and *GoToKnownMedKit, GoToMedkitInSight, GetReachableMedKit*}, that is basically the two previous ones one after the other, was the most common overall behavior of the agent. We see

that the agent makes reasonably long consistent chains of actions even though the agent makes no formal planning.
3. **Reactivity and Persistence:** We can see the sequence of actions {*Explore, GoToEnemy, FinalizeWithHammer*} as a plan to fulfill the goal *EnemyHurt*. If while going to the enemy the agent was shot, it stopped behavior *GoToEnemy*, executed *BehaviorDodge* and, having evaded the shot, resumed *GoToEnemy*. We see that the agent reacted to an event in the environment and then got back to our perceived "plan". It exhibited a good compromise between reactivity and persistence. For large values of β, the inertia, the agent took some time to dodge after perceiving a shot and only dodged when a sequence of shots happened.
4. **Resolution of conflicts among goals:** Let us take a look at figure 3 again. We see that goal *EnemyHurt* tries to make behavior *ShootEnemy* execute and goal *Not LowAmmo* tries to prevent it from executing. The goal *Not LowAmmo* has little influence until the agent starts to be with very low ammunition. When this happens, the conflicting influence of *Not LowAmmo* makes the agent switch to the hammer weapon (*FinalizeWithHammer*), because it does not need ammunition. It is an unusual, though sensible approach to ammunition saving, that emerged on interaction of the goals (note that the "designed" way to save ammo is using behavior *StopShooting*).Another case of conflict resolution happens at behavior *GoToEnemy*. To better fulfill *EnemyHurt* the agent has to get near, but to satisfy *Not IAmBeingShot* it better not. We saw in 1 and 3, the network deals with this conflict well, dodging when appropriate and resuming going to the enemy.
5. **Preference for actions that contribute to several goals:** The network always preferred *StandLookout* and *Explore* to *Stand* when they had equal executability, even when we used larger expected values for the *EnemyInSight* effect of *Stand*. The reason is simple: both *StandLookout* and *Explore* contribute to *EnemyHurt* and *HaveHighHealth*, while *Stand* just contributes to *EnemyHurt* (In fact it contributes to *ShootEnemy* that in turn contributes to *EnemyHurt*).
6. **Proper combination of concurrent actions:** We see that the agent makes good use of its resources and combine the actions properly. It shoots while dodging a bullet or running towards the enemy, it stops shooting while exploring or getting a medical kit and even continues to shoot while getting a medical kit. All combinations of actions are reasonable and the good action combinations we could conceive were observed, as the previous analysis attest.

5 The Behavior Network Agent Compared to a Completely Different Agent Based on Finite-State-Machines.

To first validate the mechanism, we used an agent implemented by other researchers, Carnagie Mellon's CMU_JBot, a Java agent based on finite-state machines that comes with the Javabots package [12]. This would prevent bias in our design of its first opponent. We made a series of 10 games of 1 minute. Fore each game we recorded the number of times the agent hit the opponent, the number of times the agent was hit, the number of times the agent was killed and the number of times the agent killed he opponent. The total score was got by giving 0.1 to each time the agent hit the opponent and 1 to each time the agent killed the opponent. Table 1 summarizes our results. The rightmost column presents the difference between the score of the agent using the extended behavior network (EBN_Bot) and the score of CMU_JBot.

We see that our agent scored much higher than the agent that used finite state machines. The low number of killings, even when many hits happened, is due to the absence of a chasing mechanism in both agents. The agents wandered through the environment, shot each other and then separated, several times.

This experiment adds evidence to the validity of behavior networks as a suitable action selection mechanism for Unreal Tournament agents, but a doubt remains: Is the better performance due to our sensors and behaviors or due to the action selection mechanism used? The next experiment sheds light on this issue.

Table 1. DeathMatch Results of EBN_Bot and CMU_JBot

Experiment #	EBNBot Hit	EBNBot Kill	CMU_JBot Hit	CMU_JBot Kill	Difference
1	0.7	0	0.2	0	0.5
2	0.1	0	0.0	0	0.1
3	0.3	1	0	0	1.3
4	0.7	0	0.1	0	0.7
5	0.9	0	0	0	0.9
6	0.4	1	0.1	0	1.3
7	0.6	0	0	0	0.6
8	0.7	1	0.0	0	1.7
9	0.9	0	0.1	0	0.8
10	0.2	1	0.2	0	1.0
Mean	0.55	0.4	0.06	0	0.8

6 The Behavior Network Agent Compared to a Plain Reactive Agent That Uses the Same Sensory-Motor Apparatus

In this experiment we compared the EBN agent to an agent that had exactly the same sensors and behaviors, but used a different action selection strategy: At each time step we disregard activation spreading for action selection and take into account only the executability of each module. This amounts to a pure reactive agent using fuzzy sensors in which the most highly likely to execute modules have priority for execution.

Now that we do not have activation we are faced frequently with situations in which two modules have the same execution-value. Let us consider for instance *FinalizeWithHammer* and *ShootEnemy*. When we have *EnemyNear*=1.0 we necessarily will have *EnemyInSight*=1.0. So, both will have identical execution-values. As these behaviors use the same resources and there are resources for just one of them to execute, we need to hard code some priority rules or insert additional conditions to decide which one to launch when appropriate. We have opted for the first approach in most cases, to differ as little as possible from the original behavior network.

Behavior *Dodge* has priority over *GoToEnemy*, behavior *GoToReachableMedkit* has priority over both *GoToMedkitInSight* and *GoToKnownMedkit*, and behavior

GoToMedkitInSight has priority over behavior *GoToKnownMedkit*. We incorporate one subtle but important rule: *FinalizeWithHammer* gets priority over *ShootEnemy*. This is needed because whenever *EnemyNear* is true *EnemyInSight* is also necessarily true, and we want the robot to hammer if the enemy is near. We changed module *Explore* to have the condition *Not IAmBeingShot*, both in the behavior network agent and in the plain reactive agent.

To overcome the low number of killings we implemented also a chasing behavior (identical) in both agents. Table 2 summarizes our results for 10 games of 30 seconds each.

Table 2. DeathMatch Results of EBN_Bot against a Reactive Agent

#	EBNBot Hit	EBNBot Kill	ReactiveBot Hit	ReactiveBot Kill	Difference (EBN-Reactive)
1	0.7	0	0.9	1	-1.2
2	0.1	1	0.1	0	1.0
3	0.3	1	0.2	0	1.1
4	0.2	0	0.3	1	-1.2
5	0.9	1	0.3	0	1.6
6	0.4	1	0.1	0	1.4
7	0.0	0	0.1	0	-0.1
8	0.7	1	0.9	0	0.8
9	0.6	0	0.6	1	-1.3
10	0.2	1	0.3	0	0.9
Mean	0.44	0.6	0.34	0.3	0.3

7 Discussion and Conclusion

We have seen that the extended behavior network was a good action selection mechanism for a complex game agent with complex goals and actions situated in a dynamic continuous environment.

We verified the properties of a good enough action selection mechanism in the 3D action game domain, namely, persistence, exploitation of opportunities, preference for actions that satisfy multiple goals, proper resolution of conflicts, performing of actions in sequences to achieve goals and sensible selection of concurrent actions.

When compared to another robot built around finite-state machines that used different sensors and behaviors but the same low-level commands, our robot performed very well.

To further validate the mechanism we measured the performance of our agent to an agent that was identical to it except for the action selection mechanism employed. This agent was totally reactive, with some priority rules to enhance its performance added. Again, our robot had significantly bigger overall scores. One interesting point is that our robot had 100% more killings but just a little over 30% more hits. This is due to the quality of its action chains. It stopped to heal itself when very hurt and dodged bullets when taking many consecutive shots. Another point that catches attention is that the mean difference in total score was much smaller in the experiment against the agent with identical sensors and behaviors. It confirms that the quality of sensors and behaviors were in great part responsible for the superior performance of our agent against CMU_JBot.

The superior performance of the robot using extended behavior networks in both experiments makes the case for extended behavior networks as a good and competitive solution to action selection for game agents. The assessment of the quality of the actions selected in section five contributes to validate extended behavior networks as an action selection mechanism for complex agents with many goals situated in complex, dynamic and continuous environments.

Our next steps are investigating ways to make the network automatically adapt its global parameters to maximize the fulfillment of its goals and make the agent adjust the expectations of the effects of the behaviors according to its experience.

References

1. Dorer, K. Extended Behavior Networks for Behavior Selection in Dynamic and Continuous Domains. In: Proceedings of the ECAI workshop Agents in dynamic domains, U. Visser, et al. (Hrsg.) Valenzia, Spanien, (2004).
2. Maes, P. How to do The Right Thing Connection Science Journal, Vol. 1, No. 3., (1989).
3. Tyrrell, Toby. An Evaluation of Maes Bottom-up mechanism for behavior selection. In Journal of Adaptive Behavior 2 (4).(1994). 307- 348.
4. Rhodes, Bradley. PHISH-Nets: Planning Heuristically in Situated Hybrid Networks . MSc Thesis. MIT. (1996).
5. Dorer, K. Extended Behavior Networks for the Magma Freiburg Team. In RoboCup-99 Team Descriptions for the Simulation League. Linkoping University Press, (1999a). 79-83.
6. Nebel, B. and Babovich,Y. Goal-Converging Behavior Networks and Self-Solving Planning Domains, or: How to Become a Successful Soccer Player. s.l. IJCAI03. (2003).
7. Tyrrell, Toby. Computational Mechanisms for Action Selection. PhD Thesis. University of Edinburgh.1993.
8. Müller,K. RoboterFussball: Multiagentensystem CS Freiburg, Diplomarbeit. Univ. Freiburg. Germany. Feb. (2001).
9. Brooks, R. A Robust Layered Control System for a Mobile Robot. IEEE Journal of Robotics and Automation. Volume RA-2, Number 1. (1986).
10. Unreal Tournament http://www.unrealtournament.com 28/03/2005
11. Kaminka, G. et al. GameBots: A Flexible Test Bed for Multiagent Team Research. Communications of the ACM Vol. 45, Issue 1. (2002). 43-45.
12. Javabots http://utbot.sourceforge.net/ 28/03/2005.

Air Pollution Assessment Through a Multiagent-Based Traffic Simulation*

Jesús Héctor Domínguez, Luis Marcelo Fernández, José Luis Aguirre, Leonardo Garrido, and Ramón Brena

Center for Intelligent Systems, Tecnológico de Monterrey,
Campus Monterrey, Monterrey, México
{A00779374, A00789695, jlaguirre,
leonardo.garrido, ramon.brena}@itesm.mx

Abstract. The present document explores how air pollution can be assessed from a multiagent point of view. In order to do so, a traffic system was simulated using agents as a way to measure if air pollution levels go down when the traffic lights employ a multigent cooperative system that negotiates the green light duration of each traffic light, in order to minimize the time a car has to wait to be served in an intersection. The findings after running some experiments where lanes of each direction are congested incrementally showed, that using this technique, there is a significant decrease in air pollution over the simulated area which means that traffic lights controlled by the multiagent system do improve the levels of air pollution.

1 Introduction

The control of vehicle traffic in big cities is an important problem in modern life. Aiming at finding a solution to this problem, several computer-based applications have been developed being traffic simulators the most common ones. A traffic simulator has the purpose of modeling, in a virtual environment, the conditions of traffic in a city so that, from the behaviours observed in the simulation, decisions can be made in order to generate better conditions for the involved entities [7].

In the last years an increasing number of simulators based on agents have been proposed. Unlike the conventional simulators where the modeling of the system is done at a macro level, in the simulators based on agents the modeling is performed at a micro level. This means that the system is made of several entities (agents) and, for each one, it is possible to define specific behaviours that indicate how those entities will respond to the events that happen in the environment in which they are immersed [1]. The behaviour of the system is not defined beforehand, but it comes out (i.e. it emerges) from the interactions among the agents of the system.

An important part of a vehicle traffic system is the operation of the traffic lights. Traditionally, each traffic light is assigned static periods of time, in which

---

* This research has been supported in part by the ITESM Research Chair CAT-011.

the lights of different colors (red, green and yellow) are turned on. An intelligent system should, however, handle those periods of time based on the present conditions of the traffic. Consequently, it is feasible to think that the vehicles' waiting time could be reduced if such traffic lights are handled intelligently. As a result of this, some other aspects, like for example air pollution levels, could be reduced.

Due to the increasing interest in mantaining good air quality in big cities [9] and the apparent relation between the vehicles' waiting time and air pollution levels, this work shows how air pollution levels diminish when the time assigned to a traffic light, when in green, is the outcome of a negotiation process that tries to diminish the vehicles' waiting time. The proposed system follows a multiagent approach aiming at reducing pollution levels.

The structure of the document is the following: Section 2 comments about some related works. Section 3 describes the multiagent system and the simulator used. Section 4 shows the conducted experiments along with the obtained results. Finally, in section 5, the conclusions and future work are mentioned.

2 Related Works

Eissfeldt et. al. [2] used a model (called Q-model) to measure air pollution levels generated in a traffic simulation. The links in the network of the simulated area were represented by priorities and output queues, each characterized by their maximum flow (capacity), length and maximal velocity allowed. The approach is not explicitly based on agents, but allows the vehicles to have individual characteristics like route destination. The work focusses on the measurement of air pollution and not in pollution reduction strategies.

Gualtieri et al. [4] presented a system that uses simulation as a way to forecast air quality on an urban area. The system uses a series of mathematical models as the basis for traffic, gas emission and gas dispersion simulation. All the models are integrated in a Geographic Information System (GIS) that allows the description of the urban areas, road networks, and pollutants distributions in the atmosphere. The work also focusses on the measurement of air pollution but from a macrolevel perspective.

France et. al. [3] presented a multiagent system for optimizing urban traffic not only in one intersection but in several. They use an interesting hierarchical organization of agents, ranging from agents that control the light patterns in one intersection to agents that coordinate groups of intersections. The work is interesting because it could be a basis for studying reductions in air pollution when there is more than one intersection. Unfortunately, they model the cars as a quantity (traffic flow) difficulting the simulation of different gas emission factors per car, which is a more realistic situation.

The work presented here is distinguished from the previous ones in that it is not only focussed in the measurement of air pollution but also on how air pollution could be reduced. Besides, each vehicle is modelled as an agent, allowing to associate individual characteristics to each one, like for example, the emission factor of the vehicles.

3 Proposed Solution

Based on the assumption that a reduction in waiting time produces a reduction on air pollution levels, our solution extends the ideas from the work of [5]. On that paper, a cooperative multiagent system was proposed for the traffic light control on an intersection in order to reduce the waiting time of a vehicle. We first describe briefly the simulator and the cooperative system used on that work, and then the extensions that are being proposed to assess gas emission.

3.1 Reducing Waiting Time

Simulator. In [5] a traffic simulator built on the synchronous engine of the MadKit Multiagent platform [6] is presented. It represents a world of a $n \times m$ grid. In this world appears an intersection of various lanes in every direction (North, East, South, West). The behaviour of cars and traffic lights is simulated not under typical units (i.e. meters, seconds) but rather as environment states (i.e. execution cycle, position on the grid). The agents of the simulator are:

Car: It is purely reactive. It has a limited "vision" that can detect in its forward direction other cars and the states of lights. It can stop, decelerate, accelerate and turn direction.
Traffic Light: This agent has several internal states that represent the green and red traffic light colors.
LightSet: Every traffic light agent belongs to a single traffic LightSet. This set is in charge of changing the state of its aggregated traffic lights. It has start and finish service times, which represent the times when the traffic lights are going to be on green state.
Traffic Manager: This agent is in charge of coordinating the different traffic LightSets in the simulation.
Source: This agent spawns cars with a predefined probability λ into the position where the agent is placed. If that position is occupied by any other vehicle, the car will not be spawned.

Cooperative system. In order to diminish the time a car has to wait to be served, they proposed a cooperative multiagent system that works in the following abstract way:

1. The LightSet checks for the worst case of congestion (i. e. the Light Agent who has the highest arrival rate of vehicles) among its aggregated lights. Then, it calculates the actual utilization rate. If this rate is greater than a "tolerance utilization rate" then it sends an *open_proposal* message to neighbor LightSets, asking them for time that they may not need. It also creates a cooperative group called *coop_group*, for which it is the manager and has the role of *leader*.
2. When the other LightSets receive the call for proposals, they subscribe to *coop_group* with the role of *providers*. They propose a time quota ($\Delta\tau$) to the *leader* in function of their actual utilization state. The proposal is send through a *reply_proposal* message.

3. The *leader* keeps track of the proposals, then it determines which of the proposals is the best once a Light cycle T has passed (The Light cycle is the sum of the service time of all the LightSets). After that, it announces to the group who was the *winner*, it increases its service time by an amount of $\Delta\tau$ and it closes the group.
4. The *winner* decreases its service time by $\Delta\tau$.

3.2 Reducing Gas Emission

Extended simulator. The following additions where made to the simulator:

1. Every Car agent can now emit a constant quantity of CO (Carbon monoxide) gas in each execution step (i.e. the emission factor). This constant quantity is assigned to the Car Agent by the Source Agent at the moment of creation of the Car. Every emission factor has the same probability of being assigned to a new Car Agent. Every Car Agent can have a different emission factor.
2. A gas emission variable is present in each cell of the entire grid. When a Car Agent emits its gas quantity, this quantity is summed over the quantity that is already present in the cell where the Car Agent is located. The emission variable is initialized with the zero value when the simulation starts.
3. The gas emission variable diffuminates over adjacent cells at a constant rate. It also evaporates at a constant rate.
4. A Gas Observer Agent is able to measure the value of the gas emission variable in each cell. Thus, it can compute the total value of the CO emission per execution cycle. It also computes the CO emission average until that moment. This agent graphs and writes to a file, both the absolute value at a particular moment and the average value until that particular moment of the total CO emission variable.

Extended cooperative system. The cooperative system presented in the last section only works when there is only one direction congested (i.e. the cooperative system is triggered only by one LightSet Agent); the reason of this is that whenever more than one direction is starting to congest, each LightSet Agent in charge of the congested direction starts a *concurrent* cooperative group as the algorithm dictates; when this occurs, due to the concurrent execution of the agents, some rare situations can happen.

Let's suppose the situation represented in figure 1. In this situation, there are four LightSet Agents engaged in two concurrent cooperative groups. In the first group, the *leader* is A. In the second group, the *leader* is B. The circle represents the Light cycle T and it must be read counterclockwise starting from A. The start time and finish time (i.e. this interval defines the service time of the LightSet) are represented as a triangle and a square respectively for each LightSet Agent. Let's suppose that A emits the *open_proposal* message. Only C answers with the *reply_proposal* message offering to A the time marked with the dotted arrow. Inmediately after that, B emits the *open_proposal* message. Again, C answers with the *reply_proposal* message offering to B the time marked with the dotted arrow. Then, A announces to its group that C is the *winner* and closes its cooperative group. C adjust its finish time as indicated with the dotted arrow. A adjust its start time in the same quantity. The service time of B is moved to the left accordingly. But, after that, B announces to its group that C is the *winner* and closes its cooperative group. C adjust its finish time in the same quantity as the first time, but in this situation, its start time will be *after* its finish time. B adjust its start time accordingly. The result is that C will mantain its green light at the same moment when D, A and B reach their green state.

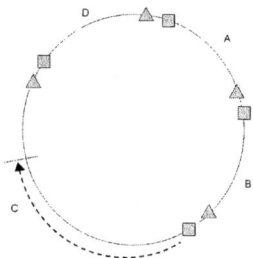

Fig. 1. Two concurrent cooperating groups using the original cooperative system that reach an akward result: at most two LightSet Agents will be in green state at the same time

As we can see, the problem arises from the fact that the Light cycle T is a *shared resource*. Then, we need some kind of monitor that ensures that the resource is being accessed by only one cooperative group at a time. Instead of blocking and activating cooperative groups, we use the simple mechanism of a *negotiation token*. A LightSet Agent can only start a cooperative group if he has the negotiation token.

So, the extensions to the cooperating system are as follow:

- The LightManager Agent is also in charge of passing the negotiation token to every LightSet Agent of the intersection. The LightManager Agent assigns the token sequentially to the LightSet Agents. When the negotiation token has passed over all LightSet Agents, the LightManager will start assigning it again.
- A LightSet Agent can only start a cooperative group if it has the negotiation token. Once the LightSet Agent closes its cooperative group, it announces to the LightManager to pass on the token.
- If a LightSet Agent recieves the token, and it doesn't need to start a cooperative group (i.e. its actual utilization rate is less than its critical utilization rate) it announces to the LightManager to pass on the token.

There will never be more than one cooperating group working at the same time. Each LightSet Agent is going to have at least one opportunity to start a cooperative group.

4 Experimentation

4.1 Simulation Environment

The objective of the experiments is to compare the total CO emission when the Light Agents at the intersection use the extended cooperative system (negotiation policy) with respect to the situation where the Light Agents use a constant time green duration (no negotiation policy). We want to know if using the negotiation policy produces a significant decrease in total CO emission.

The experiments were run over the following environment:

- A grid of 135 × 135 cells.
- One intersection consisting of 2 lanes in each direction (i.e. North, South, East, West).
- One Light Agent per lane; so there are 2 Light Agents in each LightSet.
- One Source Agent at the start of each lane. (For example, the two lanes headed to North have their two Source Agents at the South side of the lanes).
- Each Source Agent belonging to the same direction has the same spawn probability.
- Table 1 shows the CO emission factors used for the vehicles. These emission factors are based on a vehicular park study made by Rogers [8] in Monterrey city, 2003. The units are interpreted qualitatively (i.e. one minute is equivalent to one execution step in the simulator). This allowed us to use a simple real variable that represents the grams of CO emitted by the vehicles.
- The diffussion factor of the CO emission variable is set to 0.5 (or 0.5 grams per execution step). The evaporation factor of the same variable is set to 0.005 (or 0.005 grams per execution step).
- The initial green time of each LightSet is of 10 execution steps, with 2 execution steps between a change in LightSets. This initial green time defines the constant time green duration in the no negotiation policy.
- There is only one LightSet in green time at the corresponding moment, this is because the cars are able to turn right, left or go straight at the intersection.

Table 1. Average CO emission factors for some vehicle trademarks in Monterrey City. Units are: gr/(vehicle × min).

Particular vehicles				
Ford	GM	Chrysler	Dodge	Chevrolet
0.7148	0.696262	0.711	0.54931	0.51

Taxis					
Chevrolet	Volkswagen	Nissan	Ford	Chrysler	Dodge
2.4392	2.7532	2.47834	2.65486	3.20426	2.038581

4.2 Experimental Results

Using each policy, we started congesting incrementally one direction at a time: North, West, South and East. By congesting a direction we mean setting the same value to the spawn probability p_s of the Source Agents at the given direction in order to full completely all the lanes of that direction with cars (before the intersection) when the no negotiation policy is used. Experimenting with different values of λ, we found that a suitable value for congesting all the lanes of a direction is $\lambda = 0.2 = \lambda_c$ and a suitable value for maintaining a direction with a minimum quantity of vehicles is $\lambda = 0.01 = \lambda_m$.

The absolute value of the total CO emission (simulated grams) with respect to execution steps (simulated minutes) is shown in Figures 2(a), 3(a), 4(a) and 5(a). The average CO emission with respect to execution steps is shown in Figures 2(b), 3(b), 4(b) and 5(b). Each congested direction has a spawn probability of λ_c, the other directions are left free with a spawn probability of λ_m.

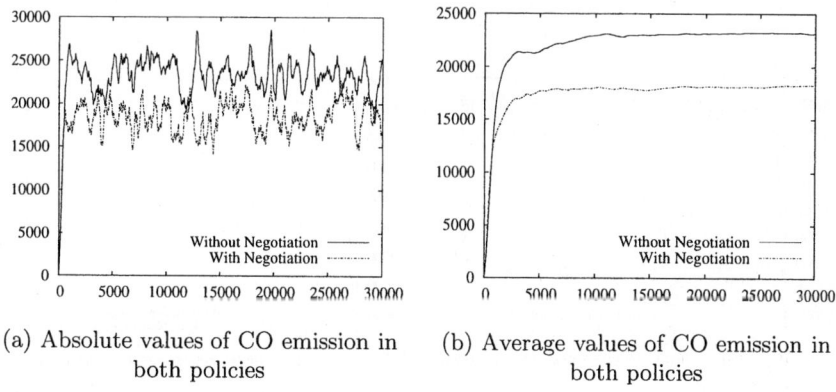

(a) Absolute values of CO emission in both policies

(b) Average values of CO emission in both policies

Fig. 2. Results for one congested direction. The congested direction was North.

The graphs show that after a considerable number of execution cycles the system tends to stabilize over the average value. We took the average value at the end of each experiment as an indicator of the air pollution level the system achieved. Then, the results for each experiment are summarized in table 2. From this, we can calculate the percentages of reduction in CO emission that the negotiation policy was able to achieve with respect to the no-negotiation policy: For one congested direction 20.95%, for two congested directions 14.71%, for three congested directions 5.12% and all directions congested 1.21%.

As we can see the extended cooperative system has the highest CO reduction when there is only one congested direction. The amount of this reduction decreases if we add more congested directions; the improvement is almost nothing when all the directions are congested. The reason for this is that when more LightSet Agents are making petitions for more time, there are less LightSet

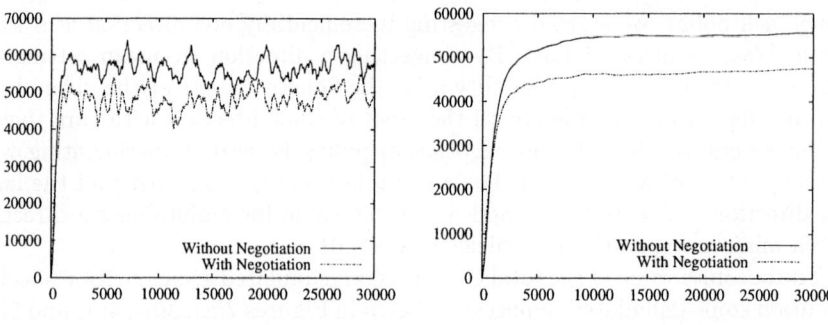

(a) Absolute values of CO emission in both policies

(b) Average values of CO emission in both policies

Fig. 3. Results for two congested directions. The congested directions were North and West.

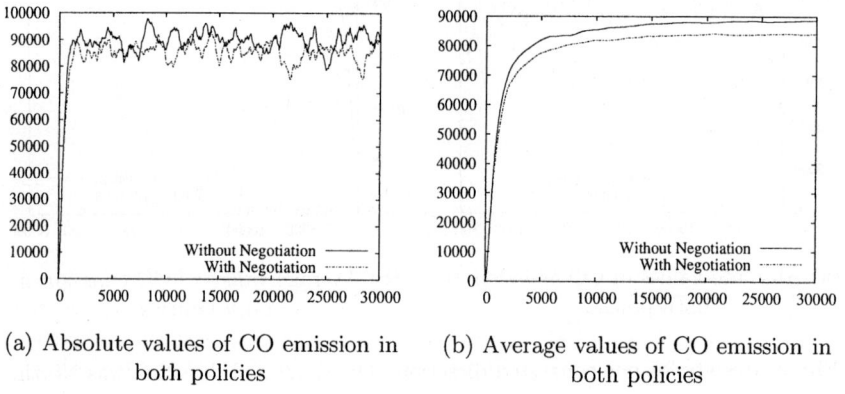

(a) Absolute values of CO emission in both policies

(b) Average values of CO emission in both policies

Fig. 4. Results for three congested directions. The congested directions were North, West and South.

Table 2. Average values of the CO emission in each congestion experiment with respect to each policy. The value was taken at the 30,000 execution step in all the experiments.

Congestion experiment	Final average CO pollution level	
	Negotiation policy	No negotiation policy
One direction	18,301 gr	23,150 gr
Two directions	47,510 gr	55,704 gr
Three directions	84,180 gr	88,725 gr
Four directions	108,500 gr	109,820 gr

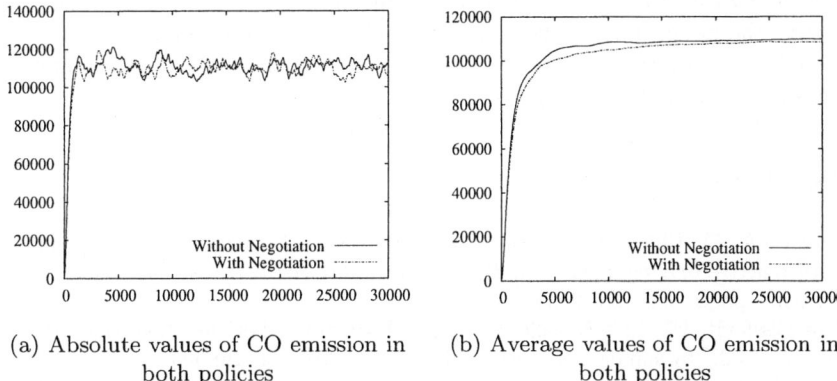

(a) Absolute values of CO emission in both policies

(b) Average values of CO emission in both policies

Fig. 5. Results when all directions are congested

Agents who can make offers. The situation becomes extreme when all the directions are congested: No LightSet Agent wants to give away green time, so it only asks for more time.

5 Conclusions and Future Work

This work presented some extensions to a multiagent cooperative system that handles vehicles' waiting time on an intersection through a negotiation process between traffic lights. The extensions allow to handle more than one congested direction using a negotiation policy among the agents that represent traffic lights; they also allow to measure vehicle CO emissions in order to assess air pollution levels. The experimental results, using the extended cooperative system, showed that attempts in reducing waiting time of vehicles in an intersection do improve the air quality in the area. The extended cooperative system has the advantage of its simplicity and modular design that permits it to be easily augmented.

More experiments can be done using another assignment policy in the negotiation process. For example, the LightManager Agent, responsible of assigning a *negotiation token* to the LightSet agents could use other assignment policies, instead of the sequential one used in this work, in order to improve the probability of a LightSet Agent to recieve time offers from other LightSet agents when it needs to start a cooperative group. So, the LightManager Agent needs to have some kind of feedback from the LightSet Agents and to be able to predict based on its probabilities model.

Also, experiments can be conducted with different values for the diffusion and evaporation factors of the CO emission variable to see their influence in the air pollution levels. Other emission gases will be incorporated in the simulator to see if the overall behaviour stays the same but with different reduction percentages for each gas. The initial green duration of the Light Agents could also be changed to explore if it produces different reduction percentages. Finally, in order to experiment with global reduction in air pollution levels, more intersections can be added to the environment where all intersections coordinate among themselves (i.e. global negotiation), or they can have their own independent cooperative system (i.e. local negotiation).

References

1. Patrick A. M. Ehlert and Leon J. M. Rothkrantz. Microscopic traffic simulation with reactive driving agents. In *Proceedings. 2001 IEEE Intelligent Transportation Systems*, pages 860–865, 2001.
2. Nils Eissfeldt, Florence-Natalie Sentuc, and Martin Luberichs. Investigating emissions of traffic by simulation. Technical report, Center for Applied Computer Science (ZAIK), April 2001.
3. John France and Ali A. Ghorbani. A multiagent system for optimizing urban traffic. In *Proceedings of the IEEE/WIC International Conference on Intelligent Agent Technology, IAT 2003*, pages 411 – 414, 2003.
4. G. Gualtieri and M. Tartaglia. Predicting urban traffic air pollution: A GIS framework. *Transportation Research Part D: Transport and Environment*, 3:329–336, 1998.
5. Francisco Guzmán and Leonardo Garrido. Towards traffic light control through a cooperative multiagent system: A simulation-based study. In *Proceedings of the 2005 Agent-Directed Simulation Symposium (ADS'05) at the 2005 Spring Simulation Multiconference (SpringSim'05)*, 2005.
6. The MadKit project. Web site. http://www.madkit.org.
7. Praveen Paruchuri, Alok Reddy Pullalarevu, and Kamalakar Karlapalem. Multi agent simulation of unorganized traffic. In *Proceedings of the first international joint conference on Autonomous agents and multiagent systems: part 1*, pages 176–183. ACM Press, 2002.
8. Tatiana Quesada Rogers. Comparación de desempeño ambiental del sector transporte en Nuevo León, a través de indicadores ambientales y energéticos. Master's thesis, Instituto Tecnológico y de Estudios Superiores de Monterrey - Campus Monterrey, 2003.
9. Matthias Schmidt and Ralf-Peter Schäfer. An integrated simulation system for traffic induced air pollution. *Environmental Modelling and Software*, 13:295–303, 1998.

A Noise-Driven Paradigm for Solving the Stereo Correspondence Problem

Patrice Delmas, Georgy Gimel'farb, Jiang Liu, and John Morris

Department of Computer Science, The University of Auckland,
Private Bag 92019, Auckland

Abstract. The conventional technique for scene reconstruction from stereo image pairs searches for the best single surface fitting identified correspondences between the the two images. Constraints on surface continuity, smoothness, and visibility (occlusions) are incorporated into a 'cost' - usually an *ad hoc* linear combination of signal similarity criteria, with empirically selected coefficients. An unsatisfactory feature of this approach is that matching accuracy is very sensitive to correct choice of these coefficients. Also, few real scenes have only one surface, so that the single surface assumption contributes to matching errors.

We propose a noise-driven paradigm for stereo matching that does not couple the matching process with choice of surfaces by imposing constraints in the matching step. We call our strategy 'Concurrent Stereo Matching' because the first step involves a high degree of parallelism (making real-time implementations possible using configurable hardware): rather than search for 'best' matches, it first identifies all 3D volumes that match within a criteria based on noise in the image. Starting in the foreground, these volumes are then examined and surfaces are selected which exhibit high signal similarity in both images. Local constraints on continuity and visibility - rather than global ones - are used to select surfaces from the candidates identified in the first step.

1 Introduction

The literature on 3D reconstruction from stereo images is extensive and dozens of strategies have been proposed [1, 2]. Invariably, a critical step is determining which points in the left and right images correspond to each other. In typical real scenes, the same pair of images could be produced by many different collections of surfaces in the scene. Formally, the correspondence problem may be characterized as ill-posed. Homogeneous textures (i.e. regions containing uniform or repetitive patterns), partial occlusions and optical signal distortions all contribute to this. Occlusions result in image areas in one image with no corresponding areas in the other image, texture homogeneity produces multiple equivalent matches and signal distortions lead to false matches. It is usual to apply constraints based on geometric properties of the features, geometric continuity and ordering of matching points[17]. Techniques for automated stereo matching has evolved from simple feature or gradient descent based algorithms (e.g. [4, 5]) to complex ones involving dynamic programming [6, 7, 8], belief propagation [9], or graph minimum-cut techniques [10, 11, 12]. However, with few exceptions, they share a common paradigm - search for a single surface yielding the best correspondence between images using constraints on surface continuity, smoothness, and visibility (or partial occlusions). These constraints are combined into a cost function - an *ad hoc* linear combination of signal similarity, surface smoothness and surface visibility criteria. With no formal theory to guide us, the coefficients used in these functions have been empirically chosen and - not surprisingly - reconstruction accuracy is very sensitive to the actual values chosen [13]. Furthermore, the single surface assumption is not met by many real scenes and thus affects reconstruction accuracy.

Kutulakos and Seitz's recent 'space carving' paradigm searches a set of images and builds a minimal photo-consistent hull in which all spatial elements (voxels) result in acceptable matches in all images [14]. Humans are also known to take a similar 'global' approach to scene interpretation: we analyse a scene by 'strokes' - moving the focus of our eyes from low to high frequency regions and then from sharp points to smooth areas and vice versa [15]. This contrasts with traditional matching algorithms which scan images line-by-line. With this background, we propose here a new reconstruction paradigm which fuses advantages and reduces disadvantages of previous methods. We call this new paradigm 'concurrent stereo matching' (CSM). We show that typical stereo pairs contain *many* admissible matches and that noise causes *minimization* algorithms (which are searching for a 'best' match rather than considering all acceptable matches) to make many incorrect decisions. Thus, our paradigm separates matching from the following search for surfaces: it first considers *all* likely matching volumes instead of singleton best matches and exploits local surface constraints rather than global continuity ones. The major features of our concurrent matching are:

- We estimate the noise at every point in the image.
- Corresponding volumes are found by image-to-image matching at each fixed depth, or disparity value. This allows mutual photometric distortions of images to be taken into account.
- Reconstruction proceeds from foreground to background in order to account for occlusions. Corresponding background volumes are enlarged at the expense of occluded portions.
- An additional region growing and continuity criterion then selects most appropriate surfaces.

Section 2 discusses the ill-posed nature of binocular stereo using artificial scene profiles and slices of one real image pair (the "Tsukuba" set). Basic steps of the concurrent paradigm are considered in Section 3, in particular, matching images to find corresponding spatial volumes and fitting surfaces to those volumes. Note that this paper aims only to illustrate the main properties of the matching paradigm we are proposing: in particular, the way in which the spatially-dependent noise is determined could be substantially improved.

2 Stereo Matching: A Fundamentally Ill-Posed Problem

An example 'scene' - consisting of a small set of separated surfaces shown in Figure 1(a) - shows how easily ambiguous matching scenarios can be built and exemplifies stereo correspondence as an ill-posed problem. Figure 1(a) shows a section through a set of surfaces: the left and right image intensity profiles are shown on the vertical and horizontal axes also. Grey shaded areas in Figures 1(b) and (c) show matching regions. In Figure 1(b) a smoothness constraint has been applied resulting in an erroneous single surface. An extreme reconstruction (from the many possible) appears in Figure 1(c). Moreover, the corresponding (precisely matching) areas do not reflect the actual scene unless occlusions are taken into account. Without additional constraints, it is impossible to discriminate between possible solutions.

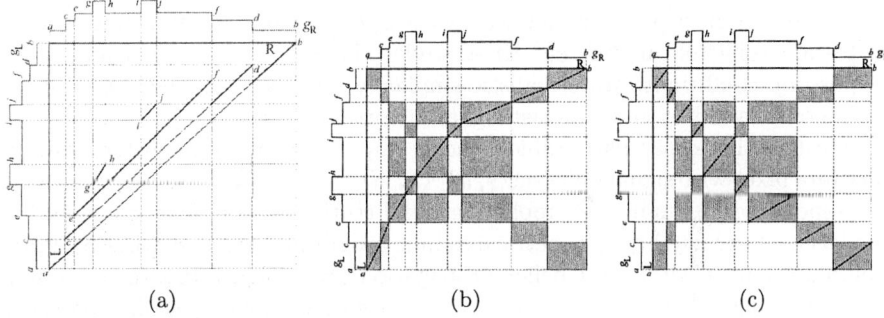

Fig. 1. Ambiguous reconstructions from a stereo pair: (a) actual surfaces, with corresponding left and right image intensity profiles shown along the vertical and horizontal axes - labels show correspondences between surfaces and segments of the images. Grey regions in (b) and (c) show possible matches. A reconstruction profile resulting from application of a smoothness constraint is shown by the dotted lines in (b). An extreme (but equally valid) profile is shown in (c).

Furthermore, even low level signal noise that is insufficient to mask major signal changes in Fig. 1 obstructs a conventional matching algorithm, because it will choose the maximum similarity between signals. Thus random noise will ensure that a random choice is made between the alternative matches (grey regions) shown in Fig. 1(b) and (c). A surface smoothness constraint might further abet a wrong choice by assigning some preference to a 'neighbour' of a wrongly matched region.

Knowing the characteristics of the image noise, a more realistic stereo matching goal is to specify an acceptable range of differences between corresponding signals. The noise model allows us to outline volumes containing all surfaces that match within this criterion. Note that we do not suppose a global noise model: we allow the noise to have spatially varying characteristics, i.e., it may be different in different regions of the image. This allows several types of radiometric and perspective distortions to be included in the 'noise' estimation. Only after delineation of the volumes is the desired surface or surfaces chosen using local surface constraints only.

Generally, stereo matching presumes that a model for signal similarity is available that accounts for changes in surface reflection with direction and for other sources of regular or random image distortions causing corresponding signals to present different intensities (grey values or colours). However, in practice, most stereo matching algorithms in computer vision, including the best-performing graph minimum-cut ones, use very simple similarity criteria such as the sum of absolute signal differences (SAD) or square differences (SSD) for all points in the common field of view of the two cameras - the 'binocularly visible' points. The signal model assumes that equal corresponding signals are distorted by an additive independent noise with the same zero-centred symmetric probability distribution. Whilst this simple model may be justified for a few stereo pairs typically used for testing algorithms, e.g., for the Middlebury data set [2], it is invalid in most practical applications, e.g. for aerial or ground stereo images of terrain collected at different times under changing illumination and image acquisition conditions. More realistic similarity models must take into account global or local offset and contrast signal distortions [6, 8].

For the "Tsukuba" pair, Table 1 shows empirical probability distributions of absolute pixel-wise signal differences, $\delta I(x,y,d) = |I_L(x,y) - I_R(x-d,y)|$, for the corresponding points in the supplied 'ground truth' and for three single-surface models reconstructed by symmetric dynamic programming stereo (SDPS), graph minimum cut (GMC), and belief propagation (BP) algorithms in a given x-disparity range $\Delta = [d_{\min} = 0, d_{\max} = 14]$. Effectively, this distribution shows the discrepancy in a real image pair from the simple signal model: sources for this 'noise' are:

1. signal-based (circuit noise, quantization, ...),
2. geometric (discrete pixel sensors, occlusions, perspective, ...) and
3. optical (non-uniform scattering, specular reflections, ...).

Table 1. Distribution of intensity differences for corresponding points in the "Tsukuba" scene: % of the corresponding points with the absolute intensity difference δI in the indicated range where x-disparities are derived from the ground truth (True) and the model reconstructed by SDPS, GMC and BP algorithms. The final column contains D, the sum of square distances between the distributions for the ground truth and the reconstructed models.

δI	0	1	2	3–	6–10	11–20	21–30	31–60	61–125	126–255	$D \times 10^{-4}$
True	18.5	29.6	19.5	19.1	6.6	3.7	1.4	1.2	0.4	0.0	
SDPS	20.9	30.9	18.1	17.9	6.7	3.7	1.2	0.6	0.0	0.0	8.5
GMC	17.2	25.3	15.5	17.3	8.9	6.9	3.3	2.2	1.4	0.0	60.9
BP	17.2	30.4	19.7	21.5	6.4	3.6	1.0	0.8	2.3	1.2	13.6

A Noise-Driven Paradigm for Solving the Stereo Correspondence Problem 311

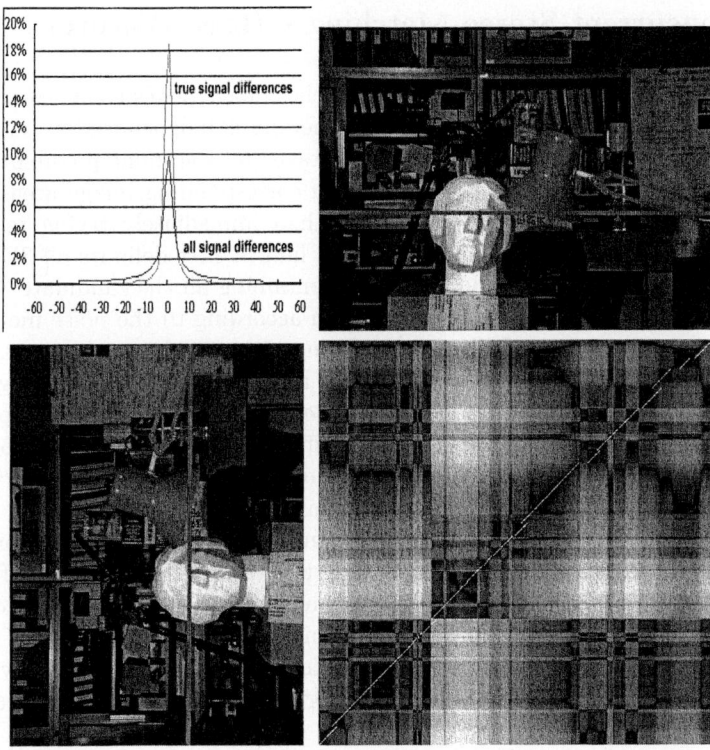

Fig. 2. "Tsukuba" stereo pair: (top left) frequency of occurence of signal differences, δI, for one pair of epipolar lines marked on the images ($y = 173$) (bottom right) grey-coded absolute signal differences, $|\delta I|$, for the whole image - black regions indicate 'perfect' matches, $\delta I = 0$. The large number of acceptable matches (dark regions) is clearly seen.

Fig. 2 (top left) plots these distributions and shows grey-coded signal correspondences for one epipolar line ($y = 173$) in terms of the pixel-wise absolute differences - black regions correspond to $\delta I = 0$. The multiplicity of possible matches is clearly seen[1]. The distribution obtained with the dynamic (SDPS) algorithm is closest to the true one. Hence, in these experiments, we used the pixel-wise absolute signal differences from SDPS as estimates of the spatially variant image noise. The overlaid true surface profiles show that in this example the single-surface approximation is close to the actual disjoint scene due to a small x-disparity range Δ.

---

[1] Scene assumptions enable the matching regions to be delimited. Assuming no 'out-of-image' matching eliminates the lower right triangle. Assuming a closest approach (or maximum disparity) eliminates much of the upper left. However, plenty of candidate matches remain!

3 Concurrent Stereo Matching – Basic Features

Concurrent stereo reconstruction first matches image pixels using a signal model to estimate random signal noise which generally is independent in both images and can be spatially variant. The model takes into account possible global or local contrast or offset deviations between corresponding image areas. In contrast to conventional paradigms, rather than immediately trying to find the single optical surface or its minimal visual hull, it first delimits all 3D volumes which are reconstruction candidates, i.e. containing all the candidate 3D points that ensure an admissible (or good) match according to the noise model[2]. The second step attempts to find surfaces fitting the candidate volumes using only smoothness and visibility constraints that rank the surfaces according to their appropriateness *for human visual perception*. The fundamentally ill-posed nature of the problem makes discovering the true surface an unrealistic goal. Thus, we set a more practical goal - to select from possible candidates a surface that closely resembles the choice that a human observer would make. In the final stage, one or more surfaces are selected and possible partial occlusions of the chosen surfaces are analyzed. In particular, this could be done by stratifying surfaces into foreground versus background and refining the occluded background after eliminating the foregrounds. By retaining all likely solutions for a given set of images, the imposition of constraints which are not always physically realistic is delayed until the final stage where they guide choices of possible solutions.

3.1 Admissible Point-Wise Correspondences

The artificial example in Fig. 1 presumes that corresponding volumes have zero matching error. If low-level noise is added to these signals, the pixel-wise correspondences for each disparity, d, have a zero-centred cluster of small signal differences that includes true matches and one or more distant clusters representing only mismatches. The noise distribution estimated from the central cluster allows us to recover the corresponding areas seen in Fig. 1.

Using the same simple model of signal distortions, natural cases such as the "Tsukuba" set (Fig. 2) produce continuous distributions of signal differences, cf. Fig. 2 (top left quadrant). Generally, the distribution of noise will be spatially variant and has to be locally estimated. For simplicity, the noise estimation process could focus on best matching scores under the same model. Table 1 shows that SDPS reconstruction along corresponding epipolar lines provides reasonably close estimates of the residual pixel-wise noise for the "Tsukuba" scene. Obviously, images with finer texture need more robust noise estimation models taking account of sub-pixel quantisation errors [16]. These noise estimates can be used to determine what is considered to be an admissible match.

As an example of the first step in our new paradigm, the middle sections of figures 3, 4 and 5 show d-slices of the candidate (x, y, d) volumes. Black points

---

[2] All good matches are equivalent with respect to the estimated noise range to within other admissible contrast / offset image deviations.

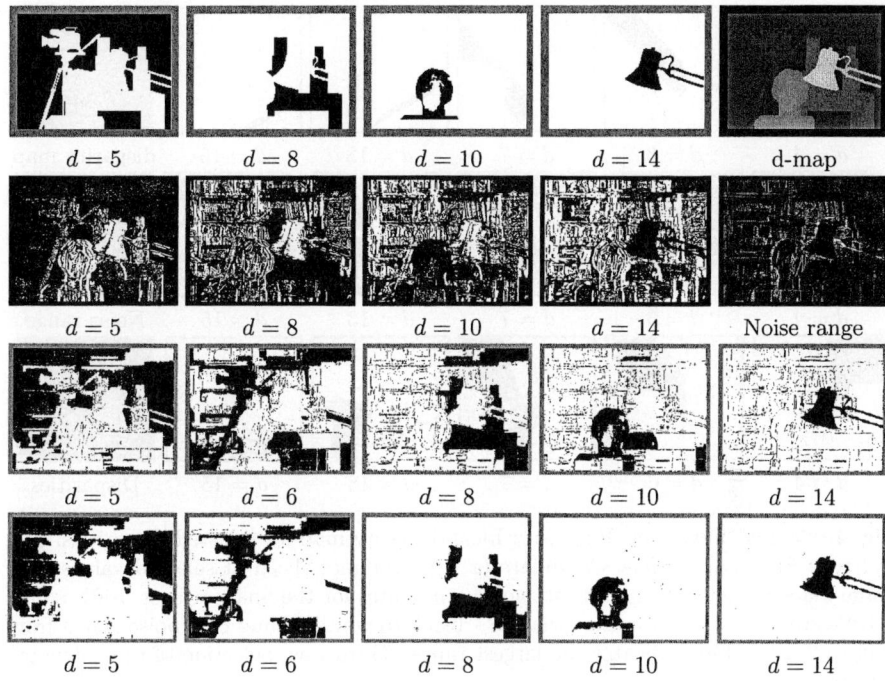

Fig. 3. "Tsukuba" image set: First row: Ideal disparity map for selected disparities. Second row: First four panels: Candidate (x,y,p) volumes sliced at selected values of d. Large black regions clearly indicate good candidates for the final surfaces. Fifth panel: SDPS-estimated spatial noise variation - black-to-white coding of a noise range from [0,0] to [0,27], with white indicating the largest range. Third row: Surface candidates. Fourth row: Selection of reconstructed surfaces which should be compared to ideal maps in the first row.

indicate candidates with signal differences within the estimated noise ranges for each (x,y)-position, i.e., acceptable matches.

3.2 Surfaces for the Corresponding Volumes

For each disparity level, likely matching pixels are merged into regions (or suppressed) using the mean shift algorithm on the left image. The steps are:

1. generate connected components based on region estimation,
2. estimate the ratio of likely matches in a connected cell versus the cell area for any given disparity slice,
3. further process the connected components borders by intra- and inter-region statistical analysis.

During the second step, each connected region is examined for good matching points at the current d value. If this proportion is above a threshhold (0.60 for the results shown), then the region is labelled a 'survivor' for this d value and the holes filled in. In the "Tsukuba" pair, only a small textureless region in

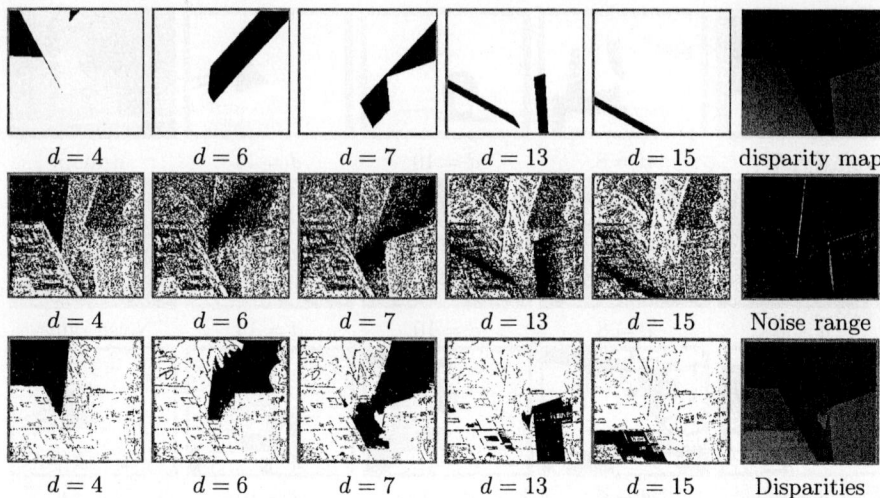

Fig. 4. "Venus" image set: First row: Ideal disparity map for selected disparities. Second row: First four panels: Candidate (x, y, p) volumes sliced at selected values of d. Large black regions clearly indicate good candidates for the final surfaces. Fifth panel: SDPS-estimated spatial noise variation - black-to-white coding of a noise range from [0,0] to [0,27], white indicates the largest range. Third row: Selection of reconstructed surfaces.

the background remained accepted after this criterion was applied. It should be noted that this threshhold is not an empirical parameter used to evaluate a cost function - as in typical 'best matching' techniques: it is a criterion established at the experiment design stage and is related to the parameters of the stereo camera configuration, including in particular, resolution in the imaging planes.

Alternative approaches based on assumptions that any detectable 'feature' must have a minimum projection (in pixels) in the image plane could be used to remove noisy outliers. Then, surfaces are sequentially fitted to each separate candidate volume working from foreground to background to within a known disparity range, Δ. In the "Tsukuba" scene, this implies that the large black region of the lamp in the $d = 14$ slice was first accepted and then propagated 'back' into the scene as occluded points. To rank surface variants in the corresponding volumes in accord with typical visual perception, we used a preference criterion based on the surface planarity, area, and its local expansion or shrinkage at the adjacent d-slices. Practically, every connected region is labelled from 1 to 6. For the slice at disparity d, the labels are:

1. regions that have no matches,
2. 'disappearing' regions with no match in the current slice that were part of connected regions in the previous slice,
3. regions 'shrinking' from slice $d-1$ to d,
4. regions or pixels 'appearing' in the current slice,

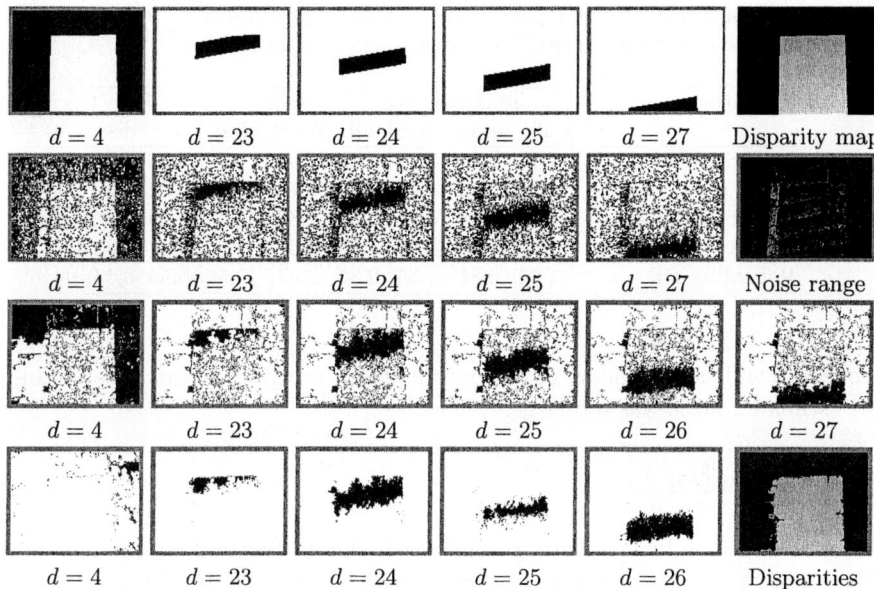

Fig. 5. "Map" image set: First row: Ideal disparity map for selected disparities. Second row: First four panels: Candidate (x, y, p) volumes sliced at selected values of d. Large black regions clearly indicate good candidates for the final surfaces. Fithh panel: SDPS-estimated spatial noise variation - black-to-white coding of a noise range from [0,0] to [0,27], white indicates the largest range. Third row: Surface Candidates. Fourth row: Selection of reconstructed surfaces.

5. identical connected regions in slice d and $d - 1$,
6. regions 'expanding' from slice $d - 1$ to slice d.

At a given disparity, region labels roughly express the likeliness of good matching and are related to the expansion or contraction of matching volumes in the $x - y - d$ space.

A selection of final volumes (represented by regions remaining at various d levels is shown in the lower row of Figs 3, 4 and 5. From Fig 2, it can be noted that our model produces very sharp, correct edges for most objects – evidenced by the very strong edges running through the signal differences plot in the lower right quadrant (in contrast to the 'fuzzy' edges of window-based correlation or 'slurred' edges of dynamic programming techniques).

In table 2, the performance of of our new algorithm is compared with the other algorithms ranked on the Middlebury dataset stereo algorithm evaluation [2] for algorithm and ground truth generation details). It can be seen that, with the exception of the "Map" set, the CSM algorithm produces very good results. The errors in the "Map" set are attributed to the original noise estimation step: the SDPS algorithm produced significant errors in the regions where there is a sharp jump in disparity. These errors translated into noise estimates for these regions that were too large. We expect that an improved noise estimation

Table 2. Comparison of CSM performance to some algorithms in the Middlebury stereo evaluation webpage (http://cat.middlebury.edu/stereo/)

Algorithm	Tsukuba			Venus			Map	
	all	untex.	disc.	all	untex.	disc.	all	disc.
MeanShiftSegm-CSM	1.15	0.80	1.86	1.18	1.04	1.48	3.08	7.34
Belief prop.	1.15	0.42	6.31	1.00	0.76	9.13	0.84	5.27
Region-Progress.	1.44	0.55	8.18	0.99	1.37	6.40	1.49	17.11
Graph cuts	1.94	1.09	9.49	1.79	2.61	6.91	0.31	3.88
Reliability-DP	1.36	0.81	7.35	2.35	2.37	13.50	0.55	6.14

procedure will remove many of the poor matches accepted in this case because the estimated noise was too large.

4 Conclusion

Analysis of stereo images with ground truth shows that each stereo pair produces a large number of equivalent (with respect to closest signal matching) solutions. Traditional stereo matching paradigms mix matching and the selection of visually most appropriate surfaces. We propose that reconstruction should be separated into two steps:

1. independent noise or signal error range estimation to outline the candidate spatial volumes which are equivalent from the standpoint of image matching and
2. selection of one or more surfaces to fit these volumes leading to more efficient stereo techniques.

This key idea in the new paradigm is the rejection of the 'best match' or minimization criterion almost universally applied to date in favour of a likely match criterion based on a local signal noise model. Our final reconstructed images exhibit excellent matching when compared to other reported algorithms – with one exception. We expect that, with an improved noise model - for example, one that could easily be derived from simple measurements with calibrated camera systems - the errors resulting from use of the SDPS generated disparity maps as noise estimators would be substantially reduced.

Finally, we observe that this new paradigm has a high level of inherent parallelism, making it well suited to efficient parallel hardware implementations permitting high resolution, accurate, real-time, 3D scene reconstruction.

References

1. D. Burschka, M. Z. Brown, and G. D. Hager, Advances in computational stereo, *IEEE Trans. PAMI*, Vol. 25, 2003, pp. 993–1008.
2. D. Scharstein and R. Szeliski, A taxonomy and evaluation of dense two-frame stereo correspondence algorithms, *Int. J. Computer Vision*, Vol. 47, 2002, pp. 7–42.

3. T. Poggio, V. Torre, and C. Koch, Computational vision and regularization theory, *Nature*, no. 317, 1985, pp. 314–319.
4. Y. C. Hsieh, D. M. Mckeown Jr, and F.P. Perlant, Performance evaluation of scene registration and stereo matching for cartographic feature extraction, *IEEE Trans. PAMI*, 1992, Vol. 14, pp. 214–238.
5. C. L. Zitnick and T. Kanade, A cooperative algorithm for stereo matching and occlusion detection, *IEEE Trans. PAMI*, 2000, Vol. 22, pp. 675–684.
6. H. H. Baker, Surfaces from mono and stereo images, *Photogrammetria*, Vol. 39, 1984, pp. 217–237.
7. Y. Ohta and T. Kanade, Stereo by intra- and inter-scanline search using dynamic programming, *IEEE Trans. PAMI*, 1985, Vol. 7, pp. 139–154.
8. G. L. Gimel'farb, Intensity-based computer binocular stereo vision: signal models and algorithms. *Int. J. Imaging Systems and Technology*, 1991, vol. 3, pp. 189–200.
9. J. Sun, N. N. Zheng, and H. Y. Dshum, Stereo matching using belief propagation, *IEEE Trans. PAMI*, Vol. 25, no. 7, 2003, pp. 787–800.
10. S. Roy, Stereo without epiploar lines: A maximum-flow formulation, *Int. J. Computer Vision*, Vol. 34, 1999, pp. 147–161.
11. Yu. Boykov, O. Veksler, and R. Zabih, Fast approximate energy minimization via graph cut, *IEEE Trans. PAMI*, Vol. 23, 2001, pp. 1222–1239.
12. J. Kim, V. Kolmogorov, and R. Zabih, Visual correspondence using energy minimization and mutual information, In: *Proc. 9th Int. Conf. Computer Vision (ICCV03), Nice, France, Oct. 2003*. IEEE Computer Society Press, 2003, pp. 1003–1010.
13. J. Liu and G. Gimel'farb, Accuracy of stereo reconstruction by minimum cut, symmetric dynamic programming, and correlation. In: *Proc. IVCNZ'04 Conf., Akaroa, New Zealand, 21-23 Nov. 2004*, pp. 65–70.
14. K. N. Kutulakos and S. M. Seitz, A theory of shape by space carving, *Int. J. Computer Vision*, Vol. 38, No. 3, 2000, pp. 199–218.
15. A. Torralba. Modeling global scene factors in attention, *J. Optical Society of America*, Vol. 20A, 2003, pp. 1407–1418.
16. S. Birchfield and C. Tomasi, A pixel dissimilarity measure that is insensitive to image sampling, *IEEE Trans. PAMI*, 1998, Vol. 20, pp. 401–406.
17. O. Faugeras, Three-Dimensional Computer Vision. A geometric Viewpoint. *MIT Press*, Cambridge, 1993.

Invariant Descriptions and Associative Processing Applied to Object Recognition Under Occlusions

Roberto Antonio Vázquez, Humberto Sossa, and Ricardo Barrón

Centro de Investigación en Computación – IPN,
Av. Juan de Dios Batíz, esquina con Miguel Otón de Mendizábal,
Ciudad de México, 07738, México
robertov@sagitario.cic.ipn.mx,
{hsossa, rbarron}@cic.ipn.mx

Abstract. Object recognition under occlusions is an important problem in computer vision, not yet completely solved. In this note we describe a simple but effective technique for the recognition objects under occlusions. The proposal uses the most distinctive parts of the objects for their further detection. During training, the proposal, first detects the distinctive parts of each object. For each of these parts an invariant description in terms of invariants features is next computed. With these invariant descriptions a specially designed set of associative memories (AMs) is trained. During object detection, the proposal, first looks for the important parts of the objects by means of the already trained AM. The proposal is tested with a bank of images of real objects and compared with other similar reported techniques.

1 Introduction

Object recognition is one of the most important problems in computer vision. The solution to this problem strongly determines the functionality of many systems, such as automatic robot guidance systems; object tracking systems; object manipulation systems; surveillance systems. In the last years, several proposals have emerged to provide a solution to this problem using invariant descriptions (refer for example to [1] and [2]) and other techniques. But, if an object is being partially occluded, the corresponding invariant description will be distorted or, in the worst case, unable to reflect the identity of the object. These systems need the development of robust recognition techniques that can handle a reasonable degree of occlusion among the objects. Several proposals have been designed to handle with partial occlusion recognition. Most of these proposals use distinctive local features of the object such as boundary information [3-7]. Despite the success achieved by these proposals, there are a number of crucial factors that limit their performance in practical applications. That is due to most of the techniques are computationally expensive requiring special hardware and high-speed processors.

In this paper we describe a simple but effective method for the recognition of objects under occlusions. Distinctive parts of objects are first detected. These parts are then described in terms of invariant features for further processing; this allows object recognition also under image transformations (translations, rotations, and so on). Object part descriptions are next used to train an associative memory (AM), the device chosen for object classification. During object detection, object parts are search for by means of swapping window connected to the AM. Each time a distinctive part of an object is detected a vote is given to that object telling that is object is present in the image. The proposal is tested with a specially designed bank of images. A first step in this direction was proposed in [13 and 14]. In [13] and [14] an AM for each object was trained. In this work an unique memory was trained for the whole set of objects. Also, the training operator was changed. In the section of experiments we will see that this new operator provides better recognition results.

The rest of the paper is organized as follows. In section 2, it is described how an object is represented for its learning and recognition. In section 3, we describe the classification tool used in this research. In section 4, we describe how the proposal is implemented, while in section 5, we present the experimental results obtained. In section 6, we finally conclude and give some directions for further research.

2 Description of an Object

For an object to be recognized in an image in the presence of occlusions we first detect its so-called *essential parts* (EP). An EP part is a part that allows to determine the presence of an object in an image. To detect an EP of an object, we get an image of the object with a background as homogeneous as possible. For an example refer to Figure 1. We then proceed as follows:

1. Manually, by means of a circular window we first select a region of the image enclosing a candidate EP the object,
2. Inside this window, we apply a standard threshold [8] to get a binary sub-image.
3. We apply to this binary circular image a connected component-labeling algorithm [9] to get all possible connected binary components.
4. We eliminate small spurious regions by means of a standard size filter [10].
5. We then compute well-known first four Hu descriptors invariant to translations and rotations, $\phi_i, i = 1,4$ to locally describe selected part. Just to remember, four Hu invariants are given as follows:

$$\phi_1 = \mu_{20} + \mu_{02}$$
$$\phi_2 = (\mu_{20} - \mu_{02})^2 + 4\mu_{11} \tag{1}$$

Fig. 1. Example of an image used to detect an essential part of an object

$$\phi_3 = (\mu_{30} - 3\mu_{12})^2 + (3\mu_{21} - \mu_{03})^2$$
$$\phi_4 = (\mu_{30} + \mu_{12})^2 + (\mu_{21} + \mu_{03})^2$$

where the μ_{ij} stand for the central moments invariants to translations. For the details refer to [1].

6. We apply steps 1 to 5 to other parts of the object.
7. We repeat this procedure (steps 1 to 6) to remaining objects.

Special attention has to be put in the selection of the set of describing parts. For example, from Figure 2, we might think that the head of the bolt and the hole of the washer could be two EPs that will allow differentiation between these two objects. However by comparing the describing features from both parts we have noticed that they could be very similar. To select an EP or a set of EPs by which we are going to perform object detection under occlusions, we have just taken from the list of pre-selected parts those that allow more discrimination with other objects. For this we have used their corresponding describing features.

Fig. 2. (a) Head of bolt selected as its essential part. (b) Whole of washer selected as it essential part

3 Basics on Associative Memories

An associative memory is a mathematical device specially designed to recall complete patterns from inputs paterns that might be altered with noise. An associative memory **M** can be viewed as an output-input system as follows: $\mathbf{x} \to \mathbf{M} \to \mathbf{y}$, with **x** and **y**, respectively the input and output patterns vectors. Each input vector forms an association with a corresponding output vector. An association beetwen input pattern **x** and output pattern **y** is denoted as $(\mathbf{x}, \mathbf{y})$ [11].

The structure of an associative memory for pattern classification is simply another way to see a neural network. In this work we use an extended associative memory useful to clasify real-valued patterns, by assigning them to the class by their index.

Let $\left(\mathbf{x}^\xi, i\right)_{\xi=1}^{p}, \mathbf{x}^\xi \in \Re^n, i = 1, m$ a set of p fundamental couples (SFC), composed by a pattern and its corresponding class-index. The problem is to build an operator $\mathbf{M}$, using this SFC, that allows to classify the patterns into their classes, i.e. $\mathbf{M}\mathbf{x}^\xi = i$ for $\xi = 1, p$ and that even in the presence of distortions it classifies them adequately, i.e. $\mathbf{M}\tilde{\mathbf{x}}^\xi = i$, where $\tilde{\mathbf{x}}^\xi$ is an altered version of $\mathbf{x}^\xi$, [12].

Matrix $\mathbf{M}$ is build in terms of a function ϕ as follows:

$$\mathbf{M} = \begin{bmatrix} \phi_1 \\ \vdots \\ \phi_m \end{bmatrix} \quad (2)$$

where each ϕ_i represents the i-th row of a matrix $\mathbf{M}$ and this function is a codification of all patterns belonging to the class i.

As specified in [12] function ϕ can take several forms. In this paper a new way to compute ϕ is proposed. Function ϕ is computing using so called "sep" operator, which allows us transform a set of relatively close ϕ_i's, into another set of more separated ϕ'_i's. This transformation, as we will next see, allows improving the associative memory's performance. In this paper, function ϕ is computed in four steps as follows:

1. Compute the maximum vector of each class:

$$\gamma_i^j = \bigvee_{\xi=1}^{p}\left(x_i^{\xi,j}\right) \quad (3)$$

2. Compute the minimum vector of each class:

$$\lambda_i^j = \bigwedge_{\xi=1}^{p}\left(x_i^{\xi,j}\right) \quad (4)$$

3. Compute the sigma vector of each class:

$$\Sigma_i^j = \gamma_i^j + \lambda_i^j \quad (5)$$

4. Finally, $\phi_i^j = \Sigma_i^{'j}$.

Pattern classification is as follows: Given a pattern $\mathbf{x} \in \Re^n$, not necessarily one of the already used to train matrix $\mathbf{M}$, class to which pattern $\mathbf{x}$ is assigned is found in two steps as:

1. First we compute the recalling vectors r_{lj} as:

$$r_{lj} = x_j + \gamma_i^j \quad (6)$$

2. Compute the index to which pattern should be associated as:

$$i = \arg_l \left[\bigwedge_{l=1}^{m} \bigvee_{j=1}^{n} |m_{ij} - r_{lj}| \right]. \tag{7}$$

4 Numerical Example

To better understand the idea of the proposal, let us look at the following numerical example.

Example 1. In a first step let us suppose we want to obtain corresponding matrix **M** from the following set of associations:

pattern	Class	pattern	class	pattern	class
(1.0, 1.0, 1.0)	1	(4.0, 4.0, 4.0)	2	(10.0, 9.0, 10.0)	3
(1.0, 2.0, 1.0)	1	(4.0, 4.0, 5.0)	2	(9.0, 9.0, 10.0)	3
(2.0, 1.0, 1.0)	1	(4.0, 5.0, 5.0)	2	(10.0, 10.0, 10.0)	3
(1.0, 1.0, 2.0)	1	(5.0, 4.0, 4.0)	2	(10.0, 11.0, 11.0)	3
(2.0, 2.0, 2.0)	1	(5.0, 4.0, 5.0)	2	(10.0, 9.0, 11.0)	3

The **max** computed from this set are: $\gamma_1 = (2,2,2)$, $\gamma_2 = (5,5,5)$ and $\gamma_3 = (10,11,11)$. In the same way, the **min** are $\lambda_1 = (1,1,1)$, $\lambda_2 = (4,4,4)$ and $\lambda_3 = (9,9,10)$. Thus $\Sigma_1 = (3,3,3)$, $\Sigma_2 = (9,9,9)$ and $\Sigma_3 = (19,20,21)$. Finally, $\phi_1 = (3.0,3.0,3.0)$, $\phi_2 = (9.0,9.0,9.0)$ and $\phi_3 = (19.0,20.0,21.0)$. Thus

$$\mathbf{M}_{sep} = \begin{bmatrix} 3.0 & 3.0 & 3.0 \\ 9.0 & 9.0 & 9.0 \\ 19.0 & 20.0 & 21.0 \end{bmatrix}.$$

Example 2. Let us now suppose we are given the following noisy version (9.3,10.5,11.5) of pattern (10.0,9.0,11.0) that we know it belongs to class 3. Verify that even in presence of noise, it is assigned to class 3.

Step 1: By applying equation (6), we have:

$$r_1 = [9.3+2 \quad 10.5+2 \quad 11.5+2] = [11.3 \quad 12.5 \quad 13.5],$$
$$r_2 = [9.3+5 \quad 10.5+5 \quad 11.5+5] = [14.3 \quad 15.5 \quad 16.5], \text{ and}$$
$$r_3 = [9.3+10 \quad 10.5+11 \quad 11.5+11] = [19.3 \quad 21.5 \quad 22.5].$$

Step 2:
Now, by applying equation (7), we have:

$l = 1: \max\left[|3.0-11.3|, |3.0-12.5|, |3.0-13.5|\right] = \max[8.3, 9.5, 10.5] = 10.5$

$l = 2: \max\left[|9.0-14.3|, |9.0-15.5|, |9.0-10.5|\right] = \max[5.3, 6.5, 7.5] = 7.5$

$l = 3: \max\left[|19.0-19.3|, |20.0-21.5|, |21-22.5|\right] = \max[0.3, 1.5, 1.5] = 1.5$

Thus

$$i = \arg_l\left[\bigwedge_{l=1}^{3}(10.5, 7.5, 1.5)\right] = \arg[1.5] = 3.$$

Thus pattern $(9.3, 10.5, 11.5)$ is assigned to class 3.

5 Implementation of the Technique

Once selected the essential feature of each object we would like to recognize, associative memory **M** is built as follows:

1. Obtain 20 images of each object in different positions and rotations.
2. To each sub-image containing the selected EP, compute the corresponding Hu's invariants as explained in section 2. Compute **max** and **min** vectors with the 20 samples as described in Section 3.
3. With these values, build corresponding associative memory as explained is Section 3.

Fig. 3. (a) Mask used to subtract form image the information to train associative memory. (b) Mask with blocked region.

In order to determine if an instance of an object is in an image we use so-called *blocking swapping* algorithm (BSA) [13 and 14]. This algorithm allows extracting information from an image to be used to operate the associative memory. Information is extracted by means of a mask **MA** with the same size as of original image; filled with circular windows of ratio of 15 pixels, see Figure 3 (a). To avoid analyzing several times the same region of the image, BSA uses a *blocking table* (BT). BT is used to decide if a window is used or not, for an example refer to Figure 3(b). BT allows blocking those regions in the image that have been selected as regions containing the distinctive part of an object.

Detection of the essential part of an object is performed in six steps as follows:

1. Clear blocking table **BT**.
2. Refresh mask **MA**.
3. Apply logical **and** operation between mask **MA** and image to be analyzed.
4. Compute first four Hu invariants to each region enclosed by circular window in the new image.
5. Apply associative memory to each obtained describing vector and if vector corresponds to essential part of one of the objects we are looking for, then give a vote for this object and block associated region in BT.
6. If whole image has been analyzed then stop algorithm, else go back to step 2.

With the aim to improve the performance of the technique, a ratio of acceptance was set. This means that an object will be assigned to a class i only if $\left[\bigwedge_{l=1}^{m} \bigvee_{j=1}^{n} \left| m_{lj} - r_{lj} \right| \right] < d_i$. For each object the acceptance ratio is chosen as:

$$d_i = \left| \frac{\phi_i}{2} - \gamma_i \right|. \qquad (8)$$

6 Experimental Results

In this section, the performance of the proposed technique is tested with images of realistic objects of varying complexity. The five objects whose images and essential parts used to test the effectiveness of the technique are shown in Figure 4.

6.1 Construction of the Memory

After applying the methodology described in section 4, for the five objects with four describing features we get:

$$\mathbf{M}_{sep} = \begin{bmatrix} 0.3599 & 0.0076 & 0.0014 & 0.0003 \\ 0.4242 & 0.0202 & 0.0006 & 0.0001 \\ 0.8884 & 0.1228 & 0.0419 & 0.0109 \\ 0.4935 & 0.0630 & 0.0027 & 0.0002 \\ 0.3847 & 0.0125 & 0.0019 & 9.7E-5 \end{bmatrix}$$

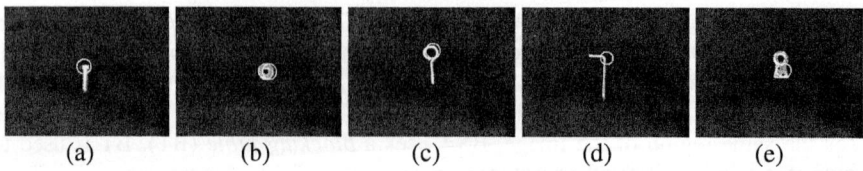

(a)　　　(b)　　　(c)　　　(d)　　　(e)

Fig. 4. The five objects used in the experiments and their essential parts. (a) A bolt. (b) A washer. (c) An eyebolt. (d) A hook. (e) A dovetail.

6.2 Results

A set of 100 images was used to test the efficiency of the proposed methodology. Some of the images of this set are shown in Figure 5. The test consisted on determining if a desired object appears or not on a given image.

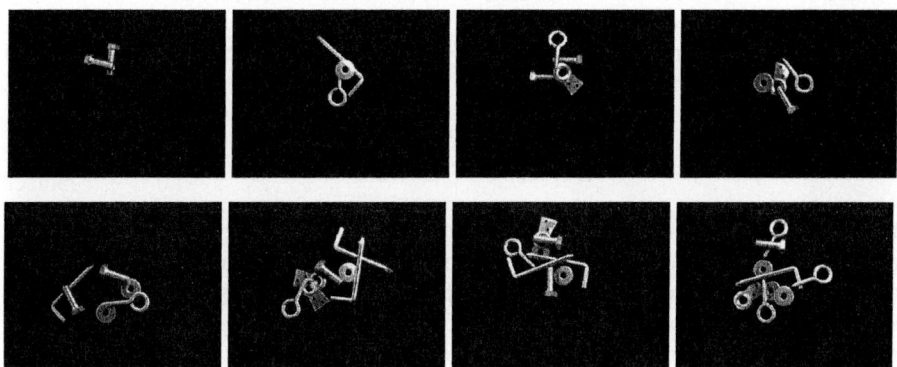

Fig. 5. Some of the images used in the experimentation

In average, the accuracy of the proposal was of **76.8%**. Table 1 summarizes the classification results for each object. In the case of the bolt, an 86% was obtained as follows: If in an image it is known that the bolt is present and if its presence is detected by the system then a positive vote a given to the bolt. In the same way, if in an image it is known that the bolt is not present and if its presence is not detected by the system then a positive vote is assigned to the bolt. In the other cases a negative vote is assigned to the bolt.

Table 1. Percentage of classification for the set of objects used

	Bolt	Washer	Eyebolt	Hook	Dovetail
% of classification	86%	70%	82%	52%	95%

Table 2. Comparison results obtained with respect to other proposals

	Operator **prom**	Operator **med**	Euclidean Distance classifier	Bayessian classifier	Proposal
Bolt	76%	70%	74%	90%	86%
Washer	67%	60%	64%	89%	70%
Eyebolt	82%	49%	80%	60%	82%
Hook	52%	52%	52%	51%	52%
Dovetail	81%	78%	83%	92%	95%
% of classification	71.6%	61.8%	71.0%	76.4%	76.8%

As you can appreciate, from Table 1, the hook presented the worst classification rate. This is due to fact that the describing features of its chosen EP are very similar to those of other EP of other objects. In others cases, as you can appreciate, classification results are reasonable good. Compared to other results reported by other works [13 and 14], Euclidean classifier, the performance of the proposal is better or comparable (Bayessian claasifier) as can be appreciated from Table 2.

As you can appreciate from this table, compared with other techniques the proposed performs better. Compared with the powerful Bayeasian classifier, the proposal presents a similar performance.

7 Conclusions and Ongoing Research

In this note we have described a simple technique for the detection of objects under occlusions by means of an associative memory and an invariant description of the so-called essential parts of an object. The proposal uses the most essential feature to describe an object. The average percentage of classification of the proposal for the set of five objects was of 76.8%. Compared with other recent techniques, the performance of our proposal was better or comparable.

Actually we are testing with other ways to describe an essential part of an object in order to improve the performance of the proposal. An immediate solution would be to obtain Hu invariants directly of the gray level image instead from the binary image.

Acknowledgements. This work was economically supported by CGPI-IPN under grants 20050156 and CONACYT by means of grant 46805. H. Sossa specially thanks COTEPABE-IPN, CONACYT (Dirección de Asuntos Internacionales) and DAAD (Deutscher Akademischer Austauschdienst) for the economical support granted during research stay at Friedrich-Schiller University, Jena, Germany.

References

[1] M. K. Hu (1962). Visual pattern recognition by moment invariants. IRE Transactions on Information Theory, 8:179-187.
[2] E. Persson and S. Fu (1977). Shape discrimination using Fourier descriptor. IEEE Transactions on SMC, 7(3):170-179.
[3] P. Tsang, P. Yuen and F. Lam (1994). Classification of partially occluded objects using 3-point matching and distance transformation. Pattern recognition, 27(1): 27-40.
[4] M. Hand and D. Yang (1990). The use of maximum curvature points for the recognition of partially occluded objects. Pattern recognition, 23(1-2):21-33.
[5] N. Pajpal, S, Chaudhury and S. Banerjee (1999). Recognition of partially occluded objects using neural network based indexing. Pattern recognition, 32(10):1737-1749.
[6] P. Tsang, P. Yuen and F. Lam (1992). Recognition of occluded objects. Pattern recognition, 25(10):1107-1117.
[7] E. Salari and S. Balaji (1991). Recognition of partially occluded objects using B-spline representation. Pattern recognition, 24(7):653-660.
[8] F. Jiulun and X. Winxin (1997). Minimum error thresholding: A note. Pattern Recognition Letters, 18(8):705-709.

[9] R. C. Gonzalez and R. E. Woods (2002). Digital Image processing. Second edition. Prentice hall, Inc 2002.
[10] R. Jain et al. (1995). Machine Vision. McGraw-Hill.
[11] H. Sossa, R. Barrón, R. A. Vázquez (2004). Transforming fundamental set of patterns to a canonical form to improve pattern recall. In proceedings of Nineth Ibero-American Conference on Artificial Intelligence (IBERAMIA-2004), LNAI 3315:687-696.
[12] H. Sossa, R. Barrón, R. A. Vázquez (2004). Real-valued pattern classification based on extended associative memory. In proceedings of Fifth Mexican Conference on Computer Science (ENC2004), IEEE Computer Society, 213-219.
[13] R. A. Vázquez, H. Sossa, R. Barrón (2004). Reconocimiento de objetos traslapados usando memorias asociativas. CICINDI 2004. Mexico City. September 7-11.
[14] R. A. Vázquez, H. Sossa, R. Barrón (2004). Reconocimiento de objetos traslapados basado en la detección de partes importantes y memorias asociativas. CNCIIC-ANIEI 2004. Nayarit, Mexico. October 20-22.

Real Time Facial Expression Recognition Using Local Binary Patterns and Linear Programming

Xiaoyi Feng[1], Jie Cui[1], Matti Pietikäinen[2], and Abdenour Hadid[2]

[1] College of Electronics and Information, Northwestern Polytechnic University,
710072 Xi'an, China
{fengxiao, cuijie}@nwpu.edu.cn
[2] Machine Vision Group, Infotech Oulu and Dept. of Electrical
and Information Engineering,
P. O. Box 4500 Fin-90014 University of Oulu, Finland
{mkp, hadid }@ee.oulu.fi

Abstract. In this paper, a fully automatic, real-time system is proposed to recognize seven basic facial expressions (angry, disgust, fear, happiness, neutral, sadness and surprise). First, faces are located and normalized based on an illumination insensitive skin model and face segmentation; then, the Local Binary Patterns (LBP) techniques, which are invariant to monotonic grey level changes, are used for facial feature extraction; finally, the Linear Programming (LP) technique is employed to classify seven facial expressions. Theoretical analysis and experimental results show that the proposed system performs well in some degree of illumination changes and head rotations.

1 Introduction

Real-time facial expression recognition plays an important role in real applications such as human-computer interaction, telecommunication and psychological research etc. However, it is a challenging problem in the computer vision literature. In the past years, only few works have addressed this issue [1-5].

Michel and R.E. Kaliouby [1] employed a feature displacement approach for expression recognition. 22 facial features were extracted from the video stream and the displacement for each feature between a neutral and a representative frame of an expression were calculated and then input to SVM classifier for training or testing. In Kotsia and Pitas' system [2], the Candide grid nodes on the face were manually placed at the first frame of one image sequence, the distance of each node's coordinates between the first and the last frame of the image sequence was used as an input to a multi-class SVM system for expression classification. Anderson and Mcowan [3] located face in scene with face tracker, then determined motion of face region only using optical flow algorithm, at last they input motion data into neural networks and determine emotion. Park [4] presented a point-wise energy based method for expression recognition. At the analysis step, they computed the motion energies of facial features and extract the dominant facial features related to each expression. At the recognition step, they performed rule-based facial expression recognition on arbitrary images using the results of analysis. Zhou et al. [5] proposed a novel network structure and parameters learning algorithm for embedded HMM based on AdaBoost and then used this optimized embedded HMM to real time facial expression recognition.

In this paper, we propose a novel, fully automatic and real time system for facial expression recognition. First, face is detected using a skin model and eyes are located based on the combination of face's geometrical structure and face segmentation; Then, the Local Binary Pattern (LBP) operator is used to efficiently describe facial expressions; Finally, the Linear Programming (LP) technique is used to classify seven basic expressions. The proposed system has no constraint on the first frame (the first frame may be with other expressions than neutral) and works well in some extent of illumination changes and head movement.

The rest of the paper is organized as follows. Face preprocessing is described in section 2 and feature extraction method is presented in section 3. In section 4, we introduce the classification method. Experimental results are described in section 5. Finally in section 6 we conclude the paper.

2 Face Preprocessing

Face preprocessing procedure includes three steps: face detection, eyes location and face normalization.

2.1 Face Detection with a Skin Locus

Martinkauppi et al. had found the Normalized Color Coordinates (NCC) combined with the skin locus most appropriate for skin detection under varying illumination [9]. To detect face-like area, the image presented in RGB color space is converted to the NCC space r, g and b. if r and b of a pixel fall into the area of the skin locus, the pixel belongs to skin. An example for skin detection is shown in Fig. 1. Considering real application, we select the largest skin component and regard it as face area (see the part inside the green box in Fig. 1).

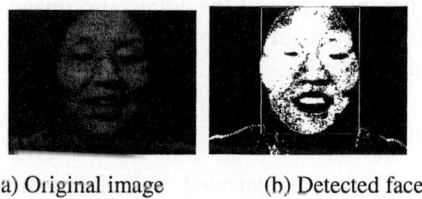

(a) Original image   (b) Detected face

Fig. 1. Face detection result

2.2 Face Segmentation

Based on the knowledge that facial features are darker than their surroundings, morphological valley detectors are usually used for eyes detection, while these feature detection methods are sensitive to illumination changes (See Fig.2).

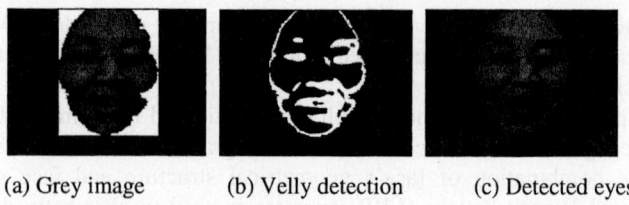

Fig. 2. Velly-based eyes detection

Here we propose a novel method for facial feature detection based on the color information, which is insensitive to illuminations. Based on the observation that eyes and eyebrows contain less and lips contain more red elements than the skin part, the color face region is converted to a grey level image named color-ratio image as follows,

$$f(x,y) = \min(255, b \times 255/r) \qquad (1)$$

Here $f(x,y)$ is the grey value of a pixel in position (x,y) in the color-ratio image and r and b are two chromaticities in NCC space. The color-ratio image corresponding to the image in Fig.1(a) is shown in Fig.3(a).

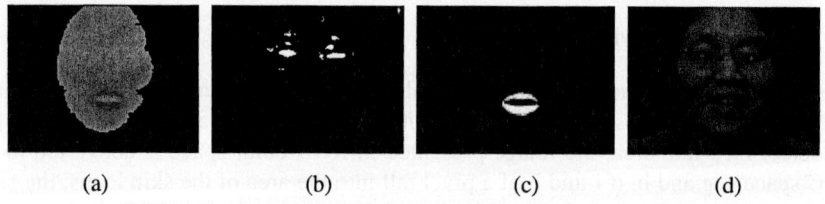

Fig. 3. Color-based eyes detection (a) Color-ratio image (b) Upper face segmentation (c) Lower face segmentation (d) Detected eyes

The upper part and the lower part of the color-ratio image are then segmented respectively, according to the rules of minimizing intra-class variance and the results are shown in Fig.3 (b) and Fig.3 (c).

2.3 Eyes Location and Tracking

After the possible facial features are detected, a similar method as proposed in [10] is applied to evaluate feature constellations, using a geometrical face model including eyes, eyebrows and mouth. Based on experiments we have modified the face model to make the tracking procedure accurate and fast.

We first select facial features locating at the upper half of face area as eyes candidates and evaluate each eye candidate pair as follows,

$$E_{eyepair} = 0.5\exp(-10(\frac{D_{eyes}-0.4B_{width}}{D})^2) + 0.25|\theta_{eyeleft}+\theta_{eyeright}-2\times\theta| \qquad (2)$$

Here B_{width} is the width of face bounding. Let $D = 0.8 B_{width}$. D_{eyes} is the real distance of an eye candidate pair. θ, $\theta_{eyeleft}$ and $\theta_{eyeright}$ indicate directions of base line (line passing through center of a eye candidate pair), left eye candidate and right eye candidate, respectively.

For each eye candidate pair, other facial features are searched for and evaluated.

$$E_{feature} = \exp(-10(\frac{d_{feature} - D_{feature}}{D})^2) \quad (3)$$

Where $features = \{mouth, eyebrows\}$, $d_{feature}$ and $D_{feature}$ are real distance and reference distance from features to base line.

The total evaluation value is a weighted sum of the values for each facial features. The weights for each pair of eyes, mouth, and eyebrows are 0.4, 0.3, 0.1 and 0.05, respectively. The constellation with the largest evaluation value is assumed to real facial features. Fig.2 (c) and Fig.3 (d) are results of eyes detection.

It should be pointed out that during eyes tracking procedure, the reference distances are replaced by corresponding real distances, which can be obtained from the just processed frame.

2.4 Face Normalization

Face normalization is based on the position of two eyes and the distance between them. After face normalization, eyes position and distance between two eyes are the same. Fig. 4 shows one face normalization result. The size of each normalized image is 150×128.

Fig.4. Normalized face

3 Face Feature Extraction

Fig.5 is an illustration of the basic LBP operator [11]. The original 3×3 neighbourhood at the left is thresholded by the value of the centre pixel, and a binary pattern code is produced. The LBP code of the centre pixel in the neighbourhood is obtained by converting the binary code into a decimal code. It is obviously that LBP is invariant to grey level changes.

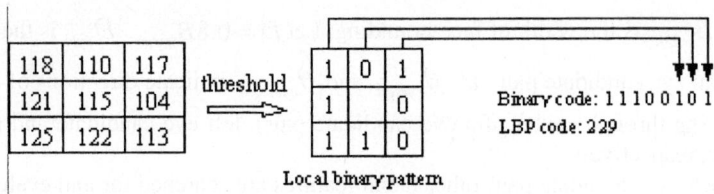

Fig. 5. The basic LBP operator

Based on this operator, each pixel of an image is labelled with an LBP code by thresholding its neighbourhood with the value of the centre pixel [11]. The 256-bin histogram of the labels (distribution of pattern codes) contains the density of each label over a local region, and can be used as a texture descriptor of the region.

The LBP operator, introduced by Ojala et al., has been shown to be a powerful measure of image texture. It has been applied to many problems with excellent performance [12, 13]. In our work, face images are seen as a composition of micropatterns, which can be well described by LBP.

Now, feature extraction is implemented with the following steps:

1. **Divide the face image into small regions.** The size of each pre-processed image is 150×128. After experimenting with different block sizes, we choose to divide the image into 80 (10×8) non-overlapping blocks (See Fig.6 (a)).
2. **Calculate the LBP histogram from each region.** The LBP histogram of each region is obtained by scanning it with the LBP operator.
3. **Concatenate the LBP feature histograms into a single feature vector.** LBP histogram of each region is combined together to form a single feature vector representing the whole image (See Fig.6 (b)).

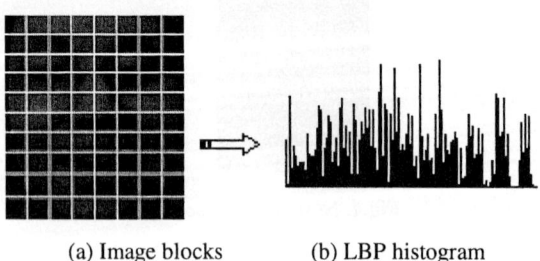

(a) Image blocks   (b) LBP histogram

Fig. 6. An example of a facial image divided into 10×8 blocks

The idea behind using our approach for feature extraction is motivated by the fact that emotion is more often communicated by facial movement, which will change visible appearance. Our feature extraction method is capable of presenting facial appearances and so it can be used for representing facial expressions.

4 Expression Classification Based on Linear Programming

In [14, 15], a single linear programming (LP) formulation is proposed which generates a plane that minimizes an average sum of misclassified points belonging to two disjoint points set. We briefly describe this LP formulation below.

Consider the two point-sets A and B in the n-dimensional real space R^n represented by the $m \times n$ matrix A and the $k \times n$ matrix B, respectively. The separating plane is as follows:

$$P := \{x \mid x \in R^n, x^T \omega = \gamma\} \quad (4)$$

Here $\omega \in R^n$ is normal to the separating plane with a distance $\frac{|\gamma|}{\|\omega\|}$ to the origin.

The separating plane P determines two open half-spaces, $\{x \mid x \in R^n, x^T \omega > \gamma\}$ containing mostly points belong to A, and $\{x \mid x \in R^n, x^T \omega < \gamma\}$ containing mostly points belonging to B. That is we wish to satisfy

$$A\omega > e\gamma, \quad B\omega < \gamma \quad (5)$$

Here e is a vector of all 1s with appropriate dimension. To the extent possible, or upon normalization

$$A\omega \geq e\gamma, \quad B\omega \leq e\gamma - e \quad (6)$$

Conditions (5) or (6) can be satisfied if and only if, A and B do not intersect, which in general is not the case. We thus attempt to satisfy (6) by minimizing some norm of the average violations of (6) such as

$$\min_{\omega,\gamma} \frac{1}{m} \|(-A\omega + e\gamma + e)_+\|_1 + \frac{1}{k} \|(B\omega - e\gamma + e)_+\|_1 \quad (7)$$

Here x_+ denotes the vector in R^n satisfying $(x_+)_i := \max\{x_i, 0\}, i = 1, 2, \ldots n$. The norm $\|\cdot\|_p$ denotes the p norm, $1 \leq p \leq \infty$.

Formulation (7) is equivalent to the following robust linear programming formulation

$$\min_{\omega,\gamma,y,z} \frac{e^T y}{m} + \frac{e^T z}{k}$$
$$-A\omega + e\gamma + e \leq y \quad (8)$$
$$B\omega - e\gamma + e \leq z$$
$$y \geq 0, z \geq 0$$

Recently, the LP framework has been extended to cope with the feature selection problem [15]. In our research, we adopt formulation (8) as a classifier to minimize wrong classification.

Since formulation (8) is only used for separating two sets points, a seven-expression classification problem is decomposed to 21 2-class classification problems. In the training stage, 21 classifiers according to 21 expression pairs are formed with 21 pairs of $\{\omega,\gamma\}$. In the testing stage, feature vector of a testing sample is imported into these classifiers for comparisons. Fig.7 shows the classification result for original image in Fig.1 (a).

Fig. 7. Classification result

5 Evaluations

In our research, a commercial digital camcorder is connected to a computer for images acquisition and the system operates at about 20 frames/second in 320X240 images on a 3GHz Pentium V. Fig.8 shows the output of the system for a test video in which the subject poses a series of facial expressions.

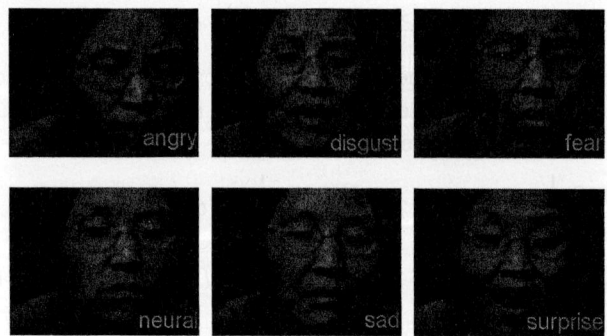

Fig. 8. Examples of correct recognition

The recognition performance of our system is tested as follows:

1) **Person-dependent recognition:** In the training stage, every one of ten individuals is required to pose seven basic expressions in from of a camcorder. Then some frames are selected from the video stream to produce expression template for this person. In the recognition stage, these individuals pose expressions again and the system recognizes them and displays the result in time. To evaluate the recognition performance, the system also save the original video stream and recognition results. When the system ends its work, each individual are asked to label his expressions in the original image sequences. Results of the system are compared to the labels and then we have the recognition rate. The average recognition accuracy is 91% (See table 1).

Table 1. Person-dependent Recognition result

Expressions	Recognizing rate
Anger	91%
Disgust	86%
Fear	82%
Happiness	99%
Neural	93%
Sadness	91%
Surprise	97%
Average	91%

2) **Person-independent recognition:** The procedure is similar to that in 1). The difference is that expressions of seven individuals are used for training and those of other three persons are used for testing. One expert who is familiar with the seven basic expressions is asked to labels the testing video streams. Results of our system are compared to the labels and then we have an average recognition rate of 78% (See table 2).

Table 2. Person-independent Recognition result

Expressions	Recognizing rate
Anger	75%
Disgust	68%
Fear	65%
Happiness	89%
Neural	78%
Sadness	81%
Surprise	87%
Average	78%

6 Conclusions

Real-time and fully automatic facial expressions recognition is one of the challenging tasks in face analysis. This paper presents a novel real time system for expression recognition. The face pre-processing is implemented based on the skin detection and face geometrical structure, which can assure correct eyes detection under large illumination changes and some degree of head movement. The Local Binary Patterns operator is used here to describe face efficiently for expression recognition. The features detection procedure is insensitive to grey level changes. The holistic features also make the proposed system insensitive to some range of head movement. At last, 21 classifiers are produced based on linear programming technique and classification is implemented with a binary tree tournament scheme, which can minimize wrong classification. The system requires no special working conditions. Besides this, experimental results demonstrate that the system performs well less constraint conditions, even in some degree of illumination changes and head movement.

Acknowledgement

The authors thank CIMO of Finland and the China Scholarship Council for their financial support for this research work. The "Talent Training Plan" of the Northwestern Polytechnic University also provides financial support to this work and should also be greatly acknowledged.

References

1. P. Michel and R. E. Kaliouby: Real time facial expression recognition in video using support vector machines, Proceedings of the 5th International Conference on Multimodal Interfaces, (2003) 258-264
2. I. Kotsia and I. Pitas: Real time facial expression recognition from image sequences using support vector machines, Proceedings of Visual Communication and Image Processing, (2005), in press
3. K. Anderson and P. w. Mcowan: Real-time emotion recognition using biologically inspired models, Proceedings of 4th International Conference on Audio- and Video-Based Biometric Person Authentication (2003) 119-127
4. H. Park and J. Park: Analysis and recognition of facial expression based on point-wise motion energy, Proceedings of Image Analysis and Recognition (2004) 700-708
5. X. Zhou, X. Huang, B. Xu and Y. Wang: Real time facial expression recognition based on boosted embedded hidden Markov model, Proceedings of the Third International Conference on Image and Graphics (2004), 290-293
6. M. Pantic, Leon J.M. Rothkrantz: Automatic analysis of facial expressions: the state of the art, IEEE Transactions on Pattern Analysis and Machine Intelligence, Vol. 22 (2000) 1424-1445
7. B. Fasel and J. Luettin: Automatic facial expression analysis: A survey, Pattern Recognition, Vol. 36 (2003) 259-275
8. Li.Stan Z & K.Anil, Handbook of face recognition, Springer-Verlag, 2004.9
9. B. Martinkauppi, Face color under varying illumination-analysis and applications, Dr.tech Dissertation, University of Oulu, Finland, 2002
10. J.Hannuksela: Facial feature based head tracking and pose estimation, Department of Electrical and Information Engineering, University of Oulu, Finland, 2003
11. T. Ojala, M. Pietikäinen, T. Mäenpää: Multiresolution grey-scale and rotation invariant texture classification with Local Binary Patterns, IEEE Transactions on Pattern Analysis and Machine Intelligence, Vol. 24(2002) 971-987
12. T. Ahonen, A. Hadid and M. Pietikäinen, Face recognition with local binary patterns. The 8th European Conference on Computer Vision (2004), 469-481
13. T. Ojala, M. Pietikäinen and T. Mäenpää. Multiresolution grey-scale and rotation invariant texture classification with Local Binary Patterns. IEEE Transactions on Pattern Analysis and Machine Intelligence Vol.24 (2002): 971-987
14. K. P. Bennett and O. L. Mangasarian, Robust linear programming discrimination of two linearly inseparable sets, Optimization Methods and software, vol.1 (1992), 23-34
15. P. S. Bradley and O. L. Mangasarian, Feature selection via concave minimization and support vector machines, Proceedings OF THE 5th International Conference on Machine Learning (1998) 82-90

People Detection and Tracking Through Stereo Vision for Human-Robot Interaction*

Rafael Muñoz-Salinas, Eugenio Aguirre, Miguel García-Silvente,
and Antonio Gonzalez

Depto. de Ciencias de la Computacion e Inteligencia Artificial,
E.T.S. Ingeniera Informática, University of Granada,
Granada, Spain
{salinas, eaguirre, M.Garcia-Silvente, A.Gonzalez}@decsai.ugr.es

Abstract. In this document we present an agent for people detection and tracking through stereo vision. The agent makes use of the active vision to perform the people tracking with a robotic head on which the vision system is installed. Initially, a map of the surrounding environment is created including its motionless characteristics. This map will later on be used to detect objects in motion, and to search people among them by using a face detector. Once a person has been spotted, the agent is capable of tracking them through the robotic head that allows the stereo system to rotate. In order to achieve a robust tracking we have used the Kalman filter. The agent focuses on the person at all times by framing their head and arms on the image. This task could be used by other agents that might need to analyze gestures and expressions of potential application users in order to facilitate the human-robot interaction.

1 Introduction

One critical aspect of the creation of certain intelligent systems is to detect the human presence and facilitate the interaction. The topic human-robot interaction has drawn a lot of attention in the last decade. The objective is to be able to create more intelligent interfaces capable of extracting information about the context or about the actions to be performed through the natural interaction with the user, for example through their gestures or voice.

One fundamental aspect in this sense is the people detection and tracking, with plenty existing literature about this topic [3, 8, 9]. The techniques to perform the detection are frequently based on the integration of different information sources such as: skin color, face detectors, motion analysis, etc.

Although the people detection and tracking with a single camera is a well explored topic, the use of the stereo technology for this purpose concentrates now an important interest. The availability of commercial hardware to resolve low-level processing problems with stereoscopic cameras, as well as lower prices for these types of systems, turns them into an appealing sensor with which intelligent

---

* This work has been supported by the the Spanish Ministerio de Ciencia y Tecnología under project TIC2003-04900.

systems could be developed. The use of stereo vision provides a higher grade of information that provides several advantages when developing human-robot applications. On one hand, the information regarding disparities becomes less sensitive to illumination changes than the images provided by a single camera, being a very advantageous factor for the environment(background) estimation. Furthermore, the possibility to know the distance to the person could be of great assistance for the tracking as well as for a better analysis of their gestures.

On this research we present an agent able to detect and track people through stereo vision. An *agent* is a process that is capable of autonomous action, interacting and cooperating in a system with another agents. The agent uses active vision to perform the tracking through a robotic head on which the vision system is installed. This agent will serve as a base for the work of other agents in charge of tasks such as gesture analysis and expressions of potential users. The detection method is based on the initial creation of a height map of the environment. This map contains information about the structure of the environment and could even be created while people are moving around. Using this structural map, it will possible to detect the objects in motion. These are potential candidates to people that would be detected through a face detector. Unlike other works that only map the environment for a static camera, our map covers the entire visible region by the stereo system. Once a person has been detected, the robotic heads allows the stereo system to rotate in order to follow them through the environment. In order to have a robust tracking we have used the Kalman filter. The tracking method is designed to maintain visible, as long as feasible, the head and arms of the person and therefore facilitate the gesture analysis.

1.1 Related Works

Among the most prestigious projects related to people detection and tracking using stereo vision we find the one by Darrel et al [1]. This paper presents an interactive display system capable of identifying and tracking several people. The detection of people is based on the integration of the information provided by a skin detector, face detector and the map of disparity of the environment. On one hand, independent objects (*blobs*) are detected on the disparity image that will be candidates to people. On the other hand, the color of the image is analyzed to identify those areas that could be related to skin. These three items are merged in order to detect the visible people. To perform the tracking, information on hair color, clothes and past history of the located people is used. In this way, the people can be identified even though they disappear from the image for a while.

In [4] it is shown a system for people detection and tracking for the interaction in virtual environments. The system allows the user to navigate in a virtual environment by just walking through the room using virtual reality glasses. In this work the face detection is a crucial aspect that has been resolved by using the face detector proposed by Viola and Jones [11]. Once the person is located, a histogram of the colors of the face and chest is used and a particle filter estimates the position of the person based on the information. The stereo information assists on knowing the position of the person in the room and therefore identifies their position on a virtual environment. On this work, the stereo process is performed by using the information gathered by different cameras located at different points of the room.

In [6] a method to locate and track people in stereo images is presented by using occupancy maps. Before the people detection process takes place, an image of the environment is created through a sophisticated image analysis method. Once the background image is created, the objects that do not belong to it are easily isolated, a map of occupancy is created, as well as a height map. The information from both maps is merged to detect people through the use of simple heuristics. The people tracking is performed by using a Kalman filter combined with deformable templates. In this work, a stereoscopic system is used and it is located three meters above the ground, on a fixed position.

On the majority of the works, elevated positions of the cameras are used [5, 6, 7]. However, on some other papers that seek the interaction with the user, the position of the camera is usually lower than the height of the person [1, 4, 10]. Besides improving the visibility of the face and arms of the person, these methods are more adequate for their implementation in robotic systems that require human-robot interaction. Studies performed show that in order to improve the acceptance of the robots by the humans it is important that they are of less height than the latter [2]. Otherwise the person could feel intimidated.

In this work we propose a method for people detection and tracking by using a movable stereoscopic system located at inferior levels from the people's height. Unlike most of the documents reviewed, that only model the environment for unmovable cameras [1, 4, 5, 6, 7], we propose a method to create a map that models all visible environment by the stereoscopic system when rotating the robotic head. A distinguished characteristic of this method is that even with movable objects present, the map can still be created. The use of this map will allows us to easily detect the objects that do not belong to the environment and narrow the people detection process to only those objects. The reduction of the information to be analyzed will enable us, besides to reduce the computer costs, to eliminate false positives produced by the face detector used. The agent that has been created uses active vision to track the person movements through all the room. This situation allows us to track the person on a wider environment, than if we had used immovable cameras, and thus makes feasible a more natural and comfortable interaction.

2 Hardware System

The hardware system is formed by a laptop to process the information, a stereoscopic system with two pinhole cameras, and a robotic head. The robotic head (Pan-Tilt Unit or PTU) has two degrees of freedom, one on the X axis (pan) of $\phi = [-139, 139]$ degrees and the other one on the Y axis (tilt) of $\psi = [-47, 31]$ degrees.

The use of our stereoscopic system enables us to capture two $320x240$ sized color images from slightly different positions (stereo pair) and to create a disparity image I_d. By knowing the internal parameters of the stereoscopic system it is feasible to estimate the three-dimensional position p_{cam} of a point in I_d. Due to the fact that the camera is subject to movements, these points are translated to a reference static system that has as a center the robotic head located at the ground level through the Eq. 1.

$$p_w = T p_{cam} \qquad (1)$$

The linear projection matrix T is created by using the intrinsic parameters of the system (provided by the manufacturer) and extrinsic ones that has been previously estimated.

3 People Detection and Tracking Process

The method for people detection and tracking proposed on this document, is an iterative process that has been outlined in Fig. 1.

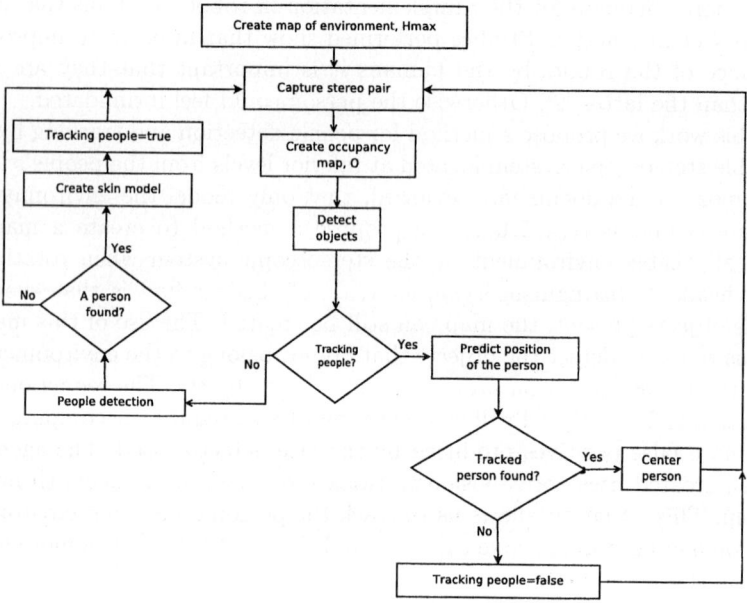

Fig. 1. Flowchart of the process

Initially, a map of the environment is created (let us denote it by $\mathcal{H}_{max}$) that registers the position of the motionless objects. This map divides the environment projected on the floor into cells of a fixed size and indicates on each one of them the maximum height of the detected objects.

Once the environment has been registered, the system begins a continuous process to capture images in order to create an instantaneous occupancy map $\mathcal{O}$. On this map we will be able to identify those objects that are in the scene but were not registered as motionless objects in $\mathcal{H}_{max}$, in other words, those objects that are in motion. The objects present in $\mathcal{O}$ are identified and analyzed to determine which of them are people. For this purpose we have applied a people detector [11] over the color image of the scene. The false positives generated by the face detector will be rejected thanks to the integration of the information of the disparity image and $\mathcal{O}$. If finally, some of the objects detected in $\mathcal{O}$ turn out to be people, the agent will begin to track the closest one.

The tracking is also an iterative process that creates on every moment a occupancy map $\mathcal{O}$ to track on it the target person. To perform the tracking the Kalman filter has been used. If the target person is located, it is determined if the PTU needs to be moved in order to center the image and in this manner have them always on sight. The objective of the centering process is to keep on the image, as long as feasible, the head and arms of the person. In the following sections the more relevant processes previously mentioned will be elaborated in more detail.

3.1 Creation of the Map of the Environment $\mathcal{H}_{max}$

Firstly on to the detection process, the environment is registered. This process aims to register the structure and motionless objects in it. This environment model will assist when separating the objects that are not part of it (in other words: the movable objects). Our approach is based on the creation of a geometrical height map of the environment $\mathcal{H}_{max}$, that divides the ground level into a group of cells with a fixed size. The points identified by the stereo system p_w are projected over $\mathcal{H}_{max}$, that stores the maximum height of the projected points in each cell. In order to avoid adding the points of the ceiling (or objects hanging from it) on $\mathcal{H}_{max}$, those that overcome the height threshold h_{max} are excluded from the process. Due to efficiency reasons for the calculation, the points below the minimum height threshold h_{min}, are also excluded. The height range $[h_{min}, h_{max}]$ should be such that the majority the person's body to be detected should fit in it. On those cells $\mathcal{H}_{max}$ (x,y) on which there are no points located, we assume that there are no objects and therefore the height is h_{min}.

Because of the stereoscopic system is subject to error, instead of only projecting the height of the point detected on a cell, it is also projected the whole uncertainty area of that point. For that purpose we have used the error model of the stereoscopic system with the parameters provided by the manufacturer.

The creation of $\mathcal{H}_{max}$ by only using a unique disparity image is subject to problems. On one hand, possible objects that do not belong to the environment (for example people passing by) could be incorrectly included as part of the environment. Also, the correlation algorithms for the stereo detection are subject to error that cause that not all the scene points are detected. Due to these reasons, instead of creating $\mathcal{H}_{max}$ from a unique disparity image, it will be done by taking several images on different instants t. For each one of this images, an instantaneous height map is created $\mathcal{H}_{max}^{t}$. Finally, the different $\mathcal{H}_{max}^{t}$ created are used to calculate $\mathcal{H}_{max}$ through a robust estimator such as the median. For that purpose, each cell of $\mathcal{H}_{max}$ will have as a maximum height value the median of all values observed on the different $\mathcal{H}_{max}^{t}$ for that particular cell using Eq. 2.

$$\mathcal{H}_{max}(x,y) = median(\mathcal{H}_{max}^{t=1}(x,y), ..., \mathcal{H}_{max}^{t=n}(x,y)) \qquad (2)$$

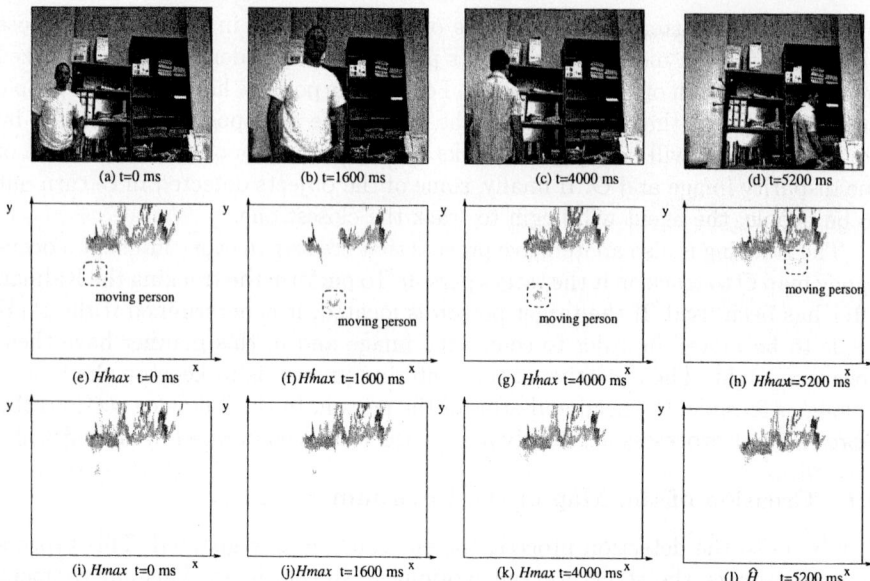

Fig. 2. Creation of the height map. Images a,b,c and d show a motion object in the $1, 4, 10$ and 13 moments. Central row (e,f,g,h) shows the instantaneous height maps $\mathcal{H}_{max}^t$ for each one of the upper images. Lower row (i,j,k,l) shows the evolution of the height map $\mathcal{H}_{max}$ created as the median of the height maps $\mathcal{H}_{max}^t$ built until that moment.

On Fig. 2 we can observe the creation of the height map of an environment. The map has been created by using a sequence of 13 images. Figure 2 only shows the images of the instants $t = \{1, 4, 10, 13\}$. On the upper row (Figs. 2 (a-d)) the images of the moments previously mentioned are shown. On the middle row (Figs. 2(e-h)), we can see the instantaneous height maps $\mathcal{H}^{\sqcup}{}_{max}$ of the upper row images. The dark areas represent the highest zones and the white areas represent the lowest ones h_{min}. On the lower row (Figs. 2(i-l)), it is shown the evolution of the height map $\mathcal{H}_{max}$ until the instant t. We can observe that for $t = 1$, $\mathcal{H}_{max}^{t=1} = \mathcal{H}_{max}$. But as we continue using more images, the height map tends to truly represent the *permanent* environment. To create these maps we have used the size of cells $\delta = 1$ cm and the range of height is $h_{min} = 0.5$ m and $h_{max} = 2.5$ m.

In order to create a complete map of the environment the camera will need to turn so it can capture information from different directions. For that purpose, the process previously described will be repeated for different values of the ϕ angle until it covers all the visible environment by the visual system. Due to space reasons, image of a complete map is not included.

3.2 Creation of the Occupancy Map $\mathcal{O}$

Once the height map $\mathcal{H}_{max}$ has been created, the people detection can begin. The first step, is to create an occupancy map $\mathcal{O}$, which will indicate on each cell the surface occupied by the objects that do not belong to the environment

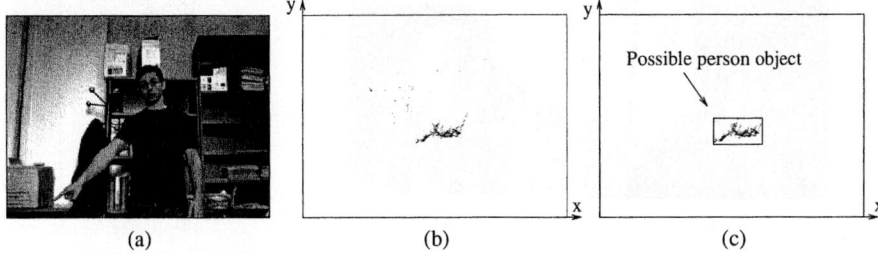

Fig. 3. (a) Right image of the pair in an instant, the environment with an object not in background. (b) Occupancy map $\mathcal{O}$ corresponding to the environment. (c) Framed information related to the object, detected using $\mathcal{O}$.

($\mathcal{H}_{max}$). For this purpose, after capturing a stereo pair of the environment, the position of the points detected p_w is calculated. For each point p_w, it is evaluated if its height is within the limits $[h_{min}, h_{max}]$ and if it exceeds the value of the corresponding cell in $\mathcal{H}_{max}$. In that case, the equivalent cell in $\mathcal{O}$ is incremented by a value proportional to the surface that occupies the registered point. Points closer to the camera correspond to small surfaces and vice versa. Therefore, the farther points will increment the value of the equivalent cell by a higher quantity than closer ones[6]. If the same increment is employed for every cell, the same object would have a lower sum of the areas the farther it is located from the camera. This scale on the increment value will compensate the difference on size of the objects observed according to their distance from the camera.

Once the dynamic map $\mathcal{O}$ is created for a determinated instant, we will analyze it to detect the objects that appear on it. On a first step, a closing process takes place with the purpose to link possible discontinuities on the objects. After this, the objects are detected by grouping cells that are connected and that their sum of areas overcomes the threshold θ_{min}. On this way, we eliminate the potential noise that appears as a consequence of the stereoscopic process.

We can observe on the Fig. 3(b) the occupancy map $\mathcal{O}$ of the environment on Fig. 3(a) using a height map $\mathcal{H}_{max}$ from Fig. 2(l). The darker values represent the areas with higher occupancy density. The image has been manually retouched to make visible the occupied areas. As it can be observed, on the upper area of Fig. 3(b) there are small dark dots that represent the noise of the stereo process. On Fig. 3(c) we can see in a frame the only object detected after the closing, grouping and thresholding processes.

3.3 Face Detection

If after the creation and analysis of $\mathcal{O}$, an object that has entered the environment has been detected, we proceed to use a face detector to determine which one could be a person's face. As face detector method we have used the one initially proposed by Viola and Jones [11]. This method consists on a general object detector based on the utilization of multiple simple classifiers arranged in cascade. The method takes as input the right image of the pair and selects the areas of the

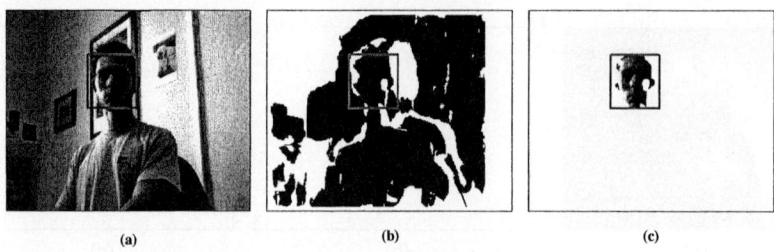

Fig. 4. Face detection. (a) Right image of the pair registered with the face framed as result of the face detector. (b) Frame translated to the disparity image. (c) Face extracted from the stereoscopic image that belongs to a person.

image where a face is detected (Fig. 4(a)). This method is only applied over the region of the right image where an object was detected in the early stage.

Due that the face detector tends to identify false positives, it is important to verify that the detected object is indeed a person's face. As a verification mechanism the points detected that could be part of a face should not be spread out among different objects in $\mathcal{O}$. For that reason, we will analyze the area of the face on the disparity image to verify if the points are part of one only object in $\mathcal{O}$. However, this area could have points that represent the background or other object even when the detector indeed identifies a face. On Fig. 4(a) we can see how a face is identified and how in the same area there are points that belong to a face and to the wall on the background. For this reason, it is very important to precisely clarify which points, on the area identified by the detector, are truly part of a face and which are not. For this mean we run a process that consists on calculating the median of the disparity values from the frame indicated by the face detector. The points with such disparity value are used as seed to perform a region growing. On 4(c) we can observe the selected region by this method for the disparity image 4(b). If after this analysis the system would identify more than one person on this environment, the system would start tracking the closest one.

3.4 Tracking

The tracking process is interactive and begins when we take a stereo pair and create its map of occupancy $\mathcal{O}$. After identifying the people present in $\mathcal{O}$ (as it has been previously explained), we need to determine which one will be tracked. To merge the available information taken in previous moments as well as the information processed on the current moment the Kalman filter has been used. This tool will allow us to merge in a proper manner the position that predicts the model with the information gathered during our search process. If the person is detected, active vision is properly used directing the visual system so the target is always centered on the image. The centering process aims to keep the subject visible on the image placing it on the best possible image position to analyze their gestures. If the subject is standing up on normal position, the goal is to capture the head and torso. If the subject raises their arms to point to any object or if he bends to pick up something from the floor, it is desirable to be able to register the action. On this work, we have contemplated the possibility of the movement sideways as well as the movements that imply changes in height (bending or sitting down). We have experimentally proven that the best option to achieve this is to keep the highest visible zone of the subject in the upper area of the image. To determine the movement that the PTU needs to perform in order to center the subject, we have used a system based on fuzzy rules that have been designed with expert knowledge and that have been adjusted according the our experimentation.

4 Experimentation

During the explanation of the model we have shown examples of its performance. A broader experimentation has been done that we are unable to show with images due to space reasons, but we will briefly explain. This experimentation refers to the detection and tracking of different people under different illumination conditions and different distances from the vision system. To perform the stereo process we have used $320x240$ sized images, by applying sub-pixel interpolation to enhance the precision.

The use of the proposed height map enables us to model the whole environment rotating the stereoscopic system on all directions. The creation method proposed (to use the median of the heights) allows to create the map even when there are people moving around in the room just as shown on Sect. 3.1. Although the height map is a partial description of the environment with much less information than the one stored in a full 3D map, it can be efficiently created, updated and does not require as much memory as the latter.

We have proven the accurate performance of the people detection method by satisfactorily eliminating the false positives produced by the face detector. The more adequate distances to detect people vary within $0, 5$ and $2, 5$ meters. However, once the person to be tracked is selected among the others, the tracking can take place in longer distances.

The time to compute is different on the detection process than on the tracking one, although the stereo process consumes most of the time (120 ms). On the tracking process, the face detector is the toughest task (81 ms), reaching ratios of $2, 5$ fps for the whole detection process (including the stereo processing). However, on the tracking process we reached ratios up to 5 fps and we have proven that it is enough in our case. These values could substantially increase if it were feasible to optimize the code of the stereo process or with the use of specific hardware, for depth computation.

5 Conclusions and Future Work

On this paper we have presented an agent capable of people detection and that uses active vision to track them. For that reason we have used a stereoscopic system installed on a robotic head. The agent initially creates a height map of the environment that registers the motionless characteristics of it. This map is later used to identify the movable objects in the environment and to search potential people among them, by using the face detector. Once a person has been detected, the agent is capable of tracking them by using a robotic head that enables the stereo system to rotate. In order to achieve a robust tracking process we have used the Kalman filter. The agent keeps the person located at all times by framing their arms and head in the image. This task could be used by other agents that might need to analyze gestures and expressions of potential users in human-robot applications.

As future projects we visualize the update of the map of the environment. For that reason, the agent should be capable of adding to the environment map those objects that are not people and stay motionless for a long period of time, and were not there when the map was initially created. Other aspect to consider is the use of the particles filter for the tracking task.

References

1. T. Darrell, G. Gordon, M. Harville, and J. Woodfill. Integrated Person Tracking Using Stereo, Color, and Pattern Detection. *Int. Journ. Computer Vision*, 37:175–185, 2000.
2. T. Fong, I. Nourbakhsh, and K. Dautenhahn. A survey of socially interactive robots. *Robotics and Autonomous Systems*, 42, 2003.
3. D. M. Gavrila. The visual analysis of human movement: A survey. *Computer Vision and Image Understanding: CVIU*, 73(1):82–98, 1999.
4. D. Grest and R. Koch. Realtime multi-camera person tracking for immersive environments. In *IEEE 6th Workshop on Multimedia Signal Processing*, pages 387–390, 2004.
5. I. Haritaoglu, D. Beymer, and M. Flickner. Ghost 3d: detecting body posture and parts using stereo. In *Workshop on Motion and Video Computing*, pages 175 – 180, 2002.
6. Michael Harville. Stereo person tracking with adaptive plan-view templates of height and occupancy statistics. *Image and Vision Computing*, 22:127–142, 2004.
7. K. Hayashi, M. Hashimoto, K. Sumi, and K. Sasakawa. Multiple-person tracker with a fixed slanting stereo camera. In *6th IEEE International Conference on Automatic Face and Gesture Recognition*, pages 681–686, 2004.
8. W. Liang, H. Weiming, and L. Tieniu. Recent developments in human motion analysis. *Pattern Recognition*, 36:585–601, 2003.
9. L. Snidaro, C. Micheloni, and C. Chiavedale. Video security for ambient intelligence. *IEEE Transactions on Systems, Man and Cybernetics, Part A*, 35:133 – 144, 2005.
10. R. Tanawongsuwan. Robust Tracking of People by a Mobile Robotic Agent. Technical Report GIT-GVU-99-19, Georgia Tech University, 1999.
11. P. Viola and M. Jones. Rapid object detection using a boosted cascade of simple features. In *IEEE Conf. on Computer Vision and Pattern Recognition*, pages 511–518, 2001.

Mapping Visual Behavior to Robotic Assembly Tasks

Mario Peña-Cabrera[1], Ismael López-Juárez[2], Reyes Rios-Cabrera[2],
Jorge Corona-Castuera[2], and Roman Osorio[1]

[1] Instituto de Investigaciones en Matemáticas Aplicadas y en Sistemas (IIMAS),
Ciudad Universitaria, Univesidad Nacional Autónoma de México,
México D.F. CP 04510
{mario, roman}@leibniz.iimas.unam.mx
http://www.iimas.unam.mx
[2] CIATEQ A.C. Centro de Tecnología Avanzada, Av. Manantiales 23-A,
CP 76246, El Marqués, Querétaro, México
{ilopez, reyes.rios, jcorona}@ciateq.mx
http://www.ciateq.mx

Abstract. This paper shows a methodology for on-line recognition and classification of pieces in robotic assembly tasks and its application into an intelligent manufacturing cell. The performance of industrial robots working in unstructured environments can be improved using visual perception and learning techniques. The object recognition is accomplished using an Artificial Neural Network (ANN) architecture which receives a descriptive vector called CFD&POSE as the input. This vector represents an innovative methodology for classification and identification of pieces in robotic tasks, every stage of the methodology is described and the proposed algorithms explained. The vector compresses 3D object data from assembly parts and it is invariant to scale, rotation and orientation, and it also supports a wide range of illumination levels. The approach in combination with the fast learning capability of ART networks indicates the suitability for industrial robot applications as it is demonstrated through experimental results.

1 Introduction

Advent of complex robotics systems in different applications such as manufacturing, health science and space, require better vision systems. This vision systems should be able to see and perceive objects and images as possible as human being does. This has led to an increased appreciation of the neural morphology of biological vision specially for the human vision system. Neuroanatomy and neurophysiology scientists, have discovered really exciting facts about visual path way from the initial point at the retina to the visual cortex in the brain using different experiments with different biological species. Scientists from disciplines such as computer science and mathematics are formulating the theories of neural functions in the visual pathway from computational and mathematics points of view. This research gives us a better understanding of how computational neural structures and artificial vision systems must be designed, showing some interesting neural paradigms, mathematics models, computational architectures and hardware implementations. We call a system composed of all these aspects a " Neuro-Vision System" and we can define it as an artificial machine that "can see" our visual world to conform applications in our daily life. Based on this, we can define two areas for a better understanding of this fascinating research field: neural morphology of biological vision and artificial neural networks paradigms used for the development of neuro-vision systems. Both approaches are necessary to deal with the development of computational strategies attempting to model attributes of human visual perception considering all constraints of existing digital computing hardware [1].

The purpose of this paper is to show a novel and simple way to consider a visual system having a machine vision with robust, flexible and easy implementation attributes for real time applications on manufacturing tasks.

2 Background and Related Work

Intelligent manufacturing cells using robots with sensorial capabilities is being investigated using Artificial Intelligence techniques such as ANN and Fuzzy Logic among others, since the mathematical and control models are simplified.

Acquiring information from multiple sensors in manufacturing systems provides robustness and self-adaptation capabilities, hence improving the performance in industrial robot applications. A few researchers have applied neural networks to assembly operations with manipulators and force feedback. Vijaykumar Gullapalli [2] used BackPropagation (BP) and Reinforcement Learning(RL) to control a Zebra robot, its neural controller was based on the location error reduction beginning from a known location, Enric Cervera [3] employed Self-Organization Map (SOM) and RL to control a Zebra robot, the location of the destination piece was unknown, Martin Howarth [4] utilized BP and RL to control a SCARA robot, without knowing the location of assembly, Lopez-Juarez [5] implemented FuzzyARTMAP to control a PUMA robot also with an unknown location. All of the above authors considered only constraint motion control during assembly; however, to complete the autonomy of the assembly system a machine vision system has to be considered. Additionally, a new concept was introduced by Hoska in 1988 [6] called "robotic fixtureless assembly" (RFA) which prevents the use of complex and rigid fixtures involving new technical challenges, but allowing very potential solutions. Ngyyuen, Mills [7] have studied RFA of flexible parts with a dynamic model of two robots with a proposed algorithm, which does not require measurements of the part deflections. Plut [8] and Bone, [9], presented a grasp planning strategy for RFA. The goal of RFA is to replace these fixtures with sensor-guided robots which can work within RFA workcells. The development of such vision-guided robots equipped with programmable grippers might permit holding a wide range of part shapes without tool changing. Using Artificial Neural Networks, an integrated intelligent vision-guided system can be achieved as it is shown by Langley et al. [10]. This job can be achieved by using 2D computer vision in different manner so that 3D invariant object recognition and POSE calculation might be used for aligning parts in assembly tasks if an adequate descriptor vector is used and interfaced in real time to a robot. Many authors have come with descriptor vectors and image transformations used as general methods for computer vision applications in order to extract invariant features from shapes, as Bribiesca [11] which developed a new chain code for shapes composed of regular cells, which has recently evolved even to represent 3D paths and knots, techniques for invariant pattern classification, like classical methods as the universal axis and invariant moments of Hu

[12], or artificial intelligence techniques, as used by Cem Yüceer and Kemal Oflazer [13] which describes an hybrid pattern classification system based on a pattern preprocessor and an ANN invariant to rotation, scaling and translation.

Applications of guided vision used for assembly are well illustrated by Gary M. Bone and David Capson [14] which developed a vision-guide fixtureless assembly system using a 2D computer vision for robust grasping and a 3D computer vision to align parts prior to mating, and Stefan Jörg et al. [15] designing a flexible robot-assembly system using a multi-sensory approach and force feedback in the assembly of moving components.

3 Original Work

Moment invariants are the most popular descriptors for image regions and boundary segments, but computation of moments of a two dimensional (2D) image involves a significant amount of multiplications and additions in a direct method. Fast algorithms has been proposed for this calculations, for binary images Philips [16]. The computation of moments can be simplified since it contains only the information about the shape of the image as proposed by Chen [17]. In many real-time industry applications the speed of computation is very important, the 2D moment computation is intensive and involves parallel processing, which can become the bottleneck of the system when moments are used as major features. This paper introduces a novel method which uses collections of 2D images to obtain a very fast feature data *"current frame descriptor vector"* of an object by using image projections and canonical forms geometry grouping for invariant object recognition, producing 3D POSE information for different pre-defined assembly parts. A fast algorithm allows calculation of a boundary object function and centroid which defines and compress 3D object information, the algorithm uses a Weight Matrix Transformation introduced by Peña [18] to generate a CFD&POSE vector which gives object recognition and pose estimation information to the robot for grasping assembly components, which in conjunction with a FuzzyARTMAP ANN forms the system called SIRIO which recognizes, learns and performs pose estimation of assembly components in the order of milliseconds, which constitutes a practical tool for real-world applications.

4 Neuro-vision Systems

The first approach that most people use for designing neuro-vision systems is called "signal to symbol paradigm", in this approach, the aim is to have meaningful scene descriptions from raw sensory data. A large computational requirement is used in this approach. If a typical time-variant visual scene has to be analyzed, there are millions of instructions to be performed for each scene, advent of faster processor today can solve partially this problem but compared with our own visual experience to perceive and provide a meaning to a complex time-variant scene in approximately 70 to 200 milliseconds and considering that many aspects of early biological vision are achieved in only 18 to 46 transformations steps [19]. It is necessary to find another method using less computational power if we want to emulate better the human visual system, and mainly because it has been estimated that 60% of sensory information in humans is by visual pathway [20].

It can be inferred that biological vision architecture is massively parallel and uses a basic hierarchical information processing [21]. Transformation and reorganization of visual data into abstract representations is similar to the "signal to symbol paradigm", that performs computations in parallel involving spatial (X-Y plane) and temporal (time-dependant) aspects of visual information processing. From engineering perspective, it is not necessary and would be practically impossible to emulate the precise electrophysiological aspects of biological vision, but it is desirable to replicate some of the neural computational structures from this biological vision concerning with processing, storing and interpretation of the spatial-temporal visual information [22].

5 Computational Neural Networks

From a computational perspective, the individual neuron layers, as the retina, can be conceptualized as one or more two-dimensional arrays of neurons that perform specific operations on the visual signals. The primary structural characteristics of a computational neural network (CNN) are: an organized morphology containing many parallel-distributed neurons, a method of encoding information within the synaptic connections of neurons and a method of recalling information when presented with a stimulus input pattern.

From a signal-processing point of view, the biological neuron has two key elements, the *synapse* and the *soma*, they are responsible for performing computaitonal tasks such as: learning, knowledge acquistion (storage or memory of past experience) and recognizing patterns. In simple terms, a neuron can be depicted as an information processing element that receives an *n-dimensional neural input vector*:

$$X(k) = [x_1(k), x_2(k), ..., x_i(k)] \in \Re^n \tag{1}$$

which represents the signal being transmited from the n-neighboring neuron from the sensory neurons. Mathematically, the information-processing ability of a neuron can be represented as a nonlinear mapping operation M_ξ (figure 1), from the input vector $X(k) \in \Re^n$ to the scalar output $Y(k) \in \Re^n$ that is:

$$M_\xi : X(k) \in \Re^n \rightarrow Y(k) \in \Re^n \tag{2}$$

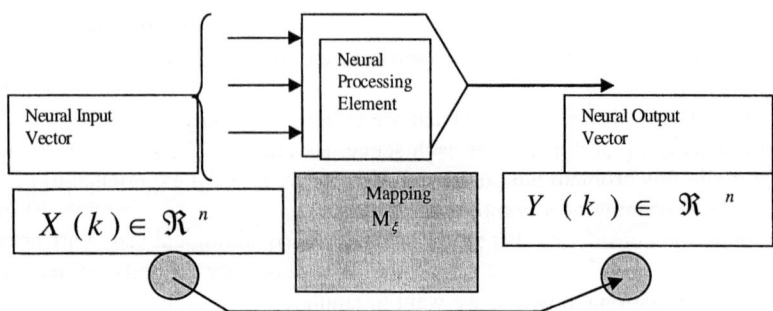

Fig. 1. A simplified model of a biological neuron (information-processing perspective)

5.1 Inspiring Ideas and ART Models

Knowledge can be built either empirically or by hand as suggested by Towell and Shavlik [23]. Empirical knowledge can be thought, as giving examples on how to react to certain stimuli without any explanation, and hand-built knowledge, where the knowledge is acquired by only giving explanations, but without examples. It was determined that in robotic systems, a suitable strategy should include a combination of both methods. Furthermore, this idea is supported by psychological evidence that suggests that theory and examples interact closely during human learning, Feldman [24].

Learning in natural cognitive systems, including our own, follows a sequential process as it is demonstrated in our daily life. Events are learnt incrementally, for instance, during childhood when we start making new friends, we also learn more faces and this process continues through life. This learning is also stable because the learning of new faces does not disrupt our previous knowledge. These premises are the core for the development of *Connectionist Models* of the human brain and are supported by psychology, biology and computer sciences. Psychological studies suggest the sequential learning of events at different stages or "storage levels" termed as *Sensory Memory* (SM), *Short Term Memory* (STM) and *Long Term Memory* (LTM).

There are different types of ANN, for this research a Fuzzy ARTMAP network is used. This network was chosen because of its incremental knowledge capabilities and stability, but mostly because of the fast recognition and geometrical classification responses. The Adaptive Resonance Theory (ART) is a well established associative brain and competitive model introduced as a theory of the human cognitive processing developed by Stephen Grossberg at Boston University. Grossberg resumed the situations mentioned above in what he called the *Stability-Plasticity Dilemma* suggesting that connectionist models should be able to adaptively switch between its plastic and stable modes. That is, a system should exhibit plasticity to accommodate new information regarding unfamiliar events. But also, it should remain in a stable condition if familiar or irrelevant information is being presented. He identified the problem as basic properties of associative learning and lateral inhibition. An analysis of this instability, together with data of categorization, conditioning, and attention led to the introduction of the ART model that stabilizes the memory of self-organizing feature maps in response to an arbitrary stream of input patterns S. Grossberg [25]. The theory has evolved in a series of real-time architectures for unsupervised learning, the ART-1 algorithm for binary input patterns G. Carpenter [26]. Supervised learning is also possible through ARTMAP G. Carpenter [27] that uses two ART-1 modules that can be trained to learn the correspondence between input patterns and desired output classes. Different model variations have been developed based on the original ART-1 algorithm, ART-2, ART-2a, ART-3, Gaussian ART, EMAP, View-NET, Fusion ARTMAP, LaminART just to mention but a few.

6 Our Approach

We think it is possible to get fast and reliable information from a simple but focused analysis of what an object might show as the very concerning, primitive and necessary information in order to have a substantial and robust cognition of what is seeing to memorize the very important aspects of the scene (we have called them "clues"), which later, can be used to retrieve memorized aspects of the object without having to recall detailed features and aspects. In someway humans do that process once an object has been seeing and learned for the very first time. We think that by learning *canonic forms* within the initial cognition process, it is possible to reconstruct the overall object cognition using primitives and perceptual grouping aspects (as the Gesttalt Laws), concerning with grouping, proximity, similarity and simplicity factors and Grossberg´s ideas about Boundary Contour System (BCS) and Feature Contour System (FCS), as shown in figure 2.

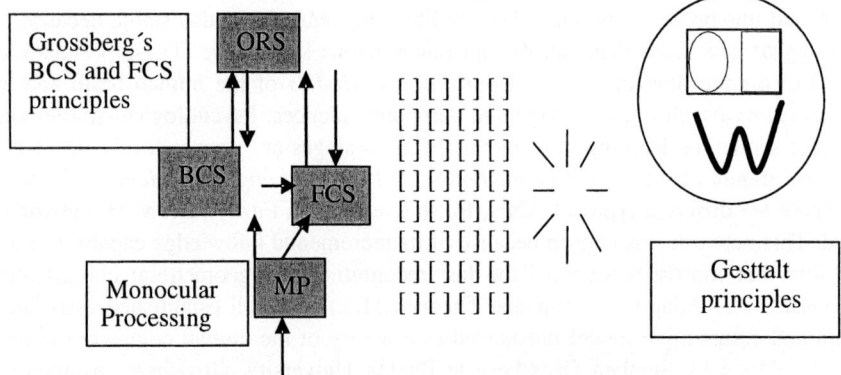

Fig. 2. Grossberg and Gesttalt principles representation

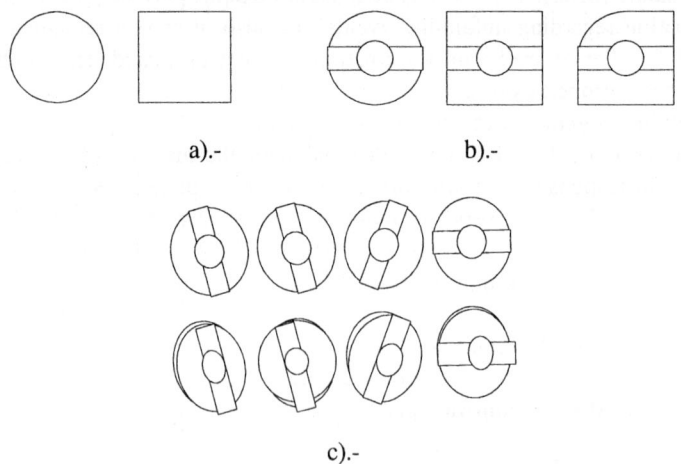

Fig. 3. a) Canonical forms for initial learning cognition. b) 2D circle, square, and radiused-square assembly pieces. c) Descriptor vector family for circle assembly part in different positions, angle, inclinations and rotations.

In this section, we will show this novel idea with simple parts that we are using in assembly applications within a manufacturing intelligent cell, we consider a circle and a rectangle as two canonical forms for the initial cognition learning as shown in figure 3a. If our system can learn this canonical forms and include them in the initial cognition (a priori knowledge), with think it is possible to provide information of objects in real world (3D) representing the assembly parts (we have called circle, rectangle and radiused-square) with 2D representations as shown in figure 3b.

The pieces, can be constructed with canonical forms grouped in different ways and following the a priori knowledge, considering "clues" this grouped forms, they can be represented by a *Descriptor Vector* containing all necessary information to achieve this idea. Having such a descriptor vector, an ANN can be trained and it is expected to have incremental knowledge to conform *descriptor vector families* which can be generated on-line with the same vision system as it is represented in figure 3c. With many learning processes and an incremental knowledge, the process will be speed up because of being just in *recall process*, once having an algorithm to create de descriptor vector, creating the *descriptor vector-component bin*, the process becomes an autonomous mechanism and the ARTMAP network sends each instance to its respective cluster.

The Boundary Object Function (BOF), is the function that describes a specific piece and it will vary according to the shape (see figure 4), this functions are showed for the circle, square and radiused-square parts used in the experiments.

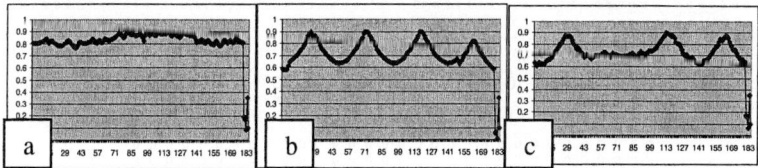

Fig. 4. BOF a).- circle b).- square c).- radiused-square

6.1 Descriptor Vector Generation and Normalization

The algorithm to generate the descriptor vector that we have called [CFD&POSE] is shown for one of the canonical forms (rectangle), a binary image is generated with some pre-processing operators and acquisition routines, applying the CFD&POSE algorithm we get an image which provide us with contour and centroid information of objects in a very novel and fast way graphically showed in figure 5.

The (H_{Wf}) Weight Transform Matrix is obtained to have a relation set of :

$$\text{Number } NWf \rightarrow [\text{coordinate numerical bin }] \qquad (3)$$

where : $\quad NWf \text{ min} \leq \sum (1's) \text{ within } (k \times k) \text{ Kernel} \leq NWf \text{ max} \quad$ for $k = 3$. $\qquad (4)$

it can be seen that *Nwfmax* provides the centroid of object and *NWf min* the boundary points of contour. For centroid calculations a summation of all *Nwfmax* is made for all X-Y's as follows:

354 M. Peña-Cabrera et al.

$$X_c = \frac{1}{No.NWf_{max-X}} \left[\Sigma\, NWf_{max} - X \right]$$
$$Y_c = \frac{1}{No.NWf_{max-Y}} \left[\Sigma\, NWf_{max} - Y \right]$$
(5)

and for boundary points we have:

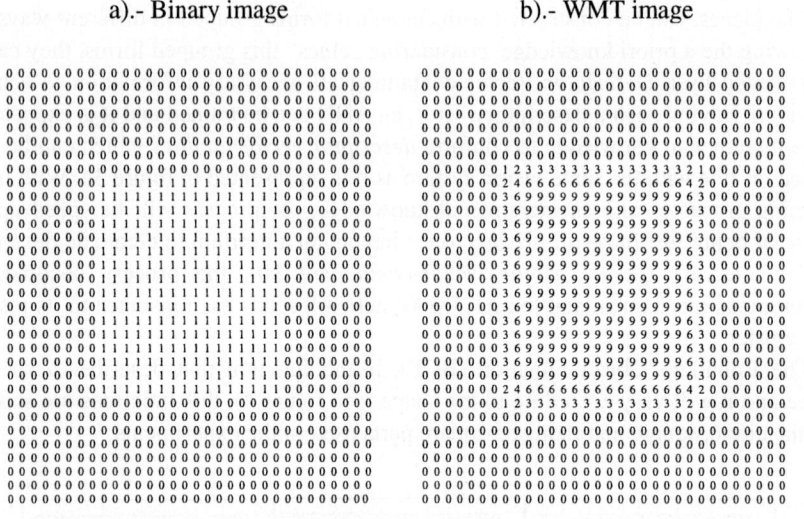

a).- Binary image　　　　　　b).- WMT image

c).- CFD & POSE image

Fig. 5. Algorithm images: a).- Binary image, b).- WMT image, c).-CFD&POSE image

$$vectorX(m) = \{x0, x1, x2,......xn\}_{NWf \min}$$
$$vectorY(m) = \{y0, y1, y2,...yn\}_{NWf \min}$$
(6)

centroid and coordinate of boundary points are obtained as well as a vector for calculations to get form feature extraction. Distances to get the BOF (boundary object function) are:

$$Dn = \sqrt{(X2-X1)^2 + (Y2-Y1)^2} \quad \forall \quad 0 \leq n \leq \text{size of angular grid} \quad (7)$$

Once the information has been processed, a descriptive vector is generated. This vector is the input for the neural network, (the vector has 185 data):
The descriptive vector is called CFD&POSE and it is conformed by:

$$[CDF \& POSE] = [D_1, D_2, D_3,..., D_n, X_c, Y_c, \theta, Z, ID]^T \quad (8)$$

D_i are the distances from the centroid to the perimeter of the object.
X_C, Y_C, are the coordinates of the centroid.
ϕ, is the orientation angle.
Z is the height of the object.
ID is a code number related to the geometry of the components.

7 Experimental Results

In order to test the robustness of the ANN, the Fuzzy ARTMAP Neural Network was trained first with 2808 different patterns and its learning capability analyzed. The percentage of recognition and the number of generated neurons are shown in figure 6.

The graph shows how the system learned all patterns in three epochs, creating only 32 neurons to classify 2808 patterns. The average time for training was 4.42 ms, and the average for testing was 1.0 ms. Results reported in this article employed 216 patterns corresponding to 72 square, 72 circle and 72 radiused-square components of the same size.

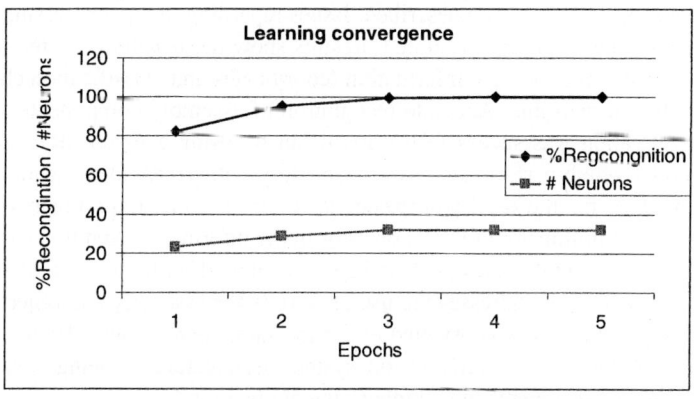

Fig. 6. Learning convergence of the neural network

With these training patterns set, the system was able to classified correctly 100% of the pieces presented on- line even if they were not of the same size, orientation or locations and for different light conditions. The average time of the total assembly cycle is 1:50.6 minutes and the minimum time is 1:46 minutes, the longest time is: 1:58 minutes. The average of the error made in both zones (grasping and assembly zones) is: 0.8625 mm, the minimum is: 0 mm while the maximum is 3.4 mm. The average of the error angle is: 4.27 ° , the minimum is: 0° and the maximum is 9°. The figure 7, shows eighteen different X and Y points where the robot might reach the male component showed as error X(mm) and error Y(mm), for the area for success grasping and assembly. See [28] for more detail.

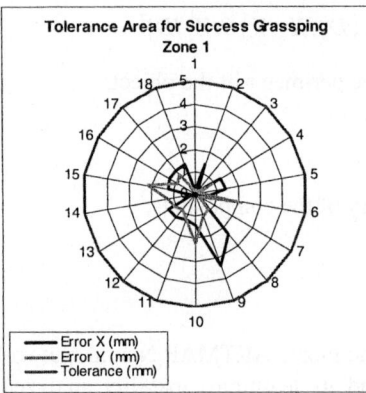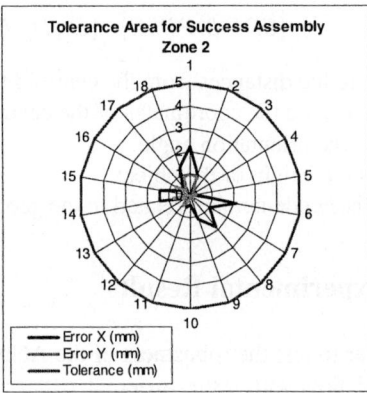

Fig. 7. Left positional error referenced to real centroid in male component. Right positional error referenced to real centroid in female component.

8 Conclusions and Future Work

A methodology for object recognition and POSE estimation for assembly components in manufacturing cells has been described. Issues regarding image processing, centroid and perimeter calculation are illustrated. Results show the feasibility of the method to send grasping and morphologic information (coordinates and classification characteristics) to a robot in real-time. Accurate recognition of assembly components and workpieces identification was successfully carried out by using a FuzzyARTMAP neural network model which performance was satisfactory with 100% identification and fast recognition times for the used workpieces lower than 5 ms. Experimental measurements showed ±3 millimeter of precision error in the information sent to the robot.

The intelligent manufacturing cell is being developed with multimodal sensor capabilities. Current work addresses the use of ANN's for assembly and object recognition separately, future work is oriented to use the same neural controller for all different sensorial modes. The SIRIO vision system architecture is being improved for handling complex 3D objects in manufacturing applications.

References

1. A. Rosenfeld,. Computer vision: a source of models for biological visual processes, Biomedical Engineering, 36,1, (1989) 93-96
2. Vijaykumar Gullapalli, Judy A. Franklin; Hamid Benbrahim: Acquiring robot skills via reinforcement learning. IEEE Control Systems, pages 13-24, February (1994)
3. Enric Cervera; Angel P. del Pobil: Programming and learning in real world manipulation tasks. IEEE/RSJ Int Conf on Inteligent Robot and Systems, 1:471-476, September (1997)
4. Martin Howarth: An investigation of task level programming for robotic assembly. PhD thesis, The Nottingham Trent University, January 1998
5. I Lopez-Juarez: On-line learning for robotic assembly using artificial neural networks and contact force sensing. PhD thesis, The Nottingham Trent University, (2000)
6. Hoska DR: Fixturless assembly manufacturing. Manuf. Eng., 100:49-54, April (1988)
7. W. Ngyuen and J.K. Mills., Multirobot control for flexible fixturless assembly of flexible sheet metal autobody parts. IEEE Int. Conf. on Robotics and Aut., , pp. 2340-2345, (1996)
8. W.J. Plut and G.M. Bone: Limited mobility grasps for fixturless assembly, In proceedings of the IEEE Int. Conf. on Robotics and Aut. , Minneapolis, Minn., pp. 1465-1470, (1996)
9. W.J. Plut and G.M. Bone: 3-D flexible fixturing using multi-degree of freedom gripper for robotics fixturless assembly. IEEE Int. Conf. on Robotics and Aut., pp. 379-384, (1997)
10. Langley C.S., et al.: A memory efficient neural network for robotic pose estimation, IEEE Int. Symp. on Computational. Intelligence on Robotics and Aut., No 1, 418-423, (2003)
11. E. Bribiesca: A new Chain Code. Pattern Recognition 32 , Pergamon, 235-251 , (1999)
12. M.K. Hu: Visual pattern recognition by moment invariants, IRE Trans Inform Theory IT-8, 179-187, (1962)
13. Cem Yüceer adn Kemal Oflazer: A rotation, scaling and translation invariant pattern classification system. Pattern Recognition, vol 26, No. 5 pp. 687-710, (1993)
14. Gary M. Bone , David Capson: Vision-guided fixturless assembly of automotive components. Robotics and Computer Integrated Manufacturing 19, 79-87 , (2003)
15. Stefan Jörg et. al. : Flexible robot-assembly using a multi-sensory approach. IEEE, Int. Conf. on Robotics and Aut., San Fco. Calif, USA (2000), pp 3687-3694
16. W. Philips: A new fast algorithm for moment com., Pattern Recog. 26, 1619-1621, (1993).
17. K. Chen: Efficient parallel algorithms for computation of two-dimensional image moments, Pattern Recognition 23, 109-119, (1990)
18. M. Peña-Cabrera, I. Lopez Juarez and R. Rios-Cabrera: A learning approach for on-line object recognition in robotic tasks, Int. Conf. on Computer Science, IEEE Computer Society Press. (2004)
19. L. Uhr: Highly parallel, hierarchical, recognition cone perceptual structures. Parallel Computer Vision, L. Uhr Ed., 249-292 (1987)
20. R.E. Kronauer, Y. Zeevi: Reorganization and diversification of signals in vision. IEEE Trans. Syst. Man, Cybern., SMC-15,1,91-101 (1985)
21. L. Uhr: Psychological motivation and underlying concepts. Structured Computer Vision, S. Tanimoto ,A. Klinger Ed. , 1-30 (1980)
22. Douglas G. Granrath: The role of human vision models in image proccesing. Proc. IEEE 69,5,552-561 (1981)
23. Geoffrey G. Towell, Jude W. Shavlik: Knowledge-based artificial neural networks Artificial Intelligence. Vol. 70, Issue 1-2, pp. 119-166. (1994)
24. Robert S. Feldman: Understanding Psychology, 3rd edition. Mc Graw-Hill, Inc., (1993).

25. Stephen Grossberg: Adaptive pattern classification and universal recoding II: Feedback, expectation, olfaction and illusions. Biological Cybernetics. Vol. 23, pp. 187-202, 1976.
26. Gail A. Carpenter et al.: A massively parallel architecture for a self-organizing neural pattern recognition. Machine, Academic Press, Inc. Pp. 54-115. (1987)
27. Gail A. Carpenter, et al: ARTMAP: supervised real-time learning and classification of nonstationary data by self-organizing neural network. Neural Networks 565-588 (1991)
28. M. Peña-Cabrera, I. López-Juárez, R. Ríos-Cabrera, J. Corona-Castuera: Machine vision learning process applied to robotic assembly in manufacturing cells. Journal of Assembly Automation Vol. 25 No. 3 (2005)

Multilevel Seed Region Growth Segmentation

Raziel Álvarez, Erik Millán, and Ricardo Swain-Oropeza

Mechatronics Research Center (CIMe),
Tecnológico de Monterrey, Campus Estado de México,
Km 3.5 Carretera al Lago de Guadalupe,
Atizapán de Zaragoza, Estado de México, Mexico, 52926
Phone: +52 55 5864 5659
{raziel, emillan, rswain}@itesm.mx

Abstract. This paper presents a technique for color image segmentation, product of the combination and improvement of a number of traditional approaches: Seed region growth, Threshold classification and level on detail in the analysis of demand. First, a set of precise color classes with variable threshold is defined based on sample data. A scanline algorithn uses color clases with a small threshold to extract an initial group of pixels. These pixels are passed to a region growth method, which performs segmentation using higher-threshold classes as homogeneity criterion to stop growth. This hybrid technique solves disadvantages from individual methods and keeps their strengths. Its advantages include a higher robustness to external noise and variable illumination, efficiency on image processing, and quality on region segmentation, outperforming the results of standalone implementations of individual techniques. In addition, the proposed approach sets a starting point for further improvements.

1 Introduction

Color image segmentation provides with an efficient and relatively simple way to identify colored objects. In Robocup's Four Legged League, it represents a typical approach for image analysis. In this league, all image processing and robot control is computed autonomously by the internal processor of an AIBO mobile robot, hence, there are strong restrictions on computing resources. Several techniques related to this type of analysis have been proposed, each trying to cope with problems such as the high processing frame rate required, sensitiveness to variable lighting conditions and the noise produced by external objects.

The techniques proposed so far belong to many categories from the classical image processing algorithms. Typical approaches analyse all pixels in the image, using predefined color classes and a simple classification method to detect regions of interest. Some techniques perform a growth of color regions based in local pixel information, such as the contrast between neighbours. Other techniques use edge detection filters and pattern matching to identify objects, achieving more tolerance to illumination changes.

From the application of these approaches to our problem, we identified two areas of improvement. The first one is concerned on how to identify accurately pixels in our environment and discard external noise. The second problem deals with efficiency, specially on the improvements obtained by processing only the regions of interest on the image, as usually objects of interest represent a small area on images. These problems are related, as focusing the algorithm on the correct areas of the image will reduce the probability on finding noise.

The use of additional information about the environment may help to better identify the important regions of the image. For instance, in our domain, the information on the objects in the environment may be combined with information on the camera perspective to predict the position of objects.

In this work, we propose a combination of image segmentation techniques already used in our domain, in order to of harness their combined advantages and minimize their disadvantages. The technique presented in this paper provides a high quality image segmentation, improving robustness to illumination changes and achieving a high processing frame rate.

The document is organized as follows. In section 2 we present an overview of related work on color image segmentation. Section 3 describes our proposed solution, starting with a multilevel color classification to discard noise, followed by a scanline processing algorithmm to segment the image, the extraction of a set of seeds from possible objects of interest, and a region growth algorithm to obtain detailed information about these objects. The description and implementation details on these components are outlined in sections 4, 5, 6, and 7 respectively. Some results obtained with the technique are provided in section 8. Finally, section 9 contains a summary of conclussions and the future work.

2   Previous Work

In the Robocup's domain, several techniques and algorithms have been proposed, corresponding to many categories of image processing theory. Common image segmentation algorithms consist on defining a set of color classes that describe the objects of interest in the environment, translating them into look-up tables [1]. This kind of methods usually perform a pixel by pixel processing, where each one is classified into one of the color classes.

Many approaches have been proposed [2, 3, 4, 5, 6] to solve the color class definition issue and achieve robustness to illumination changes. While a natural solution for adaptation to different light conditions is an on-line color class update, the large computation times required by techniques that offer good results discourages this idea. On the other hand, simplistic and fast techniques lead to misclasification problems and to poor robustness to illumination changes.

However, these techniques have some important drawbacks. First, they usually consume much processing time by reading all of the pixels in the image. Moreover, this increases the chances of classifying external noise as useful objects. Other algorithms avoid processing the whole image by extracting pixels with high probability of belonging to a color in order to start the processing from them [7, 8]. These techniques are known as Seed Region Growth (SRG) algorithms, and use those seed pixels to initiate the growth of the regions of interest according to a homogeneity criterion. The criterion substitutes the color classes and is usually replaced by a contrast metric to avoid illumination problems. However, they are highly unpredictable and very difficult to control, leading to flooding problems.

One of the most sucessfull family of algorithms consists on incorporating information about the camera perspective [9, 10, 11] to sample pixels that might contain objects of interest. Hence, it is not necessary to use the full resolution of images. Image is processed by using a set of scanlines in a layout perpendicular to the horizon. This techniques avoid areas where no objects can be found, increasing efficiency and discarding areas of noise. These algorithms may use edge detection techniques to increase their tolerance to illumination changes. However, since this method just processes the pixels along the scan lines, important information about solid objects might be lost.

3 Overview of Our Approach

The proposed segmentation algorithm implies the combination of three techniques, organized in two stages. First, scan lines are used to extract a set of color seeds. The extraction process relies in the definition of color classes. In this case, we are looking to identify pixels with a high probability of belonging to the class, so color classes are defined strictly with the implicit surfaces classification technique. From these seeds, the region growth algorithm will locate regions of interest by using a more relaxed color class as the homogeneity criterion. Thus, two classes of different probabilities are defined for each color. The following sections will describe each of the parts of this algorithm.

4 Color Classification

Color classification is a basic criteria to segment images. It consists in defining a set of color classes in the color space that characterize the known objects in the environment. In this work, color classes are used to determine which pixels in the image will be used as seeds. The usual way to create the color classes is collecting distinctive color samples and then defining each class in terms of these samples through clustering.

There are several methods to accomplish this stage. One simple approach is the definition of six thresholds for the minimal and maximal intensities of the three color channels, as proposed in [1]. However, the poor fitting of the prismatic volume to the cloud of samples may produce misclassification problems. Several other approaches have been proposed, trying to preserve properties such as simplicity, efficiency and robustness to illumination changes. For this application we used the efficient and robust method depicted in [12].

The technique is based on implicit surfaces as the limiting contour for color classes. It starts from a collection of images from which a user selects a set of color samples. Then, a number of spherical primitives are distributed uniformly along the cloud of samples using the k-means algorithm. Once located, the radius of the primitives is obtained from the standard deviation of the samples contained by each primitive. Finally, these primitives are blended to produce the final surface. The implicit function is defined by:

$$f_i(P) = \frac{(x - c_i^{(x)})^2 + (y - c_i^{(y)})^2 + (z - c_i^{(z)})^2}{r_i^2} \quad (1)$$

with the following properties:

$f(P) < \Gamma$ For all interior points $P(x, y, z)$.
$f(P) > \Gamma$ For all exterior points $P(x, y, z)$.
$f(P) = \Gamma$ For all surface points $P(x, y, z)$.

where Γ is a threshold that may be interpreted as a scale parameter.

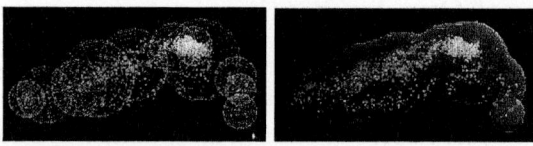

Fig. 1. Results of configuration of primitives and final color class

From the defined color classes, a look-up table is created for efficient image processing. The produced configurations and the resulting implicit surfaces fit closely the point samples used in the process, producing an accurate representation, as illustrated in Figure 1. Additional details on this technique and its advantages can be found in [12].

Multilevel. The use of strict color classes for scanning and flexible classes for region growth is a natural choice. The strict classes includes pixels with high probabilities of being part of a given color class, reducing possible noise sources; while the flexible classes support a controlled region growth, reducing flooding problems, and increasing robustness to varying illumination. The difference between these two types of color classes is shown in Figure 2.

It is important to consider that the equation of implicit surfaces can be seen as a distance metric, or a potential field. When large threshold values are selected to create the surface, there is a significantly higher risk of overlapping between different color classes. To solve this problem, pixel values will be classified into the closest class, according to the implicit function; in other words, into the class with higher probabilities.

For greater efficiency, image pixels are classified using a precalculated look-up table, built by subdividing each color component; then, a color is assigned to each combination of their values, according to our color segmentation criteria. For points on color space located over the superposed area, the winner class is

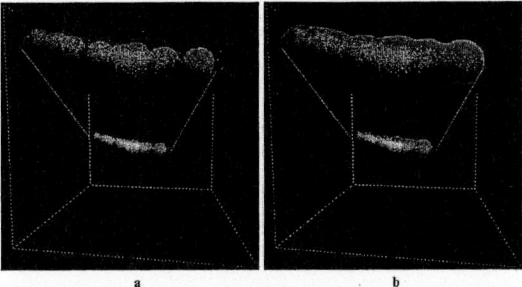

Fig. 2. Comparison in tolerance when creating color classes according to their purpose. a) Class used for scaning ($\Gamma = 0.5$). b) Class used for region growth ($\Gamma = 1.0$).

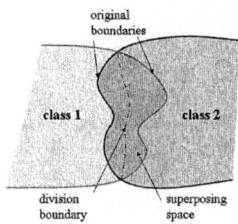

Fig. 3. Division criterion applied over two superposed classes

the one with the smallest distance to the point. Graphically, this rule is depicted in Figure 3.

5 Scanlines and Horizon Detection

The use of scanlines is a simple way to segment an image without processing every single pixel. This technique relies on a sampling pattern that selects a small set of pixels for analysis, reducing processing time.

In particular, we use the approach from Jüngel et al. [9,10], where a set of lines is used for processing. These lines are perpendicular to the horizon, and their density varies according to their distance to the camera, which is approximated based on the proximity of each pixel to the horizon line. As the pixel is closer to the horizon, it is more probable that it belongs to a distant object, so the sampling density should be higher than for pixels away from the horizon line. This density is exemplified in Figure 4.a.

However, this approach requires the horizon of the camera for each picture. This horizon is obtained from the kinematic model of the camera, using the field plane as reference. A method to calculate the horizon was proposed by Jüngel et al. [13]. In this method, the horizon line is defined as the set of pixels which are located at the same height from the field plane as the optical center of the camera. Hence, the horizon is defined as the intersection between the camera

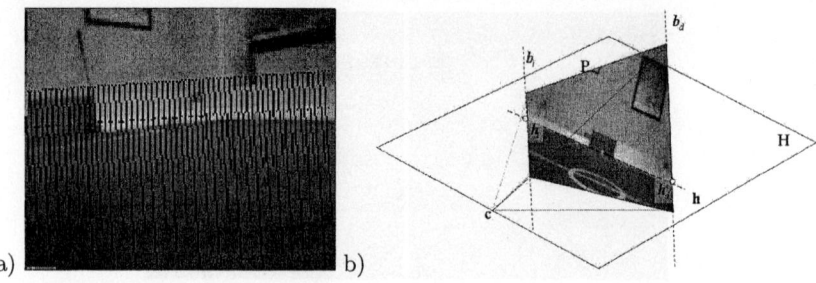

Fig. 4. a) Horizon-oriented scanlines for a sample image. Higher detail is selected for farther areas, while lower detail is chosen for closer areas. b) Planes used in the extraction of the horizon line.

projection plane P and a plane H, which is parallel to the field plane and crosses the center of projection of the camera c. This is illustrated in Figure 4.b.

6 Seed Extraction

The scanlines will be used to obtain the seeds for the region growth algorithm. In this way, just the pixels along the scanline are analyzed and coordinates stored for those with a high posibility to belong to a given color class.

Scan pattern. The scan pattern consists of a set of lines, perpendicular to the horizon, that will start from a line parallel to the horizon and go down to the field. Here, a line 8 degrees above the horizon was enough to detect objects higher than the camera, such as goals or beacons within our environment, and helped to discard sources of noise outside the field.

Scanlines of different length will be intertwined, as seen in Figure 4.a, in order to evaluate more samples at possibly distant areas of the image. Different lengths allow to control the density of the analysis. The proposed algorithm uses three different lengths, with a separation between lines of aproximately 1 degree, to guarantee that every object in the environment will be intersected by at least one scan line.

Classification. Pixels lying within these scanlines will be classified using the strict color classification previously generated in order to reduce the possibilities of identifying noise as an object of interest. In the current approach, classes are precalculated and stored in the form of a look-up table for efficiency, and remain without change during the operation of the vision system.

On theses classes, the probability threshold for classification is controlled via the surface scale parameter Γ. We call the *natural scale* of the surface when Γ is equal to 1. Values between 0 and 1 result in more tight and reduced classes, while values greater that 1 produce more flexible, tolerant classes. Thus, the classes used for this stage in our algorithm use thresholds between 0 and 1.

This routine does not need to process the entire image, just pixels on scanlines. Besides, it works as a filter to discard regions above the horizon line, which combined with the strict definition of color classes reduce significatively false positive problems caused by external noise.

During this stage it is also possible to detect field borders and lines, from transitions from green to white, which is simpler in this stage, as region growth is an unnecesary step for border detection. As no region growth is done, less strict color classes are used.

7 Seed Region Growth

Seed Region Growth is a region-based technique proposed by Wasik and Saffiotti [8] used to perform color image segmentation. This algorithm starts with a set of pixel seeds from each color class. The SRG routine takes each color set and selects a seed to start the growth. A new region is assigned to this seed.

We grow this region in a 4-pixel neighbourhood. If the neighbouring pixel already belongs to a pixel, it is ignored. If not, we use our homogeneity criterion to determine if the neighbour is similar enough to integrate it to the region. In such case, the pixel is added as a new seed for the region. Growth is interrupted when there are no more seeds for the current region. Then, a new seed is selected from the initial seed set, and the algorithm is repeated, creating new regions until there are no more initial seeds.

The homogeneity criterion is central for the algorithm. In [8], a simple threshold evaluation regarding the maximum contrast on color component values is proposed. However, the contrast criterion is very difficult to fine tune, produces variable results and it is difficult to control, so it is prone to flooding problems.

We use a different homogeneity criterion that relies on whether the pixel lies within a set of color classes with a higher tolerance than classes used for seed extraction. This classes are generated by modifying the value of the Γ parameter. Usually, the scale parameter Γ is set to 1 or greater, although the only restriction is that Γ value for classes in this stage must be bigger than the value used in past stage.

8 Results

The purpose of our technique is to achieve better segmentation results, robustness to light variations and at the same time improve the efficiency of other algorithms. For the algorithm tests, we used full resolution images from an AIBO ERS-2100, at a resolution of 176×144 pixels.

Seed extraction. This is the first stage of our algorithm and extracts a set of color pixel seeds. Color classes are defined estrictly using the implicit surfaces technique with a scale parameter $\Gamma = 0.5$. At the same time, this routine detects field lines and field borders, storing coordinates of pixels in white-green transitions for its later interpretation. Some results of this stage are shown in Figure 5. The seed extraction and lines detection processing took an average of 16ms.

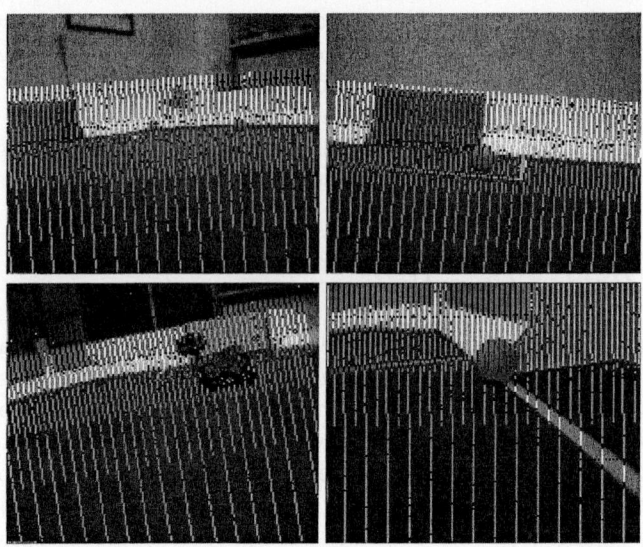

Fig. 5. Results from seed extraction and field lines and field borders (red points). Scale parameter $\Gamma = 0.5$.

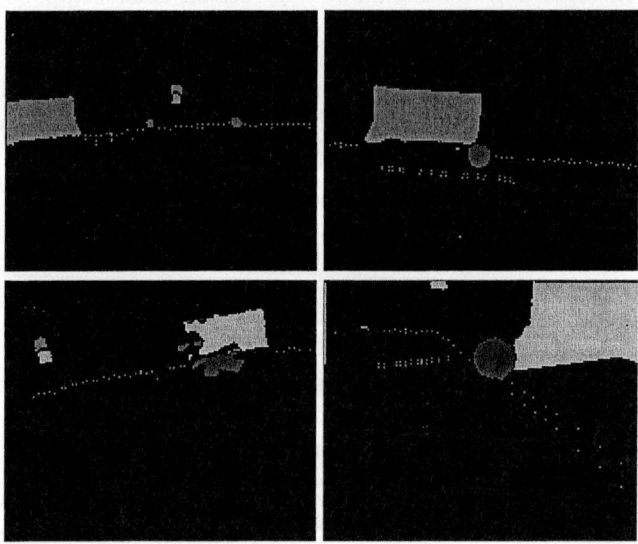

Fig. 6. Imege segmentation produced from the region growth algorithm. Scale parameter $\Gamma = 1.0$.

Region growth. Once the seeds are extracted, the second and final stage of our algorithm is run. It performs the seed region growth algorithm and it uses a set of color classes with a scale parameter $\Gamma = 1.0$. On average, it takes about 24ms to perform the segmentation of an image.

9 Conclusions and Future Work

A new technique for color image segmentation has been proposed as a result of the combination of different techniques. The technique combines the advantages of the composing methods and reduce their disadvantages. Some of the improvements from this hybrid technique are:

- A greater control on the homogeneity criterion than using the method proposed by Wasik and Saffiotti [8].
- Scanlines alone cannot identify correctly small objects on the image. The region growth increases the detected pixels, achieving a detail similar of that obtained by processing every pixel, but using less processor resources.
- The use of two levels of color classes helps to reduce the noise produced by external objects.
- It is not required that scanlines pass through an entire object to identify it, just one pixel is neccessary. Hence, a quality segmentation can be achieved using less scanlines.
- A simple variation on the scale parameter can improve tolerance to lighting conditions and control the size of the regions reached by the region growth algorithm.

These results are promising, since the efficiency and quality on segmentation objectives were fulfilled. Our future work centers on changing the look-up table segmentation for a direct evaluation of the implicit function, in order to readjust on-line our color classes accordingly to the illumination conditions. The second part of our future work would be the design of such an algorithm that, using the region-growth algorithm, recollects the new color samples necessary to update color classes. Finally, it would be significant to speed up the reconfiguration step of the implicit surfaces that describe the color classes.

References

1. Bruce, J., Balch, T., Veloso, M.M.: Fast and inexpensive color image segmentation for interactive robots. In: IEEE/RSJ International Conference on Intelligent Robots and Systems. (2000) 2061–2066
2. Oda, K., Ohashi, T., Kato, T., Katsumi, Y., Ishimura, T.: The kyushu united team in the four legged robot league. In: 6th International Workshop on RoboCup 2002 (Robot World Cup Soccer Games and Conferences), Lecture Notes in Artificial Intelligence, Springer Verlag (2002)

3. Dahm, I., Deutsch, S., Hebbel, M., Osterhues, A.: Robust color classification for robot soccer. In: 7th International Workshop on RoboCup 2003 (Robot World Cup Soccer Games and Conferences), Lecture Notes in Artificial Intelligence, Springer Verlag (2003)
4. Nakamura, T., Ogasawara, T.: On-line visual learning method for color image segmentation and object tracking. In: IEEE/RSJ International Conference on Intelligent Robots and Systems. (1999) 222–228
5. Mayer, G., Utz, H., Kraetzschmar, G.K.: Towards autonomous vision self-calibration for soccer robots. In: IEEE/RSJ International Conference on Intelligent Robots and Systems. (2002)
6. Li, B., Hu, H., Spacek, L.: An adaptive color segmentation algorithm for sony legged robots. In: 21st IASTED International Multi-Conference on Applied Informatics. (2003) 126–131
7. von Hundelshausen, F., Rojas, R.: Tracking regions. In: 7th International Workshop on RoboCup 2003 (Robot World Cup Soccer Games and Conferences), Lecture Notes in Artificial Intelligence, Springer Verlag (2003)
8. Wasik, Z., Saffiotti, A.: Robust color segmentation for the robocup domain. In: International Conference on Pattern Recognition. (2002)
9. Bach, J., Jüngel, M.: Using pattern matching on a flexible, horizon-aligned grid for robotic vision. In: Concurrency, Specification and Programming. (2002) 11–19
10. Jüngel, M., Hoffmann, J., Lötzsch, M.: A real-time auto-adjusting vision system for robotic soccer. In: 7th International Workshop on RoboCup 2003 (Robot World Cup Soccer Games and Conferences), Lecture Notes in Artificial Intelligence, Springer Verlag (2003)
11. Jüngel, M.: Using layered color precision for a self-calibrating vision system. In: 8th International Workshop on RoboCup 2004 (Robot World Cup Soccer Games and Conferences), Lecture Notes in Artificial Intelligence, Springer Verlag (2004)
12. Álvarez, R., Millán, E., Swain-Oropeza, R., Aceves-López, A.: Color image classification through fitting of implicit surfaces. In: 9th Ibero-American Conf. on Artificial Intelligence (IBERAMIA), Cholula, Mexico, Lecture Notes in Computer Science, Springer Verlag (2004)
13. Jüngel, M.: A vision system for robocup: Diploma thesis. Master's thesis, Institut für Informatik Humboldt-Universität zu Berlin (2004)

A CLS Hierarchy for the Classification of Images

Antonio Sanchez[1], Raul Diaz[2], and Peter Bock[3]

[1] LANIA, Xalapa,Veracruz, México 72820 & TCU, Fort Worth Texas 76129
asanchez@lania.mx
[2] LANIA , Xalapa,Veracruz, México 72820
[3] GWU, Washington D.C. 20006

Abstract. The recognition of images beyond basic image processing often relies on training an adaptive system using a set of samples from a desired type of images. The adaptive algorithm used in this research is a learning automata model called CLS (collective learning systems). Using CLS, we propose a hierarchy of collective learning layers to learn color and texture feature patterns of images to perform three basic tasks: recognition, classification and segmentation. The higher levels in the hierarchy perform recognition, while the lower levels perform image segmentation. At the various levels the hierarchy is able to classify images according to learned patterns. In order to test the approach we use three examples of images: a) Satellite images of celestial planets, b) FFT spectral images of audio signals and c) family pictures for human skin recognition. By studying the multi-dimensional histogram of the selected images at each level we are able to determine the appropriate set of color and texture features to be used as input to a hierarchy of adaptive CLS to perform recognition and segmentation. Using the system in the proposed hierarchical manner, we obtained promising results that compare favorably with other AI approaches such as Neural Networks or Genetic Algorithms.

"To understand is to perceive patterns"
Sir Isaiah Berlin (1909-1997)

1 Introduction

An adaptive systems such as a Neural Network and Genetic Algorithms relies on training the system using a set of samples or exemplar images, however in their case an extensive preprocess of the image is required in to order to scale the images. In this we use CLS models [13] as an alternative to other adaptive models that do not required such an extensive preprocess of the images. Instead CLS layers are used to learn color and texture features in a non-parametric fashion, mainly classifying the structure of the images. A hierarchical organization is proposed to solve various classification tasks. The higher levels in the hierarchy classify the images according to a previously learned set of classes, while the lower levels are designed to segment the images to obtain their basic components. Following this approach our application is able to accumulate a multi-dimensional histogram that estimates the probability density function of a feature space for each image and uses them as a the basis for its classification task.

In order to test the feasibility of this approach we use three examples using different sets of images. First we use satellite images to recognize different planets and then for the case of the Earth, a lower level in the hierarchy is used to segment the images in terms of land, water and cloud texture. Further down the hierarchy, the system is also able to segment type of land components such as mountains, valleys and so on. Using airplane images we are also able to segment various urban components. As a second example, we use FFT spectrograms of audio signals to distinguish various animal sounds. For this case the hierarchy is organized in four levels. One classifies images in terms of frequency range, a lower level in terms of sound duration, a third level in terms amplitude to finally have a CLS layer to determine the particular spectrogram of an animal sound. For the final example, we take regular images from ordinary pictures to train the system to recognize various types of skin texture.

1.1 Related Work

Texture analysis as a scheme to recognize and segment images has been widely used. Yet to this day, one might say that is still is very much an art. Several approaches have been tried with various levels of success. We can divide the use of texture in three main approaches: statistical where a polynomial feature vector is computed for each texture, this is the case of the EMS approach used by the EM and SVM algorithms reported in the literature, relevant to this paper is the work of Carson, C. Belongie, S. Greenspan, H. & J. Malik J [5]. A second approach is called the nonparametric structural or contextual approach, where texture is characterized by set of tone and color point features, either as RGB or HSB intensity features. As well as structural or spatial relationships among the pixels, properly named texels (texture elements). Using this approach, relevant to this paper we mention the overall review presented by Greenspan [8]. Relevant to AI, the use of neural networks and rule-based systems are needed to obtain image segmentation by means of class recognition, in a way similar to the approach we use in this paper. A final approach reported in the literature is the work of Bhanu & Wu [2] using Genetic Algorithms to obtain image segmentation by means of pseudo optimization.

1.2 Collective Learning Systems

Falling in the second approach, we present an alternative adaptive method of nonparametric texture learning. In our case we use CLS, initially proposed by Bock in 1976; conceptually is an extension of Learning Automata models [10]. The model can be defined in terms of the interaction between an Automata and its Environment {CLS, ENV} where the CLS and ENV are defined by [13]:

```
CLS   = {X, Y, STM, P, g, A}           ENV = {Y, X, T, eval}
X   = 0 .. nmax  the input set         Y the input vector Y(t)=g [Q (t)]
nmax =  state transitions              X  the output set
Y    a vector of nmax + 1 elements     T  the truth vector
     representing the outputs selected eval is the evaluation
STM  = 0 .. qmax is the state set      function X (t) = eval(Y, T)
P  is a qmax*qmax transition matrix    generates an overall X
g   is the output function             composite evaluation
A  is an compensation scheme
```

The number of incorrect outputs delivered by the CLS may determine the value of the eval function. In a CLS model, learning is achieved by means of an algedonic compensation policy to update the probabilities of the STM; a simple case is represented by [10]:

Case of a Reward (with $0 < \beta < 1$)
For the selected i -> k transition
STM(t+1)i,k =
   STM(t)i,k+ ß*(1– STM(t))i,k

For the rest of the i -> j with j=/k
STM(t+1)i,j =
   STM(t) - ß*(1– STM(t)i,k)/(n-1)

Case of a Punishment (with $0 < \beta < 1$)
For the selected i -> k transition
STM(t+1)i,k=
   STM(t)i,k - ß*STM(t)i,k

For the rest of the i -> j with j=/k
STM(t+1)i,j =
   STM(t) + ß*STM(t)/(n-1)

1.3 CLS Implementation as an ALISA Engine

For this research, we use ALISA [4] which is a multi-channel path algorithm for image classification that implements the CLS model previously described. The system is used to select an adequate set of color and texture features of an image to be used as the input of CLS. Once the feature values have been extracted from an analysis pattern, they are assembled into a feature vector that indexes the feature space of each image into a multi-dimensional histogram that functions as the State Transition

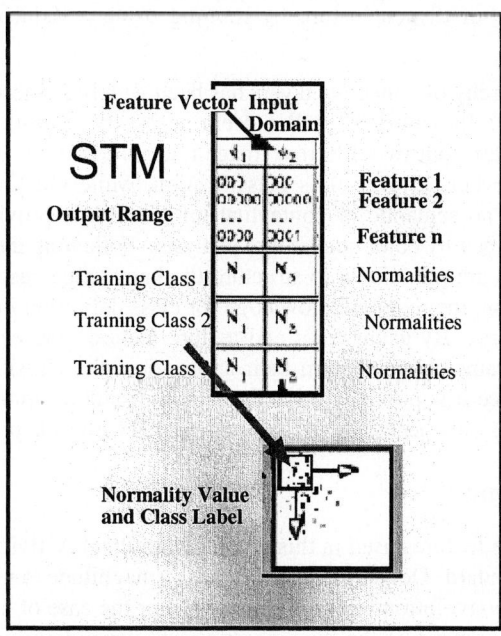

Fig. 1. The STM is the array where each training class stores the feature for each image according to the analysis of each texel (texture element) input [1]

Matrix (STM) of the CLS. Each feature histogram in the set is a row in the STM, which represents a specific class of textures to be learned. During testing, a test image is presented to the system. A multinomial-variance-based classifier is used to select the class with the highest posterior probability for that feature vector value. The unique symbol for that class is placed in a class map at the same pixel location as the center of the analysis token from which the analysis pattern was extracted; thus the class map is spatially isomorphic with the input test image. Texel by texel, the complete class map is generated for that test image, with each pixel in the class map representing the best estimate of the texture class as learned by the Texture Module during training. Figure 1 provide a conceptualization of the process.

2 Research Objectives and Implementation

2.1 Objectives and Working Hypothesis

With the previous background the objective of this paper is to validate the feasibility of classifying and segmenting diverse type of images, with as little image preprocessing as possible using only CLS layers. In order to obtain better results we propose the use of hierarchy of CLS layers to perform recognition and the classification of images before attempting image segmentation, therefore the working hypothesis of the paper is succinctly stated as follows:

Hypothesis: Using CLS layers in a hierarchical organization, it is possible to classify and segment images of diverse nature by training using a reduced sample sets of images.

The use of a hierarchy of collective layers has been widely suggested, as reported in the learning automata literature [13]. We deem necessary to work in a hierarchical fashion in order to carry out two different image recognition tasks. Thus, as proposed before, the higher levels perform class classification, while the lower levels do the segmentation. Since no semantic or contextual information is provided, the recognitions is solely performed by color and texture analysis. Following the hypothesis, sets of hierarchical levels are predefined to structure the knowledge base. As commented in the previous section, the required knowledge for class definition in a CLS models is stored in an STM array. By using color and texture features and examining the joint and marginal histograms obtained from their application, the classification process is highly enhanced, since it is possible to obtain pattern disambiguation. We have found that in most cases it is only necessary to use few features with little precision.

2.2 ALISA Configuration

The structural texture features used in this project were Pixel Activity (X, Y and combined, average, Standard Deviation and gradient (magnitude and direction). The token size for these convolutions was a 3x3 matrix. For the case of color we use RGB filters. The Dynamic ranges of the histograms varied depending on the experiments and are reported in the results. We use a standard precision of 256 discrete values for the histograms computation. In all the cases we used two different sets of images, one for training and one for testing.

2.3 Satellite and Airplane Image Segmentation

The research hypothesis is to be tested in three different sets of images. A hierarchical organization is presented for each one of them. In the first case, we use images of celestial bodies; satellite images (from ESA [7] & NASA [11]). As stated before, for our research, image size and resolution bear no importance; the only preprocessing to the images is the reduction of the pixel size to values less than 500x500 pixels to speed up the processing time and storing them on RGB mode. As it may be obvious, texture varies considerably as a function of the distance from the source. Therefore in order to maintain texture consistency, all the images used for each celestial body must come from pictures taken within the same distance range. The following hierarchy of CLS layers is used in order to recognize different images classes according to previous training. Segmentation of the distinct elements is to be done by a texel and color analysis using a cumulative histogram of the various features of the image. The hierarchy is organized as follows:

    Level 1: Solar System -> Earth
       Level 2a: Earth -> Oceans -> Depth Levels
       Level 2b: Earth -> Clouds -> Cloud Shapes
       Level 2c: Earth -> Continent -> Land Segments
         Level 3a: Land Segments -> Urban Segment
           Level 4: Urban Segment -> Building Type

The color and texture features used for this case are presented in table 2.1. There were 39 images were required for training at Level 1, 42 for Level 2, 39 for Level 3 and 20 for Level 4.

2.4 Audio Signal Testing

Considering that audio signal can be converted into Fourier Spectrograms, we decided to test the feasibility of a hierarchical arrangement to recognize different audio signals using their spectrograms. For reasons of space, we do not discuss here the issues involved with generating the FFT to compute the spectrograms; suffice it to say that for this application we relied on the use of the RAVEN [6]. As a test bed case, the spectrograms to recognize are those corresponding to animal sounds. Detecting texture features in a spectrogram may prove difficult since the image structure of the spectrogram depends on the range definition for the frequency, the time and the amplitude of the signals. In a similar fashion as in the example previously presented, in order to maintain texture consistency, all the images used for each celestial body must come from spectrograms generated with the same ranges definition for the three independent variables. Here is where the use of a hierarchy of spectrograms may become the solution to the problem. The hierarchy of CLS layers to handle the case of audio signals was organized as follows:

    Level 1: Frequency Layer (kHz) -> [Distinctive signal frequency]
      Level 2: Time Layer (sec.) -> [Typical duration of sound]
        Level 3: Amplitude Layer (RMS) -> [Standard power]
          Level 4: Recognition of the Animal Sound -> [Blue Whale, .. Parrot]

Effectively it is possible to separate signals into different frequency range values and then create an added division in time duration. Furthermore determining the RMS value for the amplitude may also help in the disambiguation of the signals. The texture features used for this case are presented in table 2.2. There were 7 images used in the training at Level 1, 11 at Level 2, 12 at Level 3 and 77 at the various CLS layers for Level 4.

2.5 Skin Recognition

Our third test deals with recognition and segmentation of specific color and texture components in an image. In this case we consider recognizing human skin from regular family pictures, with as little preprocessing as possible. We propose to train a set of CLS classes to recognize the specific colors and textures of skin. We use color and texture features independent of the context. The main problem here is to be able to reject texture patterns that closely resemble skin. Rather than using a hierarchy of classes, for this case we use a set of non-skin classes as the way to approach the problem. The texture features used for this case are presented in table 2.3. The CLS layer was trained with 24 images of texture and 65 images of non-skin textures.

3 Results

3.1 Recognition and Segmentation of Celestial Bodies

We present the results of the various levels of the hierarchy. Figure 2 shows the classification at level 1 of an image of the Sun, with 71.4% of texel acceptance. In the case of Figure 3 Level 1 classified the image as planet Earth with 66.8% while Level 2 segmented the image in three basic components. Of the 49 images given to level 1, only in two cases the system provided wrong answers, for example an image of Planet Venus was erroneously classified as the Sun.

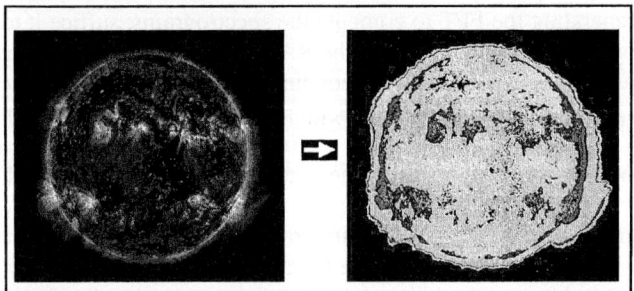

Fig. 2. Image of the Sun and the CLS recognition result at Level 1: Sun (yellow) with 71.4%

Figure 4 presents the segmentation results at Level 3 for the satellite image shown in figure 3. Figure 5 present another segmentation results. Figure 6 presents the results of an airplane image of the Earth; in this case since Level 3 classifies and segments the urban development, Level 4 segments such segment in its building type.

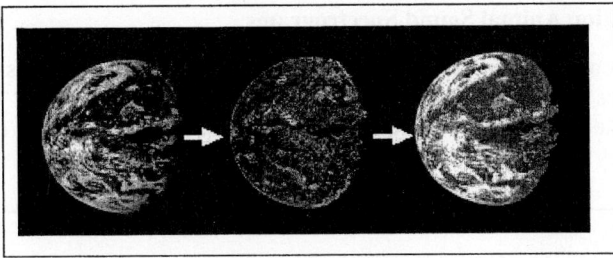

Fig. 3. Image of the Earth and the CLS recognition results: Level 1 Earth (blue) recognition with 66.8%. Level 2 Three-component segmentation.

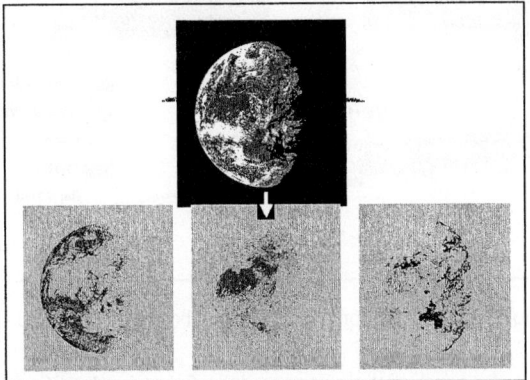

Fig. 4. Image of the Earth and the CLS recognition results: L3 subcomponents sementation

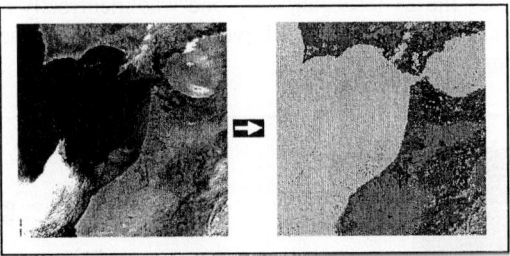

Fig. 5. Image of the Earth and the CLS recognition results: Level 3 land segmentation

Fig. 6. Airplane image and the CLS recognition: Level 3 land segment Land 4 urban segment

3.2 Recognition Animal Sound Spectrograms

Figure 7 presents the result of a fourth level hierarchy for audio signals. The Level 1 layer classifies the signal in the 1-4 kHz range (color blue); Level 2 classifies the duration of the signal in the more than 4 sec class. Finally Level 4 recognizes the spectrogram as that one of a Bearded Seal, which is the right selection.

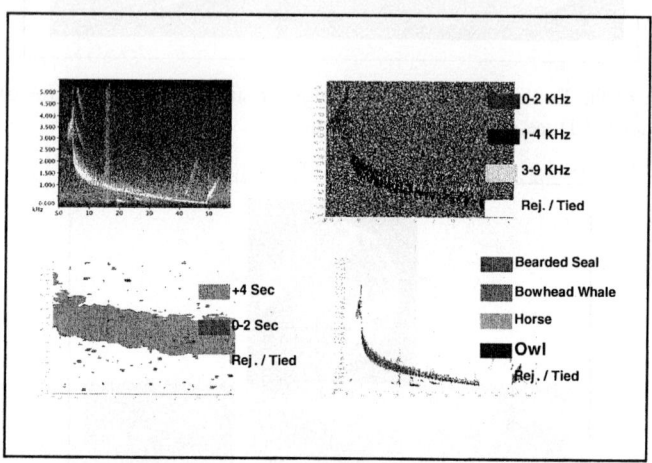

Fig. 7. Audio Signal recognition at three levels: bearded seal sound spectrogram

Figure 8 depicts the case of the spectrogram of that is classified by Level 2 in the duration of 0 to 2 seconds sending it to a different CLS layer at Level 4; in this case the spectrogram is recognized by this level as belonging to the sound of a Sheep, it is the right selection. Of the 24 tests run, only one was incorrectly recognized. Due to the few number of animal sounds tested, Level 3 for RMS amplitude values was only needed in three cases.

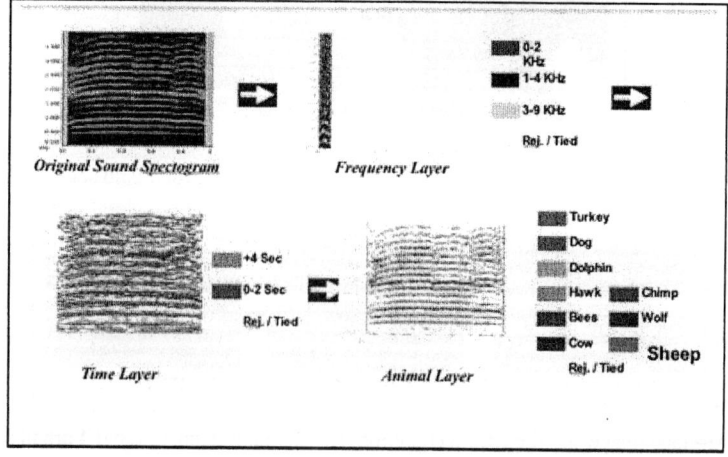

Fig. 8. Audio Signal recognition at three levels: Sheep sound spectrogram

3.3 Skin Recognition

Fig. 9 and 10 present the image segmentation of human skin texture. The case of Fig. 10 is quite interesting since, as shown in the picture, the texture of the wall, the leather vest and the wooden frame are non-skin textures that were not selected by the CLS class since those texture were trained as belonging to one of the non-skin class discussed previously.

Fig. 9. Skin segmentation of human skin

Fig. 10. Skin segmentation in contrast to non-skin textures

4 Conclusions

As stated in the results, the hierarchical organization of CLS layers proposed in the research was tested with a large set of example. Although the results suggests this approach to be a reliable and robust one for image recognition and image segmentation, it still requires to be examined under the scrutiny of a complete set of statistical tests, among them the use of confusion tables. However, the results obtained so far are similar than those reported in the literature [2], [5] using different algorithms with the added benefit of the flexibility and swift modification of the STM of the CLS architecture. Finally, through the use of accumulated histograms in learning models, image processing is greatly enhanced. Along with that, it is important to note the speed at training and testing and the small amount of space required to store an ALISA layer file.

References

1. Becker, G., Bock, P.: The ALISA Shape Module, In Proceedings of the Second International Conference on Cognitive and Neural Systems. Boston (1998)
2. Bhanu, B & Wu, X, Genetic Algorithms for Adaptive Image Segmentation In Nayar, S. K. & Poggio, T. (eds). Early Visual Learning, Oxford University Press, Oxford (1996)
3. Bock, P., Klinnert, R., Kober, R., Rovner, R., Schmidt, H.: Gray-Scale ALIAS. IEEE Transactions on Knowledge and Data Engineering, (1992) Vol. 4, No. 2
4. Bock, P.: "ALISA: Adaptive Learning Image and Signal Analysis. Proceedings of the SPIE Applied Imagery Pattern Recognition Conference, Washington D.C. (1998)
5. Carson, C. Belongie, S. Greenspan, H. & J. Malik J. Blobworld: Image segmentation using expectation-maximization and its application to image querying. IEEE Transactions on Pattern Analysis and Machine Intelligence (2002) 24(8):1026-1038
6. Cornell Lab of Ornithology: Raven Version 1.2 Ithaca, NY (2003)
7. European Space Agency: ESA Programs, National News. Available at ESA site (2004)
8. Greenspan, H.: Non Parametric Texture Learning. In Nayar, S. K. & Poggio, T. (eds) Early Visual Learning, Oxford University Press, Oxford (1996)
9. Hubshman, J., Bock, P., Achikian, M.: Detection of Targets in Terrain Images with ALIAS. Proceedings of the Twenty-Third Annual Pittsburgh Conference on Modeling and Simulation (1992) pp 927-942
10. Narendra, K.S. Thatachar, L. (eds.): Special Issue on Learning Automata. Journal of Cybernetics and Info Science (1977) Vol 1 # 2-4
11. National Auronatics and Space Administration, NASA: News and Events, Missions Exploring the Universe. Available at NASA Site (2004)
12. Pratt, W. K.: Digital Image Processing. PIKS Inside, 3rd Ed. J.Wiley, New York (2001)
13. Sanchez, A: Learning Automata: An Alternative to Neural Networks. In Rudomin, P., Arbib, M.A., Cervantes Pérez, F., and Romo, P. (Eds.). Neuroscience: From Neural Net works to Artificial Intelligence. Research Notes in Neural Computing Springer- Verlag, Heidelberg, Berlin (1993) Vol. 4.

Performance Evaluation of a Segmentation Algorithm for Synthetic Texture Images

Dora Luz Almanza-Ojeda, Victor Ayala-Ramirez,
Raul E. Sanchez-Yanez, and Gabriel Avina-Cervantes

Universidad de Guanajuato, F.I.M.E.E.
Salamanca, Mexico
{luzdora, ayalav, sanchezy, avina}@salamanca.ugto.mx

Abstract. In this paper we present the performance evaluation of a texture segmentation approach for synthetic textured images. Our segmentation approach uses a Bayesian inference procedure using co-ocurrence properties over a set of randomly sampled points in the image. We developed an exhaustive performance test for this approach that compares segmentation results to the "ground truth" images under a varying number of sampled points, in the neighborhood of each pixel used to classify it in the test images. We show our preliminary results that let us to choose the optimal number of points to analyze in the neighborhood of each pixel to assign a texture label. This method can be easily applied to segment outdoor real textured images.

1 Introduction

Image segmentation refers to the decomposition of a scene into its principal components or regions. This process makes easier the object recognition tasks and some other computer vision applications. The image segmentation process is mainly based on texture and color features taken from the scene. In this work, we are focusing in texture features because a natural or artificial object can be represented and discriminated with them. Texture features can be characterized and modeled by using filter theory or by statistical models. Besides, both approaches have proved to be efficient and useful for texture segmentation methods [1, 2]. Zhu, Wu and Mumford [3] have working on an analysis of both approaches towards a unified theory for texture modeling. Most of works have been tested with artificial texture images taken from Brodatz album [4]. Currently, a large number of works have applied these images which are considered as a benchmark to evaluate performance of texture algorithms [5]. Thus, we have also used it in order to give a comparative point of view to our algorithm.

Our work uses a texture classification method, based on a Bayesian inference and the co-ocurrence matrices [6]. We classify each pixel P taken from the test image by analyzing a square neighborhood around it. The classification process consists of random selection of a set of points (usually 10% of the neighborhood size). Each one of these points are analyzed by its co-ocurrence properties and

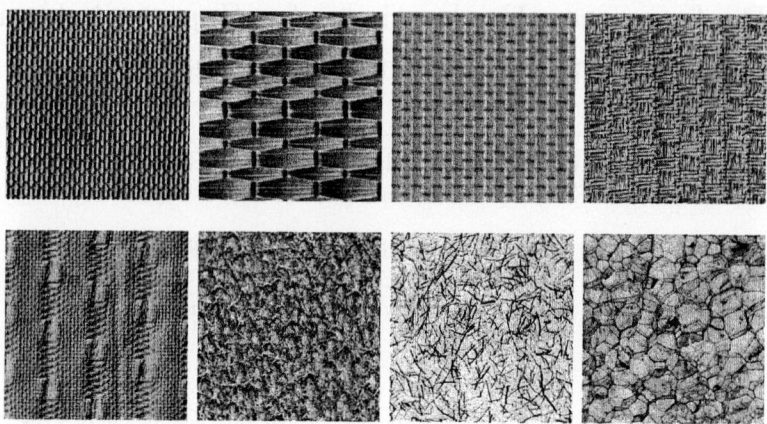

Fig. 1. Some *Brodatz* textures used in our data base

by using Bayes inference; the texture class that maximizes the *a posteriori* probability receives a vote. The class with the largest number of votes is assigned to pixel P. In the case that classification information is not good enough, an "unknown" class label is assigned for pixels where no decision about the class can be made.

The rest of this paper is organized as follows: next section explains how we used the Gray Level Co-ocurrence Matrices (GLMCs) in combination with the Bayes' Rule to classify a pixel according to a square neighborhood. Section 3, explains the segmentation process and its implementation details. In section 4, we present the performance evaluation procedures, our results with the segmented images and some evaluation graphics. Finally, in section 5 we discuss our results, the conclusions are given as well as the perspectives for this work.

2   Bayesian Texture Classification

Our segmentation approach is based on the classification of an image window composed of a square neighborhood of a pixel P. Texture classification is done by using a Bayesian inference method coupled with a voting scheme over a set of random points in texture image under test. We describe details of these procedures below.

We consider classification of a texture test image into a set of m texture classes $\{T_1, T_2, ..., T_m\}$. We compute GLMCs for a set of distances d and orientations θ

$$(d, \theta) = \{1, 2\} \times \left\{0, \frac{\pi}{4}, \frac{\pi}{2}, \frac{3\pi}{4}\right\} \tag{1}$$

to characterize each texture class. That is, we use 8 GLMCs to represent each texture class. We denote these matrices as $C_1, C_2, ..., C_8$.

As a basis for classification, we use a set R of n random points (x_i, y_i) taken from the image under test consisting of (N, M) pixels in the horizontal and vertical direction respectively. Each point in R cast a vote for a texture class based in local co-ocurrence properties for every GLMC used. Bayes' theorem is a tool for assessing how probable evidence makes some hypothesis. It makes possible to determine the probability of the cause by knowing the effect. In our case, evidence is the observation of gray level intensities for two pixels, one chosen randomly and the other at a distance following an orientation from the set of parameters (d, θ) specified above.

Firstly, a given GLMC C_k computed using parameters (d_k, θ_k) and used to computed texture classes prototypes casts a vote for the texture class that maximizes *a posteriori* probability from observed spatial arrangement. We use Bayes rule to compute this probability. If we define T_j as the event of unknown texture T belonging to class T_j, and A the event of the co-ocurrence of observing $I(R_i) = I_1$ and $I(R_i + [d_k, \theta k]) = I_2$ in the test image, we have

$$p(T_j|A) = \frac{p(A|T_j) \cdot (T_j)}{p(A)} \qquad (2)$$

In last equation, $p(A|T_j)$ can be computed from the normalized $C_{d,\theta}(I_1, I_2)$ for the parameter set under consideration and the observed gray levels I_1 and I_2. The term $p(T_j)$ is the *a priori* probability of observing texture T_j and $p(A)$ is the total probability of A. A vote v_k is given to the texture T_l that best explains observed intensities in direction (d_k, θ_k).

$$v_k = T_l \iff T_l = \max_j p(T_j|A) \qquad (3)$$

This procedure is repeated for each C_k and is selected the most voted texture label as a the vote V_i is used for choosing a winning label for the texture under test.

3 Segmentation Algorithm

A class assignment procedure is used for each pixel in the image under segmentation. We consider a square neighborhood V_p of a pixel P with coordinates (i, j), where $V_p = \{(k, l) | (k, l) \in \{i - r, ..., i + r\} \times \{j - r, ..., j + r\}\}$, with r being the half side of the neighborhood. The neighborhood patch is classified as an entire image by using the procedure described in section 2. That is, a set of n_P random points are chosen from the neighborhood set and a voting procedure is carried out. Texture label with the largest number of votes is assigned to pixel P. Nevertheless, if there is no significative differences between locally voted classes, we can assign an additional unknown class label. Subsequent step applies a statistical modal filter to the resulting image, which consists in analyzing just the pixels with unknown class and its nearest neighborhood. Thus, we find the class with the largest frequency and assign it to the pixel under test (if this class is the "unknown" class again then the class for the pixel would not change). This results in a smoother region outlining for texture classes.

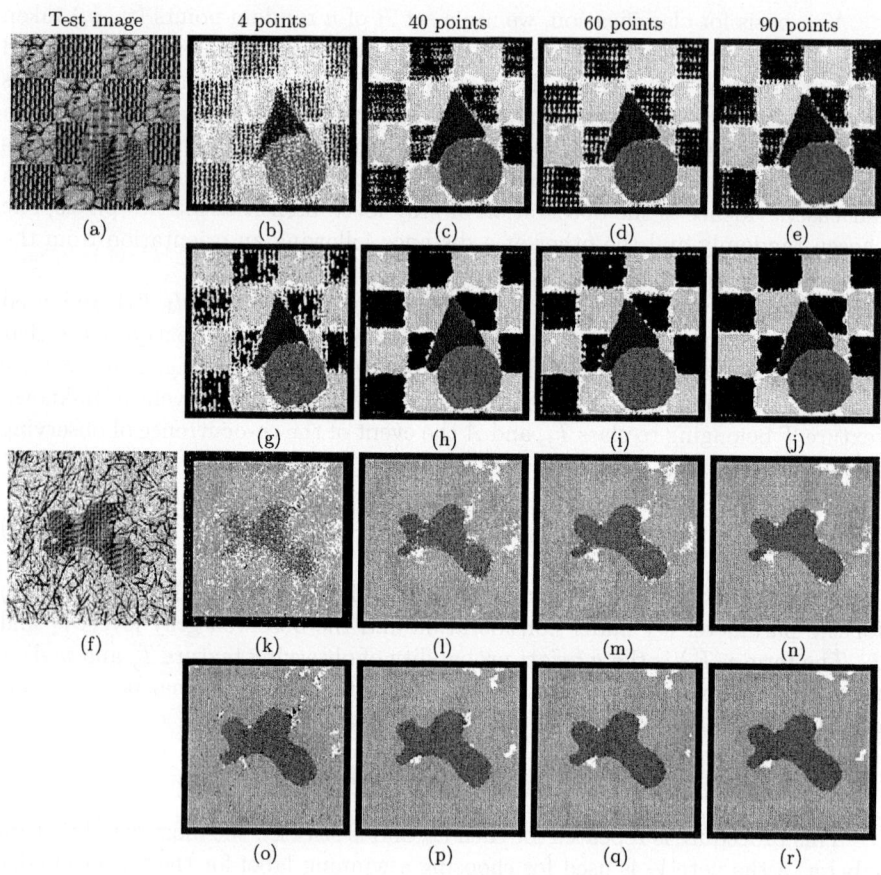

Fig. 2. Segmentation algorithm results. (a) and (f) shown test input images. In (b)-(e) and (k)-(n) shown typical segmented images. (g)-(j) and (o)-(r) shown the segmented images after applying filtered image results.

4 Experimental Results

We have tested our segmentation algorithm by using synthetic images where patches are taken from the predefined texture images shown in Fig. 1. They have been arranged to compose a set of test images (column one in Fig. 2). The size of these images is 256×256 pixels. The result of applying our segmentation algorithm for 4, 40, 60 and 90 points is shown in row one and three in Fig. 2 for two test images. In these images a same gray level implies that pixels are detected as being part of the same texture class. White pixels are associated with an unknown texture class. As we can see, segmented images present noisy borders for some of the regions and also some kind of "salt and pepper" noise inside them. To reduce this effects, we have applied a statistical modal filter. The results after application of this filter are shown in row two and four Fig. 2.

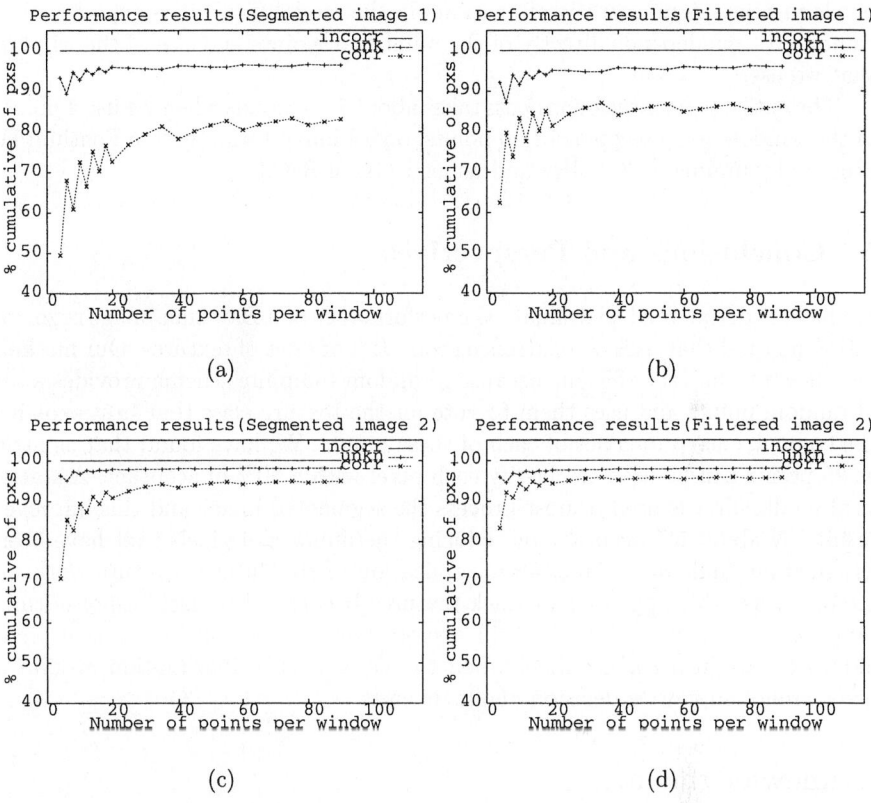

Fig. 3. Performance evaluation results. Plots a) and c) show the percentage of evaluation results to the first and third row of segmented images from Fig.2. Plots b) and d) show the results for the filtered images showed in the same Figure. By comparing a) with b) and c) with d), we observe that the space between correct and unknown pixel graphs is clearly reduced after applied the mode filter.

We made the performance evaluation test for the segmented and filtered output images. They are compared versus a "ground truth" image computed from the original image. Our algorithm depends on a half side parameter (r) for the neighborhood, and in all tests we have chosen $r=10$. This results in a 20×20 pixels neighborhood. The other parameter is the number n_P of points to be sampled from the neighborhood. This parameter is the principal variable in our algorithm and we have chosen 23 different values for it during the test.

The comparison process were made 100 times for each quantity of selected points. From each image compared, we obtain 3 numerical results: the correctly, incorrectly and unknown classified pixels. We compute the accumulated average percentage for each set of points. Finally, we made a plot with these percentage results versus the number of points taken in for the test. All of these plot results are shown in Fig. 3. As we can see, the number of correctly classified pixels increase significatively after to apply the modal filter. It is expected that computed time depends directly of the number of points and size of the window that we use.

The entire segmentation process takes about 1.5 seconds when we use 4 points in the window to 25 seconds for 90 points, on a Linux Station with a Pentium IV processor, running at 3.2 GHz and using 1 GB of RAM.

5 Conclusions and Perspectives

We have experimented to evaluate the performance of a Bayesian image segmentation method that uses co-ocurrence properties of a set of textures. Our method has shown to be very efficient because a random sampling scheme provides a set of random points and uses them to vote for the texture class that best explains the co-ocurrence properties of each of these points. We have found that as little as 25 points can be used to classify each pixel with a 80% of accuracy. A statistical modal filter is used to post-process the segmented image and this improves results by about 5% accuracy by reducing the number of pixels that have been assigned an "unknown" label after application of this filter. In future work we intend to use this approach to track textures because of its fast response time (approx. 1.5 seconds). We also will explore how to use multi-resolution techniques to assign a correct label when the co-ocurrence information around a pixel cannot support a decision about its class.

Acknowledgments

This work has been partially funded by the French-Mexican LAFMI Project "Concepción de funciones de percepción y planificación para la navegación topológica de un robot móvil en ambiente semi-estructurado interior o natural", the Mexico PROMEP project "Navegación topológica de robots usando análisis difuso de textura" and the University of Guanajuato project "Funcionalidades visuales para la navegación topológica de robots móviles".

References

1. Jain, A.K., Farrokhnia, F.: Unsupervised texture segmentation using Gabor filters. In: Proc. IEEE Int. Conf. on Systems, Man and Cybernetics, Los Angeles, CA (1990) 14–19
2. Andrey, P., Tarroux, P.: Unsupervised segmentation of Markov random field modeled textured images using selectionist relaxation. IEEE Transactions Pattern Analysis and Machine Intelligence **20** (1998) 252–262
3. Zhu, S., Wu, Y., Mumford, D.: Filters, random fields and maximum entropy (FRAME): Towards a unified theory for texture modeling. International Journal of Computer Vision (IJCV) **27** (1998) 107–126
4. Brodatz, P.: Textures: a photographic album for artist and designers. Dover Publications, New York, NY (1966)

5. Picard, R.W., Kabir, T., Liu, F.: Real-time recognition with the entire Brodatz texture database. In: Proc. of the IEEE Conf. on Computer Vision and Pattern recognition, New York, NY (1993) 638–639
6. Ayala-Ramírez, V., Obara-Kepowicz, M., Sánchez-Yáñez, R., Jaime-Rivas, R.: Bayesian texture classification method using a random sampling scheme. In: Proc. IEEE Int. Conf. on Systems, Man and Cybernetics, Washington, DC (2003) 2065–2069

Image Retrieval Based on Salient Points from DCT Domain

Wenyin Zhang[1,2], Zhenli Nie[2], and Zhenbing Zeng[1]

[1] The software engineering institute,
East China Normal University, Shanghai, P.R. China
[2] The Department of Computer Science,
Shandong Linyi Normal University, Linyi, 276005, P.R. China

Abstract. A new image retrieval method based on salient points extracted from DCT compressed domain is proposed in this paper. Using significant DCT coefficients, we provide a robust self-adaptive salient point extraction algorithm which is very robust to most of common image processing. Based on salient points, two local image features, color histogram and LBP histogram are computed to represent local properties of the image for retrieval. Our system reduces the amount of data to be processed and only needs to do partial decompression, so it can accelerate the work of image retrieval. The experimental results also demonstrate it improves performance both in retrieval efficiency and effectiveness.

Keywords: Salient Point, Image Retrieval, Discrete Cosine Transformation.

1 Introduction

Digital image databases have grown enormously in both size and number over the years [1]. In order to reduce bandwidth and storage space, most image and video data are stored and transmitted by some kind of compressed format. However, the compressed images cannot be conveniently processed for image retrieval because they need to be decompressed beforehand, and that means an increase in both complexity and search time. Therefore, it is important to develop an efficient image retrieval technique to retrieve wanted images from the compressed domain.

Nowadays, more and more attention has been paid on the compressed-domain based image retrieval techniques [2] which extract image features from the compressed data of the image. The JPEG is the image compression standard [3] and is widely used in large image databases and on the World Wide Web because of its good compression rate and image quality. However, the conventional image retrieval approaches used for JPEG compressed images need full decompression which consumes too much time and require large amount of computation. Some new researches [4, 5, 6, 7, 8, 9, 10] have recently resulted in improvements in that image features can be directly extracted in the compressed domain without full decompression.

The purpose of this paper is to propose a novel JPEG compressed image retrieval method based on *salient points* [11] computed from JPEG compressed domain. In [12], salient points are named *key points*. The salient points, where the image features are computed, are interesting for image retrieval because they are located in visual focus points and thus they can capture the local image information and reduce the amount of data to be processed. The salient points are related to the visually most important parts of the images and lead to a more discriminant image feature than *interesting points* such as corners [15], which are in general designed for robotics and shape recognition, and therefore they have drawbacks when they are applied to natural image retrieval. Visual focus points need not be corners, and a visual meaningful feature is not necessarily located in a corner. At the same time, corners may be clustered in few regions. In various natural images, regions may well contain textures, where a lot of corners are detected. Therefore, corners may not represent the most interesting subset of pixels for image indexing. The salient points may be from some kinds of interesting points, but they are related to any visual 'interesting' parts of the image. Moreover, it is interesting to have those points spread out in the whole image, and then the image features will be computed based on these salient points.

It is quite easy to understand that using a small amount of such salient points instead of all images reduces the amount of data to be processed, and obtains a more discriminating image index [11]. In this paper, based on a small part of important DCT coefficients, we provide a new salient point extraction algorithm which is of robustness. Then, we adaptively choose some important salient points to stand for the whole image, and based on these points, we extract two image features, color histogram, and LBP histogram from JPEG compressed images for retrieval.

The remainder of this paper is organized as follows. In Section 2, we introduce the works related to JPEG compression image retrieval. In Section 3, we discuss in details our new scheme, followed by the experimental results and analysis. Finally, Section 5 concludes the paper.

2 Related Works

Direct manipulation of the compressed images and videos offers low-cost processing of real time multimedia applications. It is more efficient to directly extract features in the JPEG compressed domain. As a matter of fact, many JPEG compressed image retrieval methods based on DCT coefficients have been developed in recent years.

Climer and Bhatia proposed a quadtree-structure-based method [4] that organizes the DCT coefficients of an image into a quadtree structure. This way, the system can use these coefficients on the nodes of the quadtree as image features. However, although such a retrieval system can effectively extract features from DCT coefficients, its main drawback is that the computation of the distances between images will grow undesirably fast when the number of relevant images is big or the threshold value is large. Feng and Jiang proposed a statistical parameter-based method [5] that uses the mean and variance of the pixels in each block as image features. The mean and variance can be directly computed via DCT coefficients. However, this system has to calculate the mean and variance of each block in each image, including the query image and the images in the database, and the calculation of the mean value and variance value of each block is a computationally heavy load. Chang, Chuang and Hu provided a direct JPEG compressed image retrieval technique [6] based on DC difference and the AC correlation. Instead of fully decompressing the images, it only needs to do partial entropy decoding and extracts the DC difference and the AC correlation as two image features. However, although the retrieval system is faster than the method [4,5], it doesn't do well in anti-rotation.

The related techniques are not limited to the above three typical methods. Shneier [7] described a method of generating keys of JPEG images for retrieval, where a key is the average value of DCT coefficients computed over a window. Huang [8] rearranged the DCT coefficients and then got the image contour for image retrieval. B.Furht [9] and Jose A.Lay [10] made use of the energy histograms of DCT coefficients for image or video retrieval. Most image retrieval methods based on DCT compressed domain strengthened the affectivity and efficiency of image retrieval [2]. But most of these research focused on global statistical feature distributions which have limited discriminating power because they are unable to capture the local image information.

In our proposed approach, we extract the image feature for retrieval by surrounding the image salient points computed from a small part of significant DCT coefficients. The salient points give local outstanding information, so the image features based on them have more powerful ability of characterizing the image contents.

3 The Proposed Method

In this section, we introduce in details our retrieval methods based on salient points. The content of the section is arranged with the sequence: edge point detection→ salient point extraction→image feature extraction→similarity measurement.

3.1 Fast Edge Detection Based on DCT Coefficients

Edges are significant local changes in the image and are important feature for analyzing image because they are relevant to estimating the structure and properties of objects in the scene. So edge detection is frequently the first step in recovering information from images. Now most of edge detectors make use of gradients to get edge information in pixel domain. If we extract edges by these detectors from compressed image, we have to decompress the image first, so it will take much more time. Here we provide a fast edge detection algorithm in DCT domain which directly compute the pixel gradients from DCT coefficients to get edge information. Based on it, we give the salient points extraction algorithm.

The 8 × 8 Inverse DCT formula is as follows:

$$f(x,y) = \frac{1}{4}\sum_{u=0}^{7}\sum_{v=0}^{7} C(x,u)C(y,v)F(u,v) \qquad (1)$$

$$Where: C(x,u) = c(u)\cos\frac{(2x+1)u\pi}{16}; c(0) = \frac{1}{\sqrt{2}}, c(x) = 1, x \neq 0.$$

Compute derivative to formula (1), we get:

$$f'(x,y) = \frac{\partial f(x,y)}{\partial x} + \frac{\partial f(x,y)}{\partial y} = \frac{1}{4}\sum_{u=0}^{7}\sum_{v=0}^{7} C'(x,u)C(y,v)F(u,v)$$

$$+ \frac{1}{4}\sum_{u=0}^{7}\sum_{v=0}^{7} C(x,u)C'(y,v)F(u,v) \qquad (2)$$

$$Where: C'(x,u) = -\frac{u\pi}{8}c(u)\sin\frac{(2x+1)u\pi}{16}$$

From the equation (2), we can compute the pixel gradient in (x,y), its magnitude can be given by:

$$G(x,y) = |\frac{\partial f(x,y)}{\partial x}| + |\frac{\partial f(x,y)}{\partial y}| \qquad (3)$$

In order to simplify computation, we change the angle $\frac{(2x+1)u\pi}{16}$ to acute angle [14]. Let $(2x+1)u = 8(4k+l) + q_{x,u}$, k,l and $q_{x,u}$ are integers, in which: $q_{x,u} = (2x+1)u \mod 8$, $k = (2x+1)u/32$, $l = (2x+1)u/8 \mod 4$, $0 \le q_{x,u} < 8$, $0 \le l < 4$. Then, we can do as follows:

$$\sin(\frac{(2x+1)u\pi}{16}) = \sin(\frac{(8(4k+l)+q_{x,u})}{16}) = \begin{cases} \sin(\frac{q'_{x,u}\pi}{16}) & : q'_{x,u} = q_{x,u}, l = 0 \\ \sin(\frac{q'_{x,u}\pi}{16}) & : q'_{x,u} = 8 - q_{x,u}, l = 1 \\ -\sin(\frac{q'_{x,u}\pi}{16}) & : q'_{x,u} = q_{x,u}, l = 2 \\ -\sin(\frac{q'_{x,u}\pi}{16}) & : q'_{x,u} = 8 - q_{x,u}, l = 3 \end{cases}$$

$$= (-1)^{\lceil\frac{l-1}{2}\rceil}\sin(\frac{q'_{x,u}}{16}) \qquad (4)$$

Similarly, we can get:

$$\cos(\frac{(2x+1)u\pi}{16}) = (-1)^{\lceil\frac{l+1}{2}\rceil}\cos(\frac{q'_{x,u}}{16}) \qquad (5)$$

To the formulae (4) and (5), the sign and the $q'_{x,u}$ can be decided aforehand according to x, u. Let $ss_{x,u}$ and $cs_{x,u}$ be the signs of formulae (4) and (5). The $ss_{x,u}$ and $q'_{x,u}$ can be described as follows:

$$ss_{x,u} = \begin{Bmatrix} + + + + + + + + \\ + + + + + + - - \\ + + - - - + + + \\ + + + - - + + - \\ + + - - + + - - \\ + + - + + - + + \\ + + - + - + + - \\ + + - + - + - + \end{Bmatrix} \quad q'_{x,u} = \begin{Bmatrix} 0\ 1\ 2\ 3\ 4\ 5\ 6\ 7 \\ 0\ 3\ 6\ 7\ 4\ 1\ 2\ 5 \\ 0\ 5\ 6\ 1\ 4\ 7\ 2\ 3 \\ 0\ 7\ 2\ 5\ 4\ 3\ 6\ 1 \\ 0\ 7\ 2\ 5\ 4\ 3\ 6\ 1 \\ 0\ 5\ 6\ 1\ 4\ 7\ 2\ 3 \\ 0\ 3\ 6\ 7\ 4\ 1\ 2\ 5 \\ 0\ 1\ 2\ 3\ 4\ 5\ 6\ 7 \end{Bmatrix}$$

The $cs_{x,u}$ can be given the same as $ss_{x,u}$. For more time-saving, according to Taylor formula, we extend $\sin(\frac{q'_{x,u}}{16})$ and $\cos(\frac{q'_{x,u}}{16})$ at $\pi/4$:

$$\sin(\frac{q'_{x,u}}{16}) = \sum_{k=0}^{n} \sin^{(k)}(\frac{\pi}{4}) \frac{(\frac{q'_{x,u}}{16} - \frac{\pi}{4})^k}{k!} + R_n(\frac{q'_{x,u}}{16}) \tag{6}$$

$$\cos(\frac{q'_{x,u}}{16}) = \sum_{k=0}^{n} \cos^{(k)}(\frac{\pi}{4}) \frac{(\frac{q'_{x,u}}{16} - \frac{\pi}{4})^k}{k!} + R_n(\frac{q'_{x,u}}{16}) \tag{7}$$

$$where: |R_n| < \frac{(\frac{\pi}{4})^{n+1} |\frac{q'_{x,u}-4}{4}|^{n+1}}{(n+1)!} \leq \frac{(\frac{3\pi}{16})^{n+1}}{(n+1)!}$$

When consider to extend up to second order, the equation (6) and (7) can be approximated as follows:

$$\sin(\frac{q'_{x,u}}{16}) \approx \frac{\sqrt{2}}{2}[1 - \frac{\pi}{16}(4 - q'_{x,u}) + \frac{\pi^2}{512}(4 - q'_{x,u})^2] \tag{8}$$

$$\cos(\frac{q'_{x,u}}{16}) \approx \frac{\sqrt{2}}{2}[1 + \frac{\pi}{16}(4 - q'_{x,u}) - \frac{\pi^2}{512}(4 - q'_{x,u})^2] \tag{9}$$

The residue error R_2 is more less than 0.034. This suggests that the equation (8) and (9) can be approximately decided by $q'_{x,u}$ and can be calculated off-line. As such, the $C'(x,u)$ and $C(x,u)$ in the equation (2) also can be calculated approximately by the $q'_{x,u}$, $ss_{x,u}$ and $cs_{x,u}$ off-line, which means that the coefficients of the extension of equation (2) can be computed in advance and the equation (3) is only related to the DCT coefficients $F(u,v)$. So, the computation of the equation (3) is much simplified.

Further more, because most of the DCT coefficients with high frequency are zero and do nothing to the values of edge points, so they can be omitted and then much computation is saved, which means that it is enough to use the DCT coefficients with low frequency to compute the edge points. The following Fig.1 gives an example for edge detection using different DCT coefficients. From the fig.1, we can see that the more the DCT coefficients used, the smoother the edge. With the decreasing of the number of DCT coefficients used, the 'block effect' becomes more and more obvious and many edge minutiae are lost. In a block, the more local changes in gray, the larger the value of the edge points in this block.

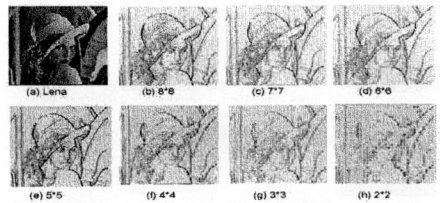

Fig. 1. an example of edge detection: (a) Lena.jpg, (b)-(h) are the edge images of Lena, which are computed respectively by first n*n DCT coefficients, $2 \leq n \leq 8$

3.2 Salient Points Computation

According to analysis in Sec.3.1 that the edge points in a block reflect the gray changes in this block, the more changes, the larger edge points value, we sum up all the edge points values in one block to stand for one salient point value, which means that one $8*8$ block corresponds to one salient point. If $M*N$ stands for the size of an image, the maximum of its salient points number is $\lceil M/8 * N/8 \rceil$. Let $Sp(x', y')$ be the salient point value in $(x', y'), 0 \leq x' < M/8, 0 \leq y' < N/8$, it can be computed as follows: (γ is a parameter, $2 \leq \gamma \leq 7$)

$$Sp(x', y') = \sum_{x=x' \times 8}^{x' \times 8 + \gamma} \sum_{y=y' \times 8}^{y' \times 8 + \gamma} |G(x, y)| \qquad (10)$$

3.3 Adaptive Selection of Salient Points

Not all salient points are important for us to image retrieval. The number of the salient points extracted will clearly influence the retrieval results. Less salient points will not mark the image; more salient point will increase the computation cost. Through experiments we have found that the gray changes in a block can be relatively reflected by the variance (denoted by σ) of AC coefficients in this block. The more changes, the larger the variance [5]. So we adaptively select more important salient points according to the variance σ.

Let M_{sp} be the mean value of $Sp(x', y')$, We adaptively select the salient points $SP(x', y')$ which satisfies the following condition:

$$\lambda \times Sp(x', y') > \mu \times M_{sp} \qquad (11)$$

$$Where: \lambda = \sigma/128, 0 \leq \lambda \leq 1; \sigma \approx \frac{1}{8}\sqrt{\sum_{x=0}^{x<8}\sum_{y=0}^{y<8}F^2(x,y)}, 0 \leq \sigma \leq 128,$$

x, y are not zero simultaneously.

The condition (11) tends to choose the salient points with larger variance σ and larger $Sp(x', y')$ values. For reducing computation cost, we also use a small part of significant DCT coefficients to compute the σ. μ is a parameter. By

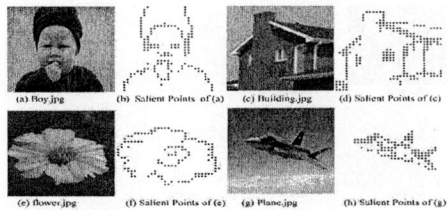

Fig. 2. Examples of images' salient points: (a),(c),(e) and (g) are the four JPEG images, (b),(d),(f) and (h) are their salient point images respectively. The parameter $\mu = 5.5$, and first $4*4$ coefficients in each 8×8 block are used to computed the variance σ and the edge points.

experiments, we give μ an estimated value 5.5 which can be suited for most of images. The Fig.2 shows some examples of images' salient points, from which we can see that the salient points actually describe the shape feature of the image.

3.4 The Feature Extraction Based on Salient Points

Color and texture are the most common used features to describe the image content. Here, based on salient points, we adopt color histogram, LBP histogram [13] as the image features for retrieval. For building the color and LBP histogram, we need decode the image block according to the salient point. As we know, JPEG adopts YCbCr color space, so color histogram needs the transformation from the YCrCb space to RGB space, we directly access the image content in compressed domain without inverse DCT transformation according to [14]. LBP histogram is directly done on the Y component for it contains more image information.

Color histogram is related to the distribution of colors in a image, which is built as follows: In RGB color space, each of the R, G and B bands is divided into four bins covering the range of $0 - 255$, resulting in a color histogram of $4 \times 4 \times 4 = 64$ bins. The color histogram H_C is computed using the following equation:

$$H_{Cm} = \frac{n_m}{N} \qquad (12)$$

where n_m is the number of pixels with color label m; and N is the number of total pixels in the image.

The Local Binary Pattern (LBP) approach proposed by Ojala et al. provides highly discriminative texture information [13]. The advantages of LBP are its invariance to any monotonic change in gray level and its computational simplicity. Here, LBP histogram is used for texture description.

3.5 Similarity Measurement

The similarity between two images P, Q is measured by following distance:

$$D(P, Q) = \lambda_1 \sum_{i=0}^{63} (H_{C_i}^P - H_{C_i}^Q) + (1 - \lambda_1) \sum_{i=0}^{256} (H_{L_i}^P - H_{L_i}^Q) \qquad (13)$$

$H_C^P, H_L^P, H_C^Q, H_L^Q$ are color histograms, LBP histograms of P and Q respectively. λ_1 is a weight parameter. In our experiments, we set λ_1 with 0.6.

4 Experimental Results and Discussions

In this section, we want to show the performance evaluation of the proposed method by experiments. Our experiments were executed on an IBM computer with P4 1.5G CPU and 256M memory. A JPEG image database which comprises 1460 images from $http://www.benchathlon.net$ and $http://sipi.usc.edu$ is used to test the proposed approach.

4.1 Performance Evaluation of Salient Point Extraction Algorithm

A good salient point extraction algorithm should be robust to noise, rotation, transition, resizing and some common image processing. In our proposed retrieval method, the salient point extraction algorithm is of great importance because it determines the local features extraction of the images. In fact, we have found in the experiments that our salient point extraction algorithm can meet most of the needs. it is very robust to noise, rotation, translation, resizing as well as other common image processing such as lighting, darkening, smoothing, compressing and so on. The main reason for its robustness is that it is done on the edge points in a block so that noise or other image precessing operations have less effect on the whole block than on one pixel. For the limitation of the paper size, much more experimental results are omitted.

4.2 Performance Evaluation of Retrieval System

Among the image database with 1460 images, nine categories of similar images including peppers, buildings, fires, airplanes, flowers, animals, birds, toys and scenes are selected by human vision to investigate the retrieval performance of the proposed method. We compared our retrieval results with the three typical JPEG image retrieval methods [4,5,6] mentioned in section 2.2. In the experiments, we use the Average Retrieval Ratio (ARR) to investigate the retrieval effectiveness of the proposed method. The ARR is defined as follow:

$$ARR = \frac{1}{N}\sum_{i=0}^{N}\frac{m_i}{N} \qquad (14)$$

where N is the total number of one group of similar images, m_i is the number of found relevant images before rank N queried by the ith image belonging to the group. Fig.3 shows the average retrieval ratio of nine image categories, from which we can see our proposed method achieves results near to the method [6] on the whole, but better than the other three methods [4,5]. From the experimental results, we can conclude that our proposed salient points can well represent the whole image and the features computed based on them have more power to character the image. Fig.4 presents a retrieval example of an image $Building119.jpg$ as the query image. The query image is the top left one, and the retrieved ones are ranked from top left to the bottom right.

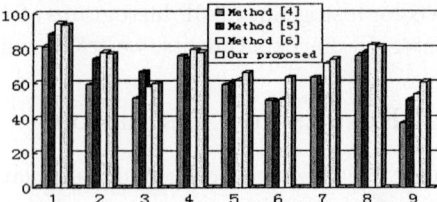

Fig. 3. The average retrieval ratio of nine image categories

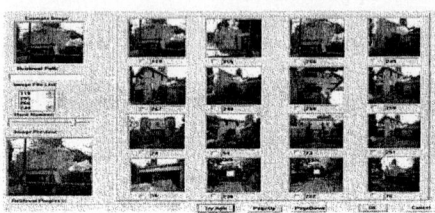

Fig. 4. An example of retrieval results using the query image "Building119.jpg", Rank≤ 16

5 Conclusions

In this paper, we provided a scheme to extract local image features based on salient points for content-based JPEG image retrieval. Because of the robustness of our salient point extraction approach in compressed domain, our retrieval system gives more improvement in efficiency and effectiveness than the compared methods shown by our experiments. The proposed salient points have more powerful ability in presenting the whole image. Based on them, we not only process more less image data without losing the image characteristic, but also extract more image features. In the future, we will go deep into our work based on the salient points for content based image retrieval.

Acknowledgements

The work was supported in part by NKBRPC-2004CB31003 and NNSFC-10471044.

References

1. R. Brunelli, O. Mich, C.M. Modena, A survey on the automatic indexing of video data, Journal of Visual Communication and Image Representation 10, 1999: 78-112.
2. M. K. Mandal, F. Idris and S. Panchanatha. A critical evaluation of image and video indexing techniques in the compressed domain. Image and Vision Computing, Vol.17,1999:513-529

3. G.K. Wallace, The JPEG still picture compression standard, ACM Communications 34(4),1991:31-45.
4. S. Climer, S.K. Bhatia, Image database indexing using JPEG coefficients, Pattern Recognition 35(11), 2002: 2479-2488.
5. G. Feng, J. Jiang, JPEG compressed image retrieval via statistical features, Pattern Recognition 36(4), 2002: 977-985.
6. C.C. Chang, J.C. Chuang, Y.S. Hu, Retrieval digital images from a JPEG compressed image database, Image and Vision Computing 22, 2004: 471-484
7. M. Shneier, M. Abdel-Mottaleb, Exploiting the JPEG compression scheme for image retrieval, IEEE Trans. Pattern Anal. Mach. Intell.18(8),1996: 849-853.
8. Huang X.L. Song L. and Shen L.X. Image retrieval method based on DCT domain. Journal of Electronics & Information Technology 12(12), 2002:1786-1789
9. B. Furht and P. Saksobhavivat, A Fast Content-Based Video and Image Retrieval Technique Over Communication Channels, Proc. of SPIE Symposium on Multimedia Storage and Archiving Systems, Boston, MA, November 1998
10. Jose A. Lay and Ling Guan, Image Retrieval Based on Energy Histograms of the Low Frequency DCT Coefficients. IEEE International Conference on acoustics, Speech, and Signal Processing, vol.6 1999: 3009-3012
11. N.Sebe, M.S.Lew, Comparing salient point detectors, Pattern Recognition Letters, v.24 n.1-3, 2003: 89-96
12. E.Loupias and S.Bres, Key points-based indexing for pre-attentive similarities: The KIWI System, Pattern Analysis and Applications, Vol.4, 2001: 200-214
13. T.Ojala, M.Pietikäinen T.Mäenpää. Multiresolution gray scale and rotation invariant texture classification with Local Binary Patterns. IEEE Transactions on Pattern Analysis and Machine Intelligence, 2002,24: 971-987
14. J. Jiang, A. Armstrong, G. Feng, Direct content access and extraction from JPEG compressed images, Pattern Recognition 35 (11), 2002: 2511-2519
15. Bres S., Jolion J.M.: Detection of Interest Points for Image Indexation. VISUAL99, Lecture Notes on Computer Science,Vol 1614(1999): 427-435

Selection of the Optimal Parameter Value for the ISOMAP Algorithm

Chao Shao and Houkuan Huang

School of Computer and Information Technology,
Beijing Jiaotong University,
Beijing, 100044, China
sc_flying@163.com, hkhuang@center.njtu.edu.cn

Abstract. The ISOMAP algorithm has recently emerged as a promising dimensionality reduction technique to reconstruct nonlinear low-dimensional manifolds from the data embedded in high-dimensional spaces, by which the high-dimensional data can be visualized nicely. One of its advantages is that only one parameter is required, i.e. the neighborhood size or K in the K nearest neighbors method, on which the success of the ISOMAP algorithm depends. However, it's an open problem how to select a suitable neighborhood size. In this paper, we present an effective method to select a suitable neighborhood size, which is much less time-consuming than the straightforward method with the residual variance, while yielding the same results. In addition, based on the characteristics of the Euclidean distance metric, a faster Dijkstra-like shortest path algorithm is used in our method. Finally, our method can be verified by experimental results very well.

1 Introduction

Nowadays, the explosive growth in the amount of data and their dimensionality makes data visualization more and more important. During the last hundreds of years, lots of approaches to visualize the high-dimensional data have been emerged, most of which fall into the following five categories: 1)use several subwindows to visually represent different subsets of the dimensions respectively, such as scatterplot matrices[1] and pixel-oriented techniques[2]; 2)rearrange the dimension axes to be non-orthogonal or even parallel, such as parallel coordinates[3] and star coordinates[4]; 3)embed the dimensions to form hierarchical partitioning of the low-dimensional space, such as dimensional stacking[5] and treemap[6]; 4)use certain objects or icons which have several visual features, each of which stands for one dimension, such as Chernoff-faces[7] and stick figures[8]; 5)reduce the dimensionality of the data to two or three dimensions, such as PCA[9], MDS[10], SOM[11], ISOMAP[12][13][14], LLE[15][16] and Laplacian Eigenmap[17], *etc.*

Unlike other methods, the dimensionality-reduction techniques consider all the dimensions as a whole, and try to preserve the high-dimensional relationship such as the (dis)similarity relationship between the data points in the low-dimensional space, which can visually represent the distribution and clustering of the data very well. As one of the nonlinear dimensionality-reduction techniques, the ISOMAP algorithm[12] extends the classical MDS algorithm by using the geodesic distance metric instead of the Euclidean distance metric in order to preserve geodesic distances between the data and thus can visualize the convex but intrinsically flat manifolds such as the swiss roll data set nicely. Its ability to preserve the global geometric properties of the manifolds in the non-iterative way makes it more and more attractive[16], in addition, one of its main advantages is that only one parameter is required, i.e. the neighborhood size or K in the K nearest neighbors method, on which the success of the ISOMAP algorithm depends[18]. Like other manifold learning techniques such as Locally Linear Embedding (LLE), It's very important for the ISOMAP algorithm to select a suitable neighborhood size, however, it's an open problem how to select a suitable neighborhood size which should be neither so large that "short-circuit" edges are introduced into the neighborhood graph, nor so small that the graph becomes disjoined or sparse so as not to approximate geodesic distances accurately[18]. A straightforward method is to select a suitable neighborhood size through estimating the "quality" of the corresponding mapping, i.e. how well the high-dimensional structure is represented in the embedded space[19], measured by the residual variance[12]. However, the straightforward method with the residual variance requires running the whole ISOMAP algorithm with every possible K and then selects the optimal K with the minimal residual variance, which makes it very time-consuming. In this paper, we present a much less time-consuming method to find a suitable neighborhood size, in which only the former part of the ISOMAP algorithm, i.e. shortest path computation, is required to run incrementally. Our method can be verified to yield the same results with the straightforward method with the residual variance by experimental results.

This paper is organized as follows: In Section 2, we recall the ISOMAP algorithm and the straightforward method with the residual variance. In Section 3, we present our method. Finally, experimental results and conclusions are given in Section 4 and Section 5 respectively.

2 The ISOMAP Algorithm and the Straightforward Method with the Residual Variance

When the global geometric structure of the high-dimensional data is unknown, we are not sure that the Euclidean distance metric is suitable to represent the dissimilarity relationship between the data. Fortunately, the Euclidean distance metric is trustworthy enough to represent the dissimilarity relationship between the data within a small enough local neighborhood. So the global geometric structure can be approximated using the local Euclidean distance information, as the ISOMAP algorithm[12] does. If the data lie on a single well-sampled manifold, it's proved that the unknown global geodesic distance between the data can be well approximated by the graph distance, i.e. the shortest path, in a suitable neighborhood graph which define a right local neighborhood structure of the data[20].

After using the geodesic distance metric approximated by the shortest path in a suitable neighborhood graph instead of the Euclidean distance metric, the ISOMAP algorithm uses the classical MDS algorithm to project the data into a low-dimensional space. So the ISOMAP algorithm can be briefly described as follows[12][13]:

1) Select n data points randomly for very large data sets to keep subsequent computation tractable;
2) Construct a suitable neighborhood graph (must be connected!) using the K nearest neighbors method with a suitable K;
3) Compute all the shortest paths in this neighborhood graph;
4) Use the classical MDS algorithm with the shortest paths to project the data into a low-dimensional space.

Given the data lying on a single well-sampled intrinsically flat manifold, the success of the ISOMAP depends on how to select a suitable neighborhood size or a suitable K in the K nearest neighbors method, by which a right local connectivity can be constructed and thus geodesic distances can be approximated accurately[18]. A straightforward method is to find a suitable neighborhood size through estimating the "quality" of the corresponding mapping, i.e. how well the high-dimensional structure is represented in the embedded space[19], measured by the residual variance[12]: $1 - \rho^2_{\hat{D}_X D_Y}$, where $\rho_{\hat{D}_X D_Y}$ is the standard linear correlation coefficient, taken over all the entries of $\hat{D}_X$ and D_Y, and where $\hat{D}_X$ and D_Y are the matrices of geodesic distances, approximated by the shortest paths, in the high-dimensional data space and Euclidean distances in the embedded space respectively. The lower the residual variance is, the better the high-dimensional data are represented in the embedded space[19]. Then the optimal K can be defined as follows:

$$K_{opt} = argmax_K (1 - \rho^2_{\hat{D}_X D_Y}) \qquad (1)$$

Due to the residual variance's use of Y, i.e. the output of the ISOMAP algorithm, and its multimodality, we must run the whole ISOMAP algorithm with every possible $K \in [K_{connection}, K_{max}]$ ($K_{connection}$ is the minimal K which can make the corresponding neighborhood graph fully connected and K_{max} is the predefined maximal K) and select the optimal K with the minimal residual variance, which makes it very time-consuming.

3 Our Method

As described above, a suitable neighborhood size should be neither so large that "short-circuit" edges are introduced into the neighborhood graph, nor so small that the graph becomes disjoined or sparse so as not to approximate geodesic distances accurately, which means that selection of the neighborhood size should depend only on the characteristics of the data, not on the specific algorithm as the residual variance does.

In fact, a suitable neighborhood size should be large enough, at the same time, shouldn't introduce "short-circuit" edges into the neighborhood graph. Obviously, under the restriction that the neighborhood graph is fully connected, the sum of all the geodesic distances, approximated by the shortest paths, drops monotonously as the neighborhood size is increased. At the same time, once "short-circuit" edges emerge, the sum of all the geodesic distances will drop sharply in contrast with the former decreasing downtrend. So we can increase K by one every time beginning with $K_{connection}$ and select the first one at which the sum of all the geodesic distances, approximated by the shortest paths, begins to drop sharply in contrast with the former decreasing downtrend as a suitable K to be used in the subsequent ISOMAP algorithm.

Unlike the residual variance, the value of our function, i.e. the sum of all the geodesic distances, approximated by the shortest paths:

$$f(K) = \sum_{all\ the\ entries} \hat{D}_X \qquad (2)$$

(as defined above, $\hat{D}_X$ is a function of the neighborhood size or K in the K nearest neighbors method) drops monotonously as the neighborhood size or K in the K nearest neighbors method is increased, and doesn't drop sharply until "short-circuit" edges emerge, which can make selection of the neighborhood size run incrementally, not with every possible K. In addition, only the former part of the ISOMAP algorithm, i.e. shortest path computation, is required to run because not the output of the ISOMAP algorithm, i.e. Y, but only geodesic distances, i.e. the entries of $\hat{D}_X$, are used. So, our method is much less time-consuming than the straightforward method with the residual variance. In addition, these two methods yield the same results, which can be verified very well by experimental results.

Although our method needn't run the latter part of the ISOMAP algorithm, i.e. the classical MDS algorithm which includes very time-consuming eigenvalue decomposition, the former part of the ISOMAP algorithm, i.e. shortest path computation, is still very time-consuming. There are two approaches to compute the shortest paths in a graph: Dijkstra's algorithm and Floyd's algorithm. Note that weights of the edges in the neighborhood graph are specified as the corresponding Euclidean distances, and the Euclidean distance metric meets the symmetry and triangular inequality conditions, so we can initialize S and T (seen in the following pseudo-code) much farther and thus quicken shortest path computation greatly based on these characteristics of the Euclidean distance metric (seen in Fig. 1). As a Dijkstra-like shortest path algorithm, its differences from Dijkstra's algorithm are listed as follows:

```
1)The shortest paths found previously need not be computed again
   and can be used to find other shortest paths;
   (use the symmetry condition)
2)For each vertex, its edges existing in the neighborhood graph
   are the shortest paths themselves, need not be computed again,
   and can be used to find other shortest paths.
   (use the triangular inequality condition)
```

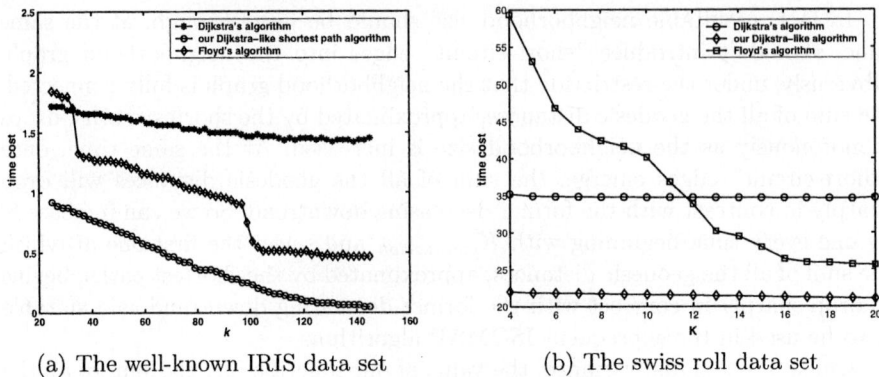

(a) The well-known IRIS data set (b) The swiss roll data set

Fig. 1. Time costs of three shortest path algorithms over different data sets with different K

We represent the i-th data point and its K nearest neighbors by x_i and $N_K(i)$ respectively, then the adjacent matrix of the corresponding neighborhood graph can be represented by $P = (p_{ij})_{n \times n}$, where

$$p_{ij} = \begin{cases} 0 & , \ j = i \\ \|x_i - x_j\| & , \ j \in N_K(i) \ or \ i \in N_K(j) \\ +\infty & , \ else \end{cases} \quad (3)$$

Consequently, we can describe our Dijkstra-like shortest path algorithm as follows:

```
initialize D̂_X = (d̂_ij)_{n×n} to be identical with P = (p_ij)_{n×n};
for each data point i
    S = {j|d̂_ij < +∞};  (S = {i} in Dijkstra's algorithm)
    T = {1,···,n} - S;
    for each data point j ∈ T
        d_j = min{d̂_il + d̂_lj|l ∈ S};  (d_j = d̂_ij in Dijkstra's algorithm)
    end
    while T ≠ Φ
        j = argmin_{l∈T}{d_l};
        d̂_ij = d_j, d̂_ji = d_j;
        S = S + {j}; T = T - {j};
        for each data point l ∈ T
            if d_l > d̂_ij + d̂_jl
                d_l = d̂_ij + d̂_jl;
            end
        end
    end
end
```

4 Experimental Results

To contrast our method with the straightforward method with the residual variance, we run the ISOMAP algorithm with our faster Dijkstra-like shortest path algorithm and different K over the following two widely used data sets: swiss roll and scurve (the corresponding manifolds are seen in Fig.2). The residual variance and our function, i.e. the sum of all the geodesic distances, approximated by the shortest paths, with different K respectively over the swiss roll data set are given in Fig.3, and over the curve data set are given in Fig.4.

In the experiments, we select 500 data points randomly from 2000 data points distributed uniformly over the corresponding manifolds, and specify the first K at which the next change of the value of our function, i.e. the sum of all the geodesic distances, approximated by the shortest paths, is one times larger than the last one as a suitable K to be used in the subsequent ISOMAP algorithm. We can see that our method obtains the same results but with much less time cost from the straightforward method with the residual variance, for example,

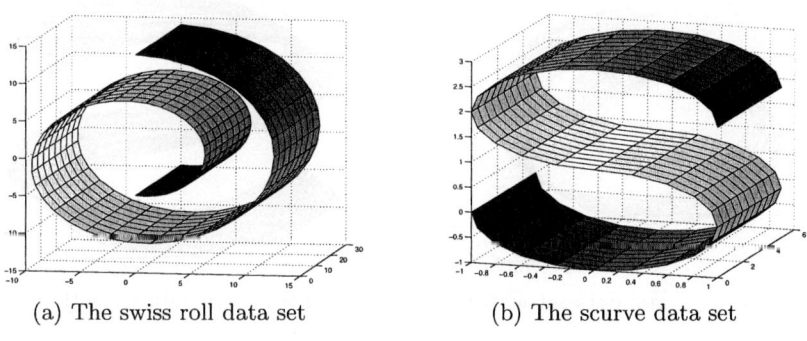

(a) The swiss roll data set   (b) The scurve data set

Fig. 2. The two data sets

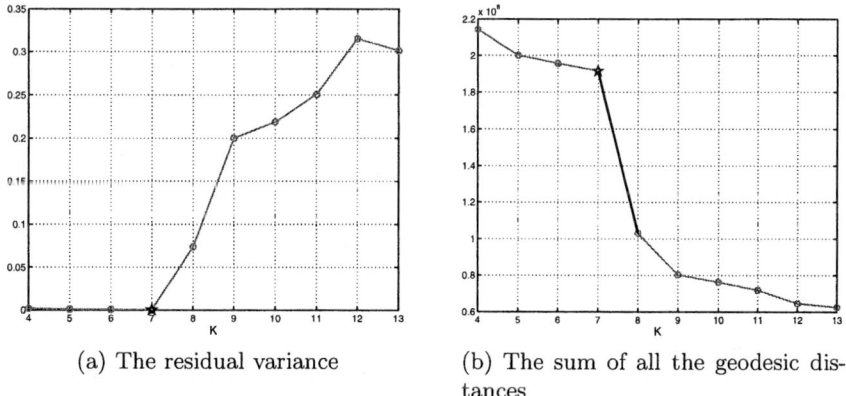

(a) The residual variance   (b) The sum of all the geodesic distances

Fig. 3. Results of these two methods over the swiss roll data set (the selected suitable K is represented by a five-pointed star)

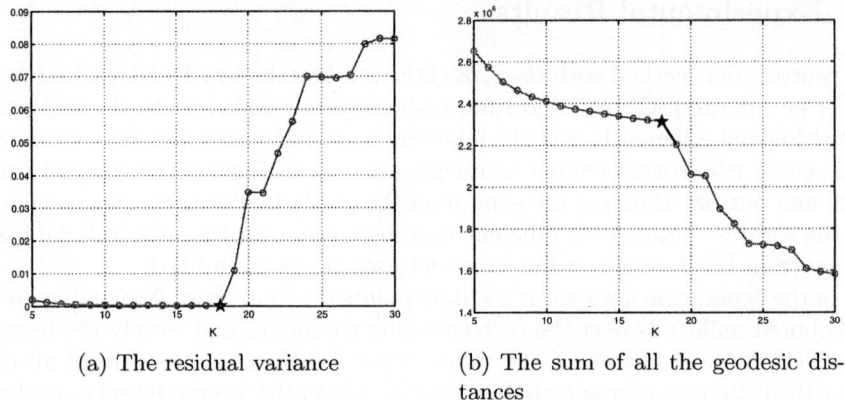

(a) The residual variance

(b) The sum of all the geodesic distances

Fig. 4. Results of these two methods over the scurve data set (the selected suitable K is represented by a five-pointed star)

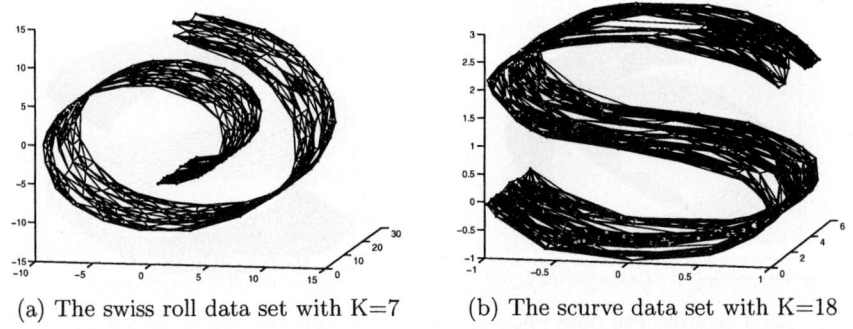

(a) The swiss roll data set with K=7

(b) The scurve data set with K=18

Fig. 5. The neighborhood graphs with the corresponding selected suitable K over the two data sets

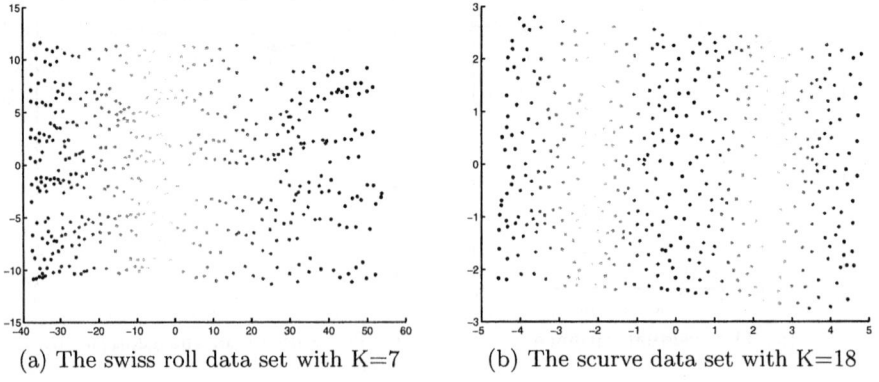

(a) The swiss roll data set with K=7

(b) The scurve data set with K=18

Fig. 6. Outputs of the ISOMAP algorithm with the corresponding selected suitable K over the two data sets

K=7 over the swiss roll data set with 144.156 seconds in our method vs. 292.204 seconds in the straightforward method with the residual variance, and K=18 over the scurve data set with 314.031 seconds in our method vs. 668.266 seconds in the straightforward method with the residual variance, and the corresponding neighborhood graphs and outputs of the ISOMAP algorithm are given in Fig.5 and Fig.6 respectively.

5 Conclusions

It's an open problem for those manifold learning techniques such as the ISOMAP algorithm to select a suitable neighborhood size in order to construct a right local connectivity. In this paper, we present an effective method to select a suitable neighborhood size or a suitable K in the K nearest neighbors method, which is much less time-consuming than the straightforward method with the residual variance because not the whole ISOMAP algorithm but only the former part of the ISOMAP algorithm, i.e. shortest path computation, is required to run not with every possible K but incrementally in our method, while yielding the same results, which can be verified by experimental results very well.

In addition, based on the characteristics of the Euclidean distance metric, i.e. the Euclidean distance metric meets the symmetry and triangular inequality conditions, a faster Dijkstra-like shortest path algorithm is used in our method.

References

1. Cleveland, W.S.: Visualizing Data. AT&T Bell Laboratories, Murray Hill, NJ, Hobart Press, Summit NJ (1993)
2. Keim, D.A.: Designing Pixel-Oriented Visualization Techniques: Theory and Applications. IEEE Transactions on Visualization and Computer Graphics, Vol. 6, No. 1 (2000) 59-78
3. Inselberg, A., Dimsdale, B.: Parallel Coordinates: A Tool for Visualizing Multi-Dimensional Geometry. Visualization'90, San Francisco, CA (1990) 361-370
4. Kandogan, E.: Visualizing Multi-dimensional Clusters,Trends,and Outliers Using Star Coordinates. Proceedings of the 7th ACM SIGKDD International Conference on Knowledge Discovery and Data Mining, San Francisco, USA (2001) 107-116
5. LeBlanc, J., Ward, M.O., Wittels, N.: Exploring N-Dimensional Databases. Visualization'90, San Francisco, CA (1990) 230-239
6. Johnson, B.: Visualizing Hierarchical and Categorical Data. Ph.D. Thesis, Department of Computer Science, University of Maryland (1993)
7. Tufte, E. R.: The Visual Display of Quantitative Information. Graphics Press, Cheshire, CT (1983)
8. Pickett, R.M., Grinstein, G.G.: Iconographic Displays for Visualizing Multidimensional Data. Proceedings of IEEE Conference on Systems, Man and Cybernetics, IEEE Press, Piscataway, NJ (1988) 514-519
9. Mao, J.C., Jain, A.K.: Artificial Neural Networks for Feature Extraction and Multivariate Data Projection. IEEE Transactions on Neural Networks, Vol. 6, No. 2 (1995) 296-317

10. Naud, A., Duch, W.: Interactive Data Exploration Using MDS Mapping. Proceedings of the 5th Conference on Neural Networks and Soft Computing, Zakopane, Poland (2000) 255-260
11. Shao, C., Huang, H.K.: Improvement of Data Visualization Based on SOM. Proceedings of International Symposium on Neural Networks, Dalian, China (2004) 707-712
12. Tenenbaum, J.B., de Silva, V., Langford, J.C.: A Global Geometric Framework for Nonlinear Dimensionality Reduction. Science, Vol. 290, No. 22 (2000) 2319-2323
13. de Silva, V., Tenenbaum, J.B.: Unsupervised Learning of Curved Manifolds. Proceedings of MSRI Workshop on Nonlinear Estimation and Classification, Berkeley, USA (2001) 453-466
14. Vlachos, M., Domeniconi, C., Gunopulos, D., Kollios, G., Koudas, N.: Non-Linear Dimensionality Reduction Techniques for Classification and Visualization. Proceedings of the 8th ACM SIGKDD International Conference on Knowledge Discovery and Data Mining, Edmonton, Canada (2002) 645-651
15. Roweis, S.T., Saul, L.K.: Nonlinear Dimensionality Reduction by Locally Linear Embedding. Science, Vol. 290, No. 22 (2000) 2323-2326
16. Hadid, A., Pietikäinen, M.: Efficient Locally Linear Embeddings of Imperfect Manifolds. Machine Learning and Data Mining in Pattern Recognition, Third International Conference, MLDM 2003, Leipzig, Germany (2003) 188-201
17. Belkin, M., Niyogi, P.: Laplacian Eigenmaps for Dimensionality Reduction and Data Representation. Neural Computation, Vol. 15, No. 6 (2003) 1373C1396
18. Balasubramanian, M., Schwartz, E.L., Tenenbaum, J.B., de Silva, V., Langford J.C.: The Isomap Algorithm and Topological Stability. Science, Vol. 295, No. 5552 (2002) 7a-7
19. Kouropteva, O., Okun, O., Pietikäinen, M.: Selection of the Optimal Parameter Value for the Locally Linear Embedding Algorithm. Proceedings of the 1st International Conference on Fuzzy Systems and Knowledge Discovery (FSKD'02), Singapore (2002) 359-363
20. Bernstein, M., de Silva, V., Langford, J.C., Tenenbaum, J.B.: Graph approximations to geodesics on embedded manifolds. Technical report, Department of Psychology, Stanford University (2000)

Proximity Searching in High Dimensional Spaces with a Proximity Preserving Order*

Edgar Chávez[1], Karina Figueroa[1,2], and Gonzalo Navarro[2]

[1] Facultad de Ciencias Físico-Matemáticas, Universidad Michoacana, México
{elchavez, karina}@fismat.umich.mx
[2] Center for Web Research, Dept. of Computer Science, University of Chile
gnavarro@dcc.uchile.cl

Abstract. Kernel based methods (such as k-nearest neighbors classifiers) for AI tasks translate the classification problem into a proximity search problem, in a space that is usually very high dimensional. Unfortunately, no proximity search algorithm does well in high dimensions. An alternative to overcome this problem is the use of approximate and probabilistic algorithms, which trade time for accuracy.

In this paper we present a new probabilistic proximity search algorithm. Its main idea is to order a set of samples based on their distance to each element. It turns out that the closeness between the order produced by an element and that produced by the query is an excellent predictor of the relevance of the element to answer the query.

The performance of our method is unparalleled. For example, for a *full* 128-dimensional dataset, it is enough to review 10% of the database to obtain 90% of the answers, and to review less than 1% to get 80% of the correct answers. The result is more impressive if we realize that a full 128-dimensional dataset may span thousands of dimensions of clustered data. Furthermore, the concept of proximity preserving order opens a totally new approach for both exact and approximated proximity searching.

1 Introduction

Kernel methods (for example k-nearest neighbors classifiers) are widely used in many AI tasks, such as recommendation systems, distance based clustering, query by content in multimedia repositories, pattern recognition, and so on. The classifying process can be abstracted as a search problem in a general metric space. A newly arrived (unknown) object is classified according to its distances to known object samples.

Kernel based methods are appealing because they are simple to design and understand. The designer only needs to define a long list of features for each object, representing the object as a high dimensional vector. The problem then translates into satisfying proximity queries in high dimensional spaces. Unfortunately, current methods for proximity searching suffer from the so-called *curse*

---

* Supported by CYTED VII.19 RIBIDI Project (all authors), CONACyT grant 36911A (first and second author) and Millennium Nucleus Center for Web Research, Grant P04-067-F, Mideplan, Chile (second and third author).

of dimensionality. In short, an efficient method for proximity searching in low dimensions becomes painfully slow in high dimensions.

The concept of high dimensionality exists on general metric spaces (where there might be no coordinates) as well. When the histogram of distances among objects has a large mean and a small variance, the performance of any proximity search algorithm deteriorates just as when searching in high-dimensional vector spaces. In sufficiently high dimensions, no proximity search algorithm can avoid comparing the query against all the database.

Such a linear complexity solution for proximity searching does not scale because the distance function is computationally expensive. To cope with the curse of dimensionality, different relaxations on the query precision have been proposed in order to obtain a computationally feasible solution. This is called *approximate similarity searching*, as opposed to the classic *exact similarity searching*. Approximate similarity searching is reasonable in many applications because the metric space modelization already involves an approximation to reality and therefore a second approximation at search time is usually acceptable.

These relaxations use, in addition to the query, a precision parameter ε to control how far away (in some sense) we want the outcome of the query from the correct result. A reasonable behavior for this type of algorithms is to asymptotically approach to the correct answer as ε goes to zero, and complementarily to speed up the algorithm, losing precision, as ε moves in the opposite direction.

There are basically two alternatives for approximate similarity searching. A first one uses ε as a distance relaxation parameter, for example they ensure that the distance to the nearest neighbor answer they find is at most $1 + \varepsilon$ times the distance to the true nearest neighbor. This corresponds to "approximation" algorithms in the usual algorithmic sense, and is considered in depth in [16, 8]. A second alternative takes ε in a probabilistic sense, for example ensuring that the answer of the algorithm is correct with probability at least $1-\varepsilon$. This corresponds to "probabilistic" algorithms in the usual algorithmic sense. A generic method to convert an exact algorithm into probabilistic is studied in [6, 3].

In this paper we present a new probabilistic proximity search algorithm. Its main idea is to order a set of samples based on their distance to each element. It turns out that the closeness between the order produced by an element and that produced by the query is an excellent predictor of the relevance of the element to answer the query. This is a completely new concept not previously explored in proximity searching. Interestingly enough, although such orders do permit exact proximity searching as well, they work much better for approximate proximity searching.

The performance of our method is unparalleled, even considering the great success of previous probabilistic methods. For example, for a *full* 128-dimensional dataset (that is, elements are uniformly distributed in 128 dimensions), it is enough to review 10% of the database to obtain 90% of the answers, and to review less than 1% to get 80% of the correct answers. The result is more impressive if we realize that a full 128-dimensional dataset usually corresponds to thousands of dimensions in clustered data.

2 Basic Concepts and Related Work

2.1 Basic Terminology

Formally, the proximity searching problem may be stated as follows: There is a universe $\mathbb{X}$ of *objects*, and a nonnegative *distance function* $d : \mathbb{X} \times \mathbb{X} \longrightarrow \mathbb{R}^+$ defined among them. This distance satisfies the three axioms that make the set a *metric space*: strict positiveness ($d(x,y) = 0 \Leftrightarrow x = y$), symmetry ($d(x,y) = d(y,x)$) and triangle inequality ($d(x,z) \leq d(x,y) + d(y,z)$). This distance is considered expensive to compute (think, for instance, in comparing two fingerprints). We have a finite *database* $\mathbb{U} \subseteq \mathbb{X}$, of size n, which is a subset of the universe of objects. The goal is to preprocess the database $\mathbb{U}$ to quickly answer (i.e. with as few distance computations as possible) *range queries* and *nearest neighbor* queries. We are interested in this work in range queries, expressed as (q, r) (a point in $\mathbb{X}$ and a tolerance radius), which should retrieve all the database points at distance r or less from q, i.e. $\{u \in \mathbb{U} \,/\, d(u,q) \leq r\}$. On the other hand, nearest neighbor queries retrieve the K elements of $\mathbb{U}$ that are closest to q.

Most of the existing approaches to solve the search problem on metric spaces are *exact algorithms* which retrieve exactly the elements of $\mathbb{U}$ at distance r or less from q. In [8] most of those approaches are surveyed and explained in detail. Additionally in [13] the techniques to optimally search for nearest neighbor queries using progressively enhanced range queries are surveyed.

2.2 Approximate Proximity Searching

In this work we are more interested in approximate and probabilistic algorithms, which relax the condition of delivering the exact solution. This relaxation uses, in addition to the query, a *precision* parameter ε to control how far away (in some sense) we want the outcome of the query from the correct result.

Approximation algorithms are surveyed in depth in [16]. An example is [1], which proposes a data structure for real-valued vector spaces under any Minkowski metric L_s. The structure, called the BBD-tree, is inspired in *kd*-trees and can be used to find "$(1 + \varepsilon)$ nearest neighbors": instead of finding u such that $d(u, q) \leq d(v, q)$ $\forall v \in \mathbb{U}$, they find u^* such that $d(u^*, q) \leq (1 + \varepsilon) d(v, q)$ $\forall v \in \mathbb{U}$.

The essential idea behind this algorithm is to locate the query q in a cell (each leaf in the tree is associated with a cell in the decomposition). Every point inside the cell is processed so as to obtain its nearest neighbor u. The search stops when no promising cells are found, i.e. when the radius of any ball centered at q and intersecting a nonempty cell exceeds the radius $d(q,p)/(1+\varepsilon)$. The query time is $O(\lceil 1 + 6k/\varepsilon \rceil^k k \log n)$, where k is the dimensionality of the vector space.

Probabilistic algorithms have been proposed both for vector spaces [1, 18, 16] and for general metric spaces [11, 6, 3].

In [3] they use a technique to obtain probabilistic algorithms that is relevant to this work. They use different techniques to sort the database according to some *promise value*. As they traverse the database in such order, they obtain more and more relevant answers to the query. A good database ordering is one that obtains most of the relevant answers by traversing a small fraction of the database. In other words, given a limited amount of work allowed, the algorithm finds each correct answer with some probability, and it can refine the answer incrementally if more work is allowed. Thus, the problem of finding good probabilistic search algorithms translates into finding a good ordering of the database.

Finally, there are approaches that combine approximation and probabilistic techniques, such as the PAC (probably approximately correct) method [9]. This also occurs with [6], where a general method based on stretching the triangle inequality offers both approximation and probabilistic guarantees.

2.3 Data Organization

All metric space search algorithms rely on an *index*, that is, a data structure that maintains some information on the database in order to save some distance evaluations at search time. There exist two main types of data organizations [8].

Pivoting Schemes. A *pivot* is a distinguished database element, whose distance to some other elements has been precomputed and stored in an index. Imagine that we have precomputed $d(p, u)$ for some pivot p and every $u \in \mathbb{U}$. At search time, we compute $d(p, q)$. Then, by the triangle inequality, $d(q, u) \geq |d(p,q) - d(p,u)|$, so if $|d(p,q) - d(p,u)| > r$ we know that $d(q,u) > r$, hence u will be filtered out without need of computing that distance.

The most basic scheme chooses k pivots $p_1 \ldots p_k$ and computes all the distances $d(p_i, u)$, $u \in \mathbb{U}$, into a table of kn entries. Then, at query time, all the k distances $d(p_i, q)$ are computed and every element u such that $D(q,u) = \max_{i=1\ldots k} |d(p_i, q) - d(p_i, u)| > r$ is discarded. Finally, q is compared against the elements not discarded.

As k grows, we have to pay more comparisons against pivots, but $D(q, u)$ becomes closer to $d(q, u)$ and more elements may be discarded. It can be shown that there is an optimum number of pivots k^*, which grows fast with the dimension and becomes quickly unreachable because of memory limitations. In all but the easiest metric spaces, one simply uses as many pivots as memory permits. There exist many variations over the basic idea, including different ways to sort the table of kn entries to reduce extra CPU time, e.g. [5, 4].

Although they look completely different, several tree data structures are built on the same pivoting concept, e.g. [17]. In most of them, a pivot p is chosen as the root of a tree, and its subtrees correspond to ranges of $d(p, u)$ values, being recursively built on the elements they have. In some cases the exact distances $d(p, u)$ are not stored, just the range can be inferred from the subtree the element u is in. Albeit this reduces the accuracy of the index, the tree usually takes $O(n)$ space instead of the $O(kn)$ needed with k pivots. Moreover, every internal node is a partial pivot (which knows distances to its subtree elements only), so we actually have much more pivots (albeit local and with coarse data). Finally, the trees can be traversed with sublinear extra CPU time.

Different tree variants arise according to the tree arities, the way the ranges of distances are chosen (trying to balance the tree or not), how local are the pivots (different nodes can share pivots, which do not belong anymore to the subtree), the number of pivots per node, and so on. Very little is known about which is best. For example, the golden rule of preferring balanced trees, which works well for exact searching, becomes a poorer choice against unbalancing as the dimension increases. For very high dimensional data the best data structure is just a linked list (a degenerate tree) [7]. Also, little is known about how to choose the pivots.

Local Partitioning Schemes. Another scheme builds on the idea of dividing the database into spatially compact groups, meaning that the elements in each group are close to each other. A representative is chosen from each group, so that comparing q against the representative has good chances of discarding the whole group without further comparisons. Usually these schemes are hierarchical, so that groups are recursively divided into subgroups.

Two main ways exist to define the groups. One can define "centers" with a covering radius, so that all elements in its group are within the covering radius distance to the center, e.g. [10]. If a group has center c and covering radius r_c then, if $d(q,c) > r + r_c$, it can be wholly discarded. The geometric shape of the above scheme corresponds to a ball around c. In high dimensions, all the balls tend to overlap and even a query with radius zero has to enter many balls.

This overlap problem can be largely alleviated with the second approach, e.g. [2, 14]. The set of centers is chosen and every database element is assigned to its closest center. At query time, if q is closest to center c_i, and $d(q, c_j) - r > d(q, c_i) + r$, then we can discard the group of c_j.

3 A New Probabilistic Search Algorithm

In this section we describe our contribution in the form of a new probabilistic algorithm based on a new indexing technique, which cannot be classified as pivot based nor compact partitioning.

We select a subset $\mathbb{P} = \{p_1, \ldots, p_k\} \subseteq \mathbb{U}$, in principle at random. Our index consists of a permutation of $\mathbb{P}$ for each element $u \in \mathbb{U}$. That is, each database element u reorders $\mathbb{P}$ according to the distances of the elements p_i to u. Intuitively, if two elements u and v are close to each other, their two permutations should be similar. In particular, if $d(u,v) = 0$, the two permutations must coincide.

At query time we compute the same permutation of $\mathbb{P}$ with respect to the query q. Then we order the database according to how similar are the permutations of the elements $u \in \mathbb{U}$ to the permutation of q. We expect that elements with orders more similar to that of q will also be spatially closer to q.

We now precise and formalize the ideas.

3.1 Index Process

Each element $u \in \mathbb{X}$ defines a *preorder* $\leq_u$ in $\mathbb{P}$. For every pair $y, z \in \mathbb{P}$ we define:

$$y \leq_u z \Leftrightarrow d(u,y) \leq d(u,z).$$

The relation $\leq_u$ is a preorder and not an order because two elements can be at the same distance to u, and thus $\exists y \neq z$ such that $y \leq_u z \wedge z \leq_u y$.

This preorder is not sufficient to derive a permutation in $\mathbb{P}$. Fortunately, preorder $\leq_u$ induces a total order in the quotient set. Let us call $=_u$ the equivalence related to preorder $\leq_u$, that is, $y =_u z$ iff $d(u,y) = d(z,u)$, and let us also define $y <_u z$ as $y \leq_u z \wedge y \neq_u z$.

We associate each preorder $\leq_u$ a permutation Π_u of $\mathbb{P}$ as follows:

$$\Pi_u = (p_{i_1}, p_{i_2}, \ldots, p_{i_k})$$

such that $\forall 1 \leq j < k$, $(p_{i_j} <_u p_{i_{j+1}}) \vee (p_{i_j} =_u p_{i_{j+1}} \wedge i_j < i_{j+1})$.

That is, elements in Π_u are essentially sorted by $\leq_u$, and we break ties using the identifiers in $\mathbb{P}$ (any consistent way to break ties would do).

Note that our index needs $nk \log k$ bits, while pivot-based index using k pivots require typically $nk \log n$ bits.

3.2 Search Process

Let (q, r) be a query with positive search radius $r > 0$. At query time we compute the permutation Π_q. Once we have the permutation induced by the query, we will sort $\mathbb{U}$ according to how much does each Π_u differ from Π_q. Then we will traverse the database in this order, hoping to find the closest elements to u soon.

To this end we use Spearman's Footrule [12] as our similarity measure between permutations, denoted $F(\Pi_q, \Pi_u)$. We sum the differences in the relative position of each element of the permutations. That is, for each $p_i \in \mathbb{P}$ we compute its position in Π_u and Π_q. We interpert $\Pi_u(p_i)$ as the position of element p_i in Π_u. Then we sum up the absolute values of the differences $|\Pi_u(p_i) - \Pi_q(p_i)|$. Formally,

$$F(\Pi_q, \Pi_u) = \sum_{1 \leq i \leq k} |\Pi_u(p_i) - \Pi_q(p_i)|$$

Thus, we traverse elements $u \in \mathbb{U}$ from smallest to largest $F(\Pi_q, \Pi_u)$.

Let us give an example of $F(\Pi_q, \Pi_u)$. Let $\Pi_q = p_1, p_2, p_3, p_4, p_5, p_6$ be the permutation of the query, and $\Pi_u = p_3, p_6, p_2, p_1, p_5, p_4$ be the permutation of an element $u \in \mathbb{U}$. A particular element p_3 in permutation Π_u is found two positions off with respect to its position in Π_q. The differences between permutations are: $3-1, 6-2, 3-2, 4-1, 5-5, 6-4$, and the sum of all these differences is $F(\Pi_q, \Pi_u) = 12$.

There are other similarity measures between permutations [12], like: Spearman's Rho and Kendall's Tau. On section 4 we will show that both have the same performance as Spearman's Footrule for our algorithm.

4 Experimental Validation

We made some experiments using uniformly distributed sets in the unitary cube. We used full dimensional dataset of 128, 256, 512 and 1024 dimensions. A full 128-dimensional dataset may span thousands of dimensions in clustered data.

The database size was 10,000 objects and the query retrieved 0.05% of database. Another parameter of our algorithm is the size of permutation. In this set of experiment we use 128 and 256 elements for $\mathbb{P}$. We compare our technique versus a classical technique of pivots using the same amount of pivots, even though this represent four more times the memory that we use in our algorithm. In other words, if we restricted the two algorithms to use the same memory, the results would be even better.

For the pivots algorithm, we calculated for each element u in the database its distance $L_\infty = \max_{p \in \mathbb{P}} |d(q,p) - d(p,u)|$. The elements in the database were sorted by this value and compared against the query taking them in this order, as in previous work [3].

In Figure 1 we show the performance of our technique. We used permutations of 128 elements and 256 for the left and right plots respectively. The x axis represents the size of the database examined, the y axis is the percentage of the answer retrieved (or the probability of returning a given answer element). Lines with the word *piv* refer to the classical pivot algorithm.

Retrieving 90% of the answer is good enough for most proximity searching applications. We observe that, as the dimension grows, a larger fraction of the database must be examined to obtain the same precision. This observation is true for the pivot based algorithm as well as for our new algorithm.

With pivots, in dimension 128, to retrieve 90% of the query we must examine 90% of the database. This is as bad as a random traversal. For the new algorithm, however we just fetch 5% of database to retrieve the same 90% of the results.

It can also be seen how the performance improves when we use larger k.

We compared other similarity measures between permutations, like Spearman's Rho and Kendall's Tau [12]. In Figure 2 we compare their relative performance. It can be seen that our algorithm has the same performance for all of them.

The AESA algorithm [15] uses the L_1 Minkowski metric as an oracle to select next-best candidates for pruning the database. We tested the L_1 distance to sort the database for a probabilistic algorithm based on pivots. That is, we repeated

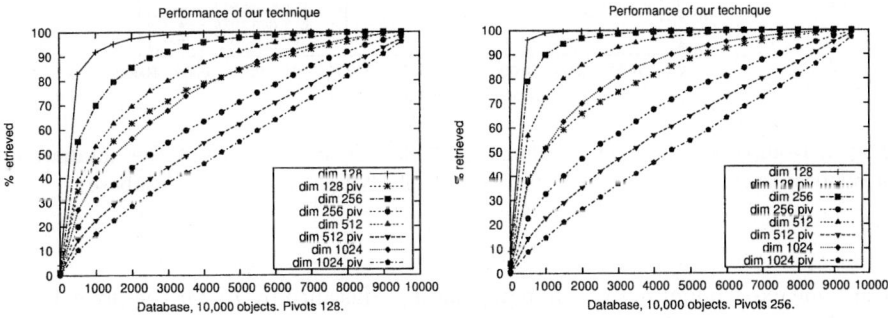

Fig. 1. Performance of the probabilistic algorithms in high dimensions. In the left side we use 128 pivots, and 256 in the right side. With our algorithm, it is possible to retrieve at least 90% of the relevant elements for the query, comparing less than 10% of the database.

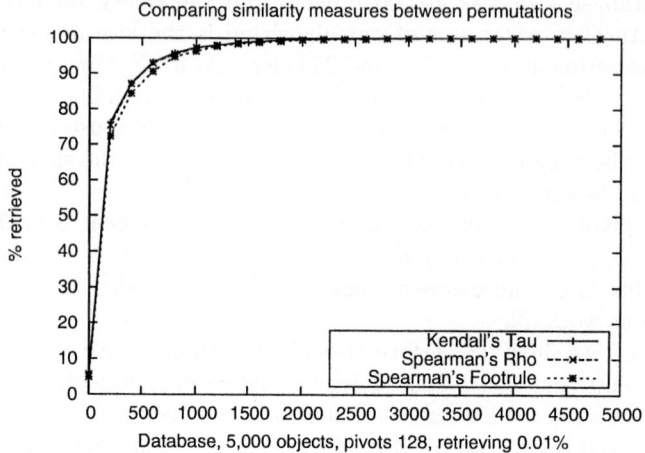

Fig. 2. Using different similarity measures between permutations. *Spearman's Footrule*, *Spearman's Rho* and *Kendall's Tau*. All of them have the same performance for our algorithm.

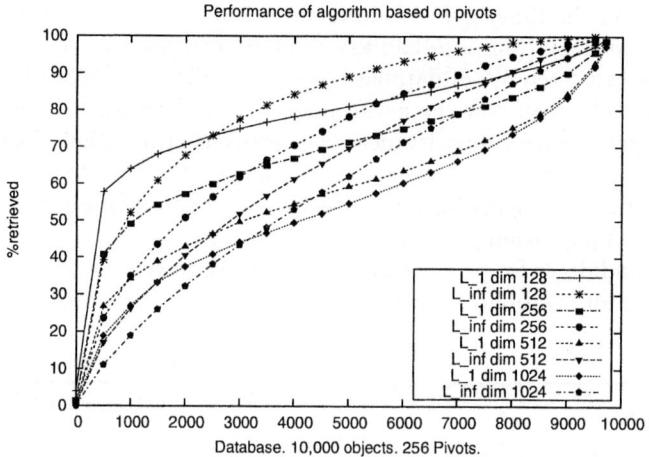

Fig. 3. Comparison between L_1 and L_∞ Minkowski metrics to sort the database on pivot-based algorithm, using 256 pivots and retrieving 0.05% of the database

the same experiment above, changing the L_∞ distance by L_1 for the pivot-based algorithm. The results were similar to those using L_∞. In Figure 3 we can observe a mixed result in the filtration power. In the first part (scanning less than 20% of the database) the L_1 distance retrieves a larger percent of the database compared to L_∞, for dimension 128. Yet, once the above point is reached, the result is reversed. The same behavior is observed in all the dimensions considered. We emphasize that, anyway, the results are very far from what we obtain with our new technique.

5 Conclusion and Future Work

In this paper we introduced a new probabilistic algorithm based on a proximity preserving order for metric range queries. We demonstrated experimentally that the proximity preserving order is an excellent oracle for selecting the best candidates. This has applications in both approximate and exact proximity searching algorithms.

We show experimentally that, even in very high dimensions, it is possible to retrieve 90% of the correct answer for the query, comparing less than 3% of the database, using just 256 bytes per database element.

AESA [15] is the best exact algorithm for proximity searching. It is seldom used because of its $O(n^2)$ memory requirements (as it requires saving the $O(n^2)$ distances between database elements), which do not scale for large databases. A rationale for the success of AESA is the use of the L_1 distance as an oracle. Since in our experiments the L_1 ordering is beaten by Spearman's Footrule, it would be very interesting to implement AESA using our proximity preserving order as the oracle for selecting the best next candidate for database pruning. We are currently pursuing this line with promising results.

Although our algorithm saves many distance computations, it still uses a linear number of *side CPU computations*. While this is fairly good in many applications because the distance computations are the leading complexity operations, we are working on a data structure that permits sublinear side computations as well.

References

1. S. Arya, D. Mount, N. Netanyahu, R. Silverman, and A. Wu. An optimal algorithm for approximate nearest neighbor searching in fixed dimension. In *Proc. 5th ACM-SIAM Symposium on Discrete Algorithms (SODA'94)*, pages 573–583, 1994.
2. S. Brin. Near neighbor search in large metric spaces. In *Proc. 21st Conference on Very Large Databases (VLDB'95)*, pages 574–584, 1995.
3. B. Bustos and G. Navarro. Probabilistic proximity search algorithms based on compact partitions. *Journal of Discrete Algorithms (JDA)*, 2(1):115–134, 2003.
4. E. Chávez and K. Figueroa. Faster proximity searching in metric data. In *Proc. of the Mexican International Conference in Artificial Intelligence (MICAI)*, Lecture Notes in Computer Science, pages 222–231. Springer, 2004.
5. E. Chávez, J.L. Marroquin, and G. Navarro. Fixed queries array: A fast and economical data structure for proximity searching. *Multimedia Tools and Applications (MTAP)*, 14(2):113–135, 2001.
6. E. Chávez and G. Navarro. Probabilistic proximity search: Fighting the curse of dimensionality in metric spaces. *Inf. Process. Lett.*, 85(1):39–46, 2003.
7. E. Chávez and G. Navarro. A compact space decomposition for effective metric indexing. *Pattern Recognition Letters*, 26(9):1363–1376, 2005.

8. E. Chávez, G. Navarro, R. Baeza-Yates, and J.L. Marroquin. Proximity searching in metric spaces. *ACM Computing Surveys*, 33(3):273–321, 2001.
9. P. Ciaccia and M. Patella. Pac nearest neighbor queries: Approximate and controlled search in high-dimensional and metric spaces. In *Proc. 16th Intl. Conf. on Data Engineering (ICDE'00)*, pages 244–255. IEEE Computer Society, 2000.
10. P. Ciaccia, M. Patella, and P. Zezula. M-tree: an efficient access method for similarity search in metric spaces. In *Proc. of the 23rd Conference on Very Large Databases (VLDB'97)*, pages 426–435, 1997.
11. K. Clarkson. Nearest neighbor queries in metric spaces. *Discrete Computational Geometry*, 22(1):63–93, 1999.
12. R. Fagin, R. Kumar, and D. Sivakumar. Comparing top k lists. *SIAM J. Discrete Math.*, 17(1):134–160, 2003.
13. G. Hjaltason and H. Samet. Index-driven similarity search in metric spaces. *ACM Trans. Database Syst.*, 28(4):517–580, 2003.
14. G. Navarro. Searching in metric spaces by spatial approximation. *The Very Large Databases Journal (VLDBJ)*, 11(1):28–46, 2002.
15. E. Vidal. An algorithm for finding nearest neighbors in (approximately) constant average time. *Pattern Recognition Letters*, 4:145–157, 1986.
16. D. White and R. Jain. Algorithms and strategies for similarity retrieval. Technical Report VCL-96-101, Visual Computing Laboratory, University of California, La Jolla, California, July 1996.
17. P. Yianilos. Excluded middle vantage point forests for nearest neighbor search. In *DIMACS Implementation Challenge, ALENEX'99*, Baltimore, MD, 1999.
18. P. N. Yianilos. Locally lifting the curse of dimensionality for nearest neighbor search. Technical report, NEC Research Institute, Princeton, NJ, June 1999.

A Neurobiologically Motivated Model for Self-organized Learning

Frank Emmert-Streib*

Institut für Theoretische Physik, Universität Bremen,
Otto-Hahn-Allee, 28334 Bremen, Germany
fes@stowers-institute.org

Abstract. We present a neurobiologically motivated model for an agent which generates a representation of its spacial environment by an active exploration. Our main objectives is the introduction of an action-selection mechanism based on the principle of self-reinforcement learning. We introduce the action-selection mechanism under the constraint that the agent receives only information an animal could receive too. Hence, we have to avoid all supervised learning methods which require a teacher. To solve this problem, we define a self-reinforcement signal as qualitative comparison between predicted an perceived stimulus of the agent. The self-reinforcement signal is used to construct internally a self-punishment function and the agent chooses its actions to minimize this function during learning. As a result it turns out that an active action-selection mechanism can improve the performance significantly if the problem to be learned becomes more difficult.

1 Introduction

The understanding of the action-perception cycle (APC) of an animal is an outstanding problem. If known, it would describe in a principle way the dynamical interplay between sensory processing, memory organization, prediction and action selection mechanism of an animal [10]. Due to the intertwined interactions of the whole system, the action-perception cycle is an systems theoretical approach to understand the neuronal organization of animals rather then a reductionistic one. Although known for a long time, we are still in the beginning to decipher its functional principle. We think, that the key to the understanding of the APC is the investigation of the action-selection mechanism, because it is by far underrepresented in the literature compared to all other parts contributing to the APC. In this paper we focus on one variant of the APC dealing with the spacial exploration of an animal in its environment.

We study the formation of an internal representation of an environment under the influence of different action-selection mechanisms. The major objective of this paper is the introduction of an action-selection mechanism which is based on

---

* Present address: Stowers Institute for Medical Research, 1000 E. 50th Street, Kansas City, MO 64110, USA.

a principle we call *self-reinforcement learning* enabling the agent to self-organized learning. In contrast to reinforcement learning [8] which is also called minimal supervised learning because a teacher is necessary to feed a qualitative signal back to the animal evaluating the last action, our self-reinforcement learning paradigm allows the animal to generate a reinforcement signal itself by comparison between predicted and perceived stimulus. For this reason, we call this signal self-reinforcement signal to emphasize that learning occurs completely unsupervised. Hence, our approach is also different to, e.g., Active Learning which was so far only used in a supervised or at least semi-supervised context [11]. We use for the remaining parts of the action-perception cycle a similar model independently invented by Herrmann et al. [4] and Oore et al. [5] introduced as hippocampus model. This paper is organized as follows: In the next section 2 we define our model and emphasize especially the part of decision making. In section 3 we present results and in 4 we conclude with a discussion.

2 The Model

2.1 Environment

The environment of the agent is an one-dimensional lattice of size N with reflecting boundary conditions. Each site of the lattice $\hat{x} \in \{1, \ldots, E\}$ is assigned an observable symbol $\hat{s} \in \{0, 1\}$, e.g. the color of the site. The position $\hat{x}$ of the agent on the grid is not directly available to the agent but only the observable symbols representing stimuli. However, there is an observation error p_s^{oe} of a symbol $\hat{s}$ on a grid position $\hat{x}$ due to an external influences, e.g. lighting conditions. We model this observation error by a Markov process given by

$$P(s|\hat{s}) = \begin{pmatrix} 1 - p_{s=1}^{oe} & p_{s=2}^{oe} \\ p_{s=1}^{oe} & 1 - p_{s=2}^{oe} \end{pmatrix} \quad (1)$$

For reasons of simplicity we assume that Eq. 1 is independent of the spatial position. The observed symbol s by the agent is obtained from

$$P(s) = \sum_{\hat{s}} P(s|\hat{s}) P(\hat{s}) \quad (2)$$

Here $P(\hat{s}) = \delta_{\hat{s}, \hat{s}=f(\hat{x})}$, with a mapping f from the position of the agent $\hat{x}$ to the observable symbol $\hat{s}$ on that site. In the following we consider only the case of a symmetric observation error $p_{s=1}^{oe} = p_{s=2}^{oe}$.

Because the environment of the agent is one-dimensional we allow the agent only to select between two different actions, $a_t \in \{-1, 1\}$. In analogy to the observation error we introduce a position error p^{pe} occurring if the agent tries to change its grid position due to an external influences, e.g. friction. Here, we assume a homogenes environment to keep things simple and additionally, we assume the transition probability $P(\hat{x}_{t+1}|\hat{x}_t', a_{t+1})$ to be stationary. The new grid position $\hat{x}_{t+1}$ is obtained by

$$P(\hat{x}_{t+1}) = \sum_{\hat{x}_t'} P(\hat{x}_{t+1}|\hat{x}_t', a_{t+1}) P(\hat{x}_t') \quad (3)$$

Here $P(\hat{x}_t') = \delta_{\hat{x}_t', \hat{x}_t}$, with $\hat{x}_t$ the actual physical position of the agent on the grid.

2.2 Dynamics of Internal States I

The inner states of the agent are given by a discrete probability distribution P_i^1, with $i \in I$. As special case we chose $I = E$. This implies that the agent knows the size of the grid. The dynamics of the inner states is again given by a Markov process [4],

$$P_{t+1}^1(i) = \sum_{i'} T_{a_t}(i|i') P_t^1(i') \qquad (4)$$

and the transition probability T_{a_t} is chosen to be

$$T_{a_t}(i|i') = N_1 \exp\left(-\frac{(i - i' + a_t)^2}{2\sigma_1^2}\right) \qquad (5)$$

N_1 is the standardization. The index a_t of the transition probability indicates that the drift direction of $T_{a_t}(i|i')$ is affected by the action of the agent. Intuitively, this couples the change of the inner states, pointing internally to a position in the representation, of the agent with its action.

2.3 Prediction and Learning

The task of the agent is to generate an internal representation of the outer environment. Because this problem shall be learned without an external teacher in a self-organized way, the agent needs a criterion to evaluates its own performance. For this reason we use the agent's prediction for the next symbol to be observed as qualitative measure of the internal self-consistency reached so far [4, 3].

$$P_{t+1}^2(s) = \sum_i P_t^S(s|i) P_{t+1}^1(i) \qquad (6)$$

$$\bar{s}_{t+1} = \operatorname{argmax}_s \left\{ P_{t+1}^2(s) \right\} \qquad (7)$$

The linear estimator in Eq. 6 is the most simple ansatz one can choose as prediction mechanism. Because P^2 is a probability distribution defined over the discrete set of observable symbols S we need an additional criterion to select the predicted symbol $\bar{s}_{t+1}$. Therefore, we use a winner-take-all mechanism 7 which selects the symbol maximizing P^2. The conditional probability $P^S(s|i)$ is the adaptive part of the agent and has to be learned. This has to be done on-line, that means every incoming sensory input is used to change $P^S(s|i)$ by a small amount.

$$P_{t+1}^S(s|i) = P_t^S(s|i) + \delta P_t^S(s|i) \qquad (8)$$

The alteration $\delta P^S_{t+1}(s|i)$ is derived from the cost function

$$E_{\text{cost}} = \frac{1}{2}\sum_s (\delta_{s_t,s} - P^S_t(s))^2 \qquad (9)$$

by gradient descent with respect to $P^S(s|i)$ [4].

$$\delta P^S_{t+1}(s|i) = \frac{\partial E_{\text{cost}}}{\partial P^S(s|i)} = \epsilon(\delta_{s_t,s} - P^S_t(s))P^1_t(i) \qquad (10)$$

Here ϵ is the learning rate which has to be chosen appropriately small.

2.4 Dynamics of Internal States II

Now, we complete the definition of the internal states of the agent. In 2.2 the internal states P^1 were effected only by the action. It seems to be plausible that P^1 should depend also on the quality of the prediction of the agent. The objective quality of the prediction is not directly accessible by the agent because there is no outer reinforcement signal to evaluate its prediction. Therefore, the conditional probability $P^S(s|i)$ seems to be useful because of two reasons. First, it is adapted by Eq. 8 and ,hence, it was learned under help of sensory input. Second, $P^S(s|i)$ is directly used for the prediction of the next symbol to be observed in Eq. 6 and hence reflects the quality of the prediction.

Formally, one can realize the feedback of the conditional probability on P^1 with the Bayesian formula [4].

$$P^1_{t+2}(i) \sim P^1_{t+2}(i|s_t) = N^{-1} P^S_{t+1}(s_t|i) P^1_{t+1}(i) \qquad (11)$$

N is a standardization.

$$N = \sum_i^I P^S_{t+1}(s_t|i) P^1_{t+1}(i) \qquad (12)$$

The new inner states $P^1_{t+2}(i)$ are approximated by $P^1_{t+2}(i|s_t)$.

2.5 Decision Making

The action-selection mechanism connects the internal model of the agent with its environment because the action is a response to the accumulated stimuli received so far which lead themselves to future stimuli. One can subdivide all possible action-selection mechanisms in two distinct classes [2], active and passive decision mechanisms. The passive decisions do not rely on the internal model of the agent in opposite to the active ones. We introduce two passive and one active decision mechanism and compare them in the results section with each other. The passive decision mechanisms are motivated by stochastic processes and represent diffusion and drift. Hence, we call them Random and Linear Walk.

The Random Walk consists just in a random selection of a possible action at each time step. The Linear Walk is given by

$$a_t = \begin{cases} a_{t-1} & : 1 < \bar{i}_t < I \\ -a_{t-1} & : \bar{i}_t = 1 \text{ or } \bar{i}_t = I \end{cases} \qquad (13)$$

with $\bar{i}_t = \lfloor \sum_i^I i P_t^1(i) \rceil$ the mean value of the internal states rounded to the nearest integer by the function

$$\lfloor n.m \rceil = \begin{cases} n & : m < 5 \\ (n+1) & : m \geq 5 \end{cases} \qquad (14)$$

for all $n, m \in \{0, 1, 2, \ldots, 9\}$.

Active Walk. The basic idea behind the Active Walk [2] we suggest, can be seen in analogy to reinforcement learning [8]. In reinforcement learning an agent tries to maximize the expected future reward by adapting the policy, which is just another name for an action-selection mechanism, appropriately. This makes sense, because the reward signal is no direct feedback of the environment on the agent responding to its actions but it is censored by a teacher which judges the quality of the actions. Hence, a reinforcement signal is reliable as well as their accumulation. Because of the presence of a teacher, reinforcement learning is also called minimal supervised learning to indicate that there is still supervision necessary. Of course, this kind of qualitative supervision is much more biological plausible then other quantitative supervised learning methods ,e.g., back-propagation [6]. On a psychological level reinforcement learning can be successfully applied to model classical conditioning, e.g., Pavlov's dog, which couples stimuli and prediction or instrumental conditioning which couples behaviour and prediction. The crucial point is, that below such a psychological level it is less plausible. For example, it is implausible to assume, that a rat in a labyrinth trying to explore its environment, receives an external reinforcement signal indicating the quality of the exploration. Where should this signal come from? Here, we exclude artificial situations in which the rat gets food after traversing the labyrinth form one point to another from a 'teacher'.

Similar to reinforcement learning we need an auxiliary function to derive actions from. We call this auxiliary function self-punishment function $P_{sp,L}^{rel}$. The self-punishment function is defined over the same space I as the internal states $P^1(i)$. The dynamics of $P_{sp,L}^{rel}$ is given by:

1. initialize $P_{sp,L}^{rel}(i; t = 0)$ randomly from the equal distribution $[0, 1]$ for all states $i \in I$
2. change $P_{sp,L}^{rel}(i; t)$ in every time step t only at the position $\bar{i}_t := \lfloor \sum_i^I i P_t^1(i) \rceil$ by $\Delta P_{sp,L}^{rel}(\bar{i}_t; t) = -\frac{r_t}{L}$, here r_t is a self-reinforcement signal and L the memory length of the self-punishment function

$$P_{sp,L}^{rel}(\bar{i}_t; t) = \begin{cases} 1 & : P_{sp,L}^{rel}(\bar{i}_t; t) > 1 \\ 0 & : P_{sp,L}^{rel}(\bar{i}_t; t) < 0 \end{cases} \qquad (15)$$

If $P_{sp,L}^{rel}(i; t) \equiv 0 \ \forall \ i \in \{1, \ldots, I\}$, reinitialize randomly.

The definition of the self-reinforcement signal is based on a comparison of the predicted $\bar{s}_t$ and perceived s_t stimulus

$$r_t = \begin{cases} 1 & : \bar{s}_t = s_t \\ -1 & : \bar{s}_t \neq s_t \end{cases} \qquad (16)$$

Here $r_t = 1$ can be interpreted as self-reward (right prediction) and $r_t = -1$ as self-punishment (wrong prediction). We call r_t self-reinforcement signal because it is generated by the agent itself without the help of a teacher. We want to mention, that in our opinion the original idea of a self-reinforcement signal, without using this notation, was introduced by [7] for studying the game of checkers.

Based on the self-punishment function, the selection of the next action is then given by:

$$a_t = \begin{cases} 1 & : i_{\max} > \bar{i}_t \\ -1 & : i_{\max} < \bar{i}_t \\ random & : i_{\max} = \bar{i}_t \end{cases} \qquad (17)$$

with $i_{\max} = \mathrm{argmax}_i P^{\mathrm{rel}}_{\mathrm{sp,L}}(i;t)$.

For L against infinity one would obtain a probability distribution

$$P_{\mathrm{sp}} = \lim_{L \to \infty} P^{\mathrm{rel}}_{\mathrm{sp,L}} \qquad (18)$$

representing the mean punishment. This limit is for real biological systems a problem because there live is finite. For this they have to decide which action to chose next on the base of the information present in the system. Hence, the self-punishment function $P^{\mathrm{rel}}_{\mathrm{sp,L}}$ introduced above is an approximation of P_{sp}.

2.6 Evaluation of the Agent

The evaluation of an agent exploring its environment is no simple task, because one has to determine a spatio-temporal error. Due to the fact, that we investigate an one-dimensional grid without orientation of the agent, the agent can predict E stimuli because this corresponds to the size of the environment. We measure the error of the agent by making a copy of the agent in each time step and put it into a test environment, which is identical to the environment the agent lived in. Then we set the learning rate $\epsilon = 0$ and delete the action-selection mechanism. Now, we control the agent from the outside in such a way, that we let it traverses the one-dimensional grid completely. The error of the agent is now given by

$$< E_{\mathrm{p}}(t) > = \frac{\#correct\ predicted\ stimuli}{E} \qquad (19)$$

Here, $<>$ is the spacial average. Because the learning process of the agent is a stochastic process the prediction error E_{p} is a random variable. We use the *first passage time* when the prediction error E_{p} of the agent reaches the first time zero as performance measure. That means, we are interested in how long does it take for the agent to learn the entire environment with prediction error zero. Due to the stochastic character of the problem it is possible, that further learning could destroy an already learned representation locally due to erroneous sensory input. But this effect will not be studied in this article. The first passage times determine its distribution p^{FPT} from which one can calculate its mean value

$$< T_{\mathrm{FPT}} >= \sum_t t p_t^{\mathrm{FPT}} \qquad (20)$$

as quantitative error measure for an ensemble of agents. Our choice of the error threshold $E_{\mathrm{p}} = 0$ to determine the first passage time means that in the following simulations we are focusing on complete convergence of our model rather then on its convergence behavior.

3 Results

3.1 Comparison of Action-Selection Mechanisms

The left Fig. 1 shows the mean first-passage time $< T_{\mathrm{FPT}} >$ for an observation and position error of $p^{\mathrm{oe}} = p^{\mathrm{pe}} = 0$ (indicated by +) and $p^{\mathrm{oe}} = p^{\mathrm{pe}} = 0.02$ (indicated by ◇) in dependence on the grid size E in a double logarithmic plot. One can see that in the case without observation and position error the curves for $< T_{\mathrm{FPT}} >$ are polynomial for all three action-selection mechanisms whereas the mean first-passage time grows exponentially for $p^{\mathrm{oe}} = p^{\mathrm{pe}} = 0.02$. This demonstrates that our algorithm is capable to form an internal representation of the environment and the dramatic increase of the mean first-passage times for non-zero observation and position error indicates that the problem of representation formation becomes more and more difficult the higher the errors are.

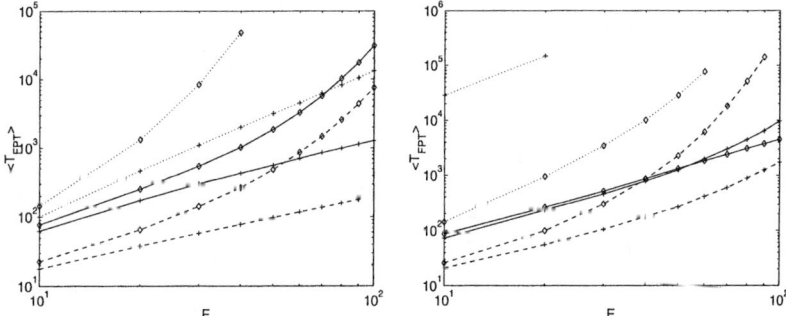

Fig. 1. Left: Mean first-passage time as function of the grid size E for the Active (full lines), Linear (dashed lines) and Random Walk (dotted lines). The memory length of the self-punishment function was $L = 10$. Left: $p^{\mathrm{oe}} = p^{\mathrm{pe}} = 0$ indicated by +, $p^{\mathrm{oe}} = p^{\mathrm{pe}} = 0.02$ indicated by ◇. Right: $p^{\mathrm{oe}} = 0$, $p^{\mathrm{pe}} = 0.02$ indicated by +, $p^{\mathrm{oe}} = 0.1$, $p^{\mathrm{pe}} = 0$ indicated by ◇.

The results for the asymmetric cases $p^{oe} = 0, p^{pe} = 0.02$ (indicated by +) and $p^{oe} = 0.1, p^{pe} = 0$ (indicated by ◊) are shown in the right Fig. 1. Interestingly, in these cases the curves grow all exponentially except for the Active Walk for $p^{oe} = 0.1, p^{pe} = 0$. For grid sizes larger than $E = 40$ the Active Walk becomes even better than the Linear Walk. From both figures one can see, that the Random Walk represents an action-selection mechanism which basically is capable exploring the environment but due to the pure diffusion this takes a long time. In contrast, the Linear Walk can be seen as a close to optimal strategy for small grid sizes and low errors. This can be best understood for the case of no position and observation error. It is clear, that any kind of diffusive walk is a waste of time for the agent because there are no errors possible. If the grid is large it would be possible, that the agent learned the complete representation except for exactly one position the agent crossed already and walks now in the 'wrong' direction. During these time steps the agent can not further improve because all other positions are already learned and, hence, it has to wait until it comes back to the unlearned spot. The smaller the grid size, the less is this effect. That means, the Random and Linear Walk can be seen as bad and good action-selection strategies.

3.2 Effect of the Memory Length L

We investigate now the influence of the memory length L of the self-punishment function. For this, we determined the mean passage times numerically for $L = 2$ and $E = 80$ and obtain $< T_{FPT} >= \{587; 1396; 5260; 9415\}$ which corresponds to $(p^{oe} = p^{pe} = 0; p^{oe} = 0.1, p^{pe} = 0; p^{oe} = 0, p^{pe} = 0.02; p^{oe} = p^{pe} = 0.02)$. This means an improvement for all cases up to $p^{oe} = 0, p^{pe} = 0.02$ as can be seen by comparison with Fig. 1. The overall effect of the memory length L is strongly

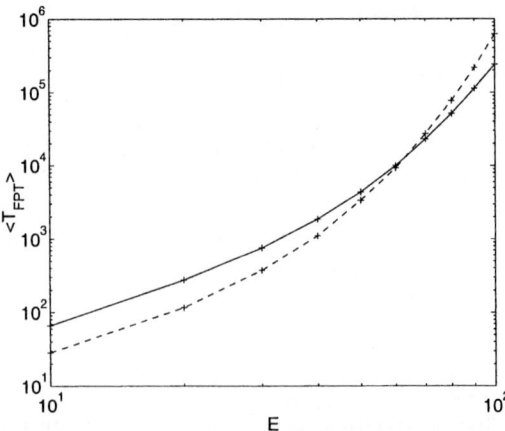

Fig. 2. Mean first-passage time as function of the grid size E for the Active (full line) and the Linear (dotted line) Walk. The memory length of the self-punishment function was $L = 2$ and the observation and position error was $p^{oe} = 0.07$ and $p^{pe} = 0.02$.

coupled to the observation and position error as well as the grid size. For this reason, one can not determine an optimal L value which gives always good or always bad results.

This is demonstrated in Fig. 2. For the curves shown there we chose $p^{oe} = 0.07$, $p^{pe} = 0.02$ and $L = 2$. Figure 2 shows the mean first-passage time $< T_{FPT} >$ of these simulations for the Active (full line) and Linear Walk (dashed line). Up to grid sizes of $E \sim 60$ the Linear Walk is better as expected. But from $E = 70$ on the mean first-passage time for the Active Walk is lower than the Linear Walk. This case demonstrates, that for difficult problems, high observation and position error and high gird sizes, an appropriately chosen action-selection mechanism can outperform a passive selection mechanism and achieve significantly better results. For the results presented in Fig. 2 this leads to a reduction of the mean learning time of about 75% for a grid size of $E = 100$.

4 Conclusion

In this article we investigated the effect of different action-selection mechanisms on the convergence of an agent in an one-dimensional grid with observation and position errors. Our results numerically proof the capability of a biologically motivated hippocampus model to learn a representation of an environment independent from the action-selection mechanism. This analysis was outstanding for the hippocampus model already introduced in [4].

The major objective of this article was the introduction of an action-selection mechanism to solve the problem of decision making for an agent based on the principle of *self-reinforcement learning*. The underlying idea is a substitution of a conventional reinforcement signal [8], which has to be provided by an teacher and is, hence, a supervised learning technique, by a more biological plausible mechanism able to be applicable to understand, e.g., the navigation of a rat in a labyrinth where doubtless no teacher is present to provide external information for the rat. We suggested to define a self-reinforcement signal as a qualitative measure of the comparison between predicted and perceived stimulus. This definition implies, that only sensory information is needed as external source of information but no teacher. We want to emphasize, that this is not just a probabilistic version of a normal reinforcement signal, because the degree of reliability of the self-reinforcement signal is not constant during learning but depends on the quality of the compositional cooperation between all parts of the action-perception cycle resulting in an impact on the prediction mechanism of the agent. If the internal model of the agent is appropriate to learn a given representation, than the reliability increases steadily during the learning process because the quality of the prediction becomes better and better. In general we think, that an actively closed action-perception cycle by an active action-selection mechanism can result in much lower learning times for a problem. Our results are first indicators for this as could be seen in the case of higher position and observation errors. This is remarkable, because the "time series analysis" part of the model, namely the hippocampus model, was not modified at all.

The lowering of the learning times can even prevent an exponential growth in dependence on the grid size as shown in the right Fig. 1 for the case $p^{oe} = 0.1$, $p^{pe} = 0.0$ and $L = 10$, at least in the parameter range investigated. Finally, we just want to mention, that the concept of self-reinforcement learning and our action selection-mechanism provide a natural starting point to investigate questions concerning the role of emotions in learning [1, 9].

Acknowledgment

We would like to thank Gökhan H. Bakir, Matthias Bethge, Ralf Der, Rolf D. Henkel, J. Michael Herrmann, Jens Otterpohl, Frank Pasemann, Klaus Pawelzik, Roland Rothenstein, Heinz Georg Schuster for fruitful discussions.

References

1. D. Döerner and K. Hille (1995), Artificial Souls: Motivated Emotional Robots. In: IEEE Conference Proceedings, International Conference on Systems Man, and Cybernetics; Intelligent Systems for the 21st Century. Vancouver, Volume 4 of 5, pp. 3828-3832.
2. F. Emmert-Streib (2003), Aktive Computation in offenen Systemen. Lerndynamiken in biologischen Systemen: Vom Netzwerk zum Organisms, Ph.D. Thesis, Universität Bremen (Germany), Mensch & Buch Verlag.
3. J.M. Herrmann, F. Emmert-Streib, and K. Pawelzik (1999), Autonomous robots and neuroethology: Emergence of behavior from a sense of curiosity. In U. Rckert A. Lffler, F. Mondada, editor, Experiments with the Mini-Robot Khepera, Proceedings of the 1st Int. Khepera Workshop, pages 89-98, Paderborn. HNI-Verlagsschriftenreihe, Bd. 64.
4. J.M. Herrmann and K. Pawelzik (1999), Self-localization of autonomous robots by hidden representations. *Autonomous Robots*, 7(1):31-40.
5. S. Oore, G. E. Hinton, and G. Dudek (1997), A mobile robot that learns its place, *Neural Computation*, 9(3):683-699
6. D. E. Rumelhart, G. E. Hinton and R. J. Williams, R. J. (1986), Learning representations by back-propagating errors. *Nature*, 323, 533–536.
7. A. Samuel (1959), Some studies in machine learning using the game of checkers. *IBM J. Res. Develop.*, 3:210-229.
8. R.S. Sutton and A.G. Burto (1998), Reinforcement Learning: An introduction. Cambridge (Mass.) MIT Press.
9. A. Tversky and D. Kahneman (1981), The framing of decisions and the psychology of choice, *Science*, 211:453-458.
10. J. von Uexküll (1920), Theoretische Biologie, Berlin Verlag von Gebrüder Paetel, 260. English translation (1926): Theoretical Biology, London: Kegan Paul, Trench, Trubner & Co.
11. X. Zhu, J. Lafferty and Z. Ghahramani (2003), Combining Active Learning and Semi-Supervised Learning Using Gaussian Fields and Harmonic Functions., In Proc. of the ICML 2003 workshop on The Continuum from Labeled to Unlabeled Data in Machine Learning and Data Mining. pp. 58-65

Using Boolean Differences for Discovering Ill-Defined Attributes in Propositional Machine Learning

Sylvain Hallé

Université du Québec à Montréal, C. P. 8888, Succ. Centre-Ville,
Montréal, Canada H3C 3P8
halle@info.uqam.ca

Abstract. The accuracy of the rules produced by a concept learning system can be hindered by the presence of errors in the data. Although these errors are most commonly attributed to random noise, there also exist "ill-defined" attributes that are too general or too specific that can produce systematic classification errors. We present a computer program called Newton which uses the fact that ill-defined attributes create an ordered error pattern among the instances to compute hypotheses explaining the classification errors of a concept in terms of too general or too specific attributes. Extensive empirical testing shows that Newton identifies such attributes with a prediction rate over 95%.

1 Introduction

Concept learning systems are aimed at the discovery of classification rules by the analysis of a set of examples described by some number of properties [1]. Frequently, a set of examples contains errors or apparent inconsistencies that hinder the learning process by provoking *classification errors*. The first and well-studied cause for these errors is the presence of random noise in the measurements; most learning systems have been adapted to generate acceptable rules under a reasonable amount of noise.

However, classification errors can also arise in the case where some of the attributes used to describe the instances are inadequate for the concept to be learned. For example, this can occur when continuous values are discretised according to ill-defined thresholds, or when attributes represent properties that are either too general or too specific for the classification task at hand.

Although such errors can be viewed as noise and treated as such, they generally leave an "error signature" among the instances that is much more coherent than mere random noise. It is based on this observation that we present in this paper a program called Newton which, by the means of Boolean differences [2], tries to build hypotheses explaining classification errors. These hypotheses suggest that one or many parameters in a case base are too loosely or too tightly defined.

The hypotheses suggested by Newton give a basis of reflection for the user of the learning system, who can better know whether the classification errors are due to noise or to something else that can be corrected by doing the observations again with attributes modified according to the suggested hypotheses. Extensive empirical testing shows that Newton identifies ill-defined attributes with an average prediction rate over 95%.

In section 2, we distinguish between random noise and ill-defined attributes. Section 3 presents a program that allows detection of non-random noise by means of Boolean differences; experimental results on sample datasets containing classification errors are given in section 4. Finally, section 5 concludes by showing some of the limits of this approach, and how it can be further studied.

2 Machine Learning and Noisy Datasets

In this section, we distinguish between the two main sources of noise found in datasets. In the following, we assume all attributes are Boolean. However, the use of Boolean attributes must not be seen as a limitation, but rather as an assumption. If a database contains discrete (nominal) attributes, these can be easily converted to Booleans by creating as many binary predicates as there are values of the original attribute. Moreover, if the instances in a dataset are divided into more than two classes, we assume the creation of a "concept" aims to provide a Boolean formula for each class C that returns 1 (*true*) when an instance is in C, and 0 (*false*) otherwise.

2.1 Sources of Noise

Following Mooney and Ourston [3], we distinguish between two primary sources of noise for examples represented as attribute-value lists.

The first is **random noise**, also called *malicious* noise. This type of noise is caused by "the occasional, non-repeatable substitution of a possibly incorrect value for the true attribute value" [4]. It can be caused by a variety of reasons including typographical errors, errors in measurement, and perception errors. Most of the work concerning noise in datasets has been interested in this particular type of noise; [5] model these errors as an adversary whose goal is to hamper learning. In [6, 7], some learning algorithms are studied with respect to their sensitivity to noise.

The second source of noise is what we call non-random (or **systematic**) noise, as has been defined in [8]. A first case of non-random noise occurs when an attribute used for describing the instances is either too general or too specific for a concept to be learned correctly. For example, if the presence of a `tail` on an animal in a dataset is represented by an attribute that takes the value 1 only when the animal has a *furred* tail, the learning system is most likely to incorrectly classify some bird specimens (which have a tail, but not a furred one) because of this overly specific attribute.

Fewer studies have been conducted concerning systematic noise. Among them, [9, 10] take into account systematic noise in the study of learning algorithms. However, contrarily to random noise, the classification error pattern in this case reveals a specific "signature". If we suppose for the moment that `tail` is the only ill-defined attribute of the dataset, then the classification errors can occur only for animals that have a tail that is *not* furred (since they should be considered as tailed but are not due to the definition of `tail`), and nowhere else. Therefore, while malicious noise is meaningless, non-random noise, as its name implies, causes classification errors in an ordered way.

One must not confuse too general or too specific attributes with too general or too specific *concepts*. An over- or under-fitting concept might be caused by a wrong definition of the attributes, but can also arise from the creation of too inclusive or too restrictive rules from correctly defined attributes.

2.2 Ill-Definition and Other Sources of Errors

This concept of ill-defined attributes can encompass many other definition problems that occur in datasets. *Ill-defined thresholds*, exposed in [1], happen when an attribute has been discretised according to the wrong boundary values. For example, an airline company might consider overweight any person over 200 kg while the dataset presented to a learning system contains a Boolean attribute `overweight` that is true whenever the passenger weighs more than 180 kg. The observations, being recorded with the wrong threshold for `overweight`, will create an error pattern that can be regarded as the Boolean attribute itself being too general.

In the same way, *residual variation* has been termed by Mingers [11] as the presence of additional factors that affect the results, but that are not recorded, either because those recording the data were unaware of the effect of the additional factors, or unable to record them. For example, a learning system might fail to get an acceptable rule predicting flu deaths if the `age of the patients` is not recorded in the observations.

This particular case where an attribute is flatly absent from a dataset can be taken into account by *coupled* error patterns. Suppose a concept to be learned is of the form $x \wedge (y \vee z)$, but that the values of x for each instance of the dataset presented to the learning system have not been recorded. It is reasonable to think that the learning system, not aware of the influence of x in the concept, will try its best and arrive at $y \vee z$ as the approximately correct concept. This formula will yield the correct value for each instance where x (not recorded) is actually true. However, when x is false, the concept will incorrectly return a false positive when $y \vee z$ is true. It all happens as if both y and z were overly general attributes identical error patterns. This reasoning can be generalised for other operators and longer formulas.

Therefore, the whole question of detecting non-random noise can be reduced to the question of detecting ill-defined attributes. For the remainder of this paper, we will concentrate ourselves on this particular question.

2.3 An Example

We illustrate the situation of ill-defined parameters by the means of a toy problem. An amusement park has a particular ride that only accepts people under

160 cm. Moreover, to prevent it from being crowded, the administration has limited its access to children under 12 and to people who have paid a VIP pass. An observer who is not aware of the regulation is asked to record data about the people who are granted access to the ride. He uses three attributes:

- y: which he sets to 1 for every person under 12
- v: which he sets to 1 for every person having a VIP pass
- s: which he sets to 1 for every person under 140 cm

For each instance, the observer also notes by the class attribute a whether the person has been granted access or turned away. He gets the results given in Figure 1(a).

y	v	s	a	a'	$\frac{\Delta^{\{0\}}a'}{\Delta y}$	$\frac{\Delta^{\{1\}}a'}{\Delta y}$	$\frac{\Delta^{\{0\}}a'}{\Delta v}$	$\frac{\Delta^{\{1\}}a'}{\Delta v}$	$\frac{\Delta^{\{0\}}a'}{\Delta s}$	$\frac{\Delta^{\{1\}}a'}{\Delta s}$
0	0	0	0	0	0	0	0	0	0	0
1	0	1	1	1	1	0	0	0	1	0
1	1	0	0	0	0	0	0	0	0	1
1	1	0	1	0	0	0	0	0	0	1
0	1	0	0	0	0	0	0	0	0	1
0	1	0	1	0	0	0	0	0	0	1
0	1	1	1	1	0	0	1	0	1	0
1	0	1	1	1	1	0	0	0	1	0
1	0	0	1	0	0	0	0	0	0	1

(a) Observations   (b) Computed Δ functions

Fig. 1. Data for the amusement park example

The concept found by the learning system he uses on this data to try to predict a, noted as a', is defined by the following formula:

$$a' = s \wedge (y \vee v)$$

Although the concept appears to be the correct one, the observer cannot explain the presence of three classification errors where a' fails to predict the correct value (in boldface in the table). The reader knows that the attribute s cuts too low (140 cm instead of the 160 cm actually used by the park), but the observer will have to wait until the next section and the presentation of Newton to find out.

3 Qualifying Non-random Noise

In this section, we present the logical foundations for the detection of possibly ill-defined attributes and show how this reasoning can be automated in a computer program called Newton.

3.1 Boolean Differences

The principle of the program is inspired from stuck-at fault analysis in combinatorial circuits [12], where the goal is to check for possibly defective logical gates that are "stuck" at the same value no matter the inputs. Instead of testing each gate individually with all possible values, one looks for an input vector on the whole circuit such that an incorrect output value can only be caused by one specific faulty gate which is then identified.

In our case, we detect that an attribute x entering in the definition of a concept f is either too general or too specific by taking the inputs, instead of the gates, to be stuck on a value. Suppose x is too general —that is, we wish it were more specific, meaning that it should return 0 on more instances than it does now. To measure the impact of a specialisation of this attribute, we suppose its value is stuck at 0 for all instances, which is the most specific it can ever get. We then compare the result of the concept formula using this "modified" attribute with that of the original concept, and in particular, on what instances a specialisation of the attribute changes the outcome.

To do so, we introduce the function $\Delta^{\{0\}}$ that we define in the following way:

$$\frac{\Delta^{\{0\}} f}{\Delta x} = f \oplus f[0/x]$$

where $\oplus$ is the exclusive-or (XOR) operator and $f[0/x]$ stands for the formula f where all occurrences of x have been replaced by 0. This function, called the "decreasing divided difference" in [2], returns 1 exactly on the instances where a specialisation of x, at a certain degree, could change the current value of f. When $\Delta^{\{0\}} f/\Delta x = 1$ for an instance where the provided concept makes a classification error, it means that a specialisation of x could eventually remove that error without having to change the formula itself.

For the case where x is supposed too general, we define the increasing divided difference:

$$\frac{\Delta^{\{1\}} f}{\Delta x} = f \oplus f[1/x]$$

Similarly, when $\Delta^{\{1\}} f/\Delta x = 1$ for an instance where the provided concept makes a classification error, it means that a generalisation of x could eventually remove that error without having to change the formula itself.

In other words, Newton attempts to give a critique of a concept by trying to explain classification errors based on ill-defined attributes. This approach bears some distant resemblance to [13, 14, 15], who attempts to give a critique of a classifier by identifying sets of cases for which a learning algorithm gives weaker predictions. In a different way, [16] use transductive inference to measure the reliability of a concept. However, the approach presented here does not involve a meta-learning of the error function, and rather tries to associate errors with specific hypotheses about the overly general or specific character of the attributes used to express the concept.

3.2 The Newton Program

Based on these findings, we developed a simple computer program called Newton that systematises this reasoning to discover particular error signatures in datasets. For each Boolean attribute x_i forming a concept f, Newton computes both $\Delta^{\{0\}}f/\Delta x_i$ and $\Delta^{\{1\}}f/\Delta x_i$ and evaluates these functions on the whole dataset. Newton then tries to cover the classification errors using a combination of these functions. The resulting covering constitutes an explanation of the classification errors in terms of possibly too general or too specific attributes.

Returning to our amusement park example of last section, we compute the two Δ functions for each attribute and evaluate them, as shown in Figure 1(b).

We see that the function $\Delta^{\{1\}}a'/\Delta s$ is the only one that can account for any of the classification errors that occurred. Moreover, it can account for all those errors. Therefore, the hypothesis that the attribute s is too specific seems appealing. The next section presents empirical results that help truly assess the validity of such an hypothesis.

4 Empirical Results

In order to validate the performance of the approach, we submitted Newton to an extensive series of tests on randomly generated classifiers. In the version used for testing, Newton is programmed to choose the Δ function that has the highest prediction rate for the classification errors as the most plausible attribute affected by systematic errors. In the case where more than one Δ function shares the highest score, Newton returns all such functions and tells the user that the attribute most likely to have been altered is among this set.

The results of these experiments show that Newton performs well at identifying one ill-defined attribute for a given concept in a dataset. In the case where more than one ill-defined attribute is present, the good performance of Newton makes it possible to work iteratively: one runs Newton to identify a first ill-defined attribute with a high confidence; once the ill-definition of this attribute is corrected, it is possible to re-run Newton that will now discover a second ill-defined attribute with again a high confidence. This process can be repeated until classification errors can no longer be reduced.

In each of these tests, a complete truth table for n Boolean variables was generated, and a classifier function $f : \{0,1\}^n \mapsto \{0,1\}$ was randomly created for the table. Then, the attributes of c randomly chosen parameters were systematically flipped with probability p, simulating overly general or overly specific attributes inducing errors in the original classification. This flipped table, along with the original classifier f, were then submitted to Newton, who was to process it and try to discover which of the parameters were the ones that had been altered by systematic bit-flipping.

The parameters n, c and p were then varied to study the response of the program under a variety of conditions. In total, the different combinations of these parameters generated 1.5 million tables on which Newton has been tested, giving extensive understanding and confidence of its behaviour.

For each test, we measured the following values:

- *prediction rate*: the average probability that Newton's prediction is actually one of the flipped parameters on a given table.
- *alternate solutions*: the average number of Δ functions returned by Newton on each generated table

A good performance of Newton should show a prediction rate as close as possible to 100%, and a number of alternate solutions as close as possible to 1.

We first tested whether the number of occurrences of distinct variables in the expression of the classifier influenced the prediction rate and number of alternate solutions. Figure 2 shows the evolution of these two numbers, in situations where the number of flipped variables ranges from 1 to 5. Each point in the graph is the average of 20,000 different classifiers.

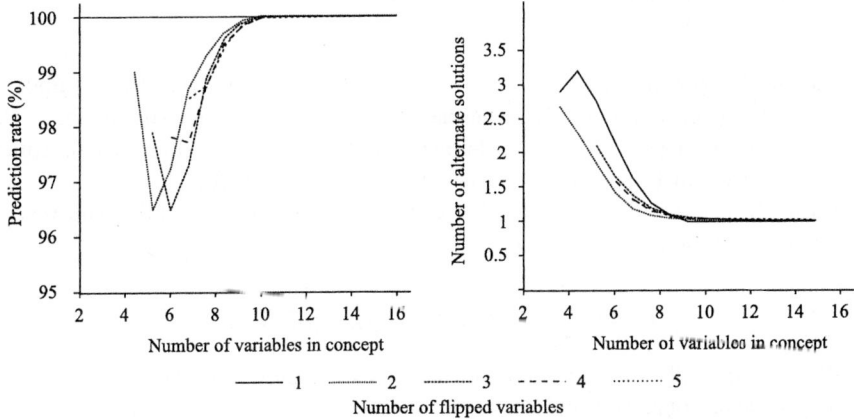

Fig. 2. Evolution of prediction rate and alternate solutions depending on the number of variables in the classifier

One can see that the prediction rate never falls below 96% and converges rather quickly to 100% for every case (this limit was even reached in the case of 1, 2, and 3 flips). Additionally, the number of alternate solutions, although it starts over 1, also quickly converges to 1. These encouraging figures suggest that Newton's results are consistently reliable as soon as the concept to evaluate reaches a minimum complexity threshold of a couple of variables.

Then, by varying the probability p of an attribute flip, we simulated different degrees of overly general or overly specific attributes. A low value for p results in an attribute where few of the values are mislabeled and simulates a subtle ill-definition; conversely, a high value for p simulates an attribute that is largely ill-defined. Figure 3 shows the evolution of prediction rate and alternate solutions when p varies from 5 to 100%.

Conformly to intuition, Newton fares slightly better when the ill-definition of the attributes is more apparent. However, even for ill-definition probabilities

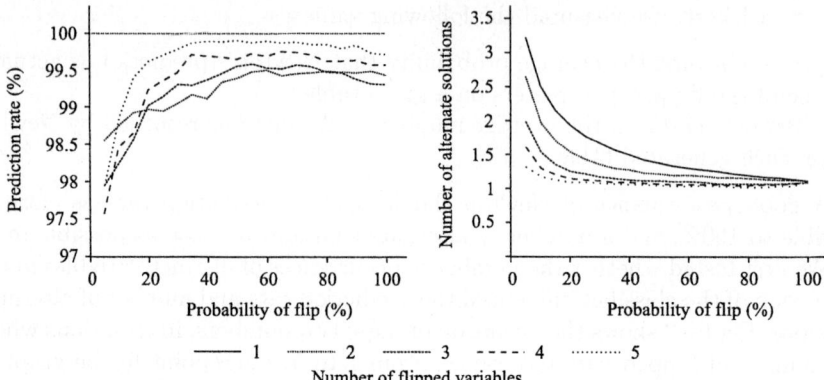

Fig. 3. Evolution of prediction rate and alternate solutions depending on the probability of a parameter flip

as low as 5%, the prediction rate stays above 97%. Moreover, the number of alternate solutions decreases as p increases; this is normal since the higher p, the more errors are induced by the ill-defined attributes, and the harder it becomes for an arbitrary Δ function to surpass one of the correct Δ's.

From these two values, we computed a compound measure called the *success rate* defined as follows:

$$\text{success rate} = \frac{\text{prediction rate}}{\text{alternate solutions}}$$

The success rate measures the probability that, if a Δ function is randomly picked in the set returned by Newton for a given table, this function is one of the

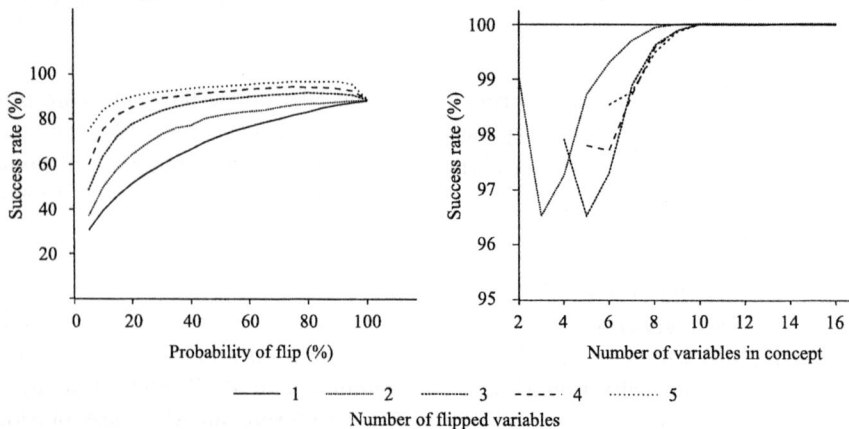

Fig. 4. Evolution of the success rate according to number of variables in the concept and probability of a bit flip

systematically altered parameters to be discovered. Of course, if Newton returns only one function, this function is picked without choice. The higher the success rate, the better the chance that a non-deterministic restriction of Newton which returns only *one* prediction is correct. Figure 4 shows the evolution of the success rate according to number of variables in the concept and probability of a bit flip.

As can be seen, success rate is on average rather good (over 96%) no matter the complexity of the concept; however, it is relatively poor for small values of p. This is due not to the fact that Δ functions fail to predict classification errors, but rather because for low systematic bit-flip probabilities, 2 to 3 alternate solutions are provided and therefore drastically cut the prediction rate by the same factor. The success rate becomes reasonable as soon as the bit-flip probability reaches 25%.

There is a good reason to believe that this figure can be improved for small probabilities. The calculations shown here assume that, when multiple Δ functions are returned by Newton, only one of them is among the variables that have actually been altered, justifying the division of the prediction rate by the number of alternate solutions. This is, however, seldom the case. In fact, in the case where Newton returns many alternate solutions, it turns out most of them are actually correct. The curves shown here therefore indicate a rather coarse lower bound to the actual success rate.

5 Conclusion and Future Work

In this paper, we have shown how ill-defined attributes can be told apart from mere random noise in sets of examples submitted to a concept learning system by the analysis of the ordered patterns of classification errors they produce. We also demonstrated by a computer program called Newton how this reasoning can be systematised by the use of Boolean derivatives and showed by extensive empirical analysis how Newton can identify with a prediction rate of more than 95% the ill-defined attributes in a dataset.

A particularly interesting application of the robustness of Newton is to search engine query refinement, where the ill-defined terms typed by a user could be intelligently tuned by using advice provided by the program. Newton's working principle could also be used directly while a concept is interactively formed by a learning system, instead of once the concept is found. The Δ functions could be used to identify the "critical zones" of a forming concept, where classification errors are most prone to occur; in turn, these Δ functions could be used to help the learning system ask questions to the user to refine its models.

In parallel to these advances, additional experiments are conducted to provide better bounds to the success rate. A newer version of Newton is also being created, in which all ill-defined attributes can be identified at once instead of iteratively.

References

1. Quinlan, J.R.: The effect of noise on concept learning. In Michalski, R.S., Carbonell, J.G., Mitchell, T.M., eds.: Machine Learning: An artificial intelligence approach. Volume 2. Morgan Kaufmann (1986)
2. Thayse, A.: Boolean calculus of differences. In Shavlik, J.W., Dietterich, T.G., eds.: Lecture Notes in Computer Science. Volume 101. Springer (1981)
3. Mooney, R., Ourston, D.: Theory refinement with noisy data. Technical Report AI 91153, Artificial Intelligence Lab, University of Texas at Austin (1991)
4. Quinlan, J.R.: Induction of decision trees. In Shavlik, J.W., Dietterich, T.G., eds.: Readings in Machine Learning. Morgan Kaufmann (1990) Originally published in *Machine Learning* 1:81–106, 1986.
5. Kearns, M.J., Li, M.: Learning in the presence of malicious errors (extended abstract). In: STOC. (1988) 267–280
6. Dietterich, T.G.: An experimental comparison of three methods for constructing ensembles of decision trees: Bagging, boosting, and randomization. Machine Learning 40 (2000) 139–157
7. Kalapanidas, E., Avouris, N., Cracium, M., Neagu, D.: Machine learning algorithms: a study on noise sensivity. In Manolopoulos, Y., Spirakis, P., eds.: BCI 2003. (2003) 356–365
8. Brazdil, P., Clark, P.: Learning from imperfect data. In Brazdil, P., Konolige, K., eds.: Machine Learning, Meta-Reasoning and Logics, Boston, Kluwer (1990) 207–232
9. Weiss, G.M.: Learning with rare cases and small disjuncts. In: International Conference on Machine Learning. (1995) 558–565
10. Provost, F.J., Danyluk, A.P.: Learning from bad data. In: ML-95 Workshop on Applying Machine Learning in Practice. (1995)
11. Mingers, J.: An empirical comparison of pruning methods for decision tree induction. Machine Learning 4 (1989) 227–243
12. Hennessy, J.L., Patterson, D.A.: Computer Organization and Design: The Hardware/Software Interface. Morgan Kaufmann (2004)
13. Bay, S.D., Pazzani, M.J.: Characterizing model errors and differences. In Langley, P., ed.: ICML, Morgan Kaufmann (2000) 49–56
14. Liu, B., Hsu, W., Ma, Y.: Discovering the set of fundamental rule changes. In: Knowledge Discovery and Data Mining. (2001) 335–340
15. Wang, K., Zhou, S., Fu, A.W.C., Yu, J.X.: Mining changes of classification by correspondence tracing. In Barbará, D., Kamath, C., eds.: SDM, SIAM (2003)
16. Kukar, M., Kononenko, I.: Reliable classifications with machine learning. In Elomaa, T., Mannila, H., Toivonen, H., eds.: ECML. Volume 2430 of Lecture Notes in Computer Science., Springer (2002) 219–231

Simplify Decision Function of Reduced Support Vector Machines

Yuangui Li[1], Weidong Zhang[1], Guoli Wang[2], and Yunze Cai[1]

[1] Department of Automation, Shanghai Jiaotong University,
Shanghai 200030, P. R. China
{li_yuangui, wdzhang, yzcai}@sjtu.edu.cn
[2] Department of Electronic and Communication Engineering,
School of Information Science and Technology, Sun Yat-Sen University,
Guangzhou 510275, P.R. China
glwang@ieee.org

Abstract. Reduced Support Vector Machines (RSVM) was proposed as the alternate of standard support vector machines (SVM) in order to resolve the difficulty in the learning of nonlinear SVM for large data set problems. RSVM preselects a subset as support vectors and solves a smaller optimization problem, and it performs well with remarkable efficiency on training of SVM for large problem. All the training points of the subset will be support vectors, and more training points are selected into this subset results in high possibility to obtain RSVM with better generalization ability. So we first obtain the RSVM with more support vectors, and selects out training examples near classification hyper plane. Then only these training examples are used as training set to obtain a standard SVM with less support vector than that of RSVM. Computational results show that standard SVMs on the basis of RSVM have much less support vectors and perform equal generalization ability to that of RSVM. ...

1 Introduction

The support vector machine(SVM) proposed by Vapnik[1] is induced according to the principle of structural risk minimization, so it performs good generalization ability, especially for small sample problems. SVM have empirically been applied to solving a wide variety of problems such as handwritten character recognition, face detection, and etc[1-4]. But two major problems confront applying SVM with nonlinear kernel on large dataset problems [5]. One is the sheer size of quadric optimization problem that needs to be solved and the training time to solve the optimization problem. The other problem is that the decision function with nonlinear kernel is dependent on the support vectors, and large number of support vectors result in large storage requirement and slow classification speed. LeeCun et al.[6] found that, for handwritten character recognition problem, the classification speed of SVM is substantially slower than that of neural networks.

Large size of quadric optimization problem require large storage space, in order to overcome this problem, several chunking methods[7-10] was proposed to decompose a large problem into smaller problems. The representative algorithm is Platt's SMO[9] which solve the large QP problem by solving a series of two multipliers sub-QP problems. For speeding up the learning of SVM, Keerthi[10] proposed improved SMO algorithm, and Li[11] proposed to train SVM with support vector candidates. The most remarkable research is reduced support vector machines proposed by Lee and Mangasarian[5], which pre-selects a subset as support vectors, and all the constraints are used to decide the region of feasible solution. The size of this subset in general is 10% of the whole training set, which remarkably decreases the size of kernel matrix and simple algorithm can obtain the SVM quickly. In general all the member of this subset will be support vectors because the square of 2-norm of slack vector is minimized instead of 1-norm as in standard SVM, which results in the loss of sparseness as that in least square SVM[12]. More support vectors will slow down the testing process and this is the second problem confronting large data classification with nonlinear SVM.

Many research focus on the reducing the number of support vector so as to improve the testing speed of SVM. The decision surface of SVM is parameterized by a set of support vectors and a set of corresponding weights. Considering a binary classification problem, the decision rule takes the form:

$$f(\mathbf{x}) = \Theta(\sum_{i}^{N_s} a_i y_i K(\mathbf{x}, \mathbf{s}_i) + b) \cdot \qquad (1)$$

where $\mathbf{s}_i$ is one of support vectors and y_i is its class attribute, a_i is corresponding Lagrange multiplier, N_s is the number of support vectors, $K(\mathbf{x},\mathbf{s})$ is kernel function, $\mathbf{x}$ is vector to be classified and Θ is a step function. After the kernel function $K(\mathbf{x},\mathbf{s})$ is chosen, the training process determines the entire parameter set $\{a_i, \mathbf{s}_i, N_s, b\}$.

From (1), we can see that the complexity of decision rule is determined by N_s and the form of kernel function. For a specific problem, after proper kernel function is chosen, the reduction in the complexity of SVM mainly relies on decrease in the number of support vectors.

In order to simplify the decision of SVM, Burges[13-14] first proposed simplified SVM to reduce the vectors representing the SVM. And Osuna[15] proposed two methods to simplify SVM, the one is to use support vector regression machine to obtain the function approximated to decision function of original SVM; the other is to obtain SVM with less support vectors by reformulation of training problems. But Osuna also stated that both solutions wouldn't always work well for every case when coefficients are strictly between the bounds.

Burges' method used a new reduced vector set to approximate the decision rule decided by all the support vectors so as to reduce the complexity of SVM. Similar but more simple method is proposed by Downs et al.[16], which deleted some unnecessary support vectors which are linearly dependent on other support vectors and changed the value of Lagrange multiplier of other support vectors so as to keep the decision function of SVM unchanged. But from the experiment results in [16], we can see that the reduction efficiency is related on specific kernel function and kernel parameter, and the reduced support vector set is not unique because the linear dependence is a collective property of all support vectors and choice of deleted vectors is subjective.

In this study, we overcome the first problem with RSVM, and then use the classification planes of RSVM to obtain a small set containing the most classification information. The small set is used to train a standard SVM which has equal generalization ability but fewer support vectors so as to simplify the decision function.

The remainder of this paper is organized as follows. We will first introduce RSVM in section 2, and then our method to simplify decision of RSVM will be described in section 3. Computational results are presented to illustrate our method in Section 4 and Section 5 concludes our work.

2 Reduced Support Vector Machines

The standard nonlinear SVM classifying a two-class train set $\{(\mathbf{x}_i, y_i)\}_{i=1}^{l} \in X^n \times R$ has the following form [2]

$$\min_{w,b} \quad J = \frac{1}{2}\|\mathbf{w}\|^2 + C\sum_{i=1}^{l} \xi_i$$
$$s.t. \quad y_i(\mathbf{w} \cdot \Phi(\mathbf{x}_i) - b) \geq 1 - \xi_i \quad (2)$$
$$\xi_i \geq 0, i = 1, \cdots, l$$

where X^n denotes the space of input vectors, ξ is the deviation between output of SVM $f(\mathbf{x}_i)$ and target output y_i and $\Phi(\cdot)$ is the map from input space into feature space, which is decided by the kernel function $K(\mathbf{x}, \hat{\mathbf{x}})$.

When the training set is large, if some optimization packages are used to solve (2), a matrix with size of $l \times l$ will be kept in storage space which always is prohibitively large. Chunking method will reduce the storage requirement for large problem, but considerably large time is required to test whether Karush-Kuhn-Tucker (KKT) conditions are satisfied by each training example and update solution gradually. The time consuming and storage space consuming process limit the use of SVM on large problems and Reduced SVM was proposed to overcome these problems. For above classification task, RSVMs solve the following optimization problem (3)

$$\min_{a,b,\xi} \quad \frac{1}{2}(\omega^T\omega + b^2) + C(\sum_{i=1}^{l} \xi_i^2)$$
$$\text{subject to} \quad y_i(\omega^T\Phi(x_i) + b) \geq 1 - \xi_i \quad (3)$$

Numeric experiments show that the accuracy does not vary much when modification of (3) on cost function is applied to solving SVM. It is known that, at the optimal solution, ω is a linear combination of training data:

$$\omega = \sum_{i=1}^{l} a_i y_i \Phi(x_i) \quad (4)$$

The most important innovation is it pre-selects a subset with m training examples to express the solution in (4), while all the l constraints still are used to determine the region of feasible solution. So (4) changes as

$$\omega = \sum_{i=1}^{m} u_i \Phi(x_i) \qquad (5)$$

Using smoothing techniques [17], optimization problem (3) can be solved quickly by a fast Newton method. The pre-selected subset with m points reduce the size of stored kernel matrix to $m \times l$ from $l \times l$, therefore the training speed is improved obviously. Computational results show that how to choose the m points has little effect on the accuracy of RSVM.

As to the size of pre-selected subset, typically m is 1% to 10% of l, and in general, m is chosen to 10% of l, or m is 200 for more large training set, while no instructions on how to choose the size of this subset are studied. But it is obvious that the large m can keep more information and obtain higher training accuracy, [18] also proved that pre-selecting a small subset instead of the whole training set to express solution would result in a little decline in test accuracy, and the computational results on three public available data sets in table 1 also can show this.

Table 1. The accuracy on training set when m is different

m	Accuracy on three training sets		
	Satimage l=4435	DNA l=2000	Mushroom l=4000
20	92.13%	88.1%	91.45%
40	92.35%	92.3%	98.35%
80	92.29%	95.9%	99.95%
200	92.72%	99.2%	100%
300	93.01%	99.15%	100%
400	93.08%	99.3%	100%

The results in table 1 show that it is safe choice that m is 10% of l. And for the square of 2-norm of slack vector ξ is minimized in (3) instead of 1-norm as in standard SVM, the sparseness will lost as that in least square SVM, so in most case the u_i in (5) for all the m points will be non-zero, therefore all the m training points should be stored for classifying new points. Our study focuses on reducing the number of support vectors and obtains a standard SVM from a RSVM.

3 Constructing Standard SVM with Less Support Vectors from Reduced SVM

For a given training set $\{(x_i, y_i)\}_{i=1}^{l} \in X^n \times R$, choose m (where m=10% of l or 200 when l>2000) training points to obtain the reduced support vector machine. The decision function of the RSVM is $f_R(x)$, and we want to obtain a standard SVM $f_s(x)$ has equal classification ability as $f_R(x)$. If $f_s(x) = f_R(x)$, then those training points make $y_i f_R(x_i) \leq 1$ will be support vectors of $f_s(x)$.

According to the definition of support vector of standard SVM, non-support vectors have little contribute on the decision function, and if only the support vectors are used as training set, same SVM can be obtained as that trained with the whole training set. So we can use $f_R(x)$ to obtain support vectors of target standard SVM and then these support vectors are used to train standard SVM $f_s(x) \cong f_R(x)$. The support vectors of $f_s(x)$ are member in the subset of training points make $y_i f_R(x_i) \leq 1$, and they can be used as training set to reduce the size of support vectors as small as possible by iterative learning.

We also note that reduced support vector machines introduce the square of 2-norm of slack vector ξ into the cost function, so the training points with positive class attribute will lie around the hyper plane $f_R(x_i) = 1$, those with negative class attribute will lie around the hyper plane $f_R(x_i) = -1$, therefore the number of training points make $y_i f_R(x_i) \leq 1$ may be large, which may make the process obtaining standard SVM become time consuming. In this case, we introduce the selecting factor γ, and those training points making $y_i f_R(x_i) \leq \gamma$ will be selected out to train standard SVM, where $0 < \gamma \leq 1$, and in most case, γ=1.

The outline of our method can be described as follows:

Step 1. Choose m training points and obtain the reduced SVM
Step 2. Obtain the training set T of standard SVM by inequality $y_i f_R(x_i) \leq \gamma$
Step 3. Use T as training set to obtain standard SVM $f_s(x)$. Denote the set of all the support vectors as S
Step 4. If the accuracy of $f_s(x)$ on original training set is acceptable or the decrease in size of S is trivial
    $T=S$, go to step 3
    Else
    Go to step 5
Step 5. End the process, output current $f_s(x)$ as substitute of $f_R(x)$.

4 Computational Results

We applied our method to four public available data sets, three of them from the university of California (UC) Irvine Machine Learning repository [19]. They are Mushroom dataset, Wisconsin Breast Cancer database, Letter Recognition problem. The one data set from [20] is SatImage dataset. For Mushroom data set, we deleted the points with missing attribute, and the 'clean' data set contain 5644 points, 4000 of them are as training set and left 1644 points are as test data. For WBC data set, the 'clean' data set contains 463 examples, 417 of them are used as training set; left 46 points are used as test set. For Letter Recognition problem, we selected out data on letter 'A' and 'N' to form a two-class problem. This subset contains 1572 training examples, 1410 of them are as training set and left 162 points are as test points. For SatImage data set, the size of training set is 4435, and that of test set is 2000. We use the code in [21] to solve the RSVM, and Keerthi's improved SMO[10] is used to solve standard SVM, the kernels for all the problems are Gaussian kernel, and the kernel parameters are chosen from a preset subset according to previous research on the same data set[10].

We first learn the RSVM with 10% training examples, then the RSVM is used to select out some points near class boundary, and these points are used as training set to obtain standard SVM. Iterative method is used to decrease the number of support vectors of standard SVM as small as possible. The test accuracy and number of support vectors for each data set are illustrated in table 2.

Table 2. Simplify decision function of RSVM by our method on 4 datasets

Data set ($l \times m$)	RSVM		Our Standard SVM	
	# SVs	Testing Accuracy	# SVs	Testing Accuracy
WBC (417×40)	40	97.83%	13	95.65%
Letter_an (1410×140)	140	90.12%	54	96.91%
Mushroom (4000×200)	200	82.4%	33	92.21%
SatImage (4435×200)	200	98.95%	63	98%

From table 2, we can see that our method can obtain a standard SVM with fewer support vectors, while the testing accuracy of the standard SVM doesn't decline obviously or even perform better. For WBC, there seem to be a 2% decline in testing accuracy, in fact, the standard SVM with our method only misclassified one point more than that of RSVM, and for the size of testing set only is 46, so the difference in testing accuracy seems obvious. As to the number of support vectors, it decreased sharply, which can improve testing speed and result in a more simple decision function of SVM. The reduction in the set of support vectors also indicates that much fewer training points need to be stored for future classification task.

For our method, the time cost of obtaining standard SVM must be small so as to make it practical in use. As we known, for the same problem, the size of training set has important impact on the training time, the size of training set used to obtain standard SVM for the four public data sets are shown in table 3.

Table 3. Size of training set for obtaining standard SVM for four public problems

Data set	WBC	Letter_AN	Mushroom	SatImage
Size of training set for RSVM	417	1410	4000	4435
Size of training set for standard SVM	155	162	101	358

From the results on table 3, we know that small portion of all the training examples are used as training points to obtain standard SVM from RSVM, which results in rapid learning process of standard SVM and makes our method practical in use.

5 Conclusion

For the training of RSVM, selecting more training points as support vectors to express RSVM results in better generalization ability, but better generalization ability is obtained at the cost of more complex decision function, slower testing speed and storing more training points for classifying new examples because sparseness of standard SVM is missing in RSVM..

In this study, we use 10% or more of all the training examples to obtain RSVM so as to assure adequate generalization ability. And then it is used to select out the training points near the class boundary. It is known that support vectors of standard SVM come from these training points near class boundary, so only these points are used to constitute a small but adequate training set to train standard SVM. Iterative method is used to decrease the number of support vectors of standard SVM as small as possible. By our method, we can obtain a standard SVM with much less support vectors and equal or better testing accuracy compared with original RSVM, which improve the testing speed and lessen the training points stored for classification task. Computational results show that our method is an effective and important improvement to RSVM.

References

1. Vapnik, V.: Estimation of Dependences based on Empirical Data: Berlin: Springer-Verlag, 1982.
2. Burges, C. J. C.: A Tutorial on Support Vector Machines for Pattern Recognition, Data Mining and Knowledge Discovery, Vol. 2, 2(1988)121-167.

3. Cristianini, N. and Taylor,J. S.: An Introduction to Support Vector Machines and other Kernel-based Learning Methods, Cambridge University Press, 2000.
4. Verzakov, B. S. A. and Frese, J. V.: A Flexible Classification Approach with Optimal Generalization Performance: Support Vector Machines, Chemometrics and Intelligent Laboratory System, 64(2002) 15-25.
5. Lee Y. J. and Mangasarian, O. L.: RSVM: Reduced Support Vector Machines. Data Mining Institute Technical Report 00-07, Computer Sciences Department, University of Wisconsin (2000).
6. LeCun, Y., Jackel, L., Bottou,L., Brunot, Cortes, A., Denker, C. J., Drucker, H., Guyon, I., Müller, U., Säckinger, E., Simard, P. and Vapnik, V.: Comparison of Learning Algorithms for Handwritten Digit Recognition, International Conference on Artificial Neural Networks, (Eds.): Fogelman, F. and Gallinari, P. (1995)53-60.
7. Osuna, E., Freund, R. and Girosi, F.: Improved Training Algorithm for Support Vector Machines, Proc. IEEE NNSP'97, Florida, USA., (1997) 276-285.
8. Joachims, T.: Making large-scale support vector machine learning practical, in (Eds): Schölkopf, B., Burges, C., Smola, A.: Advances in Kernel Methods: Support Vector Machines, MIT Press, Cambridge, MA, December 1998.
9. Platt, J. C.: Sequential Minimal Optimization: A Fast Algorithm for Training Support Vector Machines, Technical Report MSR-TR-98-14, Microsoft Research, (1998)
10. Keerthi, S. S., Shevade, S. K., Bhattacharyya , C. and Murthy, K. R. K.: Improvements to Platt's SMO Algorithm for SVM Classifier Design. Neural Computation. Vol. 13, (2001)637-649.
11. Li Yuangui, Zhang Weidong, Hu Zhonghui and Xu Xiaoming, Training Support Vector Machines with Support Vector Candidates. Journal of Harbin Institute of Technology. In press.
12. Suykens, J.A.K., Lukas, L. and Vandewalle, J.: Sparse Approximation Using Least Squares Support Vector Machines. IEEE International Symposium on Circuits and Systems. ISCAS'2000
13. Burges, C. J. C.: Simplified Support Vector Decision Rules, 13th International Conference on Machine Learning, (1996)71-77.
14. Burges, C. J. C. and Schölkopf, B.: Improving the accuracy and speed of support vector machines. In: Mozer, M., Jordan, M. and Petsche, T. (eds.): Neural Information Processing Systems, Vol. 9. MIT Press, Cambridge, MA, 1997.
15. Osuna, E. and Girosi, F.: Reducing the run time complexity of support vector machines. ICPR'98, Brisban, Australia, August 16-20, 1998.
16. Downs, T., Gates, K. E. and Masters, A.: Exact Simplification of Support Vector Solutions. Journal of Machine Learning Research. 2, (2001)293-297.
17. Lee Yuh-Jye and Mangasarian, O. L.: SSVM: A Smooth Support Vector Machine for Classification. Computational Optimization and Applications, v.20(1), (2001)5-22.
18. Lin Kuan-Ming and Lin Chih-Ien: A Study on Reduced Support Vector Machines. IEEE transactions on Neural Networks, 14(6), (2003)1449-1559.
19. Blake, C., Keogh, E. and Merz, C. J.: UCI Repository of machine learning databases, http://www.ics.uci.edu/~mlearn/MLRepository.html. Irvine, CA. University of California, Department of Information and Computer Science, 1998.
20. http://www.liacc.up.pt/ML/
21. Lee Yuh-Jye: Support Vector Machines in Data Mining. A dissertation submitted to the University of Wisconsin-Madison for degree of Doctor of Philosophy(Computer Sciences), 2001.

On-Line Learning of Decision Trees in Problems with Unknown Dynamics

Marlon Núñez, Raúl Fidalgo, and Rafael Morales

Departament of Languages and Computer Science,
Campus de Teatinos, Universidad de Málaga, 29071, Málaga, Spain
{mnunez, rfm, morales}@lcc.uma.es

Abstract. Learning systems need to face several problems: incrementality, tracking concept drift, robustness to noise and recurring contexts in order to operate continuously. A method for on-line induction of decision trees motivated by the above requirements is presented. It uses the following strategy: creating a delayed window in every node for applying forgetting mechanisms; automatic modification of the delayed window; and constructive induction for identifying recurring contexts. The default configuration of the proposed approach has shown to be globally efficient, reactive, robust and problem-independent, which is suitable for problems with unknown dynamics. Notable results have been obtained when noise and concept drift are present.

1 Introduction

An on-line concept learner is a system that learns concepts incrementally, that is to say, processes pre-classified examples one at a time. Its purpose is to find adequate hypothesis that may be used to classify future unlabeled examples. It is widely accepted that the most desirable characteristics of learning systems in general, and online concept learning systems in particular, are the following:

- *Accuracy:* The percentage of correctly classified unlabeled examples.
- *Incrementality*: The ability to construct a hypothesis by processing examples one at a time.
- *Adaptability to concept drift*: The ability to adapt current hypothesis to target concepts that change over time.
- *Robustness*: This characteristic allows an on-line learner not to be affected by noise and incompleteness of data.
- *Efficiency*: The ability to minimize the number of examples in order to support current hypothesis and to develop computationally tractable processes.
- *Adequate concept representation:* The ability to construct concepts using adequate representation descriptors (e.g. predicate expressions or symbolic/numeric attribute-value descriptors).
- *Comprehensibility of induced concept:* The ability to create comprehensible concepts, which allow users to learn something new from them.
- *Easiness and generality of configuration*: The ability to use general parameters for their configuration. A configuration based on problem-specific parameters is useless if the conditions of the problem change over time.

Current on-line concept learning methods that support concept drift [2][4][5][10][13] use several problem-specific parameters to achieve some of the desirable characteristics mentioned above. This requirement complicates the use of on-line learners because users have to discover manually an appropriate set of problem-specific parameters after a detailed study with a selected stream of examples.

The presented method, called Online Tree, uses a few general and well-known parameters that have been broadly studied [6][7][8]. We took advantage of previous research on them and used a default configuration, which was compared with several problem-specific configurations of other methods under various conditions such as hidden contexts, different rates of concept drift, noise levels and recurrent contexts.

This paper is organized as follows: section 2 explains the algorithms of the method. Section 3 shows the experimentation. In Section 4, we describe the related work and comparisons with other methods. Finally, Section 5 presents the conclusions.

2 Description of the Online Tree Method

Online Tree is a method for incremental induction of decision trees, which also supports automatic adaptability to gradual and abrupt concept drift, robustness to noise data, and the handling of symbolic and numeric attributes. This method develops a partial memory management; that is to say, it selectively forgets examples and stores a subset of them in the leaves of the tree.

Table 1. OnlineTree main algorithm

Input: *tree, example*
Output: *tree*

OnlineTree (tree, example)
    IF *root is a leaf*
        Store *(root, example)*
    ELSE
        tree=Append(root, OnlineTree (subt, example), subt2)
    ENDIF
    tree = ReviseForgeting (root, example)
    tree = RevisePruning&Expansion (root)
    RETURN *tree*

The algorithm is presented in Table 1. In this table, 'tree' is a binary decision tree, 'root' is the root of 'tree', 'subt' and 'subt2' are the hanging subtrees from 'tree', and 'example' is a vector of attribute-value pairs and a time stamp. It works as follows: given a new example and a decision tree, this algorithm drops the e*xample* down the *tree* to the appropriate leaf and stores the example there (*Store* function). Then, it starts a process in a bottom-up strategy, revising at each node the possibility of forgetting examples (*ReviseForgetting* function) and reconstructing a subtree (*RevisePruning&Expansion* function*)*.

At every recursive call, *root* is the visited node, s*ubt* is the subtree below the branch that is selected according to the value of the *example* of the splitting attribute of *root*, and *subt*2 is the other subtree. The call *OnlineTree*(*subt, example*) returns the *subt*1. Function *Append* (*root, subt*1, *subt*2) updates the tree below *root* with the returned *subt*1 and the subtree *subt*2.

In order to partition as conservatively as possible at each decision node, splits at decision nodes are always binary. Previous research [12] has shown that a binary test at a decision node produces more accurate results than multi-valued tests, in general. The generated decision tree is also comprehensible to users.

The next sections, explains the main functions of the Online Tree algorithm.

2.1 ReviseForgetting Function

The purpose of this function is to revise the performance of a subtree for taking hard decisions like forgetting or accumulating examples. This function identifies the performance state of a subtree for taking forgetting decisions.

Concept drift is identified if bad performance is detected. During this state, which we call degradation state, the node may forget various examples in order to adapt more quickly to the new context.

In general, for an incremental learner that detects bad performance it is difficult to distinguish between real concept drift and slight irregularities due to noisy in the examples. A quick reaction to the first signs of a concept drift may be misled into overreacting to noise [13].

The research on preventing overreactions for controlling very dynamic processes has received a lot of attention in other engineering disciplines. In telecommunications for instance, nodes (or routers) have to take hard decisions (e.g. discarding messages or retransmitting messages) when bad performance is detected (e.g. congestion). However, the available information in a communication node is instantaneous; it varies a lot, and therefore it is inappropriate to take decisions. In order to get more stable information, [11] sets out the *smoothing formula* for calculating a stable measure of usage throw a communication line: $LineUsage_{new} = \alpha\, LineUsage_{old} + (1-\alpha)\, InstantenousLine\ Usage$, where $\alpha \in [0, 1]$ determines how fast the node forgets recent history. The α parameter has been widely studied by Nagle and other authors [6][7][11], and the value of 7/8 is recommended. Currently, some backbone nodes of Internet with ATM technology use that formula with the recommended $\alpha=7/8$ as default value:

$$LineUsage_{new} = \tfrac{7}{8} LineUsage_{old} + \tfrac{1}{8} Instanatne\ ousLineUsa\ ge \qquad (1)$$

Where *LineUsage* is the degree of message traffic throw a communication line. A high value of *LineUsage* is interpreted as congestion in that line. Congestion in a line may force a communication node to delete messages or to ask other nodes to reduce traffic throw that line.

Another similar problem in communications occurs during a data transfer between two remote software applications throw Internet. The TCP transport level, which resides at host computers for allowing data transfer between applications, uses the formula and parameter value [6] to calculate how much a computer has to wait before retransmitting a message.

The OnlineTree learning method has also to measure learning performance from instantaneous and varying information and take hard decisions like forgetting examples. The performance measure should not be very sensitive to noise in examples.

For this reason it uses the *smoothing formula* explained above. The instantaneous performance measure is the percentage of well-classified examples under the tree node *n*. This instantaneous measure, also called *instantaneousPerf*, varies a lot at some conditions, mainly at the beginning of a subtree and after the forgetting of several examples. A careful study was carried out about the α value: 7/8 yielded the best robustness in accuracy for several problems and conditions. In conclusion the formula for calculating the performance of the subtree bellow node *n* is:

$$Performance(n)_{new} = \tfrac{7}{8} Performance(n)_{old} + \tfrac{1}{8} InstantaneousPerf(n) \qquad (2)$$

A concept drift is possible if there is a drop in *performance(n)*, but the drift is confirmed if the drop is persistent. This persistency is the key to distinguish between noise and concept drift. That is to say, a degraded performance that is persistent increments the confidence that a concept drift is real.

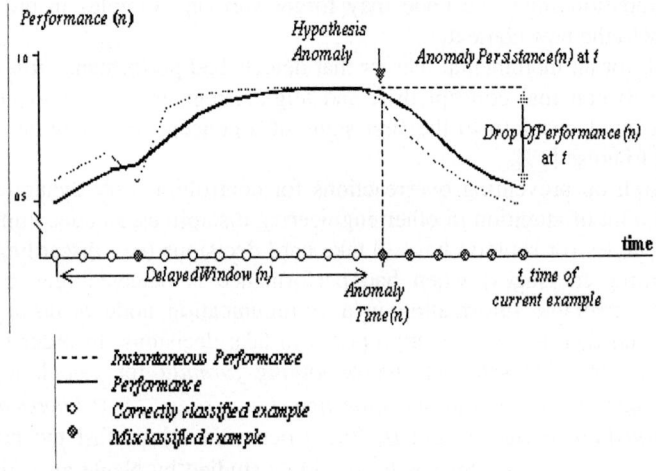

Fig.1. Detection of a hypothesis anomaly and the delayed window at a node

With the purpose of explaining *ReviseForgetting* function, some concepts need to be defined (see Figure 1): let *hypothesis anomaly* be the first detected drop in *perfomance(n)*. Let *AnomalyTime(n)* be the last time an anomaly was detected at node *n*. Let $DropOfPerformance(n)_t$ be the drop of performance at time *t* with regard to the performance at *AnomalyTime(n)* that is to say: $performance(n)_t$ - $performance(n)_{AnomalyTime(n)}$. Let *DelayedWindow(n)* be the window of node *n* whose boundaries are: the *AnomalyTime(n)* and the oldest example below the subtree.

Each node uses its delayed window for keeping the time stamps of the examples that may be forgotten, because those examples belong to an old concept. A reduction of size of this delayed window provokes the forgetting of the examples that occurred before the new window boundary. The examples that occurred after *AnomalyTime(n)* are supposed to belong to the current concept and for that reason are maintained. After AnomalyTime the node enters into *degradation state*.

In order to calculate the fraction of the delayed window to be forgotten, some concepts need to be defined. Let *AnomalyPersistence* be the measure of the persistence of bad performance. In our experiments, the best measure of anomaly persistence was the number of misclassified examples after the *AnomalyTime*, because they reflect better the number of times the deterioration has persisted. We use this number, a positive integer, as a multiplicative factor of the lost of performance as follows: *AnomalyPersistance(n)$_t$* x *DropOf Performance(n)$_t$*, which we abbreviate as *windowFraction(n)$_t$*, that is, the fraction of the delayed window to be forgotten. Thus, the new size of the delayed window, *windowSize(n)$_t$*, will be:

$$\begin{cases} windowSize(n)_{old}(1 - windowFraction(n)_t) & if \ windowFraction(n)_t \leq 1 \\ 0 & if \ windowFraction(n)_t > 1 \end{cases} \quad (3)$$

Where *windowSize(n)$_{old}$* is the size of the delayed window immediately before current time *t*. The more persistent is the bad performance, the shorter is the size of the delayed window. All examples before the delayed window are forgotten.

When performance goes up, the node enters in the *improvement state*. The delayed window disappears. In this state, the node stores every incoming example, because it needs them to learn the current concept better. The performance improves mainly because the node has already forgotten the examples that belonged to an old concept.

2.2 RevisePruning&Expansion Function

RevisePruning&Expansion(n) checks the possibility of changing the structure of the subtree below node *n* by pruning or expanding the node. The chi-squared analysis checks for the relevance of a split. The significance level of the chi-squared test is set to 5%. If a node does not pass this test, the node collects all the examples bellow it and rebuilds the subtree. Attributes are selected using the normalized entropy function. Online Tree learns dichotomic trees from examples described by symbolic and numeric attributes. In the case of numeric attributes, Online Tree analyzes the binarized form of numeric attributes (e.g. Age $\geq$ 40, Age< 40). It uses a K-means approach with K=2 for discovering two clusters. Then, a threshold between the two clusters is found easily. Online Tree treats unknown values like any other attribute value, as proposed by Quinlan [9].

With the purpose of discovering better descriptions of the target concepts, constructive induction in learning systems creates new attributes or predicates [14] applying several operations (conjunctions, disjunctions, negations). These new attributes measure the current distribution of values in recent examples. If this distribution changes, it is probable that a new context has appeared. In order to identify the distribution a new attribute is studied: *Growth (at=v | class=z)$_t$* $\in$ R, which measures the frequency of examples per a time interval such that its attribute *at* is *v* and whose class is *z*. If the number of values of *at* is *n* and the number of classes is *m*, the *ConstructiveInduction* function will create *nxm* attributes in every training example below node *n*.

3 Experimentation Results with Concepts That Change over Time

With the purpose of testing Online Tree in problems with unknown dynamics, the following section gives a presentation and analysis of the results obtained by the non-parametric Online Tree with well-known learning methods, which are parametric. Since these learning methods use parameters, they need a detailed study for obtaining good parameter values for each experiment.

Several well-known learning techniques can be ascribed a certain plasticity in the face of changes: STAGGER [10] tries to resemble the psychology of humans; some algorithms oriented to instances (for example, FLORA [13] works with a time window in a similar way to AQ-PM [4], [5], which tries to discover the boundaries of the context to be learned); and FAVORIT [3] based on ageing of knowledge.

Possibly the most important algorithms, from our point of view, are FLORA, AQ11-PM [5] and DWM-ITI [2]. The algorithm FLORA is based on the binary classification of elements and the most versatile since it can be applied to a wide range of scenarios. However, the need to manually set its configuration means that it is possibly not a good alternative for application in environments with drifting concepts with unknown conditions, because it requires a careful study to determine all its parameters. AQ algorithms are good in trying to increase accuracy without the need to store a great number of examples. Finally, DWM-ITI maintains an ensemble of ITI [12] learners, predicts using a weighted-majority vote of them, and dynamically creates and deletes those learners in response to changes on performance. The results of those methods have been obtained with the proposed parameter values on each one from the author's articles.

On each experiment, we compare our performance with the other methods over 30 runs with random seed. Moreover, a column called "Online Tree vs. The Best" on each experiment table, show if our method is better (+), equal ($\approx$) or worse (-) than the best of the others based on a t-test with 5% confidence level.

3.1 Gradual Concept Drift

The experiment set out here has been taken from [13]. Positive examples are described using a logical function that gradually and uniformly changes, during a Δt time interval, to another context. Table 2 shows the results of the gradual concept drift experimentation, varying the gradual interval (Δt = 50, 100 and 200).

Table 2 shows the results at the end of each context by the algorithms Flora and Online Tree in the experimentation carried out on abrupt symbolic concept drift. As reference we have taken the accuracy reached by the methods at the end of the

Table 2. Predictive Accuracy on gradual symbolic concept drift experimentation

	Time Step	Flora2	Flora3	Flora4	Online Tree	Online Tree vs. The Best
Gradual Δt=50	$t_1+\Delta t$	60	64	65	67	$\approx$
	$t_1+\Delta t+100$	83	84	85	99.9	+
Gradual Δt=100	$t_1+\Delta t$	63	66	72	77	+
	$t_1+\Delta t+100$	82	78	95	98	+
Gradual Δt=200	$t_1+\Delta t$	69	69	69	89	+
	$t_1+\Delta t+100$	78	83	82	99	+

gradual concept drift $(t_1+\Delta t)$ and 100 time steps later on $(t_1+\Delta t + 100)$. At the end of the gradual interval, the results are better except in the first experiment $(\Delta t=50)$, in which they are similar. 100 time steps further on from this point, we can appreciate a surprising improvement with regard to the different versions of Flora in all the experiments.

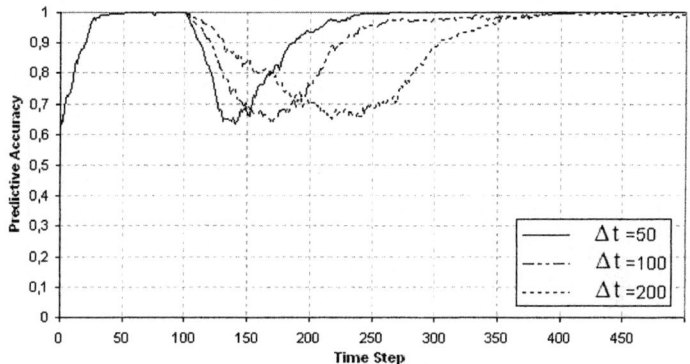

Fig. 2. Gradual concept drift for several change speeds

Figure 2 presents results of the learning curve of Online Tree with several values of Δt; 50, 100 and 200. The reaction speed of Online Tree and the achieved accuracy after this time are notably better than the method for which this experiment was prepared [13]. In these experiments, we have seen that Flora does not reach very high accuracy before time step 500, whilst Online Tree achieve it in time step 260 in the first experiment and in time step 400 in the rest.

3.2 Abrupt Concept Drift and Noise

In this section we use the dataset STAGGER [10]. The *STAGGER concepts* experiment is a synthetic problem in which the target concept changes abruptly three times. Examples are described with three symbolic attributes.

The design of the experimentation, for purposes of comparison, is identical to that which is presented in [13]. Each learning instance that appears in each time step has a determined probability ($\eta\%$) of randomly generating the label for the context it belongs to. Specifically, tests are shown that were carried out with 10%, 20% and 40% (thus in reality the number of examples badly labeled will be 5%, 10% y 20%).

Table 3 shows the comparative results while Figure 3 shows the learning curve of Online Tree for this problem. In the noise-free scenario, we can see how Flora 4, AQ11-PM and DWM-ITI obtain better results at the end of the first scenario. However, throughout the two following ones we see how the differences with our method gradually reduce, to the extent that Online Tree even has a higher convergence speed in the third state, and comparable results at the end of the second and third concept. DWM-ITI, AQ, Flora2 and 3 are not prepared to deal with noise.

Table 3. Predictive Accuracy on STAGGER Concepts with and without noise

	End of concept	Flora2	Flora3	Flora4	AQ-PM	AQ11-PM	DWM-ITI	Online Tree	Online Tree vs. The Best
Noise Free	1	100	100	100	98.6	100	98.8	99.1	-
	2	96	96	99.5	88.8	99.5	100	98.6	-
	3	96.5	96.5	98	96.3	99	100	98.7	-
10% Noise	1	94.5	94.5	94	N/A	N/A	N/A	96.3	+
	2	79	79	94	N/A	N/A	N/A	95.7	+
	3	70	78	94.5	N/A	N/A	N/A	97.2	+
20% Noise	1	89.5	89.5	98	N/A	N/A	N/A	92.9	-
	2	70	73	90	N/A	N/A	N/A	94.3	+
	3	65	67	92	N/A	N/A	N/A	91.4	≈
40% Noise	1	81	81	90	N/A	N/A	N/A	79.8	-
	2	59	60.5	80	N/A	N/A	N/A	82.8	+
	3	68	68	75	N/A	N/A	N/A	80.2	+

Compared to Flora 4, we see that in the 10% noise zone, Online Tree improves its results in the majority of measurements; this being most evident at the convergence arrived at in the second and third state. In the experimentation with 20% noise, again we see improvement but this time it is less marked. Finally, with 40% noise, whilst Flora 4 becomes tremendously irregular, Online Tree achieves better accuracy in the final states and its convergence speed is higher. "N/A" means that there are no reported results on that specific experiment with the corresponding learning method.

Figure 3 shows the learning curve of Online Tree for this problem. It shows that the degradation state is activated once a concept change is produced, thus no significant improvement in accuracy during the first instants of the context change is produced, and subsequently there is rapid and elevated accuracy thereby achieving high convergence speed. This contributes to the method reaching the final stage with sufficient time to completely construct the decision tree. With no noise in the data

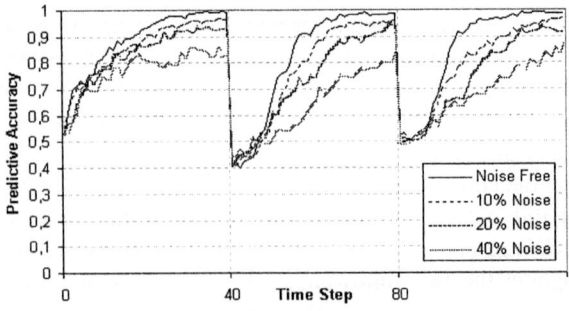

Fig. 3. Predictive accuracy of Online Tree on STAGGER concepts experiment

Online Tree achieves accuracy very close to one hundred percent in each of the contexts (99.1%, 98.6% and 98.7% respectively). Analyzing the curve with 10% noise, we see how the method suffered slightly at the end of the context (2.5% on average) mainly from the inconsistencies that are produced throughout each context.

3.3 Recurring Contexts in Abruptly Changing Concepts

The following experiment uses the STAGGER Concepts dataset periodically thorough three cycles. In Table 4, we compare the accuracy of Online Tree with Flora3 at the end of each cycle and concept. While accuracy is comparable, convergence speed is not as good as that of Flora3.

Table 4. Predictive accuracy on recurring contexts

	End of concept	Flora3	Online Tree	Online Tree vs. Flora3
Cycle 1	1	99.9	99.2	≈
	2	96	95.46	≈
	3	90.5	97.2	+
Cycle 2	1	96	97.63	+
	2	97.7	92	-
	3	96.3	95.4	≈
Cycle 3	1	98.4	95.4	-
	2	95	94.03	≈
	3	99.9	97.2	-

Figure 4 shows the learning curve of Online Tree on each cycle. As concept drifts are produced, the algorithm achieves lower fall in accuracy. This can be interpreted like Online Tree recognizes which the concept drift is, when it is produced and how to act in consequence.

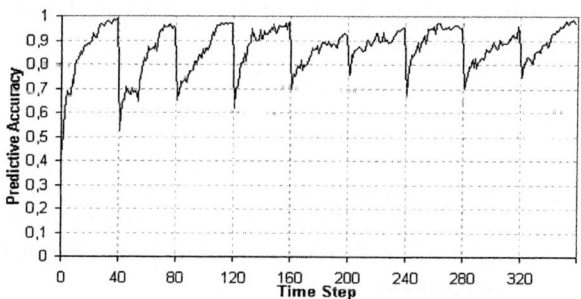

Fig. 4. Predictive Accuracy on recurrent STAGGER Concepts experiment

4 Experimentation Results with Stationary Concepts

This section deals with classic problems, in which the time dimension does not exist, obtained from the UCI Machine Learning Repository [1]. Each of the three compared methods (Online Tree, C4.5 and ITI) uses its own default configuration to tackle the datasets. C4.5 [9] is a non-incremental method and ITI [12] is an incremental method. Both are methods for induction of decision trees. The results (see table 5) of the datasets using C4.5 and ITI were obtained from [12] and [15]. Some of the ITI results were obtained using the corresponding program with its default configuration. The experiments were designed as follows: first, the examples were randomly ordered; subsequently a 10-fold cross validation was carried out. The averages and standard deviations of the ten results were calculated.

Table 5. Results obtained with C4.5, ITI and Online Tree with stationary concepts

Dataset	Number of examples	Attributes		Predictive accuracy (%)			Online Tree vs. The Best
		Simb	Num	C4.5	ITI	Online Tree	
Glass	214	0	10	69.1	66.8	85.57	+
Pima Indian	768	0	8	71.9	74.5	70.04	≈
Iris	150	0	4	94.4	94.4	92.77	≈
Balance-Scale	625	0	4	77.5	78.9	68.48	-
Ionosphere	351	0	34	91.4	92.5	90.89	≈
Wine	178	0	13	93.3	95.0	90.4	-
Mushrooms	8124	22	0	100	100	100	≈
Australian	690	8	7	84.58	83.47	82.32	≈
Chess(kr-vs-kp)	3196	36	0	99.4	99.59	94.2	-
Solar Flares	1066	10	0	81.3	79.275	82.1	≈
Nursery	12960	8	0	98.75	99.614	85.64	-
Page Block	5473	0	10	95.95	95.177	96.05	≈

As can be seen, the results obtained by our method are empirically comparable to those of the other methods under consideration. In the case of the learning of stationary concepts, Online Tree shows a typical deviation that is higher in the majority of cases with regards to the rest of the methods evaluated. The generated trees do not present great differences.

5 Conclusions

An incremental decision tree learning method has been presented which is able to learn changing concepts with the presence of noise in examples of problems with unknown conditions and which is therefore suited to be the learning mechanism of autonomic computing components.

Contrary to most of the current methods, it uses local windows. This methods uses a new strategy called a delayed window, which forces the forgetting of examples situated in a specific time interval in the past, avoiding the forgetting examples situated before or after this window.

In general, Online Tree is more robust to noise than current methods. The accuracy at the end of each context was higher than other methods in problems with noise and abrupt concept drift.

Online Tree default configuration has proved to be general and more capable of facing problems with unknown conditions, because current methods use a carefully studied configuration for each experiment.

Acknowledgments

This work was partially supported by CICYT project MOISES TIC2002-04019-C03, Spain.

References

1. Blake, C.L. & Merz, C.J.:UCI Repository of machine learning databases Irvine, University of California [http://www.ics.uci.edu/~mlearn/MLRepository.html] (1998)
2. Kolter, J. and Maloof, M.: Dynamic Weighted Majority: A new ensemble method for tracking concept drift, in Proceedings of 3rd IEEE ICDM, IEEE Press, (2003), 123-130
3. Krikazova, I., & Kubat, M.: Favorit: Concept Formation with Ageing of Knowledge, Pattern Recognition Letters, 13, (1993), 19-25
4. Maloof, M. & Michalski, R.: Selecting Examples for Partial Memory Learning, Machine Learning, 11, (2000), 27-42
5. Maloof, M. & Michalski, R.: Incremental learning with partial instance memory. Foundations of intelligent systems, LNAI, Vol. 2366, Springer-Verlag, (2002), 16-27
6. RFC-793. TCP Specification. ARPANET Working Group Requests for Comment, DDN Network Information Center, SRI Int., Postel, P. editor. Menlo Park, CA, September 1981.
7. RFC-2988. Computing TCP's transmission timer. Network Working Group Requests for Comment, Paxon, V. and Allman, M. editors, November 2000.
8. Quinlan, J. R.: Induction of Decision Trees, Machine Learning, 1, (1986), 81-106
9. Quinlan, J. R.: C4.5. Programs for machine learning. Morgan Kaufmann, (1993)
10. Schlimmer, J. & Granger, R.: Incremental Learning from Noisy Data, Machine Learning, 1, (1986), 317-354
11. Tanenbaum, A.S.: Computer Networks, Second Edition, Prentice-Hall Int., 1988, 314-315
12. Utgoff P., Berkman N. & Clouse J.: Decision Tree Induction Based on Efficient Tree Restructuring, Machine Learning 29(1), (1997), 5-44
13. Widmer, G., & Kubat, M. Learning in the Presence of Concept Drift and Hidden Contexts, Machine Learning, vol. 23, (1996), 69-101
14. Wnek, J. & Michalski, R. S. Hypothesis-Driven Constructive Induction in AQ17: A Method and Experiments, Machine Learning, 14, (1994), 139-169
15. Zupan B., Bohanec M., Bratko I., and Demsar J., Machine learning by function decomposition, Proceedings of 14th ICML, Morgan Kaufmann, (1997), 421--429

Improved Pairwise Coupling Support Vector Machines with Correcting Classifiers*

Huaqing Li, Feihu Qi, and Shaoyu Wang

Department of Computer Science and Engineering,
Shanghai Jiao Tong University,
Shanghai 200030, P.R. China
waking_lee@cs.sjtu.edu.cn

Abstract. When dealing with multi-class classification tasks, a popular and applicable way is to decompose the original problem into a set of binary subproblems. The most well-known decomposition strategy is *one-against-one* and the corresponding widely-used method to recombine the outputs of all binary classifiers is *pairwise coupling* (PWC). However PWC has an intrinsic shortcoming; many meaningless partial classification results contribute to the global prediction result. Moreira and Mayoraz suggested to tackle this problem by using *correcting classifiers* [4]. Though much better performance was obtained, their algorithm is simple and has some disadvantages. In this paper, we propose a novel algorithm which works in two steps: First the original *pairwise probabilities* are converted into a new set of *pairwise probabilities*, then *pairwise coupling* is employed to construct the global posterior probabilities. Employing support vector machines as binary classifiers, we perform investigation on several benchmark datasets. Experimental results show that our algorithm is effective and efficient.

1 Introduction

Multi-class classification is a common task in many real life problems such as face recognition and speech recognition. Two kinds of algorithms are involved; algorithms of the first kind take all classes into consideration at once [1], while algorithms of the second kind decompose the original problem into a set of binary subproblems and construct a multi-class classifier by combing all corresponding binary classifiers [2,3]. Due to their good scalability and less computational complexity, algorithms of the second kind are preferred by most researchers [3].

Among various decomposition strategies proposed, *one-against-one* is the most popular one. It trains one classifier for each pair of classes, ignoring the remaining ones. Hence for a k-class problem, $\frac{k(k-1)}{2}$ binary classifiers need to be trained. In prediction, the outputs of all binary classifiers must be recombined to construct the global result. A simple combining algorithm is *Max-Voting*, which assigns a test example to the class with the most winning two-class decisions [5].

---

* This work is supported by the National Natural Science Foundation of China under grant No. 60072029 and No.60271033.

For binary classifiers with probabilistic outputs, a more sophisticated algorithm, called *pairwise coupling* (PWC), can be employed [6]. PWC couples all *pairwise probabilities*, i.e. the probabilistic outputs of all binary classifiers, into a set of posterior probabilities. Then the test example is assigned to the class with the max posterior probability. However PWC has a shortcoming: When a test example does not belong to either class related to a binary classifier, the prediction result of this classifier is meaningless and can damage the global result.

In [4], Moreira and Mayoraz proposed an algorithm, called PWC-CC, to solve this problem, where CC stands for *correcting classifier*. A *correcting classifier* is the binary classifier trained to distinguish a pair of classes from the remaining ones. Experimental results showed that PWC-CC has much better performance than PWC. However the original PWC-CC is quite simple and has some disadvantages. In this paper, we propose a novel PWC-CC algorithm to overcome these disadvantages. The new algorithm works in two steps: First the original *pairwise probabilities* are converted into a new set of *pairwise probabilities*, then *pairwise coupling* is employed to form the global posterior probabilities. Experimental results show that our algorithm is effective and can achieve even better performance. The rest of the paper is organized as follows: In Section 2, we briefly review two different PWC methods. Section 3 describes the original PWC-CC algorithm and our novel one. Experimental results and corresponding analysis are presented in Section 4. Finally, Section 5 concludes the paper.

2 Pairwise Coupling Methods

Take for example we are dealing with a classification task involving k classes w_i, $1 \leq i \leq k$, $k \geq 3$. Then there are $\frac{k(k-1)}{2}$ binary classifiers. Suppose classifier C_{ij}, $i < j$, is trained to separate class w_i from class w_j. Given a test example x, the output of C_{ij} is a probability $r_{ij} = \text{Prob}(x \in w_i | x, x \in w_i \text{ or } w_j)$. Obviously $r_{ji} = 1 - r_{ij}$ holds, hence r_{ij} are called *pairwise probabilities*. To couple all the *pairwise probabilities* into a common set of posterior probabilities $p_i = \text{Prob}(x \in w_i | x)$, several PWC methods have been proposed.

2.1 Method by Hastie and Tibshirani

In [6], Hastie and Tibshirani introduced a new set of auxiliary variables μ_{ij}:

$$\mu_{ij} = \frac{p_i}{p_i + p_j}, \tag{1}$$

and aimed at finding p_i so that the corresponding μ_{ij} are in some sense "close" to the observed r_{ij}. In their work, the Kullback-Leibler distance between r_{ij} and μ_{ij}

$$l(\mathbf{P}) = \sum_{i<j} n_{ij} \left[r_{ij} \log \frac{r_{ij}}{\mu_{ij}} + (1 - r_{ij}) \log \frac{1 - r_{ij}}{1 - \mu_{ij}} \right]. \tag{2}$$

is selected as the closeness measurement, where n_{ij} are the weights. They pointed out that if n_{ij} are considered equal, which is reasonable when the multi-class data are balanced, $\mathbf{P}$ satisfies

$$p_i > p_j \iff \left(\tilde{p}_i = \frac{2\sum_{s:s\neq i} r_{is}}{k(k-1)}\right) > \left(\tilde{p}_j = \frac{2\sum_{s:s\neq j} r_{js}}{k(k-1)}\right) . \quad (3)$$

Therefore $\tilde{\mathbf{P}}$ is sufficient if one only requires a classification rule such as

$$\arg\max_{1\leq i\leq k} \tilde{p}_i . \quad (4)$$

Furthermore, $\tilde{\mathbf{P}}$ can be derived as an approximation to the identity

$$p_i = \sum_{j:j\neq i} \left(\frac{p_i + p_j}{k-1}\right)\left(\frac{p_i}{p_i + p_j}\right) = \sum_{j:j\neq i} \left(\frac{p_i + p_j}{k-1}\right) \mu_{ij} , \quad (5)$$

by replacing $p_i + p_j$ with $\frac{k}{2}$ and μ_{ij} with r_{ij} in (3). Thereby the differences between p_i are underestimated, which causes the method to be instable when dealing with unbalanced probabilities.

2.2 Method by Wu, Lin, and Weng

In [7], Wu et al. proposed another PWC method. They found the optimal $\mathbf{P}$ through solving the following optimization problem:

$$\min \sum_{i=1}^{k} \sum_{j:j\neq i} (r_{ji}p_i - r_{ij}p_j)^2 , \quad (6)$$

$$\text{s.t.} \sum_{i=1}^{k} p_i = 1, \quad p_i \geq 0 \; \forall i .$$

Note that (6) can be reformulated as

$$\min \; 2\mathbf{P}^T\mathbf{Q}\mathbf{P} \equiv \min \; \frac{1}{2}\mathbf{P}^T\mathbf{Q}\mathbf{P} , \quad (7)$$

where

$$Q_{ij} = \begin{cases} \sum_{s:s\neq i} r_{si}^2 & \text{if } i = j , \\ -r_{ji}r_{ij} & \text{if } i \neq j . \end{cases} \quad (8)$$

Then $\mathbf{P}$ can be obtained by solving the following linear system:

$$\begin{bmatrix} \mathbf{Q} & \mathbf{e} \\ \mathbf{e}^T & 0 \end{bmatrix} \begin{bmatrix} \mathbf{P} \\ b \end{bmatrix} = \begin{bmatrix} \mathbf{0} \\ 1 \end{bmatrix} , \quad (9)$$

where b is the Lagrangian multiplier of the equality constraint $\sum_{i=1}^{k} p_i = 1$, $\mathbf{e}$ is the $k \times 1$ vector of all ones, and $\mathbf{0}$ is the $k \times 1$ vector of all zeros. This method is easy to implement and has a more stable performance.

3 Improved Pairwise Classification with Correcting Classifiers

If a test example x is classified by classifier C_{ij}, while x belongs to neither class w_i nor class w_j, the output of C_{ij}, i.e. r_{ij}, is meaningless. Consequently considering r_{ij} in constructing the posterior probabilities $\mathbf{P}$ ($\tilde{\mathbf{P}}$) will bring in nonsense and can damage the quality of $\mathbf{P}$ ($\tilde{\mathbf{P}}$).

3.1 Algorithm by Moreira and Mayoraz

To tackle this problem, Moreira and Mayoraz proposed an algorithm called PWC-CC [4]. This algorithm trains $\frac{k(k-1)}{2}$ additional binary classifiers CC_{ij}, called *correcting classifiers*, to distinguish classes w_i and w_j from the remaining ones. For a given example x, the probabilistic output of CC_{ij} is $q_{ij} = \text{Prob}(x \in w_i \text{ or } w_j | x)$. Obviously $q_{ij} = q_{ji}$ holds. Then $\tilde{P}$ is computed using the following formula instead of (3):

$$\tilde{p}_i = \frac{2\sum_{s:s\neq i} r_{is} \cdot q_{is}}{k(k-1)} . \tag{10}$$

If an example x does not belong to either class w_i or class w_j, the output of classifier CC_{ij}, i.e. q_{ij}, is expected to be small (close to 0). Otherwise, q_{ij} is expected to be large (close to 1). Thus by using formula (10), the impact of those meaningless r_{ij} are largely weakened and the accuracy of the global prediction is improved.

3.2 A Closer Look at the PWC-CC Algorithm

Let us analyze Moreira and Mayoraz's algorithm in a more detailed way. First, we divide formula (10) into two formulas.

$$r'_{ij} = r_{ij} \cdot q_{ij} , \tag{11}$$

$$\tilde{p}_i = \frac{2\sum_{s:s\neq i} r'_{is}}{k(k-1)} . \tag{12}$$

Note that (12) has exactly the same form as (3).

Then we immediately get

$$r'_{ji} = q_{ij} - r'_{ij} \neq 1 - r'_{ij} . \tag{13}$$

and

$$\sum_{i=1}^{k} \tilde{p}_i \neq 1 . \tag{14}$$

Formula (13) indicates that r'_{ij} obtained by (11) are not real *pairwise probabilities*. Thereby sophisticated PWC method, e.g. the one described by (6), can not be applied to them. Formula (14) indicates that $\tilde{p}_i$ obtained by (12) are not posterior probabilities and the interpretation of $\tilde{\mathbf{P}}$ becomes ambiguous. We consider these the disadvantages of the original PWC-CC algorithm.

$$q_{ij}: \begin{bmatrix} - & 0.90 & 0.70 \\ 0.90 & - & 0.40 \\ 0.70 & 0.40 & - \end{bmatrix} \qquad p_i: \begin{bmatrix} 0.58 \\ 0.30 \\ 0.12 \end{bmatrix}$$

$$\text{PWC}: \quad r_{ij}: \begin{bmatrix} - & 0.60 & 0.60 \\ 0.40 & - & 0.90 \\ 0.40 & 0.10 & - \end{bmatrix} \Longrightarrow \tilde{p}_i: \begin{bmatrix} 0.40 \\ 0.43 \\ 0.17 \end{bmatrix}$$

$$\text{PWC} - \text{CC}: \quad r'_{ij}: \begin{bmatrix} - & 0.54 & 0.42 \\ 0.36 & - & 0.36 \\ 0.28 & 0.04 & - \end{bmatrix} \Longrightarrow \tilde{p}_i^O: \begin{bmatrix} 0.32 \\ 0.24 \\ 0.11 \end{bmatrix}$$

$$\text{NPWC} - \text{CC}: \quad t_{ij}: \begin{bmatrix} - & 0.83 & 0.83 \\ 0.17 & - & 0.66 \\ 0.17 & 0.34 & - \end{bmatrix} \Longrightarrow \tilde{p}_i^N: \begin{bmatrix} 0.55 \\ 0.28 \\ 0.17 \end{bmatrix}$$

Fig. 1. Comparion of NPWC-CC, PWC-CC and PWC on a 3-class problem. p_i are the real probabilities of a test example x. $\tilde{p}_i$, $\tilde{p}_i^O$, and $\tilde{p}_i^N$ are estimated by formula (3). Both PWC-CC and NPWC-CC classifies x correctly, while plain PWC behaves wrong. Note that $\tilde{p}_i^N$ is closest to p_i.

3.3 Our Algorithm

The purpose of using *correcting classifiers* is to reduce the impact those meaningless r_{ij} have on the global $\mathbf{P}$ ($\tilde{\mathbf{P}}$). The original PWC-CC algorithm achieves this purpose by weighting r_{ij} with corresponding q_{ij}. Thus the **values** of the meaningless r_{ij} are likely to be decreased, while those meaningful ones are kept nearly unchanged.

However there are other ways to achieve the same purpose. One approach is to reduce the **confidence** of meaningless r_{ij} and enhance the **confidence** of meaningful r_{ij}. We believe that in global-decision-making, the binary classifiers which have more confidence in their opinions dominate those which have less confidence in their opinions.

A classifier C_{ij} is considered to have much confidence in its output if the corresponding r_{ij} is very large (close to 1) or very small (close to 0). On the contrary, a r_{ij} around 0.5 indicates that C_{ij} is not that confident in determining which class wins. Based on these analysis, a novel PWC-CC (NPWC-CC) algorithm is proposed. NPWC-CC works in two steps:

1. r_{ij} are converted into a new set of *pairwise probabilities* t_{ij}.

$$t_{ij} = \begin{cases} \frac{1-\Delta'}{2} & r_{ij} \leq 0.5 \\ \frac{1+\Delta'}{2} & r_{ij} > 0.5 \end{cases}. \tag{15}$$

where

$$\Delta' = \begin{cases} \tanh(4\Delta) & q_{ij} \geq 0.5 \\ q_{ij}\Delta & q_{ij} < 0.5 \end{cases}. \tag{16}$$

$$\Delta = |r_{ij} - r_{ji}| = |2r_{ij} - 1| . \qquad (17)$$

2. Then a PWC method is employed to couple t_{ij} into a global $\mathbf{P}$ ($\tilde{\mathbf{P}}$).

In the first step, those meaningless r_{ij}, with expected small q_{ij}, are likely to be made more unconfident (corresponding t_{ij} are closer to 0.5). On the other hand, the confidences of the meaningful r_{ij} are likely to be strengthened (corresponding t_{ij} are farther from 0.5). A comparison of NPWC-CC, PWC-CC and PWC is illustrated in Figure 1.

From (15) (16) and (17), we immediately get $t_{ij} = 1 - t_{ji}$. This means that t_{ij} are real *pairwise probabilities*. Therefore any PWC method can be employed in NPWC-CC and the obtained p_i ($\tilde{p}_i$) are meaningful posterior probabilities. Thus the disadvantages of the original PWC-CC algorithm are overcame.

4 Experimental Results

Experiments are performed on several benchmark datasets from the Statlog collection [8]: *dna, satimage, letter,* and *shuttle*. Note that except *dna*, all data of the problems are scaled to [-1, 1]. Since *dna* has binary attributes, we leave it unchanged. Dataset statistics are listed in Table 1.

Table 1. Dataset statistics

dataset	#training data	#testing data	#class	#attributes
dna	2000	1186	3	180
satimage	4435	2000	6	36
letter	15000	5000	26	16
shuttle	43500	14500	7	9

Support vector machines (SVMs) are employed as binary classifiers to learn each binary subproblem. However standard SVMs do not produce probabilistic outputs. In [9], Platt suggested to map original SVM outputs to probabilities by fitting a sigmoid after the SVM:

$$P(y = 1|x) = \frac{1}{1 + \exp(Af(x) + B)} . \qquad (18)$$

Parameters A and B are found by minimizing the negative log likelihood of the training data:

$$\min \quad -\sum_{i=1}^{l} t_i \log(p_i) + (1 - t_i) \log(1 - p_i) , \qquad (19)$$

where

$$p_i = \frac{1}{1+\exp(Af(x_i)+B)}, \quad t_i = \frac{y_i+1}{2}. \qquad (20)$$

y_i is the target label of example x_i, $f(\cdot)$ is an SVM.

LIBSVM [10] is employed for SVMs training and testing. Experimental results are listed in Table 2. Where PWC1 is the PWC method described by formula (3), PWC2 is the method described in Section 2.2, NPWC-CC1 employs PWC1 in its second step, NPWC-CC2 employs PWC2 as its coupling method. Note that, NPWC-CC1 and PWC-CC differ only in the way they change the original *pairwise probabilities*.

Table 2. Classification performance of various algorithms

dataset	PWC1	PWC2	PWC-CC	NPWC-CC1	NPWC-CC2
dna	95.36%	95.53%	95.62%	95.62%	95.62%
satimage	90.43%	91.51%	91.92%	91.92%	92.17%
letter	97.84%	97.91%	97.98%	97.98%	98.34%
shuttle	99.89%	99.90%	99.94%	99.94%	99.93%

From Table 2, we can see that the use of *correcting classifiers* improves the classification performance of PWC on all datasets. However due to the large test datasets used, the improvements expressed in *percentage* are not that impressive as illustrated in [4]. As expected, PWC-CC and NPWC-CC1 perform exactly the same. This verifies the analysis in Section 3.3 that the impact of meaningless r_{ij} can be reduced by making them more unconfident. NPWC-CC2 performs best on all problems except *shuttle*. This highlights the virtue of NPWC-CC that more sophisticated coupling method can be employed, which is impossible for PWC-CC. In [7], it was concluded that PWC2 has a more stable performance that PWC1. Our experimental results give the same result.

5 Conclusion

Pairwise coupling (PWC) is a widely-used method in multi-class classification tasks. But it has an important drawback, due to the nonsense caused by those meaningless *pairwise probabilities*. PWC-CC tackles this problem by weighting the *pairwise probabilities* with the outputs of additional *correcting classifiers*. Though PWC-CC performs much better than PWC, it has its own disadvantages. In this paper, a novel PWC-CC (NPWC-CC) method is proposed. NPWC-CC works in two steps: First the original *pairwise probabilities* are converted into a new set of *pairwise probabilities*, wherein those meaningless probabilities are made more unconfident, while the confidences of the meaningful ones are strengthened. Then a PWC method is employed to couple the new *pairwise probabilities* into global posterior probabilities. NPWC-CC overcomes the disadvantages of PWC-CC and can achieve even better performance.

References

1. Weston, J., Watkins, C.: Support Vector Machines for Multi-Class Pattern Recognition. In: Proc. of 7th European Sympo. on Artificial Neural Networks (1999)
2. Platt, J., Cristianini, N., Shawe-Taylor, J.: Large Margin DAGs for Multiclass Classification. Advance in Neural Information Processing Systems. **12** (2000) 547-553
3. Hsu, C.-W., Lin, C.-J.: A comparison of methods for multi-class support vector machines. IEEE Trans. on Neural Networks. **13** (2002) 415-425
4. Moreira, M., Mayoraz, E.: Improved Pairwise Coupling Classification with Correcting Classifiers. In: Proc. of the 10th Europen Conf. on Machine Learning. (1998) 160-171
5. Friedman, J.: Another Approach to Polychotomous Classification. Technical report, Stanford University. (1996)
6. Hastie, T., Tibshirani, R.: Classification by Pairwise Coupling. The Annals of Statistics. **26** (1998) 451-471
7. Wu, T.-F., Lin, C.-J., Weng, R.C.: Probability Estimates for Multi-Class Classification by Pairwise Coupling. Journal of Machine Learning Research. **5** (2004) 975-1005
8. Michie, D., Spiegelhalter, D.J., Taylor, C.C.: Machine Learning, Neural and Statistical Classification. Ellis Horwood, London. (1994) Data available at ftp://ftp.ncc.up.pt/pub/statlog
9. Platt, J.: Probabilistic Outputs for Support Vector Machines and Comparison to Regularized Likelihood Methods. In: Smola, A.J., Bartlett, P.L., Schölkopf, B., Schuurmans, D. (eds.): Advances in Large Margin Classifiers. MIT Press (2000) 61-74
10. Chang, C.-C., Lin, C.-J.: LIBSVM: A Library for Support Vector Machines. (2002) Online at http://www.csie.ntu.edu.tw/~cjlin/papers/libsvm.pdf

Least Squares Littlewood-Paley Wavelet Support Vector Machine

Fangfang Wu and Yinliang Zhao

Institute of Neocomputer, Xi'an Jiaotong University,
Xi'an 710049, People's Republic of China
wffbolun@163.com, zhaoy@mail.xjtu.edu.cn

Abstract. The kernel function of support vector machine (SVM) is an important factor for the learning result of SVM. Based on the wavelet decomposition and conditions of the support vector kernel function, Littlewood-Paley wavelet kernel function for SVM is proposed. This function is a kind of orthonormal function, and it can simulate almost any curve in quadratic continuous integral space, thus it enhances the generalization ability of the SVM. According to the wavelet kernel function and the regularization theory, Least squares Littlewood-Paley wavelet support vector machine (LS-LPWSVM) is proposed to simplify the process of LPWSVM. The LS-LPWSVM is then applied to the regression analysis and classifying. Experiment results show that the precision is improved by LS-LPWSVM, compared with LS-SVM whose kernel function is Gauss function.

1 Introduction

Support vector machine (SVM) is a kind of classifier's studying method on statistic study theory [1,2]. This algorithm derives from linear classifier, and can solve the problem of two kind classifier, later this algorithm applies in non-linear fields, that is to say, we can find the optimal hyperplane (large margin) to classify the samples set. SVM can use the theory of minimizing the structure risk to avoid the problems of excessive study, calamity data, local minimal value and so on. For the small samples set, this algorithm can be generalized well [3].

Support vector machine (SVM) has been successfully used for machine learning with large and high dimensional data sets. This is due to the fact that the generalization property of an SVM does not depend on the complete training data but only a subset thereof, the so-called support vectors. Now, SVM has been applied in many fields as follows: handwriting recognition [4], three-dimension objects recognition, faces recognition [5], text images recognition, voice recognition, regression analysis and so on.

For pattern recognition and regression analysis, the non-linear ability of SVM can use kernel mapping to achieve. For the kernel mapping, the kernel function must satisfy the condition of Mercer [6]. The Gauss function is a kind of kernel function which is general used. It shows the good generalization ability. However, for our used kernel functions so far, the SVM can not approach any curve in $L_2(R)$ space (quadratic continuous integral space), because the kernel function which is used now is not the complete orthonormal base. This character lead the SVM can not approach every curve in the $L_2(R)$ space, similarly, the regression SVM can not approach every function.

According to the above describing, we need find a new kernel function, and this function can build a set of complete base through horizontal floating and flexing. As we know, this kind of function has already existed, and it is the wavelet functions. Based on wavelet decomposition, this paper propose a kind of allowable support vector's kernel function which is named Littlewood-Paley wavelet [7] kernel function, and we can prove that this kind of kernel function is existent. The Littlewood-Paley wavelet kernel functions are the orthonormal base of $L_2(R)$ space. At the same time, combining this kernel function with least squares support vector machine[8], we can build a new SVM learning algorithm that is Least squares Littlewood-Paley wavelet support vector machine (LS-LPWSVM).

In section 2, we introduce support vector machine algorithm; in section 3, we propose a new support vector's kernel function that is Littlewood-Paley wavelet kernel function; in section 4, we propose the Least squares Littlewood-Paley wavelet support vector machine (LS-LPWSVM); in section 5, we do the experiment to compare with other algorithms of SVM; finally, in section 6, we draw the conclusion.

2 Support Vector Machine

For the given samples set $\{(x_1, y_1), \ldots, (x_l, y_l)\}$, $x_i \in R^d$, $y_i \in R$, l is the samples number, d is the number of input dimension. In order to approach the function $f(x)$ with respect to this data set precisely, for regression analysis, SVM use the regression function as follows:

$$f(x) = \sum_{i=1}^{l} w_i k(x_i, x) + b \qquad (1)$$

w_i is the weight vector, and b is the threshold, $k(x_i, x)$ is the kernel function.

Training a SVM can be regarded as to minimize the value of $J(w, b)$:

$$J(w, b) = \min \frac{1}{2}\|w\|^2 + \gamma \sum_{i=1}^{l}\left(y_k - \sum_{i=1}^{l} w_i k(x_i, x) - b\right)^2 \qquad (2)$$

The kernel function $k(x_i, x)$ must be satisfied with the condition of Mercer[6]. When we define the kernel function $k(x_i, x)$, we also define the mapping from input to character's space. The general used kernel function of SVM is Gauss function, defined as follows:

$$k(x, x') = \exp(-\|x - x'\|^2 / 2\sigma^2) \qquad (3)$$

For this equation, σ is a parameter which can be adjusted by users.

3 Support Vector's Kernel Function

3.1 The Conditions of Support Vector's Kernel Function

The support vector's kernel function can be described as not only the product of point, such as $k(x,x') = k(<x \cdot x'>)$, but also the horizontal floating function, such as $k(x,x')=k(x-x')$[5]. In fact, if a function satisfied the condition of Mercer, it is the allowable support vector's kernel function.

Theorem 1[6]: The symmetry function $k(x, x')$ is the kernel function of SVM if and only if: for all function $g \neq 0$ which satisfied the condition of $\int_{R^d} g^2(\xi)d\xi < \infty$, we need satisfy the condition as follows:

$$\iint_{R^d \otimes R^d} k(x,x')g(x)g(x')dxdx' \geq 0 \tag{4}$$

This theorem proposed a simple method to build the kernel function.

For the horizontal floating function, because hardly dividing this function into two same functions, we can give the condition of horizontal floating kernel function.

Theorem 2[9,10]: The horizontal floating function is a allowable support vector's kernel function if and only if the Fourier transform of $k(x)$ need satisfy the condition as follows:

$$F[k(w)] = (2\pi)^{-\frac{d}{2}} \int_{R^d} \exp(-jwx)k(x)dx \geq 0 \tag{5}$$

3.2 Littlewood-Paley Wavelet Kernel Function

If the wavelet function $\psi(x)$ satisfied the conditions: $\psi(x) \in L_2(R) \cap L_1(R)$, and $\hat{\psi}(0) = 0$, $\hat{\psi}$ is the Fourier transform of function $\psi(x)$. The wavelet function group can be defined as:

$$\psi_{a,m}(x) = (a)^{-\frac{1}{2}} \psi\left(\frac{x-m}{a}\right) \tag{6}$$

$m \in R; a \geq 0$. For this equation, a is the flexible coefficient, m is the horizontal floating coefficient, and $\psi(x)$ is the base wavelet. For the function $f(x)$, $f(x) \in L_2(R)$, the wavelet transform of $f(x)$ defined as:

$$(W_\psi f)(a,m) = (a)^{-\frac{1}{2}} \int_{-\infty}^{+\infty} f(x)\overline{\psi\left(\frac{x-m}{a}\right)}dx \tag{7}$$

the wavelet inverse transform for $f(x)$ is:

$$f(x) = C_\psi^{-1} \int_{-\infty}^{+\infty}\int_{-\infty}^{+\infty} [(W_\psi f)(a,m)]\psi_{a,m}(x)\frac{da}{a^2}dm \tag{8}$$

For the above equation (8), C_ψ is a constant with respect to $\psi(x)$. The theory of wavelet decomposition is to approach the function $f(x)$ by the linear combination of wavelet function group.

If the wavelet function of one dimension is $\psi(x)$, using tensor theory[11], the multidimension wavelet function can be defined as:

$$\psi_d(x) = \prod_{i=1}^{d} \psi(x_i) \tag{9}$$

We can build the horizontal floating kernel function as follows:

$$k(x, x') = \prod_{i=1}^{d} \psi\left(\frac{x_i - x_i'}{a_i}\right) \tag{10}$$

a_i is the flexible coefficient of wavelet, $a_i>0$. So far, because the wavelet kernel function must satisfy the conditions of theorem 2, the number of wavelet kernel function which can be showed by existent functions is few. Now, we give an existent wavelet kernel function: Littlewood-Paley wavelet kernel function, and we can prove that this function can satisfy the condition of allowable support vector's kernel function. Littlewood-Paley wavelet function is defined as follows:

$$\psi(x) = \frac{\sin 2\pi x - \sin \pi x}{\pi x} \tag{11}$$

the above equation (11) is Littlewood-Paley wavelet function. We can prove the Fourier transform of this function is not negative, and the value of the transform is showed as follows:

$$\hat{\psi}(\omega) = \begin{cases} 1, & \pi \le |\omega| \le 2\pi \\ 0, & \text{other} \end{cases} \tag{12}$$

$\hat{\psi}(\omega) \ge 0$, and we use this wavelet to build the wavelet kernel function.

Theorem 3: Littlewood-Paley wavelet kernel function is defined as:

$$k(x, x') = k(x - x') = \prod_{i=1}^{d} \frac{\sin 2\pi\left(\frac{x_i - x_i'}{a_i}\right) - \sin \pi\left(\frac{x_i - x_i'}{a_i}\right)}{\pi\left(\frac{x_i - x_i'}{a_i}\right)} \tag{13}$$

and this kernel function is a allowable support vector kernel function.

Proof. According to the theorem 2, we only need to prove

$$F[k(w)] = (2\pi)^{-\frac{d}{2}} \int_{R^d} \exp(-jwx) k(x) dx \ge 0$$

$$F[k(w)] = (2\pi)^{-\frac{d}{2}} \int_{R^d} \exp(-jwx) k(x) dx$$

$$= (2\pi)^{-\frac{d}{2}} \int_{R^d} \exp(-jwx) \prod_{i=1}^{d} \frac{\sin 2\pi(\frac{x_i}{a_i}) - \sin \pi(\frac{x_i}{a_i})}{\pi(\frac{x_i}{a_i})} dx$$

$$= (2\pi)^{-\frac{d}{2}} \prod_{i=1}^{d} \int_{-\infty}^{+\infty} \exp(-jw_i x_i) \frac{\sin 2\pi(\frac{x_i}{a_i}) - \sin \pi(\frac{x_i}{a_i})}{\pi(\frac{x_i}{a_i})} dx_i$$

$$= (2\pi)^{-\frac{d}{2}} \prod_{i=1}^{d} \int_{-\infty}^{+\infty} \exp\left(-j(a_i w_i) \cdot (\frac{x_i}{a_i})\right) \frac{\sin 2\pi(\frac{x_i}{a_i}) - \sin \pi(\frac{x_i}{a_i})}{\pi(\frac{x_i}{a_i})} dx_i$$

$$\because \hat{\psi}(w) = \int_{-\infty}^{+\infty} \exp(-jwx) \frac{\sin 2\pi x - \sin \pi x}{\pi x} dx \geq 0$$

$$\therefore F[k(w)] \geq 0 \qquad \blacksquare$$

If we use the support vector' kernel function as Littlewood-Paley wavelet kernel function, the classifier function of SVM is defined as:

$$f(x) = \mathrm{sgn}\left(\sum_{i=1}^{l} w_i \prod_{j=1}^{d} \frac{\sin 2\pi\left(\frac{x_j - x_j^i}{a_j^i}\right) - \sin \pi\left(\frac{x_j - x_j^i}{a_j^i}\right)}{\pi\left(\frac{x_j - x_j^i}{a_j^i}\right)} + b\right) \qquad (14)$$

For regression analysis, the output function is defined as:

$$f(x) = \sum_{i=1}^{l} w_i \prod_{j=1}^{d} \frac{\sin 2\pi\left(\frac{x_j - x_j^i}{a_j^i}\right) - \sin \pi\left(\frac{x_j - x_j^i}{a_j^i}\right)}{\pi\left(\frac{x_j - x_j^i}{a_j^i}\right)} + b \qquad (15)$$

x_j^i is the value of ith training sample's jth attribute. Using the Littlewood-Paley wavelet kernel function, we can give the regression function a new concept: using the linear combination of wavelet function group, we can approach any function $f(x)$, that is to say, we can find the wavelet coefficients to decomposition the function $f(x)$.

4 Least Squares Littlwood-Paley Support Vector Machine

Least squares support vector machine is a new kind of SVM [8]. It derived from transforming the condition of inequation into the condition of equation. Firstly, we give the linear regression algorithm as follows.

For the given samples set $\{(x_1, y_1), \ldots, (x_l, y_l)\}$, $x_i \in R^d$, $y_i \in R$, l is the samples number, d is the number of input dimension. The linear regression function is defined as:

$$f(x) = w^T x + b \tag{16}$$

Importing the structure risk function, we can transform regression problem into protruding quadratic programming:

$$\min \frac{1}{2}\|w\|^2 + \gamma \frac{1}{2}\sum_{i=1}^{l}\xi_i^2 \tag{17}$$

The limited condition is:

$$y_i = w^T x_i + b + \xi_i \tag{18}$$

we define the Lagrange function as:

$$L = \frac{1}{2}\|w\|^2 + \gamma \frac{1}{2}\sum_{i=1}^{l}\xi_i^2 - \sum_{i=1}^{l}\alpha_i(w^T x_i + b + \xi_i - y_i) \tag{19}$$

According the KKT condition, we can get:

$$\frac{\partial L}{\partial w} = 0 \rightarrow w = \sum_{i=1}^{l}\alpha_i x_i \tag{20}$$

$$\frac{\partial L}{\partial b} = 0 \rightarrow \sum_{i=1}^{l}\alpha_i = 0 \tag{21}$$

$$\frac{\partial L}{\partial \xi_i} = 0 \rightarrow \alpha_i = \gamma \xi_i; \quad i=1,\ldots,l \tag{22}$$

$$\frac{\partial L}{\partial \alpha_i} = 0 \rightarrow w^T x_i + b + \xi_i - y_i = 0; \quad i=1,\ldots,l \tag{23}$$

From equation (20) to (23), we can get the following linear equation:

$$\begin{bmatrix} I & 0 & 0 & -x \\ 0 & 0 & 0 & \vec{1}^T \\ 0 & 0 & \gamma I & -I \\ x^T & \vec{1} & I & 0 \end{bmatrix} \begin{bmatrix} w \\ b \\ \xi \\ \alpha \end{bmatrix} = \begin{bmatrix} 0 \\ 0 \\ 0 \\ y \end{bmatrix} \tag{24}$$

$x=[x_1, \ldots, x_l]$, $y=[y_1, \ldots, y_l]$, $\vec{1}=[1, \ldots, 1]$, $\xi=[\xi_1, \ldots, \xi_l]$, $\alpha=[\alpha_1, \ldots, \alpha_l]$.

The equation result is:

$$\begin{bmatrix} 0 & \vec{1}^T \\ \vec{1} & x^T x + \gamma^{-1} I \end{bmatrix} \begin{bmatrix} b \\ \alpha \end{bmatrix} = \begin{bmatrix} 0 \\ y \end{bmatrix} \quad (25)$$

$w = \sum_{i=1}^{l} \alpha_i x_i$, $\xi_i = \alpha_i / \gamma$.

For non-linear problem, The non-linear regression function is defined as:

$$f(x) = \sum_{i=1}^{l} \alpha_i k(x_i, x) + b \quad (26)$$

The above equation result can be altered as:

$$\begin{bmatrix} 0 & \vec{1}^T \\ \vec{1} & K + \gamma^{-1} I \end{bmatrix} \begin{bmatrix} b \\ \alpha \end{bmatrix} = \begin{bmatrix} 0 \\ y \end{bmatrix} \quad (27)$$

$K = \{k_{ij} = k(x_i, x_j)\}_{i,j=1}^{l}$, the function $k(\cdot)$ is the Littlewood-Paley wavelet kernel function. Based on Littlewood-Paley wavelet kernel function, we can get a new learning method: Least squares Littlewood-Paley wavelet support vector machine (LS-LPWSVM). In fact, this algorithm is also Least squares support vector machine. We only use the Littlewood-Paley wavelet kernel function to represent the kernel function of SVM.

There is only one parameter γ need to be made certain for this algorithm, and the number of parameters of this kind of SVM is smaller than other kind of SVM, at the same time, the uncertain factors are decreased. Additionally, because using least squares method, the computation speed of this algorithm is more rapid than other SVM.

Because LS-SVM can not optimize the parameters of kernel function, it is hard to select $l \times d$ parameters. For convenience, we fix $a_j^i = a$, and the number of kernel function's parameters is 1. We can use the Cross-Validation method to select the value of parameter a.

5 Experiments and Results

For proving the performance of the algorithm of LS-LPWSVM, we make 3 experiments, (1) unitary function's regression, (2) binary function's regression, (3) the classifier for 5 UCI datasets. These 3 experiments will be introduced as follows.

For these 3 experiments, they were all done on an Intel P4 PC (with a 2.0GHZ CPU and 512MB memory) running Microsoft Windows 2000 Professional, Matlab6.5. For regression experiments, we use the approaching error as follows [11]:

$$E = \sqrt{\sum_{i=1}^{l}(y_i - f_i)^2 \Big/ \sum_{i=1}^{l}(y_i - \bar{y}_i)^2}, \quad \bar{y} = \frac{1}{l}\sum_{i=1}^{l} y_i \quad (28)$$

Experiment (1)
We use LS-LPWSVM to regress the following function:

$$y = x\sin(4\pi x)e^{1-x^2} + 2x^2 \tanh(10x)\cos(2\pi x) \tag{29}$$

The result of this experiment can be described as table 1, figure 1 and figure 2. In these two figures, the real line is the original function. Figure 1 is the regression result of LS-SVM which uses the Gauss kernel function. Figure 2 is the regression result of LS-LPWSVM which uses the Littlewood-Paley wavelet kernel function. From these result, we can find that the Littlewood-Paley wavelet kernel function not only has the capacity of non-linear mapping, but also inherit the characters of Littlewood-Paley wavelet's orthonormal capacity. The result of regression is more precisely.

Table 1. The regression result for unitary function y

	The parameter of kernel function	Training samples	Regression error
LS-SVM(γ=50) (Gauss kernel function)	σ=1	500	0.0637
LS-LPWSVM(γ=50)	a=2	500	0.0514

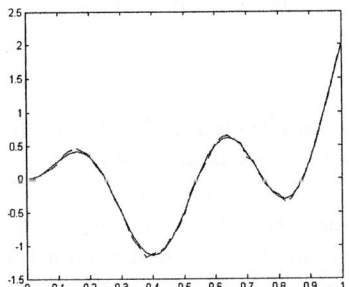
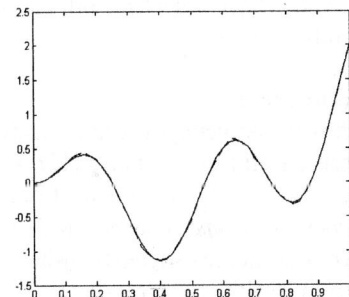

Fig. 1. The unitary regression curve based on Gauss kernel(LS-SVM)

Fig. 2. the unitary regression curve based on LS-LPWSVM

Experiment (2)
We use LS-LPWSVM to regress the following function:

$$z = (x^2 - y^2)\cdot(\cos(x)+\sin(y)) \tag{30}$$

The result of this experiment can be described as table 2, figure 4 and figure 5. Figure (3) is the original curve of binary function (30). Figure 4 is the regression result of LS-SVM which uses the Gauss kernel function. Figure 5 is the regression result of LS-LPWSVM which uses the Littlewood-Paley wavelet kernel function. From these result, we can find that the Littlewood-Paley wavelet kernel function not

Table 2. The regression result for binary function z

	The parameter of kernel function	Training samples	Regression error
LS-SVM(γ=50) (Gauss kernel function)	σ=1	2000	0.0313
LS-LPWSVM(γ=50)	a=2	2000	0.0187

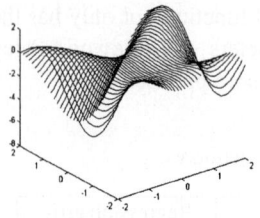
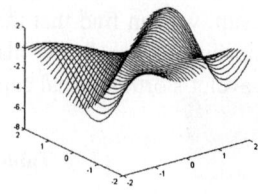

Fig. 3. The original binary function's curve

Fig. 4. The binary regression curve based on Gauss kernel

Fig. 5. The binary regression curve based on LS-LPWSVM

only has the capacity of non-linear mapping, but also inherit the characters of Littlewood-Paley wavelet's orthonormal capacity. The result of regression is more precisely.

Experiment (3)

For this experiment, we use 5 datasets to train the classifier of SVM, and these 5 datasets are all from UCI data [12]. We introduce these 5 datasets as follows.

For dataset (1), it derives from Smith, J.W., Everhart, J.E., Dickson, W.C., Knowler, W.C., and Johannes, R.S., which is named Diabetes. The diagnostic, binary-valued variable investigated is whether the patient shows signs of diabetes according to World Health Organization criteria. For this set, the kernel function of LS-SVM is Gauss function and the value of σ^2=4. The kernel function of LS-LPWSVM is Littlewood-Paley wavelet kernel function and the value of a=1.

For dataset (2), this radar data was collected by a system in Goose Bay, Labrador, which is named Ionosphere. This system consists of a phased array of 16 high-frequency antennas with a total transmitted power on the order of 6.4 kilowatts. The targets were free electrons in the ionosphere. "Good" radar returns are those showing evidence of some type of structure in the ionosphere. "Bad" returns are those that do not; their signals pass through the ionosphere. For this set, the kernel function of LS-SVM is Gauss function and the value of σ^2=5. The kernel function of LS-LPWSVM is Littlewood-Paley wavelet kernel function and the value of a=1.

For dataset (3), it derives from Dr. William H. Wolberg, and the set is nosocomial data, which is named Breast. From this data, we can tell whether the patient's breast tumour is malignant. For this set, the kernel function of LS-SVM is Gauss function and the value of $\sigma^2 = 4$. The kernel function of LS-LPWSVM is Littlewood-Paley wavelet kernel function and the value of $a=1$.

For dataset (4), it derives from spam e-mail database, which is named Spambase. From this data, we can tell whether the e-mail is a spam e-mail. For this set, the kernel function of LS-SVM is Gauss function and the value of $\sigma^2=6$. The kernel function of LS-LPWSVM is Littlewood-Paley wavelet kernel function and the value of $a=2$.

For dataset (5), it is the report of census, which is named Adult. Every data has 14 attributes. After transforming the value of each attribute between 0 and 1, we have the data set which has six numerical value attributes. The number of this data set is 32561. The set can be trained for forecasting whether man's income is over 50,000\$. In this set, there are two kinds of family's income. One kind is over 50,000\$, the number of this kind of data is 7841. The other kind is below 50,000\$, the number of this kind of data is 24720. For this set, the kernel function of LS-SVM is Gauss function and the value of $\sigma^2=10$. The kernel function of LS-LPWSVM is Littlewood-Paley wavelet kernel function and the value of $a=2$.

Table 3. The comparison precision among SVM algorithms

	N (The scale of sample set)	Accuracy (LS-SVM)	Accuracy (LS-LPWSVM)
Diabetes(γ=50)	768	99.1%	99.5%
Ionosphere(γ=50)	351	96.6%	97.7%
Breast(γ=50)	699	98.3%	98.3%
Spambase(γ=100)	4601	88.65%	91.38%
Adult(γ=100)	32561	91.79%	93.64%

Table 3 is the comparison precision among SVM algorithms. There are 2 kind algorithms as follows: LS-SVM and LS-LPWSVM. From the analysis of the data in table 3, the result of this experiment shows that the accuracy of LS-LPWSVM is better than the accuracy of LS-SVM.

6 Conclusion

For the SVM's learning method, this paper proposes a new kernel function of SVM which is the Littlewood-Paley wavelet kernel function. We can use this kind of kernel function to map the low dimension input space to the high dimension space. For the Littlewood-Paley wavelet function, because of its horizontal floating and flexible orthonormal character, it can build the orthonormal base of $L_2(R)$ space, and using this kernel function, we can approach almost any complicated functions in $L_2(R)$ space, thus this kernel function enhances the generalization ability of the SVM. At the same time, combining LS-SVM, a new regression analysis method named Least squares Littlewood-Paley wavelet support vector machine is proposed, we can compare this kind of SVM with other SVM. Experiment shows: the Littlewood-Paley wavelet kernel function is better than Gauss kernel function.

References

1. Vapnik, V. The Nature of Statistical Learning Theory. 1995. New York: Springer-Verlag 1~175.
2. Zhang, X.G. Introduction to Statistical Learning Therory and Support Vector Machines. Acta Automatica Snica. 2000, 26(1): 32~42.
3. Burges, C.J.C. A tutorial on support vector machines for pattern recognition. Data Mining and Knowledge Discovery. 1998, 2(2): 955~974.
4. Bernhard S., Sung K.K. Comparing Support Vector Machines with Gaussian Kernels to Radical Basis Fuction Classifiers. IEEE Transaction on Signal Processing. 1997, 45(11): 2758~2765.
5. Edgar O., Robert F., Federico G. Training Support Vector Machines: An Application to Face Detection. IEEE Conference on Computer Vision and Pattern Recognition. 1997. 130~136.
6. Mercer J. Function of positive and negative type and their connection with the theory of integral equations [J]. Philosophical Transactions of the Royal Society of London: A, 1909, (209):415-446.
7. Stein, E.M Topics in Harmonic Analysis Related to the Littlewood-Paley Theory, Princeton University Press and the University of Tokio Press, Princeton, New Jersey, 1970.
8. Suykens J A K, Vandewalle J. Least squares support vector machine classifiers [J]. Neural Processing Letter, 1999, 9(3): 293-300.
9. Burges C J C. Geometry and invariance in kernel based methods [A]. in Advance in Kernel Methods-Support Vector Learning[C]. Cambridge, MA: MIT Press, 1999. 89-116.
10. Smola A., Schölkopf B., Müller K R. The connection between regularization operators and support vector kernels [J]. Neural Networks, 1998, 11(4):637-649.
11. Zhang Q, Benveniste A. Wavelet networks [J]. IEEE Trans on Neural Networks, 1992, 3(6): 889-898.
12. ftp://ftp.ics.uci.edu.cn/pub/machine-learning-database/adult.

Minimizing State Transition Model for Multiclassification by Mixed-Integer Programming

Nobuo Inui and Yuuji Shinano

Tokyo University of Agriculture and Technology,
Koganei Tokyo 184-8588, Japan

Abstract. This paper proposes a state transition (ST) model as a classifier and its generalization by the minimization. Different from previous works using statistical methods, tree-based classifiers and neural networks, we use a ST model which determines classes of strings. Though an initial ST model only accepts given strings, the minimum ST model can accepts various strings by the generalization. We use a minimization algorithm by Mixed-Integer Linear Programming (MILP) approach. The MILP approach guarantees a minimum solution. Experiment was done for the classification of pseudo-strings. Experimental results showed that the reduction ratio from an initial ST model to the minimal ST model becomes small, as the number of examples increases. However, a current MILP solver was not feasible for large scale ST models in our formalization.

1 Introduction

Classification of examples is a general task which is important in many fields. For example, sentence classification is useful for a dialog system where the role of a sentence is the key for generating the next sentence and for analyzing the dialog structure[7]. The previous research often uses N-gram information and linguistic knowledge to determine sentence classes. Linguistic knowledge is effective for this purpose, since roles can be judged by the sentence structure. For example, when the sentence is a question with the first word "Do", we can classify it as a "yes-no question" on the basis of linguistic knowledge alone. However, when a system has to cope with a variety of roles and many different sentences with complicated structures, we need to collect linguistic knowledge from various examples. N-gram information and decision trees are often useful to determine sentence roles in this task. By using such statistical approaches, it is possible to automatically construct a system using corpus that can judge sentence roles with a high reliability. However, a sentence is not just a set of words but a structured sequence of words. Though cooccurrence information is effective, it is only an approximation of the sentence structure.

State transition-based methods like DFA (Deterministic Finite State Automaton), NFA (Non-deterministic Finite State Automaton) and PDFA (Probabilistic DFA) provide useful information for determining the class of a sentence.

For example, a classification automaton has been proposed for the classification of strings.[8]. In this method, the final state transition of a strings indicates its class. Let s be the final state after tracing a route on the state transition model. If the state s has state transitions with classification symbols, the string can be classified into these classes. This approach is a natural extension of the automaton that only determines whether a string is accepted or rejected. As an analogy, we use the class state which shows the string class as the final state. We also attempt to minimize such automaton using MILP (Mixed-Integer Linear Programming) technique.

This paper is organized as follows. We describe our natural language problem domain in Section 2. We present the problem definition in Section 3, and propose a solution to the minimization problem in Section 4. In Section 5, we present the experimental results for pseudo-strings and their discussion. In Section 6 we present our conclusions.

2 Problem Domain

In this paper, we focus on the problem of classifying sentences. The classification of sentences is deeply related to their meanings. The assignment of dialog acts to sentences, mentioned in Section 1, is an example where such classification is helpful. Another useful application of sentence classification is to find word meanings. It is well known that a cooccurrence relation from a word to other words often reflects the word meaning. This information can be used to build a thesaurus from the corpus. Though the cooccurrence works well in acquiring knowledge, it constitutes only a part of the information obtained from the corpus. Dependency relations (such as modifier-modified relations) between words or clauses constitute another piece of information. But almost all existing works treat dependency relations as relations between words.

State transition models, especially automaton, make it possible to express the meaning of words or sentences. For example, consider the classification of adverbs using a state transition model. Grammatically, adverbs modify various verb phrases. In a sentence such as "I have already read the book", the adverb "already" is considered to modify "have read the book". In this case, the perfect tense is used. Another sentence "I still read the book"[1], means that "I" sometimes read the book and "I" am not bored to read the book. Both "already" and "still" modify the same phrase. However "I have already finished my work" is natural, but "I have still finished my work" is not. This is because of the tense structure of the verb "finish". From this example, we can conclude that the meaning of an adverb can be classified based on the phrases modified by that adverb. In the above example, shared and non-shared parts of the strings containing "already" and "still" help to distinguish their meanings. In our previous work[4] we used word-cooccurrence information to estimate the meaning of adverbs. In contrast, here we try to find the meaning of adverbs from the resemblance of word strings.

---

[1] This sentence is present tense.

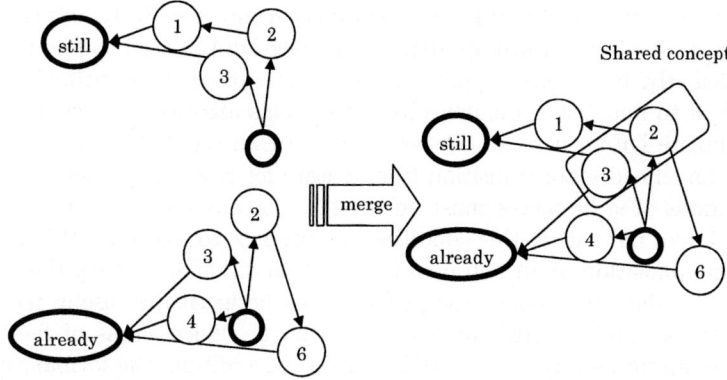

Fig. 1. Example of Merging State Transition Models

It is possible to construct an automaton that accepts an string if it can be modified by an adverb. We extend this approach to allow automata for several adverbs to be merged. In doing so, we can expect that the merged automaton expresses the meanings of several adverbs. This concept is shown in Figure 1, where two state transition models, expressing phrases modified by "still" and "already", respectively, are merged. The merged model contains a part of the state transitions shared by both models. We call this part "shared concept" to mean common phrases or word sequences between the two adverbs. If the size of the shared concepts between two adverbs is large, we generally assume that their meanings resemble based on the analogy with respect to word-cooccurrences. Thus, the merged state transition model provides a tool for analyzing adverb meanings. In addition, we posit that the minimization of a merged state transition model is important to find shared concepts. Since the set of examples from which a state transition model is derived is not complete, each state transition model is sparse. Therefore, we need to generalize the state transition models. The minimization, which is aimed at finding the least number of states to describe the given set of examples, is the key to generalization. In a previous work [2], recurrent neural networks are used to generalize the set of examples. In this work, the acceptance or rejection of a string not included in the set of examples is estimated by a neural network. In contrast to this neural network-based approach, our minimization-based approach guarantees the exact answers for all examples given. This is a benefit of our approach because there are not examples that can be ignored.

Much work has been done on the minimization of automaton. The goal of minimization is to reduce the number of states efficiently. One approach[1] uses the minimal cover automaton to reduce the size of minimum DFA. From the view of the search space reduction, an effective pruning method was proposed[5]. In this method, an initial automaton, called loop-free automaton, which is directly generated from examples, is transformed to the minimum automaton by a state-merging method. The equivalence between states is calculated using state transitions from these states, which is also used for pruning. In another approach,

NFA (Non-deterministic Finite State Automaton) are used to reduce the size of minimum DFA[6]. In a third approach[3], k-layer DFA is used to find minimum DFA efficiently. In all these approaches, the state-merging algorithm is a popular method to find the minimum automaton. This algorithm is usually applied to a complete DFA where all the next states for all inputs are known. If there exist an undefined state transition from a state for a input symbol, all possible combinations of state-merge must be tried[5]. Since our problem mentioned in Section 3 does not satisfy this condition, we propose to use the MILP approach for the minimization of an automaton in Section 4. Different with the previous approach[5] which introduced the problem-specific heuristics, useful techniques developed for solving MILP are available for the effectiveness of finding the minimum automaton by using a MILP solver. In addition, the formalization on MILP is quite simple because the problem description is obtained only giving all possible candidates of solutions. From this, we can try various variations of the minimum automaton problem by only changing the formalization.

3 Preliminary Definitions

In this section, we formally define our problem. A definition used in this paper is similar to the previous research[5].

A state transition model is denoted by $\{\Sigma, \{\epsilon\} \cup Q, q, F, \delta\}$, where Σ is a finite set of words, Q is a set of states, $q \in Q$ is an initial state, $F \subset Q$ is a set of final states and $\delta : Q \times \Sigma \rightarrow \{\epsilon\} \cup Q$ is a transition function.

ϵ in the definition means an arbitrary state. The arbitrary state is assigned for undefined words. If the action of a word is not defined on a state, an ϵ state

still : 1 2 3

already: 2 3 1

a) Example of strings modified by "already" and "still"

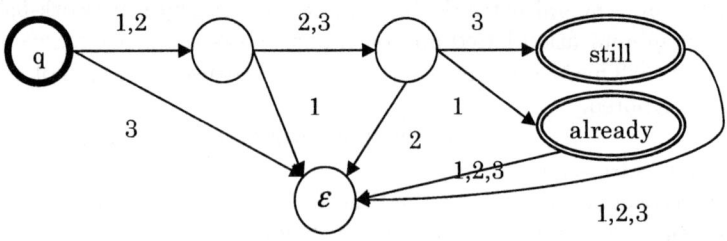

b) Merged State Transition Model

Fig. 2. Examples of state transition model

is used. In this case, the state transition to the ϵ state can be replaced to a state in Q in the minimization process. In this paper, ϵ is omitted unless necessary.

In this model, final states classify phrases into modifiable adverbs. To do so, each final state is labeled such that $F = F^1 \cup \ldots \cup F^{M_L}$ where M_L is the number of labels and $F^i \cap F^j = \phi$. For example of the classification of sentences by adverbs, the final state of a string which is modified by "already" would have the label "already". A final state can be labeled with several adverbs. If, for example, a string can be modified by "already" and "still", its final state is labeled with "already" and "still", which is not same as "already" nor "still".

Positive examples are used to learn the minimum state transition model. This is because the final states are classified into labels (adverbs). Some examples of state transition models are shown in Figure 2.

4 Classification and Mixed-Integer Programming

In this section, we describe our approach to the minimization of state transition models mentioned in Section 3.

4.1 Prefix Tree Acceptor

First, we make a PTA (Prefix Tree Acceptor) from the set of examples describing the phrases modified by adverbs. Generally PTA is a tree-shaped DFA. In our method, which we will describe later, PTA provides a temporal state number for a string and a substring of words. In PTA, a state is uniquely determined for a given string. We use the PTA shown in Figure 3. Since the number of each state is given by a natural number, we can define a set of states in PTA as $Q_p = \{1, 2, \ldots, M_{Q_p}\}$, where M_{Q_p} is the number of states required for the expression of PTA.

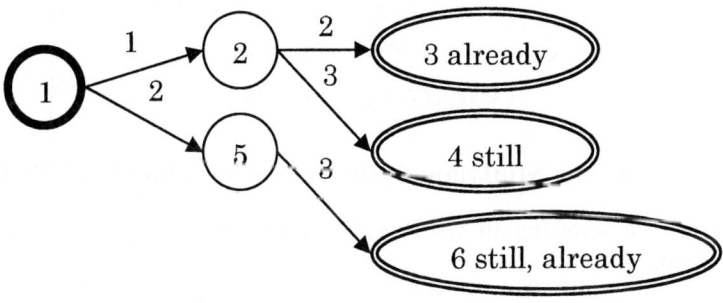

Σ={1,2,3}, Q={1,2,3,4,5,6}, q=1, F={3,4,6}

Fig. 3. Example of PTSa

4.2 Model State Transition

To use the MILP approach for the minimization of PTA given in Section 4.1, we use MSTs (Model State Transitions) for expressing the state transition models. The number of states in an MST is determined appropriately. The formulation of the MILP minimization, to be described later, tries to map a state in PTA to a state in MST so as to minimize the number of states used in MST, as shown in Figure 4. We define a set of states in MST as $Q_m = \{1, 2, \ldots, M_{Q_m}\}$. If $M_{Q_p} = M_{Q_m}$, then the existence of MST describing a given PTA is guaranteed, otherwise not. As a practical problem, M_{Q_m} controls the calculation time of MILP, since the number of expressions in it is proportional to M_{Q_m}. So we appropriately set M_{Q_m} in our experiment.

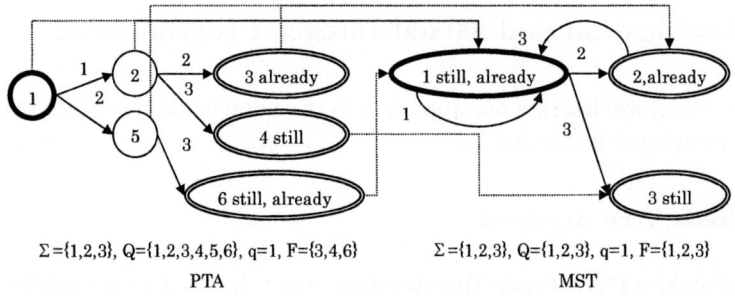

Fig. 4. Mapping a state in PTA to a state in MST for a state transition

In the next section, we formulate a mapping from a state in PTA to a state in MST. To mention the equivalence of states between PTA and MST, we use a state t in $PTA = \{\Sigma, \{\epsilon\} \cup Q_p, q_p, F_p, \delta_p\}$, a state s in $MST = \{\Sigma, \{\epsilon\} \cup Q_m, q_m, , F_m, \delta_m\}$ and a mapping function s_t from t to a state in MST. MST is said to be equivalent to PTA, if and only if:

$$t \in Q_p \rightarrow \exists s \in Q_m \text{ such that } s = s_t$$
$$t \in Q_p, s \in Q_m, s = s_t, w \in \Sigma \rightarrow \delta_m(s, w) = s_{\delta_p(t,w)}$$
$$t \in Q_p, t \in F_p^i \rightarrow s_t \in F_m^i$$

4.3 Describing the Minimum State Transition Model in MILP

The process of minimizing an MILP is shown in Figure 5. 4 parts compose this formalization:

1. Minimizing the maximum state number used in MST: (2)
2. Making mappings from states in PTA to states in MST:(3)-(7)
3. Making state transitions in MST:(8),(9)
4. Corresponding labels of states in PTA and MST:(10),(11)

In this process, the maximum number assigned to a state in MST e is minimized. The scope of e is defined in (2), where s_t shows a state in MST, which corresponds to the state t in PTA. All states are defined as positive integers in (20) and (21). L defined in (23) is used as a set of classes; each element in L represents an adverb or a set of adverbs in our problem-setting.

Expressions from (3) to (7) express mappings from the states in PTA to the states in MST. From these expressions, z_{ts} becomes 1 if $s = s_t$ and 0 if $s \neq s_t$. M_{s_t}, M_{Q_m} and M_L are constants used in expressions (20),(21) and (23).

Since a variable z_{ts} means whether a mapping from t to s is done or not, we can use a expression below, instead of (3),(4) and (7):

$$\sum_{s \in Q_m} z_{ts} = 1 \quad t \in Q_p$$

But the formalization shown in Figure 5 is better in the effectiveness from our experience.

minimize e (1)
subject to

$s_t \leq e$	$t \in Q_p$	(2)
$(M_{s_t} + 1) - (M_{s_t} + 1)x_{ts} + s - s_t \geq 1$	$s \in Q_m, t \in Q_p, s \leq t$	(3)
$(M_{Q_m} + 1) - (M_{Q_m} + 1)y_{ts} - s + s_t \geq 1$	$s \in Q_m, t \in Q_p, s \leq t$	(4)
$M_{s_t} - M_{s_t} z_{ts} + s - s_t \geq 0$	$s \in Q_m, t \in Q_p, s \leq t$	(5)
$M_{Q_m} - M_{Q_m} z_{ts} - s + s_t \geq 0$	$s \in Q_m, t \in Q_p, s \leq t$	(6)
$x_{ts} + y_{ts} + z_{ts} = 1$	$s \in Q_m, t \in Q_p, s \leq t$	(7)
$M_{s_{t'}} - M_{s_{t'}} z_{ts} + n_{sw} - s_{t'} \geq 0$	$s \in Q_m, t \in Q_p, s \leq t,$ $t' = \delta p(t, w) \in Q_p, w \in \Sigma$	(8)
$M_{Q_m} - M_{Q_m} z_{ts} - n_{sw} + s_{t'} \geq 0$	$s \in Q_m, t \in Q_p, s \leq t,$ $t' = \delta p(t, w) \in Q_p, w \in \Sigma$	(9)
$M_L - M_L z_{ts} + p_s - q_t \geq 0$	$s \in Q_m, t \in Q_p, s \leq t$	(10)
$M_L - M_L z_{ts} - p_s + q_t \geq 0$	$s \in Q_m, t \in Q_p, s \leq t$	(11)
$1 \leq n_{sw} \leq M_{Q_m}$	$s \in Q_m, w \in \Sigma$	(12)
$1 \leq s_t \leq min(t, M_{Q_m})$	$t \in Q_p$	(13)
$x_{ts} \in \{0,1\}$	$s \in Q_m, t \in Q_p, s \leq t$	(14)
$y_{ts} \in \{0,1\}$	$s \in Q_m, t \in Q_p, s \leq t$	(15)
$z_{ts} \in \{0,1\}$	$s \in Q_m, t \in Q_p, s \leq t$	(16)
$p_s \in L$	$s \in Q_m$	(17)
$q_t = l$	$t \in Q_p, l \in L,$ a state t is labeled to l in PTA	(18)
$q_t \in L$	$t \in Q_p$	(19)
$Q_p = \{1, 2, \ldots, M_{Q_p}\}$	A set of states in PTA	(20)
$Q_m = \{1, 2, \ldots, M_{Q_m}\}$	A set of states in MST	(21)
$\Sigma = \{1, 2, \ldots\}$	A set of words	(22)
$L = \{1, 2, \ldots, M_L\}$	A set of labels	(23)

Fig. 5. Classification on Minimum State Transition Model

In expressions (8) and (9), n_{sw} means the next state of s when a word w is given in MST. With this variable, a state transition model become deterministic. $\delta p(t, w)$ means the next state of t when a word w is given in PTA. Expression (10) and (11) determine the label of each state in MST. Adverbs and their combinations classify final states by using labels. If $s = s_t$, then the label of a state s in MST equals to that of the state t in MST.

By solving the problem shown in Figure 5 using the MILP solver, we obtain a set of mappings from the states in PTA to the states in MST. From this set, we can construct the minimum state transition model.

5 Experiment

We performed an experiment for the minimization of state transition models. The purpose of this experiment was to observe the feasibility of our method. We used a PC with the following specification:

- PC: Pentium 4 3.4GHz and 1GB memory
- MILP solver: CPLEX 9.1.0 (ILOG) on Windows XP (default setting of parameters)

We used pseudo-strings to evaluate our method. Pseudo-strings were randomly generated by the following parameters:

- The length of string: 5 to 10
- Words (Σ): 10 kinds
- Adverbs: 5 kinds or 10 kinds
- The number of examples: 5,10,15,20,25,30
- The size of MST: 20 states

As described in Section 4.3, the number of variables in the MILP formulation is $2M_{Q_p} + M_{Q_m} + (M_{Q_p} + M_{Q_m})M_L + 3M_{Q_p}M_{Q_m}$. Usually, the difficulty of problems on the MILP is evaluated using the number of variables and constraints (of course, usually the MILP solver solves NP-hard problems). Generally, a problem with thousands of variables is hard to solve by the MILP solver in the current state of art implementation. So a time limit of 3600 second was set for the MILP solver. The number of states in MST was set to 20, which is enough for MST to describe the given examples.

The experimental results are shown in Table 1. In this table,"Num. Exa." is the number of examples to be learned, "Num. Class" is the number of adverbs and their combinations, "Num. Sta. (PTA)" is the number of states in PTA for expressing examples. Because of our modeling constraints described in Section 4.1, the number of states is a constant, even if the number of adverbs is changed. "Calc. Time" is the calculation time for solving problems on the MILP solver. "Num. Sta. (Min. MST)" is the number of states used in MST. "*" means that the optimal solution is not found within the time limit. But, in this case, the MILP solver can sometimes find a feasible solution. We describe the number of

Table 1. Results

Num. Exa.	Num.Class	Num.Sta. (PTA)	Num.Con.	Num.Var	Calc. Time (sec)	Num.Sta. (Min. MST)
5	5	41	5539	2192	4.3	3
	10				4.1	3
10	5	77	11985	4424	14.4	5
	10				3600	*7
15	5	112	18244	6595	282.2	5
	10				3600	*8
20	5	145	24217	8640	3600	*8
	10				3600	*10
25	5	175	29575	10500	3600	*11
	10				3600	*15
30	5	207	35367	12484	3600	*
	10				3600	*

states of the feasible solution with "*". Figure 6 shows an instance where the number of examples is 5, the number of adverbs is 5, the number of words is 10.

From Table 1, the reduction rate $\frac{Num.Sta.(Min.MST)}{Num.Sta.(PTA)}$ becomes smaller as the number of states in PTA grows. This shows that our state transition model is effective with respect to reducing the number of states. Moreover, the calculation time increases as the class size increases. The class size only affects the constant in (10) and (11) in Figure 5. The number of variables is not changed, even if the class size is changed. This shows that the value of constants deeply influence the performance of the MILP solver.

As shown in our experimental results, we could not obtain the optimal or a feasible solution when there are a large number of examples. Though the main reason for this is the performance of the MILP solver, we feel that improving problem descriptions might also help.

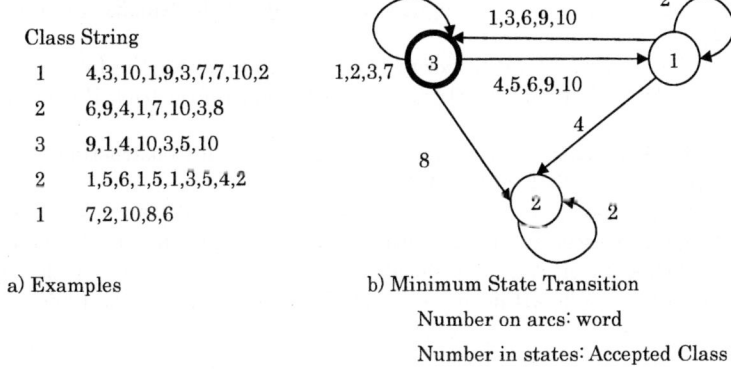

Fig. 6. An Example of Minimum State Transition Model

6 Conclusion

In this paper, we proposed a new method for the classification of strings using state transition models. In this approach, final states express the class of strings, analogous to the DFA where the final states express the acceptance of strings. In our method, a state transition is expressed in an incomplete way; for the rejection is not explicitly expressed. We apply this model to classify strings, depending on the possibility of the modification by adverbs. The minimization is described using the MILP approach. By this method, the optimal solution is guaranteed without any heuristic method. Experimental results showed that the reduction rate of states becomes smaller as the number of states in the initial state transition model (PTA) becomes larger. We, however, found that the feasibility of our method was low when the number of examples is large. In the future research, we plan to apply the minimum state transition models to analyze the meanings of adverbs.

Acknowledgments

We would like to thank Bipin Indurkha for revising our paper and giving good ideas.

References

1. Campeanu, C., Santean, N.,Yu, S: Minimal Cover-Automata for Finite Language. Theoretical Computer Science. **267** (2001) 3-16
2. Carrasco, R. C., Forcada, M. L., Valdes-Munoz, M. A., Neco, R. P.: Stable Encoding of Finite-State Matches in Discrete-Time Recurrent Neural Nets with Sigmoid Units. Neural Computation **12** (2000) 2129-2174
3. Holzmann, G. J., Puri, A.: A Minimized Automaton Representation of Reachable States. STTT '99 bf 3.2. (1999) 270-278
4. Inui,N., Kotani, Y.,Nisimura, H.: Classifying Adverbs based on an Existing Thesaurus using Corpus. Natural Language Processing Pacific Rim Symposium. (1997) 501-504
5. Oliveira, A.L., Silva, J.P.M.: Efficient Search Techniques for the Inference of Minimum Size Finite Automaton. String Processing and Information Retrieval. (1998) 81-89
6. Sgarbas, K., Fakotakis, N., Kokkinakis, G.: Incremental Construction of Compact Acyclic NFAs. ACL-2001. (2001) 474-481
7. Serafin, R., Eugenio, B.D.: FLSA: Extending Latent Semantic Analysis with features for dialogue act classification. The 42th Annual Meeting of the ACL. (2004) 692-699
8. Wang, X., Chaudhari, N.S.: Classification Automaton and Its Construction Using Learning. Advances in Artificial Intelligence: Proceedings-AI 2003. (2003) 515-519

Overview of Metaheuristics Methods in Compilation

Fernanda Kri, Carlos Gómez, and Paz Caro

Universidad de Santiago de Chile, Departamento de Ingeniería Informática,
Av. Ecuador 3659, Santiago, Chile
{fdakri, cgomez, pcaro}@diinf.usach.cl

Abstract. Compilers are nowadays fundamental tools for the development of any kind of application. However, their task gets increasingly difficult due to the constant increase in the complexity of modern computer architecture, as well as to the increased requirements imposed upon programming languages by the great diversity of applications handled at present. In the compilation process several optimization problems must be solved, some of them belonging to the NP-Hard class. The quality of the solution found for these problems has direct impact over the quality of the generated object code. To solve them, compilers do it locally through naive heuristics which might consequently lead to solutions that are far from optimal. Knowing that metaheuristics methods have recently been used massively and successfully to solve combinatorial optimization problems, similar performance in the problems found in the compilation process can be expected beforehand. Following this line of reasoning, such problems are presented in this paper and the potential use of metaheuristics techniques to find their solutions is analyzed. A review is also made of the work that has been done in this field, and finally a proposal is made of the road that this development should follow.

Keywords: Metaheuristics methods, compiler.

1 Introduction

At present, compilers are fundamental tools for the development of any kind of application. Even though compilers can be considered as black boxes into which a source program written in a high level language goes in and from which an equivalent program written in a language understandable by the machine comes out, they are highly complex tools. The constant increase in the complexity of architectures and programming languages, as well as the diversity of applications that are developed at present, are making the task of compilers more difficult every day. In the process of compilation several optimization problems must be solved, some of them NP-hard [1]. The quality of the solutions found for these problems has direct impact on the quality of the generated object code. Normally, compilers use naive heuristics and solve these problems locally, leading to solutions that are far from optimal. When we refer to a better quality object code, we understand that there is a criterion for determining whether an object code is better than another. This criterion depends on the objective sought, e.g. if the program is going to be executed in a restricted memory system (a smart card or a mobile device), we may be interested in getting the smallest possible program. On the other hand, if what we are interested in is response time, we will look for the fastest program, i.e. that which has the shortest execution time for a given architecture.

Compilers, therefore, compile for a specific architecture [2]. Thus the heuristics used consider details of the machines' organization. If we consider basic machines (Von Neumann architecture), defining heuristics that have a reasonable performance when solving these optimization problems is not so complex. Nowadays, however, with the incorporation into the architectures of cache memories, pipeline, jump speculation, out of order execution, prefetching, dynamic instruction scheduling, registry renaming, etc., the concept of efficient heuristics has become an extremely difficult task. To solve this, compilers carry out architecture simplification, generating codes that do not actually use all the advantages of the hardware.

To this complexity must be added that the speed at which changes in architecture occurs is much greater than the speed at which new compilers are built. Let us assume that a new architecture gets into the market today, and we start developing a compiler that makes use of its characteristics; it is probable that by the time the compiler is ready to go to market the architecture for which the compiler was developed will already have undergone many changes, which means that our compiler will no longer be as optimizing as we conceived it.

For example, let us think of the historical discussion of RISC (Reduce Instructions Set Computer) vs. CISC (Complex Instructions Set Computer). In recent years various benchmarking results [2] have shown that RISC is better than CISC. It is clear that for CISC machines to incorporate complex instructions in their instruction set, they have had to pay a cost in speed due to the complexity of the hardware, expecting that the use of these complex instructions will improve the machine's performance. However, what happens if the compilers do not use these new instructions? The manufacturer pays a cost (monetary and in speed) expecting a benefit that depends on the use that the compilers make of these new instructions. According to [2], when the SPECint92 benchmark is executed on a machine of the 80x86 family (a CISC machine), 96% of the instructions are executed with simple instructions (load, store, add, and y branch) that certainly exist in a RISC machine. Then complex instructions are used only 4% of the time. Apparently, the cost paid by the manufacturer is not justified. But is it a poor decision of the manufacturer or is it rather a weakness in the construction of the compilers? Nowadays it is necessary to build compilers that actually use the hardware's characteristics. All this complexity makes it necessary to change the way in which compilers are built. The use of metaheuristics methods is an alternative.

Compilers consist of two parts: analysis (front end) and synthesis (back end). The process of analysis verifies that the program has no lexical, syntactic and semantic errors. The process of synthesis generates the final code with the details inherent to the target machine. It is at this stage where the largest code optimization sources are found, since it is here where the machine's resources are limited (in the process of analysis the resources are not taken into account, with some exceptions). Within this context there is a long list of optimization problems that have been studied and others that have not. The construction of heuristics and their implementation in compilers has a long way to go, since the problem generating optimum code is undecidable [1]. The latter is what is most important to researchers, since it means that the doors will always be open for invention and application of new heuristics methods to this problem, which according to some authors is the most complex one of informatics engineering.

Metaheuristics methods have been used with great success for solving NP-hard problems [3]. It is clear that metaheuristics require usually computation times that are often significantly larger than that of heuristic. Hence, this aspect also gives an indication where the application of metaheuristics may be most useful (e. g. static problems or problems where the optimization goal is to generate a small code for smart cards, since in these cases computation time is less critical). Why not use them to solve globally the difficult problems that must be faced by the compiler? In this paper we present the compilation problems in which metaheuristics can be applied, a review of the work that has been done along this line, and finally we introduce what we believe is the road to be followed in this development.

2 Optimization Problems

The following are some of the classical optimization problems in compilers [4]:

- Instruction selection
- Instruction scheduling
- Register allocation
- Function inlining

The first three must be solved in order to generate the code; they are of great importance in performance and are largely dependent on the architecture, and that is why they are the most widely studied problems in the literature. The inlining problem, on the other hand, is considered new among the optimizations carried out by the compiler, it is dependent on the architecture, and its impact on the quality of the object code has not yet been established clearly.

2.1 Instruction Selection

Instruction selection (IS) is one of the stages in the generation of object code. In general, the IS problem consists in, given an intermediate representation of the source program, transforming it into an identical logical representation in target machine instructions (available in the form of the machine's instruction set). Multiple restrictions can also be added, such as, for example, defining the

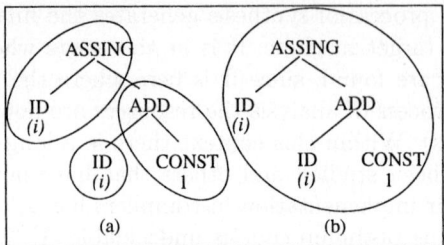

Fig. 1. Intermediate representation tree and two tiling operations for the instruction $i := i + 1$

mode of addressing the data. This problem is generally solved with tree pattern matching techniques [1]. Since generally the source program is in intermediate representation in the form of a syntactic tree, with this technique the target machine instructions are represented as *template patterns*, and what is done is to cover the source program with these patterns following some function objective, such as minimum number of instructions (smaller number of patterns). The set of *template patterns* is extracted (manually) from the set of instructions [5]. With some restrictions, optimum code is generated with dynamic programming [6].

Figure 1 shows the intermediate representation, in the form of a syntactic tree, for the instruction $i := i + 1$. Figures 1.(a) and 1.(b) show two possible *tilings* of the syntactic tree that depend completely on the *template patterns*.

The code of table 1.(a) is the one generated by the tiling of table 1.(a), and similarly, the code of table 1.(b) is the one generated by the tiling of table 1.(b). Let us take codes (a) and (b) of table 1, which correspond to the code $i := i+1$. Both are correct and are equivalent, i.e., they carry out the operation desired by the user or programmer. Also, let us assume that the code of table 1.(a) takes 3 units of time (1 unit for each instruction), and that of table 1.(b) takes 2 units of time (2 units for that single instruction). What happens if the programmer is interested in the size of the code? The answer to this is that, for that requirement, it is certainly better for the compiler to generate the code of table 1.(b). If the programmer is interested in the program's speed, then it is obvious that the second code fulfills the programmer's objective. Depending on the instruction selection scheme used, the code of table 1.(a) could be generated, and this would certainly have an effect from the standpoint of optimization. This is roughly what the compiler must do at this stage, but generally it is not done well, since compiler designers at times use a subset of instructions of the total

Table 1. Instructions generated by the tiling process

1.LOAD EAX, [i] 2.INC EAX 3.STORE [i], EAX	1.INC [i]
(a)	(b)

instructions available to the machine. If each instruction were independent of the others, the exact time for each instruction could be calculated and, with dynamic programming, an optimum solution could be obtained [6]. This involves a great simplification, since in addition to the time for each instruction the latencies of the relation between the instructions must be associated.

2.2 Instruction Scheduling

Modern CPUs can carry out instructions concurrently. Within this stage lies implicit the concept of pipeline [2]: when the instructions are divided into phases, instructions can be superposed so that they can speed up the computation (the use of resources at each stage must be examined in order to be able to superpose instructions). Within the context of the compilers we must exploit this enormous potential of the machines, using at the maximum each clock cycle and each execution phase of the instructions. The last two concepts are exploited in the instruction scheduling (ISC), which in simple words translates into obtaining a rearrangement code such that it makes use of instruction level parallelism (ILP). This generally leads to faster execution by hiding or removing latencies between the instructions. With respect to the rearrangement of instructions, not all of them can be rearranged because there are dependencies between them (data dependency and resource dependency). There are two kinds of instruction scheduling:

- **Dynamic scheduling:** It is decided at execution time and is carried out by the hardware. The idea is to get a group of instructions (usually between 8 and 64) and carry out an arrangement only of those instructions at the time of executing them. This is usually called out of order execution.
- **Static scheduling:** It is decided at compilation time. In compilation all the instructions (dependencies) are available and the arrangement is made based on that.

The scheduling problem as such NP-hard problem [7], has been studied through multiple heuristics methods such as list scheduling, tabu search, simulated annealing, and genetic algorithms, among others. With respect to the instruction scheduling problem, on the contrary, few studies have been made trying to apply the knowledge gathered on the scheduling problem to this phase of the compilation process. This problem, which is NP-hard [8], opens a great possibility of applying the gathered knowledge (mentioned previously) to optimize the compilation process. Very few heuristics methods have been proposed for this problem; they include list scheduling [9], tabu search [10], simulated annealing [11] and ant system [12]. In compiler implementation, list scheduling and some of its variations are the most widely used. When rearranging the instructions it is absolutely necessary to respect dependencies between them. There is a dependency between two instructions if the resource in instruction i that has been loaded or set is used for an operation in instruction j ($i < j$). If there is a dependency, we must not change the order of execution between the operations involved, because the resultant code would not produce the result desired by the programmer.

Table 2. Code (a) with dependencies; (b) without dependencies; and (c) code of (b) with rearrangement

1. LOAD **R0**, a	1. LOAD **R0**, a	1. LOAD **R0**, a
2. ADD **R1**, **R0**	2. ADD R1, **R0**	3. ADD R3, R2
3. ADD **R1**, R4	3. ADD R3, R2	4. LOAD R4, b
4. LOAD **R2**, **R1**	4. LOAD R4, b	5. LOAD R5, c
5. ADD **R1**, **R2**	5. LOAD R5, c	2. ADD R1, **R0**
(a)	(b)	(c)

Table 2.(a) shows an object code in which there are dependencies between the instructions, table 2.(b) shows an object code in which there are dependencies only between the first two instructions, and table 2.(c) shows a rearrangement made to code 2.(b). The first two instructions of table 2.(a) deserve further explanation. There is a data dependence between these two instructions, because the datum loaded in instruction 1 (R0) is used in instruction 2 (sum). The order of these instructions must be preserved. In these same instructions and from the viewpoint of the latencies, it should be noted that in instruction 1 a is being loaded into R0, therefore the value in R0 will not be available until the end of the execution of instruction 1. Under this context, instruction 2 can not start until instruction 1 is completely finished. Here it is said that there is a latency associated with these instructions and use is not being made of their pipeline. In code 2.(a) all the instructions have data dependencies, so the latency mentioned above can not be removed, thereby affecting the program's execution time. In table 2.(b) it is seen that there are dependencies between instructions 1 and 2 only, with the associated latency. In this case the code can be rearranged in such a way that the latencies are decreased. One way of reorganizing the code is shown in table 2.(c). If in this code rearrangement we succeed in hiding some latencies, we would be gaining some time in execution. This is roughly what must be done in this stage of the compilation process.

2.3 Register Allocation

The analysis phase produces an intermediate representation in which for each arithmetic operation, temporary variables are used. In computers there is a small number of registers (8 general purpose registers with 32 bits and 8 registers for floating point operations with 80 bits in the Pentium 80586 architecture), and in an average program there are many declared variables in the program, in addition to those created by the compiler. Under this context there is much demand and little supply. It is for that reason that efficient use of the registers is very important for the performance of the programs in execution time. All this is derived from the large difference in access time of these resources (internal register and main memory). It is important to point out that when code is generated, each variable must be allocated to a register or, in the worse case, to a memory location. When a variable is allocated to memory, instructions must be added to load this value in the register and store it in memory [4]. The life of

Table 3. (a) Code fragment in target machine instructions;(b) final code generated

(a)	(b)
1.LOAD t1,a	1.LOAD R2,a
2.LOAD t2,b	2.LOAD R1,b
3.MUL t1,w	3.MUL R2,w
4.LOAD t3,c	4.LOAD R2, c
5.LOAD t4,d	**5.STORE [MEM1],d**
6.ADD t2,x	6.ADD R1, x
7.ADD t4,y	**7.STORE [MEM2],R2**
8.ADD t3,z	**8.LOAD R2,[MEM1]**
	9.ADD R2,y
	10.STORE [MEM1],R2
	11.LOAD R2,[MEM2]
	12.ADD R2,z

a variable can be defined as the time in which it is used. The beginning of the variable's life is the moment in which it is created, usually the variable's load or initialization. The end of a variable's life is the last instruction that uses that value. This time period is called the variable's life interval. In the optimization phase the number of temporaries used, the life interval of the temporaries (or variables), and the number of registers of the target machine must be examined. With this information an allocation of variables in registers must be found. This process has been usually solved with graph coloring [13], which is NP-hard. In this model each variable a is represented by a node, and each edge of the graph between nodes a and b means that at some instant of time the life intervals of these variables intersect, i.e., they can not de allocated to the same register. The idea consists in coloring the graph with smallest number of colors (one color means one register). There are also register allocations with polynomial algorithms [14, 15], but usually they do not generate a good code.

The code of table 3.(a) is the translation of a program into its equivalent representation in instructions of the target machine. It is seen that there are only temporary values, which must be transferred or assigned to registers for the program's operation. It must also be assumed that each arithmetic instruction must have at least one operand in register. The life intervals of the variables are obtained from the examination of this code, and it is seen that, for example, the life interval of variable $t1$ is from instruction 1 (load) to 3 (use), because after this it is not used any more. The interval of variable $t3$ is from instruction 4 to 8, and so on. From this examination the interference graph, shown in figure 2, is determined.

This graph contains the relations between the life intervals of the variables. There is an edge from u to v if there is an instant in time in which variables u and v are simultaneously alive. If we have two registers in the target machine, we must color the graph with no more than 2 colors. In case the graph is not K-colorable ($K = 2$), some variables must be chosen to be loaded in memory until they are used. In the case of figure 2, temporary 1 and 3 are assigned to

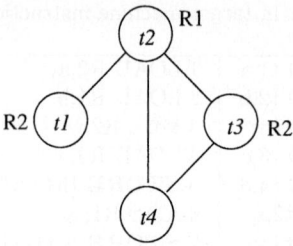

Fig. 2. Interference graph with coloring in 2 registers for code 3

register 2 and temporary 2 is assigned to register 1. Temporary 4 has been chosen to be in memory. Since temporary 4 is not assigned to a register, it must be located at a memory address for the arithmetic operation. This temporary is assigned, according to table 3.(b), to the memory position $MEM1$ (instruction 5). When it is required to use this variable in some arithmetic operation, it must be loaded in a register to perform the operation. If we choose register 2 for this purpose, then the value stored previously in this register must be stored in a memory position for it not to be lost. In the example of figure 3.(b) the value of register 2 is stored in memory position $MEM2$ (instruction 7), then memory position $MEM1$ (instruction 8) is loaded in register 2 and the arithmetic operation (instruction 9) is carried out. After performing the arithmetic operation, the content of register 2 must be transferred to $MEM1$ (instruction 10), since register 2 is not assigned to temporary 4 but to temporaries 1 and 3. Finally, the previous value that was in register 2 must be loaded to continue with the normal operation (instruction 11).

It should also be noted that the relation between the problems described above is important and is based on the order in which they are solved during the compilation process. Once the program's intermediate representation has been obtained, code must be generated for the target machine. This stage is that of instruction selection, which must be carried out before register allocation and instruction scheduling, since these two stages use the code for the target machine. The relation between the two remaining processes is rather diffuse. If we carry out the register allocation first, when instructions are added for loading and storing values in memory and register, further dependencies are created adding more restrictions and making instruction scheduling even more restrictive. If instruction scheduling is done first, the life time of one or more variables may be extended, making the register allocation problem more complex. Usually, the process is the following: first, instruction selection is executed (without hiding the latencies between the instructions and with m registers or temporary values), followed by instruction scheduling (with m registers or temporary variables), and finally register allocation (in k registers, usually $k << m$). Since in this last stage new instructions are introduced (to load values in registers and memory positions), it is a good but costly idea to carry out again the instruction scheduling to remove the possible new latencies added to the program. This is what the GCC [16] compiler does, for example.

3 State of the Art

The use of metaheuristics methods in compilation is scarce. Some of the first reports are those of Williams [17] and Nisbet [18], who used a genetic algorithm to determine how to optimize the cycles in a parallel compiler.

Later we find Beaty's work [10, 19, 20], that solves the instruction scheduling problem using a list scheduling algorithm, but to carry out the calculation of the priorities of each instruction a genetic algorithm and a tabu search algorithm are used. The idea is interesting, but no results are shown in the papers. Later, Sweany and Beaty [11] did similar work using simulated annealing, comparing it to traditional list scheduling, and they report a 6% gain.

More recently we find the work of Kri and Feeley [21], who use a genetic algorithm to solve jointly the register allocation and instruction scheduling problems. With this technique the authors show gains of up to 7% compared to traditional methods.

Mark Stephenson et. al. [22] use genetic programming to optimize two compilation heuristics: predication hyperblock formation and register allocation. For that purpose they carry out various tests with different benchmarks, getting as a result for the hyperblock heuristics an average improvement in speed of 23% for register allocation, 6% for individual applications, and 3% for general purpose heuristics.

Keith D. Cooper et. al. [23] were interested in decreasing the size of the code generated by a compiler, and they used an AG to solve ten optimization problems. They carried out various benchmarks, comparing them with traditional methods, and got improvements of up to 40% in code size, and in many cases they improved compilation speed.

Daez and Kri [24] reported gains of up to 20% for a particular case with respect to the GCC compiler using a genetic algorithm to solve the function inlining problem.

Demiroz et al. [25] report a hybrid evolutionary algorithm to solve the register allocation problem in embedded devices, showing important gains in performance and an important increase in compilation time.

Wang et al. [12] used an ant system together with list scheduling to solve the instruction scheduling problem, achieving better performance than the traditional methods, but still far from the optimum.

Finally, along a different line, we find ACOVES (analysis of compiler options via evolutionary algorithm) [26], which implements an AG to decide which of the optimization options of the GCC compiler is the most appropriate for each program.

4 Future Steps

The most direct way of applying metaheuristics methods in compilation is to replace the heuristics used to solve the optimization problems by metaheuristics that can solve the same problem. This is what has been done so far in general terms. For example, to solve the register allocation problem, the heuristics used by the compiler is replaced by metaheuristics to color the graph. The results obtained along this line are interesting, but their impact on performance is not important. We think that, along this same line, important gains can be obtained if the problems are solved globally. For instance, currently register allocation is solved at the base block or at most the procedure level, producing medium size degrees of interference, which are colored successfully with the simple heuristics used. However, if the interference graph were generated for the whole program, it would have such a large number of nodes that the heuristics would not be capable of yielding good results, and that is where the use of metaheuristics could provide an important gain. By working with the global interference graph, many accesses to memory could be avoided, for example in the backups generated in the calls for procedures and in the use of global variables. Similarly, if the other problems were solved globally, the gains could be substantial.

On the other hand, we think that metaheuristics is sufficiently powerful to solve more than one problem at a time. In view of the interrelation between the different problems, a global solution (which would consider two or more problems) would certainly achieve more important gains.

Finally, and thinking of a more aggressive approach, the idea would be to create an intermediate representation for the source program and codify it, so that (with information about the hardware) it may represent any equivalent program, i.e. that we may be able to represent all the possible programs that carry out the task defined by the source code. This would be the search space and we would use metaheuristics to search for the best solution in that space.

5 Conclusions

In this paper we have introduced briefly the main optimization problems faced by the compiler, and we have shown that the work done in the area is scarce and that the use of metaheuristics in compilation is very primitive. With this we expect to open the doors so that all the knowledge those years of use of metaheuristics for the solution of optimization problems may be applied to the process of compilation.

References

1. Aho, A.V., Ullman, J.D.: Principles of Compiler Design. Addison-Wesley (1978)
2. Hennessy, J.L., Patterson, D.A.: Computer Architecture a Quantitative Approach. Second edn. Morgan Kaufmann Publishers (1996)
3. Davis, L.: Handbook of Genetic Algorithms. Van Nostrand Reinhold, New York (1991)
4. Appel, A.W.: Modern Compiler Implementation in ML: Basic Techniques. Cambridge University Press (1997)
5. Praet, J.V., Goosens, G., Lanner, D., Man, H.D., Synthesis, H.: Instruction set definition and instruction selection for asip (1994)

6. Aho, A.V., Ganapathi, M., Tjiang, S.W.K.: Code generation using tree matching and dynamic programming. ACM Trans. Program. Lang. Syst. **11** (1989) 491–516
7. Garey, M., Johnson, D.: Computers and Intractability: A Guide to the Theory of NP-Completeness. W.H. Freman and Company, New York (1979)
8. Bernstein, D., Rodeh, M., Gertner, I.: On the complexity of scheduling problems for parallel/pipelined machines. IEEE Trans. Comput. **38** (1989) 1308–1313
9. Landskov, D., Davidson, S., Shriver, B., Mallett, P.W.: Local microcode compaction techniques. ACM Comput. Surv. **12** (1980) 261–294
10. Beaty, S.J.: Genetic Algorithms Versus Tabu Search for Instruction Scheduling. International Conference on Neural Network and Genetic Algorithms (1993) 496–501
11. Sweany, P., Beaty, S.: Instruction Scheduling Using Simulated Annealing. 3rd International Conference on Massively Parallel Computing Systems (1998)
12. G. Wang, W.G., Kastner, R.: Instruction Scheduling Using MAX- MIN Ant Colony Optimization. Great Lakes Symposium on Very Large Scale Integration (2005)
13. Chaitin, G.J., Auslander, M.A., Chandra, A.K., Cocke, J., Hopkins, M.E., Markstein, P.W.: Register Allocation Via Coloring. Computer Languages (1982) 47–57
14. Poletto, M., Sarkar, V.: Linear Scan Register Allocation. ACM Transactions on Programming Languages and Systems (TOPLAS) (1999) 895–913
15. Johansson, E., Sagonas, K.F.: Linear scan register allocation in a high-performance erlang compiler. In: PADL '02: Proceedings of the 4th International Symposium on Practical Aspects of Declarative Languages, London, UK, Springer-Verlag (2002) 101–119
16. Stallman: GNU C User and Porting Guide. Technical report, MIT (1991)
17. Williams, K., William, S.: Genetic Compilers: A New Technique for Automatic Parallelisation. 2nd European School of Parallel Programming Environments (ESPPE 96) (1996) 27–30
18. Nisbet, A.P.: GAPS: Genetic Algorithm Optimised Parallelisation. 7th Workshop on Compilers for Parallel Computing (1998) 172–183
19. Beaty, S.J.: Genetic Algorithms for Instruction Sequencing and Scheduling. Workshop on Computer Architecture Technology and Formalism for Computer Science Research and Applications (1992)
20. Beaty, S.J.: Genetic Algorithms and Instruction Scheduling. 24th Annual International Symposium on Microarchitecture (1991) 206–211
21. Kri, F., Feeley, M.: Genetic instruction scheduling and register allocation. XXIV International Conference of the Chilean Computer Science Society (2004) 76–83
22. Stephenson, M., O'Reilly, U.M., Martin, M.C., Amarasinghe, S.: Genetic programming applied to compiler heuristic optimization. In Ryan, C., Soule, T., Keijzer, M., Tsang, E., Poli, R., Costa, E., eds.: Genetic Programming, Proceedings of EuroGP'2003. Volume 2610 of LNCS., Essex, Springer-Verlag (2003) 238–253
23. Cooper, K.D., Schielke, P.J., Subramanian, D.: Optimizing for reduced code space using genetic algorithms. In: Workshop on Languages, Compilers, and Tools for Embedded Systems. (1999) 1–9
24. Baez, M., Kri, F.: Inlining de funciones con algoritmos genticos. In: Workshop de Inteligencia Artificial, Jornadas Chilenas de Computacin. (2004)
25. Demiroz, B., Topcuoglu, H., Kandemir, M.: A hybrid evolutionary algorithm for solving the register allocation problem. In Gottlieb, J., Raidl, G.R., eds.: Evolutionary Computation in Combinatorial Optimization – EvoCOP 2004. Volume 3004 of LNCS., Coimbra, Portugal, Springer Verlag (2004) 62–71
26. Ladd, S.R.: Acovea: Analysis of compiler options via evolutionary algorithm (2005)

Comparison of SVM-Fuzzy Modelling Techniques for System Identification

Ariel García-Gamboa, Miguel González-Mendoza, Rodolfo Ibarra-Orozco,
Neil Hernández-Gress, and Jaime Mora-Vargas

Intelligent Systems Research Group, Tecnológico de Monterrey,
Campus Estado de México, Km 3.5 Carretera al Lago de Guadalupe,
Col. Margarita Maza de Jurez, Atizapán de Zaragoza,
Estado de México, Mexico, 52926
Phone: +52 55 5864 5751
{ariel.garcia, mgonza, rodolfo.ibarra, ngress, jmora}@itesm.mx

Abstract. In recent years, the importance of the construction of fuzzy models from measured data has increased. Nevertheless, the complexity of real-life process is characterized by nonlinear and non-stationary dynamics, leaving so much classical identification techniques out of choice. In this paper, we present a comparison of Support Vector Machines (SVMs) for density estimation (SVDE) and for regression (SVR), versus traditional techniques as Fuzzy C-means and Gustafson-Kessel (for clustering) and Least Mean Squares (for regression), in order to find the parameters of Takagi-Sugeno (TS) fuzzy models. We show the properties of the identification procedure in a waste-water treatment database.

1 Introduction

The system identification is a very difficult task which consists of determining the mathematical model of a system or predicting its behavior even if it is a non linear system. Different approaches have been recently developed like in [1] which is based in the Takagi-Sugeno (TS) fuzzy modelling technique. The performance of this approach was improved in [2], [12], taking advantage of the support vector density estimation method.

The construction procedure of a TS model consists in two steps. First one, the fuzzy sets (membership functions) in the rule antecedents are defined by means of a priori knowledge on the process (expertise) or by data-driven techniques. Second one, the parameters of the consequent functions (typically linear) are identified by Least Mean Squares methods.

The principal problem of the construction procedure resides in the definition of the antecedent membership functions. Several efforts deal with algorithms making a fuzzy clustering in the Cartesian product-space of the inputs and outputs. With this kind of techniques, one obtains initially multidimensional fuzzy sets, which are either used in the model directly or after projection onto the individual antecedent variables. Their performance depends on the number of clusters in data, the shape and volume of every cluster, the initialization of the

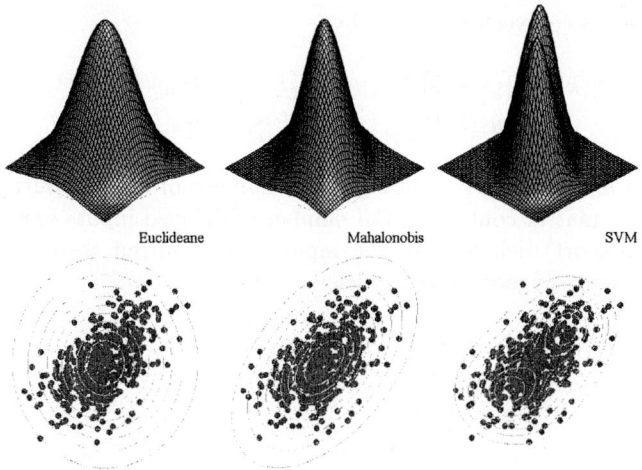

Fig. 1. Different distance norms

clustering algorithm and the distribution of the data patterns. In algorithms with point prototypes, the type distance defines the shape of the clusters. For instance, the Fuzzy C-Means (FCM) algorithm uses the Euclidean norm distance, appropriate for spherical shapes. The Gustafson-Kessel (GK) algorithm uses fuzzy covariance matrices in order to obtain a Mahalonobis norm distance [5]. SVM constructs clusters bounds from which one computes orthogonal distances, see Fig. 1.

For the estimation of the consequent functions parameters, we make a comparison of traditional Least Mean Squares versus Support Vector Machines for regression (SVR). This paper is organized as follows: the Takagi-Sugeno fuzzy model is explained is section 2. Section 3 gives a brief description of Support Vector Machines for regression and density estimation, section 4 introduces the general identification method, section 5 shows the experimental results in a waste-water treatment database and , finally, some conclusions are given.

2 Takagi-Sugeno Fuzzy Model Structure

Consider an unknown non linear MIMO system $y = f(u)$ with n_i inputs: $u_k = [u_{1k}, \ldots, u_{nik}]^T$ and n_0 outputs: $y_k = [y_{1k}, \ldots, y_{nok}]^T$ with $k = 1, \ldots, l$, respectively. Following the notation introduced in (Babuska, et al. 1998), denote q the backward operator $qy(k) = y(k-1)$ and the capital letters A and B polynomials in q, $A = a_0 + a_1q + a_2q^2 + \ldots$. Given two integers, $m < n$, define an ordered sequence of delayed samples of y as:

$$\{y(k)\}_m^n = [y(k-m), y(k-m-1), \ldots, y(k-n)]$$

The MISO model has the form:

$$y_l(k+1) = \Im_l(x_l(k)), \quad l = 1, \ldots, n_o, \qquad (1)$$

where the regression vector is given by:

$$x_l(k) = [\{y_1(k)\}_0^{n_{yl1}}, \{y_2(k)\}_0^{n_{yl2}}, \ldots, \{y_{n_o}(k)\}_0^{n_{yln_o}},$$
$$\{u_1(k)\}_{n_{dl1}}^{n_{ul1}}, \{u_2(k)\}_{n_{dl2}}^{n_{ul2}}, \ldots, \{u_{n_i}(k)\}_{n_{dln_i}}^{n_{uln_i}}].$$

Here n_y is a n_o x n_o matrix containing the number of delayed outputs n_u and, n_d are n_0 x n_i matrix containing the number of delayed inputs and the number of pure (transport) delays from the input to the output respectively. $\Im_l$ are rule-based Takagi-Sugeno fuzzy models:

$$R_{li}: If \quad x_l(k) \quad is \quad \Omega_{li} \tag{2}$$
$$then \quad y_{li}(k+1) = A_{li}y(k) + B_{li}x(k) + c_{li} \tag{3}$$
$$i = 1, \ldots, k_l, \tag{4}$$

where Ω_{li} is the antecedent fuzzy set of the ith rule, $A_{li} = [A_{li1}, \ldots, A_{lin_o}]^T$ and $B_{l_i} = [B_{li1}, \ldots, B_{lin_i}]^T$ are vectors of polynomials. K_l is the number of rules in the lth model.

The fuzzy sets can be defined by multivariate membership functions $\omega(x(k))$: $\Re^{p_l} \rightarrow [0, 1]$, where $p_l = \sum_{j=1}^{n_o} n_{ylj} + \sum_{j=1}^{n_i} n_{ulj} + 1$ is the dimension of the antecedent space. Alternatively, the antecedent of (2) can be given in the conjunctive form:

$$R_{li}: If \quad x_l(k) \quad is \quad \Omega_{li1} \quad and \quad \ldots \quad and \quad If \quad x_l(k) \quad is \quad \Omega_{lip} \tag{5}$$
$$then \quad y_{li}(k+1) = A_{li}y(k) + B_{li}u(k) + c_{li} \tag{6}$$
$$i = 1, \ldots, k_l. \tag{7}$$

The output of the TS model is computed by the weighted mean:

$$y_l(k+1) = \frac{\sum_{i=1}^{K_l} \omega_{li}(x_l(k))y_{li}(k+1)}{\sum_{i=1}^{K_l} \omega_{li}(x_l(k))} \tag{8}$$

In the product space form (2), $\omega_{li}(x(k))$ is simply the membership degree $\mu_{\omega_{li}}(x(k))$. In the conjunctive form (5), $\omega_{li}(x(k))$ is given by the product of the individual antecedent membership degrees.

3 Support Vector Machines

In agreement with the inductive principle of the structural risk minimization, [11], in the statistical learning theory, a function, which describes correctly a training set X and which belongs to a set of functions with a low VC (Vapnik-Chervonenkis) dimension, will have a good generalization capacity independently of the input space dimension. Based on this principle, the Support Vector Machines [11] have a systematic approach to find a linear function, belonging to a set of functions with a low VC dimension.

3.1 Support Vector Machines for Classification

The principal characteristic of SVMs for pattern recognition is to build an optimal separating hyperplane between two classes. If this is not possible, the second great property of this method resides in the projection of X space into a Hilbert space F of highest dimension, through a function $\varphi(x)$. One example is the internal product evaluated using kernel functions:

$$k(x_i, x_j) = \phi(x_i)^T \phi(x_j), \quad i,j = 1, \ldots, l. \tag{9}$$

satisfying Mercer conditions, like the Gaussian kernel:

$$k(x_i, x_j, \sigma) = \frac{1}{\sigma\sqrt{2\pi}} \exp\left[-\frac{(x_i - x_j)^2}{2\sigma^2}\right] \tag{10}$$

Thus, thanks to the freedom of using different types of kernels, the optimal separating hyperplane corresponds to different non-linear estimators in the original space. In the density estimation problem, we consider the training data:

$$x_1, \ldots, x_l \in X \tag{11}$$

where l is the number of observations and X is a distribution in the space R_n. The goal is to find a function $f(x)$ having a value larger than or equal to zero in an area that captures more of the learning points and a negative value in the opposite case.

3.2 Support Vector Machines for Density Estimation

For SVMs, in density estimation, we have only one class that we can separate of the origin with an optimal hyperplane (Schlkopf, et al. 1999). In order to build a SVM for the density estimation problem with a nonlinear decision function in a nonlinearly-separable case, one has to solve the following dual quadratic optimization (QP) problem:

$$\text{Maximize} \quad L_D = \sum_{i,j=1}^{l} \alpha_i \alpha_j k(x_i, x_j) - \sum_{i=1}^{l} \alpha_i k(x_i, x_i) \tag{12}$$

$$\text{subject to} \quad 0 \leq \alpha_i \leq \frac{1}{vl}, \quad \sum_i \alpha_i = 1 \tag{13}$$

where α_i are Lagrange multipliers introduced to transform the primal quadratic problem with linear constraints into the dual problem showed above. The parameter $(0,1)$ establishes an upper limit of the fraction of vectors remaining out of the learned distribution (outliers) and a lower limit of the fraction of support vectors. Thus, it is defined the decision function

$$f(x) = \text{sgn}\left(\sum_i \alpha_i k(x_i, x) - b\right) \tag{14}$$

which takes the value of +1 in a small region that captures most of the training patterns and the value −1 for other regions. The examples x_i associated with Lagrange multipliers α_i greater than zero are called support vectors, since they have a significant contribution in (5). Geometrically, these vectors are on the border of the evaluation function, so we can compute the value of b exploiting the fact that for every α_i, its corresponding x_i satisfies.

$$b = \sum_{j=1}^{l} \alpha_j k(x_i, x_j) \tag{15}$$

3.3 Support Vector Machines for Regression

SVMs consist in finding the parameters α_i^* and β_i^*, $i = 1, \ldots, l$ that maximize the functional.
Maximize

$$L_D(\alpha, \beta) = -\epsilon \sum_{i=1}^{l} (\alpha_i + \beta_i) + \sum_{i=1}^{l} y_i(\alpha_i + \beta_i) - \frac{1}{2} \sum_{i,j=1}^{l} (\alpha_i + \beta_i)(\alpha_j + \beta_j) H(x_i, x_j) \tag{16}$$

$$\text{subject to} \quad \sum_{i=1}^{l} (\alpha_i) = \sum_{i=1}^{l} (\beta_i), 0 \leq \alpha_i, \beta_i \leq C, i = 1, \ldots, l \tag{17}$$

given the training data (x_i, y_i), $i = 1, \ldots, l$, an inner product kernel H, an insensitive zone ϵ, and a regularization parameter C. The dual problem can be solved via standard quadratic programming. Once solutions α_i^* and β_i^*, $i = 1, \ldots, l$ are calculated, the regression function is constructed in terms of these values as

$$f(x) = \sum_{i=1}^{l} \gamma_i^* H(x_i, x) \tag{18}$$

where

$$\gamma_i^* = \alpha_i^* - \beta_i^*. \tag{19}$$

In the regression problem, both ϵ and C which play an important role for noise and smoothness of the function, respectively, have to be selected a priori. However, systematic selection of these parameters has not been proposed.

4 General Identification Method

It is necessary that the user defines the structure of the model, it means to determine matrices n_y, n_u and n_d, on the basis of prior knowledge and/or by comparing several candidate structures in terms of the prediction error or other suitable criteria [8].

After the definition of the structure, one must estimate the parameters of the n_o MISO models (2), the antecedent membership functions and the consequent polynomials. Perhaps, the most important parameter is the number of clusters, problem known as cluster validity problem [4]. It can be specified by the user or sought automatically by some algorithms like substractive clustering [3].

Following the method presented in [1], the identification method proceeds in four steps:

1. From the input-output sequences $\{x(k), y(k)\}_{k=1}^{n_d}$, form the nonlinear regression problem of eq. (1), using the user-specified structural parameters n_x, n_y and n_d.
2. Partition the data into a set of local sub models by using SVM clustering in the Cartesian product space XY.
3. Determine the antecedent membership functions from the cluster parameters, tested algorithms are: FCM, GK and SVMDE.
4. Given the antecedent membership functions, estimate the consequent parameters, tested algorithms are LMS and SVR.

5 Identification Example

As an example, we choose a FAMIMO [1] SIMO benchmark, simulating a continuous flow aerated lagoon for waste-water treatment in the pulp and paper industry, a process characterized by nonlinear and non-stationary dynamics [6]. The bioreactor contains a mixed microbial population, called biomass, growing on a blending of two types of pollutant substrates, an energetic and xenobiotic one. The benchmark multi-variable control objective consists in controlling, from the waste-water dilution rate, the biomass in the bioreactor outflow as well as the residual concentration of xenobiotic and energetic pollutant substrates. We have an identification database and a validation one.

Table 1. Comparison of the identification (learning phase) by means of the methods analyzed

	FCM with LMS	GK with LMS	SVDE with LMS	SVDE with SVR
Miomass concentration	99,52129 %	99,09118 %	99,7514 %	99,9975 %
Xenobiotic substrate	99,37025 %	99,2381 %	99,7024 %	99,9995 %
Energetic substrate	98,0838 %	96,5305 %	99,8371 %	99,9977 %

The structure of the SIMO model is selected in a way that every output depends on the other ones as we can see in the structure of the matrix n_y. Vectors n_x and n_d specify only a delay in the input.

---
[1] FAMIMO: Fuzzy Algorithms for the control of Multi-Input, Multi-Output Processes. LTR Project 21911 Reactive Scheme.

Table 2. Comparison of the validation (testing phase) by means of the methods analyzed

	FCM with LMS	GK with LMS	SVDE with LMS	SVDE with SVR
miomass concentration	96,6248 %	97,8446 %	98,9975 %	99,2048 %
Xwnobiotic substrate	98,4156 %	96,8206 %	99,5591 %	99,9387 %
Energetic substrate	66,2819 %	70,6666 %	99,7849 %	99,8810 %

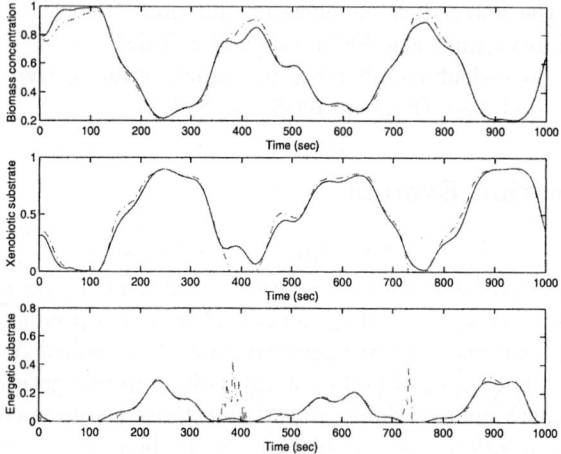

Fig. 2. Comparison of the process output, solid line, with the FCM-LMS fuzzy model, dashed line

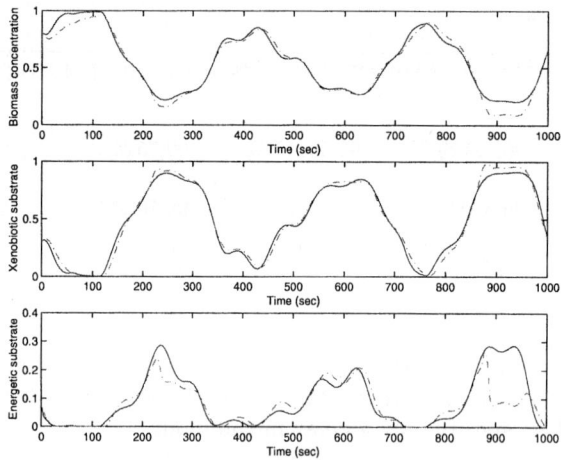

Fig. 3. Comparison of the process output, solid line, with the GK-LMS fuzzy model, dashed line

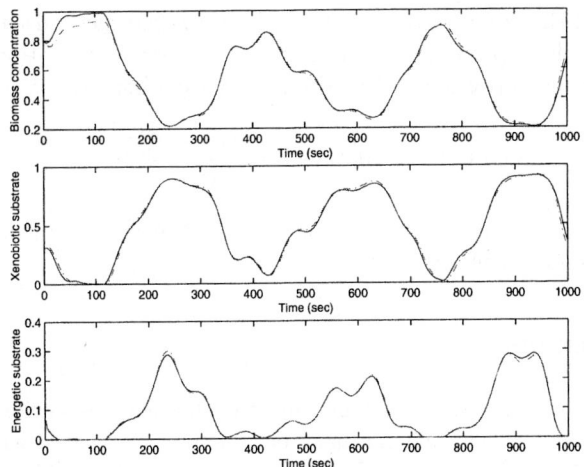

Fig. 4. Comparison of the process output, solid line, with the SVDE-LMS fuzzy model, dashed line

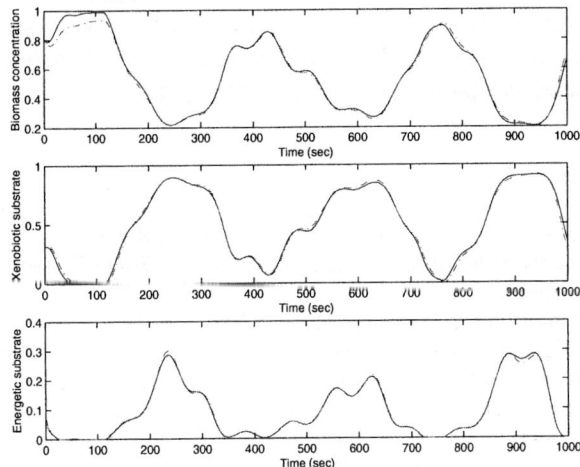

Fig. 5. Comparison of the process output, solid line, with the SVDE-SVR fuzzy model, dashed line

The fuzzy identification method, proposed by Babuska in [1], joined by three different clustering algorithms for the antecedent parameters and two methods for the consequent estimation was used. Thus, the comparisons were performed between the following methods:

1. Gustafson-Kessel and Least Mean Squares.
2. Fuzzy C-Means and Least Mean Square.
3. SVM Density Estimation and Least Mean Squares.
4. SVM Density Estimation and SVM Regression algorithms.

Table 1 shows the comparison results of the proposed methods in the learning phase and Table 2 presents the results of the system validation. The values correspond to the variance accounted for (VAF) performance index given by:

$$VAF = 100\% \left[1 - \frac{var(y-y1)}{var(y)}\right]$$

Figures 2, 3, 4 and 5 show the outputs for the validation data set of the compared Takagi-Sugeno models.

6 Conclusions

In this paper, a comparison of four different strategies is performed in order to identificate the Takagi-Sugeno fuzzy parameters. Compared with traditional methods, like Fuzzy C-means or Gustafson-Kessel and Least Mean Squares, the Support Vector Machine learning algorithm is able to make a best approximation of the clusters, see Fig. 1, and, for the estimation of the consequent functions parameters, results also show that a better approximation is obtained. Consequently, the best results were obtained by using SVM density estimation to calculate the antecedent membership functions and the SVM regression algorithm to find the consequent parameters of the fuzzy model.

References

1. Babuska, Robert et al. (1998). Identification of MIMO systems by input-output TS fuzzy models. IEEE International Conference on Fuzzy Systems. Pag. 657-662, Anchorage, Alaska.
2. Babuska, Robert and Verbruggen, H. B. (1994). Applied fuzzy modelling. In proceedings IFAC Symposium on Artificial Intelligence in Real Time Control, pag. 61-66, Valencia, Spain. Chiu, S. L. (1994). Fuzzy model identification based on cluster estimation. Journal of Intelligent Fuzzy Systems, vol. 2, pag. 267-278.
3. Chiu, S. L. (1994). Fuzzy model identification based on cluster estimation. Journal of Intelligent Fuzzy Systems, vol. 2, pag. 267-278.
4. Guillaume, S. (2001). Designing Fuzzy Inference Systems from Data: An Interpretability-Oriented Review. IEEE Transactions on Fuzzy Systems, 9(3): 426-443.
5. Gustafson, D. and Kessel, W. (1979). Fuzzy clustering with a fuzzy covariance matrix. In Proc. IEEE CDC, pag. 761-766, San Diego, USA.
6. Youssef, C. Ben (1997). Benchmark of a wastewater treatment process. LAAS Rep. 97458. Contrat FAMIMO, November.
7. Schlkopf, Bernhard et al. (1999). Estimating the Support of a High-Dimensional Distribution. Technical Report Microsoft Research. 27 November 1999.
8. Takagi, T. and Sugeno, M. (1985). Fuzzy identification of systems and its application to modelling and control. IEEE Transaction on Systems, Man and Cybernetics, 15(1):116-132.
9. Takagi, T. and Yasukawa, T. (1993). A fuzzy logic approach to qualitative modelling. IEEE Trans. Fuzzy Systems, 1:7-31, 1993.

10. Titli, A. (2001). Logique floue et systmes flous. Notes de cours de lInstitut National des Sciences Appliques, Toulouse, France.
11. Vapnik, Vladimir N. (1998). Statistical Learning Theory. Wiley-Interscience.
12. González-Mendoza, Miguel. SVM Clustering for Identification of Takagi-Sugeno Fuzzy Models. 5th IFAC International Symposium on Intelligent Components and Instruments for Control Applications (SICICA'2003), Aveiro (Portugal), 2003.

Time-Series Forecasting by Means of Linear and Nonlinear Models

Janset Kuvulmaz[1], Serkan Usanmaz[2], and Seref Naci Engin[1]

[1] Department of Electrical Engineering, Yildiz Technical University,
34349 Besiktas, Istanbul Turkey
{janset, nengin}@yildiz.edu.tr
[2] Department of Quantitative Methods, Marmara University,
34722 Goztepe, Istanbul Turkey
susanmaz@lycos.com

Abstract. The main objective of this paper is two folds. First is to assess some well-known linear and nonlinear techniques comparatively in modeling and forecasting financial time series with trend and seasonal patterns. Then to investigate the effect of pre-processing procedures, such as seasonal adjustment methods, to the improvement of the modeling capability of a nonlinear structure implemented as ANNs in comparison to the classical Box-Jenkins seasonal autoregressive integrated moving average (ARIMA) model, which is widely used as a linear statistical time series forecasting method. Furthermore, the effectiveness of seasonal adjustment procedures, i.e. direct or indirect adjustments, on the forecasting performance is evaluated. The Autocorrelation Function (ACF) plots are used to determine the correlation between lags due to seasonality, and to determine the number of input nodes that is also confirmed by trial-and-errors. The linear and nonlinear models mentioned above are applied to aggregate retail sales data, which carries strong trend and seasonal patterns. Although, the results without any pre-processing were in an acceptable interval, the overall forecasting performance of ANN was not better than that of the classical method. After employing the right seasonal adjustment procedure, ANN has outperformed its linear counterpart in out-of-sample forecasting. Consequently, it is confirmed that the modeling capability of ANN is improved significantly by using a pre-processing procedure. The results obtained from both ARIMA and ANNs based forecasting methodologies are analyzed and compared with Mann-Whitney statistical test.

1 Introduction

ANNs have been widely used as an alternative to traditional time series forecasting methods in many areas of science such as ecology, hydrology, finance, electricity and control [1-6]. During the last decade, there have been many comparative studies investigating time series analyses using ANNs and statistical methods such as Box-Jenkins ARIMA, Holtz-Winter and Multiple Regression. The findings out of those works report confusing results. While some claim that ANNs are able to model seasonal patterns effectively without any pre-processing [7-10] and also the work of Kang [11], which is a highly cited PhD dissertation, some others conclude that seasonal adjustment should be done before forecasting in order to outperform the traditional forecasting techniques mentioned above [12, 13]. In addition, there are some works on hybrid, cascade or auxiliary usage of neural networks along with traditional models [14, 15] and also several comparative reviews on the forecasting capabilities of ANNs and other statistical methods [16-18].

As the literature and the current work point out, ANNs can have superior features over conventional methods in modeling and forecasting. They can deal with complex patterns and establish models reflecting nonlinear relationships without pre-assumption about the system because of their data-driven nature. ANNs perform well even with a missing or incomplete data with their capability of generalization. Furthermore, being universal approximators, it is proven mathematically that they can approximate any continuous function to any desired accuracy. However, this is valid with the expense of the fact that there is no limit about the number of layers and nodes. Also, the underlying mechanism of ANNs is nonlinear and not predictable. Errors cannot be determined before the ANN has performed. There is no standard way for choosing the number of layers, nodes or the training algorithm. They act as a black box and, their performance inherently depends on the amount of training data [19]. All these drawbacks may cause under or over fitting problem, which make them far from being universal approximators in practice.

Alternatively, a number of statistical methods are available for dealing with times-series data. The most popular one is known as Autoregressive Integrated Moving Average (ARIMA) model suggested by Box and Jenkins in 1976 [20]. The purpose of ARIMA is to identify patterns and make predictions out of time-series data. An ARIMA model is a combination of three simple models- an autoregressive (AR), an integration (I) and a moving average model (MA). The autoregressive model tries to find relationships between the values based on how far apart they are in time. The integration isolates the absolute level of the time-series value from the differences in that level from one time point to the next. And finally, the moving average portion of the model smoothes out the quirks, making it easier to examine the underlying factors that influence the process.

The model can also accommodate seasonal components, where the series tend to move in a cyclical way over time. Such a component does not literally have to follow the seasons of the year. It can have a cycle of a day, week, or a month as well as a year. Under these circumstances, seasonal components of ARIMA can be included to make the predictions more accurate. The real strengths of ARIMA method is that it allows a proper modeling of time-series data. However, the method can be difficult to interpret and requires statistical expertise.

The current study is concerned to find out if ANNs, as being universal approximator, are able to model and forecast time-series with strong trend and seasonal fluctuations. If not, how their forecasting performance could be bettered with seasonal adjustments. Results are compared with Box-Jenkins ARIMA model.

The paper is organized as follows; the next section presents both ANN and Box-Jenkins models. In the third section seasonal adjustment methods are introduced. In the fourth section research methodology and data description is given. The fifth section includes the empirical results and their interpretation. And the conclusion is given as usual in the last section.

2 Nonlinear vs. Linear Models

This section briefly presents ANNs based forecasting methodologies considered as nonlinear, and the statistical method, ARIMA, emerging as a powerful linear time-series analyzing tool.

2.1 Neural Network Architecture

ANNs are a class of nonlinear and non-parametric models, which is inspired from the human nerve system. ANNs develop a relationship between variables using input-output mapping.

The most popular ANN architecture for time-series forecasting is the multilayer feed-forward neural network model [21, 8, 13]. The architecture is composed of an input layer with nodes which are the previous lagged observations, hidden layer(s) and output layer with linear or nonlinear activation functions. Then the network model can be described as

$$y_t = \alpha_0 + \sum_{j=1}^{n} \alpha_j f\left(\sum_{i=1}^{m} \beta_{ij} y_{t-i} + \beta_{0j}\right) + \varepsilon_t \qquad (1)$$

where m is the number of input nodes, n is the number of hidden nodes, f is the activation function and α_j is a vector of weights from the hidden nodes to the output nodes. β_{ij} are weights from the input nodes to the hidden nodes. α_0 and β_{0j} are weights coming from the bias terms.

ANN's forecasting capability predominantly depends on its architecture. Since it is not a deterministic method, constructing a most appropriate model for a particular problem is usually quite cumbersome. It must be noted that there is no exact theoretical way of selection procedure for any of the parameters. Therefore, the most common way to implement an ANN model is still using heuristic assumptions based on experimental studies and trial-errors.

Number of Input Nodes
Number of input nodes is related with learning capability of ANNs. In previous works, most of the researchers determined the number of input nodes experimentally. Besides, some of them tried to analyze time-series with various statistical and optimization methods in order to establish a sound basis for determining the number of input nodes. In this particular work reported here, ACF analyses are utilized in determining the number of input nodes, which is confirmed by trial-error based experiments.

Number of Hidden Nodes and Hidden Layers
Number of hidden nodes is an indicative criterion for the generalization capability of ANNs. The hidden nodes allow ANNs to discover the pattern in time-series and

construct a mapping function between input and output data. Indeed, several methods have been reported in literature. However, the most common way of selection procedure for number of hidden nodes is again based on trial-errors. About selecting the number of hidden layers, there is a consensus on choosing the number of hidden layers as not more than two layers to solve forecasting problems.

Number of Output Nodes
Determination of the number of output nodes depends on the forecasting problem of interest. Here, if the forecast is performed only one month into the future, one output node is employed. On contrary, if the forecast is done on multiple months, i.e. 12 months projection, 12 output nodes are used.

Activation Function
Activation function constructs a mapping between the input and output, which is mostly a nonlinear relationship. In general, logistic function is preferred for hidden nodes because of its advantageous features such as being continuous, differentiable at any points and monotonically increasing function. It also accepts inputs varying from $-\infty$ to $+\infty$ and squashes the output into a range of [0 1]. Here in this paper, logistic function is employed for hidden layers and a linear function for output layer.

Training Algorithm
The modeling capability of neural networks depends on the usage of an efficient learning algorithm. One of the most popular training algorithms is the classical back-propagation (BP) algorithm, which is based on the gradient descent method. However, standard BP has some deficiencies such as having slow convergence rate and getting stuck in local minima. Taking these shortcomings into consideration Levenberg-Marquard (LM) algorithm, which is proven as a more robust and fast learning procedure is employed. As summarized in [22], the LM algorithm is an approximation to Newton's method.

2.2 ARIMA (Box-Jenkins) Model

Autoregressive Integrated Moving Average (ARIMA) is popularized by George Box and Gwilym Jenkins [20]. The Box-Jenkins ARIMA approach primarily employs three linear filters; Integration (I), autoregressive (AR) and moving average (MA) filters. The time-series of interest is processed successively by these filters applied until no more additional characteristic feature can be extracted.

At the first stage, the aim is to identify patterns and cycles such as seasonality and the order of autoregressive and moving average terms, which display the characteristics of the data.

The AR and MA filters are used in order to generate errors in a random or white noise characteristic. Integrating all the three filters (AR, I and MA) with proper orders, identification stage is terminated. The obtained model is called Autoregressive Integrated Moving Average model of order ARIMA(p,d,q). So, a nonseasonal ARIMA(p,d,q) model can be expressed as a combination of previous observations (p), differencing (d) and previous errors (q).

Usually, economic and financial data display monthly seasonality, which is seen as periodic fluctuations correspond to one year period. The nonseasonal ARIMA model, ARIMA(p,d,q), can be extended to handle the seasonal feature as ARIMA(p, d, q) $(P,D,Q)_s$, where s represents the number of lags that the time-series repeats itself.

A seasonal ARIMA (p,d,q) $(P,D,Q)_s$ model, in general, can be expressed as,

$$\phi_p(B)\Phi_p(B^s)(1-B)^d(1-B^s)^D y_t = \theta_q(B)\Theta_Q(B^s)\varepsilon_t$$
$$\phi_p(B) = 1 - \phi_1 B - \phi_2 B^2 - \ldots - \phi_p B^p$$
$$\Phi_p(B) = 1 - \Phi_s B^s - \Phi_{2s} B^{2s} - \ldots - \Phi_{Ps} B^{Ps} \qquad (2)$$
$$\theta_q(B) = 1 - \theta_1 B - \theta_2 B^2 - \ldots - \theta_q B^q$$
$$\Theta_Q(B) = 1 - \Theta_s B^s - \Theta_{2s} B^{2s} - \ldots - \Theta_{Qs} B^{Qs}$$

where s is the seasonal length (e.g. $s = 4$ for quarterly data and $s = 12$ for monthly data), B is the back shift operator defined by $B^k y_t = y_{t-k}$ and ε_t is a sequence of white noise with zero mean and constant variance. $(1-B)^d$ and $(1-B^s)^D$ are the non-seasonal and seasonal differencing operators, respectively. The model is often referred to as the ARIMA(p,d q) $(P,D,Q)_s$ model

After the identification step for seasonal data is performed, the P, D, Q parameters must be estimated. It must be noted that even though the Autocorrelation Function (ACF) and the Partial Autocorrelation Function (PACF) are the two most useful tools for time-series model identification, trial-error and the need for human judgments are still inevitable because of the insufficient information provided by ACF and PACF plots. As confirmed by Jhee et al. [15], a systematic search through reasonable combinations of AR and MA orders is believed to form the best choice for the model. The diagnostic checking step is used to validate the model. After the model is validated by diagnostic checking, the model can be applied for forecasting.

3 Seasonal vs. Seasonally Adjusted Data

As mentioned above, seasonality can be defined as a pattern of cycles, which repeats itself regularly in a specific time period. Therefore, it is difficult to interpret if the fluctuations in the data are due to changes in the level of data itself or due to regular variations. The adjustment makes the data easier to interpret and avoids misleading that may be caused by seasonal changes.

Another issue that must be considered is the selection of seasonal adjustment method, (either direct or indirect). If a time-series is a sum of series of components that are seasonally adjusted, it is referred to as indirectly adjusted aggregate series. The alternative is the direct adjustment obtained by applying the seasonal adjustment procedure directly to the aggregate data. Under most circumstances, the direct and indirect adjustments for an aggregate series are not identical [23].

It should be noted that selecting a deseasonalizing procedure depends on various criteria, such as diversity of data sources and existence of different working day effect or dominating trends [24]. However, the choice is left to the experiences of the analyst, most of the time.

4 Methodology

Within the framework of the current study, monthly aggregate retail sales forecasts are carried out. The reason to work with the aggregate retail sales data is that it involves highly strong trend and seasonal patterns, plotted in Figure 1. The data is obtained from Economagic [25], which is an online data library presenting real world economical data from various official sources.

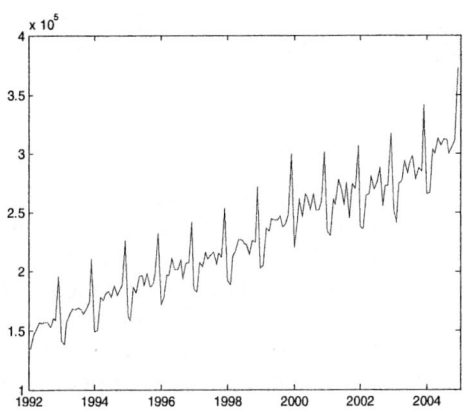

Fig. 1. The aggregate retail sales data recorded during the period of 1992-2004

As seen, the total sampling period spans from January 1992 to December 2004. The last 12 observations are held in reserve to test both the one-step and multi-step forecasting performance of the models established. The rest of the data is used to construct the model parameters.

The forecasting performances of one linear model (ARIMA) and three nonlinear models (ANNs trained with raw data, ANNs trained with directly seasonally adjusted data and ANNs trained with indirectly seasonally adjusted data) to assess one-step ahead and multi-step ahead forecasting experiments. A number of comparisons are performed by means of statistical methods, where MAPE (mean absolute percentage error) and APE (absolute percentage error) are used as performance indices.

During the time-series analysis experiments, both one-step and multi-step ahead forecasts are performed. In one step forecast, forecast only one month into the future is done. As the data got real, they were included into the computation. Forecasts for 12 months are obtained by this way. Multi-step forecasts, on the other hand, present the forecast results for 12 months projection.

In neural network based forecasting, the standard fully connected three layer feedforward neural network architecture is employed. Although various numbers of input nodes (1, 2, 3, 4, 12, 13 and 24) were experimented on trial-error basis, the final number of input nodes is determined via ACF analyses. 12 hidden node levels from 2 to 24 with an increment size of 2 are used. Consequently, 84 different networks are employed in order to find the appropriate model with a logistic and linear activation functions for hidden and output nodes respectively, and LM method is chosen as a learning algorithm. The neural network model constructions and computations are carried out in MATLAB 6.5.

To determine the effect of seasonal adjustment, both seasonal and seasonally adjusted (directly and indirectly adjusted) data are used for comparison purpose.

For ARIMA method, ACF and PACF plots are examined for the identification of the characteristics of the data. The data is differenced for one order to remove the trend pattern and again differenced for 12 orders to remove the seasonal pattern. After the trend and seasonal patterns are removed, the best fitting parameters for the model are estimated as ARIMA $(0,1,1)(3,1,3)_{12}$. All the ARIMA model fittings and forecasting are conducted on MINITAB 13.20.

5 Results

The out-of-sample forecast performance of the models for one-step forecast and for multi-step forecast are reported in Table 1. Generally, all the models performed satisfactory according to their MAPE values ranging from 0.67 to 2.04. Although the performance results are given with MAPE, the evaluation of these results can be misleading due to the extreme Absolute Percentage Error values that may arise in out-of-sample forecasts. Therefore, the paired comparison tests are realized by Mann-Whitney (M-W) tests using the Absolute Percentage Errors (APE).

Table 1. Out-of-sample (2004) forecasting error measure MAPE (%) values of the models

Model	One-Step Forecast	Multi-Step Forecast
Model 1 - ANN (Unadjusted Data)	2.04	1.83
Model 2 - ANN (Directly Adjusted Data)	1.40	1.57
Model 3 - ANN (Indirectly Adjusted Data)	0.77	0.67
Model 4 - ARIMA	1.17	1.46

Table 2. Statistical comparison of forecasting models

One-Step Forecast	M-W Test Statistics (*p-values*)	Multi-Step Forecast	M-W Test Statistics (*p-values*)
Model 1 vs. Model 2	47 *(0.149)*	Model 1 vs. Model 2	49 *(0.184)*
Model 1 vs. Model 3	34 *(0.028)**	Model 1 vs. Model 3	23 *(0.005)**
Model 1 vs. Model 4	49 *(0.184)*	Model 1 vs. Model 4	54 *(0.299)*
Model 2 vs. Model 3	59 *(0.453)*	Model 2 vs. Model 3	38 *(0.05)**
Model 2 vs. Model 4	64 *(0.644)*	Model 2 vs. Model 4	71 *(0.954)*
Model 3 vs. Model 4	49 *(0.184)*	Model 3 vs. Model 4	38 *(0.05)**

* Significant at the 0.05 level with Mann-Whitney test

The paired comparisons of four different methods are shown in Table 2 under one-step forecast and multi-step forecast titles according to Mann-Whitney (M-W) tests. The results for one-step forecast indicate that there is a significant difference in forecasting performances only between Model 1 and Model 3 (starred *p*-values). However, the M-W tests for one-step forecast display no difference among any other paired models. The results for multi-step forecasts indicate that the forecasting performance of Model 3 is superior to the other three models. On the other hand, the forecasting performances of the other three models are found as identical according to M-W tests. As seen from the first two comparisons under both one- and multi-step forecasts, the ANN models trained with different seasonally adjusted data exhibit different forecasting performances with respect to ANN model trained with unprocessed data. Figure 2 is given for comparison purpose for four models for both one-step and multi-step forecasting.

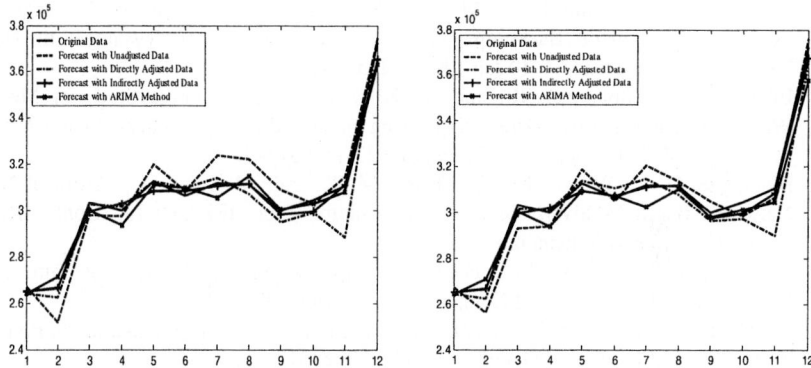

Fig. 2. Actual Data and Both One-Step and Multi-Step Forecasts

6 Conclusion

In this paper, modeling and forecasting capability of both ANNs and Box-Jenkins ARIMA methods are examined and then monthly aggregate retail sales, which exhibit strong trend and seasonal characteristics, are evaluated with one-step and multi-step forecasts for 12 months. In the light of the experimental forecasting results presented in the previous section, the following is concluded.

Even though ARIMA method gives small MAPE values for both one-step and multi-step forecasting, there is no statistically significant difference on forecasting performances of ANN trained with unprocessed data and ARIMA models.

The forecasting performance of ANNs can be improved with a proper adjustment procedure. It is shown that with the indirect adjustment method, ANN performance is significantly improved in multi-step forecasts but the improvement is not satisfactory in one-step forecasts compared to ARIMA.

Finally, the results indicate that ANNs are able to model seasonality without any adjustment. However, seasonal adjustment improves forecasting performance of ANNs significantly especially in multi-step forecasts. This confirms our expectation that not only using the seasonal adjustment procedure itself is crucial but also the way the adjustment procedure applied to improve ANNs forecasting capability. As a future work, the overall forecasting performance results should be tested and confirmed by analyzing data sets exhibiting different characteristics.

References

1. Corani, G.: Air Quality Prediction in Milan: Feed-forward Neural Networks, Pruned Neural Networks and Lazy Learning. Ecological Modeling, (2005) 1-17
2. Prybutok, V.R., Yi, J., and Mitchell, D.: Comparison of Neural Network Models with ARIMA and Regression Models for Prediction of Houston's Daily Maximum Ozone Concentrations. European Journal of Operational Research 122, (2000) 31–40
3. Atiya, A., El Shoura, S., Shaheen, and S., El-Sherif, M.: Application of Neural Networks the Problem of Forecasting the Flow of the River Nile. Neural Networks for Signal Processing. VII. Proceedings of the 1997 IEEE Workshop 24-26 Sep (1997) 598-606
4. Refenes, A.N., Azema-Barac, M., and Karoussos, S.A.: Currency Exchange Rate Forecasting by Error Backpropagation. Proceedings of the Twenty-Fifth Hawaii International Conference 7-10 Jan 1992 Volume: 4, 504-515
5. Elkateb, M.M., Solaiman, K., and Al-Turki, Y.: A Comparative Study of Medium-Weather-Dependent Load Forecasting Using Enhanced Artificial/Fuzzy Neural Network and Statistical Techniques. Neurocomputing 23, (1998) 3–13
6. Montague, G. A., Willis, M. J., Tham, M. T., and Morris A. J. : Artificial Neural Networks Based Multivariable Predictive Control. Proc. IEE 2nd Int. Conf. Artificial Neural Networks. Bournemouth, U.K. 1991
7. Tang, Z., and Fishwick, P.A.: Feedforward Neural Nets as Models for Time Series Forecasting. ORSA Journal of Computing 5 (4), (1993) 374–385
8. Sharda, R., and Patil, R.: Connectionist Approach to Time Series Prediction: an Empirical Test. Journal of Intelligent Manufacturing 3, (1992) 317-323
9. Franses, P.H., and Draisma, G.: Recognizing changing seasonal patterns using artificial neural networks. J. of Econometrics 81 (1997) 273-280
10. Alon, I., Qi, M., and Sadowski, R.J.: Forecasting aggregate retail sales: a comparison of artificial neural networks and traditional methods. Journal of Retailing and Consumer Services 8 (2001) 147}156
11. Kang, S.: An investigation of the use of feedforward neural networks for forecasting. Ph.D. Dissertation, Kent State University, Kent, Ohio, (1991)
12. Nelson, M., Hill, T., Remus, W., and O'Connor, M.: Time Series Forecasting Using Neura Networks: Should the Data be Deseasonalized First?. Journal of Forecasting 18 (1999) 359-367
13. Zhang, G. P., and Qi, M.: Neural network forecasting for seasonal and trend time series. E. J. of Operational Research 160 (2005) 501–514
14. BuHamra, S., Smaoui, N., and Gabr, M.: The Box–Jenkins analysis and neural networks: prediction and time series modelling. Applied Mathematical Modelling 27 (2003) 805–815
15. Jhee, W.C., Leef, K.C. and Lees, J.K. A neural network approach for the idenmeation of the Box-Jenkins model. Network 3 (1992) 323-339.
16. Marquez, L., Hill, T., and O'Connor, M.; Remus, W.: Neural network models for forecast: a review. System Sciences, 1992. Proceedings of the Twenty-Fifth Hawaii International Conference (1992) 494 - 498
17. Hill, T., Marquez, L., O'Connor, and M., Remus, W.; Artificial neural networks for forecasting and decision making. International Journal of Forecasting 10, (1994) 5–15.
18. Zhang, G., Patuwo, B.E., and Hu, M.Y.: Forecasting with artificial neural networks: The state of the art. Int. Journal of Forecasting 14 (1998) 35–62
19. Nam, K., and Schaefer, T., Forecasting international airline passenger traffic using neural networks. Logistics and Transportation 31 (3), (1995) 239–251
20. Box, G.E.P.,and Jenkins, G.M.: Time Series Analysis: Forecasting and Control. Holden-Day, San Francisco, CA. (1976)

21. Lapedes, A., and Farber, R.: Nonlinear signal processing using neural networks: prediction and system modeling. Technical Report LA-UR-87-2662, Los lamos National Laboratory, Los Alamos, NM. (1987)
22. Hagan, T.M., and Menhaj, M.B.: Training Feedforward Networks with the Marquardt Algorithm. IEEE Transactions on neural networks. Vol. 5, (1994)
23. Hood, C.C. and Findley, F.F.: Comparing Direct and Indirect Seasonal Adjustments of Aggregate Series. White Paper, US Census Bureau, Washington, DC
24. Atuk, O.,and Ural, B.P.: Seasonal Adjustment Methods: An Application to the Turkish Monetary Aggregates, White Paper, Central Bank of Republic of Turkey
25. www.economagic. com

Perception Based Time Series Data Mining with MAP Transform

Ildar Batyrshin and Leonid Sheremetov

Mexican Petroleum Institute, Eje Central Lazaro,
152, Mexico, D.F., 07730
{batyr, sher}@imp.mx

Abstract. Import of intelligent features to time series analysis including the possibility of operating with linguistic information, reasoning and replying on intelligent queries is the prospective direction of development of such systems. The paper proposes novel methods of perception based time series data mining using perceptual patterns, fuzzy rules and linguistic descriptions. The methods of perception based forecasting using perceptual trends and moving approximation (MAP) transform are discussed. The first method uses perception based function for modeling qualitative forecasting given by expert judgments. The second method uses MAP transform and measure of local trend associations for description of perceptual pattern corresponding to the region of forecasting. Finally, the method of generation of association rules for multivariate time series based on MAP and fuzzy trends is discussed. Multivariate time series are considered as description of system dynamics. In this case association rules can be considered as relationships between system elements additional to spatial, causal etc. relations existing in the system. The proposed methods are illustrated on examples of artificial and real time series.

1 Introduction

Time series data mining is a rapidly developing area of research. The tasks of time series data mining include indexing, clustering, classification, anomaly detection, rule discovery, summarization, forecasting etc [1, 7, 10]. Till now most of decision-making procedures in problems related with time series analysis are based on human decisions supported by statistical, data mining or data processing software. Import of intelligent features to these systems including the possibility of operating with linguistic information, reasoning and replying on intelligent queries is a perspective direction of research [12]. Computational Theory of Perceptions (CTP) [11] can serve as a basis for such extension of these systems. The methodology of CTP proposes methods of reasoning with linguistic information based on fuzzy models. The goal of perception based time series data mining (PTSDM) may be considered as a development of models and methods based on CTP that can be useful for supporting decision making procedures in problems related with the systems described by time series data bases. Generally these procedures should give replies on fuzzy queries, realize perception based inference and do perception based forecasting. Effective realization of a PTSDM system is impossible without the use of efficient time series data mining methods developed so far by data mining community. But the use of fuzzy concepts and perceptual patterns in description of time series data bases requires a development of new and adaptation of existing methods of TSDM supporting representation and processing of fuzzy and perception based information in time series data bases (TSDB). Several approaches to description of patterns and shapes of time series, generation of fuzzy rules and extraction of linguistic summaries from time series data bases were recently developed [1, 2, 4, 5, 7, 8, 10]. These methods can be used as basic methods in PTSDM.

In this paper we propose several new methods of PTSDM that use perception based functions, fuzzy rules and moving approximation (MAP) transform. Perception based fuzzy functions [3] use linguistic scaling and fuzzy granulation of trends and shapes. In Section 2 we propose the method of application of this technique to modeling expert knowledge in qualitative time series forecasting when time series history is absent. Section 3 applies MAP transform and association function based on MAP [5] to define time series forecasting method based on time series history. The proposed method of forecasting uses the pattern in time series history which has maximal similarity with prototype goal pattern. Perception based functions and MAP transform both deal with trends of time series: the first formalize expert evaluations of trends whereas the second extracts the trends from time series. Finally, in Section 4 we consider the method of construction of fuzzy association rules based on fuzzy perception based trends and MAP.

2 Perception Based Functions in Qualitative Forecasting

Here we propose the methods of perception based forecasting that use representation of qualitative expert predictions by perception based functions (PBF). PBF gives natural way to represent linguistic expert judgments in qualitative forecasting [6] and resulting fuzzy function can be easily tuned due to its parametric definition.

Qualitative forecasting methods use the opinions of experts to subjectively predict future events [6]. These methods are usually used when historical data either are not available or are scarce, for example to forecast sales for the new product. In subjective curve fitting applied to predicting sales of a new product the product life cycle is usually thought of as consisting of several stages: "growth", "maturity" and "decline". Each stage is representing by qualitative patterns of sales as follows [6]:

- *"Growth"* stage: Start Slowly, then Increase Rapidly, and then Continue to Increase at a Slower Rate;
- *"Maturity"* stage, sales of the product stabilize: Increasing Slowly, Reaching a Plateau, and then Decreasing Slowly;
- *"Decline"* stage: Decline at an Increasing Rate.

The "growth" stage is subjectively represented as S-curve, which could then be used to forecast sales during this stage. To predict time intervals for each step of "growth" stage the company uses the expert knowledge and its experience with other products. The subjective curve fitting is very difficult and requires a great deal of expertise and judgment [6]. The methods of reconstruction of perception based functions [3] can support the process of qualitative forecasting. The qualitative patterns of sales may be represented by perceptual patterns of trends and each stage may be represented by the sequence of fuzzy time intervals with different trend patterns. For example, S-curve modeling *"Growth"* stage can be represented by rules:

R_1: *If T is Start of Growth Stage then V is Slowly Increasing and Convex.*
R_2: *If T is Middle of Growth Stage then V is Quickly Increasing.*
R_3: *If T is End of Growth Stage then V is Slowly Increasing and Concave.*

In these rules, *T* denotes time intervals and *V* denotes the sale volumes. The time intervals *Start of Growth Stage* etc. define fuzzy intervals and corresponding perceptual trends of sales describe sub-shapes of *S*-curve.

Perception based functions use linguistic scaling of trend patterns and fuzzy granulation of linguistic scales. Below is an example of linguistic scale of *Increasing-Decreasing* patterns: L_D= <EXTREMELY QUICKLY DECREASING, QUICKLY DECREASING, DECREASING, SLOWLY DECREASING, CONSTANT, SLOWLY INCREASING, INCREASING, QUICKLY INCREASING, EXTREMELY QUICKLY INCREASING>. In abbreviated form this scale will be written as follows: L_D= <1:EQD, 2:QDE, 3:DEC, 4:SDE, 5:CON, 6:SIN, 7:INC, 8:QIN, 9:EQI>. The granulation of this scale may be done by suitable crisp or fuzzy partition of the set of possible slope values of linear functions approximating time series in sliding windows. For example, if perceptual pattern *4:SDE* is given by fuzzy set defined on the set of possible slope values [-10,10] then a slope value of linear function approximating time series values in some window will belong to this fuzzy set with some degree. The central slope values of perceptual patterns will define directions of the change of time series values [3]. Fig. 1 shows examples of such directions corresponding to grades *7:INC* (dashed line) and *4:SDE* (dotted line). Perceptual patterns will be given as fuzzy sets around these directions.

The scale of concave-convex patterns can have the following grades: L_{CC}= <STRONGLY CONCAVE, CONCAVE, SLIGHTLY CONCAVE, LINEAR, SLIGHTLY

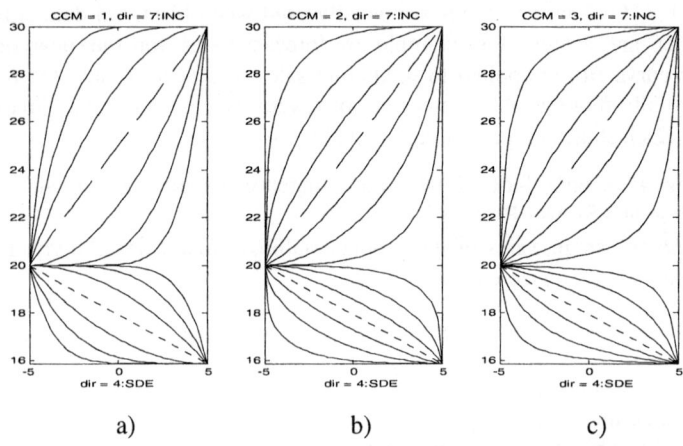

Fig. 1. Granulation of convex-concave patterns in directions 7:*INC* (dashed line) and 4:*SDE* (dotted line) obtained by a) BZ- modification; b) BY-modification, and c) BS-modification

CONVEX, CONVEX, STRONGLY CONVEX>. The possible granulation of such patterns is considered below.

The grades of these scales can be used for generation of linguistic descriptions like *"QUICKLY INCREASING and SLIGHTLY CONCAVE"*, *"SLOWLY DECREASING and STRONGLY CONVEX"* etc. Such perception based descriptions may be represented as suitable convex-concave modification of corresponding linear patterns of directions and by further fuzzification of obtained curves. Several methods of convex (CV) and concave (CC) modifications were proposed in [3].

BZ-modifications are based on Zadeh operation of contrast intensification:

$$CC(y) = y_2 - \frac{(y_2 - y)^2}{y_2 - y_1}, \quad CV(y) = y_1 + \frac{(y - y_1)^2}{y_2 - y_1},$$

where y is a modified function and y_1, y_2 are the minimal and the maximal values of $y(x)$ on considered interval of input variable x. The grades of L_{CC} scale are represented by the following patterns, respectively: P_{CC} = <*CC(CC(CC(y))), CC(CC(y)), CC(y), y, CV(y), CV(CV(y)), CV(CV(CV(y)))*>. Fig. 1a) shows these patterns applied to directions 7.*INC* and 4.*SDE*. For example, the pattern *SLOWLY DECREASING AND STRONGLY CONVEX* is represented by the undermost curve in Fig.1a) and calculated by $f= CV(CV(CV(y)))$ where y is the line corresponding to 4:*SDE*.

BY-modification uses the following CC-CV modifications of linear function y:

$$CC_t(y) = y_2 - \sqrt[t]{(y_2 - y_1)^t - (y - y_1)^t}, \quad CV_t(y) = y_1 + \sqrt[t]{(y_2 - y_1)^t - (y_2 - y)^t},$$

where t is a parameter, $t \in (0,1]$. We have: $CC_1 = CV_1 = I$, where I is the identity function: $I(y)=y$. Fig.1b) shows CC-CV patterns in directions 7:*INC* and 4:*SDE* corresponding to all grades of the linguistic scale L_{CC} and obtained by BY-modifications <$CC_{0.4}$, $CC_{0.6}$, $CC_{0.8}$, I, $CV_{0.8}$, $CV_{0.6}$, $CV_{0.4}$> respectively.

BS-modification applies the following CC-CV modifications of linear function y:

$$CC_s(y) = y_1 + \frac{(y_2 - y_1)(y - y_1)}{(y_2 - y_1) + s(y_2 - y)}, \quad CV_s(y) = y_2 - \frac{(y_2 - y_1)(y_2 - y)}{(y_2 - y_1) + s(y - y_1)},$$

where $s \in (-1,0]$. We have $CC_0 = CV_0 = I$. Fig. 1c) shows CC-CV patterns obtained by BS-modification of directions 7:*INC* and 4:*SDE* corresponding to all grades of L_{CC} scale as follows: <$CC_{-0.95}$, $CC_{-0.8}$, $CC_{-0.5}$, I, $CV_{-0.5}$, $CV_{-0.8}$, $CV_{-0.95}$> respectively.

The linear and convex-concave patterns may be used for crisp and fuzzy modeling of perception based time series patterns. Fuzzy modeling uses fuzzification of perceptual trend patterns [3]. This fuzzification may be defined parametrically depending on the type of fuzzy set used for fuzzification and on parameters of this fuzzy set. Perception based function is given by the concatenation of perceptual trend patterns defined on a sequence of connected crisp or fuzzy intervals. This PBF may be used for evaluation or forecast of function values for given values of argument.

The possible reconstruction of rules R_1-R_3 considered above is shown in Fig. 2. The resulting fuzzy function is obtained as a concatenation of fuzzy perception based patterns defined on the sequence of fuzzy intervals given in antecedents of rules R_1-R_3. The width of this fuzzy function corresponds to uncertainty of forecasting. This

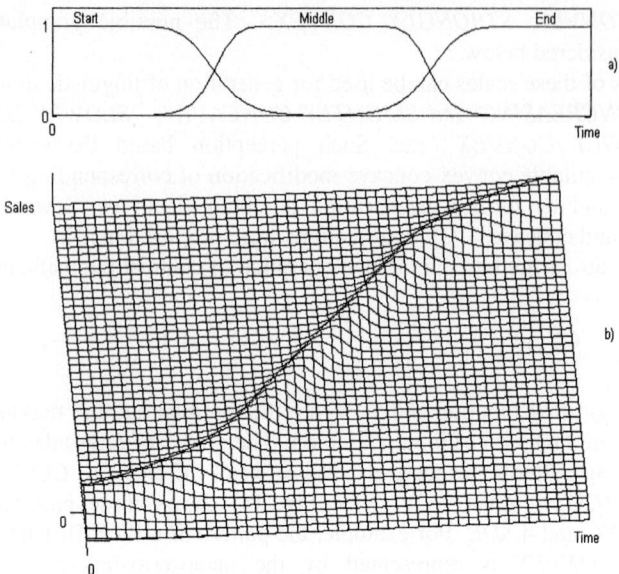

Fig. 2. Fuzzy perception based S-curve modeling product life cycle

PBF can be used for forecasting of sells of new product. Perception based functions corresponding to "Maturity" and "Decline" stages can be reconstructed similarly.

The proposed approach to qualitative forecasting reflects the style of expert linguistic judgments. It supposes a scaling and granulation of fuzzy expert evaluations. Parameterization of resulting fuzzy function gives possibility to tune it easily for adjusting the resulting curve to expert opinions.

3   Forecasting with Perceptual Patterns Defined by MAP

In this section we introduce the main definitions of MAP transform and describe its use for perception based forecasting. A time series (y,t) is a sequence (y_i, t_i), $i \in I = (1,..., n)$, such that $t_i < t_{i+1}$ for all $i = 1,..., n-1$, where y_i and t_i are real values of time series and time points, respectively. A time series (y,t) will be denoted also as y. A window W_i of a length $k > 1$ is a sequence of indexes $W_i = (i, i+1,..., i+k-1)$, $i \in \{1,...,n-k+1\}$. Denote $y_{W_i} = (y_i, y_{i+1},..., y_{i+k-1})$. A sequence $J=(W_1, W_2,..., W_{n-k+1})$ of all windows of the length k, $(1 < k \le n)$, is called a sliding (moving) window.

A linear function $f_i = a_i t + b_i$ with parameters $\{a_i, b_i\}$ that minimize the criterion

$$Q(f_i, y_{W_i}) = \sum_{j=i}^{i+k-1} (f_i(t_j) - y_j)^2 = \sum_{j=i}^{i+k-1} (a_i t_j + b_i - y_j)^2,$$

is called a linear regression or least squares approximation of y_{W_i}. It is well known that the optimal values of parameters a_i, b_i can be calculated as follows:

$$a_i = \frac{\sum_{j=i}^{i+k-1}(t_j-\overline{t_i})(y_j-\overline{y_i})}{\sum_{j=i}^{i+k-1}(t_j-\overline{t_i})^2}, \; b_i = \overline{y_i} - a_i\overline{t_i}, \text{ where } \overline{t_i} = \frac{1}{k}\sum_{j=i}^{i+k-1}t_j, \; \overline{y_i} = \frac{1}{k}\sum_{j=i}^{i+k-1}y_j.$$

Suppose $a = (a_1, ..., a_{n-k+1})$ is a sequence of slope values of linear approximations of time series (y,t) in sliding window of size k. A transformation $MAP_k(y,t) = a$ is called a moving approximation (MAP) transform of time series y. The slope values $a = (a_1, ..., a_{n-k+1})$ are called local trends. The following theorem [5] gives simple method of MAP transform calculation for time series with a fixed time step.

Theorem 1. Suppose time points $t = (t_1, ..., t_n)$ are increasing with a constant step h such that $t_{i+1} - t_i = h$ for all $i = 1, ..., n-1$. Then the values of MAP transform $MAP_k(y,t)$ can be calculated as follows:

$$a_i = \frac{6\sum_{j=0}^{k-1}(2j-k+1)y_{i+j}}{hk(k^2-1)}, \; i \in (1,2,...,n-k+1). \quad (1)$$

Suppose $y = (y_1,...,y_n)$ and $x = (x_1,...,x_n)$ are two time series, and $MAP_k(y) = (a_{y1}, ..., a_{ym})$, $MAP_k(x) = (a_{x1}, ..., a_{xm})$, $k \in \{2,...,n-1\}$, $m = n-k+1$. The function

$$coss_k(y,x) = \frac{\sum_{i=1}^{m} a_{yi} \cdot a_{xi}}{\sqrt{\sum_{i=1}^{m} a_{yi}^2 \cdot \sum_{j=1}^{m} a_{xj}^2}}$$

is called a measure of local trend associations. This measure equals to cosine of angle between two vectors of slope values $MAP_k(y)$ and $MAP_k(x)$: $coss_k(y,x) = cos(\angle(MAP_k(y), MAP_k(x)))$. From definition of this measure it follows that it takes values in real interval $[-1,1]$. The important property of this measure consists in it invariance to independent linear transformations of time series.

Theorem 2. Suppose (y,t) and (x,t) are two time series and $L_1(y,t)=(p_1y+q_1,r_1t+s_1)$ and $L_2(y,t)=(p_2y+q_2,r_2t+s_2)$, $(p_1, p_2, r_1, r_2 \neq 0)$, are their linear transformations then

$$coss_k(L_1(y,t),L_2(x,t)) = sign(p_1) \cdot sign(r_1) \cdot sign(p_2) \cdot sign(r_2) \cdot coss_k((y,t),(x,t)).$$

Corollary 3. Measure |coss| is invariant under independent linear transformations of time series.

Definition 4. Suppose $y = (y_1,...,y_n)$ and $x = (x_1,...,x_q)$ are two time series, $(n,q \geq 2)$ and $y_P = (y_i,..., y_{i+j-1})$, $i \in \{1,...,n-j+1\}$, $j \in \{2,...,min(n,q)\}$, is a pattern in y of length j. For any $k \in \{2,...,j\}$ define a fuzzy set P of TS patterns $x_F = (x_i,..., x_{i+j-1})$, $i \in \{1,..., q-j+1\}$, with membership values $\mu_P(x_F) = 0.5(coss_k(y_P,x_F)+1)$. This fuzzy set will be called a perceptual pattern of y_P in x defined by MAP_k.

From the property of *coss* it follows that the definition of fuzzy set above is consistent, i.e. $\mu_P(x_F) \in [0,1]$ and $\mu_P(x_F) = 1$ if $y_P = x_F$. From Theorem 2 it follows that the membership values $\mu_P(x_F)$ are invariant under all monotone transformations of time and time series values when $p_1, p_2, r_1, r_2 > 0$.

An important part of most problems in time series data mining is to find a time series pattern x_F most similar to pattern y_P. In terms of perception based patterns defined by *MAP* this problem is formulated as a search of patterns x_F in time series x with maximal membership value in perceptual pattern defined by y_P. The solution of this problem will use a calculation of *MAP* transforms $MAP_k(x)$ and $MAP_k(y_P)$, and then a search of subsequence $MAP_k(x)_m$ in $MAP_k(x)$ of the same length m as the length of $MAP_k(y_P)$ such that the $cos(\angle(MAP_k(y_P), MAP_k(x)_m))$ takes a maximal value. The pattern $x_F = (x_i, \ldots, x_{i+j-1})$, generating this sequence by *MAP*, such that $MAP_k(x_F) = MAP_k(x)_m$ will have maximal membership value in perceptual pattern defined by y_P. This method is used below in perceptual forecasting by MAP.

The idea of the forecasting method based on MAP consists in the following. The goal prototype pattern y_P consists of the values of time series y located directly before the time point t_k where time series value is forecasted. The method finds perceptual pattern of prototype y_P in the history of the time series. N patterns, where N is a given number, that have maximal membership values in this perceptual pattern are used for forecasting values in time point t_k. The slope values located immediately after these patterns are weighted by their membership values and weighted average of these slope values is used for calculation the forecasted value in time point t_k. This forecasted value is used as a part of new perceptual pattern for forecasting time series value in new time point t_{k+1}, etc.

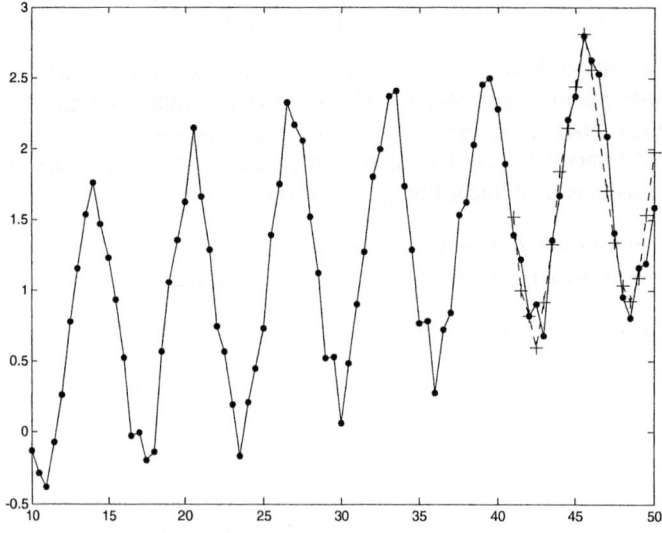

Fig. 3. Results of perceptual forecasting with prototype patterns: • - time series values, + - forecasted values

The example of application of this method to forecasting values in several sequential time points is shown in Fig. 3. In this example we used prototype pattern containing 8 points located before forecasted value. $N = 3$ patterns in time series history most similar to prototype pattern are used for forecasting slope value located after prototype. This slope value by means of formula (1) is used for calculation a time series value in time point t_k. This value is presented on Fig. 3 by leftmost "+". This forecasted value is used further as a last point in new prototype pattern for forecasting time series value (the next "+") in the following time point etc. As shown in Fig. 3 the forecasting gives good evaluation of time series values in the last 19 time points.

4 Association Rules with Perception Based Trends

Suppose $y = (y_1,\ldots,y_n)$ and $x = (x_1,\ldots, x_n)$ are two time series, $(n \geq 2)$. In this section we consider the method of construction of association rules in the form *If Y is A then X is B*, where A, B are perception based patterns like *Slowly Increasing*, etc in time series y and x. Suppose $W_1,\ldots,W_N$ is a set of windows where perception based patterns are considered and $\mu_A(W_i)$, $\mu_B(W_i)$ are membership values of y_{Wi} and x_{Wi} in perception based patterns A and B respectively.

The support and confidence measures [7,8] for considered fuzzy association rules can be defined as follows [4]:

$$supp(R) = \frac{1}{N}\sum_{i=1}^{N}(\mu_A(W_i) \wedge \mu_B(W_i)),\ conf(R) = \frac{\sum_{i=1}^{N}(\mu_A(W_i) \wedge \mu_B(W_i))}{\sum_{i=1}^{N}\mu_A(W_i)}. \tag{2}$$

Generation of association rules with considered window-wise conditions is illustrated here by an example of time series data base of 13 indicators of Mexican economics [9] shown in Fig. 4.

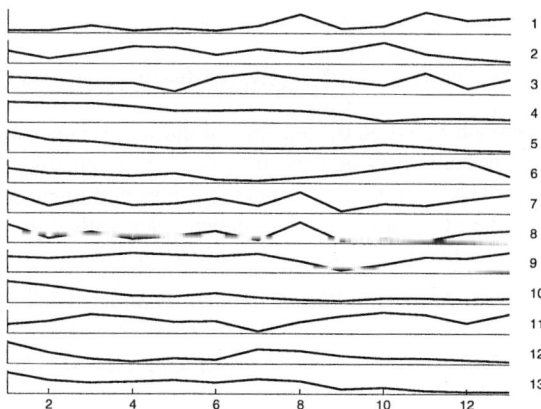

Fig. 4. Time series of 13 indicators of Mexican economics

These time series correspond to the following indicators: 1: Unemployment Rate; 2: Real average; 3: Consumer Price Index; 4: Yearly Percent change; 5: Retail sales; 6: Industrial Production; 7: Exports (Monthly % Change); 8: Imports (Monthly % Change); 9: Merchandise Trade Balance (millions of US$); 10: Interbank Cetes; 11: MSE Market Index; 12: Mexican pesos per US $; 13: Mexican pesos per Canadian $.

For each time series y we considered the set of windows $W_i = (i, i+1)$ and calculated by MAP_2 the slope values in these windows. Time series are defined on $n=13$ time points. The total number of windows and corresponding slope values equals to 12. The slope values were normalized to take values in interval [-10,10]. Fig. 5 shows membership functions of used perceptual trend patterns *Quickly Decreasing, Slowly Decreasing, Constant, Slowly Increasing, Quickly Increasing*.

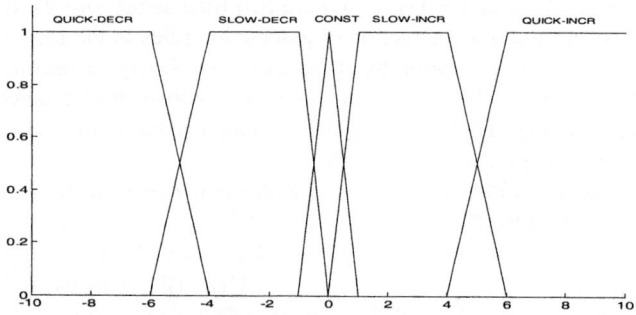

Fig. 5. Membership functions of perceptual trend patterns

The number of possible association rules for considered example equals to $N = p^2 m(m-1)/2 = 1950$, where $p = 5$ is a number of perceptual patterns and $m = 13$ is a number of time series. To decrease the number of considered association rules we have restricted by association rules with support value $supp(R)$ greater than $S_{min} = 0.3$. From (2) it follows that for each property A we can consider only time series with the value of normalized power $U_A = \frac{1}{N}\sum_{i=1}^{N} \mu_A(W_i)$ of fuzzy set A greater of equal than S_{min}. The inverse approach based on the analysis of the set of values of U_A for all time series and perceptual patterns may be used for selection of suitable minimal support value S_{min} to restrict possible number of association rules and to ensure that the set of association rules will be not empty. Some obtained rules with support value greater than 0.3 and confidence value greater than 0.7 are listed below:

If *7.Exports is Slowly Increasing* then *8.Imports is Slowly Increasing*, $S = 0.4276$, $C = 0.9593$;

If *5.Retail Sales Slowly Decreasing* then *8.Imports is Slowly Increasing*, $S = 0.3379$, $C = 0.7013$.

Note that these rules are associative but usually not causal.

5 Conclusions

Computational theory of perceptions in junction with time series data mining give the basis for development of methods modeling human expertise and supporting decision making procedures in problems related with time series analysis. The perception based TSDM tries to use in formal models the fuzzy patterns and association rules important for human decision making or underlying human experience and practice. PTSDM can be used as a model base for intelligent question answering systems in economics, finance, meteorology, petroleum industry etc.

Acknowledgment

The support for this research work has been provided by the IMP, projects D.00006 and D.00322.

References

1. Agrawal, R., Psaila, G., Wimmers, E. L., Zait, M.: Querying Shapes of Histories. In: Proc. 21st Int. Conf. Very Large Databases, Zurich, Switzerland (1995) 502-514
2. Baldwin, J.F., Martin, T.P., Rossiter, J.M.: Time Series Modelling and Prediction Using Fuzzy Trend Information. In: Proc. Int. Conf. Soft Computing Information/Intelligent Systems (1998) 499-502
3. Batyrshin, I.Z.: On Reconstruction of Perception Based Functions with Convex-Concave Patterns. In: Proc. Intern. Conf. Computational Intelligence ICCI 2004, Nicosia, North Cyprus, Near East University Press, (2004) 30 – 34
4. Batyrshin, I., Herrera-Avelar, R., Sheremetov, L., Suarez, R. Mining Fuzzy Association Rules and Networks in Time Series Databases. In.: Proc. Intern. Conf. Fuzzy Sets and Soft Computing in Economics and Finance FSSCEF, St. Petersburg, Russia, vol. I (2004) 39-53
5. Batyrshin, I., Sheremetov, L., Suarez, R., Panova, A.: Moving Approximation Transform, Local Trend Associations and Association Networks of Time Series (2005) (Submitted).
6. Bowerman, B.L., O'Connell, R.T.: Time Series and Forecasting; An Applied Approach. Duxbury Press, Massachusetts (1979)
7. Das, G, Lin, K.I, Mannila, H, Renganathan, G, Smyth, P.: Rule Discovery from Time Series. In: Proc. KDD98, (1998) 16-22
8. De Cock, M., Cornelis, C., Kerre E.E.: Elicitation of Fuzzy Association Rules from Positive and Negative Examples. Fuzzy Sets and Systems 149 (2005) 73-85
9. ICSC, Econstats Mexico, 4 (2002).
10. Sripada, S.G., Reiter, E., Hunter, J., Yu, J.: Generating English Summaries of Time Series Data using the Gricean Maxims. In: Proceedings of KDD2003, USA (2003) 187-196
11. Zadeh, L.A.: From Computing with Numbers to Computing with Words - from Manipulation of Measurements to Manipulation of Perceptions. IEEE Trans. on Circuits and Systems - 1: Fundamental Theory and Applications. 45 (1999) 105-119.
12. Zadeh, L.A.: From Search Engines to Question-Answering Systems. The Need for New Tools. In: The 12th IEEE Intern. Conf. Fuzzy Systems, vol. 2 (2003) 25-28

A Graph Theoretic Approach to Key Equivalence

J. Horacio Camacho, Abdellah Salhi, and Qingfu Zhang

University of Essex, Colchester CO43SQ, UK
{jhcama, as, qzhang}@essex.ac.uk

Abstract. This paper is concerned with redundancy detection and elimination in databases via the solution of a key equivalence problem. The approach is related to the hardening of soft databases method due to Cohen et al., [4]. Here, the problem is described in graph theoretic terms. An appropriate optimization model is drawn and solved indirectly. This approach is shown to be effective. Computational results on test databases are included.

1 Introduction

Textual databases often contain a lot of redundant information, and information that is corrupt as a result of errors such as key punch errors, scanning errors, spelling errors, to name a few.

Because of these errors, it is often hard to decide whether two entries (records) in the database refer to the same real world object. The problem is, here, considered in the context of structured databases.

This problem has been tackled under different guises as the probabilistic record linkage [1], the merge/purge problem [2], duplicate detection [3], and others. Here we focus on an approach related to the *Hardening Soft Information Sources* approach due to Cohen et al., [4]. It is related, but simpler, since as will be seen, it is formulated as a simpler optimization problem than the global optimization one suggested in [4]. This simplification follows from the fact that in [4], a record has potentially many fields each pointing to a real world object, i.e. it forms a reference. Here, we consider that the whole record however many fields it may have, points to a single object. This is an important distinction since the initial complete graph we work from is much simpler than what would be considered if the model in [4] was exactly adhered to.

In the next subsection, formal models of the problem are presented. A solution approach is given in Section 2. Examples and experimental results on test datasets are shown in Section 3. Section 4 introduces an important improvement to the basic approach. Section 5 is a comparison of the enhanced approach with a standard approach on many but small databases. Section 6 is the conclusion.

1.1 Formulation of the Key Equivalence Problem

Let *object identifier* O_i be any record in a database with fields $o_1, o_2, ..., o_m$. Each one of these fields describes a specific characteristic of O_i, such as name, address, telephone number. Let also *object* be the real target which O_i is referring to and *key* be the unique identification of the record in a database. Then, *Key equivalence* occurs when two or more O_i's in a database refer to the same *object*, [5]. As said earlier, the main difference between our formulation and that of the hardening approach, [4], is that here we consider a database as a set of O_i's, while in Cohen *et al.*'s work, a database consists of a set of *tuples*, each of which consisting of a set of *references*, or fields. Each reference points to a real world object.

Since, given a database, it is not easy to tell which records point to the same object, we initially assume that all of them point to the same object. This means that all records can potentially be represented by the same object identifier. Therefore, initially at least, we in fact assume that when all redundancy is removed, we will possibly be left with no database. This assumption may sound unreasonable, since only a small percentage of records in a database might be corrupted, but it is only necessary to motivate our method. It does not limit the application of the method suggested.

Let now each object identifier be represented by a node. Then, the *potential* redundancy of an identifier (node) may be represented by a directed arc between this identifier and another one. An incoming arc means the source node is potentially redundant. Since, as was assumed, initially they all point to each other, no direction is required, leading to a complete graph.

Let $G(V, E)$ be this graph with $V = \{v_1, v_2, ..., v_n\}$ its set of nodes each corresponding to an object identifier (record) in a given database, and $E = \{(i,j) | i, j = 1, 2, ..., n, i \neq j\}$ its set of arcs.

By some string similarity metric, such as SoftTF-IDF, [6], it is possible to find weights for all edges of graph G specifying how likely it is that two object identifiers point to the same real world object, i.e. one of them is redundant. A large weight between two O_i's says they are unlikely to point at the same object, and a small weight says otherwise, i.e. there is redundancy. In this fashion, since SoftTF-IDF scales the similarity with values between zero and one, where one is the maximum similarity, we take as a weight its inverse value (1−SoftTF-IDF). We are left with the question of how close to zero a weight has to be in order to say that one of the records is redundant. It will become clear, later, that this question is at the heart of the problem.

Clearly, a subgraph of G with minimum total weight will catch redundancy. Moreover, this subgraph must have all the nodes of G.

2 Solution Approach

A further formalization is necessary to model this situation. In particular, we consider that a subgraph of G that captures all or part of the redundancy in the database, is generated by a function from V to V. As such, it has the properties of totality and unicity. Given G, we want to find $G'(V, E')$ such that $E' \subseteq E$, and

$$z = \sum_{(i,j) \in E, i \neq j} e_{ij} w_{ij} + \left(n - \sum_{(i,j) \in E, i \neq j} e_{ij} \right) \lambda_1 + \left(\sum_{(i,j) \in E, i \neq j} e_{ij} \right) \lambda_2 \quad (1)$$

is minimized, where $e_{ij} = 1$ if $(i,j) \in E'$ and 0, otherwise, n is the size of the database, $w_{ij}, i, j = 1, 2, ..., n$ are the weights, and λ_1 and λ_2 are constants which control the size of the resulting database for the amount redundancy detected. Equivalently, they are constants which when known exactly will give a value z which is smallest for the database that has been cleaned of all its redundancy and nothing else, i.e. the perfect solution. Of course the choice of these constants will influence the effectiveness of the approach advocated here. A simple manipulation of the z expression results in

$$z = \sum_{(i,j)\in E, i\neq j} e_{ij}w_{ij} + \lambda_1 n - \lambda_1 \sum_{(i,j)\in E, i\neq j} e_{ij} + \lambda_2 \sum_{(i,j)\in E, i\neq j} e_{ij}$$

$$= \sum_{(i,j)\in E, i\neq j} e_{ij}w_{ij} + \lambda_1 n - (\lambda_1 - \lambda_2) \sum_{(i,j)\in E, i\neq j} e_{ij}$$

By constraining z with the requirements of the relation (function) between the nodes, and after a slight transformation of the expression of z, due to the fact that some terms are constants, and also by replacing $\lambda_1 - \lambda_2$ with a single parameter k, we obtain the following optimization problem.

$$\min z = \sum_{(i,j)\in E, i\neq j} e_{ij}w_{ij} - k \sum_{(i,j)\in E, i\neq j} e_{ij} \qquad (2)$$

s.t.

$$\sum_{j\in E} e_{ij} \leq 1, \forall i, i \neq j \qquad (3)$$

$$\sum_{(i,j)\in E} e_{ij} \leq n - 1 \qquad (4)$$

$$u_i - u_j \leq n - 1 - n e_{ij}, \qquad (5)$$
$$i, j = 1, ..., n, i \neq j, u_i \in R^+$$

Note that restrictions (3) imply that there is at most one edge (i,j) from each node i. Restrictions (4) and (5) eliminate cycles, [8]. From the above model, it is clear that if $k \leq 0$, the second term of z is zero or positive and so the minimum corresponds to all $e_{ij} = 0$, i.e. no edge is worth including in the solution, giving $E' = \emptyset$.

If $k > 0$ the minimum of z must be negative, i.e. $\sum_{(i,j)\in E, i\neq j} e_{ij}w_{ij} \leq k \sum_{(i,j)\in E, i\neq j} e_{ij}$ in which case the solution to the above model will be those arcs with small weights. Moreover, because we are minimizing, all these weights will be less than k.

2.1 Formalization

Parameter k is essential for trapping redundancy and its proper setting will decide on how successful the detection of redundancy will be. Set too large, a connected subgraph of G will be the solution, thus including all nodes (object identifiers). Set too low, very few if any will be included in the solution, thus leaving out genuine redundancy. It must be clear already that trees satisfy the constraints of the above optimization model. A solution to the problem is likely to be a collection of subtrees of the minimum spanning tree of G. In other words, it is likely to be a forest.

Definition 1. *A spanning forest of a connected graph G is a forest whose components are subtrees of a spanning tree of G.*

Definition 2. *A minimum spanning forest of a connected graph G is a forest whose components are minimum spanning trees of the corresponding components in G.*

Proposition 1. *The solution to the suggested optimisation model is a spanning forest. Moreover, it is a minimum spanning forest.*

Proposition 2. *For a given k, the optimal solution to model (2)-(5) can be obtained in polynomial time.*

Proof. Trim the graph of all its edges with weights greater that k. Apply a greedy algorithm to the remaining subgraph of G to find the minimum spanning tree (forest if disconnected).

Remark 1. The problem of finding the optimum k may not be solvable in polynomial time. A practical estimation of k is given below.

Remark 2. Parameter k varies from database to database.

2.2 Estimating k

The threshold constant k can be chosen arbitrarily, below 0.5, for instance. That may well work in some cases. However, in general, it is better to find an estimate directly related to the given database, (*Remark 2*). This can be done as follows.

Algorithm 1:

1. Find the weighted complete graph G corresponding to the given database;
2. Find the minimum spanning tree of G;
3. Assign the largest weight for which a good match between records is found, to k;

2.3 Detecting Redundancy

Redundant records are detected according to the following algorithm.

Algorithm 2:

1. Apply Algorithm 1 to the given database;
2. Remove all edges with weights $> k$, from the minimum spanning tree of G output by Algorithm 1;

The output is a tree (or forest) that represents the detected redundant records. Each tree of the spanning forest can be reduced to one node. The remaining nodes of the forest constitute the records of the resulting database after removing redundancy.

2.4 Illustration

Consider a database with only four records, i.e. four object identifiers. As shown in Table 1, each record is associated with a node v_i of a graph G. Now consider G as a complete graph; its set E of edges are given in Table 2. Moreover, we also compute the weights of each edge (i,j) using the SoftTF-IDF method, [6]. These weights are also included in Table 2.

Table 1. A database example

Database
$v_1 = $ Coby Lashiwn Y. 303 Main
$v_2 = $ Coby Angela 303 Main
$v_3 = $ Coby Wiliams A. 303 Main
$v_4 = $ Coby Agel 303 Main

Table 2. Set of edges and set of weights

Edge (i,j)	Weight w_{ij}
(1, 2)	$w_{12} = w_{21} = 0.329$
(1, 3)	$w_{13} = w_{31} = 0.400$
(1, 4)	$w_{14} = w_{41} = 0.329$
(2, 3)	$w_{23} = w_{32} = 0.329$
(2, 4)	$w_{24} = w_{42} = 0.250$
(3, 4)	$w_{34} = w_{43} = 0.329$

Now, applying Algorithm 1 to the graph of Fig.1 results in the graph of Fig.2. A greedy algorithm has been used to solve the minimum spanning tree problem, [8]. By consulting Fig.2, it is obvious that k must take value 0.25. Removing all edges of the minimum spanning tree with weights $> k$ leads to record v_2 (or v_4) being redundant. Thus, $E' = \{(2,4)\}$.

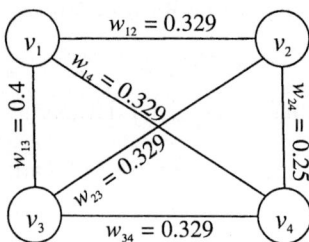

Fig. 1. The complete graph G of the dtatabase

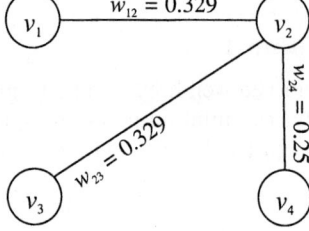

Fig. 2. The minimum spanning tree G' output by Algorithm 1

3 Experimental Results

The approach presented in this paper is tested on the datasets of Table 3. Its performance is measured via the quality of the solution it returns for each dataset. This quality is calculated as, $quality = \frac{2*precision*recall}{precision+recall}$, where, $precision = \frac{c}{|E'|}$, $recall = \frac{c}{|E^*|}$, c is the number of correctly linked rows, i.e. the number of records

Table 3. Experimental data, source [6]

Dataset	Records	Redundancies
BirdKunkel	337	38
BirdScott2	719	310
Census	841	671
Cora	923	902
Parks	654	505
Restaurant	863	228

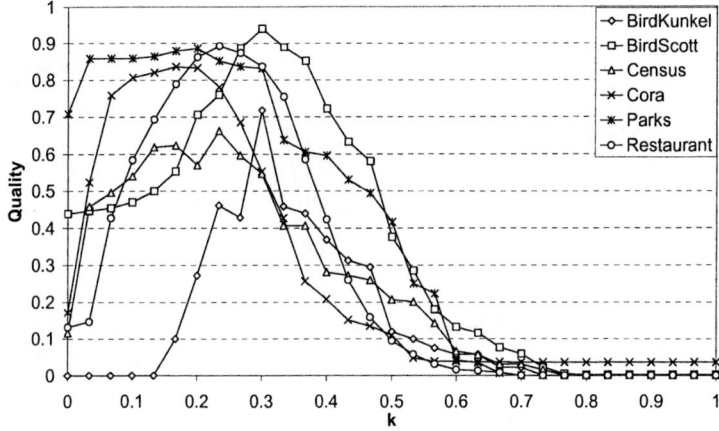

Fig. 3. Results obtained for each dataset for 31 different values of k between 0 and 1

pointing to the same real world object, $|E'|$ is number of edges (i,j) in the solution set E' and $|E^{*'}|$ is the number of redundant records in the database, [6]. In each case, the quality is computed for 31 values of k, between zero and one. The results are displayed in Fig.3.

Note that, from Fig.3, the quality of solution is not generally sensitive to the value of k. However, for dataset BirdKunkel, it is: indeed, the quality of solution drops from about 0.72 to 0.45 for values of k not near 0.3. This sensitivity to the choice of k is a serious issue, particularly when new databases are considered. In the following, a heuristic approach is suggested for reducing it.

4 Improvement: Reducing Sensitivity to Parameter k

The sensitivity to the choice of k can be reduced by the following pre-processing steps. Before choosing k, the forest (tree) representing potential redundancy is further trimmed as follows.

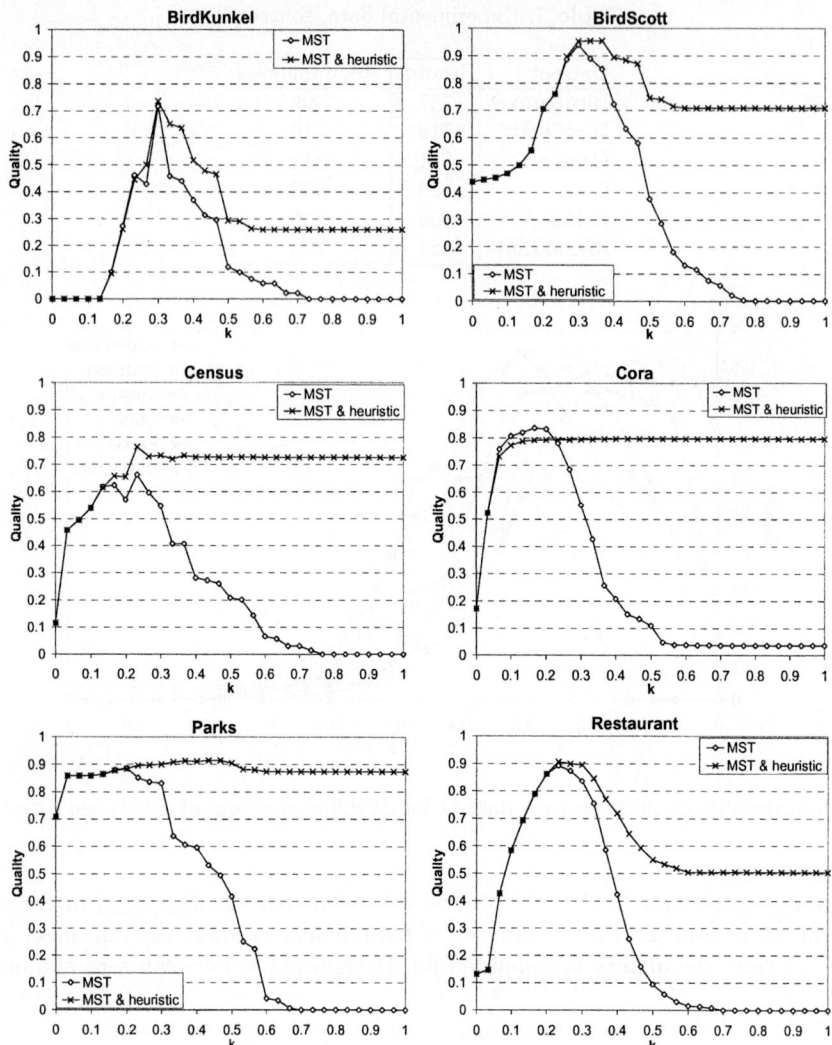

Fig. 4. Heuristic results to reduce the sensitivity of k obtained for each dataset for 31 different values of k between 0 and 1

4.1 Reduce the Degree of Each Node

For each nodes v_i such that $deg(v_i) \geq 2$ do:
Compare the weights of its incident edges $j, k, l, \ldots$ pairwise.
if $|w_{ij} - w_{ik}| > \delta_1$ then
    if $w_{ij} > w_{ik}$ then remove (i,j); else remove (i,k); endif
endif

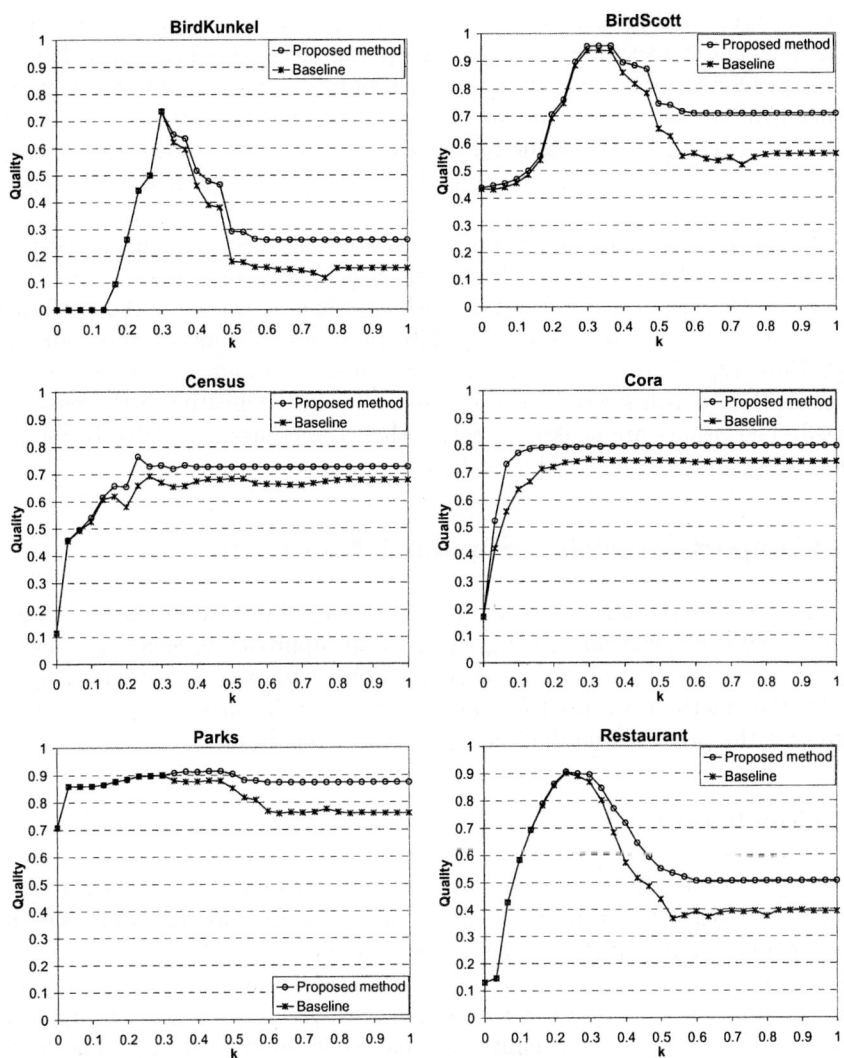

Fig. 5. Baseline results for each dataset for 31 different values of k between 0 and 1

Here, we remove edges whose weights differences are bigger than $\delta_1 = 0.05$. The value of δ_1 is empirically determined.

4.2 Reduce the Length of Branches

Often, the minimum spanning tree representing potential redundancy, shows many nodes (records) which do not seem to be similar. For instance, w_{ij} and w_{jk} are of the same order, but, w_{ik} is significantly different from both. This occurs when branches have more than two nodes. So, reducing the size of the long branches according to some difference of weights between adjacent edges criterion, enhances the accuracy of estimating parameter k. We proceed as follows.

Link each vertex in the solution to the root of its tree and obtain the weights between the actual vertex and the intermediary vertices to the root node. If a weight is bigger than some value δ_2, then remove from the branch, the edge with largest weight. Here, again, the value of δ_2 is empirically settled, and found to be 0.6.

Having incorporated the pre-processing steps suggested in this section, the results of the enhanced approach suggest in all cases, and in particular in the case of Birdkunkel, a wider interval in which k can be chosen without affecting too much the quality of redundancy detection. The results are represented in Fig4. Note, especially, that in the cases of Census, Cora and Parks datasets, the intervals from which k can be chosen are very wide, indicating little sensitivity indeed. The results are strikingly better than the earlier ones (Fig.3) obtained before the improvements to the method.

5 Comparison with a Standard Approach

In [7], manual matching of records in record-linkage is treated via the solution of an assignment problem. A comparison of our approach to this mathematical programming based method is reasonable. The same weights provided by the softTF-IDF method are used for both approaches. Results are given in Fig.5. Note that the proposed method performs better on all datasets.

6 Conclusion

We have looked at the problem of detecting and removing redundancy in structured databases. An optimization model of the integer programming type has been devised for it. Although, this model is difficult to solve directly, it turns out that a tree graph of a certain kind (a forest) provides an optimum solution, given k. This solution can be obtained in polynomial time. The approach suggested has been tried on many but small structured databases. The results are encouraging. Further efforts are currently expanded in order to improve the estimation of the threshold parameter k in the case of large databases.

Acknowledgment. This work is supported by Conacyt grant number 168588.

References

1. H. B. Newcombe, J. M. Kennedy, S. J. Axford, and A. P. James. Automatic linkage of vital records. Science, 130:954–959, 1959.
2. M. A. Hernandez and S. J. Stolfo. The merge/purge problem for large databases. In Proceedings of the 1995 ACM SIGMOD International Conference on Management of Data (SIGMOD-95), pages 127–138, San Jose, CA, May 1995.

3. A. E. Monge and C. P. Elkan. An efficient domain-independent algorithm for detecting approximately duplicate database records. In Proceedings of the SIGMOD 1997 Workshop on Research Issues on Data Mining and Knowledge Discovery, pages 23–29, Tuscon, AZ, May 1997.
4. W. W. Cohen, H. Kautz, and D. McAllester. Hardening soft information sources. In Proceedings of the Sixth International Conference on Knowledge Discovery and Data Mining (KDD-2000), Boston, MA, Aug. 2000.
5. Carlton Pu, Key Equivalence in Heterogeneous Databases, Department of Computer Science, Columbia University, New York, NY, 1991.
6. William W. Cohen, Pradeep Ravikumar, Stephen E. Fienberg, A Comparison of String Distance Metrics for Name-Matching Tasks, 2003.
7. Jaro, M. A. Advances in Record-Linkage Methodology as Applied to Matching the 1985 Census of Tampa, Florida, Journal of the American Statistical Association, 89, 414-420, 1989.
8. Nemhauser and Wolsey. Integer and Combinatorial Optimization. Willey Interscience,1988.

Improvement of Data Visualization Based on ISOMAP

Chao Shao and Houkuan Huang

School of Computer and Information Technology,
Beijing Jiaotong University,
100044 Beijing, China
sc_flying@163.com, hkhuang@center.njtu.edu.cn

Abstract. Using the geodesic distance metric instead of the Euclidean distance metric, ISOMAP can visualize the convex but intrinsically flat manifolds such as the swiss roll data set nicely. But it's well known that ISOMAP performs well only when the data belong to a single well-sampled manifold, and fails when the data lie on disjoint manifolds or imperfect manifolds. Generally speaking, as the data points are farer from each other on the manifold, the approximation of the shortest path to the geodesic distance is worse, especially for imperfect manifolds, that is, long distances are approximated generally worse than short distances, which makes the classical MDS algorithm used in ISOMAP unsuitable and thus often leads to the overlapping or "overclustering" of the data. To solve this problem, we improve the original ISOMAP algorithm by replacing the classical MDS algorithm with the Sammon's mapping algorithm, which can limit the effects of generally worse-approximated long distances to a certain extent, and thus better visualization results are obtained. As a result, besides imperfect manifolds, intrinsically curved manifolds such as the fishbowl data set can also be visualized nicely. In addition, based on the characteristics of the Euclidean distance metric, a faster Dijkstra-like shortest path algorithm is used in our method. Finally, experimental results verify our method very well.

1 Introduction

Nowadays, the explosive growth in the amount of data and their dimensionality makes data visualization more and more important. During the last hundreds of years, lots of approaches to visualize the high-dimensional data have been emerged, most of which fall into the following five categories: 1)use several subwindows to visually represent different subsets of the dimensions respectively, such as scatterplot matrices[1] and pixel-oriented techniques[2]; 2)rearrange the dimension axes to be non-orthogonal or even parallel, such as parallel coordinates[3] and star coordinates[4]; 3)embed the dimensions to form hierarchical partitioning of the low-dimensional space, such as dimensional stacking[5] and treemap[6]; 4)use certain objects or icons which have several visual features, each of which stands for one dimension, such as Chernoff-faces[7] and stick figures[8];

5)reduce the dimensionality of the data to two or three dimensions, such as PCA[9], MDS[10], SOM[11][12][13], ISOMAP[14][15][16], LLE[17][18] and Laplacian Eigenmap[19], *etc.*

Unlike other methods, the dimensionality-reduction techniques consider all the dimensions as a whole, and try to preserve the high-dimensional relationship between the data points in the low-dimensional space, which can visually represent the distribution and clustering of the data very well. As one of the dimensionality-reduction techniques, ISOMAP extends the classical MDS algorithm by using the geodesic distance metric instead of the Euclidean distance metric in order to handle with the convex but intrinsically flat manifolds such as the swiss roll data set, however, ISOMAP needs certain assumptions about the data, i.e. the data must belong to a single well-sampled manifold, not disjoint manifolds or imperfect manifolds[18][16][20]. As we know, ISOMAP uses the shortest path in a suitable neighborhood graph to approximate the global geodesic distance between the data points. Unfortunately, as the data points are farer from each other on the manifold, the approximation of the shortest path to the geodesic distance is generally worse, especially for imperfect manifolds. Generally speaking, long distances are approximated worse than short distances. What's the worst, the classical MDS algorithm used in the original ISOMAP algorithm is linear and treats all the distances equally. So, long distances which are generally worse approximated often dominate the global structure of the result maps, and short distances which are generally more trustworthy are often scarified, which often leads to the overlapping or "overclustering" of the data[18][21][20]. To solve this problem, a solution is presented in [16], but the results remain poor because some unsuitable or untrustworthy long Euclidean distances of each data point are used directly and thus the local feature is lost[18]. In this paper, we improve the original ISOMAP algorithm by replacing the classical MDS algorithm with the Sammon's mapping algorithm, which can limit the effects of generally worse-approximated long distances to a certain extent and generally more trustworthy short distances are better preserved. As a result, not only imperfect manifolds but also intrinsically curved manifolds can be visualized better by our method.

This paper is organized as follows: In Section 2, we recall the original ISOMAP algorithm. In Section 3, we present our method. Finally, experimental results and conclusions are given in Section 4 and Section 5 respectively.

2 ISOMAP

When the global geometric structure of the high-dimensional data is unknown, we are not sure that the Euclidean distance metric is suitable to represent the dissimilarity between the data. Fortunately, the Euclidean distance metric is trustworthy enough to represent the dissimilarity between the data within a small enough local neighborhood. So the global geometric structure can be approximated using the local Euclidean distance information, as ISOMAP does. If the data lie on a single well-sampled manifold, it's proved that the unknown global geodesic distance between the data points can be well approximated by the graph distance, i.e. the shortest path, in a suitable neighborhood graph which defines a local neighborhood structure of the data[22].

After using the geodesic distance metric approximated by the shortest path in a suitable neighborhood graph instead of the Euclidean distance metric, the original ISOMAP algorithm uses the classical MDS algorithm to project the data into a low-dimensional space. So the original ISOMAP algorithm can be briefly described as follows[14][15]:

```
1)Select n data points randomly for very large data sets to keep
subsequent computation tractable;
2)Construct a suitable neighborhood graph (must be connected!) using
the k nearest neighbors method;
3)Compute all the shortest paths in this neighborhood graph;
4)Use the classical MDS algorithm with the shortest paths to project
the data into a low-dimensional space.
```

ISOMAP is suitable for the data lying on a single well-sampled intrinsically flat manifold, since the global geodesic distances are well approximated and the classical MDS algorithm performs well. Unfortunately, the data often lie on imperfect manifolds, which make the global geodesic distances approximated not well, especially for the data which are far from each other on the manifold. Generally speaking, long distances are approximated worse than short distances, which makes the classical MDS algorithm unsuitable. Therefore, it's reasonable to replace the classical MDS algorithm with the Sammon's mapping algorithm which can limit the effects of long distances to a certain extent and emphasize short distances more. In addition, the nonlinear Sammon's mapping algorithm has much stronger power than the linear classical MDS algorithm. These are the thinking of our method.

3 Our Method

As described above, our method rewrites step 4 as follows:

```
4)Use the Sammon's mapping algorithm with the shortest paths to project
the data into a low-dimensional space.
```

Given a suitable neighborhood graph, shortest path computation (step 3) is very time-consuming. There are two approaches to compute the shortest paths in a graph: Dijkstra's algorithm and Floyd's algorithm. Note that weights of the edges in the neighborhood graph are specified as the corresponding Euclidean distances, and the Euclidean distance metric meets the symmetry and triangular inequality conditions, so we can initialize S and T (seen in the pseudo-code) much farther and thus quicken shortest path computation greatly based on these characteristics of the Euclidean distance metric (seen in Fig. 1). As a Dijkstra-like algorithm, its differences from Dijkstra's algorithm are listed as follows:

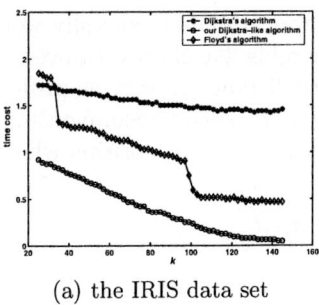 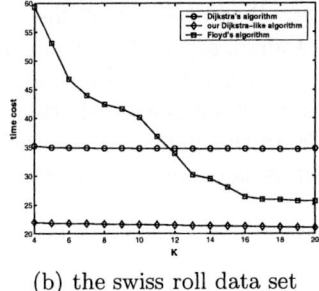

(a) the IRIS data set (b) the swiss roll data set

Fig. 1. Time costs of three shortest path algorithms over different data sets with different k

1) The shortest paths found previously need not be computed again and can be used to find other shortest paths; (use the symmetry condition)

2) For each vertex, its edges existing in the neighborhood graph are the shortest paths themselves, need not be computed again, and can be used to find other shortest paths. (use the triangular inequality condition)

We represent the i-th data point and its k nearest neighbors by x_i and $N_k(i)$ respectively, then the adjacent matrix of the corresponding neighborhood graph can be represented by $P = (p_{ij})_{n \times n}$, where

$$p_{ij} = \begin{cases} 0 &, \quad j = i \\ \|x_i - x_j\| &, \quad j \in N_k(i) \text{ or } i \in N_k(j) \\ +\infty &, \quad else \end{cases} \quad (1)$$

Consequently, we can describe our Dijkstra-like algorithm as follows:

```
for each data point i
    S = {j|p_ij < +∞};  (S = {i} in Dijkstra's algorithm)
    T = {1,···,n} - S;
    for each data point j ∈ T
        d_j = min{p_il + p_lj|l ∈ S};  (d_j = p_ij in Dijkstra's algorithm)
    end
    while T ≠ Φ
        j = argmin_{l∈T}{d_l};
        p_ij = d_j, p_ji = d_j;
        S = S + {j};  T = T - {j};
        for each data point l ∈ T
            if d_l > p_ij + p_jl
                d_l = p_ij + p_jl;
            end
        end
    end
end
```

As described above, long distances are approximated generally worse than short distances, especially for imperfect manifolds, i.e. short distances are more trustworthy generally. So we should use those distance-preserving projection algorithms which emphasize shorter distances more, such as Sammon's mapping, not MDS. In this paper, we use the Sammon's mapping algorithm whose objective function is defined as follows:

$$E = \sum_{i<j} \frac{(\delta_{ij} - d_{ij})^2}{\delta_{ij}} \quad (2)$$

Where δ_{ij} and d_{ij} represent the high-dimensional distance, i.e. the geodesic distance approximated by the shortest path here, and the low-dimensional distance, i.e. the Euclidean distance here, between the i-th and j-th data points respectively. Let x_{il} ($l = 1, \cdots, m$) be the l-th coordinate of the i-th data point in the low-dimensional space, then we have

$$d_{ij} = \sqrt{\sum_{l=1}^{m}(x_{il} - x_{jl})^2} \quad (3)$$

We recall that Sammon's mapping usually uses the steepest descent strategy to minimize the objective function iteratively, in which the choice of the learning rate is very important. To avoid the problems resulted from the unsuitable learning rate, we use the variable alternation strategy[23] to minimize the objective function (Equ. 2) iteratively as follows:

$$\forall i,l \quad \frac{\partial E}{\partial x_{il}} = \sum_{j \neq i} \frac{\partial E}{\partial d_{ij}} \cdot \frac{\partial d_{ij}}{\partial x_{il}} = 0 \quad (4)$$

$$\forall i,l \quad x'_{il} = \frac{\sum_{j \neq i}[\frac{1}{\delta_{ij}}x_{jl} + \frac{1}{d_{ij}}(x_{il} - x_{jl})]}{\sum_{j \neq i}\frac{1}{\delta_{ij}}} \quad (5)$$

Equ. 5 is used to minimize the objective function (Equ. 2) iteratively, in which the learning rate is not required any more. Experimental results show that this variable alternation strategy is feasible (seen in Fig. 2).

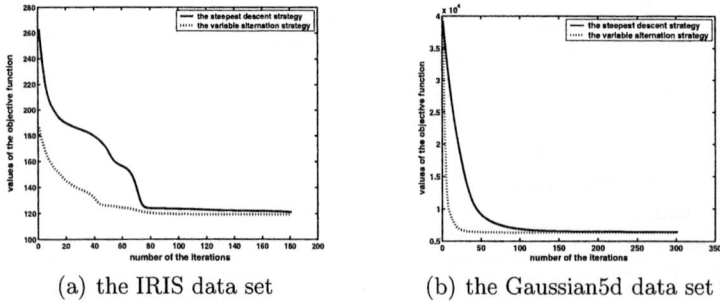

(a) the IRIS data set   (b) the Gaussian5d data set

Fig. 2. Processes of convergence of two optimization strategies over different data sets

Similar to the steepest descent strategy, this variable alternation strategy often leads to local minima or even saddle points depending on the initial layout. One general solution is to use a good initial layout. We use the linear classical MDS algorithm to provide a good initial layout for the Sammon's mapping algorithm. So our method can be described as follows:

```
1)Select n data points randomly for very large data sets to keep
subsequent computation tractable;
2)Construct a suitable neighborhood graph (must be connected!) using
the k nearest neighbors method;
3)Compute all the shortest paths in this neighborhood graph using our
Dijkstra-like algorithm;
4a)Use the classical MDS algorithm with the shortest paths to provide
the initial layout for the subsequent Sammon's mapping algorithm.
4b)Use the Sammon's mapping algorithm with the variable alternation
strategy (Equ. 5) to project the data into a low-dimensional space.
```

4 Experimental Results

Being a nonlinear variant of the original ISOMAP algorithm, our method can visualize the convex but intrinsically flat manifold such as the swiss roll data set as nicely as the original ISOMAP algorithm (seen in Fig. 3(a) and Fig. 3(c)), however, the method presented in [16] cannot visualize the swiss roll data set well (seen in Fig. 3(b)) because it uses some unsuitable or untrustworthy long Euclidean distances of each data point directly. To test if our method can also solve the problem presented in [16][18][20] well and can improve data visualization based on ISOMAP for the data lying on imperfect manifolds, we run the original ISOMAP algorithm, the method presented in [16], and our method over another two data sets: IRIS and Gaussian5d. Besides the well-known IRIS data set, we also use another widely-used data set: Gaussian5d, which consists of 6 clusters of equal size in 5 dimensions. We specify that the centers of the clusters are the points (0, 0, 0, 0, 0), (10, 0, 0, 0, 0), (0, 10, 0, 0, 0), (0, 0, 10, 0, 0), (0, 0, 0, 10, 0) and (0, 0, 0, 0, 10), and the data follow a Gaussian distribution whose covariance matrix is an identity matrix. The results of the original ISOMAP algorithm, the method presented in [16], and our method over these two data sets are given in Fig. 4 and Fig. 5 respectively.

Because our method uses the more powerful nonlinear Sammon's mapping algorithm instead of the linear classical MDS algorithm and thus emphasizes generally more trustworthy short distances more, we believe that our method can visualize more manifolds nicely. To validate this point, we also run these three algorithms over an intrinsically curved manifold – the fishbowl data set (seen in Fig. 6(a)) which the original ISOMAP algorithm cannot visualize very well, the results are given in Fig. 6.

From these results, we can see that the data lying on imperfect manifolds or intrinsically curved manifolds such as the IRIS, Gaussian5d and fishbowl data sets can be visualized much better by using our method (seen in Fig. 4(c), 5(c),

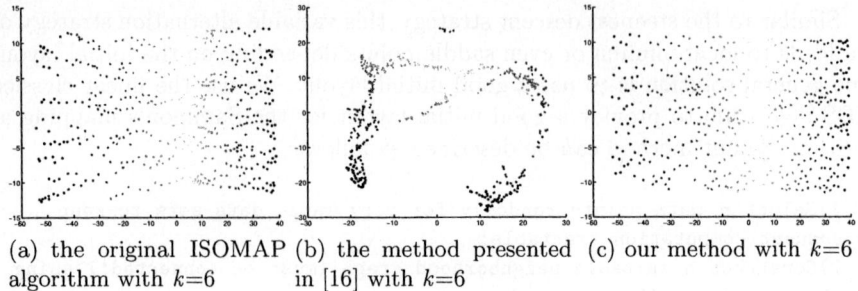

(a) the original ISOMAP algorithm with $k=6$ (b) the method presented in [16] with $k=6$ (c) our method with $k=6$

Fig. 3. The results of these three methods over the swiss roll data set

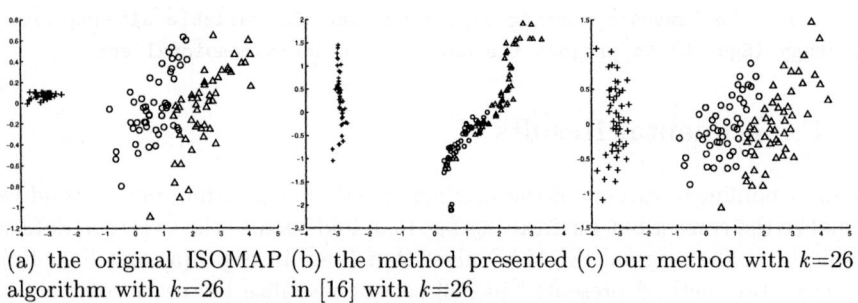

(a) the original ISOMAP algorithm with $k=26$ (b) the method presented in [16] with $k=26$ (c) our method with $k=26$

Fig. 4. The results of these three methods over the IRIS data set

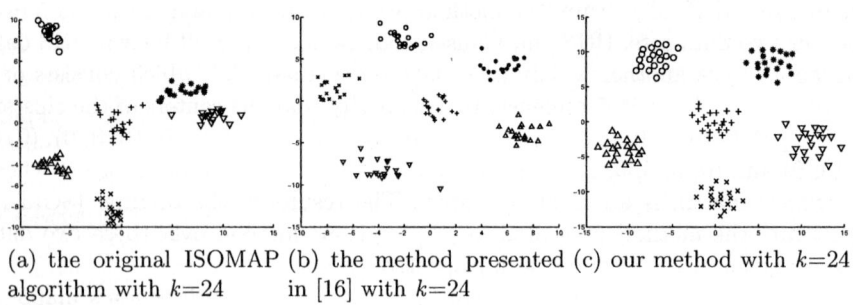

(a) the original ISOMAP algorithm with $k=24$ (b) the method presented in [16] with $k=24$ (c) our method with $k=24$

Fig. 5. The results of these three methods over the Gaussian5d data set

and 6(d)) than by using the original ISOMAP algorithm (seen in Fig. 4(a), 5(a), and 6(b)) and the method presented in [16] (seen in Fig. 4(b), 5(b), and 6(c)). So, we can say that the problem above has been solved in a sense, and better visualization results have been obtained, especially for imperfect manifolds or intrinsically curved manifolds.

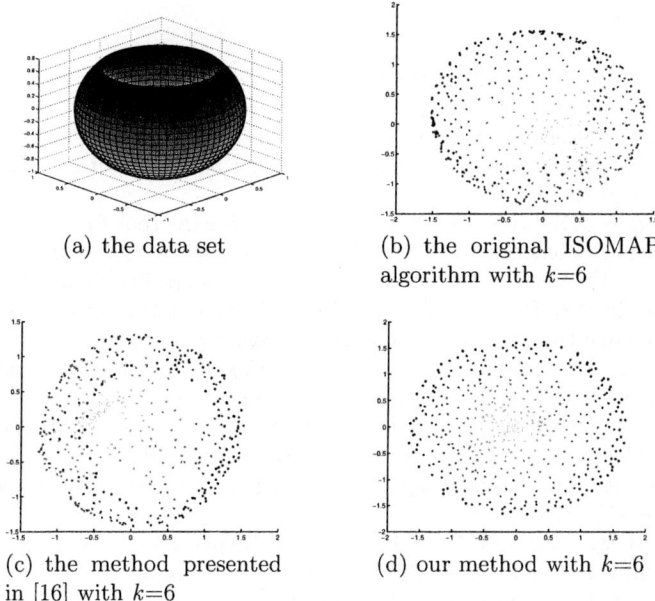

Fig. 6. The results of these three methods over the fishbowl data set

5 Conclusions

In this paper, we improve data visualization based on ISOMAP especially for the data lying on imperfect manifolds or intrinsically curved manifolds by replacing the classical MDS algorithm with the Sammon's mapping algorithm to limit the effects of generally worse-approximated long distances to a certain extent and generally more trustworthy short distances are better preserved, because as the data points are farer from each other on the manifold, the approximation of the shortest path in the neighborhood graph to the geodesic distance is generally worse, especially for imperfect manifolds, and because the nonlinear Sammon's mapping algorithm has much stronger power than the linear classical MDS algorithm. Experimental results verify our method very well.

To avoid the problems resulted from the unsuitable learning rate and local minima existing in the Sammon's mapping algorithm, we use the variable alternation strategy to minimize the objective function iteratively and the linear classical MDS algorithm to provide a good initial layout for the Sammon's mapping algorithm. In addition, based on the characteristics of the Euclidean distance metric, i.e. the Euclidean distance metric meets the symmetry and triangular inequality conditions, a faster Dijkstra-like shortest path algorithm is used in our method.

References

1. Cleveland, W.S.: Visualizing Data. AT&T Bell Laboratories, Murray Hill, NJ, Hobart Press, Summit NJ (1993)
2. Keim, D.A.: Designing Pixel-Oriented Visualization Techniques: Theory and Applications. IEEE Transactions on Visualization and Computer Graphics, Vol. 6, No. 1 (2000) 59-78
3. Inselberg, A., Dimsdale, B.: Parallel Coordinates: A Tool for Visualizing Multi-Dimensional Geometry. Visualization'90, San Francisco, CA (1990) 361-370
4. Kandogan, E.: Visualizing Multi-dimensional Clusters,Trends,and Outliers Using Star Coordinates. Proceedings of the 7th ACM SIGKDD International Conference on Knowledge Discovery and Data Mining, San Francisco, USA (2001) 107-116
5. LeBlanc, J., Ward, M.O., Wittels, N.: Exploring N-Dimensional Databases. Visualization'90, San Francisco, CA (1990) 230-239
6. Johnson, B.: Visualizing Hierarchical and Categorical Data. Ph.D. Thesis, Department of Computer Science, University of Maryland (1993)
7. Tufte, E. R.: The Visual Display of Quantitative Information. Graphics Press, Cheshire, CT (1983)
8. Pickett, R.M., Grinstein, G.G.: Iconographic Displays for Visualizing Multidimensional Data. Proceedings of IEEE Conference on Systems, Man and Cybernetics, IEEE Press, Piscataway, NJ (1988) 514-519
9. Mao, J.C., Jain, A.K.: Artificial Neural Networks for Feature Extraction and Multivariate Data Projection. IEEE Transactions on Neural Networks, Vol. 6, No. 2 (1995) 296-317
10. Naud, A., Duch, W.: Interactive Data Exploration Using MDS Mapping. Proceedings of the 5th Conference on Neural Networks and Soft Computing, Zakopane, Poland (2000) 255-260
11. Merkl, D., Rauber, A.: Alternative Ways for Cluster Visualization in Self-Organizing Maps. Proceedings of the Workshop on Self-Organizing Maps (WSOM97), Espoo, Finland, (1997) 106-111
12. Su, M.C., Chang, H.T.: A New Model of Self-Organizing Neural Networks and its Application in Data Projection. IEEE Transanctions on Neural Networks, Vol. 12, No. 1 (2001) 153-158
13. Shao, C., Huang, H.K.: Improvement of Data Visualization Based on SOM. Proceedings of International Symposium on Neural Networks, Dalian, China (2004) 707-712
14. Tenenbaum, J.B., de Silva, V., Langford, J.C.: A Global Geometric Framework for Nonlinear Dimensionality Reduction. Science, Vol. 290, No. 22 (2000) 2319-2323
15. de Silva, V., Tenenbaum, J.B.: Unsupervised Learning of Curved Manifolds. Proceedings of MSRI Workshop on Nonlinear Estimation and Classification, Berkeley, USA (2001) 453-466
16. Vlachos, M., Domeniconi, C., Gunopulos, D., Kollios, G., Koudas, N.: Non-Linear Dimensionality Reduction Techniques for Classification and Visualization. Proceedings of the 8th ACM SIGKDD International Conference on Knowledge Discovery and Data Mining, Edmonton, Canada (2002) 645-651
17. Roweis, S.T., Saul, L.K.: Nonlinear Dimensionality Reduction by Locally Linear Embedding. Science, Vol. 290, No. 22 (2000) 2323-2326
18. Hadid, A., Pietikäinen, M.: Efficient Locally Linear Embeddings of Imperfect Manifolds. Machine Learning and Data Mining in Pattern Recognition, Third International Conference, MLDM 2003, Leipzig, Germany (2003) 188-201

19. Belkin, M., Niyogi, P.: Laplacian Eigenmaps for Dimensionality Reduction and Data Representation. Neural Computation, Vol. 15, No. 6 (2003) 1373C1396
20. Li, Y.: Distance-Preserving Projection of High-dimensional Data for Nonlinear Dimensionality Reduction. IEEE Transactions on Pattern Analysis and Machine Intelligence, Vol.26, No. 9 (2004) 1243-1246
21. Li, J.X.Z.: Visualization of high-dimensional data with relational perspective map. Information Visualization, Vol. 3, No. 1 (2004) 49-59
22. Bernstein, M., de Silva, V., Langford, J.C., Tenenbaum, J.B.: Graph approximations to geodesics on embedded manifolds. Technical report, Department of Psychology, Stanford University (2000)
23. Trosset, M.W.: Extensions of Classical Multidimensional Scaling: Computational Theory. Computational Statistics, Vol. 17 (2002) 147-162

Supporting Generalized Cases in Conversational CBR

Mingyang Gu

Department of Computer and Information Science,
Norwegian University of Science and Technology,
Sem Saelands vei 7-9, N-7491, Trondheim, Norway
mingyang@idi.ntnu.no

Abstract. Conversational Case-Based Reasoning (CCBR) provides a mixed-initiative dialog for guiding users to refine their problem descriptions incrementally through a question-answering sequence. Most CCBR approaches assume that there is at most one discrete value on each feature. While a generalized case (GC), which has been proposed and used in traditional CBR processes, has multiple values on some features. Motivated by the conversational software component retrieval application, we focus on the problem of extending CCBR to support GCs in this paper. This problem is tackled from two aspects: similarity measuring and discriminative question ranking.

1 Introduction

The basic idea underlying case-based reasoning (CBR) [1, 2] is to reuse the solution to the previous most similar problem in helping solve the current problem. In traditional CBR processes, users are assumed to be able to provide a well-defined problem description, and based on such a description a CBR system can find the most appropriate previous case (base case). But this assumption is not always realistic. In some situations, users only have vague ideas about their problems at the beginning of retrieval, and tend to describe them by surface features.

Conversational Case-Based Reasoning (CCBR) [3] provides a mixed-initiative dialog for guiding users to construct their problem descriptions incrementally through a question-answering sequence. In CCBR, as illustrated in Fig. 1, a user provides her initial problem description that is to be transformed as an initial new case. The CCBR system uses the initial new case to retrieve the first set of most similar cases, and identifies a group of informative features from them to generate discriminative questions. Both the retrieved cases and identified discriminative questions are ranked and shown to the user. The user either finds out the base case to terminate the retrieval process or chooses a question to answer. An updated new case is constructed through combining the previous new case with the newly answered question. Subsequent rounds of retrieving and question-answering will iterate until the user finds her desired

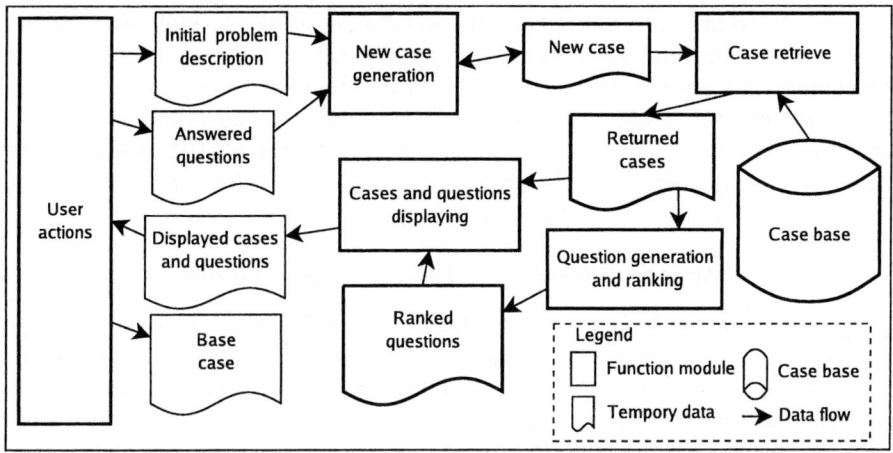

Fig. 1. Conversational Case-Based Reasoning

base case or no discriminative questions are available. CCBR applications have been successfully fielded, such as [3, 4, 5, 6].

Most of the works in CCBR assume that on each feature, there is either missing value or one discrete value (so called point cases, PC). While a GC [7] has multiple values on some features. In the CBR community, there are a considerable amount of research works concerning GCs [8, 9, 10, 11]. While to our knowledge, there are no published results about how to support GCs in CCBR. In this paper, motivated by the software component retrieval application [6], we extend CCBR process to support GCs.

The rest of this paper is organized as follows. In Section 2, we present the software component retrieval application, in which both the component query and stored software components are formalized as GCs; a formal model to represent GCs and a method to calculate the similarity between them are presented in Section 3 and Section 4, respectively; in Section 5, we analyze the feasibilities of applying the current question ranking methods in CCBR to support GCs; related works are listed in Section 6, and we draw our conclusion in Section 7.

2 Motivation to Support Generalized Cases in CCBR

2.1 Software Component Retrieval Using Conversational CBR

Software component retrieval, which is concerned with how to locate and identify appropriate components to satisfy users' requirements, is one of the major problems associated with the software component reuse. With the emergence of several component architecture standards, such as, CORBA, COM, and EJB, software components interoperation becomes more easily. Therefore, component reuse surpasses the limitation of a single software company, that is, instead of getting components from an in-house component library, users search for desired components from component markets (web-based software component collections provided by vendors or third parties). Without the knowledge about how the components are constructed and stored by others, it is very hard for users to well define their component queries. In our research, we propose a conversational software component retrieval approach using the CCBR technology, in which each component takes the form of a stored case, and a component query, as a new case, is constructed by the conversational process.

2.2 Representing Component and Query Using Generalized Cases

Comparing with the PCs used in traditional CCBR works, cases used to support component retrieval need to have multiple values on some features (GCs) for both a new case and stored cases. The semantic for a stored case (a software component) to have multiple values on one feature is that one software component has the capability to function in several situations specified by the multiple values on that feature. For instance, in the image processing domain, if a software component has three values on one feature, 'input image type': BMP, JPEG and TIFF, it means that component has the ability to process all these three different types of images. While the semantic for a new case to have multiple values on one feature is that a user demands all the requirements specified by these values to be satisfied.

3 A Formal Generalized Case Representation Method

Generally, a case in CBR can be represented by a three-item vector $< PD, SD, O >$ [2]:

—PD (Problem Description): the state of the world at the time the case was happening and, if appropriate, what problem needed to be solved at that time.

—SD (Solution Description): the stated or derived solution to the problem specified in the problem description.

—O (Outcome): the resulting state of the world after the solution has been carried out.

In our research, the PD part of a GC takes the form of a set of $< feature, value >$ pairs (fv pairs). Comparing with the fv pairs used for the PD of a PC, those for a GC have the following characteristics:

— For a PC, there is at most one fv pair for each feature. On the contrary, there may be multiple fv pairs for each feature in the PD part of a GC. Each fv pair in a generalized new case presents a specific requirement of the user on this feature, while that in the generalized stored case tells that the software component presented by this case can support the function described by this fv pair.

— For a PC, the $value$ in each fv pair takes the form of a single number (numeric feature) or a string (nominal feature). On the contrary, the $value$ in a fv pair of a GC may be either a single value (a number or a string) or a numeric interval. When the value takes the form of a numeric interval, it means, for a generalized new case, all the values existing in the interval are the demanded requirements by the user on this feature, and for a generalized stored case, the software component presented by this case can support all the functions or function variables specified by the values contained in the numeric interval.

Since the goal of the CCBR process is to identify the most similar or appropriate stored case in the case base, we use the unique tag of each case as the SD part and drop off the O information from the case description. In the software component retrieval application, we use each component's unique name as the SD part of the corresponding case.

A new case in the CCBR process has only the PD part compared with a stored case that has both the PD and SD parts.

As illustrated by Fig. 1, to complete a CCBR process, we need further defining the following two modules: case retrieve module, and question generation and ranking module.

4 Supporting Generalized Case Retrieval Using a Query-Biased Similarity Calculation Method

One important difference between CBR and CCBR lies on the content of the new case. In CBR, including that supporting GCs, a new case is assumed to be created completely in advance, and the case retrieval process is completed in one shot of retrieval. While a new case in CCBR is incrementally constructed by a sequence of question-answering processes, so it is incompletely or partially specified during the middle-stage retrieval process. There are some features that get values in stored cases, while have not be assigned values in a new case in the middle stage of the conversational retrieval process. The similarities on these features are the same, unmatched, to all the stored cases. In fact, if these features are assigned values in the end, the similarities on these features should benefit the final base case. So in order to avoid the negative influences of these features on the similarity measurement in the middle stage of the conversational retrieval, a query-biased similarity calculation method, which only takes the features appearing in the new case (query) into account, is more suitable for CCBR. The empirical efficiency of this method has been evaluated in [12]. The semantics behind this method is that to which degree the partially specified new case is satisfied by each stored case decides the possibility of that stored case to be selected and shown to the user. In our research, we compute the similarity by counting how many or to what degree the incomplete requirements specified by the fv pairs in a new case are satisfied by the fv pairs in a stored case.

In our approach, the similarity measurement is defined using the concept of distance. The greater the distance between a new case and a stored case, the less the similarity between them is.

$$distance(n, c) = \sqrt{\frac{\sum_{fv \in FVS} w_{fv} dif^2(fv, c)}{\sum_{fv \in FVS} w_{fv}}} \qquad (1)$$

In addition, $dif(fv, c)$ is a function used to compute the difference between the new case and a stored case on the fv pair or to what degree this fv pair is satisfied by the stored case, c, which is defined as follows:

$$dif(fv,c) =$$

$$\begin{cases} 1 & c \text{ has missing value on feature } f \\ 1 & f \text{ is a nominal feature, and } c \text{ has not the } fv \text{ pair} \\ & \text{in its } PD \\ 0 & f \text{ is a nominal feature, and } c \text{ has the } fv \text{ pair in its } PD \\ |v - near(f,v,c)| & f \text{ is a normalized numeric feature, and } v \text{ is} \\ & \text{a single number} \\ 1 - (\frac{len(cov(f,v,c))}{len(v)}) & f \text{ is a normalized numeric features, and v is} \\ & \text{a interval value} \end{cases}$$
(2)

where $near(f,v,c)$ is a function to find out the nearest value of v in c on feature f, $cov(f,v,c)$ is a function to return the subintervals of v covered by the values in c on feature f, and $len()$ is a function to compute the length of its parameter (interval/intervals). For example, there are three fv pairs on a normalized numeric feature f : $(f, 0.1), (f, [0.2, 0.3]), and (f, [0.6, 0.8])$ in a stored case c, and two fv pairs in a new case n, $(f, 0.55) and (f, [0.2, 0.7])$. The differences for each fv pair in n are calculated as follows:

$$dif((f, 0.55), c) = |0.55 - near(f, 0.55, c)| = |0.55 - 0.6| = 0.05$$

$$dif((f, [0.2, 0.7]), c) = 1 - (\frac{len(cov(f,[0.2,0.7],c))}{len([0.2,0.7])}) = 1 - (\frac{len(\{[0.2,0.3],[0.6,0.7]\})}{0.5})$$
$$= 1 - (\frac{0.2}{0.5}) = 0.6$$
(3)

5 Selecting a Discriminative Question Ranking Metric

In our approach, the features that appear in the currently retrieved cases, but have not been assigned values in the current new case, will be transferred as discriminative questions. For example, in the currently retrieved cases, there is a feature, 'input image dimension', which is used to describe how many dimensions the input images of the corresponding software component should have. This feature has not been assigned values in the current new case, so a discriminative question, 'how many dimensions do you want the input images of your desired component to have?'

Before all identified discriminative questions are displayed to users, they are ranked according to their capabilities of discriminating the stored cases from each other if they are answered. In fact, CCBR research is currently to a large extent focusing on the discriminative question selecting and ranking in order to minimize the cognitive load on users to retrieve the base case. We review the question ranking methods used in traditional CCBR and classify them into four categories: information metric [5, 13, 14, 15, 16], occurrence frequency metric [3, 17], importance weight metric [12], and feature selection strategies [18]. We analyze, in the following subsections, the feasibilities of applying them in the CCBR supporting GCs, and propose the necessary adjustments if they can not be used directly.

5.1 Information Metric

Information is a way of measuring the uncertainty of a user about which stored case is the base case. When there is no clear requirement specified in the query (new case), the uncertainty is highest. With more and more features get their values in a new case, the uncertainty will reduce step by step. Normally, entropy function is used to quantify the uncertainty, and information gain measurement is used to measure which feature, if it is answered or assigned values, can produce most information. In [16], the author further proved that if the SD part of each case in a case base is unique (so called irreducible case base), the information gain one feature may provide is calculated by the following equation:

$$-\sum_i p_i log p_i \qquad (4)$$

where $p_1, p_2...p_r$ are the propositions of this feature's values in the counted stored cases.

At first glance, it is impossible to apply the information metric-based feature ranking method in the CCBR supporting GCs, since the information metric requires each feature can at most have one single discrete value in a case. While through the following three steps, the generalized case base can be transferred to a state where the information metric can be applied:

—1. if there is a numeric interval value on one feature, we can use the sampling method applying on the value field of that feature to generate a set of sample numbers to represent the numeric interval.

—2. if there is a continuous-valued feature in the case base, Mitchell [19] discussed the methods transferring a continuous-valued feature into a discrete-valued feature through dynamically defining new discrete-valued features that partition the continuous attribute value into a discrete set of intervals.

—3. if there are multiple discrete values on one feature in a case, we can simply combine all these discrete values together to form a new value and add it into the value set for this feature. This step may cause a problem of combination explosion if the discrete values are combined randomly or irregularly. However, in practical application domains, the values, combined together to form a new value, normally have some semantic relations behind them. For instance, in the image processing software component retrieval application, there is a feature called 'the datatype of the input image'. On this feature, there are 12 discrete features totally, such as, byte, word, Dword, signed char, short, long, signed int, signed short, float, double, float complex, and double complex. While the number of the combination values of these discrete values is only 5, such as anyDataType, realDataType, integerDataType, unsignedIntegerDataType, and complexDataType. This is because the software component producers always provide the functions that are similar or related to each other, other than randomly selecting them in order to improve a component's function without increasing too much cost.

5.2 Occurrence Frequency Metric

In NaCoDAE (Navy Conversational Decision Aids Environment) [3], the identified discriminative questions are ranked according to their frequency appearing in the PD part of the returned cases. The larger the number of the returned cases in which one feature is assigned values, the higher ranking priority that feature gets. In this metric, it is assumed that the cases are highly heterogeneous, that is, the features appearing in one case may not appear in another case.

This metric will not deal with PCs or GCs differently, since it only count whether there is assigned value/values on one feature in a case. Therefore, this discriminative question ranking method can be directly applied in the CCBR supporting GCs.

5.3 Importance Weight Metric

One problem in case-based reasoning is the curse of the dimensionality [19], that is, not all the available features are relevant or equally important. Feature weighting method can avoid this problem by assigning different features with various importance weights according to their contributions, such as EACH [20] and Relief [21]. The rational behind the importance weight-based feature ranking method is that the most relevant or important features can provide more information than other features to discriminate cases from one another.

If we can find out features' importance weights, this metric can be used in the CCBR supporting GCs. While the fact, there are multiple values on some features in GCs, may cause difficulties in some weighting methods. For example, Relief requires computing the difference between a new case and a stored case on a particular feature as a whole. This problem can be solved by calculating the average, maximal or minimal value of all the difference values of the fv pairs sharing the same feature f, which are computed by Equation 2. Another point we need pay attention to is that some weight learning methods, for instance EACH and Relief, are supervised-learning process, that is, the cases in a case base should be able to be classified into limited number of groups or categories according to cases' SDs. If the case base is irreducible [16], such as the software component library (case base), these weighting methods are unsuitable.

5.4 Feature Selection Strategies Metric

From the perspective that whether the question ranking process can be explained, McSherry provided a new type of method, Strategist [18]. This method provided four feature-selection strategies, CONFIRM, ELIMINATE, VALIDATE, and OPPOSE, listed in order of priority. A feature supports the CONFIRM strategy, if it has a value that occurs only in the target solution class in the current returned cases, the ELIMINATE strategy if one of its values occurs in the target solution class but not in the likeliest alternative solution class, the VALIDATE strategy if one of its value is more likely in the target solution class than in any others, and the OPPOSE strategy if one of its values is less likely in the likeliest alternative solution class than in any others.

If we follow the three steps listed in the information metric subsection to transform the interval-valued features, continuous-valued, and multiple-valued features into the single-discrete-valued features, this method can be applied to the CCBR supporting GCs. In addition, this feature selection strategies metric uses a supervised process, and can not be applied to the irreducible case base.

5.5 Choosing a Suitable Discriminative Question Ranking Metric

For the software component retrieval application, we choose the information metric as the discriminative question ranking method. The rational behind our decision is that the case base storing software components is irreducible, therefore, we drop the importance weight metric and the feature selection strategies metric that incorporate supervised processes inside. In addition, the heterogeneous level of our case base is quite low, which makes it less efficient to choose the occurrence frequency metric.

6 Related Research

Recently, there are several researches [7, 22, 23] on how to calculate the similarity between GCs. The authors described a GC as a subspace in the case space, constructed by the case's features, instead of a point as in the traditional CBR. They formulate the similarity calculation problem between two GCs as a mathematical optimization problem. Comparing to their works, our method supports similarity measurement of GCs particularly for CCBR application. That is, in CCBR a new case is partially specified and incomplete, so a query-biased similarity calculation method is more suitable. In addition, we also tackle the discriminative question ranking problem in the CCBR supporting GCs.

In [24], Gupta proposed a taxonomic conversational CBR approach to solve the problems caused by the abstraction relations among feature values. In his approach, for each feature, an independent subsumption taxonomy is created by the case base designer in advance, and only the most specific fv pair in each feature taxonomy is selected to describe a case. The similarity between one fv pair in a new case and that in a stored case with the same f is calculated based on their values' relative positions in the taxonomy. The question generated from a higher level feature value in one feature taxonomy is constrained to be asked before those that come from the lower level feature values. If we consider that a higher level feature value in the feature taxonomy may implicitly contain all its lower-level feature values, this method is capable of supporting GCs in some sense. While comparing with our method, his method is unable to support a feature to have multiple values on the same abstraction level.

7 Conclusion

In this paper, we focus on the problem of supporting GCs in CCBR. This problem is tackled from two aspects: similarity measuring and discriminative question ranking. In similarity measuring, we adopt a query-biased similarity calculation method, that is, to count how many or to what degree the requirements specified by the fv pairs in a new case are satisfied by each stored cases. For discriminative question ranking, we analyze the feasibilies of applying four types of question ranking metrics, used in traditional CCBR, in the CCBR supporting GCs. In addition, from the software component retrieval application, we discuss the semantics of GCs, and exemplify how to choose a question ranking metric according to the characteristics of the application.

Recently, how to improve CCBR using knowledge-intensive methods is getting more and more attention [3, 17, 24, 25]. How to support GCs in knowledge-intensive CCBR methods is our further research direction, for instance, the multiple values assign to a feature may have overlapping or conflicting semantic relations.

References

1. Aamodt, A., Plaza, E.: Case-based reasoning: Foundational issue, methodological variations, and system approaches. AI Communications **7** (1994) 39–59
2. Kolodner, J.: Case-based reasoning. Morgan Kaufmann Publishers Inc. (1993)
3. Aha, D.W., Breslow, L.A., Munoz-Avila, H.: Conversational case-based reasoning. Applied Intelligence: The International Journal of Artificial Intelligence, Neural Networks, and Complex Problem-Solving Technologies **14** (2001) 9
4. Gupta, K.M.: Knowledge-based system for troubleshooting complex equipment. international Journal of Information and Computing Science **1** (1998) 29–41
5. Shimazu, H.: Expertclerk: A conversational case-based reasoning tool for developing salesclerk agents in e-commerce webshops. Artificial Intelligence Review **18** (2002) 223 – 244
6. Gu, M., Aamodt, A., Tong, X.: Component retrieval using conversational case-based reasoning. In Shi, Z., ed.: International Conference on Intelligent Information Systems, Beijing, China (2004)
7. Maximini, K., Maximini, R., Bergmann, R.: An investigation of generalized cases. In: 5th International Conference on Case-Based Reasoning, Trondheim, Norway (2003) 261 – 275
8. Kolodner, J.L., Simpson, R.L.: The mediator: Analysis of an early case-based problem solver. Cognitive Science **13** (1989) 507–549
9. Reinartz, T., Iglezakis, I., Roth-Berghofer, T.: Review and restore for case-based maintenance. Computational Intelligence **17** (2001) 214–234
10. Rayner, N.J.W., Harris, C.J.: Mission management for multiple autonomous vehicles. research journal of University of Southampton (1996)
11. Gebhardt, F., Vob, A., Grather, W., Schmidt-Belz, B.: Reasoning with complex cases. Kluwer Academic Publishers (1997)
12. Gu, M., Tong, X.: Comparing similarity calculation methods in conversational cbr. In: Submitted to the 2005 IEEE International Conference on Information Reuse and Integration, Hilton, Las Vegas, Nevada, USA (2005)
13. Cunningham, P., Smyth, B.: A comparison of model-based and incremental case-based approaches to electronic fault diagnosis. in. In: Case-Based Reasoning Workshop, Seattle, USA (1994)

14. Carrick, C., Yang, Q., Abi-Zeid, I., Lamontagne, L.: Activating cbr systems through autonomous information gathering. In: International Conference on Case Based Reasoning, Germany (1999)
15. Goker, M.H., Thompson, C.A.: Personalized conversational case-based recommendation. In: the 5th European Workshop on Case-Based Reasoning(EWCBR 2000), Trento, Italy (2000)
16. McSherry, D.: Minimizing dialog length in interactive case-based reasoning. In: International Joint Conferences on Artificial Intelligence. (2001) 993–998
17. Gu, M., Aamodt, A.: A knowledge-intensive method for conversational cbr. In: International Conference on Case-Based Reasoning, Chicago Illinois (2005)
18. McSherry, D.: Interactive case-based reasoning in sequential diagnosis. Applied Intelligence **14** (2001) 65–76
19. Mitchell, T.: Decision tree learning. In: Machine Learning. McGraw Hill (1997) 414
20. Salzberg, S.: A nearest hyperrectangle learning method. Mach. Learn. **6** (1991) 251–276
21. Kira, K., Rendell, L.: The feature selection problem traditional methods and a new algorithm. In: Tenth National Conference on Artificial Intelligence. (1992)
22. Mougouie, B., Bergmann, R.: Similarity assessment for generalizied cases by optimization methods. In: 6th European Conference on Case-Based Reasoning, Aberdeen, Scotland, UK (2002) 249 – 263
23. Alexander Tartakovski, Martin Schaaf, R.M., Bergmann, R.: Minlp based retrieval of generalized cases. In: 7th European Conference on Case-Based Reasoning, Madrid, Spain (2004) 404 – 418
24. Gupta, K.M.: Taxonomic conversational case-based reasoning. In: International Conference on Case-Based Reasoning, Vancouver, BC, Canada (2001) 219–233
25. Gupta, K.M., Aha, D.W., Sandhu, N.: Exploiting taxonomic and causal relations in conversational case retrieval. In: European Conference on Case Based Reasoning, Aberdeen, Scotland, UK (2002) 133–147

Organizing Large Case Library by Linear Programming

Caihong Sun[1], Simon Chi Keung Shiu[2], and Xizhao Wang[3]

[1] Information School, Renmin University of China, Beijing, 100872, P.R. China
caihongsun@vip.sina.com
[2] Computing Department, The Hong Kong Polytechnic University,
Hung Hum, Kowloon, Hong Kong
csckshiu@comp.polyu.edu.hk
[3] College of Mathematics and Computer, Hebei University,
Baoding City, Hebei Province, 071002, P.R. China
wangxz@mail.hbu.edu.cn

Abstract. In this paper we proposed an approach to maintain large case library, which based on the idea that a large case library can be transformed to a compact one by using a set of case-specific weights. A linear programming technique is being used to obtain case-specific weights. By learning such local weights knowledge, many of redundant or similar cases can be removed from the original case library or stored in a secondary case library. This approach is useful for case library with a large number of redundant or similar cases and the retrieval efficiency is a real concern of the user. This method of maintaining case library from scratch, as proposed in this paper, consists of two main steps. First, a linear programming technique for learning case-specific weights is used to evaluate the importance of different features for each case. Second, a case selection strategy based on the concepts of case coverage and reachability is carried out to select representative cases. Furthermore, a case retrieval strategy of the compact case library we built is discussed. The effectiveness of the approach is demonstrated experimentally by using two sets of testing data, and the results are promising.

1 Introduction

Nowadays, with information exploding, how to help users to locate the information what they need is a big challenge for the information providers, educators. Recently, how to build an efficient case library are proposed and discussed a lot by many researchers, especially with the rapid growth of case-based reasoning (CBR) systems both in research area and commercial use in e-business. Maintaining case libraries become more important when case-based reasoning (CBR) systems are being used to solve wide range of problems. Large-scale CBR systems are becoming more prevalent, with case library sizes ranging from thousands [1] to millions of cases [2]. With the increasing growth of the size of a case base, case retrieval takes longer time and case base maintenance, which is defined as the process of refining a case base to improve the system's performance [3], has become an active research topic. Various case base maintenance problems have been addressed in the past few years. To provide maintenance support at the case level, [4] suggested a competence preserving deletion approach. Competence (or coverage) is the range of target problems that a given system can solve, and is also a fundamental evaluation criterion of CBR system performance. In [5], the authors presented a new model of case competence, and demonstrated a way in which the proposed model of competence can be used to assist case authors. Authors in [6] used data mining techniques in a novel role of a back-end technology for CBR systems, i.e., the acquisition of cases and discovery of adaptation knowledge. [7] used advanced AI techniques such as neural networks and fuzzy methods to acquire features' importance and eliminate irrelevant features in a given dataset. One important concept in the CBR community is to distinguish the salient features from all the features in the dataset; feature selection methods can reduce the task's dimensionality when they eliminate irrelevant features [8]. In [7,8,9], for each feature, a value can be assigned to indicate the degree of importance of this feature. In [10] the authors introduced the local weight concept while investigating weighted fuzzy production rules in which a local weight is assigned to each proposition of a rule to indicate the degree of importance of the proposition in the antecedent contributing to its consequent. In this paper, we use the local weight concept to select representative cases from a large case library. A local weight called case-specific weight is assigned to each feature of each case to indicate the degree of importance of the feature contributing to its case.

Nearest neighbor (NN) algorithms are techniques used to solve Pattern Recognition and Classification problems. Nowadays NNs is used for case retrieval in CBR systems 12]. [11] demonstrated that even if cases are not explicitly classified into a set of finite groups (classes), the solution space can often be clustered into a collection of sets and each set contains similar solutions. The NN classification procedure is very straightforward: given a set of classified examples, which are described as points in an input space, a new unclassified example is assigned to the known class of the nearest example. Many researchers [13,14,15] use local metrics to compute the "nearest" relation while others use global metrics. In our paper, we use case-specific weight to compute the "nearest" relation. In order to ignore the noisy data and improve the retrieval efficiency of CBR systems, we propose a method to maintain the case base by selecting representative cases based on the coverage and reachability concepts. After applying the maintenance process, the case base contains fewer cases, and many noisy cases were deleted.

We establish an approach to transfer the original large case library to a small one with the purpose that it can significantly improve the retrieval efficiency and the performance of the system. Furthermore, the computational complexity of acquiring local specified feature weights is relative small when comparing with neuro-fuzzy feature learning. The approach integrates learning case-specific weight, computing case competence and selecting seed cases into a framework of case base maintenance. The maintaining methodology has two main steps. First, a linear programming technique is used to learn case-specific weights and evaluate the importance of different features for each case. Second, a case selection strategy based on the concepts of case coverage and reachability is used to select representative cases. Furthermore, based on the framework of case maintenance, we discuss a case retrieval strategy and a case addition strategy. In order to demonstrate the effectiveness of this approach, two experiments using the Pima Indians Diabetes and the Australian Credit Approval are carried out. The results show that the two testing case bases can be reduced by 89.96% and 90.04% respectively. The training set overall accuracy of the two smaller case bases is 100%, and the testing set overall accuracy is 73.48% and 79.71% respectively.

2 Approach of Maintaining a Case Library

Consider a case library where an individual case is represented as (Problem, Solution). The problem is assumed to be an n-dimensional vector $(p_1, p_2, \cdots, p_n)$ where each component corresponds to a feature (attribute) of the case library. The solution, without losing generality, is regarded as a cluster symbol taking values of 0 and 1 where 0 denotes positive class and 1 negative class. In other words, all cases in the case library are categorized into two classes. They are the positive class X with the individual case $x = (x_1, x_2, \cdots, x_n)$, and the negative class Y with the individual case $y = (y_1, y_2, \cdots, y_n)$.

Assume that, for each feature, a distance measure has been defined. The distance measure for the j-th feature is denoted by ρ_j, i.e., ρ_j is a mapping from $F_j \times F_j$ to $[0, \infty)$ (where F_j denotes the range of the j-th feature) with the properties:

(1) $\rho_j(a,b) = 0$ if and only if a = b;
(2) $\rho_j(a,b) = \rho_j(b,a)$ and
(3) $\rho_j(a,b) \leq \rho_j(a,c) + \rho_j(c,b)$

Usually the distance measure depends on the specific domains. In this paper, we define the distance measure as follows:

(1) $\rho_j(a,b) = |a-b|$ if a and b are real numbers;

(2) $\rho_j(a,b) = \begin{cases} 1 \text{ if } a \neq b \\ 0 \text{ if } a = b \end{cases}$ if a and b are symbols.

We now define the distance measure between two cases. For any pair of cases $x = (x_1, x_2, \cdots, x_n)$ and $y = (y_1, y_2, \cdots, y_n)$, the distance measure is defined as

$$d(x,y) = \frac{1}{M} \sum_{j=1}^{n} \rho_j(x_j, y_j) \tag{1}$$

where M is such a positive number to scale that the value range of the distance measure into [0, 1]. Usually, the number M can be determined by

$$M = \max_{x \in X, y \in Y} od(x, y). \tag{2}$$

and $od(x, y) = \sum_{j=1}^{n} \rho_j(x_j, y_j)$.

After introducing the distance measure, our methodology, which consists of two major phases, will be described in sub-sections 2.1 and 2.2 respectively. Furthermore, based on maintenance framework, section 2.3 will discuss about case retrieval strategy.

2.1 Phase One - Learning Case-Specific Weights

In this section, a feature evaluation function is defined. The smaller the evaluation value, the better the corresponding case-specific weights. Thus we would like to find the weights such that the evaluation function attains its minimum by using a linear programming technique. We formulate this optimization problem as follows. We first introduce a new distance measure based on case-specific weight, called pseudo-distance.

For any given case $p = (p_1, p_2, \cdots, p_n)$, its case-specific weight refers to a vector $w^{(p)} = (w_1^{(p)}, w_2^{(p)}, \cdots, w_n^{(p)})$ where each component is non-negative real number. When no confusion occurs, the superscript (p) can be omitted.

By incorporating the case-specific weight into the distance measure, a pseudo-distance measure for a pair of cases $x = (x_1, x_2, \cdots, x_n)$ and $y = (y_1, y_2, \cdots, y_n)$ can be defined as

$$d_x(y) = \sum_{j=1}^{n} w_j^{(x)} \rho_j(x_j, y_j) \tag{3}$$

Where $w_j^{(x)}$ is the case-specific weight corresponding to the j-th component of case x. This measure is called pseudo-distance because the symmetry $d_x(y) = d_y(x)$ generally does not hold. Here we denote $d_x(y)$ as the distance from y to x.

For a fixed case $p = (p_1, p_2, \cdots, p_n) \in X$ with case-specific weight vector $w = (w_1, w_2, \cdots, w_n)$, we consider the following function:

$$E_p(w_1, w_2, \cdots, w_n) = \sum_{x \in X} \left(\frac{\beta}{1-\beta} d_p(x)(1 - d(p, x)) - d(p, x) d_p(x) \right) \tag{4}$$

Where β is a constant in (0,1). The two measures, $d(p, x)$ and $d_p(x)$ are regarded as the old and new distance from case x to case p respectively. Noting that

$$\frac{\partial}{\partial d_p(x)} E_p(w_1, w_2, \cdots, w_n) = \sum_{x \in X} \left(\frac{\beta}{1-\beta} - \frac{1}{1-\beta} d(p, x) \right) \tag{5}$$

We have

(1) if $d(p, x) < \beta$ then $E_p(w_1, w_2, \cdots, w_n)$ monotonically increases with respect to $d_p(x)$; and

(2) if $d(p, x) > \beta$ then $E_p(w_1, w_2, \cdots, w_n)$ monotonically decreases with respect to $d_p(x)$.

It implies that, when $d(p,x) < \beta$, $d_p(x)$ approaches its minimum (or when $d(p,x) > \beta$, $d_p(x)$ approaches its maximum), the evaluation function (4) monotonically approaches its minimum. Thus, we expect that, by minimizing the evaluation function (4), $d_p(x)$ becomes small (when $d(p,x) < \beta$) or big (when $d(p,x) > \beta$). If the parameter β is regarded as a threshold, then $d(p,x) < \beta$ ($d(p,x) > \beta$ resp.) can be interpreted as that the old distance from x to p is relatively "small" ("big" resp.). By minimizing function (4), we expect that the new distance from x to p, $d_p(x)$, becomes smaller (bigger resp.). It is clear that the objective of minimizing function (4) is to make the case classification decision easy. In other words, under the principle that "The smaller the distance between cases, the more possibly the two cases belonging to the same cluster", the decision for determining whether two cases belonging to the same cluster in the new distance measure is easier than in the old distance measure.

We now focus on the minimization of function (4) under certain conditions. Let $c = d(p,x)$ and

$$\chi_j = \rho_j(x_j, p_j) \qquad (5^*)$$

Then, from equation (4), (1) and (3), we have

$$E_p(w_1, w_2, \cdots, w_n) = \sum_{x \in X} \left(\frac{\beta}{1-\beta} \left(\sum_{j=1}^n w_j \chi_j \right)(1-c) - \left(\sum_{j=1}^n w_j \chi_j \right) c \right)$$

$$= \sum_{x \in X} \left(\sum_{j=1}^n \left(\frac{\beta}{1-\beta}(1-c)\chi_j - c\chi_j \right) \right) w_j = \sum_{j=1}^n k_j w_j \qquad (6)$$

Where $k_j = \sum_{x \in X} \left(\left(\frac{\beta}{1-\beta}(1-c) - c \right) \chi_j \right), j = 1, 2, \cdots, n.$ (6*)

It is no meaning minimizing (6) if without any constraints. Suppose that the case library $X \cup Y$ has no conflicted cases, i.e., there exist no two cases $x \in X$ and $y \in Y$ such that $x = y$. The shortest distance (in old measure) from the positive case p to the negative set Y is given by:

$$\varepsilon_p = \min_{y \in Y} d(p,y) \qquad (7)$$

Thus, the inequality $\varepsilon_p > 0$ holds. We hope that, in new pseudo-distance measure, the distance from p to each negative y is not less than ε_p. That is,

$$\min_{y \in Y} d_p(y) \geq \min_{y \in Y} d(p,y) \qquad (8)$$

We attempt to find a set of case-specific weights for the case p such that the function (6) achieves minimum subject to the constraint (8). This is an optimization problem with constraints. Noting that equation (8) is equivalent to $d_p(y) \geq \varepsilon_p$ for all cases $y \in Y$, and $d_p(y) = \sum_{j=1}^{n} w_j \rho_j(p_j, y_j)$, the optimization problem becomes the following linear programming problem:

$$\min E_p(w_1, w_2, \cdots, w_n) = \sum_{j=1}^{n} k_j w_j$$
$$\text{s.t.} \quad d_p(y) = \sum_{j=1}^{n} \alpha_j w_j \geq \varepsilon_p, \quad y \in Y \qquad (9)$$
$$0 \leq w_j \leq 1 \quad j = 1, 2, \cdots, n$$

Where k_j is given by equations (6*), α_j is defined as $\alpha_j = \rho_j(p_j, y_j)$, and ε_p is specified by equation (7).

2.2 Phase Two - Representative Cases Selection Strategy

This phase aims to select representative cases from positive class X according to the case-specific weights obtained in phase one. Our selection strategy is based on a coverage concept.

After solving the linear programming (9), we can obtain a set of case-specific weights $(w_1^{(p)}, w_2^{(p)}, \cdots, w_n^{(p)})$ for each positive $p = (p_1, p_2, \cdots, p_n) \in X$. Using this set of case-specific weights, we define the coverage of a positive case. Let p be a given positive case, q be an arbitrary case, we say p covers q if

$$d_p(q) < \varepsilon_p \qquad (10)$$

where ε_p is specified by equation (7). The coverage of p, Coverage(p), is defined as

$$Coverage(p) = \{e \mid d_p(e) < \varepsilon_p\} \qquad (11)$$

From equation (7) we know that a positive example covers a negative example is impossible. In other words, the coverage of a positive case is a subset of X. Similarly, we can define the reachablity of p as

$$\text{Re} \, achibillity(p) = \{e \mid d_e(p) < \varepsilon_p\} \qquad (12)$$

The coverage of a case p represents the generalization capability of this case. The bigger the number of cases in its coverage, the more representative the selected case p. On the other hand, the reachability of a case p represents the degree to which p can be covered by another case. From equation (11) and (12), we can determine both the coverage and the reachability for each positive case p. The current objective is to select a set of positive cases with their case-specific weights such that the selected cases can cover the entire positive set X. In fact, the selected cases can exclude the entire negative set Y.

There is always a trade-off between the number of cases to be stored in the case library of a Case-Based Expert System and the performance of retrieval efficiency. The larger the case library, the more the problem space covered. However, it would also downgrade the system performance if the number of cases grows to an unacceptable high level. We expect the number of the selected representatives to be as small as possible. Thus our selection strategy is described as:

"*Finding a set of positive cases which can cover the entire positive set X such that the number of this set of cases attains minimum.*"

Finding an exact algorithm for our optimal selection problem is not realistic, since it is a NP-hard problem. An intuitive and powerful heuristic algorithm is described as follows.

The set R is initialized to be empty.

1. For each case p in X, determine Coverage(p) and Reachability(p) by equations (11) and (12).
2. Find case p* such that $|Coverage(p^*)| = Max_{p \in L}|Coverage(p)|$. If there exists more than one case such that the maximum is reached, then select a case p** from them such that $|Reachability(p^{**})| = Min_{p^*}|Reachability(p^*)|$. If there exists more than one case such that the minimum is reached, select one randomly.
3. Put $R = R \cup \{p^*\}$ and $L = L - Coverage(p^*)$, if $|L| = 0$ then stop else goto 1.

Consequently, the set R is approximately regarded as the set of selected representative cases.

2.3 Case Retrieval Strategy

After the above two phases, we obtain a case library with a group of representative positive cases and a group of representative negative cases, together with a case specific weight with each case. When a test case comes, we use Nearest Neighbor (NN) algorithm to retrieve cases in the new case library. Here we modify the NN algorithm a little, i.e. use pseudo-distance given in equation (3) to compute distance between the test case and each representative cases (with case specific weights) in the obtained compact case library.

2.4 An Example

There is a case base with 10 cases, each case has 4 attributes, 6 cases belong to positive class X, and the other 4 cases belong to negative class Y. Without losing generality, we consider case 1 to 6 as class X, and case 7 to 10 as class Y. Now we use this sample case base to demonstrate our approach.

Learning the specific weight of case p (a positive case). First we use Equation (7) to compute ε_p, then for a given constant β in (0,1), apply case p (here p=1,2,...,6) and negative cases (i.e. case 7 – case 10) in class Y to linear programming problem specified as equation (9). After solving this linear programming problem, we get a specific weight for case p.

Now we've got a set of specific weights for each positive case. Then we apply these weights to the heuristic algorithm described in section 2.2 to obtain the selected representative cases.

3 Experimental Analyses

This section presents the experimental analysis of our methodology on two real-world problems, i.e. the Pima Indians Diabetes (PID)[1] and the Australian Credit Approval (ACA)[2] problems. The PID data consist of 8 attributes with numeric values (The 8 attributes are " Number of times pregnant", "Plasma glucose concentration a 2 hours in an oral glucose tolerance test", "Diastolic blood pressure (mm Hg)", "Triceps skin fold thickness (mm)", "2-Hour serum insulin (mu U/ml)", "Body mass index (weight in kg/(height in m)^2)", "Diabetes pedigree function" and "Age (years)".), two classes (one is positive and the other is negative), and 768 instances. The ACA data consists of 14 attributes, two classes (one is positive and the other is negative) and 690 instances. Among the 14 attributes, 6 are numerical and 8 are categorical.

For the whole PID database we randomly select 70% for training and the other 30% for testing, for the whole ACA database we randomly select 80% for training and other 20% for testing. Table 1 shows the distribution of training and testing data of the PID and ACA datasets.

Table 1. Distribution of Training and Testing for PID and ACA

	PID database			ACA database		
	Total	Training	Testing	Total	Training	Testing
Positive	538	346	154	383	308	75
Negative	230	192	76	307	244	63
Total	768	538	230	690	552	138

After applying our approach mentioned in section 2 to PID database ($\beta=0.4$) and ACA database (($\beta=0.3$), the training and testing accuracy are shown in Table 2.

Table 2. PID and ACA Experimental Results

	Representatives	Deletion Rate	Training Accuracy	Testing Accuracy
PID	54	89.96%	100%	73.48%
ACA	55	90.04%	100%	79.71%

---

[1] Taken from UCI Machine Learning Repository, see website http://www.ics.uci.edu/~mlearn/MLRepository.html
[2] The dataset can be downloaded from http://www.liacc.up.pt/ML/statlog/datasets/australian/australian.doc.html

We also compare the number of selected representatives and training/testing accuracy by using case-specific weights and without using case-specific weights. We also test with different threshold β values. The comparison results are shown in Figures 1 and 2 for PID and ACA respectively. From the experimental results, one may see that by introducing the case-specific weights, the deletion rate and testing accuracy are better than without using weights. In addition, the selection of a good threshold β can base on the distribution of the old distance in the training sets, i.e., identifying a threshold to indicate if the old distance is small or big.

The result shows that the size of case bases after using our maintenance process can be reduced by almost 90% if case-specific weights are introduced. The training accuracy could be 100%, and the testing accuracy could attain 75% or more. Since the size of a case base is significantly reduced, the retrieval efficiency of the case base system could greatly be increased.

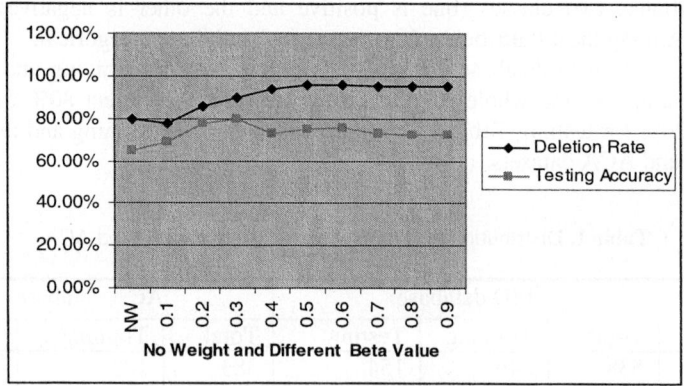

Fig. 1. PID Experiment Analysis on no weights and different Beta value

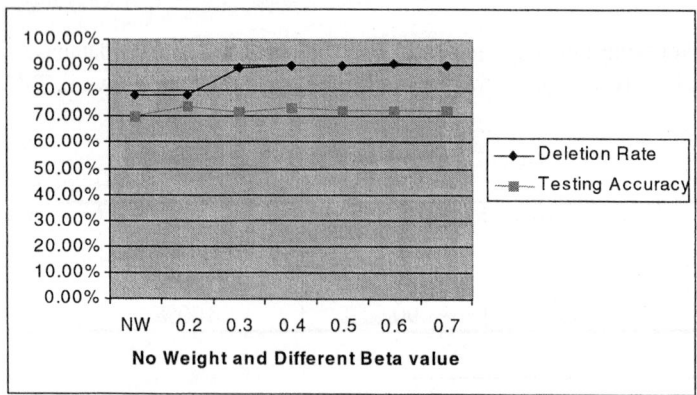

Fig. 2. ACA Experiment Analysis on no weights and different Beta value

4 Summary and Future Works

In this paper, we have developed a methodology of maintaining CBR systems by introducing the case-specific weight concept. The main idea is to transform a large case library to a small one by using a set of case-specific weights, which are obtained by solving linear programming problems. The experimental results show that both testing accuracy and retrieval efficiency of the CBR systems are increased. Besides, it shows that the computational cost of maintenance process is not high. Future works include (1) performing a computational complexity analysis and compare computational costs with other case base maintenance approaches, (2) extending this approach to solve multiple classes problems and non-classification problems (such as predication problem), (3) comparing the linear programming case-specific weight learning algorithm with weight learning algorithms, and (4) investigating the case addition strategy of our approach for on-line or periodic updates, and (5) comparing the retrieval efficiency with C4.5.

References

1. Cheetham, W. , Graf, J.: Case-Based Reasoning in Color Matching, Advances in Case-Based Reasoning, the second International Conference on Case-Based Reasoning, ICCBR(1997) 1-12.
2. Deangdej, J., Lukose, D., Tsui, E., Beinat, P. , Prophet, L. : Dynamically creating indices for two million cases: A real world problem. Advances in Case-Based Reasoning, the third European Workshop, EWCBR (1996) 105-119.
3. Leake, D.B., Wilson, C.: Categorizing Case-Base Maintenance: Dimensions and Directions. Advances in Case Based Reasoning, 4th European Workshop, EWCBR (1998) 196-207.
4. Smyth, B. , Keane, M.T.: Remembering to Forget: A Competence-Preserving Case Deletion Policy for Case-based Reasoning systems. Proceedings of the fourteenth International Joint Conference on Artificial Intelligence, IJCAI (1995) 377-382.
5. Smyth, B., Mckenna, E.: Modeling the Competence of Case-bases. Advances in Case-Based Reasoning, 4th European Workshop, EWCBR(1998) 208-220.
6. Anand, S.S, Patterson, D., Hughes, J. , Bell, G.: Discovering Case Knowledge using Data Mining. in D. A. Second Pacific Asia Conference, Australia, PAKDD (1998) 25-35.
7. Basak, J., De, R. K. ,Pal, S. K: Unsupervised feature selection using a neuro-fuzzy approach. Pattern Recognition Letters, 19 (1998) 998-1006.
8. Wettscherck, D., Aha, D.W.: Weighting Features. Case-based Reasoning Research and Development, First International Conference, ICCBR (1995) 347-358.
9. Aha, D. W.: Feature weighting for lazy learning algorithms. In H. Liu & H Motoda (Eds.) Feature Extraction, Construction and Selection: A Data Mining Perspective, Norwell MA: Kluwer (1998).
10. Yeung, D. S. , Tsang, E. C. C.: Weighted Fuzzy Production Rules. Fuzzy Sets and Systems 88 (1997) 299-313.
11. Avesani, P., Perini, A. , Ricci, F.: Interactive case-based planning for forest fire management, Applied Artificial Intelligence (1998).

12. Blanzieri, E., Ricci, F.: Probability Based Metrics for Nearest Neighbor Classification and Case-Based Reasoning. Advances in Case-Based Reasoning, the third European Workshop, EWCBR (1996) 14-28.
13. Aha, D. W., Goldstone, R. L.: Learning attribute relevance in context in instance-based learning algorithms. In proceedings of the Twelfth Annual Conference of the Cognitive Science Society, pp141-148, Cambridge, MA, (1990).
14. Short, R. D. , Fukunaga K.: A new nearest neighbor distance measure. In proceedings of the fifth IEEE International Conference on Pattern Recognition,, Miami veach, FL(1980) 81-86.
15. Racci, F. ,Avesani P.: Learning a local similarity metric for case-based reasoning. In the first international Conference on Case-Based Reasoning, ICCBR (1995) 301-312.

Classifying Faces with Discriminant Isometric Feature Mapping*

Ruifan Li[1], Cong Wang[1], Hongwei Hao[2], and Xuyan Tu[1,2]

[1] School of Information Engineering,
Beijing University of Posts and Telecommunications,
Beijing, China, 100876
smartfun@tom.com, wangc@nlu.caai.cn
[2] School of Information Engineering,
University of Science and Technology Beijing,
Beijing, China, 100083
{hhw, tuxuyan}@ies.ustb.edu.cn

Abstract. Recently proposed manifold learning algorithms, e.g. Isometric feature mapping (Isomap), Locally Linear Embedding (LLE), and Laplacian Eigenmaps, are based on minimizing the construction error for data description and visualization, but not optimal from classification viewpoint. A discriminant isometric feature mapping for face recognition is presented in this paper. In our method, the geodesic distances between data points are estimated by Floyd's algorithm, and Kernel Fisher Discriminant is then utilized to achieve the discriminative nonlinear embedding. Prior to the estimation of geodesic distances, the neighborhood graph is constructed by incorporating class information. Experimental results on two face databases demonstrate that the proposed algorithm achieves lower error rate for face recognition.

1 Introduction

In recent years, a growing interest has been shown in subspace method for face recognition [1, 2, 3, 4, 5, 6, 7]. As face images are represented as high-dimensional pixel arrays, they often belong to a subspace of intrinsically low dimension. In particular, Eigenfaces [1] and Fisherfaces [2] have, to some extent become benchmarks for this task. Eigenfaces is based on Principle component Analysis (PCA), which performs dimensionality reduction by projecting the original N-dimensional data onto the $d(<< N)$-dimensional linear subspace spanned by the leading eigenvectors of covariance matrix of the original data. For linearly embedding manifolds, PCA is guaranteed to produce a compact representation. However, since PCA is an unsupervised learning algorithm, Eigenfaces may not be optimal from the classification viewpoint.

Fisherfaces is based on Fisher Linear Discriminant (FLD), a supervised learning algorithm. Contrasted to PCA, which finds a projection direction that retains

---
* This research was partly supported by Beijing University of Posts and Telecommunications (BUPT) Education Foundation.

maximum variance, FLD finds the optimal projection direction that maximized the distances between classes and minimized the distances within classes. Generally, FLD-based methods always perform better than those of PCA-based [3]. The limitation of Fisherfaces is the singularity of with-class matrix caused by the small samples size against their high dimensions. Moreover, both approaches effectively see only the Euclidean structure failing to deal with nonlinear changes in face images caused by large pose variation, lighting, and facial expression.

As enhancements for Eigenfaces and Fisherfaces, kernel Eigenfaces [8] and kernel Fisherfaces [9, 10, 11], are proposed using kernel trick with impressive results. In these two methods, the samples are first implicitly mapped onto a high-dimensional feature space, and then linear method, i.e. PCA or FLD is applied, equivalent to extracting the nonlinear features in the original input space. Both of them can discover the nonlinear structure hidden in the face images. However, none of them explicitly considers the structure of the manifold on which the face images possibly reside.

Recently, neuroscientists emphasized the manifold ways of perception, and showed the face images may reside on a nonlinear submanifold hidden in the image space [12]. Some manifold learning methods, such as Isomap (or Isometric feature mapping) [13], LLE (Locally Liner Embedding) [14], and Laplacian Eigenmaps [15] are proposed. These methods achieve the submanifold by collectively analyzing the overlapped local neighborhoods. Experiments on some artificial data sets have shown their effectiveness on data description and visualization [13, 14]. However, they are developed based on reconstruction for data representation and are not suitable for classification tasks.

In order to cope with this problem, Yang [16] proposed an extended Isomap algorithm for face recognition and other classification tasks, briefly as Ext-Isomap. The main difference between Ext-Isomap and the original Isomap is that after geodesic distances obtained, the former uses FLD to achieve the low dimensional embedding while the latter uses Multi-Dimensional Scaling (MDS). However, the neighborhood construction is obtained without using the class information. Thus, to some extent, discriminant information may be lost.

In this paper, we propose a discriminative manifold learning method for face recognition. Our method, named as SKFD-Isomap, is much similar to Isomap and Ext-Isomap. To be specific, in the first step, the neighborhood graph of the high-dimensional data is constructed to using class information, i.e. in a Supervised manner, then in the second step, the geodesic distance is computed using the Floyd's algorithm, and in the final step, feature vectors are embedded into a low dimensional space using Kernel Fisher Discriminant (KFD). As the KFD algorithm is better for classification, the embedding can have a discriminative property.

The rest of this paper is organized as follows. In section 2, the discriminative manifold learning algorithm , i.e. SKFD-Isomap, is proposed. In section 3, experiments are reported. Section 4 ends with some conclusions.

2 Discriminative Isometric Feature Mapping

Consider a set of c disjoint subsets $X = \bigcup_{i=1}^{c} X_i$ with each element $x \in \mathbb{R}^N$, and each subset has n_i samples, i.e. $\sum_{i=1}^{c} n_i = n$. We aim to learn the discriminative manifold for pattern classification. The first step is to determine the neighbors of each sample x_i on the low dimensional manifold M based on Euclidean distance metric $d_X(x_i, x_j)$ in the input space X. Whereas, contrasted to the unsupervised nature of Isomap and Ext-Isomap, our method utilizes the class information by rescaling the Euclidean distance between two data points with a constant factor λ ($0 < \lambda < 1$) if the class labels are the same. Then, the new distance matrix between any two data points is used to determine whether two points are neighbors or not. Two simple definitions for neighborhood can be used: one is the points within some fixed radius ϵ; the other is all of its K nearest neighbors. Thus, these neighborhood relationships are represented in a weighted graph G in which $d_G(x_i, x_j) = d_X(x_i, x_j)$ if x_i and x_j are neighbors, and $d_G(x_i, x_j) = \infty$ otherwise.

For data lying on a nonlinear manifold, the "true distance" between two data points is the geodesic distance on the manifold, i.e. the distance along the surface of the manifold, rather than the straight-line Euclidean distance, as shown in Figure 1. Therefore, the next step is to estimate geodesic distance $d_M(x_i, x_j)$ between any pair of points on the manifold M. Its basic idea is that for neighboring points, input space distance provides a good approximation to geodesic distance; for faraway points, geodesic distance can be approximated by a sequence of "short hops" between neighboring data points. In other words, $d_M(x_i, x_j)$ is approximated by the shortest path between x_i and x_j on G, which is computed as

$$d_G(x_i, x_j) = min\{d_G(x_i, x_j), d_G(x_i, x_k) + d_G(x_k, x_j)\} \quad (1)$$

for each $k = 1, \cdots, n$. (This procedure is known as Floyd's algorithm). The shortest paths between any two points are represented in a matrix D where $D_{ij} = d_G(x_i, x_j)$.

Thus, each data point is represented by a feature vector of its geodesic distance to any points. In other words, the feature vector of data point x_i is an n-dimensional vector $f_i = [D_{ij}]$ where $j = 1, \cdots, n$ and $D_{ii} = 0$. Then, we apply kernel Fisher Discriminant on the feature vectors to find an optimal projection direction for classification.

In KFD, each vector f_i is projected to a high-dimensional feature space, $\mathbb{R}^f$, by a nonlinear mapping function, $\phi : \mathbb{R}^n \to \mathbb{R}^f$, $f > n$. Note that the dimensionality of the image space $\mathbb{R}^f$ can be arbitrarily large. Then, we formulate the FLD problem in the high-dimensional feature space only using dot products [17, 18, 19].

We assume the projection $\phi(f_i)$ are centered in $\mathbb{R}^f$, i.e. $\frac{1}{n}\sum_{i=1}^{n} \phi(f_i) = 0$, which could be implemented as in [18, 19]. The between-class and within-class scatter matrix are defined as

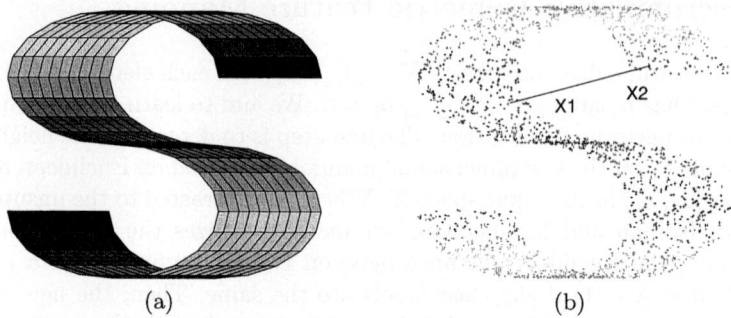

Fig. 1. S-curve and geodesic distance. (a) the original S-curve; (b) the 2000 random samples from S-curve and the straight line which represents the Euclidean distance between those two points.

$$S_B^\phi = \sum_{i=1}^{c} n_i \mu_i^\phi (\mu_i^\phi)^T \tag{2}$$

$$S_W^\phi = \sum_{i=1}^{c} \sum_{j=1}^{n_i} (\phi(f_j) - \mu_i^\phi)(\phi(f_j) - \mu_i^\phi)^T \tag{3}$$

where μ_i^ϕ is the mean of class i in $\mathbb{R}^f$. Applying FLD in feature in kernel space, we need to find eigenvalues λ and eigenvectors $\mathbf{w}^\phi$ of

$$\lambda S_W^\phi \mathbf{w}^\phi = S_B^\phi \mathbf{w}^\phi, \tag{4}$$

which can be obtained by

$$\mathbf{W}_{OPT}^\phi = \arg\max_{\mathbf{W}^\phi} \frac{(W^\phi)^T S_B^\phi W^\phi}{(W^\phi)^T W_B^\phi W^\phi} = [\mathbf{w}_1^\phi, \cdots, \mathbf{w}_m^\phi] \tag{5}$$

where $\{\mathbf{w}_i^\phi\}_{i=1}^m$ is the set of generalized eigenvectors coreesponding to the m largest generalized eigenvalues $\{\lambda_i\}_{i=1}^m$.

From the theory of reproducing kernels, any solution $\mathbf{w}^\phi \in \mathbb{R}^f$ must lie in the span of all the mapping of training samples [18], and there exist coeffieients α_i such that

$$\mathbf{w}^\phi = \sum_{i=1}^{n} \alpha_i \phi(f_i) \tag{6}$$

We define the kernel function as $k(x,y) = \phi(x) \cdot \phi(y)$, thus the kernel matrix in high-dimensional space can be denoted as K, i.e., $K_{ij} = k(f_i, f_j) = \phi(f_i) \cdot \phi(f_j)$, which is a $n \times n$ symmetric matrix. We can also define a matrix Z: $Z = (Z_i)_{i=1,\cdots,c}$, where Z_i is a $n_i \times n_i$ matrix with terms all equal to $\frac{1}{n_i}$, i.e., Z is a $n \times n$ block diagonal matrix.

Thus, the KFD problem becomes

$$\lambda KK\alpha = KZK\alpha \tag{7}$$

We can now project the vectors in $\mathbb{R}^f$ to a lower dimensional space spanned by the eigenvector. Let f be the feature vector of a test sample x, whose projection is $\phi(f)$ in $\mathbb{R}^f$, then the projection of $\phi(x)$ onto the eigenvectors as follows:

$$\mathbf{w}^\phi \cdot \phi(f) = \sum_{i=1}^{n} \alpha_i k(f_i, f) \tag{8}$$

The above procedures can learn a subspace for further classification. Note that for new test sample the estimation of its geodesic distances to other points is implicit. Therefore, some nonlinear interpolation techniques, such as Generalized Regression Neural Network (GRNN) [20] are required to learning the mapping.

To summarize, the procedure of our discriminative manifold learning, SKFD-Isomap, for classification has five steps as follows:

1. Construct neighborhood graph: Compute distances matrix between data points, and re-scale them with class information, i.e., $d_X(x_i, x_j) = \lambda d_X(x_i, x_j)$ ($0 < \lambda < 1$) if x_i and x_j belong to the same class.
2. Compute shortest paths: Estimate geodesic distances $d_M(x_i, x_j)$ between points on the manifold M using Floyd's algorithm. Thus, the feature of each point can be denoted as f_i.
3. Compute low-dimensional embedding: Apply KFD to the matrix of graph distances G, constructing a discriminative submanifold.
4. Compute maps for test samples: Approximate their images from input space onto the feature space using GRNN, and then project the obtained features onto the submanifold.
5. Classify new samples: Predict their class labels using simple classifier, such as K nearest neighbor.

3 Experiments

In this section, our method is compared with Eigenfaces [1] and Fisherfaces [2], two benchmark methods for face recognition, using the Yale and AT&T face databases[1]. In all the experiments, preprocessing to locate the faces was applied. And for the achieved subspace, a nearest neighbor classifier is utilized. The parameters of each method are determined empirically to achieve the best results. For Eigenfaces, the samples are projected to a subspace spanned by the leading eigenvectors. For Fisherfaces the samples are projected to a subspace spanned by the $c-1$ eigenvectors. For our method, the polynomial kernel function with second order, e.g. $k(x,y) = (\phi(x) \cdot \phi(y)) = (x \cdot y)^d$, in which $d = 2$ are selected; different values of λ between 0.1 and 0.5 are tested; only the ϵ neighborhood definition is considered.

---

[1] Thanks to AT&T laboratory Cambridge and Center for Computational Vision and Control at Yale University for making these two databases publicly available.

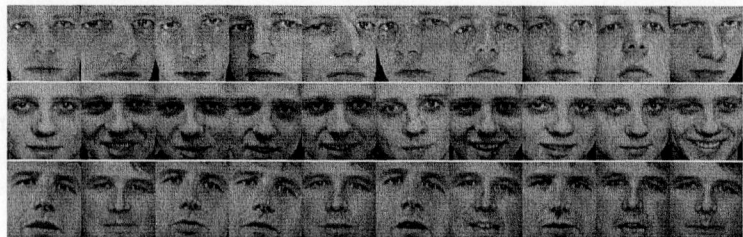

Fig. 2. Chopped facial images examples from AT&T database

The AT&T face database contains 400 images of 40 subjects, including 36 males and 4 females. It includes slight variations in illumination, facial expression (open/closed eyes, smiling/not smiling) and facial details (glasses/no glasses). Figure 2 shows images of a few subjects. To reduce computational complexity, each face image with original size 112 by 92 with 256 levels per pixel is chopped to 64 by 64 for experiments. Figure 2 shows closely cropped images of a few subjects.

This Yale database contains 165 images, each size 320 by 243, of 15 subjects in a variety of conditions including with and without glasses, illumination variation, and changes in facial expression. And every image in this database has large background. As proven in [21], statistics-based algorithms for face recognition require "pure" faces to evaluate their performance. Therefore, the original images have been cropped without containing the facial contours with size 87 by 123. Furthermore, each image has been resized to by 58 for 82 computational efficiency. Figure 3 shows closely cropped images of a few subjects.

In all experiments, each image is first represented by a raster scan vector of the intensity values, and then normalized to be zero-mean unit-variance vectors. The training set and test set are selected randomly. When performing the experiment, for each subject, five images are randomly selected for training, and the other samples are left as test samples. All the images are then projected to a reduced space and recognition is performed using a nearest neighbor classifier. To reduce the fluctuation among the results, the experiments are performed 400

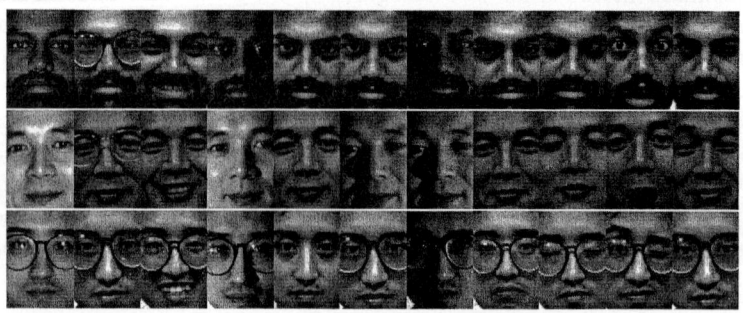

Fig. 3. Chopped facial images examples from Yale database

Table 1. Performance comparison on the AT&T Database

Method	Dims	Error Rate (%)
Eigenfaces	30	22.57
Fisherfaces	39	14.32
SKFD-Isomap	39	8.62

Table 2. Performance comparison on the Yale Database

Method	Dims	Error Rate (%)
Eigenfaces	35	25.73
Fisherfaces	14	20.21
SKFD-Isomap	14	12.38

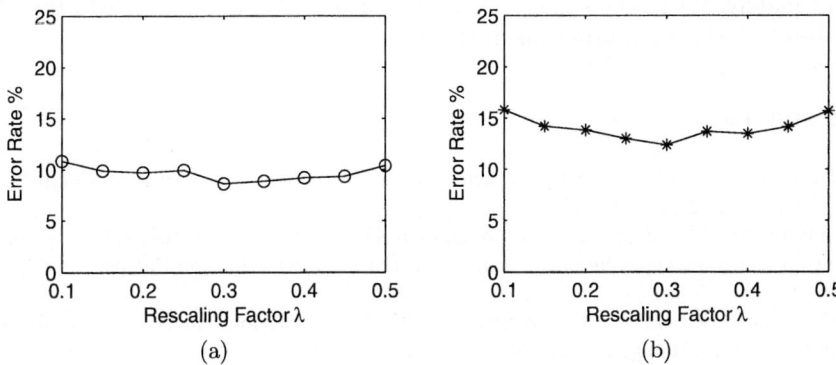

Fig. 4. Performance comparison with different rescaling factor λ. (a) different λ in AT&T database, $\epsilon = 12$; (b) different λ in Yale database, $\epsilon = 10$.

times. The average best experimental results on two face databases are given in table 1 and 2. And the parameters for AT&T database is $\epsilon = 12$ and $\lambda = 0.25$; the parameters for Yale database is $\epsilon = 10$ and $\lambda = 0.30$. And, We also test the performance of our method with different values of λ from 0.1 to 0.5. Figure 4 shows the results. As shown in figure 4, the value of λ will not be set to too large or too small. Thus, the trail and error procedure will guide the selection of different λ.

From the experimental results, our method achieved the much more classification error rate than the Eigenfaces and Fisherfaces. We could explain it as follows: the geodesic distances are better than Euclidean distances for face representation; the supervised scheme makes the discriminative information be reserved; KFD is better than linear methods for nonlinear information extraction. To be brief, the discriminative geodesic distances really reflect the true structure the submanifold, and the KFD can exactly embed it.

4 Conclusion

In this paper, we presented a novel approach for face recognition, which is based on discriminant isometric feature mapping. Similar to Isomap algorithm, our method includes three steps. First, a neighborhood is constructed using a supervised scheme. Then the geodesic distance matrix is computed using the Floyd's algorithm to obtain the feature vector. In the final step, we use KFD to embedding the feature vector into submanifold. In face recognition experiments, this method serves as a feature extraction process compared with Eigenfaces and Fisherfaces, combined with a nearest neighbor classifier. Experimental results on two publicly available face databases show that our approach excels the other two methods.

In our method, the supervised scheme of rescaling distances between points is ad hoc. Therefore, a principled approach should be considered. In addition, the construction of neighborhood graph is crucial. However, when the given data are scattered far away, the neighborhood graph of them may be disconnected. Unfortunately, our method cannot deal with such kind of data. More efforts will be taken to tackle such problems in the future.

References

1. Turk, M.A., Pentland, A.P.: Eigenfaces for recognition. Journal of Cognitive Neurosicence **3** (1991) 72–86
2. Belhumeur, P.N., Hespanha, J.P., Kriegman, D.J.: Eigenfaces vs. fisherfaces: recognition using class specific linear projection. IEEE Transactions on Pattern Analysis and Machine Intelligence **19** (1997) 711–720
3. Martinez, A., Kak, A.: Pca versus lda. IEEE Transactions on Pattern Analysis and Machine Intelligence **23** (2001) 228–233
4. Bartlett, M.S., Movellan, J.R., Sejnowski, T.J.: Face recognition by independent component analysis. IEEE Transactions on Neural Networks **13** (2002) 1450–1464
5. Vasilescu, M.A.O., Terzopoulos, D.: Multilinear analysis of image ensembles: Tensorfaces. In: Proc. European Conf. on Computer Vision and Pattern Recognition, Vancouver, B.C. (2002) 447–460
6. Vasilescu, M.A.O., Terzopoulos, D.: Multilinear independent component analysis. In: Proc. International Conf. on Computer Vision and Pattern Recognition, Vancouver, B.C. (2005) 37–40
7. He, X., Yan, S., Hu, Y., Niyogi, P., Zhang, H.J.: Face recognition using laplacianfaces. IEEE Transactions on Pattern Analysis and Machine Intelligence **27** (2005) 328–340
8. Yang, M.H., Ahuja, N., Kriegman, D.: Face recognition using kernel eigenfaces. In: Proc. IEEE International Conf. on Image Processing, Vancouver, B.C. (2000) 37–40
9. Yang, M.H.: Kernel eigenfaces vs. kernel fisherfaces: face recognition using kernel methods. In: Proc. IEEE International Conf. on Automatic Face and Gesture recognition, Washington, D.C. (2002) 215–220
10. Liu, Q., Huang, R., Lu, H., Ma, S.: Face recognition using kernel based fisher discriminant analysis. In: Proc. International Conf. on Automatic Face and Gesture recognition, Washington, D.C. (2002) 788–795

11. Liu, Q., Lu, H., Ma, S.: Improving kernel fisher discriminant analysis for face recognition. IEEE Transactions on Circuits and Systems for Video Technology **14** (2004) 42–49
12. Seung, H.S., Lee, D.D.: The manifold ways of perception. Science **290** (2000) 2268–2269
13. Silva, V., Tenenbaum, J., Langford, J.: A global geometric framework for nonlinear dimensionality reduction. Science **290** (2000) 2219–2223
14. Roweis, S., Saul, L.: Nonlinear dimensionality reduction by locally linear embedding. Science **290** (2000) 2223–2226
15. Belkin, M., Niyogi, P.: Laplacian eigenmaps and spectral techniques for embedding and clustering. In: Advances in Neural Information Processing Systems, Vancouver, B.C. (2001) 788–795
16. Yang, M.H.: Extended isomap for pattern classification. In: Proc. National Conf. on Artificial Intelligence, Edmonton, Alta., Canada (2002) 224–229
17. Scholkopf, B., Smola, A., Muller, K.: Nonlinear component analysis as a kernel eigenvalue problem. Neural Computation **10** (1998) 1299–1319
18. Mika, S., Ratsch, G., Weston, J., Scholkopf, B., Muller, K.: Fisher discriminant analysis with kernels. In: Proc. IEEE Workshop on Neural Networks for Signal Processing, Madison, W.I. (1999) 41–48
19. Baudat, G., Anouar, F.: Generalized discriminant analysis using a kernel approach. Neural Computation **12** (2000) 2385–2404
20. Specht, D.F.: A general regression neural network. IEEE Transactions on Neural network **2** (1991) 568–576
21. Chen, L.F., Liao, H.Y., Lin, J.C., Han, C.C.: Why recognition in a statistics-based face recognition system should be based on the pure face portion: a probabilistic decision-based proof. Pattern Recognition **34** (2001) 1393–1403

A Grey-Markov Forecasting Model for the Electric Power Requirement in China

Yong He and Min Huang

College of Biosystems Engineering and Food Science,
Zhejiang University, Hangzhou, 310029, China
yhe@zju.edu.cn

Abstract. This paper presents a Grey-Markov forecasting model for forecasting the electric power requirement in China. This method takes into account the general trend series and random fluctuations about this trend. It has the merits of both simplicity of application and high forecasting precision. This paper is based on historical data of the electric power requirement in China, and forecasts and analyzes the electric power requirement in China by the Grey–Markov forecasting model. The forecasting precisions of Grey-Markov forecasting model from 2002 to 2004 are 99.42%, 98.05% and 97.56%, and those of GM(1,1) grey forecasting model are 98.53%, 94.02% and 88.48%. It shows that the Grey-Markov forecasting models have higher precision than GM(1,1) grey forecasting model. The results provides scientific basis for the planned development of the electric power supply in China.

1 Introduction

The grey system theory was initially presented by Deng [1]. The grey forecasting model adopts the essential part of the grey system theory. The GM(1,1) grey forecasting model can be used in circumstances with relatively a little data and it can use a first-order differential equation to characterize an unknown system. So the GM(1,1) grey forecasting model is suitable for forecasting the competitive environment where decision makers can reference only limited historical data[2]. But the forecasting precision for data sequences with large random fluctuation is low.

The Markov-chain forecasting model can be used to forecast a system with randomly varying time series. It is a dynamic system which forecasts the development of the system according to transition probabilities between states which reflect the influence of all random factors. So the Markov-chain forecasting model is applicable to problems with random variation, which could improve the GM(1,1) model[3]. The disadvantage of the model is that it demands that the process is a stationary one, that is, the trend curve is a horizontal line. If the trend curve is non-horizontal, the forecast is less accurate because the states of the ordinary Markov probability matrix forecast are stationary. To improve the Markov-chain forecasting model, this paper builds a GM(1,1) grey forecasting model to describe the historical data of the electric power requirement in China to calculate the fluctuating trend curve first[4].

The rationale of Grey-Markov forecasting model is as follows: first a GM(1,1) grey forecasting model is built to calculate the fluctuating trend curve of the historical data series, then specify some states around the trend curve, a Markov transition matrix can be built to find out the transition probability, finally these two models should be combined to forecast accurately by the historical time series data. This forecasting method can make full use of the information given by historical data, and increase greatly the forecasting precision of random fluctuating sequences.

2 Research Methodology

2.1 GM(1,1) Grey Forecasting Model

Step 1: Assume an original series to be $X^{(0)}$,

$$X^{(0)} = \{ X^{(0)}(1), X^{(0)}(2), ..., X^{(0)}(n) \}. \tag{1}$$

Step 2: A new sequence $X^{(1)}$ is generated by the accumulated generating operation (AGO).

$$X^{(1)} = \{ X^{(1)}(1), X^{(1)}(2), ..., X^{(1)}(n) \}. \tag{2}$$

where $X^{(1)}(k) = \sum_{i=1}^{k} x^{(0)}(i)$, $k=1,2,...n$.

Step 3: Establish a first-order differential equation.

$$(dx^{(1)}/dt) + az = u. \tag{3}$$

where $z^{(1)}(k) = \alpha x^{(1)}(k) + (1-\alpha)x^{(1)}(k+1)$, $k = 1,2,...,n-1$. α denotes a horizontal adjustment coefficient, and $0 < \alpha < 1$. The selecting criterion of α value is to yield the smallest forecasting error rate[5].

Step 4: From step 3, we can have $\hat{x}^{(1)}(k+1)$ and $\hat{Y}(k)$.

$$\hat{x}^{(1)}(k+1) = (x^{(0)}(1) - \frac{u}{a})e^{-ak} + \frac{u}{a}. \tag{4}$$

where $\hat{\theta} = \begin{bmatrix} a \\ u \end{bmatrix} = (B^T B)^{-1} B^T Y$, $B = \begin{bmatrix} -z^{(1)}(2) & 1 \\ -z^{(1)}(3) & 1 \\ ... & ... \\ -z^{(1)}(n) & 1 \end{bmatrix}$,

$$\hat{Y}(k) = (x^{(0)}(2), x^{(0)}(3), ..., x^{(0)}(n))^T. \tag{5}$$

Step 5: Inverse accumulated generation operation (IAGO). Because the grey forecasting model is formulated using the data of AGO rather than original data, IAGO can be used to reverse the forecasting value.
Namely

$$\hat{x}_0^{(0)}(k) = \hat{x}^{(1)}(k) - \hat{x}^{(1)}(k-1), k=2,3,...,n. \tag{6}$$

Step 6: From step 5, a trend curve equation can be built:

$$\hat{Y}(k) = \hat{x}^{(0)}(k+1) = ge^{-ak}. \tag{7}$$

where $g = (x^{(0)}(1) - u/a)(1 - e^{\alpha})$, k=0,1, ...,n-1. $\hat{Y}(k)$ denotes the forecasting data[6].

2.2 Partition of States by Markov-Chain Forecasting Model

The values of $X^{(0)}(k+1)$ are distributed in the region of the trend curve $\hat{Y}(k)$ that may be divided into a convenient number of contiguous intervals. When $X^{(0)}(k+1)$ falls in interval i, one of S such intervals, it may be regarded as corresponding to a state E_i in an m order Markov unstable sequence, E_i can be signified as follows:

$$E_i = [E_{1i}, E_{2i}]. \tag{8}$$

Where i=1,2...S, S is the amount of states.

$$E_{1i} = \hat{Y}(k) + A_i. \tag{9}$$

$$E_{2i} = \hat{Y}(k) + B_i. \tag{10}$$

As $\hat{Y}(k)$ is a time function, so, E_{1i} and E_{2i} will vary with the time series. It means that the state E_i is dynamic. To establish S (the amount of states), E_{1i} and E_{2i}, depends on the study object and the original data series[7].

2.3 Calculate the Transition Probability P

For Markov-chain series, the transition probability from state E_i to state E_j can be established using an equation as follows:

$$P_{ij}(m) = \frac{M_{ij}(m)}{M_i} \quad (i,j=1,2,...,S). \tag{11}$$

where $P_{ij}(m)$ is the transition probability of state E_j transferred from state E_i for m steps (in this paper, 1 step stands for 1 year), m is the number of transition steps each time, $M_{ij}(m)$ is the number of original data of state E_j transferred from state E_i for m steps, M_i is the number of original data points in state E_i.

These $P_{ij}(m)$ values can be presented as a transition probability matrix $R(m)$.

$$R(m) = \begin{bmatrix} P_{11}(m) & P_{12}(m) & \cdots & P_{1j}(m) \\ P_{21}(m) & P_{22}(m) & \cdots & P_{2j}(m) \\ & & \cdots & \\ P_{j1}(m) & P_{j2}(m) & \cdots & P_{ij}(m) \end{bmatrix} (i,j=1,2,\ldots,S). \quad (12)$$

The state transition probability $P_{ij}(m)$ reflects the statistical law of each state transition in a system, which is the foundation of Markov probability matrix forecast. The future development of the system can be forecasted by studying the state transition probability matrix $R(m)$. Generally, it is necessary to observe the one-step transition matrix $R(1)$. Suppose the object to be forecasted is in state E_Q ($1 \le Q \le S$), row Q in matrix $R(1)$ should be considered. If max $P_{Qj}(1) = P_{QL}(1)$ ($j=1,2,\ldots,S$; $1 \le Q \le S$), then what will most probably happen in the system at the next moment is the transition from state E_Q to state E_L. It is difficult to determine the future transition of the state, if two or more transition probabilities in the row Q of matrix $R(1)$ are the same. Therefore the transition probability matrix of two-step transition matrix $R(2)$ or multi-step transition matrix $R(m)$, where $m \ge 3$, should be considered [8].

2.4 Calculate the Forecasting Data

After the determination of the future state transition of a system, i.e. the determination of grey elements E_{1i}, E_{2i}, the changing interval of the forecast value is between E_{1i} and E_{2i}. The most probable forecast value, $\hat{Y}(k+1)$, is considered to be the middle value of the determined state interval, that is

$$\hat{Y}(k+1) = 1/2(E_{1i} + E_{2i}) - \hat{Y}(k) + 1/2(A_t + B_t). \quad (13)$$

3 The Grey-Markov Forecasting Model for the Electric Power Requirement in China

There are many factors which could influence the electric power requirement, such as the economy, the industry framework, people's income level, the weather, the government's policy and so on. Some factors are clear, and others are not clear. So the time series of electric power requirement of a country show large random fluctuations. As Table 1 showed, the historical data series of the electric power requirement of China from 1985 to 2002 is rising, but fluctuating randomly. So this paper forecasts and analyzes the electric power requirement by Grey-Markov forecasting model [9].

Table 1. The Electric Power Requirement of China from 1985 to 2004(unit: hundred million kilowatt-hour)

Number	1	2	3	4	5
Year	1985	1986	1987	1988	1989
Amount	4117.6	4507.0	4985.2	5466.8	5865.3
Number	6	7	8	9	10
Year	1990	1991	1992	1993	1994
Amount	6230.4	6804.0	7589.2	8426.5	9260.4
Number	11	12	13	14	15
Year	1995	1996	1997	1998	1999
Amount	10023.4	10764.3	11284.4	11598.4	12305.2
Number	16	17	18	19	20
Year	2000	2001	2002	2003	2004
Amount	13471.4	14633.5	16200	18910	21735

3.1 Build the GM(1,1) Grey Forecasting Model

Based on the historical data of the electric power requirement in China from 1985 to 2001, a trend curve equation is built by GM(1,1) Grey forecasting model. It is as follows:

$$\hat{Y}(k) = \hat{X}^{(0)}(k+1) = 4331.308566 e^{0.078455k} \quad (k=1,2,3\ldots,k). \tag{14}$$

Where k is the series number of the year, and $k=1$ means that it is 1985.
The forecast value of 2002 calculated by the equation is 16438.15 hundred million kilowatt-hours.

3.2 Partition of States by Markov-Chain Forecasting Model

According to the actual electric power requirement data, four states, that is, four contiguous intervals are established about the curve of $X^{(0)}(k+1)$. According to the formula (8) and (9), the four states intervals can be got as follows:

$$E_1: \quad E_{11} = \hat{Z}(k) - 0.130\overline{Y} \qquad E_{21} = \hat{Z}(k) - 0.045\overline{Y}.$$

$$E_2: \quad E_{12} = \hat{Z}(k) - 0.045\overline{Y} \qquad E_{22} = \hat{Z}(k).$$

$$E_3: \quad E_{13} = \hat{Z}(k) \qquad\qquad E_{23} = \hat{Z}(k) + 0.045\overline{Y}.$$

$$E_4: \quad E_{14} = \hat{Z}(k) + 0.045\overline{Y} \qquad E_{24} = \hat{Z}(k) + 0.130\overline{Y}.$$

Where $\overline{Y}$ denotes the average value of the historical electric power requirement from 1985 to 2001. Fig.1 shows the historical data series, the regressed curve and the states intervals.

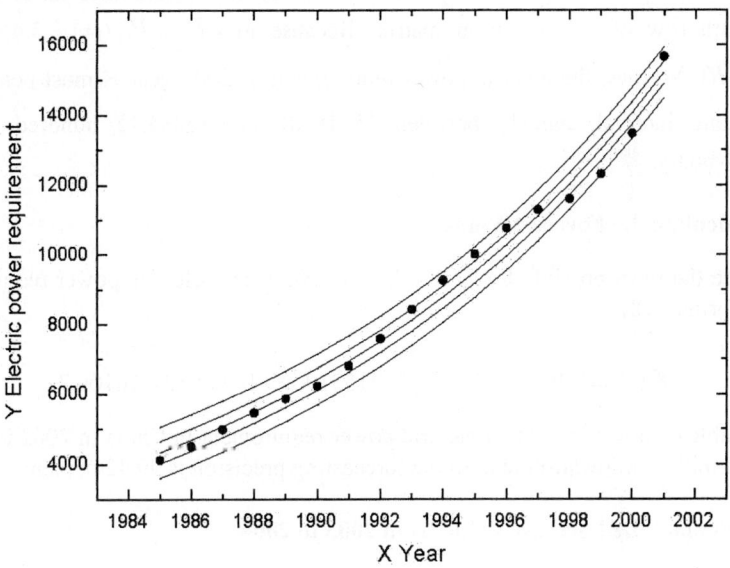

Fig. 1. The forecasting curve of the electric power requirement in China

3.3 Calculate the Transition Probability P

After observing the states intervals and the historical data series, the number of the historical data in every interval can be got. They are as follows:

$$M_1=7,\ M_2=5,\ M_3=1,\ M_4=4,$$

where M_i denotes the number of the historical data in the interval i, and $i=1,2,3,4$.

The numbers of One-step transiting to E_1, E_2, E_3, E_4 from E_1 are as follows:

$$M_{11}(1)=5,\ M_{12}(1)=2,\ M_{13}(1)=0,\ M_{14}(1)=0.$$

Next $M_{ij}(1)$, where $i=2,3,4$ and $j=1,2,3,4$ can be calculated in the same way. Then calculate the one-step transition probabilities to every states interval and present them to the transition matrix $R(1)$ as follows:

$$R(1)=\begin{bmatrix} \frac{5}{7} & \frac{2}{7} & 0 & 0 \\ \frac{2}{5} & \frac{2}{5} & \frac{7}{5} & \frac{7}{5} \\ 0 & 1 & 0 & 0 \\ 1 & 1 & 1 & 1 \\ 0 & 0 & \frac{1}{3} & \frac{2}{3} \\ \frac{3}{3} & 0 & \frac{3}{3} & \frac{3}{3} \end{bmatrix}$$

The electric power requirement of 2001 year is in the E_4 state interval, so observe the fourth row of the transition matrix. Because max $P_{4j} = P_{44}$ ($j=1,2,3,4$) as the matrix $R(1)$ shows, the electric power requirement of 2002 year is most possible in the E_4 state interval, namely between 15319.28 and 16894.12 hundred million kilowatt-hours.

3.4 Calculate the Forecast Value

Calculate the most possible forecast value of 2002 year's electric power requirement by the formula (8).

$$\hat{Y}(18) = 1/2(E_{14} + E_{24}) = 1/2(15319.28 + 16894.12) = 16106.7$$

As Table 1 shows, the actual electric power requirement in China in 2002 is 16200 hundred million kilowatt-hours. So the forecasting precision is 99.42 percent.

3.5 Calculate the Forecast Value from 2003 to 2004

Calculate the forecast value from 2003 to 2004 by Grey-Markov forecasting model following the above steps. The forecast value of 2003 is 18541.3 hundred million kilowatt-hours, and that of 2004 is 21204.7 hundred million kilowatt-hours. So the forecasting precisions are 98.05% and 97.56%.

3.6 Comparison of Forecast Values Between the Grey-Markov Forecasting Model and the GM(1,1) Grey Forecasting Model

First build a GM(1,1) Grey forecasting model to forecast the electric power requirement from 2002 and 2004. Then present the forecasting results and the results that are forecasted by Grey-Markov model in Table 2.

Table 2. Comparison of forecast values with two different methods

Year	Reality amount	GM(1,1) Value	GM(1,1) Precision	Grey-Markov Value	Grey-Markov Precision
2002	16200	16438.15	98.53%	16106.7	99.42%
2003	18910	17779.7	94.02%	18541.3	98.05%
2004	21735	19230.8	88.48%	21204.7	97.56%

Table 2 shows that the Grey-Markov forecasting model is better for forecasting the electric power requirement in China. The forecast values of Grey-Markov forecasting models are more precise than GM(1,1) grey forecasting model, for data sequence with large random fluctuation.

4 Conclusions

The Grey-Markov forecasting model can fully utilize the information of the historical time series data with large random fluctuation. As the case study shows that the accuracy of Grey-Markov forecasting model in forecast value for 2002 to 2004 is higher than those of GM(1,1) grey forecasting model in this paper. Based on the above analysis, the Grey-Markov forecasting model appeals to be intrinsically better because it has merits of both simplicity of application and high forecasting precision. This model has integrated the advantages of GM(1,1) grey forecasting model and Markov-chain forecasting model.

The forecasting result of this forecasting method is greatly dependent on state intervals partitioning. There is no standard rule to divide the states intervals. Generally speaking, the number of states should be decided according to the data and the demands of the problem. If the historical data are not abundant, the number of states should be fewer, so that the transition between the states can be clearly revealed. If the data are abundant, the number of states should be increased and the forecasting precision would be increased correspondingly.

Because the electric power requirement in China is influenced by many factors such as the economy, the industry framework, people's income level, the weather and the government's policy, there is a certain development trend for the historical time series data, and the data fluctuate randomly. So it is suitable to forecast the electric power requirement by the Grey-Markov forecasting model.

The Grey-Markov forecasting model could be applied to forecast other time series problems with large random fluctuation.

Acknowledgements

This study was supported by the Teaching and Research Award Program for Outstanding Young Teachers in Higher Education Institutions of MOE, P. R. C., Natural Science Foundation of Zhejiang (Project No: RC02067).

References

1. Deng, J.L.: Control problems of Grey System. Wuhang. Huazhong University of Science and Technology Press. Wuhang (1990) 1-2
2. Chao, H. W.: Predicting tourism demand using fuzzy time series and hybrid grey theory. Tourism Management. Vol. 25(2004) 367-374
3. He, Y., Bao, Y. D.: Grey-Markov Forecasting Model and its Application. Systems Engineering (Theory and Practice). Vol. 9. No. 4(1992) 59-63

4. Zhang, S. J., He, Y.: A Grey-Markov Forecasting Model for Forecasting the Total Power Requirement of Agricultural Machinery in Shangxi Province. Journal of Shanxi Agricultural University (Natural Science Edition). Vol.21. No.3(2001) 299-302
5. Wen, J. C., Huang, K. H., Wen, K. L.: The Study of α in GM(1,1) Model. Journal of the Chinese Institute of Engineers. Vol. 23. No. 5(2000) 583-589
6. Bao, Y. D., Wu, Y. P., He, Y.: A New Forecasting Model Based on the Combination of GM(1,1) Model and Linear Regression. Systems Engineering (Theory and Practice). Vol. 24. No. 3(2004) 95-98
7. Zhang, S. J., He, Y.: Forecast of the grain yield based on the trend-state mathematical model. Journal of Zhejiang University (Agric.& Life Sci.). Vol. 27. No. 6(2001) 673-676
8. He, Y.: A New Forecasting Model for Agricultural Commodities. J. agric. Engng Res.. Vol.60(1995) 227-235
9. National Bureau of Statistic of China: China Statistical Year Book. China Statistics Press. Beijing (2004)

A Fault Detection Approach Based on Machine Learning Models

Luis E. Garza Castañon[1], Francisco J. Cantú Ortiz[2],
Rubén Morales-Menéndez[1], and Ricardo Ramírez[1]

[1] Department of Mechatronics and Automation, ITESM Monterrey Campus,
{legarza, rmm, rramirez}@itesm.mx
[2] Research and Graduate Programs Office, ITESM Monterrey Campus,
Av. Eugenio Garza Sada Sur No. 2501,
Monterrey, N.L. 64,489 México
fcantu@itesm.mx

Abstract. We present a new approach for process fault detection based on models generated by machine learning techniques. Our work is based on a residual generation scheme, where the output of a model for process normal behavior is compared against actual process values. The residuals indicate the presence of a fault. The model consists of a general statistical inference engine operating on discrete spaces. This model represents the maximum entropy joint probability mass function (pmf) consistent with arbitrary lower order probabilities. The joint pmf is a rich model that, once learned, allows one to address inference tasks, which can be used for prediction applications. In our case the model allows the one step-ahead prediction of process variable, given its past values. The relevant past values for the forecast model are selected by learning a causal structure with an algorithm to learn a discrete bayesian network. The parameters of the statistical engine are found by an approximate method proposed by Yan and Miller. We show the performance of the prediction models and their application in power systems fault detection.

1 Introduction

The problem of fault detection in processes has received great attention during last years, and a wide variety of methods have been developed, most of them based on fault detection and isolation (FDI) techniques or in knowledge-based methods. FDI is based on the use of analytical redundancy rather than physical redundancy. In FDI the redundancy in static and dynamic relationships between process inputs and outputs is exploited [4]. The methods used by FDI can be summarized in parity space approach, state estimation approach, fault detection filtering, and parameter identification approach. In every case, a mathematical model of process is required, either in state-space or input-output form but most of the time these models are linear systems. Since many processes exhibits a nonlinear dynamics, the above methods are limited to work well in a small region around the point of operation. Other nonlinear approaches have been proposed for FDI, but they only work well for a limited class of nonlinear systems [13].

Knowledege-based methods rely on qualitative model descriptions in the form of neural networks, bayesian networks, fuzzy logic or qualitative reasoning. Neural networks are widely used in fault detection and diagnosis [12] but they represent black box models and can not deal with missing information. Bayesian networks (BNs) have been lately used in fault detection and diagnosis [8], as they represent robust models for nonlinear systems able to deal with missing information and noise. A potential problem in BNs is the time for inference process in large domains. Fuzzy logic uses a database with IF-THEN rules which use linguistic variables. The problem with fuzzy logic is that can not deal with incomplete information in explicit form and the overall dimension of rules may blow up strongly even for small processes [2]. The methods based in qualitative reasoning [9] require a set of qualitative differential equations between process variables not easy to obtain for complex processes.

A recent trend is the combination of methods to take advantage of the best aspects of every approach (see for instance [6]). Our work is mainly focus in this direction.

In our approach, we use the FDI philosophy, that is, the generation of residuals and the decision and isolation of the fault.

In the generation of residuals phase, we substitute the classical models of process normal behavior (eg. discrete linear models) with a discrete probabilistic function, whose parameters are learned offline from raw data. The probabilistic function is a general statistical inference engine, which allows inference to know future values of process variables, given their past values. In our case, we predict the one step-ahead value of process variable given a set of past process variable values. The set of relevant process variable values having direct influence on the forecast, are learned offline by using an algorithm to learn discrete bayesian networks. The output of this algorithm is a graphical causal structure, which is simplified by selecting the Markov blanket of the forecast process variable. This kind of compact probabilistic models are robust to noise, incomplete information and nonlinearities.

In the decision and isolation step, we generate residuals from the comparison between the output of the probabilistic model and actual process variable values. These residuals are filtered and compared against a table of limits to indicate the existence of a determined type of fault.

We test our approach diagnosing multiple-faults events in a large power transmission network and show promising results.

2 The Proposed Approach

A general overview of our approach is shown in fig. 1. Basically we generate residuals from the comparison between a process normal behavior model and the actual process values. The model consists of a statistical inference engine whose structure and parameters are learned offline with machine learning algorithms. The residuals behavior indicate the existence of a fault.

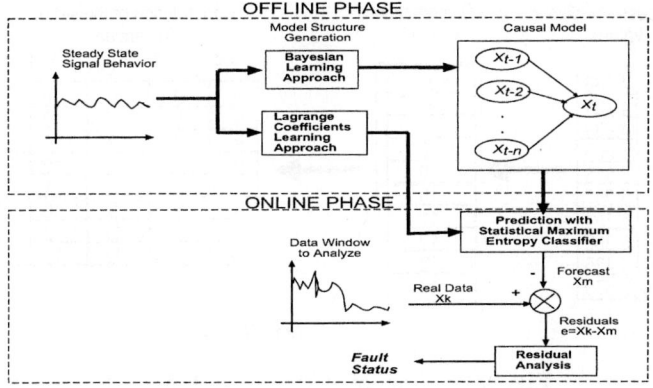

Fig. 1. An overview of the fault detection approach based on machine learning models

The architecture of the method is split in two phases: the offline phase and the online phase. The offline phase learns the model structure and parameters, and the online phase take the decision regarding the presence of a fault.

2.1 The Offline Phase

The offline phase generates a discrete process normal behavior model from data, by applying machine learning techniques which learn both: the model structure and the parameters. First, continuous variables are discretized by using fixed bins or a more elaborated technique as fuzzy clustering. The fixed interval width discretization, merely divides the range of observed values in equal sized bins. The general idea with multivariate discretization approach based on the *fuzzy C-means* algorithm [10], is that rather than discretizing independently each variable, we find the centroids of the c clusters defined by the user, and assign each instance of the multivariate series to the closest cluster[1].

The process of discretization allows the use of standard discrete bayesian networks learning algorithms and the implementation of the algorithm to learn the general statistical inference engine parameters.

Once the discretization phase has been achieved, the next issue in the construction of the model, is the specification of the set of attributes and the instances, to be supplied to the algorithm that learns the discrete bayesian network structure. This is not a trivial issue, since possibly we do not know anything about the lagged dependencies in the process variable dynamics. If we have observed a sample of N data for the variable X, the forecast or prediction variable X_t may depend on any of the past values $X_{t-1}, X_{t-2}, \ldots, X_{t-N}$. We solve this problem by selecting an initial set of attributes M_d[2] and keep adding attributes

---

[1] According to a defined metric. We use a simple Euclidean distance metric.
[2] M_d is also the size of the time window, and the instances are formed sliding the time window through the complete time series. In a time series with N data we can have $N - M_d + 1$ instances.

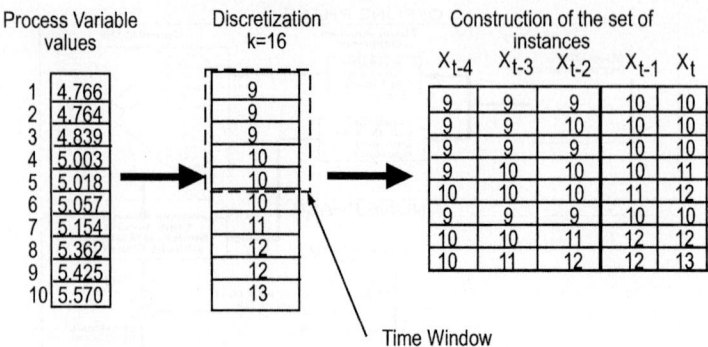

Fig. 2. Selection of attributes with $M_d = 5$

until a causal structure can be found. Although it is possible that different causal structures can be found, even a trivial structure with just two nodes, we can test each structure and select the more accurate. If a causal structure cannot be found with a discretization policy, then increase the number of bins, in fixed discretization policy, or increase the number of clusters, in the *fuzzy C-means* discretization policy, and again do the iterative selection of the size of attributes. An example of the selection of the attributes in a time series is shown in figure 2, with $M_d = 5$. The input to the discrete bayesian networks learning algorithm is thus a set of instances having the form $\{X_{t-M_d-1}, \ldots, X_t\}$. Notice we are not assuming beforehand anything regarding independence of variables or specific time dependencies. The algorithm that learns the bayesian network structure is intendend to find such dependencies.

When the causal structure of the set of M_d attributes is found, we select our model from the Markov blanket of the prediction variable. The Markov blanket in a BN consists of node's parents, its children and its children's parents. The Markov blanket forms a natural feature selection, as all features outside the Markov blanket can be safely deleted from the BN. We exploit this feature to produce a much smaller causal structure for our forecast model, without compromising the classification accuracy.

The prediction variable is the M_dth attribute, has $\mathcal{P}$ parents (variables influencing directly its value) and no children (other variables over which the forecast variable have an influence). We enforce this by specifying a variable ordering to the BN learning algorithm. Figure 3(a) shows an example of causal network learned with five attributes, and figure 3(b) shows the reduced model obtained for the forecast variable. The process variable X_t is the forecast variable and $X_{t-1}, X_{t-2}, X_{t-3}$ and X_{t-4} are the process variable past values.

After we obtain the relevant past values for the forecast variable, we learn the parameters of the statistical inference engine based on the maximum entropy principle.

Consider a random feature vector $\hat{F} = (\mathbf{F}, \mathbf{C})$, $\mathbf{F} = (F_1, F_2, \ldots, F_N)$, with $F_i \in \mathcal{A}_i$ and $\mathcal{A}_i$ the finite set $\{1, 2, 3, \ldots, |\mathcal{A}_i|\}$, and $\mathbf{C} \in \{1, 2, \ldots, K\}$. Denote the full discrete feature space by $\mathcal{G} \equiv \mathcal{A}_1 \times \mathcal{A}_2 \cdots \times \mathcal{A}_N \times \mathcal{C}$. Suppose we are

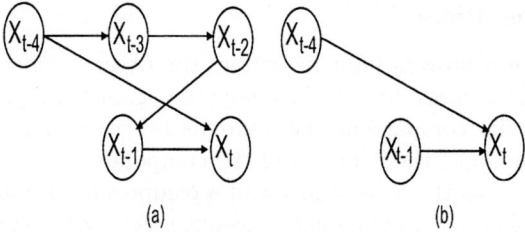

Fig. 3. (a) causal model for 5 attributes, (b) reduced model

given knowledge of all $(N(N-1)/2)$ pairwise pmf's $\{P[F_m, C], \forall m\}$ and wish to constrain the joint pmf $P[\mathbf{F}, \mathbf{C}]$ to agree with these. The pairwise probabilities typically are estimated from training set co-occurrence counts. The maximum entropy (ME) joint pmf consistent with these pairwise pmf's has the Gibbs form

$$P[C = c | F = f] = \frac{exp\left(\sum_{i=1}^{N} \gamma(F_i = f_i, C = c)\right)}{\sum_{c'=1}^{K} exp\left(\sum_{i=1}^{N} \gamma(F_i = f_i, C = c')\right)} \quad (1)$$

where

- F is the set of relevant past values for the forecast variable,
- C is the set of predicted variables.

for instance, for the model represented by fig. 3(b), $F = (X_{t-1}, X_{t-4})$ and $C = (X_t)$.

The subset of model parameters (Lagrange multipliers) $\{\gamma(C_i = c_i, F = f), i = 1, \ldots, N, c_i = 1, \ldots, K, f = 1, \ldots, K\}$ are learned with a deterministic annealing algorithm. Where N is the number of relevant past values for the prediction variable, K is the number of discretization bins.

We need to supply following inputs to the Lagrange coefficients learning algorithm:

- A training set of $\mathcal{P}+1$ attributes with M instances,
- a training set support size $\mathcal{G}_s << \mathcal{G}$,
- an annealing parameter η,
- an annealing threshold ϵ,
- an annealing initial temperature T_{max} and final temperature T_{min}
- a ρ learning-rate parameter.

A more detailed explanation about the selection of parameters for the annealing algorithm can be found in section 3.1.

The inference engine provides a probability distribution of the forecast variable, given the evidence of relevant past values of forecast variable. We select the discrete state with highest probability and to make a comparison against the real data, we substitute the state by its correspondent real value.

2.2 The Online Phase

In order to perform process fault detection, the observations or measurements obtained from the process, have to be compared against the prediction given by the model. From this comparison, the residuals are generated and then analyzed to give a decision about the behavior of the component.

If we denote X_t as the measurement of a component variable at time t, and $\hat{X}_t$ as the prediction of the component variable given by the steady state model, then the residual e_t is computed from:

$$e_t = X_t - \hat{X}_t \qquad (2)$$

The differences between the steady-state model and the real data, e_t, are transformed to a filtered version of residuals, using the equation:

$$\bar{e}_t = \bar{e}_{t-1} + \lambda * (|e_t| - \bar{e}_{t-1})$$

The value of λ, between 0 and 1, represents the smoothing factor of the residuals. We refer to the average value of a set of filtered residuals as the error weighted moving average (EWMA) index.

The fault decision is accomplished by comparing the actual filtered residuals against the previously computed limit thresholds of each fault mode. The limit thresholds were calculated from intensive simulations, which include single faults and different combinations of multiple faults.

An example of modelling for a three phases voltage behavior, in the presence of a fault in a power network, is given in fig. 4. Dotted line is the prediction of voltage normal behavior and continuous line represents the real node voltage values.

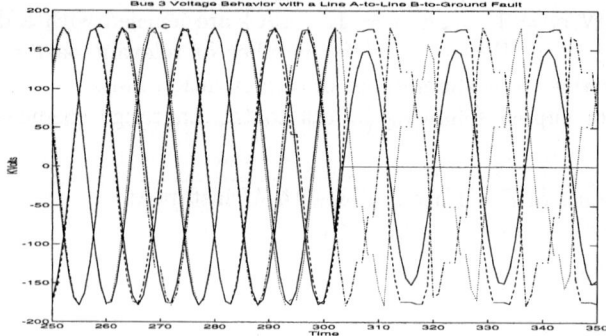

Fig. 4. Modelling of voltage behavior in a power network with a line-to-line-to-Ground fault

3 Application in Fault Diagnosis

We illustrate the application of our approach in a simulated power transmission network shown in fig. 5. The system consists of 24 nodes, 34 lines and 68 breakers. The electrical power network is supplied with the energy produced by three-phase generators. Ideally, the generators supply the energy to three-phase balanced loads, which means that every load has an identical impedance. In a balanced circuit, each phase has the same magnitude of voltage, but displaced 120 electrical degrees. In all simulations we include varying resistive-inductive loads in several nodes.

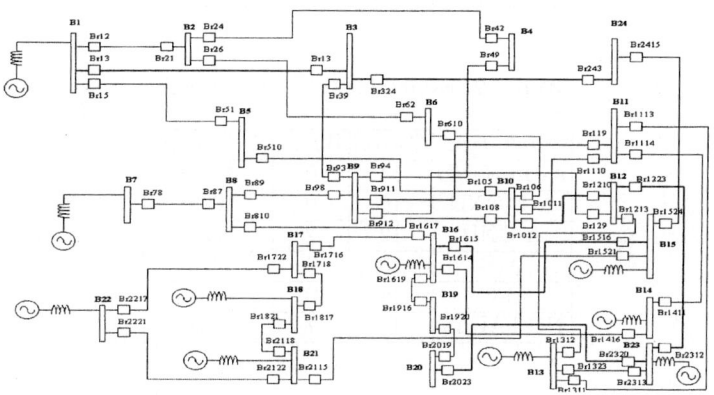

Fig. 5. Electrical power network test system

A fault in a electric network is any event that interfere with the normal flow of current. The faults in an electrical power network can be divided in two types: *symmetrical* faults and *unsymmetrical* faults. The symmetrical faults involve the three phases of the system, are relatively easy to evaluate, and represent about the 5 % of the fault cases. The unsymmetrical faults involve some kind of unbalance, and include line to ground faults and line to line faults. The line to ground faults represent about 70 % of the faults, and the line to line faults represent about 25 % of the cases [7].

The diagnosis in large power networks is a difficult task, mainly due to overwhelming amount of data, the cascaded effect, and the uncertainty in the information. The main protection breakers of a node can be opened (as a secondary protection) by faults at neighbor nodes, giving rise to ambiguous diagnoses. The voltage measurements at a given node, are also perturbed by faults at neighbor nodes.

With our modeling approach, we represent the steady state dynamics of continuous signals (e.g. voltages) in every node, and detect different types of faults: symmetrical faults (e.g. a three-phase to ground fault) and unsymmetrical faults (e.g. a line-to-ground fault).

To evaluate the degree of success in the identification of the faulty components, we ran two sets of 24 simulations in the power network. We randomly simulate simultaneous different types of faults in several nodes. To guide the

Table 1. Evaluation 1 by type of fault

Fault Type	Correct	Wrong	% Accuracy
A-B-C-GND	4	0	100.0
A-B-GND	2	0	100.0
A-GND	4	1	80.0
A-B	3	1	75.0
B-C	6	0	100.0
NO FAULT	3	0	100.0

Table 2. Evaluation 2 by type of fault

Fault Type	Correct	Wrong	% Accuracy
A-B-C-GND	14	0	100.0
A-B-GND	10	0	100.0
A-GND	12	2	85.7
A-B	15	3	83.3
B-C	16	0	100.0
NO FAULT	17	7	70.8

search for real faulted nodes, a first diagnosis, based on pure discrete signals coming from main breakers status, was applied [5]. This diagnosis delivers a subset of most likely faulted nodes, and then our fault detection approach was applied to this subset.

In the first set of 24 simulations, we selected randomly four test nodes, and simulate faults in every test node of the network (a maximum of four faults in the network) . To evaluate the performance of our method, we measure the level of accuracy to determine the correct state (normal or faulted) of test nodes. The summary of results for this set is given in table 1. Electrical phases are identified by *A,B* and *C*, and ground connection is identified by *GND*. The fault-free state is labeled as *NO FAULT*.

In the second set of 24 simulations, we apply faults only in the four test nodes (a maximum of four faults in the network), and the performance was measured by the identification of the correct state in test nodes. The summary of results for this set is given in table 2. The type of faults included *symmetrical* and *unsymmetrical* faults. we were able to determine with great accuracy the *symmetrical* faults, but we have problems with false positive detections and line-to-line faults.

We also performed the evaluation 1 with a level of 30 % of random missing information in test nodes data. The steady state models were learned with a training set of data with 10% of random missing information. The computed EWMA indices remain almost in the same values (±2%) computed without missing information. The evaluation 1 with missing information, delivered the same fault identification as the evaluation 1 without missing information.

3.1 Parameters Tuning

The parameters of the deterministic annealing algorithm we use to learn the Lagrange coefficients were obtained from [11]. The annealing parameter η was fixed at 0.9; The annealing threshold ϵ was 0.000001; The annealing initial temperature T_{max} was 1.0; the final temperature T_{min} was 0.000001; and the ρ learning-rate parameter was 0.3. We experimented with higher values on the T_{max} parameter (e.g. 10, 100) and the results obtained did not change in a significant manner. Other ρ parameter values used were 0.1, 0.2 and 0.4 and the results just vary slightly.

A main limitation of our approach, is the learning time of the statistical inference engine coefficients. When we use more discrete states, the set support size has to be increased to reach good levels of accuracy, but this also increase the learning time. We have tested our approach with different discretizations, and found that keeping the number of bins or fuzzy clusters in a low level, we still obtain good levels of accuracy.

4 Conclusions and Future Works

We have presented a new approach to detect faults based on models learned by machine learning techniques. The model represents the process normal behavior and is used in a residual generation scheme where model output is compared against actual process values. The residuals generated from this comparison are used to indicate the existence of a fault. The compact learned models are robust to noise, missing information and nonlinearities. We apply our method in a very difficult domain, as it is an electrical power network. The noise in data, the cascaded effect, and the perturbation by neighbor nodes, makes the diagnosis task hard to achieve. We have shown good levels of accuracy in the determination of the real faulted components and the mode of fault, in multiple events, multiple mode fault scenarios, where missing information was given. We determine in experimental simulations that wrong node state identifications were mainly due to the overlapping between EWMA indices thresholds, giving rise to ambiguous fault decisions. We plan to reach higher levels of success with the help of more reliable signal change detection methods.

References

1. W. Chen, Ch. Liu and M. Tsai M, "Online Fault Diagnosis of Distributions Substations Using Hybrid Cause-Effect Network and Fuzzy Rule-based Method", *IEEE Transactions on Power Delivery*, Vol. 15, No. 2, 2000, pp. 710-717.
2. R. Isermann, "On Fuzzy Logic Applications for Automatic Control, Supervision, and Fault Diagnosis", *IEEE Transactions on Systems, Man, and Cybernetics-Part A: Systems and Humans*, Vol. 28, No. 2, 1997, pp. 221-235.
3. J.Cheng , D. Bell, and W. Liu, *Learning Bayesian Networks from Data: An Efficient Approach Based on Information Theory*, Technical Report, Dept. of Computing Science, University of Alberta, Alberta CA. 1998.

4. P. Frank, "Fault Diagnosis in Dynamic Systems using Analytical and Knowledge Based Redundancy–A Survey and New Results", *Automatica* vol 30, 1990, pp. 789-804.
5. L. Garza, F. Cantú, and S. Acevedo, "A Methodology for Multiple-fault Diagnosis based on the Independent Choice Logic", In Springer *LNCS/LNAI Proc. of the IBERAMIA-SBIA*, pp. 417-426, Sao Paulo, Brasil, 2000.
6. S. Gentil, J. Montmain, and C. Combastel, "Combining FDI and AI Approaches within Causal-Model-Based Diagnosis", *IEEE Transactions on Systems, Man and Cybernetics-part B: Cybernetics*, vol. 34, No. 5 October 2004.
7. J. Grainger and W. Stevenson, *Power Systems Analysis*. McGraw-Hill, Inc., USA, 1994
8. U. Lerner, R. Parr, D. Koller and G. Biswas "Bayesian Fault Detection and Diagnosis in Dynamic Systems", *IEEE Transactions on Control Systems*, vol 9, 1999, pp. 498-503.
9. E. Manders, G. Biswas, P. Mosterman, L. Badford, V. Ram and J. Barnett, "Signal Interpretation for Monitoring and Diagnosis, a Cooling System Testbed", *IEEE Transactions on Control Systems*, vol 9, 1999, pp. 498-503.
10. L. Wang , *A Course in Fuzzy Systems and Control*, Englewood Cliffs, NJ, USA, 1997.
11. L. Yan and D. Miller, "General Statistical Inference for Discrete and Mixed Spaces by an Approximate Application of the Maximum entropy Principle", *IEEE trans. On Neural Networks*, vol 11, no 3, 2000, pp. 558-573.
12. D. Zhang, S. Dai, Y. Zheng, R. Zhang and P. Mu, "Researches and Applications of a Hybrid Fault Diagnosis System", *Proceedings of the 3r world Congress on Intelligent Control and Automation 2000*, Hefei, P.R. China, pp. 215-219.
13. A. Zhirabok and O. Preobrazhenskaya, "Robust Fault Detection and Isolation in nonlinear systems", *in Proceedings IFAC Symp. SAFEPROCESS'94*, Finland, june 1994, pp. 244-248.

A Mixed Mutation Strategy Evolutionary Programming Combined with Species Conservation Technique*

Hongbin Dong[1,2], Jun He[1,3], Houkuan Huang[1], and Wei Hou[2]

[1] School of Computer Science and Information Technology,
Beijing Jiaotong University, Beijing 100044, China
[2] Department of Computer Science, Harbin Normal University, Harbin 150080, China
[3] School of Computer Science, University of Birmingham, Birmingham B15 2TT, UK
donghongbin@263.net, j.he@cs.bham.ac.uk

Abstract. Mutation operators play an important role in evolutionary programming. Several different mutation operators have been developed in the past decades. However, each mutation operator is only efficient in some type of problems, but fails in another one. In order to overcome the disadvantage, a possible solution is to use a mixed mutation strategy, which mixes various mutation operators. In this paper, an example of such strategies is introduced which employs five different mutation strategies: Gaussian, Cauchy, Levy, single-point and chaos mutations. It also combines with the technique of species conservation to prevent the evolutionary programming from being trapped in local optima. This mixed strategy has been tested on 21 benchmark functions. The simulation results show that the mixed mutation strategy is superior to any pure mutation strategy.

1 Introduction

Evolutionary Programming (EP), inspired from biology evolution, now has been applied successfully to solving many numerical optimization problems [1], [2]. The main procedure of EP for continuous optimization is divided into two phases: (1) Each individual generates an offspring via mutation; (2) Better individuals from the parent and offspring population are selected as the next generation.

Many mutation operators, e.g., Gaussian, Cauchy, Levy, single-point and chaos mutations, have been presented to generate new individuals. Gaussian mutation is the classical mutation used in Conventional EP (CEP). Cauchy mutation is proposed as a fast evolutionary programming (FEP) [3]. It converges faster to a better solution than CEP on many multivariate functions. Levy mutation can lead to a large variation and a large number of distinct values in evolutionary search, in comparison with traditional Gaussian mutation [4],[5]. Levy mutation is said to be more general and flexible than Cauchy mutation

---

* This work is supported by National Natural Science Foundation of China under Grant (60443003).

because of its α parameter [4],[5]. The distinctions between Single-Point Mutation Evolutionary Programming (SPMEP) and the traditional evolutionary programming are that only one component of each solution is mutated in each generation and the deviation σ follows a fixed mutation scheme [6]. SPMEP is claimed to be superior to CEP, FEP on many multimodal and high-dimensional functions [6], but worse than CEP on a few low-dimensional functions with a few local optima. Chaos mutation can increase exploration and exploitation capability. Each mutation strategy is capable to tackle one class of problems very well, but may not in another one. A solution to this trouble is to mix different strategies together and benefit from the advantages from all strategies.

In order to reduce the effects of the genetic drift resulting from the selection mechanism, to allow the formation and the maintenance of different solutions and to prevent the EA from being trapped in local optima, niching (or speciation) methods have been proposed [7]. A niche can be viewed as a subspace in the environment that can support different types of life. A species is defined as a group of individuals with similar biological features capable of interbreeding among themselves but that are unable to breed with individuals outside their group. A Species Conservation GA (SCGA) has been introduced [8] and it is proved to be very effective in finding multiple solutions of multimodal optimization problems.

In this paper we don't create a new mutation operator but aim to design a mixed mutation strategy. Inspired from evolutionary game theory, we design a novel evolutionary programming, Mixed Strategy Evolutionary Programming Combined with Species Conservation Technique (SMSEP). It mixes Gaussian, Cauchy, Levy, single-point and chaos mutations. In SMSEP, each individual chooses one of these five mutation strategies to generate its offspring according to a mixed strategy distribution. This mixed strategy distribution is dynamically adjusted based on the performance of mutation strategies. In SMSEP, we also make use of species conservation technique to prevent the algorithm from being trapped in local optima.

The rest of this paper is organized as follows. In Section 2, we introduce a framework of SMSEP based on evolutionary game theory. In Section 3, we introduce the method of species conservation. In Section 4, we propose an EP algorithm using mixed mutation strategies Based Species Conservation for continuous optimization problem. In Section 5, we test the algorithm on 21 benchmark functions and report results. Section 6 is devoted to conclusions and future studies.

2 A General Framework of Evolutionary Programming Using a Mixed Strategy

In this paper EP is used to solve a continuous optimization problem. Consider the following global optimization problem

$$\begin{cases} \min f(x_1, x_2, \cdots, x_m), \\ \text{s.t. } x_i \in [a_i, b_i], \quad i = 1, \cdots, m. \end{cases} \quad (1)$$

EP using a mixed strategy is inspired from evolutionary game theory [9]. Now we describe its basic idea.

Let I be a population consisting of μ individuals. For each individual $i \in I$, it has a strategy set, written by $s = \{1, 2, ..., m\}$, where $m_i \geq 2$ is the number of strategies. A single strategy is called a pure strategy in the game theory. At each generation, an individual can choose a pure strategy from it strategy set to implement its next action. In this paper, each individual has a set of mutation operators, which consists of five different mutations. An individuals will choose one of mutations to generate new individuals based on a probability. A mixed strategy for individual i is a probability distribution over the set of its pure strategy. For each individual i, we can represent its mixed strategy distribution as a vector $\boldsymbol{\rho_i}$ whose its hth element is $\rho_{ih} \in R$. $\rho_{ih} \in R$ is the probability for the individual i to choose the hth pure strategy. How to determine the mixed strategy probability is the key issue in designing a successfully mixed strategy.

Assume at the tth generation, individual i takes strategy s_i. For the strategy s_i, we assign a payoff to it, denoted by $\pi_i(s)$. In EP, it is not easy to define a prior or explicit value for the payoff for each strategy. In this paper, this value of an individual's pure strategy is implicitly determined by whether the strategy help the individual succeed in selection process against other individuals. If the strategy used by an individual helps the individual to win the selection, then this pure strategy will be enhanced, otherwise, the individual will switch to other strategy. More details of the idea will be illustrated in the below paragraph of updating the mixed strategy.

In general, an evolutionary process combines two basic elements: a mutation mechanism that provides variety and a selection mechanism that favors some varieties over others.

The mutation process could be described as follows: Let $I(t)$ be a population at a generation t, each individual $i \in I$ will choose a pure strategy h according to the mixed strategy distribution, and then generate its offspring I'. A value of fitness f_i is also assigned to each individual in the offspring population. Each offspring individual will inherit the mixed strategy distribution from its parent.

The selection process could be described as follows: For the population $I(t)$ and its offspring population $I(t)'$, μ individuals will be selected based on their fitness values.

The updating process of each individual mixed strategy in the new generation population is described as follows: After selection, we evaluate the payoff of the used strategy for each individual in the next generation population. The payoff function for each strategy is defined as follows: assume individual i to use the pure strategy h in the mutation. The individual should belong to one of the two classes: parent population or offspring population.

If the individual i comes from offspring population, then a positive payoff is assigned to this pure strategy, because the mutation h generates a better offspring; if the individual i comes from the parent population, then a negative payoff is assigned to the strategy h, because the mutation strategy h which it used doesn't generate a better offspring.

3 Species Conservation Technique

The Species Conservation Genetic Algorithm (SCGA) achieves niching by exploiting the notion of species [8]. The definition of species, as well as the operation of the GA using species conservation, depends on a parameter we call species distance d_s (d_s is a species distance). The species distance defines the upper bound on the distance between two individuals for which they are considered to be similar. In the SCGA the species distance is used to decide which individuals are worth preserving from one generation to the next.

A species is a subset S of the population P_N (where N is the population size) in which the distance between any two individuals is less than the species distance. In the SCGA the species in a population are constructed around certain individuals called species seeds.

Let $S_1, S_2, ..., S_k$ be a partitioning of the population P_N into species. An individual $x^* \in S_i$ is the species seed in its species if, for every individual $y \in S_i$, $f(x^*) \leq f(y)$. We also say that species seed x^* dominate the species S_i. A species S_i is centered on its species seed x^*, if, for every individual $y \in S_i$, $d(x^*) < d_s/2$.

4 A Mixed Mutation Strategies Evolutionary Programming Based Species Conservation

The mixed EP will use five different mutation strategies: Gaussian, Cauchy, Levy, single-point and chaos mutations. The structure of the mixed EP is almost the same as any of traditional EPs with little extra computation cost. The EP algorithm using mixed strategy is described as follows:

Alg.1: (Mixed Strategies Evolutionary Programming)

1. Choose a set of pure strategy $\{1, 2, 3, 4, 5\}$, which are Gaussian, Cauchy, Levy, single-point and chaos mutations respectively.
2. Initialization:
   - Generate an initial population consisting of μ individuals, each of which can be represented by a set of real vectors $(\boldsymbol{x}_i, \boldsymbol{\sigma}_i)$, $i = 1, 2, \cdots, \mu$, $\boldsymbol{x}_i$ are objective variables, and $\boldsymbol{\sigma}_i$ are standard deviations. Each $\boldsymbol{x}_i$ and $\boldsymbol{\sigma}_i$ has m independent components:

   $$\begin{aligned}\boldsymbol{x}_i &= (x_i(1), x_i(2), \cdots, x_i(m)), \\ \boldsymbol{\sigma}_i &= (\sigma_i(1), \sigma_i(2), \cdots, \sigma_i(m)),\end{aligned} \qquad i = 1, \cdots, \mu.$$

   - For each individual i, assign an initial probability distribution to the mixed strategy vector:

   $$\boldsymbol{\rho}_i = (\rho_i(1), \rho_i(2), \rho_i(3), \rho_i(4), , \rho_i(5)), \qquad i = 1, \cdots, \mu.$$

3. Determine species seeds set X_s by invoking Algorithm 2.

4. Mutation: for each individual i, we choose a mutation strategy h according to the probability of its mixed strategy vector ρ. Then mutate the individual and generate a new offspring according to this chosen strategy.
The details of Gaussian, Cauchy, Levy, single-point and chaos mutations are described as follows: Given parent $(x_i^{(k)}, \sigma_i^{(k)})$,

Gaussian mutation: Create an offspring $(x_i^{(k+1)}, \sigma_i^{(k+1)})$ as follows:

$$\begin{cases} \sigma_i^{(k+1)}(j) = \sigma_i^{(k)}(j)\exp\{\tau N(0,1) + \tau' N_j(0,1)\}, j = 1, 2, \cdots, m, \\ x_i^{(k+1)}(j) = x_i^{(k)}(j) + \sigma_i^{(k+1)}(j)N_j(0,1), \qquad j = 1, 2, \cdots, m, \end{cases} \quad (2)$$

where $N(0,1)$ stands for a standard Gaussian random variable fixed for a given individual i; and $N_j(0,1)$ is the standard Gaussian random variable for each component j. Where k is the current generation number; and the parameters τ and τ' are defined as the same as [10]:

$$\tau = 1/\sqrt{2\mu}, \qquad \tau' = 1/\sqrt{2\sqrt{\mu}}.$$

Cauchy Mutation: Creates an offspring $(x_i^{(k+1)}, \sigma_i^{(k+1)})$ as follows:

$$\begin{cases} \sigma_i^{(k+1)}(j) = \sigma_i^{(k)}(j)\exp\{\tau N(0,1) + \tau' N_j(0,1)\}, j = 1, 2, \cdots, m, \\ x_i^{(k+1)}(j) = x_i^{(k)}(j) + \sigma_i^{(k+1)}(j)\delta_j, \qquad j = 1, 2, \cdots, m, \end{cases} \quad (3)$$

where δ_j is a standard Cauchy random variable and is generated anew for each value of component j.

Lévy Mutation: Creates an offspring $(x_i^{(k+1)}, \sigma_i^{(k+1)})$ as follows:

$$\begin{cases} \sigma_i^{(k+1)}(j) = \sigma_i^{(k)}(j)\exp\{\tau N(0,1) + \tau' N_j(0,1)\}, j = 1, 2, \cdots, m, \\ x_i^{(k+1)}(j) = x_i^{(k)}(j) + \sigma_i^{(k+1)}(j)L_j(\beta), \qquad j = 1, 2, \cdots, m, \end{cases} \quad (4)$$

where $L_j(\beta)$ is a random number generated anew for each individual j from Levy distribution with parameter $\beta = 0.8$.

Single-Point Mutation: Create an offspring $(x_i^{(k+1)}, \sigma_i^{(k+1)})$ as follows: j is randomly chosen from the set $\{1, 2, \cdots, m\}$. For this mutation, only one component of each solution is mutated in each iteration.

$$\begin{cases} \sigma_i^{(k+1)}(j) = \sigma_i^{(k)}(j)\exp(-\alpha), \\ x_i^{(k+1)}(j) = x_i^{(k)}(j) + \sigma_i^{(k+1)}(j)N_j(0,1), \end{cases} \quad (5)$$

where $\alpha = 1.01$, the initial value of $\sigma_i(j)$ is equal to $\frac{1}{2}(b_j - a_j)$. If $\sigma_i(j) < 10^{-4}$, then $\sigma_i(j) = (b_j - a_j)/2$.

Chaos Mutation: The Logistic Function as a mutation operator. The common and simple chaotic function, the logistic equation is: $C_{l+1} = \lambda C_l(1 - C_l)$, $C_l \in [0,1]$, where $\lambda = 4, l = 1, 2, ..., W$.

Create an offspring $(x_i^{(k+1)}, \sigma_i^{(k+1)})$ as follows:

$$\begin{cases} \sigma_i^{(k+1)}(j) = \sigma_i^{(k)}(j)\exp\{\tau N(0,1) + \tau' N_j(0,1)\}, & j=1,2,\cdots,m, \\ x_i^{(k+1)}(j) = x_i^{(k)}(j) + \sigma_i^{(k+1)}(j)C_j(0,1), & j=1,2,\cdots,m, \end{cases} \quad (6)$$

where $C_j(0,1)$ is a random number generated anew for each individual j from Logistic Function with parameter λ.

5. For μ parents and their μ offsprings, calculate their fitness value $f_1, f_2, ..., f_{2\mu}$.
6. Conserve species from set X_s by invoking Algorithm 3.
7. Define and initialize a winning function for each individual in the parent and offspring populations as $w_i = 0$, for individual $i = 1, 2, ..., 2\mu$. For each individual i, select one fitness of another individual, say f_j and compare the two fitness values. If f_i is less than f_j, the winning function for individual i is increased by one, $w_i = w_i + 1$. Perform this procedure q times for each of parent and offspring.
8. According to the winning function w_i, for each individual $i = 1, 2, ..., 2\mu$, select μ individuals that have the largest winning values from the parent population and the offspring population.
9. For each individual i in the next generation population, upgrade its mixed strategy as follows.
   - If the individual comes from the offspring population, and the pure strategy used in the mutation is h where $h \in \{1,2,3,4,5\}$, then we will enhance this pure strategy h:

$$\begin{cases} \rho_{ih}^{(k+1)} = \rho_{ih}^{(k)} + (1 - \rho_{ih}^{(k)}) * \gamma, \\ \rho_{il}^{(k+1)} = \rho_{il}^{(k)} - \rho_{lh}^{(k)} * \gamma, & \forall l \neq h. \end{cases} \quad (7)$$

   where $0 < \gamma < 1$ is a small positive as a parameter to adjust the probability distribution of mixed strategy. In this paper $\gamma = 1/4$.
   - If the individual is selected from the parent population, and the pure strategy used in the mutation is h where h takes value from $\{1,2,3,4,5\}$ then weakens the strategy h,

$$\begin{cases} \rho_{ih}^{(k+1)} = \rho_{ih}^{(k)} - \rho_{ih}^{(k)} * \gamma, \\ \rho_{il}^{(k+1)} = \rho_{il}^{(k)} + \frac{1}{m-1} * \gamma * \rho_{lk}^{(k)}, & \forall l \neq h. \end{cases} \quad (8)$$

10. Repeat step 3-9 until the stopping criterion is satisfied.

Alg.2: (The algorithm for determining the species seeds)

1. Initialize species seeds set X_s, $X_s = \emptyset$.
2. Search for the best unmarked individual $x^* \in G(k)$.
3. Mark individual x^* as processed.
   For each individual $x \in X_s$, if the distance between two individuals $(dist(x^*, x) > d_s/2)$, then let $X_s = X_s \cup \{x^*\}$.
4. Repeat step 2-3 until no more unmarked individuals in $G(k)$.

Alg.3: (The algorithm for conserving species)

1. For each individual $x \in X_s$, Select the worst unmarked $y \in S'(x, d_s)$, if y does not exists Go to Step 3.
2. If $(f(y) > f(x))$ then $y = x$ Go to Step 4.
3. Select the worst unmarked $y \in G(k+1)$, let $y = x$.
4. Mark y as processed.
5. Repeat step 1-4 until no more unprocessed individuals.

5 Experimental Results and Analysis

We apply SMSEP to a set of benchmark optimization problems. The 21 benchmark functions are given in Table 2 in the end of the paper. A more detailed description of each function is given in [3], [6]. They have the characteristics of unimodal/multimodal, low-dimensional/high-dimensional. Functions $f_1 - f_{11}$ are high-dimensional problems. Functions $f_1 - f_3$ are unimodal function. Function f_4 is the step function, which has one minimum and is discontinuous. Function f_5 is a noisy quartic function, where random $[0, 1)$ is a uniformly distributed random variable in $[0, 1)$. Functions $f_6 - f_{11}$ are multimodal functions where the number of local minima increases exponentially with the problem dimension. Functions $f_{12} - f_{21}$ are low-dimensional functions which have only a few local minima.

The experiment setting is given as follows: the initial population $\mu = 100$, and the tournament size $q = 10$, and the initial standard deviation $\sigma = 1.0$ in Gaussian, Cauchy, Levy mutations, $\sigma = \frac{1}{2}(b_i - a_i)$ in single point mutation. The value of parameter α in single point mutation strategy of function f_1, f_2, $f_3 - f_7$, f_8, f_9, f_{10}, $f_{11} - f_{21}$ is 2.31, 5.01, 1.01, 5.01, 1.01, 2.81 and 1.01 respectively in SMSEP. No single α value was the best for all different problems, so it is necessary to find different α values for different problems. The halting criterion is that the maximum number of generations Gen's is reached. The initial populations are always generated at random in the domain. All these conditions are the same as in [3], [6].

Table 1 shows the simulation results compared with those given in [3], [6]. From Table 1, we can see that the performance of SMSEP is better than or the same as SPMEP, FEP and CEP on all 21 functions. This result demonstrates that through a mixture of different mutation strategies, SMSEP has a more stable performance over different functions. This is different from EP using a single mutation strategy: it works very well on a subset of test functions, but poorly on others.

It is observed from Table 1 that SMSEP's standard deviations are smaller than those of SPMEP, FEP and GEP, which indicated the best values in all 50 runs are very close to the mean best function values. So the robustness of SMSEP is superior to FEP, CEP and SPMEP.

The success of SMSEP can be explained as follows: different mutation operators have different advantages. During different search phase and area, it is important to choose a right mutation operator.

Table 1. A comparison among: SMSEP, SPMEP, FEP and CEP on $f_1 - f_{21}$. All results have been averaged over 50 runs, where "Mean best" indicates the Mean best function values found in the last generation, and "Std dev" stands for the standard deviation.

F	Gen's	SMSEP		SPMEP		FEP		CEP	
		mean best	std dev	mean best	std dev	mean best	std dev	mean best	std dev
f_1	1500	5.24e-5	1.13e-5	1.3e-4	1.0e-4	5.7e-4	1.3e-4	2.2e-4	5.9e-4
f_2	2000	1.39e-4	2.01e-4	5.1-4	1.5e-5	8.1e-3	7.7e-4	2.6e-3	1.7e-4
f_3	5000	5.35e-3	2.05e-3	6.5e-3	2.0e-3	0.3	0.5	2	1.2
f_4	1500	0	0	0	0	0	0	577.76	1125.76
f_5	3000	6.75e-3	1.33e-3	1.0e-2	1.5e-3	7.6e-3	2.6e-3	1.8e-2	6.4e-3
f_6	9000	-12569.48	5.21e-3	-12569.48	9.1e-12	-12554.5	52.6	-7917.1	634.5
f_7	5000	2.5e-5	2.18e-6	4.7e-5	3.6e-5	4.6e-2	1.2e-2	89	23.1
f_8	1500	1.56e-3	5.82e-4	1.9e-3	4.4e-4	1.8e-2	2.1e-3	9.2	2.8
f_9	2000	1.74e-5	1.35e-5	5.6e-3	1.7e-3	1.6e-2	2.2e-2	8.6e-2	0.12
f_{10}	1500	2.59e-7	1.55e-7	8.5e-7	9.7e-9	9.2e-6	3.6e-6	1.76	2.4
f_{11}	1500	5.63e-6	2.0e-6	1.4e-5	9.2e-6	1.6e-4	7.3e-5	1.4	3.7
f_{12}	100	0.998004	0	1	1.6e-15	1.22	0.56	1.66	1.19
f_{13}	4000	3.08e-4	4.13e-7	4.5e-4	1.5e-4	5.0e-4	3.2e-4	4.7e-4	3.0e-4
f_{14}	100	-1.03	2.69e-8	-1.03	4.3e-10	-1.03	4.9e-7	-1.03	4.9e-7
f_{15}	100	0.398	0	0.398	5.7e-10	0.398	1.5e-7	0.398	1.5e-7
f_{16}	100	3	0	3	5.6e-9	3.02	0.11	3	0
f_{17}	100	-3.86	0	-3.86	1.5e-9	-3.86	1.4e-5	-3.86	1.4e-2
f_{18}	200	-3.32	6.26e-5	-3.25	5.4e-2	-3.27	5.9e-2	-3.28	5.8e-2
f_{19}	100	-10.1	1.04e-5	-6.63	3.5	-5.52	1.59	-6.86	2.67
f_{20}	100	-10.4	3.97e-5	-7.4	3	-5.52	2.12	-8.27	2.95
f_{21}	100	-10.54	2.9e-5	-6.53	4	-6.57	3.14	-9.1	2.92

In the early search phase, Cauchy mutation is more likely to generate larger jumps than Gaussian mutation and get a fast convergence rate. However, it would be less effective than Gaussian mutation near the small neighborhood of the global optimum because a relatively smaller search step is needed. So non-Gaussian mutations play a significant role in the early stages of evolution, taken as a global search, while the Gaussian mutation as a local search. Levy mutation with a smaller α converges faster initially because of its long jumps and more distinct values. However, Levy mutation with a bigger parameter α behavior more like Gaussian mutation. SPMEP searches one direction each time and this technique has been proven to be efficient for some high dimensional functions, in a sum form of one-dimensional functions. Besides increasing exploration and exploitation capability, Chaos mutation can also improve the convergence speed, resume the population diversity and prevent premature convergence.

Species conservation technique guarantees the high fitness individuals to keep in the population, at the same time, a few low fitness individuals also are survival. Although they are far from the other members of the population, possibly close to an unexplored region which is very important to the search. Species conservation preserve the "good quality" of the population.

Table 2. The 21 benchmark functions

Test function	n	S	f_{min}
$f_1(x) = \sum_{i=1}^{n} x_i^2$	30	$[-100, 100]^n$	0
$f_2(x) = \sum_{i=1}^{n} \mid x_i \mid + \prod_{i=1}^{n} \mid x_i \mid$	30	$[-10, 10]^n$	0
$f_3(x) = \max\{\mid x_i \mid, 1 \leq i \leq n\}$	30	$[-100, 100]^n$	0
$f_4(x) = \sum_{i=1}^{n} (\lfloor x_i + 0.5 \rfloor)^2$	30	$[-100, 100]^n$	0
$f_5(x) = \sum_{i=1}^{n} i x_i^4 + random[0, 1)$	30	$[-1.28, 1.28]^n$	0
$f_6(x) = \sum_{i=1}^{n} (x_i \sin(\sqrt{\mid x_i \mid}))$	30	$[-500, 500]^n$	-12569.5
$f_7(x) = \sum_{i=1}^{n} (x_i^2 - 10\cos(2\pi x_i) + 10)$	30	$[-5.12, 5.12]^n$	0
$f_8(x) = -20\exp\left(-0.2\sqrt{\sum_{i=1}^{n} x_i^2/n}\right)$			
$-\exp\left(\sum_{i=1}^{n} \cos(2\pi x_i)/n\right) + 20 + e$	30	$[-32, 32]^n$	0
$f_9(x) = \frac{1}{4000}\sum_{i=1}^{n} x_i^2 - \prod_{i=1}^{n} \cos(x_i/\sqrt{i}) + 1$	30	$[-600, 600]^n$	0
$f_{10}(x) = \frac{\pi}{n}[10\sin^2(\pi y_i)$			
$+\sum_{i=1}^{n-1}(y_i - 1)^2\left(1 + 10\sin^2(\pi y_{i+1})\right) + (y_n - 1)^2]$			
$+\sum_{i=1}^{n} u(x_i, 10, 100, 4)$			
$y_i = 1 + \frac{1}{4}(x_i + 1)$			
$u(x_i, a, k, m) = \begin{cases} k(x_i - a)^m, x_i > a, \\ 0, -a \leq x_i \leq a, \\ k(-x_i - a)^m, x_i < -a. \end{cases}$	30	$[-50, 50]^n$	0
$f_{11}(x) = 0.1[\sin^2(3\pi x_1)$			
$+\sum_{i=1}^{n-1}(x_i - 1)^2(1 + \sin^2(3\pi x_{i+1}))$			
$+(x_n - 1)(1 + \sin^2(2\pi x_n))] + \sum_{i=1}^{n} u(x_i, 5, 100, 4)$	30	$[-50, 50]^n$	0
$f_{12}(x) = \left(\frac{1}{500} + \sum_{j=1}^{25} \frac{1}{j + \sum_{i=1}^{2}(x_i - a_{ij})^6}\right)^{-1}$	2	$[-65.536, 65.536]^n$	1
$f_{13}(x) = \sum_{i=1}^{11}\left(a_i - \frac{x_1(b_i^2 + b_i x_2)}{b_i^2 + b_i x_3 + x_4}\right)^2$	4	$[-5, 5]^n$	0.0003075
$f_{14}(x) = 4x_1^2 - 2.1x_1^4 + x_1^6/3 + x_1 x_2 - 4x_2^2 + 4x_2^4$	2	$[-5, 5]^n$	-1.0316285
$f_{15}(x) = [x_2 - \frac{5.1}{4\pi}x_1^2 + \frac{5}{\pi}x_1 - 6]^2$			
$+10[1 - \frac{1}{8\pi}\cos(x_1)] + 10$	2	$[-5, 10] \times [0, 15]$	0.398
$f_{16}(x) = [1 + (x_1 + x_2 + 1)^2(19 - 14x_1 + 3x_1^2 + 6x_1 x_2$			
$+3x_2^2)] \times [30 + (2x_1 - 3x_2)^2(18 - 32x_1 + 12x_1^2 + 48x_2$			
$-36x_1 x_2 + 27x_2^2)]$	2	$[-2, 2]^n$	3
$f_{17}(x) = -\sum_{i=1}^{4} c_i \exp\left[-\sum_{j=1}^{4} a_{ij}(x_j - p_{ij})^2\right]$	4	$[0, 1]^n$	-3.86
$f_{18}(x) = -\sum_{i=1}^{4} c_i \exp\left[-\sum_{j=1}^{6} a_{ij}(x_j - p_{ij})^2\right]$	6	$[0, 1]^n$	-3.32
$f_{19} = -\sum_{i=1}^{5}\left[(x - a_i)(x - a_i)^T + c_i\right]^{-1}$	4	$[0, 10]^n$	-10
$f_{20} = -\sum_{i=1}^{7}\left[(x - a_i)(x - a_i)^T + c_i\right]^{-1}$	4	$[0, 10]^n$	-10
$f_{21} = -\sum_{i=1}^{10}\left[(x - a_i)(x - a_i)^T + c_i\right]^{-1}$	4	$[0, 10]^n$	-10

SMSEP combines these five different mutation strategies together. By the probability distribution of an individual's mixed strategy, SMSEP mutation dynamically adjusts strategy during the different search phase. This means a mixed strategy has integrated the advantages of global search and local search together, and is more efficient and stable than a pure strategy.

6 Conclusions

In this paper we propose a new way to design a mixed mutation strategy, which aims at integrating the advantages of different mutation operators, rather than creating a new mutation operator. Inspired from evolutionary game theory, SMSEP mixes five different mutation strategies: Gaussian, Cauchy, Levy, single-point and chaos mutations. We have tested SMSEP on 21 benchmark functions. The experimental results have shown that SMSEP performs better than or at least the same as the best of FEP, CEP and SPMEP on most benchmark problems tested. We have also illustrated a general framework to design a mixed strategy, and under this framework, it is easy to implement different mixed strategy scheme.

In the future, we will consider how to designing other types of mixed strategy evolutionary programming, e.g., mixed selection strategies, mixed strategy parameters. It is possible to extend the idea to other algorithms such as genetic algorithms, evolutionary strategies etc.

References

1. Fogel, L.J., Owens, A.J., Walsh, M.J.: Artificial Intelligence through Simulated Evolution Computation. John Wiley & Sons, New York, NY (1966)
2. Fogel, D.: Evolution Computation: Toward a New Philosophy of Machine Intelligence. IEEE Press, Piscataway, NJ (1995)
3. Yao, X., Liu, Y., Lin, G.: Evolutionary programming made faster. IEEE Trans. Evolutionary Computation **3** (1999) 82–102
4. Iwamatsu, M.: Generalized evolutionary programming with Lévy-type mutation. Computer Physics Computation **147** (2002) 729–732
5. Lee, C.Y., Yao, X.: Evolutionary programming using mutations based on the Lévy probability distribution. IEEE Trans. on Evolutionary Computation **8** (2004) 1–13
6. Ji, M., Tang, H., Guo, J.: A single-point mutation evolutionary programming. Information Processing Letts **90** (2004) 293–299
7. Holland, J.H.: Adaptation in Natural and Artificial System. Second edn. MIT Press, Cambridge, MA (1992)
8. Li, J.P., Balazs, M.E., Parks, G.T., Clarkson, P.J.: A species conserving genetic algorithm for multimodal function optimization. Evolutionary Computation **10** (2002) 207–234
9. Weibull, J.W.: Evolutionary Game Theory. MIT press, Cambridge, MA (1995)
10. Baeck, T., Schwefel, H.P.: An overview of evolutionary algorithms for parameter optimization. Evolutionary Computation **1** (1993) 1–24

Coevolutionary Multi-objective Optimization Using Clustering Techniques

Margarita Reyes Sierra and Carlos A. Coello Coello

CINVESTAV-IPN (Evolutionary Computation Group),
Electrical Eng. Department, Computer Science Dept.,
Av. IPN No. 2508, Col. San Pedro Zacatenco,
México D.F. 07300, México

Abstract. We propose a new version of a multiobjective coevolutionary algorithm. The main idea of the proposed approach is to concentrate the search effort on promising regions that arise during the evolutionary process as a product of a clustering mechanism applied on the set of decision variables corresponding to the known Pareto front. The proposed approach is validated using several test functions taken from the specialized literature and it is compared with respect to its previous version and another approach that is representative of the state-of-the-art in evolutionary multiobjective optimization.

1 Introduction

Despite the considerable volume of research on evolutionary multiobjective optimization [1], little emphasis has been placed on certain algorithmic design aspects such as efficiency [2, 3]. Additionally, the use of coevolutionary mechanisms has been scarce in the evolutionary multiobjective optimization literature. As in our original proposal [4], the main motivation of the work reported here is precisely to take advantage of some coevolutionary concepts to design a multi-objective evolutionary algorithm (MOEA) that can be more efficient (in terms of fitness function evaluations). The main idea of the proposed algorithm is to obtain information along the evolutionary process as to focus the search in the "promising" sub-regions, and then to use a subpopulation for each of these subregions. At each generation, these different subpopulations "cooperate" and "compete" among themselves and from these different processes we obtain a single Pareto front. The size of each subpopulation is adjusted based on their contribution to the current Pareto front. The proposed approach uses the adaptive grid proposed in [3] to store the nondominated vectors obtained along the evolutionary process, enforcing a more uniform distribution of such vectors along the Pareto front. This new version of our algorithm performs a clustering analysis on the set of decision variables of the current Pareto front to find the promising regions of the search space. In this way, the number of populations needed does not exceed the total number of members on the true Pareto front.

2 Coevolution

Coevolution refers to a reciprocal evolutionary change between species that interact with each other. The relationships between the populations of two different species can be described considering all their possible types of interactions. Such interaction can be positive or negative depending on the consequences that such interaction produces on the population. Evolutionary computation researchers have developed several coevolutionary approaches in which normally two or more species relate to each other using any of the possible relationships, mainly competitive (e.g., [5]) or cooperative (e.g., [6]). Also, in most cases, such species evolve independently through a genetic algorithm. The key issue in these coevolutionary algorithms is that the fitness of an individual in a population depends on the individuals of a different population.

3 Previous Work

Parmee and Watson [7] proposed a collaborative scheme in which they use one population to optimize each of the objective functions of a problem. The method is really created to converge to a single (ideal) trade-off solution. However, through the use of penalties the algorithm can maintain diversity in the population. These penalties relate to variability in the decision variables' values. Keerativuttitumrong et.al. [8], Tan et.al. [9] and Iorio and Li [10], proposed cooperative schemes in which one population is defined for each decision variable of the problem. In order to evaluate an individual in any population, individuals from the other populations must be selected in order to complete a solution. In [8], the evolution of each of these populations is controlled through Fonseca and Fleming's MOGA [11]. The method in [9] uses an external archive to store and update the nondominated solutions found so far and also to guide the search to the less exploded subregions of the search space. Finally, in [10] the evolution of each of the populations is controlled through the scheme of the NSGA-II [2]. After each generation, the method proposed in [10] uses a nondominated sorting over all the subpopulations of parents and offspring to determine the new parents subpopulations.

4 Description of Our Approach

As in [4], the main idea of our approach is to focus the search efforts only towards the promising regions of the search space. Such "promising" regions are determined using clustering analysis of the current Pareto front. The evolutionary process of our approach is divided in two main stages. The first stage takes place during the first quarter of the total of generations. After that, in the second stage (the rest of the generations) we perform what we call a *checkpoint* in specific moments that will be mentioned later.

First Stage. During the first stage, the algorithm is allowed to explore all of the search space, by using a population of individuals which are selected using Fonseca and Fleming's Pareto ranking scheme [11]. Additionally, the approach uses the adaptive grid proposed in [3]. At the end of this first stage, the algorithm analyses the current Pareto front (stored in the adaptive grid) in order to determine the promising regions of the search space. In this new version, we perform a clustering analysis on the set of values of the decision variables corresponding to the current Pareto front. The aim is to determine the promising regions of the search space (line 6, Figure 1). This analysis is performed independently for each decision variable. Once we know the clusters of the

```
1. gen = 0
2. populations = 1
3. while (gen < Gmax) {
       if (gen ≥ Gmax/4)
4.         if (gen = Gmax/4, Gmax/2, 3Gmax/4 or
               ∃ x ∈ pop_zero : x ∈ current Pareto front) {
5.             check_active_populations()
6.             clustering_algorithm()
7.             construct_new_subpopulations()}
8.     for (i = 1; i ≤ populations; i + +)
9.         if (population i contributes to the current Pareto front)
10.            evolve_and_compete(i)
11.    elitism()
12.    reassign_resources()
13.    gen + + }
```

Fig. 1. Pseudocode of our algorithm

values corresponding to each one of the decision variables, we proceed to form a set of new populations. This process is illustrated in Figure 2. A cluster is a set of values, so for each cluster of each variable, we obtain the limits that bound that cluster. Once that we know the limits of each cluster, we have a set of intervals for each variable. Then, a set of sub-regions is created in the following way. For each point in the current Pareto front, we proceed to locate the interval on each variable to which it belongs. This process gives us a region in the search space. For each point in the current Pareto front we first check if it belongs to any region already located. If the point belongs to an existing region, we continue with the next point. Otherwise, we proceed to create the corresponding region, and so on. After that, we assign a new population to each region created, i.e., those that have individuals in the current Pareto front (line 7, Figure 1). In this way, in the worst case we will have as many populations as points in the current Pareto front. Finally, we use one extra population (called *population zero*) that continues searching for good solutions on the whole search space. This population is initialized with an 80% of points of the current Pareto front and a 20% of random points (with the aim of generating intermediate points on the current Pareto front while adding diversity).

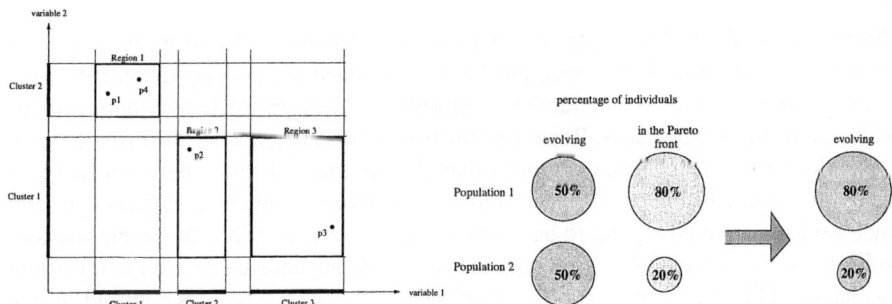

Fig. 2. (left) Mechanism used to locate the promising regions of the search space. A population will be assigned to each located promising region. (right) Resources reassignment: Each population is assigned or removed individuals such that its final size is proportional to its contribution to the current Pareto front.

Second Stage. When reaching the end of the first stage, the algorithm consists of a certain number of populations looking each at different regions of the search space. At each generation, the evolution of all the populations takes place independently and, later on, the nondominated elements from each population are sent to the adaptive grid where they "cooperate" and "compete" in order to conform a single Pareto front. After this, we count the number of individuals that each of the populations contributed to the current Pareto front. Our algorithm is *elitist* (line 11, Figure 1), because after the first generation of the second stage, all the populations that do not provide any individual to the current Pareto front are automatically eliminated and the sizes of the other populations are properly adjusted (line 12, Figure 1). Each population is assigned or removed individuals such that its final size is proportional to its contribution to the current Pareto front. These individuals to be added or removed are randomly generated/chosen. This process is illustrated in Figure 2. Thus, populations compete with each other to get as many extra individuals as possible. Note that it is, however, possible that the sizes of the populations "converge" to a constant value once their contribution to the current Pareto front no longer changes.

Checkpoint. During the second stage, we perform a *checkpoint* in specific moments of the evolutionary process (line 4, Figure 1). The checkpoint takes place as before (see Figure 1) [4], but also when the population zero includes a new individual in the adaptive grid, that is, in the current Pareto front. When the checkpoint happens, we perform a check on the current populations in order to determine how many (and which) of them can continue (i.e., those populations which continue contributing individuals to the current Pareto front, which are the "good" populations) (line 5, Figure 1). As at the end of the first stage, we perform again the clustering analysis on the set of values of the decision variables corresponding to the current Pareto front, and proceed to form a set of new populations. The non-dominated individuals from the "good" populations are kept. All the good individuals are distributed across the newly generated populations. The elitist process continues and the size of each population will be adjusted based on the same criteria as before. Note however, that we define a minimum population size and this size is enforced for all populations after each checkpoint.

Clustering Analysis. We implemented a clustering algorithm based on the nature of the *k-means* algorithm [12]. Since the *k-means* algorithm: (1) depends on the initial centroids and (2) requires the number of clusters needed, we made two modifications to overcome these drawbacks. Regarding the first disadvantage, when the distance from a given point x to its centroid is greater than the minimum distance between two centroids, the point x becomes a new centroid. To maintain the number of clusters constant, once we have selected a point to be a new centroid, we choose one of the closest centroids to be eliminated. With respect to the second disadvantage, we use the following mechanism [12]: Let x_i be a point, d_i the distance between x_i and its centroid, K the current total number of clusters and $\bar{d}_i$ the average distance between x_i and the K centroids. We create a new cluster with centroid x_i when: $|d_i - \bar{d}_i| \leq \bar{d}_i T$ where T is such that $0 < T < 1$. As big is the value of T, as big is the number of clusters created. Since the previous mechanism creates new clusters, we use a simple mechanism to also eliminate clusters when the corresponding centroids are very close: If the distance between two centroids is less that T times the average distance between centroids, one of them is eliminated.

Parameters Required. Our proposed approach requires the following parameters (The parameter T of the clustering algorithm used was fixed to $T = 1$): (1) Crossover rate (p_c) and mutation rate (p_m), (2) Maximum number of generations ($Gmax$), (3) Size of the initial population ($popsize_{init}$) to be used during the first stage and minimum size of the secondary population ($popsize_{sec}$) to be used during the second stage.

5 Results

To validate our approach, we performed both quantitative comparisons (adopting four metrics) and qualitative comparisons (plotting the Pareto fronts produced) with respect to the previous version of our approach (CO-MOEA) [4] and with respect to one MOEA that is representative of the state-of-the-art in the area: the Nondominated Sorting Genetic Algorithm II (NSGA-II) [2]. For our comparative study, we implemented the four following metrics:

Error Ratio (ER) [13]: This metric indicates the percentage of solutions (from the nondominated vectors found) that are not members of the true Pareto optimal set: $ER = \frac{\sum_{i=1}^{n} e_i}{n}$, where n is the number of vectors in the current set of nondominated vectors available; $e_i = 0$ if vector i is a member of the Pareto optimal set, and $e_i = 1$ otherwise.

Generational Distance (GD) [14]: The concept of generational distance was introduced as a way of estimating how far are the elements in the Pareto front produced by our algorithm from those in the true Pareto front of the problem: $GD = \frac{\sqrt{\sum_{i=1}^{n} d_i^2}}{n}$ where n is the number of nondominated vectors found by the algorithm being analyzed and d_i is the Euclidean distance (measured in objective space) between each of these and the nearest member of the true Pareto front.

Spacing (SP) [15]: This metric was proposed as a way of measuring the range (distance) variance of neighboring vectors in the Pareto front known:
$SP = \sqrt{\frac{1}{n-1} \sum_{i=1}^{n} (\bar{d} - d_i)^2}$ where $d_i = min_j(\sum_{k=1}^{m} |f_k^i - f_k^j|)$, $i, j = 1, ..., n$, m is the number of objectives, $\bar{d}$ is the mean of all d_i, and n is the number of vectors in the Pareto front found by the algorithm being evaluated.

Two Set Coverage (SC) [16]: Consider X', X'' as two sets of objective vectors. SC is defined as the mapping of the order pair (X', X'') to the interval $[0, 1]$: $SC(X', X'') \triangleq |\{a'' \epsilon X''; \exists a' \epsilon X' : a' \preceq a''\}|/|X''|$. If all points in X' dominate or are equal to all points in X'', then by definition $SC = 1$. $SC = 0$ implies the opposite. In general, $SC(X', X'')$ and $SC(X'', X')$ both have to be considered due to set intersections not being empty.

For each of the test functions shown below, we performed 30 runs per algorithm and a total of 10,000 evaluations. The parameters for NSGA-II were $popsize$=100 and 100 generations. All the algorithms used a bit mutation probability (p_m) equal to $1/codesize$ and a crossover probability (p_c) equal 0.8. The Pareto fronts that we will show correspond to the median of the 30 runs with respect to the ER metric. Regarding constraint-handling, we used the original scheme provided in the case of the NSGA-II. However, since our algorithm (both versions) does not have such a mechanism, we implemented a simple penalty function over the value of objective functions of each infeasible individual.

Test Function 1. Minimize $f_1(x_1, x_2) = x_1$, $f_2(x_1, x_2) = g(x_1, x_2)h(x_1, x_2)$
subject to: $g(x_1, x_2) = 11 + x_2^2 - 10cos(2\pi x_2)$
$$h(x_1, x_2) = \begin{cases} 1 - \sqrt{\frac{f_1(x_1,x_2)}{g(x_1,x_2)}} & f_1(x_1, x_2) \leq g(x_1, x_2) \\ 0 & \text{otherwise} \end{cases}$$
$0.0 \leq x_1 \leq 1.0, -30.0 \leq x_2 \leq 30.0$

In this example, our approach used: $popsize_{init} = 100$, $popsize_{rec} = 30$ (38 gen).

Test Function 2. Minimize $f_1(x) = \sum_{i=1}^{2}(-10e^{-0.2*\sqrt{x_i^2+x_{i+1}^2}})$,
$f_2(x) = \sum_{i=1}^{3}(|x_i|^{0.8} + 5sin(x_i^3))$ subject to: $-5.0 \leq x_1, x_2, x_3 \leq 5.0$
In this case, our approach used: $popsize_{init} = 100$, $popsize_{rec} = 30$ (40 gen).

Test Function 3. Minimize $f_1(x_1, x_2) = x_1$, $f_2(x_1, x_2) = x_2$
subject to: $g_1(x_1, x_2) = -x_1^2 - x_2^2 + 1 + 0.1cos(16 arctan\frac{x_1}{x_2}) \leq 0$
$g_2(x_1, x_2) = (x_1 - \frac{1}{2})^2 + (x_2 - \frac{1}{2})^2 - \frac{1}{2} \leq 0, 0.0 \leq x_1, x_2 \leq \pi$
In this example, our approach used: $popsize_{init} = 100$, $popsize_{rec} = 30$ (40 gen).
Table 1 shows the values of the metrics for each of the MOEAs compared.

6 Discussion of Results

As we can see in Table 1, in the first function the new version of our approach (CO-MOEA2) is clearly better than the previous version (CO-MOEA), with respect to all the metrics. On the other hand, although the results of the NSGA-II are better on average than the results of CO-MOEA2, the SC metric indicates that the Pareto fronts obtained by both algorithms are on average almost of the same quality.

As in the first function, in the second function CO-MOEA2 is better than CO-MOEA. However, in this case the results of the CO-MOEA with respect to the SP metric are weakly better than the results of CO-MOEA2. In this function, the results of CO-MOEA2 are better on average than the results of the NSGA-II, except for the SP metric. However, as in the first function, the SC metric indicates almost the same quality on the results of CO-MOEA2 and NSGA-II.

In the case of the third function, we can see that CO-MOEA and CO-MOEA2 obtained very similar results. CO-MOEA has better results only with respect to the SP metric. On the other hand, in this function the NSGA-II has better results on average only with respect to the ER metric. With respect to the SC metric, the NSGA-II obtained the best results, followed by CO-MOEA2 and CO-MOEA.

In general, from Table 1 and Figures 3 and 4, we can conclude that in the first two functions the new version of our approach has clearly improved the original version, and obtained very competitive results with respect to the NSGA-II. In the third function, CO-MOEA2 has obtained the same quality on the results than the CO-MOEA and NSGA-II. Finally, we can conclude that CO-MOEA2 needs to improve the results obtained with respect to the distribution (SP metric). We consider this as part of our future work.

Table 1. Comparison of results between the previous version of our approach (denoted by CO-MOEA [4]), the new version (CO-MOEA2) and the NSGA-II [2], for all the test functions

		Test Function 1				
		CO-MOEA	CO-MOEA2	NSGA-II	Two Set Coverage	
ER	best	0.54	0.02	0.00	X	SC(X,CO-MOEA)
	median	0.83	0.10	0.07	CO-MOEA	0.00
	worst	1.00	0.44	0.47	CO-MOEA2	0.67
	average	0.83	0.15	**0.13**	NSGA-II	0.83
	std. dev.	0.1223	0.1112	0.1289	Average	75%
GD	best	0.0004	0.0001	0.0047	X	SC(X,CO-MOEA2)
	median	0.7018	0.0040	0.0056	CO-MOEA	0.00
	worst	20.237	0.0910	0.0061	CO-MOEA2	0.00
	average	2.0042	0.0159	**0.0055**	NSGA-II	0.02
	std. dev.	3.9452	0.0249	0.0004	Average	1%
SP	best	0.0098	0.0045	0.0064	X	SC(X,NSGA-II)
	median	2.2077	0.0090	0.0073	CO-MOEA	0.00
	worst	47.351	0.9069	0.0084	CO-MOEA2	0.00
	average	4.8611	0.1344	**0.0073**	NSGA-II	0.00
	std. dev.	9.1779	0.2491	0.0006	Average	**0%**
		Test Function 2				
		CO-MOEA	CO-MOEA2	NSGA-II	Two Set Coverage	
ER	best	0.61	0.12	0.16	X	SC(X,CO-MOEA)
	median	0.72	0.23	0.27	CO-MOEA	0.00
	worst	0.83	0.35	0.37	CO-MOEA2	0.66
	average	0.72	**0.24**	0.28	NSGA-II	0.62
	std. dev.	0.0557	0.0578	0.0578	Average	64%
GD	best	0.0299	0.0028	0.0032	X	SC(X,CO-MOEA2)
	median	0.0311	0.0032	0.0036	CO-MOEA	0.02
	worst	0.0332	0.0038	0.0044	CO-MOEA2	0.00
	average	0.0313	**0.0032**	0.0037	NSGA-II	0.07
	std. dev.	0.0008	0.0002	0.0004	Average	5%
SP	best	0.0387	0.0519	0.0450	X	SC(X,NSGA-II)
	median	0.0980	0.1100	0.0553	CO-MOEA	0.02
	worst	0.1282	0.1534	0.1060	CO-MOEA2	0.07
	average	0.0808	0.1069	**0.0606**	NSGA-II	0.00
	std. dev.	0.0288	0.0306	0.0156	Average	5%
		Test Function 3				
		CO-MOEA	CO-MOEA2	NSGA-II	Two Set Coverage	
ER	best	0.09	0.05	0.01	X	SC(X,CO-MOEA)
	median	0.15	0.16	0.08	CO-MOEA	0.00
	worst	0.25	0.29	0.17	CO-MOEA2	0.25
	average	0.14	0.15	**0.08**	NSGA-II	0.21
	std. dev.	0.0404	0.0461	0.0339	Average	23%
GD	best	0.0009	0.0009	0.0008	X	SC(X,CO-MOEA2)
	median	0.0014	0.0012	0.0013	CO-MOEA	0.23
	worst	0.0015	0.0015	0.0016	CO-MOEA2	0.00
	average	0.0014	**0.0012**	**0.0012**	NSGA-II	0.17
	std. dev.	0.0001	0.0001	0.0002	Average	20%
SP	best	0.0051	0.0047	0.0065	X	SC(X,NSGA-II)
	median	0.0064	0.0085	0.0099	CO-MOEA	0.13
	worst	0.0077	0.0185	0.0155	CO-MOEA2	0.14
	average	0.0064	**0.0092**	0.0101	NSGA-II	0.00
	std. dev.	0.0007	0.0027	0.0022	Average	**14%**

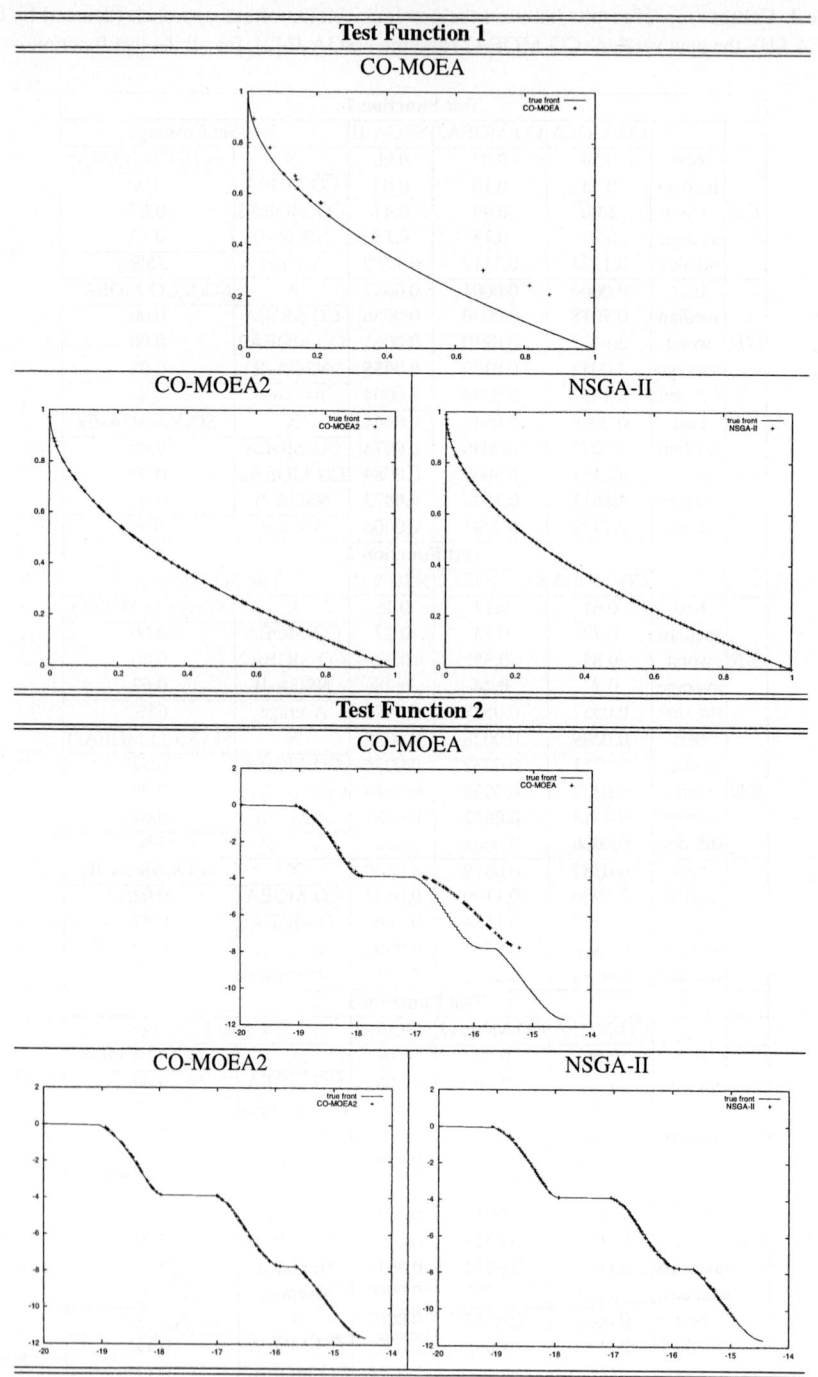

Fig. 3. Pareto fronts obtained by the previous version of our approach (CO-MOEA), the new version (CO-MOEA2) and the NSGA-II [2], for test functions 1 and 2

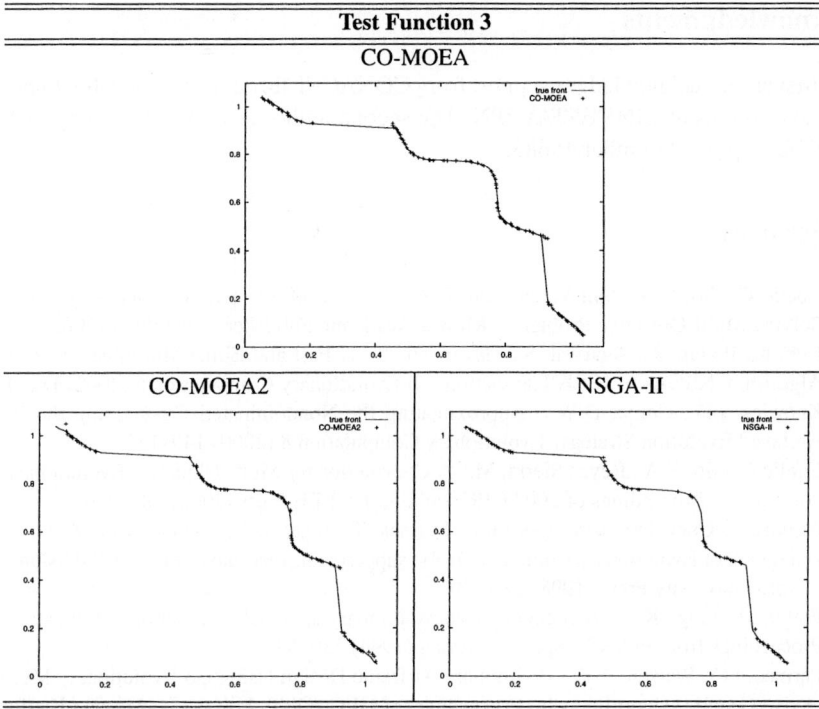

Fig. 4. Pareto fronts obtained by the previous version of our approach (CO-MOEA), the new version (CO-MOEA2) and the NSGA-II [2], for test function 3

7 Conclusions and Future Work

We have presented a new version of a coevolutionary multi-objective evolutionary algorithm whose main idea is to detect the most "promising" sub-regions of the search space and focus the search on them. With this aim, the proposed algorithm applies a clustering algorithm on the set of decision variables of the known Pareto front. The proposed approach was validated using several test functions taken from the specialized literature. Our comparative study showed that the proposed approach has improved its original version and that it is very competitive with respect to another algorithm that is representative of the state-of-the-art in the area.

Since we are proposing a coevolutionary scheme that uses MOGA as its search engine, we consider as an interesting idea to use another multiobjective algorithm in order to improve the obtained results. This is a very important advantage of coevolutionary schemes. On the other hand, we also plan to replace the adaptive grid with another more efficient mechanism in order to improve our distribution results. Finally, we need to test our approach with high-dimensional functions so that we can study possible scalability difficulties.

Acknowledgments

The first author acknowledges support from CONACyT through a scholarship to pursue graduate studies at CINVESTAV-IPN. The second author acknowledges support from CONACyT project number 45683.

References

1. Coello Coello, C.A., Van Veldhuizen, D.A., Lamont, G.B.: Evolutionary Algorithms for Solving Multi-Objective Problems. Kluwer Academic Publishers, New York (2002)
2. Deb, K., Pratap, A., Agarwal, S., Meyarivan, T.: A Fast and Elitist Multiobjective Genetic Algorithm: NSGA–II. IEEE Transactions on Evolutionary Computation **6** (2002) 182–197
3. Knowles, J.D., Corne, D.W.: Approximating the Nondominated Front Using the Pareto Archived Evolution Strategy. Evolutionary Computation **8** (2000) 149–172
4. Coello Coello, C.A., Reyes Sierra, M.: A Coevolutionary Multi-Objective Evolutionary Algorithm. In: Proceedings of 2003 CEC. Volume 1., IEEE Press (2003) 482–489
5. Paredis, J.: Coevolutionary algorithms. In Bäck, T., Fogel, D.B., Michalewicz, Z., eds.: The Handbook of Evolutionary Computation, 1st supplement. Institute of Physics Publishing and Oxford University Press (1998) 225–238
6. Potter, M., Jong., K.D.: A cooperative coevolutionary approach to function optimization. In: Proceedings from PPSN V, Springer-Verlag (1994) 530–539
7. Parmee, I.C., Watson, A.H.: Preliminary Airframe Design Using Co-Evolutionary Multiobjective Genetic Algorithms. In: Proceedings of GECCO'99. Volume 2., Morgan Kaufmann (1999) 1657–1665
8. Keerativuttitumrong, N., Chaiyaratana, N., Varavithya, V.: Multi-objective Co-operative Co-evolutionary Genetic Algorithm. In et al., J.M.G., ed.: Proceedings of PPSN VII, Springer-Verlag (2002) 288–297
9. Tan, K., Chew, Y., Lee, T., Yang, Y.: A cooperative coevolutionary algorithm for multiobjective optimization. In: IEEE International Conference on Systems, Man and Cybernetics. Volume 1., IEEE Press (2003) 390–395
10. Iorio, A., Li, X.: A cooperative coevolutionary multiobjective algorithm using non-dominated sorting. In: Proceedings of GECCO, LNCS 3102, Springer-Verlag (2004) 537–548
11. Fonseca, C.M., Fleming, P.J.: Genetic algorithms for multiobjective optimization: formulation, discussion and generalization. In: Proceedings of the Fifth International Conference on Genetic Algorithms, Morgan Kauffman Publishers (1993) 416–423
12. Jain, A.K., Dubes, R.C.: Algorithms for Clustering Data. Prentice Hall, New Jersey (1988)
13. Van Veldhuizen, D.A.: Multiobjective Evolutionary Algorithms: Classifications, Analyses, and New Innovations. PhD thesis, Department of Electrical and Computer Engineering. Air Force Institute of Technology, Wright-Patterson AFB, Ohio (1999)
14. Van Veldhuizen, D.A., Lamont, G.B.: On Measuring Multiobjective Evolutionary Algorithm Performance. In: 2000 CEC. Volume 1., IEEE Service Center (2000) 204–211
15. Schott, J.R.: Fault Tolerant Design Using Single and Multicriteria Genetic Algorithm Optimization. Master's thesis, Department of Aeronautics and Astronautics, Massachusetts Institute of Technology, Cambridge, Massachusetts (1995)
16. Zitzler, E., Deb, K., Thiele, L.: Comparison of Multiobjective Evolutionary Algorithms: Empirical Results. Evolutionary Computation **8** (2000) 173–195

A Comparison of Memetic Recombination Operators for the MinLA Problem

Eduardo Rodriguez-Tello[1], Jin-Kao Hao[1], and Jose Torres-Jimenez[2]

[1] LERIA, Université d'Angers,
2 Boulevard Lavoisier, 49045 Angers, France
{ertello, hao}@info.univ-angers.fr
[2] Mathematics Department, University of Guerrero,
54 Carlos E. Adame, 39650 Acapulco Guerrero, Mexico
jose.torres.jimenez@acm.org

Abstract. In this paper the Minimum Linear Arrangement (MinLA) problem is studied within the framework of memetic algorithms (MA). A new dedicated recombination operator called Trajectory Crossover (TX) is introduced and its performance is compared with four previous crossover operators. It is shown that the TX crossover induces a better population diversity. The MA using TX is evaluated on a set of well-known benchmark instances and is compared with several state-of-art MinLA algorithms.

Keywords: Recombination Operators, Memetic Algorithms, Linear Arrangement.

1 Introduction

The *Minimum Linear Arrangement* problem (MinLA) was first stated by Harper in [11]. His aim was to design error-correcting codes with minimal average absolute errors on certain classes of graphs. MinLA arises also in other application areas like graph drawing, VLSI layout, software diagram layout and job scheduling [3].

MinLA can be stated formally as follows. Let $G(V, E)$ be a finite undirected graph, where V ($|V| = n$) defines the set of vertices and $E \subseteq V \times V = \{\{i,j\}|i,j \in V\}$ is the set of edges. Given a one-to-one function $\varphi : V \to \{1..n\}$, called a linear arrangement, the total edge length for G with respect to arrangement φ is defined according to the equation 1.

$$LA(G, \varphi) = \sum_{(u,v) \in E} |\varphi(u) - \varphi(v)| \qquad (1)$$

Then the MinLA problem consists in finding an arrangement φ for a given G so that $LA(G, \varphi)$ is minimized.

There exist polynomial time exact algorithms for some special cases of MinLA such as trees, rooted trees, hypercubes, meshes, outerplanar graphs, and others (see [3] for a detailed survey). However, MinLA is NP-hard for general graphs [7] and for bipartite graphs [4]. Therefore, there is a need for heuristics to address this problem in reasonable time. Among the reported algorithms are a) heuristics especially developed for MinLA, such as the binary balanced decomposition tree heuristic (DT) [1], the multi-scale algorithm (MS) [13] and the algebraic multigrid scheme (AMG) [18]; and b) metaheuristics such as Simulated Annealing [16] and Genetic Algorithms [17].

In this paper, we investigate the potential of the paradigm of Memetic Algorithms (MAs), which are known to be very powerful for hard combinatorial optimization problems [12, 6, 5]. In particular, we are interested in the design of an effective mechanism to recombine solutions which constitutes one of the key elements of MAs. A recombination operator, called Trajectory Crossover (TX), is introduced. This operator is based on the path relinking technique proposed in [8] and incorporates problem specific knowledge. Its performance is compared with four other classical crossover operators.

Our MA incorporates a fast greedy heuristic used to create the initial population and a local search operator based on a fine tuned Tabu Search algorithm. The effectiveness of the MA with TX is demonstrated with a set of 21 benchmark instances taken from the literature. The computational results are reported and compared with previously published ones, showing that our algorithm is able to improve on some previous best results.

The rest of the paper is organized as follows. Section 2 presents the different components of the MA used for the comparisons. Then, the studied recombination operators are reviewed in Section 3. Section 4 is dedicated to computational experiments and comparisons with previous reported results. Last section summarizes the main contributions of this research work.

2 Memetic Algorithms for MinLA

In this section we present a Memetic algorithm for solving the MinLA problem. Next the details of its implementation are presented.

2.1 Search Space, Representation and Fitness Function

The search space $\mathcal{A}$ for the MinLA problem is composed of all possible arrangements from V to $\{1, 2, ..., n\}$. It is easy to see then, that there are $n!$ possible linear arrangements for a graph with n vertices. In our MA a linear arrangement φ is represented as an array l of n integers, which is indexed by the vertices and whose i-th value $l[i]$ denotes the label assigned to the vertex i. The fitness of φ is evaluated by using Equation 1.

2.2 The General Procedure

Our MA starts building an initial population P, which is a set of configurations having a fixed constant size $|P|$ (*initPopulation*). Then it performs a series of cycles called generations. At each generation, a predefined number of recombinations (*offspring*) are executed. In each recombination two configurations A and B are chosen randomly from the population (*selectParents*). A recombination operator is then used to produce an offspring C from A and B (*recombineIndividuals*). The local search operator (*localSearch*) is applied to improve C for a fixed number of iterations L and the improved configuration C is inserted in the population. Finally, the population is updated by choosing the best individuals from the pool of parents and children (*UpdatePopulation*). This process repeats until a stop condition is verified, usually when a predefined number of generations (*maxGenerations*) is reached. Note however, that the algorithm may stop before reaching *maxGenerations*, if a better solution is not produced in a predefined number of successive generations (*maxFails*).

2.3 The Initialization Operator

The operator $initPopulation(|P|)$ initiates the population P with $|P|$ configurations. To create a configuration, we use the binary balanced decomposition tree heuristic (DT) reported in [1], slightly adapted in order to work in a randomized form. The algorithm is based on a divide-and-conquer approach, the idea is to divide the vertices into two sets, to recursively arrange each set internally at consecutive locations, and finally to join the two ordered sets, deciding which will be put to the left of the other. Due to the randomness of the DT algorithm, the initial population is well diversified.

2.4 Selection

Mating selection ($selectParents(P)$) prior to recombination is performed on a purely random basis without bias to fitter individuals, while selection for survival ($updatePopulation(P)$) is done by choosing the best individuals from the pool of parents and children. It is done by taking care that each phenotype exists only once in the new population. Thus, replacement in our algorithm is similar to the (μ, λ) selection scheme used in [14, 5, 6].

2.5 The Recombination Operator

The main idea of the recombination operator ($recombineIndividuals(A, B)$) is to generate new diversified and potentially promising individuals. To do that, a good MinLA recombination operator should take into consideration, as much as possible, the individuals' semantic. In Section 3, several recombination operators are presented, including the new TX recombination operator for MinLA.

2.6 The Local Search Operator

The purpose of the local search (LS) operator $localSearch(C, L)$ is to improve a configuration C produced by the recombination operator for a maximum of L iterations before inserting it into the population. In our implementation, we have decided to use Tabu Search (TS) [8].

TS starts with a configuration, then it proceeds iteratively to visit a series of locally best configurations following a neighborhood function. At each iteration, a best neighbor is chosen to replace the current configuration, even if the former does not improve the current one. In order to avoid the stops at suboptimal points and the occurrence of cycles, TS introduces the notion of tabu list. The basic idea is to record each visited configuration, or generally its attributes and to forbid to visit again this configuration during the next T iterations (T is called the tabu tenure).

In our LS operator the neighbor of a given arrangement φ is obtained by swapping the labels of any pair (i,j) of different vertices. When such a move is performed the couple of vertices (i,j) is classified tabu for the next T iterations. Therefore, the vertices i and j cannot be exchanged during this period. Nevertheless, a tabu move leading to a configuration better than the best configuration found so far is always accepted (aspiration criterion). The tabu tenure T for a move is fixed to $0.10*n$. To implement the tabu list, it is sufficient to use an array of size $|V|$. The algorithm stops either if it reaches the predefined maximum of L iterations or when it ceases to make progress. In the proposed implementation a lack of progress exists when S successive iterations do not produce a better solution.

The algorithm memorizes and returns the most recent arrangement φ^* among the best configurations found: after each iteration, the current configuration φ replaces φ^* if $LA(G,\varphi) \leq LA(G,\varphi^*)$. It permits to produce a solution which is as far away as possible from the initial solution in order to better preserve the population diversity.

3 Recombination Operators

The recombination (crossover) operator plays a very important role in any Memetic Algorithm. Indeed, it is this operator that is responsible for creating potentially promising individuals. There are several crossover operators that can be applied to permutation problems [2, 9, 15, 5, 19]. In this section, we focus on four of these operators, as well as the new Trajectory Crossover dedicated to the MinLA problem.

3.1 Order Crossover

The Order Crossover (OX) operator was first proposed by Davis in [2]. It is implemented by selecting two random crossover points. The offspring inherits the elements between the two crossover points, inclusive, from the first parent in the same order and position as they appeared in it. The remaining elements are inherited from the second parent in the order in which they appear in that parent, beginning with the first position following the second crossover point and skipping over all elements already present in the offspring.

3.2 Partially Matched Crossover

The Partially Matched Crossover (PMX) operator was introduced in [9]. It is designed to preserve absolute positions from both parents. It works by selecting two crossover points in the first parent and copying the elements between them to the offspring. This transfer also defines a set of mappings between the elements that have been copied and the elements in the corresponding positions in the second parent. Then, the rest of the elements are copied in the positions they occur in the second parent. If one position is occupied by an element already copied from the first parent, the element provided by the mappings is considered. This process is repeated until the conflict is solved.

3.3 Cycle Crossover

Cycle Crossover (CX) is an operator that was proposed in [15]. It preserves the information contained in both parents in the sense that all elements of the offspring are taken from one of the parents, in other words CX does not perform any implicit mutation. In CX the offspring inherits all the elements found at the same position in the two parents. Then, starting with a randomly chosen unassigned position in the offspring, an element from one of the parents is randomly selected. After that, additional assignments are made to ensure that no implicit mutation occurs. Then, the next unassigned position to the right is processed in the same way until all the elements have been considered. In case there are still unassigned positions and we are at the end of the genome then we proceed at its beginning.

3.4 Distance Preserving Crossover

The Distance Preserving Crossover (DPX) operator reported in [5] relies on the notion of distance between solutions. DPX aims at producing an offspring that has the same hamming distance to each of its parents, and this distance is equal to the distance between the parents themselves. DPX starts by copying all the elements found at the same position in both parents to the offspring. Then, the rest of the positions in the offspring are randomly assigned with the yet unassigned elements, taking care that no assignment that is found in one of the parents is inherited into the child.

3.5 Trajectory Crossover

The new Trajectory Crossover (TX) for MinLA is inspired from the path relinking algorithm presented by Glover and Laguna as an alternative to integrate intensification and diversification strategies in the context of Tabu Search [8].

TX generates new offspring while exploring trajectories that connect two parents (A and B), by starting from one parent, called *initial solution*, and generating a trajectory in the neighborhood space that leads toward the alternate parent, called *guiding solution*. This process is accomplished by selecting moves that introduce attributes contained in the guiding solution. Please note that each new solution in the trajectory corresponds to an individual.

In the TX operator the offspring inherits any element common to both the parents. Then, starting at a random position of the parents, their elements are examined from left to right in a cyclic fashion. If the elements at the position

Parent A	2 4 [7] 1 8 9 3 5 6	Parent A	2 4 7 [1] 8 9 3 5 6
Parent B	7 4 [5] 8 3 9 1 2 6	Child X	5 4 7 [8] 3 9 1 2 6
Child W	2 4 [5] 1 8 9 3 [7] 6	Child Y	2 4 7 [8] [1] 9 3 5 6
Child X	[5] 4 [7] 8 3 9 1 2 6	Child Z	5 4 7 [1] 3 9 [8] 2 6
	(a)		(b)

Fig. 1. Trajectory Crossover example

being looked at are the same, that position is skipped; otherwise, a swap is performed between two elements in parent A or in parent B, whichever gives the fitter solution, so that the elements at the analyzed position become alike. This process is repeated until all positions have been considered. All chromosomes obtained using this process are valid offspring of A and B; out of them the fittest offspring C is returned.

An example of the TX crossover is illustrated in Fig. 1. Suppose we start at a randomly chosen position, for this example position 3. In parent A, element 7 is located at the position 3 and in parent B element 5 is located at this position. There are two ways in which the two parents can move closer to one another; by swapping the elements 5 and 7 in parent A or in parent B (Fig. 1(a)). The fitness values of these two solutions are computed, suppose that child X has the lower cost. Then child W is eliminated and the next position in the two resulting solutions (A and X) is considered. In Fig. 1(b) the children obtained by swapping the elements 1 and 8 in parent A or in children X are presented. Their fitness is calculated and the child with higher cost is eliminated, the process is repeated until all positions have been considered.

4 Computational Experiments

In this section, we present a set of experiments accomplished to evaluate the performance of the different recombination operators presented in Section 3. Their characteristics were investigated by using them within the MA framework presented in Section 2. The algorithms were coded in C and compiled with *gcc* using the optimization flag -$O3$. They were run sequentially into a cluster of 10 nodes, each having a Xeon bi-CPU at 2 GHz, 1 GB of RAM and Linux.

The test-suite used in the experiments presented in this paper is composed of the instances proposed by Petit[1] [16] and used later in [1, 13, 17]. It consists of six different families of graphs having a number of vertices between 62 and 9800.

4.1 Comparison of Recombination Operators

The purpose of the first experiment is to evaluate the performance of the different recombination operators presented in Section 3. The evaluation takes into

---
[1] http://www.lsi.upc.es/~jpetit/MinLA/Experiments

Table 1. Comparison of memetic recombination operators for MinLA

Operator	randomA1		mesh33x33		c2y	
OX	894603.0	0.031	35054.6	0.031	89088.3	0.033
PMX	916023.3	0.334	35952.3	0.218	89193.0	0.223
DPX	899313.6	0.208	34975.3	0.258	84651.3	0.296
CX	891294.0	0.331	35041.6	0.032	84673.3	0.035
TX	881023.0	0.469	34827.0	0.305	83865.0	0.277

account two aspects: the capacity to generate new potentially promising individuals and the ability to keep a diversified population. Both characteristics are very important in the whole search process because they represent the classical trade-off between exploration and exploitation. For the first criterion the average fitness is used, while the population diversity is calculated with the entropy measure proposed in [10] and shown in Equation 2, where n_{ij} represents the number of times the variable i is set to the value j in the population P. This function takes values in the interval $[0, 1]$. An entropy of 0 indicates that all the individuals in the population are identical.

$$entropy(P) = \frac{-\sum_{i=1}^{n}\sum_{j=1}^{n}(\frac{n_{ij}}{|P|})\log(\frac{n_{ij}}{|P|})}{n \log n} \qquad (2)$$

In order to enable a fair comparison all the recombination operators were tested under the same conditions on three representative instances ($randomA1$, $c2y$ and $mesh33x33$) taken from the the Petit's test-suite [16]. The following parameters were used for the MA in this experiment: a) population size $|P| = 100$, b) recombinations per generation $offspring = 50$, c) maximal number of local search iterations $L = 500$, d) maximal number of generations $maxGenerations = 1500$ and e) maximal number of successive failed generations $maxFails = 100$. A relative small number of local search iterations was used, to reduce the strong influence of the local search in the results.

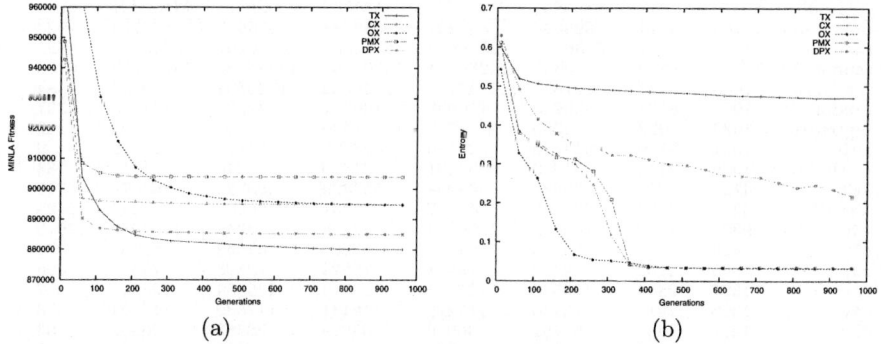

Fig. 2. Graphs representing the behavior of 5 memetic recombination operators over the $randomA1$ instance. (a) Average population fitness, (b) Population entropy.

Due to the non-deterministic nature of the algorithm, 20 independent runs were executed for each instance/operator combination. The results of these executions are summarized in Table 1. For each instance/operator combination we present the average population fitness and the average population entropy after 1500 generations. This table shows clearly that the TX operator allows us to obtain better results for the three graphs while conserving also the population diversity. In our experiments we have tested other instances and they provide similar results. This dominance is better illustrated in Fig. 2, where the behavior of the studied operators is presented over the *randomA1* instance. In Fig. 2(a) the X axis represents the number of generations, while the Y axis indicates the average population fitness. Fig. 2(b) presents the evolution of the population entropy (Y axis) with respect to the number of generations. Observe that the best trade-off between exploration and exploitation is obtained by the TX operator.

4.2 Comparison with the Best Known Results

In the second experiment we have tunned the combination of our MA and the TX operator (MA+TX). Then a performance comparison of the MA+TX procedure with the following heuristics was carried out: SS+SA [16], DT+SA [1], AMG [18] and GH [17]. In this experiment the MA+TX parameters were: a) population size $|P| = 50$, b) recombinations per generation *offspring* = 25, c) maximal number of local search iterations $L = 10000$, d) maximal number of generations $maxGenerations = 10000$ and e) maximal number of successive failed generations $maxFails = 100$.

Table 2 presents the detailed computational results produced by this experiment. The first three columns in the table indicate the name of the graph, its number of vertices and its number of edges. The rest of the columns indicate the best total edge length found by each of the compared heuristics. These results

Table 2. Performance comparison between MA+TX and several state-of-the-art algorithms

Graph	$|V|$	$|E|$	SS+SA	DT+SA	AMG	GH	MA+TX	Δ_C
randomA1	1000	4974	869648	884261	888381	878637	868724	-924
randomA2	1000	24738	6536540	6576912	6596081	6550292	6535849	-691
randomA3	1000	49820	14310861	14289214	14303980	14246646	14240538	-6108
randomA4	1000	8177	1721490	1747143	1747822	1735691	1719906	-1584
randomG4	1000	8173	150940	146996	140211	142587	141538	1327
bintree10	1023	1022	4069	3762	3696	3807	3808	112
hc10	1024	5120	523776	523776	523776	523776	523776	0
mesh33x33	1089	2112	31929	33531	31729	32040	31917	188
3elt	4720	13722	363686	363204	357329	383286	363079	5750
airfoil1	4253	12289	285597	289217	272931	306005	285429	12498
whitaker3	9800	28989	1169642	1200374	1144476	1203349	1167089	22613
c1y	828	1749	63145	62333	62262	62562	62333	71
c2y	980	2102	79429	79571	78822	79823	79420	598
c3y	1327	2844	123548	127065	123514	125654	123521	7
c4y	1366	2915	116140	115222	115131	117539	115204	73
c5y	1202	2557	97791	96956	96899	98483	96962	63
gd95c	62	144	509	506	506	506	506	0
gd96a	1096	1676	96366	99944	96249	98388	96253	4
gd96b	111	193	1416	1422	1416	1416	1416	0
gd96c	65	125	519	519	519	519	519	0
gd96d	180	228	2393	2409	2391	2391	2391	0

were taken from their corresponding papers. Finally, the last column presents the difference (Δ_C) between the best total edge length found by MA+TX and the previous best known solution reported in the literature.

From Table 2, one observes that MA+TX is able to improve on 4 previous best known solutions and to equal these results in 5 instances. For the other instances, MA+TX did not reach the best reported solution, but its results are very close to the best reported (in average 1.1%). Notice that for some instances the improvement is important; leading to a significant decrease of the total edge length (Δ_C up to -6108). With respect to the computational effort we have noted that MA+TX, given that it is a memetic algorithm, consumes considerably more computer time than some heuristics especially developed for MinLA such as DT [1], MS [13] and AMG [18].

5 Conclusions

In an extensive study, several recombination operators, including the new Trajectory Crossover (TX) operator, were compared within a Memetic Algorithm framework. From this comparison we can conclude that the best trade-off between exploration and exploitation is obtained by the TX operator. Furthermore, the performance of our MA+TX algorithm was assessed through extensive experimentation over a set of well known benchmark instances and compared with four other state-of-the-art algorithms: SS+SA [16], DT+SA [1], MS [13] and GH [17]. The results obtained by MA+TX are superior to those presented by the previous proposed evolutionary approach [17], and permit to improve on some previous best known solutions.

There are some issues for future research. For example, to investigate the behavior of MA+TX when it is applied to larger instances, like those proposed by Koren and Harel in [13], in order to study its scalability.

Acknowledgments. This work is supported by the CONACyT Mexico, the "Contrat Plan Etat Région" project COM (2000-2006) as well as the Franco-Mexican Joint Lab in Computer Science LAFMI (2005-2006). The reviewers of the paper are greatly acknowledged for their constructive comments.

References

1. R. Bar-Yehuda, G. Even, J. Feldman, and S. Naor. Computing an optimal orientation of a balanced decomposition tree for linear arrangement problems. *Journal of Graph Algorithms and Applications*, 5(4):1–27, 1996.
2. L. Davis. Applying adaptive algorithms to epistatic domains. In *Proceedings of the IJCAI*, pages 162–164. Morgan Kaufmann, 1985.
3. J. Diaz, J. Petit, and M. Serna. A survey of graph layout problems. *ACM Comput. Surv.*, 34(3):313–356, 2002.
4. S. Even and Y. Shiloah. NP-completeness of several arrangement problems. Technical Report CS0043, Technion, Israel Institute of Technology, Haifa, Israel, 1975.

5. B. Freisleben and P. Merz. A genetic local search algorithm for solving symmetric and asymmetric traveling salesman problems. In *Proc. Of the 1996 IEEE Int. Conf. On Evolutionary Computation*, pages 616–621. IEEE Press, 1996.
6. P. Galinier and J. Hao. Hybrid evolutionary algorithms for graph coloring. *Journal of Combinatorial Optimization*, 3(4):379–397, 1999.
7. M. Garey and D. Johnson. *Computers and Intractability: A guide to the Theory of NP-Completeness*. W.H. Freeman and Company, New York, 1979.
8. F. Glover and M. Laguna. *Tabu Search*. Kluwer Academic Publishers, 1997.
9. D. E. Goldberg and R. Lingle. Alleles, loci, and the travelling salesman problem. In *Proc. Of an Int. Conference on Genetic Algorithms and their Applications*, pages 154–159. Carnegie Mellon publishers, 1985.
10. J. J. Grefenstette. Incorporating problem specific knowledge into genetic algorithms. In L. Davis, editor, *Genetic Algorithms and Simulated Annealing*, pages 42–60, London, 1987. Morgan Kaufmann Publishers.
11. L. Harper. Optimal assignment of numbers to vertices. *Journal of SIAM*, 12(1):131–135, 1964.
12. W. E. Hart, N. Krasnogor, and J. E. Smith, editors. *Recent Advances in Memetic Algorithms and Related Search Technologies*. Springer-Verlag, 2004.
13. Y. Koren and D. Harel. A multi-scale algorithm for the linear arrangement problem. In L. Kucera, editor, *Proceedings of 28th Inter. Workshop on Graph-Theoretic Concepts in Computer Science (WG'02)*, volume 2573 of *LNCS*, pages 293–306. Springer Verlag, 2002.
14. P. Merz and B. Freisleben. Fitness landscapes, memetic algorithms and greedy operators for graph bi-partitioning. *Evolutionary Computation*, 8(1):61–91, 2000.
15. I. Oliver, D. Smith, and J. Holland. A study of permutation crossover operators on the travelling salesman problem. In *Proc. Of the 2nd. Int. Conference on Genetic Algorithms*, pages 224–230. Lawrence Erlbaum Associates, 1987.
16. J. Petit. *Layout Problems*. PhD thesis, Universitat Politécnica de Catalunya, 2001.
17. T. Poranen. A genetic hillclimbing algorithm for the optimal linear arrangement problem. Technical report, University of Tampere, Finland, June 2002.
18. I. Safro, D. Ron, and A. Brandt. Graph minimum linear arrangement by multilevel weighted edge contractions. *Journal of Algorithms*, 2004. in press.
19. D. Whitley, T. Starkweather, and D. Fuquay. Scheduling problems and traveling salesman: The genetic edge recombination operator. In *Proc. Of the 3rd Int. Conf. On Genetic Algorithms*, pages 133–140. Morgan Kaufmann, 1989.

Hybrid Particle Swarm – Evolutionary Algorithm for Search and Optimization

Crina Grosan[1], Ajith Abraham[2], Sangyong Han[2], and Alexander Gelbukh[3]

[1] Department of Computer Science,
Babeş-Bolyai University,
Cluj-Napoca, 3400, Romania
[2] School of Computer Science and Engineering,
Chung-Ang University,
Seoul 156-756, Korea
[3] Centro de Investigacin en Computacin (CIC),
Instituto Politcnico Nacional (IPN), Mexico
ajith.abraham@ieee.org, cgrosan@cs.ubbcluj.ro,
hansy@cau.ac.kr, gelbukh@gelbukh.com

Abstract. Particle Swarm Optimization (PSO) technique has proved its ability to deal with very complicated optimization and search problems. Several variants of the original algorithm have been proposed. This paper proposes a novel hybrid PSO - evolutionary algorithm for solving the well known geometrical place problems. Finding the geometrical place could be sometimes a hard task. In almost all situations the geometrical place consists more than one single point. The performance of the newly proposed PSO algorithm is compared with evolutionary algorithms. The main advantage of the PSO technique is its speed of convergence. Also, we propose a hybrid algorithm, combining PSO and evolutionary algorithms. The hybrid combination is able to detect the geometrical place very fast for which the evolutionary algorithms required more time and the conventional PSO approach even failed to find the real geometrical place.

1 Introduction

Evolutionary Algorithms (EA) use a population of potential solutions (points) of the search space. These solutions (initially randomly generated) are evolved using different specific operators which are inspired from biology. Through cooperation and competition among the potential solutions, these techniques often can find optima quickly when applied to complex optimization problems.

There are some similarities between PSO and Evolutionary Algorithms:

- both techniques use a population (which is called *swarm* in the PSO case) of solutions from the search space which are initially random generated;
- solutions belonging to the same population interact with each other during the search process;

– solutions are evolved (their quality is improved) using techniques inspired from the real world.

Even then, there are still many differences between these two techniques.

In what follows, we will apply both techniques for solving a well known geometrical place problems [6]. It is well known that in the case of these problems a set of points which accomplish a given condition (or a set of conditions) is explored. In many situations, the searched geometrical place consists of more than one point (solution). Evolutionary algorithms and PSO techniques are ideal candidates for this problem mainly due to their ability to deal with a population of solutions at the same time.

We propose a new particle swarm technique which is based on the basic PSO algorithm proposed by Eberhart and Kenedy in 1995. Some related work and existing variants of PSO can be found in [3], [4], [5], [8], [9], [10], [12], [13], [14].

The main scope of our paper is to perform a comparison between PSO and EA and to exploit the weakness/strength of each of them. Finally, taking into account of the results, we propose a hybrid algorithm combining PSO and EA which seems to perform better in complicated situations than each of these techniques considered separately.

The paper is structured as follows: Section 2 presents some basics of the PSO technique. Section 3 briefly describes the a new variant of the particle Swarm technique. The general evolutionary algorithm is described in Section 4. In section 5 some experiments using different test problems are performed. Conclusions and remarks are presented towards the end.

2 Particle Swarm Optimization Technique

Like other EA techniques, PSO is a population-based search algorithm and is initialized with a population of random solutions, called particles ([7]).

Unlike in the EA techniques, each particle in PSO is also associated with a velocity. Particles fly through the search space with velocities which are dynamically adjusted according to their historical behaviors. Therefore, the particles have the tendency to fly towards the better and better search area over the course of search process. The PSO was first designed to simulate birds seeking food which is defined as a 'cornfield vector' [8].

PSO is initialized with a group of random particles (solutions) and then searches for optima by updating each generation.

Each individual is treated as a volume-less particle (a point) in the D-dimensional search space. The ith particle is represented as $X_i = (x_{i1}, x_{i2}, \ldots, x_{iD})$. At each generation, each particle is updated by following two 'best' values.

The first one is the best previous location (the position giving the best fitness value) a particle has achieved so far. This value is called pBest. The pBest of the ith particle is represented as $P_i = (p_{i1}, p_{i2}, \ldots, p_{iD})$.

At each iteration, the P vector of the particle with the best fitness in the neighborhood, designated lor g, and the P vector of the current particle are combined to adjust the velocity along each dimension, and that velocity is then used to compute a new position for the particle. The portion of the adjustment to the velocity influenced by the individual's previous best position (P) is considered the *cognition* component, and the portion influenced by the best in the neighborhood is the *social* component.

With the addition of the inertia factor, ω, by Shi and Eberhart [14] (for balancing the global and the local search), these equations are:

$v_{id} = \omega^* v_{id} + \eta_x^* \text{rand}()^*(p_{id} - x_{id}) + \eta_2^* \text{Rand}()^*(p_{gd} - x_{id})$ (1)

$x_{id} = x_{id} + v_{id}$ (2)

where rand() and Rand() are two random numbers independently generated within the range of [0,1] and $\eta 1$ and $\eta 2$ are two learning factors which control the influence of the social and cognitive components.

In (1) if the sum on the right side exceeds a constant value, then the velocity on that dimension is assigned to be $\pm V_{max}$. Thus, particles' velocities are clamped to the range of [-V_{max}, V_{max}] which serves as a constraint to control the global exploration ability of the PSO algorithm. This also reduces the the likelihood of particles for leaving the search space. Note that this does not restrict the values of X_i to the range [-V_{max}, V_{max}]; it only limits the maximum distance that a particle will move during one iteration.

3 Proposed PSO Approach for Dealing with Geometrical Place Problems

The proposed PSO algorithm is similar to the classical one which uses neighborhoods but still there are some differences which are described below. We consider the PSO algorithm with neighborhoods, but not overlapping ones as usual. Thus, the particles in the swarm 'fly' in independent sub-swarms. It is just like dividing the swarm into multiple independent 'neighborhoods'[1], [11]. The dimension of each neighborhood (sub-swarms) is the same for all considered sub-swarms. The reason for not choosing overlapping neighborhoods is that for the geometrical place problems the solution consists of a set of points and not merely a single point. In the classical PSO, each solution will follow the best solution in the swarm or the best solution located in its neighborhood. This means, finally all solutions will converge to the same point. But for the geometrical place problem we need to find a set of different solutions. By considering different sub-swarms, the number of solutions which can be obtained at the end of the search process might be at most equal to the number of sub-swarms (this in case each sub-swarm will converge to a different point). Taking into account all these considerations, we will consider small sub-swarms (having usually few particles: 4 or 5) so that we have the chances to obtain, finally, a greater number of different points (which is ideal for geometrical place problems). The algorithm proposed is called Independent Neighborhoods Particle Swarm Optimization (INPSO). The main steps of the INPSO algorithm are described below:

INPSO algorithm

while *iteration* <= *max_iterations* **do**
  begin
    for each particle p **do**
    begin
      Calculate fitness value
      if the fitness value is better than the its best fitness value in history
      then Update *pbest*
      if the fitness value attained a minimum criteria
      then Stop particle p in the current *pbest* location
    end
    for each particle p**do**
    begin
      Identify the particle in the neighborhood with the best fitness value so far as the *lbest*
      Assign its index to the variable l
      if particle p is not stopped
      then Calculate particle velocity according equation (a)
      Update particle position according equation (b)
    end
  end

When a particle finds a feasible solution (its fitness value attains minimum criteria) it is obvious there is no need to continue 'flying' and thus the particle can stop at that *pBest* location. But the particle will continue to share its experience with its still 'flying' neighbors (particles belonging to the same sub-swarm).

4 Experiment Results

This section illusrates the various experiments performed using geometrical place problems. Results obtained by the INPSO are compared with the results obtained by the standard EA. The EA used in the experiments uses real encoding of solutions. Mutation and convex crossover are the genetic operators used. Parameters used by INPSO are given in Table 1 and parameters used by EA are given in Table 2.

Table 1. Parameter settings for INPSO

Parameter	Value
η_x	1.49445
η_y	1.49445
Sub-swarm size	4
V_{max}	$0.1* X_{max}$
inertia weight	[0.5+(Rnd/2.0)]

Table 2. Parameter settings for EA

Parameter	Value
Sigma	1
Crossover probability	0.5
Mutation probability	0.7

Both η_x and η_2 are set to 1.49445 [2] to make the search cover all surrounding regions which is centered at the *pBest* and *lBest*. A randomized inertia weight is used, namely it is set to $[0.5+(Rnd/2.0)]$ ([5]). V_{max} is set to $0.1*X_{max}$. The value of V_{max} is usually chosen to be $k*X_{max}$, with $0.1 \leq k \leq 1.0$ [4].

Population size is the same for both algorithms: 500 individuals and particles respectively.

4.1 Experiment 1

We consider the case in which the geometrical place of the points for which the difference (in absolute value) of the distances to two given points is equal to a given constant k. In a two dimensional space the geometrical place consists of hyperbole of focuses of the two given points. In a three dimensional space the geometrical place consists on the hyperboloid of focuses of the two given points. This problem can also be extended to higher dimensional spaces.

We consider the same population randomly generated for both algorithms. The populations obtained after 50 generations by INPSO and EA are depicted in Figure 1 (a) and Figure 1 (b) respectively. Population obtained after 200 generations by INPSO and EA is depicted in Figure 2 (a) and Figure 2(b) respectively.

As evident from these figures, INPSO algorithm has converged faster than EA. Even after 250 generations, there are some particles which did not con-

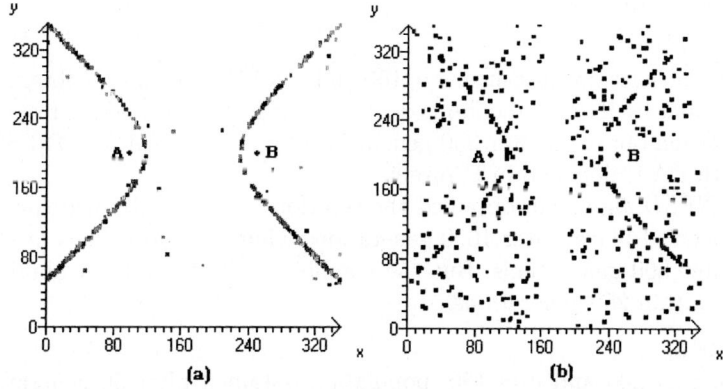

Fig. 1. Population obtained after 50 generations. (a) population obtained by INPSO, (b) population obtained by EA.

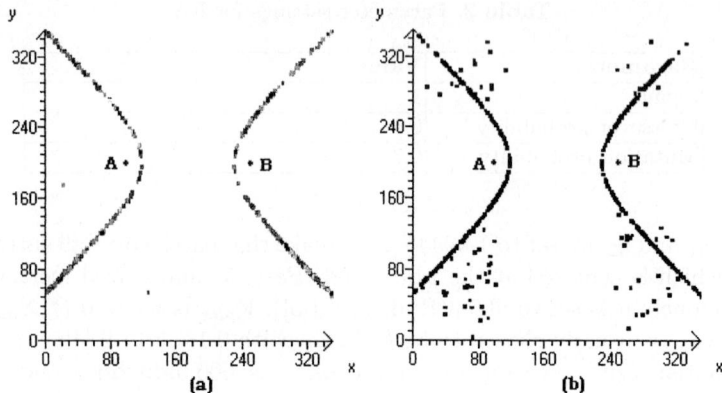

Fig. 2. Population obtained after 200 generations. (a) population obtained by INPSO, (b) population obtained by EA.

verge to the geometrical place. The EA individuals takes longer time (about 500 generations) but all the individuals finally converged to the geometrical place. Using the hybrid approach (INPSO for first 100 generations and EA after 100 generations) all solutions converged to the geometrical place in less than 250 generations. h

4.2 Experiment 2

In this experiment the geometrical place of the points M for which the product of the distances to two fixed points $F_1(-c, 0)$ and $F_2(c, 0)$ is equal to the constant a^2 is searched. This geometrical place is called *the oval of Cassiani*. The geometrical place depends on the values of a and c. Four cases can be envisaged and we will analyze two of the cases.

Case $a < c$.

Let us consider, for instance, a = 150 and c = 151. Population obtained after 50 generations by INPSO and EA is depicted in Figure 3 (a) and (b) respectively.

Population obtained after 250 generations by INPSO, EA and INPSO combined with EA is depicted in Figure 4.

The INPSO algorithm obtained the solutions (all particles will converge to the geometrical place) after 1000 generations while the individuals of EA converged after 800 generations. But the combined INPSO and EA obtained the solutions within 250 generations.

Case $a > c$.

When a = 200 and c = 150, population obtained after 50 generations by INPSO and EA is depicted in Figure 5 (a) and (b) respectively. Population obtained after 250 generations by INPSO, EA and INPSO combined with EA is depicted in Figure 6.

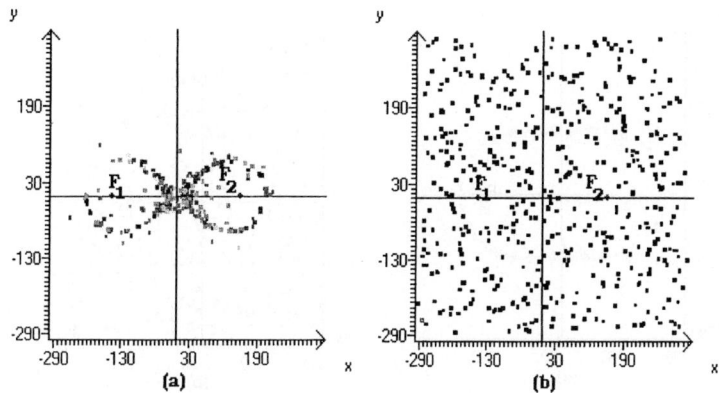

Fig. 3. Population obtained after 50 generations by INPSO (Figure 5 (a)) and by EA (Figure 5 (b))

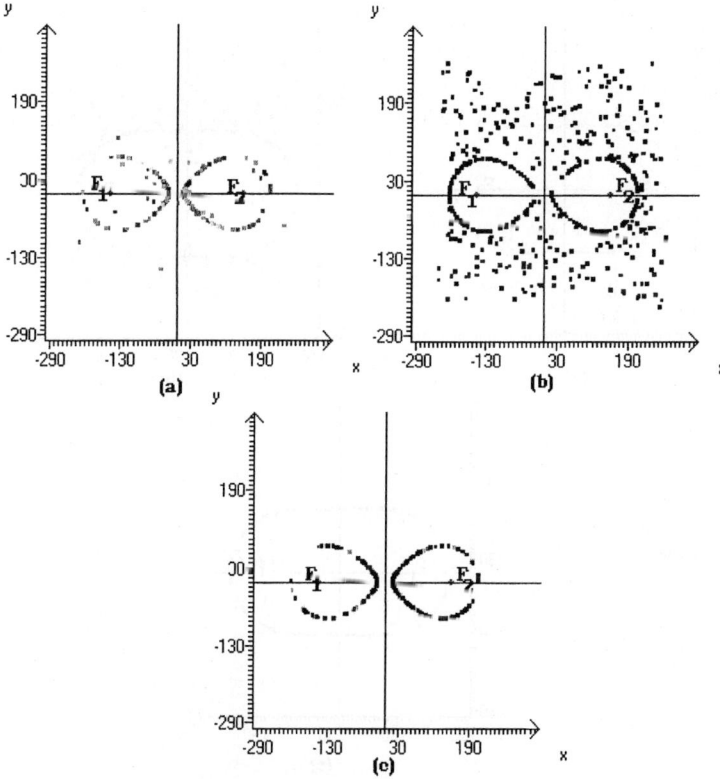

Fig. 4. Population obtained after 250 generations by INPSO (Figure 6(a)), EA (Figure 6(b) and INPSO combined to EA (Figure 6(c))

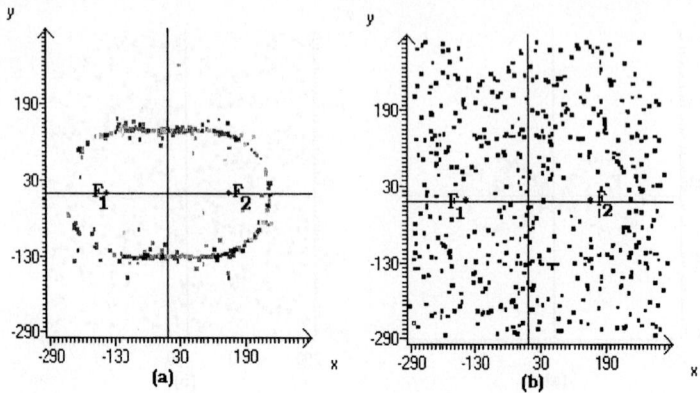

Fig. 5. Population obtained after 50 generations by INPSO (Figure 7 (a)) and by EA (Figure 7 (b))

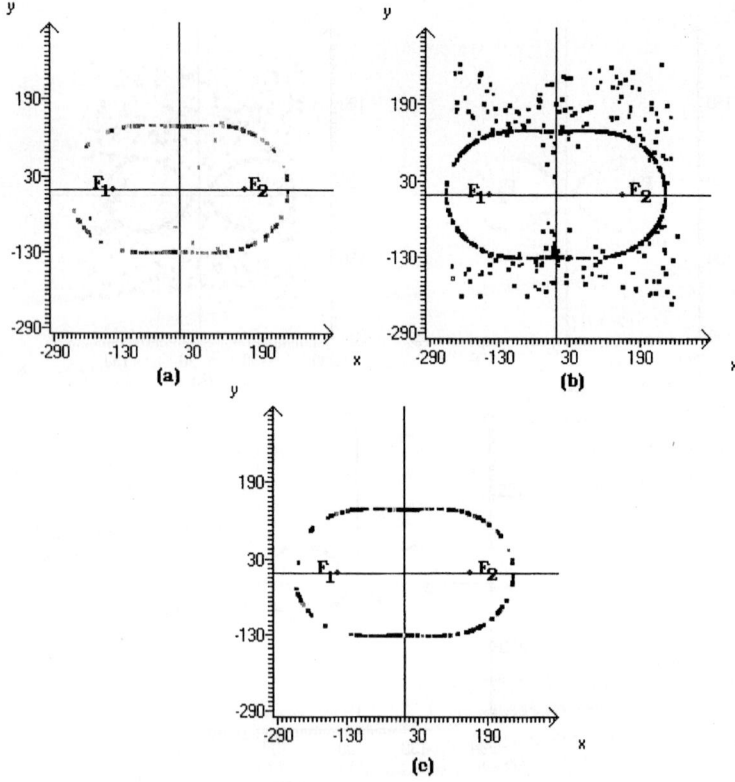

Fig. 6. Population obtained after 250 generations by INPSO (Figure 8(a)), EA (Figure 8(b) and INPSO combined to EA (Figure 8(c))

As evident from these experiments, INPSO is very fast compared to EA. For more difficult problems there can be situations where some particles could never converge to the geometrical place. EA is not very fast but with a good population size and Irsgurnumber of generations the performance could improve. Empirical results using the hybrid approach illustrate that the combination could play an important role in finding solutions with fewer number of generations when compared to the individual approaches.

5 Conclusions

In this paper a new variant of PSO called Independent Neighborhood Particle Swarm Optimization (INPSO) is proposed and used to solve geometrical place problems. INPSO uses independent sub-swarm which evolves independently with respect to the entire population. The PSO rules are applied for each sub-swarm.

Performance of INPSO is compared with the classical Evolutionary Algorithms (EA). INPSO is very fast compared to EA. But, for difficult problems, there can be some particles (a sub-swarm for instance) which could never converge. Taking into account these issues, we proposed a hybrid approach involving INPSO and EA. The key advantages of the hybrid approach are in making use of the fast convergence property of INPSO and EA's definite convergence (guaranteed solution). After a given number of INPSO generations (in our case after 100 generations) EA method was deployed. The combination obtains the solutions very fast and all individuals converged to the geometrical place with fewer iterations.

Acknowledgements

This research was supported by the MIC (Ministry of Information and Communication), Korea, under the Chung-Ang University HNRC-ITRC (Home Network Research Center) support program supervised by the IITA (Institute of Information Technology Assessment).

References

1. Bergh, F.D. and Engelbrecht, A. A Cooperative Approach to Particle Swarm Optimization, IEEE Transaction on Evolutionary Computation, 8(3): pp. 225-239, 2004.
2. Clerc, M. The swarm and the queen: towards a deterministic and adaptive particle swarm optimization. Proceedings of the IEEE Congress on Evolutionary Computation (CEC 1999), pp. 1951-1957, 1999.
3. Eberhart, R. C. and Kennedy, J. A new optimizer using particle swarm theory. Proceedings of the Sixth International Symposium on Micromachine and Human Science, Nagoya, Japan. pp. 39-43, 1995.
4. Eberhart, R. C., Simpson, P. K., and Dobbins, R. W. Computational Intelligence PC Tools. Boston, MA: Academic Press Professional, 1996.

5. Eberhart, R. C. and Shi, Y. Particle swarm optimization: developments, applications and resources. Proceedings of the IEEE Congress on Evolutionary Computation (CEC 2001), Seoul, Korea. 2001
6. Grosan, C. Solving geometrical place problems by using Evolutionary Algorithms. World Computer Congress, Student Forum, M. Kaaniche (Ed.), Toulouse, France, pp. 365-375, 2004
7. Hu, X., Shi Y., and Eberhart, R.C. Recent Advences in Particle Swarm, Congress on evolutionary Computation, Portland, Oregon, June 19-23, pp. 90-97, 2004
8. Kennedy, J. and Eberhart, R. C. Particle swarm optimization.Proceedings of IEEE International Conference on Neural Networks (Perth, Australia), IEEE Service Center, Piscataway, NJ, Vol.IV, pp.1942-1948, 1995.
9. Kennedy, J. Minds and cultures:Particle swarm implications. Socially Intelligent Agents: Papers from the 1997 AAAI Fall Symposium. Technical Report FS-97-02, Menlo Park, CA: AAAI Press, 67-72, 1997.
10. Kennedy, J. The Behavior of Particles, 7th Annual Conference on Evolutionary Programming, San Diego, USA, 1998.
11. Krohling, R.A., Hoffmann, F. and Coelho, L.S. Co-evolutionary Particle Swarm Optimization for Min-Max Problems using Gaussian Distribution, In Proceedings of the Congress on Evolutionary Computation (CEC'2004), IEEE Press, Vol. 1, pp. 959-964, 2004.
12. Shi, Y., and Eberhart, R. C. Empirical study of particle swarm optimization. Proceedings of the 1999 Congress on Evolutionary Computation, 1945-1950. Piscataway, NJ: IEEE Service Center, 1999.
13. Shi, Y., and Eberhart, R. C. Parameter selection in particle swarm optimization, Proceedings of the 1998 Annual Conference on Evolutionary Computation, 1998.
14. Shi, Y. and Eberhart, R. C. A modified particle swarm optimizer. Proceedings of the IEEE Congress on Evolutionary Computation (CEC 1998), Piscataway, NJ. pp. 69-73, 1998

Particle Swarm Optimization with Opposite Particles

Rujing Wang and Xiaoming Zhang

Institute of Intelligent Machines (IIM) of Chinese Academy of Science,
230031 Hefei, Anhui, P.R. China
rjwang@iim.ac.cn, xmzhang@ustc.edu

Abstract. The particle swarm optimization algorithm is a kind of intelligent optimization algorithm. This algorithm is prone to be fettered by the local optimization solution when the particle's velocity is small. This paper presents a novel particle swarm optimization algorithm named particle swarm optimization with opposite particles which is guaranteed to converge to the global optimization solution with probability one. And we also make the global convergence analysis. Finally, three function optimizations are simulated to show that the PSOOP is better and more efficient than the PSO with inertia weights.

1 Introduction

Particle Swarm Optimization (PSO) was first introduced by James Kennedy and Russel C.Eberrhart in 1995 and it was discovered through simulation of a simplified social model[1]. It can search the multidimensional complex space efficiently through cooperation and competition among the individuals in a population of particles[2].

When the PSO starts, a population of particles is generated first with random positions and a velocity is random assigned to each particle[3]. The fitness of each particle is then evaluated according to the objective function. Then the particles begin to search for the best solution. Each particle's trajectory is adjusted by dynamically altering the velocity of each particle, according to its own search experience and other particles' experience. The position vector and the velocity vector of particle j in the d-dimensional search space can be represented as $X_j = (x_{j1}, x_{j2}, x_{j3}, \ldots, x_{jd})$ and $V_j = (v_{j1}, v_{j2}, v_{j3}, \ldots, v_{jd})$ respectively. According to the objective function, let the best position of each particle be $P_j = (p_{j1}, p_{j2}, p_{j3}, \ldots, p_{jd})$ and the best position of all the particles be $G = (g_1, g_2, g_3, \ldots g_d)$. The formulas[4] which the particles use to adjust its position and velocity is:

$$V_j = V_j + c_1 * rand1() * (P_j - X_j) + c_2 * rand2() * (G - X_j) \qquad (1)$$

$$X_{j+1} = X_j + V_{j+1} \qquad (2)$$

where c_1 and c_2 are acceleration coefficients and are always made 2, rand1() and rand2() are random numbers in [0,1] [5].

The first part of (1) represents the previous velocity. The second part represents the personal experience. The third part represents the collaborative effect of the particles and it always pulls the particles toward the global best solution which particles found so far.

At each iteration of PSO, the velocity of each particle is calculated according to (1) and the position is updated according to (2). Generally, a maximum velocity vector is defined in order to control the V_j. Wherever a v_{jd} exceeds the defined limit, its velocity will be set to be $v_{max\ d}$. If a particle finds a better position than the previously found best position, it will be stored in memory. The algorithm goes on until the satisfactory solution is found or the predefined number of iterations is met.

In this paper, we propose a novel PSO named Particle Swarm Optimization with Opposite Particles (PSOOP). It can converge to the global optimization solution with probability one. The global convergence analysis is also made using the F.Solis and R.Wets' research result[6]. Finally several experiments are simulated to show the advantage of PSOOP.

2 Particle Swarm Optimization with Opposite Particles

In the basic PSO, the particle's velocity is an important factor. The bigger is the velocity of the particle, the larger is the searching scope and the more possible is the particle get away from the local optimization solution. But when the velocity is very big, it always neglects the better solution in the local scope and it is difficult to attain the high precision solution. At the same time the particle is prone to be fettered by the local optimization solution when the particle's velocity is small [7].

2.1 The Form of the PSOOP

In this paper, we propose the PSOOP. It can let the particles have strong globe search ability even when their velocity is very small. The trait of the opposite particles is that they do not update their position according to (2). They move to an opposite direction. You can look at the Fig. 1. They are selected randomly in the particle swarm and their new formula which will update their position is :

$$X'_j(t+1) = X_j(t) - V_j(t) \qquad (3)$$

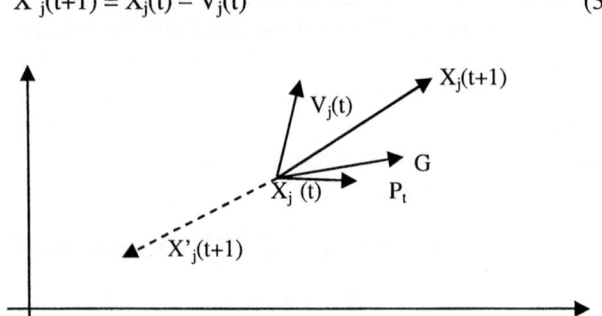

Fig. 1. Movement of Particle X_j

When this new algorithm starts, normal particles run following the formula (1) and (2) and the opposite particles run following the formula (1) and (3). If one of the opposite particles finds a better solution than G(the best position of all the particles), the opposite particle will change to be a normal particle and one particle will be selected randomly from the normal particles to become an opposite particle. If the G is acquired by the normal particles, the opposite particle will still be opposite. When the opposite particles' position reach the border of the problem space, they will be set to be the normal particles which has the best position G. The flow chart of PSOOP is depicted graphically in Fig 2.

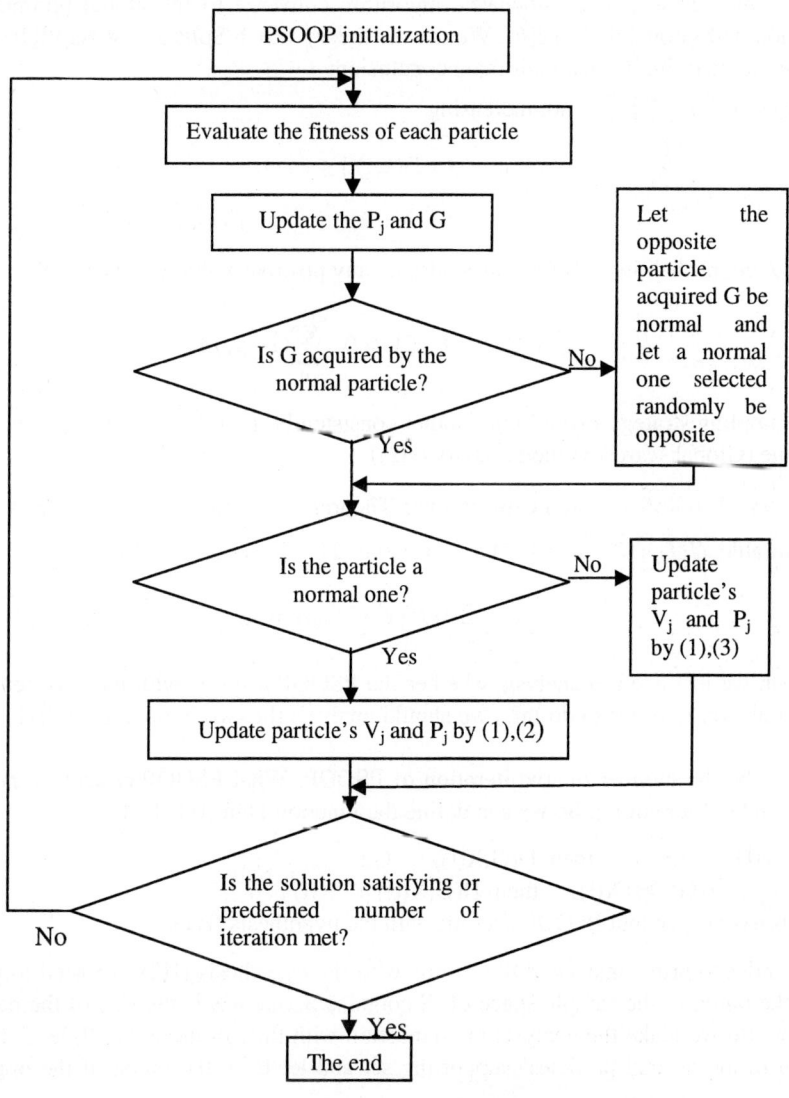

Fig. 2. The flow chart of PSOOP

It is sure that the best particle at time t actually found a better solution than others. But important information about the search space may be neglected through overemphasis on the single best neighbor[8]. But the opposite particles do not like the normal ones. They will search the space which normal particles do not think of as important. So they make the search become more global and they also make the particle swarm become more energetic.

2.2 Global Convergence Analysis of PSOOP

PSOOP is a kind of stochastic optimization algorithm. We can use the theory which is about how can a kind of stochastic algorithm converge to the global optimization solution with probability one[6]. We use the theory which Solis and Wets[9][10] have proved to be right. We list their main conclusion:

(H1) D s.t. $\{f(x^k)\}_{k=0}^{\infty}$ nonincreasing

$$f(D(x,\xi)) \leq f(x)$$

$$\xi \in S \Rightarrow f(D(x,\xi)) \leq \min\{f(x), f(\xi)\}$$

(H2) Zero probability of repeatedly missing any positive-volume subset of S.

$$\forall A \subseteq S \text{ s.t. } v(A) > 0, \sum_{k=0}^{\infty}(1-\mu_k(A)) = 0$$

i.e. sampling strategy given by μ_k cannot consistently ignore a part of S with positive volume (Global search methods satisfy (H2))

Theorem 1. (Global Search Convergence Theorem). Suppose f measurable, $S \subseteq \mathbb{R}^n$ measurable, *(H1), (H2)*, and $\{x^k\}_{k=0}^{\infty}$ generated by the algorithm. Then

$$\lim_{k \to \infty} P(x^k \in R_{\varepsilon,M}) = 1$$

Then we just need to analysis whether the PSOOP accords with the Theorem 1 as stated above. In order to do this, we should analysis the two hypothesizes (H1), (H2) first.

Let j be the number of the iteration of PSOOP. What PSOOP returns is the best solution G of iteration j. So we can define the function D in (H1) be that:

If $f(G) \leq f(X(t))$ then $D(G,X(t)) = G$;
Else if $f(G) > f(X(t))$ then $D(G,X(t)) = X(t)$.
It is easy to see that PSOOP accords with the hypothesis (H1).

In order to prove that PSOOP accords with the hypothesis (H2), we need to prove that the union of the sample space of S contains S where S is the size of the particle swarm. So we make the analysis in connection with this. In the PSOOP, let A be the union of the normal particles' supporting set and let B be the union of the opposite particles' supporting set. Because the normal particles' searching mechanism is opposed to the opposite particles', they search toward different direction. At the same time all the particles are in the same problem space and the initial position of the opposite particles is random. So we can find a natural number N. When t > N, we have A∪B ⊇ S. Let $M_{j,t}$ indicates the sample space's supporting set of the particle j of iteration t. So we can have $\bigcup_{j=1}^{S} M_{j,t} = S$. Then let C be the Borel subset of S where $C = M_{j,t}$. So we can get that $v(C) > 0$ and $\mu_t(C) = \sum_{j=1}^{S} \mu_{j,t}(C) = 1$. That means that 1-$\mu_t(C) = 0$. So we can see that PSOOP accords with the hypothesis(H2). That is to say that PSOOP accords with the Theorem 1.

Sum up all the analysis and we know that the PSOOP converges to the global optimization solution with probability one.

3 Experiments and Analyses

The PSOOP algorithm is realized by Java programming language.

3.1 Benchmark Functions

Three well-known benchmark functions are used to evaluate the performance of the PSOOP after a predefined number of iterations. Its performance is also compared with the PSO with inertia weights.

Table1. The Introduction of Benchmark functions [11]

Function Name	Mathematical Representation	Initial Range	Global Optimization Solution	Function Figure
Rosenbrock	$f(X) = \sum_{i=1}^{n} [100(x_{i+1} - x_i^2)^2 + (x_i - 1)^2]$	[-10, 10]	0	Fig. 3(left)
Rastrigin	$f(X) = \sum_{i=1}^{n} [x_i^2 - 10\cos(2\pi x_i) + 10]$	[-5.12, 5.12]	0	Fig. 3(middle)
Shaffer's F6	$f(x,y) = 0.5 + \frac{(\sin\sqrt{x^2+y^2}) - 0.5}{(1.0 + 0.001(x^2+y^2))^2}$	[-100, 100]	0	Fig. 3(right)

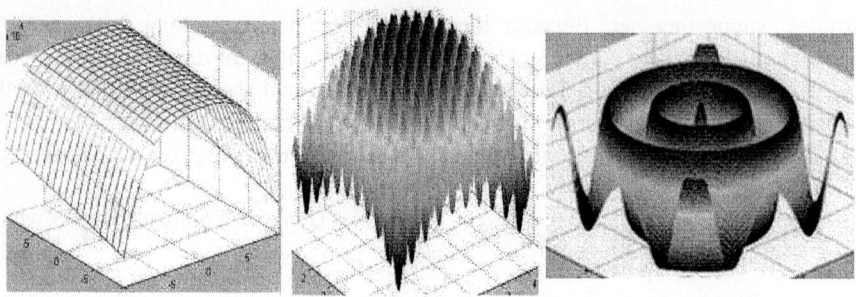

Fig. 3. Function Figure (2 dimension)

3.2 The Results

The results are given in table 2.

Table 2. Results of the experiments

Function Name	Algorithm	Size of population	P_{max}	Proportion of the opposite particles	result
Rosenbrock	PSO	20	10	0	32.978
Rosenbrock	PSOOP	20	10	10%	30.216
Rosenbrock	PSOOP	20	10	30%	30.182
Rosenbrock	PSOOP	20	10	50%	30.149
Rosenbrock	PSO	100	10	0	28.871
Rosenbrock	PSOOP	100	10	10%	27.493
Rosenbrock	PSOOP	100	10	30%	26.839
Rosenbrock	PSOOP	100	10	50%	27.611
Rastrigin	PSO	20	5.12	0	37.264
Rastrigin	PSOOP	20	5.12	10%	37.087
Rastrigin	PSOOP	20	5.12	30%	37.202
Rastrigin	PSOOP	20	5.12	50%	35.568
Rastrigin	PSO	100	5.12	0	29.472
Rastrigin	PSOOP	100	5.12	10%	30.947
Rastrigin	PSOOP	100	5.12	30%	23.456
Rastrigin	PSOOP	100	5.12	50%	28.753
Shaffer's F6	PSO	20	100	0	0.00032
Shaffer's F6	PSOOP	20	100	10%	0.00014
Shaffer's F6	PSOOP	20	100	30%	0.00022
Shaffer's F6	PSOOP	20	100	50%	0.00025
Shaffer's F6	PSO	100	100	0	0.00012
Shaffer's F6	PSOOP	100	100	10%	0.0
Shaffer's F6	PSOOP	100	100	30%	0.0
Shaffer's F6	PSOOP	100	100	50%	0.0

notation:
1. The number of iteration of every algorithm is 2000;
2. The dimension of both function Rosenbrock and function Rastrigin is 30;
3. The dimension of function Shaffer's F6 is 2;
4. The particle's maximum velocity of Rosenbrock and Rastrigin is 0.5 ;
5. The particle's maximum velocity of Shaffer's F6 is 2.0 ;
6. Every algorithm run for 50 times and the result in the table is the average result.

The same experiments were done by Maurice Clerc and James Kennedy[11]. The size of population of particles is 20 in their experiments. Their best result of Rosenbrock function is 39.118488. Their best result of Rastrigin function is 46.4689. Their best result of Shaffer's F6 function is 0.000247. Our result is better than theirs. And if the number of iteration is big enough, the result of PSOOP will be better.

3.3 The Analysis of the Result

From the results given, we can see that the PSOOP is obviously better than the PSO with inertia weights. When the number of particles is small (for example: 20 particles), the best results of function Rosenbrock and function Rastrigin are got by PSOOP with 50% opposite particles. The best results of function Shaffer's F6 is got by PSOOP with 10% opposite particles. When the number of particles is large (for example: 100), the best results are got by PSOOP with 30% opposite particles in all of the three functions. But the worst results in the experiments are all got by PSO with inertia weights. So the results show that the novel algorithm PSOOP is better than the canonical PSO and it is satisfying.

4 Conclusion

In this paper, the standard PSO is improved to be a novel algorithm-PSOOP which is guaranteed to converge to the global optimization solution. The opposite particles are add to the algorithm in order to improve the global search ability of the PSO. The global convergence analysis is also made to prove that the PSOOP can converge to the global optimization solution with probability one. At last, some experiments is carried out to show the performance of the PSOOP comparing with the PSO with inertia weights.

One aspect that we would like to explore in the future is how to get the proportion of the opposite particles in the particle swarm. In this paper, the proportion of the opposite particles is set by user. So we can not be sure that the proportion we set is the best. In the future we propose to let the algorithm set the proportion of the opposite particles automatically according to the setting of other parameters and objective function.

References

1. Kennedy J., Eberhart R.C.: Particle swarm optimisation. Proceedings of the IEEE International Conference on Neural Networks. (1995) 1942-1948.
2. Ke Jing, Qian Jixin, Qiao Yizheng: A Modified Particle Swarm Optimization Algorithm. Journal of Circuits and Systems. 5 (2003) 87-91.
3. Ratnaweera A., Halgamuge S.K., Watson H.C.: Self-Organizing Hierarchical Particle Swarm Optimizer With Time-Varying Acceleration Coefficients. IEEE TRANSACTIONS ON EVOLUTIONARY COMPUTATION. (2004) 240-255
4. Eberhart R.C., Kennedy J.: A New Optimizer Using Particle Swarm Theory. Proceedings of Sixth International Symposium Micro Machine and Human Science (1995) 39-43
5. Shi Y.H., Eberhart R.C.: Parameter Selection in Particle Swarm Optimization. Evolutionary Programming VII: Proc.EP 98. (1998) 591-600
6. Zeng J.C, Cui Z.H.: A Guaranteed Global Convergence Particle Swarm Optimizer. Journal of Computer Research and Development. 8 (2004) 1333-1338.
7. Shi Y.H., Eberhart R.C.: A Modified Particle Swarm Optimizer. IEEE International Conference on Evolutionary Computation. (1998) 69-73
8. Mendes R., Kennedy J., Neves J.: The Full Informed Particle Swarm: Simpler, Maybe Better. IEEE TRANSACTIONS ON EVOLUTIONARY COMPUTATION. (2004) 204-210
9. Solis F., Wets R.: Minimization by random search techniques. Mathematics of Operation Research. 6 (1981) 19-30
10. http://ocw.mit.edu/NR/rdonlyres/Sloan-School-of-Management/15-099Fall2003/594A2FDC-A9B1-4336-AFDC-E2298F3C0DC4/0/ses5_solis_wets.pdf
11. Clerc M., Kennedy J.: The Particle Swarm-Explosion, Stability, and Convergence in a Multidimensional Complex Space. IEEE TRANSACTIONS ON EVOLUTIONARY COMPUTATION. 6 (2002) 58-73

Particle Evolutionary Swarm Optimization with Linearly Decreasing ϵ-Tolerance

Angel E. Muñoz Zavala, Arturo Hernández Aguirre,
and Enrique R. Villa Diharce

Center for Research in Mathematics (CIMAT),
Department of Computer Science,
A.P. 402, Guanajuato, Gto. 36240, México
{aemz, artha, villadi}@cimat.mx

Abstract. We introduce the PESO (Particle Evolutionary Swarm Optimization) algorithm for solving single objective constrained optimization problems. PESO algorithm proposes two perturbation operators: "c-perturbation" and "m-perturbation". The goal of these operators is to prevent premature convergence and the poor diversity issues observed in Particle Swarm Optimization (PSO) implementations. Constraint handling is based on simple feasibility rules, enhanced with a dynamic ϵ-tolerance approach applicable to equality constraints. PESO is compared and outperforms highly competitive algorithms representative of the state of the art.

1 Introduction

In PSO algorithms, the social behavior of individuals is rewarded by the best member in the flock. The credibility on the best regulates how fast the flock is going to follow him. When the flock slowly follows the best, exploration is improved but convergence is reduced. Too much credibility on the best reduces exploration hence concentrating the flock on small areas but accelerating convergence time. In a constrained search space, that trade-off becomes harder to balance since the constraint handling mechanism may increase the pressure on the flock to follow the best member which is trying to reach the feasible region, or the function optimum if the best is already feasible.

PSO algorithms do not have an strategy to handle constraints. Out of the many approaches possible, recent results by Mezura [1] indicate that simple "feasibility rules" (F rules) are powerful if correctly blended with evolutionary algorithms. He also noted that the constraint handling mechanism should be in "harmony" as much as possible (they do not contradict each other) with the search operators (algorithm operators). In that context we propose PESO for constrained optimization, a standard PSO algorithm enhanced with two perturbation operators to keep diversity, and uses feasibility rules for constraint handling.

The remainder of this paper is organized as follows. In Section 2 we introduce the problem of interest. Section 3 presents recent approaches to enhance PSO with a constraint handling mechanism. Section 4 introduces our approach and pseudo-code of PESO algorithm. Section 5 provides a comparison of results with respect to state-of-the-art algorithms. Conclusions and future work are given in Section 6. In the Appendix, we list the 13 test problems used in our experiments, and provide the parameters used by PESO.

2 Problem Statement

We are interested in the general nonlinear optimization problem in which we want to:

$$\text{Find } x \text{ which optimizes } f(x) \tag{1}$$

subject to:

$$g_i(x) \leq 0, \quad i = 1, \ldots, n \tag{2}$$

$$h_j(x) = 0, \quad j = 1, \ldots, p \tag{3}$$

where x is the vector of solutions $x = [x_1, x_2, \ldots, x_r]^T$, n is the number of inequality constraints and p is the number of equality constraints. For an inequality constraint that satisfies $g_i(x) = 0$, we will say that is active at x. All equality constraints h_j (regardless of the value of x used) are considered active at all points of $\mathcal{F}$ ($\mathcal{F}$ = feasible region).

3 Related Work

Significant effort and progress has been reported in the literature as researchers figure out ways to enhance the PSO paradigm with a constraint handling mechanism. Parsopoulos and Vrahatis [2], proposed a dynamic penalty function approach with limited success. Coath and Halgamuge [3], proposed the "feasible solutions method" (FSA), and the "penalty function method" (PFA) for constraint handling. FSA requires initialization of all particles inside the feasible space; they reported this goal is hard to achieve for some problems. FPA requires careful fine tuning of the penalty function parameters as to discourage premature convergence. Zhang and Xie [4], proposed DEPSO, a hybrid approach that uses a reproduction operator similar to that found in differential evolution. DEPSO applies the reproduction operator only to *PBest* but in PESO a similar perturbation is applied to every particle. Toscano and Coello [5] also perturb all particles but according to a probability value that varies with the generation number (as proposed by Fieldsend and Singh [6]).

4 The PESO Algorithm

The Particle Swarm Optimization (PSO) algorithm is a population-based search algorithm based on the simulation of the social behavior of birds within a flock. In PSO, particles are "flown" through a hyperdimensional search space. The feature

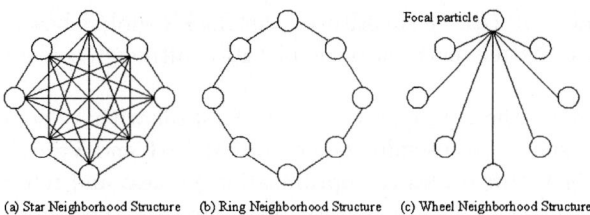

(a) Star Neighborhood Structure (b) Ring Neighborhood Structure (c) Wheel Neighborhood Structure

Fig. 1. Neighborhood structures for PSO [7]

that drives PSO is social interaction. Particles within the swarm learn from each other better regions to explore, thus based on this shared knowledge they tend to become more similar to their "better" neighbors. A social structure in PSO is determined through the formation of neighborhoods. These neighborhoods are determined through labels attached to every particle in the flock. Thus, the social interaction is modeled by spreading the influence of a "global best" all over the flock as well as neighborhoods are influenced by the best neighbor and their own past experience. Figure 1 shows some neighborhood structures studied by Kennedy [7]. Our approach, PESO, adopts the **ring** organization. In that organization each particle communicates with its n immediate neighbors, $n/2$ on each side. The neighborhood is determined through an index label assigned to every individual. This version of the PSO algorithm is called PSO-LocalBest

```
P_0 = Rand(LL, UL)
F_0 = Fitness ( P_0 )
C_0 = ConstraintSum ( P_0 )
V_0 = Rand(-(UL-LL), (UL-LL))
PBest_0 = P_0
FBest_0 = F_0
CBest_0 = C_0
Do
   LBest_i = LocalBest ( FBest_i, CBest_i )
   V_{i+1} = Velocity ( V_i, P_i, PBest_i, LBest_i)
   P_{i+1} = P_i + V_{i+1}
   F_{i+1} = Fitness ( P_{i+1} )
   C_{i+1} = ConstraintSum ( P_{i+1} )
   < PBest_{i+1}, FBest_{i+1}, CBest_{i+1} > =
       Best ( PBest_i, P_{i+1}, FBest_i, F_{i+1}, CBest_i, C_{i+1} )
End Do
```
```
Function LocalBest
For k = 0 To n
   LBest_i[k] = Best {(FBest_i[k - 1], CBest_i[k - 1]),
                      (FBest_i[k + 1], CBest_i[k + 1])}
End For
```
```
Function Velocity
For k = 0 To n
   For j = 0 To d
      r1 = c1 * U(0, 1)
      r2 = c2 * U(0, 1)
      w = U(0.5, 1)
      V_{i+1}[k, j] = w * V_{i+1}[k, j] + r1 * (PBest_i[k, j] - P_i[k, j]) +
                     r2 * (PBest_i[LBest_i(k), j] - P_i[k, j])
   End For
End For
```

Fig. 2. Pseudo-code of *PSO* algorithm with **LocalBest**

since the local best (*lbest*) substitutes the flock's global best. LocalBest has the advantage of better search space exploration although convergence has been reported slower [8].

Figure 2 shows the standard PSO-LocalBest algorithm adopted by our approach. It also shows the pseudo-code of **LocalBest** and **Velocity** functions.

The *velocity* vector drives the optimization process and reflects the socially exchanged information. The inertia weight w controls the influence of previous velocity on the new velocity. The value of constants $c1$, $c2$ and w is given in the Appendix.

```
P₀ = Rand(LL, UL)
F₀ = Fitness ( P₀ )
C₀ = ConstraintSum ( P₀ )
V₀ = Rand(-(UL-LL), (UL-LL))
PBest₀ = P₀
FBest₀ = F₀
CBest₀ = C₀
Do
    LBestᵢ = LocalBest ( FBestᵢ, CBestᵢ )
    Vᵢ₊₁ = Velocity ( Vᵢ, Pᵢ, PBestᵢ, LBestᵢ )
    Pᵢ₊₁ = Pᵢ + Vᵢ₊₁
    Fᵢ₊₁ = Fitness ( Pᵢ₊₁ )
    Cᵢ₊₁ = ConstraintSum ( Pᵢ₊₁ )
    < PBestᵢ₊₁, FBestᵢ₊₁, CBestᵢ₊₁ > =
        Best ( PBestᵢ, Pᵢ₊₁, FBestᵢ, Fᵢ₊₁, CBestᵢ, Cᵢ₊₁ )
    Temp = C-Perturbation (Pᵢ₊₁)
    FTemp = Fitness ( Temp )
    CTemp = ConstraintSum ( Temp )
    < PBestᵢ₊₁, FBestᵢ₊₁, CBestᵢ₊₁ > =
        Best ( PBestᵢ, Temp, FBestᵢ, FTemp, CBestᵢ, CTemp )
    Temp = M-Perturbation (Pᵢ₊₁)
    FTemp = Fitness ( Temp )
    CTemp = ConstraintSum ( Temp )
    < PBestᵢ₊₁, FBestᵢ₊₁, CBestᵢ₊₁ > =
        Best ( PBestᵢ, Temp, FBestᵢ, FTemp, CBestᵢ, CTemp )
    Pᵢ = Pᵢ₊₁
    Fᵢ = Fᵢ₊₁
    Cᵢ = Cᵢ₊₁
    Vᵢ = Vᵢ₊₁
End Do
```

```
Function C-Perturbation
For k = 0 To n
    For j = 0 To d
        r = U(0, 1)
        p1 = Random(n)
        p2 = Random(n)
        p3 = Random(n)
        Temp[k, j] = Pᵢ₊₁[p1, j] + r (Pᵢ₊₁[p2, j] - Pᵢ₊₁[p3, j])
    End For
End For
```

```
Function M-Perturbation
For k = 0 To n
    For j = 0 To d
        r = U(0, 1)
        If r ≤ 1/d Then
            Temp[k, j] = Rand(LL, UL)
        Else
            Temp[k, j] = Pᵢ₊₁[k, j]
    End For
End For
```

Fig. 3. Main Algorithm of *PESO*

4.1 Perturbation Operators and Constraint Handling

PESO algorithm makes use of two perturbation operators to keep diversity and exploration. PESO has three stages; in the first stage the standard PSO algorithm [8] is performed, then the perturbations are applied in the next two stages. The main algorithm of PESO is shown in Figure 3.

The goal of the second stage is to add a perturbation in a way similar to the so called "reproduction operator" found in *differential evolution* algorithm. This perturbation, called C-Perturbation, is applied all over the flock to yield a set of temporary particles $Temp$. Each member of $Temp$ is compared with its corresponding (father) member of $Pi + 1$, so the perturbed version updates $PBest_i$ if it has a better fitness value. Figure 3 also shows the pseudo-code of the **C-Perturbation** operator.

In the third stage every vector is perturbed with some probability on each dimension of the particle vector. The perturbation can be explained as the addition of random values with uniform distribution. The perturbation, called M-Perturbation, is applied to every particle to yield a temporal set of particles $Temp$. Then each member of $Temp$ is compared with its corresponding "father" and updates $PBest_i$ if it is better. Figure 3 also shows the pseudo-code of the **M-Perturbation** operator.

Constraint handling and selection mechanisms are described by a set of "feasibility rules". These rules are: 1) given two feasible particles, pick the one with better fitness value; 2) if both particles are infeasible, pick the particle with the lowest sum of constraint violation, and 3), given feasible and infeasible particles, the feasible particle must be picked. These rules are implemented by function **Best** used to update *Pbest* and *Fbest* in PESO's main algorithm. See Figure 3.

4.2 PESO with Linearly Decreasing ϵ−Tolerance

PESO's performance is improved for test problems with equality constraints, such as g03, g05, g11 and g13. By using a dynamic ϵ tolerance approach, individuals no farther than ϵ from an equality constraint are allowed to live longer, therefore improving their chance to find a better constraint value. The tolerance is linearly decremented from 0.1 to $1E - 6$ with the first 90% of the generations. For the last 10%, the tolerance is kept with no change.

5 Comparisons PESO vs SR vs Toscano's PSO

The test problems in the benchmark of Runarsson and Yao used for our experiments [9] are listed in the Appendix. A total of 50 particles were used by PESO, for 2333 generations to yield 350,000 fitness function evaluations. Constants $c1 = 0.1$, $c2 = 1$, and $w = U(0.5, 1)$. All solutions found in 30 runs were feasible.

A comparison with Runarsson and Yao's Stochastic Ranking algorithm, (SR), [9]. Results are shown in Table 1. Note that SR is better in g02, g07 and g10. Also,

Table 1. Results of PESO and SR for benchmark problems

TF	Optimal	Best Result PESO	Best Result SR	Mean Result PESO	Mean Result SR	Worst Result PESO	Worst Result SR
g01 Min	-15.000000	-15.000000	-15.000000	-15.000000	-15.000000	-15.000000	-15.000000
g02 Max	0.803619	0.792607	0.803619	0.721748	0.782715	0.614135	0.723591
g03 Max	1.000000	1.000004	1.001	1.000004	1.001	1.000003	1.001
g04 Min	-30665.539	-30665.538672	-30665.539	-30665.538672	-30665.539	-30665.538672	-30665.539
g05 Min	5126.4981	5126.498095	5126.497	5126.498095	5126.497	5126.498095	5126.497
g06 Min	-6961.81388	-6961.813876	-6961.814	-6961.813876	-6961.814	-6961.813876	-6961.814
g07 Min	24.306209	24.306921	24.306	24.371253	24.306	24.593504	24.306
g08 Max	0.095825	0.095825	0.095825	0.095825	0.095825	0.095825	0.095825
g09 Min	680.630057	680.630057	680.630	680.630057	680.630	680.630058	680.630
g10 Min	7049.3307	7049.459452	7049.248	7099.101386	7049.25	7251.396245	7049.27
g11 Min	0.750000	0.749999	0.750	0.749999	0.750	0.749999	0.750
g12 Max	1.000000	1.000000	1.000000	1.000000	1.000000	1.000000	1.000000
g13 Min	0.053950	0.053949	0.053942	0.067214	0.066770	0.447811	0.438803

Table 2. Results of PESO and Toscano's PSO for benchmark problems

TF	Optimal	Best Result PESO	Best Result PSO	Mean Result PESO	Mean Result PSO	Worst Result PESO	Worst Result PSO
g01 Min	-15.000000	-15.000000	-15.000000	-15.000000	-15.000000	-15.000000	-15.000000
g02 Max	0.803619	0.792607	0.803432	0.721748	0.790406	0.614135	0.750393
g03 Max	1.000000	1.000004	1.004720	1.000004	1.003814	1.000003	1.002490
g04 Min	-30665.539	-30665.538672	-30665.500	-30665.538672	-30665.500	-30665.538672	-30665.500
g05 Min	5126.4981	5126.498095	5126.640	5126.498095	5461.081333	5126.498095	6104.750
g06 Min	-6961.813880	-6961.813876	-6961.810	-6961.813876	-6961.810	-6961.813876	-6961.810
g07 Min	24.306209	24.306921	24.351100	24.371253	25.355771	24.593504	27.316800
g08 Max	0.095825	0.095825	0.095825	0.095825	0.095825	0.095825	0.095825
g09 Min	680.630057	680.630057	680.638	680.630057	680.852393	680.630058	681.553
g10 Min	7049.3307	7049.459452	7057.5900	7099.101386	7560.047857	7251.396245	8104.310
g11 Min	0.750000	0.749999	0.749999	0.749999	0.750107	0.749999	0.752885
g12 Max	1.000000	1.000000	1.000000	1.000000	1.000000	1.000000	1.000000
g13 Min	0.053950	0.053949	0.068665	0.067214	1.716426	0.447811	13.669500

SR average stays closer to the optimum and is better than PESO in problems g07 and g10. Nonetheless, the results are very competitive and comparable for all other problems. In brief, SR improves the results of PESO only in problems g02, g07 and g10.

In Table 2 we show the results of PESO and Toscano and Coello's PSO (TCPSO). It can be seen that PESO is clearly better than TCPSO in problems g05, g07, g10, and g13, but TCPSO is better in problem g02. Although the best results for the rest of the problems are comparable, PESO outperforms TCPSO in the average results for problems g05, g07, g10, g11 and g13, TCPSO is better than PESO in problem g02. Note that TCPSO worst values are really far from the average, an under performance not shown by PESO. Due to lack of space we can not provide additional results on minimum number of generations required to attain the optimum, but they are equiparable with TCPSO.

6 Conclusions and Future Work

We have introduced PESO, a PSO algorithm enhanced with two perturbation operators to keep diversity and feasibility rules for constrained optimization.

PESO does not need the adjustment of several control and mutation parameters. The results are highly competitive. Future work includes an extension for multiobjective optimization.

References

1. Mezura, E.: Alternatives to Handle Constraints in Evolutionary Optimization. PhD thesis, CINVESTAV-IPN, Mexico, DF (2004)
2. Parsopoulos, K., Vrahatis, M.: Particle swarm optimization method for constrained optimization problems. In: Proceedings of the Second Euro-International Symposium on Computational Intelligence, E-ISCI2002 (2002)
3. Coath, G., Halgamuge, S.K.: A comparison of constraint-handling methods for the application of particle swarm optimization to constrained nonlinear optimization problems. In: Proceedings of the 2003 Congress on Evolutionary Computation, IEEE (2003) 2419–2425
4. Zhang, J., Xie, F.: Depso: Hybrid particle swarm with differential evolution operator. In: Proceedings of IEEE International Conference on Systems, Man and Cybernetics, IEEE (2003) 3816–3821
5. Toscano, G., Coello, C.: A constraint-handling mechanism for particle swarm optimization. In: Proceedings of the 2004 Congress on Evolutionary Computation, IEEE (2004) 1396–1403
6. Fieldsend, J., Singh, S.: A multi-objective algorithm based upon particle swarm optimization, and efficient data structure and turbulence. In: Proceedings of 2002 U.K. Workshop on Computational Intelligence, The European Network on Intelligent Technologies for Smart Adaptive Systems (2002) 37–44
7. Kennedy, J.: Small worlds and mega-minds: Effects of neighborhood topology on particle swarm performance. In: IEEE Congress on Evolutionary Computation, IEEE (1999) 1931–1938
8. Kennedy, J., Eberhart, R.: The Particle Swarm: Social Adaptation in Information-Processing Systems. McGraw-Hill, London (1999)
9. Runarsson, T., Yao, X.: Search biases in constrained evolutionary optimization. IEEE Transactions on Systems, Man and Cybernetics - Part C: Applications and Reviews **35** (2005) 233–243

Appendix

1. **g01**: Minimize: $f(x) = 5\sum_{i=1}^{4} x_i - 5\sum_{i=1}^{4} x_i^2 - \sum_{i=5}^{13} x_i$
   subject to:

$$g_1(x) = 2x_1 + 2x_2 + x_{10} + x_{11} - 10 \leq 0$$
$$g_2(x) = 2x_1 + 2x_3 + x_{10} + x_{12} - 10 \leq 0$$
$$g_3(x) = 2x_2 + 2x_3 + x_{11} + x_{12} - 10 \leq 0$$
$$g_4(x) = -8x_1 + x_{10} \leq 0$$
$$g_5(x) = -8x_2 + x_{11} \leq 0$$
$$g_6(x) = -8x_3 + x_{12} \leq 0$$
$$g_7(x) = -2x_4 - x_5 + x_{10} \leq 0$$

$$g_8(x) = -2x_6 - x_7 + x_{11} \leq 0$$
$$g_9(x) = -2x_8 - x_9 + x_{12} \leq 0$$

where the bounds are $0 \leq x_i \leq 1$ ($i = 1, \ldots, 9$), $0 \leq x_i \leq 100$ ($i = 10, 11, 12$) and $0 \leq x_{13} \leq 1$. The global optimum is at $x^* = (1,1,1,1,1,1,1,1,1,3,3,3,1)$ where $f(x^*) = -15$. Constraints g_1, g_2, g_3, g_4, g_5 and g_6 are active.

2. **g02**: Maximize: $f(x) = \left| \frac{\sum_{i=1}^n \cos^4(x_i) - 2 \prod_{i=1}^n \cos^2(x_i)}{\sqrt{\sum_{i=1}^n i x_i^2}} \right|$
subject to:

$$g_1(x) = 0.75 - \prod_{i=1}^n x_i \leq 0$$

$$g_2(x) = \sum_{i=1}^n x_i - 7.5n \leq 0$$

where $n = 20$ and $0 \leq x_i \leq 10$ ($i = 1, \ldots, n$). The global maximum is unknown; the best reported solution is [9] $f(x^*) = 0.803619$. Constraint g_1 is close to being active ($g_1 = -10^{-8}$).

3. **g03**: Maximize: $f(x) = (\sqrt{n})^n \prod_{i=1}^n x_i$
subject to:

$$h(x) = \sum_{i=1}^n x_i^2 - 1 = 0$$

where $n = 10$ and $0 \leq x_i \leq 1$ ($i = 1, \ldots, n$). The global maximum is at $x_i^* = 1/\sqrt{n}$ ($i = 1, \ldots, n$) where $f(x^*) = 1$.

4. **g04**: Minimize: $f(x) = 5.3578547x_3^2 + 0.8356891 x_1 x_5 + 37.293239 x_1 - 40792.141$
subject to:

$$g_1(x) = 85.334407 + 0.0056858 x_2 x_5 + 0.0006262 x_1 x_4 - 0.0022053 x_3 x_5 - 92 \leq 0$$
$$g_2(x) = -85.334407 - 0.0056858 x_2 x_5 - 0.0006262 x_1 x_4 + 0.0022053 x_3 x_5 \leq 0$$
$$g_3(x) = 80.51249 + 0.0071317 x_2 x_5 + 0.0029955 x_1 x_2 + 0.0021813 x_3^2 - 110 \leq 0$$
$$g_4(x) = -80.51249 - 0.0071317 x_2 x_5 - 0.0029955 x_1 x_2 - 0.0021813 x_3^2 + 90 \leq 0$$
$$g_5(x) = 9.300961 + 0.0047026 x_3 x_5 + 0.0012547 x_1 x_3 + 0.0019085 x_3 x_4 - 25 \leq 0$$
$$g_6(x) = -9.300961 - 0.0047026 x_3 x_5 - 0.0012547 x_1 x_3 - 0.0019085 x_3 x_4 + 20 \leq 0$$

where: $78 \leq x_1 \leq 102$, $33 \leq x_2 \leq 45$, $27 \leq x_i \leq 45$ ($i = 3, 4, 5$). The optimum solution is $x^* = (78, 33, 29.995256025682, 45, 36.775812905788)$ where $f(x^*) = -30665.539$. Constraints g_1 y g_6 are active.

5. **g05** Minimize: $f(\boldsymbol{x}) = 3x_1 + 0.000001x_1^3 + 2x_2 + (0.000002/3)x_2^3$
   subject to:

$$g_1(\boldsymbol{x}) = -x_4 + x_3 - 0.55 \leq 0$$
$$g_2(\boldsymbol{x}) = -x_3 + x_4 - 0.55 \leq 0$$
$$h_3(\boldsymbol{x}) = 1000\sin(-x_3 - 0.25) + 1000\sin(-x_4 - 0.25) + 894.8 - x_1 = 0$$
$$h_4(\boldsymbol{x}) = 1000\sin(-x_3 - 0.25) + 1000\sin(x_3 - x_4 - 0.25) + 894.8 - x_2 = 0$$
$$h_5(\boldsymbol{x}) = 1000\sin(-x_4 - 0.25) + 1000\sin(x_4 - x_3 - 0.25) + 1294.8 = 0$$

where $0 \leq x_1 \leq 1200$, $0 \leq x_2 \leq 1200$, $-0.55 \leq x_3 \leq 0.55$, and $-0.55 \leq x_4 \leq 0.55$. The best known solution is $x^* = (679.9453, 1026.067, 0.1188764, -0.3962336)$ where $f(x^*) = 5126.4981$.

6. **g06** Minimize: $f(\boldsymbol{x}) = (x_1 - 10)^3 + (x_2 - 20)^3$
   subject to:

$$g_1(\boldsymbol{x}) = -(x_1 - 5)^2 - (x_2 - 5)^2 + 100 \leq 0$$
$$g_2(\boldsymbol{x}) = (x_1 - 6)^2 + (x_2 - 5)^2 - 82.81 \leq 0$$

where $13 \leq x_1 \leq 100$ and $0 \leq x_2 \leq 100$. The optimum solution is $x^* = (14.095, 0.84296)$ where $f(x^*) = -6961.81388$. Both constraints are active.

7. **g07** Minimize: $f(\boldsymbol{x}) = x_1^2 + x_2^2 + x_1 x_2 - 14x_1 - 16x_2 + (x_3 - 10)^2 + 4(x_4 - 5)^2 + (x_5 - 3)^2 + 2(x_6 - 1)^2 + 5x_7^2 + 7(x_8 - 11)^2 + 2(x_9 - 10)^2 + (x_{10} - 7)^2 + 45$
   subject to:

$$g_1(\boldsymbol{x}) = -105 + 4x_1 + 5x_2 - 3x_7 + 9x_8 \leq 0$$
$$g_2(\boldsymbol{x}) = 10x_1 - 8x_2 - 17x_7 + 2x_8 \leq 0$$
$$g_3(\boldsymbol{x}) = -8x_1 + 2x_2 + 5x_9 - 2x_{10} - 12 \leq 0$$
$$g_4(\boldsymbol{x}) = 3(x_1 - 2)^2 + 4(x_2 - 3)^2 + 2x_3^2 - 7x_4 - 120 \leq 0$$
$$g_5(\boldsymbol{x}) = 5x_1^2 + 8x_2 + (x_3 - 6)^2 - 2x_4 - 40 \leq 0$$
$$g_6(\boldsymbol{x}) = x_1^2 + 2(x_2 - 2)^2 - 2x_1 x_2 + 14x_5 - 6x_6 \leq 0$$
$$g_7(\boldsymbol{x}) = 0.5(x_1 - 8)^2 + 2(x_2 - 4)^2 + 3x_5^2 - x_6 - 30 \leq 0$$
$$g_8(\boldsymbol{x}) = -3x_1 + 6x_2 + 12(x_9 - 8)^2 - 7x_{10} \leq 0$$

where $-10 \leq x_i \leq 10$ ($i = 1, \ldots, 10$). The global optimum is $x^* = (2.171996, 2.363683, 8.773926, 5.095984, 0.9906548, 1.430574, 1.321644, 9.828726, 8.280092, 8.375927)$ where $f(x^*) = 24.3062091$. Constraints g_1, g_2, g_3, g_4, g_5 and g_6 are active.

8. **g08** Maximize: $f(\boldsymbol{x}) = \frac{\sin^3(2\pi x_1)\sin(2\pi x_2)}{x_1^3(x_1 + x_2)}$
   subject to:

$$g_1(\boldsymbol{x}) = x_1^2 - x_2 + 1 \leq 0$$
$$g_2(\boldsymbol{x}) = 1 - x_1 + (x_2 - 4)^2 \leq 0$$

where $0 \leq x_1 \leq 10$ and $0 \leq x_2 \leq 10$. The optimum solution is located at $x^* = (1.2279713, 4.2453733)$ where $f(x^*) = 0.095825$. The solutions is located within the feasible region.

9. **g09** Minimize: $f(x) = (x_1 - 10)^2 + 5(x_2 - 12)^2 + x_3^4 + 3(x_4 - 11)^2 + 10x_5^6 + 7x_6^2 + x_7^4 - 4x_6x_7 - 10x_6 - 8x_7$
   subject to:

$$g_1(x) = -127 + 2x_1^2 + 3x_2^4 + x_3 + 4x_4^2 + 5x_5 \leq 0$$
$$g_2(x) = -282 + 7x_1 + 3x_2 + 10x_3^2 + x_4 - x_5 \leq 0$$
$$g_3(x) = -196 + 23x_1 + x_2^2 + 6x_6^2 - 8x_7 \leq 0$$
$$g_4(x) = 4x_1^2 + x_2^2 - 3x_1x_2 + 2x_3^2 + 5x_6 - 11x_7 \leq 0$$

where $-10 \leq x_i \leq 10$ $(i = 1, \ldots, 7)$. The global optimum is $x^* = (2.330499, 1.951372, -0.4775414, 4.365726, -0.6244870, 1.038131, 1.594227)$ where $f(x^*) = 680.6300573$. Two constraints are active (g_1 and g_4).

10. **g10** Minimize: $f(x) = x_1 + x_2 + x_3$
    subject to:

$$g_1(x) = -1 + 0.0025(x_4 + x_6) \leq 0$$
$$g_2(x) = -1 + 0.0025(x_5 + x_7 - x_4) \leq 0$$
$$g_3(x) = -1 + 0.01(x_8 - x_5) \leq 0$$
$$g_4(x) = -x_1x_6 + 833.33252x_4 + 100x_1 - 83333.333 \leq 0$$
$$g_5(x) = -x_2x_7 + 1250x_5 + x_2x_4 - 1250x_4 \leq 0$$
$$g_6(x) = -x_3x_8 + 1250000 + x_3x_5 - 2500x_5 \leq 0$$

where $100 \leq x_1 \leq 10000$, $1000 \leq x_i \leq 10000$, $(i = 2, 3)$, $10 \leq x_i \leq 1000$, $(i = 4, \ldots, 8)$. The global optimum is: $x^* = (579.3167, 1359.943, 5110.071, 182.0174, 295.5985, 217.9799, 286.4162, 395.5979)$ where $f(x^*) = 7049.3307$. g_1, g_2 and g_3 are active.

11. **g11** Minimize: $f(x) = x_1^2 + (x_2 - 1)^2$
    subject to:

$$h(x) = x_2 - x_1^2 = 0$$

where: $-1 \leq x_1 \leq 1$, $-1 \leq x_2 \leq 1$. The optimum solution is $x^* = (\pm 1/\sqrt{2}, 1/2)$ where $f(x^*) = 0.75$.

12. **g12** Maximize: $f(x) = \frac{100 - (x_1 - 5)^2 - (x_2 - 5)^2 - (x_3 - 5)^2}{100}$
    subject to:

$$g_1(x) = (x_1 - p)^2 + (x_2 - q)^2 + (x_3 - r)^2 - 0.0625 \leq 0$$

where: $0 \leq x_i \leq 10$ $(i = 1, 2, 3)$ and $p, q, r = 1, 2, \ldots, 9$. The feasible region of the search space consists of 9^3 disjointed spheres. A point (x_1, x_2, x_3) is feasible if and only if there exist p, q, r such the above inequality holds. The global optimum is located at $x^* = (5, 5, 5)$ where $f(x^*) = 1$.

13. **g13** Minimize: $f(x) = e^{x_1 x_2 x_3 x_4 x_5}$
    subject to:

$$h_1(x) = x_1^2 + x_2^2 + x_3^2 + x_4^2 + x_5^2 - 10 = 0$$
$$h_2(x) = x_2 x_3 - 5x_4 x_5 = 0$$
$$h_3(x) = x_1^3 + x_2^3 + 1 = 0$$

where: $-2.3 \leq x_i \leq 2.3$ ($i = 1, 2$) and $-3.2 \leq x_i \leq 3.2$ ($i = 3, 4, 5$). The optimum solution is $x^* = (-1.717143, 1.595709, 1.827247, -0.7636413, -0.763645)$ where $f(x^*) = 0.0539498$.

Useful Infeasible Solutions in Engineering Optimization with Evolutionary Algorithms

Efrén Mezura-Montes and Carlos A. Coello Coello

CINVESTAV-IPN, Evolutionary Computation Group (EVOCINV),
Computer Science Section, Electrical Engineering Department,
Av. IPN No. 2508 Col, San Pedro Zacatenco México D.F. 07300, México
emezura@computacion.cs.cinvestav.mx
ccoello@cs.cinvestav.mx

Abstract. We propose an evolutionary-based approach to solve engineering design problems without using penalty functions. The aim is to identify and maintain infeasible solutions close to the feasible region located in promising areas. In this way, using the genetic operators, more solutions will be generated inside the feasible region and also near its boundaries. As a result, the feasible region will be sampled well-enough as to reach better feasible solutions. The proposed approach, which is simple to implement, is tested with respect to typical penalty function techniques as well as against state-of-the-art approaches using four mechanical design problems. The results obtained are discussed and some conclusions are provided.

1 Introduction

Evolutionary Algorithms (EAs) have been widely used to solve optimization problems [1]. We are interested in the general non linear programming problem in which we want to:Find x which optimizes $f(x)$ subject to: $g_i(x) \leq 0$, $i = 1, \ldots, m$ $h_j(x) = 0$, $j = 1, \ldots, p$ where $x \in \mathbb{R}^n$ is the vector of solutions $x = [x_1, x_2, \ldots, x_n]^T$, where each x_i, $i = 1, \ldots, n$ is bounded by lower and upper limits $L_i \leq x_i \leq U_i$; m is the number of inequality constraints and p is the number of equality constraints (in both cases, constraints could be linear or nonlinear). If we denote with $\mathcal{F}$ to the feasible region and with $\mathcal{S}$ to the whole search space, then it should be clear that $\mathcal{F} \subseteq \mathcal{S}$. It is well-known that, in their original versions, EAs lack a mechanism to deal with constrained search spaces. Hence, a considerable amount of research have been focused on incorporating the constraints of the problem into the fitness function of an EA. The most common approach is the use of a penalty function [2], whose aim is to decrease the fitness of infeasible solutions in order to favor the selection of the feasible ones (the fitness of a solution is calculated by merging the objective function value and the sum of constraint violation multiplied by a penalty factor). However, its main drawback is the careful fine-tuning required by the penalty factors, whose values indicate the degree of penalization [2]. In this paper, we propose to avoid the use of penalty functions; instead, we propose to handle the objective function value and the constraints of the problem separately and to use a mechanism to keep a few infeasible solutions with the lowest sum of constraint violation in the population for the next generation. These infeasible solutions must have the best objective function value among infeasible solutions. The aim is to promote the generation of solutions close to the boundaries of the feasible region in order to reach a better solution, despite its location inside or in the boundaries of the feasible set. The paper is organized as follows: Section 2 summarizes some approaches found in the literature of engineering design with evolutionary algorithms. In Section 3 we present details of the proposed approach, including a simple example to show its behavior. The experimental design, the results obtained and a discussion about them are provided in Section 4. Finally, in Section 5 we present our conclusions and future work.

2 Related Work

Many successful applications of EAs to solve engineering design problems have been reported. Ray & Liew [3] used a swarm-like based approach to solve engineering optimization problems. In their approach, a civilization was conformed by several societies, whose leaders guide the members of each society. Besides, there is a leaders' society which contains all the leaders of each society. Constraints are handled using a dominance-based approach in the constraints space [3]. To maintain diversity, the authors propose a mechanism to allow an individual not to follow its leader. The main advantage of the approach is that it requires a low number of evaluations of the objective function to obtain competitive results. However, the computational cost is increased by the ranking process and the clustering algorithm that the approach requires to initialize the societies. Hernández et al. [4] proposed PASSSS, an approach based on a multi-objective optimization algorithm called PAES [4] to solve some benchmark problems and also some structural design problems. The approach uses an external memory to store the best set of solutions found. Furthermore, PASSSS requires a shrinking mechanism to reduce the search space. Pareto dominance is used only to decide whether or not a new solution is inserted in the external memory. The authors acknowledge that the most important mechanisms of IS-PAES are its shrinking procedure and the information provided by the external memory which is used to decide the shrinking of the search space. Furthermore, despite its good performance as a global optimizer, PASSSS is an approach far from being simple to implement. An improved particle swarm optimization was proposed by He et al. [5] to solve mechanical design optimization problems. The idea is to let the particles fly only inside the feasible region. Therefore, an initial feasible population is required, which is the main disadvantage of the approach, because for some problems, even generating one single feasible solution is very difficult. Its main advantage is that its computational cost is relatively low compared with the approaches mentioned before.

3 Our Approach

The main motivation of this work is to avoid the use of a penalty function to handle the constraints of the problems and to provide a simple mechanism capable of boosting the generation of solutions close to the boundaries of the feasible region of the search space. Our proposed approach works in the following way: At each generation, the solutions are ranked based on three criteria:

1. Between 2 feasible solutions, the one with the highest fitness value wins (assuming a maximization problem/task).
2. If one solution is feasible and the other one is infeasible, the feasible solution wins.
3. If both solutions are infeasible, the one with the lowest sum of constraint violation is preferred ($\sum_{i=1}^{m} max(0, g_i(\boldsymbol{x}))$).

After the ranking process, the selected individuals for the next generation will be (1) those feasible solutions with a more promising value of the objective function and (2) infeasible solutions with the lowest value of the sum of constraint violation. As the population evolves, this selection process will lead the search to reach faster the feasible region (like a severe penalty function). However, in order to maintain infeasible solutions close to the the feasible region, at each generation, the infeasible solution with the lowest sum of constraint violation and with the best value of the objective function (taken from the μ parents or the λ offspring, each one with 50% probability) will be included in the population for the next generation. This mechanism is controlled by a user-defined parameter. Therefore, more than one copy of the same infeasible solution will be in the same population. However, it is a desired behavior because this solution will have more probabilities to generate more individuals close to it and this promising area will be explored more in-depth. As a result, the population will have, most of the time, a few infeasible solutions located in promising areas of the boundaries of the feasible region. If all the population is feasible, a random solution will be copied in the population. The parameter which controls this mechanism was called by us as Selection ratio: ($0 \leq S_r \leq 1$). We used a ($\mu + \lambda$) evolution strategy as a search engine, because its selection mechanism fits with our proposal (the selection is made to create the population for the next generation). We used typical genetic operators: self-adaptive Gaussian mutation [6] and we combined panmictic discrete/intermediate recombination for the decision variables and control variables (encoded mutation values) as well [6]. A pseudocode of the approach is provided in Figure 1.

```
Begin
    Create a random initial population of μ solutions
    For G=1 to MAX_GENERATIONS Do
        For i=1 to |λ| Do
            Choose randomly one parent from the μ available plus n other parents (one per variable)
            Generate one offspring by panmictic discrete/intermediate recombination
            Mutate the offspring
        End For
        Sort the (μ + λ) solutions using the three criteria based on feasibility
        For i=1 to |μ| Do
⇒           If flip(S_r) Then
                Move the solution at the top of the sorted (μ + λ) to the population for the next generation
            Else
⇒               Copy the best infeasible solution (from parents or offspring) to the population for the next generation
            End If
        End For
        G = G + 1
    End For
End
```

Fig. 1. Our approach. flip(W) returns 1 with probability W. Arrows indicate the steps added to maintain infeasible solutions.

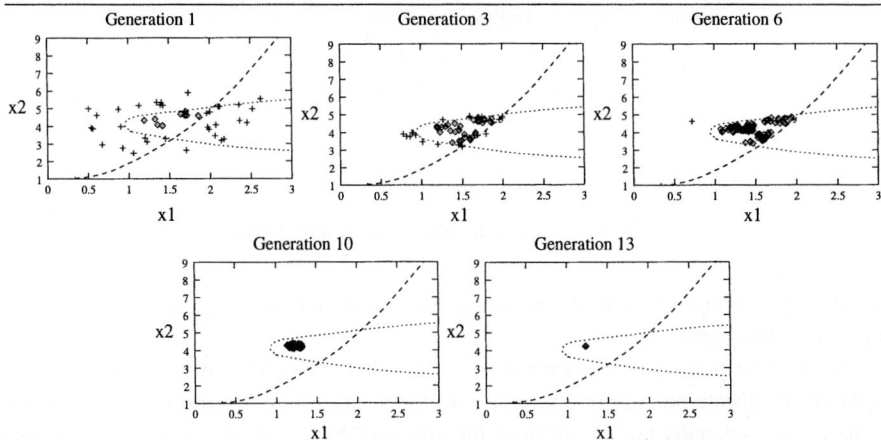

Fig. 2. Graphs showing the population behavior using our proposed mechanism. "◇" points are feasible solutions, "+" points are infeasible ones. The dashed line represents constraint $g_1(x)$ of the problem and the dotted line represents constraint $g_2(x)$.

A graphical example of the expected behavior of the approach can be found in Figure 2. We used a 2-dimensional test problem, which is a problem easy to solve by the approach; it requires about 5400 evaluations of the objective function to reach the global optimum, but it helps to visualize how our approach works. The definition of this problem is the following:

Maximize: $f(x) = \frac{\sin^3(2\pi x_1)\sin(2\pi x_2)}{x_1^3(x_1+x_2)}$

subject to: $g_1(x) = x_1^2 - x_2 + 1 \leq 0$ $g_2(x) = 1 - x_1 + (x_2 - 4)^2 \leq 0$

where $0 \leq x_1 \leq 10$ and $0 \leq x_2 \leq 10$. The global optimum is located at $x^* = (1.2279713, 4.2453733)$ where $f(x^*) = 0.095825$. As it can be observed, in generation 1 there are a few feasible as well as several infeasible solutions. The behavior of the approach can be observed in generation 3, where there are more feasible solutions than those in generation 1 and also there are infeasible solutions surrounding the feasible region. In this way, the feasible region is sampled well-enough as to find promising areas (three areas in the example). This is shown in generation 6, where there is still an infeasible solution in the population. It is worth noticing that this infeasible solution is close to the area where the global optimum is located; this can be seen in generation 10 where the infeasible solution has disappeared but the approach has found the vicinity of the constrained global optimum. Our algorithm has converged to the constrained global optimum in generation 18.

4 Experiments and Discussion

Our experimental design has two parts: (1) to compare our approach against different types of penalty function approaches and (2) to compare our results against state-of-the-art approaches. We selected four well known engineering design problems to use them

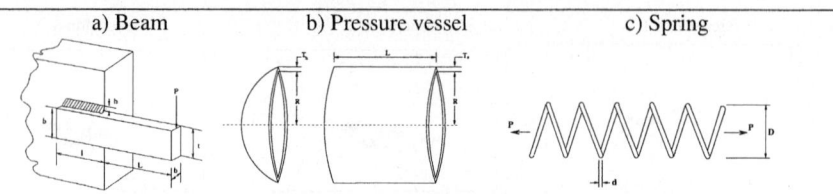

Fig. 3. Figures of the design problems adopted

in the experiments. The full description of each of them is provided in the appendix at the end of this paper.

In the first part of our experiments, we decided to implement four penalty-based approaches: Death penalty (to assign a zero fitness to infeasible solutions) [7], a static penalty (fixed penalty factor during all the process) [8], a dynamic penalty (the penalty factor is initialized with a low value and it is increased as the process evolves) [9] and an adaptive penalty (the penalty factor is adapted according to the number of feasible solutions in the population) [10]. A total of 30 runs per technique per problem were performed. The number of evaluations of the objective function was fixed to 30,000 for the four penalty-based approaches and also for our approach. For the penalty-based approaches we used a gray-coded genetic algorithm with roulette wheel selection, one point crossover and uniform mutation. The population size was 100 individuals and the number of generations 360. The rate of crossover was 0.6 and the mutation rate was 0.01. The parameters for the static, dynamic and adaptive approaches were defined after a trial-and-error process. The reported parameters were those which provided the best results and they are the following: Static approach: fixed penalty factor = 1000. Dynamic approach: $\alpha = 2$, $\beta = 2$, $C = 0.5$. Adaptive approach: $\beta_1 = 2.0$, $\beta_2 = 4.0$, $k = 50$, $\delta_{initial} = 5000$ For our approach we used a $(15 + 100)$-ES with the following initial parameters: generations = 300, $S_r = 0.97$ (which means that 3 times every 100 selections, the best infeasible solution will be copied into the population for the next generation). This small value was chosen based on conclusions found in the literature which show that only a few infeasible solutions are enough to improve performance [11]. The learning rates values were calculated using [6] (where n is the number of decision variables of the problem): $\tau = (\sqrt{2\sqrt{n}})^{-1}$ and $\tau' = (\sqrt{2n})^{-1}$. In order to favor finer movements in the search space, we initialized the mutation stepsizes for all the individuals in the initial population with only a 40% of the value obtained by the following formula (where n is the number of decision variables): $\sigma_i(0) = 0.4 \times (\Delta x_i/\sqrt{n})$ where Δx_i is approximated as follows, $\Delta x_i \approx x_i^u - x_i^l$, where $x_i^u - x_i^l$ are the upper and lower limits of the decision variable i. Discrete variables were handled by just truncating the real value to its closest integer value. The statistical results of the 30 independent runs are shown in Table 1.

As it can be seen, our approach was the only to find feasible solutions in all runs for the four problems. No penalty function was able to find feasible solutions for problem 4, the static approach could not find feasible solutions for problem 2, the dynamic approach failed to reach the feasible region in two runs for problem 1 and the adaptive approach found feasible solutions in only 27 runs for problems 1 and 2. The results in Table 1 also reflect how our approach outperforms the four penalty-based approaches in

Table 1. Statistical values obtained with each approach for the four design problem. "-" means no feasible solutions found. A result in **boldface** means a better result. "*" and "**" mean that only in 28 and 27 runs (out of 30) feasible solutions were found, respectively.

a) Welded beam design

	Death Penalty	Static	Dynamic *	Adaptive **	Our approach
Best	1.747810	1.734624	1.793387	1.776909	**1.724852**
Mean	2.021429	1.925931	2.182719	2.043387	**1.777692**
Worst	2.710572	2.320612	3.731899	3.807526	**2.074562**
St. Dev	2.3E-1	1.6E-1	4.5E-1	4.1E-1	8.8E-2

b) Pressure vessel design

	Death Penalty	Static	Dynamic	Adaptive **	Our approach
Best	6171.813965	–	6162.862793	6242.527124	**6059.701610**
Mean	7429.709001	–	7042.828564	7241.953700	**6379.938037**
Worst	9763.333984	–	7798.198242	12142.707901	**6820.397461**
St. Dev	7.9E+2	–	5.3E+2	1.2E+3	2.1E+2

c) Ten./Comp. spring design

	Death Penalty	Static	Dynamic	Adaptive	Our approach
Best	0.012727	0.012716	0.012690	**0.012684**	0.012689
Mean	0.014870	0.014319	0.013589	0.013406	**0.013165**
Worst	0.018671	0.017603	0.016827	0.015420	**0.014078**
St. Dev	1.7E-3	1.4E-3	1.0E-3	7.5E-4	3.9E-4

d) Speed reducer design

	Death Penalty	Static	Dynamic	Adaptive	Our approach
Best	–	–	–	–	2996.348094
Mean	–	–	–	–	2996.348094
Worst	–	–	–	–	2996.348094
St. Dev	–	–	–	–	0

quality (best solution found) and robustness ("best" mean, worst and standard deviation values) in all problems. The only exception was problem 3, where the adaptive penalty approach found a slightly "better" best solution. In order to analyze the convergence behavior, in Figure 4 we show the convergence graph obtained by each penalty approach and by our approach as well, for the first three test problems (the speed reducer is omitted because none penalty approach reached the feasible region). Our approach (line with black points) seems to converge really fast to a promising area (before generation 50) and the remainder of the process, this solution is slightly improved (this is truth for the three graphs). On the other hand, for problem 1 (welded beam) and problem 2 (pressure vessel), the penalty approaches got trapped in local optima or had either a very irregular convergence or did not converge at all. Finally, in problem 3 (spring) the compared techniques had problems to reach promising areas at the beginning, and at the end, they could not reach equally good solutions as those found by our algorithm.

The overall results suggest that the proposed approach was able to provide a consistent performance, while the penalty-based approaches sometimes were competitive but in other cases, their results were poor. This is due to the fact that the penalty factors must be updated according to the problem to be solved, and our approach seems to be more stable using the same set of parameters for all test problems.

The statistical results of the second part of our experiments are summarized in Table 2, where we compared our obtained solutions against those provided by the Particle Swarm Optimizer of He et al. [5] and with respect to the Civilization simulation

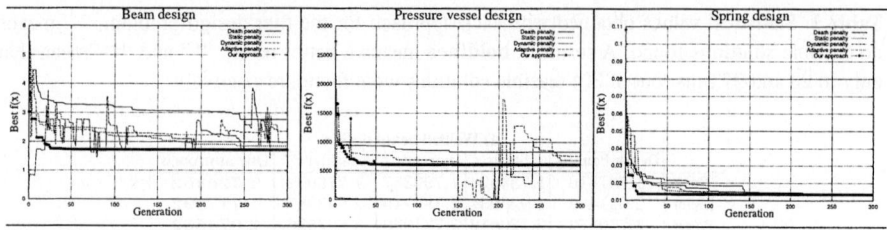

Fig. 4. Convergence graphs for three problems using the four penalty functions and our approach

Table 2. Comparison of results with respect to two state-of-the-art approaches. A result in **boldface** means a better result.

Problem	Stats	Ray & Liew [3]	He et al. [5]	Our approach
Welded beam	best	2.385435	2.380957	**1.724852**
	mean	3.255137	2.381932	**1.777692**
	St. Dev	9.6E-1	**5.2E-3**	8.8E-2
	evaluations	33000	**30000**	**30000**
Pressure vessel	best	6171.00	6059.7143	**6059.701610**
	mean	6335.05	**6289.92881**	6379.938037
	St. Dev	NA	3.1E+2	**2.1E+2**
	evaluations	**20000**	30000	30000
Ten/Comp. spring	best	0.012669	**0.012665**	0.012689
	mean	0.012923	**0.012702**	0.013165
	St. Dev	5.9E-4	**4.1E-5**	3.9E-4
	evaluations	25167	**15000**	30000
Speed reducer	best	**2994.744241**	NA	2996.348094
	mean	3001.758264	NA	**2996.348094**
	St. Dev	4.0E+0	NA	**0**
	evaluations	54456	NA	**30000**

of Ray & Liew [3]. The number of evaluations required by each approach is included. Also, in Table 3 we provide the details of the best solution found by each technique.

Based on the information in Table 2, our approach provided the best performance in problem 1 (beam design), "better" best, and mean result using a lower number of evaluations. For problem 2 (vessel design), none of the approaches was a clear winner. Ray's approach used the lowest number of evaluations of the objective function, the "best" mean value was provided by He's approach and our approach obtained the "best" best solution and the lowest standard deviation value. For problem 3 (spring design), He's approach was the most competitive. Finally, for problem 4 (speed reducer design), the best result was found by Ray's technique, but the most robust performance ("better" mean, worst and standard deviation value) and the lowest number of evaluations required was provided by our approach. He's results were not available for this problem.

From the details of the best solution found by each approach (Table 3) we emphasize the following: In the beam design problem, our approach was able to find a better result, which is located in the boundaries of the feasible region (see the values close to zero for constraints 1 and 7) and the compared approaches could not do that. For the vessel and the spring design problems, the results obtained by the compared algorithms are very similar. In the first case (vessel) our approach was able to provide the

Table 3. Details of the best solution found by each compared state-of-the-art technique

Welded	Problem 1		
beam	Ray & Liew [3]	He et al. [5]	Our approach
x_1	0.244438	0.244369	0.205730
x_2	6.237967	6.217520	3.470489
x_3	8.288576	8.291471	9.036624
x_4	0.244566	0.244369	0.205729
$g_1(x)$	−5760.110471	−5741.176933	0.000000
$g_2(x)$	−3.245428	0.000001	0.000002
$g_3(x)$	−0.000128	0.000000	0.000000
$g_4(x)$	−3.020055	−3.022955	−3.432984
$g_5(x)$	−0.119438	−0.119369	−0.080730
$g_6(x)$	−0.234237	−0.234241	−0.235540
$g_7(x)$	−13.079305	−0.000309	0.000001
f(x)	2.38119	2.380956	1.724852

Pressure	Problem 2		
vessel	Ray & Liew [3]	He et al. [5]	Our approach
x_1	0.8125	0.8125	0.8125
x_2	0.4375	0.4375	0.4375
x_3	41.9768	42.098446	42.098446
x_4	182.2845	176.636052	176.636596
$g_1(x)$	−0.0023	−0.000000	0.000000
$g_2(x)$	−0.0370	−0.035881	−0.035880
$g_3(x)$	−23420.5966	−0.000000	0.000000
$g_4(x)$	−57.7155	−63.363948	−63.363404
f(x)	6171.0	6059.701610	6059.7143

Ten./Comp.	Problem 3		
spring	Ray & Liew [3]	He et al. [5]	Our approach
x_1	0.0521602	0.051690	0.052836
x_2	0.368159	0.356750	0.384942
x_3	10.648442	11.287126	9.807729
$g_1(x)$	−0.000000	−0.000000	−0.000001
$g_2(x)$	−0.000000	0.000000	−0.000000
$g_3(x)$	−4.075805	−4.053827	−4.106146
$g_4(x)$	−0.719787	−0.727706	−0.708148
f(x)	0.012009	0.012065	0.012089

Speed	Problem 4	
reducer	Ray & Liew [3]	Our approach
x_1	3.500000	3.499999
x_2	0.700000	0.699999
x_3	17	17
x_4	7.327602	7.300000
x_5	7.715321	7.800000
x_6	3.350267	3.350215
x_7	5.286655	5.286683
$g_1(x)$	NA	−0.073915
$g_2(x)$	NA	−0.197998
$g_3(x)$	NA	−0.499172
$g_4(x)$	NA	−0.901472
$g_5(x)$	NA	−0.000000
$g_6(x)$	NA	−0.000000
$g_7(x)$	NA	−0.702500
$g_8(x)$	NA	0.000000
$g_9(x)$	NA	−0.583333
$g_{10}(x)$	NA	−0.051325
$g_{11}(x)$	NA	−0.010852
f(x)	2994.744241	2996.348094

best of them. However, for the second case (spring), our approach provided the worst of them. We argue that the approach requires (at least for this problem) more infeasible solutions in the population. This issue is part of our future work. For the last problem, our approach was able to explore the boundaries of the feasible region, but again, it did not find a better result than that found by Ray's technique. It is important to highlight that He's approach is designed to move only inside the feasible region of a given problem. Therefore, it requires a feasible initial population (which, for some problems could be very difficult to get). Ray's approach adds extra computational cost derived of clustering routines. On the other hand, our approach is based on a simple modification (to maintain the lowest infeasible solution in the population) to an EA and, therefore it is easy to implement. Besides, it does not add considerable extra computational cost. Furthermore, our approach does not require to have feasible solutions at the beginning.

We can conclude for this second part of the experiments that our approach is able to explore the boundaries of the feasible region as to reach very robust and "high" quality results. However, for some problems in some runs, the approach was trapped in local optima solutions.

5 Conclusions and Future Work

We have presented a novel approach to solve engineering design problems using evolutionary algorithms. The approach does not use a penalty function to handle constraints. Instead, it has a mechanism to allow the closest solutions to the feasible region located in promising areas of the search space to remain in the population. The selection is based on feasibility criteria and closeness to the feasible region. This mechanism does not add significant extra computational cost and it is very simple to implement. The approach was compared against penalty-function-based approaches and also against two state-of-the-art techniques providing a very competitive performance. Our future work consists on designing a mechanism to improve the local search capabilities of the approach in order to provide better results and also to apply it in the solution of dynamic/noisy optimization problems.

Acknowledgments. The first author acknowledges support from the Mexican Consejo Nacional de Ciencia y Tecnología (CONACyT) through a postdoctoral position at CINVESTAV-IPN's Electrical Engineering Department. The second author acknowledges support from (CONACyT) through project number 45683.

References

1. Michalewicz, Z., Fogel, D.B.: How to Solve It: Modern Heuristics. Springer (2004)
2. Miettinen, K., Makela, M., Toivanen, J.: Numerical comparison of some penalty-based constraint handling techniques in genetic algorithms. Journal of Global Optimization **27** (2003) 427–446
3. Ray, T., Liew, K.: Society and Civilization: An Optimization Algorithm Based on the Simulation of Social Behavior. IEEE Transactions on Evolutionary Computation **7** (2003) 386–396
4. Hernández-Aguirre, A., Botello-Rionda, S., Coello Coello, C.A.: PASSSS: An Implementation of a Novel Diversity Strategy for Handling Constraints. In: Proceedings of the Congress on Evolutionary Computation 2004 (CEC'2004). Volume 1., Piscataway, New Jersey, Portland, Oregon, USA, IEEE Service Center (2004) 403–410
5. He, S., Prempain, E., Q.H.Wu: An Improved Particle Swarm Optimizer for Mechanical Design Optimization Problems. Engineering Optimization **36** (2004) 585–605
6. Bäck, T.: Evolutionary Algorithms in Theory and Practice. Oxford University Press, New York (1996)
7. Schwefel, H.P.: Numerical Optimization of Computer Models. Wiley, England (1981)
8. Hoffmeister, F., Sprave, J.: Problem-independent handling of constraints by use of metric penalty functions. In Fogel, L.J., et al., eds.: Proceedings of the Fifth Annual Conference on Evolutionary Programming (EP'96), San Diego, California, The MIT Press (1996) 289–294
9. Joines, J., Houck, C.: On the use of non-stationary penalty functions to solve nonlinear constrained optimization problems with GAs. In Fogel, D., ed.: Proceedings of the first IEEE Conference on Evolutionary Computation, Orlando, Florida, IEEE Press (1994) 579–584
10. Hadj-Alouane, A.B., Bean, J.C.: A Genetic Algorithm for the Multiple-Choice Integer Program. Operations Research **45** (1997) 92–101
11. Mezura-Montes, E., Coello Coello, C.A.: Adding a Diversity Mechanism to a Simple Evolution Strategy to Solve Constrained Optimization Problems. In: Proceedings of the Congress on Evolutionary Computation 2003 (CEC'2003). Volume 1., Piscataway, New Jersey, Canberra, Australia, IEEE Service Center (2003) 6–13

Appendix

Full description of the four problems used in the experiments:

Problem 1: (Design of a Welded Beam) A welded beam is designed for minimum cost subject to constraints on shear stress (τ), bending stress in the beam (σ), buckling load on the bar (P_c), end deflection of the beam (δ), and side constraints. There are four design variables as shown in Figure 3a: h (x_1), l (x_2), t (x_3) and b (x_4). The problem can be stated as follows:

Minimize: $f(x) = 1.10471 x_1^2 x_2 + 0.04811 x_3 x_4 (14.0 + x_2)$

Subject to:

$g_1(x) = \tau(x) - \tau_{max} \leq 0 \quad g_2(x) = \sigma(x) - \sigma_{max} \leq 0 \quad g_3(x) = x_1 - x_4 \leq 0$
$g_4(x) = 0.10471 x_1^2 + 0.04811 x_3 x_4 (14.0 + x_2) - 5.0 \leq 0 \quad g_5(x) = 0.125 - x_1 \leq 0$
$g_6(x) = \delta(x) - \delta_{max} \leq 0 \quad g_7(x) = P - P_c(x) \leq 0$

where $\tau(x) = \sqrt{(\tau')^2 + 2\tau'\tau'' \frac{x_2}{2R} + (\tau'')^2} \quad \tau' = \frac{P}{\sqrt{2} x_1 x_2}, \tau'' = \frac{MR}{J}, M = P \left(L + \frac{x_2}{2} \right)$
$R = \sqrt{\frac{x_2^2}{4} + \left(\frac{x_1 + x_3}{2} \right)^2} \quad J = 2 \left\{ \sqrt{2} x_1 x_2 \left[\frac{x_2^2}{12} + \left(\frac{x_1 + x_3}{2} \right)^2 \right] \right\} \quad \sigma(x) = \frac{6PL}{x_4 x_3^2}, \delta(X) = \frac{4PL^3}{E x_3^3 x_4}$

$P_c(x) = \frac{4.013 E \sqrt{\frac{x_3^2 x_4^6}{36}}}{L^2} \left(1 - \frac{x_3}{2L} \sqrt{\frac{E}{4G}} \right) \quad P = 6000 \, lb, \quad L = 14 \, in, \quad E = 30 \times 10^6 \, psi, \quad G = 12 \times 10^6 \, psi \quad \tau_{max} = 13,600 \, psi, \quad \sigma_{max} = 30,000 \, psi, \quad \delta_{max} = 0.25 \, in$
where $0.1 \leq x_1 \leq 2.0, 0.1 \leq x_2 \leq 10.0, 0.1 \leq x_3 \leq 10.0$ y $0.1 \leq x_4 \leq 2.0$.

Problem 2: (Design of a Pressure Vessel) A cylindrical vessel is capped at both ends by hemispherical heads as shown in Figure 3b. The objective is to minimize the total cost, including the cost of the material, forming and welding. There are four design variables: T_s (thickness of the shell), T_h (thickness of the head), R (inner radius) and L (length of the cylindrical section of the vessel, not including the head). T_s and T_h are integer multiples of 0.0625 inch, which are the available thicknesses of rolled steel plates, and R and L are continuous. The problem can be stated as follows:

Minimize : $f(x) = 0.6224 x_1 x_3 x_4 + 1.7781 x_2 x_3^2 + 3.1661 x_1^2 x_4 + 19.84 x_1^2 x_3$

Subject to :

$g_1(x) = -x_1 + 0.0193 x_3 \leq 0 \quad g_2(x) = -x_2 + 0.00954 x_3 \leq 0$
$g_3(x) = -\pi x_3^2 x_4 - \frac{4}{3} \pi x_3^3 + 1,296,000 \leq 0 \quad g_4(x) = x_4 - 240 \leq 0$
where $1 \leq x_1 \leq 99, 1 \leq x_2 \leq 99, 10 \leq x_3 \leq 200$ y $10 \leq x_4 \leq 200$.

Problem 3: (Minimization of the Weight of a Tension/Compression String) This problem consists of minimizing the weight of a tension/compression spring (see Figure 3c) subject to constraints on minimum deflection, shear stress, surge frequency, limits on outside diameter and on design variables. The design variables are the mean coil diameter D (x_2), the wire diameter d (x_1) and the number of active coils N (x_3). Formally, the problem can be expressed as:

Minimize: $(N + 2)Dd^2$
Subject to:
$g_1(x) = 1 - \frac{D^3 N}{71785 d^4} \leq 0 \quad g_2(x) = \frac{4D^2 - dD}{12566(Dd^3 - d^4)} + \frac{1}{5108 d^2} - 1 \leq 0$
$g_3(x) = 1 - \frac{140.45 d}{D^2 N} \leq 0 \quad g_4(x) = \frac{D+d}{1.5} - 1 \leq 0$
where $0.05 \leq x_1 \leq 2, 0.25 \leq x_2 \leq 1.3$ y $2 \leq x_3 \leq 15$.

Problem 4: (Minimization of the Weight of a Speed Reducer) The weight of the speed reducer is to be minimized subject to constraints on bending stress of the gear teeth, surfaces stress, transverse deflections of the shafts and stresses in the shafts. The variables $x_1, x_2, \cdots, x_7$ are the face width, module of teeth, number of teeth in the pinion, length of the first shaft between bearings, length of the second shaft between bearings and the diameter of the first and second shafts. The third variable is integer, the rest of them are continuous.

Minimize : $f(x) = 0.7854 x_1 x_2^2 (3.3333 x_3^2 + 14.9334 x_3 - 43.0934) - 1.508 x_1 (x_6^2 + x_7^2) + 7.4777(x_6^3 + x_7^3) + 0.7854(x_4 x_6^2 + x_5 x_7^2)$

Subject to :

$g_1(x) = \frac{27}{x_1 x_2^2 x_3} - 1 \leq 0 \quad g_2(x) = \frac{397.5}{x_1 x_2^2 x_3^2} - 1 \leq 0 \quad g_3(x) = \frac{1.93 x_4^3}{x_2 x_3 x_6^4} - 1 \leq 0$

$g_4(x) = \frac{1.93 x_5^3}{x_2 x_3 x_7^4} - 1 \leq 0 \quad g_5(x) = \frac{\left(\left(\frac{745 x_4}{x_2 x_3} \right)^2 + 16.9 \times 10^6 \right)^{1/2}}{110.0 x_6^3} - 1 \leq 0$

$g_6(x) = \frac{\left(\left(\frac{745 x_5}{x_2 x_3} \right)^2 + 157.5 \times 10^6 \right)^{1/2}}{85.0 x_7^3} - 1 \leq 0 \quad g_7(x) = \frac{x_2 x_3}{40} - 1 \leq 0 \quad g_8(x) = \frac{5 x_2}{x_1} - 1 \leq 0$

$g_9(x) = \frac{x_1}{12 x_2} - 1 \leq 0 \quad g_{10}(x) = \frac{1.5 x_6 + 1.9}{x_4} - 1 \leq 0 \quad g_{11}(x) = \frac{1.1 x_7 + 1.9}{x_5} - 1 \leq 0$

where $2.6 \leq x_1 \leq 3.6, 0.7 \leq x_2 \leq 0.8, 17 \leq x_3 \leq 28, 7.3 \leq x_4 \leq 8.3, 7.8 \leq x_5 \leq 8.3, 2.9 \leq x_6 \leq 3.9$ and $5.0 \leq x_7 \leq 5.5$.

A Hybrid Self-adjusted Memetic Algorithm for Multi-objective Optimization

Xiuping Guo, Genke Yang, and Zhiming Wu

Department of Automation, Shanghai Jiaotong University,
Shanghai 200030, Shanghai, P.R. China
{gxp, gkyang, ziminwu}@sjtu.edu.cn

Abstract. A novel memetic algorithm for multi-objective optimization problems is proposed in this paper. The uniqueness of the method is that it hybridizes scalarizing selection with Pareto selection for exploitation and exploration. For extending the spread of solutions as quickly and fully as possible, the scalarizing functions defined by a wide diversified set of weights are used to go through all regions in objective space in the first phase at each generation. In the second phase, for intensifying search ability and achieving global exploration, a grid-based method is used to discover the gaps on existing tradeoff surface, and a fuzzy local perturbation is employed to reproduce additional "good" individuals in the missing areas. Both the exploitation and exploration are made dynamic and adaptive to online optimization conditions based on a function of progress ratio, ensuring better stability of the algorithm. Compared with several state-of-the-art approaches using the same set of multi-objective 0/1 knapsack problem instances, experiment results show that the proposed method perform better to some extent in terms of finding a near-Pareto front and well-extended nondominated set.

1 Introduction

The general multi-objective optimization (MOO) problem can be formulated as:

$$\begin{aligned}
\max \quad & \mathbf{y} = \mathbf{f}(\mathbf{x}) = \{f_1(\mathbf{x}), f_2(\mathbf{x}), ..., f_n(\mathbf{x})\} \\
\text{s.t.} \quad & g_c(\mathbf{x}) \leq 0 \quad c = 1, 2, ..., r \\
& \mathbf{x} = (x_1, x_2, ..., x_m) \in X
\end{aligned} \quad (1)$$

where solution $\mathbf{x}$ is a vector of decision variables, X is the space of feasible solutions, point $\mathbf{y}$ is objective vector of $\mathbf{x}$, and g_c is constraint.

For any two solutions $\mathbf{a}, \mathbf{b} \in X$, $\mathbf{a}$ is said to dominate $\mathbf{b}$ (written as $\mathbf{a} \succ \mathbf{b}$) iff

$$\forall i = \{1, 2, ..., n\} : f_i(\mathbf{a}) \geq f_i(\mathbf{b}) \quad \wedge \quad \exists i = \{1, 2, ..., n\} : f_i(\mathbf{a}) > f_i(\mathbf{b}) \ . \quad (2)$$

Point $\mathbf{f(a)}$ dominates point $\mathbf{f(b)}$ if $\mathbf{a} \succ \mathbf{b}$. A solution $\mathbf{x} \in X$ is called efficient if there is no $x' \in X$ that dominates $\mathbf{x}$. The set of all efficient solutions is called Pareto-optimal set. The image of the Pareto-optimal set is called Pareto front.

One way used to establish preference between solutions in MOO is scalarizing selection, in which all objectives are aggregated into a scalar value representing fitness. The weighted linear scalarizing function for doing this is defined as:
$$s(\mathbf{f},\lambda)=\sum_{i=1}^{n}\lambda_i f_i(\mathbf{x})\ .$$
where weight vector $\lambda=(\lambda_1,\lambda_2,...,\lambda_n)$ meets the condition: $\forall i\ \ \lambda_i \geq 0, \sum_{i=1}^{n}\lambda_i=1$.

Another alternative for the preference establishment is Pareto selection, in which a vector containing all objective values represents the fitness, and Pareto dominance is used to determine the reproduction probability of solutions.

The goal of MOO is two-sided [1], obtaining a diverse approximation as well as close to the optimal one. The implications of the two-sided goal on the notions of exploitation and exploration in multi-objective evolutionary algorithms (MOEAs) are exactly described in [1]. A competent exploitation scheme is crucial for finding diverse points near to the Pareto front as possible, and an effective exploration scheme is essential to intensify current solutions and produce new candidates from given solutions. These two phases can be split into two subprocedures aiding the search for proximity and diversity among solutions, as is an important issue that should be considered when building new MOEAs.

In the literature, various techniques have been devised to be the exploitation and exploration operators concurrently balance the diversity and proximity in MOEAs, including fitness sharing ([2]), crowding ([3],[4]), clustering ([5],[6]) and crowding-distance ([7]). Some multi-objective memetic algorithms also called genetic local search (MOGLS) that incorporate local search metaheuristics with evolutionary algorithms have been proposed recently to improve search ability of these methods. Studies in [8], [9], [10], [11] has demonstrated that the MOGLSs have high search capability to efficiently find near Pareto-optimal solutions. For example, the Pareto-based M-PAES [8] is implemented with an adaptive grid archiving technique used to achieve selection pressure and maintain solution diversity, and whether a mutant is accepted or rejected depends on the dominance relationship to the current solution and crowding degree of its grid location in the objective space. Comparatively, the diversity in the aggregation-based MOGLS [11] is ensured using variant weights, and the acceptance of a mutant relies on the scalarizing functions of it and a temporary elite population.

In this paper, we propose a hybrid self-adjusted multi-objective memetic algorithm (HSMOMA) that combines the scalarizing selection with Pareto selection aiming at: (1) Obtaining a global exploitation by using a simulated annealing to optimize the scalarizing functions defined by a wide diversified set of weights. (2) Enhancing the local search ability by genetic operations and achieving a broader exploration with a Pareto-based fuzzy incrementing strategy for perturbation. (3) Gaining better robustness for the HSMOMA via adaptively controlling the procedure based on the online feedback optimization progress ratio.

The rest of this paper is organized as follows. Section 2 describes the proposed method in detail. The computational experiments and comparisons with some prominent methods, M-PAES [8], SPEA2 [6], NSGA-II [7] and MOGLS [11], on the test instances are presented in Section 3. Section 4 offers conclusions.

2 HSMOMA

Two archives are needed in HSMOMA: the internal archive is functioned to hold nondominated solutions generated during local search, and the external archive is served to store all nondominated solutions found during optimization.

2.1 Exploitation in HSMOMA

The way to exploit global diversity in HSMOMA is straightforward: all regions in objective space are tried to be touched by optimizing the scalarizing functions defined by a set of uniform distributed weights with a simulated annealing (SA) in the first phase at each generation. Specially, the SA is not only controlled by initial temperature and cooling rate but is self-adjusted based on a progress ratio [12]. In this paper, the progress ratio pr at generation g is defined as:

$$pr(g) = \frac{|\{\mathbf{f(a)} \in nd(g); \exists \mathbf{f(b)} \in nd(g-1) : \mathbf{f(a)} \succ \mathbf{f(b)}\}|}{|nd(g)|} . \quad (3)$$

where $nd(g)$ and $nd(g-1)$ are the sets of total solutions stored in the external archive at generation g and $(g-1)$ respectively. The pr normally decreases gradually as the evolution proceeds, close to zero when approximation approaching to the Pareto front. This indicates high improvement rate at the initial stage and chromosome stagnation often occuring toward the final stage of evolution. For better improvement rate, it is desirable to tune the local search along the evolution, thus, the iterations number at each temperature in the SA is made self-adjusted based on pr, as shown in Fig.1, where "Bad ir" denotes the state with low improvement rate and "Good ir" denotes the state with high improvement rate. The iterations number $iter$ in generation g is fixed, determined as:

$$iter_g(pr) = \begin{cases} ubi, & 0 \leq pr \leq \alpha_1; \\ \frac{ubi-lbi}{\alpha_1-\alpha_2}[pr-\alpha_2] + lbi, & \alpha_1 < pr < \alpha_2; \\ lbi, & \alpha_2 \leq pr \leq 1. \end{cases} \quad (4)$$

where pr is the progress ratio at generation g, α_1 and α_2 are the boundaries of different states, ubi and lbi are the upper bound and lower bound of $iter$.

In order to ensure a stable progress ratio, the pr is taken in the study as the average pr value of the last l generations, i.e., $pr(g) = (1/l)\sum_{i=g+1-l}^{g} pr(i)$.

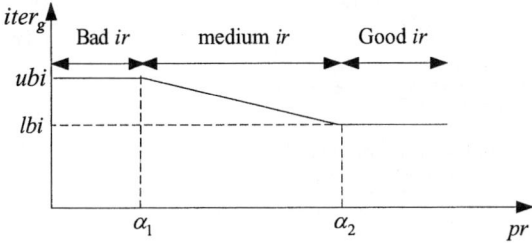

Fig. 1. Iterations number $iter_g$ at each temperature versus progress ratio pr

2.2 Exploration in HSMOMA

If diversity preserved only for maximizing approximation extent and selection pressure applied only for finding nondominated solutions, we increase the probability of obtaining discontinuous subsets of the Pareto-optimal set, thereby, an effective exploration operator should be combined with the exploitation to achieve better representation of the Pareto front. As a result, in the second phase at each generation, a Pareto-based fuzzy local perturbation (PFLP) is used for further exploration. As illustrated in Fig.2, PFLP works by dividing n dimensional objective space occupied by the points in the external archives into $G_1 \times G_2 \times \cdots \times G_n$ grids, where $G_k(k=1,2,...n)$ represents the grids number in the kth objective dimension (e.g. in Fig.2, $G_1=G_2=4$). The location of an individual in the grids is found in the way as used in [13]. The density $D(gr)$ of a grid region is defined as the number of individuals dwelling in it. The parents selected from a density-based tournament selection are perturbed to generate incrementing individuals, i.e. the parents located in the less crowded regions have higher probability to be perturbed as compared to those located in the more crowded regions. Each selected parent is perturbed with an extension of mutation, in which more than one child are produced per parent. For increasing the perturbation probability within the parents' neighborhood rather than outside the neighborhood, a solution is encoded as an m-digit chromosome $\mathbf{x}=\{x_i:i=1,2,...,n\}$, where i is coding index, $i=1$ denoting the most significant index and $i=n$ representing the least significant index of the chromosome. Perturbation probability p_i ($i=1,2,...,n;\ n>1$) for gene x_i of $\mathbf{x}$ is determined by a sigmoid function [12]:

$$p_i = \begin{cases} b[2(\frac{i-1}{n-1})^2 + a], & 0 \leq i \leq \eta; \\ b[1 - 2(\frac{i-n}{n-1})^2 + a], & \eta < i \leq n. \end{cases} \quad (5)$$

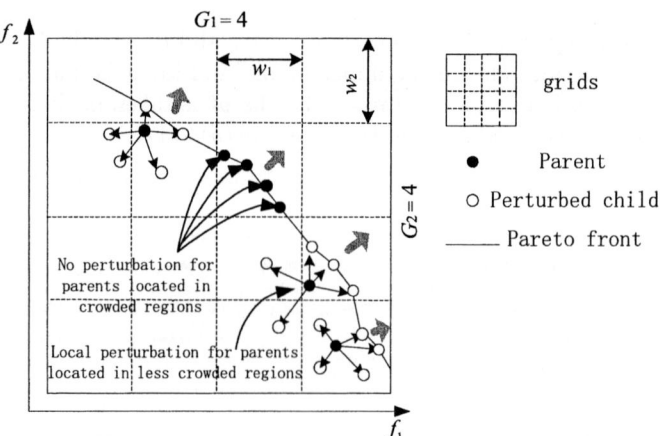

Fig. 2. Exploration for nondominated parents located in the less crowded regions

where a and b are coefficients, ab and $(ab+b)$ are the lower and upper bounds of p_i respectively, η is set as $\lceil n/2 \rceil$ in the study. As given in (5), the more significant a gene in a chromosome, the lower its perturbation probability in PFLP.

The number np of perturbations per individual in PFLP is also self-adjusted based on the online progress ratio and calculated in the same way as in [12], i.e.

$$np_g(pr) = \begin{cases} (ubnp - lbnp)[1 - 2(\frac{pr}{g})^2 + \frac{lbnp}{ubnp - lbnp}], & 0 \leq pr \leq \alpha; \\ (ubnp - lbnp)[2(\frac{pr-g}{g})^2 + \frac{lbnp}{ubnp - lbnp}], & \alpha < pr \leq 1. \end{cases} \quad (6)$$

where pr is the progress ratio at generation g, α is a satisfactory level for the pr, $ubnp$ and $lbnp$ are respectively the upper bound and lower bound of np.

2.3 Program Implementation of HSMOMA

Based on the presentation above, HSMOMA can be depicted as in Fig.3 as an feedback control scheme. The pseudocode of HSMOMA is presented as below:

1: **Initialization**
2:     Generate randomly initial population Pop of solutions
3:     Set internal archive IA and external archive EA empty: $IA \leftarrow \phi$, $EA \leftarrow \phi$
4:     Put all nondominated individuals of Pop into EA
5: **Repeat** //main loop
6:     Calculate $iter(pr)$ and $np(pr)$ at current generation g
7:     **Step 1:** Exploitation phase
8:       **For**(each individual $\mathbf{x} \in Pop$)
9:         Set IA empty and put $\mathbf{x}$ into IA: $IA \leftarrow \phi$, $IA \leftarrow IA \cup \mathbf{x}$
10:        Draw at random a scalarizing function s
11:        Optimize s using procedure SA($\mathbf{x}$,s,$iter(pr)$), returning the improved
12:           solution $\mathbf{x}'$ back to Pop
13:        Update EA with IA: $EA \leftarrow EA \cup IA$ //filtering the dominated solutions
14:     **Step 2:** Recombination phase using dominance
15:       Set tempt population $tPop$ empty: $tPop \leftarrow \phi$, $n=0$
16:       **Do**
17:         Set recombination trails $r=0$
18:         **Do**
19:           Draw at random two solutions $\mathbf{x}_1$ and $\mathbf{x}_2$ from population $Pop \cup EA$
20:           Crossover $\mathbf{x}_1$ and $\mathbf{x}_2$ obtaining $\mathbf{x}_3$, and mutate $\mathbf{x}_3$ forming child $\mathbf{x}_3'$

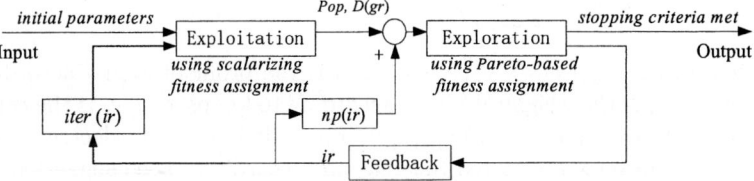

Fig. 3. Adaptive feedback control scheme for HSMOMA

21:             Compare x_3' with the solutions in EA and update EA if necessary
22:             r++
23:         **While**((x_3' is dominated by EA) and (r<MaxRecombinationTrails))
24:         **If**(x_3' is dominated by EA) {Reject x_3' and use density-based
25:             tournament to select a new offspring x_3' from EA}
26:         Place x_3' into tempt population tPop, n++
27:     **While**(n<popsize)
28:     Update population: Pop←tPop
29:     **Step 3:** Exploration phase using dominance
30:     Use density-based tournament to select population perPop from EA for
31:         perturbation
32:     Perform PFLP for each individual y∈perPop obtaining nondominated
33:         population rPop and updating EA if necessary
34:     Update Pop with rPop forming new generation
35: **Until**(stopping condition is met)

The pseudocode of local optimizer SA(**x**,s,iter(pr)) is described as below:

1: **Repeat**
2:     Set temperature: T_k←T_0, k←0
3:     **Do**
4:         Mutate **x** to generate a feasible neighbor solution **x**$'$
5:         **If**($\triangle s=\sum_{i=1}^{n}\lambda_i(f_i(\mathbf{x})-f_i(\mathbf{x}'))\leq 0$)
6:             {Accept **x**$'$ (**x**←**x**$'$) and update IA with **x**$'$}
7:         **Else If**(exp(-$\triangle s/T_k$)>rand[0,1)) {Accept **x**$'$ (**x**←**x**$'$)}
8:         k++
9:     **While**(k<iter(pr))
10:    Update temperature: T_{k+1}←γT_k //γ is cooling rate
11: **Until**(stopping condition is met)

3 Computational Experiments

3.1 Test Problems and Parameter Settings

The multi-objective 0/1 knapsack problems (MOKPs) used in [5] are tested in the study. The problem with n knapsacks and m items is formulated as:

$$\max \quad \mathbf{f}(\mathbf{x}) = \{f_1(\mathbf{x}), f_2(\mathbf{x}), ..., f_n(\mathbf{x})\}$$
$$\text{s.t.} \quad \sum_{j=1}^{m} w_{i,j} \cdot x_j \leq c_i, \quad i=1,2,...,n \ . \tag{7}$$

where $\forall i=1,2,...,n$: $f_i(\mathbf{x})=\sum_{j=1}^{m}p_{i,j}\cdot x_j$, $p_{i,j}$ is the profit of item j according to knapsack i, $w_{i,j}$ is the weight of item j according to knapsack i, c_i is the capacity of knapsack i, $\mathbf{x}=(x_1,x_2,...,x_m)\in\{0,1\}^m$, $x_j=1$ iff item j is selected, and the elements of solution **x** are sorted (decreasing) according to the suggested ratio:

$$\frac{1}{n}\sum_{i=1}^{n}\{\frac{p_{i,j}}{w_{i,j}}\}, j=1,2,...,m \ .$$

Table 1. Parameter values in our computational experiments

Instance	Initial population size		Function evaluations number		Time(sec)	
	HSMOMA	M-PAES	HSMOMA	M-PAES	HSMOMA	M-PAES
2-250	10	150	5213476	5323947	19	162
2-500	10	200	7178447	7071081	56	429
2-750	10	250	8963922	8837030	86	859
3-250	15	200	12412679	9090030	58	760
3-500	15	250	15044851	8738358	155	843
3-750	15	300	15126032	10810136	186	1590
4-250	20	250	16570223	7314780	243	1040
4-500	20	300	18454584	7796991	299	2047
4-750	20	350	20258234	5877791	522	2798

i.e. an infeasible solutions is repaired by dropping items from the solution in increasing order of the average profit/weight ratio over all knapsacks.

The tested MOKP instances (containing 2, 3 and 4 knapsacks and 250, 500, and 750 items) and the approximations generated by SPEA, SPEA2 and NSGA-II are available on the web-site[1]. The results of SPEA2 and NSGA-II are available only for instances with 750 items. The results of MOGLS [11] to the same set of instances are available on the web-site[2].

The results of M-PAES are generated here with the same parameter values as set in [8]. All computational experiments were performed on a notebook with Celeron(R) CPU 2.40 GHz and 512 M memory. HSMOMA was implemented in C++ builder, running 30 times with different random seeds on each instance for 10 generations. Some parameter values for each instance in our experiments are summarized in Table 1, which are described the initial population size, total function evaluations number and the average computational time, in second (sec), consumed by HSMOMA and M-PAES at the last two columns respectively.

One point crossover is used and mutation rate was set as $4/L$ (where L is the bits number in the chromosome) for each instance, but the mutation rate is $1/L$ in GBLP in HSMOMA. An intensive experiment was performed in order to find good combination of parameters, and the other parameters in HSMOMA for each instance were set as follows: $\alpha_1=0.01$, $\alpha_2=0.9$, $900 \leq lbi < ubi \leq 1100$, $l=3$, $ab=0.03$, $ab+b=0.83$, $\alpha=0.5$, $10 \leq lbnp < ubnp \leq 50$, the grids number G_i ($i=1,2,...,n$) for each problem are set as the same values as in M-PAES, and the parameters in the local searcher SA were chosen as: $T_0=0.0001$, $T_{end}=0.000001$ and $\gamma=0.95$.

3.2 Results Comparison

One metric used here is coverage $\tilde{C}$ [14] measuring two sets to the Pareto front:

$$\tilde{C}(A, B) = \frac{|\{\mathbf{f}(\mathbf{b}') \in B; \exists \mathbf{f}(\mathbf{a}') \in A : \mathbf{f}(\mathbf{a}') \succ \mathbf{f}(\mathbf{b}')\}|}{|B|} . \tag{8}$$

---

[1] http://www.tik.ee.ethz.ch/~ziztler/testdata.html
[2] http://www-idss.cs.put.poznan.pl/~jaszkiewicz/mokp

where A and B are two approximations. The value $\tilde{C}$ is in the interval [0,1]. In general, $\tilde{C}(A,B)\neq\tilde{C}(B,A)$, both should be considered independently.

Another metric is front spread FS [15] used for measuring the overall size of the objective space covered by an approximation. The higher the FS, the better the diversity. Let approximation A is the image of the nondominated solutions set S for n-objective problem. The FS for A is defined as:

$$FS(A) = \sqrt{\sum_{i=1}^{n} \max_{(\mathbf{x}^0,\mathbf{x}^1)\in S\times S}\{(f_i(\mathbf{x}^0) - f_i(\mathbf{x}^1))^2\}} \ . \tag{9}$$

where $f_i(\mathbf{x}^0)$ and $f_i(\mathbf{x}^1)$ are the objective values of solutions $\mathbf{x}^0$ and $\mathbf{x}^1$.

The empirical results are reported in Table 2 and 3, where each record is the average value over 30 runs. The comparison based on coverage metric is presented in Table 2, where a pair of numbers [a,b] indicates respectively the coverage values of $\tilde{C}(A,B)$ and $\tilde{C}(B,A)$, here A is HSMOMA and B is the given method. We can see from Table 2, for all instances, the HSMOMA fronts dominate a large part of the MOGLS fronts, while the MOGLS approximations dominate only a small portion of the points produced by HSMOMA. Compared with M-PAES, HSMOMA outperforms it for most of the instances according to $\tilde{C}$ metric, especially for instances with 3 and 4 objectives. In terms of Pareto optimality, HSMOMA is obviously better than SPEA2 and NSGA-II for instances with 750 items, and the coverage rates are equal to 100% for 2 and 4 knapsacks.

The average FS values are reported in Table 3. This table shows that the MOGLS tradeoff fronts with the widest spread compared to the other given algorithms. Whereas, HSMOMA is able to achieve larger FS values than MOGLS if the repair algorithm used in MOGLS for the MOKPs is employed in it, but this is at the cost of computational time. Compared with Pareto-based M-PAES, SPEA2 and NSGA-II, Table 3 presents the proposed algorithm obtains the approximations with evidently larger FS values, as means that it tends to extend the tradeoff surfaces to the new areas in objective space.

Fig.4 (a) and (b) present the fronts generated by given algorithms for instance 2-750. Clearly, the HSMOMA front are closer to the Pareto front compared to

Table 2. Coverage metric comparison of HSMOMA and other particular algorithms

Instance	MOGLS	M-PAES	SPEA2	NSGA-II
2-250	[0.76,0.09]	[0.41,0.43]	-	-
2-500	[0.79,0.06]	[1,0]	-	-
2-750	[0.84,0.05]	[0.31,0.48]	[1,0]	[1,0]
3-250	[0.78,0.07]	[0.69,0.02]	-	-
3-500	[0.81,0.01]	[0.92,0]	-	-
3-750	[0.66,0]	[0.96,0]	[0.9,0]	[0.98,0]
4-250	[0.89,0]	[0.94,0]	-	-
4-500	[0.85,0]	[1,0]	-	-
4-750	[0.65,0.01]	[1,0]	[1,0]	[1,0]

Table 3. Front spread metric comparison of HSMOMA and other particular algorithms

Instance	MOGLS	HAMOMA	M-PAES	SPEA2	NSGA-II
2-250	3465	3344	2546	-	-
2-500	5346	4490	4130	-	-
2-750	8935	8351	5796	4220	2897
3-250	4437	4089	3074	-	-
3-500	7763	7461	5332	-	-
3-750	11260	10565	4826	5796	6119
4-250	4857	4818	2680	-	-
4-500	8282	8049	4439	-	-
4-750	13498	13162	5261	8549	9982

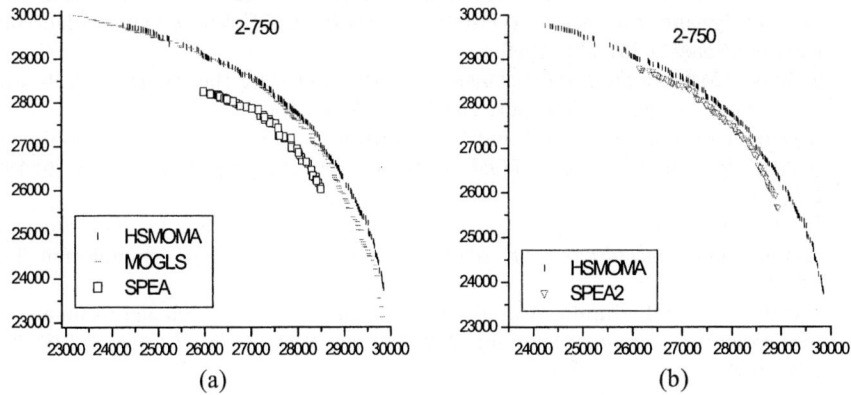

Fig. 4. Approximations obtained by particular algorithms

the approximations obtained by the other methods. Besides, Fig. 4 shows that HSMOMA performs better than the Pareto-based MOEAs in the sense of the diversity because its tradeoff surface covers larger region in the objective space.

4 Conclusions

A hybrid self-adjusted multi-objective memetic algorithm for MOO, HSMOMA, was described. It uses a local search method of simulated annealing, and combines it with the use of a population, crossover, mutation and perturbation. Scalarizing functions and Pareto dominance are employed in HSMOMA for global exploitation and exploration. Furthermore, the procedure is self-adjusted to the progress ratio for obtaining better reliability of the algorithm. The utility of HSMOMA was verified on a set of nine MOKPs. Compared with the algorithms MOGLS [11], M-PAES [8], SPEA2 [6], NSGA-II [7] on these problems, the computational results show that HSMOMA appears to be superior on the Pareto optimality, and outperforms the given Pareto-based MOEAs in terms of finding more diversified solutions.

References

1. P.A.N.Bosman and D.Thierens. The balance between proximity and diversity in multiobjective evolutionary algorithms. *IEEE Trans. on Evolutionary Computation.*,(7):174-188, 2003.
2. N.Srivivas and K.Deb. Multiobjective optimization using nondominated sorting in genetic algorithms. *Evolutionary Computation.*,(2):221-248, 1995.
3. J.D.Knowles and D.W.Corne. The Pareto archived evolution strategy: a new baseline algorithm for Pareto multiobjective optimization. *Proceedings of the 1999 Congress on Evolutionary Computation.*, 98-105, 1999.
4. Shu Min Yang, Dong Guo Shao and Yang Jie Luo. A novel evolution strategy for multiobjective optimization problem. *Applied Mathematics and Computation.*, 1-24, 2005.
5. E.Zitzler and L.Thiele. Multiobjective evolutionary algorithms: a comparative case study and the strength Pareto approach. *IEEE Trans. on Evolutionary Computation.*,(3):257-271, 1999.
6. E.Zitzler, M.Laumanns and L.Thiele. SPEA2: Improving the strength pareto evolutionary algorithm. *TIK-Report 103,Switxerland.*, 2001.
7. K.Deb, A.Pratap, S.Agarwal and T.Meyarivan. A fast and elitist multiobjective genetic algorithm: NSGA-II. *IEEE Trans. on Evolutionary Computation.*,(6):182-197, 2002.
8. J.D.Knowles and D.W.Corne. M-PAES: a memetic algorithm for multiobjective optimization. *Proceedings of the 2000 Congress on Evolutionary Computation.*,325-332, 2000.
9. H.Ishibuchi and T.Murata. A multi-objective genetic local search algorithm and its application to flowshop scheduling. *IEEE Trans. Syst., Man. & Cybern.*, (28):392-403, 1998.
10. H.Ishibuchi, T.Yoshida and T.Murata. Balance between genetic search and local search in memetic algorithms for multiobjective permutation flowshop scheduling. *IEEE Trans. on Evolutionary Computation.*, (7):204-223, 2003.
11. A.Jaszkiewicz. Genetic local search for multiple objective combinatorial optimization. *European J. of Oper. Res.*, (137):50-71, 2002.
12. K.C.Tan, T.H.Lee and E.F.Khor. Evolutionary algorithms with dynamic population size and local exploration for multiobjective optimization. *IEEE Trans. on Evolutionary Computation.*,(5): 565-588, 2001.
13. G.G.Yen and L.Haiming. Dynamic multiobjective evolutionary algorithm: adaptive cell-based rank and density estimation. *IEEE Trans. on Evolutionary Computation.*, (7):253-274, 2003.
14. J.E.Fieldsend, R.M.Everson and S.Singh. Using unconstrained elite archives for multiobjective optimization. *IEEE Trans. on Evolutionary Computation.*, (7):305-323, 2003.
15. E.Zitzler. Evolutionary algorithms for multiobjective optimization: Methods and applications. *Ph.D. dissertation, Swiss Federal Inst. Of Technol. (ETH), Zurich, Switzerland.*, 1999.

Evolutionary Multiobjective Optimization Approach for Evolving Ensemble of Intelligent Paradigms for Stock Market Modeling

Ajith Abraham[1], Crina Grosan[2], Sang Yong Han[1], and Alexander Gelbukh[3]

[1] School of Computer Science and Engineering, Chung-Ang University, Seoul 156-756, Korea
[2] Department of Computer Science, Babeş-Bolyai University, Cluj-Napoca, 3400, Romania
[3] Centro de Investigacin en Computacin (CIC), Instituto Politcnico Nacional (IPN), Mexico
ajith.abraham@ieee.org, cgrosan@cs.ubbcluj.ro,
hansy@cau.ac.kr, gelbukh@gelbukh.com

Abstract. The use of intelligent systems for stock market predictions has been widely established. This paper introduces a genetic programming technique (called Multi-Expression programming) for the prediction of two stock indices. The performance is then compared with an artificial neural network trained using Levenberg-Marquardt algorithm, support vector machine, Takagi-Sugeno neuro-fuzzy model and a difference boosting neural network. As evident from the empirical results, none of the five considered techniques could find an optimal solution for all the four performance measures. Further the results obtained by these five techniques are combined using an ensemble and two well known Evolutionary Multiobjective Optimization (EMO) algorithms namely Nondominated Sorting Genetic Algorithm II (NSGA II) and Pareto Archive Evolution Strategy (PAES)algorithms in order to obtain an optimal ensemble combination which could also optimize the four different performance measures (objectives). We considered Nasdaq-100 index of Nasdaq Stock Market and the S&P CNX NIFTY stock index as test data. Empirical results reveal that the resulting ensemble obtain the best results.

1 Introduction

Prediction of stocks is generally believed to be a very difficult task. The process behaves more like a random walk process and time varying [20],[5]. The obvious complexity of the problem paves way for the importance of intelligent prediction paradigms [21], [6]. During the last decade, stocks and futures traders have come to rely upon various types of intelligent systems to make trading decisions [1], [2],[4],[17],[13] . In this paper, we first perform a comparison between five different intelligent paradigms. Two well-known stock indices namely Nasdaq-100 index of Nasdaq^{SM} [11] and the S&P CNX NIFTY stock index [12] are used in experiments. Nasdaq-100 index reflects Nasdaq's largest companies across major industry groups, including computer hardware and software, telecommunications, retail/wholesale trade and biotechnology. The Nasdaq-100 index is a modified capitalization-weighted index, which is designed to limit domination of the index by a few large stocks while generally retaining the capitalization ranking of companies. Similarly, S&P CNX NIFTY is a well-diversified 50 stock index accounting for 25 sectors of the economy [12]. It is used for a variety of purposes such as benchmarking fund portfolios, index based derivatives and index funds. The CNX Indices are computed using market capitalization weighted method, wherein the level of the Index reflects the total market value of all the stocks in the index relative to a particular base period.

Our research is to investigate the behavior of five different techniques for modeling the Nasdaq-100 and NIFTY stock market indices so as to optimize the performance indices (different error measures and correlation coefficient) and also to find an ensemble combination of these techniques in order to further optimize the performance. The five techniques used in the experiments are: an artificial neural network trained using the Levenberg-Marquardt algorithm, support vector machine [18], difference boosting neural network [16], a Takagi-Sugeno fuzzy inference system learned using a neural network algorithm (neuro-fuzzy model) [7] and Multi-Expression Programming (MEP) [14], [15]. In order to find an optimal combination of these paradigms, the task is to evolve five coefficients (one for each technique)so as to optimize the four performance measures (objectives) namely Root Mean Squared Error (RMSE), Correlation Coefficient (CC), Maximum Absolute Percentage Error (MAP) and Mean Absolute Percentage Error (MAPE). For this purpose, the problem is formulated as a multiobjective optimization problem using NSGA II and PAES. Results obtained by the evolved ensemble are compared with the results obtained by the five techniques.

We analyzed the Nasdaq-100 index value from 11 January 1995 to 11 January 2002 and the NIFTY index from 01 January 1998 to 03 December 2001. For both the indices, we divided the entire data into almost two equal parts. In section 2, we formulate the evolutionary multiobjective approach for the ensemble design followed by experimentation setup and results in Section 3. Some conclusions are also provided towards the end.

2 Evolutionary Multiobjective Optimization Approach for Constructing Ensemble of Intelligent Paradigms

The goal is to optimize several error measures: Root Mean Squared Error (RMSE), Correlation Coefficient (CC), Maximum Absolute Percentage Error (MAP) and Mean Absolute Percentage Error (MAPE):

$$RMSE = \sqrt{\sum_{i=1}^{N} |P_{actual,i} - P_{predicted,i}|},$$

$$CC = \frac{\sum_{i=1}^{N} P_{predicted,i}}{\sum_{i=1}^{N} P_{actual,i}},$$

$$MAP = \max\left(\frac{|P_{actual,\,i} - P_{predicted,\,i}|}{P_{predicted,\,i}} \times 100\right),$$

$$MAPE = \frac{1}{N} \sum_{i=1}^{N} \left[\frac{|P_{actual,\,i} - P_{predicted,\,i}|}{P_{actual,\,i}}\right] \times 100,$$

where $P_{actual,i}$ is the actual index value on day i, $P_{predicted,i}$ is the forecast value of the index on that day and N = total number of days. The task is to have minimal values of RMSE, MAP and MAPE and a maximum value for CC. The objective is to carefully ensemble the different intelligent paradigms to achieve the best generalization performance. Test data is then passed through these individual models and the corresponding outputs are recorded. Suppose the daily index value predicted by DBNN, SVM, NF, ANN and MEP are a_n, b_n, c_n, d_n and e_n respectively and the corresponding desired value is x_n. The task is to combine a_n, b_n, c_n, d_n and e_n so as to get the best output value that maximizes the CC and minimizes the RMSE, MAP and MAPE values.

2.1 Ensemble Approach

Evolve a set of five coefficients (one for each technique) in order to obtain a linear combination between these techniques so as to optimize the values of RMSE, CC, MAP and MAPE. We consider this problem as a multiobjective optimization problem in which we want to find solution of this form: ($coef_1$, $coef_2$, $coef_3$, $coef_4$, $coef_5$), where $coef_1, \ldots, coef_5$ are real numbers between -1 and 1, so as the resulting combination:

$$coef_1{}^*a_n + coef_2{}^*b_n + coef_3{}^*c_n + coef_4{}^*d_n + coef_5{}^*e_n$$

would be close to the desired value x_n. This means, in fact, to find a solution (an array of five real numbers) so as to simultaneously optimize RMSE, CC, MAP and MAPE. This problem is equivalent to finding the Pareto solutions of a multiobjective optimization problem (objectives being RMSE, CC, MAP and MAPE). We used the two very known Multiobjective Evolutionary Algorithm (MOEA): NSGA II and PAES. For a detailed description of these techniques please refer to [3] for NSGA II and [8], [9]and [10] for PAES.

3 Experiment Results

We considered 7 year's month's stock data for Nasdaq-100 Index and 4 year's for NIFTY index. Our target is to develop efficient forecast models that could predict the index value of the following trade day based on the opening, closing and maximum values of the same on a given day. For the Nasdaq-100index the data sets were represented by the 'opening value', 'low value' and 'high value'. NIFTY index data sets were represented by 'opening value', 'low value', 'high value' and 'closing value'. The assessment of the prediction performance of the different paradigms and the ensemble method were done by quantifying the prediction obtained on an independent data set.

3.1 Parameter Settings

We used a feed forward neural network with 4 input nodes and a single hidden layer consisting of 26 neurons. We used tanh-sigmoidal activation function for the hidden neurons. The training using LM algorithm was terminated after 50 epochs and it took about 4 seconds to train each dataset. For the neuro-fuzzy system, we used 3 triangular membership functions for each of the input variable and the 27 *if-then* fuzzy rules were learned for the Nasdaq-100 index and 81 *if-then* fuzzy rules for the NIFTY index. Training was terminated after 12 epochs and it took about 3 seconds to train each dataset. Both SVM (Gaussian kernel with $\gamma = 3$) and DBNN took less than one second to learn the two data sets [2]. Parameters used by MEP are presented in Table 1.

Table 1. MEP parameter settings

Parameter		Value
Population size	Nasdaq	100
	Nifty	50
Number of iterations	Nasdaq	60
	Nifty	100
Chromosome length	Nasdaq	30
	Nifty	40
Crossover Probability		0.9
Functions set		+, - , *, /, sin, cos, sqrt, ln, lg, log2, min, max, abs

3.2 Ensemble Design Using MOEA

MOEAs Parameter Settings. The main parameters used in the experiments by the evolutionary algorithms (ensemble) are presented in Table 2.

Both NSGA II and PAES use a binary representation of solutions.

Table 2. Parameters used by NSGA II and PAES

Parameter	Value
Population size /Archive size	250
Number of function evaluations	125,000
Chromosome lenght	30

Results Analysis and Discussions. Table 3 summarizes the results achieved for the two stock indices using the five intelligent paradigms (SVM, NF, ANN, DBNN, MEP) and the ensemble approach using NSGA II and PAES. Using the MOEA- ensemble approach, we obtained a population of feasible solutions. In Table 3, we present one of the solutions from the final population obtained by NSGA II and from the archive obtained by PAES respectively.

Table 3. Performance comparison of the results obtained by the intelligent paradigms and MOEAs (NSGA II and PAES)

	SVM	NF	ANN	DBNN	MEP	NSGA II	PAES
Test results - NASDAQ							
RMSE	0.0180	0.0183	0.0284	0.0286	0.021	0.01612	0.01614
CC	0.9977	0.9976	0.9955	0.9940	0.999	0.9994	0.998
MAP	481.50	520.84	481.71	116.98	96.39	94.989	94.976
MAPE	7.170	7.615	9.032	9.429	14.33	10.559	10.542
TEST results – NIFTY							
RMSE	0.0149	0.0127	0.0122	0.0225	0.0163	0.01317	0.01319
CC	0.9968	0.9967	0.9968	0.9890	0.997	0.999	0.999
MAP	72.53	40.37	73.94	37.99	31.7	28.50	29.75
MAPE	4.416	3.320	3.353	5.086	3.72	2.933	2.910

The ensemble obtained using NSGA II for Nasdaq is:
$0.245357 * b_n + 0.77028 * c_n + 0.000978 * d_n + 0.00097 * e_n$.
The ensemble obtained using PAES for Nasdaq is:
$0.016756 * a_n + 0.242174 * b_n + 0.749939 * c_n + 0.0016604 * d_n + 0.0005028 * e_n$
The ensemble obtained using NSGA II for Nifty is:
$0.276637 * a_n + 0.220919 * b_n + 0.520039 * c_n + 0.642229 * d_n + 0.032258 * e_n$
The ensemble obtained using PAES for Nifty is:
$0.0700763 * a_n - 0.05659 * b_n + 0.4931 * c_n + 0.1541 * d_n + 0.3338 * e_n$

The best result for Nasdaq, obtained by ensemble using NSGA II for RMSE is 0.01611. The other results are: CC = 0.999, MAP = 94.99, MAPE = 10.56

The best result for Nasdaq, obtained by ensemble using NSGA II for MAP is 94.32. The other results are: RMSE = 0.0323, CC = 0.931, MAPE = 12.80

The best result for Nasdaq, obtained by ensemble using NSGA II for MAPE is 10.417. The other results are: RMSE = 0.0171, CC = 0.993, MAP = 94.68

The best result for Nasdaq, obtained by ensemble using PAES for RMSE is 0.01611. The other results are: CC = 0.999, MAP = 95.009, MAPE = 10.58

The best result for Nasdaq, obtained by ensemble using PAES for MAP is 94.49. The other results are: RMSE = 0.0538, CC = 0.877, MAPE = 17.45

The best result for Nasdaq, obtained by ensemble using PAES for MAPE is 10.51. The other results are: RMSE = 0.0163, CC = 0.995, MAP = 94.94

The best result for Nifty, obtained by ensemble using NSGA II for RMSE is 0.01245. The other results are: CC = 0.999, MAP = 45.39, MAPE = 2.81

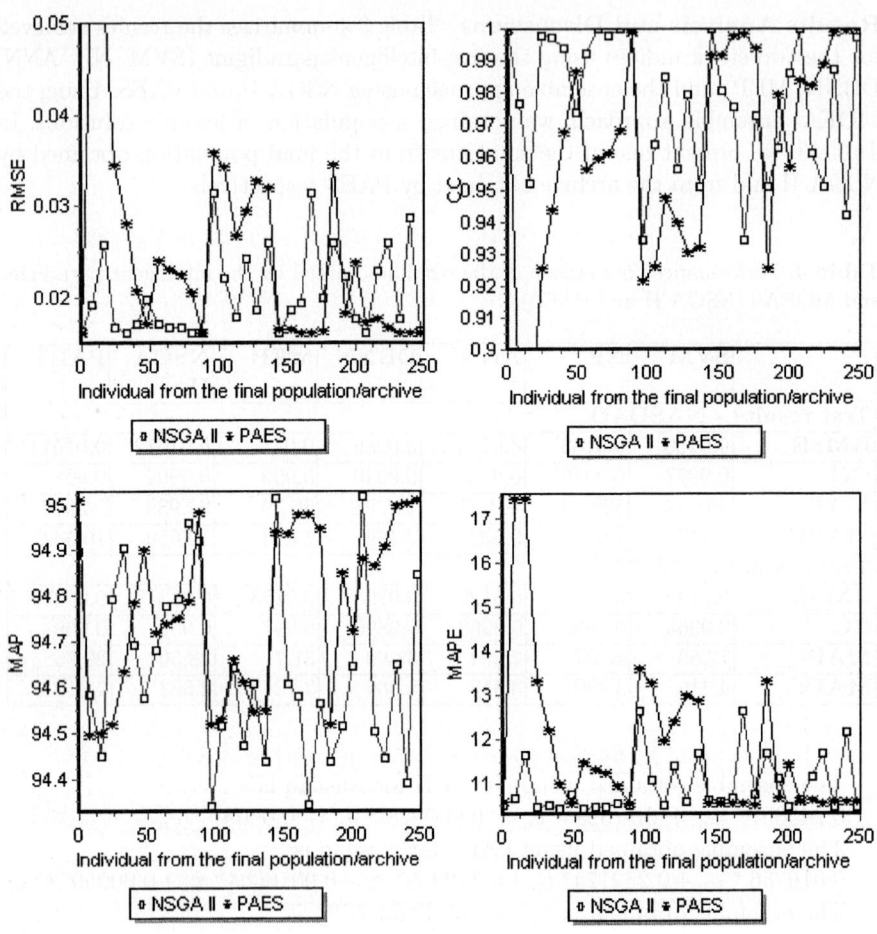

Fig. 1. Values obtained by NSGA II and PAES for RMSE, CC, MAP and MAPE for Nasdaq test data

The best result for Nifty, obtained by ensemble using NSGA II for MAP is 24.54. The other results are: RMSE = 0.0283, CC = 0.952, MAPE = 6.49

The best result for Nifty, obtained by ensemble using NSGA II for MAPE is 2.770. The other results are: RMSE = 0.0127, CC = 0.994, MAP = 45.86

The best result for Nifty, obtained by ensemble using PAES for RMSE is 0.01256. The other results are: CC = 0.999, MAP = 34.806, MAPE = 2.824

The best result for Nifty, obtained by ensemble using PAES for MAP is 24.28. The other results are: RMSE = 0.02159, CC = 0.970, MAPE = 4.94

The best result for Nifty, obtained by ensemble using PAES for MAPE is 2.780. The other results are: RMSE = 0.01266, CC = 0.997, MAP = 35.47

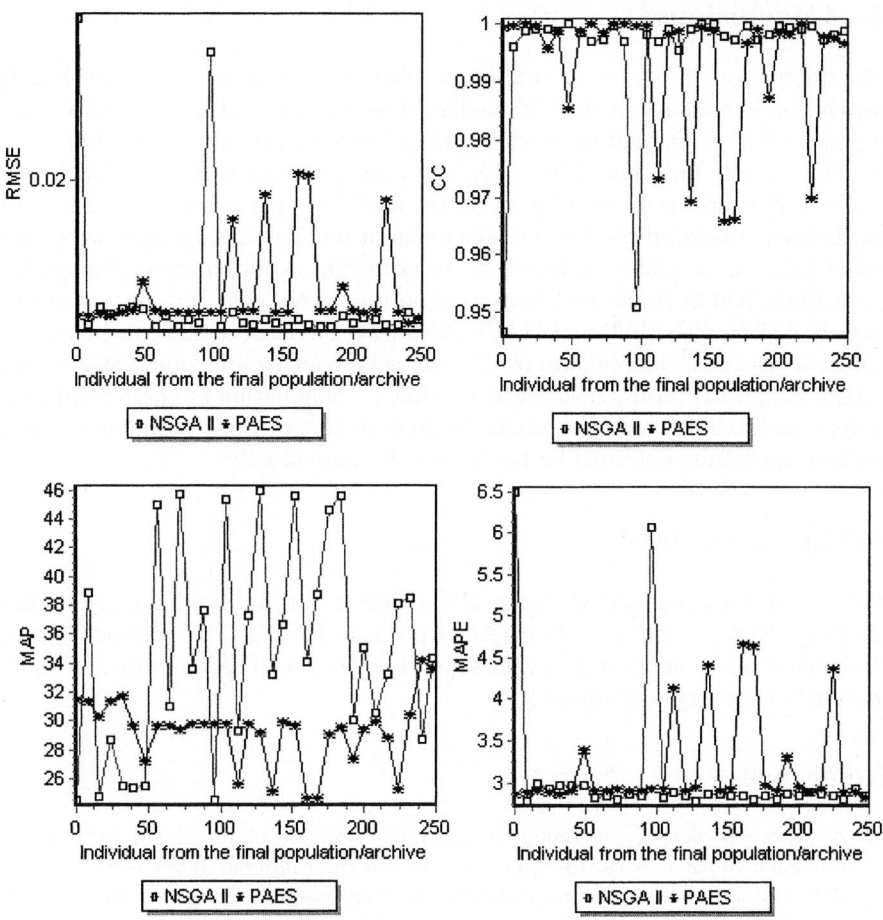

Fig. 2. Values obtained by NSGA II and PAES for RMSE, CC, MAP and MAPE for Nifty test data

The results are further graphically illustrated. In Figure 1, the values for RMSE, CC, MAP and MAPE obtained by NSGA II and PAES for Nasdaq test data are depicted. Figure 2 depicts the values for RMSE, CC, MAP and MAPE obtained by NSGA II and PAES for Nifty test data.

As evident from Figures 1 and 2, it is difficult to say one of the MOEAs could successfully obtain the best results for all indices. As an example, for Nifty, quality of solutions in the final population for RMSE obtained by NSGA II is better than the solutions obtained by PAES in the final archive. At the same time, for Nifty index, the quality of solutions in the final population for MAP obtained by NSGA II is comparatively poorer than the solutions obtained by PAES in the final archive.

4 Conclusions

The fluctuations in the stock market are chaotic in the sense that they heavily depend on the values of their immediate forerunning fluctuations. This paper presented five techniques for modeling stock indices. Taking into account of the No Free Lunch Theorem (NFL) [19], our research using real world stock data also reveals that it is difficult for one of the intelligent paradigms to perform well for different stock indices. Further the different intelligent paradigms were combined using an ensemble approach by two different evolutionary multiobjective algorithms (NSGA II and PAES) so as to optimize several performance measures namely RMSE, CC, MAP and MAPE. We evolved a set of coefficients in order to obtain a ensemble combination of the five techniques by applying NSGA II and PAES. Empirical results also illustrate that a combination of these techniques is very useful. The results obtained by an ensemble of these paradigms clearly outperform results obtained by the techniques individually.

Acknowledgements

This research was supported by the MIC (Ministry of Information and Communication), Korea, under the Chung-Ang University HNRC-ITRC (Home Network Research Center) support program supervised by the IITA (Institute of Information Technology Assessment).

References

1. A. Abraham and A. AuYeung. Integrating Ensemble of Intelligent Systems for Modeling Stock Indices, *In Proceedings of 7th International Work Conference on Artificial and Natural Neural Networks*, Lecture Notes in Computer Science- Volume 2687, Jose Mira and Jose R. Alverez (Eds.), Springer Verlag, Germany, pp. 774-781, 2003.
2. A. Abraham, N. S. Philip and P. Saratchandran. Modeling Chaotic Behavior of Stock Indices Using Intelligent Paradigms. *International Journal of Neural, Parallel & Scientific Computations*, USA, Volume 11, Issue (1&2) pp. 143-160, 2003.
3. K. Deb, S. Agrawal, A. Pratab and T. Meyarivan, A fast elitist non-dominated sorting genetic algorithms for multiobjective optimization: NSGA II. KanGAL report 200001, Indian Institute of Technology, Kanpur, India, 2000.
4. E.B. Del Brio, A. Miguel and J. Perote, An investigation of insider trading profits in the Spanish stock market, The Quarterly Review of Economics and Finance, Volume 42, Issue 1, pp. 73-94, 2002.
5. F.E.H. Tay and L.J. Cao. Modified Support Vector Machines in Financial Time Series Forecasting, *Neurocomputing* 48(1-4): pp. 847-861, 2002.
6. W.Huang, S.Goto and M. Nakamura, Decision-making for stock trading based on trading probability by considering whole market movement, European Journal of Operational Research, Volume 157, Issue 1, (16), pp. 227-241, 2004.
7. J.S.R. Jang, C.T. Sun and E. Mizutani. Neuro-Fuzzy and Soft Computing: A Computational Approach to Learning and Machine Intelligence, Prentice Hall Inc, USA, 1997.

8. J.D. Knowles and D.W. Corne, Approximating the nondominated front using the Pareto archived evolution strategies, Evolutionary Computation, 8(2), 149-172, 2000.
9. J.D. Knowles and D.W. Corne, The Pareto archived evolution strategy: A new baseline algorithm for Pareto multiobjective optimization. In *Congress on Evolutionary Computation (CEC 99)*, Volume 1, Piscataway, NJ, 98–105, 1999.
10. J.D. Knowles and D.W. Corne, M-PAES:A memetic algorithm for multiobjective optimization. In Proceedings of Congress on Evolutionary Computation, 325-332, 2000.
11. Nasdaq Stock Market^{SM}: http://www.nasdaq.com.
12. National Stock Exchange of India Limited: http://www.nse-india.com.
13. K.J. Oh and K.J. Kim, Analyzing stock market tick data using piecewise nonlinear model, Expert Systems with Applications, Volume 22, Issue 3, pp. 249-255, 2002.
14. M. Oltean and C. Grosan. A Comparison of Several Linear GP Techniques. *Complex Systems*, Vol. 14, Nr. 4, pp. 285-313, 2004
15. M. Oltean and C. Grosan. Evolving Evolutionary Algorithms using Multi Expression Programming. *Proceedings of The 7th European Conference on Artificial Life*, Dortmund, Germany, pp. 651-658, 2003.
16. N.S. Philip and K.B. Joseph. Boosting the Differences: A Fast Bayesian classifier neural network, *Intelligent Data Analysis*, Vol. 4, pp. 463-473, IOS Press, 2000.
17. R. Rodrguez, F. Restoy and J.I. Pea, Can output explain the predictability and volatility of stock returns? Journal of International Money and Finance, Volume 21, Issue 2, pp.163-182, 2002.
18. V. Vapnik. The Nature of Statistical Learning Theory. Springer-Verlag, New York, 1995.
19. D.H. Wolpert and W.G. Macready. No free lunch theorem for search. Technical Report SFI-TR-95-02-010. Santa Fe Institute, USA, 1995.
20. W.X.Zhou and D.Sornette, Testing the stability of the 2000 US stock market antibubble, Physica A: Statistical and Theoretical Physics, Volume 348, (15), pp. 428-452 , 2005
21. J.D. Wichard, C. Merkwirth and M. Ogorzalek, Detecting correlation in stock market, Physica A: Statistical Mechanics and its Applications, Volume 344, Issues 1-2, pp. 308-311, 2004

Genetic Algorithms for Feature Weighting: Evolution vs. Coevolution and Darwin vs. Lamarck

Alexandre Blansché, Pierre Gançarski, and Jerzy J. Korczak

LSIIT, UMR 7005 CNRS-ULP, Parc d'Innovation,
Boulevard Sébastien Brant, 67412 Illkirch, France
{blansche, gancarski, jjk}@lsiit.u-strasbg.fr
http://lsiit.u-strasbg.fr/afd/

Abstract. Feature weighting is a more and more important step in clustering because data become more and more complex.

An embedded local feature weighting method has been proposed in [1].

In this paper, we present a new method based on the same cost function, but performed through a genetic algorithm. The learning process can be performed through an evolutionary approach or through a cooperavive coevolutionary approach. Moreover, the genetic algorithm can be combined with the original Weighting K-means algorithm in a Lamarckian learning paradigm.

We compare hill-climbing optimization versus genetic algorithms, evolutionary versus coevolutionary approaches, and Darwinian versus Lamarckian learning on different datasets.

The results seem to show that, on the datasets where the original algorithm is efficient, the proposed methods are even better.

1 Introduction

Feature weighting is a more and more important step in data mining, because data are more and more complex: when objects are described by a large set of features, many features are correlated, some of them are noisy or irrelevent.

Many methods have been proposed for feature weighting or feature selection [2,3,4], but almost all these methods are supervised and many of them use only one set of feature weights for clustering the entire dataset. In [4] it is shown that a wrapper approach for feature weighting provides better results than a filter approach, because the wrapper approach uses a feedback from the classification algorithm to estimate the quality of feature weights. In [5] it is shown that continuous weights provide better results than binary weights (feature selection). Moreover, in agreement with [6,7], we believe that even if all features are relevant, their relative importance depends on the classes to extract.

Few methods exist for unsupervised feature weighting. The embedded method presented in [1] is based on weighted (dis)similarity measures and use a K-means clustering paradigm for local feature weighting. This method (referred here as Weighting K-means) uses hill-climbing search to minimize a cost function.

We expect better results by using the genetic approach which allows a better exploration of the seach space than hill-climbing. This can be performed through the classical genetic algorithm, but also through different strategies. Indeed, as different feature weights for each cluster are used, the cost function optimization can be divided into several sub-tasks (one per cluster), and can be performed through cooperative coevolution. Moreover, a Lamarckian approach can be used, with Weighting K-means steps as life-time learning method.

Thus, in this paper, we present five methods:

- original hill-climbing optimization (section 2);
- Darwinian evolutionary approach (section 3.1);
- Darwinian coevolutionary approach (section 3.2);
- Lamarckian evolutionary approach (section 4.1);
- Lamarckian coevolutionary approach (section 4.2).

Then, we compare all these methods on UCI repository datasets (section 5).

2 Weighting K-Means

Weighting K-means is an embedded feature weighting method, based on the well-known K-means clustering algorithm [8], that attempts to minimize the cost function defined in Equation 1, where:

- S is the dataset to classify;
- K is the number of clusters;
- n is the number of features;
- $C = \{C_1, C_2, \ldots, C_K\}$ is a set of clusters;
- $C_k(o) = 1$ if $o \in C_k$ (C_k is the k-th cluster) and $C_k(o) = 0$ otherwise;
- $c = \{c_1, c_2, \ldots, c_K\}$ and c_k is the centre of cluster C_k;
- $W = \{W_1, W_2, \ldots, W_K\}$;
- $W_k = \{w_k^1, w_k^2, \ldots, w_k^n\}$;
- $w_k^i \geq 0$ and $\sum_{i=1}^{n} w_k^i = 1$ (w_k^i is the weight on the i-th feature for the k-th cluster);
- $\beta \geq 1$ (generally $\beta = 1.8$);
- $d_i(o, o')$ is a dissimilarity measure between objects o and o' on the i-th feature.

$$f(C, c, W) = \sum_{k=1}^{K} \sum_{o \in S} \sum_{i=1}^{n} C_k(o)(w_k^i)^\beta d_i(o, c_k) \qquad (1)$$

Each step consists of three partial optimizations. The two first ones are the same as in K-means. The last optimization concerns the feature weights.

Each Weighting K-means step can be summarized as:

1. Selection of the most similar cluster for each object according to a similarity measure
2. Modification of cluster centres (defined as the centroid of all data in the cluster)
3. Modification of feature weights for each cluster as defined in Equation 2, where:
   - $sum_k^i = \sum_{o \in S} C_k(o) d_i(c_k, o)^2$;
   - $zero_k = |\{t \mid sum_k^t = 0\}|$.

$$w_k^i = \begin{cases} \frac{1}{zero_k}, & \text{if } sum_k^i = 0 \\ 0, & \text{if } sum_k^i \neq 0 \text{ and } zero_k \neq 0 \\ \dfrac{1}{\sum_{t=1}^{n} \left[\dfrac{sum_k^i}{sum_k^t}\right]^{\frac{1}{\beta-1}}}, & \text{if } zero_k = 0. \end{cases} \quad (2)$$

3 Darwinian Feature Weighting

Genetic algorithms allow a better exploration of the search space than hill-climbing. We propose an embedded feature weighting method that combine the K-means algorithm for cluster assignment and a genetic algorithm for feature weighting, which minimize the cost function (Equation 1).

The learning method can be performed through standard evolutionary algorithm or through cooperative coevolution algorithm.

The classical crossover and mutation operators are used, but weights are always normalized such that the sum of all weights for one cluster is equal to 1. A roulette-wheel method (fitness proportional selection) is used to select individuals (the inverse fitness is used, because the goal is to minimize the cost function).

3.1 Darwinian Evolutionary Approach

Each individual represents the feature weights for each cluster used by K-means to performe clustering, as shown in Figure 1. Individuals are randomly initialized such that the sum of all weights is equal to 1 for all clusters.

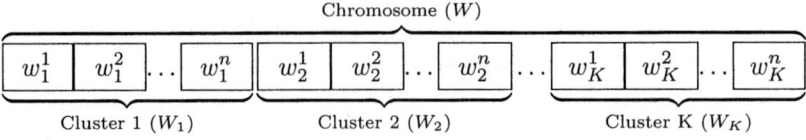

Fig. 1. A chromosome in the evolutionary approach

First, the algorithm is initialized by performing K-means with s_0 steps (with $s_0 \in \mathbb{N}^*$): the K seeds are initialized randomly (each seed is a random object o in the dataset S) and all feature weights are initialized to $\frac{1}{n}$ (where n is the number of features). The result C is defined as the current clustering.

Then, at each generation:

- K-means algorithm performs s_1 steps (with $s_1 \in \mathbb{N}^*$), for each individual, initialized by the partition of the current clustering C and using the feature weights of the individual;
- each individual is evaluated according to the cost function (Equation 1);
- K-means algorithm performes s_2 steps on the best individual of this generation (with $s_2 \in \mathbb{N}^*$) and the current clustering C is replaced if the resulting clustering is better;
- a new population is defined by reproduction.

This method is not strictly a genetic algorithm, because de fitness function evolves during learning (the current clustering C may change at each generation).

3.2 Darwinian Cooperative Coevolutionary Approach

Cooperative coevolution has been defined in [9]. It is an evolutionary algorithm which uses several populations. A population evolves in an environment which depends on the other populations and evolves with them.

In our case, each population search the best weight vector for one cluster. Individuals represent the feature weights for one cluster, as shown in Figure 2.

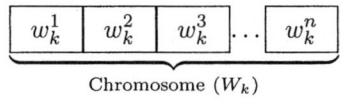

Fig. 2. A chromosome in the cooperative coevolutionary approach

As in the evolutionary approach, the algorithm is initialized by performing K-means algorithm with s_0 steps. The result C is defined as the current clustering. The feature weights are set to $\frac{1}{n}$ (where n is the number of features) for all features and all clusters. The current feature weights is called $W = \{W_1, W_2, \ldots, W_K\}$ (where W_k is the weight vector for the k-th cluster). Individuals are randomly initialized such that the sum of all weights is equal to 1. The k-th population corresponds to the k-th cluster.

Then, at each generation:

- for each individual of the k-th population:
  - K-means is initialized by the partition of the current clustering C, and performs s_1 steps using feature weights defined as follow: for the k-th cluster, the feature weights of the individual are used, and for the other clusters, the weight vector W_i is used;

- the result is used for individuals evaluation;
  (this is performed independantly for each population, eventually in parallel);
- the best individual from each population is selected;
- for all $\widetilde{W} = \left\{\widetilde{W_1}, \widetilde{W_2}, \ldots, \widetilde{W_K}\right\}$, where $\widetilde{W_k}$ can be the current weight vector W_k or $\widetilde{W_k}$ can be the weight vector of the best individual from the k-th population (there are 2^K combinations), K-means algorithm performes s_2 steps, initialized by the partition of C and the feature weights $\widetilde{W}$. C and W are replaced if a better clustering is discovered.
- a new population is defined by reproduction.

4 Lamarckian Feature Weighting

In the Lamarckian theory, individual adaptation can be communicated genetically to offspring. This theory is false in biology, but it has been succefully applied in artificial learning [10, 11, 12, 13]. The Lamarckian learning paradigm consist of a modification of chromosomes by a local search method for each individual before their evaluations.

We proposed to extend the feature weighting methods defined in sections 3.1 and 3.2 to a Lamarckian learning method, with Weighting K-means steps as life-time learning method. Like the Darwinian learning, this Lamarckian learning method can be performed through standard evolutionary algorithm or through cooperative coevolution algorithm.

The genetic operators are the same as the ones used in the Darwinian approach.

4.1 Lamarckian Evolutionary Approach

This method is almost identical to the Darwinian one except that the algorithm is initialized using Weighting K-means, and that at each generation:

- Weighting K-means algorithm performes s_1 steps, for each individual, initialized by the partition of the current clustering C and by the feature weights of the individual;
- the new weights of each individual replace the old ones;
- each individual is evaluated;
- Weighting K-means algorithm performes s_2 steps on the best individual of this generation and the current clustering C is replaced if the resulting clustering is better;
- a new population is defined by reproduction.

4.2 Lamarckian Cooperative Coevolutionary Approach

As in the Lamarckian evolutionary approach, the algorithm is initialized using Weighting K-means (s_0 steps). The result C is defined as the current result, and the obtained feature weights $W = \{W_1, W_2, \ldots, W_K\}$ are defined as the current feature weights (where W_k is the weight vector for the k-th cluster).

In Lamarckian approach, the goal of the local search method is to optimize the individuals by a modification of their chromosomes. It does not have to change the environment. But, Weighting K-means steps will change feature weights for all clusters, which corresponds to the other populations, i.e. Weighting K-means steps will change the environment. Thus, we defined a k-Weighting K-means step: it is identical to the original algorithm, except that the feature weights optimization is performed only for the k-th cluster. Then, at each generation:

- for each individual of the k-th population:
  - k-Weighting K-means is initialized by the partition of the current clustering C, and performes s_1 steps using feature weights defined as follow: for the k-th cluster, the feature weights of the individual are used, and for the other clusters, the weight vector W_i is used;
  - the weights obtained for the k-th cluster replace the ones of the evaluated individual;
  - the obtained clustering is used for individuals evaluation;
- the best individual from each population is selected;
- as for the evolutionary approach, for all $\widetilde{W}$, Weighting K-means performes s_2 steps, initialized by the partition of C and by the feature weights $\widetilde{W}$. C and W are replaced if a better clustering is discovered;
- a new population is defined by reproduction.

Remark. In the coevolutionary Lamarckian approach, for each individual, a local search initalized by C is performed. The resulting weight vector, which replace the chromosome of an individual, does not correspond to the initial clustering C, but to the clustering discovered after s_1 learning steps. However, when all the local results, from each population, are combined to obtain a global result, the new weights are used on the original clustering C, whereas nothing proves that this weights are still relevant to C.

We assume that if s_1 is small enough, there are only minor differences between C and the result clustering of each individuals. If this is true, the weight vector of an individual of the k-th population may still be relevant to the k-th cluster, and the learning will be efficient.

If s_1 is too high, there may be too much differences between C and the resulting clusterings, and the weights may become irrelevant.

This is similar to the modifications of C from one generation to another. For the same reason, we believe that a small value for s_2 must be preferred.

This alternance of modifications of the clustering and the feature weights can be considered as a form of coevolution, heterogeneous along two dimensions:

- the phenotype: the first coevolving entity is a clustering algorithm, the second one is a feature weighting algorithm;
- the paradigm: the clustering method use a hill-climbing approach, the feature weighting method a genetic algorithm.

5 Experiments

We carried out five series of tests. We compared the original Weighting K-means and the Darwinian Evolutionary Algorithm (DEA), the Dawinian Coevolutionary Algorithm (DCA), the Lamarckian Evolutionary Algorithm (LEA) and the Lamarckian Coevolutionary Algorithm (LCA). For each run of each test, the K-means seeds are randomly initialized. The parameters of the algorithms are:

- the usual parameters of genetic algorithms (number of crossovers, mutation rate, ...);
- the β parameter of Weighting K-means (set to 1.8);
- the number of Weighting K-means steps s_0, s_1 and s_2 (all set to 1);
- the number of clusters (must be known a priori).

To evaluate all the new evolutionary methods with the same number of individual at each generation, $K \times 20$ individuals are used for the evolutionary methods (where K is the number of clusters) and 20 individuals in each one of the K populations for the coevolutionary methods.

In Figure 3 is shown the average fitness (Equation 1) and the standard deviation obtained by the Weighting K-means algorithm and by the best individual discovered in 25 generations by the different evolutionary algorithms, on sev-

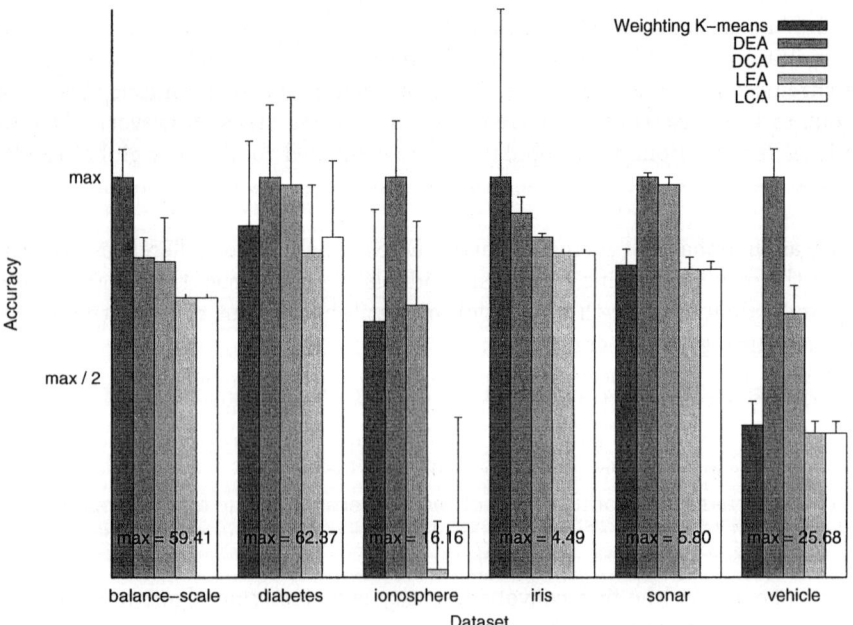

Fig. 3. Fitness obtained by the different algorithms

Table 1. Accuracy obtained by the different algorithms

Method	WG	R	J	FM
balance-scale				
K-means	0.254 ± 0.039	0.585 ± 0.027	0.298 ± 0.03	0.462 ± 0.035
WK-m	0.253 ± 0.022	0.584 ± 0.013	0.303 ± 0.015	0.468 ± 0.017
LEA	0.273 ± 0.007	0.574 ± 0.002	0.298 ± 0.002	0.462 ± 0.003
diabetes				
K-means	0.376 ± 0.012	0.554 ± 0.01	0.415 ± 0.008	0.586 ± 0.008
WK-m	0.299 ± 0.046	0.515 ± 0.022	0.368 ± 0.022	0.538 ± 0.023
LEA	0.285 ± 0.042	0.51 ± 0.019	0.362 ± 0.019	0.532 ± 0.02
ionosphere				
K-means	0.374 ± 0.001	0.554 ± 0.001	0.405 ± 0.001	0.576 ± 0.001
WK-m	0.398 ± 0.057	0.565 ± 0.032	0.439 ± 0.065	0.613 ± 0.067
LEA	0.494 ± 0.037	0.62 ± 0.021	0.556 ± 0.034	0.729 ± 0.034
iris				
K-means	0.644 ± 0.08	0.817 ± 0.055	0.595 ± 0.064	0.747 ± 0.049
WK-m	0.826 ± 0.142	0.913 ± 0.081	0.798 ± 0.132	0.883 ± 0.09
LEA	0.89 ± 0	0.95 ± 0	0.858 ± 0	0.923 ± 0
sonar				
K-means	0.303 ± 0.023	0.504 ± 0.006	0.396 ± 0.033	0.573 ± 0.038
WK-m	0.28 ± 0.023	0.504 ± 0.008	0.342 ± 0.017	0.509 ± 0.019
LEA	0.298 ± 0.02	0.511 ± 0.009	0.343 ± 0.008	0.511 ± 0.009
vehicle				
K-means	0.137 ± 0.015	0.648 ± 0.015	0.195 ± 0.014	0.326 ± 0.02
WK-m	0.174 ± 0.009	0.661 ± 0.008	0.222 ± 0.009	0.364 ± 0.013
LEA	0.17 ± 0.005	0.66 ± 0.006	0.219 ± 0.005	0.36 ± 0.008

eral datasets from the UCI repository [14][1] (the lower the fitness is the best it is supposed to be). The values are the average values over 100 runs. Since for each dataset all attributes are numerical, the difference is used as dissimilarity measure. For each dataset, we normalized each feature so that each one has an expected difference of 1. One can see that:

- the Lamarckian approach always outperforms both hill-climbing and Darwinian approach and the LEA outperforms the LCA;
- the Darwinian approach is better than the hill-climbing algorithm on the balance-scale and iris datasets, but not on all the others;
- the DCA always outperforms the DEA;
- the results with the Lamarckian approach are more stable than the ones obtained by Weighting K-means (the standard deviation is lower).

---

[1] A repository of databases used for the empirical analysis of learning algorithms.

We have also compared the accuracy of the results obtained by the standard K-means algorithm, the original Weighting K-means and the LEA (Table 1) on these datasets. For each test, several quality indices have been computed (to compare discovered and real partitions): the Wemmert and Gançarski index (WG) [15], the Rand statistic (R), the Jaccard coefficient (J), and the Folkes and Mallows index (FM) [16] (all the values are the average values over 100 runs). All these quality indices takes values in $[0; 1]$, 1 indicates that the two partitions are identical (i.e. a high value indicates a high quality). One can see that:

- on the vehicle dataset, Weighting K-means and the Lamarckian approach provide similar result, and both of them outperform K-means;
- on the ionosphere and iris datasets, Weighting K-means provides better results than K-means, but the Lamarckian learning largely outperforms the two other methods;
- on the balance-scale dataset, there are no differences between the methods;
- on the diabetes and sonar datasets K-means outperforms the two other methods that provides similar results.

It seems that, on the balance-scale, the diabetes and the sonar datasets, the cost function cannot predict the accuracy (that can lead to a bad result).

These results show that the cost function proposed in [1] is not always relevant. Our method provides better results according to this cost function, but if the minimisation of the cost function leads to a bad result, our method cannot find a good result. In summary, if the cost function is relevant for a dataset, then the coevolutionary Lamarckian method provides at least as good results as Weighting K-means. But, on the contrary, if this cost function is irrelevant, then the proposed method cannot provide better than Weighting K-means does.

6 Conclusion

In this paper we have presented genetic approaches for feature weighting. These methods are based on the feature weighting algorithm presented in [1]. The learning algorithms can be organized along two dimensions:

- the evolutionary/coevolutionary dimension, which defines whether the problem is decomposed in several sub-tasks or not;
- the Darwinian/Lamarckian dimension, which defines whether life-time learning is used or not.

This paper shows that, the Darwinian approach is not efficient for this problem, but that the Lamarckian approach provides the best results, according to the cost function. Moreover, we have shown that the cost function defined by [1] did not always provide a good estimation of clustering accuracy.

It is suprising that the LEA outperforms the LCA. This is because the lifetime learning method is global (it takes into account all the clusters), that can difficultly being applied to a local search efficiently. Another life-time learning method, adapted to coevolution should be used. We also want to try other clustering accuracy estimators.

We also want to test the efficiency of Baldwinian approach and hybrid Lamarckian/Baldwinian approach in the same framework.

Finally, as the methods are unsupervised, there may be no correspondances between clusters obtained by two different runs or algorithms, thus it is difficult to analyse similarities in the obtained weights, because local weights are used. We are working on a methodology for feature weighting comparison.

References

1. Chan, E., Ching, W., Ng, M., Huang, J.: An optimization algorithm for clustering using weighted dissimilarity measures. Pattern Recognition **37** (2004) 943–952
2. Howe, N., Cardie, C.: Weighting unusual feature types. Technical Report TR99-1735, Ithaca (1999)
3. John, G., Kohavi, R., Pfleger, K.: Irrelevant features and the subset selection problem. In: Proceedings of the Eleventh International Conference on Machine Learning. (1994) 121–129
4. Wettschereck, D., Aha, D.: Weighting features. In Veloso, M., Aamodt, A., eds.: Case-Based Reasoning, Research and Development, First International Conference, Berlin, Springer Verlag (1995) 347–358
5. Wettschereck, D., Aha, D., Mohri, T.: A review and empirical evaluation of feature weighting methods for a class of lazy learning algorithms. Artificial Intelligence Review **11** (1997) 273–314
6. Howe, N., Cardie, C.: Examining locally varying weights for nearest neighbor algorithms. In: ICCBR. (1997) 455–466
7. Frigui, H., Nasraoui, O.: Unsupervised learning of prototypes and attribute weights. Pattern Recognition **34** (2004) 567–581
8. MacQueen, J.: Some methods for classification and analysis of multivariate observations. In: Proceedings of the 5th Berkeley Symposium on Mathematical Statistics and Probability, Berkeley, CA, University of California Press (1965) 281–297
9. Potter, M., De Jong, K.: A cooperative coevolutionary approach to function optimization. In: Proceedings of the Third Conference on Parallel Problem Solving from Nature. (1994) 249–257
10. Whitley, D., Gordon, V., Mathias, K.: Lamarckian evolution, the Baldwin effect, and function optimization. In: Parallel Problem Solving from Nature (PPSN III). (1994) 6–16
11. Paredis, J.: Coevolutionary life-time learning. In: Parallel Problem Solving from Nature (PPSN IV), Springer (1996) 72–80
12. Ku, K., Mak, M.: Exploring the effects of lamarckian and baldwinian learning in evolving recurrent neural networks. In: Proceedings of the IEEE International Conference on Evolutionary Computation. (1997) 617–621
13. Ross, B.: A lamarckian evolution strategy for genetic algorithms. In Chambers, L., ed.: Practical Handbook of Genetic Algorithms: Complex Coding Systems. Volume 3. CRC Press, Boca Raton, Florida (1999) 1–16
14. Blake, C., Merz, C.: UCI repository of machine learning databases (1998)
15. Wemmert, C.: Classification hybride distribuée par collaboration de méthodes non supervisées. PhD thesis, Université Louis Pasteur, Strasbourg (2000)
16. Halkidi, M., Batistakis, Y., Vazirgiannis, M.: On clustering validation techniques. Journal of Intelligent Information Systems **17** (2001) 107–145

A Deterministic Alternative to *Competent* Genetic Algorithms That Solves to Optimality Linearly Decomposable Non-overlapping Problems in Polynomial Time

Manuel Valenzuela-Rendón, Horacio Martínez-Alfaro,
and Hugo Terashima-Marín

Centro de Sistemas Inteligentes,
Tecnológico de Monterrey, Campus Monterrey,
Av. Eugenio Garza Sada 2501 Sur,
C.P. 64849, Monterrey, N.L., Mexico
{valenzuela, hma, terashima}@itesm.mx

Abstract. David Goldberg has defined a *competent* genetic algorithm as one which "can solve hard problems, quickly, accurately, and reliably." Among other *competent* genetic algorithms that have been developed are the Bayesian optimization algorithm (BOA), the fast messy genetic algorithm (fmGA), and the linkage learning genetic algorithm (LLGA). These algorithms have been tested on problems of bounded difficulty that are additive separable formed by deceptive subproblems of order not greater than k, where $k < \ell$. BOA, fmGA, LLGA, and other *competent* genetic algorithms are stochastic, and thus, can only be assured of attaining optimality in a probabilistic sense. In this paper, we develop a deterministic algorithm that solves to optimality all linearly decomposable problems in a polynomial number of function evaluations with respect to the maximum size of the subproblems, k. The algorithm presented does not rely on a population, does not recombine individuals or apply any other *genetic* operator. Furthermore, because it is deterministic, the number of function evaluations required to find the optimum can be known in advance. The algorithm presented solves both the linkage and the optimization problems by finding the disjoint sets of related variables and the optimal values of these variables at the same time. The fact that such an algorithm can be devised has important implications for the design of GA-hard problems, and the development and evaluation of genetic optimization algorithms.

1 Introduction

Evaluation of evolutionary optimization algorithms is a difficult business. How can we say that a given algorithm is *good*? What does being a *good* evolutionary optimization algorithm precisely mean? In attempting to answer these questions, David Goldberg has put forward the concept of *competence* in genetic algorithms.

He defines a *competent* genetic algorithm as one which "can solve hard problems, quickly, accurately, and reliably" [1]. By *quickly,* he understands algorithms that, given a problem of ℓ binary variables (chromosome length), scales polynomially as $\mathcal{O}(\ell^b)$, with b as small a number as possible. *Accurately* refers to the algorithm reaching the optimum (or near optimal), and *reliably* addresses the point that genetic algorithms are stochastic, and therefore, must be evaluated in a probabilistic manner. Among other *competent* genetic algorithms that have been developed are the Bayesian optimization algorithm (BOA) [2], the fast messy genetic algorithm (fmGA) [3], and the linkage learning genetic algorithm (LLGA) [4]. Of course, these characteristics of an algorithm must be tested when solving difficult *and* worthy problems.[1] Linearly decomposable non-overlapping problems, where each part is completely deceptive has been used as a worthy and difficult test problem for genetic algorithms that use a binary representation in many occasions. In solving this type of problem, an algorithm must address, implicitly or explicitly, the *linkage problem,* i.e., it must find the relations held by loci in the chromosome. Algorithms that only solve the linkage problem have been developed [5,6]. These algorithms have been proposed as a step previous to a genetic algorithm in order to solve the optimization problem [7].

In this paper we develop a deterministic algorithm that solves linearly decomposable non-overlapping problems where the size of the subproblems is bounded. Our algorithm requires a polynomial number of function evaluations to find the optimal. Since it is deterministic, our algorithm always finds the optimal. Therefore, it complies with the requirements of *competence* of Goldberg. The algorithm presented is not genetic: it does not rely on a population, nor does it apply any type of genetic operator like recombination, mutation, or selection. In the next sections we develop *X1,* our first approach to a *competent* deterministic algorithm, and *X2,* an improved version which greatly reduces the number of function evaluations required to obtain the optimum.

2 Linearly Decomposable Non-overlapping Functions

Genetic algorithms [8,9] implicitly identify *building blocks,* low order schemata associated with individuals with high evaluation, and try to find even better individuals by recombining these building blocks. For this search strategy to work, there must be such building blocks in the structure of the problem being solved. Consequently, functions with an underlying structure where building blocks can be identified have been used as test problems for genetic algorithms.

In this paper, we are interested in algorithms capable of optimizing linearly decomposable non-overlapping (LDNO) functions. These function can be expressed as

$$f(\mathbf{x}) = f_1(\mathbf{v}_1) + f_2(\mathbf{v}_2) + \cdots + f_N(\mathbf{v}_N) \tag{1}$$

where $\mathbf{x} = [x_1, x_2, \ldots, x_\ell]$ is the complete chromosome and $U = \{x_1, x_2, \ldots, x_\ell\}$. The function f is linearly composed of N sub-functions f_i. Let S_i be the set of

---
[1] An isolated spike (also called *niddle-in-a-hay-stack*) can be a very hard problem, but it can hardly be thought as a worthy problem of being attacked.

elements of U that are the arguments of sub-function f_i. Vector $\mathbf{v}_i$ is formed by the values of the elements of S_i. Sets $S_1, S_2, \ldots, S_N$ are disjoint, $S_i \cap S_j = \emptyset\ \forall i \neq j$, and together completely cover the set of all loci U, $S_1 \cup S_2 \cup \cdots \cup S_L = U$. The cardinality of the S_i sets is bounded by k, i.e., $\max_i |S_i| = k \leq \ell$.

An example of the class LDNO functions is the following:

$$f(x_1, x_2, x_3, x_4, x_5, x_6, x_7) = f_1(x_1, x_3, x_7) + f_2(x_2, x_4, x_5, x_6), \qquad (2)$$

where $\ell = 7$, $k = 4$, $N = 2$, $S_1 = \{x_1, x_3, x_7\}$, $S_2 = \{x_2, x_4, x_5, x_6\}$. Sub-functions f_i can be deceptive, quadratic, spike, or any other non-linear function.[2]

3 Detection of Non-linearities by Random *Probes*

In order to optimize LDNO functions, an algorithm must explicitly or implicitly identify the sets S_i during or prior to the actual optimization. Once these disjoint sets are found, each sub-function can be optimized by exhaustively evaluating all its bit combinations. One possible approach to the identification of the S_i sets is to perform a series of *probes* [6] that uncover non-linear relations between pairs of bits. Munetomo and Goldberg [5] implemented an algorithm that performs randomly generated probes, or *non-linearity checks*, in the following way. A random chromosome $[x_1, x_2, \ldots, x_\ell]$ is generated; then the objective function is evaluated at the four chromosomes generated by letting two given loci i and j take all possible values:

$$f_{00} = f(\cdots x'_i, \cdots x'_j, \cdots) \qquad (3)$$
$$f_{01} = f(\cdots x'_i, \cdots x_j, \cdots) \qquad (4)$$
$$f_{10} = f(\cdots x_i, \cdots x'_j, \cdots) \qquad (5)$$
$$f_{11} = f(\cdots x_i, \cdots x_j, \cdots). \qquad (6)$$

A non-linear relation between loci i and j is detected if $f_{01} + f_{10} \neq f_{00} + f_{11}$,[3] or in other words, if the effects of changing the value of locus i and the value of locus j are non-additive. If $f_{01} + f_{10} = f_{00} + f_{11}$ then possibly there is no non-linear relation between loci i and j, *or* the background, the values of all the other loci, is such that it does not show the non-linear relation between loci i and j. This can happen because for k order non-linearities, those that depend on k loci, it might be necessary to set k loci to a specific combination of bits to uncover the non-linearity, for example, in the case the sub-function is a spike. A non-linearity check requires four function evaluations. By performing a sufficiently large number of non-linearity checks, the probability of detecting all non-linear pairwise relations can be made as close to 1.0 as desired.

---

[2] If a sub-function was linear, then it could be further decomposed into other sub-functions.

[3] To account for quasi-decomposable or noisy functions, the test is changed to $|f_{01} + f_{10} - f_{00} - f_{11}| > \epsilon$ where ϵ is a positive small constant that must be chosen appropriately [5].

4 Algorithm *X1*

Munetomo and Goldberg [5] algorithm performs random non-linearity checks to identify the S_i sets. A more efficient method can be devised by performing the probes in an ordered fashion. For example, if non-linearity is to be checked among three loci i, j, and m, the following function evaluations could be performed

$$f_{000} = f(\cdots x'_i, \cdots x'_j, \cdots x'_m, \cdots) \tag{7}$$
$$f_{001} = f(\cdots x'_i, \cdots x'_j, \cdots x_m, \cdots) \tag{8}$$
$$\vdots$$
$$f_{111} = f(\cdots x_i, \cdots x_j, \cdots x_m, \cdots), \tag{9}$$

and non-linearities would be detected if the effect of changing the values of loci i, j, and m is non-additive. In this way, only $2^3 = 8$ function evaluations are necessary, instead of the $3 \times 2 \times 4 = 24$ evaluations made if independent non-linearity checks were performed.[4]

We developed from the previous idea to create algorithm *X1* shown in Figure 1. *X1* does not perform random probes; instead, it scans the search space in an ordered fashion trying to obtain as much information as possible with the least function evaluations.

Algorithm *X1* operates in two stages. First, it detects all non-linearities and stores the arguments of the objective function where each non-linearity was detected. Second, it uses the previously stored information to construct the optimum (or one of the optima if optimizing a function with multiple optima). In the following subsections, the way the *X1* operates will be explained. To support the explanation we will take as an example the optimization of the following function:

$$f(\mathbf{x}) = f_1(x_1, x_2, x_3) + f_2(x_4, x_5, x_6, x_7) \tag{10}$$

where f_1 and f_2 will be trap functions [10], and we have arbitrarily chosen the optimum at $[010\,0111]$.

4.1 Detecting Non-linearities

Detection of non-linearities is performed in *X1* in the following manner. The objective function is evaluated at the vector of all zeros, $[000\cdots 0]$, and this value is stored in s_0. An empty matrix **G** and an empty vector **S** are created; these will store information of detected non-linearities. Points in the search space are visited in the order generated by function Next(). Function Next() returns the next vector that has the same number of ones by shifting the leftmost bit to the left one position if possible, or by adding a 1 to the right of the vector and shifting all ones to the right. Repeated calls to Next() starting from $[000\cdots 00]$ produces the sequence of all vectors with one 1, all vectors with two 1s, all the vectors with

---

[4] Notice that the three loci check detects non-linearity between loci i and j if $f_{000} + f_{110} \neq f_{010} + f_{100}$ or if $f_{001} + f_{111} \neq f_{011} + f_{101}$, i.e., the equivalent of two non-linearity checks.

```
Function X1 (f,k)
    /* Detect non-linearities and store in G and S           */
    x ← [00···0]; s₀ ← f(x);
    G ← [ ]; S ← [ ];
    x ← Next(x);
    repeat
        s ← f(x) − s₀;
        if (x, s) cannot be explained by [G S] then
            G ← [x; G]; S ← [s; S];
        x ← Next(x);
    until (number of ones in x) > k;
    Sort[G S] by S;
    /* Construct optimal from [G,S]                          */
    Identify restriction in [G S];
    Join non-contradicting restrictions that share columns;
    x* ← Form optimal solution;
    return x*, [G S]
```

Fig. 1. Implementation of algorithm *X1*

three 1s, etc. When the evaluation of a point cannot be explained by information in [G S] a non-linearity is detected and its information is stored in [G S].

A vector **x** and its incremental evaluation s can be explained if there are rows in **G** that concurrently can build **x**, *and* the addition of the corresponding entries in **S** is equal to s. For example, given the following status of [G S]

$$\begin{bmatrix} 1 & 0 & 0 & 0 & 0 & 0 & 0 & 0.3333 \\ 0 & 1 & 0 & 0 & 0 & 0 & 0 & 1.0000 \\ 0 & 0 & 1 & 0 & 0 & 0 & 0 & 0.3333 \\ 0 & 0 & 0 & 1 & 0 & 0 & 0 & 0.2000 \\ 0 & 0 & 0 & 0 & 1 & 0 & 0 & -0.2000 \\ 0 & 0 & 0 & 0 & 0 & 1 & 0 & -0.2000 \\ 0 & 0 & 0 & 0 & 0 & 0 & 1 & -0.2000 \end{bmatrix}, \quad (11)$$

an incremental evaluation of 0.0 for vector [0110000] cannot be explained because according to [G S] turning on loci 2 has an incremental evaluation of 1.0000, turning on loci 3 has an incremental evaluation of 0.3333, and this does not add up to 0.0. Figure 2 shows the status of [G S] after detecting non-linearities.

4.2 Processing Non-linearities

Sets of detected non-linearities that have 1s in the same loci can be seen as restrictions on the optimal. In our example, [G S] will contain the following rows:

A Deterministic Alternative to *Competent* Genetic Algorithms   697

$$
\begin{array}{c}
\text{Before sort} \\
\begin{bmatrix}
0\ 0\ 0\ 1\ 1\ 1\ 1 & -0.4000 \\
0\ 0\ 0\ 0\ 1\ 1\ 1 & 0.6000 \\
1\ 1\ 0\ 0\ 0\ 0\ 0 & 0.0000 \\
0\ 1\ 1\ 0\ 0\ 0\ 0 & 0.0000 \\
1\ 0\ 0\ 0\ 0\ 0\ 0 & 0.3333 \\
0\ 1\ 0\ 0\ 0\ 0\ 0 & 1.0000 \\
0\ 0\ 1\ 0\ 0\ 0\ 0 & 0.3333 \\
0\ 0\ 0\ 1\ 0\ 0\ 0 & 0.2000 \\
0\ 0\ 0\ 0\ 1\ 0\ 0 & -0.2000 \\
0\ 0\ 0\ 0\ 0\ 1\ 0 & -0.2000 \\
0\ 0\ 0\ 0\ 0\ 0\ 1 & -0.2000
\end{bmatrix}
\quad
\begin{array}{c}
\text{After sort} \\
\begin{bmatrix}
0\ 1\ 0\ 0\ 0\ 0\ 0 & 1.0000 \\
0\ 0\ 0\ 0\ 1\ 1\ 1 & 0.6000 \\
0\ 0\ 1\ 0\ 0\ 0\ 0 & 0.3333 \\
1\ 0\ 0\ 0\ 0\ 0\ 0 & 0.3333 \\
0\ 0\ 0\ 1\ 0\ 0\ 0 & 0.2000 \\
0\ 1\ 1\ 0\ 0\ 0\ 0 & 0.0000 \\
1\ 1\ 0\ 0\ 0\ 0\ 0 & 0.0000 \\
0\ 0\ 0\ 0\ 0\ 0\ 1 & -0.2000 \\
0\ 0\ 0\ 0\ 0\ 1\ 0 & -0.2000 \\
0\ 0\ 0\ 0\ 1\ 0\ 0 & -0.2000 \\
0\ 0\ 0\ 1\ 1\ 1\ 1 & -0.4000
\end{bmatrix}
\end{array}
\end{array}
$$

Fig. 2. [G S] before and after sort by incremental evaluation

$$
\begin{array}{c}
\text{After detecting restrictions} \\
\begin{bmatrix}
0\ 1\ 0\ -\ -\ -\ - & 1.0000 \\
-\ -\ -\ 0\ 1\ 1\ 1 & 0.6000 \\
-\ 0\ 1\ -\ -\ -\ - & 0.3333 \\
1\ 0\ -\ -\ -\ -\ - & 0.3333 \\
-\ -\ -\ 1\ 0\ 0\ 0 & 0.2000 \\
0\ 1\ 1\ -\ -\ -\ - & 0.0000 \\
1\ 1\ 0\ -\ -\ -\ - & 0.0000 \\
-\ -\ -\ 0\ 0\ 0\ 0 & 0.0000
\end{bmatrix}
\end{array}
\quad
\begin{array}{c}
\text{After joining restrictions} \\
\begin{bmatrix}
0\ 1\ 0\ -\ -\ -\ - & 1.0000 \\
-\ -\ -\ 0\ 1\ 1\ 1 & 0.6000 \\
1\ 0\ 1\ -\ -\ -\ - & 0.6667 \\
-\ -\ -\ 1\ 0\ 0\ 0 & 0.2000 \\
0\ 1\ 1\ -\ -\ -\ - & 0.0000 \\
1\ 1\ 0\ -\ -\ -\ - & 0.0000 \\
-\ -\ -\ 0\ 0\ 0\ 0 & 0.0000
\end{bmatrix}
\end{array}
$$

Fig. 3. [G S] after detecting restrictions implied in the non-linearities found, and after joining non-contradicting restrictions that share columns

$$
\begin{bmatrix}
0\ 1\ 0\ 0\ 0\ 0\ 0 & 1.0000 \\
0\ 1\ 1\ 0\ 0\ 0\ 0 & 0.0000 \\
1\ 1\ 0\ 0\ 0\ 0\ 0 & 0.0000 \\
\vdots &
\end{bmatrix}
\tag{12}
$$

These rows say that for the incremental evaluation of turning on locus 2 to appear in the total evaluation of the chromosome, it is necessary to have bits 1 and 3 off, this can be expressed by saying that $[010----]$ has an incremental evaluation of 1.0000, where "$-$" indicates that this positions are not defined by this restriction.

After detecting restrictions, rows of [G S] that have values on shared columns, but that do not imply a contradiction, are joined. In our example, $[-01----]$ and $[10-----]$ can be joined to $[101----]$ having an incremental evaluation of 0.6666. Figure 3 shows the status of [G S] after detecting the restrictions implied by the non-linearities found, and after joining non-contradicting restrictions that share columns.

```
Function X2 (f,k)
    /* Detect non-linearities                                          */
    k₀ ← ⌈k/2⌉;
    k₁ ← ⌊k/2⌋;
    if k₀ = 2 then k₀ ← 3;
    if k₁ = 1 then k₁ ← 2;
    [G₀ S₀] ← X1(f, k₀) starting from [00···0];
    [G₁ S₁] ← X1(f, k₁) starting from [11···1] and using 0s instead of 1s;
    /* Construct optimal                                                */
    [G₀ S₀] ← relevant rows of [G₀ S₀];
    [G₁ S₁] ← relevant rows of [G₁ S₁];
    x* ← Construct optimal from [G₀ S₀] and [G₁ S₁];
    return x*;
```

Fig. 4. Implementation of algorithm $X2$

The final step is to form a complete solutions. This is achieved starting with a vector [———————], and setting the values of loci according to that indicated by **G** giving preference to the rows with the highest incremental evaluation. For our example, we first obtain [010————] taking the first row of **G**. Then, using the second row produces [0100111]. Since all the loci are defined and all the other rows of **G** have a lower incremental evaluation, this is the optimal.

5   Algorithm $X2$

$X1$ detects all non-linearities by starting from [00···0] and evaluating in order all vectors with one 1, two 1s, three 1s, and so on up to k 1s. Algorithm $X2$, shown in Figure 4, follows a more efficient way to scan through the search space to detect non-linearities. It applies the same strategy as $X1$ and starts [00···0] but only goes up to $\lceil k/2 \rceil$ 1s. Then, it starts from [11···1] and evaluates in order all vectors of one 0, two 0s, and so on up to $\lfloor k/2 \rfloor$ 0s.

$X2$ applies $X1$ with $k = k_0$ starting from [00···0] and produces [**G₀ S₀**]. Then, it applies $X1$ with $k = k_1$ starting from [11···1] and produces [**G₁ S₁**]. Figure 5 shows the status of [**G₀ S₀**] and [**G₁ S₁**] after being sorted by incremental evaluations for our example function. $X2$ constructs the optimal from [**G₀ S₀**] and [**G₁ S₁**]. Rows in [**G₀ S₀**] which would be used to construct the optimal if $X1$ were to be used to construct the optimal from [**G₀ S₀**] are detected as *relevant* rows. In a similar manner, relevant rows in [**G₁ S₁**] are detected. Figure 8 show relevant rows in our example. Finally, a complete solution from **G₀** and **G₁** is formed by choosing first the relevant rows with the largest number of defined loci.[5] In our example, the optimal solution is [0100111].

---

[5] In case of contradicting rows with equal number of defined positions, more function evaluations are performed to decide the best solution.

$$[\mathbf{G}_0\ \mathbf{S}_0] \begin{bmatrix} 0\ 1\ 0\ 0\ 0\ 0\ 0 & 1.0000 \\ 0\ 0\ 0\ 0\ 1\ 1\ 1 & 0.6000 \\ 0\ 0\ 1\ 0\ 0\ 0\ 0 & 0.3333 \\ 1\ 0\ 0\ 0\ 0\ 0\ 0 & 0.3333 \\ 0\ 0\ 0\ 1\ 0\ 0\ 0 & 0.2000 \\ 0\ 1\ 1\ 0\ 0\ 0\ 0 & 0.0000 \\ 1\ 1\ 0\ 0\ 0\ 0\ 0 & 0.0000 \\ 0\ 0\ 0\ 0\ 0\ 0\ 1 & -0.2000 \\ 0\ 0\ 0\ 0\ 0\ 1\ 0 & -0.2000 \\ 0\ 0\ 0\ 0\ 1\ 0\ 0 & -0.2000 \end{bmatrix}$$

$$[\mathbf{G}_1\ \mathbf{S}_1] \begin{bmatrix} 1\ 1\ 1\ 0\ 1\ 1\ 1 & 1.0000 \\ 0\ 1\ 0\ 1\ 1\ 1\ 1 & 0.6667 \\ 1\ 0\ 1\ 1\ 1\ 1\ 1 & 0.3333 \\ 1\ 1\ 1\ 1\ 1\ 1\ 0 & 0.2000 \\ 1\ 1\ 1\ 1\ 1\ 0\ 1 & 0.2000 \\ 1\ 1\ 1\ 1\ 0\ 1\ 1 & 0.2000 \\ 1\ 1\ 1\ 0\ 1\ 1\ 0 & 0.0000 \\ 1\ 1\ 1\ 0\ 1\ 0\ 1 & 0.0000 \\ 1\ 1\ 1\ 0\ 0\ 1\ 1 & 0.0000 \\ 1\ 1\ 0\ 1\ 1\ 1\ 1 & -0.3333 \\ 0\ 1\ 1\ 1\ 1\ 1\ 1 & -0.3333 \end{bmatrix}$$

Fig. 5. Status of $[\mathbf{G}_0\ \mathbf{S}_0]$ and $[\mathbf{G}_1\ \mathbf{S}_1]$ after sort by incremental evaluations

$$[\mathbf{G}_0\ \mathbf{S}_1] \begin{bmatrix} 0\ 1\ 0\ -\ -\ -\ - & 1.0000 \\ -\ -\ -\ -\ 1\ 1\ 1 & 0.6000 \\ -\ 0\ 1\ -\ -\ -\ - & 0.3333 \\ 1\ 0\ -\ -\ -\ -\ - & 0.3333 \\ -\ -\ -\ 1\ -\ -\ - & 0.2000 \\ 0\ 1\ 1\ -\ -\ -\ - & 0.0000 \\ 1\ 1\ 0\ -\ -\ -\ - & 0.0000 \\ -\ -\ -\ -\ 0\ 0\ 0 & 0.0000 \end{bmatrix}$$

$$[\mathbf{G}_1\ \mathbf{S}_1] \begin{bmatrix} -\ -\ -\ 0\ 1\ 1\ 1 & 1.0000 \\ 0\ -\ 0\ -\ -\ -\ - & 0.6667 \\ -\ 0\ -\ -\ -\ -\ - & 0.3333 \\ -\ -\ -\ 1\ -\ -\ 0 & 0.2000 \\ -\ -\ -\ 1\ -\ 0\ - & 0.2000 \\ -\ -\ -\ 1\ 0\ -\ - & 0.2000 \\ -\ -\ -\ 0\ 1\ 1\ 0 & 0.0000 \\ -\ -\ -\ 0\ 1\ 0\ 1 & 0.0000 \\ -\ -\ -\ 0\ 0\ 1\ 1 & 0.0000 \\ 1\ -\ 1\ -\ -\ -\ - & 0.0000 \end{bmatrix}$$

Fig. 6. $[\mathbf{G}_0\ \mathbf{S}_0]$ and $[\mathbf{G}_1\ \mathbf{S}_1]$ after detecting restrictions implied in the non-linearities found

$$[\mathbf{G}\ \mathbf{S}] \begin{bmatrix} 0\ 1\ 0\ -\ -\ -\ - & 1.0000 \\ -\ -\ -\ -\ 1\ 1\ 1 & 0.6000 \\ 1\ 0\ 1\ -\ -\ -\ - & 0.6667 \\ -\ -\ -\ 1\ -\ -\ - & 0.2000 \\ 0\ 1\ 1\ -\ -\ -\ - & 0.0000 \\ 1\ 1\ 0\ -\ -\ -\ - & 0.0000 \\ -\ -\ -\ -\ 0\ 0\ 0 & 0.0000 \end{bmatrix}$$

$$[\mathbf{G}'\ \mathbf{S}'] \begin{bmatrix} -\ -\ -\ 0\ 1\ 1\ 1 & 1.0000 \\ 0\ -\ 0\ -\ -\ -\ - & 0.6667 \\ -\ 0\ -\ -\ -\ -\ - & 0.3333 \\ -\ -\ -\ 1\ 0\ 0\ 0 & 0.6000 \\ -\ -\ -\ 0\ 1\ 1\ 0 & 0.0000 \\ -\ -\ -\ 0\ 1\ 0\ 1 & 0.0000 \\ -\ -\ -\ 0\ 0\ 1\ 1 & 0.0000 \\ 1\ -\ 1\ -\ -\ -\ - & 0.0000 \end{bmatrix}$$

Fig. 7. $[\mathbf{G}_0\ \mathbf{S}_0]$ and $[\mathbf{G}_1\ \mathbf{S}_1]$ after joining non-contradicting restrictions that share columns

6 Number of Function Evaluations

In this section we show that algorithms *X1* and *X2* require a polynomial number of function evaluations to find the optimal.

$$\begin{array}{cc} \text{relevant rows of } [\mathbf{G}_0 \ \mathbf{S}_0] & \text{relevant rows of } [\mathbf{G}_1 \ \mathbf{S}_1] \\ \begin{bmatrix} 0 & 1 & 0 & - & - & - & - & 1.0000 \\ - & - & - & - & 1 & 1 & 1 & 0.6000 \\ - & - & - & 1 & - & - & - & 0.2000 \end{bmatrix} & \begin{bmatrix} - & - & - & 0 & 1 & 1 & 1 & 1.0000 \\ 0 & - & 0 & - & - & - & - & 0.6667 \\ - & 0 & - & - & - & - & - & 0.3333 \end{bmatrix} \end{array}$$

Fig. 8. Relevant rows of $[\mathbf{G}_0 \ \mathbf{S}_0]$ and $[\mathbf{G}_1 \ \mathbf{S}_1]$

While detecting non-linearities, *X1* performs

$$1 + \binom{\ell}{1} + \binom{\ell}{2} + \cdots + \binom{\ell}{k} = \sum_{i=0}^{k} \binom{\ell}{i} \quad (13)$$

evaluations of the objective function. Given that

$$\binom{\ell}{k} = \frac{\ell!}{k!(\ell-k)!} = \frac{\ell(\ell-1)(\ell-2)\cdots(\ell-k+1)}{k!} < \frac{\ell^k}{k!} < \ell^k, \quad (14)$$

which for a fixed k is no more than $\mathcal{O}(\ell^k)$.

Algorithm *X2* requires

$$\sum_{i=0}^{k_0} \binom{\ell}{i} + \sum_{i=0}^{k_1} \binom{\ell}{i} + \ell, \quad (15)$$

which for a fixed k is no more than $\mathcal{O}(\ell^{k_0})$.

7 Conclusions and Future Work

This paper has presented a deterministic algorithm that solves to optimality decomposable non-overlapping problems in a polynomial number of function evaluations. The fact that such an algorithm can be devised has important implications for the design of GA-hard problems, and the development and evaluation of genetic optimization algorithms. Other types of test problems should be considered. Overlapping problems have been used to test algorithms that solve the linkage problem, but overlapping problems are NP in the general case as optimization problems, and therefore, one cannot ask for polynomial order algorithms that solve them. Also, hierarchically defined functions have been used as test problems, but it could seem that there is an *ad-hoc* relation between these functions and the algorithms that solve them in polynomial time [11].

Several avenues to continue the development of the ideas that produced *X1* and *X2* can be followed. We are currently working on an algorithm that starts the detection of non-linearities from more than two points in the search space. Another line of research we are following is the development of an algorithm capable of solving hierarchically decomposable functions [12].

Acknowledgments

The work reported in this paper was supported by the Tecnológico de Monterrey, Campus Monterrey under Research Grant CAT–010.

References

1. Goldberg, D.E.: The Design of Innovation: Lessons from and for Competent Genetic Algorithms. Kluwer, Boston, MA (2002)
2. Pelikan, M.: Bayesian Optimization Algorithm: From Single Level to Hierarchy. PhD thesis, University of Illinois, Urbana-Champaign (2002) IlliGAL Report No. 2002023.
3. Goldberg, D.E., Deb, K., Karagupta, H., Harik, G.: Rapid, accurate optimization of difficult problems using fast messy genetic algorithms. Proceedings of the Fifth International Conference on Genetic Algorithms (1993) 56–64
4. Harik, G.: Linkage learning via probabilistic modeling in the ECGA. IlliGAL Report No. 99010, Illinois Genetic Algorithm Laboratory, University of Illinois, Urbana-Champaign, IL (1999)
5. Munetomo, M., Goldberg, D.E.: Identifying linkage by nonlinearity check. IlliGAL Report No. 98012, Illinois Genetic Algorithm Laboratory, University of Illinois, Urbana-Champaign, IL (1998)
6. Heckendorn, R.B., Wright, A.H.: Efficient linkage learning discovery by limited probing. Evolutionary Computation **12** (2005) 517–545
7. Munetomo, M., Goldberg, D.E.: Designing a genetic algorithm using the linkage identification by nonlinearity check. IlliGAL Report No. 98014, Illinois Genetic Algorithm Laboratory, University of Illinois, Urbana-Champaign, IL (1998)
8. Goldberg, D.E.: Genetic Algorithms in Search, Optimization, and Machine Learning. Addison-Wesley, Reading, MA (1989)
9. Holland, J.H.: Adaptation in Natural and Artificial Systems. University of Michigan Press, Ann Arbor, MI (1975)
10. Deb, K., Goldberg, D.E.: Analyzing deception in trap functions. In Whitley, D.L., ed.: Foundations of Genetic Algorithms 2. Morgan Kaufmann, San Mateo, CA (1994) 93–108
11. Pelikan, M., Goldberg, D.E.: Hierarchical problem solving by the Bayesian optimization algorithm. Proceedings of the Genetic and Evolutionary Computation Conference (GECCO-2000) (2000) 511–518 IlliGAL Report No. 2000020.
12. Watson, R.A., Hornby, G.S., Pollack, J.B.: Modeling building-block interdependency. Parallel Problem Solving from Nature (2000) 97–106

K-Dynamical Self Organizing Maps*

Carolina Saavedra[1], Héctor Allende[1],
Sebastián Moreno[1], and Rodrigo Salas[1,2]

[1] Universidad Técnica Federico Santa María,
Dept. de Informática, Casilla 110-V, Valparaíso-Chile
{hallende, smoreno, saavedra}@inf.utfsm.cl
[2] Universidad de Valparaíso, Departamento de Computación
{rodrigo.salas}@uv.cl

Abstract. Neural maps are a very popular class of unsupervised neural networks that project high-dimensional data of the input space onto a neuron position in a low-dimensional output space grid. It is desirable that the projection effectively preserves the structure of the data.

In this paper we present a hybrid model called K-Dynamical Self Organizing Maps ($KDSOM$) consisting of K Self Organizing Maps with the capability of growing and interacting with each other. The input space is soft partitioned by the lattice maps. The $KDSOM$ automatically finds its structure and learns the topology of the input space clusters.

We apply our $KDSOM$ model to three examples, two of which involve real world data obtained from a site containing benchmark data sets.

Keywords: Self Organizing Maps, Clustering Algorithms, Artificial Neural Networks.

1 Introduction

Real cases often contain many high dimensional data and the neural designer has the difficulty to decide in advance the architecture of the model, to be used to capture particular features of the data. To overcome the architectural design problem several algorithms with adaptive structure have been proposed, for example, we refer to the growing SOM [2], Growing cell Structures [5],Hierarchical Growing Neural Gas [4] and Robust Growing Hierarchical Self Organizing Map [12].

In this paper we propose a hybrid problem-dependent model based on a Kohonen's Self Organizing Maps [7] with the Bauer et al. growing variant of the SOM [2], the Martinez et al. Neural Gas (NG) [9], the K-means [11] and the Single Linkage clustering algorithm [6]. We call our hybrid algorithm K-Dynamical Self Organizing Maps ($KDSOM$). The $KDSOM$ is a hybrid model that adapts K growing self organizing maps to the input signals and introduces a soft partition to the input space. Each of the K maps of the $KDSOM$ model automatically

---

* This work was supported in part by Research Grant Fondecyt 1040365, DGIP-UTFSM, BMBF-CHL 03-Z13 from German Ministry of Education, DIPUV-22/2004 and CID-04/2003.

finds its structure to learn the topology of its respective partition and, through the interaction with the neighbors maps, it also learns the data belonging to other partitions. The number of maps and prototypes are automatically found.

The remainder or this paper is organized as follows. In the next section we briefly introduce the unsupervised clustering algorithms while in the third section the topology preserving neural models is presented. In the fourth section, our proposal of the *KDSOM* model is stated. Simulation results on synthetic and real data sets are provided in the fifth section. Conclusions and further work are given in the last section.

2 Unsupervised Clustering Algorithms

Clustering can be considered as one of the most important unsupervised learning problems. A cluster is a collection of "similar" objects and they should be "dissimilar" to the objects belonging to other clusters. Unsupervised clustering tries to discover the natural groups inside a data set.

The purpose of any clustering technique [10] is to evolve a $K \times N$ partition matrix $U(\chi)$ of the data set $\chi = \{\underline{x}_1, ..., \underline{x}_N\}$, $\underline{x}_j \in \mathbb{R}^n$, representing its partitioning into a number, say K, of clusters $\mathcal{C}_1, ..., \mathcal{C}_K$. Each element u_{kj}, $k = 1..K$ and $j = 1..n$ of the matrix $U(\chi)$ indicates the membership of pattern $\underline{x}_j$ to the cluster $\mathcal{C}_k$. In crisp partitioning of the data, the following condition holds: $u_{kj} = 1$ if $\underline{x}_j \in \mathcal{C}_k$; otherwise, $u_{kj} = 0$.

There are several clustering techniques classified as partitional and hierachical [6]. In this paper we based our model in the K-means and Single Linkage algorithms.

2.1 K-Means

The K-means method introduced by McQueen [11] is one of the most widely applied partitional clustering technique. This method basically consists on the following steps. First, K randomly chosen points from the data are selected as seed points for the centroids $\overline{z}_k$, $k = 1..K$, of the clusters. Second, assign each data to the cluster with the nearest centroid based on some distance criterion, for example, $\underline{x}_j$ belongs to the cluster $\mathcal{C}_k$ if the distance $d(\underline{x}_j, \overline{z}_k) = \|\underline{x}_j - \overline{z}_k\|$ is the minimum for $k = 1..K$. Third, the centroids of the clusters are updated to the "center" of the points belonging to the partition, for example, $\overline{z}_k = \frac{1}{N_k} \sum_{\underline{x}_j \in \mathcal{C}_k} \underline{x}_j$, where N_k is the number of data belonging to the cluster k. Finally, repeat the procedure until either the cluster centroids do not change or some optimal criterion is met.

This algorithm is iteratively repeated for $K = 1, 2, 3, ...$ until some validity measure indicates that partition $U_{K_{opt}}$ is a better partition than U_K, $K < K_{opt}$ (see [10] for some validity indices). In this work we use the F-test to specify the number K of clusters. The F-test measures the variability reduction by comparing the sum of distance squared of the data to their centroids $E_K = \sum_{j=1}^{N} \sum_{k=1}^{K} u_{kj} \|\underline{x}_j - \overline{z}_k\|^2$ of K and $K + 1$ groups. The test statistic is

$F = \frac{E_K - E_{K+1}}{E_{K+1}/(n-K-1)}$ and is compared with the F statistical distribution with p and $p(n - K - 1)$ degrees of freedom.

2.2 Single Linkage

The Single Linkage clustering scheme, also known as the nearest neighbor method, is usually regarded as a graph theoretical model [6]. It starts by considering each point as a cluster on its own. The single linkage algorithm computes the distance between two clusters $\mathcal{C}_k$ and $\mathcal{C}_l$ as $\delta_{SL}(\mathcal{C}_k, \mathcal{C}_l) = \min_{\underline{x} \in \mathcal{C}_k, \underline{y} \in \mathcal{C}_l} \{d(\underline{x}, \underline{y})\}$.

If the distance between both clusters is less than some threshold θ then they are merged into a new cluster. The process continues until the distances between all the clusters are greater than the threshold θ.

This algorithm is very sensitive to the determination of the parameter θ, for this reason we compute its value proportional to the average distance between the points belonging the same clusters, i.e., $\theta(\chi) \alpha \frac{1}{N_k} \sum_{\underline{x}_i, \underline{x}_j \in \mathcal{C}_k} d(\underline{x}_i, \underline{x}_j)$. At the beginning θ can be set as a fraction (bigger than one) of the minimum distance of the two closest points. When the algorithm is done, clusters consisting of less than l data are merged to the nearest cluster.

3 Topology Preserving Neural Models

In addition, it is also interesting to explore the topological structure of the data of each cluster. The Kohonen's Self Organizing Map [7] and their variants are useful for this task.

3.1 Self Organizing Maps

The self-organizing maps (SOM) neural model is an iterative procedure capable of representing the topological structure of the input space (discrete or continuous) by a discrete set of prototypes (*weight vectors*) which are associated to neurons of the network.

The map is generated by establishing a correspondence between the input signals $\underline{x} = [x_1, ..., x_n]^T$, $\underline{x} \in \chi \subseteq \mathbb{R}^n$, and neurons located on a discrete lattice. The correspondence is obtained by a competitive learning algorithm consisting on a sequence of training steps that iteratively modifies the weight vector $\underline{m}_k = (m_1^k, ..., m_n^k)$, $\underline{m}_k \in \mathbb{R}^n$, of the neurons, where k is the location of the prototype in the lattice.

When a new signal $\underline{x}$ arrives, every neuron competes to represent it. The best matching unit (bmu) is the neuron that wins the competition and together with its neighbors on the lattice are allowed to learn the signal. The bmu is the reference vector c that is nearest to the input and is obtained by some metric, $c = \arg\min_i \{\|\underline{x} - \underline{m}_i\|\}$.

During the learning process the reference vectors are changed iteratively according to the following adaptation rule,

$$\underline{m}_j(t+1) = \underline{m}_j(t) + \alpha(t) h_c(j, t)[\underline{x} - \underline{m}_j(t)] \qquad j = 1..M$$

where M is the number of prototypes that must be adjusted. The learning parameter $\alpha(t) \in [0,1]$ is a monotonically decreasing real valued sequence. The amount that the units learnt will be governed by a neighborhood kernel $h_c(j,t)$, which is a decreasing function of the distance between the unit j and the *bmu* c_{bmu}. The neighborhood kernel is usually given by a Gaussian function:

$$h_c(j,t) = \exp\left(-\frac{\|\underline{r}_j - \underline{r}_c\|^2}{\sigma(t)^2}\right) \quad (1)$$

where $\underline{r}_j$ and $\underline{r}_c$ denote the coordinates of the neurons c and i in the lattice. In practice the neighborhood kernel is controlled by the parameter $\sigma(t)$ and is chosen wide enough in the beginning of the learning process to guarantee global ordering of the map, and both its width and height decrease slowly during the learning process. More details and some properties of the *SOM* can be found in [7] and further improvements can be found in [1].

3.2 Neural Gas

The "Neural-Gas" (*NG*) is a variant introduced by Martinetz et al. to the *SOM* model [9]. In the *NG* the neighborhoods are adaptively defined during training by the ranking order of the distance of the codebooks to the data.

The Neural Gas consists of a set of M units: $A = (c_1, ..., c_M)$, where each unit has an associated reference vector $\underline{m}_{c_i} \in \Re^n$ indicating its position in the input space. When a data vector $\underline{x}$ is presented, the "neighborhood-ranking" $(\underline{m}_{i_0}, \underline{m}_{i_1}, ..., \underline{m}_{i_{M-1}})$ is determined, with $\underline{m}_{i_0}$ being the closest to $\underline{x}$, $\underline{m}_{i_1}$ being second closest, until $\underline{m}_{i_{M-1}}$ the most distance prototype.

If $\kappa_i(\underline{x},\underline{m})$ denotes the number κ associated with each vector $\underline{m}_i$, then the adaptation step for adjusting the $\underline{m}_i$'s is given by:

$$\underline{m}_i(t+1) = \underline{m}_i(t) + \alpha(t) h_{\lambda(t)}(\kappa_i(\underline{x},\underline{m}))(\underline{x} - \underline{m}_i) \quad i=1,..,M$$

where the neighborhood kernel $h_{\lambda(t)}(\kappa_i(\underline{x},\underline{m}))$ is one for $k_i = 0$ and decays to zero for increasing κ_i. In this paper we use the following neighborhood kernel function:

$$h_\lambda(\kappa_i(x,m)) = \exp^{\kappa_i(\underline{x},\underline{m})/\lambda(t)} \quad (2)$$

where both the learning parameter $\alpha(t) \in [0,1]$ and $\lambda(t)$ being real valued sequences that monotonically decrease in time.

4 The K Dynamical Self Organizing Maps Model

The *KDSOM* is a hybrid model that adapts K growing self organizing maps to the input signals by introducing a soft partition to the input space. Each of the K maps of the *KDSOM* model automatically finds its structure and learn the topology of its respective partitions. Due to the interaction between the maps, it also learn the data of neighboring partitions. The number of maps and prototypes are automatically found.

The training process has three stages, the first part consists in finding the possible number of clusters and their centroids. During the second stage SOM lattices are associated to each cluster and the prototypes of each grid will learn the topological structure of their partitions. Finally, in the third stage the maps grow if the topological representation is not good enough. The model iteratively adapts its parameters and grows its maps until some criterion is met.

First Stage: Clustering the data. The purpose of this stage is to find the number of clusters presented in the data. To this purpose, first we execute the K-means algorithm, presented in section 2.1, with a very low threshold in order to find more clusters than really expected. Then, the Single Linkage algorithm is executed to merge clusters that are closer to obtain, hopefully, the optimal number of clusters. When the number of clusters K and their respective centroids $\overline{z}_k$, $k = 1..K$, are obtained the first stage is considered done.

Second Stage: Topological Learning. Now, we proceed to create a grid of size 2×2 under each cluster identified in the previous stage. The maps are created randomly around the centroid $\overline{z}_k$.

Centroid neurons $\overline{m}^{[k]}$ representing the center of the $k-th$ grid and the clusters k are created as well. The position of these centroids neurons are computed by the mean value of the prototypes belonging to their map lattice, i.e., $\overline{m}^{[k]} = \frac{1}{M_k} \sum_{j=1}^{M_k} m_j^{[k]}$, where $m_j^{[k]}$ is the j-th prototype of the grid k and M_k is the number of neurons of that lattice.

During the learning process when a new signal $\underline{x}$ is presented to the model at time t the best matching map (bmm) is found as follows. Let $\mathcal{M}_k$ be the set of prototypes that belongs to the map k. The best matching units (bmu) $\underline{m}_{c_k}^{[k]}$ to the data $\underline{x}$ for each of the K maps are computed. The map that contains the closest bmu will be the bmm, i.e.,

$$\eta = \arg \min_{k=1..K} \{ \left\| \underline{x} - \underline{m}_{c_k}^{[k]} \right\|, \underline{m}_{c_k}^{[k]} \in \mathcal{M}_k \} \quad (3)$$

The prototypes will be updated iteratively according to the following learning rule:

$$\underline{m}_j^{[k]}(t+1) = \underline{m}_j^{[k]}(t) + \alpha(t) \left(h_\lambda(\kappa_\eta(\underline{x}, \overline{m}^{[k]}, t)) \right)^{\beta(t)} h_{c_k}^{[k]}(j,t)[\underline{x} - \underline{m}_j^{[k]}(t)] \quad (4)$$

where $\beta(t) \in [1, \infty]$ controls the degree of influence of neighboring maps and is a real valued sequence that monotonically increases in time. The adaptation amount of the units are given by the difference between the codebooks and the data $[\underline{x} - \underline{m}_j^{[\eta]}(t)]$ weighted by the prototype neighborhood kernel of the units belonging to the grid k, $h_{c_k}^{[k]}(j,t)$, and also weighted by the map neighborhood kernel $\left(h_\lambda(\kappa_\eta(\underline{x}, \overline{m}^{[k]}, t)) \right)^{\beta(t)}$. Both kernels are given by equations (1) and (2) respectively.

It is important to note that we are treating the maps, represented by their centroid $\overline{m}^{[k]}$, as neurons of the Neural Gas model where the neighborhoods of the maps are defined by the ranking order of the distance of the centroid neurons to the training sample. When a data vector $\underline{x}$ is presented, the "neighborhood ranking" $(\overline{m}^{[\eta]}, \overline{m}^{[\eta_1]}, ..., \overline{m}^{[\eta_K]})$ is determined, with $\overline{m}^{[\eta]}$ being the bmm, $\overline{m}^{[\eta_1]}$ the second closest map, and so on. $\kappa_\eta(\underline{x}, \overline{m}^{[\eta_i]}, t)$ denotes the number of the ranking κ associated to each vector $\overline{m}^{[\eta_i]}$.

The learning parameters $\alpha(t)$ and $\beta(t)$ are specified as follows: $\alpha(t)$ is a monotonically decreasing function of time, while $\beta(t)$ is an increasing function. For example this functions could be linear $(\alpha(t) = \alpha_0 + (\alpha_f - \alpha_0)t/t_\alpha)$ or exponential $(\alpha(t) = \alpha_0(\alpha_f/\alpha_0)^{t/t_\alpha})$, where α_0 is the initial learning rate, α_f is the final rate and t_α is the maximum number of iteration steps to reach to α_f (Analogously for $\beta(t)$, but $\beta_0 < \beta_f$).

Third Stage: Growing the Maps Lattices. In this part we introduce the variant proposed by Bauer et. al. for growing the SOM [2]. If the topological representation of the partitions of the input space is not good enough the maps will grow by increasing the number of their prototypes.

The quality of the topological representation of each map k of the *KDSOM* model is measured in terms of the deviation between the units. At the beginning we compute the quantization error $qe_0^{[k]}$ of the centroid neurons $\overline{m}^{[k]}$ over the whole data belonging to the cluster $\mathcal{C}_k$.

All units must represent their respective Voronoi polygons of data at a quantization error smaller than a fraction τ of $qe_0^{[k]}$, i.e., $qe_j^{[k]} < \tau \cdot qe_0^{[k]}$, where $qe_j^{[k]} = \sum_{\underline{x}_i \in \mathcal{C}_j^{[k]}} \left\| \underline{x}_i - \underline{m}_j^{[k]} \right\|$, $\mathcal{C}_j^{[k]} \neq \phi$ and $\mathcal{C}_j^{[k]}$ is the set of input vectors belonging to the Voronoi polygon of the unit j in the map lattice k. The units that do not satisfy this criterion require a more detailed data representation.

When the map lattice k is chosen to grow, we compute the value of $qe_j^{[k]}$ for all the units belonging to the map. The unit with the highest $qe_j^{[k]}$, called error unit e, and its most dissimilar neighbor d are detected. To accomplish this the value of e and d are computed by $e = \arg\max_j \left\{ \sum_{\underline{x}_i \in \mathcal{C}_j^{[k]}} \left\| \underline{x}_i - \underline{m}_j^{[k]} \right\| \right\}$ and $d = \arg\max_j \left(\left\| \underline{m}_e^{[k]} - \underline{m}_j^{[k]} \right\| \right)$ respectively, where $\mathcal{C}_j^{[k]} \neq \phi$, $\underline{m}_j^{[k]} \in \mathcal{N}_e$ and $\mathcal{N}_e$ is the set of neighboring units of the error unit e. A row or column of units is inserted between e and d and their model vectors are initialized as the means of their respective neighbors. After insertions, the map is trained again by using equation (4).

Clustering and labelling the data. To classify the data $\underline{x}_j$ to one of the cluster $k = 1..K$, we find the best matching map given by equation (3) and then the data receive the label of this map η, i.e, for the data $\underline{x}_j$ we set $u_{j\eta} = 1$ and $u_{jk} = 0$ for $k = \eta$. To evaluate the clustering performance we compute the percentage of right classification given by:

$$PC = \frac{1}{N} \sum_{\underline{x}_j, j=1..N} u_{jk^*} \qquad k^* = \text{True class of } \underline{x}_j \qquad (5)$$

Evaluation of the adaptation quality. To evaluate the quality of the partitions topological representation, a common measure to compare the algorithms is needed. The following metric called the mean square quantization error is used:

$$MSQE = \frac{1}{N} \sum_{M_k, k=1..K} \sum_{m_j^{[k]} \in M_k} \sum_{x_i \in C_j^{[k]}} \left\| x_i - m_j^{[k]} \right\|^2 \qquad (6)$$

5 Simulation Results

To validate the *KDSOM* model we first apply the algorithm to computer generated data and then to two real data sets obtained from a site containing benchmark data sets.

The summary of the simulation results are shown in table 1. The column *Dataset* is the experimental dataset used and *Model* is the type of model applied. The columns *Neurons* and *Grids* give the number of prototypes and maps generated respectively. Finally, the columns *PC* and *MSQE* are the percentage of right classification (5) and mean square quantization error (6) respectively, both applied to the training and test set.

The algorithms selected to compare the results are *GSOM*, *KDSOM* and *KDSOM_β*. The difference of the last two is that the update rule given by equation (4) for the *KDSOM* is with $\beta = \infty$, i.e. there is no interaction between the maps. While for the *KDSOM_β* the parameter β is greater than or equal to 1, so it induces an interaction between the maps.

To execute the simulations and to compute the metrics, all the dimensions of the training data were scaled to the unit interval. The test sets were scaled using the same scale applied to the training data (Notice that with this scaling the test data will not necessarily fall in the unit interval).

5.1 Experiment #1: Computer Generated Data

Five clusters from the two-dimensional Gaussian distribution $\underline{X}_k \sim \mathcal{N}(\mu_k, \Sigma_k)$, $k = 1, ..., 5$ were constructed, where μ_k and Σ_k are the mean vector and the covariance matrix respectively, of the cluster k. A total of 1000 training samples and 1000 test samples were drawn. The information about the parameters used to generate the clusters is given by:

Cluster	N_{train}	N_{test}	μ	Σ
1	150	150	$[0.8; 0.1]^T$	$0.03^2 * I_2$
2	150	150	$[1; -0.1]^T$	$0.03^2 * I_2$
3	200	200	$[0.1; 0.1]^T$	$0.10^2 * I_2$
4	200	200	$[0.9; 1]^T$	$0.15^2 * I_2$
5	300	300	$[0.1; 1]^T$	$0.01^2 * I_2$
Total	1000	1000		

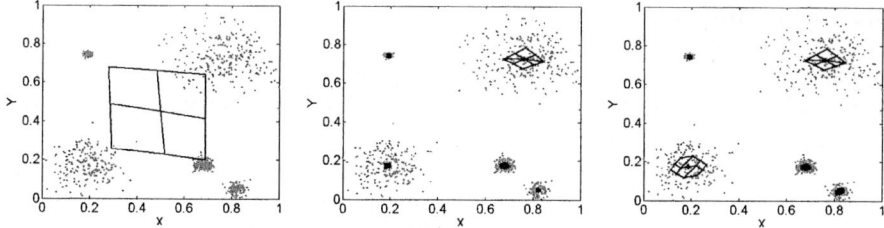

Fig. 1. Synthetic data results: Computer generated data with 1000 data. (Left) The *GSOM* modelling the data. (Middle) The *KDSOM* modelling the data (Right) The *KDSOM_β* modelling the data. The *KDSOM* and *KDSOM_β* create 5 maps lattice to model the structure of the clustered data.

In figure 1 the synthetic data set can be appreciated together with the *GSOM*, *KDSOM* and *KDSOM_β* modelling the data. The *KDSOM*s models were able to detect and learn the topology of the clusters.

The summary of the simulation results are shown in the Synthetic row of table 1. As can be noted the *KDSOM* and *KDSOM_β* obtained better classification performance than the *GSOM* model for both training and test set. For the *KDSOM* models we are able to infer the possible number of natural clusters in the data while this task is not possible for the *GSOM*. Furthermore, the *KDSOM_β* made a better topological representation than the other two models by one order of magnitude. The number of codebooks of the *GSOM* needed to model the topology of the data is much less than the number needed for the *KDSOM* models because the last implements several grids with at least four neurons. The *KDSOM_β* outperforms the *KDSOM* so for this case, the local and global adaptation of the model given by equation (4) improves the topological representation.

Table 1. Summary results showing the comparative performance of the GSOM, KDSOM and KDSOM_β models using the synthetic datasets and the real data sets composed by the Wisconsin Breast Cancer Database and the Wine Database. The growing parameter τ was set in 0.05.

Dataset	Model	Neurons	Grids	$MSQE$ Train	PC Train	$MSQE$ Test	PC Test
Synthetic	GSOM	9	1	0.021	87.8	0.024	83.7
Train: 1000	KDSOM	72	5	0.010	100	0.010	100
Test : 1000	KDSOM_β	60	5	**0.004**	100	**0.004**	100
Cancer	GSOM	18	1	2.168	83.77	1.835	83.50
Train: 369	KDSOM	49	3	0.283	86.99	0.313	91.50
Test : 200	KDSOM_β	46	3	**0.202**	90.51	**0.206**	92.50
Wine	GSOM	16	1	0.273	97.00	0.282	92.31
Train: 100	KDSOM	75	4	0.509	96.00	0.712	94.87
Test : 68	KDSOM_β	64	4	**0.188**	96.00	**0.281**	96.15

5.2 Experiment #2: Real Datasets

In the second experiment we test the algorithm with two real datasets known as the *Wisconsin Breast Cancer Database* and *Wine* datasets obtained from the UCI Machine Learning repository [3].

The *Cancer* data was collected by Dr. Wolberg, N. Street and O. Mangasarian at the University of Wisconsin [8]. The samples consist of visually assessed nuclear features of fine needle aspirates (FNAs) taken from patients' breasts. It consist in 569 instances, with 30 real-valued input features and a diagnosis (M = malignant, B = benign) for each patient. We partitioned the dataset into the Training and Test with sizes of 369 and 200 data respectively.

The *Wine* recognition data was collected by Stefan Aeberhard [3]. This data set is the result of a chemical analysis of wines grown in the same region in Italy but derived from three different cultivars. The analysis determined the quantities of 13 constituents found in each of the three types of wines. It consist in 178 instances and 13 attributes (all continuous). We partitioned the dataset into the Training and Test with sizes of 100 and 78 data respectively.

The summary of the simulation results are shown in the Cancer and Wine rows of table 1, the results are very similar to the synthetic case. As can be noted the *KDSOM* and *KDSOM_β* obtained better classification performance than the *GSOM* model for both training and test set with the exception of the *PC train* column of the *Wine* dataset. For the *KDSOM* models we are able to infer the possible number of natural clusters in the data while this task is not possible for the *GSOM*. Furthermore, the *KDSOM_β* made a better topological representation than the other two models for the train and test set, specially for the *Cancer* database. The number of codebooks of the *GSOM* needed to model the topology of the data is much less than the number needed for the *KDSOM* models because the last implements several grids with at least four neurons each. The *KDSOM_β* outperforms the *KDSOM* model, so for this cases the local and global adaptation of the model given by equation (4) improves the topological representation.

6 Concluding Remarks

In this paper we have introduced the K-Dynamical Self Organizing Maps. This model has the capability to learn the topology of clustered data by making a soft partition of the input space. The *KDSOM* is a hybrid model that automatically finds its structure to learn the topology of its respective partition and, through the interaction with the neighbor maps, it also learns the data of neighboring partitions.

The performance of our algorithm shows better results in the simulation study in both the synthetic and real data sets. In the real case, we investigated two benchmark data known as *Cancer* and *Wine* databases. The comparative study with the *GSOM* and *KDSOM* without improvement shows that our model the *KDSOM* with improvement outperforms the alternative models. The

KDSOM models were able to find the possible number of clusters and learn the topological representation of the partitions.

Further studies are needed in order to analyze the convergence and the ordering properties of the maps. Possible interesting applications of the *KDSOM* could be Web-Mining.

Acknowledgement. The authors wish to thank Prof. Dr. Claudio Moraga, Prof. Dr. Jorge Galbiati and all the unknown referees for their valuable comments.

References

1. H. Allende, S. Moreno, C. Rogel, and R. Salas, *Robust self organizing maps*, CIARP-2004. LNCS **3287** (2004), 179–186.
2. H. Bauer and T. Villmann, *Growing a hypercubical output space in a self-organizing feature map*, IEEE Trans. on Neural Networks **8** (1997), no. 2, 226–233.
3. C.L. Blake and C.J. Merz, *UCI repository of machine learning databases*, 1998.
4. K.A.J Doherty, R.G. Adams, and N. Davey, *Hierarchical growing neural gas*, To be published in proceedings of ICANNGA 2005 (2005).
5. B. Fritzke, *Growing cell structures - a self-organizing network for unsupervised and supervised learning*, Neural Networks **7** (1994), no. 9, 1441–1460.
6. A.K. Jain and R.C. Dubes, *Algorithms for clustering data*, Prentice Hall, 1988.
7. T. Kohonen, *Self-Organizing Maps*, Springer Series in Information Sciences, vol. 30, Springer Verlag, Berlin, Heidelberg, 2001, Third Extended Edition 2001.
8. O. Mangasarian, W. Street, and W. Wolberg, *Breast cancer diagnosis and prognosis via linear programming*, Operations Research **43** (1995), no. 4, 570–577.
9. T. Martinetz, S. Berkovich, and K. Schulten, *Neural-gas network for vector quantization and its application to time-series prediction*, IEEE Trans. on Neural Networks **4** (1993), no. 4, 558–568.
10. U. Maulik and S. Bandyopadhyay, *Performance evaluation*, IEEE. Trans. on Pattern Analysis and Machine Intelligence **24** (2002), no. 12, 1650–1654.
11. J. McQueen, *Some methods for classification and analysis of multivariate observations*, In Proceedings of the Fifth Berkeley Symposium on Mathematical Statistics and probability, vol. 1, 1967, pp. 281–297.
12. S. Moreno, H. Allende, C. Rogel, and R. Salas, *Robust growing hierarchical self organizing map*, IWANN 2005. LNCS **3512** (2005), 341–348.

Study of Application Model on BP Neural Network Optimized by Fuzzy Clustering

Yong He, Yun Zhang, and Liguo Xiang

College of Biosystems Engineering and Food Science, Zhejiang University,
286 Kaixuan Road, 310029 Hangzhou, P.R. China
yhe@zju.edu.cn

Abstract. A back-propagation neural network is a large-scale dynamical system, most widely-used for scientific prediction. Its application was inhibited largely by the slow convergence rate and over-prolonged training time, primarily the results of inappropriate sample preprocessing for a large initial sample domain. To solve them, this paper introduced fuzzy clustering to scale-down the learning sample set, with representativeness of the whole sample domain. The established network was tested by analyzing the correlation coefficients between measured and predicted results in the least-square one-dimensional linear regression. In the application case, 50 subsamples were clustered out of the 250-sample domain of the S195 diesel engines to train the network of topological structure 8:9:2. The convergence rate was improved approximately 6.3 times. After validating the model by another untrained 10 samples, the correlation coefficients of the working power and the diesel consumption rate were respectively 0.968 and 0.986, indicating that the optimized network was applicable for data mining from a large knowledge pool.

1 Introduction

Artificial neural network (ANN) is a large-scale parallelism nonlinear dynamical system, consisting of a series of simple processing units (artificial neurons). It processes the input knowledge by learning and analyzing samples parallelly and is characteristic of high speed calculation, abundant association, great robustness, potentiality of self-adaptive, self-organization and self-learning [1]. Back-propagation (BP) neural network, a type of artificial neural network, is thus most widely-used in the statistical computation and data mining field as a result of its high nonlinear mapping ability [2].

Several problems, however, have restrained the application of BP neural networks, e.g. the slow convergence rate and the over-prolonged training time. As a result, most scholars in the field of ANN application concentrated their studies on the amelioration of the of BP-neural-network algorithms. They selected randomly a few subsamples from the initial sample domain to train the network, expecting to accelerate the convergence rate and reduce the training duration [3]. Though the random selection of subsamples could to some extent solve the problems at the cost of losing the sample representativeness, it would potentially lead to larger errors in the model fitting results. Therefore, the sample pre-processing method should be considered as one of the most critical problems in the application of BP neural networks, since the training set has to be a representative collection of input-output patterns. Considering the similarity and comparability between samples, this paper introduced fuzzy clustering as an alternative for sample pre-processing to optimize the conventional BP neural network and thus accelerate the network convergence rate, shorten the training duration and finally improve the precision of the training results.

2 Establishment of BP Neural Network on Fuzzy Clustering

2.1 Principles of Fuzzy Clustering

Fuzzy clustering is principally to group samples of similar characteristics into the same classes (clusters), according to clustering principles and fuzzy evaluation criteria. Thus, those belonging to any clusters are of comparable properties and those in different classes correspondingly have dissimilar properties [4]. Given X as a set including N samples, i.e., $X=\{X_1, X_2, X_3, ..., X_i, ..., X_n\}$, S features of the object X_i are extracted, i.e., $X_i = \{X_{i1}, X_{i2}, ..., X_{ij}, ..., X_{is}\}$ ($i=1, 2, 3, ..., n; j=1, 2, 3, ..., S$), in which X_{ij} is the j eigenvalue of the i sample. And all eigenvalues constitutes the domain matrix $[X]$. The similarity coefficient between one another samples in $[X]$ is assigned certain value in the range of [0, 1], indicating the similarity extent between them. Accordingly, the specific steps of clustering samples of similar properties are as follows:

1. Normalize the standard deviation of each element in the domain matrix $[X]$ so as to create another matrix $[X']_{n \times n}$. The extremum values of each column element in $[X']_{n \times n}$ is normalized subsequently, resulting in a new matrix $[X'']_{n \times n}$.
2. Calculate the similarity coefficient r_{ij} between each element in the matrix $[X'']_{n \times n}$ by Euclidean distance method. The fuzzy similar matrix $[R]_{n \times n}$ is thus produced.
3. Cluster the element of similar properties in $[R]_{n \times n}$ into independent classes by establishing the confidence thresholds for the Euclidean distances, i.e. if the Euclidean distance between them is below the established threshold, the two randomly-selected samples are clustered into the same class and vice versa.

2.2 Subsamples Clustered for BP Neural Network Training

Given N initial learning samples of the BP neural network, they are clustered into n subclasses $(X_1, X_2,..., X_n)$, according to the fuzzy clustering principles mentioned above. p subsamples $(x_1, x_2, ..., x_m (p<n))$ are selected proportionally according to the subclass amount. Consequently, the amount of training samples for the network was scaled-down, i.e., a smaller set of learning samples is selected from the initial sample set after fuzzy clustering, without the loss of their representativeness of the whole training domain and the prediction accuracy of the network.

A schematic diagram of the neural network architecture was composed of one input layer, several hidden layers and an output layer [4]. Back-propagation (BP) algorithm with momentum is one of the most powerful learning algorithms in neural networks. It tries to reduce the total output error by adjusting the node weights along its gradient from output to hidden units during the network training. The typical BP neural network applies the logistic *Sigmoid* function as the neuron activation function. It can be calculated by:

$$f(x) = \frac{1}{1+e^{-x}}. \tag{1}$$

After fuzzy clustering, the m input-output subsamples (X_k, T_k) ($k=1, 2, 3, \ldots, m$) were ultimately used as the network training samples. $X_k=(x_{k1}, x_{k2}, \ldots, x_{kM})$ is the k input vector, where M is the dimensionality of input vectors, and $T_k=(t_{k1}, t_{k2}, \ldots, t_{kN})$ is the k output vector (desired), where N is the dimensionality of output vectors. The actual output vector is $O_k=(o_{k1}, o_{k2}, \ldots, o_{kN})^T$. w_{ji} is the weight that the i neuron of the former layer inputs to the j neuron in the next one. The specific BP neural network algorithm in this optimized model goes as follows:

1. Set weight and threshold values of each layer: put smaller random numbers $w_{ji}(0)$, $\theta_j(0)$, respectively, as the initial values;
2. Input training samples including the input vector X_k and the desired output vector T_k, where $k=1, 2, \ldots, m$. Each input sample should be trained iteratively in the following Steps from 3 to 5 until the network outputs are within the desired error precision;
3. Calculate the actual output and hidden unit vectors via:

$$o_{kj} = f_j(\sum_i w_{ji} o_{ki} + \theta_j). \tag{2}$$

4. Compute the training errors in the following expressions:
- Output layer:

$$\delta_{kj} = (t_{kj} - o_{kj}) \cdot o_{kj}(1 - o_{kj}); \tag{3}$$

- Input layer:

$$\delta_{kj} = o_{kj}(1 - o_{kj})\sum_m \delta_{km} w_{mj}. \tag{4}$$

Where t_{kj} is the target output of each node; the subscript k indicates a summation over all nodes in the downstream layer (the layer in the direction of the output layer) and the j subscript indicates the weight position in each node.

5. Adjust the weights and thresholds of each layer via:

$$w_{ji}(t+1) = w_{ji}(t) + \eta \delta_{kj} o_{ki} + \alpha[w_{ji}(t) - w_{ji}(t-1)]; \tag{5}$$

$$\theta_j(t+1) = \theta_j(t) + \eta \delta_j + \alpha[\theta_j(t) - \theta_j(t-1)]. \tag{6}$$

Where η is the learning step and α is the activation for each node.

6. After every iteration from 1 to m, judge whether the root mean square error E of the whole sample set is within the required tolerance via:

$$E = \frac{1}{2}\left[\sum_k \sum_j |t_{kj} - o_{kj}|^2\right]^{1/2} \leq \varepsilon. \tag{7}$$

In which ε is the specified accuracy; k ranges from 1 to M, and j from 1 to N.

7. The training stops.

In the above algorithm, each output is compared to the desired one. If there is a difference, the connection weights are altered in such a direction that the error is decreased. After the network has run through all the inputs, if the errors are still greater than the maximum desired tolerance, the network runs again until all errors are within the required tolerance. And then the weights hold constantly and the training results would be desirable for regression prediction in practices.

3 Correlation Analysis of the Training Results

The most desirable result is that the predicted values of the optimized BP neural network equal completely to the actual measured ones. Actually, this training precision is rarely possible due to the intrinsic structure imperfection of the network and its non-linear parallelism algorithm. Hence, an acceptable error tolerance is established in advance to evaluate the training results. If the differences between the network outputs and the measured values were in the given error tolerance, the learning results were considered acceptable and the model was applicable for fitting and predicting parameters interrelated with several factors; otherwise, the results were unacceptable and the network should maintain sample training until the differences were in the given error tolerance. Accordingly, the one-dimension linear regression was considered applicable to evaluate the training results of this BP neural network optimized by fuzzy clustering [5].

For the problems created by enormous training samples of multi-inputs and multi-outputs, a straight line with slope=1 could be fitted through the point (o_k, t_k) (o_k is the actual vector of the k training sample and t_k is the output vector) and the origin of the plane coordinate system. As a result, the linear regression line could be described as $y=x$, i.e., t_k equals to o_k, if no difference exists between the measured (actual) and the predicted (output) values. Actually, the predicted results are usually different from the measured values. Thus, another straight line $y'=kx'+b$ with specific slop $k\neq 1$ and intercept b could be achieved after fitting the data of t_k and o_k by the least-square one-dimensional linear regression [6]. And it is conducive to the correlation analysis between o_k and t_k. The significance of correlation coefficients was introduced in this model to evaluate the training results of the BP neural network and thus judge its topological structure stability.

4 Application to a Case

4.1 Learning Subsample Selection

A total of 10 running parameters of 260 S195 diesel engines were measured and collected in Xiaoshan District, Hangzhou, China in April, 2004. According to the pre-established confidence thresholds, 250 samples were randomly selected to cluster on the Euclidean distances between each other. The most acceptable thresholds for each subclass were calculated on condition that the Euclidean distances between samples with similar properties were all smaller than it, whereas those belonged to other groups all have larger distances than the threshold. Thus, the initial 250 samples were clustered into 50 subsamples by SPSS for windows (version 11.5.0, SPSS Inc.) as the ultimate training samples for the BP neural network (See Table 1). And the remaining 10 samples were utilized to validate the model.

8 feature parameters of the diesel engine, including the maximum oil pressure (x_1, MPa), the diesel injection pressure (x_2, MPa), the fuel supple advance angle (x_3, °CA), the cylinder pressure (x_4, MPa), the gas intake delaying angle (x_5, °CA), the gas intake lasting angle (x_6, °CA), the gas outlet advance angle (x_7, °CA) and the gas outlet lasting angle (x_8, °CA), were selected as the input nodes; the other 2 parameters, i.e., the working power (y_1, kW) and the diesel consumption rate (y_2, g/kW•h), were set as the output nodes [7].

Table 1. Several training samples pretreated by fuzzy clustering for the BP neural network (15 out of total 50 samples)

Sample	x_1	x_2	x_3	x_4	x_5	x_6	x_7	x_8	y_1	y_2
1	44.1	200	13	18	39	232	35	230	7.35	338.6
2	44.1	160	17	16	39	229	34	229	7.94	278.8
3	39.2	135	17	19	45	243	46	237	9.56	327.0
4	44.1	160	11	18	54	262	46	237	9.04	327.7
5	39.2	180	12	20	33	218	31	219	7.65	300.5
6	44.1	200	13	18	39	232	35	230	8.09	338.6
7	39.2	70	20	14	47	247	58	259	8.53	292.4
8	39.2	100	18	15	45	240	26	213	8.31	300.5
9	41.2	140	17	19	35	232	40	237	7.57	303.2
10	49.0	105	16	15	39	235	39	235	8.24	270.6
11	49.0	95	17	20	27	234	43	242	9.56	300.5
12	44.1	90	14	20	40	232	37	232	7.79	329.1
13	39.2	125	17	18	50	254	37	229	8.82	323.6
14	49.0	170	20	20	33	224	34	219	8.75	277.4
15	44.1	230	18	20	55	270	65	277	7.94	353.5

4.2 BP Neural Network Training

The determination of the amount of hidden nodes is most critical in designing the multilayer BP neural network. In the literature, it could be expressed via [8]:

$$n_1 = \sqrt{n+m} + a. \tag{8}$$

Where n_1 is the hidden unit amount; n is the input neuron amount; m is the output neuron amount; and a is a constant between 1 and 10. Thus, the hidden unit amount in this model could be calculated as:

$$\sqrt{8+2} + 1 \leq n_1 \leq \sqrt{8+2} + 10.$$

So,
$$4.16 \leq n_1 \leq 13.16$$

The network was trained to test the model precision by increasing n_1 until the errors went into the required tolerance. As a result, 9 hidden nodes were established for the highest convergence rate to the desired accuracy. And the network topological structure was 8:9:2.

After generalizing all training data in the range of [0, 1] to minimize the negative influences produced by the different units and order of magnitudes, the BP neural network was trained by a program developed in Visual Basic (version 6.0, Microsoft Corporation). On condition that the error tolerance $\varepsilon=0.0001$, the hidden nodes $n_1=9$, the learning step length $\eta=0.5$, and the activation $\alpha=0.5$, the network accuracy ran into the desired error tolerance and the nodes of each layer held their constant weights after training 79 000 times (See Tables 2 and 3).

Table 2. Weights and thresholds from the hidden nodes to the input nodes

Input layer	Hidden layer					
	1	2	3	4	5	6
1	-0.071	1.098	-1.509	-0.422	-1.408	-0.719
2	1.620	-0.384	0.145	0.415	-0.655	-0.700
3	-0.680	-0.176	-0.518	-0.525	1.452	-0.900
4	-1.087	-0.711	-0.692	1.827	-1.474	-0.389
5	-0.245	-6.382	-0.452	8.241	-1.390	-0.824
6	-1.600	-0.653	-0.353	8.072	0.351	-0.609
7	-0.311	-0.531	-0.408	-0.980	0.228	0.504
8	1.000	0.112	1.062	-0.427	-0.831	-7.530
Threshold	-0.307	-1.198	-8.755	-0.319	0.369	-0.760

Table 3. Weights and thresholds from the output nodes to the hidden nodes

Output layer	Hidden layer						Threshold
	1	2	3	4	5	6	
1	-1.708	0.850	-1.325	7.041	2.417	-0.264	0.190
2	0.318	1.389	-0.461	-0.089	-2.197	-0.672	-0.107

4.3 Model Validation

The 10 samples out of the initial training set of 250 samples were randomly selected for model validation. And the 8 feature parameters were similarly inputted to predict the working power (y_1) and the diesel consumption rate (y_2). In addition, the two output parameters were both comparatively predicted in the general BP neural network established by the initial 250 samples without pretreatment of fuzzy clustering. And the structure of the latter network was established by means similar to that of the former one (see Sec. 4.2) and trained until the convergence rates reached to the highest. The results showed that the learning rate of the network trained by all of the 250 samples was much slower than that of the one optimized by fuzzy clustering and thus its training duration was approximately 6.3 times longer. All of the predicted results were listed in Table 4.

Table 4. Measured and predicted values of BP neural network with and without fuzzy clustering for 10 S195 diesel engines

Engine No.	Working power (kW)			Diesel consumption rate (g/(kW•h)		
	Measured (x_1)	Predicted after fuzzy clustering (y_1)	Predicted without clustering (y_1')	Measured (x_2)	Predicted after fuzzy clustering (y_2)	Predicted without clustering (y_2')
1	7.87	7.36	7.04	270.6	285.5	296.1
2	8.37	8.24	7.97	272.0	288.7	304.9
3	8.24	7.98	7.52	320.2	334.7	339.6
4	7.68	7.44	6.83	331.8	354.1	361.7
5	8.96	8.88	9.06	338.6	349.8	352.3
6	8.64	8.62	8.77	273.3	290.3	326.6
7	8.88	8.56	8.14	307.3	324.8	329.8
8	7.96	7.84	7.32	273.6	295.8	312.3
9	8.97	8.68	8.46	286.9	307.2	313.7
10	7.94	7.65	7.62	312.8	331.2	342.4

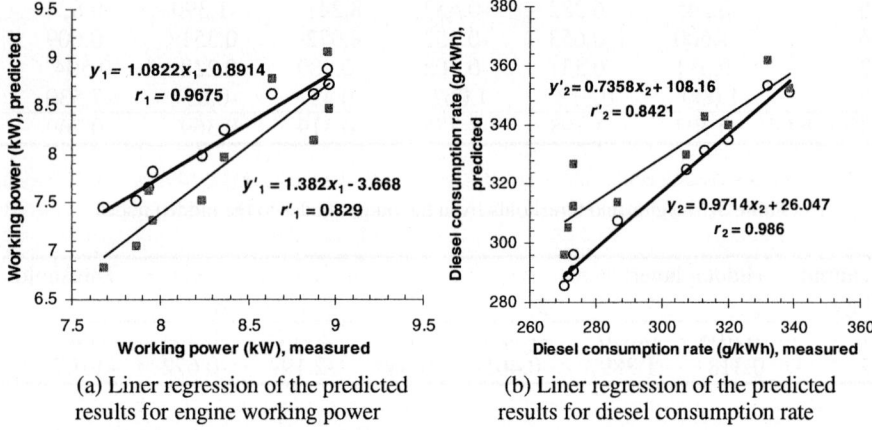

(a) Liner regression of the predicted results for engine working power

(b) Liner regression of the predicted results for diesel consumption rate

Fig. 1. One-dimensional linear regression analysis between measured and predicted results ((black ○) predicted results of BP-NN on fuzzy clustering; (gray ■) predicted results of BP-NN trained by samples without fuzzy clustering; (bold —) fitting curve for measured and predicted results of BP-NN on fuzzy clustering; (normal —) fitting curve for measured and predicted results of BP-NN trained by samples without fuzzy clustering; the linear regression functions and the corresponding correlation coefficients were illustrated respectively for engine working power ($y_1 = f(x_1), r_1$) and diesel consumption rate ($y_2 = f(x_2), r_2$))

The correlation coefficients (r) between the measured and predicted values were analyzed by the least-square one-dimensional linear regression in Fig. 1. It could be observed that the fitting curves for the predicted results of BP neural network on fuzzy clustering held higher correlation coefficients than the regression line created by the predicted values of BP neural network trained without clustering for both engine working power (r_1) and diesel consumption rate (r_2), i.e., $r_1=0.968$ was desirably higher than $r_1'=0.829$ (see Fig. 1(a)) and $r_2=0.986$ was more acceptable than $r_2'=0.842$ (see Fig. 1(b)). Additionally, the correlation coefficients of engine working power (r_1) and the diesel consumption rate (r_2) were both greater than $r_{0.05}(10)=0.5760$ and $r_{0.01}(10)=0.7079$, indicating high significance. Thus, the prediction model was prominently optimized by fuzzy clustering by reducing the redundant input samples, simplifying the network structure, increasing the convergence rate with less training time consumption and as a result improving the forecasting accuracy.

5 Conclusions

The fuzzy clustering was adopted as an alternative to preprocess the input samples of the BP neural network by grouping the initial samples of similar characteristics in the same subclass. The subsamples were then selected proportionally to the subclass amount to train the network. Thus, the amount of training samples was scaled-down, without the loss of representativeness of the whole training domain. The network was further validated by predicting untrained samples and the predicted results were analyzed by the correlation coefficients with measured values after least-square one-dimensional linear regression.

In the application example, the initial 250 S195 diesel engines of 10 running feature parameters were clustered into 5 subclasses. And a total 50 subsamples were selected as input samples to train the BP neural network of topological structure 8:9:2. Another network was then modeled with the initial 250 samples without clustering pre-processing. And its learning rate was much slower than that of the former, with training duration approximately 6.3 times longer. After validating the two established networks by another 10 untrained samples, the correlation coefficients for the working power and the diesel consumption rate of the optimized one were respectively 0.968 and 0.986, both higher than those of the latter to indicate high significance. Thus, fuzzy clustering was a promising means feasible to scale-down the large learning set of BP neural network, simplify its structure, reduce the training time consumption and improve the forecasting accuracy.

Acknowledgements

This study was supported by the Teaching and Research Award Program for Outstanding Young Teachers in Higher Education Institutions of MOE, P.R.C., Natural Science Foundation of China (Project No: 30270773), Specialized Research Fund for the Doctoral Program of Higher Education (Project No: 20040335034) and Natural Science Foundation of Zhejiang Province, China (Project No: RC02067).

References

1. Xi, G.: A Tentative Investigation of the Learning Process of a Neural Network System. Automatization Transaction, Vol. 17. No. 3. (1991) 311-316
2. Alexander, G. P.: An Accelerated Learning Algorithm for Multiplayer Perceptron Networks. IEEE Trans on Neural Networks, Vol. 5. No. 3. (1994) 493-497
3. Yang, S.: Principles and application of engineering fuzzy theory. Press of National Defense Industry, Beijing (1996) 56-69
4. Lacher, R.C., Hruska, S.I., Kuncicky, D.C.: Back-Propagation Learning in Expert Networks. IEEE Transaction on Neural Networks, Vol. 1. No. 3. (1992) 62-72
5. Chen, X., Luo, S., Wang, Z., Tao, Y.: Research on Preprocessing and Postprocessing of the Application of BP Neutral Network. Systems Engineering--Theory & Practice, Vol. 1. No. 2. (2002) 65-70
6. Hu, G.: Probability Theory and Mathematical Statistics. China Agricultural Science and Technology Press, Beijing (1994) 21-43
7. Rodriguez, C., Rementeria, S., Martin, J.I., Lafuente, A., Muguerza, J., Perez, J.: A Modular Neural Network Approach to Fault Diagnosis. IEEE Trans on Neural Networks, Vol. 7. No. 2. (1996) 326-340
8. Shang, G., Zhong, L., Chen, L.: Discussion about BP neural network structure and choice of samples training parameter. Journal of Wuhan University of Technology, Vol. 19. No. 2. (1997) 108-110

Application of Modified Neural Network Weights' Matrices Explaining Determinants of Foreign Investment Patterns in the Emerging Markets

Darius Plikynas[1] and Yusaf H. Akbar[2]

[1] Informatics department, Vilnius Management Academy,
Basanaviciaus 29a, Vilnius, Lithuania, EU
Phone: +370 69829465, Fax: +370 521336 06
d.plikynas@delfi.lt
http://www.omnitel.net/neuraleconom
[2] School of Business, Southern New Hampshire University,
2500 North River Rd, Manchester, NH 03106, USA
Phone: 603-668-2211
y.akbar@snhu.edu

Abstract. Quantitatively examining determinants of foreign direct investment (FDI) in Central and East Europe (CEE) is an important research area. Traditional linear regression approaches have had difficulty in achieving conceptually and statistically reliable results. The key tasks addressed in this research are a neural network (NN) based (i) FDI forecasting model and (ii) nonlinear evaluation of the determinants of FDI. We have explored various modified backprop NN weights' matrices and distinguished some nontraditional NN topologies. In terms of MSE and R-squared criteria, we found and checked relationship between modified NN input weights and FDI determinants weights. Results indicate that NN approaches better able to explain FDI determinants' weights than traditional regression methodologies. Our findings are preliminary but offer important and novel implications for future research in this area including more detailed comparisons across sectors as well as countries over time.

1 Introduction

There have been a number of empirical tests of the determinants of FDI in the CEE region, most of these studies have used linear primarily regression techniques to test a series of key variables and their influence on inward FDI flows in the CEE region. This paper aims to offer an alternative new methodology using NN modeling approaches to examining the determinants of FDI. It is explicitly non-linear in its approach and thus allows for the modeling of non-linear empirical phenomena without the need to impose linearity on data for the purposes of regression analyses.

There are two principle data issues that provide a significant empirical challenge to research in the CEE region. First is that consistent data for the region's countries is hard to find. Second, the time period for which reasonable time-series empirical analysis can be used is 10-15 years. These two issues mean that if we are interested in developing a rigorous analytical empirical model, we will have to maximize the explanatory value of the existing data. Arguably, linear regression techniques struggle with this paucity of data and combined with the need to achieve parsimonious regression equations, linear regression techniques require the researcher to eliminate variables and therefore reduce the use of the existing data. A holistic non-linear approach, such as the one we develop in this paper, may help in overcoming this problem.

Our paper is organized as follows. Part 2 below offers a brief literature review of FDI empirical research in the CEE region and a summary of key conceptual issues that flow from this. Part 3 describes our model and outlines the scope of the research. This section will examine the main constraints and assumptions of our interdisciplinary approach as well as how we confront the problems of data constraints on research on CEE. Part 4 develops the neural network optimization approach we used to estimate the best NN configuration. Part 5 employs the optimal NN in order to provide (in a nonlinear way) the major determinants of FDI. We introduce the novel way to extract weights for the determinants of FDI from the NN input weights matrixes. Part 6 is a concluding section which summarizes our findings and also offers future directions for related research.

2 Literature Review and Conceptual Framework

There are well-established theories of FDI that have the broad acceptance of scholars for their conceptual robustness (e.g. [1]-[2]). Indeed, Dunning's OLI paradigm has been used widely as a taxonomic framework for examining the determinants of FDI (e.g. [3]). Focusing on ownership advantages [4] examined capital intensity and FDI; Lall [5] studied technology intensity and Li and Guisinger [6] related firm size to FDI.

FDI in CEE is determined by risk, labour costs, host market size and gravity factors (e.g. proximity to trading partners [7]-[8]). Risk can be related strongly to announcements of EU membership progress. In other words when positive developments on EU membership occur for CEE countries, inward FDI flows should increase in anticipation of future membership for the recipient countries. Similar empirical results have been generated by Martin and Velazquez [9] in the context of Spanish membership of the EU.

We believe that previous research has substantially enhanced our empirical understanding of the determinants of FDI. However, we believe that few (if any) studies have attempted to integrate both firm-level strategic variables with macro-economic or 'environmental' factors in a holistic non-linear model. It is on this basis that we aim to build a model based on NN modeling. As we demonstrate in sections below, the main innovation in this paper is the use of non-linear dynamics since we believe that the phenomenon of FDI itself is neither statistically linear nor conceptually static. Standard methodologies used to examine FDI are constrained by the linear approach required for them to be operationable.

Nonlinear dynamic methods became popular in the financial investment markets after such well-known research e.g. [10]-[11] had made seminal contributions in the field. New methods were found useful only after modern information technologies and artificial intelligence systems (AIS) were capable of modeling nonlinear dynamics in real time.

More specifically, the focus of this paper is to evaluate how simple NN techniques can be employed for the investigation of non-stationary, complex and low data frequency FDI behavior. In this research, we have adopted and modified a standard MLP - multilayer perceptron NN model (error back-propagation, data feed-forward).

3 Model and Methodology

Major Constraints and Assumptions. In the previous section, we have mentioned persistent drawbacks of the linear multivariate analyses in the research of nonstationary, volatile and chaotic behavior of investment phenomena. Frequently, the statistical significance of most of the input variables (macro- and microeconomic, political and social) is too low for the inclusion in linear multivariate models. However, these statistically nonsignificant factors drastically shift the whole system away from the predicted course of events due to their chaotic, non-stationary nature. More often than not these factors become determinant, when major factors are alike or compensate each other [12]. This is especially relevant in investment markets, where investment conditions are similar across different countries or even regions.

The main reasons for a paucity of NN studies in prior research in the CEE region are related to the following problems: 1) scarcity of the available data (too short observation period; it varies between 8 to 14 years of observations, which started right after the collapse of the soviet system between 1989 and 1991); 2) insufficiently low data sampling frequency (e.g. primarily annual discrete observations are available in the data). We can overcome the those problems through the use of a bootstrap scheme, first presented by Giannerini and Rosa [13].

According to the above discussion, we have adopted a panel data approach as it partly eliminates the biases bound to the individual country FDI inflows and expands the available data set needed for NN learning. Our research consists of employment of the neural network methods: (i) design and optimization of the multilayer perceptron NN model, (ii) FDI forecasting using NN approach and (iii) estimation of the nonlinear weights for the determinants of FDI in CEE region.

We have employed NN methods, which were specially designed and optimized in order to forecast FDI and estimate nonlinear weights for the determinants of FDI (economic, financial, social and gravity-type). A panel data approach and bootstrap procedure considerably enlarged the data pool and consequently improved NN performance. We have used a MLP (multilayer perceptron) model with an error back-propagation and learning feed-forward (Levenberg-Marquet fast NN learning algorithm) method.

NN methods should satisfy a number of necessary conditions: a) to be able to approximate and predict nonlinearities, which are very common in FDI flows, b) to be very sensitive to unique and rare events, c) to have integrated complex technical and fundamental means of analyses. A review of the related literature suggests (e.g. [11], [14] and [15]) that error back-propagation (learning feed-forward) neural network method fits the investigation conditions mentioned above and is well related to the input data properties described in the sections above. To our knowledge, this method is mostly known and popular among financial analysts in the field (e.g. [11] and [16]). Therefore, we have chosen it for our research purposes.

4 Employment of the NN Methods: Experimental Setup

4.1 Research Data

The data used in this paper are extracted from the (i) UNCTAD [17]: United Nations Conference on Trade and Development, World investment directory and World investment Report [18], (ii) World Bank National Accounts Database, (iii) the IMF, (iv) OECD and (v) EBRD data sources. The final data set includes 24 variables and is assembled from and justified by several other studies see (e.g. [19]). This inquiry differs from these investigations in that its purpose is to make better prognoses and identify significant FDI factors using nonlinear NN approach.

We used batch NN training: a weights matrix was updated each time when all input data was presented to the net. All input data was normalized. Various transformation functions and learning algorithms were used. The major part of the research was executed using a multilayer perceptron NN [15]. The number of iterations used, net configurations, momentums and are described further. An effective neural net construction required employment of various optimization techniques such as the search for effective NN learning algorithms, an optimal number of iterations, an optimal data form factor, the best fit of our NN configuration and the presence of recurrence.

We investigated the following basic learning algorithms: a) gradient descent, b) batch gradient descent with momentum, c) variable learning rate, d) conjugate gradient and e) the fastest known Levenberg-Marquet (quasi-Newton method). The mean square error (MSE), the R2-determination coefficient and learning duration were the main criteria for the mutual comparison of NN learning algorithms.

The learning data set consisted of 180 panel data rows (each of 15 countries has a learning data set of 12 years beginning from 1990 ending in 2001) and testing data set consisted of 15 data rows (for forecasting the FDI flows in 2002). Data was normalized and encoded. For better NN generalization we have used early stopping procedure.

The data model can be expressed as follows from the Fig. 1. The basic data types were grouped in several categories: (a) economic (like exports, GDP, imports, inflation, trade, unemployment), (b) financial (like capital expenditure, tax revenue, taxes on goods and services, S&P credit ratings), (c) social (like health expenditure, wages and salaries, PCs per 1000 people, scientific and technical journal articles) and (d) gravity/geographical. There is also considerable evidence that geographical proximity is an important factor in observed trade and investment patterns, judging by the findings from gravity-type models like classical Leamer's [20] and neural network based on Deichmann model [19].

We have included both absolute and relative (percentage change) measures. We have also included a separate input data type: dynamic measures (on the right in the Fig. 1), which stand for the second moment variables. This offers qualitatively additional information to aid NN performance. We have to admit that some input variables correlate with each other, but we have left all of them. This is due to the fact of incompleteness and inconsistency which persists for almost all data sets.

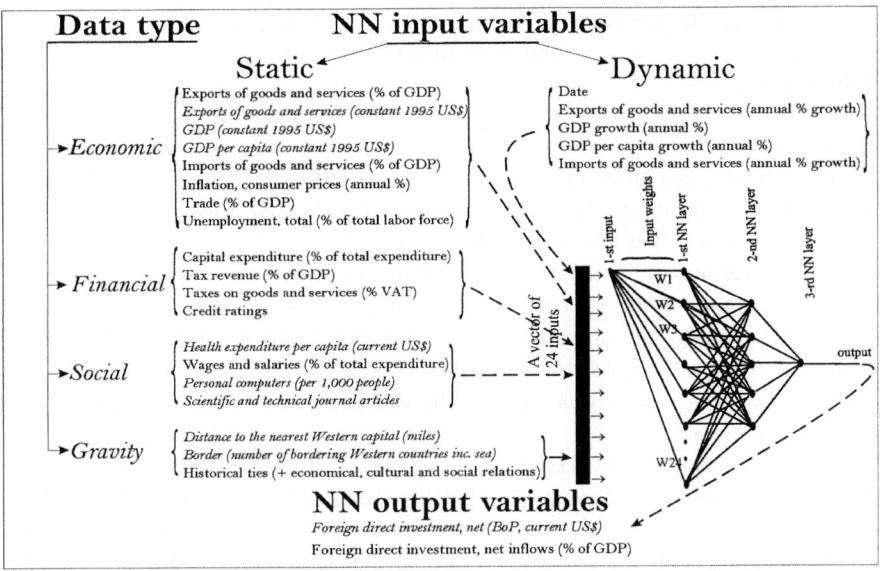

Fig. 1. The basic data types and input variables (absolute measures in italics) used for training of the NN (MLP) in order to get the best approximation and prognoses results for FDI in the CEE region

4.2 Premises for the MLP Optimization

Let us assume that the financial problem domain $\Omega(\Omega_{in}; \Omega_{out})$ is characterized by 1) sub domain Ω_{in}, which consists of the set of input data space vectors $\{I_{in}\}$ (where n denotes the input space dimensionality and $i=[1,.. k]$ indicates the input data vector); 2) sub domain Ω_{out}, which consists of the set of output data space vectors $\{O_{im}\}$ with appropriate output dimensionality m. NN is used for mapping a given input space onto the desirable output space (NN decisions). Our goal consists of investigating the mapping function Φ

$$\Phi(\{I_{in}\}) \rightarrow \{O_{im}\}. \tag{1}$$

A MLP network serves as a universal approximator, which learns how to relate the set of the input space vectors {Iin} to the set of output (solutions) space vectors $\{O_{im}\}$. The transformation function Φ is then characterized by the MLP structural parameters like weights' matrix W, biases B, number of neurons N, topology structure T, learning parameters L

$$\Phi = \Phi(W, B, N, T, L). \tag{2}$$

This is supervised learning. MLP gains experience by learning how to relate the input space vectors $\{I_{in}\}$ to the known output vectors $\{O_{im}\}$. Now we parameterize Eq. (1)

$$\Phi_{W, B, N, T, L}(\{I_{in}\}) \rightarrow \{O_{im}\}. \tag{3}$$

For the effective implementation of MLP networks, we had to investigate the major NN structural parameters like W, B, N, T and L in a decomposition manner. The investigation results are worth it, because NN optimization software, developed by our team (executable code generated on Matlab platform), reduces a substantial part of the technical work.

For the effective implementation of the NN optimization scheme we have investigated different data factors like random distribution of input cases, different set of input variables and different outputs (see Fig. 1). In the latter case, instead of using FDI measured only in absolute terms, we alternatively have used FDI measured in relative terms, i.e. FDI as a % of country's GDP.

The final result of our findings is that effectively parameterized NN exhibits the best approximating and forecasting performance. To summarize, the estimated NN MLP model finally has approached the following form: the Levenberg-Marquet learning algorithm (fast quasi-Newton method), optimal number of epochs (iterations) is 15, the best NN topology is 24:10:1, the learning rate $lr = 0.2$ and the learning momentum $mc = 0.3$.

In addition, we spot-checked a null hypothesis of the conservative approach: checking forecasting models against a model of the last observations is called a Naïve or AR(1) forecast. The idea is based on the checking whether our forecasting is any better comparing with the forecasting method than prognostic values equal to the previous period values. A number of empirical studies (e. g. [14] and [16]) have suggested that sometimes is hard to defeat this hypothesis. Despite the latter fact, in our case the obtained R-square equals to 0.294 which is much worse if compare to the average of 0.7 for NN estimations. Therefore, the authors argue that the system based on their proposed framework noticeably defeats the conservative hypothesis.

Notwithstanding the appealing power of NN methods, we have also applied MLR analyses. This gave us the estimation of the comparative validity of the NN method (the MLR method returns the least squares fit of y on X by solving the linear model).

The final comparison of MLP and MLR methods in terms of MSE for the large number of reiterations (using different NN weights' matrixes) is presented in the extended version of the current paper. Yet, our statements are supported with some more encouraging findings related with NNs weights matrixes, which have particularly well forecasted and approximated the FDI data (some results are of one order higher than MLR's in terms of MSE and R-square). These NN weights' matrixes are saved and can be simulated any time. The problem is that these static NN configurations with the appropriate weight matrixes will perfectly do for this particular data set, but not for the updated set. Especially if updated data does not follows the previous patterns. This is the main reason for the search of the optimal NN generating technique.

The reader should have in mind that we have used the standard MLR approach. Obviously, there are more sophisticated MLR optimization models (e.g. the rejection of non significant variables can decrease the MSE), which were not applied in our research due to the limited research scope. The conclusion – we still need some more evidence in order to make strong statements about better performance of MLP.

The preliminary results from this study demonstrate the fact that after the relevant NN optimization techniques have been employed, the researcher is armed with a powerful analysis tool. We believe that the system based on proposed framework will foster nonlinear analyses in FDI sector.

5 Analysis of FDI Determinants Using NN Weights Approach

5.1 "Natural" NN Topology

Finally, we have employed the optimal NN (designed in the previous section) to provide a nonlinear estimates of the major determinants of FDI. We introduce the novel way to extract weights for the determinants of FDI from the NN weight matrixes. Our experiments, discussed in this paper, focus on testing the nonlinear type of input weightings, which are driven by FDI dynamics. In fact, the simplest linear approach to this idea is MLR method, which returns the least squares fit of the FDI on input factors (e.g. Trade, GDP, Inflation etc) by solving the linear model. In this model, each input has his own weight by which it influences country based dynamics of FDI.

Our task is not only the use of NN in FDI patterns analyses and prognoses, but also the search for the NN parameters, which can estimate nonlinear weights of the investment factors leading to the observed FDI dynamics. To our knowledge, there is no experiment in the field of that would focus on the NN mechanisms of FDI input weights estimation in such an experimental setting. Technically, the task is not a trivial one, because of the complicated NN structure itself. We have to explore the mapping function Φ (see Eq. 3) in more detail.

For this purpose we found the most fitting NN model (designed using Matlab NN Toolbox, which has 26 layers with sustained 24:10:1 topology), capable to reflect the issues in the most 'natural' way. In this case, the first 24 layers have one neuron and one input connection each (every junction connects to the corresponding input factor), the 25-th layer has 24 neurons with 24x24 layer weights matrix and the 26-th layer has one output neuron with 24x1 layer weights matrix.

The "Natural" NN topology case gives us very promising average results: (i) for the learning set MSE equals 0.0015 (MLP) and 0.0046 (MLR), R-squared equals 0.9354 (MLP) and 0.8069 (MLR); (ii) for the testing set MSE equals 0.0194 (MLP) and 0.038 (MLR), R-squared equals 0.6895 (MLP) and 0.3914 (MLR).

5.2 Nonlinear Weights of the FDI Determinants: Research Results

This subsection presents research results obtained from the application of the "natural" NN topology case (see subsection 4.1), which was designed and chosen by the authors as one of the best NN models. For the effective implementation of NN approach, we have widely exploited results described in the sections 3 and 4. The subsequent experimentation took place on the Matlab software platform. Major statistical estimations of the average (20 repeated experiments under the same experimentation setup) nonlinear weights obtained for the determinants of FDI are depicted in Table 1.

From Table 1, nonlinear estimates for NN weights have positive and negative values. This is due to a manner NN is learning the relationship between input and output values. This could be avoided if NN biases (biases are additional NN parameters) were used. However, the authors purposefully trained the NN without the biases, as they are additional parameters, which could make the input weights' analysis more problematic.

Table 1. Statistical characteristics of the nonlinear weights obtained for the determinants of FDI using the NN approach (the last column stands for the comparison against linear weights)

No	FDI determinants	NN input weights' mean (m)	Var.	H0: norm*	T-test Signif. p-test** (H1: $\bar{x}=m$)	Confid. level (95.0%)	β-regr. Param. (MLR)
1	Date	0.04	0.06	0	0.098	0.21	0.03
2	Cap_Exp	0.03	0.48	0	0.064	0.58	-0.03
3	Exp_Goods	0.30	1.41	0	0.051	0.99	-0.20
4	Exp_Goods_Growth	0.11	1.23	0	**0.035**	0.93	0.10
5	Exp_Goods_Const	0.49	3.89	0	0.136	1.65	0.61
6	GDP_Const	-0.08	1.20	0	0.061	0.92	0.27
7	GDP_Growth	-0.11	0.89	0	0.059	0.79	0.04
8	GDP_Const_Per_Cap	-0.06	1.76	0	0.142	1.11	0.15
9	GDP_Per_Cap_Growth	0.37	0.35	0	0.132	0.50	-0.11
10	Health_Exp_Per_Cap	-0.37	0.42	0	0.067	0.54	-0.04
11	Imports_Goods	0.55	3.34	0	0.170	1.53	0.01
12	Imports_Goods_Growth	0.24	0.90	1	0.074	0.80	-0.01
13	Inflation	-0.21	0.18	0	0.195	0.36	0.01
14	PC_Per1000	0.10	1.77	0	0.308	1.11	-0.07
15	Scientific_Publ	-0.13	2.16	0	0.227	1.23	-0.14
16	Tax_Revenue	-0.38	0.34	0	**0.027**	0.49	0.11
17	Taxes_VAT	-0.07	0.69	0	0.059	0.70	-0.02
18	Trade	-0.06	1.20	0	0.297	0.92	0.12
19	Unemployment	0.46	5.49	0	0.139	1.96	0.16
20	Wages	0.38	1.13	0	0.121	0.89	-0.10
21	Grav_Distance	0.17	0.34	0	**0.024**	0.48	-0.12
22	Grav_Borders	-0.47	0.54	0	**0.000**	0.61	0.01
23	Grav_Historical_Ties	0.18	0.63	0	0.098	0.66	-0.20
24	Fin_Ratings	-0.01	0.70	0	0.101	0.70	0.07

Notes: NN input weights we interpret here in the same way as MLR factor weights.
* - H0: normal, we chose a Lilliefors test; 0 – means that we cannot reject the null hypothesis.
** - p- test: for a typical significance level $\alpha=0.05$ in order to reject the H1: $\bar{x} = m$ hypothesis, the probability of observing our sampled result must be less than the significance level.

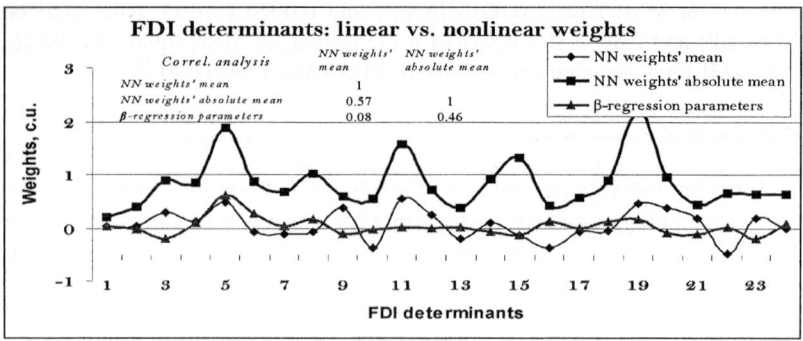

Fig. 2. Comparison of weights for FDI determinants (x axis) obtained in a linear and nonlinear way

We can also notice that NN input weights have very high variance (see Table 1), which is due to more sophisticated NN learning nature (NN can learn the same task in many different ways). The latter fact can be relatively softened by the use of NN input weights' absolute mean values. In this case we are more concerned about the deviation from the zero irrespective of whether deviation is positive or negative. In the Fig. 2, we made an attempt to compare correlations between both linear and nonlinear weights of FDI determinants.

However, amount of the obtained results and comments is too big for the inclusion in the current article. Therefore wider discussion is needed in the subsequent research papers.

6 Results and Conclusions

A number of theoretical and empirical studies have suggested that the effectiveness of a traditional quantitative FDI analysis, based on linear approach, is restricted by data problems related to transitional effects, small data sets, data incompleteness, inconsistencies, rare events and nonlinearities, which are widely present in the CEE region. Given this apparent methodological shortcoming of linear approaches, we have offered a novel non-linear methodology in this research.

We have shed new light on some conceptual novelties in application of neural network approach for improved (country-based) FDI patterns forecasting and nonlinear evaluation of the determinants of FDI. Our approach complements existing investment decision support tools aimed for MNE's FDI planning and forecasting. Moreover, the research will benefit not just MNEs, but more generally appropriate CEE public policy makers as it deals with FDI strategies and investment determinants effecting CEE countries economic development.

We additionally implemented a novel way of estimating weights for the determinants of FDI using a specially designed MLP NN method. These weights are estimated in a nonlinear manner and have very high variance, which is due to more sophisticated NN learning nature

Statistical tests do show general impression of consistency in our approach. In fact, our findings about the NN employed verify that a NN methodology is able to capture more complex nonlinear relations than those estimated by the linear analyses. This is especially relevant in times of high volatility, crises, transitional periods or chaotic behavior, which is present in the CEE market.

We are at pains to emphasize that our findings represent an initial first 'take' on FDI flows and their explanatory sources. Moreover, we have spent a considerable amount of this paper examining the methodological novelty of our work. Subsequent papers will focus more on the empirical aspects of our research once we have established the methodological importance of our work.

Future research will focus on cross-industry/sectoral analyses as well as developing panel data sets for use in the NN framework.

References

[1] Hymer, S. (1960) The International Operations of National Firms: A Study of Foreign Direct Investment, MIT Press, Cambridge, Mass. (published in 1976)
[2] Dunning, J. H. "The Prospects for Foreign Direct Investment in Central and Eastern Europe." in The Economics of Change in East and Central Europe, edited by Peter J. Buckley and Pervez N. Ghauri. Academic Press Limited, 1994.
[3] Hong M. and Lou Shou Chen, "Quantitative and Dynamic Analysis of the OLI Variables Determining FDI in China", RURDS, Vol. 13, No. 2, 2001, pp. 163-172.

[4] Pugel, T. "The determinants of Foreign Direct Investment: an Analysis of US Manufacturing Industries" Managerial and Decision Economics, Vol. 2, 1981, pp. 220-228
[5] Lall, S. "Monopolistic Advantages and Foreign Involvement by US Manufacturing Industry" Oxford Economic Papers 32: 102-122, 1980.
[6] Li J. and Guisinger S "The Globalization of Service Multinationals in the Triad Nations: Japan, Europe and North America" Journal of International Business Studies 23 (4): 675-696, 1992.
[7] Garibaldi, P., Mora, N., Sahay, R. and Zettelmeyer, J 'What Moves Capital to Transition Economies?', IMF Conference "A decade of transition", Washington, DC, February 1999.
[8] Resmini, L. 'The Determinants of Foreign Direct Investment into the CEECs: New Evidence from Sectoral Patterns', mimeo., LICOS and L.Bocconi University, 2000.
[9] Martin, C. and Velazquez, F.J. 'Determining factors of foreign direct investment in Spain and the rest of the OECD: lessons for the CEECS', Centre for Economic Policy Research discussion paper series 1637, Centre for Economic Policy Research, London, 1997.
[10] Peters, E. "Chaos and order in the capital markets". New York: John Wiley&Sons. 325 p. 2000.
[11] Freedman, R.S., Klein, A. and Lederman J. Artificial Intelligence in the Capital Markets, Probus publishing. Chicago, 1995.
[12] Chakrabarti, A. "The Determinants of Foreign Direct Investment: Sensitivity Analyses of Cross-Country Regressions", Kyklos Vol. 54 No.1, 2001, pp. 89-114.
[13] Gianerini, S. and Rosa, R. "New resampling method to asses the accuracy of the maximum Lyapunov exponent estmation". Physica D, 155, 101-111, 2001.
[14] Hiemstra, Y. "Linear Regression Versus Backpropagation Networks to Predict Quartely Excess Returns". The Second international Workshop on Neural Networks in the Capital Markets, CalTech, Pasadena. 1999.
[15] Plikynas D, Simanauskas L, B da S. "Research of Neural Network Methods for Compound Stock Exchange Indices Analysis", Informatica, Vol. 13. 2002.
[16] Trippi R.R., Lee J.K. Artificial intelligence in Finance & Investing: State-of-the-Art Technologies for Securities Selection and Portfolio Management. Chicago: Irwin. 1996.
[17] United Nations Conference on Trade and Development. World Investment Directory, Volume 8, Central and Eastern Europe 2003, www.unctad.org, 2003.
[18] United Nations Conference on Trade and Development, World investment Report.: The Shift Towards Services. United Nations, New York and Geneva 2004.
[19] Deichmann, J., Haughton, D. and Topi, H. "Geography Matters: Kohonen Classsification of Determinants of Foreign Direct Investment in Transition Economies". Journal of Business Strategies, Vol. 20, No. 1, 2003.
[20] Leamer, E.E. and Levinsohn, J. (1995) "International trade theory: the evidence" in G.Grossman and K. Rogoff (eds.) Handbook of International Economics Volume III, Elsevier, North Holland.

Neural Network and Trend Prediction for Technological Processes Monitoring

Luis Paster Sanchez Fernandez, Oleksiy Pogrebnyak, and Cornelio Yanez Marquez

Center for Computing Research, National Polytechnic Institute,
Av. Juan de Dios Batiz s/n casi esq. Miguel Othon de Mendizabal,
Col. Nueva Industrial Vallejo, CP 07738, Mexico City, Mexico
{lsanchez, olek, cyanes}@cic.ipn.mx

Abstract. The goal of this paper is to introduce an efficient predictive supervisory method for the trending of variables of technological processes and devices, with low run-time, for periodic analysis of high frequency, relatively (periods smaller than a second). This method allows to predict the time in which a process variable will arrive to an abnormal or important values. The data obtained in real time for each variable are used to estimate the parameters of a mathematical model. This model is continuous and of first-order or second-order (critically damped, overdamped or underdamped). An optimization algorithm is used for estimating the parameters. Before performing the estimation, the most appropriate model is determined by means of a feed-forward neural network.

1 Introduction

It has been estimated that the U.S. petrochemical industry loses $10 billion annually due to "abnormal" situations [1], a generic term describing departures from acceptable operating conditions. Consequently, there is considerable incentive for the development of process monitoring and fault detection techniques that can detect an abnormal situation quickly and accurately [2]. Statistically-based process monitoring techniques can detect when the plant state becomes "abnormal" by comparing current measurements with pre-determined limits. Such "alarm" limits can be calculated from the residuals of a stochastic process model, based on statistical descriptions of historical process data, or specified as acceptable bounds on process variability. If an "abnormal" operation can be predicted with a sufficient warning period, then an effective corrective action may be able to prevent the predicted operation from actually occurring [3]. In several papers, some methods are proposed that signals impending emergency limit violations by using predictions (or forecasts) from a process model [3].

This paper proposes an efficient predictive supervisory algorithm for the trending of variables of technological processes and devices, with low run-time, for periodic analysis of high frequency, relatively (periods smaller than a second). The method allows to predict the time in which the variables of technological processes will arrive to a critical or abnormal value. The critical state that may or may not be abnormal (as it happens with the operation of the hydraulic canals whose dynamics are complex).

The neural network (NN) is a very powerful mathematical tool for systems identification, and is used extensively in the presented work. The feed-forward network was chosen due to it's ability to successfully recognize diverse patterns. In our case, it is used to recognize signal patterns of first and second order dynamic systems [4] in which the dynamics of a considerable amount of technological processes can be represented with a good approximation [5], [6]. The recommended methodology consists of to recognize the most appropriate model by means of a feed-forward neural network and later, the parameters are estimated through an optimization algorithm [7] thus reducing the total processing time.

The least-squares error criterion is used as optimization index:

$$I = \sum_{i=1}^{N} ki[V(i) - Vm(i)]^2 \qquad (1)$$

Where:

I : index to be minimized.
V(i) : value at the sampling instant i.
Vm(i) : output value of model at the sampling instant i.
N : number of samples of the variable for estimating the parameters of the model.
Ki: weight coefficients (value 1 is being used).

This work bears relationship to a broad range of mathematical techniques, ranging from statistics to fuzzy logic, which have been used successfully in intelligent data analysis [8].

The transfer functions of the used models are the following:

- First order model:

$$\frac{Y(S)}{X(S)} = \frac{Ke^{-\theta S}}{T_1 S + 1} \qquad (2)$$

- Second order model:

$$\frac{Y(S)}{X(S)} = \frac{Ke^{-\theta S}}{s^2/w_n^2 + 2\zeta s/w_n + 1} \qquad (3)$$

Where the parameters to be estimated are:

T_1 : time constant.
K : gain.
w_n : natural oscillation frequency.
θ : time delay.
ζ : coefficient of damping.
    $\zeta<1$ (underdamped).
    $\zeta=1$ (critically damped).
    $\zeta>1$ (overdamped).

2 Block Chart of the Method

Fig. 1 displays the simplified flow chart of a cycle of the predictive alarm algorithm. A circular buffer of changeable dimensions is used. This cycle begins with the permanent storing of N last data of the variable of the technological process or device under supervision.

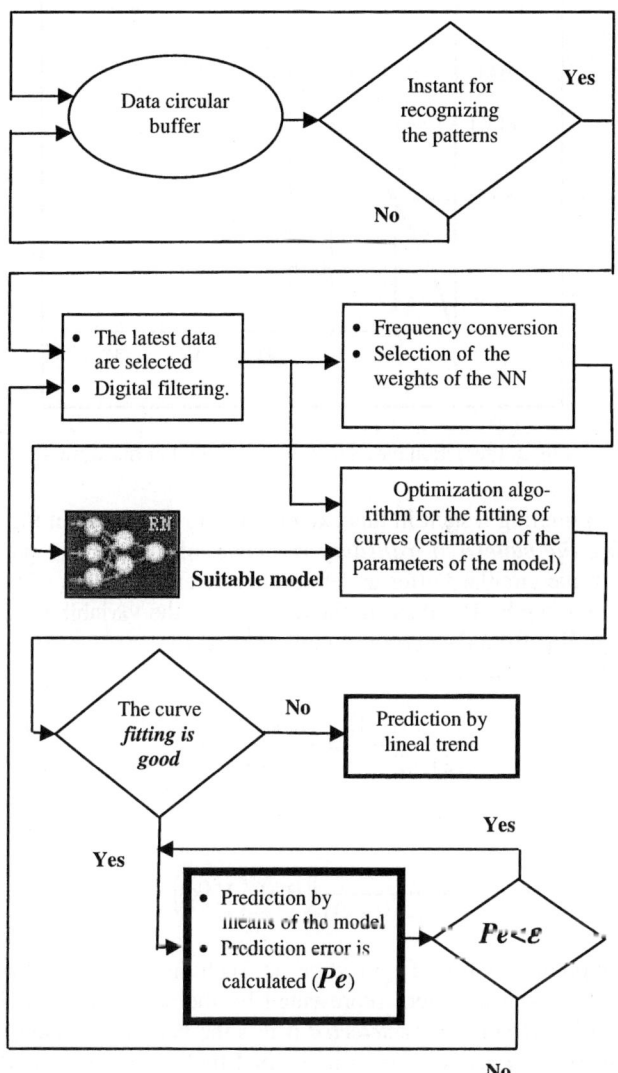

Fig. 1. Flow diagram of the predictive alarm algorithm cycle

Fig. 2 shows an example of a variable versus time plot V(t) with the following parameters:

HAL: high alarm limit. v(k): current value. v(k-1): previous value. T: sampling period. t_p: prediction time.

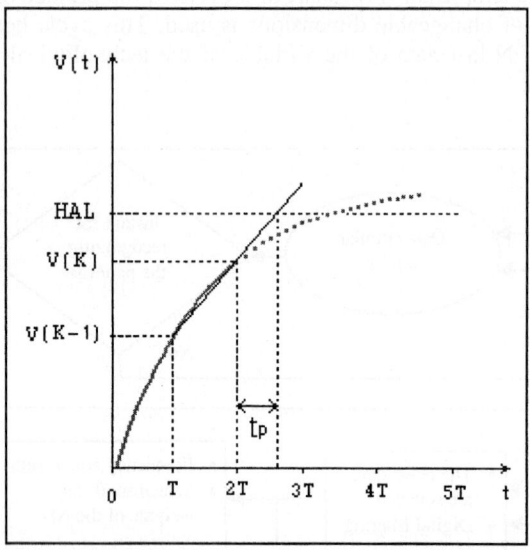

Fig. 2. Prediction based on the linear-trend of the variable

The current sampling instant in this example is 2T. As shown in Fig. 2, the *instant for recognizing the pattern of transitory response*, of the model representing by the points stored in the circular buffer is determined by an algorithm of lineal trend prediction. On predicting by lineal trend, the behavior of the variable is considered to be that of a straight line from the current sampling instant.

Regarding Fig. 2, it can be stated that:

$$\frac{V(k) - V(k-1)}{2T - T} = \frac{HAL - V(k)}{tp} \qquad (4)$$

obtaining t_p as:

$$tp = \left(\frac{T}{V(k) - V(k-1)}\right)[HAL - V(k)] \qquad (5)$$

A minimum prediction time T_{mp} must be set, such that if $t_p < T_{mp}$, then the recognition process of the signal pattern represented by the samples stored in the circular buffer begins. ***The latest data are selected*** if it is the ***instant for recognizing the pattern of transitory response***, as shown in a simplified way in Fig. 3. The oldest data are discarded until significant points indicating the beginning of a new temporary response (thick line) are found. This is shown in Fig. 3 by points 1 and 2, in response of second- and first-order systems, respectively.

Then, a *sampling frequency conversion* with a non-integer factor combining interpolation and decimation is performed [9], which makes it possible to obtain 30 points.

This is the number of input neurons of the NN. Later, the *selection of the weights of the NN* is accomplished in accordance with the sign of the 30-point-curve slope, since it was trained for the patterns with a positive and negative slope. As an output, the NN will produce the most *suitable model* with its parameters estimated through an *optimization* algorithm *for the fitting of curves* using all the selected points. Hooke and Jeeves's [10] optimization method of direct search is used.

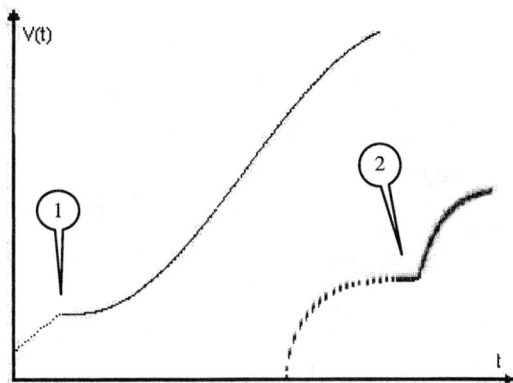

Fig. 3. The procedure for taking the points that will be used in the identification step

3 First and Second Order Systems Patterns for Training the Neural Network

The selection of the NN training patterns was based on the behavior of the dynamic responses of first- and second-order systems to step input function, because this is the most frequent type of disturbance. In other cases, even though it might not strictly be an ideal step, it can be considered as such, provided that for instance, the time constants of the process are relatively larger than the time constants of an exponential signal. For a ramp input function, the lineal trend algorithm is sufficient for a prediction with high accuracy.

Fig. 4 displays the responses of critically damped second order systems, with natural oscillation frequencies w_n equal to 1, 0.5 and 0.25, respectively, and the same sampling frequency. Fig. 5 shows 30 points for every curve. They have been taken up from sampling frequencies of 4, 2 and 1 samples per second, respectively. That is why every time interval in axis X will be the sampling period of each curve. If the points of the three curves (Fig. 5) were graphically represented using the same time interval for axis X, they would be superimposed, as shown in Fig. 6.

A similar behavior will occur in first order systems with respect to the time constant, as well as in overdamped and underdamped second order systems, in which only its coefficient of damping will show any difference (see Fig. 7). In the diagrams, it can be seen that w_n does not exert any influence on the signal pattern when each mark on axis X indicates the order in which the points were taken up rather than the time. This is the procedure to follow, since it is not of any interest to estimate the parameters of the model (time constant and gain for first order systems; gain, ζ and w_n

for second order systems). It only matters to recognize, through the neural network, the type of model that best represents the register of stored data. Therefore, for input patterns of critically damped first and second order systems, only the amplitude that varies; for overdamped and underdamped second order systems only the amplitude and the ζ vary. Fig. 8 shows as the transitory response pattern for an underdamped second order system is determined. The objective is time prediction to arrive at inferior values to stationary state.

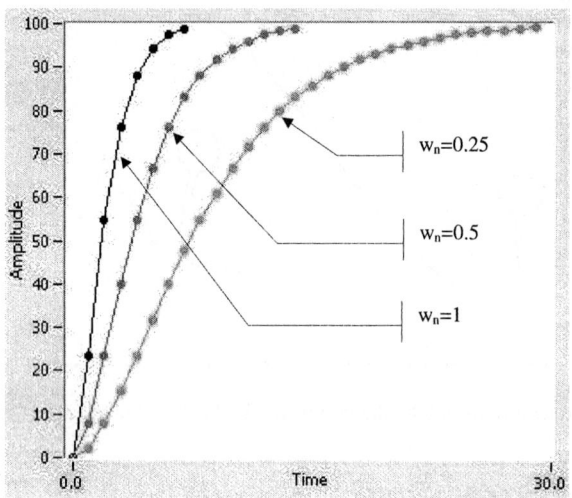

Fig. 4. Responses of critically damped systems with the same sampling frequency

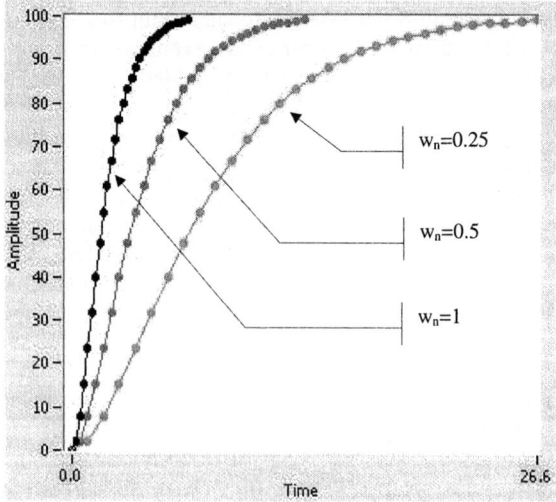

Fig. 5. Responses of critically damped systems with 30 points for every curve due to sampling frequencies of 4, 2 and 1 samples per second, respectively

Neural Network and Trend Prediction for Technological Processes Monitoring 737

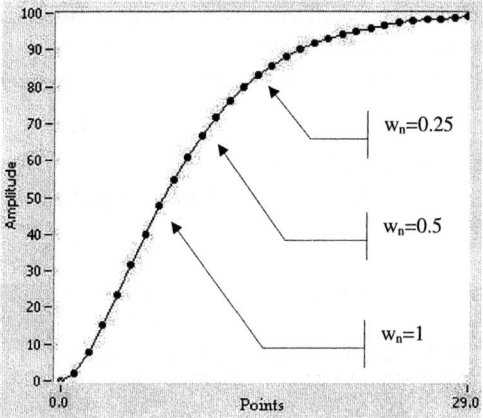

Fig. 6. The three curves of Fig. 5 superimposed

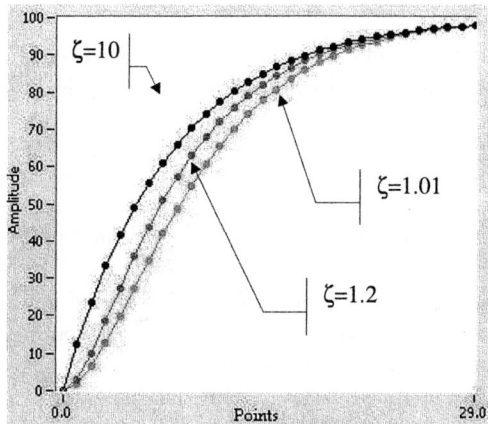

Fig. 7. Responses of an overdamped system for different coefficients of damping

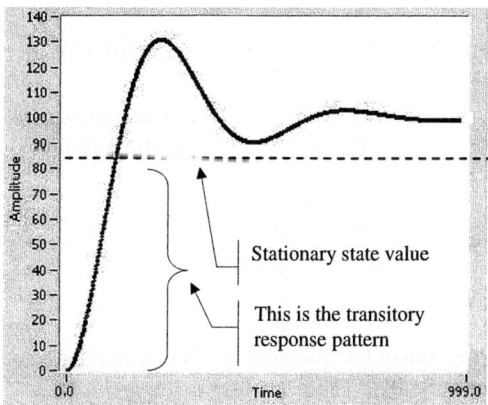

Fig. 8. Transitory response pattern for an underdamped second order system

For NN training patterns, the maximum value of signal amplitude are taken up in percents (%), standardized, from 40% to 90%.

After numerous tests, training was carried out with 858 input patterns, distributed in the following way:

- For overdamped second order systems (OSOS):
  For every ζ value, 11 patterns are obtained corresponding to the variations of the amplitude from 40 to 90, with an increase of 5 (40, 45, 50, 55, 60, 65, 70, 75, 80, 85, 90).
  The ζ varies from 1.2 to 3, with an increase of 0.09, thus obtaining a total of **220 patterns.**
  For ζ greater than 3, the behavior of the system is similar to a first order system.
- For underdamped second-order systems (USOS):
  As for every ζ value, 11 patterns corresponding to amplitude variations are obtained.
  The ζ varies from 0.1 to 0.7, with an increase of 0.0667, thus obtaining a total of **99 patterns**.
- For first- (FOS) and critically damped second-order (CSOS) systems, **11 patterns** are created, respectively, corresponding to amplitude variations from 40 to 90.

In order to have a similar number of patterns for each model and achieve a better training of the NN, the F and CSOS patterns are repeated 20 times, respectively, for a total of 440 patterns. For the USOS pattern they are repeated twice for 198 patterns. 858 PATTERNS IN ALL.

Once the patterns were chosen, varied topologies were used until the simplest with the most suitable response was obtained. Eventually, a 30-input neural network was used, 11 neurons in the hidden layer and four-output neurons.

Very good results were obtained in the training and generalization of the NN. The training error was 0.15%. Over 1000 test patterns were used, obtaining a correct response, with an error of 0.9% of failures.

4 Results Assessment of the Patterns Recognition

The Fig. 9 shows five test patterns which were well recognized by neural network. The Table 1 presents the results. The used legends are the following:

osos: Overdamped second-order systems.
usos: Underdamped second-order systems.
csos: Critically damped second-order systems.
fos : First-order systems.

The Fig. 10 shows three noisy test patterns for first-order systems which were well recognized by neural network. The Table 2 presents the results.

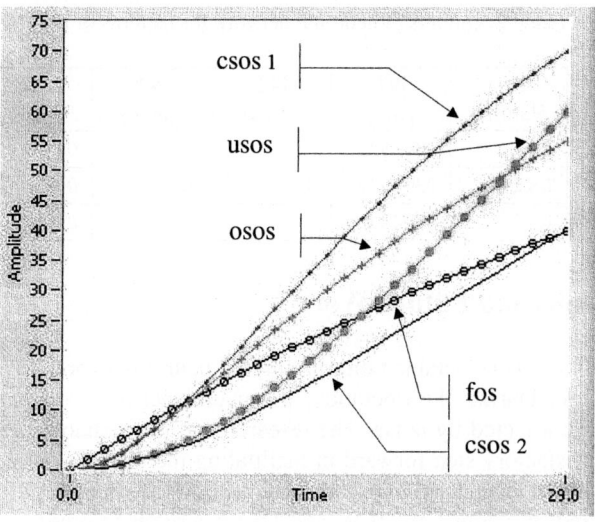

Fig. 9. Example of transitory response test patterns

Table 1. Outputs of neuronal network for patterns of Fig 9

Test Pattern	N1 (fos)	N2 (csos)	N3 (osos)	N4 (usos)
fos	**0.998687**	0	0.002310	0
csos 1	0.000027	**0.996556**	0.003431	0.000000
csos 2	0	**0.998668**	0.002008	0.000015
usos	0.000008	0	0	**0.999989**
osos	0	0	1	0

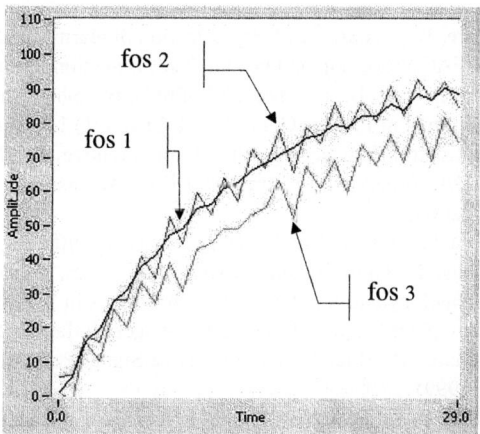

Fig. 10. Three noisy test patterns for first-order systems

Table 2. Outputs of neuronal network for patterns of Fig. 10

Test Pattern	N1 (fos)	N2 (csos)	N3 (osos)	N4 (usos)
fos 1	0.999999	0	0	0
fos 2	0.999979	0	0	0
fos 3	0.962691	0	0	0

5 Conclusions and Future Work

Satisfactory results were obtained on training the neural network, having a high level of generalization. During the operation, the neural network recognized the signals used, even those affected by noise. The research and the technological advances presented are a satisfactory step forward in facilitating the use of advanced and efficient algorithms of predictive alarm by trend, with minimum processing time. The method has been applied by using LabVIEW and DLL's written in other programming languages such as C and Delphi. The DLL's are freely available for other users to implement in their programming language of choice. The only programming required is to make a call to the subroutines exported by the DLL's. Signals affected by higher levels of noise will be used for future studies. Moreover, work has began to enhance the neural network to not only select the most appropriate model, but also make a pre-estimation of such a model. This optimization algorithm would be extremely efficient as its initial operation conditions would be the values pre-estimated by the neural network. This algorithm has been successfully applied in forecasts of temperature, level, hydraulic channels and simulation.

References

1. Nimmo, I.: Adequately address abnormal operations. Chem. Eng. Progress 91 (9) (1995) 36-45
2. Juricek, B., Larimore, W., Seborg, D.: Early detection of alarm situations using model predictions. In: Proc. IFAC Workshop on On-Line Fault Detection, Lyon, France (1998)
3. Juricek, B., Dale E., Seborg, D., Larimore, W.: Predictive monitoring for abnormal situation management. Journal of Process Control, Vol. 11 (2001) 111-128
4. Ogata, K.: Modern Control Engineering. 4th. Edition. Prentice Hall, NY (2001).
5. Boyer, S.A.: SCADA: Supervisory Control and Data Acquisition. 3rd edn. Book News, Inc., Portland, OR (2004)
6. Södertröm, T., Stoica, P.: System identification. Englewood Cliffs, NJ, Prentice-Hall (1989)
7. Edgar, T., Himmelblau, D.: Optimization of chemical processes. NY, MacGraw-Hill (1988)
8. Robins, V. et al.: Topology and Intelligent Data. Advances in Intelligent Data Analysis V, Lecture Notes in Computer Science, Vol. 2810. Springer-Verlag GmbH (2003) 275–285
9. Oppenheim, A., Schafer, R., Buck, J.: Discrete-Time Signal Processing. 2nd edn. Prentice-Hall Int. Editions (1999)
10. Hooke, R., Jeeves, T.: Direct Search Solution for Numerical and Statistical Problems. Journal ACM, vol. 8 (1961) 212-221

Underspecified Semantics for Dependency Grammars*

Alexander Dikovsky

LINA-FRE CNRS 2729, Université de Nantes,
2, rue de la Houssinière BP 92208 F 44322, Nantes cedex 3, France
Alexandre.Dikovsky@univ-nantes.fr

Abstract. We link generative dependency grammars meeting natural modularity requirements with underspecified semantics of *Discourse Plans* intended to *account for exactly those meaning components that grammars of languages mark for*. We complete this link with a natural compilation of the modular dependency grammars into strongly equivalent efficiently analysed categorial dependency grammars.

1 Introduction

Dependency grammars describe syntax in terms of dependencies: binary relations between words (see [1]). They generate dependencies explicitly, in contrast with grammars (HPSG, TAG, Type Logical Grammars etc.) calculating dependencies from other structures. Till recently, there was a common opinion that dependency grammars lack formal theory, in particular formal semantics. In recent papers, dependency grammars were defined as calculi of syntactic types: *Categorial Dependency Grammars (CD-grammars)* of [2, 3] and as generative *Dependency Structure Grammars (DS-grammars)* [4]. These grammars are weakly more powerful than CF-grammars, incomparable with mildly CS-grammars (in particular, with multi-component TAG) and expressive enough to represent discontinuous dependencies. The CD-grammars have an efficient polynomial time parsing algorithm [3] and are learnable from positive examples in rigid case [5].

Below we complete the DS-grammars meeting natural modularity requirements with underspecified formal semantics of *Discourse Plans* of [6] recently elaborated in [7], extendable to a higher order logical semantics. We demonstrate a natural morphism from the Discourse Plans to modular DS-grammars and show that these grammars are compiled into strongly equivalent CD-grammars.

2 Discourse Plans Semantics

2.1 Discourse Plans

DISCOURSE PLANS represent the course of event conceptualization by the speaker. They are *functional* in the following sense. Plans are *terms*, i. e. tree-like

---

* This work was partially supported by the grants 04-01-00565 and 05-01-01006-a of the Russian Academy of Sciences.

functional compositional structures. *All* elements (*semantemes*) of these structures, with the only exception of special empty primitives (zero values, empty lists) have arguments and are functions (proper constants are set off in bold).

Semantic types and compositionality. Semantemes have functional types, defined from primitive types, of which there are four *initial basic types*: **n** (nominators, i. e. 'things' in the most general sense), **s** (sententiators, i. e. 'actions', 'processes', 'events', 'facts', etc.), **q** (qualifiers, 'meanings qualifying nominators'), and **c** (circumscriptors, 'meanings qualifying sententiators and qualifiers'). Basic types are extended by their specific instances. Thus the complete set of basic types is partially ordered under the *specific / generic relation* $\prec$. For instance: $\mathbf{n_a} \prec \mathbf{n}$ (animated nominator, e. g. 《hearer$^{\mathbf{n_a}}$》), $\mathbf{n_{mass}} \prec \mathbf{n}$ (mass nominator, e. g. 《TV$^{\mathbf{n_{mass}}}$》, 《milk$^{\mathbf{n_{mass}}}$》), $\mathbf{q_{qnt-mass}} \prec \mathbf{q_{qnt}} \prec \mathbf{q}$ (qualifier of mass nominators, e. g. 《much$^{\mathbf{q_{qnt-mass}}}$》), $\mathbf{s_{attr}} \prec \mathbf{s}$, $\mathbf{s_{percep}} \prec \mathbf{s_{eff}} \prec \mathbf{s}$ (situations of attribution, direct perception and effect, e. g. 《be$_{attr}$$^{\mathbf{s_{attr}}}$》, 《kiss$^{\mathbf{s_{eff}}}$》, 《watch$^{\mathbf{s_{percep}}}$》).

Every basic type **u** has a corresponding *optional* version $\mathbf{u}^{(0)}$ signifying optional arguments of this type. In addition, circumscriptor and qualifier types have *iterative* versions $\mathbf{u}^{(\omega)}$ (zero or more objects of type **u**). Together, basic, optional and iterative types constitute the set of *primitive* types. Finally, the primitive types serve to form complex *functional types* $(\mathbf{u_1} \ldots \mathbf{u_k} \to \mathbf{v})$ ($\mathbf{u_1} \ldots \mathbf{u_k}$ and **v** being respectively the argument and value types). E.g. the situation 《pour out》 has the type $\left(\mathbf{c}^{(\omega)} \mathbf{n_a} \mathbf{n_{lqm}}^{(0)} \mathbf{n_{ctr}} \to \mathbf{s}\right)$, where $\mathbf{n_{lqm}}^{(0)} \prec \mathbf{n_{mass}} \prec \mathbf{n}$ is the optional liquid matter nominator and $\mathbf{n_{ctr}} \prec \mathbf{n}$ is the container nominator type.

Compositionality is restricted by the condition that a subplan with the value of type $\mathbf{t_1}$ may be substituted in another plan of type $(\mathbf{u_1} \bar{\mathbf{u}} \to \mathbf{v})$ in the place of the argument of type $\mathbf{u_1}$, to obtain a composite plan of type $(\bar{\mathbf{u}} \to \mathbf{v})$, only if $\mathbf{u_1} = \mathbf{t_2}$ or $\mathbf{u_1} = \mathbf{t_2}^{(0)}$, and either $\mathbf{t_1} = \mathbf{t_2}$ or $\mathbf{t_1}$ is a case of $\mathbf{t_2}$ (denoted $\mathbf{t_1} \leq \mathbf{t_2}$). In classical lexicographical terms, this means that the class of semantic compatibility of $\mathbf{u_1}$ is a superclass of that of $\mathbf{t_1}$, or that $\mathbf{u_1}$ is optional $\mathbf{t_1}$.

Roles, actants, circumstantials. We distinguish traditionally two basic classes of semantemes: *situations* and *monads*. A situation is a function, with one or more arguments, called *actants* and identified by their *(semantic) roles* (different arguments of the same situation have different roles)[1]. Arguments without roles are called *circumstantials*. They are grouped into a single list. So there is one generic circumstantial argument, whose iterative type is determined by the semanteme's value type: $\mathbf{q}^{(\omega)}$ for nominator-value semantemes and $\mathbf{c}^{(\omega)}$ for semantemes of other value types. Semantemes without actants are called *monads*.

Most verbs express situations: *John*$_{SBJ}$ *gave the letter*$_{OBJ}$ *to Fred*$_{DST}$; Fr. *Il*$_{SBJ}$ *me*$_{OBJ}$ *dérange par son chant*$_{INS}$ /He disturbs me by his singing/. By contrast, most names, adjectives and adverbs do not express situations, so that their meanings are represented by monads. A situation is specified by its *profile*, which

---

[1] In this short paper, we do not touch at the fundamental problem of adequate choice of roles (see [7] for details and discussion) and use quite intuitively some conventional roles, such as SBJ, OBJ, DST (destination), RCP (recipient), INS (instrument), etc.

includes the situation functor, the argument types, the situation value type and the role of each actant. E. g., the situations *give* and *déranger* have the profiles: $\langle\!\langle \text{give} \left(\text{SBJ}^{\text{na}}, \text{OBJ}^{\text{n}}, \text{RCP}^{\text{na}}\right)^{\text{S}_{\text{caus-mov}}} \rangle\!\rangle$ and $\langle\!\langle \text{déranger} \left(\text{SBJ}^{\text{n}}, \text{OBJ}^{\text{na}}, \text{INS}^{\text{n}^{(0)}}\right)^{\text{S}_{\text{eff}}} \rangle\!\rangle$. Given such a profile, one can reconstruct the complete functional type of the situation. For instance, the complete type of $\langle\!\langle \text{give} \rangle\!\rangle$ is $\left(\mathbf{c}^{(\omega)} \mathbf{n}_a \mathbf{n} \mathbf{n}_a \rightarrow \mathbf{s}_{\text{caus-mov}}\right)$ ($\mathbf{s}_{\text{caus-mov}} \prec \mathbf{s}_{\text{eff}}$ is the type of 'caused movement' situations; $\mathbf{c}^{(\omega)}$ stands for a possibly empty list of circumscriptors: circumstantial arguments of $\langle\!\langle \text{give} \rangle\!\rangle$).

Communicative ranks. Two main instruments of event conceptualization are (1) choosing semantemes from the dictionary to designate an event and reference its participants and (2) assigning the speaker's point of view on the relative salience of participants (COMMUNICATIVE STRUCTURE).

For each situation in Discourse Plan, a communicative structure is assigned to its *communicative group*: the situation's functor and *all* arguments (not exclusively actants). Each communicative group element is assigned a *communicative rank*. We distinguish two THEMATIC ranks: *topic continuation* and *implied* and three RHEMATIC ranks: *focus*, *background* and *periphery*.

Topic continuation (denoted T). Assigned to the member of the communicative group to which the new (rhematic) information will be relativized. Corresponds to a referent initialized or previously evoked in the discourse context, which becomes, in the current plan point, the main entity under consideration. E. g.: *Those girls, they$_T$ giggle when they see me.*

Implied (O). Assigned to a member of a communicative group if its referent is extremely salient due to deixis, anaphora, etc. (often elided in the surface form). E. g.: *Remember Mark?* (= *Do you$_O$ remember Mark?*).

Focus (⊙). Assigned to the member of a group, which conveys the new (as opposed to given or presupposed) information.

Background (⊕). Assigned to those members of a group, which convey other pertinent information (and so cannot be dismissed). E. g.: *I$_T$ hit the stick$_⊕$ against the fence$_⊙$.*

Periphery (⊖). Assigned to the members of a group, which become non-salient and should be dismissed. E. g. in the answer to *Do you sell your car? – Sorry, it's already been bought*, the figure of the buyer obtains the rank ⊖.

Diatheses and diathetic shifts. SEMANTIC DIATHESES [2] are discourse plan elements specifying, for a situation, the intended change in types and communicative ranks with respect to the dictionary profile and the prototypical rank assignment [3]. Every semantic diathesis is implemented by the corresponding

---

[2] Diatheses used in discourse plans are close to those of [8].
[3] The *prototypical* assignment is as follows: thematic ranks are assigned only to SBJ; ⊙ is assigned to the rightmost argument (in the order of plan points) which is not otherwise assigned a thematic rank (or to the situation functor, if no such argument exists); other arguments are assigned ⊕.

diathetic shift, i.e. the transformation of the situation profile licensed by this diathesis (a definition of possible diathetic shifts can be found in [6]). Here, we limit ourselves to several examples.

Example: English passivization occurs when the OBJ actant of an effect situation is promoted to the rank of topic. $\text{dth}_{f-passive}$ (PAGT $\curvearrowleft$ SBJ$_\odot$, SBJ $\curvearrowleft$ OBJ$_T$) is one of passivization diatheses in English. If we take the situation which, under prototypical rank assignment, has the form $Eve_{\text{SBJ:T}}$ $gave_\oplus$ *the apple*$_{\text{OBJ:}\oplus}$ *to* $Adam_{\text{RCP:}\odot}$, the diathetic shift for f-passive transforms it to *The apple*$_{\text{SBJ:T}}$ *was given*$_\oplus$ *to* $Adam_{\text{RCP:}\oplus}$ *by* $Eve_{\text{PAGT:}\odot}$.

Example: The gerund in English is brought about by the need to demote the subject actant and to change the type of the affected situation to $\mathbf{n}_{\text{ger}} \prec \mathbf{n}$. The plan in Fig. 1(a) shows the gerund diathesis $\langle\!\langle \text{dth}_{ger} (\emptyset \curvearrowleft \text{SBJ}_\ominus)^{\mathbf{n}_{\text{ger}}} \rangle\!\rangle$ being applied to the situation $\langle\!\langle \text{watch} (\text{SBJ}^{\mathbf{n}_a}, \text{OBJ}^{\mathbf{n}})^{\mathbf{s}_{percep}} \rangle\!\rangle$.

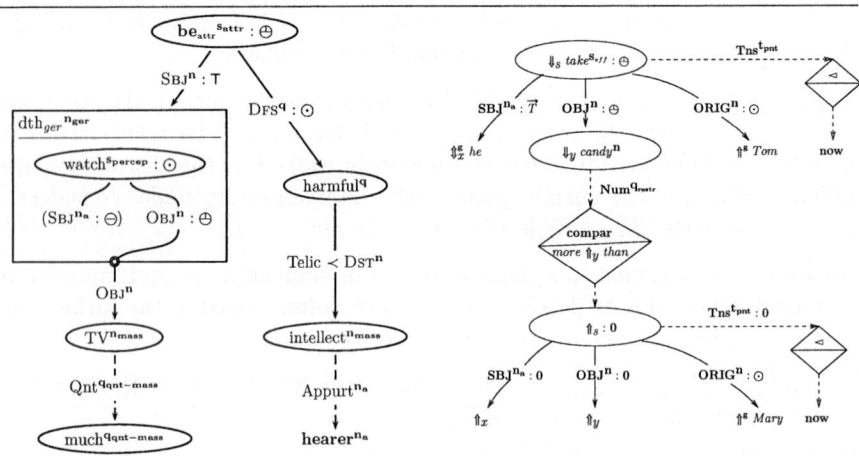

(a) *Watching much TV is harmful for your intellect*

(b) *He took more candies from Tom than from Mary*

Fig. 1. Examples of discourse plans

(1) Ellipses signify functional semantemes. (2) The box represents a diathesis (communicative ranks assignment) and the corresponding diathetic shift (the deleted actants, which are bracketed, the connections to the outside of the box, the projection of roles defined by the situation onto those defined by the diathetic shift). (3) Solid lines link actants to their situations and are labeled with roles. (4) Dashed lines link circumstantials to their governor semantemes and are labeled with names of attributes. (5) Diamonds represent embedded functions applying to attributes (e.g., $\triangleleft$: pointwise and interval time precedence).

Dynamic context. Realizable plans. In discourse plans, one can use embedded functions accessing two contexts: invariable long term *global context* and dynamic short term *local context* which is updated in the course of planning. In the plan in Fig. 1(a) we see four context access functions: $\Uparrow^g Tom$ and $\Updownarrow^g_x he$ access the referents of *Tom* and *he* in the global context (the latter also introduces local reference x), $\Downarrow_s take^{s_{eff}}$ adds to the local context local reference s to the function $take^{(c^{(\omega)}n_a nn^{(0)} \to s_{eff})}$ dereferenced by $\Uparrow_s$. The local context is a bounded resource memory: adding to it a new reference may cause deletion of some other reference. Exact reference scoping rules can be found in [6].

In order for a discourse plan to be realizable, it is necessary that all local references satisfy scoping rules and the rank assignment for every situation in the plan must match the definition of a diathesis in the dictionary and must be implementable by one of the shifts licensed by this diathesis.

2.2 Relation with Complete Semantics

Realizable plans are transformed by a semantical morphism *sem* into (meaning) λ-terms. *sem* is relativized to a signature interpretation I which interprets semantemes and embedded signature functors by 1st order λ-terms and diatheses by 2d order λ-terms. In this semantics, actants and circumstantials are translated differently:

$$sem^I\big[K(\pi_1^{\mathbf{u}}:R \mid \bar{\pi})\big] = \big((K^I \; sem^I[\pi_1]) \; sem^I[\bar{\pi}]\big),$$

if $K^{(\mathbf{u}_1 \bar{\mathbf{u}} \to \mathbf{v})}$ is either a dictionary semanteme or a semantical derivative $(S_{dth} K_0)$ of a situation K_0 through diathetic shift S_{dth} of some licensed diathesis dth of K_0, π_1 is the subplan of the plan $K(\pi_1^{\mathbf{u}}:R \mid \bar{\pi})$ for the actant of K identified by the role R and $\mathbf{u} \prec \mathbf{u}_1$. Much as the semantics of an actant is determined by its role, the semantics of a circumstantial is determined by an ATTRIBUTE. The difference is that the attributes are specified only by plans, but not by the dictionary profiles.

$$sem^I\Big[K\big([\pi_1^{\mathbf{u}}:A \mid \bar{L}]^{\mathbf{u}_1^{(\omega)}} \mid \bar{\pi}\big)\Big] = \big((A^I \; sem^I[\pi_1]) \; sem^I[K^I(\bar{L} \mid \bar{\pi})]\big),$$

if $\pi_1^{\mathbf{u}}$ is the first circumstantial in the circumstantial list $[\pi_1^{\mathbf{u}} \mid \bar{L}]^{\mathbf{u}_1^{(\omega)}}$ of $K^{\left(\mathbf{u}_1^{(\omega)} \bar{\mathbf{u}} \to \mathbf{v}\right)}$ in the plan $K\big([\pi_1^{\mathbf{u}} \mid \bar{L}]^{\mathbf{u}_1^{(\omega)}} \mid \bar{\pi}\big)$ and $\mathbf{u} \prec \mathbf{u}_1$.

Example: Appurtenance. The plan in Fig. 1(a) conceptualizes the noun phrase *your intellect* using the monad $\langle\!\langle intellect^{(\mathbf{q}^{(\omega)} \to \mathbf{n}_{mass})}\rangle\!\rangle$ whose *appurtenance* attribute *Appurt* applies to $\langle\!\langle hearer^{na}\rangle\!\rangle$. The meaning of this attribute is defined through the meaning of the preposition $\langle\!\langle of\rangle\!\rangle$ whose logical type is $(e \to t) \to ((e \to t) \to (e \to t))$. Extending underspecified types to logical, we obtain the traditional semantics :

$$sem^{log}[intellect([hearer:Appurt])] = \Big(\big(of^{log} \; hearer^{(e \to t)}\big) \; intellect^{(e \to t)}\Big).$$

3 Dependency Structure Grammars

If it were not for distant dependencies, DSG would be CF generative dependency grammars. To work with discontinuities, DSG use *generalized dependency structures (gDS)*: linear ordered graphs with labeled arcs (dependencies) and nodes (words or nonterminals), in which some maximal connected component is selected as *head component* and some node in this component is selected as *gDS head*. One-component gDS is a *dependency tree*. For instance, in two-component gDS below the underlined node is head.

$$\text{Pn}_{pers} \; \underline{V_{tr}} \; MORE \; NG_s \; Pp \; NG \; THAN \; Pp \; NG$$
(with arcs: pred, restr, prep–iobj, dobj, prepos, compar, prepos)

Each gDS δ can be seen as the structure of the string $w(\delta)$ of node labels in natural order.

DSG use the following composition $\delta[\alpha \backslash \delta_1]$ (simultaneous composition: $\delta[\alpha_1, \ldots, \alpha_n \backslash \delta_1, \ldots, \delta_n]$) of gDS. $\delta[\alpha \backslash \delta_1]$ results from gDS δ by substituting gDS δ_1 for node α of δ so that should be preserved:
(i) the order of nodes in δ, δ_1: $w(\delta[\alpha \backslash \delta_1]) = x \; w(\delta_1) \; y$, if $w(\delta) = x \; label(\alpha) \; y$,
(ii) the dependencies in δ, δ_1: the head of δ_1 inherits dependencies of α in δ [4],
as in the following example:

$$\delta_1 = A \; \underline{B} \qquad \delta_2 = a \; A \qquad \delta_3 = b \; B \; b$$

$$\delta_1[A, B \backslash \delta_2[A \backslash \delta_2], \delta_3[B \backslash \delta_3]] = a \; a \; A \; b \; b \; \underline{B} \; c \; c$$

Discontinuous dependencies are established in DSG using polarized valencies and potentials.

Definition 1. *For a finite set* **C** *of dependency types, four polarities are introduced: left and right positive:* $\nearrow, \nwarrow$ *and left and right negative:* $\swarrow, \searrow$ *. For instance, the polarities* $\nearrow$ *and* $\searrow$ *mean outgoing (respectively, incoming) from left to right. For each polarity v, there is the unique "dual" polarity $\breve{v}$:* $\breve{\nearrow} = \searrow$, $\breve{\nwarrow} = \swarrow$, $\breve{\swarrow} = \nwarrow$, $\breve{\searrow} = \nearrow$. *A polarized valency is an expression (vC), in which v is one of the four polarities and $C \in$ **C**. **V** is the set of all valencies.*

For instance, in gDS

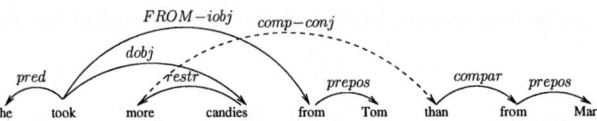

the long distance dependency *comp–conj* relating the two parts of the discontinuous comparative construction *more..than* can be defined using dual valencies $\nearrow comp-conj$ and $\searrow comp-conj$.

Definition 2. *Valency strings* $\Gamma \in \mathcal{P} =_{df} \mathbf{V}^*$ *are called* **potentials**. *Let* $\Gamma = \Gamma_1(vC)\Gamma_2(\breve{v}C)\Gamma_3$ *and* $\Gamma' = \Gamma_1\Gamma_2\Gamma_3$ *be two potentials such that* $(vC) = (\nearrow A)$, $(\breve{v}C) = (\searrow A)$ *or* $(vC) = (\swarrow A), (\breve{v}C) = (\nwarrow A)$. (vC) *is* **first available (FA)** *for $(\breve{v}C)$ in Γ and both are* **neutralized** *in Γ' (denoted $\Gamma \twoheadrightarrow_{FA} \Gamma'$) if Γ_2 has no occurrences of (vC) and $(\breve{v}C)$. This reduction of potentials $\twoheadrightarrow_{FA}$ is terminal and confluent. So each potential Γ has a unique FA-normal form denoted $[\Gamma]_{FA}$. The product $\odot$ of potentials defined by: $\Gamma_1 \odot \Gamma_2 =_{df} [\Gamma_1\Gamma_2]_{FA}$ is clearly associative. So we obtain the monoid of potentials* $\mathbf{P} = (\mathcal{P}, \odot)$ *with the unit ε.*

---

[4] We use nonterminals $label(\alpha)$ in the place of α when no conflicts.

Definition 3. *A* **Dependency Structure Grammar (DSG)** *G has the* rules $r = (A \to \delta)$ *with* $A \in N$ *and a gDS* δ, *on which* potential assignments $[\Gamma^L](r, X, \omega)[\Gamma^R]$ *may be defined,* (r, X, ω) *being an occurrence of X in δ and Γ^L, Γ^R being left and right potentials assigned to this occurrence* [5].

Derivation trees of G result from derivation trees T of cf-grammar $\{A \to w(\delta) \mid A \to \delta \in G\}$ by defining potentials $\pi(T, n)$ of nodes n :

1. $\pi(T, n) = \varepsilon$ *for every terminal node n;*
2. $\pi(T, n) = \Gamma_1 \odot \ldots \odot \Gamma_k$, *for every node n with sons $n_1, ..., n_k$ derived by rule $r = (A \to \delta)$, in which $w(\delta) = X_1...X_k$ and $\Gamma_i = \Gamma_i^L \odot \pi(T, n_i) \odot \Gamma_i^R$, where $[\Gamma_i^L](r, X_i, \omega_i)[\Gamma_i^R]$ are the rule potential assignments. A gDS is generated in the node n by the composition: $gDS(T, n) = \delta[X_1 \ldots X_k \backslash gDS(T, n_1), \ldots, gDS(T, n_k)]$. Every pair of dual valencies neutralized at this step corresponds to a long distance dependency added to this gDS.*

A derivation tree T is complete *if the potential of its root S is neutral: $\pi(T, S) = \varepsilon$. We set $G(D, w)$ if there is a complete derivation tree T of G from the axiom S, such that $D = gDS(T, S)$ and $w = w(D)$.*

$\Delta(G) = \{D \mid \exists w \in W^+ \ G(D, w)\}$ *is the* gDS-language *generated by G.*
$L(G) = \{w \in W^+ \mid \exists D \ G(D, w)\}$ *is the* language *generated by G.*

For instance, the following four-rule DSG:

$G_1: \quad S \to a[\swarrow a] \ \underline{S} \quad \mid \quad A \quad c \quad A \to [\nwarrow a]b \quad A \quad c \quad \mid \quad [\nwarrow a]b$
generates the language $L(G_1) = \{a^n b^n c^n \mid n > 0\}$.

4 Modular DSG

As expressive as they are (see [4]), the DSG are only simplified models of grammars usable in real linguistic applications. They don't support features, and propose no link with semantics. The former is easy to fix. We will suppose that terminals and nonterminals are decorated with finite-valued feature structures. We will extend terminals to *proto-terminals* (denoted $\{X\}$): classes of words with unifiable feature structures. We will also extend the rules by *constraints*: conditions of applicability in terms of feature values, and we will admit iterated dependencies (denoted $d*$). In order to link these generalized DSG ($gDSG$) with the discourse plans, we choose their subclass that we dub *modular DSG*.

Definition 4. *Modular DSG (MDSG) is a gDSG decomposable into a union of subgrammars (modules) $G = \bigcup_{(M)} G_{(M)}$ with disjoint sets of nonterminals (the nonterminal (M) serves as the axiom of $G_{(M)}$), satisfying conditions:*

$(\mathbf{m_1})$ *if several rules of $G_{(M)}$ share the same left hand nonterminal: $A \to \delta_1/c_1 \mid \ldots \mid \delta_k/c_k$, then the constraints c_i are one-to-one exclusive;*
$(\mathbf{m_2})$ *terminals of $G_{(M)}$ are proto-terminals of G or axioms of other modules;*

---

[5] For instance, $A \to [\nwarrow D_1] \underline{B} [\nearrow D_2] \ C$ denotes the rule $A \to \underline{B} \ C$ with assignment $[\nwarrow D_1] B [\nearrow D_2]$. We omit empty potentials.

(**m₃**) *in every module, no recursion is possible through the heads of right-hand gDS of its rules;*
(**m₄**) *in every rule $A \to \delta$, δ has at most one (possibly iterated) dependency.*

Example of English verb group module:

$(VG) \to VG_1$ /dist = 0 |

$\underline{VG_1}$ $(THAN-compar)$
/dist = comp−conj

$VG_1 \to \overset{pre-circ*}{\overleftarrow{(PreCG)\quad VG_2}}$

$VG_2 \to VG_3 \overset{post-circ*}{\overrightarrow{\quad (PostCG)}}$

$VG_3 \to \overset{pred}{\overrightarrow{(NG)\quad VG_4}}$
/SBJ.cr = T, SBJ.type = n_a, $\boxed{\text{SBJ=pred.subd}}$ |

VG_4 /SBJ.cr = 0
$VG_4 \to VG_5$ /asp = nperf |
$\overset{aux}{\overrightarrow{AuxG \quad (PerfG)}}$ /asp = perf

$VG_5 \to VG_6 \overset{inf-obj}{\overrightarrow{\quad}} (V_{inf}G)$
/PRED.type = s_{mph}, $\boxed{\text{OBJ=infobj.subd}}$ |

$VG_6 \overset{sent-obj}{\overrightarrow{\quad}} (Obj-cl)$
/PRED.type ≠ s_{mph}, $\boxed{\text{OBJ=sentobj.subd}}$ |

VG_6 /$\boxed{\text{OBJ=dobj.subd}}$ ∨ OBJ.cr = 0

$VG_6 \to VG_7 \overset{P-iobj}{\overrightarrow{\quad}} (P-PG)$
/role(P).type = **n**, role(P).cr = ⊙, $\boxed{\text{role(P)=Piobj.subd}}$ |

VG_7 /PRED.act < 3 ∨ role(P).cr = 0

$VG_7 \to \{V\} \overset{diobj}{\overrightarrow{\quad}} (NG)$
/$\boxed{\text{prof(PRED)=prof(V)}}$, $\boxed{\text{OBJ=dobj.subd}}$, OBJ.type = **n**,
(OBJ.cr = 0 ∨ (role(P).cr ≠ 0 = OBJ.cr) ∨
(OBJ.cr = combg ∧ role(P).cr = ⊙)) |

$\{V\}$ /$\boxed{\text{prof(PRED)=prof(V)}}$,
(PRED.act < 2 ∨ OBJ.cr = 0)

LEGEND: For a role R, $R.cr$ and $R.type$ denote the communicative rank and the type of the actant with the role R; for a preposition P, $role(P)$ is the role of the oblique actant represented by the corresponding prepositional phrase (e.g., $role(FROM) = ORIG$); $PRED$ is the situation functor's role, $PRED.act$ is the number of its actants, $prof(PRED)$ is the profile of the situation; for a dependency d, $d.subd$ is the subordinate; the boxed equations define a morphism from derivations onto discourse plans (e.g., $OBJ = dobj.subd$ maps direct objects onto actants with the role OBJ).

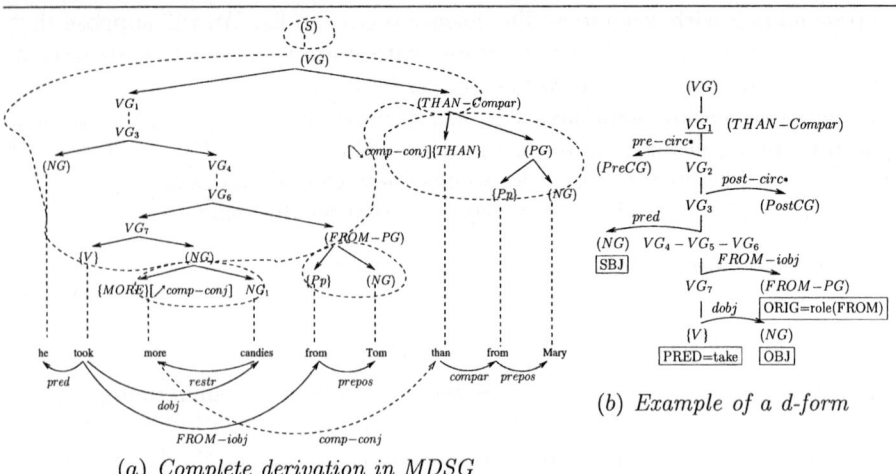

(a) *Complete derivation in MDSG*

(b) *Example of a d-form*

Fig. 2. Modular derivations

As it is clear from definition 4, due to the modularity constraints, each complete derivation of a MDSG G is a composition of derivations in modules $G_{(M)}$ (cf. example in Fig. 2(a)). These module derivations start with module axiom (M) and have in the leaves either proto-terminals of G or other modules' axioms. We call such derivations of $G_{(M)}$ *m-terminal*. m-terminal derivations are *minimal* if each iterative dependency is iterated at most once. Clearly, there are finitely many minimal derivations in each MDSG. More importantly, each minimal derivation D in a module $G_{(M)}$ is uniquely identified by the constraint σ on features, which is a composition of constraints of rules applied in D. We will call *d-form* a minimal m-terminal derivation decorated by its feature constraint: $D_\sigma =_{df} D \circ \sigma$ (see the verb group module d-form in Fig. 2(b)).

Linking Discourse Plans to MDSG. Semantical interpretation Φ of a MDSG is defined through its d-forms. As it is explained above (see the legend to the verb group module), the morphism Φ is defined through equations of the form $Role = dependency.subd$. A simplified rule of top-down construction of $\Phi(D)$ for a modular complete derivation D is as follows. 1. Determine the topmost m-terminal subderivation D_0 of D and its module $G_{(M)}$. 2. Define the d-form F of which D_0 is an instance. 3. Find the semanteme equation $PRED = Key$ in F [6]. 4. For each actant A of Key with $Key.cr \notin \{\ominus, O\}$, find the corresponding object dependency d in F and set $\Phi((d.subd)) = A$. 5. For each instance c_0 of an iterated dependency $c*$ in D_0, determine from the feature constraint the corresponding circumstantial C and the attribute a, set $\Phi((c.subd)) = C$ and decorate this argument with a in the plan. □

E.g., the d-form in Fig. 2(b) of the second topmost subderivation in Fig. 2(a) defines the topmost situation *take* and its arguments in the plan in Fig. 1(b).

5 Compiling Modular DSG into Categorial DG

Categorial dependency grammars (CDG) are simply related with the classical categorial grammars. They assign to words "curried" variants of first order types: $[l_1 \backslash \ldots \backslash m/ \ldots /r_1]$, whose left (l_i), right (r_i) and main (m) subtypes can be elementary or polarized. When a word w is assigned an elementary type l (denoted $w : l$) and a phrase p has type $[l\backslash \alpha]$ $(p : [l\backslash \alpha])$, then $l[l\backslash \alpha] \models \alpha$ $(wp : \alpha)$ and dependency l is established from the head of p to w. When two distant phrases have dual main and argument valency types, e.g. $p_1 : (\swarrow d)$ and $p_2 : [(\nwarrow d)\backslash \alpha]$, then $(\swarrow d)..[(\nwarrow d)\backslash \alpha] \models \alpha$ $(p_1..p_2 : \alpha)$ and distant dependency d is established from the head of p_2 to the head of p_1 if the two dual types are in a sense "closest". To express immediate neighborship, valency types can be decorated by two adjacency modalities: ♭ (host) and # (anchored). $p_1 : \#(\swarrow d)$ means that $p_1 : (\swarrow d)$ must be anchored immediately on

---
[6] We suppose that F has this equation. It is not always the case: in the verb group module above, the second rule for VG_4 defining perfective verb forms presumes two modules: one for the auxiliary taking the subject argument and the other for the participle taking all complement arguments and determining the semanteme key.

the left of a phrase host for left $(\swarrow d)$. $p_2 : [\flat(\swarrow d)\backslash\alpha]$ means that p_2 is host for left $(\swarrow d)$. So $\#(\swarrow d)[\flat(\swarrow d)\backslash\alpha] \models (\swarrow d)\alpha$ and $p_1 p_2 : (\swarrow d)\alpha$. For instance, $[\flat(\swarrow clit-dobj)\backslash subj\backslash S/aux]$ is one of possible types of auxiliary verbs in French, which defines them as host words for a cliticized direct object.

A calculus of dependency types in CDG and an efficient polynomial time parsing algorithm for it can be found in [3]. CDG can be transformed in *strongly* equivalent DSG and DSG can be transformed in *weakly* equivalent CDG [4]. As it turns out, MDSG are equivalent to DSG and CDG in the following sense.

Theorem 1. *For each DSG, there is a weakly equivalent MDSG.*

Theorem 2. *Each MDSG G can be transformed into a CDG G' such that $\Delta(G') = \Delta(G)$ (and so $L(G') = L(G)$).*

Construction sketch. 1. Specialization. Resolve feature constraints to construct all minimal derivations D_σ. Let D_σ be such derivation in a module $G_{(M)}$. Its head leaf is a proto-terminal $\{W\}$. Assign to all word forms $w \in \{W\}$ the types $c_\sigma =_{df} [\gamma_{l_m}\backslash \ldots \backslash \gamma_{l_1}\backslash H/\gamma_{r_1}/\ldots/\gamma_{r_m}]$ constructed as follows. **2. Subcategorization.** Let $r_1, \ldots, r_m$ be the sequence of rules applied in D_σ and $\backslash v_1 \ldots v_k =_{df} \backslash v_1 \ldots \backslash v_k$. Then $\gamma_{l_i} = \backslash \Gamma_{l_i} \backslash d_{l_i}$, if r_{l_i} defines left dependency d_{l_i} and assigns to the rule head h left potential Γ_{l_i} (similar for right subtypes). Otherwise, $\gamma_{l_i} = \backslash \flat^l(v_{l_i}) \backslash \Gamma_{l_i}$, if r_{l_i} defines no left dependency, assigns Γ_{l_i} to h and if a negative valency v_{l_i} is assigned to the head of a gDS in a minimal derivation in the module $G_{(L)}$ of the left neighbor (L) of h. **3. Main subtype definition.** $H =_{df} d$, if (M) is subordinate through dependency d in some rule of G, $H =_{df} \#^l(v)$, if isolated node (M) is assigned negative valency v at the step 2, $H =_{df} S$ otherwise. □

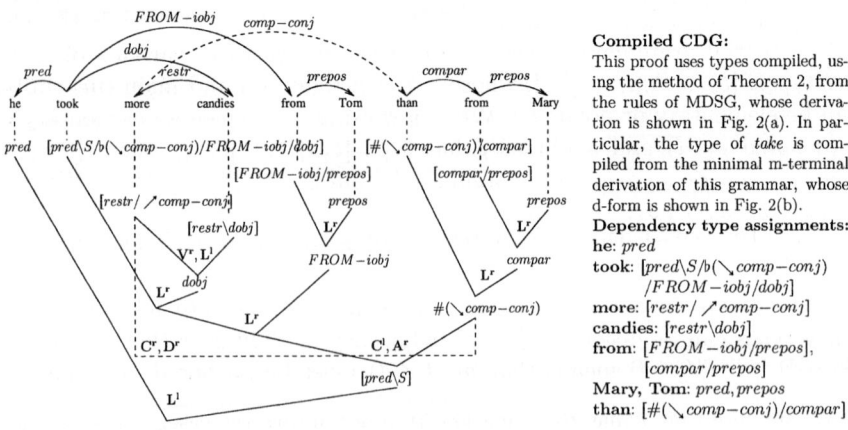

Fig. 3. A proof in CDG compiled from a MDSG.

6 Conclusion

The Discourse Plans are intended to establish a formal link between dependency syntax and referential semantics on a minimal natural language specific cognitive base. The logical aspect of this link will be presented elsewhere.

References

1. Mel'čuk, I.: Dependency Syntax. SUNY Press, Albany, NY (1988)
2. Dikovsky, A.: Dependencies as categories. In: "Recent Advances in Dependency Grammars". COLING'04 Workshop. (2004) 90–97
3. Dekhtyar, M., Dikovsky, A.: Categorial dependency grammars. In: Proc. of Intern. Conf. on Categorial Grammars, Montpellier, France (2004) 76–91
4. Béchet, D., Dikovsky, A., Foret, A.: Dependency structure grammars. In: Proc. of the 5th Int. Conf. "Logical Aspects of Computational Linguistics". LNAI 3492 (2005) 18–34
5. Béchet, D., Dikovsky, A., Foret, A., Moreau, E.: On learning discontinuous dependencies from positive data. In: Proc. of the 9th Intern. Conf. "Formal Grammar 2004". (2004) 1–16
6. Dikovsky, A.: Linguistic meaning from the language acquisition perspective. In: Proc. of the 8th Intern. Conf. "Formal Grammar 2003". (2003) 63–76
7. Dikovsky, A., Smilga, B.: Semantic roles and diatheses for functional discourse plans. In: Proc. of the 2nd International Conference "Meaning-Text Theory", Moscow, Russia (2005) 98–109
8. Padučeva, E.V.: Diathesis and diathetic displacement. Russian Linguistics **26** (2002) 179–215

Distributed English Text Chunking Using Multi-agent Based Architecture*

Ying-Hong Liang[1,2] and Tie-Jun Zhao[1]

[1] MOE-MS Key Laboratory of Natural Language Processing and Speech
in Harbin Institute of Technology, Harbin, 150001
[2] School of Information and Computer Engineering in North East Forestry University,
Harbin, 150080
{liangyh, tjzhao@mtlab.hit.edu.cn}

Abstract. The traditional English text chunking approach identifies phrases by using only one model and phrases with the same types of features. It has been shown that the limitations of using only one model are that: the use of the same types of features is not suitable for all phrases, and data sparseness may also result. In this paper, the Distributed Multi-Agent based architecture approach is proposed and applied in the identification of English phrases. This strategy put phrases into agents according to their sensitive features and identifies different phrases in parallel, where the main features are: one, easy and quick communication between phrases; two, avoidance of data sparseness. By applying and testing the approach on the public training and test corpus, the F score for arbitrary phrases identification using Distributed Multi-Agent strategy achieves 95.70% compared to the previous best F score of 94.17%.

Keywords: English text chunking; distributed architecture; Multi-Agent.

1 Introduction

Text chunking is an important strategy for Natural Language Processing. It can be applied broadly within the Natural Language Processing (NLP) fields in areas such as: machine translation, information extraction, topic content analyzing and text processing. The levels of precision and recall utilized in text chunking may impact on the correctness of the text analyzing and text processing.

Text chunking has received much attention since Abney proposed the strategy of shallow parsing [1] and consequently designed a shallow parser [2]. Skut W. and Brants T. (1998) then designed a maximum-entropy partial parser which performed well on English text chunking [3]. This technique gained further prominence in 2000 when the theme of the Conference on Computational Natural Language Learning (CONLL) was English text chunking [4]. In this conference, the open training and test corpus were delivered, and many statistical and machine learning methods were applied to English text chunking [5-6]. Tong Zhang, Fred Damerau and David Johnson (2002) introduced the Winnow method which is also a machine learning method for English text chunking [7]. The advantage of this particular method is that

---

* This work was supported by the Natural Science Foundation of China (Grant No. 60375019); the International Cooperate Project of Sino-Ireland (Grant No. CI-2003-03).

it can isolate related features within a large quantity of features. However, this method has a lower searching efficiency and needs large memory because of the large quantity of features employed. At the same time, data sparseness also occurs as it applies the feature of "word" to all phrases.

To summarize the above approaches, we can find that English text chunking has made rapid progress to a certain extent. However, as a strategy for shallow parsing, text chunking is a prerequisite step before attempting further analysis such as web information extraction or full parsing. As such higher precision, recall and faster speed are required in the process and current processes can not satisfy this requirement.

The main task of text chunking is to identify phrases within a sentence [8]. From the previous work in English text chunking, we know that only one model is applied and the same types of features are used to identify all phrases. The disadvantages of this method are as follows:

(1) Every phrase's characteristics can not be comprised within one model, so the result of analysis on some phrases for example, LST, CONJP, INTJ are not satisfactorily identified;
(2) The same types of feature are used on all phrases even though some of them are not applicable to some phrases;
(3) A better result can be achieved if more types of feature are used, but this will lead to data sparseness if the "word" type of feature is applied to all types of phrases.

In fact, different phrases have different sensitive features. For example, noun phrase and verb phrase are sensitive to the feature of "part of speech (POS)" characteristics. For example, the feature for SBAR category consists of some fixed words such as "because" and "before". The words that comprise the CONJP classification are as follows: "not only", "along with", "as well as", "but also" and so on. Therefore, the SBAR and CONJP category are more sensitive to the feature of "word" characteristics than the POS. Moreover, the quantity of words that comprise the SBAR and CONJP categories are limited. So, data sparseness can be avoided if the feature of "word" feature is only applied to those phrases that are sensitive to that particular feature of "word".

From above analysis, we can conclude that the analysis of those types of phrase that are sensitive to the "word" feature will not be satisfactory if only the POS is used to identify all phrases in an effort to avoid data sparseness. Therefore, a better outcome will occur if we select different features and different models for different phrases so as to obtain a better result by integrating the identity of each phrase.

In recent years, the theory of multi-agent and distributed processing has been applied in many fields [9, 10]. This theory effectively integrates and co-ordinates several agents to solve the problem. Therefore, we propose to apply the Distributed Multi-Agent based architecture approach to identifying English phrases. This strategy divides phrases according their sensitive features and applies an agent to identify phrases within a group. As each agent communicates with other agents the performance of the chunking is improved. This strategy remedies the shortcomings in using only one model to identify multiple types of phrases and also has several advantages:

(1) It applies the theory of multi-agent into the field of Natural Language Processing and concentrate on the characteristics of each phrase. This focus does not occur when only one model is used to identify multiple types of phrases;
(2) Different models and sensitive features are used to identify different phrase, so this not only avoids data sparseness but also improves the speed and performance of chunking;
(3) Through the communication between agents and by the restriction of phrase priority, one phrase can be identified by using the information of other phrases which improves the chunking performance.

The remainder of this paper is organized as follows: Section 2 gives the distributed architecture of English text chunking based on the Multi-Agent strategy; Section 3 describes the implementation of distributed English chunking using the Multi-Agent strategy; Section 4 illustrates the result of distributed English chunking using Multi-Agent strategy and compares to other methods; and Section 5 gives a conclusion of our present work and highlights possible future work in this area.

2 The Distributed Architecture of English Text Chunking

The function of Multi-Agent theory solves a problem in a decomposing way [9]. Task share and result share are often methods used to get to an answer. Task share appears when a task is decomposed into sub-tasks and assigned to different agents, while result share indicates that agents share the related information of sub-tasks. The procedure of getting the answer to a question is divided into three parts [9]:

(1) Decomposing the task: The task is to be decomposed into smaller sub-tasks;
(2) Getting the answer to a sub-task : To get the answer for each sub-task separately. This includes information share among the agents: One agent can help other agent if it has useful information for the other agent;
(3) Synthesizing each sub-task's answer: Integrating each sub-task's answer to get the final answer.

In this paper, a distributed architecture of English text chunking using Multi-Agent strategy is proposed and sensitive features of each phrase are considered. Through the combination of task share and result share, the information can be transferred among the agents. The distributed architecture of English text chunking using Multi-Agent strategy is shown in Figure 1.

In Figure 1, the dashed line with arrowhead represents the communication relationship between two agents. From Figure 1, the chunking task is divided into several sub-tasks, with each sub-task's answer being achieved in parallel by some agents transferring information between each other. This satisfies the task share component of Multi-Agent theory. The right hand portion of Figure1 demonstrated the synthesizing each sub-task's answer, which in return satisfies the result share in Multi-Agent theory.

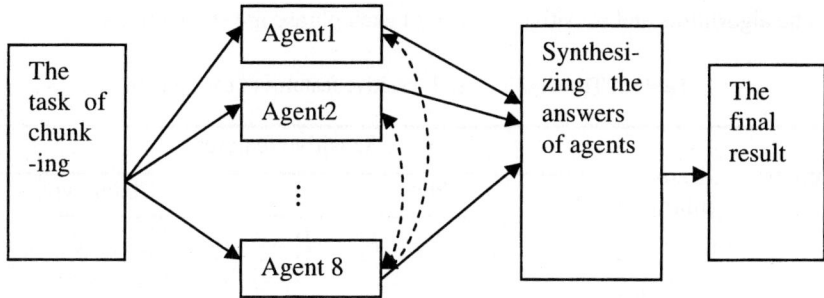

Fig. 1. The distributed architecture of English text chunking using Multi-Agent strategy

In our system, eleven types of phrases are identified (refer to Penn Treebank for definition of English phrase types). Table 1 briefly outline each agent.

Table 1. A brief introduction to each agent

Agents	Function
Agent1	To identify NP
Agent2:	To identify VP
Agent3	To identify PP, ADVP and ADJP
Agent4	To identify INTJ and LST
Agent5	To identify SBAR and CONJP
Agent6	To identify UCP and PRT
Agent7	To read a new sentence
Agent8	To synthesize each sub-task's answers so as to get the final result

3 The Implementation of Distributed English Text Chunking Using Multi-agent Architecture

3.1 The Algorithm and Sensitive Features of Each Phrase

A sensitive feature has crucial effect on chunking. Where large quantities of features exist, there are only a few features that are crucial for chunking. Those redundant features not only take up the memory space but also affect the searching efficiency. So, having larger quantities of features do not always produce a better result. The most important determinant is whether the feature is a sensitive feature.

The constituent of each phrase in training corpus was analyzed by statistical method. The sensitive features of each phrase were summarized by observing the identification performance of each phrase.

The algorithms used to identify phrases are classical. It is confirmed that these methods are effective to identify phrases by researchers.

The algorithms and sensitive features of each phrase are shown in Table 2:

Table 2. The algorithm and sensitive features of each phrase

Phrases	Algo-rithm	W	V_{-1}	P_{-1}	P_0	P_1	P_s	C_{-1}	C_1	P_b
				POS				Chunk type		
SBAR, CONJP	BS	√								
UCP	LSM						√			
PRT	LSM	√	√							
NP	CoSR						√			√
VP	LSM						√			
PP	BS	√		√						
ADVP, ADJP	LSM				√			√	√	
INTJ, LST	BS	√				√				

Notes: *BS*=binary search, *LSM*=longest string matching, *CoSR*=combination of boundary statistics and the rule revise [11], *W*=current word, V_{-1} represents that there is a verb related with PRT in this sentence before current word; P_{-1}=previous POS; =Current POS; P_1=next POS; P_s= the POS string that can compose a phrase; C_{-1}= the previous chunk type; C_1= next chunk type; P_b= boundary probability.

3.2 The Communication Between Agents and the Priority of Each Phrase

Our communication language used is KQML (Knowledge Query and Manipulation Language). Figure 2 is a sketch map detailing the communication path amongst agents.

In Figure 2, six agents (agent 1 to agent 6) begin to activate only when agent 7 reads a new sentence, and this sentence is then sent to these six agents. Agent 8 begins to synthesize the six answers so as to produce the final result when all the six agents have completed their tasks. Each agent (agent 1 to agent 6) has its own model and algorithm in accordance with its task, and communication occurs among the six agents in the course of the identification process via the communication language (KQML). Four primitives are defined, and Table 3 provides a brief outline of them.

Distributed English Text Chunking Using Multi-agent Based Architecture   757

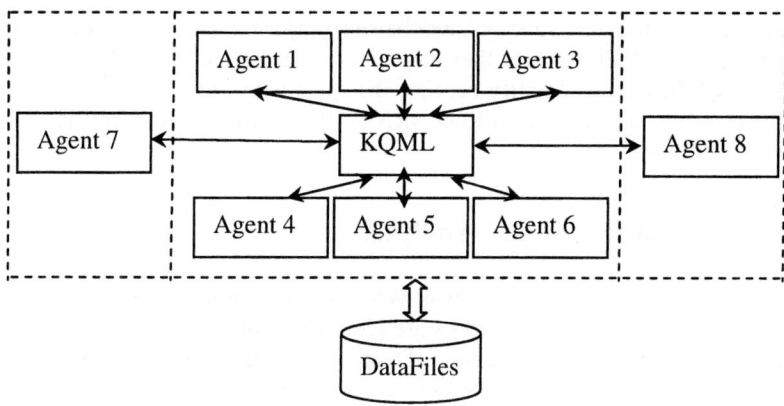

Fig. 2. The communication path amongst agents

Table 3. A brief introduction to four primitives

Primitive	Function
Inform primitive	(1) Agent 7 sends a message to six agents (agent 1 to agent 6) when it reads a new sentence. (2) Six agents send message to agent 8 when they all have completed their tasks.
Query primitive	Query primitive sends a message to the other agents during the course of identification to determine the identification situation of the other phrases.
Reply primitive	Reply primitive corresponds with query primitive. It sends message to the query agent.
Close primitive	Close primitive sends a message (agent 7 sends message) to notify other agents to remove interim information from repository and agent 7 then reads a new sentence to begin a new cycle.

The responsibility of agent 8 is to synthesize each sub-task's answers. Agent 8 obtains the last result by prioritizing each phrase. We believe that the result of higher priority result is more credible than that of the lower priority. The priority of phrases is set as follows:

INTJ=LST=CONJP>UCP>NP>VP>SBAR=PP=PRT >ADJP=ADVP.

As the features of INTJ, LST and CONJP are "word" based. There are fixed word and the quantity is limited. Therefore, serious data sparseness does not occur, and so the highest priority is set for INTJ, LST and CONJP. UCP can be easily regarded as noun phrase, so its priority was set higher than that of a noun phrase. The frequency of NP and VP in a sentence is high, so it is important to identify NP and VP. The priority of noun phrase is higher than that of verb phrase because some verbs with POS =VBG are not always verb phrases, on the contrary, they often are included within a noun phrase. SBAR, PP and PRT have communicated with each other during the course of identification, so they have the same priority. Their priorities are lower than those of NP and VP because they can not cover the result of NP and VP. ADJP and ADVP are difficult to identify because the word with POS =JJ is often within a noun phrase, while the word with POS =RB is often within a verb phrase, so their priority is the lowest.

4 Experimental Result and Analysis

We use the public corpus (Penn Treebank WSJ15-18 is training corpus and WSJ20 is the test corpus). Eleven English phrases are identified using Distributed Multi-Agent strategy. The result comparison between Distributed Multi-Agent strategy and other methods is listed in Table 4 (using the same corpus).

Table 4. The comparison of Distributed Multi-Agent strategy and other methods

method / result	SVM	Memory-based method	Winnow	Distributed Multi-Agent strategy
Precision (%)	93.45	94.04	94.28	95.31
Recall (%)	93.51	91.00	94.07	96.09
$F_{\beta=1}$ (%)	93.48	92.50	94.17	95.70

SVM, Memory-based method and Winnow are typical methods in English chunking, and their results are state of the art. The above comparison implies that Distributed Multi-Agent strategy achieves state of the art performance with less computation than previous systems. Moreover, Distributed Multi-Agent strategy has the following advantages: (1) Distributed Multi-Agent strategy only uses sensitive features, so it occupies smaller memory. (2)The time cost of the proposed method is more bearable. We tested the speed of this method within a computer whose CPU is PIV 1.5G, with 256M memory and the speed from training to test is no more than 1.5 minutes. The success of this method relies on the Distributed Multi-Agent's ability to use individual model to identify individual phrases and the communication ability among the agents.

Table 5 is the comparison between the results of Winnow and those using Distributed Multi-Agent strategy (using the same corpus).

Table 5 shows that all the results using the Distributed Multi-Agent strategy are higher than those using the Winnow method. This illuminates that Distributed Multi-Agent strategy can improve the result with all phrases. It is worthwhile to note that the improvement of INTJ, LST and CONJP is larger than other phrases as the feature "word" used by these three phrases in Distributed Multi-Agent strategy, and the quantity of these words is limited. As a result, data sparseness does not occur, and this proves that by using different feature for different phrase data sparseness can be avoided in Distributed Multi-Agent strategy. The improved scope of PRT and SBAR phrases is large too, which illuminates that the communication between these two phrases is effective. In addition, the results of other phrases are improved to a certain extent through the adoption of prioritizing results.

Table 5. The result comparison between Winnow and Distributed Multi-Agent strategy

Phrase	Winnow method			Distributed Multi-Agent strategy		
	Precision (%)	Recall (%)	$F_{\beta=1}$ (%)	Precision (%)	Recall (%)	$F_{\beta=1}$ (%)
ADJP	81.68	73.29	77.26	81.35	90.42	85.65
ADVP	82.63	81.29	81.96	93.05	88.21	90.57
CONJP	55.56	55.56	55.56	76.00	100.00	86.36
INTJ	100.00	50.00	66.67	66.67	80.00	72.73
LST	0.00	0.00	0.00	100.00	100.00	100.00
NP	94.39	94.37	94.38	94.65	95.75	95.20
PP	97.64	98.03	97.83	98.32	98.50	98.41
PRT	81.44	74.53	77.83	92.72	91.50	92.11
SBAR	91.15	88.60	89.86	92.45	95.26	93.83
VP	94.38	94.78	94.58	96.78	96.72	96.75
all	94.28	94.07	94.17	95.31	96.09	95.70

5 Conclusion and Future Work

English chunking is a core part of shallow parsing. Researchers have previously paid more attention to the various approaches for chunking. However, the characteristics of phrases and the relationship between phrases have been ignored. In this paper, a Distributed Multi-Agent English chunking strategy is proposed. As this strategy uses different models and sensitive features for different phrases, and the characteristics of each phrase are sufficiently considered. At the same time, data sparseness is avoided with sensitive features. The chunking result is improved by the communication among agents and performance and speed are also improved considerably when compared with other approaches. The proposed method offers a brand-new strategy for chunking and experimental results show that the result using the proposed method is significantly better than the current comparable state-of-the-art approach for English text chunking task.

This paper proposes and implements a chunking model with Distributed Multi-Agent strategy, and as it is in its initial stages there is obviously much scope for improvement. Our future work will focus two aspects:

(1) Searching for new suitable algorithms in the identification of each phrase (especially noun and verb phrases) to further increase the performance of the model;
(2) To identify Chinese text chunks using Distributed Multi-Agent strategy.

References

1. Abney S. : Parsing by chunks. Principle Based Parsing. Berwick, Abney and Tenny. Kluwer A. Publishers. 1991.
2. Abney S. : Partial parsing via finite-state cascades. Workshop on Robust Parsing, 8th European Summer School in Logic, Language and Information. Prague, Czech Republic. (1996) 8-15.
3. Skut W. and Brants T. : A maximum-entropy partial parser for unrestricted text. Proceedings of the 6th Workshop on Very Large Corpora. Montreal, Quebec. 1998.
4. Tjong Kim Sang E.F. : Introduction to the CoNLL-2000 Shared Task: Chunking. Proceedings of CoNLL-2000 and LLL-2000. Lisbon, Portugal. (2000) 127-132.
5. Kudoh T. and Matsumoto Y. : Use of Support Vector Learning for Chunk Identification. Proceedings of CoNLL-2000 and LLL-2000. Lisbon, Portugal. (2000) 127-132.
6. Tjong Kim Sang E. F. : Memory-Based Shallow Parsing. In proceedings of CoNLL-2000 and LLL-2000. Lisbon, Portugal. (2000) 559-594.
7. Zhang T. , Damerau F. and Johnson D. : Text Chunking based on a Generalization of Winnow. Machine Learning Research. 2 (2002) 615-637.
8. HongLin Sun and ShiWen Yu: The summarization of shallow parsing method. The linguistics of the present age. (2000) 063-073.
9. Michael W. : An Introduction to Multi-Agent Systems. Chichester. England. 2002.
10. Kargupta H. , Hamzaoglu I. and Stafford B. : Web Based Parallel/Distributed Medical Data Mining Using Software Agents. Extended Proceedings of the 1997 Fall Symposium, American Medical Informatics Association. (1997).
11. YingHong Liang and TieJun Zhao: The Identification of English Base Noun Phrase Based on the Hybrid Strategy. Computer Engineering and Application. 35 (2004) 1-4.

A Similarity-Based Approach to Data Sparseness Problem of Chinese Language Modeling

Jinghui Xiao, Bingquan Liu, Xiaolong Wang, and Bing Li

School of Computer Science and Techniques, Harbin Institute of Technology,
Harbin, 150001, China
{xiaojinghui, liubq, wangxl, bli}@insun.hit.edu.cn

Abstract. Data sparseness problem is inherent and severe in language modeling. Smoothing techniques are usually widely used to solve this problem. However, traditional smoothing techniques are all based on statistical hypotheses without concerning about linguistic knowledge. This paper introduces semantic information into smoothing technique and proposes a similarity-based smoothing method which is based on both statistical hypothesis and linguistic hypothesis. An experiential iterative algorithm is presented to optimize system parameters. Experiment results prove that compared with traditional smoothing techniques, our method can greatly improve the performance of language model.

1 Introduction

Statistical language model plays an important role in natural language processing and has a wide range of applications in many domains, such as speech recognition[1], OCR[2], machine translation[3], and pinyin-to-character conversion[4], etc. Data sparseness is an inherent problem in statistical language modeling. Because of the limitation of training corpus there always exist linguistic events that never occur or only occur few times. In such circumstances, it's impossible to accurately estimate their probabilities from the observed sequences by MLE (Maximum Likelihood Estimation) principle and other estimation schemes have to be used. The above problem is called data sparseness problem.

Data sparseness problem is very severe even using large scale of training corpus. For instance, Brown[5] constructed an English trigram model by the corpus consisting of 366 million English words and discovered that there were 14.7% word triples of the test corpus that never occurred in the training corpus. In this paper, a Chinese bigram model is constructed with the corpus of 5 million Chinese characters. In the test corpus, 23.5% word pairs are absent from the training samples.

The common solutions to data sparseness problem are smoothing techniques, such as adding one smoothing[6], Good-Turing smoothing[7], back-off smoothing[8], interpolation smoothing[9], etc. Literature[10] gives a comprehensive comparison between common smoothing techniques. All these techniques are based on some statistical hypotheses. For example, adding one smoothing assumes that all the linguistic events should be observed at least one time. Back-off smoothing adopts the lower-order model to substitute the current model when encountering data sparseness.

The above hypotheses are all based on the statistical approach, rather than the linguistic approach, which do not fit in for the realities. This paper introduces semantic information into smoothing technique and proposes a similarity-based smoothing technique. Such a linguistic assumption is made that those words with similar meanings provide similar syntax functions and should appear in similar contexts. Then such words can help to predict the current words in the smoothing process for language model. In this paper, an extensive ngram model by word similarity is firstly constructed. Then we combine it with traditional interpolation smoothing method and propose a similarity-based smoothing technique. At last an experiential iterative algorithm is presented to optimize system parameters.

This paper is organized as follows. In section 2, the similarity-based smoothing technique is presented and several relevant questions are discussed, including word similarity calculation, parameters optimization. Experiment results are described and then discussed in section 3. We outline the related works in section 4 and manage to draw the conclusions in section 5.

2 Similarity-Based Smoothing Technique

2.1 Ngram Model

A language model is aiming at estimating the probability of a sequence of words. According to the Bayesian rule, the probability of word sequence $w_1, w_2...w_m$ is typically broken down into its component probabilities:

$$P(w_1, w_2...w_m) = \prod_{i=1}^{m} P(w_i | w_1, w_2...w_{i-1}) \quad (1)$$

Since there are too many parameters to be estimated for large i, it's difficult to compute a probability of form (1). Usually a Markovian assumption on words dependencies is made: the current word's probability is only dependent on the previous n-1 words at most. Thus the probability is determined by:

$$P(w_1, w_2...w_m) = \prod_{i=1}^{m} P(w_i | w_{i-n+1},...w_{i-1}) \quad (2)$$

$w_{i-n+1},...w_{i-1}$ are called *the history words* and w_i is called *the current word* or *the predicted word*. Usually n=2 or 3. Because of its simplicity and efficiency, ngram model becomes one of the most popular language models.

2.2 Similarity-Based Ngram Model

This paper makes such a linguistical assumption that similar words should appear in similar contexts and can help to predict the probability of the current word in language modeling. In this section, an extensive ngram model by word similarity is constructed. According to the above assumption, if a word is observed in normal ngram model, its similar words should appear in the similarity-based ngram model, and vice versa. The similarity-based ngram model is formulized by:

$$P_{sim}(w_i | w_{i-n+1},...w_{i-1}) = \sum_{w_i' \in SimSet(w_i)} S(w_i, w_i') P(w_i' | w_{i-n+1},...w_{i-1}) \quad (3)$$

where $SimSet(w_i)$ is the similar word set of w_i, $S(w_i, w_i')$ is the normalized weight for word similarity, P is the normal ngram probability and P_{sim} is the similarity-based ngram probability. When data sparseness happens, P_{sim} is helpful to predict the value of P.

2.3 Similarity-Based Smoothing Technique

To deal with data sparseness problem, it is from the linguistical view for similarity-based ngram model, while it's the statistical view for traditional smoothing techniques. This paper combines the two points of views together and proposes a similarity-based smoothing technique. It is formulated by

$$P_{smoothed}(w_i | w_{i-n+1},...w_{i-1}) = \lambda \times P_{inter}(w_i | w_{i-n+1},...w_{i-1}) + (1-\lambda) \times P_{sim}(w_i | w_{i-n+1},...w_{i-1}) \quad (4)$$

where $P_{smoothed}$ is the ultimate smoothed probability and P_{inter} is the probability calculated by traditional smoothing technique. This paper adopts the interpolation smoothing technique and it can be recursively defined as below:

$$P_{inter}(w_i | w_{i-n+1},...w_{i-1}) = \theta_n \times P_{inter}(w_i | w_{i-n+2},...w_{i-1}) + (1-\theta_n) \times P(w_i | w_{i-n+1},...w_{i-1}) \quad (5)$$

where θ_k $k=1,2..n$ are the coefficients for k-order language model.

2.4 Word Similarity Calculation

There are two kinds of methods to calculate word similarity. One is the statistical method and makes use of word frequency. The other is the semantic way to use the compiled knowledge database, such as WordNet[11] and Hownet[12]. For data sparseness problem, since there are no enough words to estimate word probability, it's not enough to calculate word similarity which is usually a function of word probability. Then this paper adopts the semantic way and use Hownet2004 and "TongYiCi CiLin"[13] in word similarity calculation.

Hownet is a semantic knowledge database whose mainly descriptive object is concept. The similarity of two concepts c_1 and c_2 is defined as below:

$$Sim(c_1, c_2) = \alpha_1 ClsSim(c_1, c_2) + \alpha_2 ClsFrm(c_1, c_2) + \alpha_3 DefSim(c_1, c_2) + \alpha_4 DefInclude(c_1, c_2) \quad (6)$$

In the above formula, $ClsSim(c_1, c_2)$ is the class similarity that is calculated between the concept classes of c_1 and c_2; $ClsFrm(c_1, c_2)$ is the class framework similarity that is calculated according to the frameworks between the concept classes of c_1 and c_2; $DefSim(c_1, c_2)$ is the definition similarity which is calculated by the definitions of c_1 and c_2; And $DefInclude(c_1, c_2)$ is the similarity of the included concept definitions which is calculated between the concepts that are included in c_1 or c_2 (the sub-concepts of c_1 and c_2). $\alpha_1, \alpha_2, \alpha_3$ and α_4 are scale coefficients.

Word similarity is usually calculated through concept similarity. A word typically has several concepts and there are three ways to get word similarity from their concept similarities: 1. Take the maximum concept similarity as word similarity. 2. Take the minimum concept similarity. 3. Choose the average concept similarity. This paper adopts the last method to make good use of the information of each concept.

In word similarity computing, it's straightforward to calculate the similarity between each word in lexicon. However it'll cost too much time in real world applications. This paper decomposes similarity computation into two steps. The first step is to get some semantic subsets instead of the whole lexicon. In the second step, we calculate the similarity between each word in each subset. This paper chooses the synonym set of hownet2004 as the first subset, the antonym set of hownet2004 as the second and at last choose each word class of "TongYiCi CiLin"[1] as the rest subsets. The words in each subset all tend to be substitutable to each other. Different smoothed language models can be built up based on one or more different semantic subsets and different performances are yielded. We'll discuss it in detail in section 3.

2.5 Parameter Optimization

Besides word frequencies, there are two other kinds of parameters to estimate to construct the language model suggested by formula (4): λ for formula (4) and $\theta_k\ k=1,2..n$ for formula (5). This paper proposes an experiential iterative algorithm to optimize λ and $\theta_k\ k=1,2..n$ which adjusts them to maximize the probability of the held-out corpus. The algorithm can not be strictly deduced by mathematics, whereas it works surprisingly well in practices. Thus we call it an "experiential" one. The procedures are summarized as follows:

1. Initialize the values of λ and θ_k in the range of [0, 1].
2. Fixing θ_k, optimize λ to maximize the probability of the held-out corpus.
3. Fixing λ, optimize each θ_k in a recursive way so as to make the probability of the held-out corpus maximal.
4. Calculate the perplexity of the held-out corpus, if converged, break the iteration; otherwise, go to step (2).

We will detail the step (2) and step (3) in the rest of this section.

2.5.1 Fixing θ_k, Get the Optimal Value for λ

This step is to optimize λ so as to maximize the probability of held-out corpus. Let H denote the held-out corpus, and we try to find $\lambda = \arg\max_\lambda(\log(P_{smoothed}(H)))$.

According to the formulas (4), we can get:

---

[1] "TongYiCi CiLin" is a machine-readable lexicon which contains more than seventy thousands lemmas. These lemmas are organized by their senses and rhetoric, and they are divided into several hierarchical classes. Each class contains similar words. There are totally seven general classes and more than one thousand detailed classes.

$$\log(P_{smoothed}(H)) = \sum_{(w_1,w_2,...w_n)\in H} N(w_1,w_2,...w_n)\log(P_{smoothed}(w_n \mid w_1,w_2,...w_{n-1}))$$

$$= \sum_{(w_1,w_2,...w_n)\in H} N(w_1,w_2,...w_n)\log(\lambda \times P_{inter}(w_n \mid w_1,w_2,...w_{n-1}) \quad (7)$$

$$+ (1-\lambda) \times P_{sim}(w_n \mid w_1,w_2,...w_{n-1}))$$

Take the derivative of formula (7) with respect to λ, perform some simple arithmetic and equate the result to zero, we can get the equation below:

$$\sum_{(w_1,w_2,...w_n)\in H} N(w_1,w_2,...w_n)[\frac{P_{inter}(w_n \mid w_1,w_2,...w_{n-1}) - P_{sim}(w_n \mid w_1,w_2,...w_{n-1})}{\lambda \times P_{inter}(w_n \mid w_1,w_2,...w_{n-1}) + (1-\lambda) \times P_{sim}(w_n \mid w_1,w_2,...w_{n-1})}] = 0 \quad (8)$$

Since θ_k is assumed to be fixed and P_{inter} can be calculated, the equation (8) has a single independent variable λ. Furthermore, there is only one solution for that equation, because the second derivative of (7) is equal to

$$-\sum_{(w_1,w_2,...w_n)\in H} N(w_1,w_2,...w_n)[\lambda + \frac{P_{sim}(w_n \mid w_1,w_2,...w_{n-1})}{P_{inter}(w_n \mid w_1,w_2,...w_{n-1}) - P_{sim}(w_n \mid w_1,w_2,...w_{n-1})}]^{-2} \quad (9)$$

which is negative for all the values of λ and the left part of (8) is a decreasing function about λ. Therefore we can choose any appropriate interval search algorithm to find the root of equation (8) which is the optimal λ that make the formula (7) maximal.

2.5.2 Fixing λ, Get the Optimal Value for θ_k

This step is to optimize each θ_k $k=1,2..n$ in condition of the fixed λ. The procedure is a recursive process. We first fix all θ_k $k=1,2..n-1$ and get the optimal value of θ_n. Then we fix all θ_k $k=1,2..n-2$, together with the value of θ_n, and calculate the optimal value of θ_{n-1}. Continue the above process until we get each optimal value of θ_k $k=1,2..n$. The deductive procedures are very similar to the above procedures of getting the optimal λ value, and we can get the optimal value for θ_k $k=1,2..n$ by recursively solving the following equation:

$$\sum_{(w_1,w_2,...w_n)\in H} N(w_1,w_2,...w_n)[\frac{\lambda \times \prod_{m=k+1}^{n}\theta_m \times (P_{inter}(w_n \mid w_{n-k+2},...w_{n-1}) - P(w_n \mid w_{n-k+1},...w_{n-1}))}{\lambda \times P_{inter}(w_n \mid w_1,w_2,...w_{n-1}) + (1-\lambda) \times P_{sim}(w_n \mid w_1,w_2,...w_{n-1})}] = 0 \quad (10)$$

θ_k is hidden in the formula of $P_{inter}(w_n \mid w_1,w_2,...w_{n-1})$, we don't expand it because of the limitation of paper width.

3 Experiment and Discussion

3.1 Evaluation

This paper evaluates the smoothing algorithm by the performance of the language model which is smoothed by that method. The most common metric for language model is perplexity. Perplexity is the reciprocal of the geometric average probability assigned by language model to each word of test corpus and is defined as below:

$$PP_c = 2^{-\frac{1}{N_c}\sum_{i=1}^{N_w} \log_2 P_{smoothed}(w_i|w_{i-n},...w_{i-1})} \qquad (11)$$

where N_c and N_w are the number of characters and the number words of the test corpus respectively. It's generally regarded that lower perplexity correlates with better performance.

3.2 Results and Discussions

We take our experiments on two kinds of corpus. One is the People's Daily corpus which consists of approximately 8 million Chinese characters. The other is the tour corpus collected from some tour websites which consists of 10 million Chinese characters. For the People's Daily corpus, it's divided into three parts: the training corpus consisting of 5 million Chinese characters, the held-out corpus containing 1.5 million characters and the test corpus which is built up by the rest characters. We evaluate our algorithm by the performance of the smoothed bigram model. The results are presented in the table below:

Table 1. Perplexity on Different Smoothed Language Models on People's Daily Corpus

	Model S	Model A	Model B	Model C
Perplexity	88.63	73.72	69.73	53.78
Reduction	------	16.82%	21.32%	39.32%

Model S is the baseline language model which is smoothed by the standard linear interpolation algorithm. Model A, B and C are all smoothed by the similarity-based method this paper proposed, but they choose different semantic subsets in word similarity calculation. Model A only uses the synonym set of Hownet2004. Model B adopts both the synonym set and antonym set of Hownet2004. Model C not only uses the Hownet semantic subsets, but also adopts the word class of "TongYiCi CiLin".

For the tour corpus, it's also divided into three parts: the training corpus consisting of 8 million Chinese characters, the held-out corpus containing 1 million characters and the test corpus built up by the rest characters. The results are listed in the table below:

Table 2. Perplexity of Different Smoothed Language Models on Tour Corpus

	Model S	Model A	Model B	Model C
Perplexity	59.79	53.64	52.52	43.20
Reduction	------	10.29%	12.16%	27.75%

From the two tables we can see that the perplexities of model A, B and C are much lower than that of the baseline model. As much as 39% perplexity reduction is achieved in table 1, and 27% perplexity reduction in table 2. These models show much more predictive capability. Thus we can conclude that the similarity-based smoothing method which this paper proposes is far more effective than the traditional smoothing algorithm and higher performance language model can be achieved in this way. Meanwhile, we can also see that as the semantic subsets are increasingly adopts (from model A to C), the perplexity of language model becomes lower and lower, and more powerful model is obtained. Then the second conclusion can be made that the improvement of the performances of A, B and C is due to the increasing semantic information in the language model, which verifies this paper's linguistic hypothesis.

In the rest of this section, we check the performance of the iterative algorithm proposed in section 2.5. The results are described in figure 1 and figure 2:

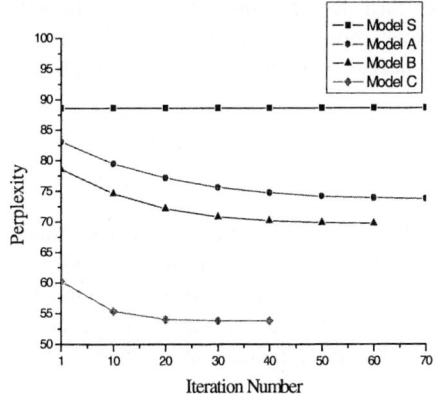 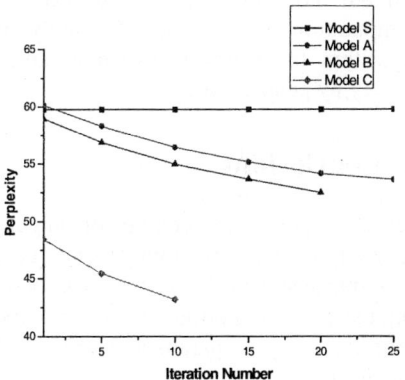

Fig. 1. Performance of Iterative Algorithm on People's Daily Corpus

Fig. 2. Performance of Iterative Algorithm on Tour Corpus

For comparison convenience, we also present Model S (which is not optimized by the iterative algorithm) in the two figures. As the figures show, Model A, B and C outperform S during the iterations, which verify our first conclusion above. And as the iteration number increases, the perplexities of A, B and C are constantly reduced, until the algorithms converge.

To further verify the effectiveness of the experiential iterative algorithm, we compare it with EM (Expectation-Maximum) algorithm and carry out the experiments on the People's Daily corpus. The results are presented in table 3:

Table 3. Perplexity of Language Models Optimized by Different Algorithms

	Model A	Model B	Model C
EI Algorithm	73.72	69.73	53.78
EM Algorithm	75.86	73.42	55.47

In table 3, we take EI algorithm as experiential iterative algorithm for short. As the table shows, the models, which are optimized by EI algorithm, achieve lower perplexities and obtain more predictive capability. Then we can make the last conclusion that the experiential iterative algorithm is effective to optimize the parameters for the similarity-based smoothing method.

4 Related Works

Essen[14] first proposed similarity-based method for data sparseness problem and introduced word similarity into language modeling. Dagan[15] extended Essen's idea and integrated word similarity into back-off framework. Essen and Dagan's ideas greatly illuminate our work. But there are two important differences between our work and Essen and Dagan's. Firstly, Essen and Dagan adopted statistical methods to calculate word similarity. But since the training corpus is already sparse to stat word frequency, it is definitely sparse to calculate word similarity which is usually a function of word frequency. Obviously the performances of these methods are limited. To avoid the above problem, we turn to semantic way in similarity computation in our work. Secondly, this paper proposes an experiential iterative algorithm to optimize system parameters, whereas Dagan determined parameters merely by people's trials.

5 Conclusions

For data sparseness problem of language modeling, this paper introduces semantic information into smoothing technique and presents a similarity-based approach to data sparseness problem, which is based on both the statistical assumption and the linguistical assumption. Then an experiential iterative algorithm is proposed to optimize system parameters. From the experiment results, we can get three conclusions:

- The similarity-based smoothing technique is far more effective than the traditional smoothing method, and high performance language model can be obtained.
- The performance improvement of the language model smoothed by similarity-based technique is duo to the increasing semantic information in the models.
- The experiential iterative algorithm is effective to optimize system parameters for similarity-based smoothing technique.

Acknowledgement

This investigation was supported emphatically by the National Natural Science Foundation of China (No.60435020) and the High Technology Research and Development Programme of China (2002AA117010-09).

We especially thank the anonymous reviewers for their valuable suggestions and comments.

References

1. F. Jelinek. Self-Organized Language Modeling for Speech Recognition. IEEE ICASSP, 1989.
2. George Nagy. At the Frontier of OCR. Processing of IEEE. 1992. 80(7).
3. Peter F. Brown, Stephen A. Della Pietra, Vincent J. Della Pietra, and Robert L. Mercer. The Mathematics of Statistical Machine Translation: Parameter Estimation. Computational Linguistics. 1992. 19(2).

4. Liu Bingquan, Wang Xiaolong and Wang Yuying, Incorporating Linguistic Rules in Statistical Chinese Language Model for Pinyin-to-Character Conversion. High Technology Letters. Vol.7 No.2, June 2001, P:8-13
5. Brown, Peter F., Vincent J. Della Pietra, Peter V. deSouza, Jenifer C. Lai, and Robert L. Mercer. Class-based n-gram models of natural language. Computational Linguistics, 18(4):467-479. 1992.
6. Harold Jeffreys. Theory of Probability. Clarendon Press, Oxford, second Edition, 1948.
7. Irving J. Good. The population frequencies of species and the estimation of population parameters. Biometrika, 40, pp. 237-264, 1953.
8. Slava M. Katz. Estimation of probabilities from sparse data for the language model component of a speech recognizer. IEEE Transactions on Acoustics, Speeech and Signal Processing, 35(3):400-401. 1987.
9. F. Jelinek and R. L. Mercer. Interpolated estimation of markov source parameters from sparse data. In Pattern Recognition in Practice, pp. 381--397, 1980.
10. Stanley F. Chen and Joshua Goodman. An empirical study of smoothing techniques for language modeling. Computer Speech and Language, 13:359-394, October 1999.
11. George A. Miller, Richard Beckwith, Christiane Fellbaum, Derek Gross, and Katherine Miller. Introduction to WordNet: An On-line Lexical Database[EB], Cognitive Science Laboratory Princeton University, 1993.
12. www.keenage.com
13. Mei Jiaju, Chinese thesaurus "Tongyici Cilin", Shanghai thesaurus Press, 1983.
14. Essen, Ute and Volker Steinbiss. Coocurrence smoothing for stochastic language modeling. In Proceedings of ICASSP, volume I, pp. 161-164. 1992.
15. Ido Dagan, Lillian Lee, and Fernando C. N. Pereira. Similarity-based models of word cooccurrence probabilities. Machine Learning, 34(1-3):43--69, 1999.

Self-training and Co-training Applied to Spanish Named Entity Recognition

Zornitsa Kozareva, Boyan Bonev, and Andres Montoyo

Departamento de Lenguajes y Sistemas Informáticos,
Universidad de Alicante, Spain
{zkozareva, montoyo}@dlsi.ua.es
{bib}@alu.ua.es

Abstract. The paper discusses the usage of unlabeled data for Spanish Named Entity Recognition. Two techniques have been used: self-training for detecting the entities in the text and co-training for classifying these already detected entities. We introduce a new co-training algorithm, which applies voting techniques in order to decide which unlabeled example should be added into the training set at each iteration. A proposal for improving the performance of the detected entities has been made. A brief comparative study with already existing co-training algorithms is demonstrated.

1 Introduction

Recently there has been a great interest in the area of *weakly supervised learning*, where unlabeled data has been utilized in addition to the labeled one. In machine learning, the classifiers crucially rely on labeled training data, which was previously created from unlabeled one with some associated cost. Self-training and co-training algorithms allow a classifier to start with few labeled examples, to produce an initial weak classifier and later to use only the unlabeled data for improving the performance.

In previous research by Collins and Singer [2], co-training was applied only to Named Entity classification, by making a split of features into contextual and spelling ones. They point as a future work the development of a complete Named Entity Recognition (NER)[1] system, which we build using self-training and co-training techniques.

We studied the already existing co-training methods and we introduce a new so called "voted co-training" algorithm. The method guarantees the labeling confidence of the unlabeled examples through a voting scheme.

The system has been developed and tested for Spanish language, but having the proper feature set for a NER system in another language, we can say that

---

[1] NER system consists in detecting the words that make up the entity and then classify these words into predefined categories such as people, organization and location names, temporal expressions etc.

the same experiments can be conducted with no restrains. For Spanish the obtained results are encouraging, 90.37% f-score for detecting 2000 entities using 8020 unlabeled examples and 67.22% f-score for entity classification with 792 unlabeled examples.

2 Named Entity Recognition

One Named Entity Recognition system plays important role in lots of natural language applications such as Information Extraction, Information Retrieval, Question Answering etc., by providing the most informative instances in a text, for instance names of people, locations, organizations. A NER task consists of two subtasks, one for entity detection and another for entity classification.

Recently there has been a great interest in entity recognition using diverse machine learning techniques such as AdaBoost, Maximum Entropy, Hidden Markov Models etc., as well as the development of the features needed by these classifiers. However the focus of our paper is NER system build on unlabeled data. For the experimental settings, we incorporated the feature set previously studied by *Kozareva et al.*, [5].

lexical
- **p**: position of w_0 (e.g. the word to be classified) in a sentence
- **c[−3, +3]**: word forms of w_0 and the words in its window ±3
- **fW**: first word making up the entity
- **sW**: second word making up the entity if present

orthographic
- **aC**: all letters of w_0 in capitals
- **iC[−3, +3]**: $w_{-3}, w_{-2}, w_{-1}, w_0, w_{+1}, w_{+2}, w_{+3}$ initiate in capitals

trigger word: w_{-1} and w_{+1} trigger word for location, person, organization
gazetteer word: w_0 belong to gazetteer list

Fig. 1. Features for NE detection and classification

For NED, we used the BIO model proposed by [7]. A word should have one of the following three tags: **B** indicating a word at the beginning of a NE, **I** for word inside a NE and **O** tag for words outside a NE.

The annotation scheme is demonstrated in the example: *Soy_O Antonio_B Guijero_I de_O Portugal_B ._O*[2]. The following features have been used for NED: p, $c[-2, +2]$[3], aC and $iC[-2, +2]$.

We classify our entities into four categories - PERson, LOCation, ORGanization and MISCellanegous. The following set of features has been considered: $c[-3, +3]$, fW, sW, aC, $iC[-3, +3]$, trigger[4] and gazetteer[5] word.

---

[2] the English meaning is: *I am Antonio Guijero from Portugal.*
[3] in our example the word form at position 0 is *Soy*.
[4] semantically significant word pointing to some of the categories person, location, organization; e.g. city is a trigger word for locations.
[5] collections of names of people, locations, organizations.

3 Weakly Supervised Algorithms

In this section we mention already existing co-training and self-training algorithms, and describe the proposed by us voted co-training.

3.1 Co-training

Blum and Mitchel [1] assume that there exists two independent and compatible feature sets or views of data, where each feature set defining a problem is sufficient for learning and classification purposes. A classifier learned on each of those redundant feature subsets can be used to label data for the other and thus expand each other's training set. However in a real-world application, finding independent and redundant feature splits can be unrealistic and this can lead to deterioration in performance [6].

From another side Goldman and Zhou [4], proposed a co-training strategy that doesn't assume feature independence and redundancy. They learn two different classifiers from a data set. The idea behind this strategy is that the two algorithms use different representations for their hypotheses and thus they can learn two diverse models that can complement each other by labeling some unlabeled data and enlarge the training set of the other. In order to decide which unlabeled examples a classifier should label, they derive confidence intervals. We adopt this co-training strategy, having two different basic classifiers and a third (external) classifier, that decides which labeled example to be included into the training data, when the initial classifiers disagree.

Collins and Singer [2] introduce the CoBoost algorithm to perform Named Entity classification, which boosts classifiers that use either the spelling of the named entity, or the context in which that entity occurs. Our approach differs from theirs by the co-training algorithm we use, the classification methods we worke with and the feature sets used for the NED and NEC modules.

3.2 Self-training

The definition for self-training could be found in different forms in the literature, however we adopted the definition of Nigam and Ghani [6]. We need only one classifier, without any split of features. For several iterations the classifier labels the unlabeled data and converts the most confidently predicted examples of each class into a labeled training example.

3.3 Voted Co-training Algorithm

After the resume of the existing co-training algorithm, here we introduce our method. Voted co-training starts with a small set of hand-labeled examples and three classifiers that learn the same pool of unlabeled examples. For each iteration the unlabeled data set is turned into labeled and instances with some growing size predefined by the user are added into the training set. In order to guarantee the labeling confidence of the unlabeled examples, for each example

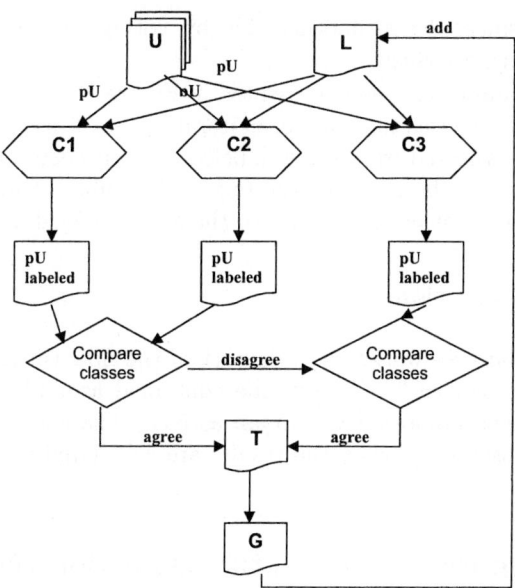

- C_1 and C_2 two different classifiers
- C_3 external different classifier used in voting
- L a set of labeled training examples
- U a set of unlabeled examples
- T a temporal set of instances

Loop for I iterations:

1. do a pool pU of P randomly selected examples e_j from U
2. use L to individually train classifiers C_1, C_2, C_3 and label examples in pU
3. $\forall e_j \in pU$ whose classes agree by C_1 and C_2, do $T = T \cup \{e_j\}$
4. $\forall e_i \in pU$ whose classes disagree by C_1 and C_2, use C_3 and apply voting; select examples whose classes agree between two classifiers and add them to T
5. take randomly G examples from T and add them to L, while maintaining the class distribution in L
6. empty T

Fig. 2. the proposed Voted Co-training Algorithm

a voting strategy has been applied. Two initial classifiers compare the predicted class for each instance. When they agree, this instance is added directly into a temporal set T, when they disagree, the prediction of an external classifier is considered and voting among them is applied. To the already existing temporal set T are added only those instance on which the external classifier agrees with at least one of the initial classifiers.

We incorporate voting, knowing that such technique is used to examine the outputs of several various models and select the most probable category predicted by the classifiers. From another side by voting, the performance of a single classifier is outperformed.

The voted co-training scheme is presented in Figure 2. For further notations in this paper, we refer to I as the number of iterations, to P as the pool size (e.g. number of examples selected from the unlabeled set U needed for annotation at each iteration), to G as the growing size (e.g. the number of most confidently labeled examples added at each iteration to the set of labeled data L).

3.4 Data and Evaluation

The experimental data we worked with is part of the Spanish Efe corpus, used in the competitions of Clef [6]. The test file contained around 21300 tokens of which 2000 have been annotated by human as NEs. The correct classes of the test file have been used only when the results are calculated with the *conlleval* [7] evaluation script.

4 Self-training for Named Entity Detection (NED)

Considering the time-performance disadvantage of self and co-training techniques, and the complexity of each one of the tasks we have to resolve, we decided to use self-training for NEDetection.

The self-training algorithm starts with small set of 20 hand-labeled instances as a training set[8]. At each iteration a pool of P unlabeled examples is made, and one single classifier turns them into labeled ones. Only the most confident examples are added into L, keeping a constant ratio in the training data, for avoiding to introduce imbalance of the class set. The classifier we used has been K-nn algorithm[9], known with its property of taking into consideration every single training example when making the classification decision and significantly useful when training data is insufficient.

4.1 Experiments and Results

The parameter settings are: growing size $G = \{10, 20, 30, 40, 50, 100, 200, 500\}$, pool $P = \{30, 50, 60, 70, 80, 200, 500, 1000\}$, $I = 40$. The constant ratio in the training data is 5:3:2 for **O**, **B** and **I** tags, due to the frequent appearance of tag **O** compared to the other two categories.

The achieved performances with these settings can be found in Table 1. Note that the exposed results are after BIO error analysis, which we discuss in section

---

[6] http://clef.isti.cnr.it/
[7] the script contained the following measures: Precision (of the tags allocated by the system, how many were right), Recall (of the tags the system should have found, how many did it spot) and $F_{\beta=1}$(a combination of recall and precision).
[8] in our case, the first sentences in the unlabeled data.
[9] with one nearest neighbour.

4.2. We indicate with G10[10] the f-score obtained for all **BIO** tags with growing size G equal to 10, for each one of the 40 iterations.

In Table 1, the best performance per setting is denoted in bold. For instance, G10 reached 81.71% with 340 training size. Comparing G10's best performance with 340 training examples to the other settings, it can be seen that performance is not the same[11]. The difference comes from the examples added to L, which for each iteration and experimental setting did not repeat. For the next growing sizes of 20, 30, 40 and 50, the maximum performance is around 80.43%, 76.9%, 79.88% and 78.88%. For $G = 100$ with 1320 training examples 82.54% have been obtained; compared to the best performance of G10 this result is higher, however the number of examples participating in the training set is bigger. For all experimental settings, the best performance of 84.41% has been reached with 1620 examples and growing size 200.

Summarizing, we can say that satisfactory results for NE detection can be reached, using small sized training data. From another side for instance-based learning, it is not necessary to be stored all training instances, rather few examples inside stable regions. It can happen that an instance correctly classified by the self-training algorithm and added to L may not contribute with new information. Thus the performance will not improve. In future, we would like to measure the informativeness of each individual instance and include only those bringing novel information.

4.2 Error Analysis of the Detected Entities

We made analysis of the obtained results and managed to resolve and correct around 16% of the occurred errors. The postprocessing consist of:

BIO substitution, applied when tag **O** is followed by **I**. We simply replace **I** by **B** when the analyzed word starts in capital letter, in the other case we put **O**. As can be seen from the example in Section 2 and regarding the definition given in [7], tag **O** cannot be followed by tag **I**. The first 6 columns in Table 1 demonstrate the performance of each individual tag (e.g. B and I). With BIO substitution, performance is improved with 10%.

Statistical representation, compares $f(w_i)$, the frequency of a word w_i starting in capital letter and tagged as **B**, versus f^*, the frequency of the same word w_i taking its lowercased variant frequency from the test file. *Tambien_B* is detected 63 times as possible entity, but its variant $f^*(tambien) = 265$, shows that the word tends to be written in lowercased letters. In this case tag B is transformed into **O**.

For entities as *La_B Mancha_I*, this substitution will be erroneous. First *La* is part of the entity and is correctly classified, but its lowercase variant *la* is

---

[10] For the other notations, the number next to G indicates the growing size per iteration. The first 5 columns represent the scores before and after postprocessing. With iB, iI and iG10 are denoted the initial results of self-training without BIO error analysis and with cB, cI and G10, the results after BIO error analysis.

[11] the comparison for the same training size with the other settings is denoted in italic in Table 1.

Table 1. *Self-training performance for NED task*

I	iB	cB	iI	cI	iG10	G10	G20	G30	G40	G50	G100	G200	G500
1	64.40	79.78	34.31	47.01	52.94	69.26	73.51	70.23	74.00	66.32	71.80	73.91	*77.76*
2	66.10	81.92	33.63	52.35	53.69	72.43	78.41	70.69	71.83	71.13	73.16	*71.93*	78.47
3	67.69	81.53	34.84	53.88	55.69	72.85	74.29	72.57	78.30	72.73	*73.91*	75.39	76.18
4	72.10	81.52	41.10	53.98	61.20	72.92	73.88	71.59	78.12	73.9	79.39	76.73	80.26
5	72.17	80.86	41.98	54.95	61.52	72.81	70.85	76.62	79.04	76.71	76.64	74.72	81.73
6	72.07	80.79	39.72	54.38	60.39	72.56	66.53	76.10	72.93	*74.93*	78.40	76.00	81.38
7	72.29	81.09	38.25	55.56	60.11	73.09	73.74	74.19	76.39	75.76	77.28	76.67	81.91
8	73.62	81.12	38.14	55.37	61.67	73.04	74.10	73.44	*78.24*	76.65	79.29	77.40	81.42
9	72.65	80.97	38.10	52.36	60.66	71.95	70.42	73.48	76.06	76.01	79.91	77.49	81.23
10	72.56	80.75	37.11	50.92	60.24	71.32	73.75	*73.94*	77.15	76.81	80.27	78.06	81.83
11	74.11	80.95	32.94	50.04	60.15	70.96	75.23	72.82	68.91	76.84	81.99	77.84	81.76
12	76.46	80.14	35.57	50.19	63.54	70.66	74.56	73.20	71.18	76.99	81.82	79.22	81.83
13	76.25	80.20	38.33	56.63	64.81	72.89	75.57	75.16	72.77	77.90	**82.54**	80.60	82.22
14	76.53	80.20	32.96	57.44	61.71	73.18	76.33	75.21	74.96	**78.88**	82.17	80.93	82.40
15	76.75	79.89	36.15	62.61	63.29	74.78	78.24	75.12	75.45	78.29	80.44	81.32	82.94
16	81.85	85.47	39.20	65.68	67.02	79.36	*78.30*	75.24	75.17	78.26	80.43	82.03	82.80
17	82.68	87.06	42.62	66.72	68.43	80.82	78.34	75.17	75.07	78.38	79.63	81.59	83.00
18	83.15	86.79	44.16	67.83	69.43	80.99	78.20	74.94	76.03	77.63	79.75	81.41	83.16
19	84.41	86.79	48.22	67.83	71.53	80.99	77.97	74.87	76.34	76.42	80.80	81.54	83.27
20	84.60	86.55	47.69	66.55	71.49	80.44	77.99	74.56	76.00	76.43	80.73	81.16	83.43
21	83.71	86.64	44.85	66.72	70.10	80.55	**80.43**	73.76	76.06	77.27	80.92	81.23	83.51
22	83.55	86.58	43.37	67.08	69.09	80.62	78.72	74.05	76.22	77.27	80.88	80.87	83.63
23	82.54	85.57	50.73	67.08	71.70	79.97	76.99	74.33	76.72	77.31	80.41	80.90	83.56
24	81.74	84.55	50.85	68.15	71.40	79.67	77.55	74.01	77.49	77.04	79.87	81.83	83.85
25	81.67	84.25	47.30	68.20	69.56	79.46	77.53	74.07	77.48	77.03	80.28	81.49	83.50
26	76.29	78.99	47.76	69.29	66.89	76.31	79.32	75.07	76.80	77.59	79.82	81.06	83.90
27	75.84	78.42	46.43	66.61	66.14	75.13	79.14	76.00	77.36	77.54	80.06	81.09	83.79
28	81.70	85.08	46.76	68.45	69.43	80.17	77.95	76.12	77.99	77.40	79.18	81.49	83.87
29	81.60	85.01	46.95	68.68	69.44	80.18	78.08	76.02	77.93	76.36	78.78	81.37	83.94
30	81.70	85.01	47.30	68.74	69.60	80.20	78.10	76.22	78.24	76.72	78.28	81.74	83.48
31	81.74	85.27	47.46	68.37	69.74	80.25	78.03	76.18	78.22	77.16	78.48	82.22	83.71
32	81.62	86.03	49.14	71.63	70.15	**81.71**	77.69	76.12	78.57	77.16	78.35	82.72	83.59
33	81.23	85.38	46.23	67.43	68.85	80.02	78.24	76.58	78.96	77.97	79.03	83.63	83.81
34	81.35	85.46	46.24	66.84	68.94	79.87	78.32	76.18	78.99	77.58	79.36	83.81	**84.39**
35	76.25	79.96	47.67	68.26	66.83	76.70	78.45	76.25	78.79	77.72	79.55	83.80	84.11
36	76.32	80.01	47.55	67.60	66.80	76.53	78.38	75.20	78.85	77.64	79.81	83.96	83.87
37	76.31	80.01	47.36	68.01	66.68	76.65	79.39	76.57	79.32	77.62	80.13	83.68	84.03
38	76.35	80.03	46.59	65.92	66.44	76.02	79.13	76.76	79.61	77.36	80.05	84.05	83.81
39	76.01	79.82	45.66	64.90	65.84	75.56	79.32	**76.90**	79.80	77.93	79.65	84.25	83.93
40	76.74	79.80	45.75	64.79	66.55	75.51	77.75	**76.90**	79.88	77.96	79.75	**84.41**	84.02

a determiner for female gender in Spanish language and has higher frequency than *La*. To avoid such substitutions, pairwise frequency of bigrams is considered. When the frequency of *La Mancha* is higher than the frequency of *la Mancha*, tag **B** for *La* is kept, otherwise is changed into *La_O Mancha_B*.

This transformation improved the f-score with 6%, for the experimental settings of P=500, G=200 at iteration 40. The final f-score for BIO classification achieved 90.37%, tag **B** was detected with 93.97% f-score and tag **I** reached 81.94%.

5 Co-training for Named Entity Classification (NEC)

The instances detected by the self-training algorithm are classified with the voted co-training method, as described in Figure 2. The learning process started with 10 hand-labeled examples in the following ratio 3:3:3:1, for ORG, PER, LOC and MISC classes. The instances representing MISC class tend to have rare appearance in text and the probability of encountering such instance is lower. As main classifiers have been used decision trees and k-nn, all implemented in TiMBL's package[3]. The HMM toolkit [8] has been developed for post tagging purposes, but we adopted it for NER purposes.

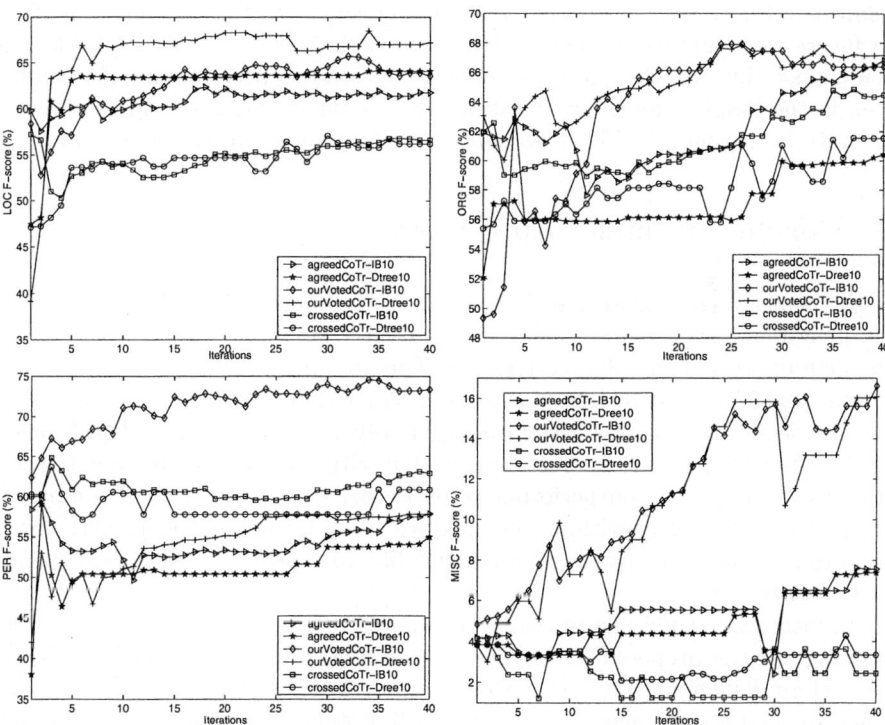

Fig. 3. From top to bottom and from left to right are represented the performances of three different co-training algorithms using k-nn and decision tree, for classifying the entities into location, organization, person and miscellaneous classes. The growing size used has been 10 for each of the 40 iterations.

5.1 Comparative Study and Discussion of the Obtained Results

A brief comparative study with other co-training algorithms has been made. The obtained results for each category are represented in separate graphics in Figure 3. By $crossedCoTr$ is denoted the co-training algorithm where two classifiers simply exchange the instances they learn, feeding each other's input. $ourVotedCoTr$ represents the proposed by us algorithm. The performance of a co-training where only the instances on which two classifiers agree and have been added into the training set L is denoted as $agreedCoTr$.

In the graphics can be seen how for each one of the four classes, our voted co-training outperforms the other two algorithms. For location class $agreedCoTr - IB10$ and $ourVotedCoTr - IB10$ start with similar efficiency, however after the 7th iteration, the curve of the voted co-training starts improving. For the same class $ourVotedCoTr - Dtree$ keeps 5% higher score than $agreedCoTr - Dtree$.

In general K-nn and decision tree dealt well with LOC and ORG classes reaching 68-70% performance. The contribution of the external classifier has been for PER and MISC classes. Compared to the other two methods, MISC class gained 8-9% better performance with $ourVotedCoTr$. This was due to the additional information provided with the agreement of the external classifier. In future we would like to work with more discriminative feature set for MISC class, since this was the class that impeded classifier's performance. As can be seen in the graphic, for many iterations two classifiers could not agree with an instance belonging to MISC class and the performance kept the same score.

6 Conclusions and Future Work

In this paper we demonstrated the building of a complete Named Entity Recognition system, using small set of labeled and large amount of unlabeled data, by the help of self-training and co-training. The obtained results are encouraging, reaching 90.37% for detection phase and 65% for classification[12].

The detection task was easily managed only with self-training. The Named Entity Classification task is more difficult, but with the proposed by us voted co-training algorithm, an outperformance of 5% per class was obtained compared to other co-training algorithms. The features used for miscellaneous class have not been so discriminative, and we would like to repeat the same experiment with a better set.

In future we would like to make a comparative study of self-training, active learning and the proposed by us voted co-training, while dealing with the NEC task. More challenging will be to investigate how voted co-training behaves compared to a supervised machine learning NER system. Finally for evaluating the effectiveness of the proposed method, it will be applied to other natural language processing task such as word sense disambiguation.

---

[12] considering the performance of person, location, organization and miscellaneous classes altogether.

Acknowledgements

This research has been partially funded by the Spanish Government under project CICyT number TIC2003-0664-C02-02 and PROFIT number FIT-340100-2004-14 and by the Valencia Government under project numbers GV04B-276 and GV04B-268.

References

1. A. Blum and T. Mitchell. Combining labeled and unlabeled data with co-training. In *COLT: Proceedings of the Workshop on Computational Learning Theory*, pages 92–100, 1998.
2. M. Collins and Y. Singer. Unsupervised models for named entity classification. In *Proceedings of the Joint SIGAT Conference on EMNLP and VLC*, pages 100–11, 1999.
3. W. Daelemans, J. Zavrel, K. Sloot, and A. van den Bosch. TiMBL: Tilburg Memory-Based Learner. Technical Report ILK 04-02, Tilburg University, 2004.
4. S. Goldman and Y. Zhou. Enhancing supervised learning with unlabeled data. In *Proceedings of the Seventeenth International Conference on Machine Learning*, pages 327–334, 2000.
5. Z. Kozareva, O. Ferrandez, A. Montoyo, R. Muñoz, and A. Suárez. Combining data-driven systems for improving named entity recognition. In *Proceedings of Tenth International Conference on Applications of Natural Language to Information Systems*, pages 80–90, 2005.
6. K. Nigam and R. Ghani. Analyzing the effectiveness and applicability of co-training. In *Proceedings of Ninth International Conference on Information and Knowledge Management*, pages 86–93, 2000.
7. T. K. Sang. Introduction to the conll-2002 shared task: Language independent named entity recognition. In *Proceedings of CoNLL-2002*, pages 155–158, 2002.
8. I. Schroder. A case study in part-of-speech tagging using the icopost toolkit. Technical Report FBI-HH-M-314/02, Department of Computer Science, University of Hamburg, 2002.

Towards the Automatic Learning of Idiomatic Prepositional Phrases*

Sofía N. Galicia-Haro[1] and Alexander Gelbukh[2]

[1] Faculty of Sciences UNAM Universitary City, Mexico City, Mexico
sngh@fciencias.unam.mx
[2] Center for Computing Research, National Polytechnic Institute, Mexico
gelbukh@cic.ipn.mx, www.Gelbukh.com

Abstract. The objective of this work is to automatically determine, in an unsupervised manner, Spanish prepositional phrases of the type preposition - nominal phrase - preposition (P–NP–P) that behave in a sentence as a lexical unit and their semantic and syntactic properties cannot be deduced from the corresponding properties of each simple form, e.g., *por medio de* (by means of), *a fin de* (in order to), *con respecto a* (with respect to). We show that idiomatic P–NP–P combinations have some statistical properties distinct from those of usual idiomatic collocations. We also explore a way to differentiate P–NP–P combinations that could perform either as a regular prepositional phrase or as idiomatic prepositional phrase.

1 Introduction

Any computational system for natural language processing must cope with the ambiguity problem. One of the most frequent ambiguities in syntax analysis is the prepositional phrase attachment. A preposition can be linked to a noun, an adjective, or a preceding verb. There are certain word combinations of the type preposition - nominal group - preposition (P–NP–P) that can be syntactically or semantically idiosyncratic in nature or both, that we called IEXP. The automatic determination of such IEXP groups should reduce the prepositional phrase attachment problem by defining three or more simple forms (since the nominal group can contain more of a simple form) as one lexical unit.

Spanish has a great number of prepositional phrases of the type P–NP–P more or less fixed. Among them: *a fin de* (in order to), *al lado de* (next to), *en la casa de* (in the house of), etc. The IEXP (*a fin de*, *al lado de*), can be analyzed assuming that these expressions behave as a syntactic unit and therefore could be included directly in a computational dictionary. Specifically, such combinations are frequently equivalent to prepositions, i.e., they can be considered as one multiword preposition: e.g., *in order to* is equivalent to *for* (or *to*) and has no relation with *order*; other examples: *in front of* (before), *by means of* (by), etc. Such dictionary can be useful in prepositional phrase attachment: given a compound preposition *in_order_to* is present in the

---

* Work partially supported by Mexican Government (CONACyT, SNI, CGPI-IPN, PIFI-IPN).

dictionary, the *to* in *John bought flowers in order to please Mary* would not be attached to *bought*.

For example, the phrase *El Tratado estableció la devolución del canal por parte de Estados Unidos* (The Treaty established the return of the canal by the United States) has the following structure according to Dependency Grammars [11]:

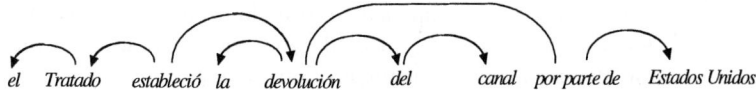

el   Tratado   estableció   la   devolución   del   canal   por parte de   Estados Unidos

In opposition, regular P–NP–P are analyzed considering the initial combination P–NP like a unit, and the second preposition as a one introducing a complement, not always linked to the preceding NP. For example, the phrase *El Senado autorizó la adopción de niños por padres del mismo sexo* (The Senate authorized the adoption of children by same sex parents) that is very similar to the previous example in the POS of most words has the following structure:

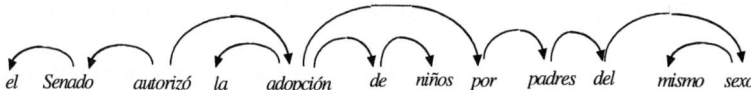

el   Senado   autorizó   la   adopción   de   niños   por   padres   del   mismo   sexo

We could observe that there are more links in a structure with regular prepositional phrases. Therefore it is necessary to distinguish which of the Spanish P–NP–P should be analyzed as a IEXP and which should be analyzed as a P–NP–P. But there is no a complete compilation of the IEXP groups. Nañez [12] compiled the most wide list but he himself considers that a prepositive relation study is something incomplete "susceptible of continuous increase". In addition, the main Spanish dictionaries [4], [14] do not contain the information necessary for a computational dictionary of this type.

The IEXP groups are used frequently in everyday language, therefore natural language applications need to be able to identify and treat them properly. Apart from syntactic analysis the range of applications where it is necessary to consider their specific non compositional semantic is wide: machine translation, question-answering, summarization, generation. But IEXP could present different uses and their meaning agree with context.

In this work, we mainly investigated corpus-based methods to obtain the prepositional phrases of the type IEXP (idiomatic expressions), and the form to differentiate their use as fixed forms from the literal ones, for example:

1. Idiomatic expression: *a fin de obtener un ascenso* (to obtain a promotion, literally: 'at end of'),
2. Free combination: *a fin de año obtendrá un ascenso* (at the end of the year she will be promoted),
3. Part of a larger idiom: *a fin de cuentas* (finally, literally: 'at end of accounts').

More precisely our aims are:

- To analyze the linguistic characteristics that differentiate IEXP groups from the regular prepositional phrases

- To find by statistical measures the IEXP groups that should be included in a computational dictionary for syntactic analysis
- To identify the different uses of the IEXP groups as idiomatic expression, free combination (literal), and part of a larger idiom.

In section 2 we present the linguistic analysis, then we present the characteristics of the corpus and some frequencies obtained from it. In section 4, we present the obtained results applying the statistical methods and our exploration to differentiate regular from idiomatic use for the same prepositional phrase.

2 Linguistic Analysis

It is important to emphasize some linguistics properties that place IEXP in a different group from the regular prepositional phrases. In Spanish grammar these groups are denominated adverbial locutions [15] or prepositional locutions [12] according to their function. As it is indicated in [15], locutions could be recognized by its rigid form that does not accept modifications and the noun that shows a special meaning, or by its global meaning, that is not the sum of the meanings of its components. For word combinations lexically determined that constitute particular syntactic structures, as it is indicated in [10], their properties are: restricted modification, non composition of individual senses and the fact that nouns are not substitutable.

1. Some features of prepositions and nouns in IEXP's

Some IEXP groups are introduced by the preposition "so". This preposition is considered old fashioned by [15]. It has a restricted use or appears in fixed forms. We found 389 cases from the corpus: *so capa de* (1 case), *so pena de* (203 cases), *so pretexto de* (177), *so riesgo de* (5), *so peligro de* (1) and one case for P-NP.

Other IEXP groups contain nouns that are rarely used outside the context of fixed expressions. Examples obtained from corpus are: *a fuer de* (in regard to, 44 cases), *a guisa de* (like, 54 cases) and *a la vera de* (to the side of, 187 cases).

2. Restricted modification

Many of the nouns found in IEXP groups cannot be modified by an adjective. For example: *por temor a* (literally: by fear of) vs. *por gran temor a* (avoiding *vs.* by great fear of), *a tiempo de* vs. *a poco tiempo de* (at the opportune moment *vs.* a short time after), etc. In some cases, the modification forces to take a literal sense of the prepositional phrase, for example in the following sentences:

- ... *por el gran temor a su estruendosa magia* (by the great fear to its uproarious magic) , *por el gran temor* has a literal meaning related to fear.
- ... *denegó hoy la libertad bajo fianza por temor a una posible fuga.* (today denied the freedom on bail to avoid a possible flight), *por temor a* has a meaning related to avoid

3. Non substitutable nouns

The noun inside the IEXP cannot be replaced by a synonym. For example in the phrase: *se tomará la decisión de si está a tiempo de comenzar la rehabilitación* (the decision will be taken on if it is the right time to begin the rehabilitation), where *a tiempo de* cannot be replaced by *a período de* (on period of), *a época de* (time of).

4. Variations in the nominal group

The nominal groups of certain IEXPs present variations due to inflection of the noun. For example, *a mano(s) de* :

- ... *tras la traición que han sufrido a mano de sus antiguos protectores argelinos.* (... after the treason that, apparently, has undergone by cause and action of their old Algerian protectors)
- ... *habitantes enardecidos por el asesinato de un profesor a manos de un policía*... (... inhabitants inflamed by the murder of a professor by cause and action of a policeman ...)

5. Different uses, meaning agree with context

Some IEXP groups initiate fixed phrases or can be literal phrases according to the context, in addition to their use as idiomatic expressions. Examples:
"*al pie de*" It appears as idiomatic expression in:

- *La multitud que esperó paciente al pie de la ladera de la sede de la administración del canal, corrió hacia arriba* ... (The patient multitude that waited at the base of the slope of the seat of the channel administration, run upwards ....)

"*al pie de*" It initiates a larger idiom: *al pie de la letra* (exactly) in:

- *Nuestro sistema de procuración de justicia se ha transformado y en vez de observar al pie de la letra las leyes* ... (Our system of justice care has been transformed and instead of observing the laws exactly ...)

"*al pie de*" It initiates a free combination in:

- *El anillo estaba junto al pie de María* (The ring was next to the foot of Maria)

3 Characteristics of the Corpus

For our analysis, we selected four Mexican newspapers that are daily published in the WEB with a considerable part of their complete publication. The texts correspond to diverse sections: economy, politics, culture, sport, etc. from 1998 to 2002. The text collection has approximately 60 million words [7].

Initially, to analyze the word groups of the type P–NP–P we used a POS tool to assign morphological annotation. We developed a program to extract the P–NP–P patterns where prepositions correspond to a very wide list of simple prepositions that was obtained from [12] which includes prepositions with liberality.

We extracted all word strings corresponding to P–NP–P using the following grammar:

```
PP      → P NP P
NP      → N | D N | V-Inf | D V-Inf
```

where P stands for preposition, N for noun, D for determinant, and V-inf for infinitive verb (in Spanish, infinitives can be modified by a determinant: *el fumar está prohibido*, literally: 'the to-smoke is prohibited').

In the complete text collection, we found 2,590,753 strings of the type P–NP–P, with 372,074 different types. The different groups with frequency greater than two were 103,009. In these strings, the above described cases for syntactic analysis were recognized: compound words of type IEXP, and the combination P–NP followed by a preposition that introduces a second prepositional phrase.

Since many IEXP are traditionally considered as complex prepositions and functional words have high frequency we obtained the frequencies of P–NP–P groups recognized with the grammar as a first approximation to determine them. Table 1 shows the frequencies of the 20 more frequent groups, where we could observe that 17 groups are IEXP type and only three phrases: *en la ciudad de* (literally: in the city of), *del gobierno de* (literally: of the government of), *del estado de* (literally: of the state of), do not correspond to IEXP type. The groups *en la ciudad de*, *del estado de* have a high score since there are two Mexican names that include the nouns 'city' (ciudad) and 'state' (estado) to differentiate them from the country: *ciudad de Mexico* (Mexico City) and *estado de México* (Mexico State). The group *del gobierno de* has a high score since 'government' has immediately an attribute related to persons and countries linked with preposition 'of'. Most of the 17 IEXPs are equivalent to a single preposition.

The sequences of words that compose the nominal groups are distributed of the following way in the text collection: NP constituted by a noun: 44,.646; NP constituted by several words: 58,363. It is observed that more than 50% contain determinants.

Table 1. Frequencies of P–NP–P patterns

Frequency	P GN P	Frequency	P GN P
11612	a pesar de	5403	en favor de
11305	a partir de	4998	a partir del
10586	de acuerdo con	4899	en el sentido de
10418	en contra de	4882	con el fin de
7982	por parte de	4779	a lo largo de
7240	en la ciudad de	4510	en caso de
6819	a fin de	4469	del gobierno de
6512	en materia de	4186	en cuanto a
5904	en el caso de	4124	del estado de
5758	por lo menos	4114	por medio de

4 Statistical Procedure

From the linguistic analysis we noted that IEXP could be classified as collocations. The extracting criteria is based on such assumption applying general methods for collocation extraction in addition to frequency. Diverse statistical measures have been used to identify lexical associations between words from corpus [2], [5], [6], [16]. The measures that we used to determine the lexical association of words are:

- Frequency (Freq),
- Point-wise mutual information (PMI),
- Log-likelihood (LL),
- Pearson measure (χ^2, or Chi-2).

We obtained these four measures for the complete collection of texts using the statistical program NSP, developed by [1]. Because of the total size of the collection we first split it in sixty parts and we applied the NSP ngram module to each part. Then we combined the results and we extracted automatically all P–NP–P groups determined by the grammar. Finally we applied each of the above four statistical measures by the corresponding NSP module and we obtained the ranked measures for them.

In order to prove the methods of idiomatic expression identification, we eliminated the P–NP–P groups that appeared less than three times, because when applying statistical methods to sparse data poor results are obtained. Since in the text collection the prepositional groups are not annotated as composed words, we compared the results against the most wide list of prepositional locutions available (LPL), that of [12].

In Figure 1 we present the learning curves automatically obtained, the horizontal axis correspond to the number of the top P–NP–P ranked by each method and the vertical axis correspond to the number of IEXP detected. In the first step we considered the top one hundred prepositional phrases ranked by the statistical measure and automatically were searched the groups considered in LPL, then we considered the top ten thousand to apply the same detection, then we considered the top twenty thousand prepositional phrases and so on augmenting ten thousand P–NP–Ps each time.

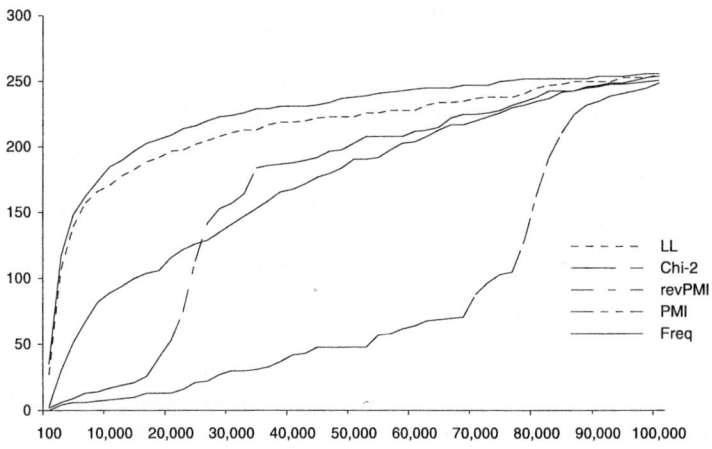

Fig. 1. Statistical measures for the P-NP-P with a minimum occurrence of 3

We considered 252 cases of LPL that correspond to specific IEXP groups, since the author considers very general cases as "a ... en" (literally: to ... in), "a ... por" (literally: to ... by), etc. An extract of LPL is the following group:

197. con ganas de	204. con motivo de
198. con idea de	205. con objeto de
199. con independencia de	206. con occasion de
200. con intención de	207. con omission de
201. con la mira en	208. con... para...
202. con miras a	209. con peligro de
203. con motivo a	210. con... por...

Since there is no generally accepted definition of the latter three measures for three elements, we applied pair-wise measures to [P–NP] and [P] of the whole combination P–NP–P: e.g., the PMI assigned to *a fin de* was the PMI of the two strings (1) *a fin* and (2) *de*. Evaluation of other possible ways of calculating the dependency between the three elements was left for our future work.

4.1 Discussion

The best measure proved to be simple frequency, and log-likelihood shows nearly the same performance. On the first 100 items the precision obtained with frequency measure was 50% (which is 20% recall on LPL).

However, manual inspection of the results revealed among the top elements new IEXP, such as *a las afueras de* (literally: 'to the outskirts of'), *bajo los auspicios de* (literally: 'under the auspices of'), *en el marco de* (literally: 'in the frame of'), *con el objetivo de* (literally: 'with the objective of'), *a efecto de* (literally: 'to effect of'), *por concepto de* (literally: 'by concept of'), etc. and variants of existing ones in LPL such as: *por la vía de* (literally: 'by the way of'), *en las manos de* (literally: 'in the hands of'). Thus, real precision of our method is better than that measured by comparison with LPL, and the method allows detection of new combinations.

PMI gives very poor results, which is in accordance with the general opinion that PMI is not a good measure of dependency (though it is a good measure of independency) [10]. What is more, PMI seems to have inverse effect: it tends to group the idiomatic examples nearer the end of the list. With this, ordering the list in *reverse* order by PMI (revPMI in Figure 1) gives better results. However, such order is much worse than Freq and LL orders: it groups most of the combinations in question around the positions from 25,000 to 35,000 in the list of 100,000. Pearson measure also shows much worse performance than LL. For a detailed comparison of the log-likelihood and chi-squared statistics, see [13].

A possible explanation for the fact that simple frequency performs in our case better than statistical dependency measures is as follows. A usual collocation is often a new term formed out of existing words, so it is more specific, and of more restricted use, than each of the two words separately. However, in our case the idiomatic (IEXP) combinations are equivalent to functional words—prepositions—which are of much more frequent use than the corresponding NP used in its literal meaning. Also, it is suggested in [9] that frequent word chains of some specific POSs (such as P–NP–N) tend to be terminological; our study can be considered as a particular case of this method.

This P–NP–P construction seems to be common across various languages, mainly among Romance languages. The work of [16] is dedicated to Dutch where less quantity of P–NP–P (34% compared with Spanish) and uses were analyzed; so the same method could be used for other languages.

The obtained results could be used to create the input databases employed by tokenizer processors such as that of [8] where authors view IEXP identification as a tokenization ambiguity problem.

4.2 Differentiating Idiomatic Expressions

We consider heuristic or filters as a form to differentiate the idiomatic expressions from the free combinations and the fixed ones. We considered to identify the grammar categories of the IEXP neighbors, based on sequences of 5 and 6 contiguous words, obtained of the total text collection with the purpose of measuring the results for the variants use.

For the group "a fin de" we obtained in an automatic form the following groups:

1. a fin de V_inf	70.3%
2. a fin de Conj (que)	21.92%
3. a fin de S	
(cuenta, cuentas,	2.8%
año,	1.6%
abril, mayo, julio, agosto, noviembre	0.066%
mes,	0.69%
milenio,	0.1%
semana	0.044%
sexenio,	0.055%
siglo)	0.38%
4. a fin de Adv (no)	1.66%

Where: **Conj** means conjunction and **Adv** means adverb. Variants 1 and 4 can be grouped since the fourth is the denied version of the first variant. In the line of "año" (year) the corresponding Spanish noun phrases to the following noun phrases are considered: year, the year, this year, the present year. In the line of "siglo" (century) the noun phrases correspond to: century, the century, this century. In "sexenio" and "milenio" the noun phrases considered are: sexenio, the sexenio, millennium, the millennium. In the line of "mes" (month) the nouns are: month, this month.

Additionally three groups exist: 1) punctuation mark (0.32%) although immediately an infinitive verb appears, 2) number (0.022%) referred to a year: 1997, 3) adverb (0.011%) followed by an infinitive verb and 4) anomalous constructions (0.033%).

As it is reported in [3] idiomatic expressions combine with a more restricted number of neighboring words than free combinations. They computed three indices on the basis of three-fold hypothesis: a) idiomatic expressions should have few neighbors, b) idiomatic expressions should demonstrate low semantic proximity between the words composing them, and c) idiomatic expressions should demonstrate low semantic proximity between the expression and the preceding and subsequent segments

Considering the first hypothesis we observed the opposite effect: *a fin de* as IEXP combines with almost any infinitive verb, whereas *a fin de* as free combination combines with few neighbors: nominal groups with semantic mark of time (year, month). The explanation could be the one suggested in the previous section. Also *a fin de* combines with few neighbors to form the fixed phrases: *a fin de cuenta y a fin de cuentas* (literally: at end of account-s).

Considering the third hypothesis: the semantic proximity between the expression and its neighbors will be high if the expression has a literal meaning, and low if it is figurative. For the example, we found in group 3 the literal variants in the context of nouns with semantic mark of time since they are semantically near to *fin* (end). We considered a simple semantic proximity to the IEXP noun, using EurowordNet[1] and looking for similar terms (synonymous) in their glosses. The forms *a fin de cuenta* and *a fin de cuenta*s were analyzed in the same form satisfying the third hypothesis.

For *fin* (end) and *año* (year) the following nouns were found: "time" (*tiempo*), "period" (*periodo*), then they form an expression with literal meaning.

Data for *fin*

09169786n 11 conclusión_8 [99%] terminio_1 [99%] terminación_4 [99%] final_10 [99%] fin_4 [99%] finalización_6 [99%]	Tiempo en el que se acaba una cosa: "el final del año académico"; "la finalización del periodo de garantía"

Data for *año*

09125664n 4 año_1 [99%]	Tiempo que tarda un planeta en completar su vuelta alrededor del sol
09127492n 10 año_2 [99%]	Periodo de tiempo que comprende 365 días

But we did not find similar terms in the glosses for *cuenta* (account) and *fin* (end), then they form an expression with figurative meaning.

Data for *cuenta*

00380975n 7 numeración_1 [99%] enumeración_1 [99%] cómputo_1 [99%] cuenta_1 [99%] conteo_1 [99%]	Acción de contar
02130199n 1 cuenta_2 [99%]	Pequeña bola atravesada por un agujero
04270113n 0 cuenta_3 [99%] nota_4 [99%]	Factura o recibo en un restaurante
08749769n 0 cuenta_4 [99%]	Dinero que se debe
08318627n 3 cuenta_5 [99%] cómputo_4 [99%] recuento_2 [99%]	El número total contado: "recuento globular"

Future work will comprise acquiring the context of all IEXP groups and we will carry out the above process. In addition, we will try to distinguish the diverse IEXP from the P–NP–P with high frequency using the same method.

5 Conclusions

Idiomatic word combinations of IEXP type, usually functioning as compound prepositions, have statistical properties distinct from those of usual idiomatic collocations. In particular, they combine with a greater number of words than usual idioms. For

---

[1] http://nipadio.lsi.upc.edu/cgi-bin/wei4/public/wei.consult.perl

their unsupervised determination from a corpus, a simple frequency measure performs better than other statistical dependence measures. In particular, among most frequent P-NP-P word chains, about 50% are idiomatic. Inspection of the most frequent chains of this type permits to detect idiomatic combinations not present in existing dictionaries. We presented an approach to differentiate them from fixed phrases and free combinations by means of semantic proximity.

References

1. Banerjee, S. & Pedersen, T.: The Design, Implementation, and Use of the Ngram Statistic Package. Proceedings of the Fourth International Conference on Intelligent Text Processing and Computational Linguistics, México (2003)
2. Church, K.W. and P. Hanks.: Word association norms, mutual information, and lexicography. In Proceedings of the 27th Annual Meeting of the Association for Computational Linguistics (1989) 76-83
3. Degand, Liesbeth & Bestgen, Yves.: Towards automatic retrieval of idioms in French newspaper corpora. Literary and Linguistic Computing (2003) 18 (3), 249-259
4. Diccionario de María Moliner.: Diccionario de Uso del Español. Primera edición versión electrónica (CD-ROM) Editorial Gredos, S. A. (1996)
5. Dunning, Ted.: Accurate methods for the statistics of surprise and coincidence" Computational Linguistics. (1993) 19(1):61-74
6. Evert, Stefan & Brigitte Krenn.: Methods for the Qualitative Evaluation of Lexical Association In Proceedings of the 39th Annual Meeting of the Association for Computational Linguistics. Toulouse, France. (2001) pp. 188-195
7. Galicia-Haro, S. N.: Using Electronic Texts for an Annotated Corpus Building. In: 4th Mexican International Conference on Computer Science, ENC-2003, Mexico, pp. 26–33.
8. Graña Gil, J., Barcala Rodríguez, F.M., Vilares Ferro, J.: Formal Methods of Tokenization for Part-of-Speech Tagging. Proceedings of the Third International Conference on Computational Linguistics and Intelligent Text Processing (CICLing-2002) Lecture Notes in Computer Science vol. 2276 Springer-Verlag (2002) pp. 240-249
9. Justeson, J. S., S. M. Katz. Technical Terminology: Some Linguistic properties and an algorithm for identification in text. Natural Language Engineering (1995) 1:9–27
10. Manning, C. D. & Schutze, H.: Foundations of Statistical Natural Language Processing. The MIT Press, Cambridge, Massachusetts. (1999)
11. Mel'cuk, Igor.: Dependency Syntax: Theory and Practice, New York: State University of New York Press. (1988)
12. Nañez Fernández, Emilio.: Diccionario de construcciones sintácticas del español. Preposiciones. Madrid, España, Editorial de la Universidad Autónoma de Madrid. (1995)
13. Rayson, P., Berridge, D., Francis, B. Extending the Cochran rule for the comparison of word frequencies between corpora. In Vol. II of Purnelle G. et al. (eds.) Le poids des mots: Proc. of 7th International Conf. on Statistical analysis of textual data (JADT 2004), Presses universitaires de Louvain (2004) pp. 926–936.
14. Real Academia Española.: Diccionario de la Real Academia Española, 21 edición (CD-ROM), Espasa, Calpe (1995)
15. Seco, Manuel.: Gramática esencial del español, introducción al estudio de la lengua, Segunda edición revisada y aumentada, Madrid, Espasa Calpe. (1989)
16. Villada, Begoña & Bouma, Gosse. A corpus-based approach to the acquisition of collocational prepositional phrases. Proceedings of EURALEX 2002, Copenhagen. Denmark (2002) pp. 153–158

Measurements of Lexico-Syntactic Cohesion by Means of Internet*

Igor A. Bolshakov[1] and Elena I. Bolshakova[2]

[1] Center for Computing Research (CIC),
National Polytechnic Institute (IPN), Mexico City, Mexico
igor@cic.ipn.mx
[2] Moscow State Lomonosov University,
Faculty of Computational Mathematics and Cybernetics, Moscow, Russia
bolsh@cs.msu.su

Abstract. Syntactic links between content words in meaningful texts are intuitively conceived 'normal,' thus ensuring text cohesion. Nevertheless we are not aware on a broadly accepted Internet-based measure of cohesion between words syntactically linked in terms of Dependency Grammars. We propose to measure lexico-syntactic cohesion between content words by means of Internet with a specially introduced Stable Connection Index (*SCI*). *SCI* is similar to Mutual Information known in statistics, but does not require iterative evaluation of total amount of Web-pages under search engine's control and is insensitive to both fluctuations and slow growth of raw Web statistics. Based on Russian, Spanish, and English materials, *SCI* presented concentrated distributions for various types of word combinations; hence lexico-syntactic cohesion acquires a simple numeric measure. It is shown that *SCI* evaluations can be successfully used for semantic error detection and correction, as well as for information retrieval.

1 Introduction

Syntactic links between content words in meaningful texts are intuitively conceived 'normal,' thus ensuring text cohesion. Nevertheless we are not aware on such numerical measure for cohesion between words syntactically linked in terms of Dependency Grammars [11] that is broadly accepted and convenient for evaluations through Internet.

In fact, the task of measurement of cohesion between words arose many years ago, in relation with information retrieval (e.g., [7, 14]) and, in the recent decades, to collocation extraction and acquisition (e.g., [10, 13]). The well-known purely statistic measure reckoning on numbers of occurrences of words and their combinations is Mutual Information [10] appropriate for text corpora evaluations.

Rapid development of Internet compels to revise the available methods and criteria oriented to text corpora [9]. In Web search engines, raw statistical data are measured in numbers of relevant pages rather then in word occurrences.

---

* Work done under partial support of Mexican Government (CONACyT, SNI, CGEPI-IPN).

A. Gelbukh, A. de Albornoz, and H. Terashima (Eds.): MICAI 2005, LNAI 3789, pp. 790–799, 2005.
© Springer-Verlag Berlin Heidelberg 2005

In this paper we propose to measure lexico-syntactic cohesion between content words with a specially introduced Stable Connection Index (*SCI*). The form of *SCI* is similar to Mutual Information, but it operates by statistics of relevant Web-pages and thus is convenient for Web measurements. It does not require iterative evaluation of the total amount of pages under search engine's control and is nearly insensitive to both quick fluctuations and slow growth of all raw Web statistics delivered by the engine. Our additional goal is to compare *SCI* with a modified version of Mutual Information introduced below.

Purposes for measuring word cohesion are at least as follows. The first is the need of computational linguistics to extract from texts stable word combinations—collocations and coordinate pairs. Being gathered into special DBs [1, 5, 12], such word combinations can be used in diverse applications. The second purpose is direct use of cohesion measurements for detection and correction of malapropisms, i.e. semantic errors of special type. It is shown that erroneous word combinations always have *SCI* values less than the intended (correct) combinations [3, 4, 6]. The third purpose is selection of sequences of words—composite terms and names—that should be used in information retrieval.

The Yandex search engine (www.yandex.ru) was used for experiments in Russian, and Google, for experiments in Spanish and English.

2 Word Cohesion

Each natural language text is a sequence of *word forms* (*tokens*), i.e. strings of letters from one delimiter to the next (e.g., *links, are, very, short*). Word forms pertaining to the morpho-paradigm with common meaning are associated into *lexemes*. One word form from a paradigm is taken as the lexeme's title for the corresponding dictionary entry, e.g. **pen** is taken for {*pen, pens*}; **go**, for {*go, going, gone, went*}. In languages with rich morphology, paradigms are broader. We divide lexemes into three categories:

- *Content words*: nouns; adjectives; adverbs; verbs except auxiliary and modal ones;
- *Functional words*: prepositions; coordinate conjunctions; auxiliary and modal verbs;
- *Stop words*: pronouns; proper names except of well known geographic or economic objects or personalities reflected in academic dictionaries and encyclopedias; any other parts of speech.

According to Dependency Grammars [11], each sentence can be represented at the syntactic level as a dependency tree with directed links "head → its dependent" between nodes labeled with word forms. Following these links in the same direction of the arcs, from one content node through any linking functional nodes down to another content node, we obtain labeled subtree structure corresponding to a word combination. In a meaningful text, we consider each revealed combination with subordinate dependencies as a collocation. E.g., in the sentence *she hurriedly went through the big forest*, the collocations are **went → through → forest, hurriedly ← went** and **big ← forest**, whereas *she ← went* and *the ← forest* are not collocations, as having stop words at the extreme nodes. The combinations may be also of coordinate type, e.g.

mom → *and* → *dad*. Thus, the syntactic links in such word combinations can be immediate or realized through functional words.

We name the defined above type of word combinability lexico-syntactic cohesion. It implies a syntactic link between components and semantic compatibility of corresponding lexemes. Such combinations are either idiomatic or free. As to their stability, thus far not defined, it is very important issue for any applications: we should primarily work with stable word combinations in computational linguistics and information retrieval.

Combinable components can be linearly separated not only by their own functional word(s) but by many others usually dependent on one of these components. In other words, a close context in a dependency tree is in no way a close linear context. This makes difference with intensively studied bigrams [9]. For example, collocation *leave position* can contain intermediate contexts in principle of any length l:

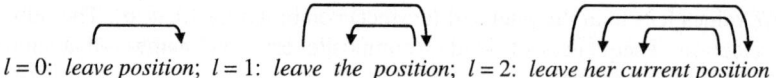

$l = 0$: *leave position*; $l = 1$: *leave the position*; $l = 2$: *leave her current position* ...

Coordinate pairs are word combination of two content words (or content word compounds) linked by a coordinative conjunction. In the most frequent case the components P_1 and P_2 of a stable coordinate pair are linked according to the formula $P_1 \rightarrow C \rightarrow P_2$, where the coordinate conjunction C is *and, or, but*.

The third type of word combinations interesting mainly for information retrieval is composite proper names. Many of them contain two word forms and can be treated as collocations (*President* → *Bush, George* ← *Bush*) or stable coordinate pairs (*Trinidad* → *and* → *Tobago*). However, numerous are names of tree and more words. For humans, the composite names can contain addressing (*Sir, Mr.*, etc.), personal name(s), family name (usually repeating father's family name), patronymic name (derived from the father's personal name—in Russian tradition: *Boris **Nikolayevich** Yeltsyn*), family name of the mother (in Hispanic tradition: *Andrés López **Obrador***). The binary decomposition for such sequences is not clear, but the usage of various shorter versions suggests corresponding dependency subtrees. For example, we take a subtree for the name of the VIP in the shape

President | George Bush.

Since one cannot say *President George,* the uniquely possible binary decomposition of the triple at the highest level is that shown by the vertical bar.

3 Numerical Criteria of Word Cohesion

Let us forget for a while about syntactic links between components of word combinations, considering their occurrences and co-occurrences in a text corpus at some limited distance between them as random events. Then their co-occurrence should be considered steady (or stable), if the relative frequency (= empirical probability) $N(P_1,P_2)/S$ of the co-occurrence of P_1 and P_2 is greater than the product of relative frequencies $N(P_1)/S$ and $N(P_2)/S$ of the components taken apart (S is the corpus size). Using logarithms, we have the criterion of word cohesion known as Mutual Information [10]:

$$MI(P_1, P_2) \equiv \log \frac{S \cdot N(P_1, P_2)}{N(P_1) \cdot N(P_2)}.$$

MI has important feature of scalability: if the sizes of all its 'building blocks' S, $N(P_1)$, $N(P_2)$, and $N(P_1,P_2)$ are multiplied by the same positive factor, *MI* conserves its value.

Other known criteria differing from *MI* but including the same building blocks, e.g., scalable Pearson Correlation Coefficient [6] or non-scalable Association Factor [13], do not seem more reasonable from statistical viewpoint, and we ignore them.

Any Web search engine automatically delivers statistics about a queried word or a word combination measured in numbers of relevant pages, and no information on word occurrences and co-occurrences is available. We can re-conceptualize *MI* with all $N()$ as numbers of relevant pages and S as the page total managed by the engine. However, now $N()/S$ are not the empirical probabilities of relevant events: the words that occur at the same a page are indistinguishable in the raw statistics, being counted only once, while the same page is counted repeatedly for each word included. We only keep a vague hope that the ratios $N()/S$ are monotonically connected with the corresponding empirical probabilities for the corresponding events.

In such a situation we may construe new criteria from the same building blocks. Since evaluation of the page total S is not simple [2], we try to avoid its use in the target criterion but to conserve its scalability. The following criterion of word cohesion named by us Stable Connection Index seems good:

$$SCI(P_1, P_2) \equiv 16 + \log_2 \frac{N(P_1, P_2)}{\sqrt{N(P_1) \cdot N(P_2)}}.$$

The additive constant 16 and the logarithmic base 2 were chosen quite empirically, analyzing a multiplicity of Russian word combinations intuitively considered cohesive. We have only tried to allocate a majority of their SCI values in the interval [0...16]. Hereafter we determine words P_1 and P_2 cohesive by the formula

$$SCI(P_1, P_2) > 0.$$

Depending on a specific search engine, the values $N(P_1)$, $N(P_2)$, and $N(P_1,P_2)$ can be got by only query (the case of Yandex) or by three sequential queries close in time (the case of Google). Anyhow the scalability spares *SCI* of the influence of slow and steady growth of the engine's resources. However, quick fluctuations of measurements from one access to Web to another implied by variations of search trajectories within the engine's resources can be automatically compensated only in the case of obtaining all values through one query (Yandex). Fortunately, the quick fluctuations usually do not exceed ±5% of the measured values, and this gives the insignificant *SCI* variations (±0.1). By the way, it means that while computing *SCI* we should retain only one decimal digit after the point.

Replacing S in the formula of *MI* by page number N_{max} valid for one of the most frequent functional words in a given language, we have constructed the criterion, which is very similar to *MI* and keeps the scalability. We name it Modified Mutual Information and intend it for comparison with *SCI*:

$$MMI(P_1, P_2) \equiv k_1 \log_2 \frac{k_2 \cdot N_{max} \cdot N(P_1, P_2)}{N(P_1) \cdot N(P_2)}$$

The constants k_1 and k_2, and the functional word met in N_{max} pages will be chosen later.

4 Correspondence of Web Statistics to Word Combinations

In all statistical considerations above, we were ignoring the issue whether a co-occurrence of two given words in a counted Web-page corresponds to a directly linked word combination or merely to a random encounter of given components. Now we should compare the number of syntactically linked pairs in the Web snippets delivered for the corresponding query with the total number automatically evaluated by the search engine. The components of a word combination met in a given text fragment are at a certain distance. For a greater generality, we should make the comparison for various distances, with especial confidence to the most probable ones. Such a comparison was made for English [3], Spanish [4], and Russian [6]. Below we shortly outline results for English.

Table 1. Statistics of co-occurrences and collocations

Collocation	Stat. type	Number of intermediate words						
		0	1	2	3	4	5
act of … force	GS	6910	3590	5470	9800	10600	10200
	TP	0.99	0.67	0.14	0.07	0.00	0.00
	CS	6840	2400	765	686	0	0
main … goal	GS	1470000	37500	19700	17200	19900	16700
	TP	0.99	0.96	0.25	0.04	0.01	0.01
	CS	1455300	36000	4920	690	200	167
lift … veil	GS	17300	38400	5970	1880	993	438
	TP	1.00	1.00	0.93	0.88	0.64	0.44
	CS	17300	38400	5550	1650	635	193
moved with … grace	GS	557	4780	3930	1980	801	191
	TP	0.96	1.00	0.96	0.94	0.81	0.37
	CS	534	4780	3770	1860	648	71
give … message	GS	6040	106000	221000	156000	96600	145000
	TP	0.73	0.85	0.73	0.63	0.27	0.03
	CS	4410	90100	161300	98300	26100	4350
bridge across … river	GS	726	37800	52800	6530	1840	753
	TP	0.99	0.96	0.97	0.85	0.55	0.54
	CS	718	36300	51200	5550	1010	407
dump … waste	GS	12800	30500	16800	13100	12900	18400
	TP	0.85	0.81	0.43	0.10	0.15	0.11
	CS	10900	24700	7220	1310	1930	2024

Google statistics of co-occurrences of two words with any *N* intermediate words in between can be gathered by a query in quotation marks containing these words separated with *N* asterisks (* wildcard operators). We took a few of commonly used collocations. The co-occurrence frequencies for each of them were automatically evaluated with N intermediate asterisks, $N = 0...5$. Since we did not dispose a dependency based syntactic analyzer of English, the counting of the syntactically linked combinations among them was done manually and only for the initial portions of deliveries. To evaluate the true portions (TP) of collocations in the automatically counted amounts, we looked through the first hundred co-occurrence snippets with various lengths of intermediate context, mentally analyzing syntax of the fragments. Multiplying the Google statistics GS by TP values, we got approximate collocation statistics (CS), cf. Table 1.

One can see that GS has one or more local maximums in the interval $N = 0...5$, while the first local maximum of CS is disposed at $N = 0$, 1 or 2. In great majority of cases the maximum of CS is unique, coinciding with the first local maximum of GS. So we can believe Google statistics in that the most probable distance between components of collocations corresponds to the first local maximum of GS, and up to this point CS is approximately equal to GS. Both maxima are to be searched in the interval [0...2] of intermediate context lengths (i.e. in the interval [1...3] of distances between components).

In other words, the majority of co-occurrences counted by the Web at the distances not exceeding 3 between components are real collocations, whereas at the greater distances they are mostly random encounters, without direct syntactic links between words. This in no way means that collocation components cannot be more distant from each other (cf. Section 2), but the Web is not suited for evaluation of the numbers of syntactically linked combinations at greater distances.

5 Main Experiment and Comparison of Criteria

Our main experimental set for *SCI* evaluations was a collection of ca. 2200 Russian coordinate pairs [5]. Similar pairs exist in any European language. This can be demonstrated by the following Russian stable coordinate pairs: *damy i gospoda* 'ladies and gentlemen'; *zhaloby i predlozheniya* 'complaints and suggestions'; *geodeziya i kartografiya* 'geodesy and cartography'; *avtobusy i avtomobili* 'buses and cars'; *amerikanskiy i britanskiy* 'American and British'; *analiz i prognoz* 'analysis and forecasting'; *bezopasnost' i obschestvennyy poryadok* 'security and social order'; *biznes i vlast'* 'business and authorities,' *etc*. Many of these pairs are sci-tech, economical or cultural terms and can be used for information retrieval.

SCI values were computed for all these pairs and in 95 percents they proved to be positive, so that the pairs that passed the test are considered stable. The distribution of *SCI* rounded to the nearest integer is given in Fig. 1. It has concentrated bell-like form with the mean value $M_{SCI} = 7.30$ and the standard deviation $D_{SCI} = 3.23$. As many as 69% *SCI* values are in the interval $M_{SCI} \pm D_{SCI}$.

Another criterion computed for the same set was Modified Mutual Information. We have selected functional word *i* 'and' as having the rank 2 among the most frequent Russian words. During the experiment we observe $N_{max} \approx 1.5 \cdot 10^9$, and constants k_1 and k_2 were chosen so that the mean values and the standard deviations for both criteria were nearly the same as for *SCI*: $k_1 = 0.7$ and $k_2 = 360$ gave $M_{MMI} = 7.09$ and $D_{MMI} = 3.32$.

The direct comparison of *SCI* and *MMI* distributions (Fig. 1 and Fig. 2) shows their proximity. Making a difference, the *SCI* distribution has strict cutoff edge 16, while the *MMI* distribution is sloping more gently to the greater values. Nevertheless, the computing of the cosine value between the two vectors of measurements gave the value .96, thus demonstrating nearly complete coincidence of the two criteria.

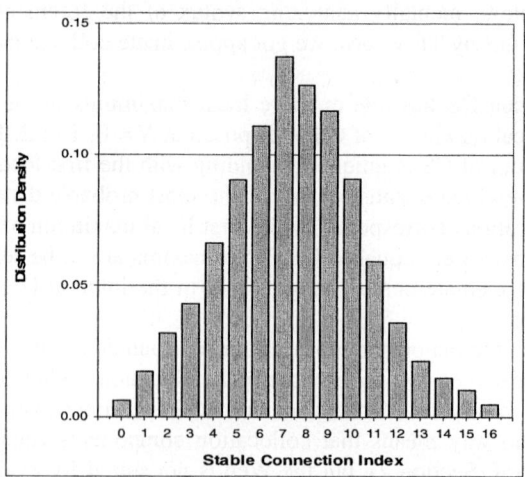

Fig. 1. Distribution for Stable Connection Index

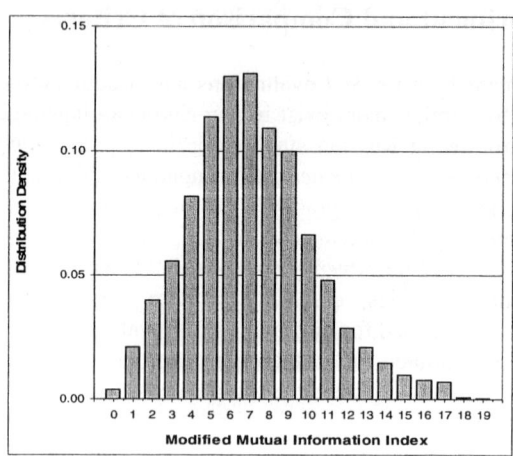

Fig. 2. Distribution for Modified Mutual Information

The comparison of *SCI* and *MMI* ranks for the same subset has shown that some interspersion does occur. E.g., the initial twenty *SCI* ranks differ from corresponding *MMI* ranks by 2 to 40, but the maximal difference constitutes only 1/50 of the whole set size. We can conclude that the compared criteria are equivalent, but *MMI* requires evaluating through the Web four numbers rather than three for *SCI*.

6 Other Experimental Results

The successful application of *SCI* is detection and correction of malapropisms. Malapropism is a type of semantic error that replaces one content word by another legitimate content word similar in sound or letters but semantically incompatible with the context and thus destroying text cohesion, e.g., the correct collocation *travel around the world* transforms to the erroneous *travel around the word*.

Experiments on malapropism detection and correction in English [3], Spanish [4], and Russian [6] have shown that nearly always *SCI* values for malapropos word combinations of various syntactic types proved to be lower then a predetermined threshold and thus can be detected, while *SCI* values for the intended (correct) collocations are always positive. Statistics of *SCI* evaluations for the three languages are rather scarce now (100 to 125 malapropisms and their corrections for each language). They are characterized by the mean values and the standard deviations given in Table 2. Malapropos combinations may give the zero number of pages with co-occurrences (65% for Russian, 57% for Spanish, and 14% for English, the language most noise prone in Internet). Such cases are represented in Table 2 by *SCI* value $-\infty$.

Table 2. SCI evaluations for malapropisms

Language	Intended collocations	Malapropos combinations
Russian	7.54 ± 3.25	$-\infty$ or 0.70 ± 2.58
Spanish	6.48 ± 2.82	$-\infty$ or −1.77 ± 2.37
English	6.14 ± 2.79	$-\infty$ or −1.72 ± 3.22

Table 3. SCI values for VIP names

| VIP | Name version | SCI values | |
		in Spanish	in Russian
Bush	George	Bush	8.3	8.4
	presidente	George Bush	6.5	5.5
	presidente	Bush	7.3	5.7
Chirac	Jacque	Chirac	4.3	8.6
	presidente	Jacque Chirac	1.8	4.6
	presidente	Chirac	5.1	3.6
Putin	Vladimir	Putin	8.5	7.5
	presidente	Vladimir Putin	5.5	6.2
	presidente	Putin	5.1	5.8
Fox	Vicente	Fox	9.1	5.9
	presidente	Vicente Fox	7.9	3.3
	presidente	Fox	4.7	0.4

These data show that *SCI* scale selected initially for Russian well suits for other languages too. All distributions are rather concentrated, and the mean values and standard deviations in various languages differ not so much.

Our recent small experiment on *SCI* evaluation consider name sequences of four present presidents in the world, namely, of USA, France, Russia, and Mexico. Each name sequence was taken in three versions. The results are given in Table 3, where vertical bars denote binary decomposition, and Cyrillic transliteration of the names used for searches in Yandex is omitted.

Table 3 shows that for all name versions *SCI* values for the two languages are comparable and usually rather high. This means that the composite names of VIPs are stable and thus selective for information retrieval, whereas their component *presidente* is so frequent that it cannot provide any selectivity. The most stable version in both languages proved to be <personal name> <family name>. Independently of versions, names of Bush and Putin are nearly equally 'popular' in both languages. Chirac is more 'popular' in Russian, while Fox is more 'popular' in Spanish. All this seems quite natural.

7 Conclusions and Future Work

We have proposed a numerical measure for lexico-syntactic cohesion between content words—Stable Connection Index. It is computed based on the raw statistics automatically delivered by a Web search engine about pages with content words and their pairs. *SCI* proved to be nearly insensitive to both slow growth of search engine's resources and quick fluctuations of raw Web statistics.

It is shown that *SCI* can be used for acquisition of new collocations from the Web, for detection and correction of semantic errors in texts, and for extraction of composite terms and names—for needs of information retrieval.

So far the experiments on *SCI* evaluations were rather limited in size, being measured in few thousands for Russian and in few hundreds for English and Spanish. However they already permit to assert that *SCI* values of collocations and stable coordinate pairs are distributed in a concentrated unimodal manner with the mean values in the interval 6 to 8 (depending on language) and with the standard deviations in the interval 2 to 3.5. The broadening of these experiments should be welcomed for any language and for any application, in order to reveal more precise statistical laws.

In the foreseeable future, we can imagine for each well-spread language a network with the nodes labeled by lexemes, and the oriented arcs labeled with types of possible syntactic links and corresponding *SCI* values. Creation of such structure is very hard task, but some operations can be automated. The network representation of language resources implemented as a special DB can facilitate numerous application of computational linguistics.

References

1. Bolshakov, I.A. Getting One's First Million…Collocations. In: A. Gelbukh (Ed.). *Computational Linguistics and Intelligent Text Processing* (CICLing-2004). Lecture Notes in Computer Science, N 2945, Springer, 2004, p. 229–242.
2. Bolshakov, I.A., S.N. Galicia-Haro. Can We Correctly Estimate the Total Number of Pages in Google for a Specific Language? In: A. Gelbukh (Ed.). *Computational Linguistics and Intelligent Text Processing* (CICLing-2003). Lecture Notes in Computer Science, N 2588, Springer, 2003, p. 415–419.

3. Bolshakov, I.A., S.N. Galicia-Haro. Web-Assisted Detection and Correction of Joint and Disjoint Malapropos Word Combinations. In: A. Montoyo, R. Muñoz, E. Metais (Eds.) *Natural Language Processing and Information Systems* (NLDB'2005). Lecture Notes in Computer Science, N 3513, Springer, 2005, p.126–137.
4. Bolshakov, I.A., S.N. Galicia-Haro, A. Gelbukh. Detection and Correction of Spanish Malapropisms by means of Internet search. In: *Text, Speech and Dialogue* (TSD'2005). Lecture Notes in Artificial Intelligence, N 3658, Springer, 2005, p. 115–122.
5. Bolshakov, I.A., A. Gelbukh, S.N. Galicia-Haro. Stable Coordinated Pairs in Text Processing. In: V. Matoušek, P. Mautner (Eds.) *Text, Speech and Dialogue* (TSD 2003). Lecture Notes in Artificial Intelligence, N 2807, Springer, 2003, p. 27–34.
6. Bolshakova, E.I., I.A. Bolshakov, A.P. Kotlyarov. Experiments in detection and correction of Russian malapropisms by means of the Web. *International Journal on Information Theories & Applications* (forthcoming).
7. Borko, H. The Construction of an Empirically Based Mathematically Derived Classification System. Proceedings of the Western Joint Computer Conference, May 1962.
8. Keller, F., M. Lapata. Using the Web to Obtain Frequencies for Unseen Bigram. *Computational linguistics*, V. 29, No. 3, 2003, p. 459–484.
9. Kilgarriff, A., G. Grefenstette. Introduction to the Special Issue on the Web as Corpus. *Computational linguistics*, V. 29, No. 3, 2003, p. 333–347.
10. Manning, Ch. D., H. Schütze. *Foundations of Statistical Natural Language Processing.* MIT Press, 1999.
11. Mel'čuk, I. *Dependency Syntax: Theory and Practice.* SUNY Press, NY, 1988.
12. *Oxford Collocations Dictionary for Students of English.* Oxford University Press, 2003.
13. Smadja, F. Retreiving Collocations from text: Xtract. *Computational Linguistics.* Vol. 19, No. 1, 1990, p. 143–177.
14. Stiles, H. E. The Association Factor in Information Retrieval. *Journal of the Association for Computing Machinery*, Vol. 8, No. 2, April 1961, pp. 271–279.

Inferring Rules for Finding Syllables in Spanish

René MacKinney-Romero and John Goddard

Departmento de Ingeniería Eléctrica,
Universidad Autónoma Metropolitana,
México D.F. 09950, México
`rene@xanum.uam.mx, jgc@xanum.uam.mx`

Abstract. This paper presents how machine learning can be used to automatically obtain rules to divide words in Spanish into syllables. Machine learning is used in this case not only as a classifier to decide when a rule is used but to generate meaningful rules which then can be used to syllabify new words. Syllabification is an important task in speech recognition and synthesis since every syllable represents the sound in a single effort of articulation. Experiments were carried out using an Inductive Logic Programming (ILP) tool. The experiments were made on different sets of words to ascertain the importance of the number of examples in obtaining useful rules. The results show that it is possible to automatically obtain rules for syllabifying.

Keywords: machine learning, syllabification, ILP, inducing rules.

1 Introduction

A syllable is a unit of speech that is made up of one or more phones. Syllabification consists of separating a word into its individual syllables. Most speakers have no difficulty in performing this separation, even though they are often unaware of the underlying rules that they have applied in order to achieve it.

Phonotactics refers to the valid sequences of sounds which are valid in a language. For instance the sound /ps/ is not valid at the start of a word in english but it is fine in greek. The study of phonotactis is usually done using data that contains information about the inflection of a particular sound in a word. Using such data, some techniques of machine learning have been used to automatically find rules for syllabification for a given language, such as genetic algorithms [1], decision trees [10], neural nets [11] and inductive logic programming [8].

Spanish provides an interesting test bed for this problem given that, unlike other languages, words are made of sequences of syllables with clear boundaries. Also, the set of rules for syllabification is known.

This paper presents ongoing work on automatically creating a syllabifying system (by inducing rules to syllabify) using machine learning on text previously syllabified by a native speaker. This text represents the positive data, the negative data is produced by automatically generating incorrect syllabifications upto a certain length. It must be noted that we use only text with no additional information.

The results are based on a corpus of a well known Spanish text syllabified by a native speaker. The first non-repetitive words of the text were then selected. Additionally the learning task was simplified by selecting only words with no diacritics. An ILP system was then used to induce rules to syllabify. The result is a theory in prolog that, with some additional predicates, is capable of syllabification of words. A differente text was used for testing purposes.

2 Machine Learning

Learning rules from examples is an important field of Machine Learning. The goal is to obtain general rules, which can be represented, for instance, as functions or first order theories. Such rules can then be used to make decisions on unseen instances of the problem.

One particular field of machine learning is adequate to our learning task: inductive logic programming (ILP) [6]. It allow us to deal with the structure of a word and provide, by means of background knowledge, tools to extract and test the elements that compose the word. In the case of ILP all examples and background knowledge are expressed as prolog predicates and clauses. Rules are generated from a given *vocabulary* which contains the predicates or functions which can be used to generate the rules.

The main issue using such a machine learning system that generates rules is the vocabulary given to it. On one hand we want to give the learning system as little information as is needed but on the other hand it is likely that unless we give the "right" information the learning system won't be able to produce anything of interest.

The work by Nerbonne and Konstantopoulos [8] focuses the impact on using different background knowledge, each based on a different approach, to learn valid affixes to a partial syllable. The results indicate that background knowledge is crucial to the learning task. Achieving different results on both accuracy and number of rules depends on the background knowledge used.

Our work focuses on a different question. We wanted to see if it is possible for a learning system to induce rules for syllabification given simple background information, not using any knowledge about known rules, and if such a system could then be used to learn rules for syllabification for other languages using the same information. This work answers the first question, whilst the second remains as future work.

3 Learning Framework

The learning task was carried out trying to investigate if useful rules can be generated using machine learning systems. Therefore, it was conducted using small corpora of only a few hundred words. Three sets of roughly 120, 200 and 300 words were used throughout the experiments.

The learning system *Aleph* was used [9], this learning system implements the PROGOL algorithm [7] and provides canonical ILP support using three files as input: *background knowledge, positive data* and *negative data*.

The background knowledge file contains the definition of predicates that can be used in the generation of hypotheses. It also has information on how a particular predicate can be used, provided in a *mode declaration* such as

:-modeb(1,hasPattern(+syllable,#pattern))?

The declaration states which are the expected inputs(+), outputs(-) and constants(#) with their type. It also indicates, in this case one, how many times the predicate can appear on the body of a clause. The type information is provided as predicates which are true if a term has a certain type.

The main issue, as was mentioned before, is which predicates should be given to the ILP system in order to induce the rules. The obvious ones are predicates that identify vowels, consonants and equalities with letters. Additionally, as a first approach, a set of general predicates were given that extracted letters from words. The problem here was that the rules generated were so complex that the system was unable to learn anything interesting.

A more standard approach was then preferred using the patterns of vowels (v) and consonants (c) in words. We say that a word *has a pattern* if the word starts with the pattern of vowels and consonants given. For example, the word "eco" has the pattern vcv (vowel, consonant, vowel) and the word "audaz" has the pattern vvc. Two predicates were provided: hasPattern(A, B), which is true if word A has pattern B, and usePattern(A, B, C), which is true if C has the letters in pattern B of word A. For instance, the following predicates are true:

hasPattern(eco, vcv).
hasPattern(aludir, vcv).
usePattern(eco,v,e).
usePattern(aludir,v,a).

Patterns can be given to the learning system using the type facility. Patterns of up-to size 5 are provided using this facility. The following predicates state that *vcv* and *v* are valid patterns.

pattern(vcv).
pattern(v).

The syllabification performed by the native speaker produced all syllables for each word. For intance, the word "olvidar" is syllabized as *ol-vi-dar*.

The positive data file contains all positive examples of correct syllabifying. These are provided as a predicate syll(A, B) where A is the word and B the first syllable obtained from the word. The following are some such examples:

syll(eco,e).
syll(audaz,au).
syll(aludir,a).

The file also contains subword syllabifying which includes a subword and the syllable that can be obtained. For instance, "olvidar" produces the following positive examples:

```
syll(olvidar,ol).
syll(vidar,vi).
syll(dar,dar).
```

This is possible since in spanish syllabification process is context free. That is, syllabification of a subword uses the same rules that for a word.

Finally the negative data file contains examples of incorrect syllabifying. These were generated simply taking all incorrect syllables. For instance given the positive example `syll(eco,e)` the following negative examples were generated:

```
:-syll(eco,ec).
:-syll(eco,eco).
```

Negative examples were limited to a length of 4 letters. Because of this, the negative data file contains almost thrice as many examples than the positive examples file.

4 Experiments

The learning corpora was obtained from "El Quijote de La Mancha"[2] by taking, as has been pointed out before, the first words with no diacritics until a certain amount of unique words had been reached. For testing a similar effort was done with "Cien años de soledad"[5].

Experiments were carried out on three different sets of words. The first one with 120 words, the second with around 200 words and the third with approximately 300. In all cases a test data set of 129 words was used.

Since Aleph uses a sequential covering algorithm [4] it seems possible that the order in which examples are presented may bias the learning of rules. An effort was made to investigate this for the smaller of the sets. No difference was encountered on the rules generated despite the reordering of examples.

5 Results and Future Work

Table 1 shows the results obtained with the test data. Accuracy is the percentage of syllables correctly obtained from subwords. In all cases accuracy for learning examples was 100%. It can be seen that accuracy does not significantly increase even thought the last set provides almost triple the amount of examples.

The system was capable of inducing the following rules

```
syll(A,B):-hasPattern(A,cvcv),
    usePattern(A,cv,B).
syll(A,B):-hasPattern(A,vcv),
```

Table 1. Syllabification Results for Test Set

Words	#Rules	Accuracy	
		Training	Test
120	69	100%	79.64%
205	116	100%	80.73%
290	179	100%	78.91%

```
    usePattern(A,v,B).
syll(A,B):-hasPattern(A,vvcv),
    usePattern(A,vv,B).
syll(A,B):-hasPattern(A,vvcc),
    usePattern(A,vvc,B).
syll(A,B):-usePattern(A,cvvc,B).
syll(A,B):-usePattern(A,cvvv,B).
syll(A,B) :-
    hasPattern(A,ccvcv),
    usePattern(A,ccv,B).
syll(A,B) :-
    hasPattern(A,cvccv),
    usePattern(A,cvc,B).
```

The first three rules represent a well known rule in spanish

> "if there is a consonant between two vowels the consonant will form a syllable with the second vowel"

meaning that anything before that consonant forms a syllable. The fourth and last also represent a well known rule

> "if there are two consonants between two vowels the second consonant will form a syllable with the second vowel"

When a hypothesis is selected the learning system clears all redundant clauses (examples covered by the hypothesis). For instance, for the example

`syll(infante,in).`

there is no rule that can be applied.

According to [3] the above rules are valid rules for syllabification in Spanish. Although the fourth and fifth rule have exceptions and can't be always applied. The exceptions in both cases are closely related to the letters which appear in the word. When the letters fall in a certain category another rule is applied.

There are two basic tasks ahead. The first is to see if it is possible for the learning system to induce the categories of letters on which exceptions are based; the second is to see how well the rules found by the system are capable of syllabifying an unseen set of words. Even if categories are not induced it may be possible to identify exceptions well enough to induce a system that is very capable to syllabify.

This work is intended only to be using Spanish as a base to see how well it can be applied to other languages. That would then allow a syllabifying system to be quickly obtained for many languages.

References

1. Anja Belz and Berkan Eskikaya. A genetic algorithm for finite state automata induction with an application to phonotactics. In B. Keller, editor, *Proceedings of the ESSLLI-98 Workshop on Automated Acquisition of Syntax and Parsing*, pages 9–17, Saarbruecken, Germany, August 1998.
2. Miguel de Cervantes Saavedra. *El Ingenioso Hidalgo Don Quijote de la Mancha.* htp://www.elquijote.com, 1605.
3. Karina Figueroa. Sintesis de voz en español, un enfoque silábico. Tesis de Licenciatura, 1998. Asesor: Leonardo Romero, Universidad Michoacana de San Nicolas de Hidalgo.
4. Tom M. Mitchell. *Machine Learning.* McGraw-Hill, New York, 1997.
5. Gabriel García Márquez. *Cien años de soledad.* Plaza & Janés Editores, 1998.
6. S. Muggleton, editor. *Inductive Logic Programming.* Academic Press, 1992.
7. S. Muggleton. Inverse entailment and Progol. *New Generation Computing, Special issue on Inductive Logic Programming*, 13(3-4):245–286, 1995.
8. John Nerbonne and Stasinos Konstantopoulos. Phonotactics in inductive logic programming. In Mieczyslaw A. Klopotek, Slawomir T. Wierzchon, and Krzysztof Trojanowski, editors, *Intelligent Information Systems*, Advances in Soft Computing, pages 493–502. Springer, 2004.
9. Ashwin Srinivasan. A learning engine for proposing hypotheses (Aleph). http://www.comlab.ox.ac.uk/oucl/research/areas/machlearn/Aleph/, 1999.
10. A. Van den Bosch. *Learning to pronounce written words. A study in inductive language learning.* PhD thesis, Universiteit Maastricht, 1997. The Netherlands.
11. Van den Bosch A. Vroomen J. and De Gelder B. A connectionist model for bootstrap learning of syllabic structure. *Language and Cognitive Processes, Special issue on Language Acquisition and Connectionionism*, 13:2/3:193–220, 1998. Ed. K. Plunkett.

A Multilingual SVM-Based Question Classification System[*]

Empar Bisbal[1], David Tomás[2],
Lidia Moreno[1], José L. Vicedo[2], and Armando Suárez[2]

[1] Departamento de Sistemas Informáticos y Computación,
Universidad Politécnica de Valencia, Spain
{ebisbal, lmoreno}@dsic.upv.es

[2] Departamento de Lenguajes y Sistemas Informáticos,
Universidad de Alicante, Spain
{dtomas, vicedo, armando}@dlsi.ua.es

Abstract. Question Classification (QC) is usually the first stage in a Question Answering system. This paper presents a multilingual SVM-based question classification system aiming to be language and domain independent. For this purpose, we use only surface text features. The system has been tested on the TREC QA track questions set obtaining encouraging results.

1 Introduction

In the last years, Question Answering (QA) has become one of the main challenges in Natural Language Processing (NLP) research. The QA task tries to obtain exact answers to questions formulated in natural language. That is the main difference between QA and Information Retrieval (IR) systems [1], which just return a list of documents that may contain the answer.

Most QA systems [2] [3] [4] [5] are based on a three-stages pipeline architecture: question analysis, document or passage retrieval, and answer extraction. Question Classification (QC) is the main task in question analysis, trying to assign a class or category to the searched answer. Answer extraction process depends on this classification as different strategies may be used depending on the question type. Consequently, the performance of the whole system depends directly on question classification. For instance, if a question like "Which is the biggest city of Germany" occurs, the system will only select city names as possible answers.

In this paper we present a multilingual Support Vector Machines (SVM) based question classification system. It uses only surface text features for language independence purposes. The system has been tested on Spanish and English corpora. Next section shows current research on question classification.

---

[*] This work has been developed in the framework of the project CICYT R2D2 (TIC2003-07158-C04) and it has been partially funded by the Spanish Government through the grant BES-2004-3935.

Section 3 describes the SVM framework. Section 4 describes in detail our system and section 5 shows the experiments carried out and the results obtained. Finally, conclusions and future work are discussed in section 6.

2 Question Classification

Question Classification is the process of mapping a question to a predefined set of answer types. This semantic restriction narrows down the set of candidate answers, facilitating this way the answer extraction stage. Different answer extraction strategies may be used depending on question class: the process to search the answer for a question like "What is nitre?" is probably different to the process carried out to answer "Who invented the radio?". The first question is asking for a *definition* while the second one expects the *name of a person*. An analysis made on the errors of open domain QA systems [6] revealed that 36% of them directly laid on the QC module.

Most QC systems are based on heuristic rules and hand made patterns [7] [8] [9] [10]. This kind of systems presents two main problems. First, the great amount of human effort needed to define the patterns as there are many different ways to query the system ("Why is Jane Goodall famous?", "What is Jane Goodall known for?", "What made Jane Goodall famous?"...). Secondly, the lack of flexibility and domain dependency of these systems: changing the domain of application or adding new classes would involve the revision and redefinition of the whole set of heuristics and patterns.

By applying Machine Learning (ML) techniques to QC modules, we expect to bypass such limitations, creating applications that can be easily adapted to changes in the process environment. With this purpose in mind we consider very important to select the features carefully when training the system because questions are often short sentences with a restricted amount of information. Moreover, using complex linguistic information like chunking, semantic analysis [11] or named entity recognition [12] seems not to fit our goal as it provides undesired language and domain dependency. This paper presents a QC system for English and Spanish based on a machine learning method, Support Vector Machines, using only surface text features. Next section briefly describes the foundations of SVM.

3 Support Vector Machines

SVM have demonstrated to perform well with high dimensional data used in many NLP tasks, like text classification. This method tries to find an optimum hyperplane (boundary) that can distinguish between two classes of samples. The nearest instances to the boundary are known as support vectors. The optimum hyperplane is the one that maximizes the margin (the distance between support vectors and the boundary). If the set is not linearly separable, SVM use a socalled "kernel function" to map the original data into a higher dimensional space where they try to find the optimum hyperplane again.

Formally, given a binary training corpora of m pairs $(x_i, y_i), i = 1..m$, where $x_i \in \mathbb{R}^n$ is the feature vector and $y_i \in \{1, -1\}$ is the tag indicating if the sample belongs or not to the class, SVM [13] [14] get the solution to this optimization problem:

$$\min_{w,b,\xi} \frac{1}{2} w^T w + C \sum_{i=1}^{m} \xi_i$$
$$\text{being } y_i(w^T \phi(x_j) + b) \geq 1 - \xi_i,$$
$$\xi_i \geq 0$$

$C > 0$ is the penalty parameter of the error term. ξ_i variables were introduced to manage non-linearly separable data sets, where a little error is permitted. The function $K(x_i, x_j) = \phi(x_i)^T \phi(x_j)$ is known as kernel. There are four well-known kernels:

- Lineal → $K(x_i, x_j) = x_i^T x_j$
- Polynomial → $K(x_i, x_j) = (\gamma x_i^T x_j + r)^d, \gamma > 0$
- RBF → $K(x_i, x_j) = \exp(-\gamma \|x_i - x_j\|^2), \gamma > 0$
- Sigmoid → $K(x_i, x_j) = \tanh(\gamma x_i^T x_j + r)$

γ, r y d are kernel parameters. Kernel selection and other model's parameters have to be set while tuning the system.

Support Vector Machines were designed to solve binary problems. This means that they could only deal with the problem of detecting if a sample belonged or not to a particular class. In order to classify into k-classes there are two basic approaches: $one - versus - all$, where k SVM are trained and each one separates one class from the others; and $one - against - one$, where $\frac{k(k-1)}{2}$ models are trained and each one separates a pair of classes. It is important to note that as one-against-one works with less number samples, it has more freedom to find a boundary that separates both classes. The training cost of one-versus-all is better than one-against-one as it has to train only k SVM. The testing cost in both strategies is similar as one-versus-all needs k evaluations and one-against-one $k - 1$.

4 System Description

Our SVM-based QC system uses the same learning features for all the languages tested. Some details about system training and evaluation are described in next subsections, as the corpora and the vectors of features employed in the task.

4.1 Corpus

When this research began, we realized that there were no free parallel and large enough corpora of questions that fitted our needs to train a machine learning system. Thus we decided to develop our own corpus. We collected 2393 questions

Table 1. Number of instances per class

Class	Examples
PROPER_NAME	362
ORGANIZATION	89
LOCATION	411
FACILITY	58
PRODUCT	131
DISEASE	9
EVENT	7
TITLE	0
LANGUAGE	7
RELIGION	2
NATURAL_OBJECT	73
COLOR	16
TIME_TOP	324
NUMEX	333
DEFINITION	563
ACRONYM	8
TOTAL	2393

from the TREC[1] QA track 1999 to 2003 in English. This set of questions was annotated with our own classification, based on the entity hierarchy described by Sekine [15]. To build the Spanish corpus we used the translations made by the UNED[2] Natural Language Processing and Information Retrieval Group[3] from TREC 1999 to 2002. We translated TREC QA 2003 questions and, in order to have a uniform translation, we reviewed translated questions from previous competitions. As a result we got a parallel corpus of 2393 questions in English and Spanish annotated using our own classification.

Our type hierarchy has three levels of annotation, beginning with a first coarse level till the third and finest one. Since there were not enough samples for some fine-grained classes, only first level types were used in the experiments. This level consists of 16 classes. Table 1 shows the classification and the number of examples pertaining to each class in the corpus.

4.2 Feature Vector

In the SVM method, every instance of the corpus is transformed into a so-called **feature vector**, an array of values representing the linguistic properties of the example and the class it belongs to. As mentioned in previous sections, our main goal is to obtain a language and domain independent system. Therefore, only surface text features are used to define the feature vector.

---

[1] Text REtrieval Conference, http://trec.nist.gov
[2] Universidad Nacional de Educación a Distancia, http://www.uned.es
[3] http://nlp.uned.es

Questions were pre-processed to detect the first feature of our feature vector: the wh-word. Obviously, when dealing with an imperative question, this feature value is void. In addition, the three words following the wh-word that are not *stopwords*[4] were used to build unigrams and bigrams by means of combinations between them: w_1, w_2, w_3, w_{12}, w_{13}, and w_{23}.

An additional feature was added in order to improve the representation of long questions: the number of words (non-stopwords) that appeared after the wh-word. This feature is very useful for discriminating "who"-questions. These questions may belong to both PROPER_NAME and DEFINITION classes. For instance, "Who is the author of 'the divine comedy'?" must be classified as PROPER_NAME, but "Who is Marlon Brando?" must belong to DEFINITION; "who"-questions that belong to DEFINITION are usually short questions, formed only by the question word and one or two additional words.

5 Experiments

Several experiments have been done to test the QC system. First group of experiments were carried out in order to evaluate the impact on accuracy when using the additional feature that represents the number of non-stopwords words in the question. We have also tested the difference between using words or stems[5], looking for a larger generalization.

Both English and Spanish experiments were carried out over the corpus described in section 4.1 using a 10-fold cross-validation. The main problem with this corpus is that for some classes there are less than 50 samples, which seems not large enough to train a machine learning application. Therefore we collected all these classes (DISEASE, EVENT, TITLE, LANGUAGE, RELIGION, COLOR, ACRONYM) in a more general one, called MIXED, and made the same experiments, this time with 10 classes instead of 16.

Finally, an additional experiment was carried out using the corpus of the *Cognitive Computation Group*[6] [11]. This experiment tried to test the flexibility of the system using another corpus and a different set of question types. This corpus has 5442 training questions and 500 for testing purpose in English that were annotated with 6 different question classes. The results obtained with this corpus allow the comparison between our approach and the *CCG* system that relies in more complex linguistic information.

For all these experiments we used the SVM implementation of WEKA [16], a set of machine learning tools written in Java. This tool uses one-against-one technique to solve multi-class problems. The optimization algorithm implemented to train SVM is the Platt's sequential minimal optimization algorithm [17]. After many experiments, we decided that the best kernel to use (the one that pro-

---

[4] Words (typically articles or prepositions) which frequency in corpus is too high and poorly informative to be used in indexing or even in training processes.
[5] A **stem** is the base part of the word including derivational affixes but not inflectional morphemes, i. e. the part of the word that remains unchanged through inflection.
[6] http://l2r.cs.uiuc.edu/~cogcomp/

duces best results and takes less time to train) was the lineal kernel, with the C parameter set to 1.

Table 2 shows a summary of the results of the experiments described above. *QA-R2D2* refers to our own corpus, while *CCG* is the corpus of the Cognitive Computation Group. Third column describes the number of classes experiments have been developed with: 16 in the original corpus, 10 when classes with less than 50 samples were unified in MIXED and 6 for the CCG corpus. Fifth column shows whether stems were used in the feature vector or not, and the last two columns show the precision with the feature vectors described in section 4.2: *feature-1* does not include the number of non-stopwords in the question whereas *feature-2* refers to experiments where such feature was used. This table shows only precision values because the system assigns a class for all the questions (100% coverage).

5.1 Discussion

The use of stems seems not to be decisive as the results fluctuate between little gains and losses depending on the experiment. With respect to the set of classes, the experiments using only 10 classes does not perform better than experiments with 16. We think this behavior is due to the fact that MIXED class is a too heterogeneous group of questions from the point of view of their respective syntactic and semantic characteristics. This way, the expected improvement was overran by the noise introduced.

On the other hand, the experiments with the *CCG* corpus were remarkably better. This behavior was not surprising for a machine learning system because of the higher number of training instances (5542 against the 2393 of QA-R2D2), whereas the number of target classes was smaller (6 against 16). If we compare our best results with *CCG* corpus, 87%, with the results obtained by [11], 91%, there isn't a great difference, taking into account that this other system uses deep linguistic information, syntactic parsing and semantic analysis, what makes the

Table 2. Precision values for experiments on Spanish and English, corpora, and sets of features

Corpus	Test type	Classes	Language	stem	*feature-1* Precision	*feature-2* Precision
QA-R2D2	10-fold cv	16	English	Yes	79.44%	81.11%
				No	79.36%	80.82%
			Spanish	Yes	80.32%	81.91%
				No	80.32%	81.91%
		10	English	Yes	79.31%	80.90%
				No	79.19%	80.48%
			Spanish	Yes	80.36%	81.61%
				No	80.11%	81.70%
CCG	train/test	6	English	Yes	85.40%	86.00%
				No	85.40%	87.00%

Table 3. Results for Spanish (16 classes + No stem)

Precision	Recall	F-Measure	Class
0.79	0.854	0.821	PROPER_NAME
0.766	0.551	0.641	ORGANIZATION
0.867	0.871	0.869	LOCATION
0.719	0.397	0.511	FACILITY
0.824	0.573	0.676	PRODUCT
0.714	0.556	0.625	DISEASE
0	0	0	EVENT
0	0	0	TITLE
0.75	0.857	0.8	LANGUAGE
0	0	0	RELIGION
0.729	0.479	0.579	NATURAL_OBJECT
1	1	1	COLOR
0.967	0.895	0.929	TIME_TOP
0.914	0.898	0.906	NUMEX
0.711	0.876	0.785	DEFINITION
1	0.25	0.4	ACRONYM

Table 4. Results for English (16 classes + No stem)

Precision	Recall	F-Measure	Class
0.791	0.826	0.808	PROPER_NAME
0.882	0.506	0.643	ORGANIZATION
0.865	0.905	0.885	LOCATION
0.552	0.276	0.368	FACILITY
0.679	0.58	0.626	PRODUCT
0.5	0.222	0.308	DISEASE
0	0	0	EVENT
0	0	0	TITLE
0.857	0.857	0.857	LANGUAGE
0	0	0	RELIGION
0.583	0.384	0.463	NATURAL_OBJECT
0.933	0.875	0.903	COLOR
0.971	0.926	0.948	TIME_TOP
0.879	0.874	0.877	NUMEX
0.714	0.856	0.779	DEFINITION
1	0.375	0.545	ACRONYM

system largely language dependent. On the contrary, obtained by our system for both English and Spanish are very similar. This fact demonstrates that our approach can manage with different languages with a similar performance.

In order to study the results in more detail, we selected the experiments with 16 classes and no stemming. Tables 3 and 4 show precision, recall and F-Measure for each class. For better understanding, we must also refer to table 1. This table shows that there are no instances for TITLE class in the training corpus, and

Table 5. Confusion matrix for Spanish (16 classes + No stem)

a	b	c	d	e	f	g	h	i	j	k	l	m	n	o	p	← classified as
3095	2	0	5	0	0	0	0	2	0	0	0	39	0			a = PROPER_NAME
18	49	4	0	2	0	0	0	0	0	0	0	0	16	0		b = ORGANIZATION
3	2	3588	0	0	0	0	1	0	1	0	0	8	30	0		c = LOCATION
7	0	10	23	2	0	0	0	0	0	0	0	1	0	15	0	d = FACILITY
19	4	4	0	75	0	0	0	0	0	1	0	0	2	26	0	e = PRODUCT
1	0	0	0	0	5	0	0	0	0	0	0	0	0	3	0	f = DISEASE
1	1	0	0	2	0	0	0	0	0	0	0	0	0	3	0	g = EVENT
0	0	0	0	0	0	0	0	0	0	0	0	0	0	0	0	h = TITLE
0	0	0	0	0	0	0	0	6	0	0	0	0	0	1	0	i = LANGUAGE
0	0	2	0	0	0	0	0	0	0	0	0	0	0	0	0	j = RELIGION
4	0	5	0	0	0	0	0	0	0	35	0	0	1	28	0	k = NATURAL_OBJECT
0	0	0	0	0	0	0	0	0	0	0	16	0	0	0	0	l = COLOR
3	0	7	0	0	0	0	0	0	0	0	0	29013	11	0		m = TIME_TOP
1	0	5	0	0	0	0	0	0	0	0	5	29923	0			n = NUMEX
25	3	15	1	5	2	1	0	1	0	9	0	4	4	4930		o = DEFINITION
0	0	1	0	0	0	0	0	0	0	0	0	0	5	2		p = ACRONYM

Table 6. Confusion matrix for English (16 classes + No stem)

a	b	c	d	e	f	g	h	i	j	k	l	m	n	o	p	← classified as
2993	5	1	11	0	0	0	0	0	1	0	2	40	0			a = PROPER_NAME
21	45	3	3	4	0	0	0	0	0	0	0	0	13	0		b = ORGANIZATION
3	0	3726	1	0	0	0	0	4	0	0	6	19	0			c = LOCATION
9	0	14	16	4	0	0	0	0	1	0	0	0	14	0		d = FACILITY
12	1	1	1	76	1	0	0	0	1	0	0	1	37	0		e = PRODUCT
1	0	0	0	1	2	0	0	0	0	0	0	0	5	0		f = DISEASE
1	0	2	0	0	0	0	0	0	0	0	0	0	4	0		g = EVENT
0	0	0	0	0	0	0	0	0	0	0	0	0	0	0		h = TITLE
0	0	0	0	1	0	0	0	6	0	0	0	0	0	0		i = LANGUAGE
0	0	1	0	0	0	0	0	0	0	0	0	0	1	0		j = RELIGION
4	0	12	0	1	0	0	0	0	28	0	0	3	25	0		k = NATURAL_OBJECT
0	0	0	0	0	0	0	0	0	1	14	0	0	1	0		l = COLOR
3	0	1	0	0	0	0	0	1	0	30013	6	0				m = TIME_TOP
2	0	8	2	0	0	0	0	0	0	6	29124	0				n = NUMEX
22	2	11	0	13	1	1	0	1	0	12	0	3	15	4820		o = DEFINITION
1	0	0	0	0	0	0	0	0	0	0	0	0	4	3		p = ACRONYM

consequently its F-Measure is 0. DISEASE, EVENT, LANGUAGE, RELIGION, COLOR, and ACRONYM have between 2 and 16 instances, so their figures are difficult to evaluate, probably not being statistically relevant.

The system works quite well for DISEASE, LANGUAGE, and COLOR class, mainly because these kinds of questions include always specific words. For example, questions about colors always include the word "color" as in "What primary *colors* do you mix to make orange?", or "What *language* is mostly spoken in

Brazil?" (for LANGUAGE class). The performance of DISEASE class decreases since there are many different ways to ask about diseases without using the word "disease" itself. For instance: "What is the most common cancer?". Again, there are no great differences between English and Spanish results.

Finally, tables 5 and 6 show the confusion matrixes for Spanish and English respectively. The higher confusion is produced between DEFINITION class and the other classes. We think this is due to the fact that we annotated questions as DEFINITION when they expected a long answer so that these questions have very different query forms and do not present a clear uniform pattern.

6 Conclusions

In this paper, a multilingual SVM-based question classification system has been presented. Question classification is one of the most important modules in a question answering system. As SVM is a machine learning method based on features, their selection is a critical issue. Opposite to other QC systems, we chose to only use surface text features in order to facilitate language and domain independency. Specifically, both English and Spanish results are not statistically different, while the overall accuracy of the system proves it to be competitive enough if compared with systems using more complex linguistic data.

Thinking of future developments, in order to improve our system we are going to collect a higher number of training samples and we are going to redefine the set of classes. As we want to test our system on other languages, new corpora will be acquired.

References

1. Salton, G., McGill, M.J.: Introduction to Modern Information Retrieval. McGraw-Hill, Inc. (1986)
2. Moldovan, D.I., Harabagiu, S.M., Girju, R., Morarescu, P., Lacatusu, V.F., Novischi, A., Badulescu, A., Bolohan, O.: Lcc tools for question answering. In: TREC. (2002)
3. Soubbotin, M.M., Soubbotin, S.M.: Use of patterns for detection of likely answer strings: A systematic approach. In: TREC. (2002)
4. Yang, H., Chua, T.S.: The integration of lexical knowledge and external resources for question answering. In: TREC. (2002)
5. Magnini, B., Negri, M., Prevete, R., Tanev, H.: Mining knowledge from repeated co-occurrences: Diogene attrec 2002. In: TREC. (2002)
6. Moldovan, D.I., Pasca, M., Harabagiu, S.M., Surdeanu, M.: Performance issues and error analysis in an open-domain question answering system. ACM Trans. Inf. Syst. **21** (2003) 133–154
7. Voorhees, E.M.: The trec-8 question answering track report. In: TREC. (1999)
8. Voorhees, E.M.: Overview of the trec-9 question answering track. In: TREC. (2000)
9. Voorhees, E.M.: Overview of trec 2001. In: TREC. (2001)
10. Hermjakob, U.: Parsing and question classification for question answering. In: Proceedings of the ACL 2001 Workshop on Open-Domain Question Answering. (2001) 17–22

11. Li, X., Roth, D.: Learning question classifiers. In: COLING. (2002)
12. Hacioglu, K., Ward, W.: Question classification with support vector machines and error correcting codes. In: HLT-NAACL. (2003)
13. Boser, B.E., Guyon, I., Vapnik, V.: A training algorithm for optimal margin classifiers. In: Computational Learing Theory. (1992) 144–152
14. Cortes, C., Vapnik, V.: Support-vector networks. Machine Learning **20** (1995) 273–297
15. Sekine, S., Sudo, K., Nobata, C.: Extended named entity hierarchy. In: Proceedings of the Language Resource and Evaluation Conference (LREC). (2002)
16. Witten, I.H., Frank, E.: Data mining: practical machine learning tools and techniques with Java implementations. Morgan Kaufmann Publishers Inc. (2000)
17. Platt, J.C.: Fast training of support vector machines using sequential minimal optimization. (1999) 185–208

Language Independent Passage Retrieval for Question Answering

José Manuel Gómez-Soriano[1], Manuel Montes-y-Gómez[2],
Emilio Sanchis-Arnal[1], Luis Villaseñor-Pineda[2], and Paolo Rosso[1]

[1] Polytechnic University of Valencia, Spain
{jogomez,esanchis,prosso}@dsic.upv.es
[2] National Institute of Astrophysics, Optics and Electronics, Mexico
{mmontesg, villasen}@inaoep.mx

Abstract. Passage Retrieval (PR) is typically used as the first step in current Question Answering (QA) systems. Most methods are based on the vector space model allowing the finding of relevant passages for general user needs, but failing on selecting pertinent passages for specific user questions. This paper describes a simple PR method specially suited for the QA task. This method considers the structure of the question, favoring the passages that contain the longer *n*-gram structures from the question. Experimental results of this method on Spanish, French and Italian show that this approach can be useful for multilingual question answering systems.

1 Introduction

The volume of online available information is growing every day. Complex information retrieval (IR) methods are required to achieve the needed information. QA systems are IR applications whose aim is to obtain specific answers for natural language user questions.

Passage Retrieval (PR) is typically used as the first step in current QA systems [1]. Most of these systems apply PR methods based on the classical IR vector space model [2, 3, 4, 5], allowing the finding of relevant passages for general user needs, but failing on selecting pertinent passages for specific user questions. These methods use the question keywords in order to find relevant passages. For instance, for the question *"Who is the president of Mexico?"*, they return a set of passages containing the words *president* and *Mexico*, but not necessarily a passage with the expected answer.

In [6, 7] it is shown that standard IR engines (such as MG and Okapi) often fail to find the answer in the documents (or passages) when presented with natural language questions. On the contrary, PR approaches based on Natural Language Processing (NLP) produce results that are more accurate [9, 10, 11, 12]. However, these approaches are difficult to adapt to several languages or to multilingual tasks.

Another common strategy for QA is to search the obviousness of the answer in the Web [13, 14, 15]. The idea is to run the user question into a Web search engine (usually Google) with the expectation to get a passage –snippet– containing the same expression of the question or a similar one. The methods using this approach suppose that due to high redundancy of the Web, the answer is written in several different ways including the same form of the question. To increase the possibility to find relevant passages they make reformulations of the question, i.e., they move or delete terms to search other structures with the same question terms. For instance, they produce the reformulation *"the president of Mexico is"* for the question *"Who is the president of Mexico?"*. Thanks to the redundancy, it is possible to find a passage with the structure *"the president of Mexico is **Vicente Fox**"*.

[14] makes the reformulations carrying out a Part Of Speech analysis of the question and moving or deleting terms of specific morph-syntactic categories. Whereas [13] makes the reformulations without doing any linguistic analysis, but just considering certain assumptions about the function of the words, such as the first or second question term is a verb or an auxiliary verb.

The problem of these methods is that not all possible reformulations of the question are considered. With these methods, it would be very costly to realize all possible reformulations, since the search engine must search for every reformulation. Our QA-oriented PR system makes a better use of the document collection redundancy bearing in mind all possible reformulations of the question efficiently running the search engine with just one question. Later the system searches for all word sequences of the question in the returned passages and weights every passage according to the similarity with the question. The passages with the more and the greater question structures will obtain better similarity values.

Moreover, given that our PR method does not involve any knowledge about the lexicon and the syntax of the specified language, it can be easily adapted to several different languages. It is simply based on the "superficial" matching between the question and the passages. As a result, it would work very well in any language with few differences between the question and the answer passages. In other words, it would be adequate for moderately inflected languages like English, Spanish, Italian and French, but not for agglutinative languages such as German, Japanese, and Nahuatl.

This paper presents the basis of our PR system and demonstrates it language independence condition with some experiments on three different languages. It is organized as follows. The section 2 describes the general architecture of the system and the equations. The section 3 discusses the experimental results of the method on Spanish, French and Italian. Finally, the section 4 presents our preliminary conclusions.

2 Passage Retrieval System

2.1 Architecture

The architecture of our PR system is shown in the figure 1.

Given a user question, it is firstly transferred to the *Search Engine* module. The Search Engine finds the passages with the relevant terms (non-stopwords), using a classical IR technique based on the vector space model. This module returns all passages that contain some relevant terms, but since the n-gram extraction is computationally expensive, it is necessary to reduce the number of passages for the *N-grams Extraction* module. Therefore, we only take, typically, the first 1000 passages (previous experiments have demonstrated that this is an appropriated number since it covers, in most of the cases, the whole set of relevant passages).

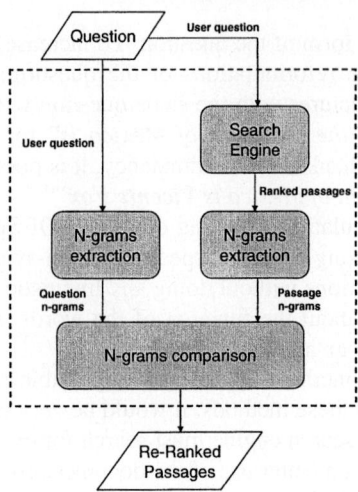

Fig. 1. Diagram of the PR system

Once the passages are obtain by the *Search Engine* module, the sets of unigrams, bigrams,..., *n*-grams are extracted from the passages and from the user question by means of the *N-grams Extraction* modules. In both cases, *n* is the number of question terms.

Then, the *N-grams Comparison* module measures the similarity between the *n*-gram sets of the passages and the user question in order to obtain the new weights for the passages. The weight of a passage is related to the lager *n*-gram structure of the question that can be found in the passage itself. The larger the *n*-gram structure, the greater the weight of the passage.

Finally, the passages with the new weights are returned to the user.

2.2 Passage Ranking

The similarity between a passage *d* and a question *q* is defined by (1).

$$sim(d,q) = \frac{\sum_{j=1}^{n} \sum_{\forall x \in Q_j} h(x, D_j)}{\sum_{j=1}^{n} \sum_{\forall x \in Q_j} h(x, Q_j)} \quad (1)$$

Where *sim(d, q)* is a function which measures the similarity of the set of *n*-grams of the question *q* with the set of *n*-grams of the passage *d*. Q_j is the set of *j*-grams that are generated from the question *q* and D_j is the set of *j*-grams of the passage *d* to compare with.

That is, Q_1 will contain the question unigrams whereas D_1 will contain the passage unigrams, Q_2 and D_2 will contain the question and passage bigrams respectively, and so on until Q_n and D_n.

The result of (1) is equal to 1 if the longest *n*-gram of the question is in the set of passage *n*-grams.

The function $h(x, D_j)$ measures the relevance of the j-gram x with respect to the set of passage j-grams, whereas the function $h(x, Q_j)$ is a factor of normalization. The function h assigns a weight to every question n-gram as defined in (2).

$$h(x, D_j) = \begin{cases} \sum_{k=1}^{n} w_k & \text{if } x \in D_j \\ 0 & \text{otherwise} \end{cases} \qquad (2)$$

Where $w_1, w_2, ..., w_{|x|}$ are the associated weights of the terms of the j-gram x.

These weights give an incentive to those terms that appear rarely in the document collection. Moreover, the weights should also discriminate the relevant terms against those (e.g. stopwords) which often occur in the document collection.

The weight of a term is calculated by (3):

$$w_k = 1 - \frac{\log(n_k)}{1 + \log(N)} \qquad (3)$$

Where n_k is the number of passages in which appears the term associated to the weight w_k and N is the total number of passages in the collection. We assume that the stopwords occur in every passage (i.e., n_k takes the value of N).

For instance, if the term appears once in the passage collection, its weight will be equal to 1 (the maximum weight), whereas if the term is a stopword, then its weight will be the lowest.

2.3 Example

Assume that the user question is *"Who is the president of Mexico?"* and that we obtain two passages with the following texts: *"Vicente Fox is the president of Mexico..."* (p_1) and *"The president of Spain visited Mexico in last February..."* (p_2).

If we split the original question into five sets of n-grams (5 is the number of question terms without the question word *Who*) we obtain the following sets:

5-gram: "is the President of Mexico".
4-gram: "is the President of", "the President of Mexico".
3-gram: "is the President", "the President of", "President of Mexico".
2-gram: "is the", "the President", "President of", "of Mexico".
1-gram: "is", "the", "President", "of", "Mexico".

Next, we obtain the five sets of n-grams from the two passages. The passage p_1 contains all the n-grams of the question (the one 5-gram, the two 4-grams, the three 3-grams, the four 2-grams and the five 1-grams of the question). If we calculate the similarity of the question with this passage, we obtain a similarity of 1.

The sets of n-grams of the passage p_2 contain only the *"the President of"* 3-gram, the *"the President"* and *"President of"* 2-grams and the following 1-grams: *"the"*, *"President"*, *"of"* and *"Mexico"*. If we calculate (1) for this passage, we obtain a similarity of 0.29, a lower value than for p_1 because the second passage is very different with respect to the original question, although it contains all the relevant terms of the question.

3 Experimental Results

This section presents some experimental results on three different languages: Spanish, Italian and French. The experiments were carried out using the CLEF-2004[1] data set. This data set contains a corpus of news documents for each language as well as a list of several questions and their corresponding answers. Table 1 shows some numbers from the document corpora.

Table 1. Corpora statistics

	# documents	# sentences	# words
Spanish	454,045	5,636,945	151,533,838
Italian	157,588	2,282,904	49,343,596
French	129,806	2,069,012	45,057,929

For the experiments detailed in this section, we considered only the subset of factual questions (the questions having a named entity, date or quantity for answer) stated on the Multi-Eight CLEF04 question set having an answer in the Spanish, Italian or French document corpora.

For the evaluation we used a metric know as coverage (for more details see [7]). Let Q be the question set, D the passage collection, $A_{D,q}$ the subset of D containing correct answers to $q \in Q$, and $R_{D,q,n}$ be the top n ranked documents in D retrieved by the search engine given a question q. The coverage of the search engine for a question set Q and a document collection D at rank n is defined as:

$$COVERAGE(Q,D,n) \equiv \frac{\left|\{q \in Q | R_{D,q,n} \cap A_{D,q} \neq 0\}\right|}{|Q|} \qquad (4)$$

Coverage gives the proportion of the question set for which a correct answer can be found within the top n documents retrieved for each question.

The figure 2 shows the coverage results on Spanish. It compares our n-gram model against the vector space model. From the figure, it is possible to appreciate the improvement of our model with respect to the classical vector model. This improvement was slightly greater for passages of one sentence, but it was also noticed when using passages of three sentences.

We can also observe that the bigger the size of the passage, the greater the resultant coverage. We believe this situation is produced by some anaphoric phenomena. It indicates that the answer is not always located in the sentence containing the n-grams of the question, but in the previous or following sentences. However, even when the bigger passages produce better coverage results, the small passages are preferred. This is because the complexity of the answer extraction (next module in the QA process) increases when dealing with bigger passages.

---

[1] The Cross-Language Evaluation Forum; http://clef.iei.pi.cnr.it/

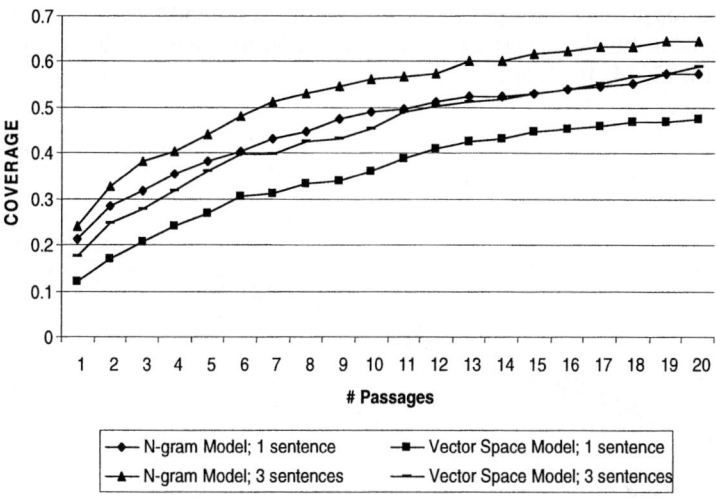

Fig. 2. Comparison against the vector space model

The figure 3 shows the coverage results on Spanish, Italian and French. These results were obtained considering passages of three sentences. It is important to notice that our *n*-gram PR model is very stable on the three different languages. In all the cases, the coverage was superior to 60% for the first twenty passages. The small differences favoring the Spanish experiment could be produced because of the size, and the possible redundancy, of the collection (see table 1).

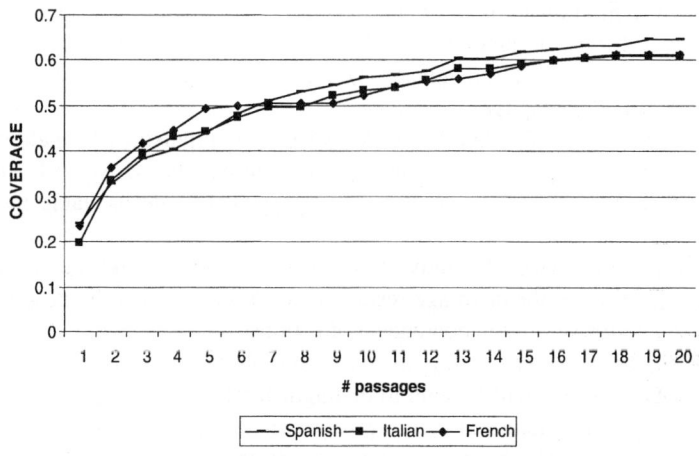

Fig. 3. Coverage on Spanish, Italian and French

Another important characteristic of our model is the high redundancy of the correct answers. The figure 4 indicates that the correct answer occurs in average four times among the top twenty passages. This finding is very important since it makes our system suitable for those current answer extraction methods based on statistical approaches [4, 13, 14, 16, 3, 5, 17].

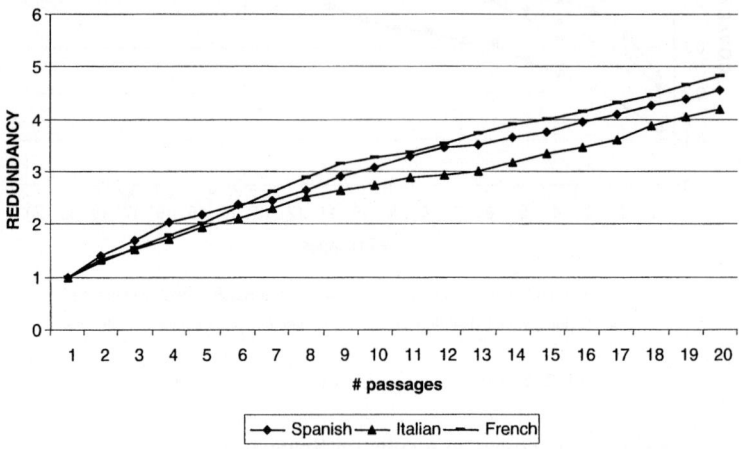

Fig. 4. Redundancy on Spanish, Italian and French

4 Conclusions

Passage Retrieval (PR) is commonly used as the first step in current QA systems. In this paper, we have proposed a new PR model based on statistical n-gram matching. This model, which allowed us to obtain passages that contain the answer for a given question, outperforms the classic vector space model for passage retrieval, giving a higher coverage with a high redundancy (i.e., the correct answer was found more than once in the returned passages).

Moreover, this PR model does not make use of any linguistic information and thus it is almost language independent. The experimental results on Spanish, Italian and French confirm this feature and show that the proposed model is stable for different languages.

As a future work we plan to study the influence of the size and redundancy of the document collection on the coverage results. Our intuition is that the proposed model is more adequate for very large document collections.

In addition, we consider that this model should allow to tackle the problem of the Multilingual QA since it will be able to distinguish what translations are better looking for their n-gram structure in the corpus, and it will discriminate the bad translations as it is very unlikely that they appear. Our further interest is to proof the above assumption using as input several automatic translations and merging the returned passages. Those passages obtained with bad translations will have less weight than those that correspond to the correct ones.

Acknowledgements

We would like to thank CONACyT for partially supporting this work under the grant 43990A-1 as well as R2D2 CICYT (TIC2003-07158-C04-03) and ICT EU-India (ALA/95/23/2003/077-054) research projects.

References

1. Corrada-Emanuel, A., Croft, B., Murdock, V.: Answer passage retrieval for question answering. Technical Report, Center for Intelligent Information Retrieval (2003).
2. Magnini, B., Negri, M., Prevete, R., Tanev, H.: Multilingual question/answering the DIOGENE system. In: 10th Text Retrieval Conference (2001).
3. Aunimo, L., Kuuskoski, R., Makkonen, J.: Cross-language question answering at the University of Helsinki. In: Workshop of the Cross-Lingual Evaluation Forum (CLEF 2004), Bath, UK (2004).
4. Vicedo, J.L., Izquierdo, R., Llopis, F., Muñoz, R.: Question answering in Spanish. In: Workshop of the Cross-Lingual Evaluation Forum (CLEF 2003), Trondheim, Norway (2003).
5. Neumann, G., Sacaleanu, B.: Experiments on robust nl question interpretation and multi-layered document annotation for cross-language question/answering system. In: Workshop of the Cross-Lingual Evaluation Forum (CLEF 2004), Bath, UK (2004).
6. Hovy, E., Gerber, L., Hermjakob, U., Junk, M., Lin, C.: Question answering in webclopedia. In: Ninth Text Retrieval Conference (2000).
7. Roberts, I., Gaizauskas, R.J.: Data-intensive question answering. In: ECIR. Lecture Notes in Computer Science, Vol. 2997, Springer (2004).
8. Gaizauskas, R., Greenwood, M.A., Hepple, M., Roberts, I., Saggion, H., Sargaison, M.: The university of Sheffield's TREC 2003 Q&A experiments. In: The 12th Text Retrieval Conference (2003).
9. Greenwood, M.A.: Using pertainyms to improve passage retrieval for questions requesting information about a location. In: SIGIR (2004).
10. Ahn, R., Alex, B., Bos, J., Dalmas, T., Leidner, J.L., Smillie, M.B.: Cross-Lingual question answering with QED. In: Workshop of the Cross-Lingual Evaluation Forum (CLEF 2004), Bath, UK (2004).
11. Hess, M.: The 1996 international conference on tools with artificial intelligence (tai'96). In SIGIR (1996).
12. Liu, X., Croft, W.: Passage retrieval based on language models (2002).
13. Del-Castillo-Escobedo, A., Montes-y-Gómez, M., Villaseñor-Pineda, L.: QA on the Web: a preliminary study for spanish language. In: Proceedings of the fifth Mexican International Conference in Computer Science (ENC'04), Colima, Mexico (2004).
14. Brill, E., Lin, J., Banko, M., Dumais, S.T., Ng, A.Y.: Data-intensive question answering. In: 10th Text Retrieval Conference (2001).
15. Buchholz, S.: Using grammatical relations, answer frequencies and the world wild web for trec question answering. In: 10th Text Retrieval Conference (2001).
16. Brill, E., Dumais, S., Banko, M.: An analysis of the askmsr question answering system (2002).
17. Costa, L.: First evaluation of esfinge: a question answering system for Portuguese. In: Workshop of the Cross-Lingual Evaluation Forum (CLEF 2004), Bath, UK (2004).

A New PU Learning Algorithm for Text Classification

Hailong Yu, Wanli Zuo, and Tao Peng

College of Computer Science and Technology, Jilin University,
Key Laboratory of Symbol Computation and
Knowledge Engineering of the Ministry of Education, Changchun 130012, China
wanli@jlu.edu.cn

Abstract. This paper studies the problem of building text classifiers using positive and unlabeled examples. The primary challenge of this problem as compared with classical text classification problem is that no labeled negative documents are available in the training example set. We call this problem PU-Oriented text Classification. Our text classifier adopts traditional two-step approach by making use of both positive and unlabeled examples. In the first step, we improved the 1-DNF algorithm by identifying much more reliable negative documents with very low error rate. In the second step, we build a set of classifiers by iteratively applying SVM algorithm on training data set, which is augmented during iteration. Different from previous PU-oriented text classification works, we adopt the weighted vote of all classifiers generated in the iteration steps to construct the final classifier instead of choosing one of the classifiers as the final classifier. Experimental results on the Reuter data set show that our method increases the performance (F1-measure) of classifier by 1.734 percent compared with PEBL.

1 Introduction

Text classification is the process of assigning predefined category labels to new documents based on the classifier learnt from training examples. In traditional classification, training examples are labeled with the same set of pre-defined category or class labels and labeling is often done manually. That is, the training examples set is composed of labeled positive examples set and negative examples set. In recent year, A number of statistical classification and machine learning techniques has been applied to text categorization, including regression models [1], nearest neighbor classifiers [2], decision tree [3], Bayesian classifiers [3], support vector machines [4], rule learning algorithm [5], voted classification [6], neural networks [7], etc.

The main problem with traditional approach is that a large number of labeled training examples are needed for accurate learning. Since labeling typically done manually, it is labor intensive and time consuming. Collecting negative training examples is especially delicate and arduous because (1) negative training examples must uniformly represent the universal set excluding the positive class, and (2) manually collected negative training examples could be biased because of human's unintentional prejudice, which could be detrimental to classification accuracy. In recent years, researchers investigated the idea of using a small-labeled set of positive class and a large unlabeled set to help learning, and this is referred as PU-Oriented text classification. It will reduce the manual labeling effort.

PU-oriented classification founds its application in topic-oriented crawling or focused crawling, where a topic-specific classifier is required to automatically identify whether the retrieved web page belongs the specific category during the crawling process. Instead of collecting negative example set for each specific domain, it is more desirable to construct a universal unlabeled example set for building any topic-specific classifiers due to the scale and diversity of negative examples.

2 Related Works

A theoretical study of Probably Approximately Correct (PAC) learning from positive and unlabeled examples was done in (Denis, 1998) [8]. The study concentrates on the computational complexity of learning and shows that function classes learnable under the statistical queries model (Kearns, 1998) is also learnable from positive and unlabeled examples. And then Denis does experiments by using k-DNF and decision trees to learn from positive and unlabeled data [9], [10]. (Bing Liu, 2002) presents sample complexity results for learning by maximizing the number of unlabeled examples labeled as negative while constraining the classifier to label all the positive examples correctly, and Bing Liu presents S-EM algorithm [11] (identifying a set of reliable negative documents by using a Spy technique and Building a set of classifiers by iteratively applying Expectation Maximization (EM) algorithm with a NB classifier) and Roc-SVM algorithm [12] (identifying a set of reliable negative documents by using a Rocchio algorithm and Building a set of classifiers by iteratively applying SVM algorithm) to learn from positive and unlabeled examples. (Bing Liu, 2003) summarize the usual method for solving the PU-oriented text classification [13]. Jiawei Han presents an algorithm called PEBL [14] that achieves classification accuracy (with positive and unlabeled data) as high as that of traditional SVM (with positive and negative data). The PEBL algorithm uses the 1-DNF algorithm to identify a set of reliable negative documents and builds a set of classifiers by iteratively applying SVM algorithm.

Besides maximizing the number of unlabeled examples labeled as negative, other methods for learning from positive and unlabeled examples are possible. (Denis, 2002) presents a NB based method [15] (called PNB) that tries to statistically remove the effect of positive data in the unlabeled set. The main shortcoming of the method is that it requires the user to give the positive class probability, which is hard for the user to provide in practice.

It is also possible to discard the unlabeled data and learn only from the positive data. This was done in the one-class SVM [16], which tries to learn the support of the positive distribution. We implement the one-class SVM. Through experiments, we show that its performance is poorer than learning methods that take advantage of the unlabeled data.

3 Our Methods

We constructed the text classifier by adopting the traditional two steps: First, identify a set of reliable negative documents from the unlabeled set by using our improved 1-

DNF algorithm. Second, build a set of classifiers by iteratively applying the SVM algorithm, and then construct the final text classifier by using the weighted voting method.

For identifying the reliable negative documents from the unlabeled examples set, we must identify the characteristics of the negative documents. For example, if the frequency of a feature occurring in the positive examples set is larger than 90% and smaller than 10% in the unlabeled examples set, then this feature can be regarded as positive. By using this method, we can obtain a positive feature set PF. If some documents in the unlabeled examples set do not contain any features in the positive feature set PF, these documents can be regarded as reliable negative examples. For describing expediently, we define the following notation: let P be the positive examples set, and U be the unlabeled examples set, and NEG_0 the reliable negative documents set produced by our improved 1-DNF algorithm, and NEG_i ($i \geq 1$) be the negative documents set produced by the ith iteration of the SVM algorithm, and PON be the training document set used by each SVM algorithm. Now we describe the process of the constructing our classifier.

In 1-DNF algorithm [14], positive feature is defined as the feature with occurring frequency in P larger than in U. We found that this definition has obvious shortcoming: it only considers the diversity of feature occurring frequency in P and U, and does not consider the absolute frequency of the feature in P. For example, the appearing rate of some feature is 1% in the positive data set and 0.5% in the unlabeled data set, this feature is obviously not positive feature. But if we use the 1-DNF algorithm to identify negative data, this feature will be regard as positive. The result is that the number of features in the PF may be much larger. So the number of documents in NEG_0 identified by 1-DNF algorithm is very less. In the extreme case, set NEG_0 may be empty. This is very disadvantageous to the iterative algorithm of the second step (Because the deviation in begin of the iterative algorithm, it will be likely to deviate more and more far). Based on the above observation, we improved the 1-DNF algorithm by considering both the diversity of the feature frequency in P and U and the absolute frequency of the feature in P.

Definition 1. A feature is regarded as positive only when it satisfies the following conditions:

1. The frequency of the feature occurring in the positive data set is greater than the frequency of the feature occurring in the unlabeled data set;
2. The absolute frequency of the feature in the positive data set is greater than $\lambda\%$, where $\lambda\%$ will be fixed through experiments.

Our improved 1-DNF algorithm can be depicted as follows, where $|P|$ is the number of the document in the positive set P, $|U|$ is the number of the documents in the unlabeled set U, and $freq\ (x_i, P)$ is the number of feature x_i occurring in the positive set P, $freq\ (x_i, U)$ is the number of feature x_i occurring in the unlabeled set U. We use our improved 1-DNF algorithm to identify the reliable negative set NEG_0. Through experiments, we prove that the number of reliable negative documents obtained by using the improved algorithm is much lager than that obtained by using the original 1-DNF algorithm.

Algorithm for identifying a set of reliable negative documents by using improved 1-DNF
```
algorithm Improved 1-DNF
  Assume the word feature set be {x₁,x₂,...,xₙ},xᵢ∈U ∪ P;
  PF = NULL;
  for(i=1, i<= n, i++){
    if (freq(xᵢ, P)/|P|>freq(xᵢ, U)/|U|&&freq(xᵢ,
        P/|P|)>λ%){
      PF=PF ∪ {xᵢ};
    }
    RN=U;
    for( each document d∈U) {
      if(∃xⱼ freq(xⱼ, d) > 0 && xⱼ∈PF ) {
        RN=RN - {d};
      }
    }
  }
```

Another distinction of our approach lies in the second step – constructing the final classifier. Unlike traditional approach where one specific classifier from the classifiers set generated during the iterative algorithm is designated as the final one, we make use of all of them to construct the final classifier based on voting method. Because we know nothing about the negative data in the PU problem, a new voting method is proposed. Through the improved 1-DNF algorithm, we obtain the reliable negative documents set NEG_0. Now the training samples set $PON = P \cup NEG_0$, and the unlabeled samples set $U = U - NEG_0$. We use SVM algorithm learnt from the training data set PON to construct the initial classifier SVM_0, and use SVM_0 to classify PP (let the precision be $accuracy_1$) and U (let the classified negative documents be NEG_1). The training example set is then augmented by adding NEG_1 to PON, that is $PON=P \cup NEG_1$, and unlabeled sample set $U=U-NEG_1$. We then use the training set PON to construct the second classifier SVM_1. SVM_1 is then used to classify PP (let the precision be $accuracy_2$) and U (let the classified negative documents be NEG_2). The training example set is then augmented by adding NEG_2 to PON, that is $PON=P \cup NEG_2$, and the unlabeled set $U=U-NEG_2$. This process iterates until no documents in U are classified as negative. Then we use the precision of each individual classifier to weight its corresponding classifier for constructing the final classifier.

Algorithm for constructing the final classifier by using weighted voting method
```
algorithm voting_final_SVM
  PP = 10% * PP; P = P - PP;
  PON = P ∪ NEG₀; U=U-NEG₀; i = 0; allAccuracy = 0;
  while(true) {
    SVMᵢ = SVM(PON);
    NEGᵢ₊₁ = SVMᵢ.classify(U);
    accuracyᵢ = SVMᵢ.predict(PP)'s precision;
    allAccuracy += accuracyᵢ;
    if (NEGᵢ₊₁==Φ)
```

```
    Break;
PON = PON ∪ NEGi+1;
U = U - NEG_{i+1};
i =i+1;
};
```

$$finalSVM = \sum_{i=0}^{n} \frac{accuracy_i}{allAccuracy} SVM_i$$

4 Experiments and Results

In our experiments we used Reuters 21578, which has 21578 documents collected from the Reuters newswire, as our training sample set. Of the 135 categories in Reuters 21578, only the most populous 10 are used. In data pre-processing, we applied *stopword* removal and *tfc* feature selection, and no *stemming* was conducted. Each category is employed as the positive class, and the rest as the negative class. For each dataset, 30% of the documents are randomly selected as test documents, and the rest (70%) are used to create training sets as follows: γ percent of the documents from the positive class is first selected as the positive set P. The rest of the positive documents (1-γ%) and negative documents are used as unlabeled set U. We range γ percent from 10%-50% to create a wide range of scenarios. The experiments results showed in the paper are the average of different γ%s.

In our experiment we used LIBSVM (version 2.71), an integrated tool for support vector classification, which can be downloaded at http://www.csie.ntu.edu.tw/~cjlin/libsvm/. We used the standard parameters of the SVM algorithm in one-class SVM classifier, PEBL classifier and our weighted voting classifier.

We used the F_1-*measure* to evaluate the performance of the classifiers, which is based on the effectiveness measure of *recall* and *precision*.

$$recall = \frac{Number\ of\ items\ of\ category\ identified}{Number\ of\ category\ members\ in\ test\ set}. \quad (1)$$

$$precision = \frac{Number\ of\ items\ of\ category\ identified}{Total\ items\ assigned\ to\ category}. \quad (2)$$

Van Rijsbergen(1979) defined the F_1-*measure* as a combination of recall(R) and precision(P) with an equal weight in the following form: $F_1(R,P) = 2RP/(R+P)$.

In the experiments, we implemented the PEBL algorithm, one-class SVM algorithm and our weighted voting classifier and compared their performance. In the step of identifying reliable negative documents from the unlabeled set U by improved 1-DNF algorithm, we ranged λ % from 10%-90%, and selected λ which results in best performance as the final value.

At first, we compared the improved 1-DNF algorithm with the 1-DNF algorithm in the number of identifying reliable negative data and the error rate. Let *SN* be the number of the reliable negative data, the ERR(%) is calculated as follows:

$$\text{ERR}(\%) = \frac{\textit{Number of the positive data in the strong negative data set}}{\textit{Number of all positive data mixed in the unlabeled data set}}. \tag{3}$$

Table 1 only gives the result when $\lambda\% = 20\%$, for which the performance of the final classifier is best. The increase of the number of strong negative data is significant, as shown in Fig. 1.

Table 1. The number of reliable negative documents and error rate

		Acq	Corn	Crude	Earn	Grain
Improved 1-DNF	SN	1003.8	343.0	1189.6	1200.4	1570.4
	ERR(%)	2.52	0.00	0.63	0.66	0.91
1-DNF	SN	161.0	203.4	116.6	269.6	128.0
	ERR(%)	0.00	0.00	0.00	0.02	0.00
		Interest	Money	Ship	Trade	Wheat
Improved 1-DNF	SN	2185.2	2087.2	2128.2	1034.2	1791.0
	ERR(%)	2.88	2.67	2.28	0.44	0.00
1-DNF	SN	299.0	269.6	324.4	70.8	200.2
	ERR(%)	0.00	0.00	0.33	0.00	0.00

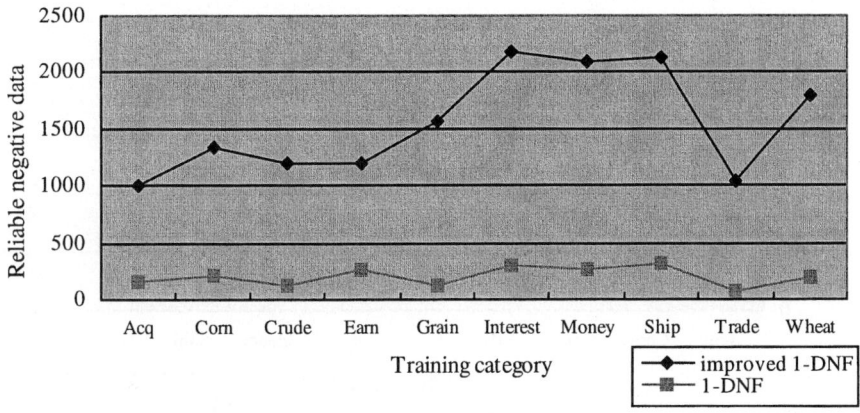

Fig. 1. Number of RN data Gained by Improving 1-DNF

From above, we know that the number of the reliable negative data identified by the improved 1-DNF algorithm is much greater than that identified by the original 1-DNF. Computing the average of reliable negative data of the 10 categories, we found that the number of reliable negative data identified by the improved 1-DNF algorithm is 7.6 times greater than that identified by the original 1-DNF. At the same time, the error rate of classifying the positive data as negative is 2%, indicating that the improved 1-DNF algorithm can identify many reliable negative data with low error rate.

The test results of the performance of the WVC (Weighted Voting Classifier), PEBL, one-class SVM (OCS) are shown in table 2 and Fig. 2, where column ALL denotes the average of the corresponding row. We observed that the performance of our WVC is best and its F_1-*measure* is higher than PEBL by 1.734 percent. The performance of OCS is worst with its F_1-*measure* lower than 22.7% and 20.9% respectively compared with WVC and PEBL. We prove that the performance of the classifier constructed only using the positive set is poorer than that takes advantage of the unlabeled data.

Table 2. Average F_1 of WVC, PEBL and OCS

	Acq	Corn	Crude	Earn	Grain	
WVC	0.9648	0.7346	0.8891	0.9813	0.9416	
PEBL	0.9538	0.7214	0.8564	0.9799	0.9083	
OCS	0.7082	0.4271	0.6766	0.914	0.6641	
	Interest	Money	Ship	Trade	Wheat	ALL
WVC	0.8528	0.8856	0.8067	0.8836	0.7971	0.87372
PEBL	0.8390	0.8686	0.7749	0.8633	0.7880	0.85538
OCS	0.7131	0.7180	0.422	0.6945	0.5210	0.64586

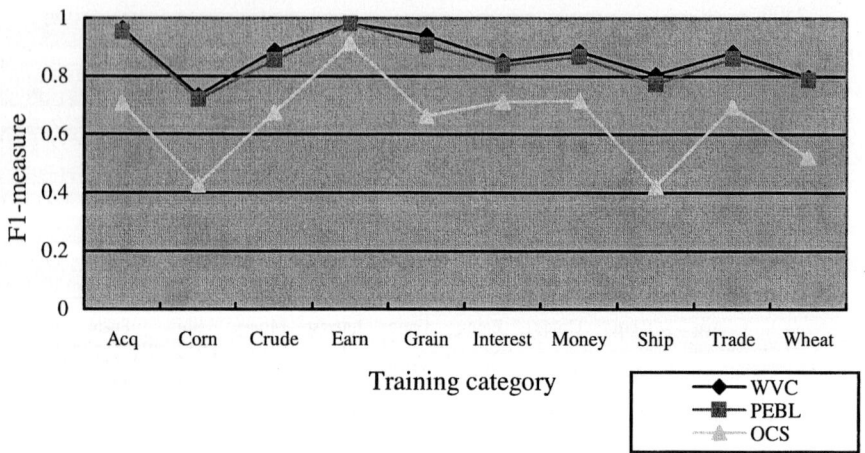

Fig. 2. Performance of Different Algorithms

5 Conclusions and Feature Work

This paper studied the PU-oriented text classification problem. A new algorithm based on modified 1-DNF and weighted voting method to solve PU classification problem in the text domain is proposed. Experimental results draw three important conclusions: First, the performance of the classifiers which discard unlabeled data set and learn only from positive data set (one-class SVM algorithm) is much poorer than the classifiers which take advantage of the unlabeled data set. Second, compared with 1-DNF algorithm, the improved 1-DNF can obtain more negative data with lower error rate. Third, applying the weighted voting method to the PU-oriented text classification can increase the performance of the classifier.

But, there are several shortcomings in our weighted voting classifier: First, our final classifier is made up of some "small" classifiers, and the weight of these "small" classifiers is only valued by the precision of classifying part of the positive P (because we know nothing about the negative documents). Second, there are not many documents in the training set "Reuters 21578", so the number of classifiers which constitute the final classifier is not very large, and the speed of the classifying is fast enough. But when used in web page classification where the number of classifiers may be very large, the speed of the classification system could be a problem. So how to select some classifiers of the classifiers set to construct the final classifier deserve further research. Third, it may be possible to improve our approach by using a continuous measure for classification instead of binary labels.

Acknowledgements

This work is sponsored by the national Natural Science Foundation of China (NSFC) under grant number 60373099.

References

1. Y. Yang and J. P. Pedersen.: Feature selection in statistical learning of text categorization. In Proceedings of the Fourteenth International Conference on Machine Learning (1997), 412-420
2. E.S. Han, G. Karypis, and V. Kumar.: Text categorization using weight adjusted k-nearest neighbor classification, Computer Science Technical Report TR99-019 (1999)
3. D. Levis and M. Ringuette.: A comparison of two learning algorithms for text classification. In Third Annual Symposium on Document Analysis and Information Retrieval (1994) 81-93
4. C. Cortes and V. Vapnik.: Support vector networks, Machine learning (1995)volume 20, 273-297
5. W. J. Cohen and Y. Singer.: Context-sensitive learning methods for text categorization. In SIGIR'96: Proc. 19th Annual Int. ACM SIGIR Conf. on Research and Development in Information Retrieval (1996) 307-315
6. S. M. Weiss, C. Apte and F. J. Damerau.: Maximizing Text-Mining Performance. IEEE Intelligent Systems (1999) 2-8
7. E. Wiener, J. O. Pedersen and A. S. Weigend.: A neural network approach to topic spotting. In Processing of the Fourth Annual Symposium on Document Analysis and Information Retrieval (SDAIR) (1995) 22-34
8. F. Denis.: PAC learning from positive statistical queries. In Workshop on Algorithmic Learning Theory (ALT) (1998)

9. F. Letouzey, F. Denis, and R. Gilleron.: Learning from positive and unlabeled examples. In Workshop on Algorithmic Learning Theory (ALT) (2000)
10. F. DeComite, F. Denis, and R. Gilleron.: Positive and unlabeled examples help learning. In Workshop on Algorithmic Learning Theory (ALT) (1999)
11. Bing Liu, Wee Sun Lee, Philip S. Yu, Xiaoli Li.: Partially supervised classification of text documents. The Nineteenth International Conference on Machine Learning (ICML) (2002) 384-397
12. Xiaoli Li, Bing Liu, Learning to classify text using positive and unlabeled data. The International Joint Conference on Artifical Intelligence (IJCAI) (2003)
13. Bing Liu, Yang Dai, Xiaoli Li, Wee Sun Lee, Philip S. Yu, Building Text Classifiers Using Positive and Unlabeled Examples. Proceedings of the Third IEEE International Conference on Data Mining (ICDM) (2003) 179-187
14. Hwanjo Yu, Jiawei Han, Kevin Chen-Chuan Chang, PEBL: Positive example based learning for Web page classification using SVM. The international conference on Knowledge Discovery and Data mining (KDD) (2002)
15. F. Denis, R. Gilleron, and M. Tommasi, Text classification from positive and unlabeled examples. Conference on Information Processing and Management of Uncertainty in Knowledge-Based Systems (IPMU) (2002)
16. Larry M. Manevitz, MalikYousef, One-Class SVMs for document classification. Journal of Machine Learning Research, volume 2 (2001) 139-154

A Domain Independent Natural Language Interface to Databases Capable of Processing Complex Queries*

Rodolfo A. Pazos Rangel[1], Joaquín Pérez O.[1], Juan Javier González B.[2],
Alexander Gelbukh[3], Grigori Sidorov[3], and Myriam J. Rodríguez M.[2]

[1] National Center for Investigation and Technological Development (CENIDET)
{pazos, jperez}@cenidet.edu.mx
[2] Technological Institute of Cd. Madero, México
{jjgonzalezbarbosa, myriam_rdz}@hotmail.com
[3] Center for Computing Research(CIC), National Polytechnic Institute(IPN), México
{gelbukh, sidorov}@cic.ipn.mx

Abstract. We present a method for creating natural language interfaces to databases (NLIDB) that allow for translating natural language queries into SQL. The method is domain independent, i.e., it avoids the tedious process of configuring the NLIDB for a given domain. We automatically generate the domain dictionary for query translation using semantic metadata of the database. Our semantic representation of a query is a graph including information from database metadata. The query is translated taking into account the parts of speech of its words (obtained with some linguistic processing). Specifically, unlike most existing NLIDBs, we take seriously auxiliary words (prepositions and conjunctions) as set theory operators, which allows for processing more complex queries. Experimental results (conducted on two Spanish databases from different domains) show that treatment of auxiliary words improves correctness of translation by 12.1%. With the developed NLIDB 82of queries were correctly translated (and thus answered). Reconfiguring the NLIDB from one domain to the other took only ten minutes.

1 Introduction

Access to information in a fast and reliable way is very important for modern society. Natural Language Interfaces to Databases (NLIDBs) permit users to formulate queries in natural language, providing access to information without requiring knowledge of programming or database query languages.

However, despite the achievements attained in this area, present day NLIDBs do not guarantee correct translation of natural language queries into database languages [1]. Moreover, queries are limited to the database domain configured by the database administrator. A Survey [9] on the importance of natural language processing (NLP) systems, conducted on 33 members of the "Pittsburgh

---
* This research was supported in part by COSNET and RITOS2.

Large User Group" professional society, mentions that:(1) NLIDBs are the most useful application for organizations among all NLP systems, (2) The five most desirable capacities of NLIDBs are: efficiency, domain independence, pronoun handling, understanding of elliptical entries (i.e., implied words), and processing of sentences with complex nouns, and (3) 50% of the best NLIDBs are those that offer domain independence.

This paper describes an approach that uses database semantic metadata to perform the analysis of nouns and auxiliary words (prepositions and conjunctions). This allows for translation of queries expressed in natural language (Spanish in our case) into SQL, with easy adaptation to different domains.

2 Related Work

Most existing NLIDBs do not carryout any real semantic processing of the user's input. They just look for keywords in the sentence [6] and focus their analysis on nouns and verbs, ignoring any auxiliary words in the query [7, 8].

In some NLIDBs, the semantic analyzer uses syntactic structure (obtained through a syntactic parser) to extract the meaning of the sentences [10]. However, no significant success is achieved yet in this direction. Semantic analysis of sentences is still a very complex task [11]: say, just determining the meaning of words is difficult due to their polysemy; for example, *file* is a tool and also a place for keeping documents.

In many NLIDBs that do use semantic analysis of a natural language query, it involves looking for keywords in the input sentence using a predefined pattern through multiple database mappings. Still, this approach is not sufficiently specific to give good results. In other systems, semantic analysis is based on probabilistic models [3, 4, 6]. Such systems rely on a corpus labeled with semantic information; however, there are no sufficiently large semantically marked corpora for use in NLIDBs.

Some NLIDBs use semantic graphs. However, the database relationships have to be defined by the user [6]. These approaches are subjective and require considerable manual effort. Such techniques have been applied to specific tasks in restricted semantic domains. They use a semantic representation, usually case frames [5].

Thus, no existing approach achieves good results in semantic analysis. That is why methods for its improvement are very important. In particular, auxiliary words (like prepositions and conjunctions) are not well-studied for tasks of processing natural language queries.

3 Assumptions

We assume that the database satisfies the following conditions, reasonable in well- designed databases: (C1) Relational, entity-relationship or a similar model is used; (C2) Each table has an explicit primary key; (C3) Each table column is explicitly associated to a domain (a named set of legitimate values for column values); (C4) Referential relationships between tables are explicitly expressed through foreign keys; (C5) Each table and column has a textual description; (C6) All tables are in second normal form; (C7) Information on conditions (C2) to (C5) can be extracted from the database metadata. Since descriptions of tables and columns are crucial for correct interpretation and translation of queries. Thus we additionally assume the following conditions: (C8) Descriptions of tables and columns are lexically and syntactically correct; (C9) Descriptions of tables and columns are short but meaningful phrases that consist of at least one noun and optionally of several meaningful words (nouns or adjectives; we do not take verbs into account), and optionally several auxiliary words (such as articles, prepositions, and conjunctions); (C10) The most meaningful word in the description of a table or a column is a noun; (C11) The description of each table is different from that of any other table or column; (C12) The description of each column is different from that of any other column of the same table (columns in different tables may have the same description); (C13) The description of each column that participates in a foreign key includes the description of the table referred to by the foreign key; (C14) The description of each column that participates in a primary key includes the description of the table, except for columns participating in a foreign key; (C15) The description of a column that does not participate in a primary or foreign key does not include the description of any table.

Though conditions (C8) to (C15) might seem restrictive, most of them would be required by humans to understand a database and correctly formulate SQL queries. Additionally, we make the following assumptions: (A1) Query sentences are lexically and syntactically correct (which can be checked by a syntactic analyzer); (A2) Queries are expressed in interrogative form.

We propose automatic creation of a domain dictionary from a synonym dictionary and metadata of the target database, using some linguistic processing. This technique performs the translation process independently of the NLIDB working data, thus avoiding reprogramming the NLIDB to port it to a database of different domain.

4 Generation of the Domain Dictionary

Dictionaries used by existing NLIDBs are created manually or semi-automatically [2]. We suggest automatic generation of the domain dictionary from a synonym dictionary and the database metadata with the help of some linguistic processing.

Synonym dictionary. In our case, we extracted a general synonym dictionary from a digital encyclopedia. It currently has 20,000 words with their synonyms and antonyms. This dictionary can be immediately used for most domains; however, it has an interface that permits to add more words.

Metadata dictionary. Database metadata can be used as a resource for interpretation of a query in a restricted domain [12]. The metadata dictionary stores database information such as number of tables, number of columns, and their location; additionally, for each table it stores the name of each column along with its data type and description.

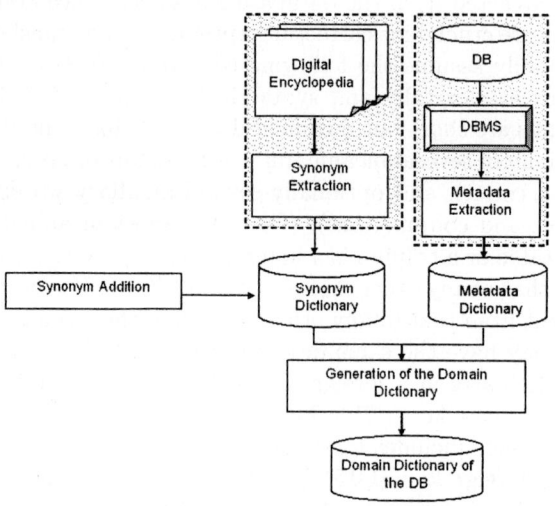

Fig. 1. Generation of the Domain Dictionary

Domain dictionary. For automatic generation of the domain dictionary, the description of each column from the metadata dictionary is processed to obtain the lemma and the part of speech (POS) of each word in the description (a POS tagger or a syntactic analyzer is used to resolve POS ambiguity). Then each noun is associated with columns and tables whose description includes this noun or its synonym. Notice that it is easier to provide meaningful descriptions for columns and tables (so that the interface can be configured automatically using this information) than to manually configure the interface dictionaries and modules for it to recognize and relate each column and table with some word in the domain dictionary.

5 Query Preprocessing

The preprocessing consists of analyzing each word of the natural language query to obtain its lexical, syntactic, and semantic information. Lexical information consists of the lemma of each word; the syntactic information consists of its part of speech (verb, noun, preposition, etc.). Semantic information is obtained from the domain dictionary in such a way that each noun is related to a set of columns and tables to which it may refer. Table 1 shows an example of a tagged query.

A Domain Independent Natural Language Interface to Databases Capable   837

Table 1. Semantic information obtained after preprocesing

QUERY: *cuáles son los nombres y las direcciones de los empleados* (what are the names and addresses of the employees)					
Word	Lema	Morphosyntactic information	Columns	Tables
cuáles(what)	cuál (which)	interrogative pronoun		
son (are)	ser (be)	verb, indicative, 3rd person, plural		
los (the)	el (the)	plural, masculine, determinative		
nombres (names)	nombre (name)	plural, masculine, noun	Categories.CategoryName, Customers.CompanyName, Employees.FirstName, Orders.ShipName,...	
y (and)	y (and)	conjunction		
direcciones (addresses)	dirección (address)	plural, femenine, noun	Employee.Address, Orders.ShipAddress, Suppliers.Address, Customers.Address	
de (of)	de (of)	preposition		
los (the)	el (the)	plural, masculine, determinative		
empleados (employees)	empleado (employee)	plural, masculine, noun	Employee.EmployeeID, Orders.EmployeeID	Employee

6 Main Algorithm

The translation process is carried out in three phases: (1) identification of the `select` and `where` phrases; (2) identification of tables and columns, and (3) construction of the relational graph.

Phase 1: Identification of the select and where phrases. The query phrases that define the SQL `select` and `where` clauses are identified in order to pinpoint the columns (and tables) referred to by these phrases. Since these clauses always involve table columns, then, according to assumption (C9) above, the phrases are query subphrases that include at least one noun (and possibly prepositions, conjunction, articles, adjectives, etc.). Additionally, from assumption (A2) it follows that the phrase that defines the `select` clause always precedes the phrase that defines the `where` clause. In Spanish, the words that separate these phrases are: verbs, *cuyo* (whose), *que* (that), *con* (with) *de* (from, with), *donde* (where), *en* (in, on, at), *dentro de* (inside), *tal que* (such that), etc.

Phase 2: Identification of tables and columns. Usually each noun in the `select`/`where` phrases refers to several database columns or tables (see Table 1), which would yield several translations of the query. Therefore, in order to pinpoint the columns and tables referred to, it is usually necessary to analyze the preposition *de* (of) and conjunction *y* (and), since they almost always appear in select/where phrases expressed in Spanish [8]. Examination of prepositions and conjunctions permits, besides considering the meaning of individual nouns, to determine the precise meaning of a select/where phrase that involves nouns related by prepositions and conjunctions. For this, preposition *de* (of) and conjunction *y* (and) are represented by operations using set theory, because of the role they play in queries.

Preposition *de* (of) establishes a close relationship between a word and its complement [14], such that, if there exists a select/where phrase that includes two nouns p and q related by preposition *de* (of), then the phrase refers to the common elements (columns or tables) referred to by p and q. Formally, $S(p\ prep\_de\ q) = S(p) \cap (q)$, where $S(x)$ is the set of columns or tables referred to by phrase x. Conjunction *y* (and) expresses the notion of addition or accumulation [14], such that if there is a select phrase that involves two nouns p and q related by conjunction *y* (and), then the phrase refers to all the elements referred to by p and q. Formally, $S(p\ conj\_y\ q) = S(p) \cup (q)$. Conjunction *y* (and) in a where phrase is treated as a Boolean operation.

For example, consider the query: *cuáles son los nombres y direcciones de los empleados* (which are the names and addresses of the employees), see Table 1. Consider the select phrase *nombres y direcciones de los empleados* (names and addresses of the employees). According to the above explanation, to extract the meaning of the select phrase it is necessary to apply two set operations: a union, corresponding to the conjunction *y* (and), and an intersection, corresponding to the preposition *de* (of). A heuristics is applied to determine the order of the two operations. In this case the preposition *de* (of) applies to the two nouns (*names and addresses of the employees = names of the employees and addresses of the employees*), therefore, the intersection operation has precedence above the union.

The output of Phase 2 is the semantic interpretation of the select and where phrases (i.e. the columns and tables referred to by these phrases), which will be used in Phase 3 to translate them into the select and where clauses of the SQL statement. The process for determining the tables and columns is the following (we rely on conditions (C8) to (C15)):

1. If a major POS word (usually noun) in the select phrase refers only to a table (and not to another table or column) then the table is permanently marked and associated to this word. If it refers to several tables, then distinguishing major POS words are extracted from the table descriptions and looked for in the select phrase in order to find out which table(s) are referred to by the first major POS word. If only one table is found, it is permanently marked and associated with the first word; otherwise the tables found are temporarily marked and associated to the first word.
2. If a major POS word in the select phrase refers only to a column (and not to another table or column), then the column is permanently marked and associated to the word and the corresponding table is also permanently marked and associated to the word. Otherwise, if the major word refers to several columns, then the analysis of preposition *de* (of) and conjunction *y* (and) described above is carried out to determine which column(s) are

referred to by the first major POS word. If only one column is found, it is permanently marked and associated to the first word; otherwise the columns found are temporarily marked and associated to the first word.
3. If a major POS word in the `where` phrase refers only to a table (and not to another table or column), then the table is permanently marked and associated to this word. Otherwise, if the word refers to several tables, then distinguishing major POS words are extracted from the table descriptions and looked for in the `select` phrase to determine which table(s) are referred to by the first major POS word. If only one table is found, it is permanently marked and associated to the first word; if several tables are found but one of them has been permanently marked, it is associated to the first word; otherwise the tables found are temporarily marked and associated to the first word.
4. If a major POS word in the `where` phrase refers only to a column (and not to another table or column), then the column is permanently marked and associated to the word and the corresponding table is also permanently marked and associated to the word. Otherwise, if the word refers to several columns, then the analysis of preposition *de* (of) and conjunction *y* (and) described in the previous paragraphs is carried out in order to find out which column(s) are referred to by the first major POS word. If only one column is found, it is permanently marked and associated to the first word; if several columns are found but one of them has been permanently marked, it is associated to the first word; otherwise the columns found are temporarily marked and associated to the first word.

At the end of this process, if there are no temporarily marked columns and tables, then we can proceed with the analysis; otherwise the analysis is aborted.

Phase 3: Construction of the relational graph. The process for constructing the relational graph is as follows:

1. Considering condition (C1), a non-directed graph is constructed from the relational or entity-relationship model of the database. Each node represents a table and each arc represents a referential relationship between tables (from condition C4). We assume binary relationships (involve two tables); this is not a serious limitation since a relationship involving more than two tables $(T_1, T_2, ..., T_n)$ can always be substituted by an auxiliary table T_a with binary relationships with tables $T_1, T_2, ..., T_n$.
2. The nodes corresponding to the tables permanently marked in Phase 2 are marked. Afterwards, for each simple selection condition in the `where` phrase that involves one column of a table (for instance: *con órdenes para el barco Mercury* (with orders for Mercury ship)), the node corresponding to the table is labeled with its corresponding simple selection condition. Finally, each marked node is labeled with the columns (of the corresponding table) referred to in the `select` phrase.
3. For each simple selection condition in the `where` phrase that involves columns of two tables, the arc incident to the nodes representing the tables is marked;

if no such arc exists, it is added to the graph and marked. Each arc marked at this step is labeled with its corresponding simple selection condition.
4. If all the selection conditions are explicitly stated in the query phrase then the subgraph consisting of all marked nodes and arcs must be a connected graph. From this sub-graph it is easy to obtain the translation into an SQL expression.
5. A disconnected sub-graph means that there exist implicit selection conditions in the query or the query is incorrectly stated. In the first case, the NLIDB has to guess the implicit selection conditions. For this a heuristics is used which based on the following assumption: all the implicit selection conditions refer to natural joins that involve tables and columns participating in a referential relationship. Therefore, a connected sub-graph is constructed by adding unmarked arcs to the disconnected sub-graph so that the number of unmarked arcs added is minimal. From this sub-graph the translation into an SQL expression is straightforward. If no connected sub-graph can be constructed, then the query is reported as incorrect.

7 Experimental Results

There is no standard evaluation method for comparing and assessing NLIDBs. The most used criterion is the translation success; i.e., the semantic equivalence between the natural language query and the SQL statement [13]. Up to now most NLIDBs can satisfactorily translate queries involving several tables if they are explicitly mentioned in the query, or queries involving one table that is not mentioned explicitly. For the experiment, the Northwind and the Pubs databases of SQL Server 7.0 were used, and 50 users were asked to formulate queries in Spanish. The resulting corpus consists of 198 different queries for the Northwind database and 70 different queries for the Pubs database. For formulating their queries the users only were allowed to see the databases schemas (definitions). The queries were classified according to difficulty (which depends on the amount of implicit column and table information in the query and special functions) and were divided into six types: (1) explicit table and column information, (2) explicit table information and implicit column information, (3) implicit table information and explicit column information, (4) implicit table and column information, (5) special functions required, and (6) impossible or difficult to answer. Table 2 shows the results obtained for the Northwind database with all the queries, which involve one, two, or more tables; in this case the success rate was 84%. Similar experiments were conducted on the Pubs database. Table 3 shows the results considering all the queries; in this case the success rate is 80%, which is very similar to that for the Northwind database. It is worth mentionary that most of the queries to the Pubs database involve two or more tables.

Additional experiments were conducted in order to assess the impact of the analysis of prepositions and conjunctions (described in Phase 2 in Section 5) on the translation success. When this analysis was excluded from the translation process, the success rate was 72.6% for the Northwind database and 67.1% for the

Table 2. Results obtained for the Northwind database

Query Results	Query Type						Total	%	%
	1	2	3	4	5	6			
Answered correctly	31	57	19	49	0	0	156	79	84
Answered with additional information	0	0	5	5	0	0	10	5	
Incorrect answer	0	0	0	1	23	5	29	15	16
Unanswered	0	0	0	3	0	0	3	1	
Total	31	57	24	58	23	5	198	100	100

Table 3. Results obtained for the Pubs database

Query Results	Query Type						Total	%	%
	1	2	3	4	5	6			
Answered correctly	7	29	8	12	0	0	56	80	80
Answered with additional information	0	0	0	0	0	0	0	0	
Incorrect answer	0	0	0	1	10	1	12	17	20
Unanswered	0	0	0	0	1	2	3	20	
Total	7	29	8	13	11	2	70	100	100

Pubs database. When the analysis was enabled, the success rate increased 11.4% for the Northwind database and 12.9% for the Pubs database. Some examples of queries that could not be satisfactorily translated are the following: *cuál es la fecha del último envío* (what is the date of the last shipment) and *cuáles son los nombres de los empleados que nacieron en febrero* (what are the names of the employees born in February). The first query could not be answered because *last shipment* is not defined in the domain and the second because it needs a special function for extracting the month from a date in the where clause of an SQL statement.

8 Conclusions

The translation approach presented favors domain independence, since the NLIDB does not need to be manually configured with a set of keywords for carrying out specific actions. It is important to point out that configuring the NLIDB for another domain (from Northwind to Pubs) took only ten minutes. The tests conducted so far have shown that the proposed approach permits: (1) avoiding the wearisome process of configuring the NLIDB for a given domain and (2) obtaining good results in translating natural language queries into SQL statements. The databases used for the tests have been used by other NLIDBs [13], which sets the foundation for designing a metric to compare the results of our NLIDB versus others. Prepositions and conjunctions play a key role in extracting the meaning of a query in Spanish. Taking them into account as set operations (intersection and union) in-creases the success rate by 12.1%.

References

1. Popescu, A.M., Etzioni, O., Kautz, H.: Towards a Theory of Natural Language Interfaces to Databases. In: Proceedings of the 2003 International Conference on Intelligent User Interfaces. ACM Press, 2003.
2. Zarate, A., Pazos, R., Gelbukh, A., Padrón, I.: A Portable Natural Language Interface for Diverse Databases Using Ontologies. LNCS 2588, 2003.
3. Stallard, M.S., Bobrow, D., Schwartz, R.: A Fully Statistical Approach to Natural Language Interfaces. In: Proc. 34th Annual Meeting of the Association for Computational Linguistics. 1996. http://citeseer.nj.nec.com/miller96fully.html.
4. Minker, W.: Stochastically-Based Natural Language Understanding across Task and Languages. In: Proc of EuroSpeech97, Rodas, Greece. 1997. http://citeseer.nj.nec.com/ minker97stochasticallybased.html.
5. Moreno, L., Molina, A.: Preliminares y Tendencias en el Procesamiento del Lenguaje Natural. Departamento de Sistemas Informáticos y Computación. Universidad Politécnica de Valencia. http://www3.unileon.es/dp/dfh/Milka/MR99b.pdf.
6. Meng, F., Chu, W.W.: Database Query Formation from Natural Language Using Semantic Modeling and Statistical Keyword Meaning Disambiguation. Computer Science Department. University of California. www.cobase.cs.ucla.edu/tech-docs/ucla-990003.ps.
7. InBase-Online. English Queries to Personnel DB. Russian Research Institute of Artificial Intelligence. 2001. http://www.inbase.artint.ru/nl/kadry-eng.asp.
8. Montero, J.M.: Sistemas de Conversión Texto Voz. B.S. thesis. Universidad Politécnica de Madrid. http://lorien.die.upm.es/ juancho.
9. Sethi, V.: Natural Language Interfaces to Databases: MSI Impact, and Survey of their Use and Importance. 1986. University of Pittsburgh.
10. AVENTINUS - Advanced Information System for Multinational Drug Enforcement. http:// www.dcs.shef.ac.uk/nlp/funded/aventinus.html.
11. Sidorov, G.: Problemas Actuales de Lingüística Computacional. In: Revista Digital Universitaria, Vol. 2, No. 1. 2001. http://www.revista.unam.mx/vol.2/num1/art1.
12. Stratica, N., Kosseim, L., Desai, B.: NLIDB Templates for Semantics Parsing. In: Proceedings of Applications of Natural Language to Data Bases (NLDB 2003). pp 235-241. http//www.cs.concordia.ca/ kosseim/research.html.
13. ELF Software Co.: Results from the Head to Head Competition. 2001. http://elf-soft.com/ns/demos.htm.
14. Real Academia Española: Gramática Descriptiva de la Lengua Española. Espasa Calpe, 1999.

An Efficient Hybrid Approach for Online Recognition of Handwritten Symbols

John A. Fitzgerald, Bing Quan Huang, and Tahar Kechadi

Department of Computer Science,
University College Dublin,
Belfield, Dublin 4, Ireland
`john.fitzgerald@ucd.ie`

Abstract. This paper presents an innovative hybrid approach for online recognition of handwritten symbols. The approach is composed of two main techniques. Firstly, fuzzy rules are used to extract a meaningful set of features from a handwritten symbol, and secondly a recurrent neural network uses the feature set as input to recognise the symbol. The extracted feature set is a set of basic shapes capturing what is distinctive about each symbol, thus making the network's classification task easier. We propose a new recurrent neural network architecture, associated with an efficient learning algorithm derived from the gradient descent method. We describe the network and explain the relationship between the network and the Markov chains. The approach has achieved high recognition rates using benchmark datasets from the Unipen database.

1 Introduction

The majority of recognisers for handwritten symbols have been built upon rule based methods or statistical methods, such as motor model [4], elastic matching [5], time-delay neural network [6], and hidden Markov models [11]. The problem with rule based methods is that it is in most cases impossible to design an exhaustive set of rules that model all possible ways of forming all symbols.

Generally, a recognizer that employs statistical methods is more flexible and reliable. However, the common static methods - curve/feature matching, Markov Model and Neural Network based approaches, have their own disadvantages. The difficulty with the curve/feature matching approaches is that they are computationally intensive and impractical for large vocabulary handwriting [6]. Hidden Markov Models (HMMs) have been successfully applied firstly to speech recognition and have been used to solve sequence learning problems, including online handwriting recognition [11]. However, to achieve a reliable executable HMM requires a human expert to choose a number of states with initial estimates of the model parameters and transition probability between the states.

Time-delay neural network (TDNN) trained with Back-propagation algorithm [7] requires the setting of less parameters. The limitation of TDNN is that the input fixed time window can render it unable to deal with varying length sequence. Another type of network is the recurrent neural network, which successfully deal with temporal sequences such as formal language learning problems.

This network solves the problems of TDNN, and is easy to use as a recognizer. The two common types of recurrent networks are the Elman network [2] and fully recurrent networks [14]. Elman networks face difficulties due to their own architecture: the network's memory consists of one relatively small context layer, and there is additional computation cost due to the need for more hidden neurons. The main problem with the fully recurrent network with real time recurrent learning (RTRL) is its computational complexity. Therefore, a new truncated recurrent network with a new dynamic learning algorithm is proposed here, with less computational complexity than RTRL.

The recognition process begins with feature extraction. The purpose of feature extraction is to translate the raw symbol data, initially a sequence of points, into something meaningful before using it as input to the network. Also, reducing the input size is beneficial in terms of efficiency. For each symbol, a set of features is generated whereby each feature is one of three types: *Line*, *C-shape* or *O-shape*. We believe that by representing each symbol in this manner, we are capturing the essence of the symbol and what distinguishes it from other symbols, thus making classification easier. The feature extraction result is used as input to the network, which classifies the symbol.

The paper is organized as follows. Section 2 gives an overview of the feature extraction phase. In section 3 the network is presented. Section 4 describes the network learning algorithm. Section 5 shows experimental results and section 6 contains conclusions and future work.

2 Feature Extraction

Feature extraction is a process which transforms the input data into a set of features which characterise the input, and which can therefore be used to classify the input. This process has been widely used in automatic handwriting recognition [12]. Due to the nature of handwriting with its high degree of variability and imprecision, obtaining these features is a difficult task. A feature extraction algorithm must be robust enough that for a variety of instances of the same symbol, similar feature sets are generated. Here we present a feature extraction process in which fuzzy logic is used. Fuzzy logic is particularly appropriate for this task, given the amount of imprecision and ambiguity present in handwritten symbols. Our feature extraction technique [9] consists of a pre-processing phase called *chording* followed by the main feature extraction phase.

Chording Phase: Each handwritten symbol is represented by a set of *strokes* $\{s_0, \ldots, s_v\}$, where each stroke is a sequence of points. Chording transforms each stroke s into a chord vector $\vec{C} = \langle c_0, \ldots, c_{n-1} \rangle$, where each chord c_i is a section of s which approximates a sector of a circle. This phase simplifies the input data so that feature extraction rules can be written in terms of chords rather than sequences of points. Furthermore, chording identifies the locations in the stroke where new features may begin, so the number of sections of the stroke which need to be assessed as potential features is drastically reduced.

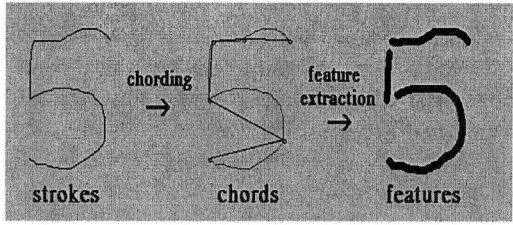

Fig. 1. Feature Extraction process for a handwritten digit

Feature Extraction Phase: The chord vectors $\langle \vec{C}_0, \ldots, \vec{C}_v \rangle$ are the input to the feature extraction phase, in which the objective is to identify the feature set which best describes the symbol. This feature set will be the set of substrokes $F = \{f_0, \ldots, f_{m-1}\}$ encompassing the entire symbol which is of a higher *quality* than any other possible set of substrokes. Each substroke f_j is a sequence of consecutive chords $\{c_a, \ldots, c_b\}$ from a chord vector $\vec{C}_i = (c_0, \ldots, c_{n-1})$, where $0 \leq a \leq b \leq n$ and $0 \leq i \leq v$.

The quality of a set of substrokes, represented by $q(F)$, is dictated by the membership values of the substrokes in F in sets corresponding to feature types. We distinguish three types of feature: *Line*, *C-shape* and *O-shape*. The membership value of a substroke f_j in the set *Line*, for example, is expressed as $\mu_{Line}(f_j)$ or $Line(f_j)$, and represents the confidence that f_j is a line. In the definition of $q(F)$ below, T is whichever of the fuzzy sets *Line*, *C-shape* or *O-shape* f_j has highest membership in.

$$q(F) = \frac{\sum_{j=0}^{m-1} \mu_T(f_j)}{m} \quad (1)$$

Fuzzy Rules: Membership values in fuzzy sets are determined by *fuzzy rules*. The fuzzy rules in the rule base can be divided into *high-level* and *low-level* rules. Membership values in fuzzy sets corresponding to feature types are determined by high-level rules. Each high level fuzzy rule defines the *properties* required for a particular feature type, and is of the form:

$$T(Z) \leftarrow P_1(Z) \cap \ldots \cap P_k(Z) \quad (2)$$

This means that the likelihood of a substroke Z being of feature type T is determined by the extent to which the properties P_1 to P_k are present in Z. Typical properties include *Straightness* and *Smoothness*. Memberships in fuzzy sets corresponding to properties are determined by low-level fuzzy rules. In each low-level rule the fuzzy value $P_i(Z)$ is defined in terms of values representing various aspects of Z. To express varying degrees of these aspects we use *fuzzy membership functions*.

The strength of our feature extraction technique is therefore dependent on an appropriate choice of requisite properties for each feature type, and low-level fuzzy rules which accurately assess the extent to which these properties are present. These properties and rules were continually updated and improved over time until the memberships being produced for the feature types were deemed accurate. The fuzzy rules form the basis of a feature extraction algorithm which determines the best feature set using numerous efficiency measures.

Example: For the symbol shown in Figure 1, the effect of feature extraction is a partition of the input $\vec{C} = \{c_0, \ldots, c_4\}$ into a set of features $F = \{(c_0, c_1), (c_2), (c_3, c_4)\}$, where $\mu_{Line}(c_0, c_1) = 0.66$, $\mu_{Line}(c_2) = 0.98$, and $\mu_{Cshape}(c_3, c_4) = 0.93$.

By using the feature extraction method described above rather than feature template matching, there will be more similarity between the feature sets extracted from a variety of instances of the same symbol, thus aiding the network's classification task. Other feature extraction methods have also extracted a set of shapes [8], but these methods attempted to match sections of the symbol against fixed, predefined versions of each shape, whereas our rule-based definitions are more flexible and allow for the wide variety of e.g. C-shapes which occur in handwriting.

3 The Recurrent Network

A new recurrent neural network has been proposed in [1], based on the Elman network architecture [2]. This network constitutes an improvement of the Elman network, with two additional features. It has a multi context layer (MCL) [15], which can keep more states in memory. The second feature is the feed forward connections from the MCL to the output layer, which can reduce the number of neurons in the hidden layer [10]. The network architecture is shown in Fig. 2.

3.1 Basic Notations and Definitions

- **Net inputs and Outputs:** Let n_{in}, n_{out} and m denote the number of input, output, and hidden layer units respectively. Let n_{con} be the number of active context layers, and let the total number of context layers be denoted by q. Let t be the current time step. $I_i(t)$ is the ith neuron input in the input layer, $\tilde{h}_j(t)$ is the input neuron j in the hidden layer, and $\tilde{o}_k(t)$ is the input neuron k in the output layer. The neuron output of the hidden and output layers are $H_j(t)$ and $O_k(t)$ respectively. The neuron output l of context layer p is denoted by $C_l(t-p)$, and $d_k(t)$ is the target of unit k in the output layer.
- **Connection weights:** Let v_{ji} be the weight connection from the input layer to the hidden layer and u_{kl}^p be the weight connection from the pth context layer to the hidden layer. Let woc_{kl}^p be the weight connection from the pth context layer to the output layer and w_{kj} be the weight connection from the hidden layer to the output layer.

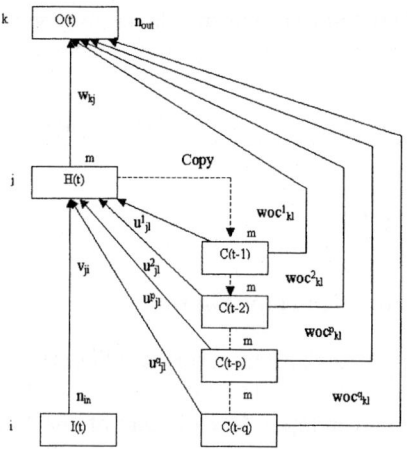

Fig. 2. The network architecture

The softmax function and logistic function are selected as the activation functions for the output layer and the hidden layer respectively, written below:

$$f_{SM}(x_i) = \frac{e^{x_i}}{\sum_{i'=1}^{N} e^{x_{i'}}} \qquad f(x_i) = \frac{1}{1+e^{x_i}}$$

where x represents the ith net input, and N is the total number of net inputs. The derivatives of the activation functions can be written respectively as follows:

$$f'_{SM}(x_i) = (1 - f_{SM}(x_i))f_{SM}(x_i) \qquad f'(x_i) = (1 - f(x_i))f(x_i)$$

According to the architecture of the network, the output of the hidden layer and the output layer are calculated at every time step, while the outputs of the context layers are obtained by shifting the information from p to $p+1$ for ($p = 1$ to q). The first context layer is updated by the hidden layer, as shown in Fig. 2. This is done in a feed-forward fashion:

1. The net input and output of the hidden layer units are calculated respectively as follows:

$$\tilde{h}_j(t) = \sum_{i=1}^{n_{in}} I_i(t)v_{ji}(t) + \sum_{p=1}^{n_{con}} \sum_{l=1}^{m} C_l(t-p)u_{jl}^p(t) \qquad (3)$$

$$H_j(t) = f(\tilde{h}_j(t)) \qquad (4)$$

where $C_l(t-p)$ are the outputs of the context layers obtained by copying the output of its predecessor. The context layer gets the previous output of the hidden layer. The following equations summarise this operation:

$$C_j(t-p) = C_j(t-p+1), p = 2, ..., q \qquad (5)$$

$$C_j(t-1) = H_j(t) \qquad (6)$$

2. The net input and output of the output layer are given respectively as follows:

$$\tilde{o}_k(t) = \sum_{j=1}^{m} H_j(t) w_{kj}(t) + \sum_{p=1}^{n_{con}} \sum_{l=1}^{m} C_l(t-p) woc_{kl}^p(t) \quad (7)$$

$$O_k(t) = f_{SM}(\tilde{o}_k(t)) \quad (8)$$

3.2 The Network and Markov Chain

A system based on our network architecture predicts the current state depending on the previous states window $[(t-1) \to (t-p)]$. However, the Markovian assumption of conditional independence is one of the limitations. The network tries to predict a more accurate current state based on more historical states. Thus, the network expresses an extended probability model based on the Markov chain.

In Markov models (MMs), the transition matrix $A = \{a_{ij}\}$, the observation symbol probability distribution in state j is $X(t) = \{x_j(t)\}$, that is, $X(t) = \{x_1(t), x_2(t), \cdots, x_n(t)\}$, where $0 \le x_j(t) \le 1$. The formulae of the Markov chain can be written as follows.

$$x_j(t+1) = \sum_{i=1}^{m} a_{ji} x_i(t), \quad j = 1, \cdots, m. \quad (9)$$

$$X(t+1) = AX(t), \quad (10)$$

$$A \ge 0, \sum_{j}^{m} a_{ij} = 1. \quad (11)$$

This can be rewritten as:

$$X(t) = A^t X(0), \quad (12)$$

where $X(0) = [x_1(0), ..., x_m(0)]$ is the initial probability vector and t represents the time step. Let $I(t) = \{I_1(t), \cdots, I_{in}(t)\}$, $H(t) = \{H_1(t), \cdots, H_m(t)\}$, $C(t-p) = \{C_1(t-p), \cdots, C_m(t-p)\}$, and $O(t) = \{O_1(t), \cdots, O_{out}(t)\}$. We write the state-transition and output functions, defined by (3), (4), (7), and (8), as:

$$H(t) = f(I(t), C(t-1), \cdots, C(t-p)) = f(I(t), H(t-1), \cdots, H(t-p)) \quad (13)$$

and

$$O(t) = f_{SM}(H(t), C(t-1), \cdots, C(t-p)) = f_{SM}(H(t), H(t-1), \cdots, H(t-p)) \quad (14)$$

According to the formulaes (3), (4), (5), (6) and (13), the state-transition map f can be written as a set of maps parameterised by input sequence s as follows:

$$f_s^p(x) = f(\phi_1(s), \cdots, \phi_p(s), x) \qquad (15)$$

Given an input sequence $S = \{s_1, s_2, \cdots, s_t\}$, the current state after t step is

$$H(t) = f_{s_p \cdots s_t}^p(H(0)) = f_{S_1^t}^p(H(0)) \qquad (16)$$

4 The Network Learning Algorithm

The training algorithms which are often used for recurrent networks (RNN) are based on the gradient descent method, to minimise the error output. With Back-propagation through time (BPTT) [7] one needs to unfold a discrete-time RNN and then apply the back-propagation algorithm. However, BPTT fails to deal with long sequence tasks due to the large memory required to store all states of all iterations. The RTRL learning algorithm established in [14] for a fully recurrent network computes the derivatives of states and outputs with respect to all weights at each iteration. It can deal with sequences of arbitrary length, and requires less memory storage proportional to sequence length than BPTT. Here we summarise our learning algorithm [1] which is similar to RTRL. As this is a multinomial classification problem, the cross-entropy error for the output layer is expressed by the following:

$$E(t) = -\sum_{k=1}^{n_{out}} d_k(t) \ln O_k(t) \qquad (17)$$

The goal is to minimise the total network cross-entropy error. This can be obtained by summing the errors of all the past input patterns:

$$E_{total} = \sum_{t=1}^{T} E(t) \qquad (18)$$

Up to this point we have introduced how the network works and is evaluated. Now, we use the gradient descent algorithm to adjust the network parameters, called the weight matrix W. Firstly, we compute the derivatives of the cross-entropy error for each net input of the output layer, the hidden layer, and the context layer. These are called local gradients. The equations for the output layer, hidden layer, and context layer are written respectively as follows:

$$LG_k(t) = d_k(t) - O_k(t) \qquad (19)$$

$$LG_j(t) = \sum_{k=1}^{n_{out}} LG_k(t) w_{kj}(t) \qquad (20)$$

$$LG_l^p(t) = \sum_{k=1}^{n_{out}} LG_k(t) woc_{kl}^p(t) \tag{21}$$

The partial derivatives of the cross-entropy error with regard to the weights between the hidden and output layers ($w_{kj}(t)$) and the weights between output layer and multi-context layer ($woc_{kl}^p(t)$) are as follows:

$$\frac{\partial E(t)}{\partial w_{kj}(t)} = LG_k(t) H_j(t) \tag{22}$$

$$\frac{\partial E(t)}{\partial woc_{kl}^p(t)} = LG_k(t) C_l(t-p) \tag{23}$$

The derivation of the cross-entropy error with regards to the weights between the hidden and multi-context layer is

$$\frac{\partial E(t)}{\partial u_{jl}^p(t)} = -\sum_{j'=1}^{m} \left[LG_{j'}(t) \frac{\partial H_{j'}(t)}{\partial u_{jl}^p(t)} + \sum_{p'=1}^{n_{con}} \sum_{r=1}^{m} LG_r^{p'}(t) \delta_{rj'} \frac{\partial H_{j'}(t-p')}{\partial u_{jl}^p(t)} \right] \tag{24}$$

where

$$\frac{\partial H_{j'}(t)}{\partial u_{jl}^p(t)} = f'(\tilde{h}_{j'}(t)) \left[\delta_{j'j} \sum_{p''=1}^{n_{con}} \delta_{pp''} H_l(t-p'') + \sum_{p'=1}^{n_{con}} \sum_{j''=1}^{m} \sum_{l'=1}^{m} u_{jl'}^{p'}(t) \delta_{l'j''} \frac{\partial H_{j''}(t-p')}{\partial u_{jl}^p(t)} \right] \tag{25}$$

where δ is the Kronecker symbol defined by $\delta_{ab} = 1$ if $a = b$, and $\delta_{ab} = 0$ if $a \neq b$. The partial derivative of the cross-entropy error for the weights between hidden layer and input layer $\partial E(t)/\partial v_{ji}(t)$ can be expressed by:

$$\frac{\partial E(t)}{\partial v_{ji}(t)} = -\sum_{j'=1}^{m} \left[LG_{j'}(t) \frac{\partial H_{j'}(t)}{\partial v_{ji}(t)} + \sum_{p'=1}^{n_{con}} \sum_{l=1}^{m} LG_l^{p'}(t) \delta_{lj'} \frac{\partial H_{j'}(t-p')}{\partial v_{ji}(t)} \right] \tag{26}$$

and

$$\frac{\partial H_{j'}(t)}{\partial v_{ji}(t)} = f'(\tilde{h}_{j'}(t)) \left[\delta_{j'j} I_i(t) + \sum_{p'=1}^{n_{con}} \sum_{j''=1}^{m} \sum_{l=1}^{m} u_{j'l}^{p'} \delta_{j'j} \frac{\partial H_{j''}(t-p')}{\partial v_{ji}(t)} \right] \tag{27}$$

5 Experimental Results

In order to evaluate our recurrent neural network's performance for handwritten symbol recognition, we trained the network with the new dynamic learning algorithm described in the previous section. The feature extraction result F is encoded in order to serve as input to the network. Each feature $f \in F$ is represented by five attributes: *type* (*Line*, *C-shape* or *O-shape*), *length* (as a fraction of the symbol length), *x-center* and *y-center* (indicating f's position in the symbol), and *orientation*. The latter represents the direction in which f was drawn

Table 1. The recognition rates of all digits from each network configuration

		Hidden neurons				
		20	25	30	35	40
Digit Rec. Rate (%)	0	92.80	95.68	94.10	95.54	96.26
	1	90.93	93.38	93.52	95.10	94.10
	2	88.20	91.94	91.08	96.40	96.12
	3	92.09	95.25	97.98	96.12	96.98
	4	91.80	92.52	93.53	94.53	95.11
	5	89.49	92.66	94.53	90.94	92.23
	6	94.96	93.09	94.82	97.41	97.12
	7	93.24	92.66	94.10	94.10	95.97
	8	88.20	89.93	93.53	94.10	91.08
	9	87.91	93.09	91.08	93.52	93.52
Ave. Rec Rate(%)		90.96	93.02	93.82	94.77	94.85

if f is a *Line*, or the direction in which f is facing if f is a *C-shape*. *O-shapes* have no orientation.

The method was tested on the digits $(0, \cdots, 9)$. So for this application the network is composed of five input neurons and ten output neurons. The attribute values were normalised and each attribute is assigned one input neuron. Similarly, each output neuron is assigned to a target symbol, so that the neuron is fired only if its corresponding target is recognised. Therefore the softmax function was chosen (3) as the activation function for the output layer and formula (17) was selected for the cross-entropy error measure. We noticed that 20 hidden neurons are sufficient to reach an accuracy of 91%, while 40 hidden neurons results in an extra 4% accuracy (see Table 1). However, this usually increases the network overhead during the training phase.

6950 isolated digits taken from section *1a* of the Unipen Train-R01/V07 dataset [13] were used for the training phase, and 6950 isolated digits from the same section were used for the testing phase. The recognition rates achieved by the approach are high, although higher rates have been achieved for Unipen digits [5]. Our recognition rates will be improved upon through a number of actions. Firstly, the feature extraction rules need to be optimised, as most errors were due to an undesirable feature extraction result. Incidentally, it was often the case that the desired feature extraction result was the second or third most likely feature set; therefore, submitting multiple feature extraction results to the network and taking the most likely result should yield improvements. Another measure which could be taken would be to combine the network classification approach with a rule-based classification approach we have developed [3].

6 Conclusions and Future Work

The disadvantage of using only rule-based methods is that it is impossible to design an exhaustive set of rules that model all possible ways of forming every symbol. The statistical and neural network models have their own disadvantages too. For instance, we have already used a fully recurrent network with RTRL on the same application. The network accuracy was very high, but was only reached with a very large computational overhead on small training datasets.

We have used a rule-based approach for feature extraction only, thus avoiding the aforementioned disadvantages of such methods, as fuzzy rules need only be written for a limited number of feature types and properties. The features sets extracted are robust, and capture what is distinctive about each symbol, making classification easier for the network. Also, using these feature sets as input is more efficient than using the raw symbol data. Using the network for classification is a far more extendable approach than using fuzzy classification rules [3].

Recognition of handwritten symbols is a hugely important and challenging problem in computer science, requiring that a variety of approaches be investigated. Here we have presented an innovative new approach to the problem. Although our recognition rates are currently slightly less than the state of the art, making the aforementioned improvements will increase our recognition rates significantly. Furthermore, we will study our system's scalability with regard to the number of symbols to be recognised, and we will continue to explore and implement more networks with different context layers and study their behaviour.

References

1. B.Q. Huang, T. Rashid, and T. Kechadi, "A New Modified Network based on the Elman Network," *The IASTED Int'l. Conf. on Artificial Intelligence and Applications (AIA 2004)*, February 2004.
2. J. Elman, "Finding Structure in Time," *Cognitive Science*, 14(2):179–211, 1990.
3. J.A. Fitzgerald, F. Geiselbrechtinger, and T. Kechadi, "Application of Fuzzy Logic to Online Recognition of Handwritten Symbols", *The Ninth Int'l. Workshop on Frontiers in Handwriting Recognition (IWFHR 9)*, Tokyo, Japan, pp. 395-400, 2004.
4. L. Schomaker and H. Teulings, "A handwriting recognition system based on properties of the human motor system," *The Int'l. Workshop on Frontiers in Handwriting Recognition (IWFHR)*, pp. 195-211, 1990.
5. H. Mitoma, S. Uchida, and H. Sakoe, "Online character recognition using eigendeformations," *The 9th Int'l. Workshop on Frontiers in Handwriting Recognition (IWFHR 9)*, Tokyo, Japan, pp. 3-8, 2004.
6. M. Schenkel, I. Guyon, and D. Henderson, "On-Line Cursive Script Recognition Using Time Delay Neural Networks and Hidden markov Models," *Int'l. Conf. on Acoustics, Speech, and Signal Processing*, Volume 2, pp. 637-640, 1994.
7. R.J. Williams and D. Zipser, "Gradient-based learning algorithms for recurrent networks and their computational complexity," *Backpropagation: theory, architectures, and applications*, pp. 433-486, 1995.
8. N. Gomes and L. Ling, "Feature extraction based on fuzzy set theory for handwriting recognition," *6th Int'l. Conf. on Document Analysis and Recognition*, pp. 655-659, 2001.
9. J. A. Fitzgerald, F. Geiselbrechtinger, and T. Kechadi, "Feature Extraction of Handwritten Symbols Using Fuzzy Logic", *The Seventeenth Canadian Conference on Artificial Intelligence (AI 2004)*, Ontario, Canada, pp. 493-498, 2004.

10. D.Y. Yeung and K.W. Yeung, "A locally recurrent neural network model for grammatical inference," *Int'l. Conf. on Neural Information Processing, pp. 1468-1473*, 1994.
11. J. Hu, M.K. Brown, and W. Turin, "HMM Based On-Line Handwriting Recognition," *IEEE Transactions on Pattern Analysis and Machine Intelligence, Volume 18, Issue 10, pp. 1039-1045*, 1996.
12. O.D. Trier, A.K. Jain, and T. Taxt, "Feature extraction methods for character recognition - A survey," *Pattern Recognition, 29:641-662*, 1996.
13. I. Guyon, L. Schomaker, R. Plamondon, M. Liberman, and S. Janet, "Unipen project of on-line data exchange and recognizer benchmarks," *The 12th Int'l. Conf. on Pattern Recognition, pp. 29-33*, 1994.
14. R. Williams and D. Zipser, "A learning algorithm for continually running fully recurrent neural networks," *Neural Computation, 1(2):270-280*, 1989.
15. W.H. Wilson, "Learning Performance of Networks like Elman's Simple Recurrent Networks but having Multiple State Vectors," *Cognitive Modelling Workshop of the Seventh Australian Conf. on Neural Networks*, 1996.

Environment Compensation Based on Maximum a Posteriori Estimation for Improved Speech Recognition[1]

Haifeng Shen[1], Jun Guo[1], Gang Liu[1], Pingmu Huang[1], and Qunxia Li[2]

[1] Beijing University of Posts and Telecommunications, 100876, Beijing, China
shen_hai_feng@126.com, guojun@bupt.edu.cn, lg@pris.edu.cn,
pmhuang@pris.edu.cn
[2] University of Science and Technology Beijing, 100083, Beijing, China
kellylqx@163.com

Abstract. In this paper, we describe environment compensation approach based on MAP (maximum a posteriori) estimation assuming that the noise can be modeled as a single Gaussian distribution. It employs the prior information of the noise to deal with environmental variabilities. The acoustic-distorted environment model in the cepstral domain is approximated by the truncated first-order vector Taylor series(VTS) expansion and the clean speech is trained by using Self-Organizing Map (SOM) neural network with the assumption that the speech can be well represented as the multivariate diagonal Gaussian mixtures model (GMM). With the reasonable environment model approximation and effective clustering for the clean model, the noise is well refined using batch-EM algorithm under MAP criterion. Experiment with large vocabulary speaker-independent continuous speech recognition shows that this approach achieves considerable improvement on recognition performance.

1 Introduction

The performance of speech recognition will be drop drastically in the adverse acoustical environment due to the environment mismatch between the training and test conditions. The state-of-the-art recognition systems employ various environment compensation algorithms. These algorithms estimate the pseudo-clean speech from the noisy observation using different environment models in different signal domains (e.g. time domain and spectral domain) or the feature domains (e.g. log spectral domain, cepstral domain) and recognize their corresponding final acoustic feature coefficients with an acoustic model pre-trained in a clean condition to realize possible acoustic match. For instance, the spectral subtraction algorithm firstly introduced by Boll [1] compensates the additive noise corruption environment and attempts to obtain the power spectrum of clean speech from the noisy power spectrum by subtracting the noise spectrum. The drawbacks of this approach are that it introduces the musical noise and "over-subtraction" which significantly influence on the recognition per-

---

[1] This research was sponsored by NSFC (National Natural Science Foundation of China) under Grant No.60475007, the Foundation of China Education Ministry for Century Spanning Talent and BUPT Education Foundation.

formance. Cepstral mean normalization (CMN) is a technique used to reduce distortions that are introduced by the transmission channel. Since the cepstrum is the discrete cosine transform (DCT) of the log spectrum, the logarithm turns the multiplication into a summation. The cepstral mean calculated from each utterance is an estimate of the channel. By subtracting the mean cepstral vector, the channel is thus removed from the cepstrum. CMN had applied in most recognition systems with the merits of better recognition performance and low computation load. The model-based approaches play an important role in most recognition systems applied in the real condition and become the most successful technique which attracts many researchers to deeply investigate [2]-[6]. VTS (Vector Taylor Series) [2] [3] and SLA (Statistical Linear Approximation) [4] [5], apply different strategies to approximate the nonlinear environment model, e.g. in the log spectral domain. VTS can be viewed as a particular case of SLA. They make full use of different approximation strategies to approach to the nonlinear environment model in the log spectral domain. Both of them generally use a Gaussian mixture model (GMM) with diagonal covariances pre-trained in the clean conditions for reducing subsequent computation load in noise estimation. Based on the well-trained clean GMM, they iteratively estimate the noise parameters on the whole test sentence using EM algorithm in the framework of ML (maximum likelihood). However, log-filterbank coefficients are highly correlated. Using the GMM with diagonal covariances, the noise estimation in the log domain is not very effective. It is noticeable that the cepstral coefficients are nearly incorrelate which are calculated from the log-filterbank coefficients with discrete cosine transform. Hence, the use of cepstral environment compensation in this case is virtually mandatory if further improve the system performance. In this paper, we investigate the cepstral environment compensation based on MAP criterion. MAP estimation has been studied in recent years [7]-[9] and has been experimentally proven to be effective since the prior information of the noise can be incorporated in the estimation procedure, which is particularly useful to estimate the noise parameters when there is large speech data corrupted by the noise. Assuming that the prior of the noise belongs to a conjugate density, EM algorithm can be applied to the MAP estimation. The prior density parameters can be obtained in the absence of the speech of the test data. Due to the cepstral features are nearly incorrelate, it is more effective to cluster the clean speech in the cepstral domain into Gaussian mixtures model with diagonal covariance matrices. In this paper, the clean model can be trained by using the Self-Organizing Map (SOM) neural network [10]. The whole procedure can be divided into three steps. Firstly, the cepstral environment is modeled as a nonlinear model, and by utilization of the piecewise linear approximation methods, e.g. VTS approximation [2], the environment model can be simplified. Secondly, assuming that the noise is a Gaussian distribution, the noisy speech can be described as a GMM with diagonal covariances obtained by combining the statistical models of the clean speech and the noise according to the above approximated environment model. Lastly, based on the revised EM algorithm under MAP criterion, the noise is well estimated and the compensated cepstral coefficients are sent into the speech recognition system for achieving robust performance. The experiments are conducted on the large vocabulary speaker-independent continuous speech recognition system. The approach described in this paper achieves significant improvement in the system performance.

The rest of the paper is organized as follows. The next section briefly describes the MAP decision rule. In section 3, we train the clean speech with SOM neural network and estimate the noise statistics using MAP estimation in detail based on VTS environment approximation. The experimental results are given in section 4 and some conclusions are drawn in section 5.

2 MAP Decision Rule

Given the observation feature sequence $Y = \{y_1, y_2, \cdots, y_T\}$ and the noise parameter λ in the cepstral domain, the Bayes theorem gives the posterior probability of the noise,

$$p(\lambda | Y) = \frac{P(Y | \lambda) p(\lambda)}{\int_\Omega P(Y | \lambda) p(\lambda) d\lambda}, \tag{1}$$

where Ω denotes an admissible region of the parameter space, $p(\lambda)$ is a known prior of the noise, $P(Y | \lambda)$ is the likelihood of the data Y given the noise parameter λ.

In the denominator of Eq.(1), called the evidence, just is a constant that is independent of the values of the parameter λ and can thus be ignored. Hence the noise parameter λ can be estimated in a posterior distribution obtained by the product of the assumed prior distribution and the conditional likelihood. By maximizing the posterior distribution, noise estimate $\hat{\lambda}_{MAP}$ can be obtained as follows

$$\begin{aligned}\hat{\lambda}_{MAP} &= \arg\max_{\lambda} p(\lambda | Y) = \arg\max_{\lambda} P(Y | \lambda) p(\lambda) \\ &\propto \arg\max_{\lambda} \{\log P(Y | \lambda) + \log p(\lambda)\}.\end{aligned} \tag{2}$$

As can be seen, ML estimation is a special case of MAP estimation. If the prior of the noise is uniform distribution which is constant, as shown in the above Eq.(2), the noise estimation can be interpreted as the equation with maximum likelihood (ML) estimation which can generally be realized by using the expectation-maximization (EM) algorithm. EM algorithm can also be applied for MAP estimation by resorting to the assumed prior of the noise belongs to conjugate probability family [7]-[9]. However, in the MAP estimation, it is very difficult to define the prior distribution of the noise and specify the parameters for the prior.

3 Cepstral Environment Compensation

3.1 VTS Environment Approximation

Due to the noise is additive in the linear spectral domain, the speech corruption in the cepstral domain will be nonlinear. Denote the noisy feature, the clean feature and the noise in the cepstral domain by y, x and n, the nonlinear acoustic-distorted model in the cepstral domain can be represented as

$$y = x + D \cdot \log\{1 + \exp(D^{-1} \cdot (n - x))\} = x + f(x, n), \tag{3}$$

where D^{-1} is the inverse of the discrete cosine transformation matrix D and $f(x,n)$ is a nonlinear function.

Given an independent and identical distributed (i.i.d.) sequence $X = \{x_1, x_2, \cdots, x_T\}$, we assume that each feature vector x can be represented as a mixture of multivariate Gaussian distributions which is written as

$$p(x) = \sum_{j=1}^{M} p_j G(x; \mu_{xj}, \Sigma_{xj}), \quad (4)$$

where M denotes the total number of mixture components, p_j, μ_{xj} and Σ_{xj} denote the mixture gain, the mean vector and the diagonal covariance matrix for the mixture component j, respectively. The Gaussian distribution with mean vector μ and diagonal covariance matrix Σ is represented by $G(\cdot \mid \mu, \Sigma)$.

We further assume that noise n can be well represented as a single Gaussian distribution $G(n; \mu_n, \Sigma_n)$ with mean vector μ_n and diagonal covariance matrix Σ_n and independent from the clean speech x. Unfortunately, the noisy speech is not a Gaussian mixture model (GMM) due to the nonlinear environment characteristics in Eq.(3). In order to effectively estimate the noise parameters from the acoustic-distorted feature sequence $Y = \{y_1, y_2, \cdots, y_T\}$ using EM algorithm, we utilize the truncated first-order VTS expansion to linearize $f(x,n)$ in Eq.(3) around the mean vector μ_{xj} in mixture component j of the clean model and the initial mean vector μ_n^0 of the noise model. This gives the linearized acoustic-distorted model in the mixture component j:

$$y = A_j x + B_j n + C_j, \quad (5)$$

where the coefficients A_j, B_j and C_j are dependent on the mixture component j, which satisfy

$$\begin{cases} A_j = D \cdot \dfrac{1}{1 + \exp\{D^{-1} \cdot (\mu_n^0 - \mu_{xj})\}} \cdot D^{-1} \\ B_j = 1 - A_j \\ C_j = f(\mu_{xj}, \mu_n^0) - (A_j - 1)\mu_{xj} - B_j \mu_n^0 \end{cases} \quad (6)$$

With VTS environment approximation, the distribution of the noisy feature is a GMM where the mean vector and the covariance of each mixture component are obtained as follows

$$\begin{cases} \mu_{yj} = A_j \mu_{xj} + B_j \mu_n + C_j \\ \Sigma_{yj} = A_j \Sigma_{xj} A_j' + B_j \Sigma_n B_j' \end{cases} \quad j = 1, 2, \cdots, M. \quad (7)$$

3.2 Clean GMM Trained with SOM

The clean GMM can be trained by using SOM neural network. In Fig.1, SOM developed by Kohonen is an unsupervised clustering network [10], which has two layers structure: the input layer and the competition layer. Each input neuron i is connected with each output neuron j with the synaptic weight w_{ij}. In Fig.2, for each representative c, we define three neighborhoods $C(k), k = 0,1,2$. Each has a different learning rate η_k. The value η_k will be greater if the neighborhood is closer to the representative c. If output neuron c wins when D dimensional input vector $x(l) = \{x_1(l), \cdots, x_D(l)\}'$ and the weight $w_j(l) = \{w_{1j}(l), \cdots, w_{Dj}(l)\}'$ satisfies [10]

$$\|x(l) - w_c(l)\| = \min \|x(l) - w_j(l)\|, \qquad (8)$$

then update the synaptic weight vector according to

$$w_j(l+1) = \begin{cases} w_j(l) + \eta_k(l)(x(l) - w_j(l)), j \in C(k) \\ w_j(l), j \notin C(k) \end{cases}. \qquad (9)$$

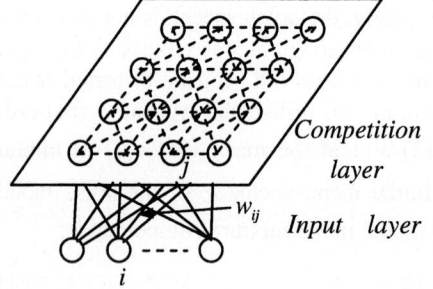

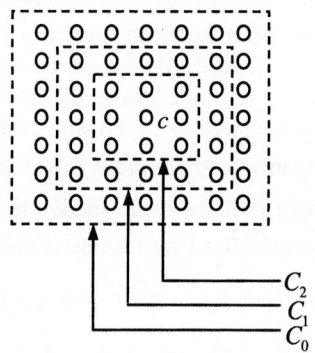

Fig. 1. SOM Network Structure **Fig. 2** Topological Neighborhoods

3.3 Noise Estimation

Based on the noisy GMM and the assumed Gaussian prior distribution, the noise estimate can be obtained using batch-EM algorithm. The batch-EM algorithm is an iterative procedure, estimating the parameter from the whole utterance. The auxiliary function $\theta_{MAP}(\hat{\lambda} \mid \lambda)$ based on MAP can be defined as follows [11]

$$\theta_{MAP}(\hat{\lambda} \mid \lambda) = E\{\log P(Y, J \mid \hat{\lambda}) \mid Y, \lambda\} + \log p(\hat{\lambda}). \qquad (10)$$

where $\hat{\lambda}$ and λ are respectively the new noise estimate and the old noise estimate.

For simplicity, in this paper, we only estimate the noise mean vector using EM algorithm which corresponds to $\lambda = \{\mu_n\}$ in Eq.(10). The diagonal covariance matrix Σ_n of the noise can be directly estimated from the incoming nonspeech frames. It is expected that we assume the prior of the noise mean vector is a diagonal Gaussian distribution $G(\mu_n; m_n, \Gamma_n)$ where m_n and Γ_n respectively are the mean vector and the diagonal covariance matrix. Eq.(10) can be rewritten as:

$$\theta_{MAP}(\hat{\lambda}\mid\lambda) = \sum_{t=1}^{T}\sum_{j=1}^{M} p(j_t = j\mid y_t,\lambda)\log\{G(y;\hat{\mu}_{yj},\Sigma_{yj})\} + \log\{G(\hat{\mu}_n;m_n,\Gamma_n)\}, \quad (11)$$

where T is the number of frames in current utterance, $J = \{j_1, j_2, \cdots, j_T\}$ is the mixture gain sequence, $\hat{\mu}_n$ is the new mean estimate corresponding to the old estimate μ_n, the noisy mean vetor $\hat{\mu}_{yj}$ is the function of $\hat{\mu}_n$ described in Eq.(7), $p(j_t = j\mid y_t,\lambda)$ is a posterior probability which can be written as

$$p(j_t = j\mid y_t,\lambda) = \frac{p_j G(y_t;\mu_{yj},\Sigma_{yj})}{\sum_{j=1}^{M} p_j G(y_t;\mu_{yj},\Sigma_{yj})}. \quad (12)$$

Taking derivative of the auxiliary function with respect to $\hat{\lambda} = \{\hat{\mu}_n\}$, the noise mean estimate can be obtained according to

$$\hat{\mu}_n = \frac{\sum_{t=1}^{T}\sum_{j=1}^{M} p(j_t = j\mid y_t,\lambda) B_j' \Sigma_{yj}^{-1}(y_t - A_j\mu_{xj} - C_j) + \Gamma_n^{-1} m_n}{\sum_{t=1}^{T}\sum_{j=1}^{M} p(j_t = j\mid y_t,\lambda) B_j' \Sigma_{yj}^{-1} B_j + \Gamma_n^{-1}}. \quad (13)$$

Eq.(13) is a noise estimation equation based on MAP estimation by taking into account the prior of the noise. With EM algorithm, this estimation procedure can do several iterations until the auxiliary function reaches convergence. Due to the ML estimation is a special case of MAP estimation, hence the noise estimate based on ML estimation can be expressed as a formulation which only omit second items both in the denominator and the numerator of the above Eq.(13).

4 Experiments

We use the large vocabulary continuous speaker-independent speech recognition system to evaluate the described approach. And we use 61 sub-syllable units as the monophone units and apply the simple left-to-right structure to obtain the well-trained monophone HMMs. Then the system builds the context-dependent triphone HMMs by connecting the corresponding sub-syllable HMMs. After tying and re-estimation with several steps, the trained models with three emitting states, 16 mixtures per state are achieved. To obtain the acoustic features, 12 MFCCs (Mel-scaled frequency cepstral coefficients) and one log-energy, along with their time derivatives are used, thus creating 39 dimensional feature vector. Then further applying CMN approach and log-energy normalization for removing the distortion in the static feature vector which is introduced by the transmission channel (e.g. microphone), these static coefficients with the preceding computed dynamic coefficients are used for training the acoustic model. The training data includes the 42690 utterances of 82 speakers (41 males and 41 females) taken from the mandarin Chinese corpus which is provided by the 863 plan (China High-Tech Development Plan) [12]. The clean 900 utterances of 9 speakers in the corpus are used for artificially contamination. The white and babble noise from NoiseX92 [13] are added to the clean test set according to different SNR from 0dB to 20dB. Then following the aforementioned approach, the static cepstral coefficients are compensated. The log-energy feature is compensated by using improved SS (Spectral Subtraction) approach which can overcome the music noise and "over-subtraction". Then all of the compensated feature vector plus their corresponding dynamic feature vector are obtained. After the static coefficients are further compensated with CMN and log-energy normalization, the feature vector is sent into the system for recognition. In this paper, we only estimate the mean vector of the noise. Assuming that the prior of the noise is assumed to be a diagonal Gaussian density, the moment method can be used to estimate the prior parameters of the noise in the absence of speech from the test data. In addition, the clean speech in the training set is trained in the cepstral domain to obtain 128 mixture Gaussian components using SOM neural network with 24 input neural nodes.

In order to effectively evaluate the described approach, we conduct a number of experiments with different approaches, such as the baseline without any compensation (using 12 MFCCs plus one log-energy feature and their corresponding delta and acceleration coefficients during the acoustic model training and recognition procedures), the CMN approach, the ML-based log environment compensation approach, the ML-based cepstral environment compensation approach and the approach described in this paper, that is, the MAP-based cepstral environment compensation approach. These approaches are respectively titled as "baseline", "CMN", "VTS+log+ML", "VTS+cep+ML" and "VTS+cep+MAP" in Table 1 and Table 2.

Firstly, we test this approach in the stationary white noisy environments. From Table 1, the speech recognition performance degrades drastically from 85.61% recognition rate in the clean condition to 0.32% in the 0dB condition. With the traditional CMN approach, the system improvement is averagely achieved with about 7% recognition rate, than that of "baseline". It demonstrates that CMN is very important approach to reduce the mismatch between the acoustic models and the test data. It can reduce the distortion introduced by the microphone used for recording the utterances. In "VTS+log+ML", the clean GMM model is trained in the log domain using the SOM neural network with 25 input neuron nodes, respectively representing 25 dimensional feature vector (24 log-filterbank coefficients and one log-energy feature). After ignoring off-diagonal elements in the covariance matrices of the clean model, they are jointly compensated using batch-EM algorithm under ML criterion [5]. It can be seen that environment compensation in the log domain is not better that those in the cepstral domain. There exists averagely about 7% recognition rate gap under ML criterion. Those results are easily explained. The noise parameter will be effectively estimated in the cepstral domain because the noisy speech can be effectively modeled the diagonal GMM after employing VTS approximation. We can further improve the system performance by using MAP criterion. In Table 1, the MAP noise estimation embedded in the cepstral environment compensation shows the effectiveness of its algorithm in all the white noisy conditions besides the clean condition.

Table 1. Recognition rates (%) for the white noise

SNR	0dB	5dB	10dB	15dB	20dB	clean	avg.
baseline	0.32	2.54	11.14	30.00	56.04	85.61	30.94
CMN	3.31	10.98	29.99	36.94	61.65	86.61	38.26
VTS+log+ML	5.18	16.16	36.16	61.24	71.63	84.14	45.75
VTS+cep+ML	9.05	24.42	47.37	68.33	79.60	86.64	52.57
VTS+cep+MAP	10.27	24.59	48.33	69.23	80.00	86.88	53.22

We also test this approach in the nonstationary babble noisy environments. The babble noise is one of the most representative noises, which is produced in the noisy room where there are a lot of people to chat. It is observed From Table 2 that with the described approach, the system also obtains further improvements at most noisy conditions compared with those compensated by "VTS+cep+ML". The system under the distortion environment only achieves 52.02% recognition rate without any compensation technique. The described approach, "VTS+cep+MAP" predominately achieves the best performance, averagely with 60.16% recognition rate, averagely outperforms "VTS+cep+ML" with 0.51% recognition improvement.

Table 2. Recognition rates (%) for the babble noise

SNR	0dB	5dB	10dB	15dB	20dB	clean	avg.
baseline	3.87	24.61	54.84	62.98	80.23	85.61	52.02
CMN	11.16	32.38	55.95	71.04	80.31	86.61	56.24
VTS+log+ML	15.77	37.19	60.77	74.73	81.07	84.14	58.95
VTS+cep+ML	15.80	35.38	60.29	76.57	83.22	86.64	59.65
VTS+cep+MAP	15.80	36.79	61.44	77.26	82.80	86.88	60.16

5 Conclusions

In this paper, we describe an environment compensation approach in the cepstral domain based on MAP estimation. The environment model in the cepstral domain is linearized by the truncated first-order vector series Taylor expansion. Batch-EM algorithm can be applied to MAP estimation assuming the prior of the noise is a conjugate density. The Gaussian mixtures model of the clean speech is achieved by using SOM neural network. Due to the cepstral features are nearly independence, experiment simulation demonstrates that this approach achieves significant improvement.

References

1. Boll, S. F.: Suppression of Acoustic Noise in Speech Using Spectral Subtraction. IEEE Trans. Acoustics, Speech and Signal Processing, (1979)113-120
2. Moreno, P.J., Raj, B., Stern, R.M.: A Vector Taylor Series Approach for Environment-Independent Speech Recognition. In the Proceedings of IEEE (1995)733-736

3. Kim, N.S., Kim, D.Y., Kong, B. G., Kim. S. R.: Application of VTS to Environment Compensation with Noise Statistics. In: ESCA workshop on Robust Speech Recognition, Pont-a-Mousson, France (1997) 99-102
4. Kim, N.S.: Statistical Linear Approximation for Environment Compensation. IEEE Signal Processing Letters, 1(1998)8-10
5. Shen, H., Liu, G., Guo, J., Li, Q.: Two-Domain Feature Compensation for Robust Speech Recognition. In: Wang, J., Liao, X., and Yi, Z. (eds.): Advance in Neural Network- ISNN 2005. Lecture Notes in Computer Science 3497, Springer-Verlag, Berlin Heidelberg New York(2005)351–356
6. Shen H., Guo, J., Liu, G., Li, Q.: Non-Stationary Environment Compensation Using Sequential EM Algorithm for Robust Speech Recognition. In: the 9th European Conference on Principles and Practice of Knowledge Discovery in Databases (PKDD 2005), Lecture Notes in Artificial Intelligence 3721, Springer-Verlag, Berlin Heidelberg New York(2005)264-273
7. Gauvain, J.L., Lee, C.H.: Maximum A Posteriori Estimation for Multivariate Gaussian Mixture Observation of Markov Chains. IEEE Transactions on Speech and Audio Processing, 2 (1994) 291-298
8. Huo, Q., Lee, C.H.: On-Line Adaptive Learning of the Continuous Density Hidden Markov Model Based on Approximate Recursive Bayes Estimate. IEEE Transactions on Speech and Audio Processing, 2(1997)161-172
9. Huo, Q., Chan, C., Lee, C.H.: Bayesian Adaptive Learning of the Parameters of Hidden Markov Model for Speech Recognition. IEEE Transactions on Speech and Audio Processing, 5(1995)334-345
10. Kohonen, T.: The self-Organizing Map. In: the Proceedings of the IEEE, Vol.78, (1990)1464-1480
11. Dempster, A.P., Laird, N. M., Rubin, D.B.: Maximum likelihood from incomplete data via the EM algorithm. Journal of the Royal Statistical Society B, (1977)1-38
12. Zu, Y. Q.: Issues in the Scientific Design of the Continuous Speech Database. Available: http://www.cass.net.cn/chinese/s18_yys/yuyin/report/report_1998.htm.
13. Varga, A., Steenneken, H. J. M., Tomilson, M., Jones, D.: The NOISEX–92 Study on the Effect of Additive Noise on Automatic Speech Recognition. Tech. Rep. DRA Speech Research Unit(1992)

ASR Based on the Analasys of the Short-MelFrequencyCepstra Time Transform

Juan Arturo Nolazco-Flores

Computer Science Department, ITESM, Campus Monterrey,
Av. Eugenio Garza Sada 2501 Sur, Col. Tecnológico,
Monterrey, N.L., México, C.P. 64849
jnolazco@itesm.mx

Abstract. In this work, we propose to use as source of speech information the Short-MelfrequencyCepstra Time Transform (SMCTT), $c_\tau(t)$. The SMCTT studies the time properties at quefrency τ. Since the SMCTT signal, $c_\tau(t)$, comes from a nonlinear transformation of the speech signal, $s(t)$, it makes the STMCTT a potential signal with new properties in time, frequency, quefrency, etc. The goal of this work is to present the performance of the SMCTT signal when the SMCTT is applied to an Automatic Speech Recognition (ASR) task. Our experiment results show that important information is given by this SMCTT waveform, $c_\tau(t)$.

1 Introduction

In a pattern classification system, a signal is preprocessed to emphasise signal features, reduce noise, etc.; the next step, in order to reduce the data, the feature extraction step is performed; finally, the features are then passed through a classifier that makes a decision. In the speech recognition problem, we usually use the acoustic speech time signal obtained from the sound pressure in the lips, although visual speech information such as lip movement, can also be used; if acoustic speech is used, in the preprocessing step, we preemphasise acoustic speech to convert speech sound pressure, $s(t)$, to velocity of the volume air of the speech [11], enhance the spectrum to remove additive noise, etc.; in the features extraction step, either the MFCC [1], lp-cepstra, plp [2, 3] coefficients are calculated; and in the classification step, hmm based systems are generally used.

In this work, we propose to obtain the features from the Short-MelFrequency-Cepstra Time Transform (SMCTT), $c_\tau(t)$, instead of calculating them from the sound pressure in the lips, $s(t)$. The aim of this work is to explore how well the SMCTT performance in an ASR task.

In the future, we would also like to analyse the SMCTT signal performances in noisy enviroments. In addition, it can also be usefull to know how well it discriminates different categories; moreover, we also would like to know if the information obtained with the SMCTT signal can be combined with the features obtained from the lips' sound pressure signal. In the same way that video speech is combined with audio signal to improve ASR, specially in noisy environments [16] [15] [12]. This improvement is achieved because it can be shown that acoustic and visual information can interact to improve the perception of speech in noise [13, 14].

This paper is organized as follows. In section 2, we review some time-frequency concepts and definitions. In section 3, we define the Short-MelFrequencyCepstrum Time Transform (SMCTT). In section 4, the speech signal pre-processing is described. The system architecture description is defined. In section 5, the experiments environment as well as the results are given. Finally in section 6, the comments and conlus ions are given.

2 Time-Frequency Speech Analysis

When we speak, we are continuously changing the physical shape of our speech production system (tongue, mouth, lips, etc). It happens that the values of each of the frequencies of the speech at least depend on the shape and the position of each of the elements of the system. Therefore, since features of the speech change with time, we then need a joint time-frequency representation of the speech. A combined time-frequency analysis tell us the contribution of the frequencies in a particular time, t.

Short-time Fourier transform has been the time-frequency representation used for speech analysis since the 1940s [5]. Actually, it is the most widely method for studying nonstationary signals[1]. The short-time Fourier Transform breaks up the signal into small time segments and calculate the Fourier transform for each of the time segments and it is defined as follows

$$S_t(\omega) = \tfrac{1}{\sqrt{2\pi}} \int e^{-j\omega\tau} s_t(\tau)\, d\tau$$

$$S_t(\omega) = \tfrac{1}{\sqrt{2\pi}} \int e^{-j\omega\tau} s(\tau) h(\tau - t)\, d\tau$$

where $s(t)$ is the acoustic speech time signal, $h(t)$ is the time window. Time segments are usually called frames. The frames can overlap adjacent frames, depending on both frames length and frame ratio. For the speech signal obtained from the lips' sound pressure, the frame length is usually 25ms and the frames ratio is 100ms.

The Short-Time Fourier transform (STFT), $S_t(\omega)$, studies the frequency properties at time t. On the other hand, the Short-Frequency Time Transform (SFTT), $s_\omega(t)$, studies the time properties at frequency f. The SFTT is defined as [5]:

$$s_\omega(t) = \tfrac{1}{\sqrt{2/pi}} \int e^{-j\omega' t} S_\omega(\omega')\, d\omega'$$

$$s_\omega(t) = \tfrac{1}{\sqrt{2/pi}} \int e^{-j\omega' t} S(\omega') H(\omega - \omega')\, d\omega'$$

---

[1] other methods have also been proposed, for example the Cohen, Wigner, Margenau-Hill, Kirkwood, Choi-Williams, etc. [5, 7, 8, 9]

It can be shown that spectrogram can be used to study the behavior of time properties at a particular frequency, ω [5].

3 Short-MelfrequencyCepstrum Time Transform (SMCTT)

Based on the definitions of the cepstral coefficients [11] and the SFTT, we will define the Short-Cepstrum Time Transform (SCTT) as follows:

$$c(t,\tau) = \frac{1}{2\pi} \int_{w=0}^{2\pi} \log |S(t,\omega)| e^{j\omega n} d\omega$$

where $|S(t,\omega)|$ is the magnitude spectrum of the speech signal. In the same way that SFTT study the time properties at frequency ω, the SCTT study the time properties at quefrency τ.

In the same way we defined the SCTT, now based on the definitions of the MFCC [1] and the SFTT we will define the Short-MelfrequencyCepstrum Time Transform (SMCTT) as follows:

$$c_n(t) = \sum_{k=1}^{20} S_k(t) \cos\left(n\left(k - \tfrac{1}{2}\right)\tfrac{\pi}{20}\right)$$

where $S_k(t) = ln(fbank_k)$ for $k = 0, 1, 2, ...20$, $fbank_k$, is the ouput of the mel filter k, mel filter is the weighted sum of the FFT magnitude spectrum values in each band of the filter. Each mel filter in the filterbank is a Triangular, half-overlapped window. In the same way that SFTT study the time properties at frequency ω, the SMCTT study the time properties at melcepstra n.

4 Digital Speech Signal Processing

Figure 1 shows the calculation needed to obtain a speech database with signal $c_t(n)$. An example of the $c_n(t)$ for different values of n is shown in Fig. 2. The

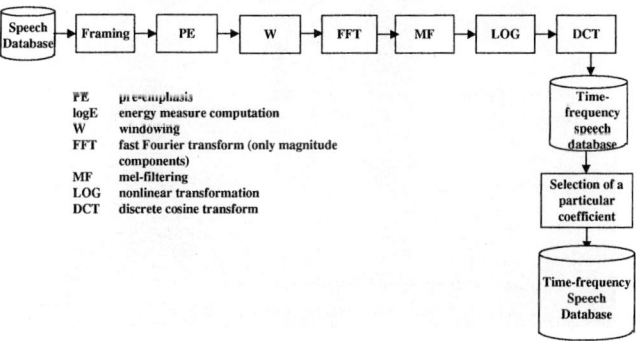

Fig. 1. Signal Speech Processing

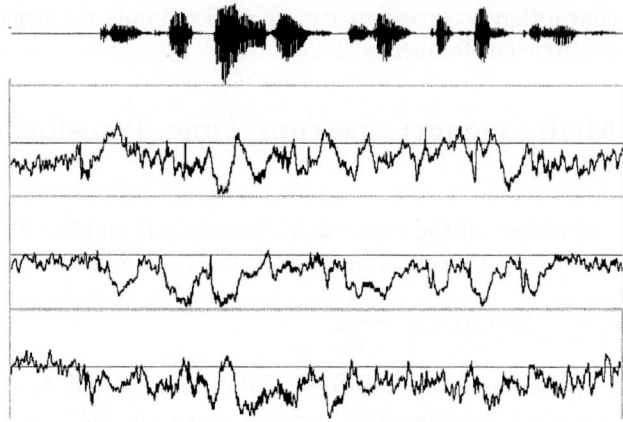

Fig. 2. $s(t)$, $c_3(t)$, $c_4(t)$ and $c_5(t)$

selection of the quefrency can be based on the noise features, for example if a melcepstral coefficient is less corrupted in a noisy environment. The $c_n(t)$ signal is the one that will be used to calculate the MFCC for the ASR system.

5 System Architecture Description

Since we are planning to explore how well the SMCTT performs in a ASR tasks, this section explains teh Architecture we used. The CMU SPHINX-III systems

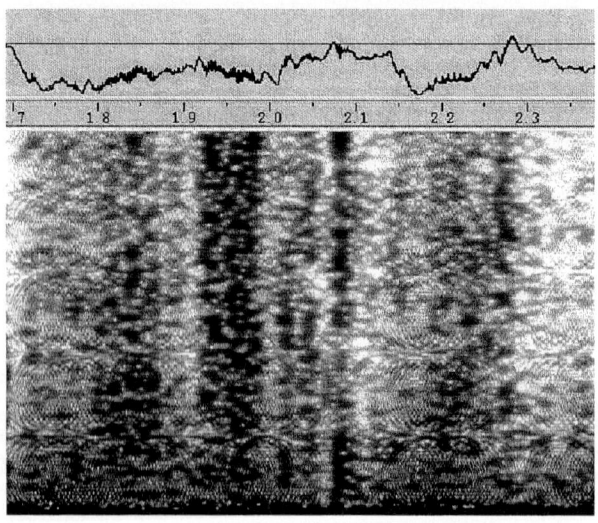

Fig. 3. $c_5(t)$ spectrogram, $c_5(\Omega)$

[10] is a HMM-based speech recognition system able to handle a large vocabulary. The architecture of this system is shown in Fig. 4. As can be observed in this figure the MFCC of $c_n(t)$ are calculated, then the MFCC's first and second derivaties are concatenated [11], i.e. if the number of MFCC is 13 then the total dimension of the feature vector would be 39.

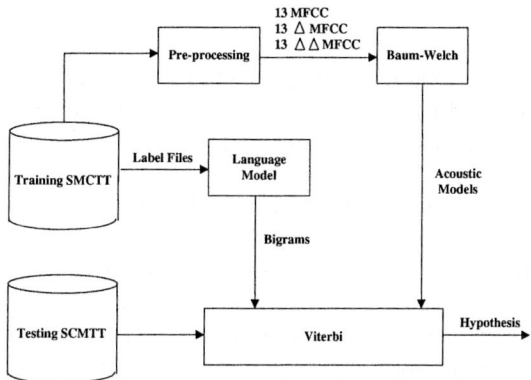

Fig. 4. CMU SPHINX-III ASR architecture

The acoustic models are also obtained using the SPHINX-III tools. These tools use a Baum-and-Welch algorithm to train this acoustic models[?]. The Baum-and-Welch algorithm needs the name of the word units to train as well as the label and feature vectors. The SPHINX-III system allows us to model either discrete, semicontinuous or continuos acoustic models. Furthermore, it allows the selection of acoustic models: either a phone set, a trigram set or a word set.

6 Experiments

In this section the configuration of the SPHINX-III system is described. Thirteen mel-frequency cepstral coefficients (MFCC) were used. First and Second deritatives were calculated, therefore each feature vector is formed by 39 elements. The speech lower frequency was 300 Hz and the speech higher frequency was 3,500 Hz. The frame rate was set to 100 ms and a 30 ms Hamming window was employed. A 512 samples FFT length was used and the number of filterbans was set to 31. Five states continuous HMM was used as acoustic modeling technique and bigrams were used as a language modeling technique. The language models are obtained using the CMU-Cambridge statistical language model toolkit version 2.0. As a discount model Good Turing was used.

Using an acoustical model and a language model a Viterbi decoder obtain the best hypothesised text. Table 1 shows the results. As expected the Witten-Bell discount strategy was the one with better results.

Table 1. WER results over several gaussian distributions and language model configurations

Coefficient	Accuracy
C3	67.699%
c4	65%
c5	67.324%

7 Conclusions

In this work, we defined Short-MelfrequencyCepstra Time Transform (SMCTT), $c_\tau(t)$, and we described the experimental results obtained when the SMCTT is used in an ASR task. The results show the important information is in this signal.

As next step is to demonstrate how well this signal complements the information of the time signal of the presion flow. A future step in this research is to analyse the robustness of this signal in presence of noisy environments.

As in the AVSR systems, we expect that by combining the information obtained by SMCTT signal with the information of the signal based on the lips' sound pressure, we will obtain better performance in a ASR task.

Since the SMCTT generates a signal with unique features, then more studies need to be developed to properly process this signal.

We are also planning to define and develop experiments with the Short-Frequency Time Transform (SFTT), the short-lpc time transform (SLPCTT), the short-ReflectionCoefficients time transform (SRCTT), the short-PLP Time Transform (SPLPTT), etc.

Acknowledgements

The authors also would like to acknowledge CONACyT, project CONACyT-2002-C01-41372, who partially supported this work.

References

1. S. Davis & P. Mermelstain, Comparasion of parametric representations for monosyllabic word recognition in continuously spoken sentences IEEE Trans. ASSP, ASSP-28, 357-366, 1980
2. Hermansky, H., Hanson, B., and Wakita, H. Perceptually based linear predictive analysis of speech,Acoustics, Speech, and Signal Processing, IEEE International Conference on ICASSP '85. Volume 10, Apr 1985 Page(s): 509-512.
3. Hermansky, H. "Perceptual Linear Predictive (PLP) Analysis for Speech," Journal of Acoustic Society of America, 1990, pp: 1738-1752
4. Zbancioc, M., Costin, M., Using neural networks and LPCC to improve speech recognition, Signals, Circuits and Systems, 2003. SCS 2003. International Symposium on Volume 2, 10-11 July 2003 Page(s):445
5. Cohen, L., Time-Frequency analysis, Prentice Hall, 1995

6. Tahir, S.M. and Sha 'ameri, A.Z., A comparison between speech signal representation using linear prediction and Gabor transform, Communications, 2003. APCC 2003. The 9th Asia-Pacific Conference on Volume 2, 21-24 Sept. 2003 Page(s):859-862
7. W. Martin, & P. Flandrin, Winger-ville Spectral Anaysis of Nonstationary Process, IEEE Proc. ASSP, Vol. ASSP-33, No. 6, Dec., 1985.
8. L.M. Kadra, The smoothed pseduo Wigner Distribution in Speech Processing, Int. J. Electronics, Vol. 65, No. 4, 1988, pp. 743-755.
9. Graudari, Speech Signal Analysis using the Wigner distribution, IEEE Pacific Rim Conference on Communications, Computers and Signal Processing, Conference Proceeding., Volume 1, 13-16 Oct. 1996 Page(s):497-501, 1989.
10. A. V. Oppenheim & R.W. Schafer, Digital Signal Processing, Prentice Hall, 1975. sphinxLee, K., Large Vocabulary Speaker-Independent Continuous Speech Recognition: The SPHINX System. .PhD thesis, Computer Science Department, Carnegie Mellon University, April 1988.
11. Deller, J.R., Proakis, J.G., Hansen, J.H.L., Discrete-Time Processing of Speech Signals, Comparasion of parametric representations for Prentice Hall, Sec. 6.2, 1993.
12. Chu, S.M.; Libal, V.; Marcheret, E.; Neti, C. Multistage information fusion for audio-visual speech recognition Multimedia and Expo, 2004. ICME '04. 2004 IEEE International Conference on Volume 3, 27-30 June 2004 Page(s):1651 - 1654 Vol.3
13. Rao, R.A.; Mersereau, R.M.; Lip modeling for visual speech recognition Signals, Systems and Computers, 1994. 1994 Conference Record of the Twenty-Eighth Asilomar Conference on Volume 1, 31 Oct.-2 Nov. 1994 Page(s):587 - 590 vol.1
14. Kaynak, M.N.; Qi Zhi; Cheok, A.D., Sengupta, K.; Zhang Jian; Ko Chi Chung; Analysis of lip geometric features for audio-visual speech recognition, Systems, Man and Cybernetics, Part A, IEEE Transactions on Volume 34, Issue 4, July 2004 Page(s):564 - 570.
15. Yuhas, B.P.; Goldstein, M.H., Jr.; Sejnowski, T.J.; Integration of acoustic and visual speech signals using neural networks, IEEE Communications Magazine, Volume 27, Issue 11, Nov. 1989 Page(s):65 - 71
16. Say Wei Foo; Yong Lian; Liang Dong; Recognition of visual speech elements using adaptively boosted hidden Markov models, Circuits and Systems for Video Technology, IEEE Transactions on Volume 14, Issue 5, May 2004 Page(s):693 - 705

Building and Training of a New Mexican Spanish Voice for Festival

Humberto Pérez Espinosa and Carlos Alberto Reyes García

Instituto Nacional de Astrofísica Óptica y Electrónica
Luis Enrique Erro No. 1, Tonantzintla, Puebla, México

Abstract. In this paper we describe the work done to build a new voice based on diphone concatenation in the Spanish spoken in Mexico. This voice is compatible with the Text to Speech Synthesis System Festival. In the development of each module of the system the own features of Spanish were taken into account. In this work we hope to enhance the naturalness of the synthesized voice by including a prosodic model. The prosodic factors taken into consideration by the model are: phrasing, accentuation, duration and F0 contour. Duration and F0 prediction models were trained from natural speech corpora. We found the best prediction models by testing several machine learning methods and two different corpora. The paper describes the building, and training process as well as the results and their respective interpretation.

1 Text to Speech Synthesis Systems

A Text to Speech (TTS) Synthesis System is a computer based system that must be able to read any text aloud [1]. There are two main goals in a text to speech system. The first one is to produce a natural sounding voice, which must sound as similar as possible to human voice. The second one is to provide the synthesized voice with a suitable intonation, to allow the listener to understand the meaning of what is being spoken. If these two goals are not accomplished, the result is a robotic and monotone voice. Such a kind of voice causes that applications of these systems are not so well accepted by users. They even generate certain discomfort or distrust in people who interact with these systems, since listening a robotized voice is not as comfortable as listening to a human voice.

Even though TTS systems can use several synthesis approaches they share a common architecture that can be divided in two large modules which are, the natural language processing module and the signal processing module. In Figure 1 are shown these two modules. The natural language processing module produces a phonetic transcription of the input text, along with the desired intonation and rhythm (prosody). The digital signal processing module transforms the received symbolic information into speech.

2 Festival

Festival is a TTS Synthesis System that offers a general framework to build TTS systems in any language. Several voices in different languages are already

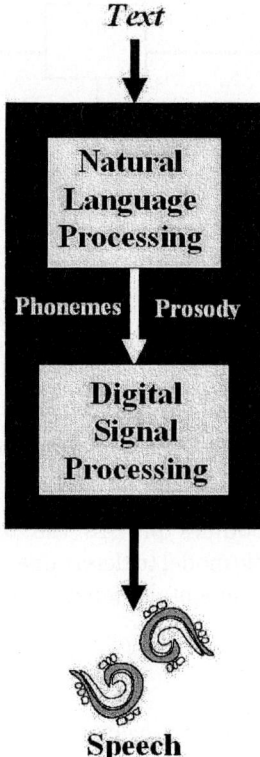

Fig. 1. Text to Speech System General Architecture

built and available to serve as reference to build new ones. In addition, it is offered the set of tools FestVox which helps in building and training new voices [2]. The philosophy of Festival is that it should not be necessary to build a whole TTS system to test an implementation of some of the modules of a TTS system. Festival offers all the needed tools to make TTS conversion in a flexible environment allowing to modify the existing modules and to add new ones. This makes Festival an excellent tool to test new models for language processing, prosody modelling and signal synthesis in any language.

Festival system is made up of the following elements [3]:

- System Control: The language for the writing of scripts is Scheme. The Festival control system includes modules in C/C++ to interface with the modules in Scheme. Object oriented representation of utterances, audio input - output, and access to audio devices are also included.
- Data Structures: They allow accessing to each one of the useful data in each stage of TTS conversion process, and also allow to model different aspects of speech (see Figure 2). The main data structure in Festival is the utterance. The utterance consists of a set of items, where each of them has one or more relations and a set of features [4].

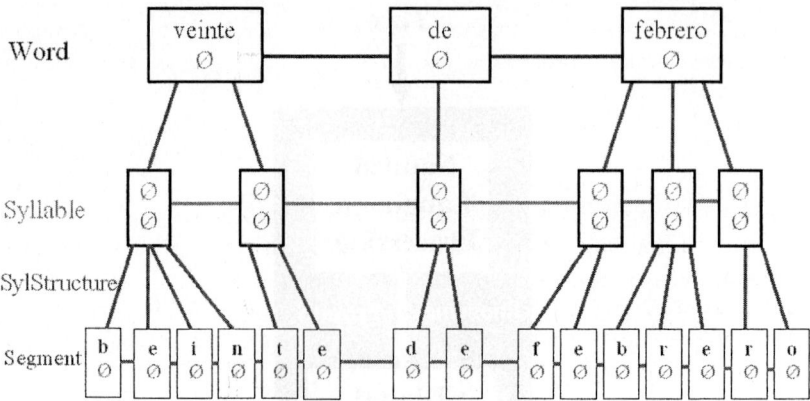

Fig. 2. Utterances structure

- TTS Modules: These modules process the text before translating it to phonemes, apply a prosodic model to determine pauses between phrases, durations of phonemes and fundamental frequency. And finally, generate the signal.

3 Voice Building

The built voice is based on diphone concatenation. A diphone is the central part of the union of two phonemes. A diphone begins in the middle of the first phone and finishes in the middle of the second phone. Diphone synthesis tries to solve the problem of coarticulation making the assumption that this kind of effects never goes beyond two phones. In order to build a diphone database a list with all the possible combinations phoneme - phoneme is needed. Next, only the diphones used in the studied language are selected.

The new voice building process included the following stages [5]:

- Corpus Recording: In order to record the diphone corpus, a list of nonsense words is created. Each one of these nonsense words includes a diphone. The list of diphones and words used in this work were taken from [6].

Table 1. Nonsense Word Examples

Nonsense Word	Diphone
ataata	a - a
ataeta	a - e
ataita	a - i

The corpus of 613 nonsense words was recorded in a professional studio and was read by a Mexican native professional radio presenter. It was recorded

at a 44.1 KHz sampling frequency and using 16 bits of representation. The output was mono channel.
- Corpus Segmentation: The result of the recording process was a file in wav format. This file was split in 613 files, each one containing a nonsense word.
- Nonsense words labelling: This labelling is at phoneme level and consists of specifying the end of each of the phonemes in the word. Festival offers a script to do the labelling automatically, however, it is not perfect and it must be corrected manually. A Index file that identifies what diphone corresponds to what file is then created.
- Text processor: Rules to handle punctuation, abbreviations, reading of numbers, spelling, etc. were included. In addition, a lexicon was included. In this lexicon the pronunciation of words that contain phonemes which are exceptions of the text to phoneme rules is specified. The algorithms for Spanish syllabification and accentuation proposed in [6] was implemented.

4 Building of a Prosodic Model

To build a prosodic model we need 4 modules [7]:

- Phrasing: It is the grouping of words in a spoken phrase dividing it in one or more prosodic groups [8]. Phrasing in voice synthesis makes the speech more understandable. To build a trained phrasing model it is recommended to use a corpus with 37,000 words. Since the size of our corpora is not enough (less than 2000 words) to train a phrasing model, we use a heuristic model, based on punctuation detection, counting of words before and after punctuation and word classification.
- Accents: In this module it is predicted what will be the accent shape of an accented syllable. For training an accent model the size of our corpora could be enough. The problem here is that the corpus must be labelled with several kind of accents, which is a very laborious task. In this work we choose to implement a tree which only differentiate between accented and not accented syllables.
- F0: After predicting accents location and their shape a pitch contour is built based on those predictions. Pitch contour, or F0 contour, is defined as the temporary variation in fundamental frequency [9]. We built a trained model for F0 prediction. This model is described in next section.
- Duration: Here the durations of phonemes and syllables in words are predicted. The experiments made to built a trained duration model are described in next section.

5 Experiments

In this work, in addition to describing the voice building process for Festival, the training and building of two of the modules of the prosodic model is also presented. These modules predicts phoneme duration and f0 contour. The experiments made using two speech corpora and several learning machine methods. The building of this two modules are described and discussed in this section.

5.1 Description of Corpora

The experiments were made using two different corpora of Mexican Spanish speech recordings. The first corpus is called Fraga and was recorded in 1998 by TLATOA UDLA laboratory in collaboration with the CSLU (for Center Spoken Language Understanding). This corpus consists of 824 recorded utterances sampled at 16 KHz. Only 110 recording were used from this corpus. The second corpus is the Corpus DIMEx100 sampled at 44.1 KHz. This corpus is described in [10]. We use 60 recordings from this corpus. For prediction we used WEKA [11] that include several prediction methods, and the tool for data manipulation WAGON which is supported by Festival and predict using CART trees.

5.2 Machine Learning Methods

Since the predicted attributes in the case of durations and F0 are continuous, the learning algorithms must support numerical prediction. After testing several prediction methods we selected those that gave better results, which are: CART Tree (Classification and Regression Tree), Linear Regression, M5P (based on linear regression) and REPTree (Fast Decision tree learner). The performance measures used in the experiments and shown in results Tables are: RMSE Root Mean Squared Error, MAE Mean Absolute Error and CORR Correlation Coefficient. The best result is the one who has higher Correlation Coefficient, lower Mean Absolute Error, and lower Root Mean Squared Error.

6 Results

6.1 Results for Duration Prediction

For the phonemes duration prediction experiments we extracted from utterances the features suggested in [5] which are at segment level and include features such as phoneme name, its preceding phoneme name and its successive phoneme name, among other 91 features. Festival supports two ways of phoneme duration modelling. One way is Zscores, that is the number of standard deviations from the mean. We made experiments predicting Zscores and also experiments predicting phoneme duration directly. In Table 2 we can see some statistics of both corpora used in duration modelling.

These instances were used to train and test the duration prediction models. Each instance corresponds to the appearance of a phoneme in the corpus. In Table 3 we can see the results for Zscores prediction. The best model for Zscores prediction was obtained using the Fraga corpus trained with the CART Tree method. In the case of corpus DIMEx100 a significant difference between MAE and RMSE can be appreciated which indicates that in corpus DIMEx100 there are instances whose prediction errors are significantly greater than the mean prediction error of the instance set. The reason of this could be that the corpus DIMEx100 was labelled automatically for these experiments and the manual correction could not be meticulous enough. Better results were obtained using

Table 2. Corpora Statistics

Statistic	DIMEx100 Zscores	DIMEx100 Duration	Fraga Zscores	Fraga Duration
Instances	2567	2567	9887	9887
Atributes	92	92	92	92
Maximum	5.452	0.205	5.433	0.220
Minimum	-4.644	0.001	-2.85	0.01
Std. Dev.	0.996	0.026	0.998	0.028
Mean	0	0.061	0	0.063

corpus Fraga since with all the prediction methods a greater correlation between real and predicted values were obtained.

Table 3. Zscores Prediction

Method	DIMEx100 RMSE	DIMEx100 MAE	DIMEx100 CORR	Fraga RMSE	Fraga MAE	Fraga CORR
CartTree	0.914	0.546	0.264	0.799	0.515	0.550
Linear Regresion	0.952	0.747	0.313	0.921	0.723	0.386
M5'	0.948	0.745	0.319	0.854	0.652	0.533
REPTree	0.987	0.762	0.289	0.888	0.666	0.493

In phoneme duration prediction, just as in Zscroes prediction, the best model for phoneme duration prediction was obtained using the corpus Fraga trained with the CART Tree method. The results obtained by predicting directly the phonemes durations were better than the obtained ones by predicting Zscores. In Table 4 we can see the results for phoneme duration prediction. In the case of durations prediction the best correlation coefficient obtained was 0.7832, whereas in the case of Zscores prediction the best correlation coefficient was 0.55. The duration prediction model built by the CART Tree using the corpus Fraga, was packed into a Scheme file to be used by our Mexican Spanish voice, since it had the best results.

Table 4. Phoneme Duration Prediction

Method	DIMEx100 RMSE	DIMEx100 MAE	DIMEx100 CORR	Fraga RMSE	Fraga MAE	Fraga CORR
CartTree	0.0234	0.0144	0.3307	0.0177	0.0114	0.7832
Linear Regresion	0.0237	0.0183	0.4269	0.0199	0.0153	0.6941
M5'	0.0238	0.0184	0.4207	0.0175	0.013	0.7788
REPTree	0.0243	0.0182	0.411	0.0181	0.0134	0.7615

At the bottom of Figure 3 it is shown a part of the signal amplitude of a phrase from corpus Fraga. The phrase is: *La generación de los sentidos*. This phrase has a total duration of 1.827 seconds. This same phrase synthesized without the prosodic trained models is shown at the top of Figure 3. Its total duration is 1.540. At middle part of Figure 3 is shown the synthesized phrase using the trained model. In this case the total duration is 1.558 segs.

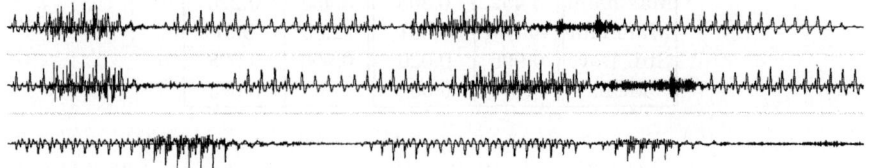

Fig. 3. Recorded and Synthesized Phrases Amplitude

In Table 5 are listed the durations in seconds of the first 9 phonemes of the phrase. We can see that the phonemes durations of the phrase synthesized with the trained duration model is closer to the phonemes duration of the phrase extracted from corpus than the phonemes durations of the phrase synthesized with a duration model based on the Zscores default CART Tree for phoneme duration prediction of Festival and the phoneme duration data proposed in [6].

Table 5. Phoneme Duration in Synthesized and Recorded Phrases

Phrase	l	a	j	e	n	e	r	a	s	i
Synthesized Old	0.044	0.067	0.032	0.059	0.049	0.059	0.058	0.067	0.071	0.060
Synthesized New	0.048	0.071	0.096	0.058	0.053	0.061	0.038	0.064	0.094	0.054
Recorded		0.120	0.090	0.100	0.040	0.050	0.060	0.040	0.060	0.140	0.080

6.2 F0 Results

For F0 prediction we used 21 features at syllable level. Some of the features are: the number of phonemes in the syllable, the number of syllables since the last pause between phrases and the position of the syllable in the word. We obtained three predictions which are: pitch at the beginning, at the middle and at the end of the syllable. We got 4303 instances from corpus Fraga and 1140 from corpus DIMEx100. The results of predictions for start pitch, middle pitch and end pitch are shown in Table 7. In Table 6 are shown the frequency ranks in Hz, means and standard deviations for both corpora.

The best Correlation Coefficients for the predictions of f0 were obtained by the CART Tree method with both corpora. All the methods used obtained better results using corpus DIMEx100 to train. We can see that final pitch data are not so consistent since the average of all the RMSE of end pitch predictions for both corpora is 19.12, whereas for initial and middle pitch is 12.304 and 9.506

Table 6. Corpora Statistics

Statistic	DIMEx100			Fraga		
	Start Pitch	Mid Pitch	End Pitch	Start Pitch	Mid Pitch	End Pitch
Minimum	72.072	72.072	36.531	73.056	73.747	36.531
Maximum	173.912	173.908	173.908	173.922	173.936	173.922
Mean	123.29	122.943	86.188	120.537	122.388	101.778
Std. Dev.	17.402	16.568	33.406	19.468	19.593	31.707

respectively. This could be due to the abnormally low end pitches extracted from corpora. In Table 6 we can see that for both corpora the lowest end pitch is 36.531 Hz.

Table 7. F0 Prediction

Method	DIMEx100			Fraga		
	RMSE	MAE	CORR	RMSE	MAE	CORR
CartTree Start	10.0812	8.0681	0.8141	13.9406	9.4689	0.6985
CartTree Mid	9.0126	7.0536	0.8559	8.4304	5.9788	0.9069
CartTree End	13.9530	9.8464	0.9117	19.8291	14.8885	0.7758
Linear Reg Start	10.397	6.293	0.801	14.1129	10.5062	0.6888
Linear Reg Mid	9.133	6.373	0.834	12.9108	9.989	0.6888
Linear Reg End	21.273	17.92	0.770	23.9241	18.7474	0.6562
M5' Start	10.406	6.096	0.802	13.7564	10.13	0.7071
M5' Mid	8.034	4.930	0.874	8.9073	5.7078	0.8907
M5' End	16.156	10.285	0.875	20.2531	13.2607	0.7694
REPTree Start	11.130	6.743	0.770	14.611	10.713	0.6659
REPTree Mid	9.229	5.759	0.831	10.3904	6.5693	0.8497
REPTree End	17.008	10.656	0.861	20.5879	12.5843	0.7679

We compare by subjective means the two best sets of f0 prediction models to determine the best one. Although we obtained a better correlation average coefficients with CART Tree and corpus DIMEx100, we decide to use the f0 prediction models obtained with CART Tree and corpus Fraga since it gives a more natural frequency variation. In Figure 4 are shown the pitch contour of the same phrase used as example in previous section. From top to down we can see: the pitch contour of the natural sentence, the pitch contour of the sentence synthesized with the default intonation model provided by festival, the pitch contour of the sentence synthesized with the model trained with corpus DIMEx100 using CART Tree, the pitch contour of the sentence synthesized with the the model trained with corpus Fraga using CART Tree.

The utterances synthesized with the default f0 model have an almost flat contour which decreases along time. These generate a monotone sounding voice. The utterances synthesized with the trained model using corpus DIMEx100 have more frequency variation, but it has some sharp changes, which generate a trembling sounding voice. Finally, using the model trained with corpus Fraga presents smooth variations of frequency and gives a more natural sounding voice.

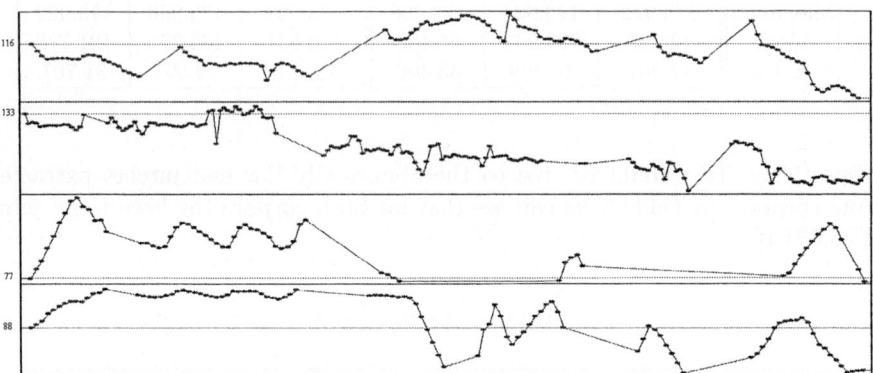

Fig. 4. Pitch Contours extracted from Synthesized Phrases and form Natural Phrase

7 Conclusions

A new voice based on diphones concatenation for the Spanish spoken in Mexico was built taking advantage of the general framework offered by Festival. We used two corpora and tested several machine learning methods for the training of a phoneme duration prediction model which predicts durations more accurately than the prediction model used before.

Also, a trained model for f0 prediction was built. This model seems to approach the f0 of the synthetic phrases to the one observed in the recorded, nonetheless, it does not modify very well the pitch contour at phrase level. It was observed from the prediction results of both corpora that end pitch prediction is more difficult than start pitch and middle pitch prediction due to data inconsistency.

We could appreciate different behaviors of results obtained from corpora. Training Zscores and phoneme duration prediction models we obtained better results using corpus Fraga. We think that it was due to a better phoneme labelling in corpus Fraga and due to its larger number of instances. In the case of F0 predictions, the corpus DIMEx100 gave better results. Since features used in F0 predictions are not at phoneme level, the corpus DIMEx100 results were not so affected by errors in labelling. However, we decided to adopt a model trained with corpus Fraga since it gave the most natural sounding voice.

After incorporating the built trained models to the Festival prosody assignation module, we obtained a voice with a more natural intonation. We thought that this improvement could be greater if we enhance the pitch extraction process, since we detected that some instances used in the f0 prediction training seems to be erroneous. We also planned to add more data from Fraga corpus to the training sets. By doing this we hope to improve the veracity and accuracy of our predictions and the quality of our models. Also we plan to improve intonation at phrase level.

References

1. Dutoit T. : An Introduction to Text-to-Speech Synthesis. Dordrecht: Kluwer Academic Publishers (Text, Speech and Language Technology, 3) (1997)
2. The Centre for Speech Technology Research (CSTR): The University of Edimburgh. Internet Page http://www.cstr.ed.ac.uk/projects/festival/
3. Meza, H. : Modelos Estadsticos de Duraciones de los Fonemas en el Espaol Mexicano. Master Thesis, Universidad de las Amricas - Puebla, Dept. of Computer Systems Engineering.(1999)
4. Black, A., Taylor, P., Macon, M. : Speech Synthesis in Festival A practical course on making computers talk Edition 2.0, for Festival Version 1.4.1 (2000)
5. Black, A., Lenzo, K. : Building Synthetic Voices for FestVox 2.0 Edition. (2003)
6. Barbosa, A. : Desarrollo de una nueva voz en Espaol de Mxico para el Sistema de Texto a Voz Festival, Master Thesis, Universidad de las Amricas - Puebla, Dept. of Computer Systems Engineering. (1997)
7. Black, A., Taylor, P., Macon, M. : The Festival Speech Synthesis System: System documentation. Technical Report HCRC/TR-83, Human Communciation Research Centre, University of Edinburgh, Scotland, UK, (1997)
8. Jun, Sun-Ah. : Prosodic Phrasing and Attachment Preferences, Journal of Psycholinguistic Research **32(2)** (2003) 219–249.
9. Schtz, S.: Prosody in Relation to Paralinguistic Phonetics - Earlier and Recent Definitions, Distinctions and Discussions. Term paper for course in Prosody, Lund University, Dept. of Linguistics and Phonetics.(2003)
10. Pineda, L., Villaseor, L., Cuetara, J., Castellanos, H., Lopez, I. : A New Phonetic and Speech Corpus for Mexican Spanish. Lecture Notes in Artificial Intelligence **3315**, Springer-Verlag. ISSN: 0302-9743, ISBN 3-540-23806-9. (2004) 974–983.
11. The University of Waikato: Hamilton, New Zealand Web Page http://www.cs.waikato.ac.nz/ ml/ 1999-2004.

A New Approach to Sequence Representation of Proteins in Bioinformatics

Angel F. Kuri-Morales[1] and Martha R. Ortiz-Posadas[2]

[1] Departamento de Computación,
Instituto Tecnológico Autónomo de México
[2] Laboratorio de Informática Médica. Departamento de Ingeniería Eléctrica,
Universidad Autónoma Metropolitana Iztapalapa
akuri@itam.mx, posa@xanum.uam.mx

Abstract. A method to represent arbitrary sequences (strings) is discussed. We emphasize the application of the method to the analysis of the similarity of sets of proteins expressed as sequences of amino acids. We define a pattern of arbitrary structure called a *metasymbol*. An implementation of a detailed representation is discussed. We show that a protein may be expressed as a collection of metasymbols in a way such that the underlying structural similarities are easier to identify.

1 Introduction

Bioinformatics has been defined as "The science of managing and analyzing biological data using advanced computing techniques. Especially important in analyzing genomic research data" [20]. The problem of sequence alignment is one of the most important issues in Bioinformatics.

Sequence alignment is the procedure of comparing two (pair wise alignment) or more (multiple sequence alignment) sequences by searching for a series of individual characters or character patterns that are in the same order in the sequence. Sequence alignment is particularly interesting when focused on problems related with molecular biology. Within this realm it is useful for discovering patterns related with functional, structural and/or evolutionary information present in biological data. Sequences that are very similar probably relate to structures having the same cellular function, or a similar biochemical function, or a similar three dimensional structure. However, the methods presently in use imply the adoption of a series of criteria which are typically subjective and *a aprioristic*. In this article we focus on the representation of proteins (the algorithms discussed may be applied, however, to other fields as well). In this context there are two types of sequence alignment: global and local. In global alignment, an attempt is made to align the entire sequence, using as many characters as possible, up to both ends of each sequence. In local alignment, stretches of sequences with the highest density of matches are aligned, thus generating one or more islands of matches or sub-alignments in the aligned sequence. In either case, however, the mainstream [1–10] has only considered that the elements of the purported sequences are contiguous, i.e. there are no gaps between such elements or *symbols*. In this paper we will introduce a generalization by considering "sequences" with gaps, whose symbols are no necessarily consecutive. This generalization will be called *metasymbol* in the rest of paper. A similar concept is used in [11] for approximate string matching and is analogous to the concept of motif commonly used in bioinformatics [12]. Our contention is that if a) the proteins under scrutiny may be re-expressed as sequences of metasymbols and b) we are able to find similar metasymbols in sets of proteins, then the similarity to which we alluded above will be simpler to determine. Our efforts will be focused, therefore, on making precise under what conditions the said representation with metasymbols is plausible and how to achieve it. In part 2 we discuss the concept of metasymbol and its representation. In part 3 we illustrate the method by meta representing two hypothetical proteins and stressing the ease of identification of the patterns embedded in proteins thusly expressed. In part 4 we present our conclusions.

2 Metasymbols

Metasymbols (Ms), as stated, are sequences of symbols in some alphabet, probably interspersed with don't-care symbols or gaps of arbitrary length. The symbol used to specify a gap is not in the alphabet and is called the *gap symbol*. Those symbols in a Ms that are in the alphabet are called solid symbols or defined symbols. Hence, every string of one or more symbols in the alphabet is a Ms, and every string that begins and ends with symbols in the alphabet, and has an arbitrary sequence of gap symbols and alphabet symbols in between, is also a Ms. We can establish the formal definition of Ms as follows:

Definition 1. Given a finite alphabet of symbols Σ, and a special symbol $\gamma \notin \Sigma$, called gap symbol, a metasymbol (say m) in Σ^+ is any string generated by the regular expression:

$$\Sigma + \Sigma(\Sigma + \gamma)^*\Sigma$$

There are several features associated with every Ms:

- The order of m, denoted $o(m)$, is the number of solid or defined symbols in m.
- The Ms size, denoted $|m|$, is the total length of the Ms considering both, the solid and gap symbols.

A Ms can be specified in several ways. One possible representation is made up by two vectors that describe, respectively, the contents, and the structure of the Ms. For example, if we use the underscore as the gap symbol, the following is an order 5 and size 10 Ms:

$$m_1 = \text{EL\_M\_E\_ \_ \_A}$$

that appears in the string: $S_1 = GTELKMIELAMAEPGLARTELVMWEQYYA$ as shown in Figure 1.

Such Ms is specified by:

- The contents vector $c(m)$ of the defined symbols in m in the order they appear. In our example $c(m_1) = [E, L, M, E, A]$. The size (number of entries) of this vector is: $|c(m)| = o(m)$.

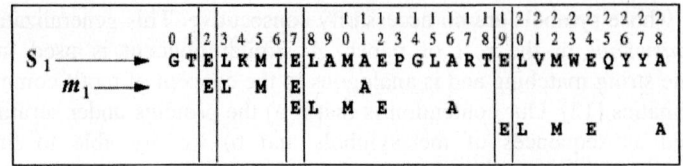

Fig. 1. Metasymbol m1 appears 3 times in string S1

- The structure vector d of the distances between every consecutive symbol in c. In our example $d(m_1) = [0, 1, 1, 3]$. The size of this vector is: $|d(m)| = o(m)-1$.

We are interested in the search of Ms's that occur frequently in longer strings of symbols in Σ. We will call *sample* to any string in Σ^+ where the Ms search takes place. Hence we will require additional features in order to characterize a Ms relatively to the sample. Given a Ms m that appears in a sample S we define:

- The Ms *occurrence list*, denoted $L(m)$, as the increasing ordered list of absolute positions where m appears in S (the first symbol in a sample is at position zero). In our previous example $L(m_1) = \{2, 7, 19\}$.
- The *Ms frequency*, denoted $f(m)$, as the number of times the Ms m appears in sample S. In our example: $f(m_1) = 3$.
- The *rough coverage*, denoted $Cov(m)$, as the formal number of symbols in S, generated (or covered) by all the appearances of Ms in the sample. That is, the product of frequency times the Ms order. In the example $Cov(m_1) = 5 \times 3 = 15$.
- The *effective coverage*, denoted $Cov_{eff}(m)$, as the actual number of symbols in the sample covered by all the appearances of Ms. This is the rough coverage defined above, minus the number of symbols in sample covered more than once by different Ms occurrences. In our example, since the letter **E** in position 7 is covered twice by two different occurrences of m_1, we have: $Cov_{eff}(m_1) = 14$.
- The *Position* of Ms_i is defined by the i-th offset (the number of symbols intervening between the first symbol of Ms_i and the first symbol of Ms_{i+1}). By convention the offset of the Ms_1 is relative to the first symbol found in m. The position of all the symbols in Ms_i is completely specified by these offsets. Since the structure of the Ms is fixed, when we specify the offset of Ms we implicitly specify the position of all of its symbols.

Our goal is to find the combination of Ms's such that a given protein (call it p) is re-expressed in its most compact way. In order to do so, we must propose a detailed representation of the compressed string. In this regard, the following further definitions are in order:

- The *Structure* of a Ms is the enumeration of its gaps.
- The *Content of a metasymbol* is the enumeration of the values of all the symbols in the Ms. In general, p is not fully covered by all instances of the different Ms, i.e. there are symbols which are not accounted for by a collection of Ms.
- The *Filler* is the enumeration of those symbols not covered by a Ms in p.

In general, the steps to express p as a collection of Ms [13] are: 1) Find an adequate set of Ms, 2) Express p as a sequence of Ms, 3)

Describe the position, structure and contents of each of the Ms, 4) Describe the contents of the filler. Now:

(1) To describe the positions of the instances of the metasymbols we use a binary sequence. Every number in the sequence represents the distance between the i-th and $(i+1)$-th Ms.
(2) To define the structure of all the Ms we use a binary sequence which represents as a collection of gaps: one for every Ms. Since the symbols are unknown, code '0' is reserved to indicate the end of the structure of a particular Ms. The structure of Ms_i is, thus, a collection of gaps plus a '0'. Furthermore, since it is possible to have a gap of size 0, every gap is encoded as its actual size +1.
(3) We proceed to define the binary contents of every metasymbol. For instance, the contents of m_1 are defined as the ASCII representation of the letters in 'ELMEA'.

Once this is done we will have defined all necessary elements: order, position, structure and contents, for every Ms in p. As stated, there are symbols which are not accounted for by the collection of Ms defined. However, the exact positions of all undefined symbols in p are, at this point, known.

(4) We enumerate the binary contents of undefined localities to complete the cover.

Under this representation $|r|$ (the size of the metasymbolic representation, in bits) is given by:

$$|r| = \mu(1+\sum_{i=1}^{M} N_i) + \omega \sum_{i=1}^{M} N_i + (\gamma + \lambda) \sum_{i=1}^{M} S_i + L - \lambda \sum_{i=1}^{M} S_i N_i$$

Where N_i denotes the number of instances of Ms_i; M = number of different Ms; $\mu = \lceil \log_2(M) \rceil$; $\omega = \lceil \log_2[\text{max. offset } Ms_i] \rceil$; $\gamma = \lceil \log_2[\text{max. gap } Ms_i] \rceil$; $\lambda = \lceil \log_2 |Ms_i| \rceil$; $S_i = \lceil \log_2(\text{max. symbols } Ms_i) \rceil$ and $L = |p|$ in bits (for a detailed derivation of the expression above, see [19]).

In the process outlined above two questions remain: a) Is the set of Ms unique? and, if such is not the case, b) How to select the best cover? The answer to (a) is clearly negative. There may be many combinations of symbols yielding different sets of Ms. The answer to (b) depends on which set of Ms we decide to consider. Each of the two questions gives rise to problems which may be shown to be very complex (in fact, they may be shown to be NP-complete) [15]. In tackling these issues we have followed the simplest path and developed a strategy which looks for the set of Ms which maximizes the algorithmic information [16] of the data. This is equivalent to finding the most compact representation of such data. In other words, we select the combination of Ms which allows the expression of a protein in its most compact form. Furthermore, it can also be formally shown that the similarities between groups of re-expressed (or *transformed*) proteins are easier to identify. Because of this reason, among others, the effort to compress proteins has been attempted in the past. At least one such attempt led to failure [17]. In that case, traditional data compression techniques were applied and the reported negative results were to be expected.

To solve issues (a) and (b) we have developed two algorithms (to which we will refer as A1 and A2, respectively) which rely on AI techniques [18]. A1 (for which see [14]) performs on-line and focuses on directly finding the best $Cov_{eff}(m_i) \forall i$ in the sequence. A2 performs off-line by tackling the problem in two steps; first, it produces a set of j plausible metasymbols in p; then, it selects the best $Cov_{eff}(m_j)$ $\forall j$ in the set. We have shown [21] that algorithms A1 and A2 have an analogous statistical behavior and, furthermore, that the re-expressed data resulting from the application of our method out-performs other alternatives. Thus, the best selection of the set of MS in p is the one minimizing $|r|$. Our intent is not to discuss the algorithms leading to such selection, but to remark the advantages of re-expressing p as above. We refer the reader interested in the algorithms to [19].

3 Metasymbolic Representation of a Protein

Our method consists of analyzing the protein sequence (p) as a string of symbols (a protein may be canonically expressed as a string of amino acids) and to identify a set of the (possible) underlying Ms's. The metasymbols, as opposed to the symbols implied in the methods discussed in the introduction, are structurally not restricted. If metasymbolic sets are found, one may pose a similarity measure between different p's which is based on the Ms's and, hence, independent of an a priori criterion. Once the protein is re-expressed in its accordance, it will appear simple to envision a similarity measure between metasymbols rather than between symbols. In what follows we illustrate with two examples.

3.1 Illustration of the Method

We apply the method to a hypothetical protein (Hyp1) herein expressed as a string of amino acids (AAs) called *AA representation*:

> Hyp1
MSMQETQVQHFRKDRQARRAERAQAKDNRFQAHQQTIQMRDMEKQVK
KQYKDHHDQMKESETHVDNIKKDDKHAIEEDQMDKDNRTSYKSHIIRHL
QMHTQQHQQYMQHQDQAKKEKTHGAIKGALKA

In order to facilitate the visualization of the metasymbols, the protein was rearranged in a 16 x 8 matrix (see figure 2). In this protein we may identify 5 metasymbols. The first metasymbol (Ms_1) consists of 12 symbols (see figure 3), and it appears 3 times. The position of the first symbol (S_1) in Ms_1's first instance is (1, 1), in its second instance is (7, 3) and in its third instance is (9, 4). To identify the position of the next instances of the Ms_1 refer to the entire amino acids sequence of the protein in the matrix of Figure 2.

1	2	3	4	5	6	7	8	9	10	11	12	13	14	15	16	
M	S	M	Q	E	T	Q	V	Q	H	F	R	K	D	R	Q	1
A	R	R	A	E	R	A	Q	A	K	D	N	R	F	Q	A	2
H	Q	Q	T	I	Q	M	R	D	M	E	K	Q	V	K	K	3
Q	Y	K	D	H	H	D	Q	M	K	E	S	E	T	H	V	4
D	N	I	K	K	D	D	K	H	A	I	E	E	D	Q	M	5
D	K	D	N	R	R	S	Y	K	S	H	I	I	R	H	L	6
Q	M	H	T	Q	Q	H	Q	Q	Y	M	Q	H	Q	D	Q	7
A	K	K	E	K	T	H	G	A	I	K	G	A	L	K	A	8

1	2	3	4	5	6	7	8	9	10	11	12	13	14	15	16	
M				E		V							D			1
				E						D	N					2
				I				M								3
Y				H								T				4
																5
																6
																7
																8

Fig. 2. Protein arranged in a 16X8 matrix   **Fig. 3.** First instance of Ms_1

Metasymbol Ms_2 consists of 8 symbols and it appears 2 times. Figure 4 shows its first instance with its initial position at (1, 3). The second instance appears at position (15, 4). Metasymbol Ms_3 consists of 3 symbols and it appears 9 times. Its first instance is shown in figure 5. Observe that its initial position is (15, 1). For instances 2 to 9 the positions are (2, 2), (3, 2), (6, 2), (13, 2), (8, 3), (5, 6), (6, 6), (14, 6) respectively (refer to Figure 2). The fourth metasymbol (Ms_4) consists of 2 symbols and it appears 7 times. In Figure 5 is shown its first instance at (4, 1). For instances 2 to 7 its positions are (7, 1), (9, 1), (16, 1), (1, 7), (9, 7), (16, 7) respectively (refer to figure 2). The last metasymbol (Ms_5) consists of 3 symbols and it appears 2 times. Figure 5 shows its first instance at (15, 6). The second instance appears at position (3,7).

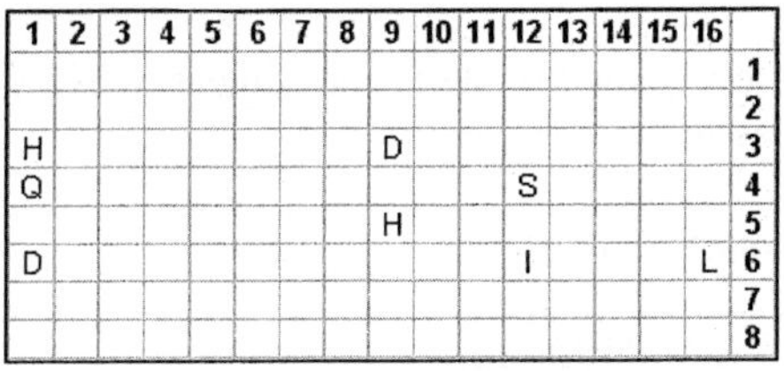

Fig. 4. First instance of Ms_2

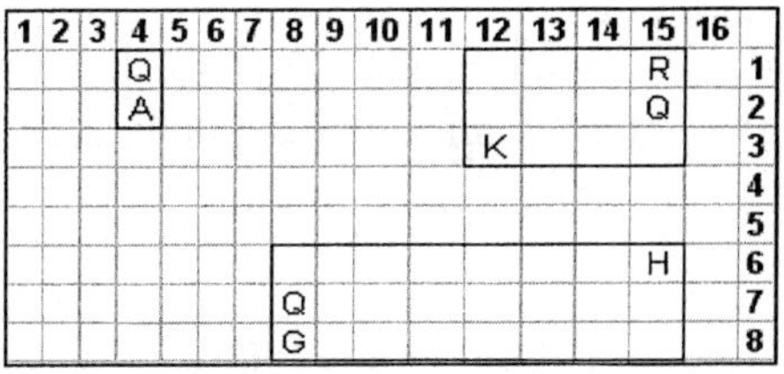

Fig. 5. First instances of Ms_3, Ms_4 and Ms_5

The symbols of all instances of Ms_i, $i=1, \ldots, 5$ account for 99 of the 128 symbols in Hyp1 (77.34%). The rest of the symbols are not covered by any Ms and make up the filler. It is shown in figure 6.

For clarity, we assign the Greek letters $\alpha, \beta, \gamma, \delta,$ and ε to $Ms_1, \ldots, Ms_5$ respectively. Then we may put protein Hyp1 in its *Ms representation* as follows:

>Hyp1: $\alpha\,\delta\,\delta\,\delta\,\gamma\,\delta\,\gamma\,\gamma\,\gamma\,\gamma\,\beta\;\alpha\,\gamma\,\alpha\,\beta\;\gamma\,\gamma\,\gamma\,\varepsilon\,\delta\,\varepsilon\,\delta\,\delta$

Notice the striking difference between the AA and Ms representations of Hyp1. We may re-express each of a set of proteins as a sequence of Ms rather than as a sequence of AAs. Once given a set in which every protein is expressed as above, the similarities between them become more readily apparent and one may replace the subjective similarity measures currently in use (which we mentioned in the introduction) by simpler, more intuitive ones.

However, without an explicit definition of the position, structure and contents of the various Ms the metasymbolic expression of the protein is meaningless. Therefore, we proceed as follows.

First, we describe the positions of all instances of the different metasymbols. In Hyp1. This corresponds to the following sequence: 0 2 2 1 5 0 1 0 2 6 3 5 0 16 5 21 0 7 0 1 1 5 6.

Every number in the sequence represents the distance between the i-th and $(i+1)$-th Ms. In Hyp1, Ms_1 starts on the position of the first symbol (1, 1); then the first instance of Ms_4 is two symbols away from Ms_1; the second instance of Ms_4 appears 2 symbols away from its first instance. Likewise, the first instance of Ms_3 is 5 symbols away from the second instance of Ms_4, and so on (see Figure 7).

1	2	3	4	5	6	7	8	9	10	11	12	13	14	15	16	
	S	M			T				H	F	R	K				1
A								Q		K				F		2
			T													3
						H	D									4
		I	K			K		A		E		D				5
	K						S		K							6
											M					7
					E	K	H						A		K	8

1	2	3	4	5	6	7	8	9	10	11	12	13	14	15	16	
Ms1	-	-	Ms4	-	-	Ms4	-	Ms4	-	-	-	-	-	Ms3	Ms4	1
-	Ms3	Ms3	-	-	Ms3	-	-	-	-	-	-	Ms3	-	-	-	2
Ms2	-	-	-	-	-	-	Ms1	Ms3	-	-	-	-	-	-	-	3
-	-	-	-	-	-	-	-	-	Ms1	-	-	-	-	Ms2	-	4
-	-	-	-	-	-	-	-	-	-	-	-	-	-	-	-	5
-	-	-	-	Ms3	Ms3	-	-	-	-	-	-	Ms3	Ms5	-	-	6
Ms4	-	Ms5	-	-	-	-	-	-	Ms4	-	-	-	-	-	Ms4	7
-	-	-	-	-	-	-	-	-	-	-	-	-	-	-	-	8

Fig. 6. The filler of protein Hyp1   **Fig. 7.** Positions of all instances of Ms_i

Next, we define the structure of all the Ms as a sequence of gaps, one for every Ms. As an example, the structure of Ms_1 is specified by the sequence: 4 3 6 7 6 1 9 5 8 3 9. The gap between S_1 and S_2 is 3 (4-1), the gap between symbols S_2 and S_3 is 2 (3-1), and so on.

Now we proceed to define the contents of every metasymbol. The content of every Ms in Hyp1 is defined by one of the sequences shown in table 1.

Table 1. Contents of Ms_i in Hyp1

Metasymbol	Contents
Ms_1	{MEVDEDNIMYHT}
Ms_2	{HDQSHDIL}
Ms_3	{RQK}
Ms_4	{QA}
Ms_5	{HQG}

As stated, there are symbols which are not accounted for by the collection of Ms defined. The exact positions of all undefined symbols in Hyp1 are, at this point, known. Therefore, a simple enumeration of the contents of these localities completes the cover. The following sequence is the filler of Hyp1:

SMTHFRKAQKFTHDIKKAEDKSKMEKHAK

3.2 Common Patterns in Proteins

The reader is reminded that our goal is to facilitate the identification of patterns common to sets of proteins and that, to this effect, we should compare at least two of these. In what follows we consider two hypothetical proteins denoted as Hyp1 and Hyp2. Hyp1 is the one discussed above; Hyp2 is a new protein. These are shown next as their respective AA representations.

>Hyp1
MSMQETQVQHFRKDRQARRAERAQAKDNRFQAHQQTIQMRDMEKQVKKQ
YKDHHDQMKESETHVDNIKKDDKHAIEEDQMDKDNRTSYKSHIIRHLQMHT
QQHQQYMQHQDQAKKEKTHGAIKGALKA

>Hyp2
MNQMQCEENDVQKQFGDHAMALHEKMVQDADKDWTFFMQEPEMAVDNS
WSDQYHQIYEVAMTHDNRKAYEDHQIQDNDMTTIYAILYIAHARQQWKYV
TCQHKHQGCEAQTQTYWTAPFMAKKILIHA

A New Approach to Sequence Representation of Proteins in Bioinformatics   887

In protein Hyp2 we may identify 3 metasymbols: Ms_1, Ms_2 and Ms_4 which are identical to the corresponding ones from Hyp1. Ms_1 appears 2 times; the position of the first symbol (S_1) of its first instance is (2, 4); the second instance is at (3, 6). To identify the position of the instances of Ms_1 refer to the entire amino acids sequence of the protein in the matrix of figure 8. Metasymbol Ms_2 appears just one time at (2,7) (see figure 9). Ms_4 appears 8 times; its first instance at (1, 3). Instances 2 to 8 are at (1, 14), (2, 12), (4, 4), (5, 11), (6, 13), (7, 5) and (7, 16) respectively (refer to figure 10). The rest of the symbols follow no pattern and make up the filler. It is shown in Figure 11.

	1	2	3	4	5	6	7	8	9	10	11	12	13	14	15	16
1	M	N	Q	M	Q	C	E	E	N	D	V	Q	K	Q	F	G
2	D	H	A	M	A	L	H	E	K	M	V	Q	D	A	D	K
3	D	W	T	F	F	M	Q	E	P	E	M	A	V	D	N	S
4	W	S	D	Q	Y	H	Q	I	Y	E	V	A	M	T	H	D
5	N	R	K	A	Y	E	D	H	Q	I	Q	D	N	D	M	T
6	T	I	Y	A	I	L	Y	I	A	H	A	R	Q	Q	W	K
7	Y	V	T	C	Q	H	K	H	Q	G	C	E	A	Q	T	Q
8	T	Y	W	T	A	P	F	M	A	K	K	I	L	I	H	A

Fig. 8. First instance of Ms_1

	1	2	3	4	5	6	7	8	9	10	11	12	13	14	15	16
1	M	N	Q	M	Q	C	E	E	N	D	V	Q	K	Q	F	G
2	D	H	A	M	A	L	H	E	K	M	V	Q	D	A	D	K
3	D	W	T	F	F	M	Q	E	P	E	M	A	V	D	N	S
4	W	S	D	Q	Y	H	Q	I	Y	E	V	A	M	T	H	D
5	N	R	K	A	Y	E	D	H	Q	I	Q	D	N	D	M	T
6	T	I	Y	A	I	L	Y	I	A	H	A	R	Q	Q	W	K
7	Y	V	T	C	Q	H	K	H	Q	G	C	E	A	Q	T	Q
8	T	Y	W	T	A	P	F	M	A	K	K	I	L	I	H	A

Fig. 9. Metasymbol Ms_2

	1	2	3	4	5	6	7	8	9	10	11	12	13	14	15	16
1	M	N	Q	M	Q	C	E	E	N	D	V	Q	K	Q	F	G
2	D	H	A	M	A	L	H	E	K	M	V	Q	D	A	D	K
3	D	W	T	F	F	M	Q	E	P	E	M	A	V	D	N	S
4	W	S	D	Q	Y	H	Q	I	Y	E	V	A	M	T	H	D
5	N	R	K	A	Y	E	D	H	Q	I	Q	D	N	D	M	T
6	T	I	Y	A	I	L	Y	I	A	H	A	R	Q	Q	W	K
7	Y	V	T	C	Q	H	K	H	Q	G	C	E	A	Q	T	Q
8	T	Y	W	T	A	P	F	M	A	K	K	I	L	I	H	A

Fig. 10. Eight instances of Ms_4

	1	2	3	4	5	6	7	8	9	10	11	12	13	14	15	16
1	M	N		M	Q	C	E	E	N	D	V	Q	K		F	G
2	D	H		A	L				K	M			D			K
3		W	T	F	F				P		M					S
4	W				Y	H	Q		Y		V	A		T		
5		R	K			E			Q			D	N	D		T
6			Y	A	I			I	A			R		Q	W	K
7	Y	V		C		H	K	H	Q	G	C	E			Q	T
8	T	Y	W	T		P	F	M	A	K	K	I	L	I	H	

Fig. 11. The filler of Hyp2

Now we are able to compare the AA sequence representation and the metasymbolic one for Hyp1 and Hyp2.

>Hyp1: $\alpha \delta \delta \delta \gamma \delta \gamma \gamma \gamma \gamma \beta \alpha \gamma \alpha \beta \gamma \gamma \gamma \epsilon \delta \epsilon \delta \delta$
>Hyp2: $\delta \delta \alpha \beta \delta \alpha \delta \delta \delta \delta \delta$

It is almost trivial to detect the underlying similarities under this re-expressed form, as opposed to the original one, as the reader may verify. The fillers for Hyp1 and Hyp2 are also exposed:

Filler for Hyp1:
SMTHFRKAQKFTHDIKKAEDKSKMEKHAK

Filler for Hyp2:
MNMQCEENDVQKFGDHALKMDKWTFFPMSWHQYVATRKEQDNDYAIIAQ
WKYVCHKHGCEQTTYWTPFMAKKILIH

Now one more interesting issue arises: Is it possible that the biological behavior of different proteins is related NOT to their similarities but also to their deep dissimilarities? This matter has not received proper attention and it remains as an open issue whose mere statement would have been impossible without the concepts herein discussed.

4 Conclusions

Protein classification, as discussed above, has been attempted looking for similarities between sequences of, for instance, amino acids. These sequences are assumed to consist of simple one dimensional arrays of consecutive basic symbols. We have abandoned such a naive approach and determined to look for "sequences" of Ms which, by definition, have unspecified structure. The underlying complexity of this kind of search is not to be dismissed.

With the algorithms (A1 and A2) which we have developed and tested, large sets of proteins in *S. cerevisiae* are being scanned. The experiments being conducted seem to prove that protein compression is achievable (on the order of 25%) and metasymbolic structures have emerged.

The next step will be to detect sets of similar Ms or sequences of Ms in other known genomes (such as the human genome) which will, hopefully, enlighten the way towards determination of protein similarity, its resulting classification and, ultimately, a reasoned explanation of the proteins' biological similarities.

References

1. Gibbs AJ and McIntyre GA, The diagram, a method for comparing sequences. Its use with amino acid and nucleotide sequences. *Eur. J Biochem.* Vol. 16, 1970, pp. 1–11.
2. Needleman SB and Wunsch CD, A general method applicable to the search for the similarities in the amino acid sequence of two proteins. *J Mol Biol.* Vol. 48, 1970, pp. 443–453.
3. National Center for Biotechnology Information, *www.ncbi.nlm.nih.gov*; last access: 30-04-05.
4. Mount DW, *Bioinformatics. Sequence and genome analysis.* Cold Spring Harbor Laboratory Press, New York, 2001.
5. Lipman DJ, Altschul SF and Kececioglu JD, A tool for multiple sequence alignment. *Proc. Natl. Acad. Sci.* Vol. 86, 1989, pp. 4412-4415.
6. Higgins DG, Thompson JD and Gibson TJ, Using CLUSTAL for multiple sequence alignments. *Methods Enzimol.* Vol. 266, 1996, pp. 237-244.
7. Corpert F, Multiple sequence alignment with hierarchical clustering. *Nucleic. Acids. Res.*, Vol. 16, 1988, pp. 10881-10890.
8. Morgenstern B, Frech K, Dress A and Werner T, DIALING: finding local similarities by multiple sequence alignment. *Bioinformatics*, Vol. 14, 1998, pp. 290-294.
9. Notredame C and Higgins DG, SAGA: Sequence alignment by genetic algorithm. *Nucleic Acids Res*, Vol. 24, 1996, pp. 1515-1524.
10. Gribskov M, Luethy R and Eisenberg D, Profile analysis. *Methods Enzimol.* Vol. 183, 1990, pp. 146-159.
11. Burkhardt, Stefan and Juha Kärkkäinen, "Better Filtering with Gapped q-Grams", *Proceedings of 12th Annual Symposium on Combinatorial Pattern Matching CPM 2001*, Amihood Amir and Gad M. Landau (editors), Lecture Notes in Computer

12. Science, No. 2089, 2001, pp. 73-85.
13. Parida, L. *Algorithmic Techniques in Computational Genomics*, Doctoral Dissertation, Courant Institute of Mathematical Sciences, University of New York, 1998.
14. Kuri A, "Pattern based lossless data compression", *WSEAS Transactions on communications*, Issue 1, Vol. 3, 2004, pp. 22–29.
15. Kuri A and Herrera O, "Efficient lossless data compression for nonergodic sources using advanced search operators and genetic algorithms", *Advances in Artificial Intelligence, Computing Science and Computer Engineering*, J. Nazuno, A. Gelbukh, C. Yañez, O. Camacho (editors), ISBN: 970-36-0194-4, ISSN: 1665-9899, Vol. 10, 2004, pp. 243–251.
16. Kuri A and Galaviz J, "Pattern-based data compression", *Lecture Notes in Artificial Intelligence* LNAI 2972, 2004, pp. 1–10.
17. Li M and Vitányi P, *An introduction to Kolmogorov complexity and its applications*, Springer Verlag, New York, 2nd Ed, 1997.
18. Nevill-Manning CG and Witten IH, "Protein is incompressible", *Proc. Data Compression Conference*, J.A. Storer and M. Cohn (editors), IEEE Press, Los Alamitos, CA, 1999, pp. 257-266.
19. Kuri-Morales A, Herrera O, Galaviz J, Ortiz M, "Practical Estimation of Kolmogorov Complexity using Highly Efficient Compression Algorithms", *cursos.itam.mx/akuri/- 2005/tempart*; last access: 04/30/05.
20. Kuri A, "Lossless Data Compression through Pattern Recognition", *cursos.itam. mx/akuri/2005/tempart*; last access: 04/30/05.
21. Definition of Bioinformatics in the Web, *www.google.com.mx/search?hl- =es&lr=&oi=defmore&q=define:Bioinformatics*, last access: 01/02/05.
22. Kuri A, Galaviz J, "Data Compression using a Dictionary of Patterns", *cursos.itam. mx/akuri/2005/tempart*; last access: 05/02/05.

Computing Confidence Measures in Stochastic Logic Programs

Huma Lodhi and Stephen Muggleton

Department of Computing, Imperial College,
180 Queen's Gate, London, SW7 2AZ, UK
{hml, shm}@doc.ic.ac.uk

Abstract. Stochastic logic programs (SLPs) provide an efficient representation for complex tasks such as modelling metabolic pathways. In recent years, methods have been developed to perform parameter and structure learning in SLPs. These techniques have been applied for estimating rates of enzyme-catalyzed reactions with success. However there does not exist any method that can provide statistical inferences and compute confidence in the learned SLP models. We propose a novel approach for drawing such inferences and calculating confidence in the parameters on SLPs. Our methodology is based on the use of a popular technique, the bootstrap. We examine the applicability of the bootstrap for computing the confidence intervals for the estimated SLP parameters. In order to evaluate our methodology we concentrated on computation of confidence in the estimation of enzymatic reaction rates in amino acid pathway of Saccharomyces cerevisiae. Our results show that our bootstrap based methodology is useful in assessing the characteristics of the model and enables one to draw important statistical and biological inferences.

1 Introduction

Modelling metabolic pathways is an important and challenging problem in system biology. Stochastic logic programs (SLPs) [1] can provide an efficient representation for enzyme catalyzed reactions in the pathways. The estimation of reaction rates and quantification of the precision and confidence in the estimated rates are key problems. Behaviour of enzymes in metabolic pathways can be studied using the Michaelis-Menten (MM) enzyme kinetic function, however the well-known method, namely Lineweaver-Burk or double reciprocal method [2] is not free of problems. Dowd and Riggs [3] have reported discouraging and poor results. Ritchie and Pravan [4] have questioned the statistical validity of the results using the method. Moreover it is computationally exhaustive to solve the MM equation using numerical methods [5, 6]. In recent years a number of probabilistic logic learning techniques [7, 8] have been proposed. Such methods have been applied for the estimation of the reaction rates of enzymes successfully [8]. In some applications the interest lies only in the estimation but challenging tasks such as modelling metabolic pathways require the quantification of the accuracy of the estimated unknown variables. The complexity of the metabolic networks establishes a need to evaluate, analyze and present methodologies for the computation of confidence in the learned models. This paper focuses exclusively on computation of confidence in the learned SLPs models as there does not exist any method that computes confidence in the parameters on SLPs. We present a methodology based on Efron's bootstrap [9] to quantify the confidence in the learned parameters on an SLP.

Experimental and theoretical results have demonstrated ensemble methods' (such as bagging [10] and boosting [11]) ability to generate highly effective predictors in propositional learning [12, 13] and also in relational learning[14, 8]. Therefore we apply a bagging [10] type ensemble ranbag [8] for estimating the reaction rates in metabolic pathways. Ranbag uses a base learner such as failure adjusted maximization (FAM) [7] and works by iteratively setting the priors of FAM randomly and obtaining the base models using the original learning set. The intuition for selecting ranbag is its way of construction of an ensemble. SLPs' parameters learnt by ranbag can be more reliable as it estimates the parameters when we perturb the priors. Once the parameters have been estimated, the key problem is the computation of confidence in estimated parameters.

Confidence intervals(CIs) provide a useful way to compute confidence in the estimated parameters on the SLPs. They specify a range of values that comprise the true parameters at given probability. CIs have many properties that make them a suitable choice for confidence computation for complex tasks such as modelling metabolic pathways. They can be easily understood and interpreted. Generally there is uncertainty in the learned parameters due to random noise in the data. Confidence intervals quantify the uncertainty in the learned parameters. They provide a reliable answer to a particular problem. For example in metabolic pathways there are a huge number of enzymes with unknown reaction rates. Our interest lies in calculating the confidence intervals for the estimated reaction rates of such enzymes. A learning algorithm can estimate the enzymatic reaction rates but does not tell the accuracy of the estimation. Confidence intervals provide a solution by giving a range of values and we can be confident that the true enzymatic reaction rates will fall within this range at a given probability.

Resampling and Bayesian inferences are two commonly used methods to draw the confidence intervals in learning methods such as neural networks (NN) and Bayesian networks (BN) [15, 16] . In resampling, a set of instances are randomly drawn with replacement from an original dataset. These replicates are then used for confidence estimation. Bayesian techniques to compute confidence intervals are different than the frequentist methods. Initially a prior is set (on the weights of the network in NN or features in BN) and then the Bayesian methods estimate posterior distribution. The variance of each output and standard deviations are computed for confidence estimation. The posterior distribution can be obtained by running a very large number of Markov Chain Monte Carlo simulation that pose computational limitations for Bayesian methods. Hence we will focus on resampling methods for confidence estimation.

We consider and present a methodology to quantify our confidence in the learned parameters on an SLP. Our approach is based on the use of Efron's bootstrap [9] in

Fig. 1. Single-substrate-enzyme catalyzed reaction (left). An SLP for the reaction (right)

probabilistic logic based methods. We evaluate the applicability of resampling methods in SLPs to construct confidence intervals. We describe two methods, the parametric bootstrap and the non-parametric bootstrap for the computation of confidence in the learned stochastic logic models. Our results show that the bootstrap based methodology is useful in the analysis of the complex data as it provides an insight into different questions. It quantifies our confidence in the estimation of reaction rates. It measures the power of an induction method. Length of the interval can guide us in the selection of the size of the dataset. Moreover it provides us a way to estimate the accurate reaction rates with confidence at a given probability.

The paper is organized as follows. SLPs and learning algorithms (FAM and ranbag) have been summarized in section 2. The bootstrap based methodology for deriving confidence intervals has been presented in section 3. Section 4 explains experimental methodology and results.

2 Stochastic Logic Programs (SLPs)

In this section we will briefly review SLPs that extend standard logic programs by combining logic and probability. An SLP is a definite labelled logic program. In an SLP all or some of the clauses are associated with parameters (labels). An SLP can be categorized into pure SLP and impure SLP depending upon the nature of the parameterization of the clauses. In a pure SLP all of the clauses are labelled whereas an impure SLP is a set of both labelled and unlabelled clauses. An SLP is a normalized SLP if labels of the clauses with same predicate symbol in the head sum to one that is any set S of clauses of the form $p : K$ where $p \in [0, 1]$ is a probability label or parameter and K is a range-restricted definite clause. In an unnormalized SLP summands, labels of clauses whose head have the same predicate symbols, do not add to one.

Examples: SLPs provide an efficient representation for metabolic pathways as they can capture the whole dynamics and can account for enzyme kinetics. For example, in SLPs representation of a pathway, the set of clauses can describe enzymes and probability labels can account for reaction kinetics. Figure 1 shows a simple single-enzyme-substrate reaction and also tells how an SLP models the kinetics of the reaction. Clauses assert that in a reaction R the reactant O is transformed into the product P and the formation is under the control of enzyme E. The product of reaction R is generated with rate z. However the formation of the product can be hindered due to factors such as reduc-

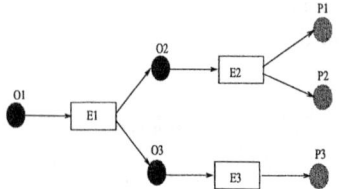

enzyme($E1,R1,[O1],[O2,O3]$).
$0.75 :: R1(y,y,y). 0.25 :: R1(y,n,n)$.
enzyme($E2,R2,[O2],[P1,P2]$).
$0.65 :: R2(y,y,y). 0.35 :: R2(y,n,n)$.
enzyme($E3,R3,[O3],[P3]$).
$0.93 :: R3(y,y). 0.07 :: R3(y,n)$.

Fig. 2. Hypothetical metabolic pathway (left).SLPs for the pathway (right)

tion in enzyme and reactant concentration or/and defective enzyme. The clause, $1 - z :: R(y, n)$, illustrates such scenarios. Figure 2 shows a simple hypothetical metabolic pathway and SLPs for the pathway. $O1$, $P1$, $P2$ and $P3$ are external metabolites, where pathway starts with $O1$ and $P1$, $P2$ and $P3$ are end products. $R1$, $R2$, $R3$ are reactions with attached rates directed by enzymes $E1$, $E2$ and $E3$ respectively.

Learning Stochastic Logic Programs

Learning of SLPs can be carried in parametric estimation tasks or in structure (underlying logic program) induction scenarios. In this work, we focus on computing confidence in the parameters on SLPs assuming that the structure of SLPs is fixed and given.

Failure Adjusted Maximization (FAM): In order to learn parameters on SLPs FAM [7] uses a method based on expectation maximization (EM). FAM uses EM [17] algorithm to perform maximum likelihood parameter estimation for the SLPs. Given a logic program and a set of initial (prior) parameters FAM computes the maximum likelihood estimates in a two step (expectation (E) step and maximization (M) step) iterative learning process. In the E-step, FAM computes the expected frequency for the clause given the current estimates of the parameters and the observed data. In the next step (M-step) the contribution of the clause is maximized. The value associated with each clause is normalized and it becomes an input for the next iteration of FAM. This process is repeated till convergence.

Random Prior Aggregating (ranbag): Ranbag [8] is a bagging [10] type method that performs statistical parameter learning of SLPs. It is based on the use of ensemble learning in probabilistic logic based methods. Ranbag uses a base learner such as FAM. Ranbag exploits the characteristic of randomness in maximum likelihood estimators such as FAM. It performs parameter learning by perturbing the priors and obtaining the base model using the original learning set in an iterative fashion. The construction of the ensemble using ranbag can be viewed as a two stage learning process. In the first stage the prior parameters of the base predictor are set according to a random distribution. In the second stage ranbag calls the base learner. The base learner is provided with the original learning set L, an underlying logic program LP and a set of prior parameters P_t. The obtained base models, $h_t = BL(L, LP, P_t)$, can be substantially diverse because base learners such as FAM depend on the selection of priors. These two stages are repeated T times. Ranbag perform the parameter estimation task by averaging the diverse predictions produced by the base models. Ranbag's estimation for ith parameter is $h_{ranbag}(i) = 1/T \sum_{t=1}^{T} h_t(i) = \hat{p}_i$. At the end of learning process ranbag returns a set of estimated parameters on SLPs, $\hat{P} = \{\hat{p_1}, \ldots, \hat{p_N}\}$.

3 The Bootstrap for Confidence Estimation

Statistical intervals such as confidence intervals provide a way to specify and quantify the precision and confidence in the estimation produced by an SLPs learning algorithm.

We now present our approach for computing confidence in the parameters on the SLPs. Our methodology is based on the use of the parametric bootstrap and the non-parametric bootstrap [9]. Consider a learning set L of instances of the form, $L = \{x_1, \ldots, x_n\}$, where the instances are coded in a relational way. Let the sample L is generated independently from an SLP S. Let $P = \{p_1, \ldots, p_N\}$ be the set of (true) parameters on the SLP and $\hat{P} = \{\hat{p_1}, \ldots, \hat{p_N}\}$ be the set of parameters estimated by a learning algorithm. In our setting an SLP represent enzymatic reactions in metabolic pathways and the parameters on the SLP represent rates of the reactions. We now make another assumption that the SLP learner estimates the parameters with very low bias. Our observation about FAM's and ranbag's bias is as follows. FAM is not a biased predictor. It computes parameters with low bias and high variance and an ensemble of FAM such as ranbag decreases the variance. The bias component either remains unchanged or there is further reduction in it. For ranbag, our conjecture is that the bias component of the statistical interval is too small to have any significance and variance is the main component of the confidence interval. Hence we can assume that bias is negligible or zero. For biased estimators there exists techniques that performs bias correction. These techniques suffer from some problem. They may not provide reliable confidence calculation for small datasets. Furthermore the number of required bootstrap replicates can be high [9].

In order to evaluate the application of the bootstrap in SLPs we present two algorithms that are based on the non-parametric bootstrap and the parametric bootstrap. The non-parametric bootstrap approach works by iteratively drawing bootstrap samples from the data. The bootstrap sample is constructed by randomly drawing, with replacement, n instances from the learning set of size n. It replaces the distribution D (according to which data is generated) by empirical distribution $\hat{D}$ that is a discrete distribution and assigns probability of $\frac{1}{n}$ to each instance. The bootstrap replicate may not contain all of the instances from the original learning set and some instances may occur many times. The probability that an instance is not included in the bootstrap sample is $(1 - 1/n)^n$. For large sample sizes the probability is approximately $1/e = 0.368$. On average bootstrap replicate contains 63.2% of the distinct instances in the learning set. Since the bootstrap sampling described above is carried out without using any parametric model, therefore it is called nonparametric bootstrap. The non-parametric bootstrap approach for uncertainty estimation is as follows.

1. for $r = 1$ to b do
    - Randomly draw with replacement n instances from the learning set L. The resulting set of instances is the non-parametric bootstrap replicate L^{B^r}.
    - Apply the SLP learner to bootstrap replicate L^{B^r} and obtain an estimate of parameters $\hat{P}_r = \{\hat{p}_{1r}, \ldots, \hat{p}_{nr}\}$
2. For each parameter i compute the average $\hat{p}_i^m = \frac{1}{r} \sum_{r=1}^{b} \hat{p}_{ir}$

We now measure the uncertainty in each of the estimated parameter. The variance for each parameter i is defined by,

$$\text{variance} = \sigma^2 = \frac{1}{b-1} \sum_{r=1}^{b} (\hat{p}_{ir} - \hat{p}_i^m)^2.$$

Given that the variance in each of the estimated parameter has been computed, the confidence interval (CI) is given by

$$\text{CI} = [\hat{p}_i{}^m - CV\sigma, \hat{p}_i{}^m + CV\sigma]$$

where CV is critical value that is derived from the desired confidence level $(1 - \alpha)$. CV can be obtained from a t-distribution table with degrees of freedom equal to the number of bootstrap samples. The nonparametric bootstrap lower limit for a parameter on the SLP is $LL = \hat{p}_i{}^m - CV\sigma$ and the upper limit is given by $UL = \hat{p}_i{}^m + CV\sigma$.

Uncertainty in an SLP learner's estimation can also be measured by another similar procedure that is based on the parametric bootstrap. In this procedure the samples are generated in a parametric fashion. The instances comprising the bootstrap replicates are sampled from the learned parametric model instead of resampling from the original learning set. The parametric bootstrap procedure is as follows.

1. Learn a stochastic logic model using a learning algorithm such as ranbag.
2. for $r = 1$ to b do
   - Generate a sample of size n from the learned SLPs to obtain a parametric bootstrap replicate L^{B^r}.
   - Apply the SLP learner to parametric bootstrap replicate L^{B^r} and obtain an estimate of parameters $\hat{P}_r = \{\hat{p}_{1r}, \ldots, \hat{p}_{n_r}\}$
3. For each parameter i compute the average $\hat{p}_i{}^m = \frac{1}{r}\sum_{r=1}^{b} \hat{p}_{ir}$

We now can calculate the variance and define confidence intervals for each parameter i as described in the preceding paragraphs (for the non-parametric bootstrap). Generally the number of bootstrap samples in any of the bootstrap procedure can be between 20 and 200, $20 \leq b \leq 200$. For complicated methods setting a value of b equal or nearer to the lower limit (20) provide sound results [18]. Both the parametric bootstrap and the non-parametric bootstrap perturbs the data but the method of perturbation is different. In the non-parametric bootstrap data is resampled from the original learning set whereas in the parametric bootstrap data is generated from the learned SLP. Furthermore, there is inherent discreteness in the non-parametric bootstrap and it can converge to uniform distribution asymptotically. There can be an asymptotic convergence to the underlying model for the parametric bootstrap.

4 Experimental Results and Analysis

In this section we describe a series of extensive and systematic experiments. We carried out the quantification of our confidence in the estimation of enzymatic reaction rates of amino acid pathway of Saccharomyces cerevisiae (baker's yeast, brewer's yeast. Figure 3 shows the aromatic amino acid pathway of yeast. We used the pathway and its stochastic logical encoding given in [19]. In our setting the underlying logic program incorporates information about enzymes, metabolites (reactants and products) and enzyme catalyzed reactions. The stochastic labels represent the reaction rates. The probability labels are assigned in a way so as the reaction rates are consistent with the biological literature. Twenty one enzymatic reactions in the metabolic pathway are represented

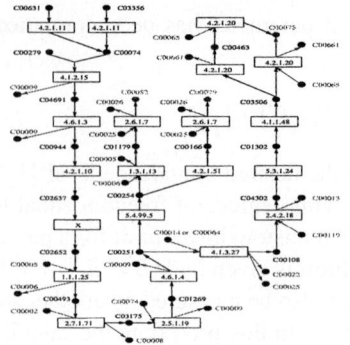

A chemical reaction is represented by a rectangle with its adjacent circles where rectangles represent enzymes and circles represent metabolites. In the figure metabolites are labelled by their KEGG accession numbers and enzymes by the EC number.

Fig. 3. The aromatic amino acid pathway of yeast

by the stochastic clauses. We used the implementation of FAM available at[1]. As our experimental methodology we generated the data from SLPs representing the pathway. We conducted experiment with a range of sample sizes n. Sample sizes considered are $n = 100$, 250 and 500. For each sample size we generated 5 datasets. For each dataset we used 25 bootstrap samples for both the parametric and the non-parametric method. We report the average results. The coordinates such as convergence criterion for FAM and stopping criterion for ranbag can control the performance of FAM and ranbag. We set FAM's convergence criterion to the log likelihood of 0.1. For ranbag we specified the number of models T to 100.

Table 1. Average coverage probabilities and length for 90% confidence intervals for different sample sizes

n	Method	Average Coverage Probability	Average Length
100	parametric	0.810	0.204
	non-parametric	0.742	0.214
250	parametric	0.810	0.139
	non-parametric	0.791	0.137
500	parametric	0.952	0.108
	non-parametric	0.881	0.101

In order to evaluate the applicability of the bootstrap in SLPs and to compare the performance of the parametric bootstrap and non-parametric bootstrap we used the following criteria. We compared the performance of both the methods for constructing 90% two-sided confidence intervals.

- We computed the average coverage probability. Coverage probability is given by the relative frequency of the true parameter p_i (rates of reactions) when the confidence interval contains the parameter p_i. We averaged the coverage probability over the total number of parameters N.

[1] http://www-users.cs.york.ac.uk/~nicos/sware/

- We measured average length of the intervals. The length of an interval is given by, $l = (\hat{p}_i{}^m + CV\sigma) - (\hat{p}_i{}^m - CV\sigma)$. We also observed the shape of the interval that is given by $s = \frac{(\hat{p}_i{}^m + CV\sigma) - \hat{p}_i{}^m}{\hat{p}_i{}^m - (\hat{p}_i{}^m - CV\sigma)}$.
- We computed the average number of true parameters that do not fall within the confidence intervals. We measured the number of true parameters with values above the confidence intervals and the average number of true parameters with values below the confidence intervals. We repeated the process for generated datasets for each sample size and then averaged the results. The criteria shows the induction power of the algorithm for estimation of reaction rates in metabolic pathways. The smaller the average number of true parameters that do not fall within the intervals the better the induction method is.

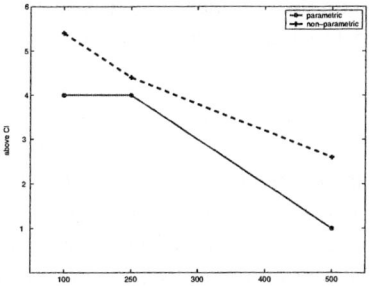
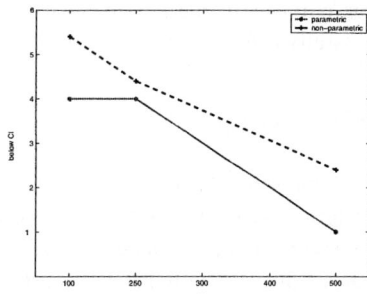

Fig. 4. Average number of true parameters (reaction rates) with values above CI (left) and with values below CI (right)

An ideal method will show the average coverage probability of 0.9. The average number of true parameters with values above the confidence intervals should be equal to the average number of true parameters that fall below the confidence intervals. Furthermore the average number of true parameters that do not fall within the confidence intervals should be small.

Table 1 shows the results for 90% two-sided confidence intervals for the enzymatic reaction rates in the pathway using the parametric and the non-parametric method. The table also shows the performance of the techniques as a function of sample size. The results show that the coverage probability of the parametric and the non-parametric method is comparable. However the coverage probability of the non-parametric bootstrap is nearer to the desired probability for small datasets (for $n = 100, 250$). It seems that the non-parametric bootstrap performs worse than the parametric bootstrap due to its inherent discreteness that add noise for very small sample sizes. However the effect of discreteness becomes insignificant for reasonable sized dataset. The non-parametric method shows better coverage for reasonable sized dataset. We infer that the parametric bootstrap is the preferable method to compute the enzymatic reaction rates for very small sample sizes.

The length of the interval for both the methods is approximately same. The length is small for large n and big for small n. It shows that reasonable sized samples provide better confidence estimation as compared to small sample sizes. We also observed the shape of the intervals. It appears that the intervals are symmetric.

Figure 4 illustrate the average number of true parameters that do not fall within the confidence interval. In figure 4 (left and right) the x-axis show the sample size n. In figure 4 (left) the y-axis shows the average number of true parameters whose values are above the confidence interval whereas figure 4 (right) shows the average number of true parameters having values below the confidence intervals. The figure illustrates the accuracy of our methodology. Large number of true parameter values fall within the confidence intervals and a very small fraction of true parameters values are above/below the confidence intervals. It is worth to be noting that the figures show the number of true parameters with values falling above and below the confidence intervals are almost equal. The results show that our bootstrap's based methodology has several advantages. The average coverage probability is much nearer to desired coverage probability and a large number of true parameter values fall within the confidence intervals. It can be successfully used to compute confidence in the estimated enzymatic reaction rates.

5 Conclusion

We have presented a methodology to compute the confidence in the predictions of an SLP learner. We evaluated the applicability of bootstrapping in probabilistic logic based methods for calculating accurate confidence intervals. We addressed an important problem of estimating confidence in learned enzymatic reaction rates. SLPs provides efficient representation for metabolic pathways where the probability labels on an SLP account for enzyme kinetics. In order to compute confidence in learned rates we applied the parametric bootstrap and the non-parametric bootstrap. Generally, the results of both the methods are comparable but the performance of the parametric bootstrap is better for small datasets and can be a preferable method for limited amount of data. Future work will consider a theoretical analysis of the bootstrap in SLP learning. Also more experimental work is required to evaluate the methodology for a range of related problems.

Acknowledgements

The authors would like to acknowledge the support of the DTI Beacon project "Metalog - Integrated Machine Learning of Metabolic Networks Applied to Predictive Toxicology", Grant Reference QCBB/C/012/00003.

References

1. Muggleton, S.H.: Stochastic logic programs. In de Raedt, L., ed.: Advances in Inductive Logic Programming. IOS Press (1996) 254–264
2. Lineweaver, H., Burk, D.: The determination of enzyme dissocistion constants. J. Am. Chem. Soc. **56** (1934) 658–666
3. Dowd, J.E., Riggs, D.S.: A comparison of estimates of michaelis-menten kinetic constants from various linear transformation. The Journal of Biological Chemistry **240** (1965)

4. Ritchie, R.J., Prvan, T.: A simulation study on designing experiments to measure the km of michalelis-menten kinetics curves. J. Theor. Biol. **178** (1996) 239–254
5. Duggleby, R.G.: Analysis of enzyme progress curves by nonlinear regression. Methods in Enzymology (1995) 61–90
6. Schnell, S., Mendoaz, C.: A fast method to estimate kinetic constants for enzyme inhibitors. Acta Biotheoretica **49** (2001) 109–113
7. Cussens, J.: Parameter estimation in stochastic logic programs. Machine Learning **44** (2001) 245–271
8. Lodhi, H., Muggleton, S.: Modelling metabolic pathways using stochastic logic programs-based ensemble methods. In Danos, V., Schachter, V., eds.: Second International Conference on Computational Methods in System Biology (CMSB-04). LNCS, Springer-Verlag (2004) 119–133
9. Efron, B., Tibshirani, R.: An introduction to bootstrap. Chapman and Hall (1993)
10. Breiman, L.: Bagging predictors. Machine Learning **24** (1996) 123–140
11. Schapire, R.E.: A brief introduction to boosting. In: Proceedings of the Sixteenth International Conference on Artificial Intelligence. (1999) 1401–1406
12. Bauer, E., Kohavi, R.: An empirical comparison of voting classification algorithm: bagging, boosting and variants. Machine Learning **36** (1999) 105–142
13. Lodhi, H., Karakoulas, G., Shawe-Taylor, J.: Boosting strategy for classification. Intelligent Data Analysis **6** (2002) 149–174
14. Dutra, I.C., Page, D., Shavilk, J.: An emperical evaluation of bagging in inductive logic programming. In: Proceedings of the International Conference on Inductive Logic Programming. (2002)
15. Friedman, N., Goldszmidt, M., Wyner, A.: On the application of the bootstrap for computing confidence measures on features of induced bayesian networks. In: Seventh International Workshop on Artificial Intelligence and Statistics. (1999)
16. Zhang, L., Kasiviswanathan, K.: Energy clearing price prediction and confidence interval estimation with cascaded neural networks. IEEE Transactions on Power Systems **18** (2003) 99–105
17. Dempster, A.P., Laird, N.M., Rubin, D.B.: Maximum likelihood from incomplete data via the em algorithm. J. Royal statistical Society Series B **39** (1977) 1–38
18. Tibshirani, R.: A comparison of some error estimates for neural network models. Neural Computation **8** (1996) 152–163
19. Angelopoulos, N., Muggleton, S.: Machine learning metabolic pathway descriptions using a probabilistic relational representation. Electronic Transactions in Artificial Intelligence **6** (2002)

Using Inductive Rules in Medical Case-Based Reasoning System

Wenqi Shi and John A. Barnden

School of Computer Science,
The University of Birmingham,
Edgbaston, Birmingham, B15 2TT, UK
W.Shi@cs.bham.ac.uk

Abstract. Multiple disorders are a daily problem in medical diagnosis and treatment, while most expert systems make an implicit assumption that only single disorder occurs in a single patient. In our paper, we show the need for performing multiple disorders diagnosis, and investigate a way of using inductive rules in our Case-based Reasoning System for diagnosing multiple disorder cases. We applied our approach to two medical casebases taken from real world applications demonstrating the promise of the research. The method also has the potential to be applied to other multiple fault domains, e.g. car failure diagnosis.

1 Introduction

Diagnosis problem was one of the first subjects investigated since digital computers became available and the Medical Diagnosis problem has absorbed lots of the attention of AI researchers. Since the middle of the 1970s, many medical expert systems have been investigated. The MYCIN System [4] was possibly one of the first expert systems which used the concepts of AI, i.e. production rules to help diagnosis in the domain of bacteremias and meningitis. However the need to generate rules and the static knowledge structure highlights the knowledge acquisition problem which most expert systems suffered from. Case-based Reasoning (CBR) methodology employs previous cases to support problem solving without necessarily understanding the underlying principles of application domain, and thus reduces the costs of knowledge acquisition and maintenance. It therefore becomes popular in weak theory domains, e.g. medical domain [7].

Multiple disorders are a frequently occurring problem in daily medical diagnosis and treatment. However, due to a common diagnosis assumption (single-fault assumption [9]) in the diagnostic problem-solving domain, majority of the work using CBR for diagnosing has focused on diagnosing single disorder [7].

Moreover, case-based diagnosis handling multiple disorders is still a challenging task. For instance, for a single disorder casebase dealing with 100 disorders, the chance of reusing a case is roughly one in a hundred. But the chance of reusing a case with even 3 independent diagnoses from 100 alternatives is roughly just one in a million. A naive case-based method was only able to solve about 3% of the cases on one real world dataset [1].

In this paper, we present an approach using inductive rules, which include Diagnostic Rules and Interaction Rules, in our case-based reasoning system to target multiple disorder problems. This approach has been evaluated on two medical casebases taken from real world applications and has been demonstrated to be promising.

2 Multiple Disorder Problem

2.1 The Need for Performing Multiple Disorder Diagnosis

Most previous medical expert systems follow a single disorder assumption, which stems from the fact that finding minimal sets of disorders that cover all symptoms for a given patient is generally computationally intractable (NP-hard) [15]. But in spite of the difficulty for expert system implementation, reality needs to be faced in the real world application.

As medical documentation becomes more and more structured, it is not rare to see more than one disease in a patient record. This is especially true for old people and those with many chronic diseases (e.g. diabetes, high brood pressure) or a syndrome (e.g. Aids). One of the casebases we got from the real world contains an overall number of 221 diagnoses and 556 symptoms, with a mean $M_D = 6.71 \pm 04.4$ of diagnoses per case and a mean $M_F = 48.93 \pm 17.9$ of relevant symptoms per case. Disorders in this casebase include diseases such as Fat liver/Liver greasing (K76.0), Illness of the Thyroid (E07.9) etc, and in the casebase, the diseases are finely divided. Moreover, multiple disorders occur in psychiatric cases as well: approximately 63.3% of incarcerated adolescents had 2 or more psychiatric disorders [14]. In this context, the observed set of the symptoms for a given patient may be better explained by more than one disorder.

2.2 Previous Work on Multiple Disorder Problem

INTERNIST matches symptoms and diseases based on forward and backward conditional probabilities in general internal medicine [10]. But it does not deal with the interacting disorders properly because it only consider one finding should be explained by one disorder, no matter how this finding could also lead to diagnosis of another disorder.

HYDI decomposes knowledge from the causal models of heart diseases into diagnosis units [9]. But the diagnosis units in HYDI largely rely on the causal models built in Heart Failure Program (HF). Only when all the causal models for other disorders are available could HYDI's method be applied to diagnose other disorders.

HEPAR∏ [11] extends the structure of Bayesian network and also [6] uses belief networks to diagnose multiple disorders, but they are both based on the medical literature and conversations with medical domain experts, which highlights the knowledge acquisition problem.

In SONOCONSULT, Set-Covering Theory [12] has been combined with CBR, and the partition class method was used to solve a multiple disorder problem [3]. Since these two methods are recent work and use CBR, we will compare our method with them in a later section.

2.3 Multiple Disorder Notation

We define necessary notions concerning our knowledge representation schema as follows: Let Ω_D be the set of all possible diagnoses, and $d \in \Omega_D$ be a disease a patient may have. Let Ω_A the set of all attributes. To each attribute $a \in \Omega_A$ a range $dom(a)$ of values is assigned. Further we assume Ω_F to be the (universal) set of findings, and a finding $f \in \Omega_F$ is $(a = v)$, where $a \in \Omega_A$ is an attribute and $v \in dom(a)$ is an assignable value to attribute a (for example, a could be 'Liver,Observableness', and v could be 'right intercostal;sub to the Xiphoid').

Let CB be the case base containing all available cases that have been solved previously. A case $c \in CB$ is defined as a tuple as follows

$$c = (\mathcal{F}_c, \mathcal{D}_c, I_c) \qquad (1)$$

$\mathcal{F}_c \subseteq \Omega_F$ is the set of findings observed in the case c. The set $\mathcal{D}_c \subseteq \Omega_D$ is the set of diagnoses for this case. I_c contains additional information, like therapy advices or prognostic hints.

3 Using Inductive Rules in a CBR System Handling the Multiple Disorder Problem

Rules are one of wide spread formalisms for medical decision-making. But for most of expert systems, the rules are difficult to get. In our method, to reduce the knowledge elicitation costs, we use an inductive learning method to generate these inductive rules, which in our approach include Diagnostic Rules and Interaction Rules. They can be refined by applying different types of background knowledge.

In this section, we explain in detail how we learn these inductive rules, and how we use Diagnostic Rules in case-abductive adaptation and Interaction Rules in case-interaction adaptation in our case-based reasoning system.

3.1 Similarity Measure

The similarity measure we are applying is the Manhattan distance for continuous or scaled parameters and Value Difference Metric (VDM) for discrete parameters[16].

We measure the final similarity between query case and a retrieved case by adding up all the weighted Manhattan Distance for the continuous or scaled findings, and all the weighted Value Difference Metric for discrete findings. The equation is showed as follows:

$$\text{Sim}(c, c') = \frac{1}{m} \sum_{i=1}^{m} w_i md(x_i, x'_i) + \frac{1}{n} \sum_{j=1}^{n} \varpi_j vdm(x_j, x'_j) \qquad (2)$$

where c is query case and c' is the case retrived, m is the number of continuous or scaled findings, n is the number of discrete findings, w_i is the weight for attribute i, and ϖ_j is the weight for attribute j.

3.2 Inductive Learning of Inductive Rules

Inspired by [2], we apply the χ^2 *test for independence* [17] to identify dependencies between finding f and diagnoses d. For small sample sizes, the Yates' correction has been applied for a more accurate result.

For those tuples $< f, d >$ with $\chi^2(f, d) > th1$ (threshold $th1 = 3.84$ when $p = .05, df = 1$), we measure the quality of the dependency by using the ϕ correlation coefficient [17]

According to Cohan's guidelines for effect size, we consider the pairs $< f, d >$ with $\phi_{fd} > 0.25$ as a strong relation effect. We then define the diagnostic rules on those tuples $< f, d >$ with a strong relation effect, which means the finding f is significantly important for diagnosing disorder d.

Definition 1 (Diagnostic Rule). *A diagnostic rule R is defined as follows:*

$$R : f \xrightarrow{\phi_{fd}} d \qquad (3)$$

where $f \in \Omega_F$ and $d \in \Omega_D$. For each rule, the coefficient ϕ_{fd} (defined in equation 6) is marked as the effect of the dependency ($\phi_{fd} > 0.25$). Finding f is called a significant finding for disorder d.

We outline the inductive learning procedure of Diagnostic Rules as follows:

1. Construct all the finding-disorder pairs $< f, d >$ for those f and d that occur in cases of the casebase CB
2. For each finding-disorder pair, compute $\chi^2(f, d)$.
3. If $\chi^2_{fd} > th1$, we define f as a significant finding for diagnosis d.
4. For each significant finding f of each diagnosis d, compute the correlation $\phi_{fd} = \phi(f, d)$.
5. For those tuples $< f, d >$ with $\phi_{fd} > 0.25$, define corresponding Diagnostic Rules.

We noticed that some disorders have more chance to happen together than the others. We believe that there exists interactions between these disorders and the interactions may change the value of some symptoms, or even mask some symptoms, which should be present in single disorder case. This is also one of the main issues that multiple disorder problems differ from single disorder problem. In our research, we do consider this kind of interactions and take these interactions into account during case-interaction adaptation.

Definition 2 (Interaction Rule). *An Interaction Rule IR is defined as follows:*

$$IR: f_1, \ldots, f_n \longrightarrow d_i \cap d_j \tag{4}$$

where $f_1, \ldots, f_n \in \Omega_F$ *and* $d_i, d_j \in \Omega_D$, *and for each* $k \in [1 \ldots n]$, *there are Diagnostic Rules* $f_k \xrightarrow{\phi_{f_k d_i}} d_i$ *and* $f_k \xrightarrow{\phi_{f_k d_j}} d_j$. *Findings* $f_1, \ldots, f_n$ *are called Interaction Findings for disorder* d_i, d_j.

The inductive learning process of Interaction Rules is as follows:

1. Construct all the disorder pairs $< d_i, d_j >$ for those d_i and d_j that occur in cases of the casebase CB
2. For each disorder pair, compute $\chi^2(d_i, d_j)$
3. If $\chi^2_{d_i d_j}$ is greater than $th1$, then define diagnose d_i is dependant with diagnose d_j and there are some interaction between these two disorders
4. Tracking the diagnostic rules DR, figure out those significant findings which both support disorder d_i and d_j, and construct Interaction Rule IR for disorder pair (d_i, d_j)

3.3 Using Diagnostic Rules in Case Abductive Adaptation

After case retrieval, we got suggested solutions. To revise the difference between the query case and the similar cases, we need to do some adaptation. In this section, we perform Case Abductive Adaptation by using our diagnostic rules to match observed findings, and calculating the possibilities of each disorder occurrence in the casebase ($PhiSet(d) = \sum_{i=1}^{t} \phi_{f_i d}$, where $f_1 \ldots f_t$ are observed significant findings to disorder d).

The higher the $PhiSet(d)$ is, the more confidently d should be included into final solution. Those disorders with $PhiSet(d) > \phi$ will be suggested as solution as the result of abductive adaptation. Here we set ϕ be a high threshold, thus only those disorders which abductive adaptation very much recommends will be considered. The Abductive Adaptation procedure is very similar to Rule-based Reasoning, which uses Diagnostic Rules inductively learnt from casebase to match symptoms and infer the final solution.

3.4 Using Interaction Rules in Case Interaction Adaptation

In this section, we introduce another adaptation to revise the result. We learnt the interaction between disorders through inductive learning described before, and then we apply those interactions to adaptation processing to improve accuracy in the following way:

1. Look through the observed symptoms and each Interaction Rule, and check whether there are interaction findings available in query case.
2. If there are interaction findings available, compare the solutions generated after case retrieval, with the interaction disorders of the interaction rules

- if there is no intersection between those solutions and the interaction disorders, then the two disorders proposed by each interaction rule will be added into the system solutions.
- if there is one disorder in common between those solutions and the interaction disorders, then we suggest that this disorder has explained the findings somehow, thus we won't add any more disorder into system solution.
- if there are two disorders in common between those solutions and the interaction disorders, then we believe that the solutions generated by the system are confirmed by the interaction rules.

3.5 Using Inductive Rules in Case-Based Reasoning System

In this section, we briefly outline the algorithm we are using to combine Abductive Adaptation and Interaction Adaptation with the previous Compositional-CBR method in our system [13].

Using Inductive Rules in CBR System algorithm
{ Given a query case C_q and casebase CB,
$DiagnosticRules = $ **ConstructDRules**(CB);
$InteractionRules = $ **ConstructIRules**(CB);
$SimSet = $ **AllFinding**(C_q);
$Fqc = $ **CompositionalCBR**$(C_q, CB, SimSet, k)$;
$PhiSet = $ **AbductiveAdaption**(C_q);
for each disorder d in casebase CB
{ if $((Fqc(d) >= \epsilon) \;||\; (PhiSet(d) > \phi))$
{ **InteractionAdaptation** $(d, InteractionRules)$;
Add_Solution $(d, solution)$;}}
return $solution$;}

Given a query case C_q and a casebase CB, we first construct Diagnostic Rules and Interaction Rules as illustrated in section 3.2, for the sake of Abductive and Interaction Adaptation procedure. Then the finding set of query case C_q is abstracted as $SimSet$ for the sake of CompositionalCBR method. Then we apply CompositionalCBR method to generate all those potential diagnosis d by computing the Similarity-Weighted Frequency [13] ,and compute ϕ value for each d in AbductiveAdaptation process. Only those disorders which satisfy corresponding thresholds and processed by Interactoin Adaptation would be included into the final solution.

4 Evaluation

This section presents the evaluation of our approach. We applied two casebases from the knowledge-based documentation and consultation system for sonography SONOCONSULT [8]. We are using 10 fold cross validation and Intersection Accuracy to evaluate how the performance changes after using Inductive Rules, and a comparison of the performances of our method and three other approaches. The evaluations have been established for both of the two casebases.

4.1 Experimental Setup

Casebase 1 consists of 1370 cases which contains an overall number of 137 diagnoses and 286 symptoms, with a mean $M_d = 7.60 \pm 4.12$ of diagnoses per case, a mean $M_f = 52.99 \pm 15.89$ of relevant findings per case and a mean $M_{d/f} = 8.80 \pm 5.65$ of findings per diagnosis per case.

The second evaluation casebase (we call *Casebase 2*) consists of 744 cases. The casebase contains an overall number of 221 diagnoses and 556 symptoms, with a mean $M_D = 6.72 \pm 04.40$ of diagnoses per case and a mean $M_F = 71.13 \pm 23.11$ of relevant findings per case, a mean $M_{d/f} = 15.46 \pm 12.52$ of findings per diagnosis per case.

4.2 Evaluation Metrics

In the usual task of assigning an example to a single category, the accuracy is just the percentage of cases which are correctly classified. But to quantitatively measure the accuracy of multiple disorder diagnosis, the simple accuracy measurement does not fit.

We adopt the Intersection Accuracy [5], as a measure for multiple disorder problems. Intersection accuracy is derived by the two standard measures: *sensitivity* and *Specificity*.

Definition 3 (Intersection Accuracy). *The Intersection Accuracy $\mathcal{IA}(c, c')$ is defined as*

$$\mathcal{IA}(c, c') = \frac{1}{2} \cdot \left(\frac{|\mathcal{D}_c \cap \mathcal{D}_{c'}|}{|\mathcal{D}_c|} + \frac{|\mathcal{D}_c \cap \mathcal{D}_{c'}|}{|\mathcal{D}_{c'}|} \right) \quad (5)$$

where c is a query case and c' is a case from the casebase, $\mathcal{D}_c \subseteq \Omega_D$ is the set of correct diagnoses, and $\mathcal{D}_{c'} \subseteq \Omega_D$ is the set of diagnoses generated by the system.

Besides Intersection Accuracy, we also measure *Standard Accuracy* which is defined as $(T^+ + T^-)/N$, where T^+ (True Positives) is the number of disorders in the correct diagnosis that are also in the system diagnosis ($|\mathcal{D}_c \cap \mathcal{D}_{c'}|$), T^- (True Negatives) is the number of disorders which are neither in the correct diagnosis nor in the system diagnosis, and N is the total number of disorders.

Moreover, *Sensitivity* is defined by (T^+/C^+), where C^+ is the number of disorders in the correct diagnosis. Sensitivity measure accuracy over the disorders actually present. *Specificity* is defined as (T^-/C^-), where C^- is the number of disorders not in the correct diagnosis. Specificity measures the accuracy over disorders which are not present.

When our system makes diagnoses for patients, it will estimate the confidence level for the results it generates. To those cases with low confidence level, the system will mark these cases as unsolved cases and seek the doctor's help.

4.3 Performance After Using Inductive Rules

We compared the performance of using naive Case-based Reasoning [1], CompositionalCBR with the performance after using Inductive Rules in Fig.1:

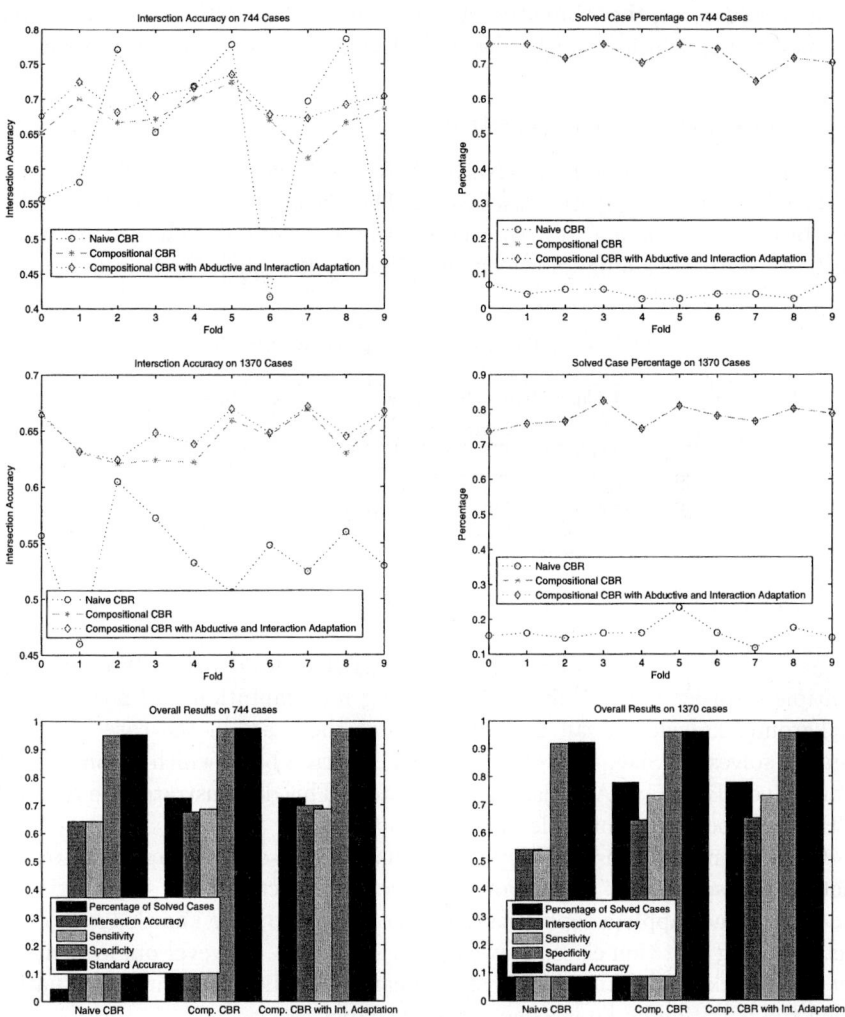

Fig. 1. Results on Two Casebases

- Naive CBR can not cope with multiple disorder problem efficiently: percentage of solved cases stays below 20% on both casebases, and overall percentage of solved case is 3% on 744 cases and 16% on 1370 cases.
- Compositional CBR significantly improved the performance, in both 10 fold measure (top four graphs) and the overall results (last two graphs), which demonstrates the relevance of this method in the multiple disorder situation.
- After using the inductive rules, the Intersection Accuracy improved for most folds, although the percentage of solved cases keeps the same. This is due to the fact that adaptation process doesn't involve the selection procedure

of solved cases, the Abductive Adaptation and Interaction Adaptation only modify the solution which affects the Intersection Accuracy in the end.

4.4 Ours vs. Set-Covering Strategy

We compared our method with Naive CBR, Set-Covering method [3] and Partition Class method [1] on *Casebase 2*. The set-covering approach combined case-based reasoning and set-covering models for diagnosis. The partition class method uses partitioning knowledge provided by the expert to help diagnosis.

Table 1. Comparison of the approaches on 744 cases

744 Cases from the SonoConsult Case Base		
Approach	solved cases (percentage)	mean IA
Naive CBR	20 (3%)	0.66
Set-Covering	502 (67%)	0.70
Our CBR System	537 (73%)	0.70
Partition Class	624 (84%)	0.73

As we can see from Table.1, the Naive CBR method performs poorly with multiple disorder cases. Naive CBR utilising no adaptation and no additional background knowledge can only solve 3% of the cases in the case base. Our method solves 537, i.e., 73% of the cases in the case base, which is much better than naive CBR (The IA is also slightly better). This demonstrates the relevance of this method in the multiple disorder situations.

Our system was considerabley better than the set-covering approach on percentage of cases solved. This is probably due to the fact that the set-covering approach does not apply a sophisticated adaptation step. The knowledge-intensive method using partition class knowledge performs best. However our system does not need background knowledge, and so can be applied in arbitrary situations when the partitioning knowledge is not available.

5 Conclusion and Future Work

In this paper, we introduce an approach using inductive rules in a case-based reasoning system. We apply Diagnostic Rules in Abductive Adaptation and Interaction Rules in Interaction Adaptation procedures. Using real medical data, this method has been demonstrated to be promising.

There are also many opportunities for future work. Firstly, we believe that interactions between disorders can be captured more effectively by investigating how many findings are changed or masked in the interacting circumstance. Secondly, experiments in other domains are desirable. Our work has the potential to be used to diagnose multiple faults in other diagnostic problem areas, such as diagnosis problems concerning machine faults.

References

1. Martin Atzmueller, Joachim Baumeister, and Frank Puppe. Evaluation of two strategies for case-based diagnosis handling multiple faults. In *Proceedings of the 2nd German Workshop on Experience Management(GWEM 2003)*, Luzern, Switzerland, 2003.
2. Martin Atzmueller, Joachim Baumeister, and Frank Puppe. Quality measures for semi-automatic learning of simple diagnostic rule bases. In *Proceedings of the 15th International Conference on Applications of Declarative Programming and Knowledge Management (INAP 2004)*, Potsdam, Germany, 2004.
3. Joachim Baumeister, Martin Atzmueller, and Frank Puppe. Inductive learning for case-based diagnosis with multiple faults. In S.Craw and A.Preece, editors, *Advances in Case-based Reasoning (ECCBR2002)*, pages 28–42. Springer Verlag, 2002. Proceedings of the 6th European Conference on Case-based Reasoning.
4. Bruce G. Buchanan and Edward H. shortliffe, editors. *Rule-Based Expert Systems The MYCIN Experiments of the Stanford Heuristic Programming Project*. Addison-Wesley Publishing Company, 1984.
5. Thompson Cynthia A and Raymond J. Mooney. Inductive learning for abductive diagnosis. In *Proc. of the AAAI-94*, volume 1, pages 664–669, 1994.
6. Linda Gaag and Maria Wessels. Efficient multiple-disorder diagnosis by strategic focusing. In A Gammerman, editor, *Probabilistic Reasoning and Bayesian Belief Networks*, pages 187–204, London, 1995. UCL Press.
7. Lothar Gierl, Mathias Bull, and Rainer Schmidt. Cbr in medicine. In Mario Lenz etc., editor, *Case-based Reasoning Technology:From Foundations to Applications*, pages 273–297. Springer-Verlag, 1998. ISBN 3-540-64572-1.
8. Matthias Huettig, Georg Buscher, Thomas Menzel, Wolfgang Scheppach, Frank Puppe, and Hans-Peter Buscher. A Diagnostic Expert System for Structured Reports, Quality Assessment, and Training of Residents in Sonography. *Medizinische Klinik*, 99(3):117–122, 2004.
9. Yeona Jang. *HYDI: A Hybrid System with Feedback for Diagnosing Multiple Disorders*. PhD thesis, Massachusetts Institute of Technology, 1993.
10. R. A. Miller, H. E. Pople, and J. D. Myers. Internist-1:an experimental computer-based diagnostic consultant for general internal medicine. *New england Journal of Medicin*, 8(307):468–476, 1982.
11. Agnieszka Onisko, Marek J. Druzdzel, and Hanna Wasyluk. Extension of the heparii model to multiple-disorder diagnosis. In M. Klopotek etc., editor, *Intelligent Information Systems*, pages 303–313. Physica-Verlag, 2000.
12. Yun Peng and James A. Reggia. *Abductive Inference Models for Diagnostic Problem-Solving*. Springer-Verlag, 1990.
13. Wenqi Shi and John A. Barnden. A compositional case adaptation approach to multiple disorder diagnostic problem solving. In Brian Lee, editor, *Proc of the 8th UK Workshop on Case-based Reasoning, UKCBR*, 2003.
14. Thaddeus PM Ulzen and Hayley Hamiton. The nature and characteristics of psychiatric comorbidity in incarcerated adolescents. *Original Research*, 43(1), 1998.
15. Staal Vinterbo and Lucila O. Machado. A genetic algorighm approach to multi-disorder diagnosis. *Artificial Intelligence in Medicine*, 18(2):117–132, 2000.
16. D. Randall Wilson and Tony R. Martinez. Improved heterogeneous distance functions. *Journal of Artificial Intelligence Research*, 1997.
17. Robert S. Witte and John S. Witte. *Statistics*. John Wiley & Sons, Inc, 2004.

Prostate Segmentation Using Pixel Classification and Genetic Algorithms

Fernando Arámbula Cosío

Lab. de Análisis de Imágenes y Visualización, CCADET, UNAM,
México, D.F., 04510
arambula@aleph.cinstrum.unam.mx

Abstract. A Point Distribution Model (PDM) of the prostate has been constructed and used to automatically outline the contour of the gland in transurethral ultrasound images. We developed a new, two stages, method: first the PDM is fitted, using a multi-population genetic algorithm, to a binary image produced from Bayesian pixel classification. This contour is then used during the second stage to seed the initial population of a simple genetic algorithm, which adjusts the PDM to the prostate boundary on a grey level image. The method is able to find good approximations of the prostate boundary in a robust manner. The method and its results on 4 prostate images are reported.

Keywords: Boundary segmentation, Genetic algorithms, Point distribution models.

1 Introduction

Automatic segmentation of the boundary of an organ, in ultrasound images, constitutes a challenging problem of computer vision. This is mainly due to the low signal to noise ratio typical of ultrasound images, and to the variety of shapes that the same organ can present in different patients. Besides the theoretical importance of the problem, there are potential practical gains from automatic segmentation of ultrasound images, since ultrasound is a portable, low cost, real time imaging modality. It is particularly suitable for intraoperative image guidance of different surgery procedures.

In this work is reported the automatic segmentation of the prostate boundary in transurethral ultrasound images. The final objective is to measure the prostate of a patient intraoperatively during a Transurethral Resection of the Prostate (TURP) for image guided surgery purposes. Transurethral images provide the same shape of the prostate during ultrasound scanning as well as during resection of the prostate, since the ultrasound probe is inserted through the same transurethral sheath of the resection instrument [1]. We could then reconstruct the 3D shape of the prostate accurately from a set of annotated transurethral images. Previous work on automatic segmentation of the boundary of the prostate in ultrasound images includes the following.

Aarnik et al., [2] reported a scheme based on edge detection using second derivatives, and edge strength information obtained from the gradient at each edge location. Using the edge location and strength information, an edge intensity image is obtained. A complete boundary of the prostate in transrectal images is constructed from the edge intensity image using rules and *a priory* knowledge of the prostate shape. The boundary construction algorithm used was not reported.

A segmentation scheme based on a variation of a photographic technique has been reported by Liu *et al.* [3], for prostate edge detection. The scheme does not produce a complete prostate boundary, it produces partial edge information from which the transrectal prostate boundary would need to be constructed.

Dinggang *et al.* [4] report a statistical shape model for segmentation of the prostate boundary in transrectal ultrasound images. A Gabor filter bank is used to characterize the prostate boundaries in multiple scales and multiple orientations. Rotation invariant Gabor features are used as image attributes to guide the segmentation. An energy function with an external energy component made of the real and imaginary parts of the Gabor filtered images, and an internal energy component, based on attribute vectors to capture the geometry of the prostate shape was developed. The energy function is optimized using the greedy algorithm and a hierarchical multiresolution deformation strategy. Validation on 8 images is reported.

A semi-automatic method is described by Pathak *et al.* [5]. Contrast enhancement and speckle reduction is performed using an edge sensitive algorithm called sticks. This is followed by anisotropic diffusion filtering and Canny edge detection. During image annotation a seed is placed inside the prostate by the user. False edges are discarded using rules, the remaining probable edges are overlaid on the original image and the user outlines the contour of the prostate by hand.

Another semiautomatic method is reported in Gong *et al.* [6]. Superellipses are used to model the boundary of the prostate in transrectal images. Fitting is performed through the optimization of a probabilistic function based on Bayes theorem. The shape prior probability is modeled as a multivariate gaussian, and the pose prior as a uniform distribution. Edge strength is used as the likelihood. Manual initialization with more than two points on the prostate boundary, is required from the user.

We have previously reported a simple global optimization approach for prostate segmentation on transurethral ultrasound images, based on a statistical shape model and a genetic algorithm, which optimizes a grey level energy function. The method was able to find accurate boundaries on some prostate images however the energy function used showed minimum values outside of the prostate boundary for other images [1].

In this paper we report a two stage method for global optimization of a statistical shape model of the prostate. During the first stage pixel classification is performed on the grey level image, using a Bayes classifier. A point distribution model [7] of the prostate is then fitted to the binary image, using a multipopulation genetic algorithm (MPGA). In this way a rough approximation of the prostate boundary is produced which takes into account the typical shape of the gland and the pixel distribution on the image. During the second stage of the process, the initial population of a simple genetic algorithm (SGA) is seeded with the approximate boundary previously found. The SGA adjusts the PDM of the prostate to the gaussian filtered grey level image. In the following sections are described the method and its results.

2 Pixel Classification of Prostate Images

Bayes discriminant functions [8] (eq.1) were used to classify prostate from background pixels.

$$y_k = lnP(x|C_k) + lnP(C_k) \qquad (1)$$

where:

$P(x|C_k)$ is the class conditional probability of class k, with $k=\{$prostate, background$\}$;
$P(C_k)$ is the *a priory* probability of class k.

Two mixture of gaussians models (MGM) of the class conditional probability distributions of the prostate and the background pixels were constructed, using the expectation maximization algorithm [8]. Each pixel sample (x) is a three-component vector (x, y, g) of the pixel coordinates (x, y) and its corresponding grey value (g). The training set consisted of: Np= 403010 prostate pixels; and Nb= 433717 background pixels. From the training sample proportions we can estimate the prior probability of class k as: $P(C_{prostate})$=403010/(403010+433717), and $P(C_{background})$=433717/(403010+433717). In figure 1 are shown two (non-training) prostate images and the corresponding pixel classification results, where a pixel is 255 if, for that pixel $y_{prostate} > y_{background}$, otherwise the pixel is zero.

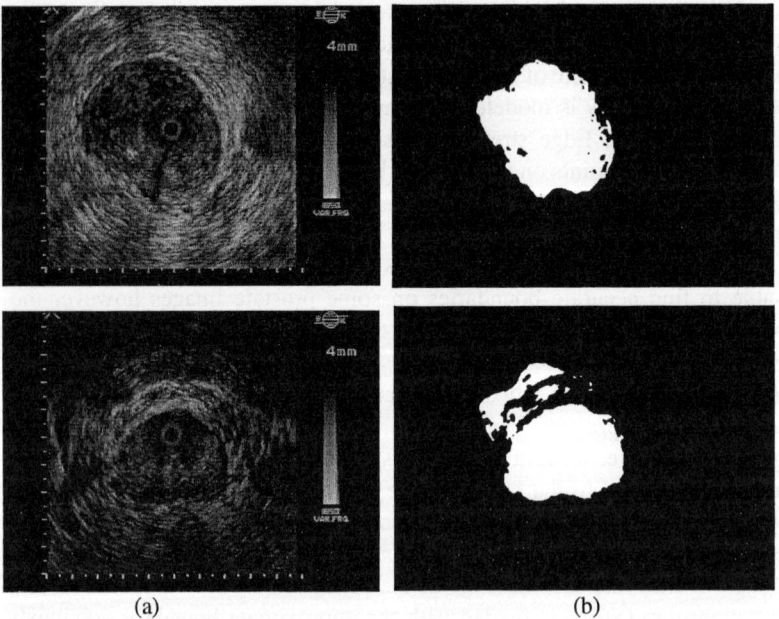

(a)   (b)

Fig. 1. Results of pixel classification a) original images; b) Corresponding binary images

3 Prostate Model Optimization

A Point Distribution Model (PDM) [7] of the shape of the prostate in transurethral images was constructed with a training set of 50 prostate shapes. The pose and shape of the model can be adjusted with 4 pose and 10 shape parameters [1]. The model is first adjusted to the binary image produced by pixel classification, using a multipopulation genetic algorithm (MPGA), with the following parameters: Probability of crossover (Pc = 0.6); Probability of mutation (Pm = 0.001); Number of subpopulations (Nsub =10); Number of individuals per subpopulation (Nind = 10); generation gap (GG = 0.9). The theory of genetic algorithms is presented in [9].

3.1 Model Fitting to the Binary Image

An energy function for model fitting was constructed based on pixel profiles, 61 pixels long, perpendicular to the prostate model and located at regular intervals along the model, as shown in Fig. 2. The energy function e_{bw} (eq.2) is minimum for model instances continuously located around white regions and surrounded by the black background.

$$e_{bw} = \frac{1}{n}\sum_{1}^{n} Gbw_i \qquad (2)$$

where:

$Gbw_i = 255 - inside + outside$

$$inside = \frac{1}{30}\sum_{-30}^{-1} p_i$$

$$outside = \frac{1}{30}\sum_{1}^{30} p_i$$

n is the number of pixel profiles sampled;
and p_i is the value (0 or 255) of pixel i.

An MPGA showed to be able to find the global minimum of the energy function e_{bw} in a consistent manner, while the single population genetic algorithm (SGA) is more sensitive to local minima. In figure 3 are shown the results of ten experiments using the MPGA and the SGA, to adjust the PDM of the prostate to a binary image produced by pixel classification.

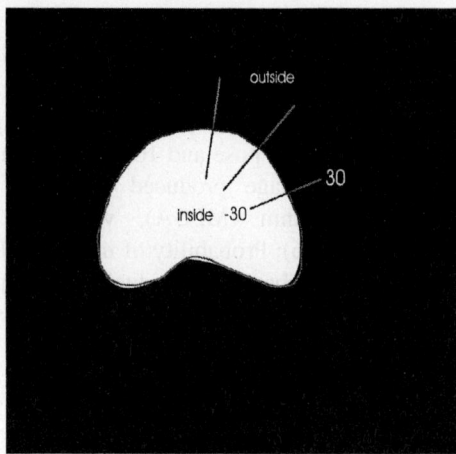

Fig. 2. Pixel profile sampling during prostate model fitting

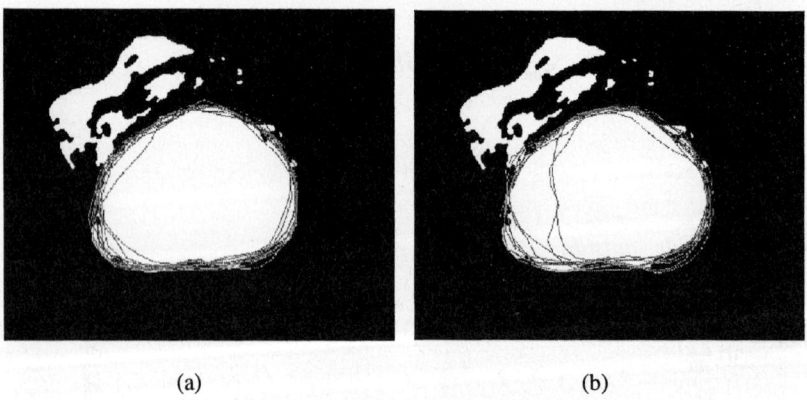

Fig. 3. Results of ten experiments of boundary fitting to a binary image, using: a) MPGA; b) SGA

3.2 Model Fitting to the Grey Level Image

The boundary obtained during model fitting to the binary image, is then used to seed the initial population of an SGA (Pc=0.6, Pm=0.001, N=50, GG=0.85) which is used to adjust the PDM to a gaussian filtered (σ^2 = 64 pixels) grey level image of the prostate. A grey level energy function was constructed (as shown in eq.3.) based on short (21 pixels long) grey level profiles sampled as shown in Fig. 2.

$$e_{grey} = \frac{1}{n\sqrt{OUT}} \sum_{i}^{n} G_i \qquad (3)$$

where:

$$OUT = \sum_{1}^{n} outside_i$$

$$G_i = 255 - outside + inside$$

$$inside = \frac{1}{10} \sum_{-10}^{-1} p_i$$

$$outside = \tfrac{1}{10} \sum_{1}^{10} p_i$$

n is the number of grey level pixel profiles sampled;
and p_i is the grey level value of pixel i.

e_{grey} is designed to produce minimum values when a boundary is placed around a dark (hypoechoic) region which is surrounded by a bright (hyperechoic) halo. In Fig. 1a can be observed that the prostate appears on ultrasound images as a dark region surrounded by a bright halo, however some prostates also show dark regions inside the gland (see Fig. 1a, bottom), which could produce minimum values of e_{grey} in some cases. Pixel classification and boundary fitting to the binary image help to avoid dark regions inside the prostate as shown in the next section.

4 Results

The method described was implemented using MATLAB (Mathworks Inc.). In Fig. 4 are shown the results obtained, for 4 different ultrasound images, compared to the corresponding expert annotated images.

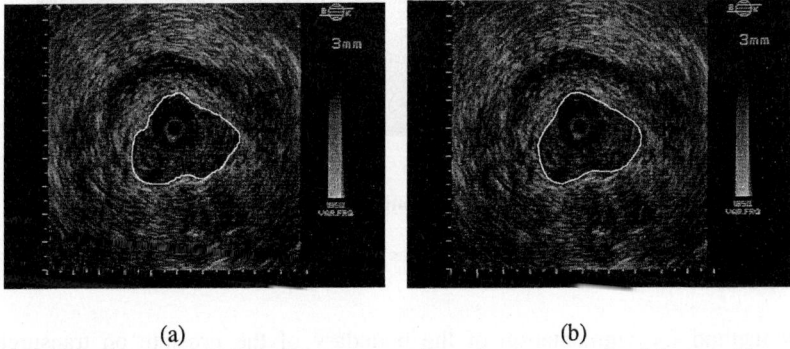

(a) (b)

Fig. 4. Results of automatic boundary segmentation: a) expert annotated images; b) computer annotated images

In the images shown in Fig. 4a, the black circle in the middle corresponds to the position of the transurethral transducer. Around the transducer a dark (hypoechoic) region inside the prostate can be observed. These dark regions inside the prostate could produce minimum values of e_{grey} (eq. 3). However the rough approximation of the prostate contour produced by the MPGA on the binary image produced by pixel classification (section 3.1) helps to avoid these dark regions and helps the SGA to find the correct boundary in the grey level image, as shown in Fig. 4b.

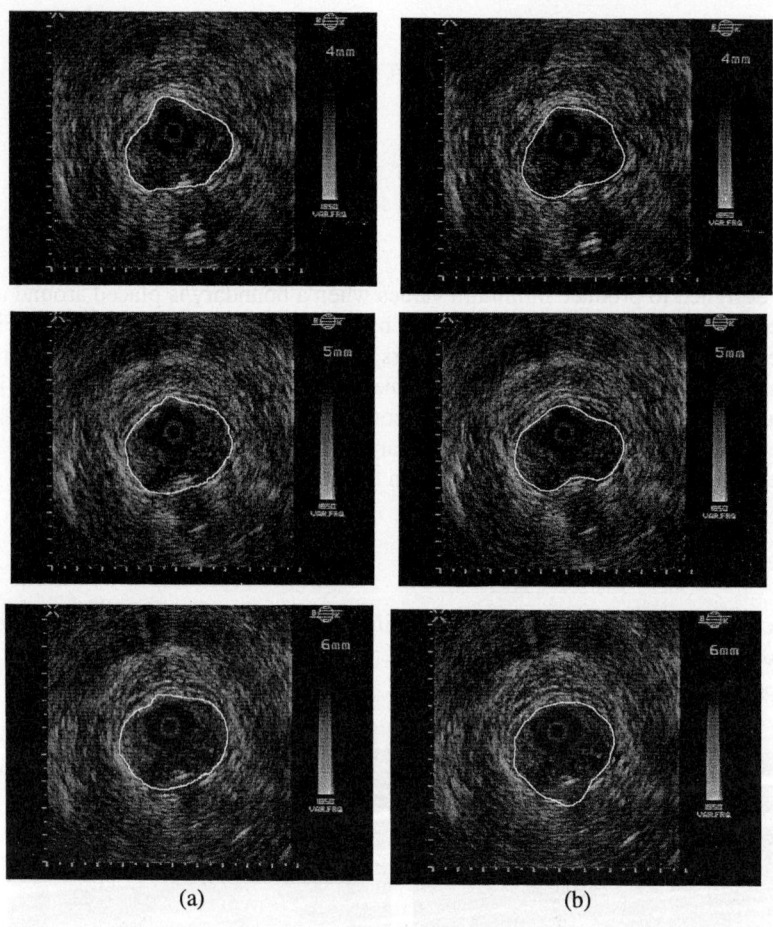

(a)   (b)

Fig. 4 (continued)

5 Conclusions

A new method for segmentation of the boundary of the prostate on transurethral ultrasound images is being developed. The method is based on a PDM of the prostate boundary, which can only deform into shapes typical of the prostate, in this way reducing significantly the search space during model fitting. A rough approximation of the prostate shape and pose, on a digital image, is produced through pixel classification and model fitting to the resulting binary image. An MPGA showed to be robust during optimization of the binary energy function.

During the second stage of the method, the PDM is adjusted using a SGA (which performs faster than the MPGA) on a gaussian filtered grey level image. The initial population of the SGA is seeded with the rough boundary previously obtained, this biases the search of the prostate boundary to the neighborhood of the initial estimate. This in turn, helps to avoid minimum values of the grey level energy function (eq. 3), that can produce gross errors in model fitting. Preliminary results showed that the method reported is able to find good approximations of the prostate boundary in different transurethral ultrasound images. It is a fully automatic scheme which does not require any user intervention.

Our method constitutes a systematic approach to boundary segmentation in transurethral images, which show characteristic dark regions inside of the prostate that can produce boundary segmentation errors. These dark regions are not characteristic of transrectal prostate images, in which most of the boundary segmentation work has been performed. Further research will include an extensive evaluation of the robustness of our method with different image conditions, and the development of a final boundary refinement stage based on edge detection.

References

1. Arámbula Cosío F., Davies B.L.: Automated prostate recognition: A key process of clinically effective robotic prostatectomy. Med. Biol. Eng. Comput. 37 (1999) 236-243.
2. Aarnik R.G., Pathak S.D., de la Rosette J. J. M. C. H., Debruyne F. M. J., Kim Y., Wijkstra H.: Edge detection in prostatic ultrasound images using integrated edge maps. Ultrasonics 36 (1998) 635-642.
3. Liu Y.J., Ng W.S., Teo M.Y., Lim H.C.: Computerised prostate boundary estimation of ultrasound images using radial bas-relief method. Med. Biol. Eng. Comput. 35 (1997) 445-454.
4. Dinggang S., Yiqiang Z., Christos D.: Segmentation of Prostate Boundaries From Ultrasound Images Using Statistical Shape Model. IEEE Trans. Med. Imag. 22 No.4 (2003) 539-551
5. Pathak S.D., Chalana V., Haynor D.R., Kim Y.: Edge-guided boundary delineation in prostate ultrasound images. IEEE Trans. Med. Ima. 19 No.12 (2000) 1211-1219.
6. Gong L., Pathak S.D., Haynor D.R., Cho P.S., Kim Y.: Parametric shape modelling using deformable superellipses for prostate segmentation. IEEE Trans. Med. Imag. 23 No. 3 (2004) 340-349.
7. Cootes T.F., Taylor C.J., Cooper D.H., Graham J.: Active shape models -Their training and application. Comput. Vision Image Understanding. 61 (1995) 38-59.
8. Bishop C.M.: Neural networks for pattern recognition. Oxford University Press (1995).
9. Golberg D. E.: Genetic algorithms in search optimization and machine learning. Addison-Wesley (1989).

A Novel Approach for Adaptive Unsupervised Segmentation of MRI Brain Images

Jun Kong[1], Jingdan Zhang[1], Yinghua Lu[1, 2], Jianzhong Wang[1], and Yanjun Zhou[1]

[1] Computer School, Northeast Normal University, Changchun, Jilin Province, China
[2] Computer School, Jilin University, Changchun, Jilin Province, China
{Kongjun, zhangjd358, luyh, wangjz019}@nenu.edu.cn

Abstract. An integrated method using the adaptive segmentation of brain tissues in Magnetic Resonance Imaging (MRI) images is proposed in this paper. Firstly, we give a template of brain to remove the extra-cranial tissues. Subsequently, watershed algorithm is applied to brain tissues as an initial segmenting method. Normally, result of classical watershed algorithm on gray-scale textured images such as tissue images is over-segmentation. The following procedure is a merging process for the over-segmentation regions using fuzzy clustering algorithm (Fuzzy C-Means). But there are still some regions which are not partitioned completely, particularly in the transitional regions between gray matter and white matter. So we proposed a rule-based re-segmentation processing approach to partition these regions. This integrated scheme yields a robust and precise segmentation. The efficacy of the proposed algorithm is validated using extensive experiments.

1 Introduction

In recent years, various imaging modalities are available for acquiring complementary information for different aspects of anatomy. Examples are MRI (Magnetic Resonance Imaging), Ultrasound, and X-ray imaging including CT (Computed Topography). Moreover, with the increasing size and number of medical images, the use of computers in facilitating their processing and analyses has become necessary [1].

Many issues inherent to medical image make segmentation a difficult task. The objects to be segmented from medical image are true (rather than approximate) anatomical structures, which are often non-rigid and complex in shape, and exhibit considerable variability from person to person. Moreover, there are no explicit shape models yet available for capturing fully the deformations in anatomy. MRI produces high contrast between soft tissues, and is therefore useful for detecting anatomy in the brain. Segmentation of brain tissues in MRI images plays a crucial role in three-dimensional (3-D) volume visualization, quantitative morphmetric analysis and structure-function mapping for both scientific and clinical investigations.

Because of the advantages of MRI over other diagnostic imaging [2], the majority of researches in medical image segmentation pertains to its use for MRI images, and there are a lot of methods available for MRI image segmentation [1-7, 12-20]. Niessen et al. roughly grouped these methods into three main categories: classification methods, region-based methods and boundary-based methods. Just as pointed out in

[14], the methods in the first two categories are limited by the difficulties due to intensity inhomogeneities, partial volume effects and susceptibility artifacts, while those in the last category suffer from spurious edges.

In this paper we address the segmentation problem in the context of isolating the brain tissues in MRI images. An integrated method using an adaptive segmentation of brain tissues in MRI images is proposed in this paper. Firstly, we give a template of brain to remove the extra-cranial tissues. Subsequently, watershed algorithm is applied to the brain tissues as an initial segmenting method. Normally, result of classical watershed algorithm on gray-scale textured images such as tissue images is over segmented. The following procedure is a merging process for the over segmented regions using fuzzy clustering algorithm (here, we take Fuzzy C-Means). But there are still some regions which are not partitioned completely, particularly in the transitional regions between gray matter and white matter. So we proposed a rule-based re-segmentation processing approach to partition these regions.

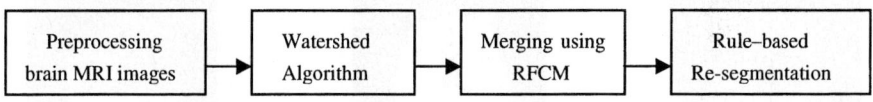

Fig. 1. The diagram of proposed method

The rest of this paper is organized as follows (shown in Fig. 1). Section 2 describes the preprocessing of MRI brain images. Watershed algorithm is briefed in Section 3. In Section 4, we give the merging process using region-based Fuzzy C-Means (RFCM) clustering. Section 5 presents the proposed rule-based re-segmentation processing approach. Experimental results are presented in Section 6 and we conclude this paper in Section 7.

2   Image Preprocessing

2.1   Extra-Cranial Tissue Removing

The horizontal and vertical projection information obtained from the binary image of MRI will be used to remove the extra-cranial tissues of brain image. At first, the binary image $B(x, y)$ shown in Fig. 2b is obtained from the gray image $I(x, y)$ in Fig. 2a. Then, the horizontal and vertical projections of the binary image, shown in Fig. 2c and Fig. 2d, are calculated as follows

$$H_x(y) = \sum_{x=1}^{M} B(x, y) \cdot \quad (1)$$

$$H_y(x) = \sum_{y=1}^{N} B(x, y) \cdot \quad (2)$$

where M is the row number of $I(x, y)$, and N is the column number of $I(x, y)$.

The projection curves will have a large number of fine peaks produced by noise (see Fig. 2c and d), so it is difficult to choose the valuable peaks. Under this condition, we use some apriori knowledge to enhance the ability of judging the valuable peaks by computing the horizontal and vertical projections within a certain range to obtain the primary special values.

According to values obtained from the image's horizontal and vertical projections, we can constitute a coarse contour of the brain MRI image shown in Fig. 2e.

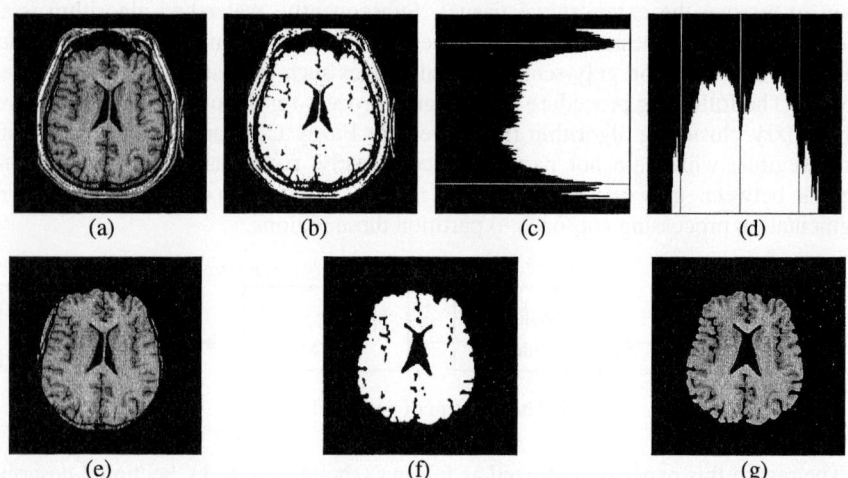

Fig. 2. Preprocessing MRI transverse image. (a) Original image. (b) Binary image. (c) Horizontal projection. (d) Vertical projection. (e) Coarse contour. (f) Binary template. (g) Preprocessed result.

2.2 Removal of Thin Connectors Using Morphological Operations

There are some redundant connectors between brain tissues and the cranium in MRI image after using the processing method mentioned above (see Fig. 2e). In this section, we remove the thin connectors using morphological operations and obtain the binary template of brain MRI image shown in Fig. 2f. Using this template, we can get Fig. 2g as the result of preprocessing.

3 Watershed Algorithm

The input to watershed algorithm is a gray-scale gradient image. Sobel edge detection is applied to get this gradient magnitude image, denoted by I_G. The gradient image is considered as a topographic relief. We apply the Vincent and Soille [9] version of watershed algorithm, which is based on immersion simulation: the topographic surface is immersed from its lowest altitude until water reaches all pixels. The output of watershed algorithm is the segmentation of I_G into a set of non-overlapping regions. Fig. 3a demonstrates the watershed result of the source image shown in Fig. 2g.

The watershed transformation constitutes one of the most powerful segmentation tools provided by mathematical morphology. But there are two disadvantages in the watershed algorithm. Firstly, result of classical watershed algorithm on gray images such as tissue images is over-segmentation, as shown in Fig. 3a. Secondly, there are some regions which are not partitioned completely particularly in the transitional regions of gray matter and white matter. It is also clearly shown in Fig. 3b obtained from one part of Fig. 3a zoomed in. In Section 4 and Section 5, we will focus our attention on these questions respectively.

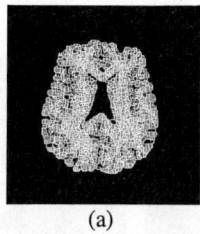
(a)

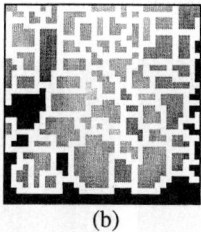
(b)

Fig. 3. (a) Partition result after using watershed algorithm. (b) Some regions that aren't divided completely.

4 Merging the Over-Segmentation Regions

After watershed algorithm being used, there are too many regions because of natural attribute of watershed algorithm -- over segmentation. To overcome this problem, a region-based FCM (RFCM) clustering approach is used to merge these regions over segmented in this section.

4.1 FCM Segmentation

The FCM clustering algorithm assigns a fuzzy membership value to each data point based on its proximity to the cluster centroids in the feature space. Let x be the set of pixels in the image I. The FCM algorithm is formulated as the minimization of the objective functional J_{FCM} with respect to the membership values U and cluster centroids v

$$J_{FCM}(U, v) = \sum_{i \in I} \sum_{k=1}^{C} u_{ik}^m \| x_i - v_k \|^2 \text{ subject to } \sum_{k=1}^{C} u_{ik} = 1, \forall x_i \in I. \tag{3}$$

where the matrix $U = \{u_{ik}\}$ is a fuzzy c-partition of I, $v = \{v_1, v_2, ..., v_c\}$ is the set of fuzzy cluster centroids, $m \in (1, \infty)$ is the fuzzy index, C is the total number of clusters, and u_{ik} gives the membership of pixel x_i in the kth cluster c_k.

The FCM objective function is minimized when high membership values are assigned to x that are close to the centroid for their particular class, and low membership values are assigned when they are far from the centroid. Let the first derivatives of J_{FCM} with respect to u and v equal to zero, which yields the two necessary conditions for minimizing J_{FCM}. The FCM algorithm is implemented by iterating the two necessary conditions until a solution is reached. After FCM clustering, each data sample will be associated with a membership value for each class. By assigning the data sample to the class with the highest membership value, a segmentation of the data can be obtained [10].

4.2 Region-Based FCM (RFCM) Clustering

The output of watershed algorithm is the segmentation of I_G into a set of non-overlapping regions denoted by R_i, $i = 1, 2, ..., n$ where n is the number of regions. To implement the merging of similar regions, we proposed a region-based FCM (RFCM) clustering method. The mean value, denoted by m_i, $i = 1, 2, ..., n$ of each region R_i, is needed.

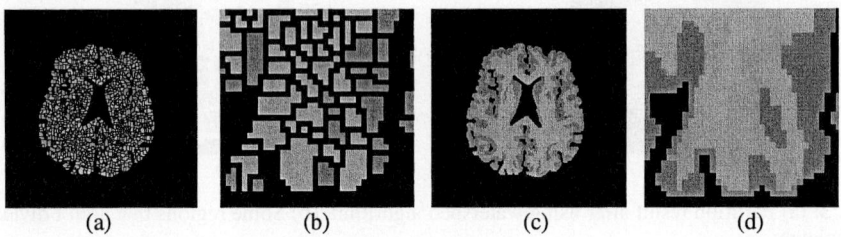

Fig. 4. (a) Image after using RFCM. (b) A partial image of (a) zoomed in. (c) Watershed lines removed from (a). (d) Watershed lines removed from (b).

The RFCM clustering algorithm in this paper is formulated as

$$J_{RFCM}(U, v) = \sum_{i \in \Omega} \sum_{k=1}^{C} u_{ik}^m \| m_i - v_k \|^2 \text{ subject to } \sum_{k=1}^{C} u_{ik} = 1, \ \Omega = \{1, ..., n\}. \quad (4)$$

where $c = 3$ (because three brain tissues are of interest: Cerebrospinal Fluid (CSF), Gray Matter (GM), and White Matter (WM) in our work), the matrix $U = \{u_{ik}\}$ is a fuzzy c-partition of I_G, $v = \{v_1, v_2, v_3\}$ is the set of fuzzy cluster centroids, and v_1, v_2, v_3 denote the centroids of CSF, GM and WM respectively, the fuzzy index $m=2$, and u_{ik} gives the membership of region R_i in the kth cluster c_k in our study.

If the difference of intensity mean value of region R_i and v_k is small, region R_i will be assigned to a high membership value for the kth cluster c_k. By assigning a region to the class with the highest membership value, a segmentation of the region can be obtained. The result image after using RFCM on Fig. 3a is shown in Fig. 4a. We can see the result of some regions which are not partitioned completely obviously in Fig. 4b obtained from a part of the image after Fig. 4a zoomed in. Fig. 4c and d are images after watershed lines removed form Fig. 4a and b respectively. From these images (see Fig. 4), the disadvantage of watershed algorithm – segmentation incompletely and inaccurately in some regions is shown clearly.

5 The Rule-Based Re-segmentation Processing

Though the image is partitioned into too many regions after the operation of watershed algorithm, there are still some regions which have not been separated completely and accurately particularly in the transitional regions of gray matter and white matter.

A Novel Approach for Adaptive Unsupervised Segmentation of MRI Brain Images

So a rule-based re-segmentation processing method to partition these regions is proposed in this section.

Searching for the Re-segmentation Regions

Because the regions needed to be segmented again are almost lying in the transitional regions of GM and WM in MRI images, the characters of these regions are considered. To determine these re-segmented regions, both the mean value and variance of each region are needed in our study. Let σ_i, © = 1, 2, ..., n denote the variance of region R_i. Three criterions provided to search for the re-segmentation regions as follows:

Let m_{gray}, m_{white} denote the mean value of GM and WM, and be set to v_2 and v_3 respectively in our experiments. Let $\Delta m_0 = (m_{white} - m_{gray})/2$, $\sigma_0 = v_3 - v_2$ and $u_{i\max} = \max(u_{i1}, u_{i2}, u_{i3})$.

Criterion 1: $m_{gray} - \Delta m_0 < m_i < m_{white} + \Delta m_0$

Criterion 2: $\sigma_i > \sigma_0$

Criterion 3: $u_{i\max} < 0.95$

If the parameters in region R_i are satisfied with these criterions mentioned above, the partition result in this region after segmentation of watershed algorithm is decided as incomplete and inaccurate segmentation, and this region should be partitioned again.

Re-segmentation Rules

Since the regions needed to be partitioned again are almost lying in the transitional regions of GM and WM, we only separate these regions into two classes: GM and WM. Suppose region R_i denotes one of these regions needed re-segmentation operating. Let p be one of the pixels in region R_i and $h(p)$ denote the intensity of p. We proposed some rules to partition the regions needed re-segmentation as follows:

Rule1: In region R_i, if $h(p) < m_i$, p is likely to be GM.

Rule2: In region R_i, if $h(p) > m_i$, p is more similar to WM than GM.

Rule3: In region R_i, if $h(p) > m_{gray}$ and $h(p) - m_{gray} < \Delta m_0$, p is possibly belonging to GM.

Rule4: In region R_i, if $h(p) < m_{white}$ and $m_{white} - h(p) < \Delta m_0$, p is likely belonging to WM.

If rule 1 and rule 3 are satisfied for pixel p in region R_i, p should be partitioned into GM. Otherwise, when rule 2 and rule 4 are satisfied for pixel p in region R_i, p ought to belong to WM.

After using the rule-based re-segmentation method processing on Fig. 4a, the re-segmentation result is shown in Fig. 5a. Fig. 5b is the finial result image. The GM and WM are shown in Fig. 5c and Fig. 5d respectively.

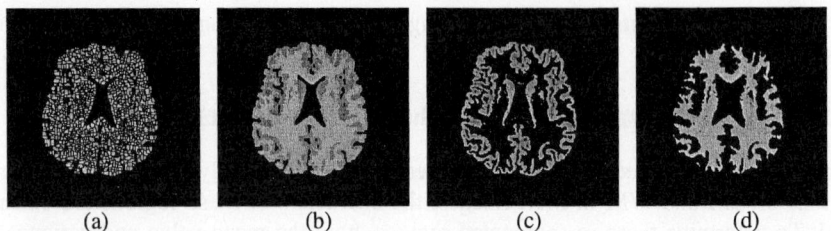

Fig. 5. (a) Result image after re-segmentation. (b) The finial result. (c) GM. (d) WM.

6 Experimental Results

6.1 Results Analyzing

Fig. 6a is a part of Fig. 3a zoomed in, and it clearly shows that some regions are partitioned incompletely after the operation of watershed algorithm. This disadvantage of watershed algorithm is obviously shown in Fig. 6b obtained from a part of Fig. 4a zoomed in. Fig. 6c is the same part image with watershed lines removed from Fig. 6b. Using our rule-based re-segmentation approach, the regions partitioned incompletely are divided again, and the result image is shown in Fig. 6d. The same part image with watershed lines removed is shown in Fig. 6e. Compared these results (Fig. 6b and d) with watershed segmentation result in Fig. 6a, the precise and veracity of our method is obviously validated.

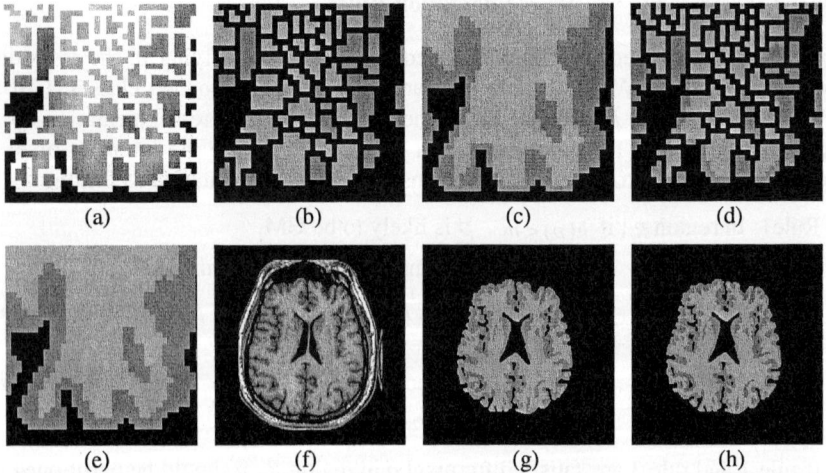

Fig. 6. (a) A part of the image after Fig. 3a zoomed in. (b) Same part of the image after Fig. 4a zoomed in. (c) Same part of (b) with watershed lines removed. (d) Same part of the image after Fig. 5a zoomed in. (e) Same part of (d) with watershed lines removed. (f) Original image. (g) Result after using RFCM. (h) The finial result.

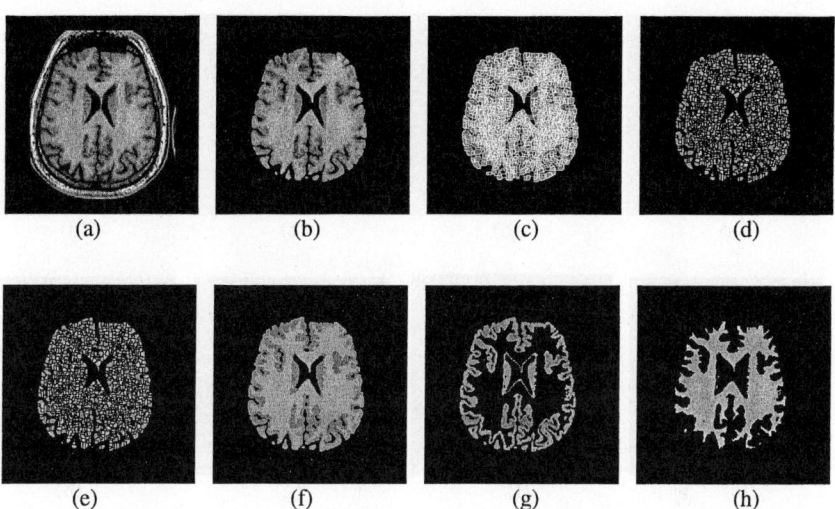

Fig. 7. Experimental results. (a) Original Image. (b) Image obtained after preprocessing. (c) Partition result after using watershed algorithm. (d) Image after using RFCM. (e) Re-segmentation image. (f) Result image obtained using our method. (g) GM. (h) WM.

In following we compare the segmentation results among original image, image after using RFCM and finial result after re-segmentation in Fig. 6f, g and h. This integrated scheme yields a robust and precise segmentation.

6.2 Executing Our Algorithm Step-by-Step

The efficacy of the proposed algorithm is validated using extensive experiments. Fig. 7 and 8 demonstrate the intermediate results of the segmentation process step-by-step. Different brain MRI images are chosen in order to demonstrate the advantages of our novel integrated method.

One of brain MRI images is shown in Fig. 7a. We remove the extra-cranial tissues from the MRI image using the preprocessing method, shown in Fig. 7b. Fig. 7c is over segmented by the application of watershed algorithm. Fig. 7d shows the image after merging regions using RFCM. The result image after re-segmentation processing is shown in Fig 7e. Fig. 7f, g and h are finial result images.

6.3 Final Results

The proposed algorithm was implemented in Matlab on a Pentium 4 2.40GHz computer. Table 1 shows execution time of the algorithm on different images and the main variables of the algorithm: the image size (N), the number of regions (wn) that is generated by watershed segmentation, the number of re-segmentation regions (sn), the centroids of GM (v_{GM}), WM (v_{WM}) and CSF (v_{CSF}) obtained from RFCM, and the centroids of GM (v'_{GM}) and WM (v'_{WM}) after re-segmentation.

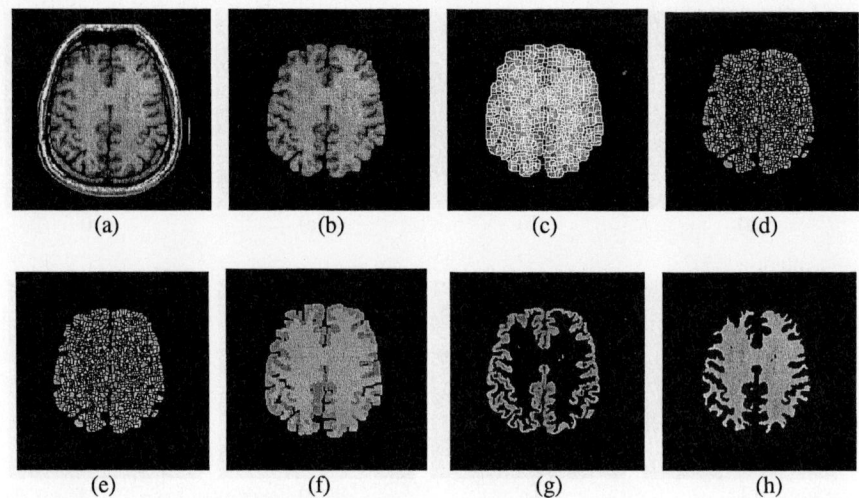

Fig. 8. Experimental results. (a) Original Image. (b) Image obtained after preprocessing. (c) Partition result after using watershed algorithm. (d) Image after using RFCM. (e) Re-segmentation image. (f) Result image obtained using our method. (g) GM. (h) WM.

Table 1. Image size (N), the number of regions (wn) generated by the watershed segmentation, the number of re-segmentation regions (sn), the centroids of GM (v_{GM}), WM (v_{WM}) and CSF(v_{CSF}) obtained from RFCM, the centroids of GM(v'_{GM}) and WM (v'_{WM}) after re-segmentation, and execution time

Image	Image size(N)	WN	SN	v_{GM}	v_{WM}	v_{CSF}	v'_{GM}	v'_{WM}	Total time(s)
Fig.2(a)	256*256	1223	375	144.53	198.99	60.83	141.00	196.00	1.1560
Fig.7(a)	256*256	1263	366	143.96	199.59	71.51	136.00	197.00	0.9590
Fig.8(a)	256*256	1196	331	136.69	197.56	60.02	133.00	194.00	0.9220

7 Conclusions

We propose a novel approach for segmenting brain tissues in MRI images, which is based on the combination of watershed algorithm, RFCM and a rule-based re-segmentation processing approach. As a result, the quality of the segmentation is improved. The algorithm is composed of four stages. In the first stage, we give a template of brain image to remove the extra-cranial tissues. Subsequently, watershed algorithm is applied to brain tissues as an initial segmenting method. Normally, result of classical watershed algorithm on gray-scale textured images such as tissue images is over-segmentation. The following procedure is a merging process for the over segmentation regions using RFCM clustering. But there are still some regions which are not partitioned completely, particularly in the transitional regions between gray matter and white matter. So we proposed a rule-based re-segmentation processing approach to divide these regions. This integrated scheme yields a robust and precise segmentation.

References

1. Pham DL, Xu CY, Prince JL: A survey of current methods in medical image segmentation. Ann. Rev. Biomed. Eng. 2 (2000) 315—37 [Technical report version, JHU/ECE 99—01, Johns Hopkins University].
2. Wells WM, Grimson WEL, Kikinis R, Arrdrige SR: Adaptive segmentation of MRI data. IEEE Trans Med Imaging, 15 (1996) 429—42.
3. LORENZ C, KRAHNSTOEVER N: 3D statistical shape models for medical image segmentation [J]. Proceedings of the Second International Conference on 3-D Digital Imaging and Modeling (3DIM)'99, (1999)394-404.
4. Tina Kapur, W.Eric L. Grimson, William M.Wells III: Segmentation of brain tissue from magnetic resonance images [J]. Medical Image Analysis, 1996, 1 (2): 109- 127.
5. Bezdek J., Hall L., Clarke L.: Review of MR image segmentation techniques using pattern recognition. Med. Phys. 20 (4), (1993) 1033–1048.
6. Clark M., Hall L., Goldgof D., Clarke L., Velthuizen R., Silbiger M.: MRI segmentation using fuzzy clustering techniques. IEEE Eng. Med. Biol. Mag. 13 (5), (1994)730–742.
7. Clarke L., Velthuizen R., Camacho M., Heine J., Vaidyanathan M., Hall L., Thatcher R., Silbiger M.: MRI segmentation: methods and application. Magn. Reson. Imaging 13 (3), (1994)343–368.
8. Yeon-Sik Ryu, Se-Young Oh: Automatic extraction of eye and mouth edges from a face image using eigenfeatures and multilayer perceptions, Pattern Recognition 34 (2001) 2459 – 2466.
9. Luc Vincent, Pierre Soille: Watersheds in Digital Spaces: An Efficient Algorithm Based on Immersion Simulations, IEEE Transaction on Pattern Analysis And Machine Intelligence, vol 13, No 6, (1991).
10. Alan Wee-Chung Liew, Hong Yan: An Adaptive Spatial Fuzzy Clustering Algorithm for 3-D MR Image Segmentation, IEEE Transaction on Medical Imaging, vol 22, No 9 (2003).
11. Ety Navon, Ofer Miller, Amir Averbuch: Color image segmentation based on adaptive local thresholds, Image and Vision Computing 23 (2005) 69-85.
12. Kollokian V.: Performance analysis of automatic techniques for tissue classification in MRI of the human brain, Master's thesis, Concordia University, Montreal, Canada (1996).
13. Kwan R.-S., Evans A., Pike G.: MRI simulation-based evaluation of image-processing and classification methods. IEEE Trans. Med. Imaging 18 (11), (1999)1085–1097.
14. Niessen W., Vincken K., Weickert J., Haar Romeny B., Viergever M.: Multiscale segmentation of threedimensional MR brain images. Internat. J. Comput. Vision 31 (2/3), (1999)185–202.
15. Nowak R.: Wavelet-based Rician noise removal for magnetic resonance imaging. IEEE Trans. Image Process. 8(10), (1999) 1408–1419.
16. Otsu N.: A threshold selection method from graylevel histograms: IEEE Trans. Systems-ManCybernet. 9 (1), (1979) 62–66.
17. Pal N., Pal S.: A review on image segmentation techniques. Pattern Recognition 26 (9), (1993)1277–1294.
18. Pham D., Xu C., Prince J.: Current methods in medical image segmentation. Annu. Rev. Biomed. Eng. 2, (2000)315–337.
19. Pizurica A.: Image denoising using wavelets and spatial context modeling. Ph.D. thesis, Ghent University, Gent, Belgium (2002).
20. Pizurica A., Philips W., Lemahieu I., Acheroy M.: A versatile wavelet domain noise filtration technique for medical imaging. IEEE Trans. Med. Imaging 22 (3), (2003)323–331.

Towards Formalising Agent Argumentation over the Viability of Human Organs for Transplantation

Sanjay Modgil,[1] Pancho Tolchinsky[2], and Ulises Cortés[2]

[1] Advanced Computation Lab, Cancer Research UK
[2] Universitat Politècnica de Catalunya

Abstract. In this paper we describe a human organ selection process in which agents argue over whether a given donor's organ is viable for transplantation. This process is framed in the CARREL System; an agent-based organization designed to improve the overall transplant process. We formalize an argumentation based framework that enables CARREL agents to construct and assess arguments for and against the viability of a donor's organ for a given potential recipient. We believe that the use of argumentation has the potential to increase the number of human organs that current selection processes make available for transplantation.

1 Introduction

Human organ transplantation constitutes the only effective therapy for many life-threatening diseases. However, while the increasing success of transplants has led to increase in demand, the lack of a concomitant increase in donor organ availability has led to a growing disparity between supply and demand. Hence, much research has focussed on definition and implementation of policies for increasing donor availability, identification of suitable recipients for organs, and procedures to increase the chances of successful transplantation. Furthermore, the scarcity of donors has led to the creation of national and international coalitions of transplant organizations. This has resulted in requirements for managing and processing vast and complex data, and accommodation of a complex set of, in some cases conflicting, national and international regulations and protocols governing exchange of organs and tissues. Hence, in [17] an agent-based architecture - CARREL - is proposed for managing the data to be processed in carrying out recipient selection, organ and tissue allocation, ensuring adherence to legislation, and following approved protocols and preparing delivery plans.

In this paper we focus on CARREL's support for donor organ (rather than tissue) transplantation. In particular, we formalise a framework for agent argumentation over organ viability for transplantation with the aim of increasing the number of human organs that current selection processes make available for transplantation. In §2 we briefly describe CARREL and the current organ selection and assignation process in which an agent representing the hospital in which the donor is located (the donor agent) initially identifies an organ as viable or non-viable for transplantation. If identified as non-viable, then the organ is discarded (not extracted from the potential donor) rather than being offered to agents representing potential recipients. However, this process does not account for the fact that doctors may disagree as to whether any given set of criteria constitute an acceptable justification for identifying an organ as viable or non-viable. For example, while a donor agent may argue that an organ is non-viable, it may well be that a recipient agent provides a stronger argument for considering the organ as viable. On the other hand, a donor agent may argue that an organ is viable, and this argument may be stronger than a recipient agent's argument for non-viability. Hence, in §2 we describe an extension to the current CARREL architecture and a new organ selection and assignation process, so as to facilitate agent argumentation over the viability of organs. In this way, organs that ordinarily would be discarded having been deemed non-viable by the donor agent, may now be successfully transplanted to a recipient with a winning argument for viability. Organs that ordinarily would be discarded if deemed non-viable by all recipient agents, may now be successfully transplanted to a recipient whose argument for non-viable is defeated by the donor's argument for viability.

In §3 we formalise a framework for the required agent argumentation over the viability of organs. We formalise a logic programming style approach to argument construction and describe and motivate how our formalism differs from existing logic programming style approaches [12, 6]. We also define conflict based interactions between the constructed arguments and relations that additionally account for some relative valuation of the strength of arguments in order that one argument may defeat its conflicting counterpart. We then describe Dung's seminal *calculus of opposition* [4] for determining the preferred (winning) arguments on the basis of the ways in which they interact. Finally, §4 concludes with a discussion and programme for future work.

2 The Carrel Institution and the Organ Selection and Assignation Process

CARREL is an electronic institution in which the interactions among a group of agents are governed by a set of norms expressed in the ISLANDER specification language [5]. CARREL is formalized as an electronic institution; a type of dialogical system where all the interactions are compositions of message exchanges, or illocutions, structured through agent group meetings called scenes or rooms. Each agent can be associated with one or more roles, and these roles define the rooms the agent can enter and the protocols it should follow. Figure 1a) shows the CARREL institution and the hospitals $UCT_1...UCT_n$ that are members of CARREL. Each $UCTx$ is modelled as an agency. The roles the different agents play in this agency are described in [3]. Here we focus on donor (DA) and recipient agent (RA) associated with each $UCTx$, and describe their roles in the organ selection and assignation process. In particular, fig.1a) shows the donor and recipient agents DA_1 and RA_1 for $UCT1$, and only the recipient agents $RA_2...RA_n$ for hospitals $UCT_2...UCT_n$. Encoded in CARREL are sets of legislation and protocols governing the exchange of organs and tissues. These are based on two physical institutions representing examples of best practice: the OCATT (Organització CATalana de Trasplantaments) [8] and ONT (Organización Nacional de Transplantes) [9] organ transplantation organizations for Catalonia and Spain respectively. A hospital becomes a member of CARREL in order to make use of the services provided. In so doing, it commits to respecting the norms that rule the interactions inside CARREL. The current selection and assignation process begins when DA_1 detects a potential

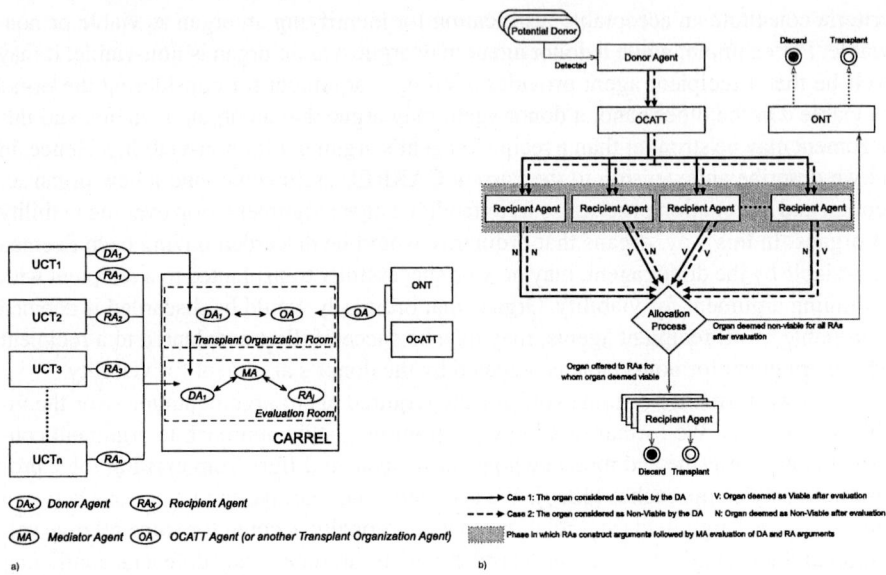

Fig. 1. a) The CARREL Institution b) Flow of the proposed human organ selection process

donor. DA_1 informs OCATT (assuming all UCT_i are in Catalonia) only if the donor's organs are deemed viable for transplantation. Organs deemed as non-viable are discarded. OCATT then offers organs to potential recipients in a prioritised queue. Once an organ is accepted, CARREL agents are then deployed to coordinate extraction of the organ and delivery to the highest prioritised recipient that accepts the organ as viable (an organ accepted by an RA may subsequently be discarded, eg. when a surgeon deems the organ non-viable at the time of operation). However, if no potential recipients are found, then OCATT offers the organ to the ONT, and a similar process takes place, this time embracing the whole of Spain. In case of refusal, the organ is then offered to transplant organizations in Europe. If every organization fails to allocate the organ, then the organ will be discarded. Currently, in Catalonia, between 15 and 20% of livers, 20% of kidneys, 60% of hearts, 85% of lungs and 95% of pancreases are discarded [8].

We now describe a new organ selection and assignation process (illustrated in fig.1b) that aims to decrease the number of discards and therefore reduce the disparity between supply and demand of organs. To facilitate this process, the roles of the DAs and RAs have been extended to include construction, sending and retrieving of arguments. A mediator agent (MA) is also defined with the role of constructing further arguments, assigning strengths to arguments and evaluating the status of interacting arguments. In addition, two new scenes or rooms are defined: a Transplant Organization Room (TOR) and an Evaluation Room (ER). Having identified a potential donor, DA_1 enters the TOR (see fig 1a) and communicates basic organ data (such as the organ type) and donor data (such as the donor's clinical history) to the OA agent representing the transplant organizations (e.g., OCATT or ONT). DA_1 also sends its arguments for whether it considers the organ to be viable or non-viable to the MA in the ER. The OA agent contacts each RA identified as a potential recipient on the basis of basic organ and donor data. Each contacted RA then constructs its own arguments for either the viability or non-viability of the organ, and communicates these arguments to the MA. In the case that some RA_j and DA_1 disagree as to the viability of the organ, MA evaluates RA_j and DA_1's arguments in order to determine the *winning* argument, and so decide whether the organ is viable or not for RA_j. We now formalise the above described argumentation.

3 Arguing over the Viability of Organs

The organ assignment process illustrates the ubiquity of disagreement and conflict of opinion in the medical domain. What may be a sufficient reason for discarding an organ for some qualified professionals may not be for others. Different policies in different hospitals and regions exist, and requiring a consensus among medical professionals is not feasible. Hence, contradictory conclusions may be derived from the same set of facts. For example, suppose a donor with a smoking history of more than 20-30 packs a year and no history of *chronic obstructive pulmonary disease* (COPD). Some would cite a donor's smoking history as sufficient reason for labelling a donor's lung as non-viable [8]. However, there are qualified physicians that reason that the donor's lung is viable given that there is no history of COPD [7].

We propose the use of argumentation [13] to formalise the required reasoning and arbitration in the presence of conflict. Argumentation involves logic based inference of arguments followed by definition of the status of arguments on the basis of the ways in which they interact. In what follows we define the agents' inference of arguments, built from a first order logic-programming style language $\mathcal{L}$, and define evaluation of the status of arguments on the basis of conflict based interactions that additionally account for the relative strengths of arguments.

3.1 Inference of Arguments

A wff of $\mathcal{L}$ is an atomic first order formula or such a formula preceded by strong negation $\neg$. Let us call such formulae *strong* literals. An agent's knowledge base Δ consists of the union of a set $\mathcal{K}$ of ground strong literals and a set $\mathcal{R}$ of defeasible rules also written in $\mathcal{L}$. The antecedent of such a rule is built from a conjunction of strong literals and/or *weak* literals of the form $\sim L$, where L is a strong literal and $\sim$ represents weak negation, i.e., L cannot be shown to be true (negation as failure).

Definition 1. *A defeasible rule is of the form:*
1) $L_1 \wedge \ldots \wedge L_m \Rightarrow L_{m+1}$, *or*
2) $L_1 \wedge \ldots \wedge L_m \Rightarrow \neg R$
where L_i ($0 \leq i \leq m$) is a strong or weak literal and R is a rule of type 1) or 2).

An example of a rule of type 1) is $p(X) \wedge \sim \neg q(X) \Rightarrow s(X)$. Note that a rule of type 2) with consequent $\neg R$ represents a challenge to any inference obtained by application of R. For instance, $r(X) \Rightarrow \neg(p(X) \wedge \sim \neg q(X) \Rightarrow s(X))$ and $t(X) \Rightarrow \neg(r(X) \Rightarrow \neg(p(X) \wedge \sim \neg q(X) \Rightarrow s(X)))$. The rationale for these non-standard rules with (possibly nested) negations of rules as consequents, will be discussed later. In the following definition of argument inference we write $\Theta(\alpha)$ to denote the application of a substitution $\Theta = \{X_1/t_1, \ldots X_n/t_n\}$ to a first order formula or rule α, where X_i are the variables in α and t_i are terms (constants or variables).

Definition 2. *Let $\Delta = (\mathcal{K} \cup \mathcal{R})$ be an agent knowledge base and α denote a strong literal, or an expression of the form R or $\neg R$ where R is a defeasible rule. Then:*

- $\Delta \mathrel{|\!\sim} \alpha$ *iff*
  - $\alpha \in \Delta$, *or*
  - *there exists a rule* $r = L_1 \wedge \ldots \wedge L_n \Rightarrow \alpha' \in \mathcal{R}$, *and a substitution* $\Theta = \{X_1/t_1, \ldots X_n/t_n\}$ *on* r *such that* $\alpha = \Theta(\alpha')$, *and for* $i = 1 \ldots n$, $\Delta \vdash \Theta(L_i)$ *where each variable in* $\Theta(L_i)$ *is assumed existentially quantified*
- $\Delta \mathrel{|\!\sim} \sim L$ *iff it is not the case that* $\Delta \mathrel{|\!\sim} L$

Definition 3. *An argument based on $\Delta = (\mathcal{K} \cup \mathcal{R})$ is a tuple (H, h) where:*

- $H \subseteq \Delta$
- $H \mathrel{|\!\sim} h$
- H *is minimal w.r.t set inclusion* ($\neg \exists H' \mid H' \subseteq H$ *and* $H' \mathrel{|\!\sim} h$)

The above defines the standard support-claim structuring of an argument [14] in which H is the support and h the claim of argument (H, h). A sub-argument of (H, h) is of the form (H', h') where H' is a subset of H. From hereon we assume $\mathcal{R}$ in Δ to be finite, in which case the arguments inferred from Δ will be finite (up to renaming of variables). Also, we use upper case letters to denote variables and lower case letters to denote constants. Note that by definition, each rule $R \in \mathcal{R}$ is the claim of an argument $(\{R\}, R)$, and if $\neg R$ is the consequent of a rule R' whose antecedent can be inferred from Δ, then R' will be in the support of an argument with claim $\neg R$ ($\{R'\}, \neg R$).

Example 1. Let r be a potential recipient for the donor d's lung. Let d_p stand for 'donor property', d_o for 'donor organ' s_h for 'smoking history', *copd* for 'chronic obstructive pulmonary disease', v for 'viable' and *contra* for 'contraindication'. Suppose DA's knowledge base Δ_d containing:

d1 = $d\_o(d, lung)$, d2 = $d\_p(d, s\_h)$, d3 = $\neg d\_p(d, copd)$,
d4 = $d\_o(D, lung) \wedge d\_p(D, s\_h) \Rightarrow contra(D, lung)$,
d5 = $contra(D, O) \Rightarrow \neg v(D, O)$

and the recipient agent's knowledge base Δ_r containing:
r1 = $d\_o(d, lung)$, r2 = $d\_p(d, s\_h)$, r3 = $\neg d\_p(d1, copd)$, r4 = $match(d, r)$
r5 = $\neg d\_p(D, copd) \Rightarrow \neg(d\_o(D, lung) \wedge d\_p(D, s\_h) \Rightarrow contra(D, lung))$,
r6 = $d\_o(D, O) \wedge match(D, R) \wedge \sim contra(R, O) \Rightarrow v(D, O)$
From Δ_d one can construct arguments:
- A1 = $(\{d4, d1\}, d\_o(d, lung) \wedge d\_p(d, s\_h) \Rightarrow contra(d, lung))$
- A2 = $(\{d1, d2, d4\}, contra(d, lung))$
- A3 = $(\{d1, d2, d4, d5\}, \neg v(d, lung))$
and from Δ_r the arguments:
- B1 = $(\{r3, r5\}, \neg(d\_o(d, lung) \wedge d\_p(d, s\_h) \Rightarrow contra(d, lung)))$
- B2 = $(\{r1, r4, r6\}, v(d, lung))$

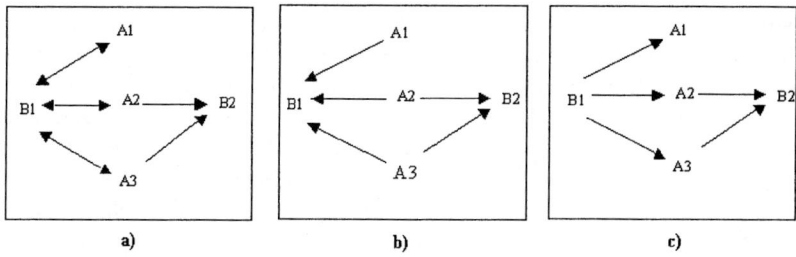

Fig. 2. The arguments' defeat relations for the smoking history example

Notice that we do not formulate $r5$ as $d\_o(D, lung) \land d\_p(D, s\_h) \land \neg d\_p(D, copd)$ $\Rightarrow \neg contra(D, lung)$, as this would result in a RA's argument for $\neg\ contra(d, lung)$ which would challenge **any** DA's argument for $contra(d, lung)$, and not just DA's arguments constructed on the basis of the donor's smoking history. That is, $B1$ represents a possible challenge to any argument for $contra(d, lung)$ **constructed using** $d4$.

3.2 Defining Defeat among Arguments and Evaluating the Status of Arguments

We now define the binary relation of *defeat* on pairs of conflicting arguments. This relation also accounts for a relative valuation of arguments encoded as a partial ordering.

Definition 4. *Let $Args$ be the set of arguments $\{(H_1, h_1) \ldots (H_n, h_n)\}$ inferred from a knowledge base Δ, and $\preceq$ a partial ordering on $Args$. Then $Defeat \subseteq (Args \times Args)$ where $((H, h), (H', h')) \in Defeat$ iff there exists a sub-argument (G, g) of (H, h) and a sub-argument (G', g') of (H', h') such that:*

- *there exists a $L_1 \land \ldots \land L_n \Rightarrow \alpha \in G'$ such that for some i, $L_i = \sim g$. In this case we say that (H, h) undercut defeats (H', h')*
- *$g \equiv \neg g'$, and it is not the case that $(H', h') \succ (H, h)$ or that (H', h') undercut defeats (H, h). In this case we say that (H, h) rebut defeats (H', h')*

Note that rebut defeats can be symmetrical in the absence of a partial order on $Args$, or when the rebutting arguments have equal strength. Note also the special case of rebut defeats between arguments with claims R and $\neg R$ where R is a defeasible rule. These are related to the notion of a *Pollock undercut* defeat [11]: $A1$ (with claim $\neg R$) denies the relation between premises and conclusion of R used in argument $A2$, and thus undercut defeats $A2$ if $A1 \succeq A2$. However, if $A2 \succ A1$ then neither argument defeats each other and so both can inappropriately co-exist in a conflict free set of arguments. One solution is to say that $A1$'s undercut defeat on $A2$ always succeeds (irrespective of their relative strength). This is the approach that is effectively adopted in other logic programming based approaches (e.g. [12]) whereby a Pollock undercut is simulated by an argument $A1$ with claim $\neg applicable\_R(X)$ undercut defeating $A2$ by disproving the non-provability assumption $\sim \neg applicable\_R(X)$ in the antecedent of $A2$'s rule R.

Our approach is to change the nature of the attack from an undercut to a rebut, so as to allow for the rule R to 'repel' and indeed defeat it's attacker $\neg R$. It is partly for this reason that rules and negations of rules can be the claims of arguments in our formalism [1]. Example 1 illustrates our motivation. We not only want that the recipient's argument $B1$ can defeat a donor argument's use of $d4$, but also that an argument using $d4$ can defeat $B1$. Hence, we do not include $\sim \neg d\_p(D, copd)$ as an exception in the antecedent of d4 as this would preclude construction of the DA's argument $A3$ for non-viability and its subsequent possible evaluation as a wining argument over $B2$.

Referring to example 1, fig.2a) shows the defeat relations between the union of Δ_d and Δ_r's arguments (where no partial ordering on the arguments is given). A unidirectional arrow indicates that the argument at the tail defeats the argument at the head of the arrow. A bidirectional arrow indicates a symmetric defeat. Note that $A3$ rebut defeats $B2$, but not vice versa, as $A3$ also undercut defeats $B2$ (see [12]).

The final stage in defining an argumentation system is to determine which arguments are preferred on the basis of the ways in which they interact. We employ Dung's seminal 'calculus of opposition' [4] to determine the preferred arguments from an *argumentation framework* $(Args, Defeat)$. Firstly, we give Dung's definition of a preferred extension:

Definition 5. *Let AF be an argumentation framework (Args, Defeat). Then for any set $S \subseteq Args$:*
- *S is **conflict free** iff no argument in S is defeated by an argument in S.*
- *An argument A is **acceptable** w.r.t. S iff each argument defeating A is defeated by an argument in S.*
- *A conflict free set of arguments S is **admissible** iff each argument in S is acceptable with respect to S.*
- *A conflict free set of arguments S is a **preferred extension** iff it is a maximal (w.r.t. set inclusion) admissible set.*

Definition 6. *Let $S_1, \ldots, S_1$ be the set of all preferred extensions of $(Args, Defeat)$. Then $\bigcap_{i=1}^{n} S_i$ is the set of preferred arguments of AF*

Referring to e.g.1, the preferred extensions are $\{A1, A2, A3\}$ and $\{B1, B2\}$, and so there are no preferred arguments. It is the role of the mediator agent (MA) to assign a partial ordering on the arguments in order to decide a preferred set of arguments. The MA can valuate (and thus order) arguments on the basis of case based reasoning and agents' reputations (see [16]). An example of the latter is when the hospital represented by RA has performed several unsuccessful lung transplants from donors with a smoking history who did not have COPD. The mediator can use this information to now prioritise $d4$ over $r5$, and hence for $i = 1 \ldots 3$: $Ai \succ B1$ and defeat(Ai,$B1$) (see fig.2b). Hence, $A1$, $A2$ and $A3$ will be preferred arguments and the organ will be labelled as non-viable.

3.3 Use of Argument Schemes and the Role of the Mediator Agent

The defeasible rules in eg. 1 can be described in terms of argument schemes, and associated critical questions [18] that help identify arguments for attacking these schemes.

---
[1] Also, it seems quite reasonable to us that a rule or its negation is the claim of an argument - "I would argue that if X and Y are the case then Z is the case".

Rules $d4$ and $d5$ formalise the non-viability scheme:

(1) If D is donor of organ O (2) and D has property C (3) and C is a contraindication for donating organ O (4) Then organ O is non-viable.

and a critical question for this scheme - *Is it the case that C is a contraindication for donating organ O?* - is addressed by formalisation of $r5$. Conceptualisation of argumentation knowledge in terms of schemes and critical questions provided a useful means for eliciting the required knowledge from doctors. At present we have upwards of thirty schemes and questions [15]. We give another example below.

Example 2. Let r be a potential recipient for the donor d's kidney k. Let sve denote *streptococcus viridans endocarditis*, svi denote *streptococcus iridans infection*, r_p denote 'recipient property', and $results\_r\_p$ denote 'results in recipient property'. Suppose the DA's knowledge base Δ_d containing rules formalising the non-viability scheme:

(1)If D is donor of organ O (2) and D has property P1 (3) and property P1 will result in a recipient having property P2 which is a contraindication for donating O (4) Then organ O is non-viable.

$d1 = d\_o(d,k)$, $d2 = d\_p(d,sve)$, $d3 = d\_o(D,k) \wedge d\_p(D,sve) \Rightarrow results\_r\_p(R,svi)$, $d4 = d\_o(D,k) \wedge results\_r\_p(R,svi) \Rightarrow contra(D,k)$, $d5 = contra(D,O) \Rightarrow \neg v(D,O)$

The recipient agent's knowledge base Δ_r contains $r1 = d\_o(d,k)$ and
$r2 = r\_p(R,svi) \Rightarrow \neg(d\_o(D,k) \wedge results\_r\_p(R,svi) \Rightarrow contra(D,k))$
$r3 = urgency(R,0) \Rightarrow \neg(d\_o(D,k) \wedge results\_r\_p(R,svi) \Rightarrow contra(D,k))$
$r4 = plan\_action(R,penicillin) \Rightarrow \neg results\_r\_p(R,svi)$
$r6 = d\_o(D,O) \wedge match(D,R) \wedge \sim contra(R,O) \Rightarrow v(D,O)$

Rules r2 and r3 are used to construct arguments addressing the critical question *'Is it the case that a transplant resulting in recipient having property P2 is a contraindication for donating O?'*. In particular r2 argues that if a recipient already has streptococcus viridans infection then it is not a contraindication, and r3 argues that if a recipient is at maximum urgency level 0 then it is not a contraindication. Rule r4 is used to construct an argument addressing the critical question *'Can the recipient be prevented from having property P2'*, by positing administration of prophylactic penicillin.

We conclude with some remarks on the role of the mediator agent (MA). As discussed in eg.1 the MA may assign an ordering to arguments on the basis of an agent's reputation. As well as assigning an ordering to arguments, an MA can construct new arguments to decide a preference. To illustrate, consider e.g.2 in which the arguments constructed will interact in the same way as in e.g.1. DA can construct an argument $A3$ for non-viable based on a donor's medical condition resulting in a recipient being infected, as well as $A1$ based on rule d4, and $A2$ based on d3,d4. $A1$, $A2$ and $A3$ rebut defeat and are rebut defeated by an RA argument $B1$ that the recipient is already infected (based on rule r2). $A2$ and $A3$ undercut defeat RA's argument $B2$ for viability based on r6. We thus obtain the same framework shown in fig.2a). In certain cases the issue may be more properly resolved not on the basis of whether RA or DA's arguments are stronger, but rather on the basis of legislation specific to the area of jurisdiction represented by the donor organisation. For example, in the case where a donor has the HIV virus and a recipient is already infected with the HIV virus, legislation may vary as to whether a transplant in such circumstances is legal or not. This legislation can be encoded for use by the MA to construct arguments to resolve the issue. For example, an argument $C1$ that is built from the rule $recipient\_jurisdiction(R, spain) \Rightarrow \neg(r\_p(R, hiv) \Rightarrow \neg(d\_o(D,O) \wedge results\_r\_p(R,hiv) \Rightarrow contra(D,O)))$ will be stronger (given that legislative arguments are given highest priority) and so asymmetrically defeat $B1$. Consequently, $C1$, $A1$, $A2$ and $A3$ will now be preferred.

4 Conclusions and Future Work

In this paper we have described an extension to the CARREL agent-based organization. The extension describes a novel application of argumentation theory in that we have formalised a framework for agent argumentation over the viability of organs for transplantation. We believe that our approach solves complex problems in the transplantation domain through efficient exchange of information and argumentation based reasoning over this information to support decision making. In particular, we believe our work has the potential to increase the number of human organs that current selection and assignation processes make available for transplantation, and thus reduce the growing disparity between supply of, and demand for, organs. Of further benefit is that a record of the agents' argumentation provides an explanatory audit trail for future reference by medical researchers, as well as a justification (that may be required in a legal context) for what are often potentially life threatening decisions.

The argumentation framework described in this paper differs from related formalisms [12, 6] in that it allows for rules and their negations to be the claims of arguments, enabling formulation of Pollock's style defeats [11] as rebut rather than the standard undercut defeats. Note that future work will allow for use of strict rules in the construction of arguments; complications arising from their use (see [2]) have motivated the restriction to defeasible rules in the work presented here. Evaluation of the preferred status of arguments may require that a mediator agent assign a partial ordering on arguments, or indeed construct further arguments. An immediate goal for future work is to formalise our proposals described in [16] for the mediator agent's use of Case-Based Reasoning, an 'Acceptability Criteria Knowledge Base' and agent reputations in the evaluation phase. Note that we have described a process whereby DA and RA arguments are submitted to the mediator without an option for making further counter-arguments in response. For example, suppose the DA and RA having submitted arguments as described in e.g. 1. Assuming that the DA has received information about the location of the potential recipient, it may instantiate and submit another argument for non-viability on the grounds that there are logistical contraindications given the RA's location and the organ's ischaemia time. This further 'round of argumentation' suggests formalisation in terms of an argumentation based dialogue. Indeed, there is a considerable body of work on formalising multi-agent argumentation based persuasion dialogues (e.g.,[10]) in which one agent attempts to persuade the other of the validity of its claim though multiple exchanges of attacking arguments. Recent work on persuasion dialogues also illustrates persuasion over action (e.g.,[1]) rather than beliefs. In this work, an argument scheme for action and its associated critical questions are used as the basis for definition of a dialogue protocol. An argument for action instantiating the proposed scheme can be attacked by arguments identified by critical questions such as: *does the action have an undesirable side-effect?* and *is there an alternative action that realises the same goal?* In future work we will need to consider such argumentation over actions given that donor and recipient agents submit arguments referencing planned actions that result in some world state supporting their claim for viability (as described in e.g. 2)

Acknowledgments. This paper was supported in part by the Grant FP6-IST-002307 (ASPIC). Thanks also to H. Prakken for useful discussion on the content of this paper.

References

1. K. M. Atkinson, T. J. M. Bench-Capon, and P. McBurney. A dialogue game protocol for multi-agent argument for proposals over action. In *Proc. First International Workshop on Argumentation in Multi-Agent Systems (ArgMAS 2004)*, 2004.
2. M. Caminada and L. Amgoud. An axiomatic account of formal argumentation. In *Proceedings of the AAAI-2005*, 2005.
3. U. Cortés, J. Vázquez-Salceda, A. López-Navidad, and F. Caballero. UCTx: a multi-agent approach to model a transplant coordination unit. In *Proceedings of the 3rd. Congrés Català dIntelligència Artificial*, 2000.
4. P. M. Dung. On the acceptability of arguments and its fundamental role in nonmonotonic reasoning, logic programming and n-person games. *Artificial Intelligence*, 77:321–357, 1995.
5. M. Esteva, D. de la Cruz, and C. Sierra. Islander: an electronic institutions editor. In *AAMAS*. ACM, 2002.
6. A.J. García and G.R. Simari. Defeasible logic programming: an argumentative approach. *Theory and Practice of Logic Programming*, 4(1):95–138, 2004.
7. A. López-Navidad and F. Caballero. Extended criteria for organ acceptance: Strategies for achieving organ safety and for increasing organ pool. *Clin Transplant, Blackwell Munksgaard*, 17:308–324, 2003.
8. OCATT. Organització Catalana de Transplantaments (OCATT). http://www10.gencat.net/catsalut/ocatt/en/htm/index.htm.
9. ONT. Organización Nacional de Transplantes. http://www.msc.es/ont.
10. S. Parsons, M. Wooldridge, and L. Amgoud. On the outcomes of formal inter-agent dialogues. In *Proceedings of the Second International Joint Conference on Autonomous Agents and Multi-Agent Systems (AAMAS 2003)*, 2003.
11. J. L. Pollock. Defeasible reasoning. *Cognitive Science*, 11:481–518, 1987.
12. H. Prakken and G. Sartor. Argument-based extended logic programming with defeasible priorities. *Journal of Applied Non-Classical Logics*, 7:25–75, 1997.
13. H. Prakken and G. Vreeswijk. *Handbook of Philosophical Logic, second edition*, chapter Logics for Defeasible Argumentation. Kluwer Academic Publishers, 2002.
14. G.R. Simari and R.P. Loui. A mathematical treatment of defeasible reasoning and its implementation. *Artificial Intelligence*, 53:125–157, 1992.
15. P. Tolchinsky and U. Cortés. Argument Schemes and Critical Questions for deciding upon the Viability of a Human Organ for transplantation. Technical report, Technical University Of Catalonia, 2005. http://www.lsi.upc.edu/~tolchinsky/sch-list.pdf.

16. P. Tolchinsky, U. Cortés, J.C. Nieves, F. Caballero, and A. López-Navidad. Using arguing agents to increase the human organ pool for transplantation. In *3rd Workshop on Agents Applied in Health Care (IJCAI-05)*, 2005.
17. J. Vázquez-Salceda, U. Cortés, J. Padget, A. López-Navidad, and F. Caballero. The organ allocation process: a natural extension of the CARREL Agent-Mediated Electronic Institution. *AiCommunications. The European Journal on Artificial Intelligence*, 3(16), 2003.
18. D. N. Walton. *Argumentation Schemes for Presumptive Reasoning*. Lawrence Erlbaum Associates, Mahwah, NJ, USA, 1996.

A Comparative Study on Machine Learning Techniques for Prediction of Success of Dental Implants

Adriano Lorena Inácio Oliveira[1], Carolina Baldisserotto[1], and Julio Baldisserotto[2]

[1] Department of Computing Systems, Polytechnic School of Engineering,
Pernambuco State University,
Rua Benfica, 455, Madalena, Recife – PE, Brazil, 50.750-410
[2] Faculdade de Odontologia, Universidade Federal do Rio Grande do Sul,
Rua Ramiro Barcelos, 2492, Porto Alegre – RS, Brazil, 90.040-060
adriano@dsc.upe.br, carol_baldi@yahoo.com.br, bjulio@ghc.com.br

Abstract. The market demand for dental implants is growing at a significant pace. In practice, some dental implants do not succeed. Important questions in this regard concern whether machine learning techniques could be used to predict whether an implant will be successful and which are the best techniques for this problem. This paper presents a comparative study on machine learning techniques for prediction of success of dental implants. The techniques compared here are: (a) constructive RBF neural networks (RBF-DDA), (b) support vector machines (SVM), (c) k nearest neighbors (kNN), and (d) a recently proposed technique, called NNSRM, which is based on kNN and the principle of structural risk minimization. We present a number of simulations using real-world data. The simulations were carried out using 10-fold cross-validation and the results show that the methods achieve comparable performance, yet NNSRM and RBF-DDA produced smaller classifiers.

1 Introduction

Dental implants have been used successfully to replace lost teeth with very high success rates [3]. Nevertheless, oral rehabilitation through dental implants presents failure risks related to the different phases of the *osseointegration* process (the integration of the implant to the adjacent bone) [14]. A number of risk factors may be related to the failure of dental implants, such as the general health conditions of the patient, the surgical technique employed, the use of smoke by the patient and the type of implant [11]. In this work, a dental implant is considered successful if it presents characteristics of osseointegration in the different phases of the process, including the prosthetic loading and its preservation. We considered that a failure took place whenever any problem related to the implant motivated its removal.

The features of the patients considered in this work were carefully chosen by an oral surgeon specialist in dental implants. The features considered here were:

1) age of the patient, 2) gender, 3) implant type, 4) implant position, 5) surgical technique, 6) an indication whether the patient was a smoker of not and 7) an indication whether the patient had a previous illness (diabetes or osteoporosis) or medical treatment (radiotherapy). These features are best described in the remaining of the paper. Some of these features, also referred to as *risk factors*, were also considered in a recent studied which used statistical techniques to analyze the risk factors associated with dental implants [11]. The data for the present study were collect between the years 1998 and 2004 by a single oral surgeon. The data set consists of 157 patterns which describe dental implants.

In the period in which data were collected there were implants carried out less than five years before. Therefore, instead of classifying the outcome of an implant simply as success or failure, we have classified our data into seven classes: (1) success confirmed until one year; (2) success confirmed between 1 and 2 years; (3) success confirmed between 2 and 3 years; (4) success confirmed between 3 and 4 years; (5) success confirmed between 4 and 5 years; (6) success confirmed for more than 5 years; and (7) failure. In general, the longer the number of years of confirmed success, the greater is the likelihood of definitive success of an implant.

Nowadays the prediction of success of failure of a dental implant is almost always carried out by the oral surgeons through clinical and radiological evaluation. Therefore, the accuracy of such predictions is heavily dependent on the experience of the oral surgeon. This works aims to help predicting the success or failure of a dental implant via machine learning techniques, thereby hoping to improve the accuracy of the predictions.

We have considered four machine learning techniques for our comparison, namely, (a) RBF-DDA with θ^- selection [18], (b) support vector machines (SVMs) [7,8,1], (c) k-nearest neighbors (kNN) [2], and (d) NNSRM (*nearest neighbors with structural risk minimization*) [12,13]. kNN is a classical classifier and was chosen because it is often used as a basis for comparison with more recent classifiers. SVMs are a more recent powerful class of machine learning techniques based on the principle of structural risk minimization (SRM). SVMs have been applied successfully to a wide range of problems such as text classification and optical character recognition [8,19]. The two remaining classifiers have been proposed recently in the literature. DDA (dynamic decay adjustment) is a fast training method for RBF and PNN neural networks [5,4]. RBF-DDA with θ^- selection uses cross-validation to select the value of parameter θ^- thus improving performance in some classification problems [18]. NNSRM uses the principle of SRM in order to build nearest neighbors (NN) classifiers with less training prototypes stored in their reference sets [12,13]. We decided to use these last two classifiers in order to assess their performance in a task different from those considered in the papers in which they were proposed [18,12]. Thus this paper also contributes by further exploring these classifiers on different data sets.

This paper is organized as follows. Next section reviews the machine learning techniques considered in this work. Section 3 describes the experiments carried out along with the results and discussion. Finally, section 4 presents our conclusions and suggestions for further research.

2 The Machine Learning Techniques Compared

2.1 Constructive RBF Neural Networks

The DDA algorithm is a very fast constructive training algorithm for RBF and probabilistic neural networks (PNNs) [5, 4]. In most problems training is finished in only four to five epochs. The algorithm has obtained good performance in a number of problems, which has motivated a number of extensions to the method recently proposed in the literature [18, 17, 16].

An RBF trained by DDA is referred as RBF-DDA. The number of units in the input layer represents the dimensionality of the input space. The input layer is fully connected to the hidden layer. RBF-DDAs have a single hidden layer. The number of hidden units is automatically determined during training. Hidden units use Gaussian activation functions. RBF-DDA uses 1-of-n coding in the output layer, with each unit of this layer representing a class. Classification uses a winner-takes-all approach, whereby the unit with the highest activation gives the class. Each hidden unit is connected to exactly one output unit. Each of these connections has a weight A_i. Output units uses linear activation functions with values computed by

$$f(\vec{x}) = \sum_{i=1}^{m} A_i \times R_i(\vec{x}) \qquad (1)$$

where m is the number of RBFs connected to that output.

The DDA training algorithm is constructive, starting with an empty hidden layer, with units being added to it as needed. The centers of RBFs, $\vec{r_i}$, and their widths, σ_i are determined by DDA during training. The values of the weights of connections between hidden and output layers are also given by DDA.

The complete DDA algorithm can be found in [5, 18]. The algorithm is executed until no changes in the parameters values (number of hidden units and their respective parameters and weights values) are detected. This usually takes place in only four to five epochs [5]. This natural stopping criterion leads to networks that naturally avoid overfitting training data [5, 4].

The DDA algorithm relies on two parameters in order to decide about the introduction of new prototypes (RBF units) in the networks. One of these parameters is a *positive threshold* (θ^+), which must be overtaken by an activation of a prototype of the same class so that no new prototype is added. The other is a *negative threshold* (θ^-), which is the upper limit for the activation of conflicting classes [5, 4].

Originally, it was assumed that the value of DDA parameters would not influence classification performance and therefore the use of their default values, $\theta^+ = 0.4$ and $\theta^- = 0.1$, was recommended for all datasets [5, 4]. In contrast, it was observed more recently that, for some datasets, the value of θ^- considerably influences generalization performance in some problems [18]. To take advantage of this observation, a method has been proposed for improving RBF-DDA by carefully selecting the value of θ^- [18].

In the RBF-DDA with θ^- selection method, the value of the parameter θ^- is selected via cross-validation, starting with $\theta^- = 0.1$ [18]. Next, θ^- is decreased by $\theta^- = \theta^- \times 10^{-1}$. This is done because it was observed that performance does not change significantly for intermediate values of θ^- [18]. θ^- is decreased until the cross-validation error starts to increase, since smaller values lead to overfitting [18]. The near optimal θ^- found by this procedure is subsequently used to train using the complete training set [18].

2.2 Support Vector Machines

Support vector machine (SVM) is a recent technique for classification and regression which has achieved remarkable accuracy in a number of important problems [7,19,8,1]. SVM is based on the principle of *structural risk minimization* (SRM), which states that, in order to achieve good generalization performance, a machine learning algorithm should attempt to minimize the *structural risk* instead of the *empirical risk* [8,1]. The empirical risk is the error in the training set, whereas the structural risk considers both the error in the training set and the complexity of the class of functions used to fit the data. Despite its popularity in the machine learning and pattern recognition communities, a recent study has shown that simpler methods, such as kNN and neural networks, can achieve performance comparable to or even better than SVMs in some classification and regression problems [15].

The main idea of support vector machines is to built optimal hyperplanes - that is, hyperplanes that maximize the margin of separation of classes - in order to separate training patterns of different classes. An SVM minimizes the first equation below subject to the condition specified in the second equation

$$\min_{w,b,\xi} \quad \frac{1}{2} w^T w + C \sum_{i=1}^{l} \xi_i$$

$$\text{subject to} \quad y_i(w^T \phi(x_i) + b) \geq 1 - \xi_i, \quad (2)$$

$$\xi_i \geq 0.$$

The training vectors x_i are mapped into a higher (maybe infinite) dimensional space by the function ϕ. Then SVM finds a linear separating hyperplane with the maximal margin in this higher dimensional space. A kernel $K(\vec{x}, \vec{y})$ is an inner product in some feature space, $K(\vec{x}, \vec{y}) = \phi^T(\vec{x})\phi(\vec{y})$. A number of kernels have been proposed in the literature [19,8,1,2]. In this work we use the radial basis function (RBF) kernel, which is the kernel used more frequently. The kernel function $K(x_i, x_j)$ in an RBF kernel is given by $K(x_i, x_j) = \exp(-\gamma ||x_i - x_j||^2), \gamma > 0$.

SVMs with RBF kernels have two parameters, namely, C, the penalty parameter of the error term ($C > 0$) and γ, the width of the RBF kernels. These parameters have great influence on performance and therefore their values must be carefully selected for a given problem. In this work, model selection is carried out via 10-fold cross-validation on training data. A grid search procedure on C and γ is performed, whereby pairs of (C, γ) are tried and the one with the best cross-validation accuracy is selected [10]. A practical method for identifying good parameters consists in trying exponentially growing sequences of C and γ. In our experiments, the sequence used was $C = 2^{-5}, 2^{-3}, \cdots, 2^{15}$, and $\gamma = 2^{-15}, 2^{-13}, \cdots, 2^3$ [10].

2.3 k-Nearest-Neighbors (kNN)

kNN is a classical prototype-based (or memory-based) classifier, which is often used in real-world applications due to its simplicity [2]. Despite its simplicity, it has achieved considerable classification accuracy on a number of tasks and is therefore quite often used as a basis for comparison with novel classifiers.

The training phase of kNN consists simply of storing all training patterns. kNN has a parameter k which is the number of neighbors to be considered for classification. For $k = 1$, kNN is also referred as *nearest neighbor* (NN). NN classifies a given pattern as belonging to the same class of the nearest pattern of the training set (also called reference set). There are a number of distances used in this process, yet Euclidean distance is by far the most frequently used [2]. We have used this distance in this work.

When $k > 1$, kNN first computes the distances of the novel pattern to be classified to all patterns of the reference set. Subsequently, the algorithm considers the k patterns of the training set with the smallest distances. Finally, the novel pattern is classified as belonging to the class of the majority of the k nearest patterns of the reference set.

In this work we have considered kNN with $k = 1$, $k = 3$ and $k = 5$ in our simulations.

In spite of its simplicity, kNN has two important disadvantages: 1) it stores all training patterns as prototypes, thereby consuming a great amount of memory and 2) the time to classify a novel pattern may be large, since the distance to all training patterns must be computed.

2.4 NNSRM

The NNSRM algorithm was recently proposed in the literature and was developed by explicitly applying the SRM principle to NN (nearest neighbor) classification [12, 13]. The main motivation was to produce NN classifiers which store much less prototypes in their reference set, thereby addressing one of the main disadvantages of the original NN. Another motivation was to develop an algorithm with comparable classification accuracy to SVMs and smaller training and classification times [12, 13].

The main idea of NNSRM consists in creating the reference set by considering only those training patterns of regions where pairs of data points of opposite classes have the smallest distances, since most classification errors occur in those regions [12, 13]. The original version of the NNSRM uses the original input space [12]. Later, a new version of the algorithm, which considers the mapping of input space via a kernel, was proposed in the literature [13]. In this work we consider only the original version of the NNSRM algorithm [12].

Consider the case of classification problems with only two classes. Suppose the training set is given by $\{\mathbf{x}_i, y_i\}$ and assume that the class labels are given by $y_i = -1$ or $y_j = 1$. Let J be the reference set and R^{emp} be the empirical risk, that is, the error on the training set. Firstly compute the pairwise distances $\rho(\mathbf{x}_i, \mathbf{x}_j) = d_{(k)}$, such that $y_i = -1, y_j = 1$ and generate a set d_k of these distances in descending order. Let $d_{(k)}$ be the kth element of this set. The NNSRM algorithm for two classes is given below [12, 13].

1) initialize $J = \emptyset, k = 1$;
2) while $R^{emp}(f_J) > 0$ do

   a) find $\mathbf{x}_i$ and $\mathbf{x}_j$ so that $\rho(\mathbf{x}_i, \mathbf{x}_j) = d_{(k)}, y_i = -1, y_j = 1$;
   b) if $\{i, j\} \not\subset J$, update $J \leftarrow J \cup \{i, j\}$;
   c) increment $k \leftarrow k + 1$.

Note that the algorithm starts with an empty reference set J and the training patterns are added to it until the training error (R^{emp}) is null. The idea of the algorithm is to include in the reference set only a number of training patterns necessary to obtain classification error equal to zero in the training set. The first pair of training patterns included in the reference set are those from different classes with the smallest distance. The algorithm proceeds considering pairs of training patterns from different classes in the order given in the set d_k.

The version of the NNSRM algorithm for N classes follows a similar idea. The detailed description of this algorithm can be found in [12].

Note that the NNSRM algorithm always obtains 100% classification accuracy in the training set. In contrast, SVMs, which are also based on the SRM principle, do not. This can be a problem for NNSRM, since the algorithm can learn noise and outliers which are common in some data sets [13]. This means that SVMs can, in most cases, achieve better generalization performance.

3 Experiments

3.1 Data Set

The input variables considered in this work were chosen by an expert (oral surgeon) based on his previous experience. According to the expert, the most important factors which influence the success or failure of a dental implant are those shown in table 1. Some of those factor were also considered in a recent study which used statistical techniques for analyzing dental implant failure [11]. Table 1 shows the input variables together with their possible values in our data set.

The distribution of the dependent variable in our problem is shown in table 2. This is a classification problem with seven classes. One of the classes indicates

Table 1. Input variables

Name	Possible values
Age (years)	from 17 to 74
Gender	{male, female}
Implant position	{ posterior maxilla, anterior maxilla, posterior mandible, anterior mandible }
Implant type	{conventional, surface treatment}
Surgical technique	{conventional, complex}
Smoker?	{yes, no}
Previous illness or medical treatment?	{no, yes (diabetes), yes (osteoporosis), yes (radiotherapy) }

Table 2. Distribution of dependent variable

Class	Frequency	Percentage
1 (success - up to 1 year)	2	1.27%
2 (success - from 1 to 2 years)	24	15.29%
3 (success - from 2 to 3 years)	25	15.92%
4 (success - from 3 to 4 years)	21	13.38%
5 (success - from 4 to 5 years)	16	10.19%
6 (success - five years or more)	62	39.49%
7 (failure)	7	4.46%
Total	157	100%

failure whereas the remaining six classes indicate success, with a variable period of time.

3.2 Experimental Setup

Due to the small number of examples in our data set we have used 10-fold cross-validation in order to compare the machine learning techniques. This is a well known technique widely used to compare classifiers whenever data is scarce [2]. In 10-fold cross-validation the data set is divided in ten disjoints subsets (folds) [2]. Subsequently, the classifier is trained using a data set composed of nine of these subsets and tested using the remaining one. This is carried ten times, always using a different subset for testing. Finally, the cross-validation error is computed as the mean of the ten test errors thus obtained.

In order to improve even more our comparison, we have firstly generated ten versions of our data set by randomly distributing the patterns. Therefore, each data set contains the same patterns yet in different orders. This means that the subsets used in 10-fold cross-validation are different for each random distributed version of our original data set.

We have performed 10-fold cross-validation using each of the ten randomly ordered versions of our data set. Hence, for each classifier, one hundred simulations were carried out (including the training and test phases).

Table 3. Comparison of classifiers: 10-fold cross-validation errors

	RBF-DDA with θ^- selection	SVM	kNN (k=1)	NNSRM
Random set 1	26.03%	25.64%	24.20%	26.75%
Random set 2	22.09%	24.36%	25.47%	27.38%
Random set 3	23.61%	23.08%	22.92%	27.38%
Random set 4	24.09%	23.08%	24.84%	28.02%
Random set 5	22.73%	24.36%	22.29%	26.11%
Random set 6	24.52%	24.36%	22.92%	26.11%
Random set 7	24.94%	23.72%	22.92%	29.93%
Random set 8	26.97%	24.36%	26.75%	27.38%
Random set 9	26.06%	24.36%	23.56%	27.38%
Random set 10	24.06%	23.08%	24.84%	31.84%
mean	24.51%	24.04%	24.07%	27.82%
st.dev	1.53%	0.81%	1.40%	1.78%

Table 4. Comparison of classifiers: number of prototypes stored (10-fold cross-validation)

	RBF-DDA with θ^- selection	SVM	kNN (k=1)	NNSRM
Random set 1	73.9	111.6	141	54
Random set 2	73.9	101.0	141	53
Random set 3	73.2	108.7	141	54
Random set 4	73.7	102.5	141	55
Random set 5	73.7	106.5	141	57
Random set 6	73.7	101.6	141	57
Random set 7	73.9	101.6	141	52
Random set 8	73.7	97.5	142	51
Random set 9	73.2	107.2	142	54
Random set 10	73.9	102.3	142	52
mean	73.68	104.05	141.3	53.9
st.dev	0.27	4.27	0.48	2.02

3.3 Results and Discussion

In this study we are interested in comparing the machine learning techniques in our problem regarding the classification error and the complexity of the classifiers, that is, the number of training prototypes stored by each of them. The simulations using RBF-DDA with parameter selection [18] were carried out using SNNS [20], whereas SVM simulations used LIBSVM [6]. We used our own implementations of kNN and NNSRM to obtain the results presented below.

Table 3 compares the classifiers with respect to 10-fold cross-validation errors. Each line of this table shows the 10-fold cross validation error obtained by each classifier using a different version of our data set (with random order of the patterns). The table also presents the mean and standard deviation of the error over the ten versions of our data set obtained by each classifiers. Table 4 presents a similar comparison of the classifiers, this time, however, regarding the number of training prototypes stored by each classifier.

The results of table 3 show that RBF with θ^- selection, SVM and kNN with $k = 1$ achieved equivalent classification performance (around 24% mean error). NNSRM, on the other hand, obtained a larger error (around 28% mean error). The best results obtained by RBF with θ^- selection (shown in table 3) used $\theta^- = 0.01$. We have carried out simulations using kNN with $k = 3$ and $k = 5$ as well, yet the smaller classification error was achieved with $k = 1$ (24.07%, as shown in table 3). With $k = 3$, the mean error was 33.04%, whereas, $k = 5$ obtained 47.44% mean classification error.

In spite of the similar accuracies obtained, the three first classifiers of tables 3 and 4 are quite different with respect to complexity, as shown in table 4. The kNN classifier produces the larger classifier, since all training patterns are stored. NNSRM was indeed able to considerably reduce the complexity of the classifier compared to NN, yet at the expense of an important decrease in accuracy. Finally, in this problem RBF-DDA with θ^- selection achieved the best trade-off between accuracy and complexity among the classifiers considered.

4 Conclusions

We have presented a comparative study on four machine learning techniques for prediction of success of dental implants. The data set consisted of 157 examples concerning real-world clinical cases. The input variables concerned risk factors for dental implants chosen by an expert (oral surgeon). The simulations were carried out using ten versions of the data set with different random orders of the patterns. For each random data set, the simulations were carried out via 10-fold cross-validation, due to the small size of the data set. The techniques compared were a) RBF-DDA with θ^- selection, b) support vector machines (SVMs), c) k-nearest neighbors (kNN) and d) NNSRM, a recently proposed technique based on kNN and the structural risk minimization principle.

The RBF-DDA, SVM and kNN classifiers achieved roughly the same classification performance (around 24% of mean cross-validation error). Yet RBF-DDA with θ^- selection obtained smaller classifiers (73.68 mean number of prototypes) than SVM (104.05 mean number of prototypes) and kNN (141.3 mean number of prototypes). The NNSRM classifier was outperformed by the other classifiers (its mean error was 27.82%), on the other hand, this method produced the smaller classifiers (with 53.9 mean number of prototypes). For our problem, which has few data, this advantage of NNSRM is not significative since it comes with an important degradation in classification accuracy.

Future work includes considering other classifiers for this problem such as the multilayer perceptron (MLP) and SVM with other kernel functions as well as evaluating the classification accuracy per class. Another research direction consists in determining the influence of each risk factor (input) on the classification accuracy, such as was done in [9].

References

1. V. David Sanchez A. Advanced support vector machines and kernel methods. *Neurocomputing*, 55:5–20, 2003.
2. A.Webb. *Statistical Pattern Recognition*. Wiley, second edition, 2002.
3. M. Barry, D. Kennedy, K. Keating, and Z. Schauperl. Design of dynamic test equipment for the testing of dental implants. *Materials & Design*, 26(3):209–216, 2005.
4. M. Berthold and J. Diamond. Constructive training of probabilistic neural networks. *Neurocomputing*, 19:167–183, 1998.
5. Michael R. Berthold and Jay Diamond. Boosting the performance of RBF networks with dynamic decay adjustment. In G. Tesauro, D. Touretzky, and T. Leen, editors, *Advances in Neural Information Processing*, volume 7, pages 521–528. MIT Press, 1995.
6. Chih-Chung Chang and Chih-Jen Lin. *LIBSVM: a library for support vector machines*, 2001. Software available at http://www.csie.ntu.edu.tw/~cjlin/libsvm.
7. C. Cortes and V. Vapnik. Support-vector network. *Machine Learning*, pages 273–297, 1995.
8. N. Cristianini and J. Shawe-Taylor. *An Introduction to Support Vector Machines*. Cambridge University Press, 2000.
9. Dursun Delen, Glenn Walker, and Amit Kadam. Predicting breast cancer survivability: a comparison of three data mining methods. *Artificial Intelligence in Medicine*, 34(2):113–127, 2005.
10. C.-W. Hsu, C.-C. Chang, and C.-J. Lin. *A Practical Guide to Support Vector Classification*, 2004. Available at http://www.csie.ntu.edu.tw/~cjlin/libsvm.
11. Donald Hui, J. Hodges, and N. Sandler. Predicting cumulative risk in endosseous dental implant failure. *Journal of Oral and Maxillofacial Surgery*, 62:40–41, 2004.
12. B. Karaçali and A. Krim. Fast minimization of the structural risk by nearest neighbor rule. *IEEE Transactions on Neural Networks*, 14(1):127–137, 2003.
13. B. Karaçali, R. Ramanath, and W. E. Snyder. A comparative study analysis of structural risk minimization by support vector machines and nearest neighbor rule. *Pattern Recognition Letters*, 25:63–71, 2004.
14. P. Laine, A. Salo, R. Kontio, S. Ylijoki, and C. Lindqvist. Failed dental implants - clinical, radiological and bacteriological findings in 17 patients. *Journal of Cranio-Maxillofacial Surgery*, 33:212–217, 2005.
15. D. Meyer, F. Leisch, and K. Hornik. The support vector machine under test. *Neurocomputing*, 55:169–186, 2003.
16. A. L. I. Oliveira, B. J. M. Melo, and S. R. L. Meira. Improving constructive training of RBF networks through selective pruning and model selection. *Neurocomputing*, 64:537–541, 2005.
17. A. L. I. Oliveira, B. J. M. Melo, and S. R. L. Meira. Integrated method for constructive training of radial basis functions networks. *IEE Electronics Letters*, 41(7):429–430, 2005.
18. A. L. I. Oliveira, F. B. L. Neto, and S. R. L. Meira. Improving RBF-DDA performance on optical character recognition through parameter selection. In *Proc. of the 17th International Conference on Pattern Recognition (ICPR'2004)*, volume 4, pages 625–628, Cambridge,UK, 2004. IEEE Computer Society Press.
19. J. Shawe-Taylor and N. Cristianini. *Kernel Methods for Pattern Analysis*. Cambridge University Press, 2004.
20. A. Zell. *SNNS - Stuttgart Neural Network Simulator, User Manual, Version 4.2*. University of Stuttgart and University of Tubingen, 1998.

Infant Cry Classification to Identify Hypo Acoustics and Asphyxia Comparing an Evolutionary-Neural System with a Neural Network System

Orion Fausto Reyes Galaviz[1] and Carlos Alberto Reyes García[2]

[1] Universidad Autónoma de Tlaxcala, Calzada Apizaquito S/N,
Apizaco, Tlaxcala, 90400, México
orionfrg@ingenieria.uatx.mx
[2] Instituto Nacional de Astrofísica, Óptica Electrónica, Luis E. Erro 1,
Tonantzintl, Puebla, 72840, México
kargaxxi@inaoep.mx

Abstract. This work presents an infant cry automatic recognizer development, with the objective of classifying three kinds of infant cries, normal, deaf and asphyxia from recently born babies. We use extraction of acoustic features such as LPC (Linear Predictive Coefficients) and MFCC (Mel Frequency Cepstral Coefficients) for the cry's sound waves, and a genetic feature selection system combined with a feed forward input delay neural network, trained by adaptive learning rate back-propagation. We show a comparison between Principal Component Analysis and the proposed genetic feature selection system, to reduce the feature vectors. In this paper we describe the whole process; in which we include the acoustic features extraction, the hybrid system design, implementation, training and testing. We also show the results from some experiments, in which we improve the infant cry recognition up to 96.79% using our genetic system. We also show different features extractions that result on vectors that go from 145 up to 928 features, from cry segments of 1 and 3 seconds respectively.

Keywords: Feature Selection, Evolutionary Strategies, Classification, Infant Cry Analysis, Pattern Recognition, Hybrid System.

1 Introduction

The cry sound produced by an infant is the result of his/her physical and psychological condition and/or from internal/external stimulation. It has been proved that crying caused by pain, hunger, fear, stress, etc. shows different cry patterns. An experimented mother can be able of recognizing the difference between different types of cry, and with this, react adequately to her infant's needs. The experts in neurolinguistics consider the infant cry as the first speech manifestation. It is the first experience on the production of sounds, which is followed by the larynx and oral cavity movements. All of this, combined with the feedback of the hearing capability, will be used for the phonemes production. Children with hearing loss, identified before their first 6 months of life, have a significant improvement in the speech development compared to those whose hearing loss was identified after their first 6 months of age. In the case of the infants that have passed through an asphyxiating period at birth, they are exposed to changes at a neurological level, depending on the asphyxiating range they had suffered. According to the American Academy of Pediatrics (AAP), from 2 to 6 out of 1000 recently born babies present asphyxia and 60% of the babies prematurely born and presenting low weight, also suffer an asphyxiating period. From them, 20 to 50% die during their first days of life. From the survivors, 25% develop permanent neurological sequels.

2 State of the Art

Recently, some research efforts on infant cry analysis (ICA) had been made; showing promising results, and highlights the importance of exploring this field. In [1], Reyes & Orozco classified samples of deaf and normal babies, obtaining recognition results that go from 79.05% up to 97.43%. Petroni used neural networks to differentiate pain and no-pain cries [2]. Tako Ekkel tried to classify newborn crying sound into two categories normal and abnormal (hypoxia), and reports a correct classification result of 85% based on a radial basis neural network [3]. Also, using self organized maps methodologies, Cano et al, in [4] report some experiments to classify infant cry units from normal and pathological babies.

3 Infant's Cry Automatic Recognition Process

The automatic infant cry recognition process (Fig. 1) is basically a problem of pattern recognition, and it is similar to speech recognition. The goal is to take the baby's cry sound wave as an input, and at the end obtain the kind of cry or pathology detected. Generally, the Speech or Infant Cry Recognition Process is done in two steps; the first step is the acoustic processing, or features extraction, while the second is known as pattern processing or classification. In the proposed system, we have added an extra step between both of them, called feature selection. For our case, in the acoustic analysis, the infant's cry signal is processed to extract relevant features in function of time. The feature set obtained from each cry sample is represented by a vector, and each vector is taken as a pattern. Next, all vectors go to an acoustic features selection module, which will help us; to select the best features for the training process, and at the same time to efficiently reduce the input vectors. The selection is done through the

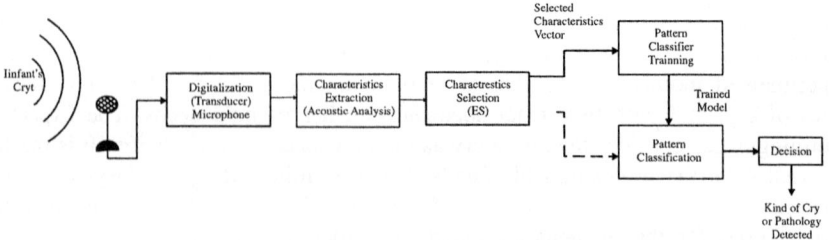

Fig. 1. Infant's Cry Automatic Recognition Process

use of evolutionary strategies. As for the pattern recognition methods, four main approaches have been traditionally used: pattern comparison, statistical models, knowledge based systems, and connectionist models. We focus in the use of the last one.

4 Acoustic Processing

The acoustic analysis implies the application and selection of filter techniques, feature extraction, signal segmentation, and normalization. With the application of these techniques we try to describe the signal in terms of its fundamental components. One cry signal is complex and codifies more information than the one needed to be analyzed and processed in real time applications. For this reason, in our cry recognition system we use a feature extraction function as a first plane processor. Its input is a cry signal, and its output is a vector of features that characterizes key elements of the cry's sound wave. We have been experimenting with diverse types of acoustic features, emphasizing by their utility Mel Frequency Cepstral Coefficients (MFCC) and Linear Predictive Coefficients (LPC).

4.1 Linear Predictive Coefficients

Linear Predictive Coding (LPC) is one of the most powerful techniques used for speech analysis. It provides extremely accurate estimates of speech parameters, and is relatively efficient for computation. Based on these reasons, for some experiments, we are using LPC to represent the crying signals. Linear Prediction is a mathematical operation where future values of a digital signal are estimated as a linear function of previous samples. In digital signal processing, linear prediction is often called linear predictive coding (LPC) and can thus be viewed as a subset of filter theory [1].

4.2 Mel Frequency Cepstral Coefficients

The low order cepstral coefficients are sensitive to overall spectral slope and the high-order cepstral coefficients are susceptible to noise. This property of the speech spectrum is captured by the Mel spectrum. High order frequencies are weighted on a logarithmic scale whereas lower order frequencies are weighted on a linear scale. The Mel scale filter bank is a series of L triangular band pass filters that have been designed to simulate the band pass filtering believed to occur in the auditory system. This corresponds to series of band pass filters with constant bandwidth and spacing on a Mel frequency scale. On a linear frequency scale, this spacing is approximately linear up to 1 KHz and logarithmic at higher frequencies (Fig. 2) [5].

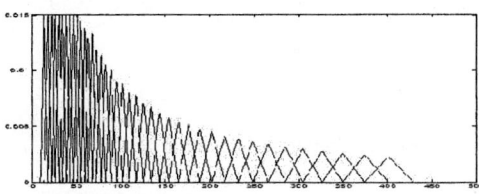

Fig. 2. Mel Filter Bank

5 Cry Pattern Classification

The acoustic features set obtained in the extraction stage, is generally represented as a vector, and each vector can be taken as a pattern. These vectors are later used to make the acoustic features selection and classification processes. For the present work we are using a classifier corresponding to the type of connectionist models known as neural networks, they are reinforced with evolutionary strategies to select features in order to improve their learning process. Having as a result a *Genetic-Neural* hybrid system.

5.1 Evolutionary Strategies

The evolutionary strategies are proposed to solve continuous problems in an efficient manner. Its name comes from the German *"Evolutionstrategien"*, so we may frequently see them mentioned as "ES". Their origin was an stochastic scaled method (in other words, following the gradient) using adaptive steps, but with time it has converted in one of the most powerful evolutionary algorithms, giving good results in some parametric problems on real domains. The Evolutionary Strategies make more exploratory searches than genetic algorithms [6].

The main reproduction operator in evolutionary strategies is the mutation, in which a random value is added to each element from an individual to create a new descendant [7]. The selection of parents to form descendants is less strict than in genetic algorithms and genetic programming.

5.2 Neural Networks

In a study from DARPA [8] the neural networks are defined as systems composed of many simple processing elements, that operate in parallel and whose function is determined by the network's structure, the strength of its connections, and the processing carried out by the processing elements or nodes. We can train a neural network to execute a function in particular, adjusting the values of the connections (weights) between the elements. Generally, the neural networks are adjusted or trained so that an input in particular leads to a specified or desired output (Fig.3). Here, the network is adjusted based on a comparison between the actual and the desired output, until the network's output matches the desired output [9].

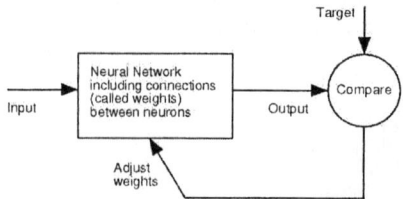

Fig. 3. Training of a Neural Network

Generally, the training of a neural network can be supervised or not supervised. The methods of supervised training are those used when labeled samples are available. Among the most popular models are the feed-forward networks, trained under supervision with the back-propagation algorithm. For the present work we have used variations of these basic models, which we describe briefly on the next sections.

5.3 Feed-Forward Input Delay Neural Network

Cry data are not static, and any cry sample at any instance in time is dependent on crying patterns before and after that instance in time. A common flaw in the traditional Back-Propagation algorithm is that it does not take this into account. Waibel et al. set out to remedy this problem in [12] by proposing a new network architecture called the "Time-Delay-Neural Network" or TDNN. The primary feature of TDNNs is the time-delayed inputs to the nodes. Each time delay is connected to the node via its own weight, and represents input values in past instances in time. TDNNs are also known as Input Delay Neural Networks because the inputs to the neural network are the ones delayed in time. If we delay the input signal by one time unit and let the network receive both the original and the delayed signals, we have a simple time-delay neural network. Of course, we can build a more complex one by delaying the signal at various lengths. If the input signal is n bits and delayed for m different lengths, then there should be nm input units to encode the total input [9].

5.4 Gradient Descent with Adaptive Learning Rate Back Propagation

The training by gradient descent with adaptive learning rate back propagation, proposed for this project, can be applied to any network as long as its weights, net input, and transfer functions have derivative functions. Back-propagation is used to calculate derivatives of performance with respect to the weight and bias variables. Each variable is adjusted according to gradient descent. At each training epoch, if the performance decreases toward the goal, then the learning rate is increased. If the performance increases, the learning rate is adjusted by a decrement factor and the change, which increased the performance, is not made [10].

The training stops when any of these conditions occurs: *i)* The maximum number of epochs (loops) is reached, *ii)* The maximum amount of time has been exceeded, or *iii)* The performance error has been minimized to the goal.

5.4.1 Hybrid System

The hybrid system was designed to train the Input Delay Neural Network with the best features selected from the input vectors. To perform this selection, we apply Evolutionary Strategies, which use real numbers for coding the individuals. The system works as follows.

Suppose we have an original matrix of size $s \times q$, where s is the number of features that each sample has and q is the number of samples available, and we want to select the best features of that matrix to obtain a smaller matrix. For doing so, a population of n individuals is initialized, each having a length of m; these individuals represent n matrices with m rows, and q columns (Fig. 4). Each row corresponds to m random numbers that go from 1 to s.

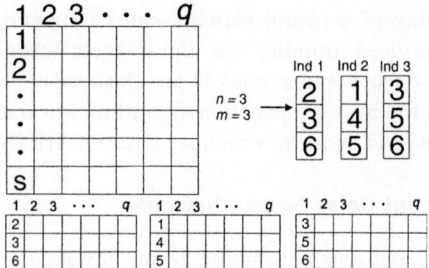

Fig. 4. Individuals Initialization

Once the matrices are obtained, n neural networks are initialized, and we train each one with one matrix, at the end of training each network, we measure the efficiency by using confusion matrices. After all the results are obtained, we select the matrices yielding the best results (Fig. 5).

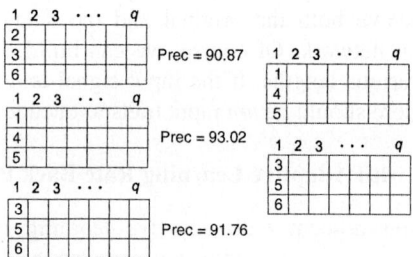

Fig. 5. Selection of the best individuals

Next, the best matrices selected are sorted and ordered from the highest to the lowest efficiency value. Next we apply tournament to them, where we generate n random numbers that go from 0 to the number of selected matrices. In Fig. 6 we show that only two matrices where selected, so we generate n (in this case 3) random numbers from 0 to 2. Since there is no matrix with a 0 index, all 0s randomly generated become 1. As a result the number 1 has twice the probability to be randomly generated than any of the other indexes, which is seen as a reward for best efficiency to the matrix in position 1, getting the highest probabilities to be chosen.

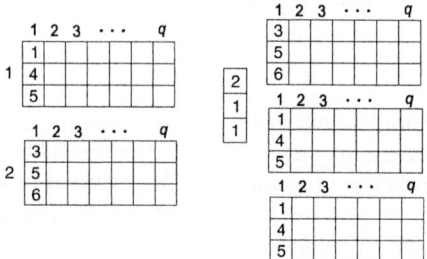

Fig. 6. Generation of a new population with the best individuals

Once the new generation of individual has been obtained, they suffer a random mutation, in each generation. First we choose a mutation factor (we used a mutation rate of 0.2), and when a new descendant is born, we generate a random number that goes from 0 to 1. If it's smaller than 0.2 the individual is mutated, if it's larger, we pass the individual as it is. When the individual is selected to be mutated, we generate a random number that goes from 1 to m, this is done to select which chromosome will be mutated. After we have this position, another random number from 1 to s (e.g. 1 – 928) is generated, which represents a new feature to be selected. When the individual is not selected to be mutated, it goes to the next generation to compete with the others as an exact copy of its parent. This process is repeated for a given number of generations stated by the user.

6 System Implementation for the Cry Classification

On the first stage, the infant's cries are collected by recordings obtained directly from doctors of the Mexican National Institute of the Human Communication (INCH), and the Mexican Institute of Social Security (IMSS, Puebla). The cry samples are labeled with the kind of cry that the collector states at the end of each cry recording. Later, we divide each cry recording in segments of 1 and 3 seconds; these segments are then labeled with a previously established code, and each one represents one sample.

By this way, for the present experiments, we have one corpus made out of 1049 samples from *normal* babies, 879 from hypo acoustics (deaf), and 340 with asphyxia, all this from 1 second segments samples. We also have another corpus composed by 329 samples of *normal* babies, 291 samples from hypo acoustics, and 111 from asphyxiating babies, all these from 3 second segment samples. The two corpuses were used for separate experiments, as it is later explained. On the next step the samples are processed one by one extracting its LPC and MFCC acoustic features, this process is done with the freeware program Praat 4.2 [11]. The acoustic features are extracted as follows: for each segment we extract 16 or 21 coefficients for every 50 or 100 milliseconds, generating vectors that go from 145 up to 1218 features for each 1 second or 3 second sample. The evolutionary algorithm was designed and programmed using Matlab 6.5 R13, the neural network and the training algorithm where implemented using the Matlab's Neural Network Toolbox.

In order to compare the behavior of our proposed hybrid system, we made a set of experiments where the original input vectors were reduced to 50 components by means of Principal Component Analysis (PCA). When we use evolutionary strategies for the acoustic features selection, we search for the best 50 features. In this way, the neural network's architecture consists of a 50 nodes input layer, a 20 nodes hidden layer (60% less nodes than the input layer) and an output layer of 3 nodes. The implemented system is interactively adaptable; no changes have to be made to the source code to experiment with any corpuses.

To perform the experiments we first made 16 different experiments, 8 experiments for each kind of segmentation, as follows; for 1 or 3 seconds we extract:

- 16 features for each 50 millisecond window
- 21 features for each 50 millisecond window

- 16 features for each 100 millisecond window
- 21 features for each 100 millisecond window

Extracting LPC and MFCC feature vectors; this is 4 different extractions using 2 different feature extractions, and 2 different segment samples, which gives us 16 different kinds of experiments. After doing all these experiments [13] we concluded that the best features, which were the ones we used to test our hybrid system are:

- For 1 second samples
  - 16 features for each 100ms, LPC (145 Features)
  - 16 features for each 100ms, MFCC (145 Features)
- For 3 second samples
  - 16 features for each 100ms, LPC (448 Features)
  - 16 features for each 50ms, MFCC (928 Features)

In all of our experiments, since we only have 340 one second, and 111 three seconds from asphyxiating babies samples, we will only choose 340 one second samples, and 111 three seconds samples from deaf and normal babies.

The training is done up to 6000 epochs or until a 1×10^{-8} error is reached. Once the network is trained, we test it using different samples from each class separated previously for this purpose (we used from each corpus 70% for training and 30% for testing). The recognition precision is shown along with the corresponding confusion matrices.

7 Experimental Results

We experimented first with the simple neural network reducing the input vectors to 50 principal components and later with our hybrid system to compare the obtained results. In these experiments we use the same input parameters, in other words, 50 input nodes and 1 time delay unit.

In the case of the simple neural network system, we perform three experiments and choose the best result. As for the hybrid system, to search for the best solution in a multi solutions space, only one experiment is done. We do so because we use 20 individuals as the initial population, 20 generations to perform the features search, and the size of the individuals was of 50 chromosomes. With all these input parameters, there are 400 different training processes needed, which takes much more time to perform each experiment. The results are shown in Table 1, where the first column corresponds to the results obtained from vectors reduced with PCA, and the second one with vectors reduced by selecting features with the evolutionary strategy presented. In both cases, the same kind of input delay neural network was utilized. The only difference being that in the first case the reduction of vectors is done before any processing by the neural network. While in the second case, feature selection is made concurrently to the neural network training. On this basis, we are presenting our model as an evolutionary-neural hybrid system.

Table 1. Results using different feature extractions, comparing a simple neural network with a hybrid system

	Neural System	Hybrid System
1 sec. LPC 16f 100ms	55.15%	86.75%
1 sec. MFCC 16f 100ms	93.33%	**96.79%**
3 sec. LPC 16f 50ms	68.79%	85.72%
3 sec. MFCC 16f 100ms	92.33%	95.56%

8 Conclusions and Future Works

The application of feature selection methods, on different kinds of pattern recognition tasks, has become a viable alternative tool. Particularly for those tasks which have to deal with input vectors of large dimensions. As we have shown, the use of evolutionary strategies for the selection of acoustic features, in the infant cry classification problem, has allowed us, not only to work with reduced vectors without losing classification accuracy, but also to improve the results compared to those obtained when applying PCA. On the other side, from the results shown, we can conclude that the best acoustic features to classify infant cry, with the presented hybrid system, are the MFCC.

For future works, in order to improve the performance of the described evolutionary-neural system, we are planning to do more experiments using other neural network configurations, different number of individuals, different number of generations and different individual size. We are also looking for adequate models to dynamically optimize the parameters of the hybrid model, in order to adapt it to any type of pattern recognition application.

As for the automatic infant cry recognition problem, we will continue experimenting with some different types of hybrid systems, such as instance and feature selection hybrid models, boosting neural network ensemble and boosting ensemble of support vector machines. And once we can be sure that our system is robust enough to identify the mentioned pathologies, we will try to increment our infant cry corpus with the same kind and some other kinds of pathologies. Particularly with the type of pathologies related to the central nervous system (CNS) This is done firstly because with more cry samples from deaf and asphyxiating babies, we can assure a more reliable learning and recognition of those cry classes. Secondly, by adding cries from infants with other pathologies, we can direct the early diagnosis to identify such pathologies. We want to concentrate on pathologies related to the CNS, because the infant cry, as a primary communication function, is naturally regulated by the CNS. So, any pathology which can be associated to the CNS should have some identifiable particular alterations on the cry signal features.

References

1. Orozco Garcia, J., Reyes Garcia, C.A. (2003), Mel-Frequency Cepstrum coefficients Extraction from Infant Cry for Classification of Normal and Pathological Cry with Feedforward Neural Networks, ESANN 2003, Bruges, Belgium.
2. Marco Petroni, Alfred S. Malowany, C. Celeste Johnston, Bonnie J. Stevens, (1995). Identification of pain from infant cry vocalizations using artificial neural networks (ANNs), The International Society for Optical Engineering. Volume 2492. Part two of two. Paper #: 2492-79.
3. Ekkel, T, (2002). "Neural Network-Based Classification of Cries from Infants Suffering from Hypoxia-Related CNS Damage", Master's Thesis. University of Twente, The Netherlands.
4. Sergio D. Cano, Daniel I. Escobedo y Eddy Coello, "El Uso de los Mapas Auto-Organizados de Kohonen en la Clasificación de Unidades de Llanto Infantil", Voice Processing Group, 1st Workshop AIRENE, Universidad Católica del Norte, Chile, 1999, pp 24-29.
5. Gold, B., Morgan, N. (2000), Speech and Audio Signal Processing. Processing and perception of speech and music. John Wiley & Sons, Inc.
6. Santo Orcero, David. Estrategias Evolutivas, http://www.orcero.org/irbis/disertacion/node217.html. 2004.
7. Hussain, Talib S., An Introduction to Evolutionary Computation, Department of Computing and Information Science Queens University, Kingston, Ont. K7L 3N6. 1998.
8. DARPA Neural Network Study, AFCEA International Press, 1988, p. 60.
9. Limin Fu., Neural Networks in Computer Intelligence. McGraw-Hill International Editions, Computer Science Series, 1994.
10. Neural Network Toolbox Guide, Matlab V.6.0.8, Developed by MathWoks, Inc.
11. Boersma, P., Weenink, D. Praat v. 4.0.8. A system for doing phonetics by computer. Institute of Phonetic Sciences of the University of Amsterdam. February, 2002.
12. A. Weibel, T. Hanazawa, G. Hinton, K. Shikano, and K.J. Lang, "Phoneme Recognition Using Time Delay Neural Networks," *IEEE Trans. Acoustics, Speech, Signal Proc.*, ASSP-37: 32'339, 1989.
13. Orion F. Reyes Galaviz. "Clasificación de Llanto de Bebés para Identificación de Hipoacúsia y Asfixia por medio de un Sistema Híbrido (Genético – Neuronal)" Master's Thesis on Computer Science, at the Apizaco Institute of Technology (ITA), March, 2005. http://solar6.ingenieria.uatx.mx/~orionfrg/tesis.pdf

Applying the GFM Prospective Paradigm to the Autonomous and Adaptative Control of a Virtual Robot

Jérôme Leboeuf Pasquier

Departamento de Ingeniería de Proyectos,
Centro Universitario de Ciencias Exactas e Ingenierías,
Universidad de Guadalajara,
Apdo. Postal 307, CP 45101, Zapopan, Jalisco, México
jleboeuf@dip.cucei.udg.mx

Abstract. A prospective paradigm, named Growing Functional Modules (GFM) has been introduced in a recent publication. Based on the epigenetic approach, the GFM paradigm is conceived to automatically generate "artificial brains" that are able to build, through interaction, their own representation of their environments. The present application consists in designing an artificial brain for a simple virtual mushroom shaped robot named hOnGo. This paper describes this initial implementation and its preliminary results.

1 Introduction

A previous paper [7] introduces a prospective paradigm named "Growing Functional Modules" (GFM) founded on the epigenetic approach. The central postulate of this paradigm states that the architecture of the artificial brain is based on the interconnection of growing functional modules. Such modules' interconnection results from the previous design phase of the robot's brain. In order to illustrate that assertion, this paper presents an initial application consisting in generating the artificial brain of a simple mushroom shaped robot named hOnGo[1] that has been introduced in a previous paper [10].

Our purpose is to exhibit the functionality and evaluate the efficiency of the artificial brain that results from the design of a GFM architecture.

Historically, hOnGo has been fashioned to give support to the development of the paradigm; the real brain design process was more chaotic than what is described in this paper. Furthermore, all subsequent results are related to a virtual version of the robot.

2 Description of the Application

2.1 The hOnGo Robot

Figure 1 shows a schematic representation of hOnGo consisting of three main parts: a single leg, a body and a hat. An actuator is placed at each of the axis of rotation J2, J3

---

[1] Spanish word for mushroom.

and J4. A fourth actuator placed at J1 that is in charge of stabilizing the hat in a horizontal position, is not considered in this version. Besides, to avoid dealing with unstable equilibrium[2], the axis J3 is positioned above hOnGo's centre of gravity.

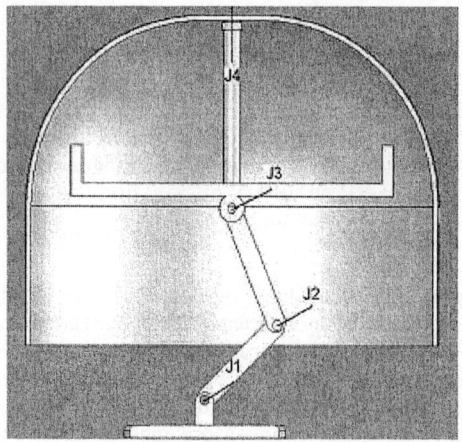

Fig. 1. Schematic representation of the mushroom shaped robot hOnGo

Motion is obtained when the robot leans on the brim of its hat and repositions its leg to take advantage of a new point of contact with the ground, as shown figure 2. Change of direction or orientation of the hat, are achieved by rotating the internal body; both effects are mutually exclusive, and depend on the contact between the hat and the ground as shown figure 3.

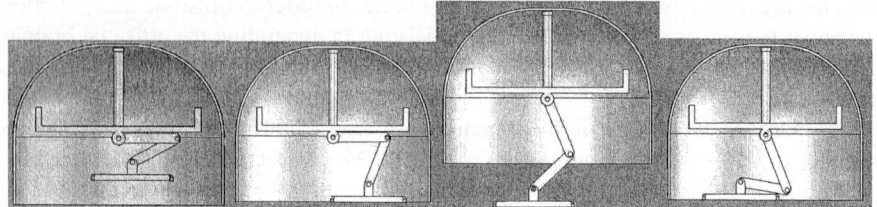

Fig. 2. Obtaining motion through leaning on the hat

2.2 The Proposal

At this point, hOnGo may be considered as a minimalist robot easy to program. Nevertheless our proposal consists in leaving out such a programming phase and substituting it with the implementation of the GFM paradigm. According to this paradigm, at least one global goal is required to trigger learning within the growing modules architecture. Therefore, hOnGo will have to permanently focus on

---

[2] A GFM module specialized in real time regulation is under study to take in charge such control tasks.

phototaxis[3], a single goal that will be implemented at the highest level of the GFM architecture.

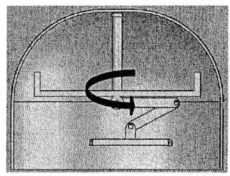 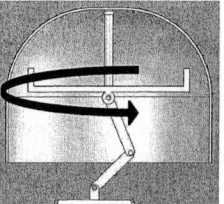

Fig. 3. Obtaining change of direction or rotation of the hat, depending of the contact between the hat and the ground

The robot structure and its actuators conform a kind of premise, thus the primary task consists in determining which functional modules should be connected to form the brain's architecture and, also, which sensors should be attached to the structure. Connecting these selected elements characterizes the GFM design phase[4] [7]. The resulting design of the brain architecture is compiled and constitutes the control system of the robot.

2.3 The Paradigm

According to Epigenesis [1], to efficiently gain autonomous control, a system must fulfill three essential characteristics: its embodiment, its situatedness in an environment and its involvement in an epigenetic developmental process [2], [3], [4], [5] and [6]. The first two requirements are satisfied by basic robotics and the GFM paradigm fulfills the requirement for the third one. GFM offers an alternative to rigid representations, which usually present a lack of perception and a shortage of learning, prevalent in most computer science paradigms. The major return would be to free the robot realization from a commonly huge programming task, replacing it by learning, which comes from the internal structure of each interconnected growing module.

Each GF module is conceived and implemented to achieve a generic task consisting in reaching a specific goal[5], generating a sequence of actions. In particular, the adaptation of these sequences is accomplished due to the feedback provided in response to these actions. From this ultimate assertion, the outcome is that, to exhibit the role played by a particular module, its task, input, output and feedback must be supplied.

At this stage, the robot's designer has available a reduced library of GF modules to elaborate the architecture of the artificial brain. Optionally, new elements may be appended to this library as long as: firstly, the interconnection scheme common to all modules is observed; and secondly, a permanent learning process is internally implemented.

---

[3] Light seeking.
[4] In fact, there is a previous phase named Behavior Prediction Analysis that has been omitted in this paper to simplify the exposition.
[5] Mostly a floating point value.

3 The Design Phase

3.1 Methodology

Learning results from an emerging process, which involves all modules concurrently. Nevertheless, the modules whose position in the architecture is closest to the actuators present a faster adaptation, since they receive more requests from others, and more feedback from sensors. As a consequence, the learning process of the brain expands hierarchically from the lowest modules to the upper ones.

Currently no methodology has been elaborated to facilitate the design phase; however, considering the nature of the previously mentioned learning process, a bottom-up approach seems convenient.

3.2 The Control of the Leg

According to the previous paragraph, the first step should consider the control of the robot's leg. A convenient solution contemplates the integration of the NAC architecture described in [8], optimized in [9] and implemented as a module in [10]. The NAC module operates building an internal growing and adaptative network of cells designed to memorize stochastic correlations between local input and output spaces. After a while, this module is able to generate the optimum sequence of actions to reach the requests of upper modules.

Figure 4 shows the architecture of hOnGo's artificial brain. Two NAC modules A1 and A2 are configured to trigger sequences of elementary actions $-\delta\theta, \delta\theta, -\delta\psi, \delta\psi$ (in output) that alter the angles of joints J2 and J3 of the robot's leg. As feedback, A1 and

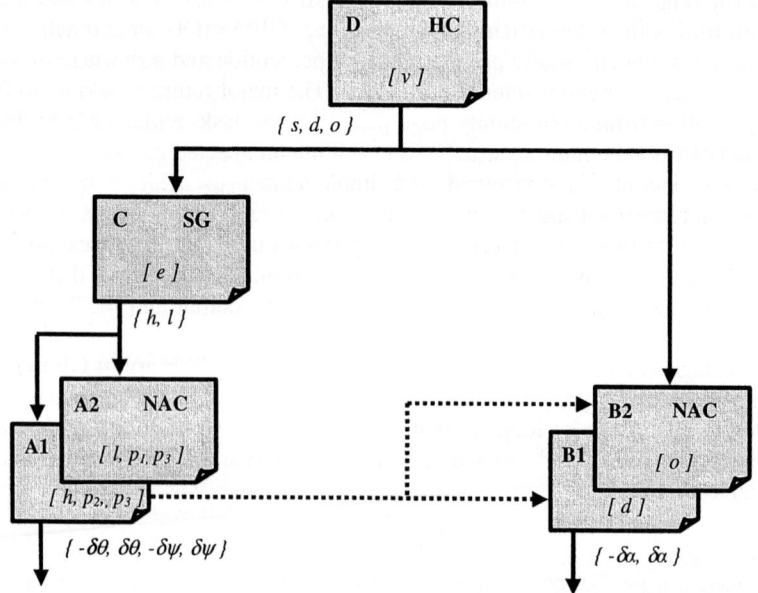

Fig. 4. Schematic representation of hOnGo's artificial brain

A2 respectively receive the current height h and length l of a step, in addition to p_2 and p_3, which correspond to the positions of joints J2 and J3. For that reason, concurrent actions on joints J2 and J3, produced simultaneously by modules A1 and A2, would generate chaotic acting and confused feedback, preventing thus respective adaptations. Therefore, these modules A1 and A2 must be implemented as "levels" represented by their superposition in figure 4; such configuration prohibits concurrent activation while it allows simultaneous learning.

At this stage, an upper module may request a specific value of height to A1 or length to A2, triggering thus an internal propagation; this propagation produces a sequence of actions that modify the angles of joints J1 and J2 toward reaching the requested input value. When failing in this attempt, an internal learning mechanism is activated to improve the internal representation that produced the sequence.

A few parameters must be provided to allow the creation of modules A1 and A2 including: the number of assigned actions, the quantity of steps between the minimum and maximum opening of each angle, a value indicating roughly the expected precision and the initial positions of joints J1 and J2.

3.3 The Control of the Hat and the Body

The control of the orientation o of the hat and of the direction d of the motion is achieved in a similar way: two NAC modules B1 and B2, control the stepper motor placed on joint J4 which monitors their relative positions. For reasons similar to those mentioned in the case of the leg, both modules cannot be solicited simultaneously and thus, are, in a similar manner, organized in levels. Furthermore, the feasibility of such solicitude depends of the position of the leg: the effect of an action on the motor will affect the direction of the motion or the orientation of the hat, depending on whether the hat makes contact with the ground or not (figure 3). To capture this physical property, an inhibition connection, symbolized by the doted arrows, is aggregated to connect module A1 to modules B1 and B2. Thus, the height, provided in input, is correlated through time with the effects observed on modules B1 and B2. Gradually, the module A1 generates inhibition through this connection to evidence the previously described phenomenon.

The required initial parameters provided to B1 and B2, are similar to those of A1 and A2, but describe the actuator in charge of joint J4.

3.4 The Control of the Steps

Steps are the result of a sequence of alternative values of heights and lengths requested to modules A1 and A2 and generated by an upper module C. Though, this is apparently not the simplest solution, it is in fact a functional one; otherwise, bypassing modules Ax would produce conflicts between concurrent modules soliciting the same actuators.

To generate an efficient sequence of alternative requests on A1 and A2, the SG module C integrates some mechanisms that produce random sequences and gradually refine them to grant the most successful combinations.

As feedback, the module C requires a unique value e that reflects the efficiency, calculated as the ratio between the length of a step and the energy spent to produce it.

3.5 The Control of the Behavior

As mentioned earlier, the unique global goal is positive phototaxis; and so, hOnGo will stay active (in motion) until maximizing the amount of incident light v captured by its (virtual) photocell. Consequently, the task of the higher module D consists in generating requests of steps s, orientation o and direction d to the modules B1, B2 and C respectively. These requests are aimed at increasing the feedback value of incident light v. As the source of light randomly changes in intensity and position over the time, the robot is continuously obliged to update its position.

The internal mechanism of this current module emulates a kind of Hill Climbing heuristic and is implemented as a network of cells, similarly to all GFM modules. Presently, this constitutes an inefficient strategy, as it repeatedly obliges the robot to evaluate all possible elementary moves before selecting the optimal one. The unique advantage of implementing such a short-term decision strategy, is to facilitate the evaluation of the robot behavior. Smarter architectures that implement strategies that take advantage of the continuity and predictability of the input space are under study. The aim of these enhancements is to increase the GFM library and thus offer generic solutions to similar optimization problems.

3.6 The Generation of the Brain

At this stage, all required feedback values must be associated to some accurate sensors and transmitted to the brain according to a protocol provided at the issue of the design phase.

Then, all characteristics of the resulting architecture, including the selected modules, together with their interconnection, parameters, feedback values and external actions are codified in a C++ file that constitutes the constructor of the artificial brain. Compiling the resultant application and linking it with the GFM library generates the corresponding artificial brain. Finally, connecting it through a serial port to a robot, virtual or not, initiates activity.

3.7 Concerning Sensing

In fact, the previous design is just concerned with the Acting Area of the brain: as the simple task entrusted to hOnGo does not require superior perception, sensors are directly connected to Acting modules.

Otherwise, the design of the Sensing Area would be achieved in a similar manner as its counterpart. Then, before being submitted to the Acting Area, more complex external stimuli should be processed by a set of "sensing" growing modules. Such modules would extract specific characteristics among external stimuli and learn the corresponding associations and discriminations to gradually produce significant patterns. The term "significant" may, for example, reflect the specificity or frequency of a pattern occurring concurrently with a positive or negative global goal.

3.8 Concerning Design

In practice, the kind and the combination of treatments, a designer decides to apply, define the types and the interconnections of GF modules forming the architecture.

The design phase may be considered as a substitute of the evolutionary process, that is, responsible to set up the appropriate "functions" to perform a coherent behavior. Against appearances, Genetic Programming does not constitute an alternative to this design phase as an accurate fitness evaluation would requires the robot to perform in a real environment, leading thus to an extremely slow process, comparable with the natural one.

The design process described in this paper is neither unique nor optimum; in particular, the NAC modules selected present a high computational cost in comparison to their diminutive functionality in regards to this specific application. Nevertheless, their capacity would allow satisfying further potential requests from additional higher modules. Besides, the HC module constitutes a very inefficient choice to head the architecture, as it forces the robot to evaluate almost any alternatives before selecting the optimal one. Better options of modules have been proposed, but not implemented yet as, rather than efficiency of the robot's behavior; the purpose of these tests was to evaluate the viability of the architecture, the skills of the robot and its aptitude at learning.

The difficulty of carrying out such design may be compensated by the fact that those dynamic functions or operations are reusable for different robots. So, specific functionalities may be extracted from the global design to form a functional subsystem. Technically, a subsystem holds only three connections with the rest of the architecture to allow input, output and feedback communications. For example, any standard four-legged robot should be roughly operated thanks to the corresponding subsystem whose feedback is given by body balance and foot pressure sensors, while output is applied on actuators placed on each joint. In figure 4, such a subsystem corresponding to hOnGo's leg is outlined with a doted line frame, but has not been transposed yet to another robot.

Additionally, this design process may be facilitated thanks to a Graphical User Interface allowing, first, the design of GFM architectures (similar to the illustration of figure 4) and then, the generation of the corresponding C++ file constituting the constructor of the artificial brain (as mentioned in section 3.6) jointly with its header file that contains the description of the communication protocol.

4   The Simulation of the Robot

As mentioned, though a real version of hOnGo is under development, all the descriptions and results published in this paper concern a simulation of the robot that, in particular, ignores the problem of stabilizing the hat. The reason is that no module able to perform this functionality had been programmed at this time. But, excepting this simplification, the simulation reproduces mostly the behavior of the robot, carrying out the commands generated by the brain and providing it with the required feedback.

Each input command modifies the angle of a specific joint; randomly and occasionally, some noise is added that causes the command to be ignored or modified. On the other hand, each of the feedback values, introduced from sections 3.2 to 3.5, is obtained by computing the matching equation described below:

- Position of joint J2: p_2 is incremented or decremented depending the command.
- Position of joint J3: p_3 is incremented or decremented depending the command.
- Direction of the robot: d incremented or decremented depending the command but required the hat to be in contact with the floor.
- Orientation of the hat: o incremented or decremented depending the command but required the hat not to be in contact with the floor.
- Elevation of the body: $h = l_{32}.\sin(p_3) + l_{21}.\sin(p_3 + p_2 - \frac{\pi}{2})$

  where l_{32} and l_{21} represents the length of the segments [J3,J2] and [J2,J1].
- Length of a step: this value is obtained by calculating the difference between the final position x_f of the foot (relatively to its zero-position) and the initial position x_i. The initial position is set when the hat looses contact with the floor; reciprocally, the final position is set when the hat enters in contact with the floor. Both values are calculated as follows:

  $l = x_f - x_i$ and $x = l_{32}.\cos(p_3) + l_{21}.\cos(p_3 + p_2 - \frac{\pi}{2})$
- Efficiency e: is calculated as the ratio between the length of a step and the energy spent to produce it. The energy is the number of elemental commands applied on joints J2 and J3 between the initial and final positions.
- Incident light v is calculated proportionally to: first, the distance between the source of light and the photocell, second, to the angle between the perpendicular of the photocell and the direction of the light. In practice, the sensitivity of the photocell is not linearly proportional to the distance but exponentially; nonetheless this facilitates the interpretation of results without affecting their quality.

The simulation of the robot may be run either on the same computer as the artificial brain or, on another computer connected to the first one through its serial port. The "two computers" alternative, though more in accordance with the concept of a remote application, has been discarded for the tests. The reason is that the RS-232 connection, even when configured at 115,200 bauds, reduces almost by a factor four the processing time of the application and so, masked the performance of the artificial brain. In the case of a real robot, this limitation, caused by the serial communication, does not affect the velocity, as the response of a servomotor is much slower than those of the simulation.

5 The Evaluation of the Application

For both following tests, the whole application has been run on a single computer equipped with a 1000 MHz Pentium III processor and 512 MB random access memory.

5.1 First Test

The first test consists in running the application with all the characteristics described in the previous sections; additionally, each time the robot cannot increase the amount of incident light, the position of this source of light is randomly modified. The purpose of this test is to exhibit the functionality of the artificial brain and thus the plausibility of the GFM approach.

At the beginning the robot's conduct is confused and chaotic, however after roughly half an hour, efficient actions are performed and, soon, a coherent behavior is obtained. At this moment, learning or adaptation becomes scarce since hOnGo is able to efficiently fulfill its single global goal, phototaxis.

5.2 Second Test

The second test consists in monitoring the growing structures of the modules. The HC module is replaced by a process that emits random but balanced requests to all modules. Figure 5 shows the evolution of the growing structures of modules Ax, Bx and C. The vertical axis represents the percentage of its final size, attained by the structure, throughout the emission of a total of three hundred requests. Each request may trigger numerous learning phases as reflected by the "steps" that present the associated curves.

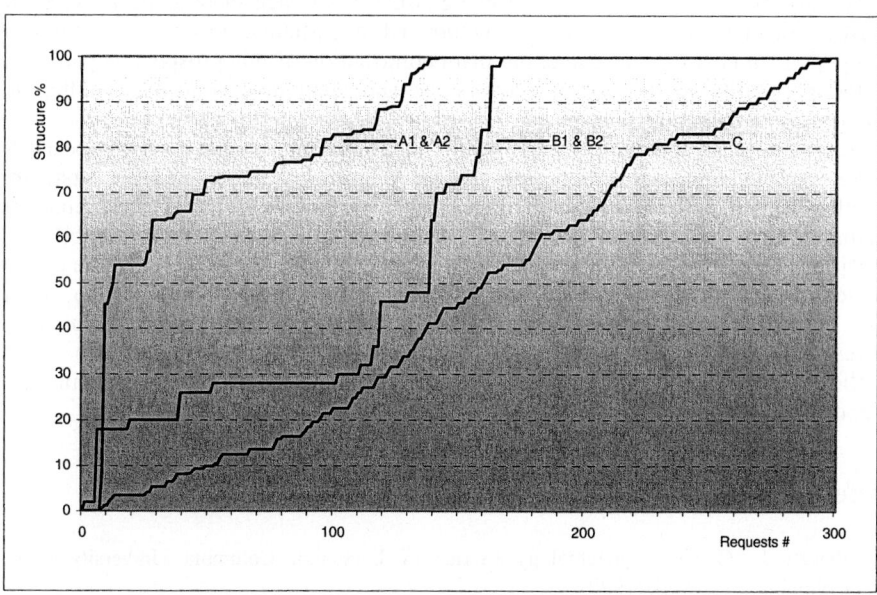

Fig. 5. Each curve represents the growing percentage of a module's structure in function of the number of requests received

The first two curves associated to modules Ax and Bx show that the structures of these modules quickly reached their optimum size: more than nine hundred cells are created in less than fifteen minutes. The last curve shows that the SG module does not perform optimally as its learning rate presents some endless growing, creating a large amount of cells; and this, despite of the stability of the environment. This almost certainly results from an error in the implementation that currently remains unresolved; however, this module complies with its task.

To stock the structures of all NAC modules, 674 Kbytes of memory are required; the SG module is not taken into account due to the lack of convergence of its structure.

In the case of a real robot, the corresponding learning time to carry out the actual number of triggered actions is evaluated to roughly four and a half hours. Yet, the servo-motors of the corresponding robot have been programmed to perform a complete rotation of Pi within thirty steps. Increasing this number of steps rises the learning precision but also the learning time. When setting the number of steps to 60, the estimated learning time exceeds seven hours.

5 Conclusions

The purpose of this paper was first of all to illustrate the GFM prospective paradigm providing an initial example of the design phase. As a result, the current experiment shows the feasibility of generating an artificial brain capable of managing a minimalist robot by applying the Growing Functional Modules paradigm. Moreover, some basic results concerning the growing structure of each module are provided to illustrate the development of the architecture and, in particular, to show its reasonable computational cost. At this stage, the main contribution of this prospective paradigm is the possibility to set up an autonomous and adaptative controller eluding its traditional programming task.

Furthermore, in this paper, some additional considerations have been exposed to make explicit the expectations of the GFM project, these include: first, the development of a real version of hOnGo; second, the necessity of combining the Acting Area with its counter part, the Sensing one; third, the potential reusability of specific subsystems; fourth, the development of adequate tools to facilitate the design phase and fifth, the expectation of expanding the low-level acquired abilities to form a high-level behavior. All these points except the second one constitute the actual axes of research of the GFM project; to fulfill this sketch, six real robots and two virtual applications are under development with the aim of testing and expanding the proposed paradigm.

References

1. Piaget, J.: Genetic Epistemology (Series of Lectures). Columbia University Press, Columbia, New York (1970)
2. Prince, G. and Demiris, Y.: Introduction to the Special Issue on Epigenetic Robotics, International Society for Adaptative Behavior (2003) Vol. 11(2) 75-77
3. Brooks, R.: Intelligence without Representation, Artificial Intelligence No. 47 (1991) 139-159
4. Grupen, A.: A Developmental Organization for Robot Behavior, Proceedings of the third International Workshop on Epigenetic Robotics IEEE, Massachusetts USA (2003)
5. Berthouze, L. and Prince G.: Introduction: the Third International Workshop on Epigenetic Robotics. In Prince, Berthouze, Kozima, Bullock, Stojanov and Balkenius (Eds.). Proceedings of the Third International Workshop on Epigenetic Robotics: Modeling Cognitive Development in Robotic Systems. Lund University Cognitive Studies Vol. 101. Lund Sweden (2003)

6. Lindblom, J. and Ziemke, T.: Social Situatedness: Vygotsky and Beyond. In Prince, Christopher G. and Demiris, Yiannis and Marom, Yuval and Kozima, Hideki and Balkenius, Christian Eds, Proceedings of the Second International Workshop on Epigenetic Robotics, Modeling Cognitive Development in Robotic Systems 94, Edinburgh, Scotland (2002) 71-78
7. Leboeuf, J.: Growing Functional Modules, a Prospective Paradigm for Epigenetic Artificial Intelligence. Lecture Notes in Computer Science 3563. Larios, Ramos and Unger eds. Springer (2005) 465-471
8. Leboeuf, J.: A Self-Developing Neural Network Designed for Discrete Event System Autonomous Control. Mastorakis, N. (eds.): Advances in Systems Engineering, Signal Processing and Communications, Wseas Press (2002) 30-34
9. Leboeuf, J.: Facing Combinatory Explosion in NAC Networks. Advanced Distributed Systems, Lecture Notes in Computer Science 3061. Larios, Ramos and Unger eds. Springer (2004) 252-260
10. Leboeuf, J.: NAC, an Artificial Brain for Epigenetic Robotics. Robotics: trends, principles and applications Vol. 15. Jamshidi, Ollero, Martinez de Dios eds. TSI Press Series (2004) 535-540

Maximizing Future Options: An On-Line Real-Time Planning Method

Ramon F. Brena and Emmanuel Martinez

Center for Intelligent Systemsm,
Monterrey Institute of Technology
ramon.brena@itesm.mx, A00588294@itesm.mx

Abstract. In highly dynamic environments with uncertainty the elaboration of long or rigid plans is useless because the constructed plans are frequently dismissed by the arrival or new unexpected situations; in these cases, a "second-best" plan could rescue the situation. We present a new real-time planning method where we take into consideration the number and quality of future options of the next action to choose, in contrast to most planning methods that just take into account the intrinsic value of the chosen plan or the maximum valued future option. We apply our method to the Robocup simulated soccer competition, which is indeed highly dynamic and involves uncertainty. We propose a specific architecture for implementing this method in the context of a player agent in the Robocup competition, and we present experimental evidence showing the potential of our method.

1 Introduction

Real-time soccer is a complex game, involving a great deal of coordination between team members, and the development of strategies leading to marking as many goals as possible and receiving as few goals as possible.

Robocup simulated soccer represents that complexity to a certain degree, meaning that many interesting soccer complexities are present in the simulated soccer as provided by the soccerserver system [3], like limited vision and hearing, noise, etc.

Thus, simulated soccer is a challenging problem from the standpoint of coordination, communication, uncertainty handling, learning, planning, and so on [9].

Many Robocup teams have applied techniques issued from the Artificial Intelligence (AI) field [16] to develop sophisticated skills. Among those AI-related techniques we find Neural Nets, Reinforcement Learning and Probabilistic Reasoning for low-level skills [17], and decision trees [18], Reinforcement Learning [19] and Multiagent Coordination methods like Coordination Graphs [11], for high-level skills.

One area that perhaps has not reached a high degree of development in Robocup is planning [1]. Due to the very dynamic nature of simulated soccer, long-term planning is pointless, as almost any long plan will fail when facing unexpected conditions. Thus, most teams are highly reactive and rely on very polished low-level skills like ball interception and shooting more than on clever playing ideas. Very few teams have applied a planning method to Robocup; in [15], a planning method using opponent modelling is applied for the Coach league team from Carnegie Mellon University. Using bayesian networks, the coach models the opponent's behavior and generates a plan. Finally, the coach communicates the plan to the players. In [5] players have different plans in their memory and they search for one plan to arrive to the opponent goal; their plans consist of dribbles and passes. The cited works use traditional planning methods where the starting point and the ending point of the plan are defined before its execution starts.

In most planning methods [20], when a plan is interrupted at execution time due to unexpected events, players have to start over from scratch a new plan -which will be most probably interrupted as well.

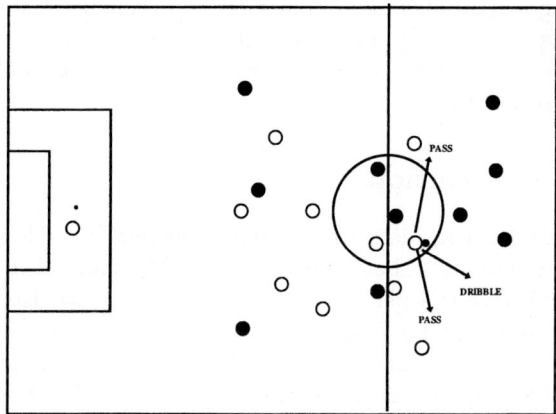

Fig. 1. Example of the problem of decision making in Robocup

Let us examine an example. Fig.1 shows a game situation where the agent with the ball must take a decision between giving the ball to a well-positioned, but lonely partner, or filtering a long pass to the right, or even to continue dribbling, as indicated by the arrows in the figure. We can see that after passing to the left, the lonely player will have almost no options other than advance and shoot, but could be blocked by many enemies in that part of the field. If instead it dribbles to the right, it still has the other options. The point here is not that dribbling is better that passing, but that under uncertainty it is good to have options for cases where what seemed to be the best option just fails and has to be dropped. In our method we stress the importance of having as many open *options* as possible.

The basic idea in our planning method is to take into consideration, when evaluating a particular possible move, how many and how good *options* the action keeps open after executing it. The advantage of doing this, instead of just selecting the best possible plan or action at a given moment according to some metric, is that in a highly dynamic environment like Robocup, plans often get stuck due to unexpected events, so the agent has to replan from scratch. In our system, for the contrary, when a plan gets stuck, it is more probable that there is another remaining option -precisely because the planning method has been fostering good options all the time.

Our planning method belongs to the class of on-line planning [8]. On-line planning interleave planning and execution whereas in traditional planning a plan is made and then executed. Agent-centered search [10] is a technique that implements on-line planning, restricting planning to the part of the domain where the current state of the agent is found. Agent-centered search decide on the local search space, search an action, and execute it. This process is repeated until the goal state is reached.

In the next section we will detail our planning method. In section 3 we will describe the Robocup application of our method in our Robocup team, then we present some experiments supporting our claims, and finally in section 5 we will discuss pros and cons of our planning method, list some results of the team, and draw some future work lines.

2   Method Description

Our planning method considers a collection of current possible actions and the next cycle future actions. [1] Let a specific play (like pass, clearball, etc.) be a triple (p, π, τ), where p is a play identifier, and π and τ are lists of parameters, π for player identifiers and τ for numeric parameters. Each τ_i has either a numerical value or the "undefined" value $\perp$. A parameter with value $\perp$ is said to be "uninstantiated". A similar convention is used for π. For instance, a pass is a triple $(pass, [passer, receiver], [direction, force])$. Partial instantiation is possible, for example, the parameters *passer* and *receiver* could have a value, but not *direction* nor *force*. A "playbook" [2] P is just a set of all uninstantiated plays.

The collection of current possible actions (CPA) is a subset of the playbook P where the π parameters are instantiated to team members identifiers. This represents the plays that are supposed to be applicable to the current situation. Of course the CPA could have every possible instantiation of every play in P, but we use heuristics to reduce its size. This is equivalent to assign to each play in P a precondition that should be satisfied in order to appear in the CPA. Plays satisfying these heuristics are called "plausible".

Preconditions are of two kinds:

- Static preconditions, which refer to the situation in the playing field, like the proximity of enemies and teammates; for instance, we can avoid passes to teammates not in the neighborhood.

---

[1] We decided not to consider more than one future cycle, so our planning trees are just two levels deep, see section 5.

- Sequencing preconditions, which refer to the possibility of executing two given plays in sequence. We say that two plays p_1 and p_2 are *compatible* if p_2 can "reasonably" follow p_1, which is determined by heuristics. For instance, after a "clearball" it is not reasonable to play a dribble, as the ball will be very far from the given player.

The playbook have the following offensive plays: [2] Pass, Filtered Pass, Dribble, Outplay (a very long dribble), Clearball (a kick to certain position), and Shoot to goal. [3]

We use a *search tree* for evaluating the playing options, defined as follows:

- The root R represents the current situation.
- For each plausible partially instantiated play p_i from the playbook P, create a brach leading to a son labeled with the action p_i. We denote by $s_i(p)$ the i-th successor of play p in the tree.
- The preceding step is repeated for the sons, giving a two-level tree. [4]

Of course the search tree defined above is classical of AI methods, but we use an original way of evaluating the tree's nodes. Each action p_i of the tree will be associated to a numeric value $E(p_i)$, as described in the following.

Our evaluation of possible plays is based on their *expected utilities*, i.e. the product of their benefit (in case they are successful) by their probability of success; this is why we call it *combined evaluation*:

$$e(p) = bf(p) * pf(p) \qquad (1)$$

where bf is the *evaluation of benefit* function (basically a heuristic taking into account the position of ball and players, see [13]), and pf the *feasibility* function, which returns a number between 0 and 1. The feasibility function is supposed to correspond to the fraction of times a given play could be successful in the given situation.

Next, the original idea we are presenting consists of using for action evaluation not only the best-evaluated son, like in minimax procedures, but a combination taking into consideration the accumulated benefit of all the future actions that will be possible to execute after the current one. The result of this is to give some weight to the quantity and quality of future options generated by a given action.

The formula used to calculate the combined evaluation $E(p)$ of a first-level play p is as follows:

$$E(p) = pf(p)(k_1 bf(p) + k_2 \max\{e(s_i(p))\} + k_3 \frac{\sum\{e(s_i(p))\}}{N}) \qquad (2)$$

where N is the total number of successors of action p, $e(s_i(p))$ are the evaluations with respect to the feasibility and utility of the future actions $s_i(p)$ of the current

---

[2] So far we have limited our attention to the options of the player with the ball. This is not a limitation of our method, but of our current experimentation.
[3] Parameter details for each play are described in [13].
[4] See the discussion section for justification of the two-level tree.

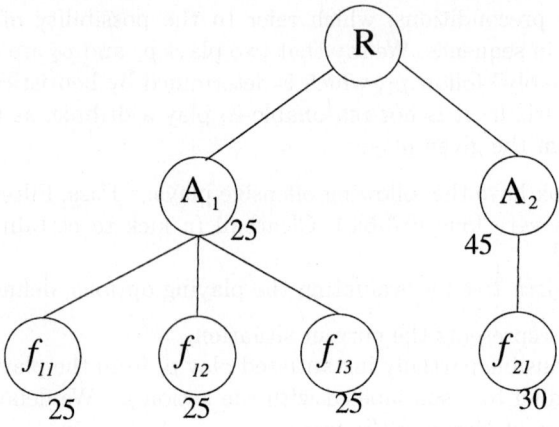

Fig. 2. A simple two-level tree

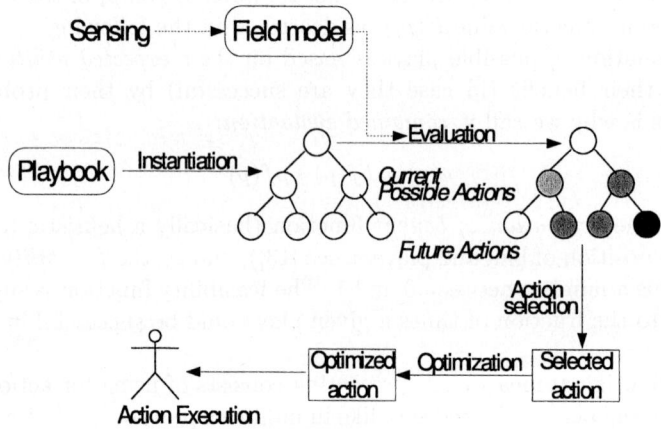

Fig. 3. Robocup prototype architecture

possible action p, and finally k_1, k_2 and k_3 are constants for fine-tuning the relative importance of the three terms in the equation's right-hand side.

We illustrate the application of this formula to a simple tree presented in figure 2, where the nodes direct evaluation [5] are written near them. We will assume for this example that $k_1 = k_2 = k_3 = 1$. In conventional maximum-driven tree evaluation, the branch to the right would be selected, either evaluating just the next move, the following one, or both combined. But applying our formula, the evaluations are different. According to our formula the evaluation of node

---

[5] We are calling "direct evaluation" the assessment of the resulting position itself, without regard to possible future plays.

A_1 is:

$$E(A_1) = pf(A_1)*(bf(A_1)+\max\{e(f_{11}), e(f_{12}), e(f_{13})\}+\frac{\sum\{e(f_{11}),e(f_{12}),e(f_{13})\}}{3})$$
$$E(A_1) = 0.9*(25+\max\{25,25,25\}+\frac{\sum\{25,25,25\}}{3})$$
$$E(A_1) = 0.9*(25+25+25) = 67.5$$

Whereas the evaluation of the node A_2 is:

$$E(A_2) = pf(A_1)*(bf(A_2)+\max\{e(f_{21})\}+\frac{\sum\{e(f_{21})\}}{1})$$
$$E(A_2) = 0.6*(45+\max\{30\}+\sum\{30\})$$
$$E(A_2) = 0.6*(45+30+30) = 63$$

So, applying our method, we select the branch to the left, where the action A_1 is chosen to be optimized and then executed.

3 Implementation

Our prototype, the "Borregos" team [12] is based in the UvA Trilearn 2003 team source code [4], on top of which we have implemented some specific skills, like goal-shooting, etc.

In the prototype we also introduced an additional *optimization* step, in which several variations of the action are generated, for instance changing slightly the direction, speed, etc., in order to choose the exact point yielding a maximum utility with respect to its list of future actions. This step is not essential to the general planning method we are presenting, and details of it can be consulted in [13].

Figure 3 illustrates the way the planning method is implemented. The basic steps involved in our prototype are:

- First we construct the two-level *play tree* as described above.
- We apply the evaluating procedure described above.
- The best evaluated first-level possible action is chosen from the CPA with its list of future actions.
  The selected first-level action is refined through the optimization process. This is the final decision of the agent.

In the current prototype, our planning method is applied just to the agent with possession of the ball; teammates apply reactive heuristics aiming to help the player with the ball, like to stay far from opponents while attacking, etc. Of course, in principle the planning method could be applied to every single player, and most probably we will do it in future versions (see section 6).

The feasibility function has been adjusted in such a way that it corresponds to the average success rate of plays. Taking a particular play, say "Pass", the prototype calculates the average success of passes throughout an entire game, let it be μ_{real}. Then, we compare it with the average success μ_{pred} predicted by the feasibility evaluation for passes, also during the complete game. They should be equal if predictions are accurate, but of course in practice this is not the case. So, we make an adjustment in the feasibility evaluation for passes, as follows:

$$pf_{new}(pass) = pf_{old}(pass) * \mu_{real}/\mu_{pred}$$

In this way we ensure that at least the average success estimation for passes correspond to the "real" probability, considered as the average success rate. This could be considered as a form of learning.

Another component links our decision mechanisms to a soccerserver command through the use of the UvA Trilearn code [4].

4 Experiments

We validated our strategy by playing games against our team disabling the use of future plays consideration. With the use of the proxyserver package [6] we generated statistics to compare the performance of the team with the simultaneous tactics. Methodologically it is important to isolate the variable we want to measure -which is our planning method's performance- from other possible sources of difference. This is why we ran matches between two versions of the same team, because if we, for instance, compare our team with other teams, the difference in performance could be attributed to other factors, like low-level skills, etc. So, we ran games between the following two versions of our team:

- The "Planning" version, which implements the planning method we are proposing, that is, it chooses the action with best combined evaluation according to formula 2.
- The "Control" version, which takes into consideration just the next possible moves, and not the possible following ones; this accounts as reducing the right-hand side of formula 2 to the term $pf(a)(k_1 bf(a))$.

For these experiments we eliminated one source of uncertainty by giving to players complete information about their current environment; this is achieved by putting "on" the "fullstate" soccerserver parameter (see discussion).

Accumulated results in 40 matches are presented in table 1. The statistical parameters are the following:

- Total goals scored (GS in the table)
- Earned Points (Points)
- Average points (AP)
- Average Goal Difference (AGD)

As we can see in table 1, the goals scored by "Planning" team was clearly greater than the received ones (scored by "Control"). Other parameters show a great obtained points percentage ("Planning" obtained 98 percent of the points played), and also a great average goal difference.

Table 1. Statistical parameters

TEAM	GS	Points	AP	AGD
Planning	172	118	2.95	3.93
Control	15	1	0.25	-3.93

5 Discussion

We are aware that our construction of the play tree with just our moves, and not the opponent ones, assuming the opponent is doing nothing relevant in the meantime, could sound like a huge simplification. Our point is that in some situations it could be too difficult to consider explicitly the opponent moves in the tree, either because there are too many or because we have too little information about the opponent's behavior. We indeed think this is partially the case in Robocup simulation, though it is sometimes possible to apply adversarial modeling techniques [14, 7]. Some evidence about our claim is shown in the experimental results presented above.

One critical aspect of our method is the accuracy of evaluation functions. Indeed, bad estimations of either utility or probability would lead to completely erroneous play evaluations. Actually we had to work a lot on these functions before the planning method delivered acceptable results, and yet we have much work to do refining those functions.

Also critical is the information about the players and the ball's position, and this is why for running the experiments we left the soccerserver parameter "full-state" on, which means that complete information about the current situation is given to players by the soccerserver. We did so, at least for basic experimentation purposes, because inaccuracy in modeling the current situation would affect as "noise" the plays' evaluation by formula 2. We plan to investigate the application of the planning method with more uncertainty involved (see section 6)

Formula 2 itself could need some adjustments for a specific application; for instance we started with a version where the third term in the right-hand side was $k_3 \sum \{e(s_i(p))\}$, that is, taking the sum instead of the average, but experimental results were much weaker. The explanation could be that in Robocup to have too many weak options is not convenient, so dividing by the number of options made the correction. We think similar adjustments could be necessary for other applications.

One potential disadvantage or our method is its high computational cost, because we need to perform many evaluations and then one optimization –involving even more evaluations. We relied on heuristics to reduce the search space for making the complexity manageable.

6 Conclusions and Future Work

We have presented a novel real-time planning method for highly dynamic domains. In our method, possible actions evaluation is based not on the maximum in the search tree, but on a metric considering the quantity and quality of the future options left available by the actions being considered.

An implementation of our method in the domain of the Robocup competition has been presented, which is at the heart of our Robocup team.

Preliminary experimental results are presented. We have shown that our planning method outperformed traditional (maximum immediate evaluation) planning.

Current research is focused on carefully refining utility and feasibility functions, as well as investigating the effect of varying the constants k_i in the evaluation formula. We plan also to provide better field modeling for keeping track of the current situation without needing the "fullstate" parameter on. Future research will include adapting our planning method to applications outside the Robocup competition, like electronic auctions, client-driven dynamic manufacturing, and aerial combat real-time decisions.

Acknowledgements

This work was supported by the Monterrey Tech's Research Grant CAT011. We would like to thank the anonymous reviewers for their insightful comments.

References

1. James Allen, James Hendler, and Austin Tate. *Readings in Planning*. Representation and Reasoning Series. Morgan Kaufmann, San Mateo, California, 1990.
2. Michael Bowling, Brett Browning, and Manuela Veloso. Plays as effective multiagent plans enabling opponent-adaptive play selection. In *Proceedings of International Conference on Automated Planning and Scheduling (ICAPS'04)*, 2004.
3. Mao Chen, Klaus Dorer, Ehsan Foroughi, Fredrik Heintz, ZhanXiang Huang, Spiros Kapetanakis, Kostas Kostiadis, Johan Kummeneje, Jan Murray, Itsuki Noda, Oliver Obst, Patrick Riley, Timo Steffens, Yi Wang, and Xiang Yin. Users manual: Robocup soccer server (for soccerserver version 7.07 and later).
4. R. de Boer and J. Kok. The incremental development of a synthetic multi-agent system: The uva trilearn, 2001.
5. Ahmad Farahany, Mostafa Rokooey, Mohammad Salehe, and Meisam Vosoughpour. Mersad 2004 team description, 2004.
6. Ian Frank, Kumiko Tanaka-Ishii, Katsuto Arai, , and Hitoshi Matsubara. The statistics proxy server. In Peter Stone, Tucker Balch, and Gerhard Kraetszchmar, editors, *RoboCup-2000: Robot Soccer World Cup IV*, pages 303–308. Springer Verlag, Berlin, 2001.
7. L. Garrido, R. Brena, and K. Sycara. Towards modeling other agents: A simulation-based study. In Jaime S. Sichman, Rosaria Conte, and Nigel Gilbert, editors, *Proceedings of the 1st International Workshop on Multi-Agent Systems and Agent-Based Simulation (MABS-98)*, volume 1534 of *LNAI*, pages 210–225, Berlin, July 4–6 1998. Springer.
8. Lise Getoor, Greger Ottosson, Markus Fromherz, and Bjoern Carlson. Effective redundant constraints for online scheduling. In *Proceedings of the 14th National Conference on Artificial Intelligence (AAAI-97)*, pages 302–307, Providence, Rhode Island, July 1997. AAAI Press / MIT Press.

9. Frans Groen, Matthijs Spaan, and Nikos Vlassis. Robot soccer: Game or science. In *Proceedings CNR-2002. Editura Universitaria Craiova*, October 2002.
10. Sven Koenig. Agent-centered search. *AI Magazine*, 22(4):109–131, 2001.
11. J. Kok, M. Spaan, and N. Vlassis. Non-communicative multi-robot coordination in dynamic environments. *Robotics and Autonomous Systems*, 50(2-3):99–114, 2005.
12. E. Martinez and R. Brena. Simultaneous planning: A real-time planning method. *Research on Computer Science*, 13:3–11, 2005.
13. Emmanuel Martinez. A real-time planning method for Robocup (in spanish). Master's thesis, Tecnologico de Monterrey, Mexico, 2005.
14. Patrick Riley and Manuela Veloso. On behavior classification in adversarial environments. In Lynne E. Parker, George Bekey, and Jacob Barhen, editors, *Distributed Autonomous Robotic Systems 4*, pages 371–380. Springer-Verlag, 2000.
15. Patrick Riley and Manuela Veloso. Planning for distributed execution through use of probabilistic opponent models. In *IJCAI-2001 Workshop PRO-2: Planning under Uncertainty and Incomplete Information*, 2001.
16. Stuart Russell and Peter Norvig. *Artificial Intelligence: A Modern Approach*. Prentice-Hall, Englewood Cliffs, NJ, 2nd edition edition, 2003.
17. Peter Stone. Layered learning in multiagent systems. In *AAAI/IAAI*, page 819, 1997.
18. Peter Stone and Manuela Veloso. Using decision tree confidence factors for multi-agent control. In Katia P. Sycara and Michael Wooldridge, editors, *Proceedings of the 2nd International Conference on Autonomous Agents (Agents'98)*, pages 86–91, New York, 9–13, 1998. ACM Press.
19. Peter Stone and Manuela M. Veloso. Multiagent systems: A survey from a machine learning perspective. *Autonomous Robots*, 8(3):345–383, 2000.
20. M. Zweben and M. S. Fox. *Intelligent Scheduling*. Morgan Kaufmann, 1994.

On the Use of Randomized Low-Discrepancy Sequences in Sampling-Based Motion Planning

Abraham Sánchez and Maria A. Osorio

Facultad de Ciencias de la Computación, BUAP,
14 Sur esq. San Claudio, CP 72550,
Puebla, Pue., México
asanchez, aosorio@cs.buap.mx

Abstract. This paper shows the performance of randomized low-discrepancy sequences compared with others low-discrepancy sequences. We used two motion planning algorithms to test this performance: the expansive planner proposed in [1], [2] and SBL [3]. Previous research already showed that the use of deterministic sampling outperformed PRM approaches [4], [5], [6]. Experimental results show performance advantages when we use randomized Halton and Sobol sequences over Mersenne-Twister and the linear congruential generators used in random sampling.

Keywords: Sampling-based motion planning, deterministic sampling, randomized Halton sequence.

1 Introduction

Robot motion planning refers to the ability of a robot to automatically plan its own motions to avoid collision with the physical objects in its environment. Such a capability is crucial, since a robot accomplishes tasks by physical motion in the real world. This capability would be a major step toward the goal of creating autonomous robots.

The most popular paradigm for sampling-based motion planning is the Probabilistic Roadmap Method (PRM) [7]. Recent research has focused on designing efficient sampling and connection strategies [7], [8], [9], [10], [2]. Many of these strategies require complex geometric operations, which are difficult to implement in high-dimensional configuration space ($\mathcal{C}$).

Deterministic sampling sequences or low-discrepancy sequences have the advantages of classical grid search approaches, i.e. a lattice structure (that allows to easily determine the neighborhood relations) and a good uniform coverage of the $\mathcal{C}$. Deterministic sampling sequences applied to PRM-like planners are demonstrated in [4], [5] to achieve the best asymptotic convergence rate and experimental results showed that they outperformed random sampling in nearly all motion planning problems. The work presented in [6] for nonholonomic motion planning proposes the use of different low-discrepancy sequences: Sobol, Faure, Niederreiter. Deterministic sampling ideas have improved computational methods in many areas [11].

Section II briefly describes deterministic sampling theory and presents the randomized Halton sequence. Section III explains expansive and SBL planners. Section IV presents our experimental results and finally in Section V the conclusions.

2 Deterministic Sampling

From a theoretical point of view a lot of effort has been spent by mathematicians to construct well-distributed sequences in multidimensional spaces.

The classical approach to generate random numbers, which should be uniformly distributed on the unit interval, is the linear congruential generator. This type of algorithm is the standard way to produce random numbers on a computer and most of the internal subroutine packages work with this kind of generator. The use of linear congruential methods may occur in the construction of multidimensional sequences. The uniformity of those sequences may be very poor.

Low-discrepancy sequences (LDS) generation is based in the successive (spread) generation of points located as far as possible of the previous points. This principle precludes the formation of clusters. LDS have been successfully applied to diverse fields such as physics, computational graphics, finances, and more recently to motion planning [5], [12] among others [11]. Their advantages in lower dimension problems has been well established, nevertheless Sánchez [12] pointed out that precision and efficiency diminish as the dimensionality increases (this study was made in the field of motion planning, other studies present the same observation in other fields [13]). This deterioration occurs due to the dependence of the points locations in higher dimensions.

Next subsections present the construction of Sobol sequence and randomized Halton sequences; they are easily implemented and fast to be computed in practice.

2.1 Sobol Sequence

In order to describe the construction, let us fix the dimension $d \geq 2$; we will construct points $x_0, x_1, x_2, \ldots$ in the unit cube I^d, and for every $k \in \mathbb{N}$ and $i \in \{1, \ldots, d\}$ let x_k^i denote the i-th coordinate of x_k, i.e., $x_k = (x_k^1, \ldots, x_k^d)$. We first need d different irreducible polynomials $p_i \in \mathbb{F}_2[x]$, where $\mathbb{F}_2$ is the finite field with two elements (such polynomials can be found in lists). For convenience we set an a priori upper bound 2^m for the length of the computed part of the sequence (this bound is absolutely not necessary, but it makes the construction easier to be implemented). Now we construct for every $i \in \{1, \ldots, d\}$ the sequence $x_0^i, x_1^i, x_2^i, \ldots, x_k^i, \ldots$ for $k < 2^m$ in the same way:

Let be i fixed and $p_i(x) = x^r + a_1 x^{r-1} + \cdots + a_{r-1} x + 1$ the i-th of the given polynomials, then we choose arbitrary $v_1, \ldots, v_r$ with $1 \leq \frac{v_j}{2^{m-j}} \leq 2^j - 1$ and odd integer, e.g. $v_j = 2^{m-j} \cdot (2^j - 1)$. After this we compute for $j = r+1, \ldots, m$ (in this order)

$$v_j = a_1 v_{j-1} \oplus a_2 v_{j-2} \oplus \cdots a_{r-1} v_{j-r+1} \oplus v_{j-r} \oplus \frac{v_{j-r}}{2^r},$$

where $\oplus$ is the bitwise xor-operation (remark: for every j is $\frac{v_j}{2^{m-j}}$ an odd integer). Having once computed $v_1, ..., v_m$, we can compute x_k^i in two ways,

- either directly by $x_k^i = \frac{g_1 v_1 \oplus \cdots \oplus g_m v_m}{2^m}$, where $g_j = b_j \oplus b_{j+1}$ and $b_j \in \{0,1\}$ the coefficients in the binary representation of $k = \sum_{j \geq 1} b_j 2^{j-1}$,
- or, when x_{k-1}^i is given, by $x_k^i = \frac{(x_{k-1}^i \cdot 2^m) \oplus v_c}{2^m}$, where $c = min\{j | b_j = 1\}$ and $b_j \in \{0,1\}$ the coefficients in the binary representation of $k = \sum_{j \geq 1} b_j 2^{j-1}$.

2.2 Randomized Low-Discrepancy Sequences

Theoretical as well as empirical research has shown that Quasi-Monte Carlo methods (QMC) can significantly increase the uniformity over random draws. Randomized QMC methods combine the benefits of deterministic sampling methods, which achieve a more uniform exploration of the sample space, with the statistical advantages of random draws.

We present the Halton sequences proposed by Halton (1960) and its randomization developed by Wang and Hickernell (2000) [14]. Halton sequences are similar to (t, s)-sequences in that they manipulate the digits of numbers in certain base representations.

Halton Sequences. First, we show how Halton sequences are defined in one dimension and then extend it to several dimensions. For any nonnegative integer n we write n in base b as

$$n = \phi_m \ldots \phi_0 = \sum_{k=0}^{m} \phi_k b^k, \qquad (1)$$

where $\phi_k \in \{0, 1, \ldots, b-1\}$ for $k = 0, 1, \ldots, m$. The n-th member of the base b Halton sequence is defined by

$$H_b(n) = 0.\phi_0 \ldots \phi_m (\text{in base } b) = \sum_{k=0}^{m} \phi_k b^{-k-1}. \qquad (2)$$

That is, we write the base b representation of the number n, reverse the order of its digits and put a decimal point in front of them. The result is a number between 0 and 1 that is by definition the n-th member of the one-dimensional, base b, Halton sequence.

The multi-dimensional Halton sequence can be obtained by generating several one-dimensional Halton sequences corresponding to bases that are prime numbers. More precisely, we take the first d prime numbers $p_1, \ldots, p_d$, generate the corresponding one-dimensional Halton sequence and use these to form the d-dimensional Halton sequences:

$$x_n = (H_{p_1}(n), \ldots, H_{p_d}(n)), \ n = 0, 1, \ldots \qquad (3)$$

As noted by Niederreiter [11], all the one-dimensional components of this sequence are $(0, 1)$-sequences in the corresponding bases. Since the one-dimensional Halton sequences are generated taking bases that are prime numbers, and hence mutually relative primes, the Halton sequence is expected to have lower correlations between its one-dimensional components.

Randomization of Halton Sequences. The randomization of Halton sequences as introduced by Wang and Hickernell [14] is based on a recursive relation that holds for the Halton sequence. This recursive relation translates the recursion from n to $n+1$ into $H_b(n)$ and $H_b(n+1)$ in a natural way.

Formally, let $x_0 \in [0,1)$ with the base b representation $x_0 = \sum_{k=0}^{\infty} \phi_k b^{-k-1}$. Define the expression that is the sum of $1/b$ and x_0 in base b

$$T_b(x_0) = (1 + \phi_h)b^{-h-1} + \sum_{k \geq h} \phi_k b^{-k-1}, \qquad (4)$$

where $h = \min\{k : u_k \neq b-1\}$. Then we can define the sequence $(T_b^n(x_0))$ by

$$\begin{aligned} T_b^n(x_0) &\equiv T_b(T_b^{n-1}(x_0)) \text{ for } n \geq 1 \text{ and} \\ T_b^0(x_0) &\equiv x_0. \end{aligned} \qquad (5)$$

Note that with $x_0 = 0$ the above sequence is exactly the one-dimensional Halton sequence in base b. Further, if the starting term can be written as a finite sum $x_0 = \sum_{k=0}^{m} \phi_k b^{-k-1}$ yielding $x_0 = 0.\phi_0 \ldots \phi_m$ (in base b) and denoting the corresponding integer $n_0 = \phi_m \ldots \phi_0$ (in base b) then $x_0 = h_b(n_0)$ and $T_b^n(x_0) = h_b(n_0 + n)$ for $n \geq 1$. That is, if the starting term of the sequence $(T_b^n(x_0))$ can be written as a finite sum, then the sequence is the same as the Halton sequence in which first n_0 elements are skipped.

Randomized Halton sequences are defined as the above sequences having their starting point randomly generated. More precisely, let $x_0 \in [0,1)^d$ have the uniform distribution. The randomized Halton sequence is defined by

$$x_n = (T_{p_1}^n(x_{0_1}), \ldots, T_{p_d}^n(x_{0_d})) \text{ for } n = 1, 2, \ldots \qquad (6)$$

Note that according to the previous paragraph randomized Halton sequences can also be defined as the deterministic Halton sequences described above by randomly skipping a number of initial terms. Wang and Hickernell showed that the elements of a randomized Halton sequence with a uniform random starting point are uniform.

Proposition 1. *If $x_0 \in [0,1)^d$ is a uniform random vector then x_n defined by 6 has the uniform distribution on $[0,1)^d$ for any $n \geq 1$.*

In practice one cannot use a uniformly distributed starting point since its base representation b generally has infinite number of digits. However, if b^m is sufficiently large, where m is the number of digits used in base representation b, to truncate each starting uniform random number by omitting its digits from $m+1$ on, we obtain numbers that approximate uniform numbers fairly well.

3 Expansive and SBL Planners

While multi-query planners use a sampling strategy to cover the whole free-space, a single-query planner applies a strategy to explore the smallest portion of free-space ($\mathcal{F}$) needed to find a solution path. For example, see the planners presented in [2], [1] and [3].

Hsu et al. introduced a planner for "expansive" $\mathcal{C}$ in [1]. The notion of expansiveness is related to how much of $\mathcal{F}$ is visible from a single free configuration or connected set of free configurations. The expansive-space planner grows a tree from the initial configuration. Each node q in the tree has an associated weight, which is defined to be the number of nodes inside $N_r(q)$, the ball of radius r centered at q. At each iteration, it picks a node to extend; the probability that a give node q will be selected is $1/w(q)$, in which w is the weight function. Then N points are sampled from $N_r(q)$ for the selected node q, and the weight function value for each is calculated. Each new point q' is retained with probability $1/w(q')$, and the planner attempts to connect each retained point to the node q.

The current implementation of the algorithm uses a fixed-size neighborhood around an existing node to sample new configurations. The neighborhoods size has a big impact on the nodes distribution. If the size is too small, the nodes tend to cluster around the initial and the goal configuration and leave large portions of the free space with no samples. If the size is very large, the samples will tend to distribute more evenly in the free space, but the rejection rate also increases significantly. The main drawback of the approach is that the required r and N parameters may vary dramatically across problems, and they are difficult to estimate for a given problem.

The planner in [3] searches $\mathcal{F}$ by building a roadmap made of two trees of nodes, T_i and T_g. The root of T_i is the initial configuration q_i, and the root of T_g is the goal configuration q_g (bi-directional search). Every new node generated during the planning is installed in either one of the two trees as the child of an already existing node. The link between the two nodes is the straight-line segment joining them in $\mathcal{CS}$. This segment will be tested for collision only when it becomes necessary to perform this test to prove that a candidate path is collision-free (lazy collision checking).

4 Experimental Results

Algorithms were written in Java. The running times given below were gathered on a 2.6 GHz Pentium IV processor with a 512 Mb of main memory running Windows.

The environments in Figures 1 and 2 are among those we used to test both algorithms. These algorithms were tested with planar articulated robots and implemented with the same parameters (the distance threshold ρ was set to 0.15 and the collision checking resolution ε to 0.001).

Fifty tests were performed with every algorithm. We used the Sobol's deterministic sequence, the randomized Halton's sequence, and the random linear congruential and Mersenne-Twister [15] generators.

Tables 1, 2 and 3 show the results of experiments performed on two difficult scenes for planar articulated robots.

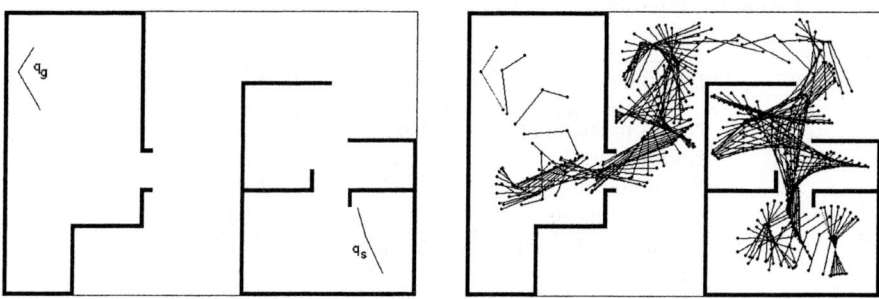

Fig. 1. A first motion planning environment and a path found for a planar manipulator

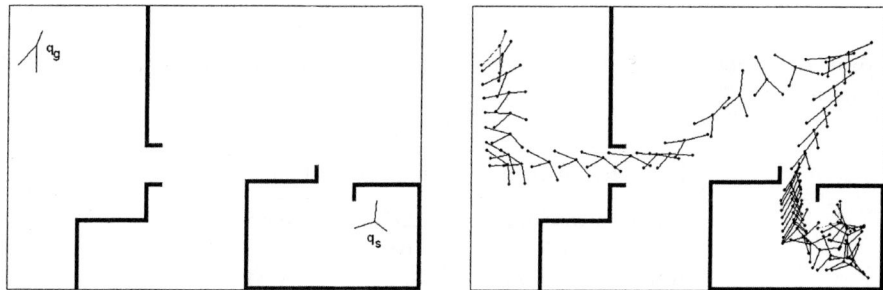

Fig. 2. Another motion planning environment and a path found for a planar manipulator

Table 1 reports results obtained with the random linear congruential generator. Results obtained with the random Mersenne-Twister generator are not reported because of its bad quality.

As we can see in these Tables, the randomized Halton and Sobol sequences outperform the random option. Improvement relative percentages in the number of collisions go from 41.27% to 77.67% while the improvement relative percentages in running times goes from 20.75% to 43.99%.

The results obtained point out that an adequate utilization of the Sobol sequence outperforms over classical Halton, Faure and Niederreiter's sequences due to the impact of dimension. The results obtained with Faure and Niederreiter's sequences are not reported in this paper because of the extremely bad quality of the results obtained.

We believe that randomization is useful in many contexts. Its value, nevertheless, depends greatly on the paradigm within it is used. Randomization does not appear to be advantageous in the PRM context, according to our experiments and the theoretical analysis presented by the authors in [5]. Deterministic sampling enables the expansive planner (Hsu/Sobol) and SBL/Sobol to be *resolution complete* [5]: if it possible to solve the query, they eventually solve it. According to our obtained results, randomized Halton sequences can be used

Table 1. Statistics for the two environments, using random sampling

First environment	Hsu/Random	SBL/Random
Nodes in roadmap	3568	8178
Nodes in path	59	107
Running time (secs)	114.97	2.12
Collision checks	598,342,368	4,774,440
Second environment	Hsu/Random	SBL/Random
Nodes in roadmap	3190	10030
Nodes in path	47	70
Running time (secs)	126.82	4.66
Collision checks	484,234,889	7,553,080

Table 2. Statistics for the two environments, using deterministic sampling (Sobol sequence)

First environment	Hsu/Sobol	SBL/Sobol
Nodes in roadmap	2286	6268
Nodes in path	67	97
Running time (secs)	40.22	1.84
Collision checks	143,258,754	3,552,236
Second environment	Hsu/Sobol	SBL/Sobol
Nodes in roadmap	1603	5764
Nodes in path	45	65
Running time (secs)	30.94	2.45
Collision checks	118,624,858	5,050,913

Table 3. Statistics for the two environments, using randomized Halton

First environment	Hsu/RH	SBL/RH
Nodes in roadmap	2222	4292
Nodes in path	59	81
Running time (secs)	76.69	1.68
Collision checks	133,611,588	2,581,166
Second environment	Hsu/RH	SBL/RH
Nodes in roadmap	2158	5299
Nodes in path	40	74
Running time (secs)	97.01	2.61
Collision checks	192,104,457	4,435,292

Table 4. Sequences Performance respect to running time, collision checks, path and roadmap number of nodes

Random sampling	Deterministic sampling	Deterministic + Random sampling
Linear congruential Mersenne Twister	Sobol	Randomized Halton
→	→	→

Table 5. Relative increment percentages respect to random sampling

First environment.	Hsu	SBL
Running time (secs)	33.30	20.75
Collision checks	77.67	45.94
Second environment.	Hsu	SBL
Running time (secs)	23.51	43.99
Collision checks	60.63	41.27

in motion planning to obtain both probabilistic analysis and the deterministic guarantees proposed in [5].

5 Conclusions

Sampling-based motion planners have proven to the best current alternative to solve difficult motion planning problems with many degrees of freedom. A crucial factor in the performance of those planners is how samples are generated. Sampling sequences should satisfy the following requirements: an uniform coverage that can be incrementally improved as the number of samples increases, a lattice structure that reduces the cost of computing neighborhood relationships, and a locally controllable degree of resolution that allows to generate more samples at the critical regions.

Discrepancy is interesting in many respects, but its computation is known to be very difficult. The complexity of the well-known algorithms is exponential. One might have hoped that these difficulties are partially counterbalanced by the existence of upper bounds for some especial types of low-discrepancy sequences. Unfortunately, the minimum number of points for which these classical bounds become meaningful grows exponentially with the dimension. We claim that deterministic sampling is suitable to capture the connectivity of configuration spaces with narrow passages [12].

Numerous low-discrepancy point sets and sequences have been proposed. They can be generated easily and quickly. For practical use, there are three different types of low-discrepancy sequences or point sets: Halton sequences, lattice rules, and (t, k)−sequences. The last one includes almost all important sequences such as Sobol sequence, Faure sequence, Niederreiter-Xing sequence, etc.

Low-discrepancy samples were developed to perform better than random samples for numerical integration (using an inequality due to Koksma-Hlawka). Low-dispersion samples were developed to perform better than random samples in numerical optimization (using an inequality due to Niederreiter).

Based in our comparative analysis we can observe that Sobol sequence is independent on the problem dimension while the classical Halton, Faure and Niederreiter's sequences are impacted by the number of dimensions confirming the analysis presented in [12]. Besides, the best results were always obtained with the randomized Halton sequences.

This fact open a new research topic in the sampling-based motion planning field, due to the random and deterministic characteristics of this sequence. The combination of random and deterministic benefits are already an important research field in Quasi-Monte Carlo simulation's community.

As thoroughly argued in [17], the achievements of sampling-based motion planners are mainly due to their sampling-based nature, not due to the randomization (usually) used to generate the samples. Therefore, efforts should better be directed towards the study of deterministic and controllable ways of generating samples, rather than towards the proposal of heuristically guided randomization variants.

This work is the first attempt to analyze the performance of the low discrepancy sequences in the single query planners context, our experiments confirm that it is possible to obtain important benefits.

The future study of different ways to improve sampling-based motion planners will benefit the solution of many practical problems as multi-robot coordination, nonholonomic planning, manipulation planning, etc.

References

1. Hsu D., Latombe J. C., Motwani R.: "Path planning in expansive configuration spaces", Int. J. of Computational Geometry and Applications, Vol. 9, (1999), 495-512
2. Hsu D.: "Randomized single-query motion planning in expansive spaces", PhD thesis, Stanford University, (2000)
3. Sánchez G. and Latombe J. C.: "On delaying colllision checking in PRM planning: Application to multi-robot coordination", The International Journal of Robotics Research, Vol. 21, No. 1, (2002), 5-26
4. Branicky M., Lavalle S. M., Olson K., Yang L.: "Quasi-randomized path planning", IEEE Int. Conf. on Robotics and Automation, (2001), 1481-1487
5. Lavalle S. M., Branicky M., Lindemann S. M.: "On the relationship between classical grid search and probabilistic roadmaps", The International Journal of Robotics Research, Vol. 23, No. 7-8, (2004), 673-692
6. Sánchez A., Zapata R., Lanzoni C.: "On the use of low-discrepancy sequences in non-holonomic motion planning", IEEE Int. Conf. on Robotics and Automation, (2003), 3764-3769

7. Kavraki L., Švestka P., Latombe J. C., Overmars M.: "Probabilistic roadmaps for path planning in high-dimensional configuration spaces", IEEE Transactions on Robotics and Automation. Vol 12, No. 4, (1996), 566-579
8. Amato N. M., Burchan B. O., Dale L. K, Jones C., Vallejo D.: "OBPRM: An obstacle-based PRM for 3D workspaces", Proc. of the Workshop on Algorithmic Foundations of Robotics, (1998), 155-168
9. Boor v., Overmars m., Van der Steppen F.: "The gaussian sampling strategy for probabilistic roadmap planners", IEEE Int. Conf. on Robotics and Automation, (1999), 1018-1023
10. Bohlin R. and Kavraki L.: "Path planning using lazy PRM", IEEE Int. Conf. on Robotics and Automation, (2000)
11. Niederreiter H.: "Random number generation and quasi-Monte Carlo methods". Society for Industrial and Applied Mathematics, Philadelphia, Pennsylvania, (1992)
12. Sánchez A.: "Contribution à la planification de mouvement en robotique: Approches probabilistes et approches déterministes", PhD thesis, Université Montpellier II (2003)
13. W. J. Morokoff and R. E. Caflisch, "Quasi-Monte Carlo integration", Journal of Computational Physics, 122, pp. 218-230, 1995.
14. Wang X., and Hickernell F. J.: "Randomized Halton sequences", Mathematical and Computer Modelling, Elsevier, Vol. 32, Issues 7-8, (2000), 887-899
15. Matsumoto M., and Nishimura T.: "Mersenne Twister: A 623-dimensionally equidistributed uniform pseudo-random number generator", ACM Transactions on Modeling and Computer Simulation, Vol. 8, No. 1, (1998), 3-30
16. Kavraki L., Latombe J. C., Motwani R., Raghavan P.: "Randomized query processing in robot motion planning", Journal of Computer and System Sciences, Vol. 57, No. 1, (1998), 50-60
17. Lindemann S., and LaValle S. M.: "Current issues in sampling-based motion planning", In P. Dario and R. Chatila, editors, Proc. Eighth International Symposium on Robotics Research, Springer-Verlag, Berlin, (2004)

A Framework for Reactive Motion and Sensing Planning: A Critical Events-Based Approach

R. Murrieta-Cid[1], A. Sarmiento[2], T. Muppirala[2], S. Hutchinson[2], R. Monroy[1], M. Alencastre[1], L. Muñoz[1], and R. Swain[1]

[1] Tec de Monterrey Campus Estado de México,
{rafael.murrieta, raulm, malencastre, lmunoz, rswain}@itesm.mx
[2] University of Illinois at Urbana-Champaign
{asarmien, muppiral, seth}@uiuc.edu

Abstract. We propose a framework for reactive motion and sensing planning based on critical events. A critical event amounts to crossing a critical curve, which divides the environment. We have applied our approach to two different problems: i) object finding and ii) pursuit-evasion. We claim that the proposed framework is in general useful for reactive motion planning based on information provided by sensors. We generalize and formalize the approach and suggest other possible applications.

1 Introduction

We propose a framework for reactive motion and sensing planning based on critical events. A critical event amounts to crossing a critical curve, which divides the environment. We work at the frontiers of computational geometry algorithms and control algorithms. The originality and the strength of this project is to bring both issues together.

We divide the environment in finitely many parts, using a discretization function which takes as input sensor information. Thus, in our approach, planning corresponds to switching among a finite number of control actions considering sensor input. This approach naturally allows us to deal with obstacles.

We have applied our approach to several different problems, here for lack of space we only present two: i) object finding and ii) pursuit-evasion. In object finding, our approach produces a continuous path, which is optimal in that it minimizes the expected time taken to find the object. In pursuit-evasion, we have dealt with computing the motions of a mobile robot pursuer in order to maintain visibility of a moving evader in an environment with obstacles.

Our solutions to these two problems have been published elsewhere. In this paper we show that these solutions actually rely on the same general framework. We claim that the proposed framework is in general useful for reactive motion planning based on information provided by sensors. We generalize and formalize the approach and suggest other possible applications.

2 A General Framework

The crux of our approach consists of relating critical events with both the controls to be applied on the robot and the robot environment representation. A *critical event* signals that the robot has crossed a critical curve drawn on the robot workspace, W. It corresponds to changes in the sensors information readings, driving our algorithms.

We use C and U to respectively denote the robot configuration space and the robot control space (velocity vectors applied to the robot). $P \subset C \times U$, the robot phase space, is the cross product of C and U. Critical curves are projections on the workspace of P. This means that even if a configuration is valid to accomplish a task, it may not be valid due to the velocity related with that configuration. Hence, the critical curves may change their location according to a given robot velocity.

Let Y denote the observation space, which corresponds to all possible sensor readings. The robot state space is $X \subset C \times E$, in which E is the set of all possible environments where the robot might be [12]. Evidently, there is a relation between the robot state $x(t)$ and the robot observation state $y(t)$ which is a function of time. Thus, $y(t) = h(x(t))$, where $y \in Y$ and $x \in X$. The robot information state is defined as $i_t = (u_0, \ldots, u_{t-1}, y_0, \ldots, y_t)$. i_t is the history of all sensor readings up to time t and all controls that have been applied to the robot up to time $t-1$ [2]. The *information space* I is defined as the set of all possibles information states [12]. We underline that the critical events and the robot objective lie over I. That is, a robot objective amounts to achieving a specific task defined on the information state. Two example robot objectives are maintaining visibility of a moving evader and reaching a robot configuration given in terms of a specific robot sensor reading.

Critical events may be of several types. A type of critical event is systematically associated to a type of control. Mainly, to accomplish a robotic task means to answer the following question: what control should be applied on the robot given some i_t?. Thus, planning corresponds to a discrete mapping $ce : i_t \to u$ between i_t and u, triggered by the critical event ce. The output controls correspond to at the very worst case locally optimal polices that solve the robotic task.

Note that instead of using the robot state space, X, we use the critical events to make a decision on control should be applied. ce actually encodes the most relevant information on X. In addition, it relates observations with the best control that can be applied. ce is built using local information but, if necessary, it may involve global one.

We want to use our framework to generate, whenever possible, optimal controls to accomplish a robotic task. As mentioned earlier, planning corresponds to relate a critical events with a control. However, some problems may be history dependent. That means that the performance of a control to be applied not only depends on the current action and a sensor reading, but it also depends on all previous sensor readings and their associated controls. In history dependent problems, the concatenation of locally optimal controls triggered by independent critical events does not necessarily generate a globally optimal solution. For instance, we have shown that object finding is history dependent and moreover NP-hard.

To deal with history dependent problems, we have proposed a two layer approach. The high level, *combinatoric* layer attempts to find a "suitable" order of reaching critical events. The low level, *continuous* layer takes an ordering input by the upper one and finds how to best visit the regions defined by critical curves. This decoupling approach makes the problem tractable, but at the expense of missing global optimality. For the combinatorial level, we have proposed to use a *utility function based heuristic*, given as the ratio of a gain over a cost. This utility function is used to drive a greedy algorithm in a reduced search space that is able to explore several steps ahead but without evaluating all possibles combinations.

In no history dependent problems, such as finding a minimal length path in an environment without holes [11], the Bellman's principle of optimality holds and thus the concatenation of locally optimal paths will result in a globally optimal one. The navigation approach presented in [11] is also based on critical events. But, differently to the ones presented in this paper, it is based on closed loop sensor feed-back.

3 Object Finding

We have used critical events to finding time optimal search paths in known environments. In particular, we have searched a known environment for an object whose unknown location is characterized by a known probability density function (pdf).

In this problem, we deal with *continuous sensing* in a continuous space. We assume that the robot is sensing the environment as it moves. A continuous trajectory is said to *cover* [9] a polygon P if each point $p \in P$ is visible from some point along the trajectory. Any trajectory that covers a simple (without holes) polygon must visit each subset of the polygon that is bounded by the aspect graph lines associated to non-convex vertices of the polygon.

We call the area bounded by these aspect graph lines the *corner guard regions*. A continuous trajectory that covers a simple polygon needs to have at least one point inside the region associated to "outlying" non-convex vertices (non-convex vertices in polygon ears), like A and C in Fig. 1 a). Since these points need to be connected with a continuous path, a covering trajectory will cross all the other corner guard regions, like the one associated to vertex B.

Since a continuous trajectory needs to visit all the corner guard regions, it is important to decide in which order they are to be visited. The problem can be abstracted to finding an specific order of visiting nodes in a graph that minimizes the expected value of time to find an object. [6] shows that the discrete version of this problem is NP-hard. For this reason, to generate continuous trajectories we propose an approach with two layers that solve specific parts of the problem. This one is described below (see 3.4).

3.1 Continuous Sensing in the Base Case

The simplest case for a continuous sensing robot is that shown in Fig. 1 b). Then, the robot has to move around a non-convex vertex (corner) to explore the unseen area A'. For now, we assume that this is the only unseen portion of the environment.

As the robot follows any given trajectory S, it will sense new portions of the environment. The rate at which new environment is seen determines the expected value of the time required to find the object along that route. In particular, consider the following definition of expectation for a non-negative random variable [5]:

$$E[T|S] = \int_0^\infty P(T > t)\, dt. \qquad (1)$$

3.2 Expected Value of Time Along any Trajectory

In the simple environment shown in Fig. 1 b) the robot's trajectory is expressed as a function in polar coordinates with the origin on the non-convex vertex. We assume that the robot will have a starting position such that its line of sight will only sweep the horizontal edge E_1. As mentioned before, the expected value of the time to find an object depends on the area A' not yet seen by the robot.

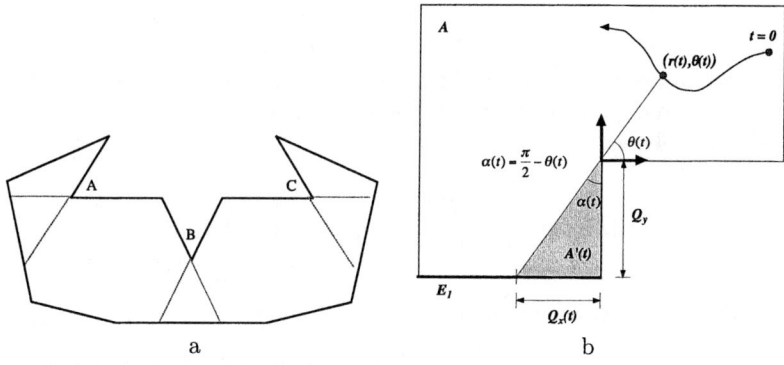

Fig. 1. a) convex corners   b) base case

Assuming that the probability density function of the object's location over the environment is constant, the probability of not having seen the object at time t is

$$P(T > t) = \frac{A'(t)}{A} = \frac{Q_y^2}{2A\,\tan(\theta(t))}, \qquad (2)$$

where A is the area of the whole environment (for more details, see [7]). Note that the reference frame used to define the equation 2 is *local*. It is defined with respect to the reflex vertex (this with interior angle larger than π). From (1) and (2),

$$E[T|S] = \frac{Q_y^2}{2A} \int_0^{t_f} \frac{dt}{\tan(\theta(t))}. \qquad (3)$$

Equation (3) is useful for calculating the expected value of the time to find an object given a robot trajectory S expressed as a parametric function $\theta(t)$.

3.3 Minimization Using Calculus of Variations

The Calculus of Variations [3] is a mathematical tool employed to find stationary values (usually a minimum or a maximum) of integrals of the form

$$I = \int_a^b F(x, y, y') \, dx, \qquad (4)$$

where x and y are the independent and dependent variables respectively.

The integral in (4) has a stationary value if and only if the Euler-Lagrange equation is satisfied,

$$\frac{\partial F}{\partial y} - \frac{d}{dx}\left(\frac{\partial F}{\partial y'}\right) = 0. \qquad (5)$$

It is possible to express the differential of time as a function of a differential of θ. This will allow us to rewrite the parametric equation as a function in which θ and r are the independent and dependent variables respectively, The resulting equation is as follows:

$$E[T|S] = \frac{Q_y^2}{2A} \int_{\theta_i}^{\theta_f} \frac{1}{\tan(\theta)} \left(r'^2 + r^2\right)^{\frac{1}{2}} d\theta. \qquad (6)$$

To find stationary values of (6), we use (5) with $x = \theta$, $y = r$ and $F = \frac{1}{\tan\theta}\left(r'^2 + r^2\right)^{\frac{1}{2}}$. After simplification, this yields the following second order non-linear differential equation,

$$r'' = r + \frac{2r'^2}{r} + \frac{2}{\sin(2\theta)}\left(r' + \frac{r'^3}{r^2}\right). \qquad (7)$$

This equation describes the route to move around a non-convex vertex (corner) to search the area on the other side optimally (according to the expected value of time). We have solved equation (7) numerically using an adaptive step-size Runge-Kutta method. The Runge-Kutta algorithm has been coupled with a globally convergent Newton-Raphson method [7].

3.4 Choosing an Ordering of Regions

To cover a simple polygon, it is sufficient that a trajectory visits at least one point inside each corner guard region (as defined in section 3) associated to reflex vertices of the polygon. The high level, combinatoric layer attempts to find an ordering for the robot to visit these corner guard regions such that the expected value of the time to find an object in the environment is reduced. Note that the discretization defined with critical events is needed because the form of the integral that define the expected value of the time may change according to the shape of the region. To find a suitable ordering, we have defined a point guard inside each corner guard region and used the approach of [6] for sensing at specific locations. The algorithm yields an ordering for visiting corner guard regions (associated to non-convex vertices) that attempts to reduce the expected value of the time to find an object.

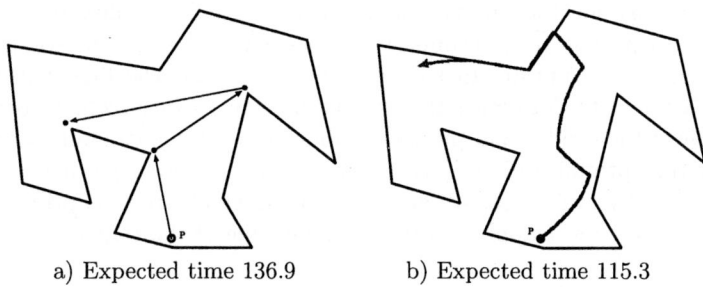

a) Expected time 136.9   b) Expected time 115.3

Fig. 2. a) concatenation of straight line paths b) concatenation of locally optimal paths

Once an ordering has been established, the lower level, continuous layer uses the sequence of non-convex vertices to perform locally optimal motions around each of them, thus generating a complete trajectory that covers the polygonal environment. We know that any trajectory generated in this fashion will not be globally optimal in the general case. The main reason of lacking global optimality is that any partition of the problem into locally optimal portions does not guarantee global optimality (Bellman's principle of optimality does not apply). However, through simulation experiments, we have found that the quality of the routes generated by our algorithm is close to the optimal solutions (more details can be found in [6] and [7]).

Figure 2 shows two routes for exploring the environment. The first one, 2 a), is composed by straight lines. The second one, 2 b), is based on the concatenation of locally optimal path generated through an appropriate ordering of reaching critical events defined with our approach. The path generated with our approach produces a smaller average time to find the object. Note that a zig-zag motion is not necessarily bad because a good trajectory must find a compromise between advancing to the next guard and sensing a larger portion of the environment as soon as possible.

4 Pursuit-Evasion

In this section, we consider the surveillance problem of maintaining visibility at a fixed distance of a mobile evader (the target) using a mobile robot equipped with sensors (the observer).

We address the problem of maintaining visibility of the target in the presence of obstacles. We assume that obstacles produce both motion and visibility constraints. We consider that both the observer and the target have bounded velocity. We assume that the pursuer can react instantaneously to evader motion. The *visibility between the target and the observer is represented as a line segment and it is called the rod (or bar)*. This rod is emulating the visual sensor capabilities of the observer. The constant rod length is modeling a fixed sensor range.

This problem has at least two important aspects. The first one is to find an optimal motion for the target to escape and symmetrically to determine the optimal strategy for the observer to always maintain visibility of the evader. The second aspect is to determine the necessary and sufficient conditions for the existence of a solution. In this section, we address the first aspect of the problem. That is, to determine the optimal motion strategy, which corresponds to define how the evader and pursuer should move. We have numerically found which are the optimal controls (velocity vectors) that the target has to apply to escape observer surveillance. We have also found which are the optimal controls that the observer must apply to prevent the escape of the target.

4.1 Geometric Modeling

We have expressed the constraints on the observer dynamics (velocity bounds and kinematics constraints) geometrically, as a function of the geometry of the workspace and the surveillance distance. Our approach consists in partitioning the phase space P and the workspace in non-critical regions separated by critical curves. These critical curves define all possible types of contacts of the rod with the obstacles [8]. These curves bound forbidden rod configurations. These rod configurations are forbidden either because they generate a violation of the visibility constraint (corresponding to a collision of the rod with an obstacle in the environment) or because they require the observer to move with speed greater than its maximum.

In order to avoid a forbidden rod configuration, the pursuer must change the rod configuration to prevent the target to escape. We call this pursuer motion the rotational motion. If the observer has bounded speed then the rotational motion has to be started far enough for any forbidden rod configuration. The pursuer must have enough time to change the rod configuration before the evader brings the rod to a forbidden one. There are *critical events* that tell the pursuer to start changing the rod configuration before it is too late. We have defined an escape point as a point on a critical curve bounding forbidden rod configuration sets (escapable cells), or a point in a region bounding an obstacle. This region is bounding either a reflex vertex or a segment of the polygonal workspace. We use D^* to denote the distance from an escape point such that, if the evader is further than D^* from the escape point, the observer will have sufficient time to react and prevent escape. Thus, it is only when the evader is nearer than D^* to an escape point that the observer must take special care. Thus, the critical events are to D^* distance from the escape points.

4.2 Optimal Target and Observer Motions

Thus, the optimal control problem is to determine D^*. We solve it using the Pontryagin's minimum principle with free terminal time [1].

Take the global Cartesian axis to be defined such that the origin is the target's initial position, and the x-axis is the line connecting the target's initial position and the escape point. Note that the *reference frame is local*. It is defined with respect to the escape point. The target and observer velocities are saturated at V_t and V_o respectively, and because the rod length must be fixed at all times, the relative velocity V_{ot} must be perpendicular to the rod. This information yields the following velocity vector diagram (see figure 3 a)). θ is the angle between the rod and x axis, α represents the direction of the evader velocity vector used to escape. The rate of change of θ can be found to be [4]:

$$\frac{d\theta}{dt} = \frac{Vot}{L} = \frac{-V_t \sin(\alpha + \theta) \pm \sqrt{V_o^2 - V_t^2 \cos^2(\alpha + \theta)}}{L} \tag{8}$$

Because the boundary conditions of the geometry are defined in terms of x, a more useful derivative would be:

$$\frac{d\theta}{dx} = \frac{d\theta}{dt}(\frac{dx}{dt})^{-1} = \frac{-R\sin(\alpha + \theta) \pm \sqrt{1 - R^2 \cos^2(\alpha + \theta)}}{LR\cos(\alpha)} \quad \text{Where} \quad R = \frac{V_t}{V_o} < 1 \tag{9}$$

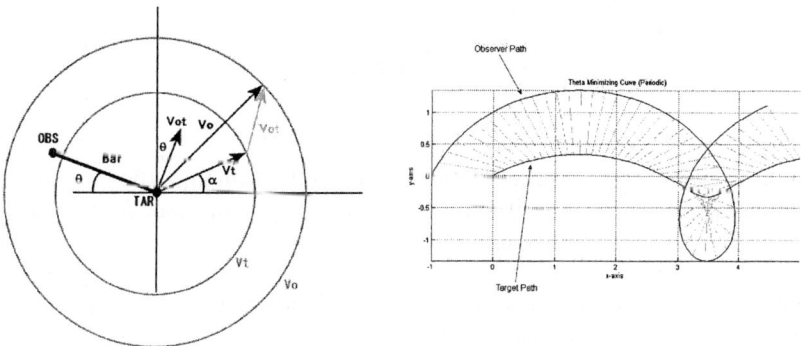

a) Velocity vector diagram   b) Optimal pursuer and evader paths

Fig. 3. Pursuit-evasion

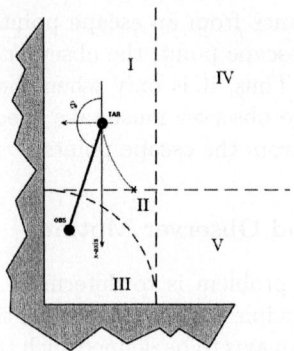

Fig. 4. The evader tries to confine the pursuer in a corner

The optimal path for the target can be defined as follows: Find for a given initial rod angle θ_0, the distance D^* to an escape point x_1 such that the final rod configuration is at a specified final angle θ_1 and the corresponding target motion $\alpha(x)$, $x \in [0, x_1]$.

The natural representation would be:

$$\frac{d\theta}{dx} = \frac{-R\sin(\alpha + \theta) \pm \sqrt{1 - R^2 \cos^2(\alpha + \theta)}}{LR\cos(\alpha)} = f_1 \quad \frac{dy}{dx} = V_t \tan \alpha = f_2 \quad (10)$$

$$\theta(0) = \theta_0, \theta(x_1) = \theta_1, y(0) = y(1) = 0 \tag{11}$$

To maximize x_1, the appropriate cost function is:

$$V = -\int_0^{x_1} dx \tag{12}$$

The minimum principle establishes:

$$u(*) = argmin\ H(x^*(t), p(t), u, t)$$

$$H = l + p^T f, \quad \dot{p} = -\nabla_x H$$

Where p is the co-state vector, H the system Hamiltonian, l the cost function, f the function state and $u(*)$ the optimal control. The optimal control problem can be stated using 4 conditions:

1. There exists two functions of x, p_1 and p_2 such that $\alpha^* = argmin[p_1 f_1 + p_2 f_2 - 1]$ is satisfied pointwise for all x.
2. The state vector satisfies the state equations and 4 boundary conditions above.
3. The final value x_1 satisfies $p_1(x_1)f_1(x_1) + p_2(x_1)f_2(x_1) - 1 = 0$.
4. The state equations for are given by:

$$\frac{dp_1}{dx} = -\frac{\partial f_1}{\partial \theta}p_1 = \frac{R\cos(\alpha+\theta) \pm \frac{R^2\cos(\alpha+\theta)\sin(\alpha+\theta)}{\sqrt{1-R^2\cos^2(\alpha+\theta)}}}{LR\cos\alpha}p_1 \quad (13)$$

$$\frac{dp_2}{dx} = -\frac{\partial f_2}{\partial y}p_2 \equiv 0 \rightarrow p_2(x) = p_2 \; (constant) \quad (14)$$

If we set p_2 to zero, the minimization condition 1 simplifies to

$$\alpha^*(x) = argmin[p_1 f_1 + p_2 f_2 - 1] \rightarrow \frac{\partial}{\partial \alpha}[p_1 f_1 - 1] = 0 \rightarrow \frac{\partial f_1}{\partial \alpha} = 0 \quad (15)$$

In the case when the escape condition (critical event) is defined by a straight line (such as when the evader tries to run the pursuer into a wall, see figure 4), a strategy to generate the solution to the boundary value problem is as follows. Generate the θ-Minimizing Curve by integrating the observer and target positions forward in x, choosing the minimizer α^* at every step Δx. Select two points on the curve and let the line through them represent the new x-axis. The two points can be chosen so that the initial and final angle conditions are satisfied (as measured with respect to the new x-axis), and the optimal path is then the section of the θ-Minimizing Curve connecting the two points. The distance between the two points is x_1, the critical distance D^* to the escape point.

Note that the optimal path for the evader to escape is not a straight line (see figure 3 b). This happens because of the kinematic constraints (bounded speeds and fixed surveillance distance), there is a trade-off between minimizing the time taken for the target to reach the escape point and maximizing the time taken for the observer to change the rod configuration. Therefore, the optimal target path is the one that minimizes the amount of angle that the observer can make in its rotation up until the target reaches the escape point. Figure 4 shows a case when the evader tries to escape pursuer surveillance by confining it against a wall in a concave corner. The critical curves are the dashed lines.

5 Discussion and Future Work

We proposed a framework for reactive motion and sensing planning based on critical events. In this approach planning corresponds to associate critical events with controls. The resulting controls correspond to locally optimal polices for history dependent problems and globally optimal polices for no history dependent ones.

The techniques used to compute optimal paths are open loop methods. However, because of the manner we are using them, a global reference frame is not required. The reference frames are local. For object finding the local reference frame is fixed with respect to the reflex vertices. For pursuit evasion the local reference frame is defined respect to escape points. Therefore, we can compute the controls and resulting paths based on information obtained online directly from the sensors. The required information to compute the controls lies on the information space I.

We underline that there is a similarity between our approach and techniques that have been reported in the literature to compute optimal paths to accomplish robotic tasks. For instance in [10], an approach to compute minimal length paths in the absence of obstacles for non-holonomic robots is presented. The optimal paths correspond to the concatenation of locally optimal ones delimited by critical curves. Those critical curves correspond to the saturation on the admissible robot controls. One important difference is that our robotic tasks are focused on sensing the environment (sensing planning) and we can base our approach on the critical events detected by the sensors.

For future work we want to consider uncertainty in both sensing and control. We believe the use of local reference frames and robot motion planning based on information obtained directly from sensors will result in a robust manner of dealing with uncertainty. We also want to extent our approach to 3D environments. A first effort in the research topic has been already published.

References

1. T. Başar, S.P. Meyn, and W.R. Perkins. *Control system theory and desing*. University of Illinois, 2004.
2. D-P. Bertsekas. *Dynamic Programming: Deterministic and Stochastic Models*. prentice, 1987.
3. Gelfran. I.M. and S.V. Fomin. *Calculus of Variations*. Prentice Hall, 1963.
4. T. Muppirala, R. Murrieta-Cid, and S. Hutchinson. Optimal motion strategies based on critical events to maintain visibility of a moving target. In *IEEE Int. Conf. on Robotics and Automation*, 2005.
5. S.M. Ross. *Introduction to Probability and Statistics for Engineers and Scientists*. Wiley, 1987.
6. A. Sarmiento, R. Murrieta-Cid, and S. Hutchinson. An efficient strategy for rapidly finding an object in a polygonal world. In *IEEE/RSJ Int. Conf. on Intelligent Robots and Systems*, 2003.
7. A. Sarmiento, R. Murrieta-Cid, and S. Hutchinson. Planning expected-time optimal paths for searching known environments. In *IEEE/RSJ Int. Conf. on Intelligent Robots and Systems*, 2004.
8. J.-T. Schwartz and M. Sharir. On the piano movers problem: I. the case of a two-dimensional rigid polygon body moving amidst polygonal barriers. *Communications on Applied Mathematics*, 36:345–398, 1983.
9. T.C. Shermer. Recent results in art galleries. *Proc. of the IEEE*, 80(9), 1992.
10. P. Souères and J.-P. Laumond. Shortest paths synthesis for a car-like robot. *IEEE Transactions on Automatic Control*, 41(5):672–688, May 1996.
11. B. Tovar, S. LaValle, and R. Murrieta-Cid. Optimal navigation and object finding without geometric maps or localization. In *IEEE Int. Conf. on Robotics and Automation*, 2003.
12. B. Tovar, S. Yershova, J. O'Kane, and S. LaValle. Information spaces for mobile robots. In *Fifth International Workshop on Robot Motion and Control*, 2005.

Visual Planning for Autonomous Mobile Robot Navigation

Antonio Marin-Hernandez[1], Michel Devy[2], and Victor Ayala-Ramirez[3]

[1] Facultad de Física e Inteligencia Artificial, Universidad Veracruzana,
Sebastián Camacho No. 5, Centro, 91000, Xalapa, Ver., Mexico
anmarin@uv.mx
[2] LAAS - CNRS, 7 avenue Colonel Roche,
31077 Toulouse, Cedex 04, France
michel@laas.fr
[3] FIMEE, Universidad de Guanajuato,
Tampico 912, 36730, Salamanca, Gto., Mexico
ayalav@laas.fr

Abstract. For autonomous mobile robots following a planned path, self-localization is a very important task. Cumulative errors derived from the different noisy sensors make it absolutely necessary. Absolute robot localization is commonly made measuring relative distance from the robot to previously learnt landmarks on the environment. Landmarks could be interest points, colored objects, or rectangular regions as posters or emergency signs, which are very useful and not intrusive beacons in human environments. This paper presents an active localization method: a visual planning function selects from a free collision path and a set of planar landmarks, a subset of visible landmarks and the best combination of camera parameters (pan, tilt and zoom) for positions sampled along the path. A visibility measurement and some utility measurements were defined in order to select for each position, the camera modality and the subset of landmarks that maximize these local criteria. Finally, a dynamic programming method is proposed in order to minimize saccadic movements all over the trajectory.

1 Introduction

Autonomous mobile robot navigation is a very complex task. Complexity relies on several factors, for example, noisy data acquisition, moving obstacles, etc. To go from a specific point to another, the robot can follow a planned path. However, whatever control strategy, the robot always executes motion commands with small errors. It is very important to integrate on the embedded system a localization method in order to maintain the robot on its planned path. A variety of localization methods have been proposed on literature. Many of them use visual landmarks, as interest points, regions of interest, or specific designed beacons.

Optimal landmarks selection for robot localization has been tackled on different works. Many of these works are focused on detection of robust landmarks [1], [2]. These frameworks are very important to handle the kidnapped robot problem, namely to recognize the current robot position without any prediction. Such a method was developed in the LAAS robotics team [3], for a robot equipped with a single camera on indoor environments. Quadrangular planar landmarks, like posters or emergency signs, are very common on public buildings; they are non-intrusive and a very useful source of information. These landmarks are automatically detected and characterized during a learning step, and then, recognized to initialize the current robot position. Then, these visual landmarks are tracked using template matching [4], and used to update the robot position along a path. This procedure is totally passive: the robot exploits only visible landmarks from a given robot position; the camera is controlled only when tracking a landmark, to keep it in the view field.

On autonomous robot navigation, perception should be an active and generative process [5]. That is to said, perception needs to be considered as a part of the generated actions, namely as a planned and controlled process.

Many works have been devoted to the choice of the Next Best View (NBV) for a sensor used to model an environment. In [6], a geometrical approach is proposed to compute, from the current scene model, the visibility volume from where occluded areas could be seen. In [7], non linear optimization is used to find the NBV for a 5 dof 3D sensor, maximizing utility criteria and minimizing costs. Other works [8] deal only with the NBV problem for the construction of a 2D model using a Laser Range Finder with only a horizontal scanning.

In [9], the museum keeper problem is solved. Here also, it is supposed that a polygonal map is already known; a non-optimal solution is proposed to find the minimum set of sensors and their respective positions in the scene from which the whole workspace is visible. This paper deals with the problem of landmark selection. If the robot needs to go from a given point to another, a free collision trajectory is generated by a path planner. In order to control the motion on this path, the robot will detect and track landmarks from a monocular vision system, equipped with a pan/tilt unit, with zooming possibilities. The visual planning task consists in selecting along the path, the landmarks and the camera modalities, which will minimize the cost of detection and tracking [10]. In order to achieve this task, it is assumed that a global map of the environment, made with a set of visual planar landmarks and their respective positions in the world, has been previously learnt.

In [11], some preliminary results were presented, using an exhaustive search of the optimal solution. This paper proposes a more realistic strategy to select, for a set of points sampled on the path, the best-adapted camera modalities, in order to detect and track landmarks. As an active process, camera modalities and landmarks are selected in function of the complete generated path. That is to say, utility of landmarks is maximized while saccadic movements are minimized.

In order to incorporate the active perception framework, different *visibility* and *utility* measurements have been proposed. On this framework, object utilities are defined by their situation in the world, and also from the robot and the camera states in the world reference frame.

The organization of this paper is as follow. Section II presents the visibility measurement used for planar landmarks. Section III tackles the problem of measuring the utility with respect to the robot state in the world and to the possible camera configurations. Section IV details the strategy used to avoid saccadic movements. Section V presents our results and finally, Section VI gives our conclusions with on the way extensions of this work.

2 Landmark Visibility

Visibility is commonly computed as a bi-valued function. Function values depend on the existence of a line of sight between the observer (robot) and the objects (landmarks). As we can notice, these binary values are not always useful, because it is supposed that the visibility of a given point is the same for every point in the 3D space from which it exists a line of sight [12]. In a physical world, the visibility of a point depends on its orientation as well as on the observer position. Commonly, a normal vector can be used to define point's orientation, and then visibility should depend on this value, e.g. when line of sight is closer to a perpendicular line to the normal vector, the visibility should be closer to zero.

In order to integrate previous considerations, it is proposed to compute the visibility V from an observer position **x**, of a given point **p** with normal vector **N**, as:

$$V = \begin{cases} -\cos(\phi) & \text{if } \phi < \frac{\pi}{2} \\ 0 & \text{other way} \end{cases} \quad (1)$$

where ϕ is the minimal angle between the vectors **d** = **p** - **x** and **N** (Fig 1a).

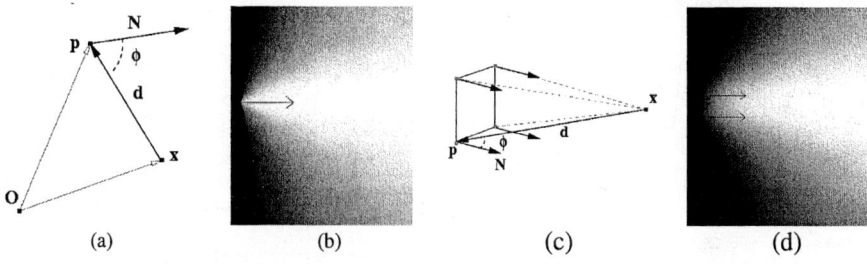

Fig. 1. Visibility: a) vectors and quantities considered for visibility computation of point **p** from a position **x** with respect to a global reference frame in **O**. b) Visibility map of a point with a horizontal normal vector from different positions. c) Corners and vectors considered for visibility computation of a plane target, d) visibility map of a line target.

It is important to note that, on this definition, the visibility depends only on the angle between the orientation (normal vector) and the observer position, whatever will be its distance to the target point. This takes into account mainly the fact that, proper visual characteristics of the observer (e.g. the visual sharpness) are not considered to compute it. Therefore, depending on camera parameters, a point can be visible but not perceptible. Proper visual characteristics will be incorporated later for utility measurements on section III.

Fig. 1b, shows visibility values of a target point from different observer positions. Only 2D visibility is considered here; the current measurement concerns the 3D visibility. Here we can see that, visibility has the same value for radial lines centered on the target point.

Most of the time, a rectangular planar landmark cannot be considered as a point in space. However, its visibility can be computed from a small set of points.

Be $\mathbf{L}_i = \{\mathbf{p}_{i1}, \mathbf{p}_{i2}, \mathbf{p}_{i3}, \mathbf{p}_{i4}\}$, the set of corners of a landmark i and $\mathbf{N}_{Li}$ the normal vector to its planar surface (Fig. 1c). Then, the visibility V_{Li} of the landmark is calculated as:

$$V_{Li} = \frac{\sum_{j=1}^{n_p} V_{ij}}{n_p} \quad (2)$$

where V_{ij} is the visibility of the j-th corner of the landmark i, and n_p is the number of points (corners) considered, here $n_p = 4$.

To reduce visual complexity, of the 3D image of the visibility map, Fig. 1d shows the visibility map of a line target (two corner points). We can notice that there is a region very near the front of target and between its corners where the visibility is very low. This implies that when the observer is very close to the target, in this case a single line, it is not able to perceive the complete target.

It is important to note that, for a planar landmark (2) gives its optimal value (V_{Li} = 1.0), in a frontal position to the normal vector and at an infinite distance from target. However, as it could be tested, in a frontal view, when the distance from observer to target is greater than the target dimensions on one order of magnitude, visibility values are close to 0.995, so very acceptable values.

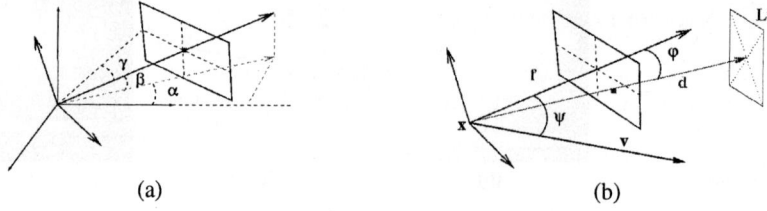

Fig. 2. Camera model: a) internal angles, α = pan angle, β = tilt angle and γ = field of view (zoom), b) external angles φ angle between $\mathbf{f}$ and $\mathbf{d}$, ψ angle between $\mathbf{v}$ and $\mathbf{f}$

3 Landmark Utility

The utility function of a given landmark $\mathbf{L}_i$ is the product of various terms K. Each one of these K terms is joined to some criterion that depends on some characteristics: viewer orientation, visual sharpness, landmark size and/or specific criteria for the given task. The K terms are normalized between 0 (null utility) and 1 (optimal utility).

Two terms are mainly used at this step: the first one to qualify the size of the landmark on viewer's image, and the other one to compare the alignment between the line of sight and the focal vector (camera orientation). The number of utility terms could be expanded to include more criteria: some other characteristics (robot orientation) will be included on section IV. In Fig. 2, it is shown the camera model and variables used for utility computation.

3.1 Size of Landmark

The size of the landmark projected on the image depends on the dimensions of the landmark, and then directly on the possible configurations of the field of view, namely the zoom parameter γ. The field of view angle is measured on the horizontal line on the camera reference frame. Vertical angle is typically 3/4 of it.

This criterion K_1 is defined by:

$$K_1^{Li} = 1 - \frac{|\gamma - \gamma_i^*|}{\max_{\gamma} |\gamma - \gamma_i^*|} \qquad (3)$$

where | | represents the absolute value, γ is the field of view of the camera (Fig. 2a) and γ_i^* is the optimal field of view at the current distance for the landmark i. Optimal field of view depends on the visual task, here the landmark localization and tracking. It must be defined from a statistical analysis of many experiments: typically, γ_i^* will be selected so that the landmark projection must be large enough to improve the localization accuracy, but cannot be too large to make more efficient the tracking. This term could be modified to give a penalty for extreme positions of the zoom, so that the system will prefer a close landmark with a mean zoom, than a further one with a minimal view field.

3.2 Camera-Landmark Alignment

It is important to notice that, although exists a line of sight between observer and landmark where visibility is not zero; the focal vector could be pointing to another direction (Fig 2b). Our second utility term considers the angle between these two vectors, and then is defined as:

$$K_2^{Li} = \cos \varphi_i \qquad (4)$$

where φ is the angle formed between the focal vector $\mathbf{f}$ and the line of sight vector of the i-th landmark $\mathbf{d}_{Li}$. The utility is maximal when the two vectors are aligned (no specularity).

3.3 Total Utility

The utility function is a product of the different K terms. Therefore, the utility of the landmark $\mathbf{L}_i$ at position $\mathbf{x}_t$ (the robot position on the path and the camera configuration: pan, tilt and zoom) will be calculated by:

$$U_i^{xt} = \left(\prod_{j=1}^{m} K_j^{Li} \right) V_i(\mathbf{x}_t) \qquad (5)$$

where m is the number of utility terms, in our case $m = 2$. A better visibility of $\mathbf{L}_i$ from configuration $\mathbf{x}_t$, improves the utility of this couple ($\mathbf{L}_i$, $\mathbf{x}_t$).

If two or more landmarks are visible from a given position $\mathbf{x}_t$, then the set of landmarks utility is the sum of utility functions for each one of them, as:

$$U_c^{xt} = \sum_{i=1}^{n} U_i^{xt} \qquad (6)$$

where U_i is the individual utility of the landmark L_i.

In Fig. 3, are shown three oriented planar landmarks and a utility map, computed only for the focal alignment term K_1 from position **x**. For easily visualization, utility values are calculated only for pan angle configuration ($\alpha_{min} < \alpha < \alpha_{max}$). Individual landmark utility in Fig 3b is presented with the same color as landmarks in Fig 3a. Color combination gives us an idea about global utility. On this configuration, landmark L_3 has null utility due to its orientation. On Fig 3b, we can see clearly, that for the right half part of the image, utility values are given mainly by L_2. While, on the opposite side, as focal alignment goes from $\alpha = 0$ (middle point) to $\alpha = \alpha_{min}$, utility values varies from a combination of L_1 and L_2 utility values to a mainly value of L_1.

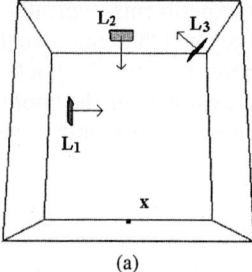
(a)

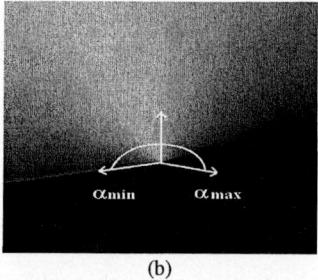
(b)

Fig. 3. Set of landmarks utility: a) oriented landmarks configuration and, b) utility map of focal alignment term for all possible pan angle (α) configurations

4 Visual Planning

To find the best modality configuration for each position **x** on the path with motion vector **v**, on [11] the complete configuration space is swept. The complexity of this approach depends explicitly on the configuration space discretization and on the number of landmarks. The approach proposed in this paper, take into account the fact that, as we can easily test, there are many regions on the configuration space where the utility value is null; where it is not, a direct computation could give us directly the best parameter configuration.

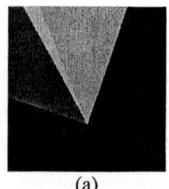
(a)

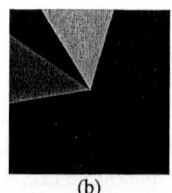
(b)

(c)

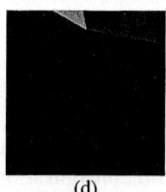
(d)

Fig. 4. Utility maps with maximal field of view restrictions

On Fig 4b, there is no restriction about the maximal field of view of the camera. It is to say that for any value of the pan angle (α) it is possible to see all visible targets, what is not at all true, due to limited camera zoom possibilities.

If the utility sum (6) is restricted to those landmarks inside the maximum field of view of the camera γ_{max}, the valid regions on the configuration space are reduced. In Fig 4, the restriction of maximal field of view is applied to the same landmarks configuration, shown on Fig 3a.

We note on Fig. 4a, three very well delimited regions. Two regions with similar color as landmarks, where only one of these landmarks contributes to the global utility function (6). And a small region in the middle, where utilities values from landmarks L_1 and L_2 are superposed. This implies that, on the first two regions only one landmark is visible with the maximal field of view. On the region in the middle, the two landmarks are visible. The third landmark is not visible from this point.

As position x moves forward, these regions change. On Fig 4b, there is no more superposed region. On Fig 4c, landmark L_3 appears on utility map with a very low value, and finally on Fig 4d, the region from L_1 disappears and utility for L_3 is higher.

Considering this example, it is possible to generate all the subsets of visible landmarks from a point of view, and then calculate the utility for each one. The maximal number of elements on subset can be fixed, in order to limit the computation. We use three as the maximal number of desired planar landmarks perceived in one image.

After some mathematical manipulation, the optimal Camera-Landmark alignment for pan and tilt angles, for the general case, is obtained by:

$$\alpha = \tan^{-1}\left(\frac{\sum_{i=1}^{n_v} C_i \sin\alpha_i}{\sum_{i=1}^{n_v} C_i \cos\alpha_i}\right), \quad \beta = \tan^{-1}\left(\frac{\sum_{i=1}^{n_v} C_i \sin\beta_i}{\sum_{i=1}^{n_v} C_i \cos\beta_i}\right) \quad (7)$$

where n_v is the number of landmarks on subset, $C_i = K^{Li}{}_1 V_{Li}$, and α_i and β_i are the pan and tilt angles of d_i.

Once utility computation is made, for all subsets of each sampled point along the path, it is possible to find the set of camera modalities for the entire path that maximizes utilities. However, this modality plan does not assure a smooth transition between modalities and therefore does not avoid saccadic movements.

In order to avoid erratic motions of the camera or of its zoom (saccadic movements), which could perturb landmarks tracking and detection, the modality plan is improved by a dynamic programming algorithm.

On this approach, each of the points over the path will be a *stage*; the utility of subset of landmarks will be a *state*; and the *decision stage* will be a minimizing function over the camera modalities (Fig 5).

The complete strategy is resumed as follow:

```
Generation of the planned path
Path sampling (x ={x₁,…,xₜ,…})
For each xₜ
  Calculate the subsets C of visible landmarks
  For each subset
    Calculate the total utility Uc
    If t > 0 then
      Compute the cost to go from all subsets
      at t-1 to current subset
Apply dynamic programming to get the optimal visual path.
```

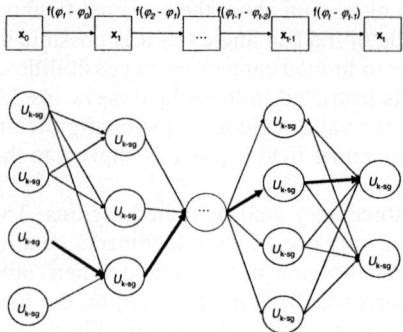

Fig. 5. Generation of the perceptual plan by a dynamic programming algorithm, darkest arrows represent the optimal path

5 Results

On Fig 6 is shown an example of visual planning for a virtual environment. On (a) we can see the planned path, and the set of planar landmarks. On next images, robot position and movement are represented by a small vector over the path. The coloured landmarks are the landmarks visible from the current position. The camera modality is represented by a thin vector (orientation = pan/tilt, size=zoom).

This example is interesting because as we can notice on (b), only three of the landmarks are visible from the initial point. On this point, landmarks L_3 and L_5 have the same visibility and utility. However, L_3 is chosen because, it will be useful on next points over the path and therefore avoiding saccadic movements. On (c) one more landmark is added to the previous one, because this configuration is more useful for localization. Finally, on (d) only the front face landmark is selected.

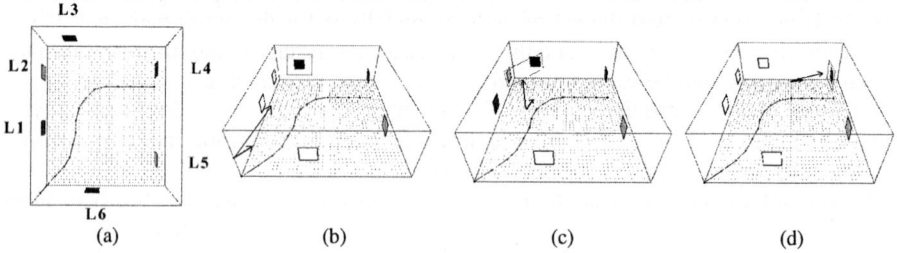

Fig. 6. Visual planning example on a virtual environment

This method was partially applied for indoor navigation. Landmarks were learnt and located with respect to a 2D map built using a SLAM approach from laser data. On Fig.7a, the visibility area of each learnt landmarks are presented; the area are computed off line, what make simpler and faster the visual planning algorithm.

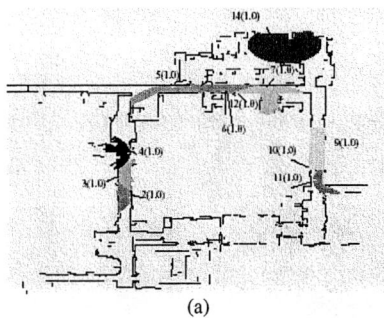 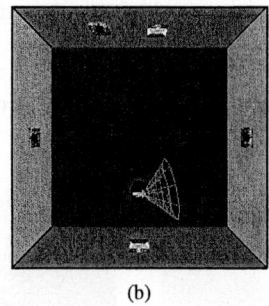

Fig. 7. a) Learnt landmarks and their visibility areas, b) aerial view of the virtual environment

On Fig.7b, we show a virtual environment used to test the visual planning. On this environment virtual robot must find and track different posters fixed on the walls. From this virtual model, synthetic images are generated and visual tracking is achieved using the template differences method described in [4].

On Fig. 8, we can see different stages of the simulation, on top synthetic images from the virtual camera, and bottom aerial views with the robot and the camera modalities. The virtual robot must follow a circular path. Wired cone represent virtual camera parameters: orientation = pan/tilt (α and β), and diameter of the base = field of view (γ). Images a) and e) correspond to the initialization step. b) and f) executes the first step of the modality plan; the field of view is reduced to get optimal image size. On images c) and g) a configuration with two landmarks is chosen, and finally on d) and h) due to the camera and movement restrictions only one landmark is conserved.

6 Conclusions and Future Work

We have presented in this paper, a strategy for visual plan generation. This strategy fulfills the requirements of a well-posed physical system, maximizing entropy (information in images) while minimizing energy (camera movements). In order to achieve the task, some measurements have been defined: (a) visibility in function of the oriented normal to the object and to the camera position, and (b) utility in function of specific observer parameters as the maximal field of view. A direct computation of optimal modalities has been proposed. Finally, a dynamic programming method has been used to generate the path in the camera configuration space, avoiding saccadic movements. This method has been validated on a virtual robot; then a visual plan has been executed by a real robot, without any execution control. On line planning has been partially applied for indoor navigation, using off line computation of the visibility areas of each landmarks. This work is on the way and a complete decisional system for active visual localization, including visual planning and control, is going to be implemented on the robot.

Here only planar landmarks and only geometrical criteria have been considered during the planning task. In fact, all landmarks have not the same utility for visual tracking and visual localization; moreover this utility depends on some environment characteristics (ambient lights, overcrowding...). In [13], we have proposed some measurements on objects and on the environment, in order to automatically select the best tracking algorithm that must be used to track a given object in a given context. Our visual planning method will use this information on the predicted tracking performance, to include in the visual plan, with the landmarks and the camera modalities, the tracker methods to be used.

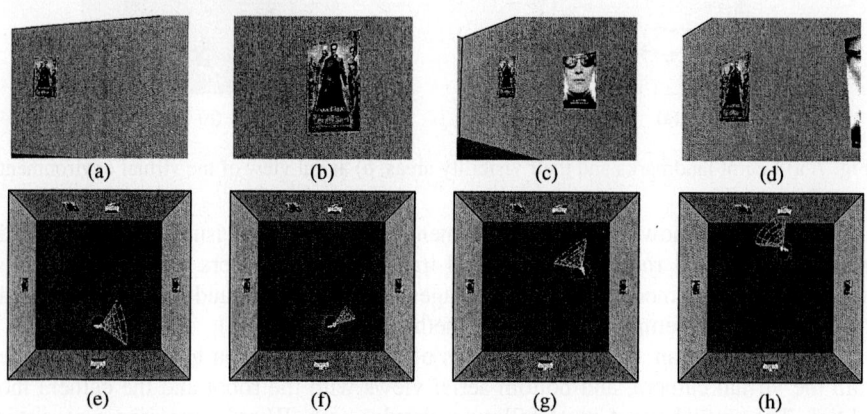

Fig. 8. Visual planning and tracking simulation: on top images from the virtual image, and on bottom top views, wired cone for the camera

Finally, when a landmark is occluded or removed from the environment, or when the path has been modified (e.g. obstacles) a new visual plan has to be made. A visual plan with an average of 400 sampled points along the path takes less than 1 second on a Sun Blade 100.

References

1. D. Burschka, J. Geiman, and G. Hager, "Optimal landmark configuration for vision-based control of mobile robots", Proc. of 2003 IEEE ICRA, Taipei, Taiwan, September 14-19, 2003, pp. 3917-3922
2. Madsen C.B., C. S. Andersen, "Optimal landmark selection for triangulation of robot position", Robotics and Autonomous Systems, vol. 23, No. 4, 1998, pp. 277-292.
3. J.B. Hayet, F.Lerasle, and M.Devy., "Visual Landmarks Detection and Recognition for Mobile Robot Navigation", in Proc. 2003 IEEE *Conf. on Computer Vision and Pattern Recognition* (CVPR'2003), Vol.II, pp.313-318, Madison (Wisconsin, USA, June 2003.
4. F.Jurie, M.Dhome, "Hyperplane Approximation for Template Matching", in IEEE. *Trans. on Pattern Analysis and Machine Intelligence*, vol. 24, No. 7, pp. 996-1000, July 2002.
5. Ralf Möller, "Perception through Anticipation - An Approach to Behaviour-based Perception", in Proc. New Trends in Cognitive Science, 184-190, Vienna, 1997
6. K.A. Tarabanis, R.Y. Tsai, and A.Kaul, "Computing occlusion-free view-points", IEEE Transactions on Pattern Analysis and Machine Intelligence, 18(3), pages 279-292, 1996.
7. K. Klein and V. Sequeira, "View planning for the 3D modelling of Real World Scenes", 2000 IEEE/RSJ IROS, volume II, pages 943-948, 2000.

8. B.Tovar, R.Murrieta-Cid and C.Esteves, "Robot Motion Planning for Map Building", in Proc. IEE/RSJ IROS'2002, Lausanne (Switzerland), Nov.2002.
9. H. González-Banos and J.C. Latombe. "A randomized art-gallery algorithm for sensor placement", ACM Symposium on Computational Geometry, SCG'01, 2001.
10. X. Deng, E. Milios, A. Mirzaian ``Landmark selection strategies for path execution", Robotics and Autonomous Systems, 17 (1996) pp. 171-185.
11. V. Ayala-Ramirez, M. Devy, "Active selection and tracking of multiple landmarks for visual navigation", in 2nd Int. Sym. on Robotics and Automation (ISRA'2000), Monterrey (Mexico), 10-12 November 2000, pp.557-562.
12. P. L. Sala, R. Sim, A. Shokoufandeh and S.J. Dickinson "Landmark Selection for Vision-Based Navigation", accepted in *IEEE IROS*, Sendai, Japan, Sep 28 – Oct 2, 2004.
13. A. Marin Hernandez, M. Devy, "Target and Environments Complexity Characterization for Automatic Visual Tracker Selection in Mobile Robotic Tasks", in Proc. 4th Int. Sym. on Robotics and Automation (ISRA'2004), Queretaro, Mexico, August 2004

Gait Synthesis Based on FWN and PD Controller for a Five-Link Biped Robot

Pengfei Liu and Jiuqiang Han

School of Electronics and Information Engineering, Xi'an Jiaotong University,
Xi'an, 710049, P.R.China
pfliu77@yahoo.com.cn

Abstract. A new reference walking trajectory for a planar five-link biped, considering both the SSP and the DSP, is presented firstly. A new combined controller to generate walking gaits following the reference trajectory is designed subsequently. The controller of five-link biped is consisted of PD controller and a fuzzy wavelet neural network controller. The scalable and shiftable coefficients of the wavelet function and weights of the network can be acquired by training the network by back-propagation algorithm online. The simulation results of the reference trajectory show that the proposed reference trajectory have good stability, repeatability and continuity during both SSP and the DSP, and when given the different initial conditions, the compatible trajectories can be achieved correspondingly. The simulation results of the trained controller show that the controller can generate the walking gaits to track the reference trajectory as close as possible.

1 Introduction

The study of humanoid robot is one of the most difficult and complex embranchment in the field of robot research. A biped robot is a class of walking robots that imitates human locomotion. The design of reference trajectory for gait cycle is a crucial step for biped motion control. However, there is a lack of systematic methods for synthesizing the gait and most of the previous work has been based on trial and error [1]. Vukobratovic [2] have studied locomotion by using human walking data to prescribe the motion of the lower limbs. Hurmuzlu [3] developed a parametric formulation that ties together the objective functions and the resulting gait patterns. Hurmuzlu's method requires the selection of specific initial conditions to assure to have continuous and repeatable gait. But this selection can be extremely challenging. This problem of selection proper initial conditions to generate repeatable gait can be remedied by using numerical methods by approximating the reference trajectories through time polynomial functions [4] or periodic interpolation [5].

From the prevailing studies on biped walking pattern design, it has been noticed that two important issues need to be regarded. Firstly, most studies have focused on motion generation during the single support phase (SSP), and the double support phase (DSP) has been neglected. But the DSP plays an important role in keeping a biped walking stably with a wide range of speeds, and thus can't be neglected. Secondly, impact, occurring at the transition between the SSP and the DSP, makes control task difficult due to the discontinuity of the angular velocity and may have destabilizing effects on biped motion.

Many researchers have shown that fuzzy set and neural network theory can solve dynamic biped locomotion problems. Murakami [6] used a set of parameters to decide the static gain of the fuzzy controller. Shin [7] developed a fuzzy variable gain force control system for a biped robot in the DSP. Juang [8] presented a three-layered neural network controller with the back-propagation through time algorithm to generate robotic walking gaits. The drawback of this method is that the number of needed hidden layers and units is uncertain. In his subsequent work [9], Juang used fuzzy neural networks to generate walking gaits successfully, however the DSP was neglected.

After the reference trajectories including both the SSP and the DSP are presented, this paper presents a new control scheme by using a fuzzy wavelet neural network and PD as the controller. The presented control scheme can generate the gait that satisfies specified constraints such as the step length, maximum height and walking speed. Simulation results are given for a five-link biped robot.

2 Biped Robot Model and Reference Trajectory

In order to demonstrate the proposed control scheme and the reference trajectories, the walking machine BLR-G1 robot [10] is used as the simulation model. As shown in Fig.1, this robot consists of five links, namely, a torso, two lower legs and two upper legs, and its hip and knee joints are driven by four DC servomotors. This robot has no feet (no ankle). A steel pipe at the tip each leg is used to maintain the lateral balance. Thus, the motion of the biped is limited to only the sagittal plane (X-Z plane). The ground condition is assumed to be rigid and nonslip. The contact between the tip and the ground is assumed to be a single point.

2.1 Dynamic Equations

The dynamic equations of the motion of the biped model are given in [10] as follows:

$$A(\theta)\ddot{\theta} + B(\theta)h(\dot{\theta}) + Cg(\theta) = DT \tag{1}$$

Where $\theta = [\theta_1, \theta_2, \theta_3, \theta_4, \theta_5]^T$, $T = [\tau_1, \tau_2, \tau_3, \tau_4]^T$, $h(\dot{\theta}) = [\dot{\theta}_1^2, \dot{\theta}_2^2, \dot{\theta}_3^2, \dot{\theta}_4^2, \dot{\theta}_5^2]^T$, $g(\theta) = [\sin\theta_1, \sin\theta_2, \sin\theta_3, \sin\theta_4, \sin\theta_5]^T$, $A(\theta) = \{q_{ij} \cos(\theta_i - \theta_j) + p_{ij}\}$, $B(\theta) = \{q_{ij} \cos(\theta_i - \theta_j)\}$, $C = diag\{-h_i\}$, τ_i is the torque at the i Th joint, and θ_i and $\dot{\theta}$ are the position and velocity of link i. The parameters D, q_{ij}, p_{ij} and h_i are constants [10]. Other useful values of the parameter are given in the table 1.

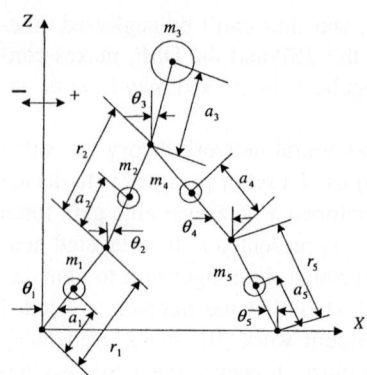

Fig. 1. Five-link Biped model   **Fig. 2.** Full gait cycle of a planar five-link biped

Table 1. Values of the parameters

Link	Mass (Kg)	Moment of Inertia (Kg · m²×10⁻²)	Length (m)	Center of Mass from Lower joint (m)
Torso	14.79	3.30	0.486	0.282
Upper leg	5.28	5.40	0.302	0.236
Lower leg	2.23	4.14	0.332	0.189

2.2 Reference Trajectory

A complete step can be divided into a SSP and a DSP [11]. The SSP is characterized by one limb (the swing limb) moving in the forward direction while another limb (the stance limb) is pivoted on the ground. This phase begins with the swing limb tip leaving the ground and terminates with the swing limb touching the ground. Its time period is denoted as T_s. In the DSP, both lower limbs are in contact with the ground while the upper body can move forward slightly. The time period of this phase is denoted as T_d. In the following step, the roles of swing limb and the stance limb are exchanged. Mu [11] presented a method for gait synthesis of a five-link biped walking on level ground during SSP and DSP, but it can't keep the continuity when switching the swing limb. The joint angle profiles can be determined when compatible trajectories for hip and the tip of the swing limb can be known. We prescribe that both knees only bend in one direction, thus, the joint angle profiles can be uniquely determined by the given hip and swing limb trajectories. From the viewpoint of the human walking pattern, the torso is kept at the upright position that the trajectory $\theta_3(t) = 0$ in both the SSP and the DSP. We design the trajectory for the swing limb firstly. From the definitions of the SSP and DSP, we just need to design the trajectory of the swing limb during the SSP. The trajectory of the tip of the swing limb is denoted by the vector $X_a : (x_a(t), z_a(t))$, where $(x_a(t), z_a(t))$ is the coordinate of the swing limb tip position in the coordinate system in Fig.2. We use a third order polynomial and a fifth order polynomial functions for x_a and z_a separately. The order of polynomial functions is determined by number of the constraint equations. They are shown below:

$$\begin{cases} x_a(t) = a_0 + a_1 t + a_2 t^2 + a_3 t^3 \\ z_a(t) = b_0 + b_1 t + b_2 t^2 + b_3 t^3 + b_4 t^4 + b_5 t^5 \end{cases}, 0 \leq t \leq T_s \quad (2)$$

Next we present constraint equations that can be used for solving the coefficients. There are four basic quantities in the SSP: step length S_l, step period for the SSP T_s, maximum height of the tip of the swing limb H_m and its location S_m. The constraint equations are described as follows:

(1) Geometrical constraints:

$$x_a(0) = -\frac{S_l}{2}, x_a(T_s) = \frac{S_l}{2}, z_a(0) = 0, z_a(T_s) = 0 \quad (3)$$

(2) Maximum height of the tip of the swing limb:

$$x_a(T_m) = S_m, z_a(T_m) = H_m, \dot{z}_a(T_m) = 0 \quad (4)$$

(3) Repeatability of the gait: The requirement for repeatable gait imposes the initial angle posture and angular velocities to be identical to those at the end of the step.

$$\dot{x}_a(0) = 0, \dot{z}_a(0) = 0 \quad (5)$$

(4) Minimizing the effect of impact: In order to minimize the effect of impact, we should keep the velocities of the swing tip zero before impact.

$$\dot{x}_a(T_s) = 0, \dot{z}_a(T_s) = 0 \quad (6)$$

Equations (3-6) can be used to solve the coefficients a_i, b_j and T_m:

$$a_0 = -\frac{S_l}{2}, a_1 = 0, a_2 = \frac{3S_l}{T_s^2}, a_3 = -\frac{2S_l}{T_s^3}, b_0 = b_1 = b_5 = 0, b_2 = \frac{16H_m}{T_s^2},$$

$$b_3 = -\frac{32H_m}{T_s^3}, b_4 = \frac{16H_m}{T_s^4}. \text{ If } S_m = 0, T_m = \frac{T_s}{2}.$$

Next the trajectory of the hip is designed. The trajectory of the hip should be divided into the SSP and the DSP, which are separately denoted by the coordinate as $X_{hs} : (x_{hs}(t), z_{hs}(t))$ in the SSP and $X_{hd} : (x_{hd}(t), z_{hd}(t))$ in the DSP. Two third order polynomial functions are used to describe $x_{hs}(t)$ and $x_{hd}(t)$.

$$x_{hs}(t) = c_0 + c_1 t + c_2 t^2 + c_3 t^3, 0 \leq t \leq T_s \quad (7)$$

$$x_{hd}(t) = d_0 + d_1 t + d_2 t^2 + d_3 t^3, 0 \leq t \leq T_d \quad (8)$$

For minimizing the vertical motion of the gravity center, we assume $z_{hs}(t)$ and $z_{hd}(t)$ as a constraint Z_h during the whole step cycle.

Considering the constraints of repeatability, continuity and stability of the gait, we can develop the constraint equations as follows:

$$x_{hs}(0) = -S_{s0}, \; x_{hd}(T_d) = \frac{1}{2}S_l - S_{s0}, \; \dot{x}_{hs}(0) = V_{h1}, \; \dot{x}_{hd}(T_d) = V_{h1}, \; x_{hd}(0) = S_{d0}$$

$$, \; x_{hs}(T_s) = S_{d0}, \; \dot{x}_{hs}(T_s) = V_{h2}, \; \dot{x}_{hd}(0) = V_{h2} \qquad (9)$$

Where S_{s0} and S_{d0} are positions of the hip at the beginning of the SSP and DSP, we assume S_{s0} as $-\frac{S_l}{4}$; V_{h1} is the hip velocity at the beginning of the SSP and V_{h2} is the hip velocity at the beginning of the DSP. V_{h1} And V_{h2} can be determined by obtaining the largest stability margin through ZMP criterion [11].

Equation (9) can be used to solve the coefficient:

$$c_0 = -\frac{1}{4}S_l, \; c_1 = V_{h1}, \; c_2 = \frac{3S_{d0} + \frac{3}{4}S_l - (V_{h1} + 2V_{h2})T_s}{T_s^2}, \; c_3 = \frac{(V_{h1} + V_{h2})T_s - 2S_{d0} - \frac{1}{2}S_l}{T_s^3}; \; d_0 = S_{d0},$$

$$d_1 = V_{h2}, \; d_2 = \frac{\frac{3}{4}S_l - 3S_{d0} - (V_{h1} + 2V_{h2})T_d}{T_d^2}, \; d_3 = \frac{(V_{h1} + V_{h2})T_d + 2S_{d0} - \frac{1}{2}S_l}{T_d^3}.$$

With the designed hip and swing tip trajectories and the biped model, the joint angle profiles can be determined by the following equations:

$$\begin{cases} \theta_1(t) = \arcsin(\dfrac{A_1 C_1 - B_1\sqrt{A_1^2 + B_1^2 - C_1^2}}{A_1^2 + B_1^2}) \\ \theta_2(t) = \arcsin(\dfrac{A_1 C_2 + B_1\sqrt{A_1^2 + B_1^2 - C_2^2}}{A_1^2 + B_1^2}) \\ \theta_3(t) = 0 \\ \theta_4(t) = \arcsin(\dfrac{A_4 C_3 - B_4\sqrt{A_4^2 + B_4^2 - C_3^2}}{A_4^2 + B_4^2}) \\ \theta_5(t) = \arcsin(\dfrac{A_4 C_4 + B_4\sqrt{A_4^2 + B_4^2 - C_4^2}}{A_4^2 + B_4^2}) \end{cases} \qquad (10)$$

Where $C_1 = \dfrac{A_1^2 + B_1^2 + r_1^2 - r_2^2}{2r_1}$, $C_2 = \dfrac{A_1^2 + B_1^2 + r_2^2 - r_1^2}{2r_2}$, $C_3 = \dfrac{A_4^2 + B_4^2 + r_2^2 - r_1^2}{2r_2}$, $C_4 = \dfrac{A_4^2 + B_4^2 + r_1^2 - r_2^2}{2r_1}$, $B_4 = Z_h$. For the SSP: $A_1 = x_{hs}(t) - x_a(t)$, $B_1 = Z_h - Z_a(t)$, $A_4 = x_{hs}(t)$, and for the DSP: $A_1 = -\frac{1}{2}S_l + x_{hd}(t)$, $B_1 = Z_h$, $A_4 = x_{hd}(t)$.

3 FWN Control System

In order to generate the gait in the reference trajectory given above, a control system is presented, as shown in Fig.3. θ_d and $\dot{\theta}_d$ are expected joint angle and angular velocities, θ and $\dot{\theta}$ are actual value of joint angle and angular velocities. θ_d and $\dot{\theta}_d$ can be acquired from the reference trajectory.

The controller can be separated into 4 sub-controllers for each joint. The sub-controllers have the same architecture, which is consisted of a PD feedback controller and a neural network feed-forward controller. The feedback controller can keep the biped robot stable, and the feed-forward controller can accelerate the control process. The PD feedback controller plays an important role in the beginning step of the control process, but the neural network controller dominates along with the training of the network by using the feedback error. Finally, the feed-forward network controller plays a role of inverse model of the biped robot approximately.

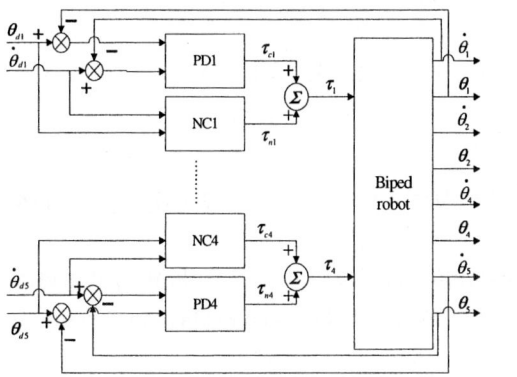
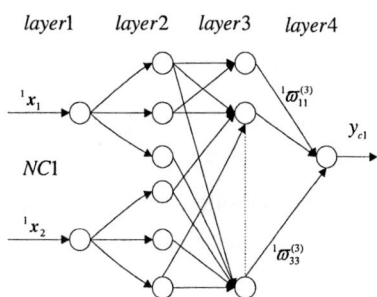

Fig. 3. Control system for five-link biped   **Fig. 4.** Architecture of FWN controller

The joint torque of biped robot is

$$\tau_k = \tau_{ck} + \tau_{nk} = K_{pk}(\theta_d - \theta) + K_{vk}(\dot{\theta}_d - \dot{\theta}) + \Phi_k(\theta_d, \dot{\theta}_d, W), (k=1,2,3,4) \quad (11)$$

where K_p and K_v are proportional and differential vector, $\Phi_k(\bullet)$ is the nonlinear mapping function of the network, W is the weight matrix of the network.

The neural network in the designed controller is a fuzzy wavelet neural network. The architecture of FWN controller is shown as Fig.4. The four networks have the same architecture. FWN controller should be trained online in BP algorithm, and the training sets can be given by equations (1) and (10). The whole network consists of four sub-networks, which denotes network controller of one joint respectively. Let $^k I_j^{(i)}$ be input of the j Th node of layer i in sub-network k. Let $^k O_j^{(i)}$ be output of the jTh node of layer i in sub-network k. The FWN is consisted of four layers. The inputs of the network are $\dot{\theta}_d$ and θ_d, which must be normalized.

Layer 1 is the input layer,

$$^kO_i^{(1)} = {}^kI_i^{(1)} = {}^kx_i, {}^kx_i \in [-1\ 1], (k=1,2,3,4; i=1,2) \tag{12}$$

Layer 2 is the fuzzification layer in which each node represents a fuzzy set. There are three fuzzy sets for each component of x, namely, P, Z and N. We choose mother wavelet function as

$$\psi(x) = (1-x^2)e^{-\frac{x^2}{2}} \tag{13}$$

$$^kO_{ij}^{(2)} = {}^kI_{ij}^{(2)} = 2^{{}^km_{ij}/2}\psi(2^{{}^km_{ij}}\ {}^kx_i - {}^kn_{ij}), (k=1,2,3,4; i=1,2; j=1,2,3) \tag{14}$$

Where ${}^km_{ij}$ are scalable coefficients, and ${}^kn_{ij}$ are shiftable coefficients.

The third layer deals with the minimum operation, which is replaced by multiplication in the network.

$$^kO_{ij}^{(3)} = {}^kI_{ij}^{(3)} = {}^kO_{1i}^{(2)}\ {}^kO_{2j}^{(2)}, (k=1,2, i=1,2,3; j=1,2,3) \tag{15}$$

The forth layer is defuzzization layer.

$$^kI^{(4)} = \sum_{i,j=1}^{3}({}^kI_{ij}^{(3)}\ {}^k\varpi_{ij}^{(3)}),\ y_k = {}^kO^{(4)} = {}^kI^{(4)}/\sum_{i,j=1}^{3}{}^kO_{ij}^{(3)}, (k=1,2,3,4) \tag{16}$$

In this controller, we learn in BP algorithm online. In the network, the parameters ${}^k\varpi_{ij}^{(3)}$, ${}^km_{ij}$ and ${}^kn_{ij}$ need to be trained in the algorithm. The evaluation function is chosen as

$$J_k = \frac{1}{2}(\tau_k - \tau_{nk})^2, (k=1,2,3,4) \tag{17}$$

The parameters of FWN controller can be trained by

$$^k\varpi_{ij}^{(3)}(t+1) = {}^k\varpi_{ij}^{(3)}(t) - \eta_1 \frac{\partial J_k}{\partial\ {}^k\varpi_{ij}^{(3)}}, (k=1,2,3,4; i=1,2,3; j=1,2,3),$$

$$^km_{ij}(t+1) = {}^km_{ij}(t) - \eta_2 \frac{\partial J_k}{\partial\ {}^km_{ij}}, (k=1,2,3,4; i=1,2; j=1,2,3), \tag{18}$$

$$^kn_{ij}(t+1) = {}^kn_{ij}(t) - \eta_3 \frac{\partial J_k}{\partial\ {}^kn_{ij}}, (k=1,2,3,4; i=1,2; j=1,2,3)$$

Where η_1, η_2 and η_3 are positive constant which is known as learning rate, and

$$\frac{\partial J_k}{\partial\ {}^k\varpi_{ij}^{(3)}} = -(\tau_k - \tau_{nk})\cdot {}^kO_{ij}^{(3)}/\sum_{i,j}{}^kO_{ij}^{(3)}, (k=1,2,3,4; i=1,2,3; j=1,2,3) \tag{19}$$

$$\frac{\partial J_k}{\partial {}^k m_{1i}} = \sum_{j=1}^{3}\left[-(\tau_k - \tau_{nk}) \cdot \frac{{}^k\varpi_{ij}^{(3)} - y_k}{\sum_{i,j}{}^k o_{ij}^{(3)}} \cdot {}^k o_{2j}^{(2)} \cdot d_1\right],$$

$$d_1 = {}^k m_{1i} \ln 2\left[\frac{1}{4}\psi(h_1) + 2^{\frac{{}^k m_{1i}}{2}}(h_1^3 - 3h_1)e^{-\frac{h_1^2}{2}} \cdot {}^k x_1\right], h_1 = 2^{{}^k m_{1i}} \cdot {}^k x_1 - {}^k n_{1i},$$
(20)

$$\frac{\partial J_k}{\partial {}^k n_{1i}} = \sum_{j=1}^{3}\left[-(\tau_k - \tau_{nk}) \cdot \frac{{}^k\varpi_{ij}^{(3)} - y_k}{\sum_{i,j}{}^k o_{ij}^{(3)}} \cdot {}^k o_{2j}^{(2)} \cdot v_1\right],$$

$$v_1 = \frac{\ln 2}{4}{}^k m_{1i}\psi(h_1) - 2^{\frac{{}^k m_{1i}}{2}}(h_1^3 - 3h_1)e^{-\frac{h_1^2}{2}}, (k=1,2,3,4; i=1,2,3)$$

$$\frac{\partial J_k}{\partial {}^k m_{2j}} = \sum_{i=1}^{3}\left[-(\tau_k - \tau_{nk}) \cdot \frac{{}^k\varpi_{ij}^{(3)} - y_k}{\sum_{i,j}{}^k o_{ij}^{(3)}} \cdot {}^k o_{1i}^{(2)} \cdot d_2\right],$$

$$d_2 = {}^k m_{2j} \ln 2\left[\frac{1}{4}\psi(h_2) + 2^{\frac{{}^k m_{2j}}{2}}(h_2^3 - 3h_2)e^{-\frac{h_2^2}{2}} \cdot {}^k x_2\right], h_2 = 2^{{}^k m_{2j}} \cdot {}^k x_2 - {}^k n_{2j},$$
(21)

$$\frac{\partial J_k}{\partial {}^k n_{2j}} = \sum_{i=1}^{3}\left[-(\tau_k - \tau_{nk}) \cdot \frac{{}^k\varpi_{ij}^{(3)} - y_k}{\sum_{i,j}{}^k o_{ij}^{(3)}} \cdot {}^k o_{1i}^{(2)} \cdot v_2\right],$$

$$v_2 = \frac{\ln 2}{4}{}^k m_{2j}\psi(h_2) - 2^{\frac{{}^k m_{2j}}{2}}(h_2^3 - 3h_2)e^{-\frac{h_2^2}{2}}, (k=1,2,3,4; j=1,2,3)$$

4 Simulations

In this section, the joint profiles for five-link biped walking on level ground during both the SSP and the DSP are simulated based on the reference trajectory given in Section 2. The parameters are given as follows: $S_l = 0.72m$, $T_s = 0.6s$, $T_d = 0.1s$, $H_m = 0.08m$, $S_m = 0m$, $S_{d0} = 0.14m$, $V_{h1} = 1m/s$, $V_{h2} = 1m/s$, $Z_h = r_1 + r_2 - H_m$.

Fig.5 shows joints angle profiles in Mu's method during the SSP and the DSP. It is seen that the joint angles have a little problem with repeatability and continuity when switching the swing limb. Fig.6 shows the joint profiles in our method. The simulation shows that the presented reference trajectory has good continuity and repeatability. Fig.7 (a) is the stick diagram of the biped robot with the prescribed conditions above, Fig.7 (b) is the diagram with the conditions:

$S_l = 0.72m$, $H_m = 0.05m$, $V_{h1} = 0.5m/s$, $V_{h2} = 0.5m/s$.

Let $\eta_1 = \eta_2 = \eta_3 = 0.3$, $K_p = [60,60,60,60]$, $K_v = [50,50,50,50]$, the network is trained by the error back-propagation presented above. Fig.8 is the errors of θ_1 and θ_2 generated by the trained controller. The results show that the error between the expected angle profile and the actual angle profile is very small, $e_{max} \leq 0.003 \, rad$. The simulation results show that the designed combined controller can generate the gait according to the reference trajectories well.

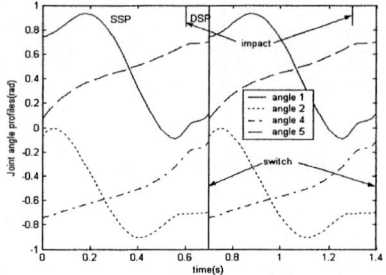

Fig. 5. Joint angle profiles in Mu's method

Fig. 6. Joint angle profiles in our method

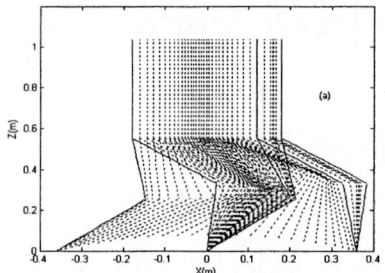

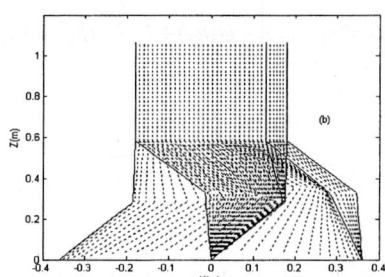

Fig. 7. Stick program of the biped robot

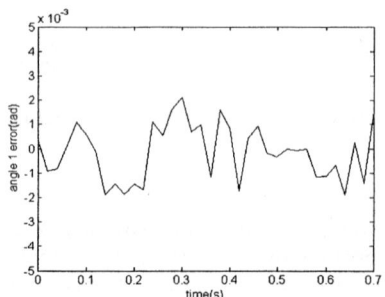

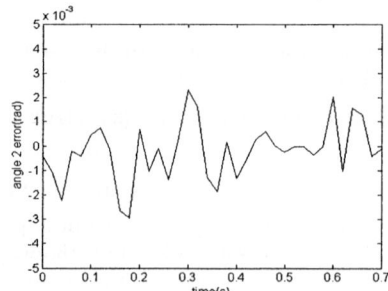

Fig. 8. Angle error of θ_1 and θ_2

5 Conclusion

In this paper, systematic reference trajectories are developed for five-link biped walking in the sagittal plane. Unlike the previous work focusing on the SSP, our reference trajectories include both the SSP and the DSP, which gives the biped a wider range of walking speeds and more stable locomotion. Furthermore, a combined controller for gait synthesis, which consisted of a fuzzy wavelet neural network controller and a PD controller, is presented in this paper. The uncertainty of the network size in the conventional neural network learning scheme has been overcome by the use of FWN. The trained controller can generate control sequences and drive the biped along the reference trajectories given In the Section 2, including both the SSP and the DSP. The proposed learning scheme trains the controller to follow reference trajectory as closely as possible.

References

1. 1 Tzafestas, S., Raibert, M., Tzafestas, C.: Robust Sliding-mode Control Applied to a 5-Link Biped Robot. Journal of Intelligent and Robotic Systems 15, (1996) 67-133
2. Vukobratovic, M., Borovac, B., Surla, D.: Scientific Fundamentals of Robotics Biped Locomotion: Danamics Stability, Control and Application. Springer-Verlag, New York (1990)
3. Hurmuzlu, Y.: Dynamics of Bipedal Gait: Part 1-objective Functions and the Contact Event of a Planar Five-Link Biped. Journal of Applied Mechanics 60, (1993) 331-336
4. Chevallereau, C., Aoustinm, Y.: Optimal Reference Trajectories for Walking and Running of a Biped Robot. Robotica19, (2001) 557-569
5. Huang, Q., Yokoi, K., Kajita, S.: Planning Walking Patterns for a Biped Robot. IEEE Transactions on Robotics and Automation 17, (2001) 280-289
6. Murakami, S., Yamamoto, E., Fujimoto, K.: Fuzzy Control of Dynamic Biped Walking Robot, Pro.IEEE.Conf.Fuzzy Systems, vol.1, no.4 (1995) 77-82
7. Shih, C.L., Gruver, W.A., Zhu, Y.: Fuzzy Logic Force Control for a Biped Robot. Proc.IEEE.Int.Symp. Intelligent Control, (1991) 269-274
8. Juang, J.G., Lin, C.S.: Gait Synthesis of a Biped Robot Using Backpropagation through Time. Proc. IEEE.Int.Conf.Neural Networks, vol.3 (1996) 1710- 1715
9. Juang, J.G.: Fuzzy Neural Network Approaches for Robotic Gait Synthesis. IEEE Transactions on System, Man, Cybernetics, vol.30 (2000) 594-601
10. Furusho, J., Masubuchi, M.: Control of a Dynamical Biped Locomotion System for Steady Walking. Journal of Dynamic Systems, Measurement, and Control, vol.108 (1986) 111-118
11. Mu Xiuping, Wu Qiong: Sagittal Gait Synthesis for a Five-Link Biped Robot. Pro. Of the 2004 American Control Conference, (2004) 4004-4009

Hybrid Fuzzy/Expert System to Control Grasping with Deformation Detection

Jorge Axel Domínguez-López and Gilberto Marrufo

Centro de Investigación en Matemáticas (CIMAT),
Guanajuato CP36240, MEXICO
{axel, marrufo}@cimat.mx

Abstract. Robotic end effectors are used over a diverse range of applications where they are required to grip with optimal force to avoid the object be either dropped or crushed. The slipping state can be easily detected by the output of the slip sensor. When the output has a non-zero value, the object is slipping. Conversely, detecting the deformation (crushing) state is more difficult, especially in an unstructured environment. Current proposed methodologies are *ad hoc* and specialised to the particular object or objects to be handled. Consequently, the gripper can only manipulate prior known objects, constraining the gripper application to a small set of predetermined objects. Accordingly, in this paper, it is proposed a hybrid approach of fuzzy and expert systems that permits to detect when an unknown object is being deformed. To determinate when the gripped object is being deformed, the fuzzy/expert system uses information from three sensors: applied force, slip rate and finger position. Several objects of different characteristics were used to prove the effectiveness of the proposed approach.

1 Introduction

Robotic effectors are required to be capable of considerable gripping dexterity, within an unstructured environment. To achieve a satisfactory grip, optimal force control is required to avoid the risk of the object slipping out of the end effector as well as any possible damage to the object. The use of a force sensor together with a slip sensor allows the end effector to grip with minimum fingertip force, reducing the risk of crushing (deforming) the object.

During grasping operation, it is possible to identify four main states of the gripped object: not touching, slipping, crushing and OK. The grasped object is at the state OK when the other three states are not activated. The states not touching and slipping are easily detected. The gripper is not touching the object when the output of the force sensor is zero. And the gripped object is slipping when the output of the slip sensor is non-zero. Now, the state crushing is not trivially defined, even with prior knowledge of the object. Reference [1] proposes incorporating electric field sensors on the object in order to measure object deformation, position and orientation. Nonetheless, the manipulator can only grip objects equipped with that sensor. This means that the system will be limited to gripping a small set of predetermined objects.

The use of sensors mounted only on the end effector will allow the manipulator to grip any kind of object. Accordingly, other approaches have been proposed, like infrared (IR) and sonar sensors. However, their effectiveness of deformation detection is poor due to several uncertainties inherent in theses sensors [2]. Other possible to solve the deformation detection is machine vision. Nevertheless, this approach increases considerably the system complexity as it requires a camera and visual perception algorithms. Therefore, it is desirable to detect object deformation using simple sensors (i.e., force, slip and position sensors) fitted on the end effector. Accordingly, the proposed approach uses the information from the applied force, slip rate and finger position sensors to determine when the object is being deformed. Several objects of different characteristics were used to prove the effectiveness of the methodology.

2 Two-Fingered End Effector

The experimentation reported in this paper has been undertaken on a simple, low-cost, two-finger end effector (Figure 1). This has just one degree of freedom; the fingers work in opposition. Although, this limits the size and shape of the objects that can gripped, this kind of gripper is widely used because the kinematics remain simple [3].

Fig. 1. End effector used for the experiments

The end effector is fitted with a slip, force and position sensors as follows:

- The slip sensor is located on one finger and is based on a rolling contact principle. An object slipping induces rotation of a stainless steel roller, which is sensed by an optical shaft encoder. The slip sensor has an operational range of 0 to $110\,\text{mm.s}^{-1}$ and sensitivity of $0.5\,\text{mm.s}^{-1}$.
- The applied force is measured using a strain gauges bridge on the other finger. The force sensor have a range of 0 to 2.5 N, with a sensitivity of 1.0 mN.

- The position of the fingers is determined using a linear potentiometer mounted on the end effector's lead screw actuator. The distance between the fingers is calculated using the information of this sensor.

3 Controller Implementation

To perform the control actions of the two-fingered end effector, a fuzzy controller was implemented. Fuzzy controllers are typically preferred over conventional approaches when the system to be controlled is highly non-linear, very complex or its mathematical model is unavailable. Grasping dynamics are frequently considered as their properties give a great influence to the success of grasping. However, fuzzy controllers have shown an excellent performance without the provision of the grasping dynamics [4]. For many complex processes, high levels of precision are unobtainable nor are they required for effective system operation. In fact, the inexactness of the description is not a liability in fuzzy systems; on the contrary, it is useful in that sufficient information can be conveyed with less effort [5].

Using the available knowledge (or experience) about the plant to be controlled, a set of control rules can be developed to express that knowledge [6]. Fuzzy controllers are less sensitive to parameter changes or disturbances compared to conventional controllers [7], as fuzzy controllers have been proved to be commonly more robust than traditional PID controllers [8]. Furthermore, fuzzy control has the advantage that its parameters can be easily updated if the plant operating points change [9]. Figure 2 shows the structure of the implemented fuzzy controller. It has two inputs, the object's slip and the applied force, and one output, the required motor voltage. The operational range of each of these variables was determined experimentally, allowing thus the database and rule-base to be manually created. The Center of Sums (CoS) was the defuzzification approach used because it has some advantages over the Center of Gravity method. In particular, CoS is faster because it is simpler [10].

The linguistic variables used for the term sets are just value magnitude components. They are Zero (*Z*), Almost Nil (*AN*), Small (*S*), Medium (*M*) and Large (*L*) for the fuzzy set slip while for the fuzzy set applied force they are *Z*, *S*, *M* and *L*. The applied motor voltage term has the set members Negative Very Small (*NVS*), *Z*, Very Small (*VS*), *S*, *M*, *L*, Very Large (*VL*) and Very Very Large (*VVL*). The latter has more set members so as to have a smoother output.

The rule-base was designed manually considering the following [11]: If the object is not slipping, the end effector should not apply more force; On the other hand, if the object is slipping, the end effector has to apply additional force proportional to the slip rate but bearing in mind the amount of force already applied. Now, if the applied force is high, it is convenient to relax (open) the fingers to reduce both the applied force and the risk of crushing the object. The developed rules are given in Table 1.

4 Deformation Detection

The fuzzy controller described earlier is able to perform an optimal grasp (without slip or deformation) for non-fragile objects. However, fragile objects are repeatedly

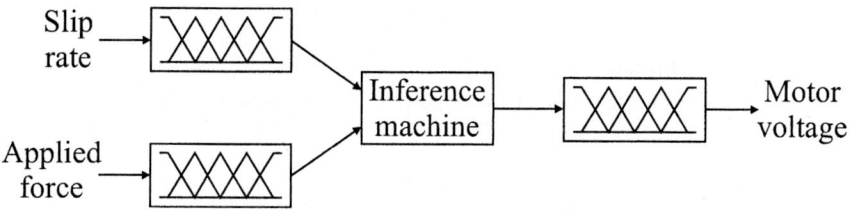

Fig. 2. Structure of the fuzzy controller

Table 1. Manually-designed fuzzy rule-base

		Fingertip force			
	Voltage	Z	S	M	L
	Z	S	VS	Z	NVS
	AN	M	S	VS	Z
Slip	S	L	M	S	VS
	M	VL	L	M	S
	L	VVL	VL	L	M

deformed and even broken, as the finger position from optimal grasp to failure is narrow. This uncomplete success is due to the incapability of the controller to detect when the object starts to suffer deformation. Thus, if the fuzzy controller knows when it is about to crush the object, its performance can be considerably improved. Accordingly, to allow the fuzzy controller to detect deformation, an expert system (ES1) is added. This expert system is capable to detect all the states (i.e., OK, slipping, crushing and not touching). A second expert system (ES2) is used to determine if the fuzzy controller output shall be utilised or not. That is, if deformation has been detected, the ES2 allows the gripper only to keep steady or relax the fingers but not to squeeze more. The ES2 decision is based on the information given by ES1. Figure 3 illustrates the proposed architecture.

The output of the ES1 is boolean: When deformation is detected, ES1 sends a 'high' level signal to the ES2, otherwise, ES1 sends a 'low' level signal to ES2. Now, the Motor voltage is equal to the Suggested motor voltage (i.e., fuzzy controller output) when no deformation exists. On the contrary, when deformation has been detected, ES2 limits the motor voltage to be less or equal to $0 V$. Hence, the gripper can only keep steady or relax the fingers, avoiding thus crushing the object. The output of the ES1 is boolean because at the current stage of development we are only considering the ES1 as a deformation detector. However, the ES1 has been designed to be used in a more complex architecture, for instance, in a reinforcement learning scheme [12] as the ES1 can provide the reward and failure signals to tune the fuzzy controller.

The rules of the ES1 are developed using several performances of the end effector using only the fuzzy controller. Figure 4 shows a typical performance of the end

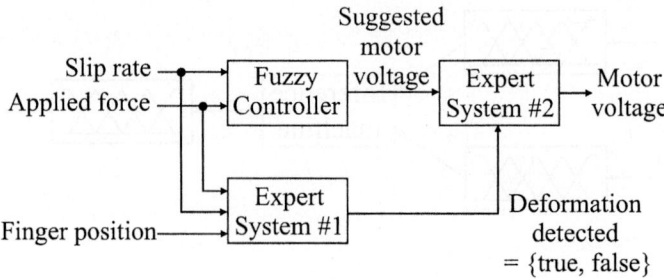

Fig. 3. Block diagram of the proposed methodology for deformation detection

effector. From 0 to 0.6 s, the system is at the `not touching` state (i.e., applied force is null). After the object has been touched but not completely grasped, the object slips. So, the system is at `slipping` state. At 1.0 s, the object has been correctly grasped and thus the system is at the `OK` state. From this point, the end effector keeps periodically closing and relaxing the fingers, being at the `slipping`, `OK` and `crushing` states several times. The system was at `crushing` state at 1.4, 1.9 and 2.9 s. When the object starts to be deformed, the applied force drops despite the fingers close. At 1.7 s the object slipped because the end effector relaxed the fingers too much. And, at 2.3 s slip is induced manually by pulling on the object. The intervention is of sufficient magnitude to cause the force applied to the object to drop suddenly, after which the fuzzy controller increases the applied force to regain stable grasping. Finally, the system is at the `OK` state the rest of the time. As said previously, `slipping` and `not touching` states can be easily detected: When the output of the slip sensor is non-zero the object is slipping, and when the output of the force sensor is zero the gripper is not touching the object. Accordingly, using this knowledge, the rules for the ES1 and ES2 were manually developed. The rule-bases of the ES1 and ES2 are given in Tables 2 and 3, respectively. The set of 'Situations' in the ES1 rule base are not used by the proposed approach but they can be used to tune the rule base of the fuzzy system [13], providing information of when the system fails. Finally, it could be argued to include the ES1 rules into the fuzzy controller, eliminating both expert systems. This can indeed be done but the final model would not be as transparent as the reported one. Although the system would not suffer from the curse of dimensionality, having three simple rule bases allows the operator to understand easier the controller than having one complex rule base.

5 Performance of the Methodology

To measure the effectiveness of the architecture depicted by Figure 3 and the three rule bases described above, they were tested with several objects of different characteristics. Due to space limitations, only the performance with three objects are explicitly shown here. These objects are: an egg (fragile), a glass of wine (breakable, non-deformable), and a metal can (non-breakable, deformable). The egg tolerates '*small*' extra force before breaking (failure), the glass tolerates a '*large*' excess of force before breaking,

Hybrid Fuzzy/Expert System to Control Grasping with Deformation Detection

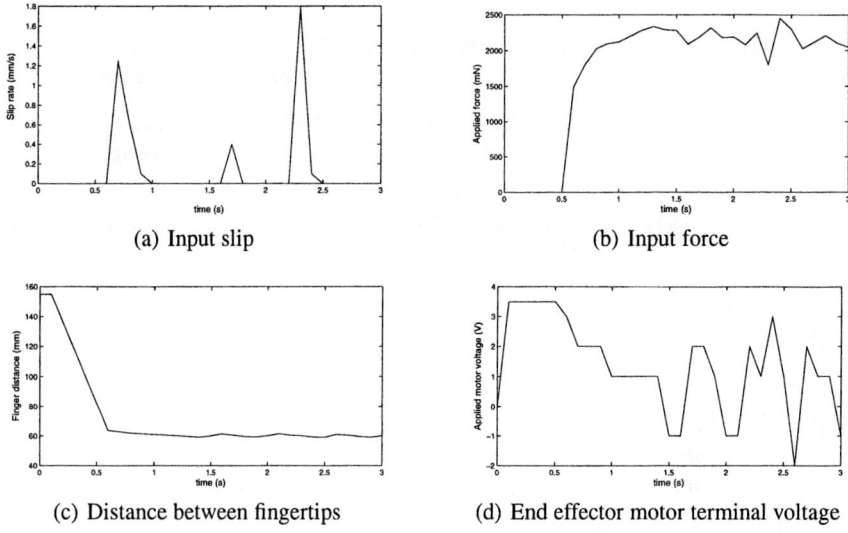

(a) Input slip

(b) Input force

(c) Distance between fingertips

(d) End effector motor terminal voltage

Fig. 4. Performance of the end effector using the fuzzy controller

Table 2. Expert system #1 rule base

Rule.1	IF applied force=0	THEN system is at `not touching` state
Rule.2	IF applied force≠0 AND slip rate≠0	THEN system is at `slipping` state
Rule.3	IF applied force drops AND slip rate=0	THEN system is at `crushing` state
Rule.4	IF applied force increases AND finger position change is '*nil*' or '*small*'	THEN system is at `crushing` state
Rule.5	IF applied force≠0 AND slip has become zero	THEN system is at OK state AND do not squeeze more
Rule.6	IF system is NOT at `not touching` state AND system is NOT at `slipping` state AND system is NOT at `crushing` state	THEN system is at OK state
Situation.1	IF applied force has become zero AND slip is zero	THEN system has failed: object broken
Situation.2	IF applied force has become zero AND slip was ≠0	THEN system has failed: object dropped
Situation.3	IF distance between fingers reduces considerably AND applied force≠0	THEN system has failed: object crushed

Table 3. Expert system #2 rule base

Rule.1 IF system is not at crushing state	THEN 'Motor voltage'= 'Suggested motor voltage'
Rule.2 IF deformation has been detected AND 'Suggested motor voltage' ≤ 0	THEN 'Motor voltage'= 'Suggested motor voltage'
Rule.3 IF deformation has been detected AND 'Suggested motor voltage' > 0	THEN 'Motor voltage'=0

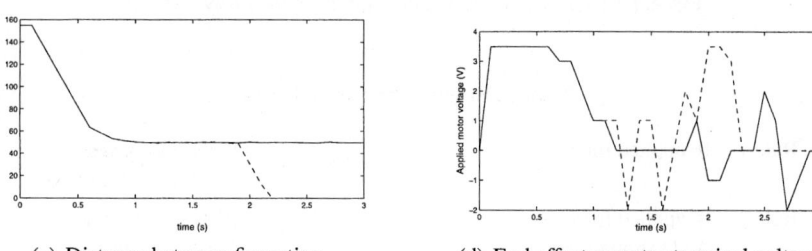

(a) Input slip (b) Input force

(c) Distance between fingertips (d) End effector motor terminal voltage

Fig. 5. Comparison of typical results of the hybrid fuzzy/expert system (solid line) and the fuzzy controller (dashed line) when the end effector grasps an egg

and the can tolerates a '*small*' excess of force before being deformed and a '*very large*' excess of force before failure. Also, consider the difference in failure mode between the egg and the glass, and the metal can — the egg and glass will break while the can will crumble (i.e., force is still present) after a period of increasing force with no change of gripper position. Their opposed characteristics allow a proficient and proper evaluation of the proposed methodology.

Figures 5, 6 and 7 illustrate typical performances of the end effector grasping an egg, a glass of wine and a metal can, respectively. The figures show the performance of the hybrid fuzzy/expert system (solid line) and compare it with the performance of the fuzzy controller (dashed line). Notice, that, especially in the Figures 6(a) and 7(a), the solid line overlaps the dashed line, as both approaches have a similar performance in some regions. After the objects have been grasped, the system operates without external disturbances until 2.5 s when slip is induced manually by applying an external force on the gripped object. Figures 5(a), 6(a) and 7(a) show such

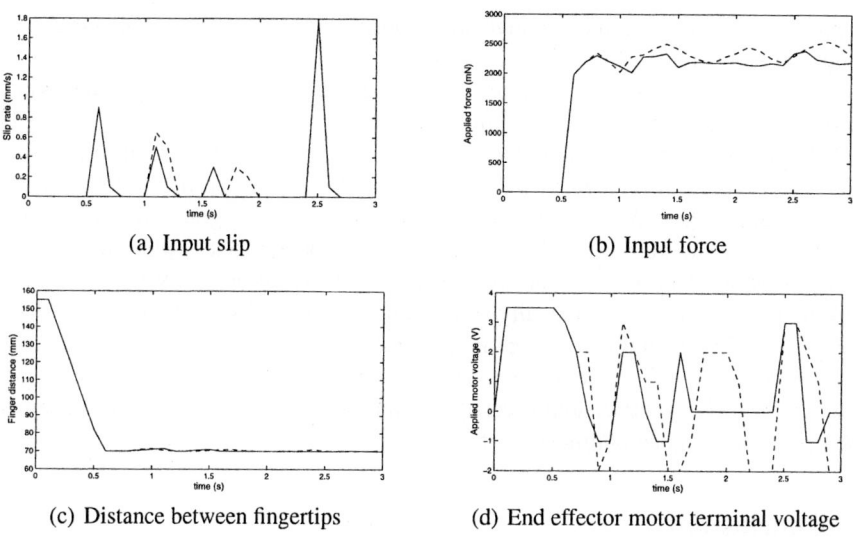

Fig. 6. Comparison of typical results of the hybrid fuzzy/expert system (solid line) and the fuzzy controller (dashed line) when the end effector grasps a glass of wine

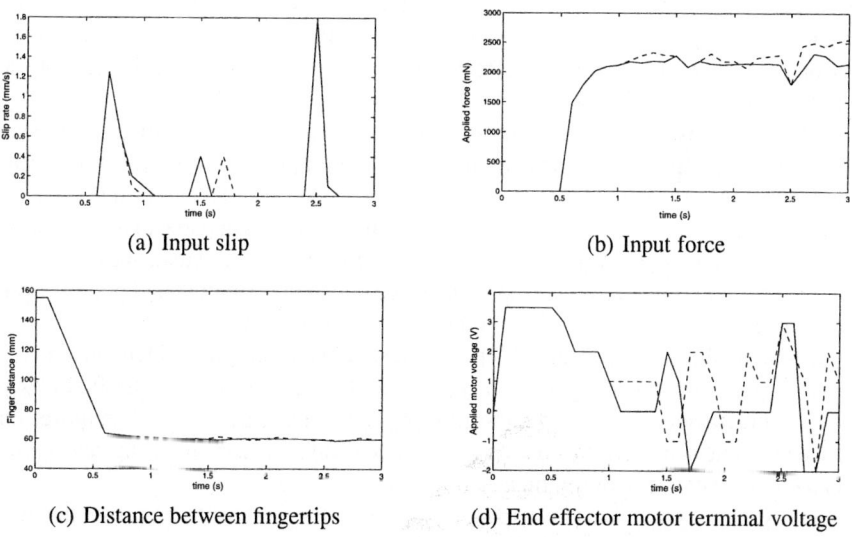

Fig. 7. Comparison of typical results of the hybrid fuzzy/expert system (solid line) and the fuzzy controller (dashed line) when the end effector grasps a metal can

intervention, which is of sufficient magnitude to cause the system to lose control of the object. Subsequently, the system increases the applied force to regain control. The other occurrences of slippage are because the end effector relaxes too much the fingers in its search for the optimal finger position (i.e., grasping with no slip and minimum applied force).

When the system reaches a good finger position, the hybrid fuzzy/expert system keeps its fingers at that position. While the fuzzy controller keeps closing, exceeding the applied force. This leads the system to the `crushing` state. To reduce the applied force, the fuzzy controller relaxes the fingers but it exceeds and the system is now at the `slipping` state. Accordingly, the fuzzy controller cycles, going from `slipping` to `crushing` and vice versa. This repels in the fuzzy controller failing in two cases: the egg was broken and the metal can was considerably deformed. When the egg was broken, the force drops dramatically and becomes zero — observe Figure 5(b) (dashed line) at 2 s. The mental can suffers its major deformation when the fuzzy controller confuse a force drop due to deformation with a force drop due to a poor grasping at 2.5 s. The hybrid fuzzy/expert system is capable to make this distinction and consequently it success, performing an optimal object grasping.

6 Conclusions

In many applications, robotic end effector are required to grasp object optimally, without dropping or crushing them. This has to be achieved even in the presence of disturbance force acting on the object. The variety of objects that can be handled makes impractical to program the system with all the objects it can grasp as well as to fit sensors on the objects. Ideally, the robot should be able to operate in a truly unstructured environment. Therefore, the end effector should be capable to grasp properly any unknown object.

A hybrid approach of fuzzy and expert systems has been described. The system uses information from tactile sensors fitted on the end effector to perform the control action. Comparing the performances of the fuzzy controller and the hybrid fuzzy/expert system, the latter is superior in all the tests. The fuzzy block is capable to detect the `not touching` and `slipping` states. Now, the expert system #1 detects the `crushing` state by differentiating between drop in the force due to deformation and poor grasping. This is the key for the success of the hybrid fuzzy/expert system.

Although, the proposed approach was tested on a simple 1 DOF gripper, the described approach could be used in more complex mechanisms as the fuzzy/expert system is independent of end effector grasping dynamics. The controller requires only to have the same sensorial information, i.e., it needs information about slip rate, applied force and the distance between fingers.

Finally, this system can be expanded to allow the system to improve the fuzzy rule base by learning. The ES1 can provide information of the gripper current state as well as failure situation. Moreover, the ES1 can also be in charge of giving the reward/punishment signal. Thus, the fuzzy controller can be tuned using some kind of learning. Actually, replacing the fuzzy controller for neurofuzzy controller with on-line learning, the system will be more robust and have the capability to adapt to different object shapes.

References

1. Thomas G. Zimmerman, Joshua R. Smith, Joseph A. Paradiso, David Allport, and Neil Gershenfeld. Applying electric field sensing to human-computer interfaces. In *Proceedings of ACM Conference on Human Factors in Computing Systems (CHI '95)*, pages 280–287, Denver, CO, 1995.
2. Ulrich Nehmzow. *Mobile Robotics: A Practical Introduction*. Springer-Verlag, London, UK, 2000.
3. A. Bicchi. Hands for dexterous manipulation and powerful grasping: A difficult road towards simplicity. *IEEE Transactions on Automatic Control*, 45(9):652–662, 2000.
4. Venketesh N. Dubey. *Sensing and Control Within a Robotic End Effector*. PhD thesis, University of Southampton, Southampton, UK, 1997.
5. J. A. Goguen. On fuzzy robot planning. In Lotfi A. Zadeh, King-Sun Fu, Kokichi Tanaka, and Masamichi Shimura, editors, *Fuzzy Sets and their Applications to Cognitive and Decision Processes*, pages 429–448. Academic Press, New York, NY, 1975.
6. C. W. de Silva. Applications of fuzzy logic in the control of robotic manipulators. *Fuzzy Sets and Systems*, 70(2-3):223–234, 1995.
7. D. Kim and S. Rhee. Design of a robust fuzzy controller for the arc stability of CO_2 welding process using Taguchi method. *IEEE Transactions on Systems, Man, and Cybernetics – Part B: Cybernetics*, 32(2):157–162, 2002.
8. E. H. Mamdani. Twenty years of fuzzy control: experiences gained and lessons learnt. In *Proceedings of IEEE International Conference on Fuzzy Systems*, volume 1, pages 339–344, San Francisco, CA, 1993.
9. Jan Jantzen. Design of fuzzy controllers. Technical Report 98-E-864 (design), Technical University of Denmark, Department of Automation, Lyngby, Denmark, 1998.
10. D. Driankov, H. Hellendoorn, and M. Reinfrank. *An Introduction to Fuzzy Control*. Springer-Verlag, New York, NY, 1993.
11. Venketesh N. Dubey, Richard M. Crowder, and Paul H. Chappell. Optimal object grasp using tactile sensors and fuzzy logic. *Robotica*, (17):685–693, 1999.
12. Richard S. Sutton and Andrew G. Barto. *Reinforcement Learning: An Introduction*. MIT Press, Cambridge, MA, 2000.
13. C. J. Harris, X. Hong, and Q. Gan. *Adaptive Modelling, Estimation and Fusion from Data: A Neurofuzzy Approach*. Springer-Verlag, Berlin and Heidelberg, Germany, 2002.

Adaptive Neuro-Fuzzy-Expert Controller of a Robotic Gripper

Jorge Axel Domínguez-López

Centro de Investigación en Matemáticas (CIMAT),
Callejon de Jalisco s/n,
Guanajuato CP36240, Mexico
axel@cimat.mx

Abstract. Advanced robotic systems require an end effector capable of achieving considerable gripping dexterity in unstructured environments. A dexterous end effector has to be able of dynamic adaptation to novel and unforeseen situation. Thus, it is vital that gripper controller is able to learn from its perception and experience of the environment. An attractive approach to solve this problem is intelligent control, which is a collection of complementary 'soft computing' techniques within a framework of machine learning. Several attempts have been made to combine methodologies to provide a better framework for intelligent control, of which the most successful has probably been that of neurofuzzy modelling. Here, a neurofuzzy controller is trained using the actor-critic method. Further, an expert system is attached to the neurofuzzy system in order to provide the reward signal and failure signal. Results show that the proposed framework permits a transparent-robust control of a robotic end effector.

1 Introduction

Robotic end effectors work in a diversity of applications in which they are required to perform dexterous manipulation of various objects under a diverse range of conditions. Ideally, they should be capable of considerable gripping dexterity in a truly unstructured environments, where novel and unforeseen situations frequently arise. Accordingly, the robot gripper should have dynamic adaptation to these situations as well as to environmental changes. In addition, the end effector should be insensitive to external disturbances. To achieve this flexibility is necessary to apply a control strategy based on automatic learning through interaction between the end effector and its environment. Reinforcement learning, a direct adaptive control method for optimal control problems, is the learning approach used here for on-line adaptation. In addition, a neural network, a neurofuzzy control and an expert system are fused into a hybrid framework to combine the advantages of these techniques. The union of neural network methods with fuzzy logic, which is termed neurofuzzy systems, is probably the most successful combination of 'soft computing' techniques [1, 2]. Neurofuzzy systems embodies the well established modelling and learning capabilities of NNs with the transparent knowledge representation of fuzzy systems. The fuzzy system is defined as a neural network type structure keeping its fundamental components. The addition of the expert system to the neurofuzzy controller is proposed in order to provide the reward and failure signals, which are required for reinforcement training.

2 Neurofuzzy Controller

Fuzzy systems have a number of advantages over traditional techniques that make them an attractive approach to solve several problems. Some of these general advantages are their ability to model complex and/or non-linear problems, mimic human decisions handling vague concepts, capacity to deal with imprecise information, etc. Nevertheless, they have also several disadvantages including mathematical opaqueness, they are highly abstract and heuristic, they need an expert (or operator) for rule discovery, the set of rules is often very difficult to determine and lack of self-organising and self-tuning mechanisms. To overcome these disadvantages but keeping the advantages, different approaches based on the idea of applying learning algorithms to fuzzy systems have been considered. Probably, the most successful approach is that of neurofuzzy modelling [1, 2], which incorporates a fuzzy system with artificial neural networks. The result is an approach that embodies the well established modelling and learning capabilities of NNs with the transparent knowledge representation of fuzzy systems. The fuzzy system is defined as a neural network type structure keeping its fundamental components. Figure 1 shows the implementation of a neurofuzzy system. Each circle represent a fuzzy neuron, i.e., the neuron activation function is a fuzzy operation (e.g., fuzzification, inference, defuzzification).

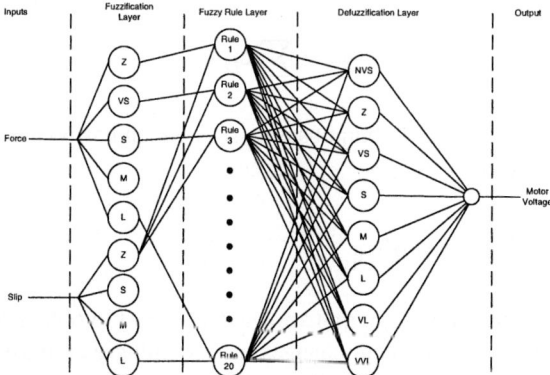

Fig. 1. Neurofuzzy network used for the gripper controller problem. Connections between the fuzzification layer and the rule layer have fixed (unity) weight. Connections between the rule layer and the defuzzification layer have their weights adjusted during training.

Once, the neurofuzzy controller has been designed and constructed, the objective of the selected learning algorithm is to determine the appropriate values for the parameters of the membership functions and the linking weights. The weights of the antecedent and consequent require as many parameters as modifiable parameters of the membership. So, it is common that instead of a weight vector, $\overline{w}$, it is a weight matrix, w. For instance, the triangular membership functions have three parameters that can be updated. This leads to have several free parameters to update, slowing the learning process. In addition, the resulted membership distribution may not be as transparent as with the designer's distribution. For example, in [3], before learning, the membership 'positive small' is in the positive region of the universe of discourse but, after learning, it is in the negative region, losing its meaning. This can be corrected if the system is able to correct inappropriate definitions of the labels. Contrarily, if the neurofuzzy system has only one modifiable weight vector (i.e., the rule confidence vector), leaving the other vectors and the fuzzy memberships fixed, it can still describe completely the input-output mapping for a nonlinear arbitrary non-linear function [1]. Moreover, the neurofuzzy system has a faster learning than a neurofuzzy system with several modifiable weight vectors.

Now, the use of rule confidences rather than a weight vector allows the model to be represented as a set of transparent fuzzy rules [1]. However, using a rule weight vector reduces considerable the storage requirements and the computational cost [2– p. 92]. Nevertheless, it is possible to alternate between the rule weight vector and the rule confidence without losing any information. The transformation from the weight vector, w_i, to the vector of rule confidence, $\mathbf{c}_i$, is a one-to-many mapping. The weight vector can be converted into confidences by measuring its grade of membership to the various fuzzy output sets, $\mu_{B^j}(\cdot)$:

$$\mathbf{c}_{ij} = \mu_{B^j}(w_i)$$

The inverse transformation, from $\mathbf{c}_i$ to w_i, is given by:

$$w_i = \sum_j \mathbf{c}_{ij}\, y_j^c$$

where y_j^c is the centre of the jth output set $\mu_{B^j}(u)$ which has bounded and symmetric membership functions.

3 Reinforcement Learning

There are occasions when input-output knowledge is hard to obtain or is not available at all. Also, when the environment changes, new training data must be obtained and the system retrained. If training is off-line (stopping the execution of the activity), the system misses the opportunity for self-retuning and reorganisation, so as to adapt to environmental changes. As manipulators and end effector work in unstructured environments where novel and unforeseen situations frequently arise, their controller should be able of dynamic adaptation, that is, learning should be on-line and unsupervised. Reinforcement learning (RL) is the natural framework for the solution of the on-line learning problem. The system trained with RL is capable to automatically learn appropriate behaviour based on continued feedback from the environment. Evaluating whether the previous action was *good* or not, the system receives a reward or punishment; this is known as the reinforcement signal [4]. The behaviour can be learned once for all or the learning algorithm can keep on adapting as time goes by.

There are many different algorithms that tackle this issue. As a matter of fact, a specific type of problem defines reinforcement learning, and all its solutions are classed as reinforcement learning algorithms. In the problem, a system is supposed to decide the best action to select based on its current state. When this step is repeated, the problem is known as a Markov decision process [5]. In fact, the environment is expressed as a Markov decision process (MDP), i.e., a stochastic environment where the changes are described by transition probabilities. A MDP has a sequence of times-termed decision points. At each decision point, the controller has to choose an action based on the environmental information (i.e., state). After performing the action a_t, the system receives an immediate reinforcement, r_t. The taken action affects the subsequent state s_{t+1}. The probability distribution of the reinforcement r_t and the subsequent state s_{t+1} depends only on the starting state s_t and the taken action a_t. The objective of the system (controller or agent) is to maximise the sum of discounted rewards [6].

RL has the advantage of being a *natural approach* to learning because it mimics the way humans and animals learn: optimising the action selection mechanism (task, performance) through trial and error while interacting with the environment. Other advantages of RL strategies are: they minimise the need for human intervention; they converge to an optimal policy, at least under certain assumptions [7].

4 Actor-Citric Method

Actor-critic methods are temporal-difference learning techniques that have two separate memories in order to represent the policy independently of the value functions [7]. One is the policy structure, which is the *actor*, and the other is the estimated value function, which is the *critic*. The former learns to choose the optimal action in each state while the latter estimates the long-term reward for each state. Figure 2 shows the architecture of the actor-critic method. The critic generates a scalar signal (i.e., TD error) that drives all the learning in both actor and critic. TD error is used to strengthen or weaken the tendency to select action a_t.

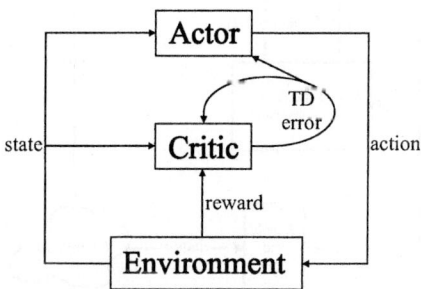

Fig. 2. Actor-critic architecture

5 Neuro-Fuzzy-Expert Framework

The implementation of the actor-critic is based on the well-known GARIC architecture [3]. Figure 3 shows the proposed framework which combines neural methods, fuzzy logic and expert systems in an actor-critic structure. It consists of a neurofuzzy controller (actor) and a neural network that criticises the actions made by the neurofuzzy controller. The neurofuzzy controller is an expansion to the original GARIC architecture. In addition, an expert system augments the conventional GARIC architecture to provide the reward and failure signals needed for reinforcement training both the actor and critic. The output of the actor and critic feed into the Stochastic Action Modified (SAM), which gives a stochastic deviation to the output of the fuzzy controller, so the system can have a better exploration of the state space and a better generalisation ability [3]. The numerical amount of deviation, which is used as a learning factor for the neurofuzzy controller, is given by:

$$s(t) = \frac{y^{*\prime}(t) - y^*(t)}{e^{-\hat{r}(t-1)}}$$

Instead of using $y^*(t)$ as output, the control action applied to the system is $y^{*\prime}(t)$, a Gaussian random variable with mean $y^*(t)$ and standard deviation $e^{-\hat{r}(t-1)}$. This leads to the action having a large deviation when the last taken action was *bad*, and vice versa. In this way, the SAM solves stochastically the exploration-exploitation dilemma: Neither exploration of the parameter space to learn new capabilities nor exploitation of what has already been learned can be pursued exclusively.

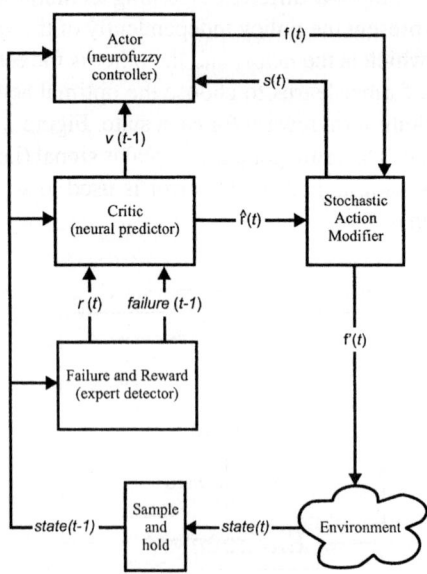

Fig. 3. Framework of the Neuro-Fuzzy-Expert controller

5.1 Determining Reward and Failure Signals

The majority of modern reinforcement learning is based on finite Markov decision processes [7]. A finite MDP is defined by the state and action sets, and by the one-step dynamics of the environment. For the controller of a robotic gripper, the state set is $S = \{$nottouching, slipping, crushing, OK$\}$, and the system decisions are grip, release and keep steady. To determine the current and the next state as well as to provide the reward and failure signals, a expert system is proposed. The expert system utilises the information from three sensors (i.e., slip rate, applied force and finger position) to produce the outputs (i.e., reward and failure signals).

The design of the expert system is based on our experience from previous works in fuzzy and neurofuzzy controllers for robotics grippers. The states slipping and not touching are easily detected: When the output of the slip sensor is non-zero the object is slipping, and when the output of the force sensor is zero the gripper is not touching the object. Crushing is considerably more difficult to detect in a truly unstructured environment. Current approaches to detect deformation are *ad hoc* and limited to a small set of predetermined objects [8]. To allow the expert system to estimate when the grasped object is being crushed, we use the following knowledge from our experimentation: When the object starts to be deformed, the applied force drops despite the fingers close; when slip is induced (either by a external force acting on the object or end effector acceleration) the applied force drops. In this way, the expert

Table 1. Expert system rule base with reward values

Rule.1	IF applied force=0	THEN system is at not touching state	R_{not}
Rule.2	IF applied force$\neq$0 AND slip rate$\neq$0	THEN system is at slipping state	R_{slip}
Rule.3	IF applied force drops AND slip rate=0	THEN system is at crushing state	R_{crush}
Rule.4	IF applied force increases AND finger position change is '*nil*' or '*small*'	THEN system is at crushing state	R_{crush}
Rule.5	IF applied force$\neq$0 AND slip has become zero	THEN system is at OK state AND do not squeeze more	R_{OK}
Rule.6	IF system is NOT at not touching state AND system is NOT at slipping state AND system is NOT at crushing state	THEN system is at OK state	R_{OK}
Situation.1	IF applied force has become zero AND slip is zero	THEN system has failed: object broken	R_{fail}
Situation.2	IF applied force has become zero AND slip was $\neq$0	THEN system has failed: object dropped	R_{fail}
Situation.3	IF distance between fingers reduces considerably AND applied force$\neq$0	THEN system has failed: object crushed	R_{fail}

system can identify a drop in the force due to deformation and a drop in the force due to poor grasping. Accordingly, Table 1 shows the manually developed rule-base of the expert system. R_{state} is the reward for being at that state.

5.2 Learning in the Critic

The critic is implemented as a neural predictor, which has a structure like the one shown in Figure 4. The critic is a predictor that indicates the current state 'goodness'. The critic maps the input state vector to the external error signal $r(t)$. This mapping gives a scalar score, $\hat{r}(t)$, which is used to update the actor weight vector:

$$\hat{r}(t) = \begin{cases} 0 & \text{start state} \\ -r(t) - v(t-1) & \text{failure state} \\ -r(t) + \gamma v(t) - v(t-1) & \text{otherwise} \end{cases} \quad (1)$$

where $v(t)$ is the network output, which is used as a *prediction of future reinforcement* (a measure of state goodness), and γ is a discount rate used to control the balance between long-term and short-term consequences of the system's actions [9]. The failure state indicates that the system has to be restarted, i.e., the gripper has to grip the object anew because it either crushed it or dropped it. The system detects that it has dropped the object when the force signal changes from a positive value to zero, while for the failure situation of crushing, the operator indicates to the system that it has crushed the object.

This network fine-tunes the rule confidence vector. Its input variables are the normalised measurements of the slip rate, the applied force to the object and the applied motor voltage. The hidden layer activation function is a sigmoidal function:

$$y_j(t) = \frac{1}{1 + \exp \sum_{i=1}^{3} a_{ij}(t) x_i(t)}$$

$$b_i(t) = b_i(t-1) + \beta_1 \hat{r}(t) x_i(t-1)$$
$$c_j(t) = c_j(t-1) + \beta_1 \hat{r}(t) z_j(t-1)$$
$$a_{ij}(t) = a_{ij}(t-1) + \beta_2 \hat{r}(t) Z'_j(t-1) x_i(t-1)$$
$$\text{for } i = 1, 2, 3 \text{ and } j = 1, \ldots, 5$$

where $Z'_j(t-1) = z'_j(t-1)\text{sgn}(c_j(t-1))x_i(t-1)$. In this work β_1 and β_2 were 0.3 and 0.4, respectively.

5.3 Learning in the Actor

The actor is implemented by a neurofuzzy controller that performs all the control operations. Its structure is shown in Figure 1. Its parameters are updated according the signal received from the critic. As said previously, we prefer to learn in the rule weight vector because the learning process is faster, less memory is required, and the meaning of the linguistic tags are not lost. Now, we want to maximise $v(t)$, the output

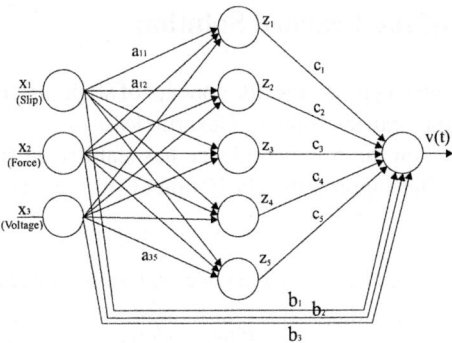

Fig. 4. The critic consists of a neural network predicting future reward, $v(t)$, which is combined with the reward signal, $r(t)$, from the expert system to produce an 'internal' reward signal, $\hat{r}(t)$, as described by Equation 1

of the critic. As the change in the rule weight vector is proportional to $\frac{\partial v(t)}{\partial w_i(t)}$, the updating of its modifiable parameters (i.e., rule confidence vector) is in the direction which increases $v(t)$:

$$\Delta w_{ij}(n) = \eta \sum_{t=0}^{n} \alpha^{n-t} \hat{r}(t) s(t) \frac{\partial v}{\partial w_{ij}(n)}$$

where both η is the learning-rate parameter and α is a momentum constant.

6 Experimental Set-Up

The experimentation has been undertaken on a simple, two-fingered end effector. The end effector was fitted with a slip, force and finger position sensors. The slip sensor is located at the left finger and is based on a rolling contact principle. The slip sensor has an operational range of 0 to 80 mm.s^{-1} and sensitivity of 0.5 mm.s^{-1}. The applied force is measured using strain gauges on the end effector structure. The force sensors have a range of 0 to 3.0 N, with a resolution of 1 mN. The position of the fingers is determined using a slider potentiometer mounted on the end effector's lead screw actuator. This sensor has a range of 0 to 154 mm with a resolution of 5 mm.

The implemented neurofuzzy control system has two inputs, the object's slip rate and the applied force, and one output, the required motor voltage. Triangular membership functions were chosen for all signals because of their simplicity and economy. The linguistic variables used for the term sets are simply value magnitude components: Zero (*Z*), Almost Nil (*AN*), Small (*S*), Medium (*M*) and Large (*L*) for the fuzzy set slip while for the applied force they are *Z*, *S*, *M* and *L*. The output fuzzy set, i.e., the applied motor voltage, has the set members Negative Very Small (*VS*), *Z*, Very Small (*VS*), *S*, *M*, *L*, Very Large (*VL*) and Very Very Large (*VVL*). This set has more members in order to have a smoother output.

7 Performance of the Learned Solution

Since reinforcement learning is on-line, the concept of stopping criterion does not apply, as learning, in principle, carries forever. Nevertheless, to access results, the learning process was stopped when the rule confidence has stabilised. Thus, the rule-base and confidences achieved after (approximately 10 min of) training are given in Table 2.

Table 2. Rule-base and (in brackets) rule confidences found after training

		\multicolumn{4}{c}{Fingertip force}			
	Voltage	Z	S	M	L
Slip	Z	L (0.1) VL (0.6) VVL (0.3)	S (0.1) M (0.4) L (0.5)	NVS (0.4) Z (0.6)	NVS (0.8) Z (0.2)
	AN	L (0.2) VL (0.8)	S (0.3) M (0.5) L (0.2)	Z (0.2) VS (0.5) S (0.3)	NVS (0.1) Z (0.7) VS (0.2)
	S	M (0.1) L (0.9)	M (0.3) L (0.7)	S (0.3) M (0.7)	VS (0.5) S (0.5)
	M	L (0.2) VL (0.8)	L (0.3) VL (0.7)	M (0.4) L (0.6)	S (0.4) M (0.6)
	L	VL (0.3) VVL (0.7)	L (0.2) VL (0.8)	L (0.7) VL (0.3)	M (1.0)

A typical performance of the gripper controller is shown in Figure 5. After the object has been grasped, slip is induced manually by pulling on it at 2.5 and 3.0 s. Figure 5(a) shows such interventions of various degrees of intensity. When the interventions are of sufficient magnitude, they cause the force applied to the object to drop suddenly. The system recognise that these drops in the force is due to *bad* grasping and so it increases the applied force to regain control. Now, the system was at `crushing` state at 1.4 and 1.9 s. When the object starts to be deformed, the force applied to the object drops despite the fingers close. The system responds relaxing (opening) the fingers. Once the applied force has stabilised, the system reaches the `OK` state and then it keeps the fingers steady. The system remains at `OK state` until a external disturbance acts on the object. Thus, the system achieves a satisfactory grip, avoiding the risk of the object slipping out of the end effector and any possible damage to the object.

8 Conclusions

Many applications required a robotic end effector capable of handling unknown object in an optimal way, without dropping or crushing them. The variety of object and the unpredictable environmental conditions make impossible to foreseen all the possible situations and so to program the end effector controller in advance. Consequently, such robotic systems need to learn on-line from interaction from their environment.

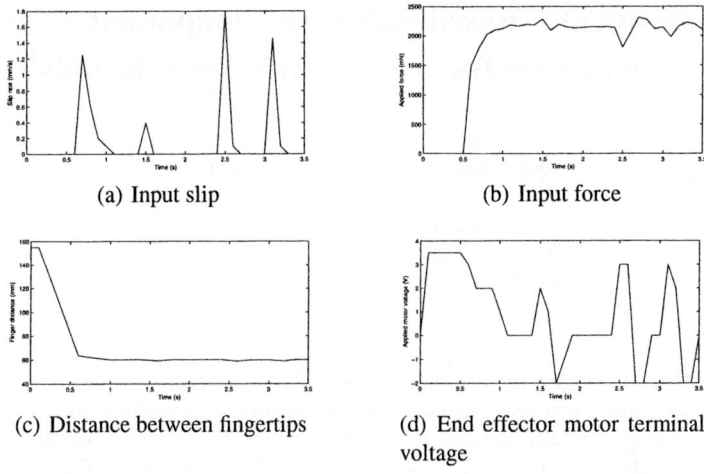

Fig. 5. Performance of the end effector using the fuzzy controller

To achieve robust and transparent control we have described the application of unsupervised reinforcement learning together with a hybrid control system. Results show that the system performs a satisfactory grip with minimum risk of slippage and crushing thanks to the ability of the expert system to detect the difference between drop in the force due to *bad* grasping and deformation. In addition, the system is able to react to external disturbances. This ability to react to external disturbances was observed in Figure 5 where object suffer induced slippage (see Figure 5(a)) and the gripper was able to regain control by increasing the applied force (see Figure 5(b)).

References

1. Martin Brown and Chris J. Harris. *Neurofuzzy Adaptive Modelling and Control*. Prentice Hall International, New York, NY, 1994.
2. C. J. Harris, X. Hong, and Q. Gan. *Adaptive Modelling, Estimation and Fusion from Data: A Neurofuzzy Approach*. Springer-Verlag, Berlin and Heidelberg, Germany, 2002.
3. H. Berenji and P. Khedkar. Learning and tuning fuzzy logic controllers through reinforcements. *IEEE Transactions on Neural Networks*, 3(5):724–740, 1992.
4. D. De Ridder. *Shared Weights Neural Networks in Image Analysis*. Master's thesis, Delft University of Technology, Delft, The Netherlands, 1996.
5. S. Singh, P. Norving, and D. Cohn. A tutorial survey of reinforcement learning. *Sadhana*, 19(6):851–889, 1994.
6. C. J. C. H. Watkins. Automatic learning of efficient behaviour. In *Proceedings of First IEE International Conference on Artificial Neural Networks*, pages 395–398, London, UK, 1989.
7. Richard S. Sutton and Andrew G. Barto. *Reinforcement Learning: An Introduction*. MIT Press, Cambridge, MA, 2000.
8. Ulrich Nehmzow. *Mobile Robotics: A Practical Introduction*. Springer-Verlag, London, UK, 2000.
9. Simon Haykin. *Neural Networks A Comprehensive Foundation*. Prentice-Hall, Upper Saddle River, NJ, 1999.

A Semantically-Based Software Component Selection Mechanism for Intelligent Service Robots[1]

Hwayoun Lee, Ho-Jin Choi, and In-Young Ko

Information and Communications University,
119 Munjiro, Yuseong-gu, Daejeon, 305-732, Korea
{leehy, hjchoi, iko}@icu.ac.kr

Abstract. Intelligent service robots (ISRs) adapt to unpredictable environments by determining how to resolve the problems occurred in a troubled situation. As a way to successfully and continuously provide services, we envisage the software system embedded in a robot to dynamically reconfigure itself using new components selected from component repositories. This paper describes a component selection mechanism, which is an essential function to support such dynamic reconfiguration. We adopt a semantically-based component selection mechanism in which situational information around ISRs is represented as critical semantic information for the service robots to select software components.

1 Introduction

Intelligent service robots (ISRs) sense environments, recognize problems in a troubled situation, determine how to resolve the problems and perform relevant behaviors to overcome the difficulty. The real environment around an ISR is highly unstructured and unknown. In order to adapt to such an unpredictable environment, an ISR aims to execute multiple tasks for multiple purposes, thus requires an extremely complex system of diverse software components [1]. For this kind of ISRs, it would be impossible to pre-code all the robot behaviors. In case of single-purpose and fixed-architecture systems, a robot can perform well a set of specific tasks which are known under a static environment, but may not perform well on some other tasks under different environments. In a dynamic environment, a robot with the ability to reconfigure its software to suit to the environment is more likely to succeed than one having software with fixed architecture [2].

However the software in an ISR cannot have all sorts of functionality for diverse situations since it is impossible to anticipate all unexpected situations. Therefore, an ISR should be able to reconfigure its software dynamically. Here, dynamic reconfiguration means that an ISR reconfigures its software during execution without interruption of its services.

This paper describes a component selection mechanism, which is an essential function to support such dynamic reconfiguration. When an ISR recognizes a troublesome

---

[1] This research was performed for the Intelligent Robotics Development Program, one of the 21st Century Frontier R&D Programs funded by the Ministry of Commerce, Industry and Energy of Korea.

situation through its environment recognition part, it searches component repositories for appropriate components to adapt to the situation, and reconfigures its software system. In this paper, a software component represents one specified non-complex robot behavior. We develop the "Component" ontology tree with reference to specifications of real robot software components.

Existing component selection mechanisms have limitations of low recall and precision rates because they do not take into account relevant domain information. To improve the inefficiency, semantically-based approaches of component selection are proposed in [6, 9]. For the component selection in the ISR domain, we follow the semantically-based approach which utilizes situational information around ISRs to minimize the inefficiency in the existing mechanisms. However, it was difficult to apply the techniques in these approaches directly to our ISR domain because of the difference of required information for component selection.

The remainder of this paper is organized as follows. Section 2 describes related works and limitations of existing component selection mechanisms. Section 3 proposes our semantically-based approach for component selection, and presents the mechanism and an illustrative example. Section 4 concludes the paper.

2 Limitations of Existing Selection Mechanisms

There have been many efforts to support search and retrieval mechanisms for component services. The existing approaches can be classified into four types [3]: the simple keyword and string based search [4], faceted classification and retrieval [5, 6], signature matching [7], and behavioral matching [8]. Although these approaches provide models to represent essential properties of component services, and support mechanisms to match services against a set of requirements, they cannot be universally applied to different domains. The main reason is that they need to be customized or extended based on domain knowledge.

Application of an existing component selection mechanism to a domain without any extension based on domain-specific knowledge may result in lowering the recall and precision rates of component search [9]. The *recall rate* means the ratio between the number of relevant components retrieved and the number of relevant components that are available in a library. The *precision rate* is defined as the ratio between the number of relevant components found and the number of trials of retrieving components. The existing approaches also do not support a *query relaxation* mechanism (see Section 3.3 for more details), which is one of the key factors to improve the performance of component search.

Although there exist semantically-based component selection mechanisms developed in the areas of component based software and Web services [9, 10, 11], it is hard to apply the methodologies to the ISRs domain. It is because, to use the approaches, users must participate in selecting components during the design and development of software systems. The existing approaches mostly focus on representing user requirements and matching them against component descriptions. The work presented in this paper also adopts a semantically-based component selection mechanism. However, we mainly focus on modeling, representing and utilizing situation information around a robot. In the ISRs domain, it is critical to consider situation information (internal status and environmental conditions) in selecting appropriate components to overcome the situation. In this approach, when a robot encounters a problem, the component broker searches for components based on the situation information without user's intervention. Especially, we use an ontology-based approach to represent semantically enriched situation information for ISRs.

3 A Component Selection Mechanism for Intelligent Service Robots

3.1 A Semantically-Based Approach

To enable service robots to recognize a situation that they face, it is essential to extract a set of semantic elements from a sensed environment, and to combine them together to formulate an integrated semantics of the situation. Based on the situational semantics recognized, an ISR can plan for a series of actions to overcome the situation.

We use an ontology-based approach to represent the semantics of situations around a service robot and the functionalities of component services. We analyzed possible navigational scenarios of service robots to identify a set of essential properties to characterize the situations that may occur. In addition, we analyzed a set of software components developed for controlling the navigational behaviors of service robots, and produced a model to represent functionalities of the components. Based on these analyses, we have defined the 'Situation' and 'Component' ontologies to represent the semantics of situations and component functionalities, respectively. We also have defined the 'Reconfiguration Strategy' ontology to connect the situational semantics identified to a type of software components that can be used to handle the situation. This makes the component selection mechanism flexible and scalable by loosely coupling component functionalities from situations.

The main focus of this paper is in the models that we developed for describing the three ontologies (called the ISRs ontologies), and the semantic relaxation mechanism that we used to improve the recall and precision rates in selecting components. Fig. 1 shows the hierarchies of the ISRs ontologies that we defined.

During the process of developing the semantic description models, we analyzed the possible scenarios of using the ontologies to dynamically determine the action of reconfiguring robot software to handle a certain set of situations. For instance, when a robot faces an obstacle while navigating to a destination, the robot needs to consider the distance between the obstacle and the wall to decide an appropriate action to avoid the obstacle. To handle this kind of situation, the Situation ontology need to have a property that represents the distance between objects in consideration.

All three ontologies have the 'name' property that is for representing the name of an ontology node in the hierarchies. Situation and Reconfiguration Strategy ontologies include generic properties such as 'geometry', 'kinematics', 'dynamics' and 'task' that are necessary to characterize the types of situations. The 'geometry' property can be used to represent geometrical characteristics such as points, lines, angles, surfaces and solidity of the robot itself and other objects in the environment [12]. The 'kinematics' property represents the basic motions of a robot in handling a subject

[13]. The 'dynamics' property describes the forces and their relations primarily to a motion [12]. The 'task' property is for describing a robot task which is a sequence of unit behaviors such as exploration and searching for an object.

There are properties that describe relationships between ontologies. The 'required strategy' property in the Situation ontology is for specifying an appropriate reconfiguration strategy for a situation, and the 'support strategy' property in the Component ontology is for describing the reconfiguration strategies that a component can support.

3.2 The ISRs Ontologies

The ISRs ontologies consist of the Situation, Reconfiguration Strategy and Component ontologies (Fig. 1). The ontologies are described in RDF (Resource Description Framework), which is the framework for representing semantic information on the Web [14]. We also used the Protégé tool to edit the ontologies. The Protégé tool provides a set of graphical user interfaces that allow users to construct domain ontologies, to customize data entry forms, and to enter data for ontology definitions [15].

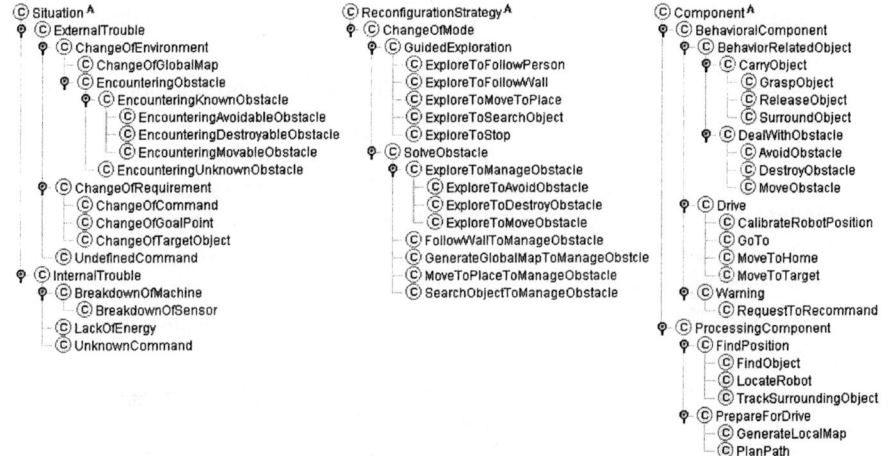

Fig. 1. The ISRs Ontologies

The Situation ontology conceptualizes situations around ISRs in a dynamic environment. There are two types of situations: external and internal situations. An *external situation* is normally caused by a set of conditions that are monitored from the external environment of a robot, and an *internal situation* is generated by an exceptional condition occurred in the robot software system.

The Reconfiguration Strategy ontology describes the possible solutions to the exceptional situations. A reconfiguration strategy describes an action to switch between tasks to handle a situation. For example, when an ISR meets an obstacle while exploring, the Reconfiguration Strategy ontology suggests changing its task from exploration to manipulation of the obstacle. As we discussed earlier, the indirect connection between Situation and Component ontologies via the Reconfiguration Strategy ontology gives flexibility to the component selection.

The Component ontology classifies functionality of unit behaviors of a robot. There are two main branches in the Component ontology: behavioral and processing components. *Behavioral components* represent the navigational and manipulation actions of a robot. *Processing components* represent the functionalities to collect and analyze information around an ISR. There are other ontologies that we defined to represent the geometry, kinematics, dynamics, and task properties. We do not explain about them in details in this paper due to the limited space.

3.3 Component Selection Steps

When a situation is identified by matching the internal and external conditions monitored against the Situation ontology, a set of reconfiguration strategies are selected based on the predefined connections between the Situation and Reconfiguration Strategy ontologies. A set of candidate components that support the reconfiguration strategies are then collected based on the relationships between the Reconfiguration Strategy and Component ontologies. The following explains the detail steps of component selection, and Fig. 2 illustrates these steps graphically:

i. A situation, s_i is located in the Situation ontology based on the conditions monitored from an environment.

ii. A reconfiguration strategy, r_i that are directly related to the situation (s_i) is identified in the Reconfiguration Strategy ontology.

iii. The reconfiguration strategy, r_i is relaxed to include the most general node, r_j, which has the same set of properties as r_i. All child nodes of r_j, r_c (c = 1... n) including r_i itself are selected as possible reconfiguration strategies.

iv. For all the possible reconfiguration strategies, semantic distances (ISR_SemDist, which will be explained later in this section) are measured.

v. A reconfiguration strategy, r_k, which has the smallest semantic distance (the ISR_SemDist value), is selected.

vi. A component, c_k, which is corresponded to the selected reconfiguration strategy, is identified as the most suitable component to solve the situation recognized at the first step.

In the information and knowledge management area, it has been an issue that queries given by users often fail to specifically describe their information needs. The *query relaxation* is the mechanism that was developed to extend users queries such that more relevant results can be gathered even though users' queries are not specific enough to cover what users really want [17]. We have adopted the query relaxation mechanism to our ontology-based component selection mechanism so that a wider range of components can be retrieved and evaluated even though the situation identified based on the environmental conditions does not represent the exact situation that the robot actually faced.

Among the several relaxation techniques, we use the *edge relaxation* method which relaxes an edge of a query ontology tree to make the query less restrictive. Especially, we modified the method by restricting the relaxation based on shared properties of nodes in an ontology hierarchy. In the modified relaxation method (*semantic relaxation*), an ontology node is relaxed to a node that has the same set of properties as the node that was originally selected by a query. The following paragraphs define our component selection mechanism (including the semantic relaxation) in a formal way.

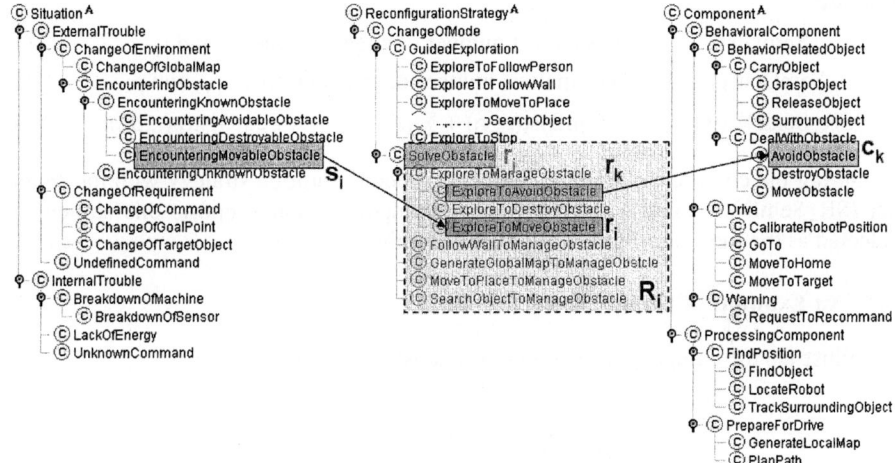

Fig. 2. An Example of Component Selection

Let s_i is a node in the Situation ontology (S), r_i is a node in the Reconfiguration Strategy ontology (R), and c_i is a node in the Component ontology (C). For all $s_i \in S$, $r_i \in R$, $c_i \in C$ in the ISRs ontologies, there are relations such as 'required strategy' between S and R, and 'support strategy' between R and C. In addition, we apply the relaxation technique to the Reconfiguration Strategy ontology, R such that for $r_i \in R$, r_c (c=1, ..., n) are selected as candidate reconfiguration strategies.

If we do not apply the relaxation method and semantic distance measure (see below for details), s_i is directly mapped to r_i, and r_i is mapped to c_i. When the semantic relaxation is applied, for r_i, r_c (c = 1, ..., n) are considered as candidate reconfiguration strategies. Then, an element of r_c (c = 1, ..., n) which has the smallest semantic-distance value (the ISR_SemDist value) is determined as the reconfiguration strategy to be used, and in turn, a component corresponding to r_k becomes the component to be selected in the Component ontology. r_k can be r_i or one of r_c (c = 1, ..., n).

The *semantic distance* is the topological distance between related concepts in an ontology hierarchy [18]. In this paper, semantic distances are measured between nodes in the Reconfiguration Strategy ontology, and between properties. We use a simple semantic-distance measure that counts the number of edges in the shortest path between two nodes in an ontology hierarchy. The shorter the distance, more semantically similar the nodes are.

To formally define the semantic-distance measure, let us assume that r_i is a reconfiguration strategy that is corresponded to a situation detected, and r_j is one of the nodes in the relaxed reconfiguration strategies. Also, let us assume that n is the number of common properties between the situation node and the relaxed reconfiguration strategies, and P_k is one of the common properties. p_{ks} is the value of P_k for the situation, and p_{kj} is the value of P_k for r_j. A weight value is assigned to each of the properties, and w_k is the weight value for the property P_k. We also define w_r as the weight value to be considered when the semantic distance between reconfiguration strategies are measured. We define the functions to calculate semantic distances as follows:

$$\text{SemDist}(r_i, r_j) = \text{the smallest number of edges between } r_i \text{ and } r_j \qquad (1)$$

$$\text{SemDist}(p_{ks}, p_{kj}) = \text{the smallest number of edges between } p_{ks} \text{ and } p_{kj} \qquad (2)$$

$$\text{ISR\_SemDist}(r_j) = w_r \times \text{SemDist}(r_i, r_j) + \sum_{(k=1,\ldots,n)} w_k \times \text{SemDist}(p_{ks}, p_{kj}) \qquad (3)$$

During the component selection process, a reconfiguration strategy with the smallest ISR_SemDist value is selected, and a component that supports this strategy is selected as the most appropriate component for the situation.

3.4 An Example of Component Selection

We illustrate the component selection mechanism using an example.

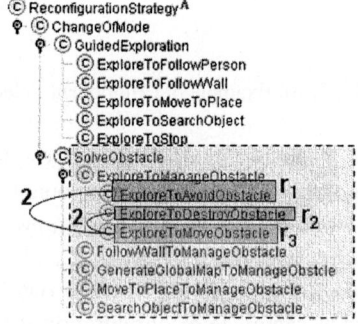

Fig. 3. Semantic Distance Measurement in the Reconfiguration Strategy Ontology

Let us consider the case when an ISR hits an obstacle while exploring a place, and recognizes the obstacle as a movable object. The situation perceived in this case is EncounteringMovableObstacle (s_i in Fig. 2) in the Situation ontology. Encountering-MovableObstacle is then mapped to ExploreToMoveObstacle (r_i in Fig. 2) in the Reconfiguration Strategy ontology. ExploreToMoveObstacle has a set of dynamics properties such as weight, size, and velocity, and geometry properties such as distance. ExploreToMoveObstacle is relaxed to SolveObstacle (r_j in Fig. 2) and thus all subnodes of SolveObstacle are considered as possible reconfiguration strategies, r_c (c = 1... n). However, since the task that the robot was performing before hitting the situation is the Exploration task, only the strategies that can switch this task into other tasks will be selected. Therefore, the children of ExploreToManageObstacle, ExploreToAvoidObstacle (r_1 in Fig. 3), ExploreToDestroyObstacle (r_2 in Fig. 3) and ExploreToMoveObstacle(r_3 in Fig. 3) are selected as candidate reconfiguration strategies. In the next step, to measure ISR_SemDist, we firstly calculate the semantic distances between the candidate strategies as represented in Fig. 3.

$$\text{SemDist}(r_1, r_3) = 1+1=2, \ \text{SemDist}(r_2, r_3) = 1+1=2, \ \text{SemDist}(r_3, r_3) = 0 \qquad (4)$$

Semantic distances between properties are also calculated. We measure the semantic distance between the value of a property of the situation identified and the value of the same property defined for each of the candidate reconfiguration strategies. Let us assume that there are four properties to compare: weight (p_1), size (p_2), velocity (p_3), and distance (p_4). For the situation selected, the property values are defined like: p_{1s}, p_{2s} and p_{3s}. For the reconfiguration strategies, r_1, r_2 and r_3, the property values are defined like: p_{11}, p_{21}, p_{31} and p_{41} for r_1; p_{12}, p_{22}, p_{32} and p_{42} for r_2; and p_{13}, p_{23}, p_{33} and p_{43} for r_3. The semantic distances between property values of the situation and reconfiguration strategies can be calculated as follows (Fig. 4):

$$\text{SemDist}(p_{1s}, p_{11})=2, \ \text{SemDist}(p_{2s}, p_{21})=0, \ \text{SemDist}(p_{3s}, p_{31})=1, \ \text{SemDist}(p_{4s}, p_{41})=0$$
$$\text{SemDist}(p_{1s}, p_{12})=2, \ \text{SemDist}(p_{2s}, p_{22})=2, \ \text{SemDist}(p_{3s}, p_{32})=4, \ \text{SemDist}(p_{4s}, p_{42})=3$$
$$\text{SemDist}(p_{1s}, p_{13})=2, \ \text{SemDist}(p_{2s}, p_{23})=4, \ \text{SemDist}(p_{3s}, p_{33})=4, \ \text{SemDist}(p_{4s}, p_{43})=4 \qquad (5)$$

Finally, the ISR_SemDist values between reconfiguration strategies are measured as follows. In this example we assign weight values intuitively based on the priority of considering the properties in the ISRs domain.

$$\text{ISR\_SemDist}(r_1) = 5 \times \text{SemDist}(r_1,r_3) + 4 \times \text{SemDist}(p_{1s},p_{11}) + 3 \times \text{SemDist}(p_{2s},p_{21})$$
$$+ 2 \times \text{SemDist}(p_{3s},p_{31}) + 1 \times \text{SemDist}(p_{4s},p_{41}) = 20$$

$$\text{ISR\_SemDist}(r_2) = 5 \times \text{SemDist}(r_2,r_3) + 4 \times \text{SemDist}(p_{1s},p_{12}) + 3 \times \text{SemDist}(p_{2s},p_{22})$$
$$+ 2 \times \text{SemDist}(p_{3s},p_{32}) + 1 \times \text{SemDist}(p_{4s},p_{42}) = 35$$

$$\text{ISR\_SemDist}(r_3) = 5 \times \text{SemDist}(r_3,r_3) + 4 \times \text{SemDist}(p_{1s},p_{13}) + 3 \times \text{SemDist}(p_{2s},p_{23})$$
$$+ 2 \times \text{SemDist}(p_{3s},p_{33}) + 1 \times \text{SemDist}(p_{4s},p_{43}) = 23 \qquad (6)$$

Since r_1 has the smallest semantic distance among candidate reconfiguration strategies, ExploreToAvoidObstacle is selected as a reconfiguration strategy to be used. Finally, the component, AvoidObstacle, which supports the strategy, is selected as the most suitable component for the situation.

4 Conclusions

In this paper, we have presented an approach to a semantically-based component selection mechanism for ISRs. In a dynamically changing environment, a robot needs to adapt to the environment by reconfiguring its software components in order to cope with troublesome situations.

We regard the situation information around a robot as a critical factor to consider for the reconfiguration and have proposed to represent the information as semantic information using ontology. The ISR ontologies express situations, reconfiguration strategies, and components. We have also proposed techniques of relaxation and semantic distance measure which provide flexibility of component selection based on the ISR ontologies.

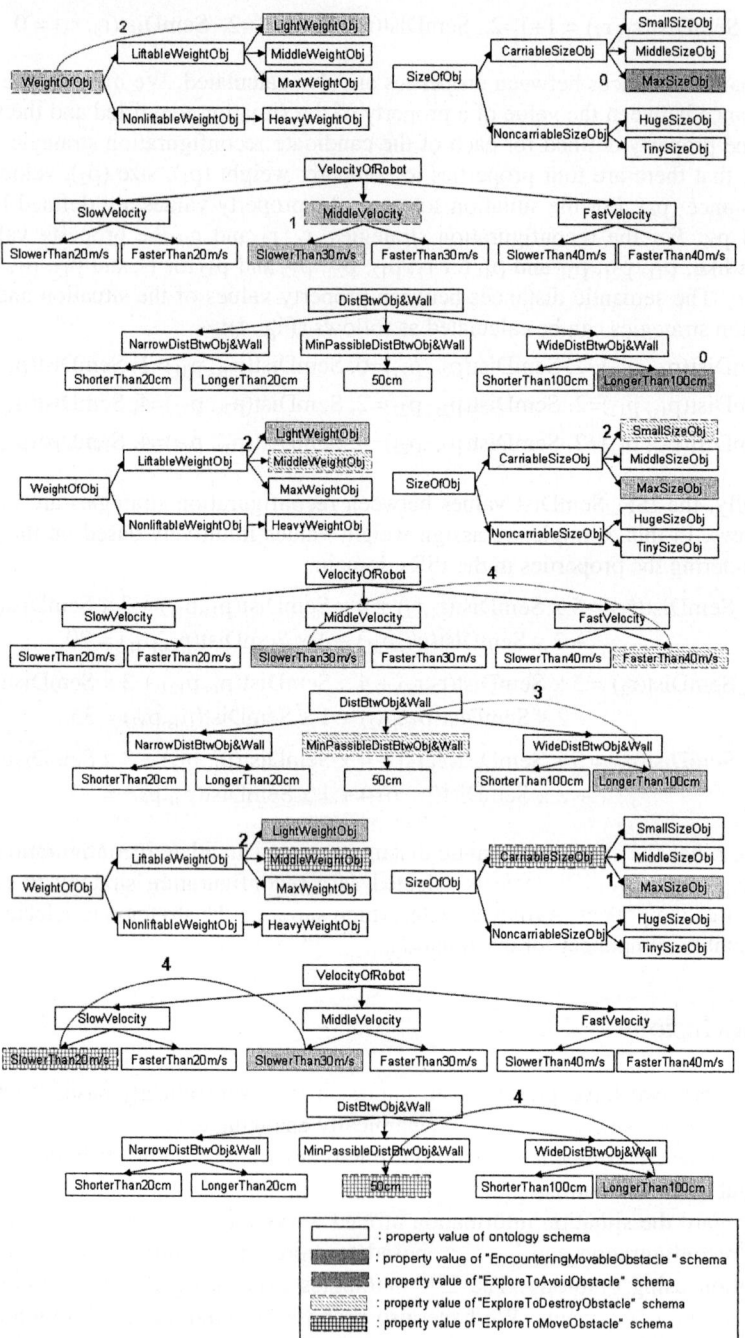

Fig. 4. Semantic Distances between the Properties of the Situation and Reconfiguration Strategy Ontologies

References

1. Lars P., David A., Danica K., Henrik I. C.: Towards an Intelligent Service Robot System. Accepted for International Conference on Intelligent Autonomous Systems (2000)
2. David J. C.: Morphology and Behavior in Distributed Robotic Systems. Ph.D. Thesis Proposal (2004)
3. Hafedh M., Petko V., Anne-Marie D. S., Philippe G.: Automating the Indexing and Retrieval of Reusable Software Components. Proceedings of the 6th International Workshop NLDB'01 Spain (2001) 75-86
4. Mili, A., Mili, R., Mittermeir, R.: Storing and Retrieving Software Components: A Refinement-Based System. IEEE Transactions on Software Engineering, Vol. 23. No. 7, (1997) 445–460
5. Prieto-Díaz R., Freeman, P.: Classifying Software for Reuse. IEEE Software, Vol. 4. No. 1, (1987) 6-16
6. Ostertag, E., Hendler, J., Prieto-Diaz, R., and Braum, C.: Computing Similarity in a Reuse Library System: An AI-based Approach. ACM Transactions on Software Engineering and Methodology, Vol. 1. No. 3, (1992) 205 – 228
7. Zaremski A. M., Wing, J. M.: Signature Matching: A Key to Reuse. Software Engineering Notes, Vol. 18. No. 5, (1993) 182–190.
8. Hall R.J.: Generalized Behavior-Based Retrieval. Proceedings of the Fifteenth International Conference on Software Engineering, Baltimore (1993) 371–380
9. Vijayan S., Veda C. S.: A Semantic-Based Approach to Component Retrieval. ACM SIGMIS Database, Vol. 34. No. 3, (2003) 8-24
10. Paolucci M., Kawamura T., Payne T., Sycara K.: Semantic Matching of Web Services Capabilities. In I. Horrocks and J. Hendler (eds.), Proceedings of the First International Semantic Web Conference, Sardinia, Springer (2002) 333–347
11. Kaarthik S., Kunal V., Amit S., John M.: Adding Semantics to Web Services Standards. In Proceedings of the 1st International Conference on Web Services (2003)
12. Merriam-Webster Online. http://www.m-w.com/dictionary.htm
13. John J. Craig: Introduction to Robotics Mechanics and Control. 3rd edn. Pearson Prentice Hall (2005)
14. Graham K., Jeremy J. C.: Resource Description Framework Concepts and Abstract Syntax. http://www.w3.org/TR/rdf-concepts
15. What is Protégé?. http://protege.stanford.edu/overview
16. Sihem A., SungRan C., Divesh S.: Tree Pattern Relaxation. International Conference on Extending Database Technology (2002)
17. Yangjun C., Duren C., Karl A,: On the efficient evaluation of relaxed queries in biological databases. Proceedings of the Eleventh International Conference on Information and Knowledge Management (2002)
18. Valerie C.: Fuzzy Semantic Distance Measures between Ontological Concepts. Fuzzy Information Processing NAFIPS '04 IEEE, Vol. 2 (2004) 635-640

An Approach for Intelligent Fixtureless Assembly: Issues and Experiments

Jorge Corona-Castuera[1], Reyes Rios-Cabrera[1], Ismael Lopez-Juarez [1],
and Mario Peña-Cabrera[2]

[1] CIATEQ A.C. Advanced Technology Center, Manantiales 23A,
Parque Industrial Bernardo Quintana, 76246 El Marques, Queretaro, Mexico
{jcorona,reyes.rios,ilopez}@ciateq.mx
http://www.ciateq.mx
[2] Instituto de Investigaciones en Matematicas Aplicadas y Sistemas IIMAS-UNAM,
Circuito Escolar, Cd. Universitaria 76246, DF, Mexico
mario@leibniz.iimas.unam.mx
http://www.iimas.unam.mx

Abstract. Industrial manufacturing cells involving fixtureless environments require more efficient methods to achieve assembly tasks. This paper introduces an approach for Robotic Fixtureless Assembly (RFA). The approach is based on the Fuzzy ARTMAP neural network and learning strategies to acquire the skill from scratch without knowledge about the assembly system. The vision system provides the necessary information to accomplish the assembly task such as pose, orientation and type of component. Different ad-hoc input vectors were used as input to the assembly and the vision systems through several experiments which are described. The paper also describes the task knowledge acquisition and the followed strategies to solve the problem of automating the peg-in-hole assembly using 2D images. The approach is validated through experimental work using an industrial robot.

1 Introduction

The main concern in robot programming while dealing with unstructured environments lies in achieving the tasks despite of uncertainty in the robot's positions relative to external objects. The use of sensing to reduce uncertainty significantly extends the range of possible tasks. One source of error is that the programmer's model of the environment is incomplete. Shape, location, orientation and contact states have to be associated to movements within the robot's motion space while it is in constraint motion. A representative method for achieving constrained motion in the presence of position uncertainty is well illustrated by Mason [1] and De Schutter [2]. Compliant motion meets external constraints by specifying how the robot's motion should be modified in response to the forces generated when the constraints are violated. Generalizations of this principle can be used to accomplish a wide variety of tasks involving constrained motion, e.g., inserting a peg into a hole or following a weld seam under uncertainty.

The goal of Robotic Fixtureless Assembly (RFA) is to replace constraining features by sensor-guided robots. The term was introduced by Hoska in 1988 [3] which also encourages the use of sensor-guided robots in unstructured environments avoiding costly fixtures. In this paper we present an RFA approach that uses vision and force sensing for robotic assembly when assembly components geometry, location and orientation is unknown at all times. The assembly operation resembles the same operation as carried out by a blindfold human operator. The approach is divided in four stages as suggested by Doersam and Munoz [4] and Lopez Juarez [5]:

Pre-configuration: From an initial configuration of the hand/arm system, the expected solutions are the required hand/arm collision-free paths in which the object can be reached. To achieve this configuration, it is necessary to recognize invariantly the components and determining their location and orientation.

Grasp: Once the hand is in the Pre-configuration stage, switching strategies between position/force control need to be considered at the moment of contact and grasping the object. Delicate objects can be broken without a sophisticated contact strategy even the Force/Torque (F/T) sensor can be damage.

Translation: After the object is firmly grasped, it can be translated to the assembly point. The possibility of colliding with obstacles has to be taken into account.

Assembly Operation: The assembly task requires robust and reactive positions/force control strategies. Mechanical and geometrical uncertainties make high demands on the controller.

Our proposal contains all steps mentioned above using vision and force contact sensing. The following section presents related work and outlines our contribution. In Section 3, the robotic testbed is described followed by the description of the assembly methodology provided in Section 4. The pre-configuration for recognition and location of components and the assembly operation are described. Both of them are based on FuzzyARTMAP neural network architecture. The training for assembly operations is autonomously acquired using fuzzy rules with minimum information from real force contacts. The experimental results and analysis which validate our approach are provided in Section 5. Finally, in Section 6 conclusions and future work is presented.

2 Related Work

Some researchers have used neural networks for assembly operations, mapping F/T data to motion direction. Gullapalli, [6] used Reinforcement Learning (RL) to control assembly operations with a Zebra robot, where the fixed component position was known. Cervera, [7] employed Self-Organizing Maps (SOM) and RL for assembling different part geometry with unknown location. Howarth, [8] worked with Backpropagation (BP) and RL to control assembly using a SCARA robot, Lopez Juarez [5] implemented Fuzzy ARTMAP to guide and learn insertions with a PUMA robot. Skubic [9] presented a sensor-based scheme for identifying contact formations (CF) which does not use geometric models of the workpieces. The method uses fuzzy logic to model and recognize the sensory patterns and also resolve the inherent ambiguities. In [10], Skubic focus the problem of teaching robots force-based assembly skills from human demonstration to avoid position dependencies. The learning of an assembly skill involves the learning of three functions: 1) The mapping of sensor signals to Single-Ended Contact Formations (SECFs) acquired using supervised learning;

2) The sequences of SECFs; and 3) The transition velocity commands which move the robot from the current SECF to the next desired SEFC. The operator demonstrates each SEFC while force data is collected and used to train a state classifier. The classifier is used to extract the sequence of SECFs and transitions velocities which comprise the rest of the skill. On the other hand, the integration of vision systems to facilitate the assembly operations in uncalibrated workspaces is well illustrated by the work of Jörg [11] and Baeten [12] using eye-in-hand vision for different robotic tasks.

2.1 Original Work

The grounding idea for the work reported in this paper was to learn the assembly skill from scratch, without any knowledge just asking to do task i.e. "assembly". For compliant motion, we present an autonomous system to acquire knowledge for task-level programming. The initial mapping between contact states and corrective motions is based on fuzzy rules.

Some of the reviewed work in the previous section has been done in simulations and a few with industrial robots. In our approach the generalisation for assembling different types of components is demonstrated as well as the robustness to perform the task since the assembly has always been successful, which is especially important when dealing with real-world operations under extreme uncertainty. It is important to note that the required knowledge for assembly is embedded into the Neural Network Controller (NNC) from the beginning through the contact states of the mating pairs and no supervision is needed. The generalisation of the NNC has been demonstrated by assembling successfully different part geometry using different mechanical tolerances and offsets using the same acquired knowledge base, which has provided an important foundation towards the creation of truly self-adaptive industrial robots for assembly.

3 Workplace Description

The manufacturing cell used for experimentation is integrated by a KUKA KR15/2 industrial robot. It also comprises a visual servo system with a ceiling mounted camera as shown in figure 1. The robot grasps the male component from a conveyor belt and performs the assembly task in a working table where the female component is located. The vision system gets an image to calculate the object's pose estimation and sends the information to the robot from two defined zones: **Zone 1** which is located on the conveyor belt. The vision system searches for the male component and determines the pose information needed by the robot. **Zone 2** is located on the working table. Once the vision system locates the female component, it sends the information to the NNC.

The NNC for assembly is called SIEM (*Sistema Inteligente de Ensamble Mecánico*) and is based on a FuzzyARTMAP neural network working in fast learning mode [13]. The vision system, called SIRIO (*Sistema Inteligente de Reconocimiento Invariante de Objetos*), also uses the same neural network to learn and classify the assembly components. The SIRIO was implemented with a high speed camera CCD/B&W, PULNIX 6710, with 640x480 resolution; movements on the X and Y axis were implemented using a 2D positioning system.

An Approach for Intelligent Fixtureless Assembly: Issues and Experiments 1055

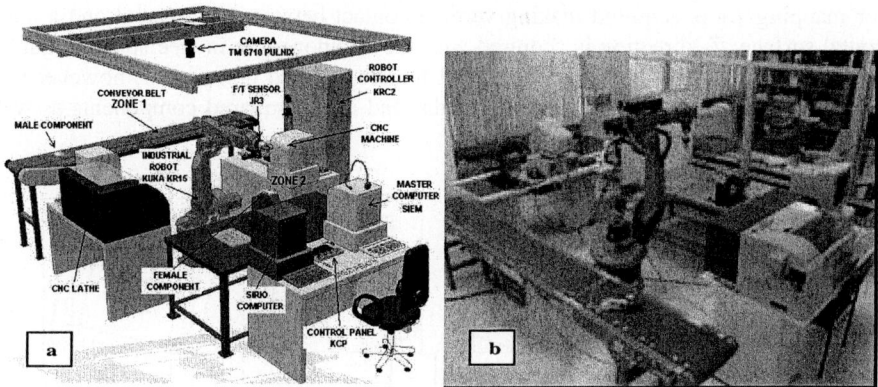

Fig. 1. a) Manufacturing Cell. b) Real picture.

For experimental purposes three canonical peg shapes were used: circular, square and radiused-square as it is shown in figure 2. Both, chamfered and chamferless female components were employed during the work reported in this paper.

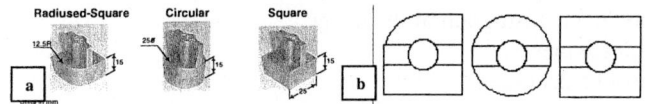

Fig. 2. a) Assembly components, b) Top view

4 Assembly Methodology

4.1 Pre-configuration

Starting from scratch. Initially, the robot system does not have any the knowledge on how to perform the assembly task. To accomplish the very first assembly the robot has to acquire a Primitive Knowledge Base (PKB) using an interactive method. We propose a behaviour-based approach to learn the initial mapping between contact states to motion commands employing fuzzy rules, as the one shown in expression (1) [14]. By using this mapping an Acquired-PKB (ACQ-PKB) is created and later used and refined on-line by the NNC.

IF *(Fx is pos)and(Fy is med)and(Fz is pos)and(Mx is med)and(My is pos)and(Mz is med)* THEN *(Dir is X+)*   (1)

There are 12 defined motion directions (X+, X-, Y+, Y-, Z+, Z-, Rz+, Rz-, X+Y+, X+Y-, X-Y+ and X-Y-) and for each one there is a corresponding contact state. An example of these contact states is shown in figure 3. The contact states for linear motion X+, X-, Y+, Y-, and linear combined motions X+Y+, X+Y-, X-Y+, X-Y- are shown in figure 3(a). In figure 3(b), it is shown a squared component having four contact points. Figures 3(c) and 3(d) provide additional patterns for rotation Rz- and Rz+ respectively when the component has only one point of contact. The contact state for mapping Z+ is acquired making vertical contact between component and a horizontal surface, Z- direction is acquired with the component is in free space. Figure 3 shows only contact states in a chamfered female squared component, however this approach applies also for chamfered circular and radius-squared components as well as the chamferless components.

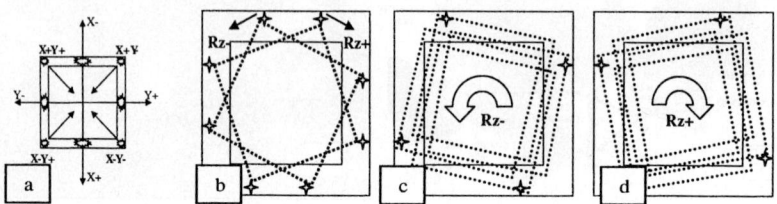

Fig. 3. Contacts between chamfered components while acquiring the primitive knowledge base, a) Linear movements, b) Pure rotation Rz+ and Rz-, c) Rotation Rz-, d) Rotation Rz+

Acquiring location and component type. The SIRIO system employs the following methodology:

1. Finding the region of interest (ROI).
2. Calculate the histogram of the image.
3. Search for pieces.
4. Centroid calculation.
5. Piece orientation.
6. Calculate Boundary Object Function (BOF), distances between the centroid and the perimeter points.
7. Descriptor vector generation and normalization (CFD&POSE).
8. Information processing in the neural network.

The descriptive vector is called CFD&POSE (Current Frame Descriptor and Pose) and it is conformed by (2):

$$[CDF \& POSE] = [D_1, D_2, D_3, ..., D_n, X_c, Y_c, \theta, Z, ID]^T \qquad (2)$$

where: D_i are the distances from the centroid to the perimeter of the object. (180 data)

X_C, Y_C, are the coordinates of the centroid.

ϕ, is the orientation angle.

Z is the height of the object.

ID is a code number related to the geometry of the components.

With this vector and following the above methodology, the system has been able to classify invariantly 100% of the components presented on-line even if they are not of the same size, orientation or location and for different light conditions. There are several components patterns to train/recognize as it is illustrated in figure 4. The reader is referred to [15] for complete details.

The CFD&POSE vector is invariant for each component and it is used for classification. The vector is normalized to 185 data dimension and normalized in the range [0.0 – 1.0]. The normalization of the BOF is accomplished using the maximum divisor value of the vector distance. This method allows to have very similar patterns as input vectors to the neural network, getting a significant improvement in the operation system. In our experiments, the object recognition method used the above components having 210 patterns as primitive knowledge to train the neural network. It was enough to recognize the assembly components with $\rho_a = 0.2$ (base vigilance), $\rho_{map} = 0.7$ (vigilance map) and $\rho_b = 0.9$ parameters, however, the SIRIO system can recognize more complex components as it is shown in figure 5, where several different animal shapes were used for testing. Same results for invariance and object recognition were obtained.

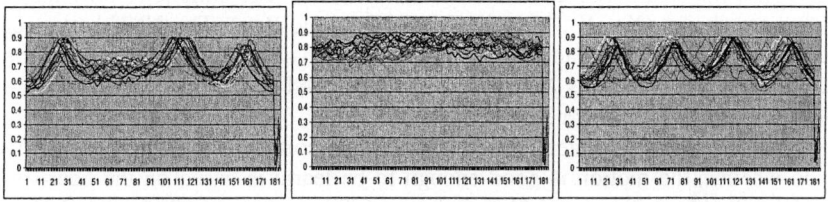

Fig. 4. Several component representation for training/testing. Left, radiused-square; Middle, circular; Right, square.

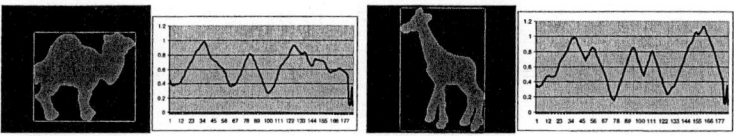

Fig. 5. Complex components for testing and their corresponding CFD&POSE vectors

4.2 Grasp

At this stage, the PKB has been acquired and the location information sent to the robot. The motion planning from Home position to zone 1 uses the male component given coordinates provided by SIRIO. The robot uses this information and the F/T sensor readings to grasp the piece and to control the motion in Z direction.

4.3 Translation

The translation is similar to the translation to grasp the component in zone 1. The path to move the robot from zone 1 to zone 2 (assembly point) is done by using the coordinates given by the SIRIO system. The possibility of collision with obstacles is avoided using bounded movements.

4.4 Assembly Operation

The assembly operation is achieved by the SIEM. The system interacts directly with the robot and F/T readings in real-time. It provides the robot the *"touch sense"*, and works when the robot has to grasp the piece or assembly it. The robot carries out the assemblies with incremental straight and rotational motions of 0.1 mm and 0.1°, respectively. Rotation around the X and Y axes was avoided so that only straight directions were considered which means that only compliant motion in XY plane and rotation around the Z axis was considered. In order to get the next motion direction the forces are read, normalized and classified using the NNC on-line. The F/T pattern obtained from the sensor provides a unique identification. The F/T vector (3), comprises 12 components given by the 6 data values (positive and negative).

$$[Current\ F/T] = [fx, fx-, fy, fy-, fz, fz-, mx, mx-, my, my-, mz, mz-]^T \qquad (3)$$

The normalized pattern is used as input to the NNC which associates it with the corresponding motion direction. Figure 6 illustrates some patterns for the initial mapping (PKB) for chamfered and chamferless insertions. For simplicity only major directions are shown (X+, X-, Y+, Y-, Z+, Z-, Rz+ and Rz+). The NNC have security software limits from -40 N to 40 N in force and from -20 N·dm to 20 N·dm in torque. The complete PKB consists 24 patterns for chamfered components and 24 for chamferless components as indicated in section 4.1.

Having an assembly system which is guided by compliant motion, the criterion to decide whether the motion is good enough to be learnt is based on the heuristic expression (4), where $F_{initial}$ and F_{after} is a merit figure measured before and after the corrective motion is applied and F is computed using equation (5) as in Ahn's work [16]. This means that if expression (4) is satisfied then the pattern is learnt.

$$(F_{initial} - F_{after}) \geq 10 \qquad (4)$$

$$F = \sqrt{fx^2 + fy^2 + fz^2 + mx^2 + my^2 + mz^2} \qquad (5)$$

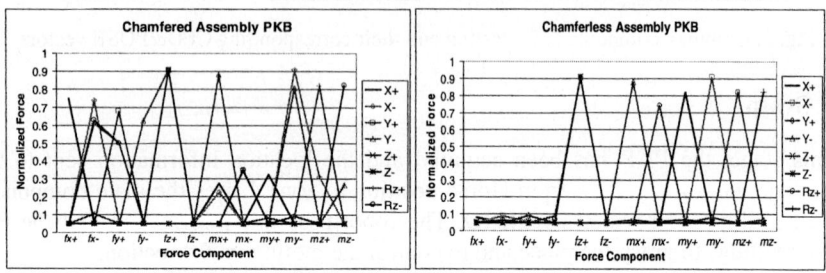

Fig. 6. ACQ-PKB obtained from chamfered and chamferless components

5 Assembly Cycles and Results

Several tests were carried out to asses the performance. The diameter of the male components was 24.8 mm whereas the diameter of female components were 25 mm, the chamfer was set to 45° and 5 mm width. Results are contained in table 1. In zone 2 the SIRIO only provides location (X,Y) because the female component orientation was fixed, however an error occurs and it is related to the component's tolerance. The error for the chamfered square component is 0.8°, 0.5° for the chamfered radiused-square and 0.4° for the chamferless square and 0.6° for the chamferless radiused-square. Error recovery is illustrated in figure 8. The assembly operation ends when ¾ of the body of male component is in the hole, this represents 14 mm. The FuzzyARTMAP NNC parameters were: $\rho_a = 0.2$, $\rho_{map} = 0.9$ and $\rho_b = 0.9$.

Table 1. Eighteen diferent assembly cycles, where IN= Insertion, P=piece, Ch=chamfer present, Time=Assembly cycle time, Time A= Insertion time, NC=correct neural classification, S=square, R=radiused-square, C=circle, N=no and Y=yes

# IN	P	Ch	Time (min)	Time A (sec)	ZONE 1			Error zone 1			ZONE 2		Error zone 2		NC
					Xmm	Ymm	RZ°	Xmm	Ymm	RZ°	Xmm	Ymm	Xmm	Ymm	
1	S	Y	1:15	32.5	62.4	144.1	10	0.2	-1.3	0	84.6	102.1	0.3	-1	Y
2	S	Y	1:15	30.4	62.4	45.7	12	1.8	0.2	2	85.6	101.1	-0.7	0	Y
3	S	Y	1:15	31.8	178.7	47.7	23	0.9	-0.8	3	84.7	100.9	0.2	0.2	Y
4	R	Y	1:11	30.1	181.6	147	29	-0.3	-0.7	-1	84.7	100.6	0.2	0.5	Y
5	R	Y	1:14	29.4	62.4	145.1	36	0.2	-0.3	-4	84.9	100.7	0	0.4	Y
6	R	Y	1:19	29.6	67.3	44.8	48	3.1	-0.7	-2	85.3	101.6	-0.4	-0.5	Y
7	C	Y	1:15	29.6	180.6	49.6	57	1	1.1	-3	84.6	102.4	0.3	-1.3	Y
8	C	Y	1:13	30.2	180.6	148	77	-0.7	0.3	7	84.3	101	0.6	0.1	Y
9	C	Y	1:14	30.2	61.5	146	79	-0.7	0.6	-1	83.9	101.6	1	-0.5	Y
10	S	N	1:18	29.9	63.4	45.7	83	-0.8	0.2	-7	85.4	100.5	-0.5	0.6	Y
11	S	N	1:19	30.4	179.6	48.6	104	0	0.1	4	83.2	100.8	1.7	0.3	Y
12	S	N	1:22	34.6	180.6	147	104	-0.7	-0.7	-6	83.2	101.8	1.7	-0.7	Y
13	R	N	1:22	38.3	61.5	146	119	-0.7	0.6	-1	84.8	102.8	0.1	-1.7	Y
14	R	N	1:22	36.8	63.4	43.8	126	-0.8	1.7	-4	83.6	101.8	1.6	-0.7	Y
15	R	N	1:24	36.6	179.6	47.7	138	0	-0.8	-2	83.2	101.7	1.7	-0.6	Y
16	C	N	1:17	30.5	182.6	149	150	1.3	1.3	0	83.7	101.2	1.2	-0.1	Y
17	C	N	1:15	28.3	63.4	146	155	1.2	0.6	-5	84.6	100.7	0.3	0.4	Y
18	C	N	1:15	29.7	64.4	47.7	174	0.2	2.2	4	83.9	101.1	1	0	Y

Table 1 shows the position errors in zone 2 which is represented in figure 7 as the trajectory followed by the robot. The minimum time of assembly cycle was 1:11 min, the maximum was 1:24 min and the average time was 1.17 min. The system has an average angular error of 3.11° and a maximum linear position error from -1.3 mm to 3.1 mm due to the camera positioning system in Zone 1. We improved the results presented in [15].

The force levels in chamferless assemblies are higher than the chamfered ones. In the first one, the maximum value was in Z+, 39.1 N for the insertion number 16, and in the chamfered the maximum value was 16.9 N for the insertion number 9.

In chamfered assembly, in figure 7, it can be seen that some trajectories were optimal like in insertions 2, 5, 7, 8 and 9, which was not the case for chamferless assembly; however, the insertions were correctly completed.

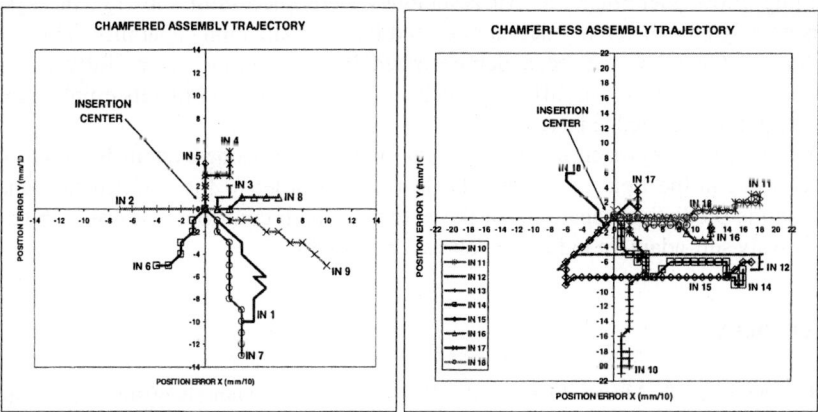

Fig. 7. Assembly trajectory in top view for each insertion in zone 2. The trajectory starts with the labels (INx) and ends at 0,0 origin coordinate.

In figure 8, each segment corresponds to alignment motions in other directions different from Z-. The radial lines mean the number of Rz+ motions that the robot performed in order to recover the positional error for female components. The insertion paths show how many rotational steps are performed. The maximum alignment motions were 22 for the chamfered case in comparison with 46 with the chamferless component.

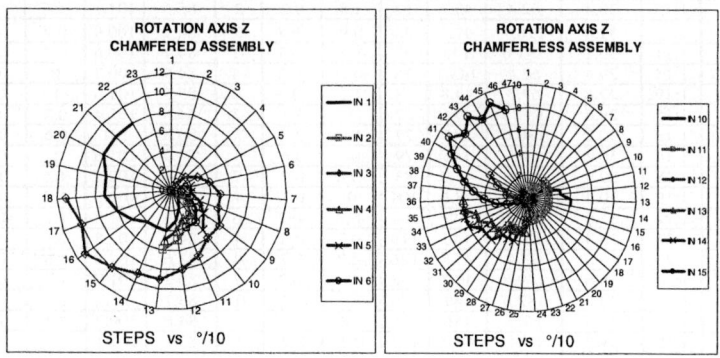

Fig. 8. Compliant rotational motions (only Rz+) for each insertion in zone 2

6 Conclusion

An approach for peg-in-hole automated assembly was presented. The proposed methodologies were used to achieve the tasks and tested successfully in the real world operations using an industrial manipulator. The robot is able to perform not only the assembly but also it can start working without initial knowledge about the environment, and it can increase its PKB at every assembly if it is necessary.

Accurate recognition of assembly components was successfully carried out by using FuzzyARTMAP neural network model which was initially trained with 210 patterns, and its performance was completely satisfactory for the whole experiments obtaining 100% identification. All assemblies were successful showing the system robustness against different uncertainties and its generalization capability. The generalisation of the NNC has been demonstrated by assembling successfully different component geometry using different mechanical tolerances and offsets employing the same acquired knowledge base.

The presented approach using the vision and force sensing system has envisaged further work in the field of multimodal learning in order to fuse information and to increase the prediction capability of the network which contributes towards the creation of truly self-adaptive industrial robots for assembly.

References

1. Lozano-Perez T., Mason, M.T., Taylor R. H.: Automatic synthesis of fine motion strategies. Int. Journal of Robotics Research Vol. 3 No. 1 (1984) 3-24
2. De Schutter, J., Van Brussel, H.: Compliant robot motion I, a formalism for specifying compliant motion tasks. Int. Journal of Robotics Research. Vol. 7 No. 4 (1988) 3-17

3. Hoska, D.R.: Fixturless assembly manufacturing. Manuf Eng. No.100 (1988) 49-54
4. Doersam, T., Munoz Ubando, L.A.: Robotic hands: modelisation, control and grasping strategies. Meeting annuel de L'Institute Fanco-Allemand pour les Application de la recherche IAR (1995).
5. Lopez-Juarez Ismael: On-line learning for robotic assembly using artificial neural networks and contact force sensing. PhD thesis, Nottingham Trent University, (2000).
6. Gullapalli, V., Franklin, J.A., Benbrahim, H.: Control under uncertainty via direct reinforcement learning. Robotics and Autonomous Systems. (1995) 237-246
7. Cervera, E., Del Pobil, A.P.: Programming and learning in real world manipulation tasks. In: Int. Conf. on Intelligent Robot and Systems (IEEE/RSJ). Proc. 1 (1997) 471-476
8. Howarth, M.: An investigation of task level programming for robotic assembly. PhD thesis. The Nottingham Trent University (1998)
9. Skubic, M., Volz, R.A.: Identifying single-ended contact formations from force sensor patterns. IEEE Transactions on Robotics and Automation. Vol. 16 (2000) 597-603
10. Skubic, M., Volz, R.A.: Acquiring robust, force-based assembly skills from human demonstration. IEEE Trans. on Robotics and Automation. Vol. 16 No. 6 (2000) 772-781
11. Jörg, S., Langwald, J., Stelter, J., Natale, C., Hirzinger, G.: Flexible robot assembly using a multi-sensory approach. In: Proc. IEEE Int. Conference on Robotics and Automation. San Francisco, CA (2000) 3687-3694
12. Baeten, J., Bruyninckx, H., De Schutter, J.: Integrated vision/force robotic servoing in the task frame formalism. Int. Journal of Robotics Research. Vol. 22. No. 10-11 (2003) 941-954
13. Carpenter, G.A., Grossberg, J., Markunzon, N., Reynolds, J.H., Rosen, D.B.: Fuzzy ARTMAP: a neural network architecture for incremental learning of analog multidimensional maps. IEEE Trans. Neural Networks Vol. 3 No. 5 (1992) 678-713
14. Driankov, D., Hellendoorn, H., Reinfrank, M.: An introduction to fuzzy control. 2nd ed. Springer Verlag. (1996)
15. M. Peña-Cabrera, I. López-Juárez, R. Ríos-Cabrera, J. Corona-Castuera: Machine vision learning process applied to robotic assembly in manufacturing cells. Journal of Assembly Automation Vol. 25 No. 3 (2005)
16. Ahn, D.S., Cho, H.S., Ide, K.I., Miyazaki, F., Arimoto, S.: Learning task strategies, in robotic assembly systems. Robotic Vol. 10, (1992) 409–418

On the Design of a Multimodal Cognitive Architecture for Perceptual Learning in Industrial Robots

Ismael Lopez-Juarez[1], Keny Ordaz-Hernández[1,2] Mario Peña-Cabrera[3], Jorge Corona-Castuera[1], and Reyes Rios-Cabrera[1]

[1] CIATEQ A.C. Advanced Technology Centre, Manantiales 23A,
Parque Industrial Bernardo Quintana, 76246. El Marques, Queretaro, Mexico
{ilopez, kordaz, jcorona, reyes.rios}@ciateq.mx
http://www.ciateq.mx

[2] Laboratoire en Ingénierie des Processus et des Services Industriels LIPSI-ESTIA,
Technopôle Izarbel; 64210 Bidart, France
k.ordaz@estia.fr
http://www.estia.fr

[3] Instituto de Investigaciones en Matemáticas Aplicadas y Sistemas IIMAS-UNAM,
Circuito Escolar, Cd. Universitaria 76246, DF, Mexico
mario@leibniz.iimas.unam.mx
http://www.iimas.unam.mx

Abstract. Robots can be greatly benefited from the integration of artificial senses in order to adapt to changing worlds. To be effective in complex unstructured environments robots have to perceive the environment and adapt accordingly. In this paper, it is introduced a biology inspired multimodal architecture called $M_2ARTMAP$ which is based on the biological model of sensorial perception and has been designed to be a more versatile alternative to data fusion techniques and non-modular neural architectures. Besides the computational overload compared to FuzzyARTMAP, $M_2ARTMAP$ reaches similar performance. This paper reports the results found in simulated environments and also the observed results during assembly operations using an industrial robot provided with vision and force sensing capabilities.

1 Introduction

The manufacturing industry requires the development of flexible assembly cells, which in turn require flexible and adaptive industrial robots. Neural network software has proved to provide flexibility and adaptability to a number of robotic systems. Also, recent research in industrial robotics aims at the involvement of additional sensory devices to improve robustness, flexibility and performance of common robot applications [1]. Unfortunately, most industrial robotic systems are designed to perform activities based on a single sensorial modality. Only a few benefit from multisensorial perception, possibly because sensor integration with data fusion techniques tends to be hard-established in the control subsystem.

These reasons have motivated the development of a multimodal neural architecture to enhance industrial robots' sensing abilities. This sort of architecture provides the ideal mechanism to incorporate multiple sensors into the robotic system. The architecture, called Multimodal ARTMAP (M$_2$ARTMAP), presented in this work is based on the adaptive resonance theory (ART) developed by G.A. Carpenter and S. Grossberg [2] and it accomplishes its goal by means of a modular structure and a *prediction fusion* technique, as it has been shown in simulations.

2 Related Work

The common approach to face multimodality in robotic systems is the employment of data fusion or sensor fusion techniques [3, 4]. Multimodal pattern recognition is presented in [5] using Multi-Layer Perceptron (MLP).

The ART family is considered as an adequate option, due to its superior performance found over other neural network architectures [6].

The adaptive resonance theory has provided ARTMAP-FTR [7], MART [8], and Fusion ARTMAP [9] —among others— to solve problems involving inputs from multiple channels. Nowadays, G.A. Carpenter has continued extending ART family to be employed in information fusion and data mining [10], among other applications.

The Mechatronics and Intelligent Manufacturing Systems Research Group (MIMSRG) performs applied research in intelligent robotics, concretely in the implementation of machine learning algorithms applied to assembly labors —using contact forces and invariant object recognition. The group has obtained adequate results in both sensorial modalities (tactile and visual) in conjunction with voice recognition, and continues working in their integration within an intelligent manufacturing cell (see [11]). In order to integrate other sensorial modalities into the assembly robotic system, an ART-Based multimodal neural architecture is desired.

3 ART-Based Multimodal Neural Architecture

3.1 ART Architectures

Since it is desired to attend at least two sensorial modalities of an industrial robotic system, the architecture is designed with a modular approach as MART [8] and Fusion ARTMAP [9] architectures, in an opposite manner to Martens et al. [3] using a vector concatenation approach with Fuzzy ARTMAP [12, 13] architecture.

Neither MART nor Fusion ARTMAP seem to provide the degree of autonomy desired (at the component level) in an industrial environment, as presented in Table 1.

3.2 Biology-Inspired Architecture

As Waxman [14] states, multimodality appears in nature as a strategy of great relevance to a variety of applications. It is a mean by which multiple sensing modalities provide complementary evidence supporting or negating a decision (e.g. the recognition of an object).

The architecture's structure is inspired by the biological model of sensorial perception: sensory neurons conducting impulses inwards to the brain or spinal cord, as shown in Fig. 1a. The architecture achieves this by assigning dedicated Fuzzy ARTMAP modules to each modality (as "sensory neurons") and conducting the output of each module to an Integrator (as "superior colliculus"[1]), which makes the prediction fusion of all modules.

Table 1. ART-based architectures for multi-channel problems

Architecture	Building Block	Function	Comments
Fuzzy ARTMAP	Fuzzy ART	Classification, recognition, and prediction	Non-modular. Requires vector concatenation. It is not possible to know the predictive power of each sensor or modality
MART	ART 2 [13]	Classification	Does not provide recognition (obviously nor prediction)
Fusion ARTMAP	Fuzzy ART	Classification, recognition, and prediction	Modular. Identical performance as Fuzzy ARTMAP, Fuzzy ART only provides unsupervised learning, thus autonomy is reduced
M_2ARTMAP	Fuzzy ARTMAP	Classification, recognition, and prediction	Similar to Fusion ARTMAP, but the employment of Fuzzy ARTMAP modules permits a higher level of autonomy

Finally, the fused prediction is passed to a superior Fuzzy ARTMAP neural network, called Predictor, (as "multisensory neurons") to obtain the final prediction (see Fig. 1b). For a description of the participation of the superior colliculus in multimodality, see [14].

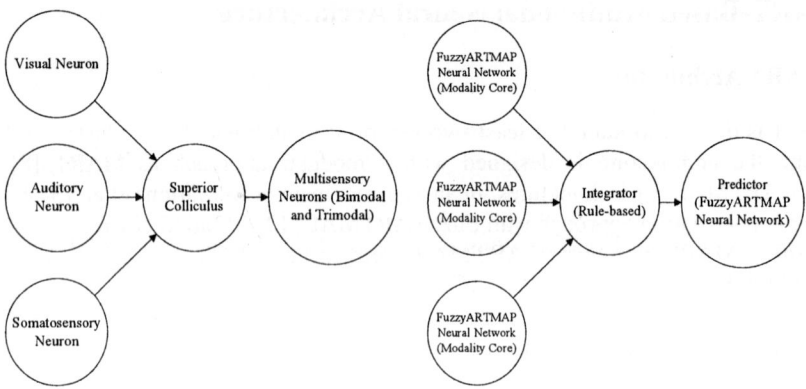

Fig. 1. Schematics of the biological model (a) and the M-ARTMAP model (b) of multimodal sensorial perception

---

[1] The superior colliculus (SC) integrates the maps from visual, auditory and somato-sensory neurons. SC appears in mammals such as cats, monkeys, humans, etc.

3.3 M₂ARTMAP Architecture

The M$_2$ARTMAP architecture is composed of Fuzzy ARTMAP neural networks as hierarchical architecture. M$_2$ARTMAP has a mechanism of multimodal work that is established by prediction fusion; i.e. data fusion is taken to a higher level of abstraction: instead of merging perception data from each modality, the predictions from each corresponding neural network are combined accordingly to the current task. This is also a different approach to voting systems, given that in voting systems all neural networks are receiving exactly the same input.

The maximum number of possible combinations of predictions, given n modalities with at least one modality at a time, is:

$$\sum_{i=0}^{n}\binom{n}{i}-\binom{n}{0}=2^n-1 \quad (1)$$

Given this, it is necessary to set in a configuration component the semantic category to which each combination belongs, in order to settle the rules that establish the valid combinations.

M$_2$ARTMAP Model. The process modeled in M$_2$ARTMAP is given by the following mappings:

Let E, S, P, I, C and η be the environment states space, the perceptions space, the predictions space, the neural networks' internal states space, the neural networks' configurations space and the quantity of modalities —respectively.

The activities sensing ζ, training η, predicting κ and multimodality predicting K are given by the mappings:

$$\zeta : E \rightarrow S \quad (2)$$
$$\eta : S \times P \rightarrow I \quad (3)$$
$$k : I \times S \rightarrow P \quad (4)$$
$$K : P^n \times C^m \rightarrow P \quad (5)$$

Accordingly to the diagram exposed in Fig. 2, the components of M$_2$ARTMAP are:

- *Predictor* is the final prediction component that uses modalities' predictions.
- *Modality* is the primary prediction component that is composed by an artificial neural network (ANN), an input element (Sensor), a configuration element (CF), and a knowledge base (KB).
- *Integrator* is the component that merges the modalities' predictions by inhibiting those that are not relevant to the global prediction activity, or stimulating those who are considered of higher reliability —in order to facilitate the Predictor's process.

Process Description. The process, firstly introduced in [15], is easily carried out. Given an instance of the M$_2$ARTMAP system —conformed by three modalities m_1, m_2, and m_3 — the process is stated as follows:

Let us suppose that all modalities are working simultaneously and that their neural networks have already been trained. At time τ, the identifiable states of the environment for each modality are e_1, e_2, and e_3—respectively. The three states produce (by means of sensor$_1$, sensor$_2$, and sensor$_3$) the perceptions s_1, s_2, and s_3; i.e.

$$\forall\, e_i \in E\, \exists\, s_i \in S : s_i = \zeta(e_i),\ 1 \leq i \leq 3 \qquad (6)$$

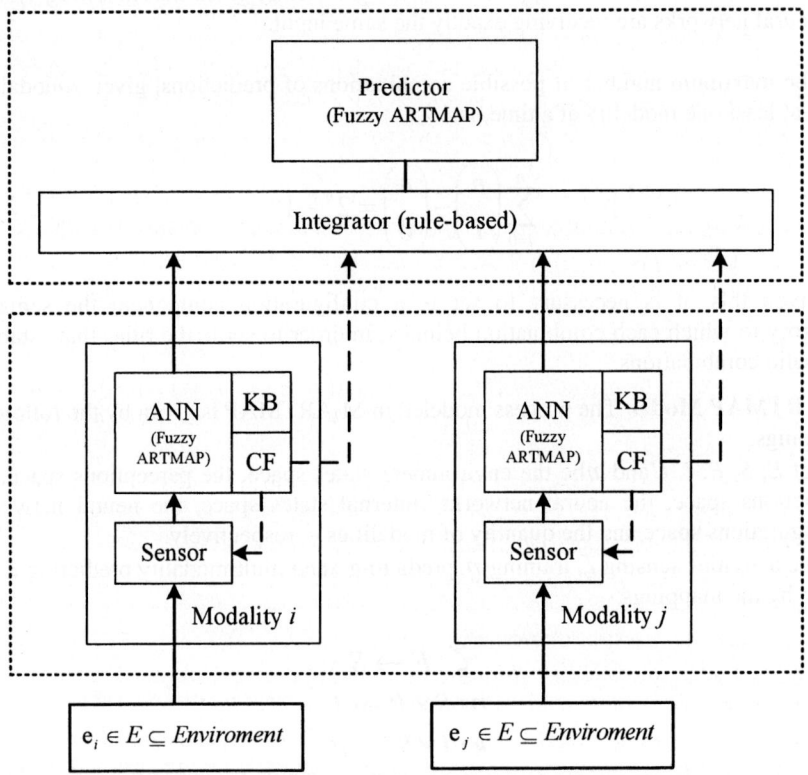

Fig. 2 Multimodal neural architecture, M_2ARTMAP, integrated by three main components organized in two layers: *Modality* (several found at the lower layer), *Predictor* and *Integrator* (at the upper layer)

Next, each ANN receives the perception corresponding to its sensorial modality and outputs its prediction; i.e.

$$\forall\, s_i \in S\, \exists\, p_i \in P : p_i = K(_\tau \ell_i, s_i),\ _\tau \ell_i \in I,\ 1 \leq i \leq 3 \qquad (7)$$

Where the internal state $_\tau \ell_{i\psi}$ corresponds to modality i at time τ. Then, the Integrator gathers all predictions, performs their fusion using the associated configuration of each modality, and provides the Predictor with a pattern (resulting from prediction fusion) in order to yield the final prediction; i.e.

$$p_\tau = K((p_1, p_2, p_3), (c_1, c_2, c_3)), \quad c_i \in C \tag{8}$$

4 Results

4.1 Quadruped Mammal Database Simulations

Fuzzy ARTMAP and M_2ARTMAP systems were simulated using the *Quadruped Mammal* database [16] which represents four mammals (dog, cat, giraffe, and horse) in terms of eight components (head, tail, four legs, torso, and neck). Each component is described by nine attributes (three location variables, three orientation variables, height, radius, and texture), for a total of 72 attributes. Each attribute is modeled as a Gaussian process with mean and variance dependent on the mammal and component (e.g. the radius of a horse's neck is modeled by a different Gaussian from that of a dog's neck or a horse's tail). At this point, it is important to mention that Quadruped Mammal database is indeed a structured quadruped mammal instances generator that requires the following information to work: animals <seed> <# of objects>.

For this experiment, the M_2ARTMAP system weakly couples the information provided by each component in the global prediction since none of the processing modules (*Modality*) in the lower layer (see Fig. 2) is affected by other processing module, as stated by Clark and Yuille [17].

In the first set of simulations, both Fuzzy ARTMAP and M_2ARTMAP where trained (in one epoch) and tested with the same set of 1000 exemplars produced with seed = 1278. Both architectures achieved 100% prediction rates.

In the next set of simulations, Fuzzy ARTMAP and M_2ARTMAP where applied to a group of 384 subjects (91 variations of the choice parameter and 4 variations of the base vigilance), both architectures where trained (again in one epoch) using the set of 1000 exemplars produced with seed = 1278 and tested using the set of 1000 exemplars produced with seed = 23941. Once again, both achieved 100% prediction rates. Nevertheless, M_2ARTMAP's recognition rates where slower than expected. Thus, a t-Student paired test was conducted to constrain the difference between both architectures. It was confirmed that M_2ARTMAP's recognition rate was at most 5% slower than Fuzzy ARTMAP's recognition rate, by rejecting the null hypothesis with a 1-tail *p*-value less than 0.0001.

Considering the latter results, a new set of simulations was conducted. But in this case, the previous group was separated into four groups of 728 subjects, each one conformed of 8 subgroups (having from 1 to 8 modalities) of 91 subjects. The simulations were realized over these 32 subgroups of subjects. Fig. 3 shows that the average performance difference between Fuzzy ARTMAP and M_2ARTMAP varies along with the quantity of modalities employed.

Evidently, M_2ARTMAP outperforms Fuzzy ARTMAP in the training phase when less than 3 modalities are taken (see Fig. 3a), and in the testing when less than 6 modalities are taken (see Fig. 3b).

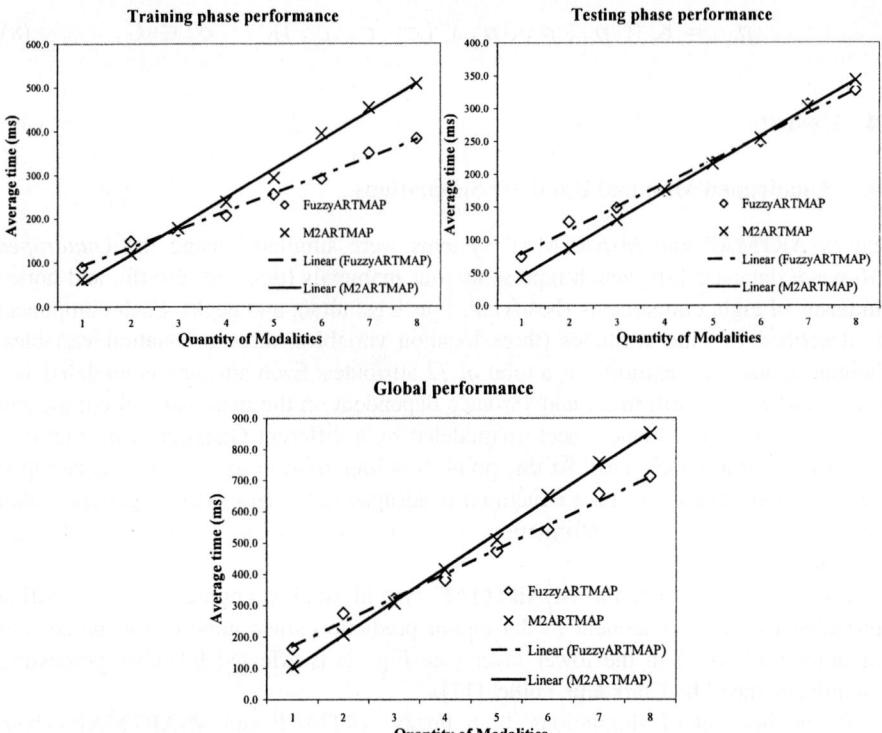

Fig. 3. Performance comparison of Fuzzy ARTMAP vs. M-ARTMAP. (a) Training phase. (b) Testing phase. (C) Global performance.

In these simulations' scenario, M_2ARTMAP globally outperforms Fuzzy ARTMAP only when less than 4 modalities are taken (see Fig. 3c). We should take into account that normally in a working neural network the training phase occurs once and the testing or recognition phase occurs indefinitely. Under real-world conditions, in unstructured environments, an industrial robot normally operates in recognition phase. The training occurs only at the beginning and a few more times if on-line learning is allowed [19].

4.2 On-Line Control

The model has been conceived to be used in industrial environments, giving to robots the self-adapting ability. As an early approach, this model has been implemented with Visual C++ 6.0 as part of the KUKA KR15 industrial robot control, whose tactile perception is acquired by a JR3 6 DOF force/torque sensor positioned at the wrist of the robot.

The test operation consists in a typical "peg-in-hole" insertion[2] (see Fig. 4), in which the exact position of assembly is unknown to the robot. In order to succeed in

---

[2] Peg-in-hole insertion is not only a longstanding problem in robotics but the most common automated mechanical assembly task [18].

the insertion, the robot receives *a priori* exemplars of tactile perception. It learns such exemplars and forms its Primitive Knowledge Base (PKB) as shown in Fig. 5.

Figures 5 and 6 show the initial force/torque patterns and the ones acquired at the end of the task, respectively. The values in the vertical axis correspond to the normalized patterns magnitude (see [19]). At the present time, a unimodal version of the model has been validated, so that its predictions drive to successful insertions. The time to complete them oscillates around 1 minute.

Fig. 4. KUKA KR15 industrial robot with JR3 force/torque sensor

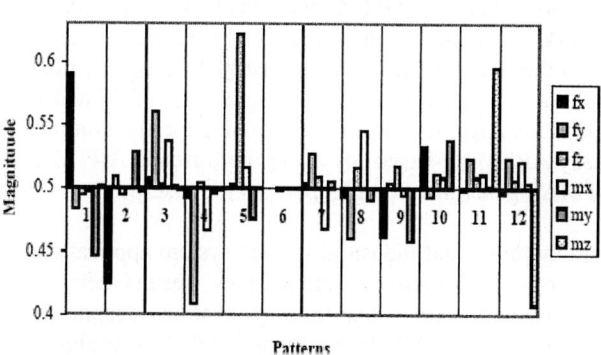

Fig. 5. Tactile perception

During this time, the robot learns the whole operation, improving its dexterity as it performs more insertions. By the end of the task, new knowledge (Fig. 6) is reused by the manipulator so that initial mistakes are not made again, demonstrating its adaptability.

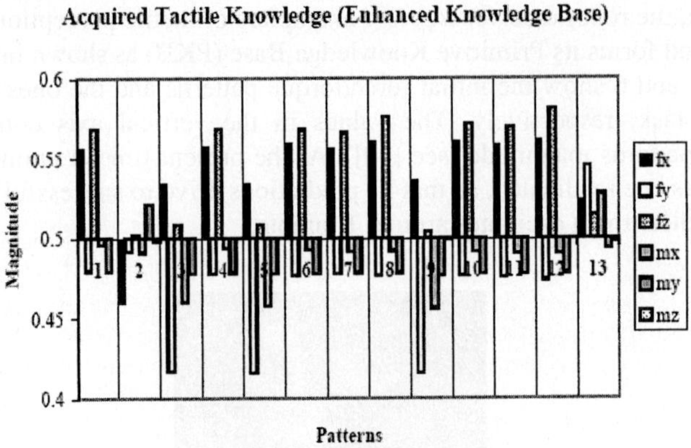

Fig. 6. Acquired tactile knowledge

5 Conclusions and Future Work

We have presented a new ART-based neural architecture that enhances and facilitates multi-sensor integration to industrial robotic systems, by providing multimodal pattern recognition and prediction capabilities. The architecture's main building blocks are Fuzzy ARTMAP modules.

M_2ARTMAP has a computational overload over Fuzzy ARTMAP, and probably over Fusion ARTMAP too (since the latter uses Fuzzy ART modules and the former uses Fuzzy ARTMAP ones). Despite that, M_2ARTMAP reaches similar performance to Fuzzy ARTMAP, as Fusion ARTMAP claims to do [9, p. 158].

As future work, it has been considered to replace the low-layer Fuzzy ARTMAP components by other variants that achieve Fuzzy ARTMAP's functionality with only one Fuzzy ART module instead of two (Category ART [20] and Fuzzy ARTvar [21] are good candidates). Also, it is desired to combine the Integrator (rule-based) and the Predictor (Fuzzy ARTMAP-based) by using the Cascade ARTMAP [22] architecture (a Fuzzy ARTMAP generalization that permits the insertion of rule-based knowledge explicitly).

Results from the unimodal industrial robotic system application show the practical viability of the model, whereas the simulations' results demonstrate that it has a potential for being employed in real-time applications despite its relative slowness compared to Fuzzy ARTMAP. In real-world robot operations we are expecting M_2ARTMAP be robust with its multimodal prediction capability. M_2ARTMAP's training and testing time in comparison with Fuzzy ARTMAP could be unimportant considering its improved confidence. Finding more than three modalities in practical work is unlikely since at most, visual and tactile sensing are found in robotic applications. Other sensors like collision avoidance and presence sensors are just discrete type value sensor not considered as inputs to the M_2ARTMAP architecture. The performance of M_2ARTMAP has to be tested experimentally using visual and tactile sensing as the principal modalities.

The visual modality has been integrated into the trial robotic system so that we will be in a position to experimentally validate the architecture's capabilities. A distributed system is being developed which will fusion all sensors in a single workstation computer.

References

1. Jörg, S.M., Langwald, J., Stelter, J., Natale, C., Hirzinger, G.: Flexible robot-assembly using a multi-sensory approach. In: Proc. IEEE Int. Conference on Robotics and Automation. (2000) 3687–3694
2. Carpenter, G.A., Grossberg, S.: Adaptive Resonance Theory. In Arbib, M.A., ed.: The Handbook of Brain Theory and Neural Networks. 2nd edn. MIT Press, Cambridge, Massachusetts (2003) 87–90
3. Martens, S., Gaudiano, P., Carpenter, G.A.: Mobile robot sensor integration with fuzzy ARTMAP. In: IEEE ISIC/CIRA/ISAS Joint Conference, IEEE (1998)
4. Thorpe, J., McEliece, R.: Data fusion algorithms for collaborative robotic exploration. Progress Report 42-149, California Institute of Technology (2002)
5. Yang, S., Chang, K.C.: Multimodal pattern recognition by modular neural network. Optical Engineering 37 (1998) 650–659
6. Carpenter, G.A., Grossberg, S., Iizuka, K.: Comparative performance measures of fuzzy ARTMAP, learned vector quantization, and back propagation for handwritten character recognition. In: International Joint Conference on Neural Networks. Volume 1., IEEE (1992) 794–799
7. Carpenter, G.A., Streilein, W.W.: ARTMAP-FTR: a neural network for fusion target recognition with application to sonar classification. In: AeroSense: Proceedings of SPIE's 12th Annual Symposium on Aerospace/Defense Sensing, Simulation, and Control. SPIE Proceedings, Society of Photo-Optical Instrumentation Engineers (1998)
8. Fernandez-Delgado, M., Barro Amereiro, S.: MART: A multichannel art-based neural network. IEEE Transactions on Neural Networks 9 (1998) 139–150
9. Asfour, Y.R., Carpenter, G.A., Grossberg, S., Lesher, G.W.: Fusion ARTMAP: An adaptive fuzzy network for multi-channel classification. In: Third International Conference on Industrial Fuzzy Control and Intelligent Systems [IFIS-93], IEEE Press (1993) 155–160
10. Parsons, O., Carpenter, G.A.: Artmap neural networks for information fusion and data mining: Map production and target recognition methodologies. Neural Networks 16 (2003)
11. Lopez-Juarez, I., Peña, M., Corona, J., Ordaz Hernández, K., Aliew, F.: Towards the integration of sensorial perception in industrial robots. In: Fifth International Conference on Application of Fuzzy Systems and Soft Computing [ICAFS], Milan, IT (2002) 218–223
12. Carpenter, G.A., Grossberg, S., Markuzon, N., Reynolds, J.H., Rosen, D.B.: Fuzzy ARTMAP: A neural network architecture for incremental supervised learning of analog multidimensional maps. In: IEEE Transactions on Neural Networks. Volume 3., IEEE (1992) 698–713
13. Carpenter, G.A., Grossberg, S.: ART 2: Selforganisation of stable category recognition codes for analog input patterns. Applied Optics 26 (1987) 4919–4930
14. Waxman, A.M.: Sensor fusion. In Arbib, M.A., ed.: The Handbook of Brain Theory and Neural Networks. 2 edn. MIT Press, Cambridge, Massachusetts (2003) 1014–1016
15. Ordaz Hernández, K., Lopez-Juarez, I.: Hacia M- ARTMAP: una arquitectura neuronal multimodal para percepción sensorial en robots industriales. In Sossa Azuela, J.H., Pérez Cortés, E., eds.: Advances on Computer Sciences (IV International Congress Computer Sciences ENC 2003). CIC-IPN/SMCC, Apizaco, Tlax., MX (2003) 319–324

16. Ginnari, J.H., Langley, P., Fisher, D.: Quadruped mammals. Found as *Quadraped Animals Data Generator* at UCI Machine Learning Repository http://www.ics.uci.edu/~mlearn/MLRepository.html (1992)
17. Clark, J.J., Yuille, A.L.: Data Fusion for Sensory Information Processing Systems. Kluwer Academic, Nowell, Massachusetts (1990)
18. Paulos, E., Canny, J.: Accurate insertions strategies using simple optical sensors. In: Proc. IEEE International Conference on Robotics and Automation. Volume 2. (1994) 1656–1662.
19. Lopez-Juarez, I., Howard, M.: Knowledge acquisition and learning in unstructured robotic assembly environments. Information Sciences 145 (2002) 89–111
20. Weenink, D.: Category art: A variation on adaptive resonance theory neural networks. In: Proc. of the Institute of Phonetic Sciences. Volume 21., Amsterdam, NL (1997) 117–129
21. Dagher, I., Georgiopoulos, M., Heileman, G.L., Bebis, G.: Fuzzy ARTvar: An improved fuzzy ARTMAP algorithm. In: International Joint Conference on Neural Networks (IJCNN-98). Volume 3., Alaska, IEEE (1998) 1688–1693
22. Tan, A.H.: Cascade ARTMAP: Integrating neural computation and symbolic knowledge processing. IEEE Transactions on Neural Networks 8 (1997) 237–250

CORBA Distributed Robotic System: A Case Study Using a Motoman 6-DOF Arm Manipulator

Federico Guedea-Elizalde, Josafat M. Mata-Hernández,
and Rubén Morales-Menéndez

ITESM, Campus Monterrey,
Center for Innovation in Design and Technology,
Eugenio Garza Sada 2501,
64849 Monterrey, Nuevo León, México
fguedea@itesm.mx, jmatahdez@yahoo.com.mx, rmm@itesm.mx

Abstract. We present a remote operated robot application based on a standard CORBA distributed system to control a MOTOMAN 6-DOF arm manipulator. The robot is based on XRC2001 robot controller. Current approach could be extented to other Yaskawa controllers (e.g. ERC, ERCII, MRC, MRCII) without major changes. The main idea is to define a set of generic IDL interfaces that can be used to integrate commercial proprietary libraries hiding the intricate of low level components. The challenge is to create a remote client-server application which facilitates the integration of one or several arm manipulators based on mentioned controllers independently from computer system or different platforms.

Keywords: robotic, distributed systems, CORBA.

1 Introduction

CORBA provides the opportunity to use software components that can be implemented by using different programming languages and running in different platforms. ORB technology is both middleware and a component technology. As a middleware technology it supports local/remote transparency to clients. As a component technology, it supports the definition of APIs and run time activation of executable modules [1]. The CORBA programming model allows programmers to extend existing interfaces polymorphically, replace instances of objects, and add new objects to an existing system. Furthermore, CORBA supports implementations that address the performance and footprint issues of scalability [2].

Software for manufacturing systems are often constructed by integrating pre-existing software components. Accurate specification of the component interactions in these systems is needed to ensure testability and maintainability. Moreover, standards for manufacturing systems must specify the interactions to achieve inter-operability and substitutability of components [3].

Besides, components usage through their explicit interfaces and interoperability between different languages, allows increase reuse, quality of result and outsourcing capabilities [4].

We present a case study to integrate one Motoman industrial robot arm manipulator to a CORBA distributed system, introduced in [5]. It is important to mention that the project arise as a necessity to find new solutions to collaborative work between robot arm manipulators in a manufacturing environment and trying to find new approaches on more complex tasks, such as packaging, dispensing, handling, material removal applications, among others.

Although XRC 2001 robot controller offers standard networks for DeviceNet, ControlNet, Profibus-DP, and Interbus-S, these approaches need to acquire several hardware and software modules, which only works under limited specifications and *ad-hoc* characteristics closely related with the supplier. At the end, this produces high cost solutions to customers and low interoperability across devices.

Motoman provides commercially available software to their robot controllers for calibration, off-line programming and communications tasks. Nevertheless, these do not provide enough customization to more specialized applications. As an example, VDE suite (Visual Data Exchange) which provides Ethernet communications on MRC and XRC controllers and standard RS-232C serial communications to run on the three mentioned controllers, works only under Windows platform. The program is limited to copy files between the robot controller and a PC, delete job files, and provide expanded storage area for robots jobs.

Probably, the most advanced communications software available for the XRC controller is MotoView. This program provides an interactive web interface to XRC robot controllers which allow the user to remotely monitor robot status, data and I/O. Likewise provides the user with robot file operation and manipulation capability. This approach has good advantages due to java platform usage but do not provide all the capabilities and advantages a distributed system must accomplish.

In this work we are using the concept of function encapsulation to create a set of generic objects that facilitate the development and integration of a distributed system using CORBA specification [6]. This goal is achieved using wrapper functions [7] which deal with the specific details of each equipment but give a more simple and powerful functionality to other components over the system.

The paper is organized as follows: Section II describes the main components used. In Section III, the architecture and implementation to integrate these modules are presented. Section IV provides an analysis of important issues. Finally, comments on future research is presented in section V.

2 Robotic System Description

We present a brief description of the main components used in this project. The components are as follows (see Fig. 1):

1. A Motoman UP6 robot arm manipulator (XRC2001 controller)
2. Two Pentium Computers
3. MotoCom SDK software library

We have as final goal to create a remote client-server application which facilitates the integration of one or several arm manipulators based on mentioned controllers independently from computer system or different platforms.

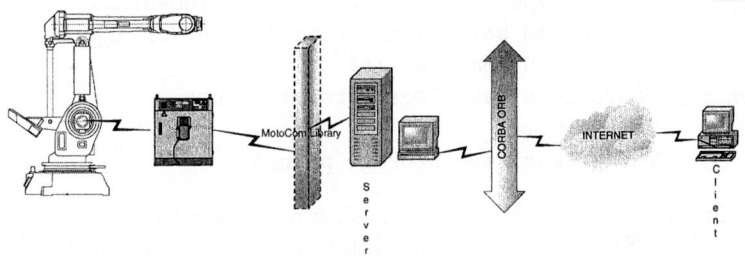

Fig. 1. UP6 CORBA-based system

Arm Manipulator. The arm manipulator is a Motoman UP6 manufactured by Yaskawa. High speed transmission can be achieved using an Ethernet I/F board in the XRC or MRC controller. Table 1 shows the basic operation limits for this robot arm.

Table 1. Physical limit and name of axes for UP6 robot arm manipulator

Axis	UP6	
	Maximum Motion Range	Maximum Speed
S-Axis (Turning/sep)	±170°	140°/s
L-Axis (Lower Arm)	+155°/-90°	160°/s
U-Axis (Upper Arm)	+190°/-170°	170°/s
R-Axis (Wrist Roll)	±180°	335°/s
B-Axis (Bend/Pitch/Yaw)	+225°, -45°	335°/s
T-Axis (Wrist Twist)	±360°	500°/s

Computers. Two computers are used for experimentation, one for GUI client and other one for robot server. First one is a Pentium Centrino at 1400MHz with 512 MB on RAM, the operating system is Windows XP-2002. Second one has similar characteristics.

MotoCom library. We are using MotoSoft SDK library. This component provides data transmission between a PC and Motoman controllers. The library is composed in the form of Windows DLL (Dynamic Link Library). It includes several functions for robot communication, file data transmission, status reading, robot control, read and write of I/O signals and other related characteristics. Below a representative C++ function definition is shown. This function moves the robot a specified motion from a current position to a target position.

```
BscMov (short nCid, char *movtype, char *vtpe, double spd, char
*framename, short rconf, short toolno, double *p);
```

```
nCid         Communication handler ID
*movtype     Motion type (joint, linear or incremental)
*vtype       Move speed selection (control point or angular)
spd          Move speed (mm/s or /s)
*framename   Coordinate name (base, robot or user)
toolno       Tool number
*p           Target position storage pointer
```

One limitation of this DLL usage is that requires a hardware key supplied with MotoCom SDK which must be installed on the PC parallel port (robot server) in order to work.

3 Integration

The communication between with the PC and the robot controller is made via Ethernet or standard RS-232C. Depending on robot controller evaluation (ERC, MRC or XRC), RS-232C internal port or teach pendant parameters must be first initialized. In case of Ethernet communication being preferred, proper Ethernet board must be installed in the robot controller so the device can communicate using TCP/IP protocol. Controller parameters must be initialized for an IP address, Subnet Mask, Default Gateway and Server Address. After proper setup, robot server only requires the robot IP address to establish a correct communication.

In this proposal, using CORBA, there are two main components which communicate each other using the following approaches: a) Naming Services and b) IDL interfaces. The first approach is useful to connect or reconnect the different modules through the network, without being concern with resolving IOR references. The client modules only need the name of the servers and the reference of the Naming Server, which is predefined in the system. The second approach convey the object paradigm, and the client applications use this interface to command or monitor the servers.

Robot server. This is a wrapper component [7], which process all calls to the arm manipulator from different clients. Function calls are listed in table 2. The robot server first gets the control of the arm robot to which is connected and based on several internal calls, it sets up the specific axis to be controlled [5].

Robot GUI. This is a client application which communicates with the robot server using the IOR reference provided by the Naming Service. Through this application the user or operator can manipulate the robot with basic movements.

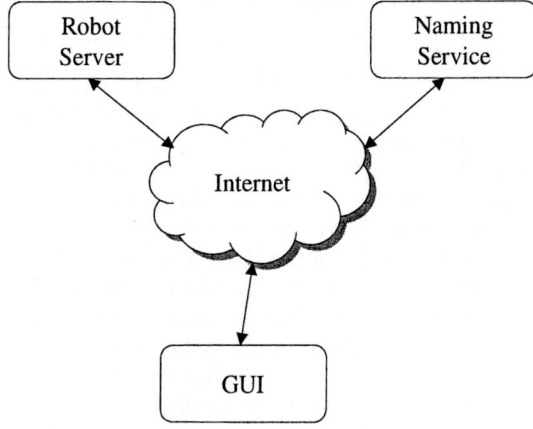

Fig. 2. Client and server components for UP6 CORBA-based system

3.1 Implementation

Robot Server.
The robot server is a software component, which links the Robot GUI interface with the robot controller. Main functions are as follows:

1. connect to the robot controller and get control access of the arm,
2. create its own reference and
3. register on the naming service

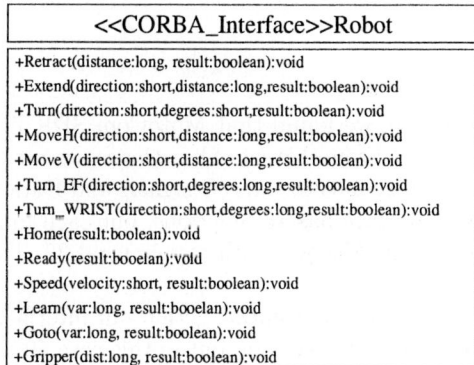

Fig. 3. Robot IDL Class represented in UML

After this, the robot server gets into an infinite loop waiting for commands to execute from the client side. If several clients want to have access to the

Table 2. Main Functions for robot arm manipulators

Functions	Arguments	Description
Extend	Distance	Extend the arm a specific distance
Retract	Distance	Retract the arm a specific distance
Move-H	Distance,Direction	Move the arm over the track a specific distance
Move-V	Distance,Direction	Move the arm UP or DOWN a specific distance
Turn	Degrees,Direction	Turn the base of the arm a specific angle
Turn-G	Degrees,Direction	Turn the End-Effector a specific angle
Turn-W	Degrees,Direction	Turn the Wrist a specific angle
MoveTo	Position	Move to a previous defined position
Learn	Position	Save the current arm position in a variable
Ready	NA	Move arm to Ready position
Home	NA	Move arm to Home position
Gripper	Position	Open/Close Gripper
Speed	Velocity	Set the speed for all movements

arm, then a FIFO policy is held to give control only one client a time. The IDL interface represented in UML, is shown below (Fig. 3). Although the number of functions is limited, they can move the End-Effector to different positions.

Tables 3 and 4 show all C++ functions available in MotoCom SDK library and the way several of these ones were encapsulated through CORBA wrapper components. This is done in order to implement the previously defined IDL interface. Some of these functions are wrapped in more than one component in order to accomplish the status or movement required. Likewise, there are several approaches to produce a specific movement, which one to use, depends on the specific task to realize. The approach that produces the best and more efficient result is selected.

4 Analysis

From previous information, we found that MotoCom SDK library has 74 functions categorized in 5 areas. From this set of functions, two areas are not managed by our interface; this corresponds to the I/O signals and Data File management. In the other hand our interface has 13 functions, but each function make use of one or more functions of the MotoCom library, in total 32. This gives a 43 % of utilization.

One important issue in this information is that our interface does not have an explicit query status of the robot system, but in this case 50 % of them (reading status) is used implicitly in our functions. Furthermore, the way these functions are called requires a specific sequence and data format that could change from one robot system to another. In short, our interface definition frees the client developer from dealing with many kinds of robots. The client developer is focus in a small number of functions which provides the functionality required for most kind of robot systems.

Table 3. MotoCom Functions implemented in CORBA Wrapper Functions. Adapted from [8].

Function	MotoCom Function Name	CORBA Wrapper Component
File data transmission function	BscDownload	-
	BscUpload	-
Robot Control Function or Reading Status	BscFindFirst	-
	BscFindFirstMaster	-
	BscFindNext	-
	BscGetCtrlGroup	-
	BscDownLoad	-
	BscGetError	Used in All
	BscGetFirstAlarm	Used in All
	BscGetStatus	Learn
	BscGetUFrame	-
	BscGetVarData	Learn
	BscIsAlarm	Ready
	BscIsCtrlGroup	-
	BscIsCycle	-
	BscIsError	Used in All
	BscIsErrorCode	Used in All
	BscIsHold	Ready
	BscIsJobLine	-
	BscIsJobName	-
	BscIsJobStep	-
	BscIsLoc	All except Speed
	BscIsPlaymode	Ready
	BscIsRemoteMode	Ready
	BscIsRobotPos	All except Speed
	BscIsTaskInf	-
	BscIsTeachMode	Ready
	BscJobWait	-

Another important issue is that many kinds of robots provide an extensive number of functions to manage the robot, and many of them use the same arguments or only vary in a few ones. Our interface is designed to manage with a variable number of similar functions by using flexible parameters. This method is similar to have a list of predefined functions or capacities and only the functions supported by the current robot system are enabled. As an example, some robots can manage a track where the robot can be displaced. This represent another degree of movement, in such case the MoveH() function deal with this movement, using the track if it exists or using a linear movement if this extra axis doesn't exist. Other typical example, is the exchange between robots of 5 DOF and 6 DOF. In this example, the last DOF corresponds to the wrist axis, and for the client developer is transparent. He doesn't have to bother which is the number of axis to move.

Table 4. MotoCom Functions implemented in CORBA Wrapper Functions, continuation

Function	MotoCom Function Name	CORBA Wrapper Component
Control of System	BscCancel	-
	BscChangeTask	-
	BscContinueJob	-
	BscConvertJobP2R	-
	BscConvertJobR2P	-
	BscDeleteJob	-
	BscHoldOff	Ready
	BscHoldOn	-
	BscImov	Extend, Retract, Speed
	BscMDSP	-
	BscMov	Move H, Move V, Speed
	BscMovj	Home, MoveTo, Move H, Move V, Speed
	BscMovl	Home, MoveTo, Gripper, Speed
	BscOPLock	-
	BscOPUnLock	-
	BscPMov	Turn, Turn-G, Turn-W, Speed
	BscPMovj	Turn, Turn-G, Turn-W, Speed
	BscPMovl	Turn, Turn-G, Turn-W, Speed
	BscPutUFrame	-
	BscPutVarData	Learn
	BscStartJob	-
	BscSelectJob	-
	BscSelectMode	Ready
	BscSelLoopCycle	-
	BscSelOneCycle	-
	BscSelStepCycle	Ready
	BscSetLineNumber	-
	BscSetMasterJob	-
	BscSetCtrlGroup	-
	BscServoOff	Ready
	BscServoOn	Ready
	BscUpload	-
Support of DCI function	BscDCILoadSave	-
	BscDCILoadSaveOnce	-
	BscDCIGetPos	MoveTo
	BscDCIPutPos	Learn
Read/Write of I/O signals	BscReadIO	-
	BscWriteIO	-
Other Functions	BscClose	Ready
	BscCommand	Ready
	BscConnect	Ready
	BscDisconnect	Ready
	BscDiskFreeSizeGet	-
	BscGets	-
	BscInBytes	-
	BscIsErrorCode	Ready
	BscOpen	Ready
	BscOutBytes	-
	BscPuts	-
	BscSetBreak	Ready
	BscSetComm	Ready
	BscSetCondBSC	Ready
	BscStatus	-

5 Conclusions

A commercial MOTOMAN arm manipulator is remotely operated using the Client-Server concept, Object encapsulation and CORBA middleware software. This work shows how with a few number of methods (or functions) but flexible designed interfaces, previous components from other applications can be reused without changes or just minor changes. There is a tradeoff between function encapsulation and robot performance. The first one allows easy integration in the client side but increases the complexity or programming effort in the server side. In the other hand, with a one-to-one mapping of robot functionality to robot interface, the integration effort becomes bigger on the client side. If the client side has the task to command the robot then the complexity of the client program increases according to the number of functions to deal with.

In future research we must include in the interface more functions to deal with I/O signals and Data File management, due to these concepts are managed by most of the commercial robots.

Acknowledgments. This work was supported by the TEC de Monterrey, Campus Monterrey.

References

1. L.G. Österlund, "Component Technology," in *Proceedings of the IEEE Computer Applications in Power.*, Vol 13, no. 1, pp. 17-25. January 2000.
2. J. N. Pires and J.M.G. S da Costa "Object-Oriented and Distributed Approach for Programming Robotic Manufacturing Cells," in *IFAC Journal Robotics and Computer Integrated Manufacturing*, Vol.16 no. 1 pp. 29-42, March 2000.
3. D. Flater, "Specification of Interactions in Integrated Manufacturing Systems," NISTIR, 6484, March 2000.
4. G. Beneken, U. Hammerschall, M.V. Cengarle, J. Jürgens, B. Rumpe, M. Schoenmakers, and M. Broy, "Componentware - State of the Art 2003," in *Understanding Component* Workshop of the CUE Initiative at the Univeritá Ca' Foscari di Venezia Venice, October 7-9, 2003.
5. F. Guedea, I. Song., F. Karray, R. Soto, "Enhancing Distributed Robotics Systems using CORBA," in *Proceedings of the First International Conference on Humanoid, Nanotechnologies, Information Technology, Communication and Control, Environment and Management 2003* " Manila, Philippines, March 27-29, 2003.
6. OMG, "Common Object Request Broker Architecture and specification," Technical Report, Object Management Group, Fall Church, USA, 2000 Release 2.4.
7. F. Guedea, I. Song., F. Karray, R. Soto, R. Morales, "Wrapper Component for Distributed Robotics Systems," in *Mexican International Conference on Artificial Intelligence 2004* " Mexico City, April 26-30, 2004, pp. 882-891.
8. MOTOMAN, "MotoCom SDK ," Function Manual, Motoman YASKAWA Electric Manufacturing, USA, 2002.

An Integration of FDI and DX Techniques for Determining the Minimal Diagnosis in an Automatic Way

Rafael Ceballos, Sergio Pozo, Carmelo Del Valle, and Rafael M. Gasca

Departamento de Lenguajes y Sistemas Informticos, Universidad de Sevilla,
Escuela Tcnica Superior de Ingeniera Informtica,
Avenida Reina Mercedes s/n 41012 Sevilla, Spain

Abstract. Two communities work in parallel in model-based diagnosis: FDI and DX. In this work an integration of the FDI and the DX communities is proposed. Only relevant information for the identification of the minimal diagnosis is used. In the first step, the system is divided into clusters of components, and each cluster is separated into nodes. The minimal and necessary set of contexts is then obtained for each cluster. These two steps automatically reduce the computational complexity since only the essential contexts are generated. In the last step, a signature matrix and a set of rules are used in order to obtain the minimal diagnosis. The evaluation of the signature matrix is on-line, the rest of the process is totally off-line.

1 Introduction

Diagnosis allows us to determine why a correctly designed system does not work as expected. Diagnosis is based on a set of integrated sensors which obtain a set of observations. The aim of diagnosis is to detect and identify the reason for any unexpected behaviour, and to isolate the parts which fail in a system. The behaviour of components is stored by using constraints. Inputs and outputs of components are represented as variables of the component constraints. These variables can be observable and non-observable depending on the allocation of the sensors.

Two communities work in parallel, although separately, in model-based diagnosis: FDI (from Automatic Control) and DX (from Artificial Intelligence). Nevertheless, the integration of FDI with DX theories has been shown in recent work [1],[2]. Within the DX community the work of Reiter [3] and De Kleer and Willians [4] introduce the basic definitions and foundations of diagnosis. A general theory was proposed to explain the discrepancies between the observed and the correct behaviour by using a logical-based diagnosis process. In the FDI community, [5] and [6] presented the formalization of structural analysis, the process to obtain the ARRs (Analytical Redundancy Relation) of the system.

In this work an integration of FDI theories with the DX community is proposed, in order to improve the minimal diagnosis determination. This integration has three phases. The structural pre-treatment in the first phase and the reduction of the model in the second phase enables the improvement of the computational complexity. The minimal diagnosis is obtained by applying an observational model to a signature matrix together with a set of compilation rules. The evaluation of the signature matrix is on-line, however the rest of the process is totally off-line.

Our paper has been organized as follows. First, definitions and notations are established in order to clarify concepts. Section 3 shows an example of the validation of this approach. Section 4 describes the advantages of the structural pretreatment. After that, in Section 5, the process for the definition of the context network is explained. Section 6 describes the determination of the minimal diagnosis. Finally, conclusions are drawn and future work is outlined.

2 Definitions and Notation

In order to clarify the diagnosis process some definitions must be established.

Definition 2.1. *System Model*: A finite set of polynomial equality constraints (P) which determine the system behaviour. This is done by means of the relations between non-observable (V_i) and observable variables (sensors) of the system (O_j).

Definition 2.2. *Observational Model*: A tuple of values for the observable variables.

Definition 2.3. *Context*: A collection of components of the system, and their associated constraints. The number of possible contexts is $2^{nComp} - 1$, where $nComp$ is the number of components of the system.

Definition 2.4. *Context Network*: A graph formed by all the contexts of the system in accordance with the way proposed by ATMS[7]. The context network has a natural structure of a directed graph for set inclusion.

Definition 2.5. *Diagnosis Problem*: A tuple formed by a system model and an observational model. The solution to this problem is a set of possible failed components.

3 Example

Figure 1a shows a polybox system. This polybox system is derived from the standard problem used in the diagnosis community [4]. The system consists of fifteen components: nine multipliers, and six adders. The observable variables are represented by shaded circles in Figure 1a.

4 Structural Pretreatment

The first part of this section shows the way to divide the diagnosis problem into independent diagnosis subproblems. The second part of this section explains the

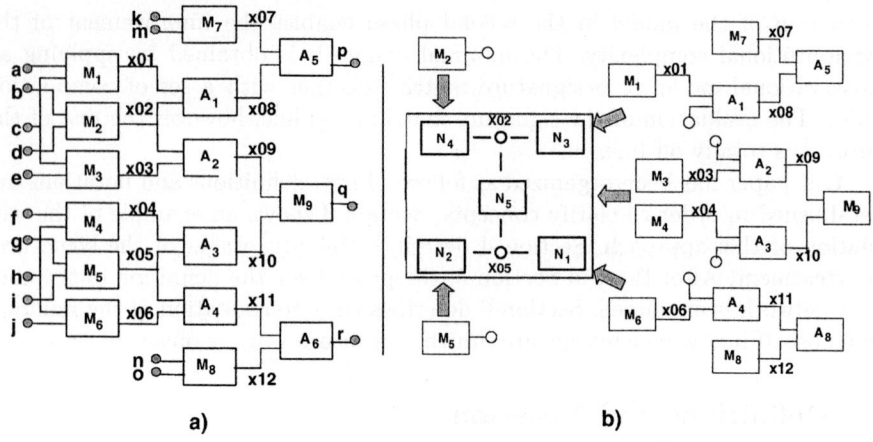

Fig. 1. a) Polybox example b) Nodes of the polybox example

way of grouping the components into nodes in order to reduce the number of non-observable variables to be considered in the system.

4.1 Identification of the Clusters

The objective of this section is the partition of the system into independent subsets of components. This partition reduces the computational complexity of the diagnosis process since it enables the generation of the diagnosis of the whole system based on the diagnosis of the subsystems.

Definition 4.1. *Cluster of components*: A set of components T is a cluster, if it does not exist a common non-observable variable of any component of the cluster with any component outside the cluster, and if for all $T' \subset T$, T' is not a cluster of components. In a cluster, all common non-observable variables among the components belong to the same cluster, therefore all the connections with components which are outside the cluster are monitored. A cluster of components is totally monitored, and for this reason the detection of faults inside the cluster is possible without information from other components which do not belong to the cluster. A more detailed explanation and the cluster detection algorithm appears in [2].

The diagnosis space for a system initially consists of 2^{nComp} diagnoses [4], where $nComp$ is the number of components of the system. Therefore the computational complexity for the diagnosis process is always smaller for an equivalent system divided into clusters, due to the reduced number of possible diagnoses.

4.2 Obtaining Relations Without Non-observable Variables

In the diagnosis process it is necessary to produce new relations without non-observable variables, in order to monitor the system behaviour by using only the observational model. Our approach uses a function named *NewRelations* (NR) which takes a set of constraints and obtains a set of new constraints without a set of non-observable variables. Example: NR({x-a·c, y-b·d, f-x-y}, {x ,y}) = {a·c + b·d - f = 0}.

This function can be implemented using different techniques. The Gröbner Basis algorithm [8] is used here. Gröbner basis theory is the origin of many symbolic algorithms used to manipulate equality polynomials. It is a combination of Gaussian elimination (for linear systems) and the Euclidean algorithm (for univariate polynomials over a field). The Gröbner basis can be used to produce an equivalent system which has the same solution as the original, and without having non-observable variables.

4.3 Obtaining the Nodes of Each Cluster

The main assumption in this paper is to suppose that only one constraint is associated to each component. If it is necessary to apply this methodology to components with n constraints (where $n > 1$), it is then possible decoupling the component x into n virtual components x_i with one constraint each.

Our approach provides the minimal set of constraints to detect all the possible diagnoses of a system. The introduction of new definitions is necessary in order to efficiently generate this set of constraints:

Definition 4.2. *Dispensable variable*: A non-observable variable v_i is dispensable if there exist only two components x_i and x_j which include this variable in their related constraints. In the polybox example the variable x04 and the variable x08 are dispensable variables.

Definition 4.3. *Node of components*: A single component could be a node of components if none of its non-observable variables is a dispensable variable. Two components, or, a component and a node of components, belong to the same node of components if they have a common dispensable variable.

Algorithm: The algorithm for the identification of the nodes of a cluster begins by creating n nodes, where n is the number of components of the cluster. All these nodes have initially one component. When a dispensable variable v is detected, the two nodes, which include v in their constraints, are merged into one node. The process ends when all the disponsable variables are detected. Each node contains a set of constraints and a set of dispensable variables.

When all the nodes are identified, new set of constraints, without the dispensable variables is obtained, by applying the *NewRelations* function to the set of constraints of each node. If the node of components have no dispensable variables it is not necessary to apply the *NewRelations* function.

In the DX community diagnoses are determined by conflicts. Many methodologies try to use the structural description of the system, those methods are known as compilation methods. In [9] the Possible Conflicts (PCs) concept is proposed as a compilation technique. Each PC represents a subsystem within system description containing minimal analytical redundancy and being capable

Table 1. Improvements obtained using structural pretreatment in the examples

Example	Clusters	Nodes	No pretreatment			With pretreatment		
			Vars.	Ctxs.	Elapsed time	Vars.	Ctxs.	Elapsed time
Polybox	1	5	12	$2^{15}-1$	32 seconds	2	31	31 milliseconds

of becoming a conflict. Computing Analytical Redundancy Relations (ARRs)[5] is the compilation technique of FDI methodology.

Our approach provide the minimal set of contexts which include an overdetermined system of constraints that can detect a conflict in a cluster. The contexts are built by using nodes of components instead of components, since it is impossible to generate constraints without non-observable variables by using a subset of a node, because it will be impossible to substitute a dispensable variable of the node, which only appears in one component of the context.

Example: Figure 1b shows the partition of the polybox example into nodes. Table 1 shows the results obtained in the proposed example. The column *Nodes* shows the addition of all the nodes included in the clusters of the system. The column *Vars* shows the initial number of non-observable variables, and the final number of non-observable variables after the structural pretreatment. The column *Ctxs* shows the total number of possible contexts of the system, and the final number of possible contexts by using the structural pretreatment. The column elapsed time shows the necessary time to process the set of contexts of the system if the time to process one context is supposed to be 1 millisecond. In the polybox example 1 cluster is obtained. The non-observable variables are reduced from 12 to 2. Table 2 shows the list of nodes of the polybox example, and the constraint obtained in each node by eliminating the dispensable variables.

5 Determination of the Context Network

Our approach provide the minimal set of contexts which can detect a conflict in a cluster. The minimality issue was not guaranteed in the original ARR approach, but its guaranteed in our approach. In [9] approach the PCs are obtained directly by using components, but our approach use nodes instead of components,

Table 2. Nodes for the polybox example

Nodes	Components	Constraints	Dispensable var.	Non-Obs var.
N_1	$M_6M_8A_4A_6$	$h \cdot j + n \cdot o - r + x05$	{x06, x11, x12}	{x05}
N_2	M_5	$g \cdot i - x05$	{}	{x05}
N_3	$M_1M_7A_1A_5$	$a \cdot c + k \cdot m - p + x02$	{x01, x07, x08}	{x02}
N_4	M_2	$b \cdot d - x02$	{}	{x02}
N_5	$M_3M_4M_9A_2A_3$	$q - (f \cdot h + x05) \cdot (x02 + c \cdot e)$	{x03, x04, x09, x10}	{x02, x05}

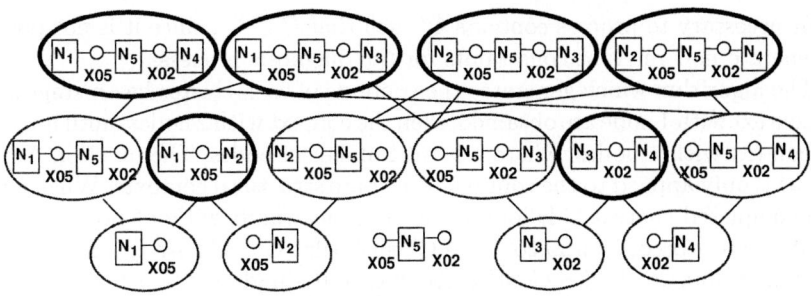

Fig. 2. Context network of the polybox example

therefore the size of the problem is reduced from 2^c, where c is the number of components, to 2^n, where n is the number of nodes.

A context network, in accordance with the way proposed by ATMS[7], is generated in order to obtain all the relevant contexts for the diagnosis process. In order to establish the smallest set of contexts it is necessary to introduce the following definitions.

Definition 5.1. *Structural context*: This is a context where all the nodes are connected, that is, they compose a connected graph, and all the non-observable variables appear in at least two constraints. The function to determine which are structural contexts is named *isAStructural* and takes a context C and returns a true value if it is a structural context.

Definition 5.2. *Minimal completed context*: A structural context C is a completed context if the set of constraints of the nodes of the context is an overdetermined system of constraints, and, if it is possible to generate new constraints without non-observable variables by using the set of constraints of the context. A completed context is minimal if no context C' $\subset$ C exists such that C' is a completed context.

If C is a minimal completed context then all the context C' exists, where C $\subset$ C', can only generate constraints which can be generated with context that contains fewer nodes. Therefore, if a context C is a minimal completed context it

Table 3. CARCs obtained in the polybox example

Index	Context	CARC
1	N_1N_2	h·j + n·o - r + g·i
2	N_3N_4	a·c + k·m - p + b·d
3	$N_1N_3N_5$	q - (f·h - h·j - n·o + r)·(-a·c - k·m + p + c·e)
4	$N_1N_4N_5$	q - (f·h - h·j - n·o + r)·(b·d + c·e)
5	$N_2N_3N_5$	q - (f·h + g·i)·(-a·c - k·m + p + c·e)
6	$N_2N_4N_5$	q - (f·h + g·i)·(b·d + c·e)

is not necessary to process contexts C' such that C ⊂ C', since it is not possible to generate new relevant constraints for the diagnosis process.

The algorithm which generates the contexts of each cluster has n stages, first the context with 1 node are obtained, then the context with 2 nodes, until it reaches the context with n nodes, where n is the number of nodes. The function *NewRelations* is only applied to the contexts which are structural contexts. When a minimal completed context C is found, the new constraints without non-observable variables are stored, and no contexts C', such that C ⊂ C', are generated. These new constraints are named Context Analytical Redundancy Constraint.

Definition 5.3. *Context Analytical Redundancy Constraint (CARC)*: A constraint obtained from a minimal completed context in such a way that only the observed variables are related.

Example: In order to clarify this section, Tables 2 and 3 shows the results obtained for the polybox example. This system includes only one cluster with 15 components. The number of possible contexts is reduced from $2^{15}-1$ to 2^5-1. By applying the rules and the algorithm proposed in this section, 14 contexts of the possible 31 (2^5-1) are generated, however only 6 are minimal completed contexts. These 6 contexts generate 6 CARCs. Figure 2 shows the context network of the polybox example. Only the treated contexts are circled. The minimal completed contexts are circled in bold.

6 Determination of the Minimal Diagnoses

The last step is the determination of the minimal diagnoses using the set of CARCs. In order to clarify the methodology, we suppose that the sensor observations are correct. We propose using a signature matrix as in FDI, but in order to obtain the same minimal diagnoses as in DX approach, it is necessary to apply a set of rules which guarantee the no-exoneration case in the solution.

Definition 6.1. *Fault signature*: Given a set of n CARCs, denoted CARC= {$CARC_1$, $CARC_2$, ..., $CARC_n$}, and a set of m faults denoted F = {F_1,...,F_m}, the signature of a fault F_j is given by $FS_j = [s_{1j},..., s_{nj}]^T$ in which $s_{ij} = 1$ if the context which generated the $CARC_i$ involves the nodes included in the fault F_j, and $s_{ij} = 0$ otherwise.

Definition 6.2. *Signature matrix*: All the signatures for the set of possible faults constitute the signature matrix.

Definition 6.3. *Signature of an observation*: This is given by OS=[OS_1,...,OS_n] where OS_i=0 if the $CARC_i$ is satisfied, and OS_i=1 otherwise.

Definition 6.4. *Diagnosis set*: The set of faults whose signatures are consistent with the signature of the observational model. Our approach assumes that an observation signature OS is consistent with another signature FS_j if $OS_i = s_{ij}\ \forall$ i.

Definition 6.5. *Minimal diagnosis*: A fault F_j is a minimal diagnosis if F_k is not a diagnosis $\forall$ faults $F_k \subset F_j$.

Table 4 shows the signature matrix for the polybox example in order to clarify these definitions and the process to obtain the minimal diagnoses. The signature $OK = [0, ..., 0]^T$ represents the no-fault case. The signature matrix is very similar to the corresponding matrix in the FDI methodology. However in our approach, the faults involve nodes instead of components.

In this example it is necessary to expand the number of columns of the signature matrix in order to consider multiple faults. Each fault F_j, which involves n nodes, is obtained using a fault F_k, which involves $n-1$ nodes, and a simple fault F_s which is not involved in F_k. The multiple fault signature F_j is given by $FS_j = [s_{1j}, ..., s_{nj}]^T$ in which $s_{ij} = 0$ if $s_{ik} = s_{is}$, and $s_{ij} = 1$ otherwise. The multiple fault signature F_j is not added to the signature matrix if $\forall\, s_{ij} : s_{ij} = 1 \rightarrow s_{ij} = s_{ik}$, due to the implication that the new multiple fault is a superset of a previously obtained fault which involves fewer nodes, and therefore cannot be part of a minimal diagnosis. The generation of the signature matrix stops when it is impossible to generate new signatures of faults which involve n nodes, with the faults which involve $n-1$ nodes.

In FDI, the exoneration assumption [1] is implied, that is, given an observational model, each component of the support of a satisfied CARC is considered as functioning correctly, that is, it is exonerated. In the DX approach, the exoneration is not considered by default.

In order to obtain the same results as in the DX approach by using a signature matrix, it is necessary to apply a new definition of consistency. In the no-exoneration case an observation signature OS is consistent with another signature FS_j if $\forall\, OS_i = 1$ then $s_{ij} = 1$. That is, only the non-satisfied CARCs are used, and F_j must have the value 1 in each non-satisfied CARC. When the diagnosis set is obtained by using the new definition of consistency, we propose the application of a set of rules in order to detect which of the faults are minimal diagnoses, since many faults will be consistent with the observational model although they are not a minimal diagnosis. The following algorithm generates the rules to obtain the minimal diagnoses.

Algorithm: Let CS(OS,FS) be a function which evaluates whether the signature OS is consistent with signature FS. For each possible fault F_j in the signature matrix, let MD_{Fj} be a Boolean variable which holds information on whether a fault F_j is a minimal diagnosis, and let VC_{Fj} be a Boolean variable which holds information on whether a fault F_j is a valid candidate for the generation of new faults that could be a minimal diagnosis. For each possible fault F_j it is initially supposed that $VC_{Fj} = true$.

The first step is to validate if the OK (no fault case) is a minimal diagnosis: $MD_{OK} = CS(OS, OKS)$, and, for any simple fault F_j, the equality $VC_{Fj} = \neg MD_{OK}$ must be satisfied.

If OK is not a minimal diagnosis, the following rules must be evaluated for all the possible faults (except OK) in the same sequential order as they appear in

Table 4. The signature matrix of the polybox example

CARC	OK	F_1	F_2	F_3	F_4	F_5	F_{12}	F_{13}	F_{14}	F_{15}	F_{23}	F_{24}	F_{25}	F_{34}	F_{35}	F_{45}	F_{xxx}
1	0	1	1	0	0	0	1	1	1	1	1	1	1	0	0	0	1
2	0	0	0	1	1	0	0	1	1	0	1	1	0	1	1	1	1
3	0	1	0	1	0	1	1	1	1	1	1	0	1	1	1	1	1
4	0	1	0	0	1	1	1	1	1	1	0	1	1	1	1	1	1
5	0	0	1	1	0	1	1	1	0	1	1	1	1	1	1	1	1
6	0	0	1	0	1	1	1	0	1	1	1	1	1	1	1	1	1

$F_{xxx} \subset \{F_{123}, F_{124}, F_{134}, F_{135}, F_{145}, F_{234}, F_{235}, F_{245}\}$

	OK	F_1	F_2	F_3	F_4	F_5	F_{12}	F_{13}	F_{14}	F_{15}	F_{23}	F_{24}	F_{25}	F_{34}	F_{35}	F_{45}	F_{xxx}
VC	1	1	1	1	1	1	1	1	1	0	1	1	0	1	0	0	0
MD	0	0	0	0	0	1	1	0	0	0	0	0	0	1	0	0	0

VC and MD values for the observation signature OS = $[0, 0, 1, 1, 1, 1]^T$

Table 5. A subset of the rules for the polybox example

MD_{OK} = CS(OS,OKS)	$MD_{F1} \Rightarrow VC_{F14}$ = false	$MD_{F13} \Rightarrow VC_{F123}$ = false
$VC_{F1} = \neg MD_{OK}$	...	$MD_{F13} \Rightarrow VC_{F134}$ = false
...	$MD_{F1} \Rightarrow VC_{F15}$ = false	$MD_{F13} \Rightarrow VC_{F135}$ = false
$VC_{F5} = \neg MD_{OK}$	$MD_{F2} = VC_{F2} \wedge$ CS(OS,FS$_2$)	$MD_{F14} = VC_{F14} \wedge$ CS(OS,FS$_{14}$)
$MD_{F1} = VC_{F1} \wedge$ CS(OS,FS$_1$)	...	...
$MD_{F1} \Rightarrow VC_{F12}$ = false	$MD_{F13} = VC_{F13} \wedge$ CS(OS,FS$_{13}$)	$MD_{F245} = VC_{F245} \wedge$ CS(OS,FS$_{245}$)

the signature matrix. These rules guarantee the correct detection of the minimal diagnoses for an observational model:

- For each fault F_j with the signature FS_j, the equality $MD_{Fj} = VC_{Fj} \wedge$ CS(OS,FS$_j$) must be satisfied.
- For each fault F_k which involves n + 1 nodes, where n $\geq$ 0, and which can be obtained using the fault F_j (that involves n nodes) and a simple fault F_s (which is not involved in F_j) then $MD_{Fj} \Rightarrow VC_{Fk}$ = false.

Example: Table 5 shows a subset of the rules for the polybox example. The generation of the rules for the verification of whether a fault is a minimal diagnosis can be done off-line, because these rules are the same for all the observational models. The bottom of Table 4 shows the VC and MD evaluation results for the observation signature OS = $[0, 0, 1, 1, 1, 1]^T$. Only the evaluation of the rules must be done on-line. This part of the process is a simple propagation of Boolean values.

The evaluation of the signature matrix is very similar to the FDI methodology. However in our approach, the faults involve nodes instead of components. Hence, the last step is the substitution of each node with one of its components. In the polybox example, fault F_3 is equivalent to the faults in $\{\{M_1\}, \{M_7\},$

$\{A_1\}, \{A_5\}\}$; fault F_{12} is equivalent to faults $\{\{M_6M_5\}, \{M_8M_5\}, \{A_4M_5\}, \{A_6M_5\}\}$; and so on.

The information of all the possible minimal diagnoses is stored in a matrix and as a set of rules. Therefore, it is only necessary to calculate this matrix and rules once. As happens in FDI methodology, this work can be done off-line, only the evaluation of the signature matrix and rules is on-line. Our approach provide always the minimal diagnoses set of the system by using an observational model. The minimality issue was not guaranteed in the original FDI approach since only the signature matrix is used, but it is guaranteed in our approach since the compilation rules are added to the diagnosis process.

7 Conclusions and Future Work

This paper proposes a new approach to automation of and improvement in the determination of minimal diagnosis. The approach is based on FDI and DX theories. The structural pre-treatment in the first phase and the reduction of the model in the second phase enable improvement in the computational complexity. All the possible minimal diagnoses are represented as a signature matrix and as a set of rules. It is only necessary to calculate this matrix and rules once. The minimal diagnosis is obtained by using an observational model, the signature matrix and a set of compilation rules. Only the evaluation of the compilation rules and signature matrix is on-line, the rest of the process can be done off-line.

The methodology was applied to an standard example, and the results were very promising. As future work we suggest extending the methodology to include dynamic systems and to include more complex and real problems, where the application of the methodology could be more complicated.

Acknowledgment

This work has been funded by the M. de Ciencia y Tecnología of Spanish (DPI2003-07146-C02-01) and the European Regional Development Fund.

References

1. Cordier, M., Lévy, F., Montmain, J., Travé-Massuyés, L., Dumas, M., Staroswiecki, M., Dague, P.: A comparative analysis of AI and control theory approaches to model-based diagnosis. In: 14th European Conference on Artificial Intelligence. (2000) 136–140
2. Ceballos, R., Gómez López, M. T., Gasca, R., Pozo, S.: Determination of Possible Minimal Conflict Sets using Components Clusters and Grobner Bases. In: DX04, 15th International Workshop on Principles of Diagnosis, Carcassonne, France (2004) 21–26
3. Reiter, R.: A theory of diagnosis from first principles. Artificial Intelligence 32 **1** (1987) 57–96

4. de Kleer, J., Mackworth, A., Reiter, R.: Characterizing diagnoses and systems. Artificial Intelligence **2-3** (1992) 197–222
5. Staroswiecki, M., Declerk, P.: Analytical redundancy in non linear interconnected systems by means of structural analysis. In: IFAC Advanced Information Processing in Automatic Control (AIPAC-89), Nacy, France (1989) 51–55
6. Cassar, J., Staroswiecki, M.: A structural approach for the design of failure detection and identification systems. In: IFAC-IFIP-IMACS Conf. on Control of Industrial Processes, Belfort, France. (1997)
7. de Kleer, J.: An assumption-based truth maintenance system. Artificial Intelligence **2** (1986) 127–161
8. Buchberger, B.: Gröbner bases: An algorithmic method in polynomial ideal theory. Multidimensional Systems Theory, N. K. Bose, ed. (1985) 184–232
9. Pulido, B., González, C.A.: Possible conflicts: A compilation technique for consistency-based diagnosis. IEEE Transactions on Systems, Man, and Cybernetics **34** (2004) 2192–2206

Evolutionary Dynamic Optimization of a Continuously Variable Transmission for Mechanical Efficiency Maximization

Jaime Alvarez-Gallegos[1], Carlos Alberto Cruz Villar[1], and Edgar Alfredo Portilla Flores[2]

[1] CINVESTAV-IPN,
Electrical Engineering Department,
Apdo. Postal 14-740, 07300,
Mexico DF, Mexico
{jalvarez, cacruz}@cinvestav.mx

[2] Universidad Autónoma de Tlaxcala,
Engineering and Technology Department,
Calz. Apizaquito S/N Km. 15, 90300, Apizaco, Tlax. Mexico
eportilla@ingenieria.uatx.mx

Abstract. This paper presents a dynamic optimization approach based on the differential evolution (DE) strategy which is applied to the concurrent optimal design of a continuously variable transmission (CVT). The structure-control integration approach is used to state the concurrent optimal design as a dynamic optimization problem which is solved using the Constraint Handling Differential Evolution (CHDE) algorithm. The DE strategy is compared with the sequential approach. The results presented here demonstrate that the DE strategy is less expensive than the sequential approach from the computational implementation point of view.

1 Introduction

The traditional approach for the design of mechatronic systems, considers the mechanical behavior and the dynamic performance separately. Usually, the design of the mechanical elements involves kinematic and static behaviors while the design of the control system uses only the dynamic behavior; therefore, from a dynamic point of view this approach cannot produce an optimal system behavior [1], [2]. Recent works on mechatronic systems design propose a concurrent design methodology which considers jointly the mechanical and control performances [3].

In this paper an alternative methodology to formulate the system design problem of mechatronic systems is to state it in the dynamic optimization framework. In order to do so, the parametric optimal design and the proportional and integral (PI) controller gains of a pinion-rack continuously variable transmission (CVT) is stated as a dynamic optimization problem (DOP). The kinematic and dynamic models of the mechanical structure and the dynamic model of the controller are jointly considered, besides a system performance criterion and a set of constraints which states the mechanical structure and the controller specifications. The methodology goal is to obtain a set of optimal mechanical and controller parameters which can produce a simple system reconfiguration.

Methods usually employed to solve the resulting DOP belong to the nonlinear programming field. However, these classical methods need a point to initialize the optimization search, then consequently the convergence of the algorithm depends on the chosen point. Moreover, the nonlinear programming approach is able to produce only one possible solution. On the other hand, a recently population-based evolutionary optimization algorithm the so called Differential Evolution (DE) has been successfully applied on mechanical design optimization [4], [5]; however in these papers the mechanical design problem is stated as a static optimization problem.

The DE strategy is very similar to standard evolutionary algorithms, the main difference is in the reproduction step. An arithmetic operator is used in this step, which means that the DE algorithm can directly operate on genes (design variables). In this paper the DE algorithm named CHDE (Constraint Handling Differential Evolution) presented in [11] is used, because the standard DE algorithms lack of a mechanism to bias the search towards the feasible region in constrained spaces. The CHDE algorithm proposes a constraint-handling approach, which relies on three simple selection criteria based on feasibility to bias the search towards the feasible region. These constraint-handling approach produces a very powerful search for constrained optimization problems.

The paper is organized as follows: In Section 2 the description and the dynamic CVT model are presented. The design variable, performance criteria and constraints to be used in the concurrent optimal CVT design are established in Section 3. A brief description of the algorithms used in this paper is presented in Section 4. Section 5 presents some optimization results and discuss them. Finally, in Section 6 some conclusions and future work are presented.

2 Description and Dynamic CVT Model

Current research efforts in the field of power transmission of rotational propulsion systems, are dedicated to obtain low energy consumption with high mechanical efficiency. An alternative solution to this problem is the so called continuously variable transmission (CVT), whose transmission ratio can be continuously changed in an established range. A pinion-rack CVT which is a traction-drive mechanism is presented in [7], this CVT is built-in with conventional mechanical elements as a gear pinion, one cam and two pair of racks. The conventional CVT manufacture is an advantage over other existing CVT's.

In order to apply the design methodology proposed in this paper, the pinion-rack CVT is used. In [8] a dynamic model of a pinion-rack CVT is developed. Ordinary differential equation system (1) describes the CVT dynamic behavior. There, T_m is the input torque , J_1 is the mass moment of inertia of the gear pinion, b_1 is the input shaft coefficient viscous damping, r is the gear pinion pitch circle radius, T_L is the CVT load torque, J_2 is the mass moment of inertia of the rotor, R is the planetary gear pitch circle radius, b_2 is the output shaft coefficient viscous damping and θ is the angular displacement of the rotor. On the other hand, L, R_m, K_b, K_f and n represent the armature circuit inductance, the circuit resistance, the back electro-motive force constant, the motor torque constant and the gearbox gear ratio of the DC motor, respectively. Parameters r_p, λ and b_c denote the pitch radius, the lead angle and the viscous damping coefficient of the lead screw, respectively. $J_{eq} = J_{c2} + Mr_p^2 + n^2 J_{c1}$ is the equivalent mass moment of inertia and $d = r_p \tan \lambda$, is a lead screw function. Moreover, $\theta_R(t) = \frac{1}{2} \arctan\left[\tan\left(2\Omega t - \frac{\pi}{2}\right)\right]$ is the rack angle meshing. The combined mass to be translated is denoted by M and $P = \frac{T_m}{r_p} \tan \phi \cos \theta_R$ is the loading on the gear pinion teeth, where ϕ is the pressure angle. The state variables $x_1 = \dot{\theta}$, $x_2 = i$, $x_3 = e$ and $x_4 = \dot{e}$ are the angular speed of the rotor, the input current of the DC motor, the CVT offset and the displacement speed of the offset, respectively. The control signal $u(t)$ is the input voltage to the DC motor.

$$\dot{x}_1 = \frac{T_m A + \left[J_1 A \frac{x_3}{r} \sin \theta_R\right] x_1^2 - \left[b_2 + b_1 A^2 + J_1 A \frac{x_4}{r} \cos \theta_R\right] x_1 - T_L}{J_2 + J_1 A^2}$$

$$\dot{x}_2 = \frac{u(t) - \left(\frac{nK_b}{d}\right) x_4 - Rx_2}{L} \qquad (1)$$

$$\dot{x}_3 = x_4$$

$$\dot{x}_4 = \frac{\left(\frac{nK_f}{d}\right) x_2 - \left(b_l + \frac{b_c}{r_p d}\right) x_4 - \frac{T_m}{r_p} \tan \phi \cos \theta_R}{M + \frac{J_{eq}}{d^2}}$$

$$y = x_1$$

where

$$A = 1 + \frac{x_3}{r} \cos \theta_R; \quad \theta_R(t) = \frac{1}{2} \arctan\left[\tan\left(2x_1 t - \frac{\pi}{2}\right)\right] \qquad (2)$$

3 Concurrent Optimal Design

In order to apply the design methodology proposed in this work, two criteria are considered. The first criterion is the mechanical CVT efficiency which considers the mechanical parameters and the second criterion is the minimal energy consumption which considers the controller gains and the dynamic system behavior.

3.1 Performance Criteria and Objective Functions

The performance of a system is measured by several criteria, one of the most used criterion is the system efficiency because it reflects the energy loss. In this work, the first criterion used in order to apply the design methodology is the mechanical efficiency criterion of the gear system. This is because the racks and the gear pinion are the principal CVT mechanical elements.

In a previous work we have stated that in order to maximize the mechanical CVT efficiency, the $\Phi_1(\cdot)$ function given by (3) must be minimized. Equation (3) states the design problem objective function, where N_1, e and r represent the gear pinion teeth number, the CVT offset and the pitch pinion radius respectively.

$$\Phi_1(\cdot) = \frac{1}{N_1}\left(\frac{2r + e\cos\theta_R}{r + e\cos\theta_R}\right) \qquad (3)$$

On the other hand, in order to obtain the minimal controller energy, the design problem objective function given by (4) is used.

$$\Phi_2(\cdot) = \frac{1}{2}\left[-K_p(x_{ref} - x_1) - K_I\int_0^t (x_{ref} - x_1)d\right]^2 \qquad (4)$$

In (4), a proportional and integral (PI) controller structure is used, this is because in spite of the development of many control strategies, the proportional, integral and derivative (PID) controller remains as the most popular approach for industrial processes control due to the adequate performance in most of such applications.

3.2 Constraint Functions

The design constraints for the CVT optimization problem are proposed according to geometric and strength conditions for the gear pinion of the CVT.

To prevent fracture of the annular portion between the axe bore and the teeth root on the gear pinion, the pitch circle diameter of the pinion gear must be greater than the bore diameter by at least 2.5 times the module [10]. Then, in order to avoid fracture, the constraint g_1 must be imposed. To achieve a load uniform distribution on the teeth, the face width must be 6 to 12 times the value of the module [1], this is ensured with constraints g_2 and g_3. To maintain the CVT transmission ratio in the range $[2r, 5r]$ constraints g_4, g_5 are imposed. Constraint g_6 ensures a teeth number of the gear pinion equal or greater than 12 [1]. A practical constraint requires that the gear pinion face width must be equal or greater than $20mm$, in order to ensure that, constraint g_7 is imposed. To constraint the distance between the corner edge in the rotor and the edge rotor, constraint g_8 is imposed. Finally to ensure a practical design for the pinion gear, the pitch circle radius must be equal or greater than $25.4mm$, then constraint g_9 is imposed.

On the other hand, it can be observed that J_1, J_2 are parameters which are function of the CVT geometry. For this mechanical elements the mass moments of inertia are defined by (5), where ρ, m, N, h, e_{max}, r_c and r_s are the material density, the module, the teeth number of the gear pinion, the face width, the highest offset distance between axes, the rotor radius and the bearing radius, respectively.

$$J_1 = \frac{1}{32}\rho\pi m^4 (N+2)^2 N^2 h; \quad J_2 = \rho h \left[\frac{3}{4}\pi r_c^4 - \frac{16}{6}(e_{max} + mN)^4 - \frac{1}{4}\pi r_s^4\right] \tag{5}$$

3.3 Design Variables

In order to propose a vector of design variables for the concurrent optimal CVT design, the standard nomenclature for a gear tooth is used.

Equation (6) states a parameter called module m for metric gears, where d is the pitch diameter and N is the teeth number.

$$m = \frac{d}{N} = \frac{2r}{N} \tag{6}$$

The face width h, which is the distance measured along the axis of the gear and the highest offset distance between axes e_{max} are parameters which define the CVT size. The above design variables belong to the mechanical structure. On the other hand, the gain controllers belong to the dynamic CVT behavior. Therefore, the vector p^i which considers mechanical and dynamic design variables is proposed in order to carry out the concurrent optimal CVT design.

$$p^i = [p_1^i, p_2^i, p_3^i, p_4^i, p_5^i, p_6^i]^T = [N, m, h, e_{max}, K_P, K_I]^T \tag{7}$$

3.4 Optimization Problem

In order to obtain the optimal values of the mechanical CVT parameters and the controller gains, we propose a dynamic optimization problem, as follows

$$\min_{p \in R^6} F(x, p, t) = \int_0^{10} \Phi_n dt \quad n = 1, 2 \tag{8}$$

subject to

$$\dot{x}_1 = \frac{AT_m + \left[J_1 A \frac{2x_3}{p_1 p_2}\sin\theta_R\right]x_1^2 - T_L - \left[b_2 + b_1 A^2 + J_1 A \frac{2x_4}{p_1 p_2}\cos\theta_R\right]x_1}{J_2 + J_1 A^2}$$

$$\dot{x}_2 = \frac{u(t) \quad (\frac{nK_b}{d})x_4 - Rx_2}{L} \tag{9}$$

$$\dot{x}_3 = x_4$$

$$\dot{x}_4 = \frac{(\frac{nK_f}{d})x_2 - (b_l + \frac{b_c}{r_p d})x_4 - \frac{T_m}{r_p}\tan\phi\cos\theta_R}{M + \frac{J_{eq}}{d^2}}$$

$$u(t) = -p_5(x_{ref} - x_1) - p_6 \int_0^t (x_{ref} - x_1)dt \tag{10}$$

$$J_1 = \frac{1}{32}\rho\pi p_2^4 (p_1+2)^2 p_1^2 p_3 \qquad (11)$$

$$J_2 = \frac{\rho p_3}{4}\left[3\pi r_c^4 - \frac{32}{3}(p_4+p_1 p_2)^4 - \pi r_s^4\right] \qquad (12)$$

$$A = 1 + \frac{2x_3}{p_1 p_2}\cos\theta_R \qquad (13)$$

$$d = r_p \tan\lambda \qquad (14)$$

$$\theta_R = \frac{1}{2}\arctan\left[\tan\left(2x_1 t - \frac{\pi}{2}\right)\right] \qquad (15)$$

$$\begin{aligned}
g_1 &= 0.01 - p_2(p_1 - 2.5) \le 0 \\
g_2 &= 6 - \frac{p_3}{p_2} \le 0 \\
g_3 &= \frac{p_3}{p_2} - 12 \le 0 \\
g_4 &= p_1 p_2 - p_4 \le 0 \\
g_5 &= p_4 - \frac{5}{2}p_1 p_2 \le 0 \\
g_6 &= 12 - p_1 \le 0 \\
g_7 &= 0.020 - p_3 \le 0 \\
g_8 &= 0.020 - \left[r_c - \sqrt{2}(p_4 + p_1 p_2)\right] \le 0 \\
g_9 &= 0.0254 - p_1 p_2 \le 0
\end{aligned} \qquad (16)$$

4 Algorithms

In order to apply the design methodology, two solution algorithms to solve the dynamic problem given by (8)–(16) are used.

Differential Evolution. The Constraint Handling Differential Evolution (CHDE) algorithm is used in this paper. This algorithm proposes an approach based on the idea of preserving the main DE algorithm and to add only a simple mechanism to handle the constraint.

In standard DE algorithms an arithmetic operator is used, this operator depends on the differences between randomly selected pairs of individuals. An initial population of NP individuals is randomly generated, then for each parent (individual) C_i^G of the generation G, an offspring C_i^{G+1} is created, where the number of the generations on the algorithm are stated by the $MaxGenerations$ parameter. The way of generating an offspring is to select randomly three individuals from the current population $C_{r_1}^G$, $C_{r_2}^G$, $C_{r_3}^G$ where $r_1 \ne r_2 \ne r_3 \ne i$ and $r_1, r_2, r_3 \in [1, ..., NP]$. Select a random number $j_{rand} \in [1, ..D]$ where D is the number of genes or design variables of the system to optimize. Then, for each gene $j = 1, .., D$, if $rand_j < CR$ or $j = i$, let

$$C_i^{j,G+1} = C_{r_3}^{j,G} + F(C_{r_1}^{j,G} - C_{r_2}^{j,G}) \qquad (17)$$

otherwise, let

$$C_i^{j,G+1} = C_i^{j,G} \qquad (18)$$

where CR is the probability of reproduction, F is a scaling factor and $C_i^{j,G}$ is the $j-th$ gene of the $i-th$ individual of the $G-th$ generation. In order to select the individual of the next generation between the corresponding parent and offspring, three selection criteria are applied. These criteria guide the population towards a feasible zone, improve the algorithm convergence and bound the design variables. Moreover, they carry out the constraint handling. A more detailed explanation about these criteria is given in [11].

The CHDE approach only use the evaluated function, which is obtained by solving the four differential equations of the dynamic system and the objective function equation. The evaluated constraints and the constraint handling guide the population towards the feasible region, this represents an advantage when additional constraints are added to the original problem because the gradient information is not necessary.

Nonlinear Programming Method. A DOP can be solved by converting it into a Nonlinear Programing (NLP) problem, two transcriptions methods exist for the DOP: the sequential and the simultaneous methods [12]. In the sequential method, only the control variables are discretized; this method is also known as a control vector parameterization. The resulting problem can be solved using conventional NLP method. A vector p^i which contains the current parameter values is proposed and the NLP problem given in (19) and (20) subject to (9) to (16) is obtained. There B_i is the Broyden-Fletcher-Goldfarb-Shanno (BFGS) updated positive definite approximation of the Hessian matrix, and the gradient calculation $\nabla F^T(p^i)$ is obtained using sensitivity equations. Hence, if d^i solves the subproblem (19) and $d^i = 0$, then the parameter vector p^i is an optimal solution to the original problem. Otherwise, we set $p^{i+1} = p^i + d^i$ and with this new vector the process is done again.

$$\min_{d \in R^4} QP(p^i) = F(p^i) + \nabla F^T(p^i) d + \frac{1}{2} d^T B_i d \qquad (19)$$

subject to

$$g_j(p^i) + \nabla g_j^T(p^i) d \leq 0 \quad j = 1, ..., 9 \qquad (20)$$

The NLP approach needs the gradient calculation and to solve sensitivity equations to obtain the necessary information to establish a subproblem. The number of sensitivity equations is the product between the number of state variables and the number of parameters, in this case the sensitivity equations are twenty four. Additionally, six gradient equations and one equation in order to obtain the value of the objective function must be solved. Besides, fifty four gradient equations of the constraints must be calculated.

5 Optimizations Results

The system parameters used in the optimization procedure were: $b_1 = 1.1Nms/rad$, $b_2 = 0.05Nms/rad$, $r = 0.0254m$, $T_m = 8.789Nm$, $T_L = 0Nm$, $\lambda = 5.4271$, $\phi = 20$, $M = 10Kg$, $r_p = 4.188E-03m$, $K_f = 63.92E-03Nm/A$, $K_b = 63.92E-03Vs/rad$, $R = 10\Omega$, $L = 0.01061H$, $b_l = 0.015Ns/m$, $b_c = 0.025Nms/rad$ and $n = ((22*40*33)/(9*8*9))$.

The initial conditions vector was $[x_1(0), x_2(0), x_3(0), x_4(0)]^T = [7.5, 0, 0, 0]^T$. In order to show the CVT dynamic performance for all simulations, the output reference was considered to be $x_{ref} = 3.2$. The parameters used in the CHDE algorithm are the following: Population number $NP = 50$, $MaxGenerations = 250$; the parameters F and CR were randomly generated. The parameter F was generated per generation between $[0.3, 0.9]$ and CR was generated per run between $[0.8, 1.0]$. In table 1 the mean computational time is the average of the time of five runs of the CHDE algorithm.

The results obtained with the NLP and the CHDE algorithms are shown in table 1. The values of the mechanical CVT parameter and the controller gains for each objective function with both algorithms are shown in table 2.

Table 1. Optimization results

Item	$F(\Phi_1)$		$F(\Phi_2)$	
	NLP	CHDE	NLP	CHDE
Optimum	0.4281	0.4282	721.17	555.52
Mean computational time [seg]	1558	18345	1055	17965
Iteration number	6	250	4	250

Table 2. Results for the CVT parameters

Parameter	$F(\Phi_1)$		$F(\Phi_2)$	
	NLP	CHDE	NLP	CHDE
p_1	38.1838	38.1767	12.00	13.44
p_2	0.0017	0.0017	0.0030	0.0019
p_3	0.0200	0.0200	0.0200	0.0200
p_4	0.0636	0.0636	0.0909	0.0631
p_5	10.0000	9.9933	5.0000	5.0000
p_6	1.0000	0.9996	0.0100	0.0100

5.1 Discussion

In table 1, it can be observed that for $F(\Phi_1)$, similar results for both algorithms are obtained. On the case of $F(\Phi_2)$, the CHDE approach obtains a better result than the NLP approach. It can be said that the CHDE algorithm reaches the *best* optimum of the function. On both objective functions, despite the low computational time of the NLP approach, the CHDE algorithm presents a higher performance, because in all runs carried out the population presents convergence towards the global optimum.

For the NLP approach, the whole system equation was simultaneously solved to establish the subproblem until the stop criteria of the subproblem were satisfied. The initial point to search the optimum is $p^1 = [13, 0.0019, 0.02, 0.0629, 5, 0.1]^T$ for both functions. However, on the $F(\Phi_2)$ case, that optimum is only reached starting the search from p^1.

The results for the CHDE algorithm were achieved with 12500 evaluations of the objective function for each run, approximately. For the NLP approach, evaluations of the objective function were 4 for each run. Despite the computational cost of the CHDE algorithm, it can be observed that the algorithm ensures convergence towards one *best* solution.

In table 2, it can be observed that for $F(\Phi_1)$, the optimal solution presents a more compact CVT size, because the value of the p_2 parameter is lower than the value of the initial point. On the other hand, the controller gains p_5 and p_6 for both algorithm present a similar value. For the $F(\Phi_2)$ function, the optimal solution of the CHDE presents a better result than the optimal solution of the NLP algorithm, because the optimal solution obtained presents a minimal energy controller besides a more CVT size. This can be observed on the same value of the p_5, p_6 parameters and the smallest value of the p_2 parameter.

6 Conclusions

In this paper a concurrent optimal design of a CVT was carried out. A novel approach based on the Differential Evolution method was used to solve the resulting problem. The performance of the CHDE algorithm was compared versus a NLP approach and the results provided a competitive performance. A CHDE advantage is that the arithmetic operator is applied to the design variables in order to give an easier implementation. On the other hand, because the CHDE presents a suitable handle of the constraints, it can be observed that the algorithm converges towards the feasible zone in each generation. From the optimization results it can be observed that the CHDE algorithm is a very powerful algorithm for solving dynamic optimization problems.

Further research includes the statement of the concurrent optimal design as a multiobjective dynamic optimization problem and to apply the CHDE algorithm to obtain the Pareto optimal solutions.

References

1. Norton R.: Machine Design. An integrated approach. Prentice Hall Inc., Upper Saddle River, NJ 07458; 1996.
2. van Brussel H., Sas P., Nemeth I. Fonseca P.D., van den Braembussche P.: Towards a Mechatronic Compiler. IEEE/ASME Transactions on Mechatronics. **6** (2001) 90–104

3. Li Q., Zhang W.J., Chen L.: Design for Control–A concurrent Engineering Approach for Mechatronic Systems Design. IEEE/ASME Transactions on Mechatronics. **6** (2001) 161–168
4. Deb K., Jain S.: Multi-Speed Gearbox Design Using Multi-Objective Evolutionary Algorithms KanGal Report No. 2002001
5. Shiakolas P.S., Koladiya D., Kebrle J.: On the Optimum Synthesis of Six-Bar Linkages using Differential Evolution and the Geometric Centroid of Precision Positions Technique. In Mechanism and Machine Theory **40** (2005) 319–335
6. Shafai E., Simons M., Neff U., Geering H.: Model of a Continuously variable transmission. In First IFAC Workshop on Advances in Automotive Control. (1995) 575–593
7. De Silva C., Schultz M., Dolejsi E.: Kinematic analysis and design of a continuously variable transmission. In Mech. Mach. Theory, **29** (1994) 149–167
8. Alvarez Gallegos J., Cruz Villar C.A., Portilla Flores E.A.: Parametric optimal design of a pinion-rack based continuously variable transmission In IEEE/ASME International Conference on Advanced Intelligent Mechatronics. (2005) 899–904
9. Spotts M.: Mechanical design Analysis. Prentice Hall Inc., Englewood Cliffs, NJ; 1964.
10. Papalambros P., Wilde D.: Principles of optimal design. Modelling and computation. Cambridge University Press., The Edinburg Building, Cambridge CB2 2RU, UK; 2000.
11. Mezura-Montes E., Coello Coello C.A., Tun-Morales I.: Simple Feasibility Rules and Differential Evolution for Constrained Optimization. In R Monroy, G. Arroyo-Figueroa, L.E. Sucar, and H. Sosa, editors, Proceedings of the Third Mexican International Conference on Artificial Intelligence (MICAI'2004), 707–716, Heidelberg, Germany, April 2004. Mexico City, Mexico, Springer Verlag. Lecture Notes in Artificial Intelligence No. 2972.
12. Betts J.T.: Practical Methods for Optimal Control Using Nonlinear Programming. SIAM, Philadelphia; 2001.

Performance Improvement of Ad-Hoc Networks by Using a Behavior-Based Architecture

Horacio Martínez-Alfaro[1] and Griselda P. Cervantes-Casillas[2]

[1] Center for Intelligent Systems, Tecnológico de Monterrey,
Monterrey, N.L. 64849 México,
hma@itesm.mx
[2] Motorola Nogales IESS
Nogales, Son. Mexico
griscervantes@motorola.com

Abstract. This paper presents a new approach to improve performance in wireless ad-hoc networks with the DSR protocol using a Behavior-Based Architecture. Four levels of competence based on strategies to improve the cache were implemented for the Behavior-Based Architecture: sort routes, prefer fresher routes, selection, and disperse traffic. A conflict solver was implemented to solve counter level commands. Three different activation criteria for the conflict solver were developed, generating instances of the architecture. Two metrics were used to evaluate the performance of the ad-hoc network: end-to-end delay and dropped packet average for voice and data services, respectively. Six scenarios were analyzed showing the improvement of the network performance with respect to the original DSR protocol.

1 Introduction

An ad-hoc network is a collection of wireless mobile host forming a temporary network without the aid of any established infrastructure or centralized administration [1]. In ad-hoc networks all nodes cooperate in order to dynamically establish and maintain routing in the network, forwarding packets for each other to allow communication between nodes which are not directly within the wireless transmission range. Rather than using the periodic or background exchange of routing information, common in most routing protocols, an on-demand routing protocol is one that searches for and attempts to discover a route to some destination node only when a sending node originates a data packet addressed to that node. Several routing protocols with an on-demand mechanism for wireless ad-hoc networks have been used, including DSDV [2], TORA [3, 4], DSR [5, 1], and AODV [6].

The *Dynamic Source Routing* protocol (DSR) adapts quickly to routing changes when host moves frequently and delivers better performance than other on-demand protocols like AODV, TORA, DSDV, under low mobility conditions. The key characteristic of the DSR [5, 1] is the use of source routing. That is, the sender knows the complete hop-by-hop route to the destination. These routes are stored in a route cache. The data packets carry the source route in the packet header.

The DSR protocol has a *Route Discovery* and a *Route Maintenance* mechanisms; each one operates using entirely an on-demand behavior. When a node in the ad-hoc network attempts to send a packet to some destination, if it does not already know a route to that destination, it uses Route Discovery to dynamically discover one. The route is cached an used as needed for sending subsequent packets, each one using the Route Maintenance mechanism to detect if the route has broken.

DSR does not contain any explicit mechanism to expire stale routes in the cache, or prefer fresher routes when faced up with multiple choices [7]. Picking stalled routes causes some problems: consumption of additional network bandwidth, full interface queue slots although the packet is eventually dropped or delayed and possible pollution of caches in other nodes.

Our objective is to design a *Behavior-Based Architecture* (BBA) to improve routing in ad-hoc networks, using the DSR routing protocol; its main goal is to have better global performance network, improving delays and drecreasing dropped packets. The proposed solution scheme is based on BBA implemented in softbots [8], which are software robots working in a simulated environment. In our case each softbot represents one network node.

The *Behavior-Based architecture* was inspired by insects [9, 10, 11]. These organisms own a primitive degree of intelligence, even so they are able to survive in hostile environments. BBA has been only implemented for mobile robots. In BBA, the global performance of the softbot emerges from specific performance of every integrating system, unlike the hierarchical architecture, the sensor data is distributed in parallel to each system. The way in which the system process the sensor data will define a single behavior; every behavior incorporates some degree of competence. This type of architecture provides a very reactive performance in the softbot acquiring a high degree of robustness due the parallel data distribution. In this way if one of the systems is down, the other behaviors still work allowing the softbot to achieve its task [8].

2 Methodology

We use a detailed simulation model based on *NS-2 Network Simulator*, extended with our support for realistic modeling of mobility and wireless communication [12].

We simulated six different scenarios with two types of services: data and voice, since both are the most commonly used services nowadays. The data service was implemented over the TCP transport protocol for all scenarios. The voice service was implemented for scenarios 1, 2, and 3 over TCP and scenarios 4, 5, and 6 over UDP.

Two performance metrics were evaluated for each scenario:
- **Data packets end-to-end delay.** This includes all possible delays caused by buffering during route discovery latency, queuing at the interface queue, retransmission delays at the MAC, and propagation and transfer times.
- **Dropped packet average.** The ratio of the data packets delivered to the destinations to those data packets forwarded. Dropped packets key cause is due to queuing at the interface queue and collisions.

The end-to-end delay metric was used for the voice service and the dropped packet average for the data service.

The main feature of the DSR is the use of source routing [5]; that is, the sender knows completely the route by which the packet will pass in order to arrive to the final destination node. All these routes are stored in the route cache in two different ways, paths and links. This route cache has a primary route cache and a secondary route cache. We worked with the primary route cache and with paths. As mention before, the DSR protocol has a Route Discovery and Route Maintenance mechanisms. The Route Discovery mechanism sends a route request packet to every node inside its transmission range that started the discovery; if none is the destination, those nodes retransmit the route request packet, and the process continues until the route request packet reaches its destination node. This process generates a lot of traffic in the network and uses network bandwidth, which increases the packet delivery delay and dropped packets.

One way in which DSR avoids route discovery every time that needs one to a destination node or when sending subsequent packets to the same destination node by checking its cache if it has a saved route to the requeste destination node. This is why route caching is a key part of every on-demand routing protocol. This caching implies a good cache managing strategy selection. By caching and making effective use of this collected network state information, the amortized cost of route discoveries can be reduced and the overall performance of the network can be significantly improved.

2.1 Behavior-Based Architecture

A Behavior-Based Architecture (BBA) was designed and implemented to establish good cache managing strategies with four levels of competence (see Figure 1); this has a direct effect on the DSR primary cache managing of every node in the network.

First Level of Competence: Sort
The first level of competence is to sort every node's cache yielding a faster route search. As more time takes for a packet to get a route, delay and dropped packets increase. Three different sorting bahaviors are implemented: sort by minimum number of nodes, sort by minimum send time, and no sorting. The standar functionality of the DSR protocol when receiving a route request packet is to search in the route cache a route to that destination and choose the first route with minimum number of nodes scanning the entire route cache. In the first two sorting behaviors, when adding a route, the route cache is sorted by minimum number of nodes or by minimum send time to same destination.

Second Level of Competence: Prefer Fresher Routes
It is possible to find a route with this behavior in the sorted route cache; however, the sorted route cache could find the freshest route and therefore the route may be broken. These routes do contribute unnecessarily to the load in the routing layer. High routing load usually has a significant performance impact in low bandwidth wireless link. This increases problems with delay and dropped packets.

The Prefer Fresher Routes behavior scans all the route cache to find the route with minimum number of nodes or minimum send time to a specific destination and when faced to multiple choices, it selects the fresher route. When the route cache is sorted, the search for fresher route is faster.

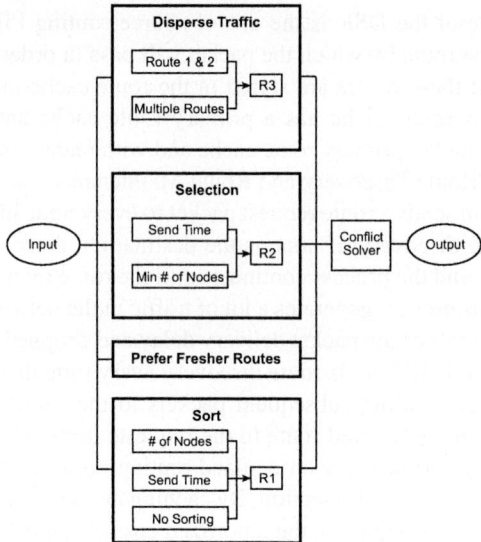

Fig. 1. A Behavior-Based Architecture for wireless ad-hoc networks

Third Level of Competence: Selection

This behavior is designed for nodes that have both types of traffic: voice and data. Its goal is to have the possibility to choose the route based on the packet to be sent, i.e., it could be chosen to use minimum send time routes for voice packets and minimum number of nodes for data packets.

Fourth Level of Competence: Disperse Traffic

This behavior disperses traffic in the network by sending different routes every time one is requested unlike the original DSR which always sends the first route with the minimum number of nodes found without caring if there are more routes with the same minimum number of nodes. Two ways to disperse traffic were implemented: multiple routes (same destination node) with one same characteristic and two routes with different characteristics. The first one selects every route that satisfies a selection criteria. If the Prefer Fresher Routes is active, the newest route in the route cache is first selected, then the second newest, and so on until every route has been used. If there is only one route that satisfies the selection criteria (second way of to disperse traffic), the traffic is dispersed with the first route that does not satisfy those criteria, either minimum number of nodes or minimum send time.

Conflict Solver

Every competence level generates an output command and sometimes these commands could be set opposite; due to this, a Conflict Solver (CS) is implemented. The CS activates the Sort level when adding a route to the route cache and when one is requested, it decides whether or not to activate the other three levels. These two calling types could be in parallel form. There is a global CS and a CS for the first, third, and fourth level of competence. All these CSs establish which behaviors are active and which criteria is used to apply them. By establishing different activation criteria in the CS, different instances of the BBA are generated.

2.2 Architecture Instances

Based on the advantages offered by the BBA parallel scheme and behavior activation/deactivation in every level, three instances of the BBA were generated to evaluate the network performance. *BBA1* instance is focused to use routes based on the type of service of every node. *BBA2* is focused to use routes with minimum number of nodes without caring for the type of application used. *BBA3* is focused to use routes with minimum send time without caring for the type of service used. Not every behavior is active in every level of the *BBA2* and *BBA3* instances.

2.3 Experiments

The simulation process is divided in experiments with two transport protocols: TCP and UDP. For every set of experiments, both types of services were evaluated: end-to-end delay was evaluated for voice and dropped packets for data.

For every TCP scenario, the original DSR and the one modified with the architecture instances *BBA1*, *BBA2*, and *BBA3* were analyzed. For the UDP scenarios the original DSR and the architecture instances *BBA2* and *BBA3* were analyzed.

2.4 Delay Performance Metrics

We used the following metrics for the performance analysis of the end-to-end delay in ad-hoc network: (a) Average $\bar{x} = \frac{1}{n}\sum_{i=1}^{n} x_i$, (b) Variance $\sigma^2 = \frac{1}{n}\sum_{i=1}^{n}(x_i - \bar{x})^2$, (c) Standard deviation $\sigma = \sqrt{\sigma^2}$, and (d) Burst factor $f_b = \sigma^2/\bar{x}$.

The burst factor gives an idea of the traffic type in the network: $f_b > 1$ peak traffic, $f_b < 1$ soft traffic, $f_b = 1$ Poisson traffic. When there is peak traffic, there are traffic bursts very intense, not advisable. Ideally, it is better to have f_b closer to 1 since Poisson traffic represents an infinite number of buffers yielding minimum delay [13].

3 Simulation Results

The scenarios used to evaluate the ad-hoc network performance included two types of services: data and voice. We implemented two types of transport protocols, TCP and UDP, and two types of mobility, constant node motion and no node motion. The data service was implemented only in the TCP transport protocol, but the voice service was implemented in both transport protocols to see performance differences. The traffic sources used are continuos bit rate (CBR) and voice. The voice source was simulated using an exponential traffic with burst time 1.004s and idle time 1.587s [14]. Only 512-byte data packets were used. The number of source-destination pairs and the packet sending rate in each pair is varied to change the offered load in the network. The mobility model uses the random waypoint model [15] for 5 ms and 300 ms in a rectangular field, 400 m × 400 m and 600 s of simulation time. Twenty nodes were used: 4 source-destination pairs for voice, 4 source-destination pairs for data, and 2 source-destination pairs with voice and data services. The source-destination pairs are spread randomly over the network.

The DSR protocol maintain a send buffer of 64 packets. It contains all data packets waiting for a route. Such packets are the ones for which route discovery has started but no reply has arrived yet. To prevent buffering of packets indefinitely, packets are dropped if they wait in the send buffer for more then 30 s. All packets (both data and routing) send by routing layer are queued at the interface queue until the MAC layer can transmit them. The interface queue has a maximum size of 50 packets and it is maintained as a priority queue with two priorities each one served in FIFO order. Routing packets get higher priority than data packets.

3.1 Dropped Packets Results with TCP

The three architecture instances shown in Table 1 show a significant improvement in the general dropped packet average compare to the original DSR. This is due to the focus of the architecture to manage the route cache of every node in the network, preferring better and newer routes than the original DSR. Instance *BBA3* is the one with the best performance, mainly in the scenarios with mobility. This instance is focused in using routes with minimum send time and newer in the cache, contributing to lower the discovery route time and to decrease the possibility of deleting packets from the send buffer.

Table 1. Dropped packet average from all 20 nodes with TCP

Scenario	Original DSR	Instance BBA1	Instance BBA2	Instance BBA3
1	2.56%	2.79%	2.07%	2.55%
2	4.66%	4.08%	4.29%	3.61%
3	3.83%	2.89%	3.38%	2.84%

Figures 2 and 3 show dropped packets for the original DSR and the modified DSR with instance *BBA3* of the scenario 2.

Figure 2 shows the performance of the scenario 2 for the original DSR. Figure 2(a) shows total packets sent, received, and dropped for every node in the network. Figure 2(b) shows a detail of the total dropped packets. The main problems in networks that generate dropped packets are due to dropped packets in the queue and collisions.

Figure 3 shows the performance of the scenario 2 with instance *BBA3*. Figure 3(a) shows total packets sent, received, and dropped for every node in the network. Figure 3(b) shows total dropped packets.

3.2 End-to-End Delay Results with TCP

Table 2 shows the results of the end-to-end delay for the voice service for the three scenarios with TCP. It includes original DSR, and modified DSR with instances *BBA1*, *BBA2*, and *BBA3*. A source-destination pair is denominated a *session*. Two sessions

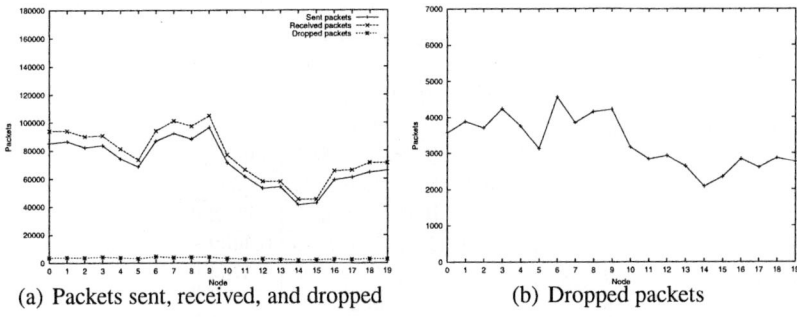

(a) Packets sent, received, and dropped   (b) Dropped packets

Fig. 2. Scenario 2 for original DSR with TCP

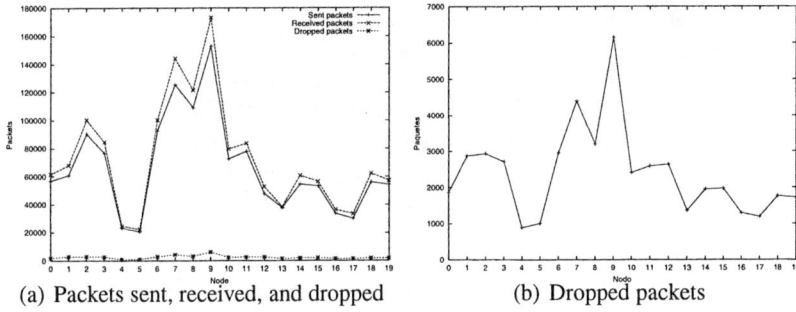

(a) Packets sent, received, and dropped   (b) Dropped packets

Fig. 3. Scenario 2, instance BBA3 with TCP dropped packets

were analyzed for the TCP experiments but, due to the lack of space, only results for one session are shown.

We focused on the average to compare the end-to-end delay in the ad-hoc network. In all scenarios the three architecture instances show a considerable improvement in the end-to-end delay average compared to the original DSR. This is due to the cache managing strategies implemented for every node assuring that fresher routes are used and a more disperse traffic is happening over several routes, making more trustable options to send packets yielding a decrease in packet delivery time.

Comparing the improvement in the performance metrics of the network for the two session, instance BBA2 shows a higher improvement than the other two instances, compared to the original DSR. Instance BBA2 is focused on finding routes with the minimum number of nodes and when it finds them, selects the freshest one. In addition to this, it disperses traffic over more than one route generating less crowded routes and decreasing packet delivery time keeping an enhanced performance of the network.

Figure 4 shows the scenario 2 performance for a session and it includes the original DSR and instance *BBA2*.

As one can see in Figure 4, instance BBA2 (Figure 4(b)) shows a major improvement in all statistics metrics compared to the original DSR.

Table 2. End-to-end delay metrics for a network session

Metric	Original DSR	Instance BBA1	Instance BBA2	Instance BBA3
Scenario 1				
min	0.0102	0.0001	**0.0000**	0.0001
$\bar{x}$	0.9820	0.9278	**0.7592**	0.9056
max	8.0387	**46.0931**	5.0857	5.9868
σ^2	0.4814	1.3197	**0.2346**	0.3409
f_b	0.4902	1.4224	0.3090	**0.3764**
Scenario 2				
min	**0.0048**	0.0049	**0.0048**	**0.0048**
$\bar{x}$	0.6800	0.5112	**0.2889**	0.3432
max	16.1109	**31.4180**	5.5558	24.9125
σ^2	1.0376	2.1451	**0.1947**	0.5423
f_b	1.5259	4.1940	**0.6740**	1.5803
Scenario 3				
min	0.0049	0.0049	**0.0000**	0.0002
$\bar{x}$	0.7810	0.5936	0.6496	**0.4038**
max	10.8735	**13.9272**	12.0237	10.2866
σ^2	1.4703	1.5242	0.9338	**0.8463**
f_b	1.8824	2.5677	**1.4376**	2.0961

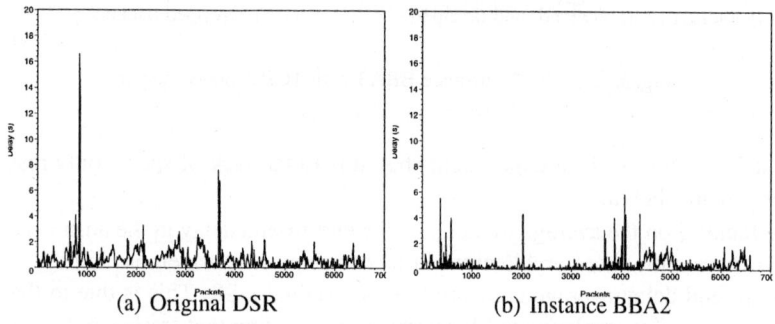

(a) Original DSR (b) Instance BBA2

Fig. 4. Scenario 2 with TCP End-to-end delay

4 Results with UDP

After performing the TCP experiments, only instances *BBA2* and *BBA3*, which showed the best performance improvement, were evaluated with UDP.

Both architecture instances show an improvement in the general average dropped packets compared to the original DSR for the three scenarios; however, this improvement was not as high as the one shown with the TCP experiments. This is mainly due to the functionality characteristics of each protocol. UDP protocol sends packets continuously without knowing if a packet has been received by the following node; then, if there is no route to the destination in the cache, it will be continuously requesting Route Discovery. While TCP when sending a packet, it waits for the acknowledge packet before sending another, using less Route Discovery. The proposed BBA is focused on managing the cache of every node in the network giving as a result better and fresher routes than the original DSR. However, it is not focused directly on the Route Discovery mechanism, yielding not as good results as the the ones with TCP. Instance *BBA3* with UDP had the best performance improvement in dropped packets metric (similar results with TCP).

Both architecture instances had a small improvement for all scenarios. The statistics metrics used show that is not a very stable traffic since there is peak traffic in all scenarios. This type of traffic is formed of very intense burst generating more problems in the network, like more packets waiting for a route and more use of Route Discovery.

5 Conclusions

Most on-demand routing protocols for wireless ad-hoc networks use route caching to reduce the overload of routing information and the route discovery latency. In wireless ad hoc networks, the routing changes happen frequently due the mobility of the nodes. Unless route caching adapts well to frequent routing changes, it could affect the network performance adversely. This work was motivated by previous studies where it is demonstrated that the DSR performance is degraded due to stalled caching routes. The DSR protocol is a good candidate for the study of suitable caching strategies since this makes aggressive use of the route caching.

This paper has presented a performance analysis in wireless ad-hoc networks using a Behavior-Based Architecture. The analysis is based on the DSR protocol and is divided in analysis with the TCP transport protocol and analysis with the UDP transport protocol.

Based on the experiments performed, it is demonstrated that the proposed and implemented BBA improves the performance in wireless ad-hoc networks up to 50% in end-to-end delay and up to 25% in dropped packets. Up to date, this is the first reported research results that proves that BBA can be adapted and implemented to these type of networks.

Three instances of the architecture were implemented and showed better performance than the original DSR. This proves the robustness of the designed architecture. It will also allow that the instances can be chosen according to the required improvement needs. For both TCP and UDP transport protocols analyzed, instance BBA3 produces less dropped packets; whereas instance BBA2 causes less end-to-end delay. These two instances can be interpreted as heuristics, improving the performance in wireless ad-hoc networks: to use routes with minimum send time to decrease dropped packets and to use routes with minimum number of nodes to decrease delay.

Instances *BBA2* and *BBA3* are implemented by means of better managing cache strategies: Sort routes, Prefer Fresher routes, Selection, and Disperse Traffic; which all of them are small changes in the way cache is managed. This confirms one of the main advantages of BBA, small changes could generate great results. Although the simulator does not report the processing time for each node in the network, we consider that the implemented algorithms does not represent a noticeable CPU time increase. Keeping in mind that another basic idea of the BBA is to keep simple and practical the algorithms for each behavior.

In addition, although the experiments were performed using the DSR routing protocol, the BBA developed can be adapted to any protocol that handles route caching.

Acknowledgment. The first two authors wishes to acknowledge the support for this research work granted by CONACYT, México under the project "Performance optimization in ad-hoc networks".

References

1. Johnson, D.: Routing in ad-hoc networks of mobile host. Proceedings of Workshop on mobile computing systems and applications **1** (1994) 1–6
2. Perkins, C.E., Bhagwat, P.: Highly dynamic destination sequenced distance-vector routing (DSDV) for mobile computers. ACM SIGCOMM '94 Conference on Communications Architectures, Protocols and Applications (1994) 234–244
3. Park, V.D., Corson, M.S.: A highly adaptive distributed routing algorithm for mobile wireless networks. Procceedings of INFOCOM'97 (1997) 1405–1413
4. Park, V.D., Corson, M.S.: Temporally-ordered routing algorithm (TORA) version 1: Functional specification. Internet-Draft (1997)
5. Johnson, D.B., Maltz, D.A.: Dynamic source routing in ad-hoc wireless networks. Mobile Computing (1996)
6. Perkins, C.: Ad-hoc on distance vector (AODV) routing. Internet-Draft (1997)
7. Perkins, C.E., Royer, E.M., Das, S.R., Marina, M.K.: Performance comparison of two on-demand routing protocols for ad-hoc networks. IEEE Personal Communications (2001)
8. Uribe-Gutiérrez, S., Martínez-Alfaro, H.: An application of behavior-based architecture for mobile robots design. Proceedings of MICAI 2000: Advances in Artificial Intelligence (2000) 136–147
9. Brooks, R.: A robust layered control system for a mobile robot. Technical Report AI MEMO 864, Massachussetts Institute of Technology, E.U. (1985)
10. Brooks, R.: Achieving artificial intelligence through building robots. Technical Report AI MEMO 899, Massachussetts Institute of Technology, E.U. (1986)
11. Brooks, R.: The behavior language; users guide. Technical Report AI MEMO 1227, Massachussetts Institute of Technology, E.U. (1990)
12. Martínez-Alfaro, H., Vargas, C., Cervantes-Casillas, G., Rosado-Ruiz, A.M.: Contribuciones al simulador NS-2. Congreso de Investigaci=n y Extensi=n del Sistema Tecnológico de Monterrey (2002)
13. Leijon, H.: Overflow from full availability group. Available from http://www.itu.int/itudoc/itu-d/dept/psp/ssb/planitu/plandoc/ovfull.html (1998)
14. Chuah, C., Subramanian, L., Katz, R.: A scalable framework for traffic policing and admission control. Report No. UCB//CSD-1-1144, Computer Science Division (EECS) University of California Berkeley (2001) 1–28
15. Fall, K., Varadhan, K.: Ns notes and documentation. Available from http://www.isi.edu/nsnam/ns/ (1999)

Analysis of the Performance of Different Fuzzy System Controllers

Patrick B. Moratori[1], Adriano J.O. Cruz[1], Laci Mary B. Manhães[1,2],
Emília B. Ferreira[1], Márcia V. Pedro[1], Cabral Lima[1], and Leila C.V. Andrade[1,3]

[1] Instituto de Matemática / NCE - Universidade Federal do Rio de Janeiro (UFRJ),
Caixa Postal 68.530 - 21945-970 - Rio de Janeiro - RJ - Brasil
{moratori, mmanhães, emiliabf, marciavp}@posgrad.nce.ufrj.br
{adriano, clima}@nce.ufrj.br
[2] Faculdade Salesiana Maria Auxiliadora (FSMA),
Rua Monte Elísio s/n° - Macaé - RJ - Brasil
[3] Escola de Informática Aplicada da
Universidade Federal do Estado do Rio de Janeiro (UNIRIO),
Avenida Pasteur 458 - Urca – Rio de Janeiro - RJ - Brasil
leila@uniriotec.br

Abstract. The main goal of this work is to study the reliability of fuzzy logic based systems. Three different configurations were compared to support this research. The context used was to guide a simulated robot through a virtual world populated with obstacles. In the first configuration, the system controls only the rotation angle of the robot. In the second one, there is an additional output that controls its step. In the third one, improvements were included in the decision process that controls the step and the rotation angle. In order to compare the performance of these approaches, we studied the controller stability based on the removal of rules. We measured two parameters: processing time and the amount of step necessary to reach the goal.

This research shows that simplicity and easiness of the design of fuzzy controllers don't compromise its efficiency. Our experiments confirm that fuzzy logic based systems can properly perform under adverse conditions.

1 Introduction

The design of systems that simulate real conditions is a very complex process, both for hardware and software solutions. Computer Science presents many different possibilities of constructing very reasonable approaches. Fuzzy logic reduces the difficulties of implementation because even when the designer doesn't have complete knowledge about the problem, it is still possible to write simple and efficient controllers. This characteristic proved to be true after the comparisons of different configurations, in order to define the controller robustness. The results indicate that fuzzy logic based systems can contribute to robotic and industrial automation areas providing simple and efficient solutions.

The fuzzy logic based system described in this work guides a simulated robot through a virtual world populated with randomly placed obstacles. This model simulates a real situation where a robot tries to move through a complex environment.

The sensors used to acquire information are simple, so its knowledge of the environment is limited. Three different approaches were simulated in order to test their performance. In the first approach the system controls only the direction in which the robot moves at a constant speed, which was simulated as a constant step. In the second configuration another output controls the robot speed. The variation of speed was simulated as a variable step. In the third configuration, modifications were done in the fuzzy module in order to apply optimizations in the system controls. The entire system is based on a model previously tested [1] [2] [3] [4]. The main goal of this work is to compare the performance of these controllers considering the cost of processing and the quantity of steps necessary to achieve the goal. The tests show that the optimized approach presents an improved performance without an increase on processing time, which will be important when the system is moved to the controller of the real robot. The tests also shown that modifications applied to fuzzy module inference allowed a proper control to a variable step. So, it is possible to incorporate a velocity control to the system, without compromising its general efficiency.

2 Model Description

The fuzzy controller has to move the robot from the left sidewall to right sidewall avoiding the fixed obstacles randomly distributed as well as the other sidewalls. Fig. 1 shows the simulated robot and the virtual world.

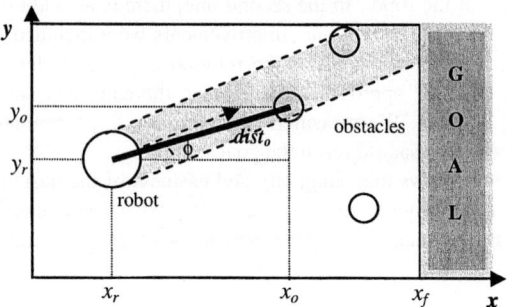

Fig. 1. Diagram of simulated robot and the virtual world

The radius of the robot is equal to 6 units and the radius of each obstacle is equal to 3 units. The virtual world corresponds to the plane [0x200], [0x100]. The robot has to arrive at the right sidewall defined at the position $x_f=200$ at any coordinate y.

Three variables x_r, y_r and ϕ determine the exact position of the robot. The robot has sensors that detect and measure the distances to the obstacles that lay on its path. Fig. 2 shows the detection of possible collisions and measurements used by the sensors. Should more than one obstacle be detected only the closest one is considered by the algorithm ($dist_o$).

At each stage of the simulation the robot moves using information from the horizontal angle (ϕ), the y_r coordinate of the robot and the distance to the closest obstacle ($dist_o$). In the first approach the system generates as the only output the rotation angle of the robot (θ) that moves at a fixed step (Δ_c). In the second approach, the controller outputs are the angle of rotation (θ) and a variable step (Δ_v). In the third configuration, two outputs were also generated, angle of rotation (θ) and an optimized variable step (Δ_{ov}). The results of the last approach benefited the task of guiding efficiently the simulated robot through a virtual world.

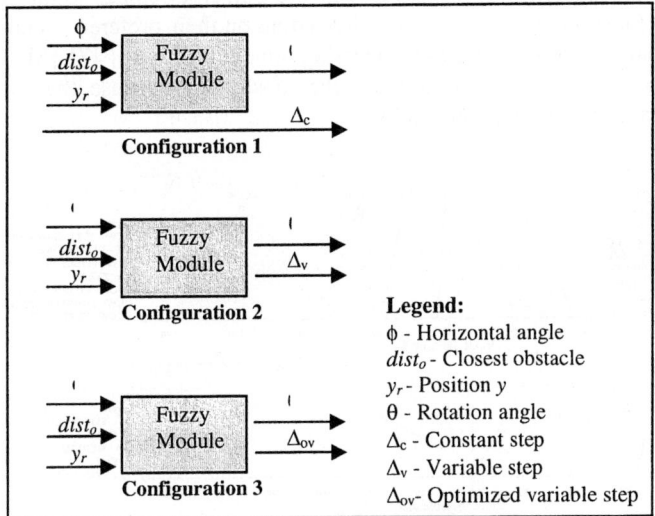

Fig. 2. The fuzzy controllers

We use simple kinematics equations similar to the ones described by Kosko and Kong [9], and used to solve the problem of backing up a truck. The equations that describe the movement of the robot at every stage of the simulation are:

$$\phi' = \phi + \theta \\ x_r = x_r + \Delta \cos(\phi') \\ y_r = y_r + \Delta \sin(\phi') \qquad (1)$$

Note that Δ represents the value of the distance moved by the robot at every stage of the simulation and it is also a function of ϕ, y_r and $dist_o$. The range of the variables, or their universe of discourse, is:

$$0 \le dist_o, x_r \le 200 \\ 0 \le y_r \le 100 \\ -180^o \le \phi \le +180^o \\ -30^o \le \theta \le +30^o \\ -0.3 \le \Delta \le 10 \qquad (2)$$

In the first configuration, Δ is a constant equals to 1.3 units while in the second and the third, Δ varies in the interval, shown on equation (2). Negative values defined to Δ allow little backward movements. Positive values of ϕ and θ represent counter clockwise rotations and negative values clockwise rotations. Therefore, usual geometric conventions are used.

The universes of discourse of the "linguistic variables" associated to the input variables are divided into fuzzy sets that represent the semantic of linguistic terms. Fuzzy sets represent the semantic of their labels using functions that assign a real number between 0 and 1 to every element x in the universe of discourse X. The number µÃ (x) represents the degree to which a object x belongs to the fuzzy set Ã. Designers of fuzzy logic based systems depending on their preference and experience have used many different fuzzy membership functions [5] [6] [7] [8]. In practice, triangular and trapezoidal functions are the most used because they simplify the computation and give very good results.

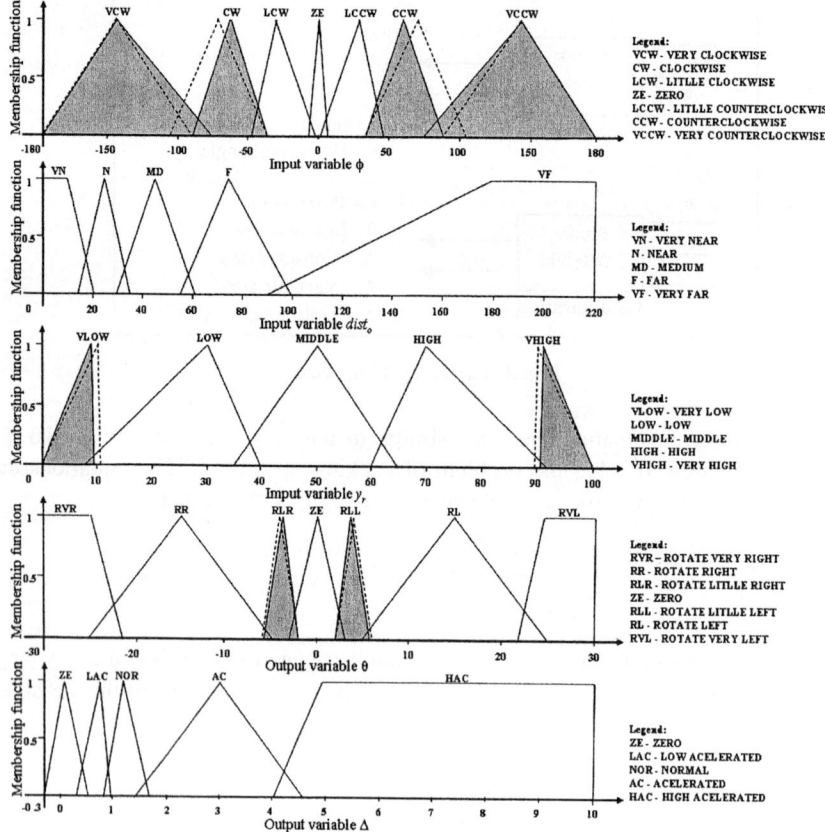

Fig. 3. Fuzzy membership functions for each linguistic fuzzy set value

The items (a), (b), (c) and (d) of Fig. 3 show all the functions representing the membership functions used on all configurations of the controller. The item (e) of Fig. 3 shows the membership functions used with variable Δ, which is used on the second and third configuration. The sets ZE, LCW and LCCW (from φ) and the sets

RLR, ZE and RLL (from θ) are narrower than the others. This characteristic allows a finer control around the horizontal direction, avoiding large changes when the robot is heading in the right direction. Wider sets were used at the extremes of the universe of discourse in order to obtain faster changes of direction when the robot is in the wrong direction. The sets VN, N and MD (from $dist_o$) are also represented by narrower sets by the same reason. The sets ZE, LAC and NOR (from Δ) are narrower than the others in order to apply refined velocity control in situations of eminent crashes.

In the Fig. 3, we highlight the changes implemented in the optimization (third approach) by using shaded sets and the hatched lines show previous configurations.

The controller under normal conditions operates based mainly on information from the distance to the nearest obstacle or wall ($dist_o$) and the angle to the horizontal (φ). So this part of the rule base is composed of 35 rules that allows the robot to turn to the right or to the left and to move at a fixed step of size equal to 1.3 units (configuration 1) or at a variable speed (configuration 2 and 3) that is simulated by the variable step (Δ). Table 1 shows the optimized rule base, identifying on each cell the output pair (θ, Δ). The shaded cells show where the modifications occurred.

Table 1. Rule base matrix for the robot controller

φ / $dist_o$	VCW	CW	LCW	ZE	LCCW	CCW	VCCW
VN	(RVL, ZE)	(RVL, ZE)	(RVL, ZE)	(RL, ZE)	(RL, ZE)	(RL, ZE)	(RVR, ZE)
N	(RVL,LAC)	(RVL,NOR)	(RVL,NOR)	(RL,NOR)	(RL,NOR)	(RL,NOR)	(RVR,LAC)
MD	(RVL,NOR)	(RL, AC)	(RLL, AC)	(RLL,HAC)	(RLR,AC)	(RR, AC)	(RVR,NOR)
F	(RVL, AC)	(RL, AC)	(RLL, AC)	(RLR,HAC)	(RLR,AC)	(RR, AC)	(RVR, AC)
VF	(RVL, AC)	(RL, AC)	(RLL, AC)	(RLR,HAC)	(RLR,AC)	(RR, AC)	(RVR, AC)

The following rules were applied in the previous configurations:

Table 2. Rules applied in the previous configurations

φ / $dist_o$	LCCW	CCW
VN	(RLL, ZE)	(RLL, ZE)
N	(RLL, NOR)	(RLL,NOR)

There are particular situations, where the robot is closer to the upper or lower walls in which the rules shown above do not guide the robot correctly. In order to solve this problem, two rules, that take the y_r position of the robot into account, were added. These rules, that are independent from the other two input variables, use only two fuzzy sets (variable y_r) and are shown in (3):

$$\text{if } (y_r \text{ is VLOW}) \text{ then } (\theta \text{ is RVL}) \text{ and } (\Delta \text{ is ZE}) \qquad (3)$$
$$\text{if } (y_r \text{ is VHIGH}) \text{ then } (\theta \text{ is RVR}) \text{ and } (\Delta \text{ is ZE})$$

The controller has finer control rules when near to obstacles or walls, it can move at very slow speed in these situations, therefore it was decided to set a maximum number of simulation cycles (500) in order to avoid longer processing times.

3 Testing Stability and Performance

It was necessary to define the context and reference parameters to measure and compare the performance of different configurations. In order to compare the performance of these configurations we studied the robot stability based on the removal of rules [9] [10]. Using this background we measured processing times and quantity of steps done during the trajectory. A smaller quantity of steps means that the robot was able to reach its goal in less time.

First the controller was tested in different situations in order to evaluate its ability to guide the robot through the virtual world. This was done in order to define the adequate parameters to the remaining experiments. In this first experiment, the number of obstacles was varied between 1 and 5, randomly distributed over the virtual world. For each of these arrangements, we tested different starting positions (10 positions) and starting angles (5 angles) evenly distributed over the universe of discourse of each variable. Note that the robot always started at the left sidewall. The controller was able to guide the robot correctly to its goal in all of these randomly generated situations.

In order to test the stability of the controller we choose to gradually remove rules from the rule base and check the behaviors of the robot. The idea is to verify whether it is possible to obtain a stable and efficient system even when the entire scope of the problem is unknown.

To guarantee the validity of the remaining comparisons, we choose from the previous experiment a fixed distribution of the obstacles. The five fixed obstacles are shown in the Fig. 4(a), 5(a), 6(a).

Initially we defined 50 initial positions, combining initial values of ϕ (-90°, -45°, 0°, 45°, 90°) and y_r (6, 15, 25, 35, ... , 85, 94). However, four of these combinations (-45°, 6), (-90°, 6), (45°, 94), (90°, 94) were not tested because the robot would start at a virtually impossible position. Each one of these remaining 46 initial positions, that we called a sample, was first processed using the complete rule base. At each step of the experiment one rule was removed, according to a predefined criterion, and all of the 46 initial configurations were reprocessed. The Fig. 4(a), 5(a) and 6(a) show for each configuration, one example of a complete trajectory of the robot starting at $y_r = 45$ and $\phi=50°$, as well as the graphics about the behavior of the variables θ (4(b), 5(b), 6(b)) and Δ (4(c), 5(c), 6(c)).

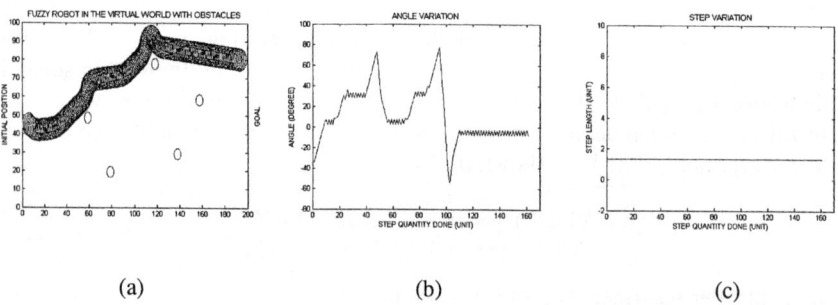

(a) (b) (c)

Fig. 4. Constant step configuration represented in (a), (b) and (c), respectively

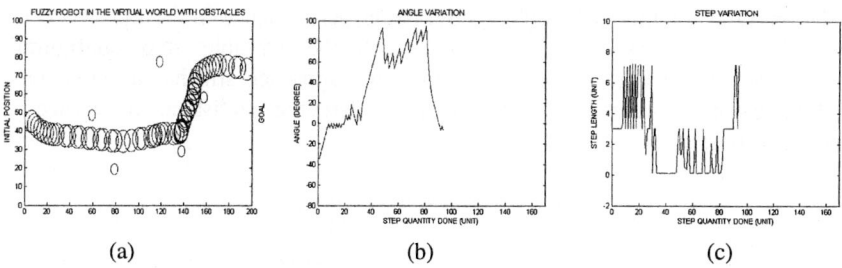

Fig. 5. Variable step configuration represented in (a), (b) and (c), respectively

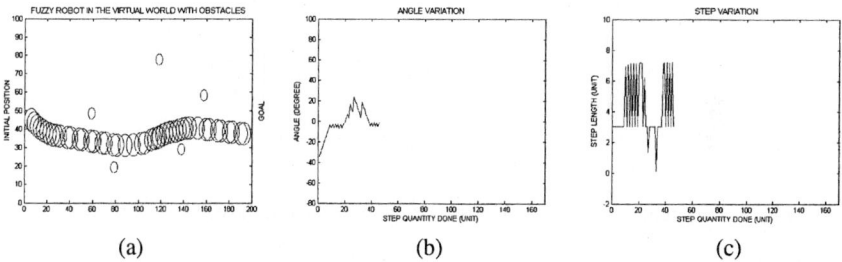

Fig. 6. Optimized variable step configuration represented in (a), (b) and (c), respectively

The Fig. 4, 5 and 6 show the model evolutions in which a more adequate information treatment was done. In each new approach, the step quantity to develop the trajectory was decreased, as in 4(b), 5(b) and 6(b). A better trajectory line, Fig. 4(a), 5(a) and 6(a), has been obtained from the different configurations.

We defined a total of 24 different ways of removal of rules. Of these ways, 20 used random removal and the other four used the following order of removal: (1) sequential removal using column-wise order; (2) reverse sequential column-wise, meaning that the rules from the last column will be removed first; (3) central rules first (outlined cells in the Table 1) and then peripheral rules; (4) peripheral rules first then central rules. Combining all these different possibilities, in our experiment we have a total of 122544 final samples processed.

The resulting figures for processing time and number of steps were stored for all samples and compared. The tests were done on a computer equipped with a processor Intel Pentium© M 710(1.40 GHz) with 512 MB of DDR SDRAM using Matlab© 7.0.

4 Simulations and Results

The stability and robustness of the controller was analyzed as the rules were removed counting the number of samples that achieved the right wall. Figure 7 shows these results for all configurations of the controller. These figures are important because they are a direct measurement of the degree of success of the systems as information control was removed. They show that even when the designer does not have entire knowledge about the problem it is still possible to write an efficient controller.

The optimized approach has obtained a better performance in the most part of the removed rule process, when compared with the variable step configuration. We observed in the Fig. 7 that the constant step approach still has a better general stability. Even so it is important to note that the statistical differences are comparatively small.

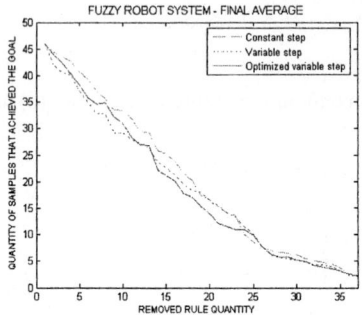

Fig. 7. Different controllers performance in successive removed rules process

The controller performance was analyzed using the following criteria: processing time and quantity of steps executed during the entire trajectory. In order to obtain a more complete vision, we analyzed not only the behavior of the samples but also the performance of the ones that achieved their goal.

In the analysis of all samples, we measured (1) the average of the number of steps done in all the simulations, (2) the average processing time of each sample, (3) the average processing time to simulate all samples on each one of the criteria used to remove the rules, (4) the total time spent in all simulations and (5) quantity of stagnated samples during its trajectory.

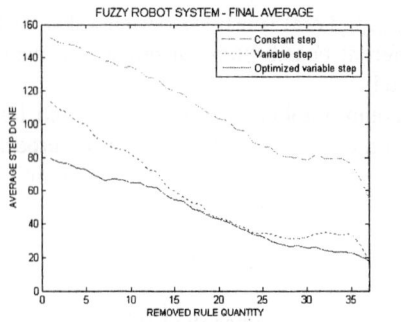 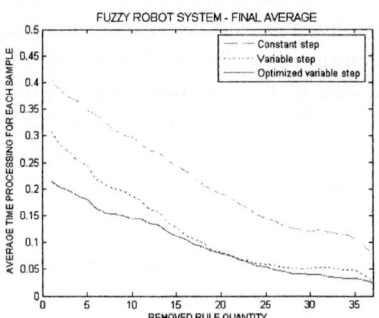

Fig. 8. Average number of steps executed   **Fig. 9.** Processing time of each sample

The Fig. 8 and 9 show the average number of steps executed and processing time of each sample, respectively, for the three model approaches. The obtained results identify the evolution of these parameters in each approach. A relevant improvement was observed comparing the constant step (hatched line), the variable step (doted line) and the optimized variable step (line). Other details of this analysis can be seen on Table 3.

Table 3. Analysis of all samples

	Characteristics	Constant step	Variable step	Optimized variable step
Time (seconds)	Average processing time to simulate all samples on each one of the criteria used to remove the rules	375,8	214,1	171,8
	Total time spent in all simulations	9018,8	5139,5	4124,1
Samples (unit)	Quantity of stagnated samples during its trajectory, limited by 500 simulation cycles.	69	53	None

Comparatively, the values related to the time feature show a better performance when the optimized variable step was applied. The quantity of samples that spent long time at obstacles, which we called stagnated samples, indicates that the controller had not wasted much time processing eminent crashes, avoiding compromising its efficiency.

In the analysis of the samples that reached the goal we considered the following aspects: (1) the average number of steps to reach the goal, the lowest and the highest values; (2) the average time spent to simulate a single sample, its shortest and widest value.

Table 4. Analysis of samples that reached the goal

	Characteristics	Constant step	Variable step	Optimized variable step
Step done (unit)	Average number of steps to reach the goal	155	79	65
	Lowest quantity of movements done by the controller in simulations of the experiment	143	36	35
	Highest quantity of movements done by the controller in simulations of the experiment	498	437	298
Time (seconds)	Average time spent to simulate a single sample	0,34	0,18	0,15
	Shortest time for a sample	0,18	0,05	0,05
	Longest time for a sample	1,88	0,65	0,67

It is possible to note an improved performance of the system that has an optimized variable step for all analyzed experiments except for the stability analysis (Fig. 6), where it showed more sensitivity to the removal of rules. This approach generates a low average of number of steps to reach the goal, comparing with the others configurations. Additionally, it spent a reduced time to process all samples.

Based on the obtained results in all analyzed aspects, an increased efficiency was observed in the system overall performance. The optimizations were effective, because the stability and efficiency of the controller were not compromised. The comparison among different approaches shows the reliability of the fuzzy logic based systems.

5 Final Considerations

This work analyzed the performance of a fuzzy controller used to guide a simulated robot through a virtual world populated with obstacles randomly placed. We tested three different controller configurations. We used a criteria based on the removal of rules to test the stability and sensitivity of the controller at the same time. The measurement of the performance of the controller was based on the following parameters: processing time and quantity of steps to reach the goal. In the majority of the experiments the performance of the optimized variable step controller was better than the other ones. The quantity of stagnated samples indicates that the controller had not wasted much time processing eminent crashes. The properly speed treatment brought improvements in time processing and number of steps to reach the goal, without compromising the simplicity of the system design. The optimizations were effective because the stability and efficiency of the controller were not compromised. The comparison among different approaches indicated the reliability of the fuzzy logic based systems.

References

1. Moratori, P. *et al.*: Análise de Estabilidade e Robustez de um Sistema de Controle Fuzzy Otimizado desenvolvido para guiar um robô simulado. In: Proceedings of XXXII SEMISH: Brazilian Software and Hardware Seminars, São Leopoldo, RS, Brazil, (2005) pp. 1704-1715.
2. Moratori, P. *et al.*: Analysis of stability of a Fuzzy Control System developed to control a simulated robot, In: Proceedings of FUZZ-IEEE 2005: The 14th IEEE International Conference on Fuzzy Systems, Reno, Nevada, USA, (2005) pp. 726-730.
3. Moratori, P. *et al.*: Analysis of the performance of a Fuzzy Controller developed to guide a simulated robot, In: Proceedings of ICCC 2005: The IEEE 3rd International Conference on Computational Cybernetics, Mauritius, (2005).
4. Moratori, P. *et al.*: Analysis of Sensitivity and Robustness to a Fuzzy System developed to guide a Simulated Robot through a Virtual World with Obstacles, In: Proceedings of ISDA 2004: The IEEE 4th International Conference on Intelligent Systems Design and Applications Conference, Budapest, Hungary, (2004) pp. 283-286.
5. Setnes, M. and Roubos, H.: GA-Fuzzy Modeling and Classification: Complexity and Performance, IEEE Transactions and Fuzzy Systems. v.8, n° 5, October (2000) pp. 509-521.

6. Yen, J. and Langari, R.: Fuzzy Logic: Intelligence, Control and Information, Prentice Hall, Englewod Cliffs (1999).
7. Mamdani E.: Application of Fuzzy Logic to Approximate Reasoning using Linguistic Synthesis, IEEE Transactions on Computers, vol. C-26, n° 12, (1997) pp. 1182- 1191.
8. Kosko, B.: Fuzzy Thinking: The New Science of Fuzzy Logic. London: Flamingo (1993).
9. Kosko, B. and Kong, S.: Comparison of Fuzzy and Neural Truck Backer-Upper Control Systems, In: Neural Networks and Fuzzy Systems: A Dynamical Systems Approach to Machine Intelligence", Prentice Hall, Englewod Cliffs (1992) p.339.
10. Langari, G. and Tomizuka, M.: Stability of fuzzy linguistic control systems. In: Proceedings of the 1990 29th Conference on Decision and Control (1990) pp. 2185-2190.

Discrete-Time Quasi-Sliding Mode Feedback-Error-Learning Neurocontrol of a Class of Uncertain Systems

Andon Venelinov Topalov[1] and Okyay Kaynak[2]

[1] Control Systems Department, Technical University of Sofia, branch Plovdiv, 25,
Canko Dustabanov str.,4000, Plovdiv, Bulgaria
`topalov@tu-plovdiv.bg`
[2] Electrical & Electronic Engineering Department,
Mechatronics Research and Application Center, Bogazici University,
Bebek, 34342 Istanbul, Turkey
`okyay.kaynak@boun.edu.tr`

Abstract. The features of a novel dynamical discrete-time algorithm for robust adaptive learning in feed-forward neural networks and its application to the neuro-adaptive nonlinear feedback control of systems with uncertain dynamics are presented. The proposed approach makes a direct use of variable structure systems theory. It establishes an inner sliding motion in terms of the neurocontroller parameters, leading the learning error toward zero. The outer sliding motion concerns the controlled nonlinear system, the state tracking error vector of which is simultaneously forced towards the origin of the phase space. It is shown that there exists equivalence between the two sliding motions. The convergence of the proposed algorithm is established and the conditions are given. Results from a simulated neuro-adaptive control of Duffing oscillator are presented. They show that the implemented neurocontroller inherits some of the advantages of the variable structure systems: high speed of learning and robustness.

1 Introduction

The applications of neural networks in closed-loop feedback control systems have only recently been rigorously studied. When placed in a feedback system, even a static neural network becomes a dynamical system and takes on new and unexpected behaviors. Hence, such properties of the neural structures as their internal stability, passivity, and robustness must be studied before conclusions about the closed-loop performance can be made.

Variable structure systems (VSS) with sliding mode were first proposed in the early 1950s [1]. The best property of the sliding mode control (SMC) scheme is its robustness. Broadly speaking, a system with an SMC is insensitive to parameter changes or external disturbances. Recent studies have emphasized that the convergence properties of the gradient-based training strategies widely used in artificial neural networks can be improved by utilizing the SMC approach. A sliding mode learning approach for analog multilayer feedforward neural networks (FNNs) has been presented in [2], by defining separate sliding surfaces for each network layer. A further contribution to the subject can be found in [3] in which the approach presented in [4] for Adaline neural networks is extended to allow on-line learning in FNNs with a scalar output.

Although from a theoretical point of view the development of VSS-based learning algorithms for analogue (i.e. continuous time) neurons seems easier and straightforward, the discrete-time algorithms are more convenient for practical implementation. The discrete-time sliding mode control (DTSMC) design issues have been addressed in [5, 6]. The stability issues in DTSMC have been presented in [7] and the sufficient conditions for convergence have been determined. The first results on adaptive learning in discrete-time neural networks, for both single and multilayer perceptrons, based on the theory of the quasi-sliding modes in discrete time dynamical systems are presented in [8]. These algorithms constitute the basis of the later proposed identification and control schemes in [9]. Another learning algorithm for FNNs is recently developed in [10]. It may be considered as the discrete time counterpart of the continuous time algorithm earlier proposed in [2].

The feedback-error-learning approach, initially proposed in [11] and applied to control of robot manipulators, has been based on the neural network (NN) realization of the computed torque control, plus a secondary proportional plus derivative (PD) controller. The output of the PD controller has been also used as an error signal to update the weights of a NN trained to become a feedforward controller. Subsequently this approach has been extended for learning schemes where NN has been applied as an adaptive nonlinear feedback controller [12].

In the present paper the feedback-error-learning approach is further investigated by applying a newly developed VSS-based discrete-time on-line learning algorithm to the NN feedback controller (NNFC). An inner quasi-sliding motion in terms of the NNFC parameters is established, leading the output signal of the conventional feedback controller (CFC) toward zero. The outer quasi-sliding motion concerns the nonlinear system under control, the state tracking error vector of which is simultaneously forced towards the origin of the phase space.

Section 2 presents the developed discrete-time on-line learning algorithm, the proposed sliding mode feedback-error-learning control scheme and introduces the equivalency constraints on the sliding control performance for the plant and the learning performance for the NNFC. Results from a simulated control of Duffing oscillator by using this neurocontrol strategy are shown in section 3. Finally, section 4 summarizes the findings of the work.

2 The Quasi-Sliding Mode Feedback-Error-Learning Approach

2.1 Initial Assumptions and Definitions

The proposed control scheme is depicted on Figure 1. The system under control is considered as nonlinear and nonautonomous, described by Eq. (1).

$$\theta^{(r)} = \psi\left(\theta, \dot{\theta},...,\theta^{(r-1)}, t\right) + \tau \qquad (1)$$

where $\psi(\cdot)$ is an unknown function, $\underline{\theta} = \left[\theta, \dot{\theta},...,\theta^{(r-1)}\right]^T$ is the state vector, τ is the control input to the system and t is the time variable.

A PD controller (the CFC block on Figure 1) is provided both as an ordinary feedback controller to guarantee global asymptotic stability in compact space and as an inverse reference model of the response of the system under control.

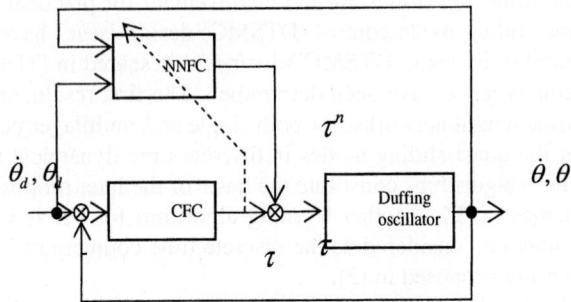

Fig. 1. Block diagram of nonlinear regulator sliding mode feedback-error-learning scheme

Consider a two-layered feedforward NN implemented as NNFC where $X = [x_1, x_2, ... x_p]^T \in \mathbb{R}^p$ is the augmented by a bias term input vector (input pattern) which is assumed fixed during the learning iterations, $T_H(k) = [\tau^n_{H1}(k), ... , \tau^n_{Hn}(k)]^T \in \mathbb{R}^n$ is the vector of the output signals from the neurons in the hidden layer, where k is the time index or iteration. $netT_H(k) = [net\,\tau_{H_1}(k), net\,\tau_{H_2}(k), ..., net\,\tau_{H_n}(k)]^T$ is the vector of the net input signals of the hidden neurons. It is computed as $netT_H(k) = W1(k)X$, where $W1(k) \in \mathbb{R}^{n \times p}$ is the matrix of the time-varying weights of the connections between the neurons of the input and the hidden layer. Each element $w1_{i,j}(k)$ of this matrix represents the weight of the connection of the corresponding hidden neuron i from its input j. $\tau^n(k) \in \mathbb{R}$ is the time varying network output. It can be calculated as follows:

$$\tau^n(k) = W2(k)\Phi[netT_H(k)] = W2(k)T_H(k) \qquad (2)$$

where $W2(k) \in \mathbb{R}^{1 \times n}$ is the vector of the weights of the connections between the neurons in the hidden layer and the output node. Both $W1(k)$ and $W2(k)$ are considered augmented by including the bias weight components for the corresponding neurons. $\Phi[netT_H(k)] = [f_1(net\,\tau_{H_1}(k)), ..., f_n(net\,\tau_{H_n}(k))]^T$, $\Phi: \mathbb{R}^n \to \mathbb{R}^n$ is an operator which elements $f_i(\cdot)$ are the activation functions of the neurons in the hidden layer. It will be assumed here that $f_i(\cdot): \mathbb{R} \to \mathbb{R}$ is such that $f_i(-net\,\tau_{H_i}) = -f_i(net\,\tau_{H_i})$ for $i = 1,...,n$. The so called tan-sigmoid activation function $\left(tan\text{-}sig(x) = \frac{1 - e^{-x}}{1 + e^{-x}}\right)$, common to neural networks, has been used in the experiments. The neuron in the output layer is considered with a linear activation function. The output signal of the PD controller $\tau^c(k)$ represents the learning error for the neurocontroller at the time step k.

2.2 The VSC-Based Discrete-Time On-Line Learning Algorithm

A VSC-based discrete-time learning algorithm is applied to the NNFC. The zero adaptive learning error level for the neurocontroller $S_c(k)$ and the sliding surface for the nonlinear system under control $S_p(k)$ are defined as $S_c(k) = \tau^c(k) = \tau^n(k) + \tau$ and $S_p(k) = \Delta e(k) + \lambda e(k)$ respectively with $e(k) = \theta(k) - \theta_d(k)$, and λ being a constant determining the slope of the sliding surface.

In the continuous SMC design the well known stability condition to be satisfied for a sliding mode to occur is [13]:

$$S(t)\dot{S}(t) < 0 \qquad (3)$$

In the discrete-time implementation of the sliding mode methodology a non-ideal sliding (quasi-sliding) regime will inevitably appear, since the control input is computed and applied to the system at discrete instants. It is clear that the condition (3) which assures the sliding motion is no longer applicable in discrete-time systems. Thus, a discrete-time sliding mode condition must be imposed. The simplest approach is to substitute the derivative by the forward difference as in (4)

$$\left[S(k+1) - S(k)\right] S(k) < 0 \qquad (4)$$

but this represents the necessary, not sufficient condition for the existence of a quasi-sliding motion, [7]. It does not assure any convergence of the state trajectories onto the sliding manifold and may result in an increasing amplitude chatter of the state trajectories around the hyperplane, which means instability. A necessary and sufficient condition assuring both sliding motion and convergence onto the sliding manifold is given in the following form [7]:

$$|S(k+1)| < |S(k)| \qquad (5)$$

The above condition can be decomposed into two inequalities as:

$$\left[S(k+1) - S(k)\right] \text{sign} S(k) < 0 \qquad (6)$$

and

$$\left[S(k+1) + S(k)\right] \text{sign} S(k) > 0 \qquad (7)$$

where (6) and (7) are known as sliding condition and convergence condition, respectively.

The network should be continuously trained in such a way that the sliding mode conditions (6) and (7) will be enforced. To enable $S_c = 0$ is reached, the following theorem is used:

Theorem 1: If the adaptation laws for the weights $W1(t)$ and $W2(t)$ are chosen respectively as

$$\Delta W1(k) = -\frac{2 netT_H(k) X^T}{X^T X} \quad (8.a)$$

$$W1(k+1) = W1(k) + \Delta W1(k) \quad (8.b)$$

and

$$\Delta W2(k) = -2W2(k) + \frac{T_H^T(k)}{T_H^T T_H} \alpha \, sign \, \tau^c(k) \quad (9.a)$$

$$W2(k+1) = W2(k) + \Delta W2(k) \quad (9.b)$$

with $\alpha \in \mathbb{R}$ being the adaptive reduction factor satisfying $0 < \alpha < 2|\tau^c(k)|$, then, for any arbitrary initial condition $\tau^c(0)$, the learning error $\tau^c(k)$ will converge asymptotically to zero and a quasi-sliding motion will be maintained on $\tau^c = 0$.

Proof: One can check that the following string of equations is satisfied.

$$\begin{aligned}\Delta \tau^c(k+1) &= \tau^c(k+1) - \tau^c(k) = \tau^n(k+1) - \tau^n(k) = \\ &= W2(k+1) T_H(k+1) - W2(k) T_H(k) = \\ &= [W2(k) + \Delta W2(k)] T_H(k+1) - W2(k) T_H(k) = \\ &= W2(k)[T_H(k+1) - T_H(k)] + \Delta W2(k) T_H(k+1) = \\ &= W2(k)\{\Phi[netT_H(k+1)] - \Phi[netT_H(k)]\} + \Delta W2(k) \Phi[netT_H(k+1)]\end{aligned} \quad (10)$$

Note that

$$netT_H(k+1) = W1(k+1) X = [W1(k) + \Delta W1(k)] X = netT_H(k) + \Delta W1(k) X \quad (11)$$

Substituting (11) and (8.a) into (10) yields

$$\begin{aligned}\Delta \tau^c(k+1) &= W2(k)\{\Phi[netT_H(k) + \Delta W1(k) X] - \Phi[netT_H(k)]\} + \\ &+ \Delta W2(k) \Phi[netT_H(k) + \Delta W1(k) X] = \\ &= W2(k)\{\Phi[-netT_H(k)] - \Phi[netT_H(k)]\} + \Delta W2(k) \Phi[-netT_H(k)]\end{aligned} \quad (12)$$

Since Φ is odd by assumption, the previous error equation becomes

$$\begin{aligned}\Delta \tau^c(k+1) &= -2W2(k) \Phi[netT_H(k)] - \Delta W2(k) \Phi[netT_H(k)] = \\ &= -[2W2(k) + \Delta W2(k)] T_H(k)\end{aligned} \quad (13)$$

Substituting (9.a) into the above equation gives

$$\Delta \tau^c(k+1) = \left[-2W2(k) + 2W2(k) - \frac{T_H^T(k)\alpha \, \text{sign}\, \tau^c(k)}{T_H^T(k)T_H(k)}\right] T_H(k) = \\ = -\alpha \, \text{sign}\, \tau^c(k) \quad (14)$$

By multiplying both sides of Eq. (14) by $\tau^c(k)$ it follows that

$$\Delta \tau^c(k+1)\tau^c(k) = -\alpha |\tau^c(k)| < 0 \quad (15)$$

which means that the sliding condition (4) or (6) is satisfied.
Eq. (14) can be also rewritten as follows

$$\tau^c(k+1) = \tau^c(k) - \alpha \, \text{sign}\, \tau^c(k) \quad (16)$$

By adding to the both sides of Eq. (16) $\tau^c(k)$ and subsequent multiplication with $\text{sign}\, \tau^c(k)$ the following equation can be obtained

$$\left[\tau^c(k+1) + \tau^c(k)\right] \text{sign}\, \tau^c(k) = 2|\tau^c(k)| - \alpha \quad (17)$$

It follows from Eq. (17) that the convergence condition (7) will be satisfied for all $0 < \alpha < 2|\tau^c(k)|$ and $\tau^c(k) \neq 0$. This proof is a sufficient condition for the quasi-sliding mode to occur.

Remark 2: Note that Eq. (16) describes the neurocontroller error dynamics.
In particular if $\alpha = \beta |\tau^c(k)|$ with $0 < \beta < 2$ is used it follows that

$$\tau^c(k+1) = (1-\beta)\tau^c(k) \quad (18)$$

which coincides with the result obtained by Sira-Ramirez and Zak (1991), and shows that the learning error will converge asymptotically to 0 at a rate of $1-\beta$.

2.3 Relation Between the Discrete-Time VSC-Based Learning of the Controller and the Quasi-Sliding Motion in the Behavior of the Controlled System

The relation between the sliding line $S_p(k)$ and the zero adaptive learning error level $S_c(k)$, when λ is taken as $\lambda = \frac{K_P}{K_D}$, is determined by the following equation:

$$S_c(k) = \tau^c(k) = K_D \Delta e(k) + K_P e(k) = K_D \left[\Delta e(k) + \frac{K_P}{K_D} e(k)\right] = K_D S_p(k) \quad (19)$$

where K_D and K_P are the PD controller gains.

For a quasi-sliding regime to occur for the system under control conditions (4)-(7) must be satisfied.

Theorem 3. If the adaptation strategy for the adjustable parameters of the NNFC is chosen as in equations (8)-(9) then an outer quasi-sliding motion of the nonlinear system under control will have place and its state tracking error vector will be simultaneously forced towards the origin of the phase space.

Proof: One can check that the following two strings of equations are satisfied:

$$\Delta S_p(k+1) S_p(k) = \frac{1}{K_D^2} \Delta S_c(k+1) S_c(k) =$$

$$= \frac{1}{K_D^2} \Delta \tau^c(k+1) \tau^c(k) = -\alpha \frac{1}{K_D^2} |\tau^c(k)| < 0 \qquad (20)$$

which means that the sliding condition (4) or (6) is satisfied.

$$\left[S_p(k+1) + S_p(k) \right] \operatorname{sign} S_p(k) = \frac{1}{|K_D|} \left[S_c(k+1) + S_c(k) \right] \operatorname{sign} S_c(k) =$$

$$= \frac{1}{|K_D|} \left[\tau^c(k+1) + \tau^c(k) \right] \operatorname{sign} \tau^c(k) = 2 \left| \frac{\tau^c(k)}{K_D} \right| - \alpha \qquad (21)$$

which means that the convergence condition (7) will be satisfied for all $0 < \alpha < 2 \left| \frac{\tau^c(k)}{K_D} \right|$.

Remark 4. The obtained results mean that, assuming the VSC task is achievable, utilization of τ^c as the learning error for the NNFC together with the tuning laws of (8)-(9) enforces the desired reaching mode followed by the quasi-sliding regime for the system under control. It is straightforward to prove that the hitting occurs in finite time.

3 Quasi-Sliding Mode Control of Duffing Oscillator

In the simulations, we test the effectiveness of the proposed approach on the control of a Duffing oscillator which is described by the following differential equation:

$$\ddot{\theta} = -p_1 \theta - p_2 \theta^3 - p \dot{\theta} + q \cos(\omega_d t) + \tau \qquad (22)$$

where, $p_1 = 1.1$, $p_2 = 1$, $p = 0.4$, $q = 2.1$ and $\omega_d = 1.8$. The control problem is to enforce the states to the periodic orbit described as $\ddot{\theta}_d = \sin(\theta_d)$ with $\theta_d(0) = 1$ and $\dot{\theta}_d(0) = 0$. The identification and control of the system in Eq. (22) have previously been studied in [14]. It must be noted that the enforced trajectory is radically different from the stable limit cycle of the system dynamics, and this fact requires continuous control effort.

The block diagram of the control system is depicted in Figure 1 in detail. In Figure 2, the phase space behavior is demonstrated. The plot seen figures out that $S_p = 0$ line is the attracting invariant. Clearly the error vector is guided towards the sliding manifold and due to the design presented, it is forced to remain in the vicinity of the attracting loci without explicitly knowing the analytical details of the function $\psi(\cdot)$. However, it can fairly be claimed that the sliding manifold is most probably a locally invariant subspace as the results strongly depend upon the unknown function $\psi(\cdot)$.

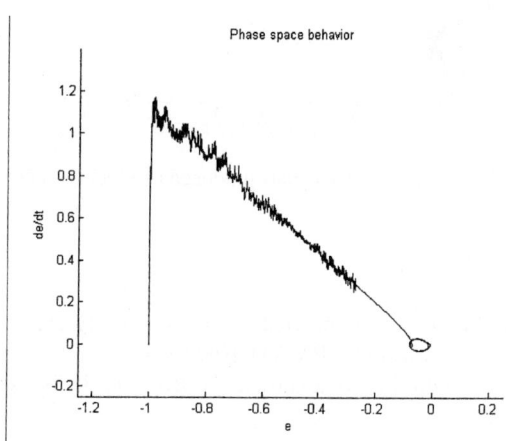

Fig. 2. Phase space behavior

In Figure 3, the applied control signals produced by CFC and NNFC are illustrated. Although the exact use of the $sign(\cdot)$ function in Eq. (9.a) introduces some amount of high-frequency components in the NNFC control signal, the produced control sequence is sufficiently smooth and reasonable in magnitude.

It can be seen that the CFC control signal is suppressed by the NNFC and the required trajectory is closely followed demonstrating the good performance of the control scheme.

4 Conclusion

A novel approach for generating and maintaining quasi-sliding regime in the behavior of a system with uncertainties in its dynamics is introduced. The system under control is under a closed-loop simultaneously with a conventional PD controller and an adaptive variable structure neurocontroller. The presented results from a simulated control of Duffing oscillator have demonstrated that the predefined quasi-sliding regime could be generated and maintained if the NNFC parameters are tuned in such a way that the reaching is enforced. Another prominent feature that should be emphasized is the computational simplicity of the proposed approach.

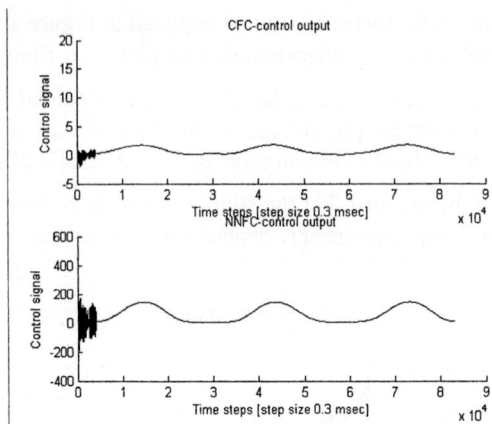

Fig. 3. Applied control signals produced by CFC and NNFC

Acknowledgements

The first author would like to acknowledge Ministry of Education and Science of Bulgaria Research Fund Project No: BY-TH-108/2005.

The second author would like to acknowledge Bogazici University Research Fund Project No: 03M109.

References

1. Utkin, V.I.: Sliding Modes in Control and Optimization. Springer-Verlag, Berlin Heidelberg New York (1992)
2. Parma, G.G., Menezes, B.R., Braga, A.P.: Sliding Mode Algorithm for Training Multilayer Artificial Neural Networks. Electronic Letters, Vol. 34, No. 1 (1998) 97-98
3. Shakev, N.G., Topalov, A.V., Kaynak, O.: Sliding Mode Algorithm for On-Line Learning in Analog Multilayer Feedforward Neural Networks. In: Kaynak et al. (eds.): Artificial Neural Networks and Neural Information Processing. Lecture Notes in Computer Science, Springer-Verlag, Berlin Heidelberg New York (2003) 1064-1072
4. Sira-Ramirez, H., Colina-Morles, E.: A Sliding Mode Strategy for Adaptive Learning in Adalines. IEEE Trans. on Circuits and Systems-I: Fundamental Theory and Applications, Vol. 42, No. 12 (1995) 1001-1012
5. Gao, W., Wang, Y., Homaifa, A.: Discrete-Time Variable Structure Control Systems. IEEE Trans. on Indust. Electr., Vol. 42 (1995) 117-122
6. Sira-Ramirez, H.: Non-linear Discrete Variable Structure Systems in Quasi-sliding Mode. International Journal of Control, Vol. 54 (1991) 1171-1187
7. Sarpturk, S.Z., Istefanopulos, Y., Kaynak, O.: On the Stability of Discrete-Time Sliding Mode Control Systems. IEEE Trans. on Automatic Control, Vol. 32 (1987) 930-932
8. Sira-Ramirez, H., Zak, S.H.: The Adaptation of Perceptrons with Applications to Inverse Dynamics Identification of Unknown Dynamic Systems. IEEE Trans. Syst. Man and Cybern., Vol. 21, No. 3 (1991) 634-643

9. Kuschewski, J.G., Hui, S., Zak, S.H.: Application of Feedforward Networks to Dynamical Systems Identification and Control. IEEE Trans. Cont. Syst. Techn., Vol. 1, No. 1 (1993) 37-49
10. Parma, G.G., Menezes, B.R., Braga A.P.: Neural Network Learning with Sliding Mode Control: The Sliding Mode Backpropagation Algorithm. Int. Journal Neural Syst., Vol. 9, No. 3 (1999) 187-193
11. Kawato, M., Uno, Y., Isobe, M., Suzuki, R.A.: Hierarchical Model for Voluntary Movement and with Application to Robotics. IEEE Contr. Syst. Mag., Vol. 8, No. 2 (1988) 8-16
12. Gomi, H., Kawato, M.: Neural Network Control for a Closed-Loop System Using Feed-Back-Error-Learning. Neural Networks, Vol. 6 (1993) 933-946
13. Edwards, C., Spurgeon, S.K.: Sliding Mode Control: Theory and Applications, Taylor & Francis, Ltd. (1998)
14. Poznyak, A.S., Yu, W., Sanchez, E.N.: Identifcation and Control of Unknown Chaotic Systems via Dynamic Neural Networks. IEEE Transactions on Circuits and Systems—I: Fundamental Theory and Applications, Vol. 46, No.12 (1999) 1491–1495

Stable Task Space Neuro Controller for Robot Manipulators Without Velocity Measurements

Gerardo Loreto and Rubén Garrido

Departamento de Control Automático,
CINVESTAV-IPN, Av.IPN 2508 México D.F., 07360, México
(gloreto, garrido)@ctrl.cinvestav.mx.

Abstract. In this work a stable task space neuro algorithm for set-point control of robot manipulators with uncertain parameters is proposed. A depart from current approaches is the fact that a Wavelet Neural Network with on-line real-time learning seeks to explicitly compensate both the unknown gravity terms and the mismatch between the true and the estimated Jacobian matrix and the fact that it does not need velocity measurements. Linear position filtering is used to estimated the robot joint velocity in the control law and the properties of the Wavelet Neural Network are employed for avoiding velocity measurements in the learning rule. It is shown that all the closed loop signals are uniformly ultimately bounded. Experimental results in a two degrees of freedom robot are presented to evaluate the proposed controller.

1 Introduction

In order to move the robot end-effector to the desired position using task information, *a priori* knowledge about robot kinematics and dynamics may be required. One way to alleviate the above difficulty is to identify or calibrate the robot parameters; however, it would be a time-consuming task. Several approaches have been proposed in the literature to address the above problem. For instance, Miyazaki and Masutani [6] provided the first rigorous stability analysis of task space based feedback controller in spite of an uncertain image Jacobian. A practical drawback of this approach is the fact that it requires exact knowledge of both the robot Jacobian matrix and the gravitational torques. The above requirements were partially overcome using adaptive techniques in [1] where the linear in the parameters property of the gravity terms is exploited and the structure of the gravity terms in the form of a gravity regressor must be known. Recently, in [10] exact knowledge of the gravity regressor was relaxed and the proposed approach unifies adaptive proportional derivative (PD) plus gravity compensation and proportional, integral and derivative (PID) controllers. Moreover, it does not require any knowledge about the gravitational terms. It is worth remarking that in [1] and [10] exact knowledge of the entire robot Jacobian matrix is relaxed. A disadvantage of the PID controllers proposed in [10] is that they may cause a large overshoot in the transient response due to the fact that the error in estimating the gravitational terms is large at the beginning. It is also worth noting that in the above approaches the closed loop system remains stable in spite of imprecise knowledge on the robot Jacobian matrix but no explicit effort is done for compensating the lack of knowledge about this matrix. Moreover, all the above approaches require the measurements of robot joint velocity which are often contaminated by a considerable amount of noise or they are not available.

In the last few years several neural network (NN) controllers for robot manipulators, derived through Lyapunov stability theory, have been proposed to deal with the robot dynamics uncertainties [4], [5], [7]. Justification for using NN for robot control lies in their excellent capability of learning a nonlinear model without any *a priori* knowledge on their parameters and structure.

The present paper proposes a neuro-based controller for robot manipulators in task space. The proposed scheme does not need an *a priori* knowledge on the robot gravity terms structure and parameters. Further, exact knowledge of the robot Jacobian matrix is not needed. A depart from previous works is the fact that the proposed control law seeks to explicitly compensate both the unknown gravity terms and the mismatch between the true and the estimated Jacobian matrix and it does not need velocity measurements. The learning rule for Wavelet Neural Network (WNN) training is obtained from a Lyapunov stability analysis and no off-line training phase is required. Linear position filtering is used for estimating the robot joint velocity in the control law, moreover, the properties of the WNN are exploited in order to avoid velocity measurements in the learning rule. To the best of the authors' knowledge this is the first time that these properties of the WNN are employed in this way. It is proved that all the closed-loop signals are *uniformly ultimately bounded* (UUB) and converge to a compact set which can be made arbitrarily small. Experimental results are shown in order to assess the performance of the proposed controller and a comparative study is made where the proposed controller is compared against adaptive and PID based controllers.

2 Background

Throughout this paper, we use the notations $\lambda_m\{\mathbf{A}\}$ and $\lambda_M\{\mathbf{A}\}$ to indicate the smallest and largest eigenvalues respectively of a symmetric positive definite bounded matrix $\mathbf{A}(\mathbf{x}) \in \Re^{n \times n}$, for any $\mathbf{x} \in \Re^n$. The vector norm is defined as $\|\mathbf{x}\| = \sqrt{\mathbf{x}^T \mathbf{x}}$, and the matrix norm is defined as the corresponding induced norm $\|\mathbf{A}\| = \sqrt{\lambda_M\{\mathbf{A}^T\mathbf{A}\}}$. Given $\mathbf{A}=[a_{ij}]$, $\mathbf{B} \subset \Re^{m \times n}$ the Frobenius norm is defined by $\|\mathbf{A}\|_F^2 = tr(\mathbf{A}^T \mathbf{A})$ with $tr(\cdot)$ the trace of a matrix. The Frobenius norm is compatible with the two-norm so that [8] $\|\mathbf{A}\mathbf{x}\| \le \|\mathbf{A}\|_F \|\mathbf{x}\|$.

2.1 Wavelet Neural Networks

Consider the WNN with N_2 hidden neurons and N_3 output neurons. Given the input vector $\mathbf{x} = [x_1 \cdots x_{N1}]^T \in \Re^{N_I}$, then, the output vector $\mathbf{y} = [y_1 \cdots y_{N3}]^T \in \Re^{N_3}$ is given by

$$\mathbf{y} = \mathbf{W}^T \sigma(\mathbf{x}) \tag{1}$$

where $\mathbf{W}^T=[w_{kj}] \in \Re^{N_3 \times (N_2+1)}$ with w_{kj} the weight connecting the hidden neuron j and the output neuron k and $\sigma(\mathbf{x})=[1\ \sigma_1(\mathbf{x})\ ...\ \sigma_{N2}(\mathbf{x})]^T \in \Re^{N_2+1}$ with $\sigma_j(\mathbf{x}) = \prod_{i=1}^{N_1} \sigma_j(x_i)$ an activation function generated by dilating and translating the mother wavelet function which we select it as the first derivative of a Gaussian function, i.e. $\sigma_j(x_i) = -x_i \exp\left(-\dfrac{(x_i - c_{ji})^2}{2 p_{ji}^2}\right)$ where c_{ji} is the translation and p_{ji} is a dilation parameters.

2.2 Robot System Model

The dynamics of the n-revolute links rigid robot manipulator can be expressed as [8]

$$\mathbf{M(q)\ddot{q}} + \mathbf{C(q,\dot{q})\dot{q}} + \mathbf{B\dot{q}} + \mathbf{G(q)} = \tau(t) \qquad (2)$$

where $\mathbf{q}(t) \in \Re^n$ is the joint angular displacement vector, $\mathbf{\dot{q}} \in \Re^n$ is the joint velocity vector, $\mathbf{M(q)} \in \Re^{n \times n}$ is the inertia matrix, $\mathbf{C(q,\dot{q})\dot{q}} \in \Re^n$ is the centrifugal and Coriolis term, $\mathbf{B} \in \Re^{n \times n}$ is the positive semidefinite diagonal matrix accounting for joint viscous friction, $\mathbf{G(q)} \in \Re^n$ is the gravity term and $\tau(t) \in \Re^n$ is the control torque. The main properties of revolute joint manipulator dynamics are as follows [8]

1. Matrix $\mathbf{\dot{M}(q)} - 2\mathbf{C(q,\dot{q})}$ is skew-symmetric.
2. There exists a positive constant k_c such that $\|\mathbf{C(q,\dot{q})}\| \le k_c \|\mathbf{\dot{q}}\|$

One possible definition for the elements of $\mathbf{C(q,\dot{q})}$ for which property 1 holds is

$$\mathbf{C}_{ij}(\mathbf{q},\mathbf{\dot{q}}) = \dfrac{1}{2}\left[\mathbf{\dot{q}}^T \dfrac{\partial M_{ij}}{\partial \mathbf{q}} + \sum_{k=1}^{2}\left(\dfrac{\partial M_{ik}}{\partial q_j} - \dfrac{\partial M_{jk}}{\partial q_i}\right)\dot{q}_k\right] \qquad (3)$$

$i, j = 1, \ldots, n$

where M_{ij} are the elements of the $\mathbf{M(q)}$. This definition implies that

$$\mathbf{\dot{M}(q)} = \mathbf{C(q,\dot{q})} + \mathbf{C(q,\dot{q})}^T \qquad (4)$$

In a large number of applications, the desired position of the end-effector is given in the task space coordinates $\mathbf{x} \in \Re^m$ such as Cartesian or Visual coordinates. The kinematics and the differential kinematics maps between the end-effector position coordinates $\mathbf{x} \in \Re^m$ and the joint space coordinates $\mathbf{q} \in \Re^n$ can be written as

$$\mathbf{x} = \mathbf{h(q)}, \qquad \mathbf{\dot{x}} = \mathbf{J(q)\dot{q}} \qquad (5)$$

where $\mathbf{h} : \Re^n \to \Re^m$, $\mathbf{J(q)} = \dfrac{\partial \mathbf{h(q)}}{\partial \mathbf{q}}$ is the Jacobian matrix. An important property of the Jacobian matrix $\mathbf{J(q)}$ for revolute joint robot is the following

Property 1. The robot Jacobian matrix is bounded for all $\mathbf{q} \in \Re^n$, i.e., there exists a finite constant k_J such that $\|\mathbf{J}(\mathbf{q})\| \le k_J \quad \forall \mathbf{q} \in \Re^n$

3 Stability Analysis

Many well-known results state that any continuous function can be approximated in a compact set using a neural network with appropriate weights [4]. Using the neural network universal approximation property, an unknown function $\Psi(\mathbf{q})$ can be approximated by a WNN as

$$\Psi(\mathbf{q}) = \mathbf{W}^T \sigma(\mathbf{q}) + \varepsilon \tag{6}$$

where $\mathbf{W}^T \in \Re^{N_3 \times (N_2+1)}$, $\sigma(\cdot) \in \Re^{N_2+1}$ and ε is the neural network approximation error. For some unknown constant optimal ideal weights $\mathbf{W}$, the reconstruction error is bounded by $\|\varepsilon\| < k_\varepsilon$. In order to implement neural network (6) the following assumption on the ideal weights is needed [4]

Assumption 1. *The optimal ideal weights $\mathbf{W}$ are bounded by positive values k_w so that $\|\mathbf{W}\|_F \le k_w$*

An estimate of the function $\Psi(\mathbf{q})$ denoted as $\hat{\Psi}(\mathbf{q})$ is

$$\hat{\Psi}(\mathbf{q}) = \hat{\mathbf{W}}^T \sigma(\mathbf{q}) \tag{7}$$

where $\hat{\mathbf{W}}^T \in \Re^{N_3 \times (N_2+1)}$ are estimates of the ideal neural network weights $\mathbf{W}$ and provided by some on-line weight tuning algorithm.

Motivated by the Jacobian transpose control philosophy introduced in [9], the proposed control law is

$$\tau = \hat{\mathbf{J}}(\mathbf{q})^T \mathbf{K}_p \tilde{\mathbf{x}} - \mathbf{K}_d \dot{\hat{\mathbf{q}}} + \hat{\mathbf{W}}^T \sigma(\mathbf{q}) \tag{8}$$

$$\dot{\hat{\mathbf{q}}} = -\mathbf{L}_1 \hat{\mathbf{q}} - \mathbf{K}_d \tilde{\mathbf{q}} \tag{9}$$

where $\mathbf{K}_p = k_p \mathbf{I}$ and $\mathbf{K}_d$ are symmetric positive definite diagonal proportional and derivative gain matrices and $\hat{\mathbf{J}}(\mathbf{q})$ is an estimate of the uncertain Jacobian matrix $\mathbf{J}(\mathbf{q})$ such that

$$\left\| \mathbf{J}(\mathbf{q}) - \hat{\mathbf{J}}(\mathbf{q}) \right\| \le k_\Delta \tag{10}$$

where k_Δ is a positive constant. The goal of the control law (8) in closed loop with the robot model (2) is to drive the position $\mathbf{x}$ to a neighborhood of the desired position $\mathbf{x}^*$ with a certain precision

$$\|\mathbf{x}^* - \mathbf{x}\| \le B; \quad B > 0 \tag{11}$$

In order to perform the stability analysis of the closed loop system we proceed as follows. Adding and subtracting $\mathbf{J}(\mathbf{q})^T \mathbf{K}_p \tilde{\mathbf{x}}$ on the right hand side of (2) and substituting the above control law (8), the closed-loop system dynamics is obtained as

$$\mathbf{M(q)\ddot{q}+C(q,\dot{q})\dot{q}+B\dot{q}+G(q)+\Delta K}_p\tilde{\mathbf{x}}=\mathbf{J(q)}^T\mathbf{K}_p\tilde{\mathbf{x}}-\mathbf{K}_d\dot{\hat{\mathbf{q}}}+\hat{\mathbf{W}}^T\sigma(\mathbf{q}) \quad (12)$$

where $\Delta = \mathbf{J(q)} - \hat{\mathbf{J}}(\mathbf{q})$. Then, by defining

$$\Psi(\mathbf{q}) = \mathbf{G(q)} + \Delta \mathbf{K}_p \tilde{\mathbf{x}} \quad (13)$$

and using (6), the closed-loop system becomes

$$\mathbf{M(q)\ddot{q}+C(q,\dot{q})\dot{q}+B\dot{q}}+\tilde{\mathbf{W}}^T\sigma(\mathbf{q})+\varepsilon=\mathbf{J(q)}^T\mathbf{K}_p\tilde{\mathbf{x}}-\mathbf{K}_d\dot{\hat{\mathbf{q}}} \quad (14)$$

where $\tilde{\mathbf{W}} = \mathbf{W} - \hat{\mathbf{W}}$ is the weight estimation error.

Remark 1. In the regulation control problem, the point $\mathbf{x}^*$ is a constant position and the point $\mathbf{x}$ is attached to the robot arm end-effector, then, the term $\Delta \mathbf{K}_p \tilde{\mathbf{x}}$ can be considered as a function of the robot end effector position and then, using the forward kinematics, is also a function of the joint positions $\mathbf{q}$. Note also from (13) that the NN approximates simultaneously the gravity terms $\mathbf{G(q)}$ and the term $\Delta \mathbf{K}_p \tilde{\mathbf{x}}$ containing the error between the true and the estimated Jacobian matrix.

The following theorem shows how to adjust the weights of neural network (7) to guarantee closed-loop stability in spite of uncertain gravity terms and Jacobian matrix.

Theorem 1. *Consider the closed-loop system (14) where the updating law for the weights of neural network (7) is given by*

$$\dot{\mathbf{W}} = -\mathbf{K}_w \sigma(\mathbf{q})\left[\dot{\mathbf{q}} - \mu \hat{\mathbf{J}}(\mathbf{q})^T \mathbf{f}(\tilde{\mathbf{x}})\right]^T - \kappa \mathbf{K}_w \|\tilde{\mathbf{x}}\|\mathbf{W} \quad (15)$$

where $\mathbf{K}_w$ is positive defined diagonal matrix, κ is a positive constant and function $\mathbf{f}(\tilde{\mathbf{x}})$ is defined as $\mathbf{f}(\tilde{\mathbf{x}}) = \dfrac{\tilde{\mathbf{x}}}{1+\|\tilde{\mathbf{x}}\|}$. *If μ is chosen such that*

$$\min\left\{\sqrt{\frac{k_p}{\lambda_M\{\bar{\mathbf{M}}(\mathbf{q})\}}}, \frac{\lambda_m\{\mathbf{B}\}}{c}\right\} > \mu > 0 \quad (16)$$

with

$$\begin{aligned}\bar{\mathbf{M}}(\mathbf{q}) &= \hat{\mathbf{J}}(\mathbf{q})\mathbf{M}(\mathbf{q})\hat{\mathbf{J}}(\mathbf{q})^T \\ c &= 2\lambda_M\{\mathbf{M(q)}\}k_j k_j + \lambda_M\{\mathbf{M(q)}\}d_j + k_j k_c\end{aligned} \quad (17)$$

where k_j and d_j are positive constants, then, $\tilde{\mathbf{x}}$, $\dot{\mathbf{q}}$, $\dot{\hat{\mathbf{q}}}$ and $\tilde{\mathbf{W}}$ are Uniform Ultimately Bounded (UUB).

Proof. Define a Lyapunov function candidate as

$$\begin{aligned}V &= \frac{1}{2}\dot{\mathbf{q}}^T\mathbf{M(q)}\dot{\mathbf{q}} + \frac{1}{2}\tilde{\mathbf{x}}^T\mathbf{K}_p\tilde{\mathbf{x}} + \frac{1}{2}\dot{\hat{\mathbf{q}}}^T\dot{\hat{\mathbf{q}}} - \mu \mathbf{f}(\tilde{\mathbf{x}})^T\hat{\mathbf{J}}(\mathbf{q})\mathbf{M(q)}\dot{\mathbf{q}} \\ &+ \frac{1}{2}\operatorname{tr}\left(\tilde{\mathbf{W}}^T\mathbf{K}_w^{-1}\tilde{\mathbf{W}}\right)\end{aligned} \quad (18)$$

Equation (18) is positive definite since by hypothesis $\sqrt{\frac{k_p}{\lambda_M\{\bar{\mathbf{M}}(\mathbf{q})\}}} > \mu$. Substituting closed-loop system (14), using definition (4) and using the robot model properties shown in section 2, the time derivative of the Lyapunov function (18) yields

$$\begin{aligned}\dot{V} &= \dot{\mathbf{q}}^T\left[-\mathbf{B}\dot{\mathbf{q}}-\varepsilon\right]-\dot{\mathbf{q}}^T\mathbf{L}_1\dot{\hat{\mathbf{q}}}-\mu\dot{\mathbf{f}}(\tilde{\mathbf{x}})^T\hat{\mathbf{J}}(\mathbf{q})\mathbf{M}(\mathbf{q})\dot{\mathbf{q}}-\mu\mathbf{f}(\tilde{\mathbf{x}})^T\dot{\hat{\mathbf{J}}}(\mathbf{q})\mathbf{M}(\mathbf{q})\dot{\mathbf{q}}\\
&\quad -\mu\mathbf{f}(\tilde{\mathbf{x}})^T\hat{\mathbf{J}}(\mathbf{q})\mathbf{C}(\mathbf{q},\dot{\mathbf{q}})^T\dot{\mathbf{q}}-\mu\mathbf{f}(\tilde{\mathbf{x}})^T\hat{\mathbf{J}}(\mathbf{q})\left[\mathbf{J}(\mathbf{q})^T\mathbf{K}_p\tilde{\mathbf{x}}-\mathbf{K}_d\dot{\mathbf{q}}-\mathbf{B}\dot{\mathbf{q}}-\varepsilon\right]\\
&\quad +\mathrm{tr}\left\{\tilde{\mathbf{W}}^T\left[\mathbf{K}_w^{-1}\dot{\tilde{\mathbf{W}}}-\sigma(\mathbf{q})\dot{\mathbf{q}}^T+\mu\sigma(\mathbf{q})\mathbf{f}(\tilde{\mathbf{x}})^T\hat{\mathbf{J}}(\mathbf{q})\right]\right\}\end{aligned} \quad (19)$$

using neural network weight update law (15), the time derivative (19) becomes

$$\begin{aligned}\dot{V} &= \dot{\mathbf{q}}^T\left[-\mathbf{B}\dot{\mathbf{q}}-\varepsilon\right]-\dot{\mathbf{q}}^T\mathbf{L}_1\dot{\hat{\mathbf{q}}}-\mu\dot{\mathbf{f}}(\tilde{\mathbf{x}})^T\hat{\mathbf{J}}(\mathbf{q})\mathbf{M}(\mathbf{q})\dot{\mathbf{q}}-\mu\mathbf{f}(\tilde{\mathbf{x}})^T\dot{\hat{\mathbf{J}}}(\mathbf{q})\mathbf{M}(\mathbf{q})\dot{\mathbf{q}}\\
&\quad -\mu\mathbf{f}(\tilde{\mathbf{x}})^T\hat{\mathbf{J}}(\mathbf{q})\mathbf{C}(\mathbf{q},\dot{\mathbf{q}})^T\dot{\mathbf{q}}-\mu\mathbf{f}(\tilde{\mathbf{x}})^T\hat{\mathbf{J}}(\mathbf{q})\Delta\mathbf{K}_p\tilde{\mathbf{x}}-\mu\mathbf{f}(\tilde{\mathbf{x}})^T\hat{\mathbf{J}}(\mathbf{q})\hat{\mathbf{J}}(\mathbf{q})^T\mathbf{K}_p\tilde{\mathbf{x}}\\
&\quad -\mu\mathbf{f}(\tilde{\mathbf{x}})^T\hat{\mathbf{J}}(\mathbf{q})\left[-\mathbf{K}_d\dot{\mathbf{q}}-\mathbf{B}\dot{\mathbf{q}}-\varepsilon\right]+\kappa\mathrm{tr}(\tilde{\mathbf{W}}^T\hat{\mathbf{W}})\|\tilde{\mathbf{x}}\|\end{aligned} \quad (20)$$

We now provide upper bounds on the following terms

$$-\dot{\mathbf{q}}^T\mathbf{B}\dot{\mathbf{q}} \leq -\lambda_m\{\mathbf{B}\}\|\dot{\mathbf{q}}\|^2$$

$$-\dot{\mathbf{q}}^T\varepsilon \leq k_\varepsilon\|\dot{\mathbf{q}}\|$$

$$-\dot{\mathbf{q}}^T\mathbf{L}_1\dot{\hat{\mathbf{q}}} \leq -\lambda_m\{\mathbf{L}_1\}\|\dot{\hat{\mathbf{q}}}\|^2$$

$$-\mu\dot{\mathbf{f}}(\tilde{\mathbf{x}})^T\hat{\mathbf{J}}(\mathbf{q})\mathbf{M}(\mathbf{q})\dot{\mathbf{q}}-\mu\mathbf{f}(\tilde{\mathbf{x}})^T\dot{\hat{\mathbf{J}}}(\mathbf{q})\mathbf{M}(\mathbf{q})\dot{\mathbf{q}}-\mu\mathbf{f}(\tilde{\mathbf{x}})^T\hat{\mathbf{J}}(\mathbf{q})\mathbf{C}(\mathbf{q},\dot{\mathbf{q}})^T\dot{\mathbf{q}} \leq \mu c\|\dot{\mathbf{q}}\|^2$$

$$-\mu\mathbf{f}(\tilde{\mathbf{x}})^T\hat{\mathbf{J}}(\mathbf{q})\Delta\mathbf{K}_p\tilde{\mathbf{x}} \leq \mu k_j k_\Delta k_p\|\tilde{\mathbf{x}}\|$$

$$-\mu\mathbf{f}(\tilde{\mathbf{x}})^T\hat{\mathbf{J}}(\mathbf{q})\hat{\mathbf{J}}(\mathbf{q})^T\mathbf{K}_p\tilde{\mathbf{x}} \leq -\frac{\mu}{1+\|\tilde{\mathbf{x}}\|}k_p\lambda_m\{\hat{\mathbf{J}}(\mathbf{q})\hat{\mathbf{J}}(\mathbf{q})^T\}\|\tilde{\mathbf{x}}\|^2 \quad (21)$$

$$\mu\mathbf{f}(\tilde{\mathbf{x}})^T\hat{\mathbf{J}}(\mathbf{q})\mathbf{K}_d\dot{\mathbf{q}} \leq \mu k_j\lambda_M\{\mathbf{K}_d\}\|\dot{\mathbf{q}}\|$$

$$\mu\mathbf{f}(\tilde{\mathbf{x}})^T\hat{\mathbf{J}}(\mathbf{q})\mathbf{B}\dot{\mathbf{q}} \leq \mu k_j\lambda_M\{\mathbf{B}\}\|\dot{\mathbf{q}}\|$$

$$\mu\mathbf{f}(\tilde{\mathbf{x}})^T\hat{\mathbf{J}}(\mathbf{q})\varepsilon \leq \frac{\mu}{1+\|\tilde{\mathbf{x}}\|}k_j k_\varepsilon\|\tilde{\mathbf{x}}\|$$

$$\mathrm{tr}\left(\tilde{\mathbf{W}}^T(\mathbf{W}-\tilde{\mathbf{W}})\right) \leq -\left[\left(\|\tilde{\mathbf{W}}\|_F-\frac{k_w}{2}\right)^2-\frac{k_w^2}{4}\right]$$

where k_j and d_j denotes the norm bound for $\hat{\mathbf{J}}(\mathbf{q})$ and $\dot{\hat{\mathbf{J}}}(\mathbf{q})$, respectively. In the bounds obtained previously we have used robot model properties and the following inequalities $\|\mathbf{f}(\tilde{\mathbf{x}})\| \leq 1$; $\|\dot{\mathbf{f}}(\tilde{\mathbf{x}})\| \leq 2\|\dot{\tilde{\mathbf{x}}}\| \leq 2k_J\|\dot{\mathbf{q}}\|$. Due to the inequalities (21), (20) becomes

$$\dot{V} \leq [\gamma_B \|\dot{\mathbf{q}}\| - (k_\varepsilon + \mu k_j \lambda_M\{\mathbf{B}\})]\|\dot{\mathbf{q}}\| - (\lambda_m\{\mathbf{L}_1\}\|\ddot{\mathbf{q}}\| - \mu k_j \lambda_M\{\mathbf{K}_d\})\|\ddot{\mathbf{q}}\|$$

$$-\frac{\mu}{1+\|\tilde{\mathbf{x}}\|}(k_p \lambda_m\{\hat{\mathbf{J}}(\mathbf{q})\hat{\mathbf{J}}(\mathbf{q})^T\}\|\tilde{\mathbf{x}}\| - k_j k_\varepsilon)\|\tilde{\mathbf{x}}\| \qquad (22)$$

$$-\left[\kappa\left[\left(\|\tilde{\mathbf{W}}\|_F - \frac{k_w}{2}\right)^2 - \frac{k_w^2}{4}\right] - \mu k_j k_\Delta k_p\right]\|\tilde{\mathbf{x}}\|$$

where $\gamma_B = \lambda_m\{\mathbf{B}\} - \mu c$ is a positive constant. Then, the time derivative of Lyapunov function (18) is guaranteed to be negative definite as long as

$$\|\tilde{\mathbf{x}}\| > \frac{k_j k_\varepsilon}{k_p \lambda_m\{\hat{\mathbf{J}}(\mathbf{q})\hat{\mathbf{J}}(\mathbf{q})^T\}}; \quad \|\dot{\mathbf{q}}\| > \frac{k_\varepsilon + \mu k_j \lambda_M\{\mathbf{B}\}}{\gamma_B};$$

$$\|\ddot{\mathbf{q}}\| > \frac{\mu k_j \lambda_M\{\mathbf{K}_d\}}{\lambda_m\{\mathbf{L}_1\}}; \quad \|\tilde{\mathbf{W}}\|_F > \frac{k_w}{2} + \sqrt{\frac{\mu k_j k_\Delta k_p}{\kappa} + \frac{k_w^2}{4}} \qquad (23)$$

According to the standard Lyapunov theory extension [4], the above demonstrates that $\tilde{\mathbf{x}}$, $\dot{\mathbf{q}}$, $\ddot{\mathbf{q}}$ and $\tilde{\mathbf{W}}$ are Uniformly Ultimately Bounded (UUB).

Remark 2. The parameter learning law (15) contains an unknown quantity $\dot{\mathbf{q}}$. The learning law (15) can be rewritten as

$$\dot{\hat{\mathbf{W}}} = -\mathbf{K}_w\left[\dot{\Phi}(\mathbf{q},\dot{\mathbf{q}}) + \dot{\Sigma}(\mathbf{q},\tilde{\mathbf{x}})\right] \qquad (24)$$

where

$$\Phi = \sigma(\mathbf{q})\mathbf{q}^T; \qquad \Sigma = \mu\sigma(\mathbf{q})\mathbf{f}(\mathbf{x})^T \mathbf{J}(\mathbf{q}) - \kappa\|\tilde{\mathbf{x}}\|^2 \hat{\mathbf{W}} \qquad (25)$$

By integrating both sides of (24) an equivalent version of (24) is obtained, where $\dot{\mathbf{q}}$ is eliminated

$$\hat{\mathbf{W}} = -\mathbf{K}_w\left[\Phi(\mathbf{q}) + \Sigma(\mathbf{q},\tilde{\mathbf{x}})\right] \qquad (26)$$

Definition (25) implies that

$$\frac{d}{dt}\Phi(q_i) = \Phi(q_i,\dot{q}_i) = \sigma(q_i)\dot{q}_i \qquad (27)$$

note that

$$\frac{d}{dt}\exp\left(-\frac{q_i^2}{2}\right) = q_i \exp\left(-\frac{q_i^2}{2}\right)\dot{q}_i = \sigma(q_i)\dot{q}_i \qquad (28)$$

then, the function $\Phi(\cdot)$ which satisfies (27) is

$$\Phi(q_i) = \exp\left(-\frac{q_i^2}{2}\right) \qquad (29)$$

which time derivative correspond to a WNN activation function.

Remark 3. The stability analysis presented in Theorem 1 may be easily reacted to take into account external bounded disturbance. In this case, if the external disturbance d with $\|d\| \leq k_d$ and the approximation error ε are considered as a single term $E=\varepsilon+d$, then, this new term replaces ε in the analysis and the following upperbound $\|E\| \leq k_E = k_\varepsilon + k_d$ instead of k_ε should be used.

Compared with the approach presented in [1], the proposed controller in this work (8) has the advantage that it compensates explicitly for errors in the Jacobian matrix, it does not need any *a priori* knowledge about the structure of gravity term and the stability conditions make tuning easier in practice, i.e., chose a sufficiently small gain μ. Furthermore, controllers proposed in [1] and [10] require the measurements of robot joint velocity.

4 Experimental Results

The experimental setup used to show the performance features of the controller (8) corresponds to robot arm having two degree of freedom moving in the vertical plane. The end-effector position is measured using a Dalsa camera, model CA-D1-128A, capable of 800 frames per second. Joint angles are obtained from two incremental encoders located on the motors driving the robot links. The camera is placed parallel to the plane where the robot moves with some distance away in a fixed-camera configuration [3]. Complete information regarding this visual servoing system can be found in [2]. Let us consider a thin lens without aberration and a perspective transformation as an ideal pinhole camera model [3], then, the Jacobian matrix $\mathbf{J}(\mathbf{q})$ from the joint space to image space is obtained as

$$\mathbf{J}(\mathbf{q}) = \mathbf{J}_i \mathbf{J}_r(\mathbf{q}) \tag{30}$$

where $\mathbf{J}_i$ is the image Jacobian matrix and $\mathbf{J}_r(\mathbf{q})$ is the robot Jacobian matrix and they are given by

$$\mathbf{J}_i = \alpha \frac{\lambda}{\lambda - z} \begin{bmatrix} \cos(\theta) & -\sin(\theta) \\ \sin(\theta) & \cos(\theta) \end{bmatrix}; \quad \mathbf{J}_r(\mathbf{q}) = \begin{bmatrix} l_1 \cos(q_1) & l_2 \cos(q_2) \\ l_1 \sin(q_1) & l_2 \sin(q_2) \end{bmatrix} \tag{31}$$

where α is the scale factor of length in *pixels/m*, λ is the focal length and z is the distance between camera and robot. When the kinematics and camera parameters of the robot system are uncertain, the approximate robot and image Jacobian matrices are

$$\hat{\mathbf{J}}_i = \hat{\alpha} \frac{\hat{\lambda}}{\hat{\lambda} - \hat{z}} \begin{bmatrix} \cos(\hat{\theta}) & -\sin(\hat{\theta}) \\ \sin(\hat{\theta}) & \cos(\hat{\theta}) \end{bmatrix}; \quad \hat{\mathbf{J}}_r(\mathbf{q}) = \begin{bmatrix} \hat{l}_1 \cos(q_1) & \hat{l}_2 \cos(q_2) \\ \hat{l}_1 \sin(q_1) & \hat{l}_2 \sin(q_2) \end{bmatrix} \tag{32}$$

where $\hat{\alpha}, \hat{\lambda}, \hat{z}, \hat{\theta}, \hat{l}_1$ and $\hat{l}_2$ are the estimated of α, λ, z, θ, l_1 and l_2 respectively. The estimate length values and camera parameters used in the experiment to calculate the Jacobian matrix are $\hat{l}_1 = 0.25$, $\hat{l}_2 = 0.1$, $\hat{\theta} = 30°$ and $\hat{\alpha} \frac{\hat{\lambda}}{\hat{\lambda} - \hat{z}} = 1$, while the exact values for the manipulator lengths are $0.21\ m$ and camera orientation is $\theta = 10°$. The WNN was formed with 8 neurons, fed with joint information, their centers and their widths are assumed to be fixed. We choose the centers evenly spaced between $[4, 4]^T$ to $[-4, -4]^T$, their widths were set to $p = [0.5, 0.5]$ and all the initial weights values were set to zero. The control law (8) was compared against the PID controller [10].

$$\tau = -\hat{\mathbf{J}}(\mathbf{q})^T \mathbf{K}_p \mathbf{s}(\mathbf{e}) - \mathbf{K}_d \dot{\mathbf{q}} + \mathbf{K}_I \int_0^t \left(\dot{\mathbf{q}} + \alpha_1 \hat{\mathbf{J}}(\mathbf{q})^T \mathbf{s}(\mathbf{e}) \right) d\tau \tag{33}$$

and the adaptive PD controller [10]

$$\tau = -\hat{\mathbf{J}}(\mathbf{q})^T \mathbf{K}_p \mathbf{s}(\mathbf{e}) - \mathbf{K}_d \dot{\mathbf{q}} + \mathbf{Z}(\mathbf{q}) \hat{\psi} \tag{34}$$

$$\dot{\hat{\psi}} = -\mathbf{L} \mathbf{Z}(\mathbf{q})^T \left(\dot{\mathbf{q}} + \alpha_2 \hat{\mathbf{J}}(\mathbf{q})^T \mathbf{s}(\mathbf{e}) \right) \tag{35}$$

where $\mathbf{K}_I$ and $\mathbf{L}$ are positive definite matrices, $\mathbf{s}(\mathbf{e})$ is a scalar potential function defined in [10]. In the case of the robot employed in the experiments the gravity regressor $\mathbf{Z}(\mathbf{q}) \in \Re^{n \times p}$ is given by

$$\mathbf{Z}(\mathbf{q}) = \begin{bmatrix} \sin(q_1) & 0 \\ 0 & \sin(q_2) \end{bmatrix} \tag{36}$$

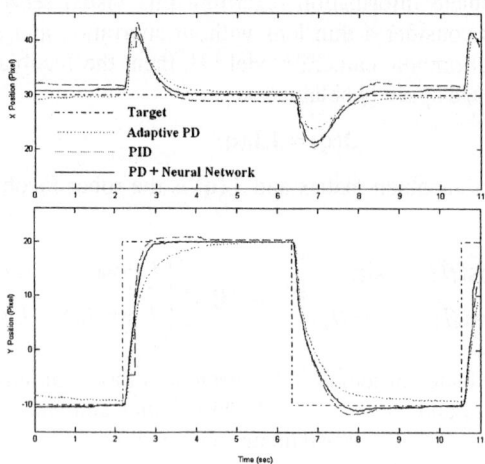

Fig. 1. Image position under uncertainties in the Jacobian matrix

In the experiment the feedback gains were selected as $\mathbf{K}_p$=diag$\{0.3\}$, $\mathbf{K}_d$= diag$\{0.1\}$ and $\mathbf{K}_I$ = diag$\{0.004\}$. Update law parameters were chosen as $\mathbf{L}$ = diag$\{0.3\}$, $\mathbf{K}_w$ = diag$\{0.05\}$, α_1=10, α_2=3, κ=0.001 and μ=0.2. The desired image position was set to $\mathbf{x}^* = [30 \; x_2^*]^T$ *pixels*, where x_2^* was a square wave signal of 15 *pixels* of amplitude centered at 5 *pixels* and at a frequency of 0.12 *Hertz*. Fig. (1) depicts the experimental results. From the above result it is clear that the NN controller has an improved performance compared with the adaptive and the PID controllers. In the case of the adaptive controller, since it is designed to compensate only for unknown gravity terms, then, it can not deal adequately with the effects of an uncertain Jacobian matrix. The PID controller exhibited overshoots when the Jacobian matrix was uncertain. The above behavior could be explained since the goal of the integral part is only to compensate for the gravity terms evaluated at the unknown desired joint position. Note also that the integral part can not compensate the whole term (13) since $\Delta K_p \tilde{x}$ is zero at the desired position x^* whereas the NN part of control law (8) tries to approximate this nonlinear term regardless if the joint positions q do correspond or do not to the desired unknown position q^*.

5 Conclusions

In this paper we have presented theoretical and experimental results for stable task space control for robot manipulators and shown that all the closed-loop signal are UUB. The robot gravity term and a Jacobian matrix are assumed to be unknown. A novelty of the proposed approach is the fact that a WNN with on-line real-time learning was employed for compensating simultaneously the robot gravitational terms and the error due to the mismatch between the true and the estimated Jacobian Matrix. Velocity measurements are avoided by using a linear high-pass filter in the control law and by exploiting the WNN properties in the learning law. This approach is believed to be new. Experimental results on a two degrees of freedom manipulator are presented to evaluate the proposed controller and performance is experimentally compared against controllers encountered in the literature which shown the effectively of the control law proposed.

References

1. Cheah, C. C., M. Hirano, S. Kawamura & S. Arimoto, Approximate Jacobina Control for Robots with Uncertain Kinematics and Dynamics, *IEEE Trans. On Robotics and Automation*, Vol. 19, No. 4, pp 692-702, Aug. 2003.
2. Garrido, R., A. Soria, P. Castillo & I. Vásquez, A Visual Servoing Architecture For Controlling Electromechanical Systems, in Proc. IEEE Int. Conf. Control Applications & Int. Symp. Intelligent Control, pp. 35-40, Sept. 2001.
3. R. Kelly, Robust Asymptotically stable visual servoing of Planar Robots, IEEE Trans. On Robotics and Automation, vol. 12, No. 5, 759-766, 1996.
4. Lewis, F. L., S. Jagannathan & A. Yesildirek, Neural Network Control of Robot Manipulators and Nonlinear Systems, Taylor & Francis, Philadelphia 1999.
5. G. Loreto, Wen Yu and R. Garrido, Stable Visual Servoing with Neural Network Compensation, Proc. IEEE International Symposium on Intelligent Control, pp. 183-188, Sep. 2001.
6. F. Miyazaki and Y. Masutani, Robustness of sensory feedback control based on imperfect jacobian, in Proc. Robotics Research: 5th Int. Symposium, H. Miurna and S. Arimoto. Eds., Cambridge, MA, pp. 201-208, 1990.

7. Shuzhi S. Ge, C. C. Hang. & L. C. Woon, "Adaptive Neural Network Control of Robot Manipulator in Task Space", IEEE Transactions on Industrial Electronics, Vol.44, No.6, 1997.
8. M. Spong, M. Vidyasagar, Robot Dynamics and Control, New York, Wiley, 1989.
9. M.Takegaki and S.Arimoto, A New Feedback Method for Dynamic control of Manipulator, ASME J. Dynamic Syst. Measurement, and Contr., Vol.103, 119-125, 1981.
10. Yazarel, H. & C. C. Cheah, Task-Space Adaptive Control of Robotic Manipulators with Uncertainties in Gravity Regressor Matrix and Kinematics, IEEE Trans. on Automatic Control, Vol 47, No. 9, pp. 1580-1585, Sep. 2002.

Input-Output Data Modelling Using Fully Tuned RBF Networks for a Four Degree-of-Freedom Tilt Rotor Aircraft Platform

Changjie Yu[1,2], Jihong Zhu[1], Jianguo Che[2], and Zengqi Sun[1]

[1] State Key Lab of Intelligent Technology and Systems,
Department of Computer Science and Technology,
Tsinghua University, Beijing 100084, China
[2] Air Defence Command College, Zhengzhou 450052, China
yu-cj03@mails.tsinghua.edu.cn

Abstract. Input-Output data modelling using fully tuned radial basis function networks(RBF) for a tilt rotor aircraft experimental platform is presented in this paper. The behavior of the four degree-of-freedom platform exemplifies a high order nonlinear system with significant cross-coupling between longitudinal, latitudinal directional motions, and tilt rotor nacelles rolling movement. This paper develops a practical algorithm coupled with model validity tests for identifying nonlinear autoregressive moving average model with exogenous inputs(NARMAX). It is proved that input-output data modelling using fully tuned algorithm is suitable for modelling novelty configuration air vehicles. A procedure for system modelling was proposed in the beginning of this paper and the subsequent sections provided detailed descriptions on how each stage in the procedure could be realized. The effectiveness of this modelling procedure is demonstrated through the tilt rotor aircraft platform. The estimated model can be utilized for nonlinear flight simulation and control studies.

1 Introduction

Neural network offers a powerful tool in modelling nonlinear systems over a compact set rather than a small neighborhood around the origin of the linear system approximation. Neural network as a powerful tool for learning complex input-output mappings has stimulated many studies for identification of dynamical systems with unknown nonlinearities [1], [2], [3], [4], [5]. For neural-based identification, there are two main issues that stand out: One is the choice of the model architecture to be adopted for system identification, and the other is the choice of the learning algorithm. The classical weights-tuning algorithms are based on the assumption that the hidden units' centers and widths are selected properly *a priori*. In practice, it is important to choose the centers and widths according to either a preliminary training or through an *ad hoc* procedure. To avoid the off-line training, an alternative way to estimate the centers is to use supervised algorithms such as multivariate clustering algorithm[5]. However, as reported, all these efforts can not guarantee finding the correct center locations, especially when identifying time-varying dynamic systems.

With the use of inaccurate centers, deterioration in performance is observed which in turn unavoidably increase the number of the hidden neurons.

In classical aircraft applications, the role of system identification is to estimate the parameters of nonlinear or linearized 6 DOF equation of motion from flight or wind tunnel data, having a known structure. Recently, neural networks have been employed for estimating the aerodynamic coefficients of unmanned air vehicles (UAV's) [6]. RBF networks were used to capture variations in aircraft mach number. Neural networks were utilized by [7], [8] for dynamic modelling and control of supermanoeuvring delta wing aircraft. Lately, B-splines have been investigated in modelling and identification of nonlinear aerodynamic functions [9]. In all these cases the model structure is known. However, in the present study, no model structure was assumed *a priori* i.e. black-box modelling. Such an approach yields input-output models with neither a prior defined model structure nor specific parameter settings reflecting any physical aspects. This is an important contribution of this work. In this study, fully tuned RBF networks are used to demonstrate these concepts by successfully modelling the dynamical behaviour of the tilt rotor aircraft platfrom. Such a high fidelity nonlinear model is often required for the nonlinear flight simulation studies. Since, there is no reliance on the mathematical model, the estimated RBF model has to be thoroughly verified using rigorous time and frequency domain tests. If the model structure and the estimated parameters are correct then the residuals (difference between model and system output) should be unpredictable from all linear and nonlinear combinations of past inputs and outputs. This is ensured by carrying out higher order cross-correlation tests, proposed by [10].

The tilt rotor aircraft combines the hover performance and control of a helicopter with the cruise speed and efficiency of a turboprop airplane. As shown in Fig.1, the tilt rotor aircraft feature wing tips are mounted proprotors that can be rotated from a vertical orientation to a horizontal position for high speed cruise.

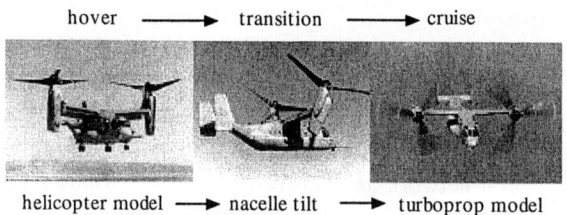

Fig. 1. Tilt rotor aircraft configuration

The experimental platform simulates similar problems and challenges encountered in real systems. These include complex dynamics leading to both parametric and dynamic uncertainty, unmeasurable states, sensor and actuator noise, saturation and quantization, bandwidth limitations and delays. From the control point of view, it exemplifies a high order nonlinear system with significant cross-coupling between longitudinal, latitudinal directional motions, and tilt rotor nacelles rolling movement.

2 Experimental Setup

The experimental platform is shown in Fig. 2. The tilt rotor aircraft platform is mounted on a base E as shown in Fig. 3. The arm BF can rotate around the center O freely, and ψ and θ are the yaw and the pitch angles, respectively. The wing LR can also rotate freely on the axis BF, and ϕ is the roll angle. The left and right nacelles can tilt around L, R, and the nacelle tilting angle is equal at the same time. n_t denotes nacelle tilting angle. Thus, the model has four degree-of-freedom. The rotors are driven separately by two DC motors, measured by tachogenerators coupled to the points of L, R, respectively. Rotary encoders are mounted on the joint O and L, R to measure the angles ψ, θ and nacelle tilting angle n_t, respectively. The tilting of left nacelle and right one is driven by DC motor in F. The encoder for the roll angle ϕ is mounted on the position F.

 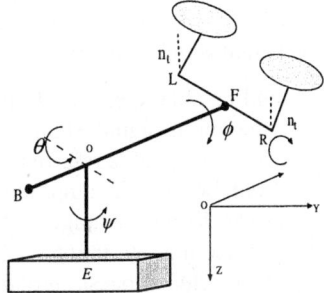

Fig. 2. Tilt rotor aircraft platform experimental setup **Fig. 3.** Tilt rotor aircraft platform scheme

We must emphasize the main differences between the tilt rotor aircraft and the experimental platform: There are no cyclical controls in the experimental platform. Cyclic is used for directional control in a tilt rotor aircraft. In tilt rotor aircraft, lift is generated via collective pitch control, i.e. pitch angles of all the blades of the two rotors are changed by an identical amount at every point in azimuth, but at the constant rotor speed. However, in case of the experimental platform, pitch angles of all the blades are fixed and speed control of the two rotors is employed to achieve longitudinal, latitudinal directional controls. But the behavior of the tilt rotor aircraft platform, in certain aspects, resembles that of a tilt rotor aircraft.

3 Input-Output Data Modelling for Tilt Rotor Platform

The objective of input-output data modelling is to find exact or approximate models of the tilt rotor aircraft platform. The procedure is shown in Fig. 4. Once the model is obtained, it is required to verify whether the model is good enough to represent the platform. A number of validation tests are available in the literatures.

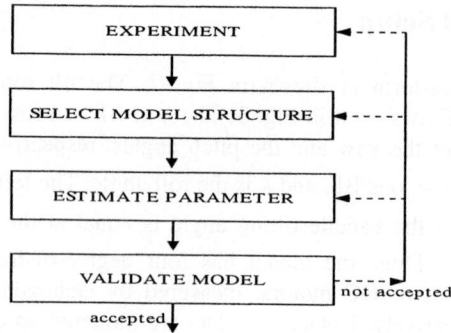

Fig. 4. System identification procedure

3.1 Experimental Input-Output Data

In input-output data modelling, the type of input signal to be used plays a crucial role and has a direct bearing on the fidelity of the resulting identified model. The excitation signal should have two important characteristics:

1) it should be able to excite all the dynamic modes of interest, that is, the spectral content of the input signal should be rich in frequency corresponding to system bandwidth. Such a signal is referred to as persistently exciting.

2) it should be rich in amplitude level, that is, have different levels of input amplitudes over the whole range of operation. These two conditions can generally be fulfilled by selecting an input such as sine wave, Guassian signal, independent uniformly distributed process, ternary pseudorandom sequence and the N-samples-constant signal. In order to excite the system modes of interest, we use the N-samples-constant signal as the input excitation one[11].

The N-samples-constant signal is defined by:

$$u(t) = e\left(\text{int}\left[\frac{t-1}{N}\right] + 1\right) \qquad t=1,2,\ldots \tag{1}$$

where $e(t)$ is a white noise signal with variance σ_e^2, at each N th sampling instant (*int* denotes the integer part). Its covariance function is

$$R_u(\tau) = \frac{N-\tau}{N}\sigma_e^2 \tag{2}$$

corresponding to the spectral density

$$\chi(\omega) = \frac{\sigma_e^2}{2\pi N}\frac{1-\cos N\omega}{1-\cos\omega} \tag{3}$$

Input signal, platform and neural networks outcomes, prediction error are shown in Fig. 5. sample time is 0.05 second.

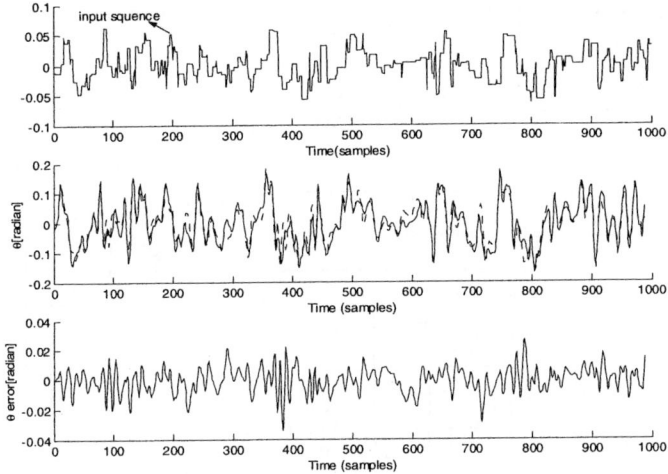

Fig. 5. Input signal, platform and neural networks outcomes, θ prediction error. In the second part, the real curve denote the tilt rotor aircraft platform output, dashed curve is RBF networks output.

3.2 Select Model Structure and Model Order Determination

In this investigation, a nonlinear autoregressive moving average model with exogenous inputs (NARMAX) is employed. The model is of the form:

$$y(t) = f(y(t-1),...,y(t-n_y),u(t-1),...,u(t-n_u),e(t-1),...,e(t-n_e)) + e(t) \qquad (4)$$

where, $y(t)$, $u(t)$ and $e(t)$ are the output, input and noise, respectively. n_u, n_y and n_e are the maximum lags in the input and the output and noise, respectively, and $\{e(t)\}$ is assumed to be a zero mean white sequence. The system noise $e(t)$ is generally unobserved, it can only be replaced by the prediction error or residual $\varepsilon(t)$, and eqn. (4), can be re-written as:

$$y(t) = f(y(t-1),...,y(t-n_y),u(t-1),...,u(t-n_u),\varepsilon(t-1),...,\varepsilon(t-n_e)) + \varepsilon(t) \qquad (5)$$

Neural network architecture based on RBF networks is depicted in Fig. 6. The nonlinear functional form $f(.)$ in the RBF expansion, used in this study is the Guassian function. The cascade correlation algorithm described by[12], provides an elegant method for parameter estimation. The basic idea of the cascade correlation algorithm is iteratively to reduce the error made by the output unit by inserting hidden units that correlate (or anti-correlate) well with the error signal. The networks are frozen while optimizing the new hidden unit candidate. The algorithm avoids the moving targets problem of standard back-propagation algorithm.

A RBF networks can be regarded as a special two layer network which is linear in the parameters provided all the RBF centres are prefixed. Given fixed centres i.e. no adjustable parameters the first layer or the hidden layer performs a fixed nonlinear transformation, which maps the input space onto a new space. With n inputs and m

hidden neurons is shown in Fig. 7. h_i is the output of hidden unit i. Such a network can be represented as

$$\hat{y}(t) = w_0 + \sum_{i=1}^{m} w_i h_i \qquad (6)$$

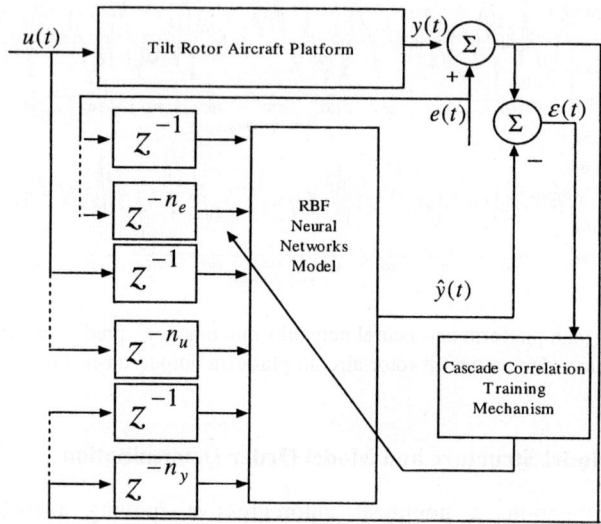

Fig. 6. NARMAX model architecture with RBF networks and cascade correlation learning algorithms

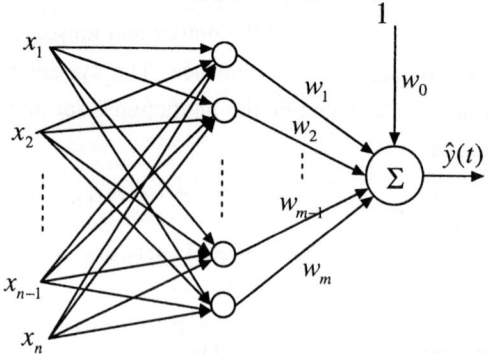

Fig. 7. Radial basis function networks structure

The output layer then implements a linear combiner on this new space and the only adjustable parameters are the weights of this linear combiner. These parameters can therefore be determined using the linear least square method, which is an important advantage of this approach. This is basically how an RBF network works.

The model order can be determined by the Lipschitz method which estimates the model order from the experimental data without estimating the values of the parameters of the model. The main idea of the method is that we can estimate the maximal gradient of an unknown mapping from the experimental input-output data or in other words we can estimate the smoothness of an unknown mapping. While smooth mapping (less maximal gradient) is a desirable feature of a model, we determine the order of the model to create the smoothest mapping between the input and the output data. To achieve this we calculate the following quotient [13]:

$$L^{(n)} = \left(\prod_{k=1}^{p} \sqrt{n} L^{(n)}(k) \right)^{1/p} \tag{7}$$

where $L^{(n)}(k)$ is the k-th largest gradient of the function calculated from the known experimental input-output data. This quotient has the property: if n_0 is the optimal order, that $L^{(n_0-1)}$ is much larger than $L^{(n_0)}$ and $L^{(n_0+1)}$ is very close to $L^{(n_0)}$, so we can find the sharpest breakpoint in the graph of $L^{(n)}$ vs. n. shown in Fig. 8.

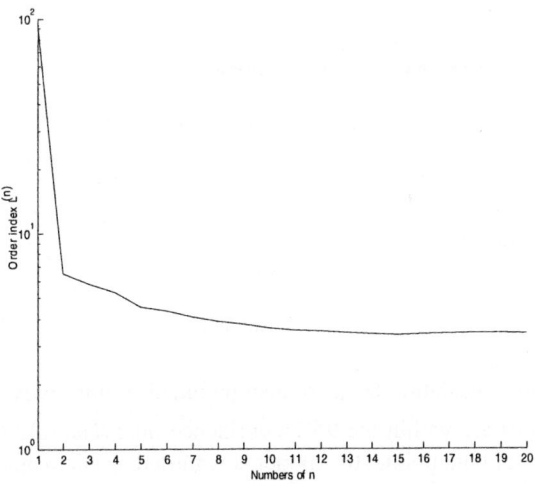

Fig. 8. The relation between $L^{(n)}$ and n, The best result is achieved with $n_u = n_y = 12$

3.3 Correlation Test

A more convincing method of the identification model validation is to use correlation tests. If the model of a system is adequate then the residuals or prediction errors $\varepsilon(t)$ should be unpredictable from (uncorrelated with) all linear and nonlinear combinations of past inputs and outputs. The derivation of simple tests that can detect these conditions is complex, but it can be shown that the following conditions should hold[11]:

$$\xi_{\varepsilon\varepsilon}(\tau) = E[\varepsilon(t-\tau)\varepsilon(t)] = \delta(\tau) \tag{8}$$

$$\xi_{u\varepsilon}(\tau) = E[u(t-\tau)\varepsilon(t)] = 0 \qquad \forall \tau \tag{9}$$

$$\xi_{u^2\varepsilon}(\tau) = E[u^2(t-\tau) - \overline{u}^2(t)\varepsilon(t)] = 0 \quad \forall \tau \tag{10}$$

$$\xi_{u^2\varepsilon^2}(\tau) = E[u^2(t-\tau) - \overline{u}^2(t)\varepsilon^2(t)] = 0 \quad \forall \tau \tag{11}$$

$$\xi_{\varepsilon(\varepsilon u)}(\tau) = E[\varepsilon(t)\varepsilon(t-1-\tau)u(t-1-\tau)] = 0 \quad \tau \geq 0 \tag{12}$$

where, $\xi_{u\varepsilon}(\tau)$ indicates the cross-correlation function between $u(t)$ and $\varepsilon(t)$, $\varepsilon u(t) = \varepsilon(t+1)u(t+1)$, $\delta(t)$ is an impulse function. This test result is shown in Fig. 9.

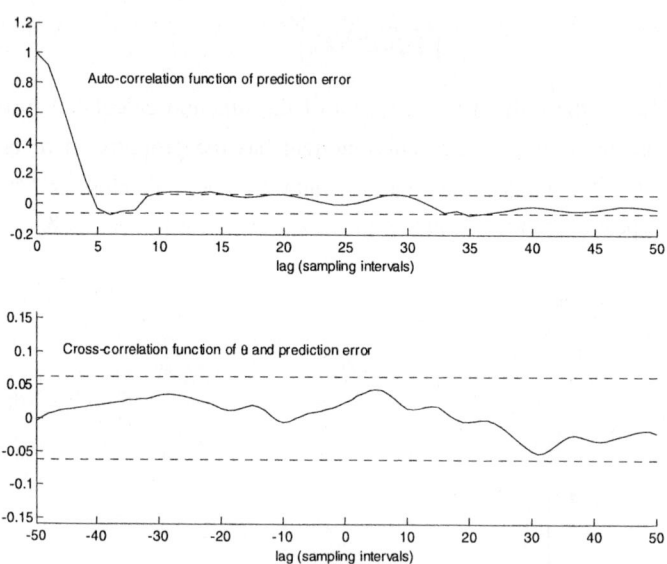

Fig. 9. Residual test

The higher-order correlation tests are also included in this study. In general, if the correlation functions are within the 95% confidence intervals, $\pm 1.96/\sqrt{N}$, where, N is the total number of data points, the model is regarded as adequate. It is important to note that only the first few lags are significant.

Having accomplished the structure selection and model order determination, the final important step is model verification.

3.4 Experiment Validate Model

Validation model is a key final step. It is assumed that the body resonance modes of the platform lie in a low frequency range of 0-10 Hz, while two rotor dynamics are at significantly higher frequencies. The physical constants of the experimental platform are shown in Table 1.

The transition between helicopter and airplane flight modes is vital for a variety of flight missions, and necessitates a change in control strategy. Yet maintaining a station is one of the difficult problems. In helicopter mode, thrust is used for vertical

Table 1. Physical constants of the experimental platform

Symbol	Values
The mass of each rotor (m)	0.1365
The mass of arm BF(m_{bf})	1.220
The distance of arm LR(r_{lr})	0.428
The distance of arm BF(r_{bf})	1.290

control while pitch attitude is used for velocity control. In airplane mode, these roles are exchanged, with thrust controlling airspeed and pitch attitude controlling vertical flight path angle. The exchanging uses of pitch attitude and thrust control combined with gross changes in aircraft response with flight condition present challenges to the control system designer. The Input-output data come from this transition. The experimental validation result is shown in Fig. 10.

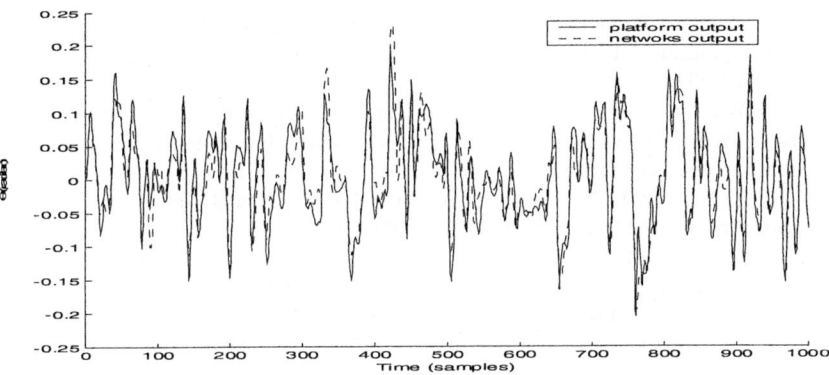

Fig. 10. Platform output and networks output

4 Conclusions

The suitability of input-output data modelling technique to model a four degree-of-freedom of unknown dynamics, has been successfully demonstrated. Standard back-propagation algorithm has two disadvantages. First, it is difficult to select the exact network structure. Second, with the option of only tuning the weights, the performance is poor with the use of inaccurate centers and widths. But, cascade correlation fully tuned RBF networks are ideal candidates for modelling this complex engineering systems. Careful selection of excitation signal is an important part for the input-output data modelling. Without due consideration to this issue, the obtained model would not be able to capture the system dynamics, resulting in a poor model. Since no mathematical model is available, extensive model validation is imperative. The proposed method provides a powerful and fast approach to model next generation air vehicles such as UAV's, X-wing and delta-wing aircraft, whose flight dynamics are not well understood or not easy to establish from first principles. And the identification model can be utilized for nonlinear flight simulation and control studies.

References

1. Narendra, K.S., Parthasarathy, K.: Identification and Control of Dynamical Systems Using Neural Networks. IEEE Trans. Neural Networks. 1(1990) 4–26
2. Ahmad, S.M., Chipperfield, A.J., Tokhi, M.O.: Parametric Modelling and Dynamic Characterization of a Two-degree-of-freedom Twin Totor Multi-input Multi-ouput System. Proc. Instn Mech. Engrs, Part G, Journal of Aerospace Engineering. 215(G2), (2001)63–78
3. Ahmad, S.M., Chipperfield, A.J., Tokhi, M. O.: Dynamic Modelling and Open Loop Control of a Twin Rotor MIMO System. Proc. Instn Mech. Engrs, Part I: J. Systems and Control Engineering. 216(I6), (2002)477–496
4. Elanayar, S., Shin, Y.: Radial Basis Function Neural Network for Approximation and Estimation of Nonlinear Stochastic Dynamic Systems. IEEE Trans. Neural Networks. (1994)594–603
5. Chen, S., Mulgrew, B., Grant, P.M.: A Clustering Technique for Digital Communications Channel Equalization Using Radial Basis Runction Networks. IEEE Trans. Neural Networks 4 (1993)570-579
6. Blythe, P.W., Chamitoff, G.: Estimation of Aircrafts Aerodynamic Coefficients Using Recurrent Neural Networks. In Proc. Second Pacific International Conference on Aerospace Science and Technology. 1995
7. Kim, B.S., Calise, A.J.: Nonlinear Flight Control Using Neural Networks. Journal of Guidance, Control, and Dynamics. Vol. 20(1)(1997)26-33
8. Rokhsaz, K., Steck, J.E.: Use of Neural Networks in Control of High-Alpha Maneuvers. Journal of Guidance, Control, and Dynamics. Vol. 16(5) (1993)934-939
9. Bruce, P.D., Kellet, M.G.: Modelling and Identification of Nonlinear Aerodynamic Functions Using B-splines. Proc. Instn. of Mech. Engrs. Vol 2, Part G,(2000)27-40
10. Billings, S. A., Voon, W.S.F.: Correlation Based Validity Tests for Nonlinear Models. Int. J. Control, Vol. 44(1) (1986)235-244
11. Nørgaard, M. O. Ravn, N.K., Poulsen, L. K.: *Neural Networks for Modelling and Control of Dynamic Systems.* London: Springer-Verlag(2000)
12. Lehtokangas, M., Saarinen, J., Kaski, K.: Accelerating Training of Radial Basis Function Networks with Cascade-Correlation Algorithm. Neurocomputing. vol. 9(2)(1995)207-213
13. He, X., Asada, H.: A New Method for Identifying Orders of Input-output Models for Nonlinear Dynamic Systems. Proc. of the American Contr. Conf. San Francisco, California. June(1993)2520-2523

A Frugal Fuzzy Logic Based Approach for Autonomous Flight Control of Unmanned Aerial Vehicles

Sefer Kurnaz[1], Emre Eroglu[1], Okyay Kaynak[1,2], and Umit Malkoc[2]

[1] Aeronautics and Space Technologies Institute, Turkish Airforce Academy,
Yesilyurt, 34807 İstanbul,Turkey
kurnazsefer@yahoo.com; emreroglu@gmail.com
[2] Bogazici University, Department of Electrical and Electronic Engineering,
Bebek, 34342 Istanbul, Turkey
kaynak@boun.edu.tr, umit.malkoc@boun.edu.tr

Abstract. This paper proposes a fuzzy logic based autonomous flight controller for UAVs (unmanned aerial vehicles). Three fuzzy logic modules are developed for the control of the altitude, the speed, and the roll angle, through which the altitude and the latitude-longitude of the air vehicle are controlled. The implementation framework utilizes MATLAB's standard configuration and the Aerosim Aeronautical Simulation Block Set which provides a complete set of tools for rapid development of detailed 6 degree-of-freedom nonlinear generic manned/unmanned aerial vehicle models. The Aerosonde UAV model is used in the simulations in order to demonstrate the performance and the potential of the controllers. Additionally, Microsoft Flight Simulator and FlightGear Flight Simulator are deployed in order to get visual outputs that aid the designer in the evaluation of the controllers. Despite the simple design procedure, the simulated test flights indicate the capability of the approach in achieving the desired performance.

1 Introduction

This paper addresses the design of a simple fuzzy-logic controller for the autopilot of Unmanned Aerial Vehicles. UAVs are remotely piloted or self-piloted aircraft that can carry many different types of accessories such as cameras, sensors and communications equipment. They have a very wide range of applications including both civil and military areas. Some important features that make them very popular are their low cost, smaller size and their extended maneuver capability because of the absence of a human pilot.

In literature, there can be found many different approaches related to the autonomous control of UAVs; some of the techniques proposed include fuzzy control [1], adaptive control [2], [3], neural networks [4], [5], genetic algorithms [7] and Lyapunov Theory [8]. In addition to the autonomous control of a single UAV, research on other UAV related areas such as formation flight [6] and flight path generation [9] are also popular.

The approach proposed in this paper is fuzzy logic based. Three fuzzy modules are designed, one module is used for adjusting the bank angle value to control the latitude and the longitude coordinates, and the other two are used for adjusting the elevator and the throttle controls to obtain the desired altitude value.

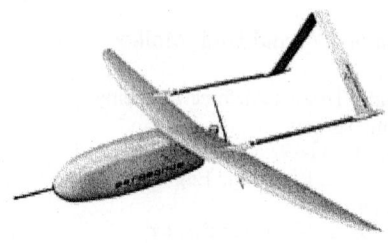

Fig. 1. Aerosonde UAV

Table 1. UAV Specifications

Weight	27-30 lb,
Wing Span	10 ft
Engine	24 cc, 1.2 kw
Flight	Fully Autonomous / Base Command
Speed	18 – 32 m/s
Range	>1800 miles
Altitude Range	Up to 20,000 ft
Payload	Maximum 5 lb with full fuel

The performance of the proposed system is evaluated by simulating a number of test flights, using the standard configuration of MATLAB and the Aerosim Aeronautical Simulation Block Set [11], which provides a complete set of tools for rapid development of detailed 6 degree-of-freedom nonlinear generic manned/unmanned aerial vehicle models. As the test air vehicle, a model which is called Aerosonde UAV [12] is utilized. The great flexibility of the Aerosonde, combined with a sophisticated command and control system, enables deployment and command from virtually any location.

The paper is organized as follows. Section 2 starts with a basic introduction to fuzzy control and then explains the design of the fuzzy controllers which are used for the autonomous control of the UAV. The inputs and the outputs of each controller are described and the membership functions used in their fuzzification are given. Simulation results are presented in Section 3, and finally concluding remarks and information about future work are given in Section 4.

2 Fuzzy Logic Control System

Basically, a fuzzy logic system consists of three main parts: the fuzzifier, the fuzzy inference engine and the defuzzifier. The fuzzifier maps a crisp input into some fuzzy sets. The fuzzy inference engine uses fuzzy IF-THEN rules from a rule base to reason for the fuzzy output. The output in fuzzy terms is converted back to a crisp value by the defuzzifier.

In this paper, Mamdani-type fuzzy rules are used to synthesize the fuzzy logic controllers, which adopt the following fuzzy IF-THEN rules:

$$R^{(l)}: If(x_1 \text{ is } X_1^l) \text{ AND....AND } (x_n \text{ is } X_n^l) \text{ THEN } y_1 \text{ is } Y_1^l,....,y_k \text{ is } Y_k^l \quad (1)$$

where R^l is the lth rule $x = (x_{l_1},....,x_n)^T \in U$ and $y = (y_{l},...,y_k)^T \in V$ are the input and the output state linguistic variables of the controller respectively, $U, V \subset \Re^n$ are the universe of discourse of input and output variables respectively,

$(X_{l_1},....,X_n)^T \subset U$ and $(Y_1,....,Y_k)^T \subset V$ are the labels in linguistic terms of the input and the output fuzzy sets, and n and k are the numbers of the input and the output states respectively.

We consider a multi-input and single-output (MISO) fuzzy logic controller $(k=1)$, which has singleton fuzzifier. Using triangular membership functions, algebraic product for logical AND operation, product-sum inference and Centroid defuzzification method, the output of the fuzzy controller has the following form:

$$y_j = \frac{\sum_{l=1}^{M}(\prod_{i=1}^{N}\mu x_i^l(x_i))y_j}{\sum_{l=1}^{M}\prod_{i=1}^{N}\mu x_i^l(x_i)} \qquad (2)$$

where N and M represent the number of input variables and the total number of rules respectively. μx_i^l denote the membership function of the lth input fuzzy set for the ith input variable.

The aerial vehicle considered in this paper as the test vehicle is a 6 degree-of-freedom nonlinear aerial vehicle, called Aerosonde UAV, for which a model is provided in *Aerosim Aeronautical Simulation Block*.

Three fuzzy logic controllers are designed for Aerosonde in order to control the altitude and the latitude-longitude as shown below. These three controllers acting in combination enable the navigation of the aerial vehicle.

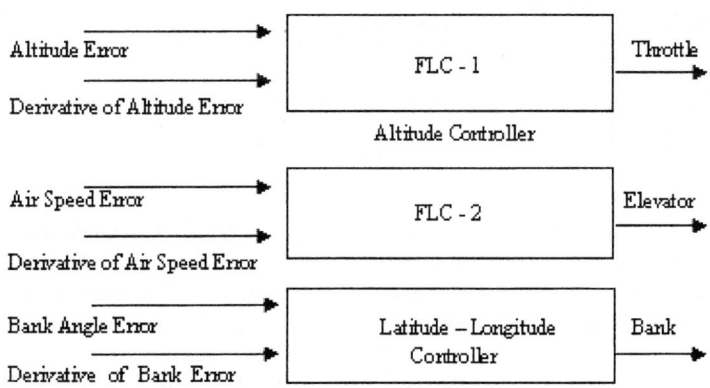

Fig. 2. Fuzzy Logic Controllers

The altitude controller has two sub-control systems, namely the throttle controller and the elevator controller. The throttle fuzzy logic controller has two inputs: the altitude error (i.e. the difference between the desired altitude and the actual altitude) and its rate of change. The latter indicates whether the UAV is approaching to the desired altitude or diverging away. Like the throttle controller, the elevator control has two inputs, the air speed error and its derivative. The control outputs of the block are the throttle and the elevator respectively, responsible for the head going up or down.

If the fuzzy controller types in literature are reviewed, it can be seen that there are two main classes of fuzzy controllers: one is the position-type fuzzy controller which generates the control input (u) from the error (e) and the error rate (Δe), and the other is the velocity-type fuzzy logic controller which generates incremental control input (Δu) from the error and the error rate. The former is called PD Fuzzy Logic Controller and the latter is called PI Fuzzy Logic Controller according to the characteristics of information that they process. Fig.3 shows the general structure of these controllers.

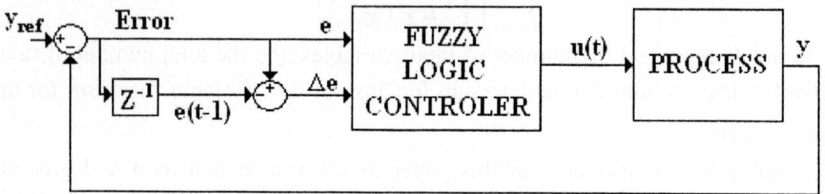

Fig. 3.a. PD Type Fuzzy Logic Controller

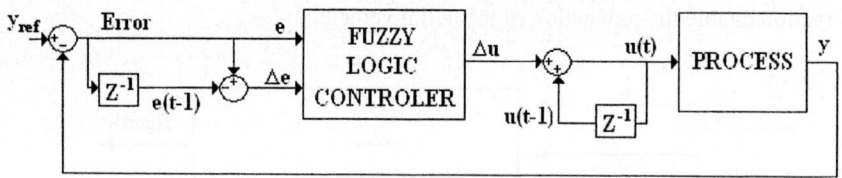

Fig. 3.b. PI Type Fuzzy Logic Controller

In this work, PI type fuzzy controllers were preferred for the bank angle and the altitude controllers. Because of the highly nonlinear nature of the UAV model and the inference between the controlled parameters, it is easier to derive the required change in the control input instead of predicting its exact value. This was the main reason for the choice.

PI Fuzzy Logic Controller system has two inputs, the error e(t) and the change of error $\Delta e(t)$, which are defined by

$$e(t) = y_{ref} - y \tag{3}$$

$$\Delta e(t) = e(t) - e(t-1) \tag{4}$$

where y_{ref} and y denote the applied set point input and the plant output, respectively. The output of the Fuzzy Logic Controller is the incremental change in the control signal $\Delta u(t)$. The control signal is therefore obtained by

$$u(t) = u(t-1) + \Delta u(t) \tag{5}$$

The PI controller (also PI FLC) is known to give poor performance in transient response due to the internal integration operation. On the other hand, in the case of a PD controller (also for a PD FLC) it may not be possible to remove the steady state error. So, in the cases when the required performance cannot be achieved by using only a PD or a PI type controller, it is better to combine them and construct a PID type fuzzy controller. This was the case for the elevator control in this work and therefore it was decided to adopt a PID type for this controller to control of the airspeed. The structure used is shown in Fig.4, which is a very popular one [10].

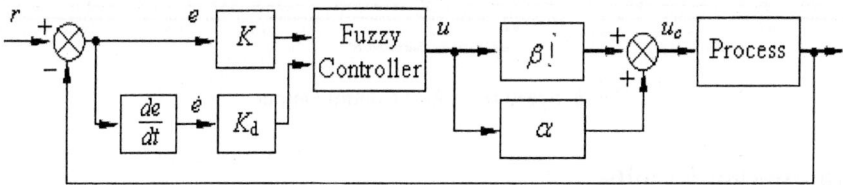

Fig. 4. PID Type Fuzzy Logic Controller

While developing the fuzzy logic controllers, simple rule tables are preferred by taking into account the specialist knowledge and the experience. The control output surfaces shown in Fig. 5.a and Fig.5.b are the typical ones, resulting from 25 and 49 rules respectively.

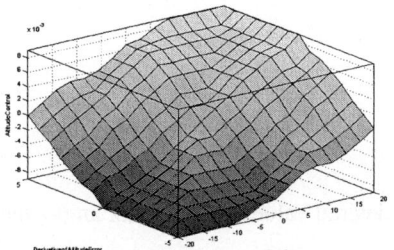 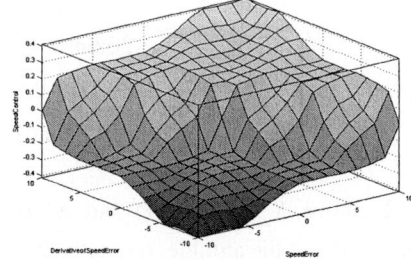

Fig. 5.a. Rule Surface of Air Speed   **Fig. 5.b.** Rule Surface of Altitude

The membership functions used for each input of the fuzzy logic controllers are triangular types. As the membership functions of the altitude error and its derivative, five triangular functions were chosen, dividing the ranges [-20,20] (m) and [-5,5] (m/s) equally in a symmetrical fashion, the functions at the either end being open ended ones as is common. For the air speed and the bank angle and their derivatives, 7 (to get better performance) similar functions were used in the ranges [-10, 10] (m/s), [-40, 40] (deg), [-10, 10] (m/s^2) and [-10, 10] (deg/s) respectively.

As the output membership functions, the bank angle and the throttle control outputs were represented with seven membership functions in the ranges of [-0.02, 0.02] (*deg*) and [-0.01, 0.01] (*frac*) respectively. The membership functions used for the elevator control were rather special however, as shown in Fig. 6.

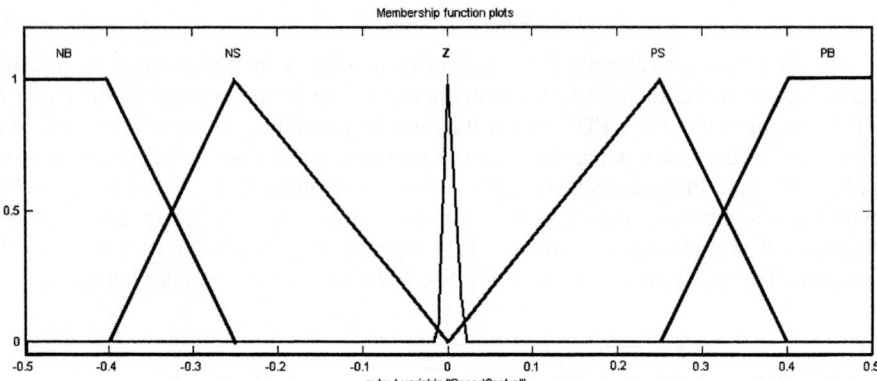

Fig. 6. Speed (Elevator) Control Output

3 Simulation Results

The Simulink model that is used for the simulation studies is depicted in Fig.7. A number of studies were carried out for different flight scenarios. For the results reported in this paper, a worst case approach was adopted, in which the reference signals for all the controlled variables are allowed to change simultaneously as shown in Eq.6. Additionally, $[W_N \ W_E \ W_D]^T = [2 \ 2 \ 0]^T$ (m/s) wind effects are included to the simulation environment.

$$[X_d(t)] = \begin{bmatrix} X_{d1}(t) \\ X_{d2}(t) \\ X_{d3}(t) \end{bmatrix} = \begin{bmatrix} 20\sin(0.001\pi t) \\ 23 + 5\sin(0.001\pi t) \\ 1000 + 50\sin(0.001\pi t) \end{bmatrix} \tag{6}$$

In above, $X_{d1}(t)$, $X_{d2}(t)$ and $X_{d3}(t)$ are the desired values for the bank angle, the airspeed and the altitude, respectively.

In order to have a better idea about the performance of the fuzzy controllers, similar simulation studies were carried out with well tuned conventional PI type controllers (PID in the case of elevator control) and it was seen that the fuzzy logic based controllers for the bank angle and the airspeed (elevator controller) resulted in better performances. In the case of the altitude controller, there could not be seen an appreciable difference.

In Fig. 8, the controllers are fuzzy type during the first period of the simulation (first 1250 seconds of simulation) and then conventional PI types are switched in.

In Fig.9, the settling times and the overshoots are compared when the controllers are switched in. Even though the settling times of the fuzzy logic controllers are quite satisfactory, there is room for improvements in the overshoots.

A Frugal Fuzzy Logic Based Approach for Autonomous Flight Control of UAVs 1161

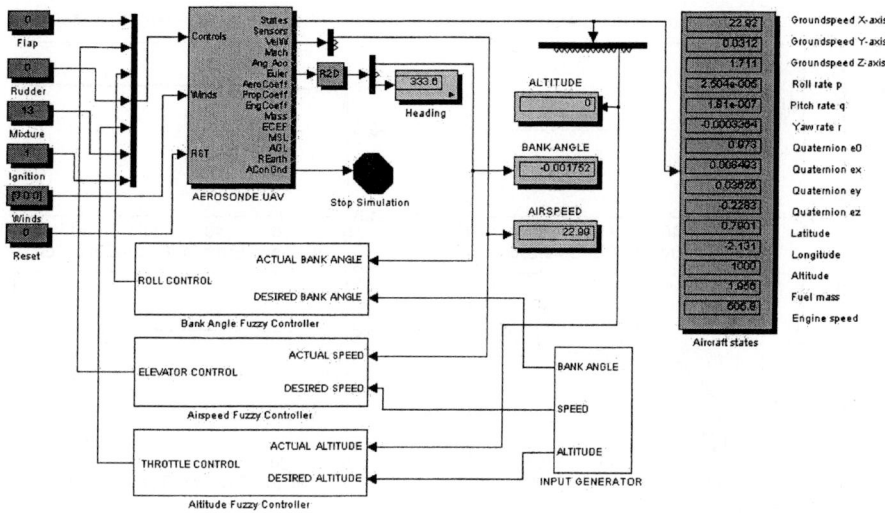

Fig. 7. Simulink Model that is used during Simulation Studies

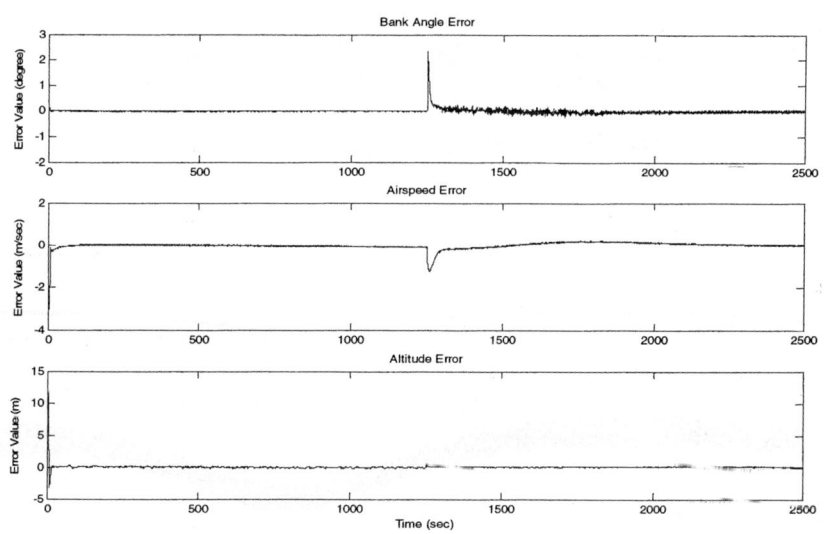

Fig. 8. Error for Bank Angle, Air Speed and Altitude

Under the given simulation conditions, the steady state tracking errors of the fuzzy logic controllers for the bank angle, the air speed and the altitude change in a ranges [-0.065, 0.055], [-0.48, 0.35] and [-0.88, 1.135] respectively. The outputs of bank angle, air speed and altitude fuzzy logic controllers presented in Fig.10.

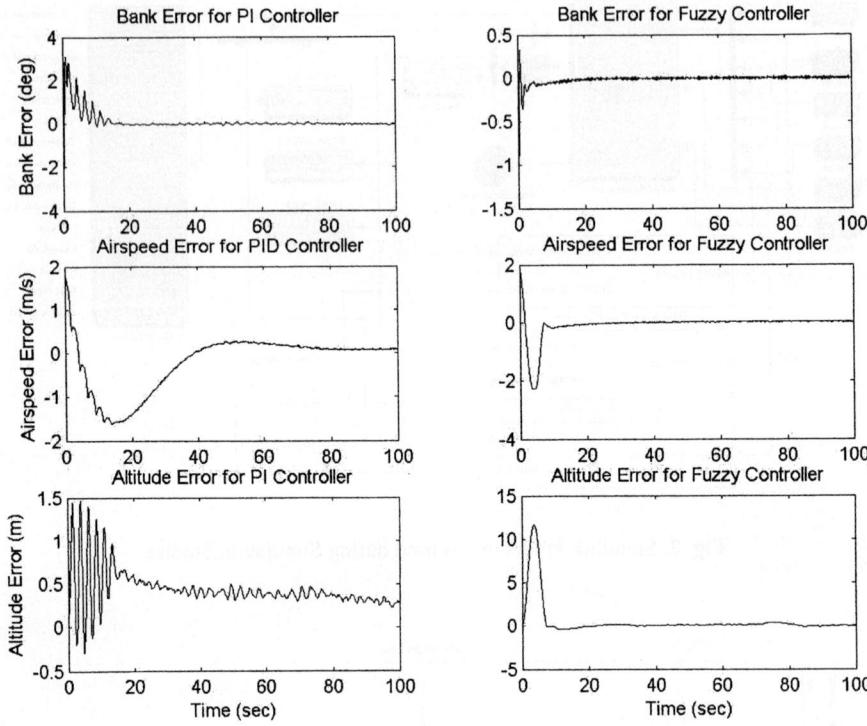

Fig. 9. Error for Bank Angle, Air Speed and Altitude

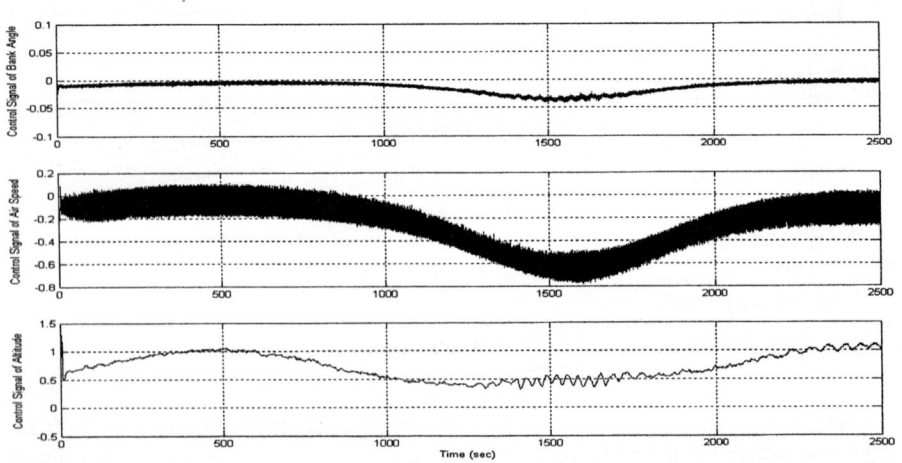

Fig. 10. Control Signals of Bank Angle, Air Speed and Altitude

4 Conclusion

In this paper, a fuzzy logic based autonomous flight controller for UAVs is proposed. The simulation studies presented verify that the UAV can follow the pre-defined trajectories despite the simplicity of the controllers. However, as seen by the simulation results, there exist some oscillations and errors when wind effects are added to the simulation environment. In search of a better performance, it is planned to utilize the well known ANFIS (Adaptive Neuro Fuzzy Inference Systems) approach in future works for a better tuning of the membership functions, the parameter adaptation rules being based on Variable Structure Systems theory.

References

[1] L.Doitsidis, K.P. Valavanis, N.C. Tsourveloudis, M. Kontitsis: A framework for fuzzy logic based UAV navigation and control. Proceedings of the International Conference on Robotics and Automation, Volume 4, Page(s):4041 – 4046, (2004)

[2] C.J.Schumacher, Rajeeva Kumar: Adaptive control of UAVs in close-coupled formation flight. Proceedings of the American Control Conference, Volume 2, Page(s):849 – 853, (2000)

[3] B.Andrievsky, A.Fradkov: Combined adaptive autopilot for an UAV flight control. Proceedings of the 2002 International Conference on Control Applications, Volume 1, Page(s):290 – 291, (2002)

[4] W.R.Dufrene, Jr,.: Application of artificial intelligence techniques in uninhabited aerial vehicle flight. The 22nd Digital Avionics Systems Conference, vol.2, Page(s):8.C.3 - 8.1-6, (2003)

[5] Y.Li, N. Sundararajan, P. Sratchandran: Neuro-Controller Design for Nonlinear Fighter Aircraft Maneuver using Fully Tuned RBF Networks. Automatica, Vol.37, pp. 1293-1301, (2001)

[6] F.Borrelli, T.Keviczky, G.J.Balas: Collision-free UAV formation flight using decentralized optimization and invariant sets. 43rd IEEE Conference on Decision and Control, Vol.1, Page(s):1099 - 1104, (2004)

[7] J.A.Marin, R.Radtke, D.Innis, D.R.Barr, A.C.Schultz: Using a genetic algorithm to develop rules to guide unmanned aerial vehicles. Proceedings of the IEEE International Conference on Systems, Man, and Cybernetics, vol.1, Page(s):1055 - 1060, (1999)

[8] W.Ren, R.W.Beard: CLF-based tracking control for UAV kinematic models with saturation constraints. Proceedings of the 42nd IEEE Conference on Decision and Control, vol.4, Page(s):3924 - 3929, (2003)

[9] D.Dathbun, S.Kragelund, A.Pongpunwattana, B.Capozzi: An evolution based path planning algorithm for autonomous motion of a UAV through uncertain environments. Proceedings of the 21st Digital Avionics Systems Conference, vol.2, Page(s):8D2-1 - 8D2-12, (2002)

[10] Qiau, W. and Muzimoto, M.: PID Type Fuzzy Controller and Parameter Adaptive Method. Fuzzy Sets and Systems 78, pp 23-35, (1995)

[11] Aerosim, Aeronautical Simulation Block Set v1.1, Users Guide, www.u-dynamics.com

[12] Aerosonde – Global Robotic Observation System, www.aerosonde.com

Sensor-Fusion System for Monitoring a CNC-Milling Center

Rubén Morales-Menéndez, Sheyla Aguilar M, Ciro A. Rodríguez,
Federico Guedea Elizalde, and Luis E. Garza Castañon

ITESM Monterrey campus,
Av. Garza Sada # 2501, 64,489 Monterrey NL, México
{rmm, A00792459, ciro.rodriguez, fguedea, legarza}@itesm.mx

Abstract. Industrial CNC-milling centers demand adaptive control systems for better product quality. Surface roughness of machined parts is a key indicator of product quality, as it is closely related to functional features of parts such as fatigue life, friction, wear, etc. However, on-line control systems for surface roughness are not yet ready for industrial use. One of the main reasons is the absence of sensors that provide measurements reliably and effectively in a hostile machining environment. One potential solution is to combine readings from several different kinds of sensors in an intelligent sensor-fusion monitoring system. We implemented such a system and compared three modelling approaches for sensor-fusion: multiple regression, artificial neural networks (ANNs), and a new probabilistic approach. Probabilistic approaches are desirable because they can be extended beyond simple prediction to provide confidence estimates and diagnostic information as to probable causes. While our early experimental results with aluminum show that the ANN approach has the greatest predictive power over a variety of operating conditions, our probabilistic approach performs well enough to justify continued research given its many additional benefits.

1 Introduction

Milling is a very important operation among CNC industrial machining processes. Turning and end milling are the most common operations. Milling is widely used in a variety of manufacturing industries in which quality is an important factor. Surface roughness is an important indicator of quality, as it is closely related to fatigue life, friction, wear, etc.

Surface roughness is influenced by several factors including cutting parameters such as spindle speed, feed rate, and depth of cut. Cutting parameters can be defined in advance, but other process conditions such as coolant, workpiece diameter, tool wear, chips loads, and material properties are uncontrolled.

Intelligent control techniques could be very useful for controlling surface roughness. However, no industrial applications for monitoring surface roughness exist because there are no sensors that can provide accurate online measurements in this harsh machining environment.

Sensors are currently too inaccurate and too unreliable for effective use in many machining applications. Direct sensors are impractical due to vibration and chips loads. Non-contacting sensors have interference from the environment. This makes indirect sensing methods such as sensor fusion attractive.

Sensor fusion refers to a class of mathematical methods for integrating several sensor signals into one fused measurement. These integrated measurements can predict relevant states such as surface roughness more accurately than single sensor measurements. Artificial neural nets and statistical multiple regression are established sensor-fusion techniques. However, we are also interested in probabilistic models for their ability to incorporate the many stochastic variables which are classical in machining processes. We are also interested in probabilistic models because they can be naturally extended to provide diagnostic information.

The paper is organized as follows. Section 2 reviews previous work and the main concepts which have been exploited. It also describes our probabilistic model. Section 3 describes experimental conditions in the CNC machining center. Section 4 discusses the performance of the different models. Finally, section 5 concludes the paper and discusses future work.

2 Background

State of the art. Several researchers have worked on machining monitoring systems. In surface roughness, important work had been done[1]. However, this work has yet to reach industrial applications. Reasons for this include narrow applicability of techniques and/or problems with online updating.

[4] classifies modelling techniques into four groups: *machining theory* based approaches [2], [10], [12]; *experimental investigation* approaches [16], [7]; *designed experiments* approaches [8], [11]; and *artificial intelligence (AI)* approaches [3], [6], [9], [13], [14], [15], [17]. Machining theory approaches attempt to model the complexities of the machining process. This is quite difficult, and such models typically perform poorly. The other approaches are empirical, based on experimental data. This paper focuses on the *AI* approach.

In [1] a sensor fusion technique based on neural networks is used for the on-line prediction of surface roughness in turning of low carbon steel.

[17] developed an online surface recognition system based on neural networks to predict the surface roughness of machined parts in the end milling process. Using spindle speed, feed rate, depth of cut, and the average vibration per revolution as the four input neurons, an artificial neural network model was developed to predict the surface roughness. [13] replicated this work for turning operations. They found that the radial direction of vibration between tool and workpiece during the cutting process was the most significant predictor.

In [3] a neural network approach is given for the prediction of surface roughness in CNC face milling. The approach exploits the theory of face milling and the mechanism of surface roughness formation based on principles of Taguchi experimental design.

---

[1] See this seminal paper [1].

[15] modeled experimental results using Response Surface roughness Methodology (*RSM*). *RSM* is a collection of mathematical and statistical techniques that are useful for modelling and analyzing problems in which the response of interest is influenced by several variables, and where the goal is to obtain the response. The mathematical model used a genetic algorithm to optimize an objective function, thus obtaining the machining conditions for the required surface roughness.

In [9] (based on [6]), a down milling machining process for Alumic was modelled. An adaptive neuro-fuzzy inference system was developed to predict the effect of the machining variables on the surface roughness. This work focussed more on optimization than modelling.

[14] utilized a neural network and a regression model to predict surface roughness and tool flank wear over time for a variety of cutting conditions in finish hard turning.

To make an impact on industrial applications, we believe more realistic models are required, particularly models capable of incorporating stochastic information.

Sensor fusion. Our experiments will focus on CNC face milling. The factors most likely to influence the surface roughness in CNC face milling are [3]: *d: the depth of cut* influences quality in an indirect way. Increasing the depth of cut increases the cutting resistance and the amplitude of vibrations. Cutting temperature also rises. It is expected that surface roughness will deteriorate. *f: the feed rate.* Generally, as feed rate increases, surface roughness also increases. **s**: the cutting speed. When cutting speed exceed the range of built-up edge formation, an increase in cutting speed generally improves surface quality.

There are other important factors such as the *engagement of the cutting tool, cutting tool wear, use of cutting fluid*, and the *three components of the cutting force*. We focus only on the three cutting parameters (s,d,f) described above, plus one recorded cutting phenomenon: the vibration signal $(v)^2$.

Sensor fusion is an indirect measuring method which extracts key unmeasurable information from several readily available measurements. This is an attractive choice for machining's harsh environment which permits few sensors. Selecting the right variables (sensors) and an effective model are the keys to making sensor fusion work, but no hard guidelines exist for making these choices in the field of machining.

Basically, the problem can be defined as follows: *given some independent variables, find the model that best predicts the dependent variable.* We know our independent variables (s,d,f,v) affect our dependent variable (Ra)[3]; however, we do not know the model. We consider three different modelling approaches: statistical multiple regression, an artificial neural network, and a probabilistic

---

[2] All experiments were conducted without chatter phenomena.
[3] Roughness average is universally recognized and the most frequently used parameter of roughness.

model. In the following subsections we briefly describe the principles of these modelling approaches.

Statistical Multiple Regression Model. We chose independent variables (s,d,f,v) which have the greatest influence on the dependent variable (Ra). A multiple regression model was developed using these variables. We propose two multiple regression structures:

Multiple regression structure I. We exploited a model described by eqn (1):

$$Ra_i = b_0 + b_1 s_i + b_2 f_i + b_3 d_i + b_4 v_i + b_5 s_i f_i + \cdots + b_{10} d_i v_i$$
$$+ b_{11} s_i f_i d_i + \cdots + b_{14} f_i d_i v_i + b_{15} s_i f_i d_i v_i + \varepsilon_i \qquad (1)$$

where $\varepsilon_i \sim \mathcal{N}(0, \sigma^2)$, $\{b_j\}_{j=0}^{15}$ are unknown parameters. We assume that Ra_i follows a normal distribution for every combination of the values of (s_i, f_i, d_i, v_i). This model contains the main effects and interactions of the independent variables.

Multiple regression structure II. Eqn (2), uses definitions similar to eqn (1):

$$Ra_i = b_0 (s_i)^{b_1} (f_i)^{b_2} (d_i)^{b_3} (v_i)^{b_4} + \varepsilon_i \qquad (2)$$

where $\{b_j\}_{j=0}^{4}$ are unknown parameters.

Artificial Neural Networks. *ANNs* are a form of multiprocessing computer system based on the parallel architecture of the human brain. The application of *ANNs* to online process monitoring systems has attracted great interest due to their learning capabilities, noise suppression, and parallel computability. Multi-layer feed-forward networks are the most common architecture. These networks can consist of any number of neurons arranged in a series of layers. Layer *0* of the network is the input data; the outputs of the last layer *n* of artificial neurons is the output of the network. Layers between *0* and *n* are called hidden layers. At the moment, no definite rules exist for determining the number of neurons required at each level for a given application – we will try several configurations. Although any number of layers may be used, more than 3 layers are usually not required.

There are several learning algorithms for training neural networks, including Backpropagation and Radial Basis Function training. Both of these methods are derived from the well-known Delta rule for single layer networks. Backpropagation has proven successful in many industrial applications and is easily implemented. The backpropagation algorithm can be described as follows: (1) Inputs are presented to the network and errors are computed, (2) Changes are propagated from the output layer to the first layer, and (3) Weights and biases are updated.

The above steps are iterated to minimize an error index on the training set. Methods such as *Bayesian regularization* and *Levenbery-Marquardt* are often exploited to improve this process, and can also help with the problem of determining the optimum number of neurons in hidden layers.

While bias and variance can be computed easily in linear regression models, the choice between bias and variance in *ANNs* is not an easy task because they have several free parameters. A biased model results when the model is under-parameterized. However, an over-parameterized model will have high variance.

Probabilistic Model. Our proposed probabilistic model consists of a general statistical inference engine operating in discrete spaces. This model represents the maximum entropy joint probability mass function (*pmf*) consistent with arbitrary lower order probabilities. Instead of using previous classical models, we are proposing a discrete probabilistic function whose parameters are learned off-line from experimental data. We can predict dependent process variable (Ra) values given independent process variable (s,d,f,v) values. The set of relevant process variables having direct influence on the prediction is learned by a discrete Bayesian network learning algorithm. The generated graphical causal structure is simplified by selecting the Markov blanket of the predicted process variable (Ra). This compact probabilistic model is robust to noise, incomplete information and nonlinearities.

The basic modelling procedure can be divided into four basic steps. First, continuous variables are discretized into K fixed bins[4] or a fuzzy clustering. We developed a multivariate discretization approach based on the fuzzy C-means algorithm [18]. Second, the causal structure is computed [5]. Third, a simplification of the causal structure is derived using the Markov blanket. Markov blankets perform natural feature selection, as all features outside the Markov blanket can be safely deleted from the Bayesian network. We exploit this feature to produce a much smaller causal structure for the model without compromising the classification accuracy. Finally, in the fourth step we learn the statistical inference engine parameters based on the maximum entropy principle [19].

Maximum Entropy Principle. The maximum entropy joint probability mass function has the Gibbs form given by eqn (3):

$$P[C=c|F=f] = \frac{exp\left(\sum_{i=1}^{N}\gamma(F_i=f_i,C=c)\right)}{\sum_{c'=1}^{K}exp\left(\sum_{i=1}^{N}\gamma(F_i=f_i,C=c')\right)} \quad (3)$$

where F is the set of relevant independent process variables (s,d,f,v) and C is the set of dependent process variables (Ra). The subset of model parameters, Lagrange multipliers ($\gamma(\cdot,\cdot)$), are learned via a *deterministic annealing* algorithm.

3 Experiments

Numerous factors influence surface roughness. As discussed above, we focussed on three preliminary cutting parameters (**feed rate, spindle speed, depth of cut**) and one measured cutting phenomenon (the **vibration signal**). Table 1 shows the different cutting parameters tested.

---

[4] This step was proposed by [19] to get an approximated solution with joint *pmf* support restricted to a subset of the full discrete feature space.

Table 1. Experimental operating conditions

Spindle speed, RPM	Feed rate, mm/min	Depth of cut, mm
1,000 1,500 2,000	200 400	0.5 1 2
2,200 2,400 2,700 3,000	600 800 1000	

CNC Machining Center. The experimental tests were conducted on a KX10 HURON machining center with a capacity of 20 KW, three axes, having a SIEMENS open-Sinumerik 840D controller. This machining center possesses high-precision sideways that allow all three axes to reach a speed of up to 30 m/min. The machine has high-rigidity, high-precision features and there is no interference between the workpiece and the moving parts.

The cutting tool was an Octomill $R220.43 - 03.00 - 05$ face mill of SECO Carboloy with diameter 80 mm, depth of cut 3.5 mm, and six inserts of the SECO Carboloy OFEX-05T305TN-ME07 T250M type. This cutting tool is shown in Fig. 1 (left).

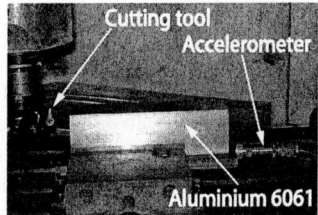

Fig. 1. Cutting tool and cutting tool-accelerometer system

Vibration signals (v) were measured online by an accelerometer installed on the flat metal support (Fig. 1, right). We analyzed each vibration signal as a Power Spectral Density (PSD), where the spectral estimation describes the power density contained in the signal. We computed the PSD of a signal using the periodogram nonparametric method, in which the power spectrum of a signal is obtained from the squared magnitude of its discrete Fourier transform. Based on this result, we computed the average power. The surface roughness was measured using a shop-floor type surface roughness measuring instrument.

4 Results

For computing, input data (s,d,f,v) was normalized and output data (Ra) was mapped to $[-1, 1]$. All models were trained using two sets of training data. The first training set consisted of 100% of the experimental data to obtain the best possible fit. The second set consisted of 75% of the data with 25% left over for testing, in order to guage the models' generalization capacity. Splitting was done using a uniform sampling process.

Table 2. Experimental model performance (multiple regression and ANN)

#	Variables				Least Square Error				ANN neurons hidden layer				
	s	f	d	v	Structure I		Structure II						
					100%	75-25%	100%	75-25%	4	5	6	7	8
1	0	1	1	1	1.39	2.56	16.94	5.67	0.872	0.652	0.559		
2	1	0	1	1	2.14	2.46	4.58	2.48	0.993	1.180	0.773		
3	1	1	0	1	0.83	1.42	0.75	0.77	0.400	0.659	0.361		
4	1	1	1	0	0.59	1.33	0.67	0.80	0.223	0.088	0.078		
5	1	1	1	1	0.40	0.91	0.68	0.78	0.079	0.077	0.088	0.062	0.042

We also wanted to test whether all our input variables (s,d,f,v) were actually needed. All 15 possible subsets of the inputs were tested; table 2 shows only the best 5. The last row corresponds to the complete set of variables. (Most of the following discussion focusses only on the results in this row.)

The LSE (least square errors) are shown as $\frac{1}{n}\sum e^2$ (in μm^2 per sample); e is the error between the computed and the measured surface roughness obtained from the offline stylus profile.

For the multiple regression models (structures I and II) we show the LSE for both training sets (100% and 75-25% split). For the 100% training set, we used all the data to both train and evaluate the model. For the 75-25% case, the LSE is evaluated on the remaining 25% of the data.

We evaluated several ANN models containing different numbers of hidden layer neurons. Table 2 shows only the 100% train/test results for the ANN models.

Statistical Multiple Regression. As can be seen in table 2, structure I performed better than II. Structure I had these performance parameters[5]: $r = 0.915$, $r^2 = 0.837$, $r_a^2 = 0.826$. Fig. 2 shows the predicted behavior of structure I.

In order to validate the 25% LSE, we recomputed it with 10 different 75%-25% splits. The average LSE for structure I was 0.71 with variance 0.21. (Structure II was 1.72 ± 1.12.)

Using a standard ANalysis Of VAriance (ANOVA), some of the terms in the general equation for structure I can be eliminated, giving a simplified equation with only a slightly higher LSE (0.44 instead of 0.40 μm^2).

$$Ra_i = 0.017 - 0.432(s_i) + 0.665(f_i) - 0.211(s_i f_i) + 0.151(s_i d_i) - 0.127(f_i d_i)$$
$$+ 0.159(d_i v_i) - 0.250(s_i d_i v_i) + 0.178(f_i d_i v_i) + \varepsilon_i \quad (4)$$

Artificial Neural Network Models. We tested a number of feed-forward networks having four input neurons, n-m neurons in 1-2 hidden layers, and 1 output neuron. The hidden layers used tanh activation functions. Very good performance was obtained using eight neurons in one hidden layer (4-8-1): $\frac{1}{n}\sum e^2 =$

---

[5] r = coefficient of correlation, r^2 = coefficient of determination, r_a^2 = adjusted coefficient of determination.

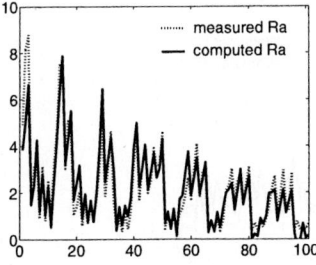 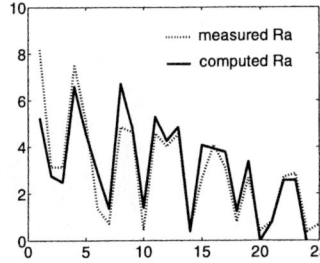

Fig. 2. Performance of regression model I. The left model was trained/tested with full data. The right model was trained with 75% and tested with 25% of the data.

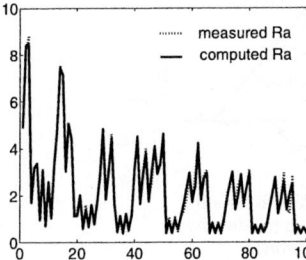 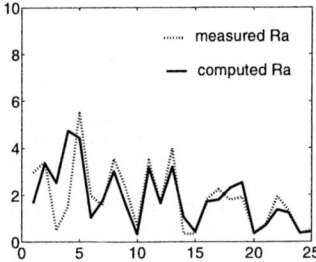

Fig. 3. Performance of the 4-8-1 ANN. The left model was trained/tested with full data. The right model was trained with 75% and tested with 25% of the data.

0.042 μm^2 per sample. Fig. 3 shows the performance of this ANN. The LSE for 75-25% was 0.113.

Probabilistic Model. The LSE for the maximum entropy joint *pmf* model described in section 2 was $\frac{1}{n}\sum e^2 = 1.47$ μm^2 per sample. Fig. 4 shows the performance when the model was trained/tested with the full dataset using $K = 32$ bins.

As Fig. 4 shows, there are some regions in which this probabilistic model works very well. Nevertheless, considerable errors appear in regions of greater nonlinear behaviour. Some potential solutions are: (1) increases the number of bins during the discretization step, (2) use more data for the training step, and (3) smooth the function.

Discussion. Successful implementation of an online monitoring system depends on two subsystems, the sensors and the modelling approach. We must choose the type and number of sensors used, and we must also choose the technique for associating the sensory information to the process state.

Regarding the sensor subsystem, there are many in-process sensing techniques, direct and indirect, but any technique has its own advantages and draw-

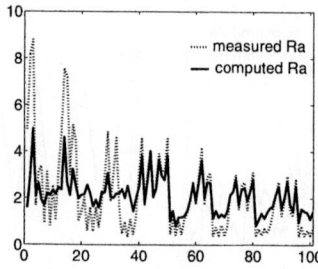

Fig. 4. Performance of the probabilistic model

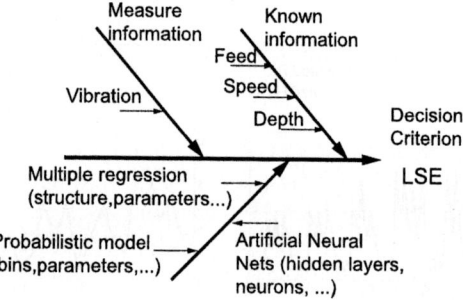

Fig. 5. Input variables and models for sensor-fusion monitoring system

backs. No single technique has proven to be completely reliable over a wide range of operating conditions. Hence, a sensor fusion system which uses more than one sensor is attractive since the loss of sensitivity in one sensor domain can be offset by information from other sensors.

In choosing among our three modelling approaches, multiple regression, artificial neural networks, and probabilistic models, attention must be paid to the highly non-linear characteristics of complex machining processes. Currently, ANN-based algorithms seem to possesses the most flexibility in integrating the multiple sensing information.

A monitoring system operates on a simple principle: *all machine actions have distinct and repeatable patterns or signatures that sensors can measure.* However, the quality of sensing information is affected very significantly by the environmental conditions. Stochastic phenomena occur during the machining process due to the many uncontrolled variables. This makes probabilistic models attractive.

We selected the best combination of input variables for the sensor fusion system by minimizing the modelling error, LSE, across 15 different subsets of input variables and three modelling approaches, Fig. 5. We define our performance index as $IP(Sensor_j) = P(Model_i, ON(Sensor_j)) - P(Model_i, OFF(Sensor_j))$, where $P(\cdot, \cdot)$ represents the average performance with (without) the $Sensor_j$ for the $Model_i$. Table 2 shows only the best 5 subsets. Only the sensors that improve the performance of the sensing system are selected. Validating the sensing system against another test set is recommended to check accuracy, overfitting and generalization.

5 Conclusions

Our final sensor fusion system successfully selected the best subset of inputs (all four) for the model: spindle speed, feed rate, depth of cut and vibration. The surface roughness could be effectively predicted.

This sensor fusion approach is relatively economical. The sensors used in the proposed surface roughness system are low-cost compared to optical-based or acoustic-based sensors. For varying types of material, cutting tools, and cutting parameters, data sets could be built for reconfigurable systems. Adaptation features allowing the system to learn parameters for new configurations could be even more useful.

ANNs have better prediction performance than statistical multiple regression and our probabilistic model, and have the ability to model more complex nonlinearities and interactions. However, the maximum entropy joint pmf works well enough to justify continued interest. Ultimately, probabilistic models are better suited to diagnosis and decision-making frameworks and to modelling stochastic variables in the machining domain. The multiple regression models are the most efficient in terms of computing time and online adaptation.

Future work. Our next goals for this research are to improve the predictive performance of the probabilistic model and to test all the models on larger datasets that encompass more of the stochastic phenomena. We also want to exploit the decision-making capabilities of the probabilistic model.

Acknowledgment. The authors wish to thank Jim Mutch (University of British Columbia, Canada) for his careful reading of the manuscript and his suggestions.

References

1. R. Azouzi and M. Guillot. On-line prediction of surface finish and dimensional deviation in turning using neural network based sensor fusion. *Mach. Tools Manufacture*, 37(9):1201–1217, 1997.
2. D. K. Baek, T. J. Ko, and H. S. Kim. Optimization of feedrate in a face milling operation using a surface roughness model. *Int. J. of Machine Tools and Manufacture*, (41):451–462, 2001.
3. P. G. Benardos and G. C. Vosniakos. Prediction of surface roughness in CNC face milling using neural networks and taguchi's design of experiments. *Robotics and Computer Integrated Manufacturing*, pages 343–354, 2002.
4. P. G. Benardos and G. C. Vosniakos. Predicting surface roughness in machining: a review. *Int. J. of Machine Tools and Manufacture*, pages 833–844, 2003.

5. J. C. Cheng, D. Bell, and W. Liu. Learning bayesian networks from data: An efficient approach based on information theory. Technical report, Dept. of Computing Science, University of Alberta, Alberta, CA, 1998.
6. J. C. Cheng and M. Savage. A fuzzy net based multilevel in-process roughness recognition system in milling operations. *Int. J. Adv. MAnuf. Technology*, 9(17):670–676, 2001.
7. S. A. Coker and Y. C. SHIN. In-process control of surface roughness due to tool wear using a new ultrasonic system. *Int. J. Math. Tools Manufact.*, 36(3):411–422, 1996.
8. J. P. Davim. A note on the determination of optimal cutting conditions for surface finish obtained in turning using design of experiments. *J. of Materials Processing Technology*, (116):305–308, 2001.
9. F. Dweiri, M. Al-Jarrah, and H. Al-Wedyan. Fuzzy surface roughness modeling of CNC down milling of alumic-79. *J. of Materials Processing Technology*, (133):266–275, 2003.
10. K. F. Ehmann and M. S. Hong. A generalized model of the surface generation process in metal cutting. *CIRP Annals*, (43):483–486, 1994.
11. K. H. Fuh and C. F. Wu. A proposed statistical model for surface quality prediction in end milling of al alloy. *Int. J. of Machine Tools and Manufacture*, (35):1187–1200, 1995.
12. H. Kim and C. N. Chu. Texture prediction of milled surfaces using texture superposition method. *Computer Aided Design*, (31):485–494, 1999.
13. S. S. Lee and J. C. Chen. On-line surface roughness recognition system using artificial neural networks system in turning operations. *Int. J. of Advanced Manufacturing Technology*, 22:498–509, 2003.
14. T. Özel and Y. Karpat. Predictive modeling of surface roughness and tool wear in hard turning using regression and neural networks. *Machine tools and Manufacture*, (45):467–479, 2005.
15. P. V. S. Suresh, P. Venkateswara Rao, and S. G. Deshmukh. A genetic algorithmic approach for optimization of surface roughness prediction model. *Int. J. of Machine Tools and Manufacture*, 42:675–680, 2002.
16. J. D. Thiele and S. N. Melkote. Effect of cutting edge geometry and workpiece hardness on surface generation in the finish hard turning of aisi 52100 steel. *J. of Materials Processing Technology*, (94):216–225, 1999.
17. Y. H. Tsai, J. C. Chen, and S. J. Lou. An in-process surface regression system based on neural networks in end milling cutting operations. *Int. J. of Machine Tools and Manufacture*, (39):583–605, 1999.
18. L. Wang. *A Course in Fuzzy Systems and Control*. Englewood Cliffs, NJ, USA, 1997.
19. L. Yan and D. Miller. General statistical inference for discrete and mixed spaces by an approximate application of the maximum entropy principle. *IEEE trans. On Neural Networks*, 11(3):558–573, 2000.

A Probabilistic Model of Affective Behavior for Intelligent Tutoring Systems

Yasmín Hernández[1], Julieta Noguez[2], Enrique Sucar[3],
and Gustavo Arroyo-Figueroa[1]

[1] Instituto de Investigaciones Eléctricas, Gerencia de Sistemas Informáticos,
Reforma 113, Col. Palmira,
62490 Cuernavaca, Morelos, México
{myhp, garroyo}@iie.org.mx
[2] Tecnológico de Monterrey, Campus Cd. de México,
Calle del Puente 222, Col. Ejidos de Huipulco, Tlalpan
14380 México, D. F., México
jnoguez@itesm.mx
[3] Tecnológico de Monterrey, Campus Cuernavaca,
Paseo de la Reforma 182-A, Col. Lomas de Cuernavaca,
62589 Temixco, Morelos, México
esucar@itesm.mx

Abstract. We propose a general affective behavior model integrated to an intelligent tutoring system with the aim of providing the students with a suitable response from a pedagogical and affective point of view. The affective behavior model integrates the information from the student cognitive state, student affective state, and the tutorial situation, to decide the best pedagogical action. The affective model is implemented as a decision network with a utility measure on learning. For the construction of the affective behavior model, we are using personality questionnaires and emotions models. An initial evaluation of the model is presented, based on questionnaires applied to experienced teachers. We present the initial results of this evaluation.

1 Introduction

We have developed a virtual laboratory as a complementary tool for learning mobile robotics. Since the main goal of the virtual laboratory is to serve as learning tool for students, we have incorporated an intelligent tutoring system (ITS). In most developments of ITS, the tutor-student interaction has been unnatural. However, in the last few years, researchers in computer science have turned towards emotions which were originally believed to be unrelated to computer systems performance [1]. Scientific studies have demonstrated the influence of emotions in human communication [2]; and, a hypothesis is that it can also take place in the human-machine interaction [1]. In an ITS, this hypothesis becomes stronger, since emotions have been identified as important players in motivation, and motivation is very important for learning [3]. When a tutor recognizes the affective state of the student and responds accordingly, he may be able to motivate students. Several authors have proposed to use the affective state of the student to give him a more suitable response that fits with his affective and cognitive state [4, 5, 6, 7]. However, the affective state has not yet been used to decide the pedagogical response. This is due there are still many questions about emotions without response, such as which affective states are relevant for learning.

We propose a model of affective behavior for a tutor, which combines the affective and cognitive state of the student to establish the affective and pedagogical actions. The affective behavior model integrates an affective student model based on the OCC cognitive model of emotion [8], represented as a Bayesian network. In the construction of the affective student model we use personality questionnaires based on the five factor model [9]. For the affective behavior model, we propose the use of a decision network with a utility measure on learning. By using the decision network, the tutor selects the best pedagogical and affective response given the current state of the student. We have conducted an initial evaluation of our model, by means of questionnaires presented to university teachers. In the questionnaires we presented several scenarios of tutoring and we asked the teachers to select the appropriate pedagogical action for each scenario. We present preliminary results in the construction of the affective behavior model; and also we present the results of evaluation of the model.

2 Architecture of an Affective ITS

An ITS is a computer-based educational system that provides individualized instruction like a human tutor, based on knowledge about the student (student model), about teaching (tutor module), and about specific domains (expert module). It also has an interface module, which decides how to present the material to the student in the most effective way. An ITS decides how and what to teach based on the student cognitive state. However, it has been demonstrated that an experienced human tutor manages the emotional state of the student in order to motivate him and to improve his learning process. Therefore, the student model structure needs to be augmented to include knowledge about the affective state. Also, an ITS needs the ability of reasoning about the affective state in order to provide the students with an adequate response from a pedagogical and affective point of view. In this sense, a model of affective behavior for the tutor is required; this model has to establish parameters that enable a mapping from affective and cognitive student model to pedagogical responses of the tutor.

We propose an *affective behavior model* which is being integrated to an ITS coupled to a virtual laboratory for teaching mobile robotics. In Fig. 1 the ITS architecture is presented, the affective components are shown shaded.

The affective analysis module obtains the indicators used to infer the affective state and to update the affective student model. With this last structure, the affective behavior model will determine the affective action to be delivered by the tutor. We take the indicators for the affective state from the interaction and performance of the student in the ITS. In next section, we describe the affective student model, and then we present the affective behavior model.

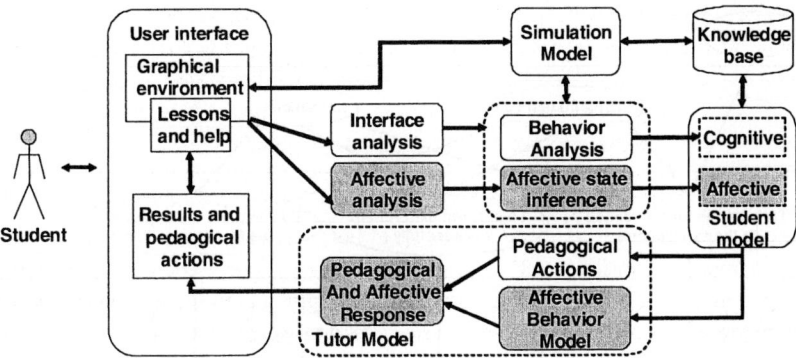

Fig. 1. Architecture of the ITS. The indicators of the affective state are obtained from the interaction of the student; and then the affective behavior model establishes the pedagogical action.

3 Affective Student Model

The student model must contain knowledge about the affective state of the student, in addition to knowledge about his cognitive state, in order to give him an affectively adequate response and at the pedagogically appropriate time. Several ways to evaluate the emotional state have been proposed; some are based on the detection of physical and biological signs [10], other implementations are based on the use of personality and emotion models [4], and others are based in student interaction [5]. We use the OCC cognitive model of emotion [8] to establish the affective state. The OCC model establishes the emotional state as a result of a comparison between goals and situation, i.e. how the situation fits with goals. The OCC model is also used by [4]. For representing the affective state, we are using Bayesian networks [11] because the process of establishing the affective state involves uncertainty [4].

To determine the student affective state we use the following factors: 1) student personality traits, 2) student knowledge state, 3) goals and 4) tutorial situation. We represent the affective student model by a Bayesian network as it is shown in Fig. 2. The dependency relations have been established based on literature [12, 13]. This way to represent the affective state is similar to one proposed by [4].

The OCC model establishes emotional state as a cognitive appraisal between goals and situation. We represent this comparison with nodes *goals* and *tutorial situation*, propagating evidence to nodes *goals satisfied*, and with these last nodes propagating evidence to the nodes *affective state*. According to the OCC model, the goals are fundamental to determine the affective state. To establish the student goals, we have two options: to ask the student, or to infer them. We think that asking the student is not a good option because people, in general, tend to be kind and to give kinder responses, even if the counterpart is a computer [14]. Therefore, we infer goals by means of personality traits.

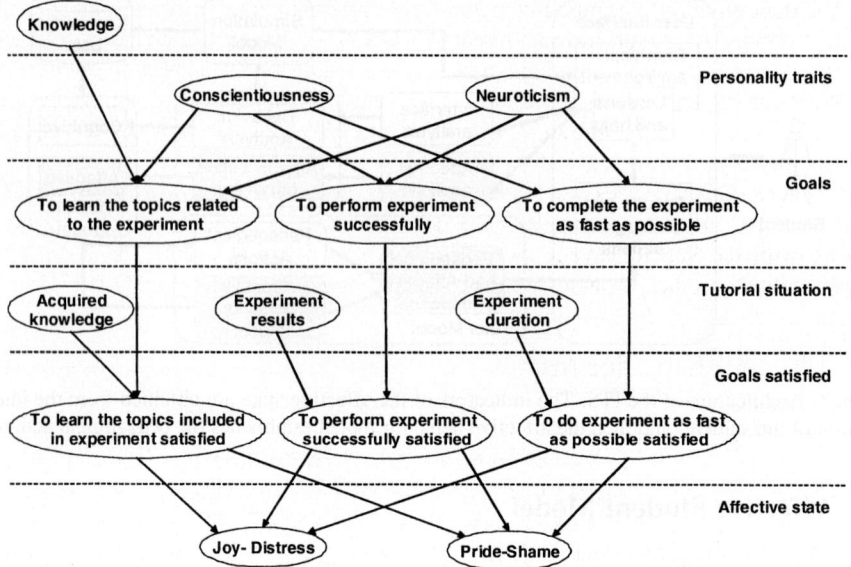

Fig. 2. Bayesian network that represents the affective student model. We infer the affective state from goals satisfied, which are a comparison between goals and situation.

We based personality traits on the five factor model [9], which considers five dimensions for personality: *openness, conscientiousness, extraversion, agreeableness,* and *neuroticism*. Currently, we use only two of them (*conscientiousness, neuroticism*) to establish goals because a relationship exists between these two dimensions and learning [13]. Also, a relation between learning and *openness* has been stated, but it has not been proved [13]. Although we use only two personality dimensions to infer goals, we think that all five dimensions influence the affective state.

The application domain for our model is a virtual laboratory for teaching mobile robotics, where the students perform experiments about different aspects of robotics. The goals for our domain are: 1) to learn the topics related to the experiment, 2) to perform experiment successfully, and 3) to complete the experiment as fast as possible. In order to know if a goal has been satisfied, we include the nodes *goals satisfaction* (one for each goal), and they are influenced by the nodes *goals* and *tutorial situation* (see Fig. 2). The nodes *goals satisfied* represent the comparison between goals and situation as established by the OCC model. The nodes *tutorial situation* are variables which have the outcomes of the student actions, and their values are obtained from the performance of the student on the virtual laboratory.

From the emotion set proposed by the OCC model [8], we consider four possible emotional states: *joy, distress, pride, shame*. We use these emotions because they emerge as a consequence of the actions of the students. Although at present, we are not using mood to infer the affective student state, we think that mood influences the emotional state too. Sometimes emotional state and mood are used interchangeably, but we distinguish them. Mood represents the longer term emotional state, while affective state represents the instantaneous emotional state. Mood has an arousal level higher than emotion, i.e. mood changes slower than emotion [15]. We consider that both, emotion and mood, have an effect on each other. Currently, we are working on how to obtain the student mood and how to use it to determine the affective state.

We have established the initial and conditional probabilities for the affective student model based on the literature, and from personality questionnaires. We applied a personality questionnaire based on the five factor model to a group of 58 students. From these questionnaires we obtained the *a priori* probabilities for the personality variables, but the aim is to apply the personality questionnaire to each student interacting with the ITS to have a more accurate personality measure. The conditional probabilities for other variables were established based in the literature [12, 13].

4 Affective Behavior Model

Once the affective student model has been obtained, the tutor has to respond accordingly, and in order to do that, the tutor needs a model of affective behavior (ABM) which establishes parameters that enable a mapping from affective and cognitive student model to responses of the tutor. Fig. 3 shows a block diagram for the ABM. The ABM receives information from three components: the affective student model, the cognitive student model and the tutorial situation. The proposed model translates these components into affective actions towards the tutor and interface modules. The affective action contains knowledge about the overall situation that will help the tutor module to determine the next response to the student, and also it will advise the interface module to express the response in a suitable way.

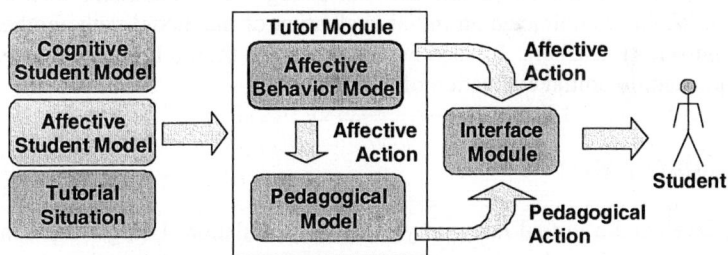

Fig. 3. Block diagram of the ABM. The ABM receives information from the affective student model, the cognitive student model and the tutorial situation.

Based on the affective action, the tutor module can decide if it is necessary to provide another exercise or to change the topic in turn. For example, if the student's response is incorrect and his affective state is happy, the tutor can encourage the student with another exercise more suitable to the situation in order to maintain motivation in a high level.

We represent the ABM by means a decision network. In Fig. 4, we present a high level representation for the ABM using a decision network [11]. This decision network establishes the pedagogical action considering a utility on learning. The affective action is influenced directly by the affective state; and with the affective action and the acquired knowledge, the pedagogical action is established. The pedagogical action is chosen with the maximum utility in learning of the student. The nodes *affective state* and *acquired knowledge* corresponds to nodes *affective state* and *acquired knowledge*, respectively, on the Bayesian network for the affective student state (see Fig. 2).

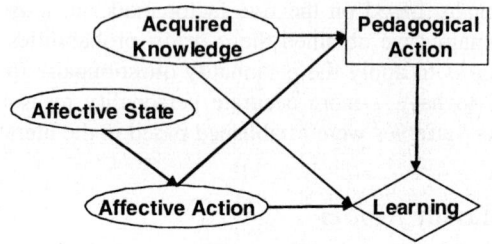

Fig. 4. A high level decision network for the ABM. The pedagogical action considers a utility on learning.

In order to establish the pedagogical action, the affective action and the acquired knowledge is needed. The acquired knowledge is the knowledge the student has after the experiment; and it receives evidence from the knowledge that the student had before the experiment and from the results of the experiment. The affective action receives evidence from the affective state.

The pedagogical action has utility in student learning. We established the utility measure with base on the experience as a teacher of our group of research, a group of five teachers. We asked them to rate the four pedagogical actions for each affective state. Also, We have conducted an initial evaluation of the model with another group of seven university teachers. In section 5, we present the preliminary results in the construction and the initial evaluation of the model.

5 Preliminary Results

We have developed a virtual laboratory based on simulation. Using a 3-D simulator, the students can explore the basic concepts in the course *mechanical design*, as well as sensors and control, before they start to build a physical robot. An intelligent tutoring system guides the students during their interactions with the virtual laboratory, providing the student with the opportunity to learn through exploration and giving him personalized help. In Fig. 5 we present a screenshot of the virtual laboratory, a student is performing an experiment on following the way.

We have implemented and evaluated a first version of the ABM. We have motivating results in the estimation of the affective state and in establishing the pedagogical action. This first version of the model has been implemented in the Elvira system [16]. For evaluating the model we constructed several scenarios of tutoring. A tutoring scenario consists of the personality of the student, the knowledge that the student has before the experiment, and the tutorial situation, i.e. the results of the experiment. In Table 1 we present the tutoring scenarios that we use as evidence.

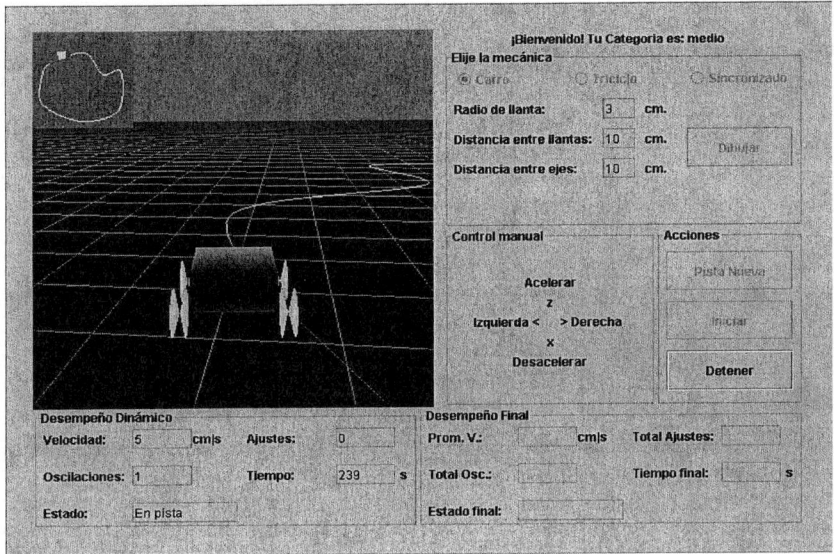

Fig. 5. A screenshot of the virtual laboratory. A student is performing an experiment on following the way.

The variable knowledge has these two values: *the student knows* and *the student does not know*. The personality variables have three values: *low*, *average* and *high*. The variables *tutorial situation* have two values: *positive* and *negative*. We established two basic situations: the student knows the current topic and the student does not know the current topic. We set the two personality variables to a high value. For the two situations, we consider four cases: 1) the student has a high value for the three variables representing the tutorial situation; 2) the student has a high value for two variables; 3) the student has a high value for one variable; 4) the student has not high value for none variable. In sum, we have eight cases.

The tutoring scenarios were used as evidence to predict the goals of the student, how much satisfied is a goal, the affective state of the student, and to establish the affective and the pedagogical actions. In Table 2 we present the inferences on the affective state, goals and satisfied goals for the evidence on Table 1. We only present one value for the variables *goals*, *goals satisfied*, *joy-distress* and *pride-shame*, because their other values are the complement.

We can observe that the student has high probability for the value *present* for the three goals, because he has a value *high* for both personality dimensions. Also we can observe that the probabilities for the value *joy* of the variable *joy-distress* increase if the goals are satisfied and they decrease if the goals are not satisfied. *Pride-shame* has the same effect; the probabilities for the value *pride* increase if the goals are satisfied. In general, the distributions obtained for the affective state variables seem reasonable, thus we are currently validating them with a psychologist. The inferences presented in Table 2 are intermediate results in the performance of the complete ABM. In table 3, we present the pedagogical and affective actions established by the model for the same eight cases. The variable *affective action* has three values: *neutral*, *moderate* and *strong*. The variable *pedagogical action* has four values: 1) Present another exercise with lower difficulty level, 2) Present another exercise with same difficulty level, 3) Present another exercise with higher difficulty level, and 4) Explain the topic again, in another way.

Table 1. Tutoring scenarios used as evidence to the ABM. The column *knowledge* represents the knowledge the student has before to perform the experiment.

Cases	Knowledge	Personality Dimensions		Tutorial Situation		
		Conscientiousness	Neuroticism	Acquired knowledge	Experiments results	Experiment duration
1	Knows	High	High	Positive	Positive	Positive
2	Knows	High	High	Positive	Positive	Negative
3	Knows	High	High	Positive	Negative	Negative
4	Knows	High	High	Negative	Negative	Negative
5	Does not know	High	High	Positive	Positive	Positive
6	Does not know	High	High	Positive	Positive	Negative
7	Does not know	High	High	Positive	Negative	Negative
8	Does not know	High	High	Negative	Negative	Negative

Table 2. Inferences for the tutoring scenarios. These three goals correspond to the three goals of the affective student model.

Cases	Goals			Goals Satisfied			Affective State	
	Goal 1	Goal 2	Goal 3	Goal 1 Satisfied	Goal 2 satisfied	Goal 3 satisfied	Joy-Distress	Pride-Shame
	Present	Present	Present	Present	Present	Present	Joy	Pride
1	0.50	0.98	0.99	0.80	0.98	0.99	0.97	0.97
2	0.50	0.98	0.99	0.80	0.98	0.01	0.86	0.86
3	0.50	0.98	0.99	0.80	0.02	0.01	0.57	0.57
4	0.50	0.98	0.99	0.21	0.02	0.01	0.17	0.17
5	0.97	0.98	0.99	0.98	0.98	0.99	0.99	0.99
6	0.97	0.98	0.99	0.98	0.98	0.01	0.89	0.89
7	0.97	0.98	0.99	0.98	0.02	0.01	0.69	0.69
8	0.97	0.98	0.99	0.02	0.02	0.01	0.05	0.05

Table 3. Pedagogical and affective actions for the eight cases. The affective action is inferred from the affective state; the pedagogical action receives evidence from the knowledge of the student and the affective action.

Cases	Affective Action	Pedagogical Action
1	Neutral	Present another exercise with higher difficulty level
2	Moderate	Present another exercise with same difficulty level
3	Moderate	Present another exercise with same difficulty level
4	Strong	Present another exercise with lower difficulty level
5	Neutral	Present another exercise with higher difficulty level
6	Neutral	Present another exercise with same difficulty level
7	Moderate	Present another exercise with same difficulty level
8	Strong	Explain the topic again, in another way

We can observe that the affective action has the value *neutral* (cases 1, 5 and 6) when the affective state is good (the variable *joy-distress* has a high probability for the value *joy*), in these cases the tutor can establish to give student an exercise with same or higher difficulty; and, the affective action has the value strong (cases 4 y 8) when the affective state is not good.

In order to validate the results of the model, we presented the eight cases to a group of seven professors with experience in teaching between 8 and 26 years. In this study, the professors could choose one of the four possible pedagogical actions, or they could determine another pedagogical action. In this last case, we asked the professor to explain the other pedagogical action, and the reasons to establish it. Therefore, we have three possible results for each case: 1) the professor selects the same pedagogical action than the model, 2) the professor selects another pedagogical action included in the model, and 3) the professor selects a pedagogical action not included in the model.

We compared the results of model with the teachers' answers; and in the 57% of the cases, the pedagogical action established by the teachers agreed with the pedagogical action established by the model. In the 38% of the cases, the pedagogical action established by the professors was different to the established by the model, but the pedagogical action established by the professor is one of the pedagogical actions included in the model. And, in the 5% of the cases the professors established a pedagogical action not included in the model. An interesting finding is that there are more matches in cases where the professor has less years of experience in teaching. We are analyzing in detail the professors' answers for each case in order to obtain some insight to improve the affective behavior model.

6 Conclusions and Future Work

In this paper, we proposed an affective behavior model for an intelligent tutoring system. Our main contribution is establishing a pedagogical response given an affective state. We have presented an affective student model based on the OCC model, and an initial affective behavior model. We have presented some preliminary results of affective and pedagogical responses under different situations, and an initial evaluation of the affective behavior model. The intelligent tutoring system for the virtual laboratory without affective components is already in use. The next phase is to integrate the affective behavior model to the ITS. Then, we will conduct some experiments to compare the improvements in learning of the students with the incorporation of the affective components against the ITS without affective components.

References

1. Picard, R.W.: Affective Computing. MIT Press (1997).
2. Damasio, A.R.: El error de Descartes. Andrés Bello, Santiago, Chile (1996).
3. Johnson, W.L., Rickel, J.W., Lester, J.C.: Animated Pedagogical Agents: Face-to-Face Interaction in Interactive Learning Environment. International Journal of Artificial Intelligence in Education, 11 (2000) pp. 47-78.
4. Conati, C., Zhou, X.: Modeling students' emotions from Cognitive Appraisal in Educational Games. 6th International Conference on Intelligent Tutoring Systems (2002).
5. de Vicente, A., Pain, H.: Informing the Detection of the Students' Motivational State: An Empirical Study. 6th International Conference on Intelligent Tutoring Systems (2002).
6. Johnson, W.L., Rizzo, P.: Politeness in Tutoring Dialogs: "Run the Factory, That's What I'd Do". 7th International Conference on Intelligent Tutoring Systems (2004).
7. Moore, J.D., Porayska-Pomsta, K., Varges, S., Zinn, C.: Generating Tutorial Feedback with Affect. 17th International FLAIRS Conference (2004) Miami Beach, Florida.
8. Ortony, A., Clore, G.L., Collins, A.: The Cognitive Structure of Emotions. Cambridge University Press (1988).
9. Costa, P.T., McCrae, R.R.: Four Ways Five Factors are Basic. Personality and Individual Differences, 13(1) (1992) pp. 653-665.
10. Nkambou, R., Héritier V.: Facial Expression Analysis for Emotion Recognition in ITS. 7th International Conference on Intelligent Tutoring Systems, (2004).
11. Pearl, J.: Causality: Models, Reasoning, and Inference. Cambridge University Press (2000).
12. Boeree, G.: Personality Theories. (1998) http://www.ship.edu/~cgboeree/
13. Heinström, J.: The impact of personality and approaches to learning on information behaviour, Information Research, Vol. 5 No. 3, April 2000, http://informationr.net/ir
14. Reeves, B. Nass, C.: The Media Equation: How people treat computers, television and new media like real people and places. Cambridge University Press (1996).
15. Velásquez, J.D.: Modeling Emotions and Other Motivations in Synthetic Agents. Fourteenth National Conference on Artificial Intelligence (1997).
16. Diez, J.: The Elvira Project. (2004) http://www.ia.uned.es/investig/proyectos/elvira

A Semi-open Learning Environment for Virtual Laboratories

Julieta Noguez[1] and L. Enrique Sucar[2]

[1] Tecnológico de Monterrey, Campus Ciudad de México,
Calle del Puente 222, Col. Ejidos de Huipulco, Tlalpan
14380 México, D.F., México
jnoguez@itesm.mx
http://doc.mor.itesm.mx:8181/jnoguez
[2] Tecnológico de Monterrey, Campus Cuernavaca,
Paseo de la Reforma 182-A, Col. Lomas de Cuernavaca,
62589 Temixco, Morelos, México
esucar@itesm.mx
http://dns1.mor.itesm.mx/~esucar

Abstract. Open learning environments often involve simulation where learners can experiment with different aspects and parameters of a given phenomenon to observe the effects of these changes. These are desirable in virtual laboratories. However, an important limitation of open learning environments is the effectiveness for learning, because it strongly depends on the learner ability to explore adequately. We have developed a semi-open learning environment for a virtual robotics laboratory based on simulation, to learn through free exploration, but with specific performance criteria that guide the learning process. We proposed a generic architecture for this environment, in which the key element is an intelligent tutoring system coupled to a virtual laboratory. The tutor module combines the performance and exploration behaviour of a student in several experiments, to decide the best way to guide his/her. We present an evaluation with an initial group of 20 students. The results show how this semi-open leraning environment can help to accelerate and improve the learning process.

1 Introduction

A *virtual laboratory* provides a way to perform experiments with equipment that is not physically present in the same place as the user. There are two types of virtual labs: (i) remote and (ii) simulated. In a remote lab the user interacts with equipment that is physically in another place via sensors and actuators, using a computer and a communication network (i.e. internet). A simulated lab has a computer model of the equipment and its environment, and the user interacts with these models to perform experiments [6].

The quality of the interaction environment enables the acquisition of skills and the learning of concepts when using a virtual laboratory. Student needs free exploration of different aspects and parameters to improve his understanding and learning. The simulated laboratories respond to the student's actions to extend the student's understanding of his actions in the context of specific situations.

Open learning environment often involve simulation where learners can experiment with different aspects and parameters of a given phenomenon to observe the effects of these changes [9]. A substantial limitation of these systems is their effectiveness for learning. It strongly depends on the learner, on the specific features that influence the learner ability to explore adequately, and the lack of a clear definition of what constitutes effective exploration behavior [1]. However, this hypothesis necessitates further studies before drawing stronger conclusions.

We considered important to maintain an open learning environment in the virtual laboratory, because the student has free exploration of different parameters to observe their effects inside the environment; but we add specific objectives for each experiment which the student needs to achieve, enabling an intelligent tutor to assess the effectiveness of the exploration behavior and the acquired knowledge.

2 Generic Architecture

We proposed a generic architecture for semi-open learning environments providing several advantages: flexibility, it allows to consider different models for each student in a common framework, adaptability, by obtaining an initial model of a new learner from similar student models, and modularity, it can be easily extended to other domains, to include more students, more knowledge objects and more experiments.

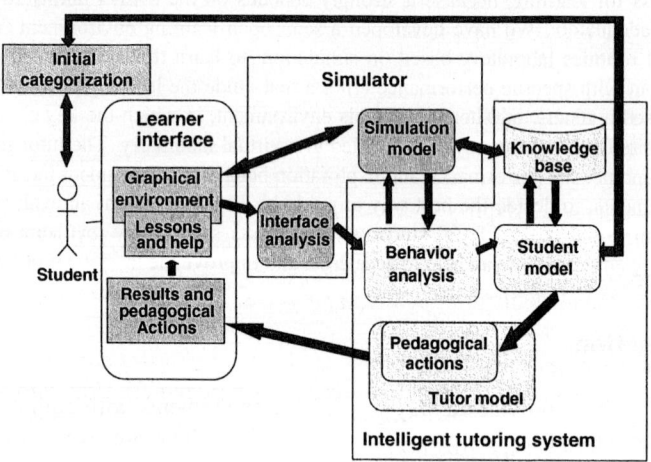

Fig. 1. Generic architecture for semi-open learning environments. It includes 3 main modules: (i) the learner interface, (ii) the simulator, and (iii) the intelligent tutoring system which includes an initial categorization of the student.

A block diagram of the generic architecture is depicted in figure 1. Next, we will describe briefly each generic element of this architecture.

Learner Interface. We considered important aspects of open learning environments, because the student needs explore different parameters to observe their effects inside the simulated lab, but each experiment has specific objectives the student needs to achieve, enabling an effective assessment of the exploration behavior and learning goals. This element is an important key of the system and we will describe it with more detail in the next section.

Simulator. This module contains a set of models of the domain with which the student interacts in the experiments, and these are displayed in a graphical way for visualization and interaction by the students. It includes the student interaction analysis, the experiment performance, and the exploration behavior results.

Intelligent Tutoring System. The ITS guides and evaluates the students during his/her interaction with virtual laboratory. It includes a student for adapting the interaction for each individual student.

Initial Categorization. We design an approach what increase the possibilities of learning environment interacting in an appropriate way with student. Following the idea of virtual laboratories have non invasive process, we used the previous student information like academic background and data from previous student interaction. In this application we defined three categories of students: novice, medium and expert. This category is used later to define the exercise complex, the different kind of help required by the student, etc.

The architecture and the semi-open learning environment are generic. It means they can be able applied to several domains. But, in order to clarify the functionality of the semi-open learning environment, we present, as a case of study, a robotics virtual laboratory based on simulation.

3 A Semi-open Learning Environments

We have developed a virtual laboratory based on simulation. Using a 3-D simulator, the students can explore the first concepts in a robotics course: mechanical design, as well as sensors and control, before they start building a physical robot [10]. An intelligent tutoring system guides the students during their interactions with the virtual lab, providing the student with the opportunity to learn through exploration and giving him/her personalized help.

Based on some questionnaires and interviews with instructors of robotics, we defined the main characteristics for free explorations in combination with the simulator and experiment behavior. We defined an interface with this information. The main elements of the interface are shown in figure 2.

3.1 Simulated Experiments

We have developed a simulated virtual laboratory for mobile robotics. It is used in an undergraduate robotics course, which integrates three developments. Firstly, the students interact with the virtual laboratory based on a 3-D simulation, which lets students explore the first concepts in the course: mechanical design, sensors, and control, before they start building a physical robot. Secondly, an intelligent tutoring system guides the students during their interactions with the virtual lab. Finally, the students form teams to build a small mobile robot for a competition.

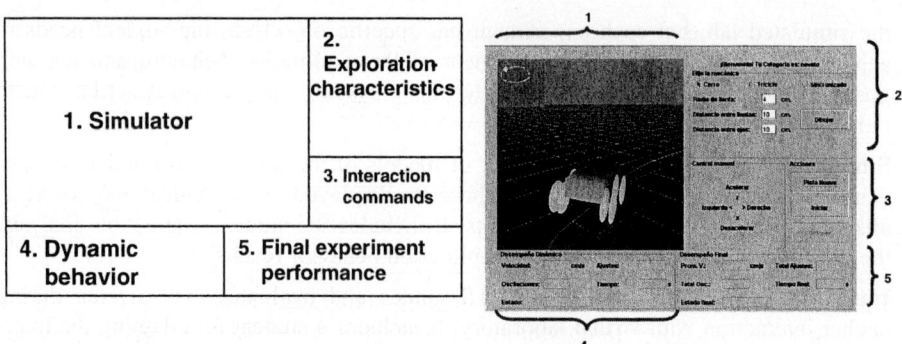

Fig. 2. Main elements of virtual laboratory interface

The experiments are related to a line following competition for mobile robots, which requires some basic knowledge in mechanical design, sensors, control theory and programming from the students. We defined a sequence of specific experiments to enable the assessment of the knowledge items, step by step.

- The first experiment involves robotics' mechanical design concepts. The educational goals are: (i) to learn mechanical aspects of mobile robotics, and (ii) to practice with cinematic models using manual control.
- The second and third experiments are designed to explore basic properties of infrared (IR) sensors (which help to change speed and direction).
- The fourth experiment is related with actuators and control theory. We defined a set of robot basic instruction to control the mobile robot. We construct an interpreter to simulate an automatic control program. The student writes his control program previously, taking care of the mechanical and sensor position defined in experiments three and four.

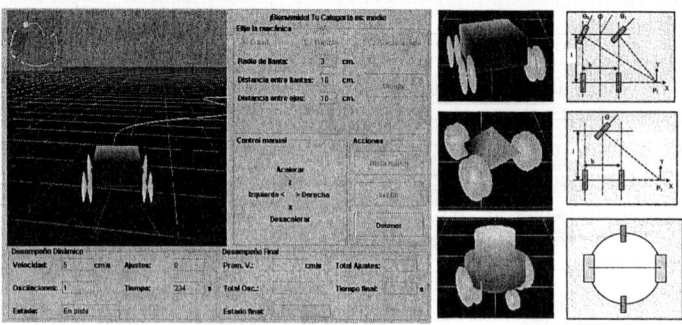

Fig. 3. Experiment 1: Kinematics and mechanical aspects of mobile robots are explored by students in this experiment

3.2 Exploration Characteristics

Different aspects should be explored by students for each experiment. The exploration characteristics are related with the experiments goals. For example, the first experiment involves robotics' mechanical design concepts. Students are able to explore three kinematics models, and several parameters for each model like distance between axles, wheel radius, distance between wheels, etc. as shown in figure 3.

3.3 Interaction Commands

The first, second and third experiments are designed to practice with cinematic models using manual control. In these experiments students can change robot directions using the arrow keys and other keys to increase or decrease the speed of the robot. The fourth experiment is related with actuators and control theory. We defined a set of robot basic instruction to control the mobile robot, with which the student can design and test a control program.

3.4 Dynamic Behavior and Final Experiment Performance

The interface shows the dynamic behavior of the mobile robot according to the exploration parameters and student interaction during the experiments. The results of each experiment, in terms of exploration and performance, are considered in the intelligent tutoring system to select the best pedagogical response.

4 Relational Student Model

The student model adapts the learning experience to suit the learner's perceived needs [8]. The cognitive state of a learner is inferred from two parts: the previous data about the student and student's behavior during the interaction with the system [1]. Both involve uncertainty, so a model that considers it is required. Thus, we developed a student model representation for intelligent tutoring systems coupled to virtual laboratories, using probabilistic relational models [3].

Probabilistic relational models (PRM) provide a new approach for student modeling, integrating the expressive power of Bayesian networks and the facilities of relational models. Friedman states in [2] "...The basic entities in a probabilistic relational models are objects or domain entities. Objects in the domain are partitioned into a set of disjoint classes $X_1,...,X_n$. Each class is associated with a set of attributes $A(X_i)$. Each attribute $A_j \in A(X_i)$ takes on values in some fixed domain of values $V(A_j)$". The dependency model is defined at the class level, allowing it to be used for any object in the class. PRM's explicitly use the relational structure of the model, so the attributes of an object depend on attributes of related objects. A PRM specifies the probability distribution using the same underlying principles used in specifying Bayesian networks [5]. PRM's allow a compact and natural representation of student models for virtual laboratories. An example is shown in figure 4.

The main advantages of PRM's can be extended to relational student models. First, each class model allows the definition of several Bayesian nets with different conditional probabilistic values. Second, it is easy to organize the classes by levels to improve the understanding of the model. Third, it let organize by several structures of levels of this evidence propagation giving facilities to communicate Bayesian nets. A bayesian net derived from PRM of figure 4 is shown in figure 5.

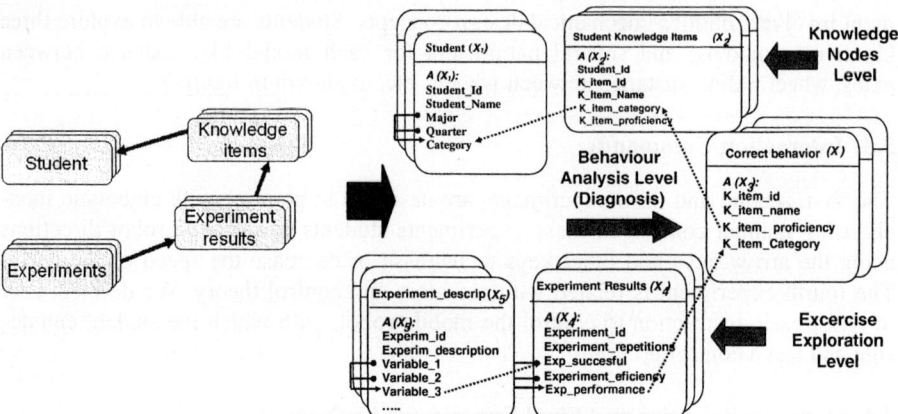

Fig. 4. Conditional probabilistic dependencies between some classes and their attributes related with experiments. Left picture shows probabilistic dependency between classes related with experiments. Right picture shows conditional probabilistic dependencies between some attributes of these classes.

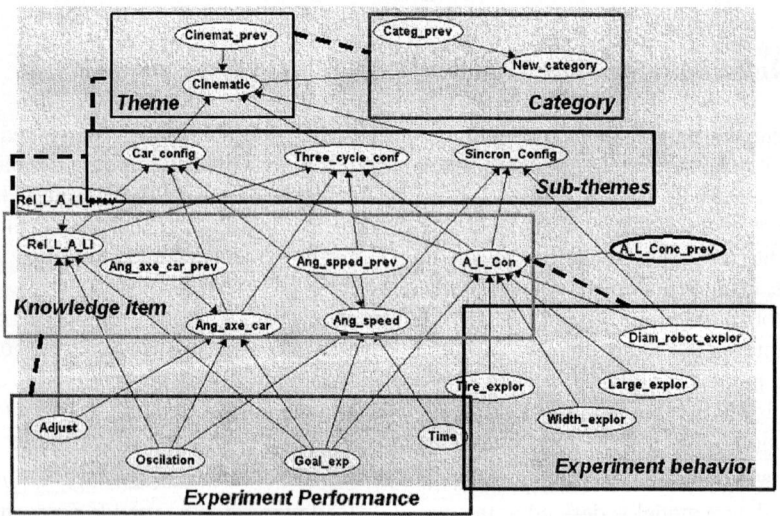

Fig. 5. A bayesian net derived from relational student model. Experiment performance and experiment results attributes belong to Experiment results class. Knowledge items, Sub-themes and Themes are concerned to Knowledge items class, and Category belongs to Students class.

This student model has several advantages: flexibility, user adaptability, high modularity and facility for model construction for different scenarios. The model keeps track of the students' knowledge at different levels of granularity, combining the performance and exploration behavior in several experiments, in order to decide the best way to guide the student in the subsequent experiments, and to re-categorize the students based on the results. For more detailed explanation of the student model see [4].

5 The Tutor Module

The tutor model keeps track of the students' knowledge at different levels of granularity, combining the performance and exploration behavior in several experiments, to decide the best pedagogical action. We defined an influence diagram [7] to decide the best pedagogical action. See figure 6.

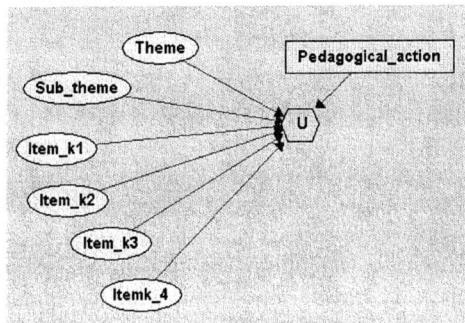

Fig. 6. Influence diagram for pedagogical action selection. The pedagogical action considers utility on learning of the student.

The utility function defined for this model is:

$$U(Pedagogical\_action) = -C_1 * Cost(Kw\_Obj) + C_2(P(Kw\_Obj=unknown)) \quad (1)$$

Where:
U(Pedagogical_action) = Utility of the pedagogical action.
C_1, C_2 = Constants related with type of knowledge object.
Cost(Kw_Obj) = Cost of the object help (The cost is proportional to the "size" of the explanation).
P(Kw_Obj=unknown) = Probability that the students does not has the concept.

After each experiment, the tutor selects the pedagogical actions with highest utility. The possible actions are: present another experiment with higher difficulty level, present another experiment with lower difficulty level, present another experiment with same difficulty level, display some help, display a lesson, apply a quiz, and present another experiment of the next type. We are currently improving the utility function according to the evaluation experiments.

6 Evaluation Process

We have concluded a user study with the semi–open learning environment, in particular we evaluated the tutor and the student model, using a virtual robotics laboratory. By analyzing the learner's exploration as they used the system gave insight on the general effectiveness of experiment performance. We obtained some quantitative and qualitative results that give some measure of the prediction capabilities of the proposed student model, and of the utility of the tutor in a semi–open learning environment.

- **Participants.** The subjects were university students in computer system engineering between 5th and 8th semester. A total of 20 subjects enrolled in a robotics basic course participated in the study. We decided to divide the subjects into a control and an experimental group, 50% each.
- **Experiment Design.** In the experiment, all subjects used the robotics virtual laboratory. We introduced the academic background of each student to the system. It applied the initial categorization process for them. The pre-test phase included a 60 minutes lecture on basic robotics concepts and a paper and pencil test designed to evaluate the learners' knowledge of the concepts targeted by the virtual laboratory. The pre-test consisted of 25 questions organized in a same way as the knowledge objects in the PRM for experiments 1 to 4. Both, control and experimental groups participated in a session (30 to 60 minutes) performing experiments with the virtual laboratory. The experimental group had the support of the tutor during the experiments, while the control group explored the virtual lab without tutor. The post-phase consisted of a test analogous to the pre-test and of a ten item questionnaire targeted at students' opinions about their virtual laboratory experience. In addition, the system produced log files that capture the sessions at the level of basic exploration actions and experiment performance results.
- **Study Results.** Figure 7 shows the initial categorization results versus pre-test for the first knowledge objects targeted by experiment 2 (the graphs show the averages of the 20 students), The values for the initial categorization model were defined based only on academic background. For the novice students (left graph), we found that in general the predictions are below the test results. However, a lecture was given just before the pre-test was applied, so we think that this affected the results in particular for the novices. For the students categorized at the intermediate level (right graph), the predictions of the model are very good for almost all the knowledge items.

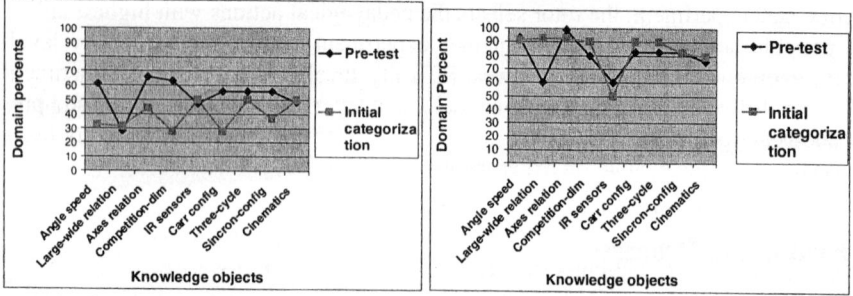

Fig. 7. Initial categorization vs. pre-test (left graph for novice students, right graph for intermediate students). Each graph shows the average knowledge (in percentage) for each concept related to experiments 2.

Figure 8 summarizes the results after experiments 2,3 and 4 for the control and experimental groups. For the group supported by the tutor, the average of number of repetitions of experiment 2 was 8 and 70% of the learners increase the categorization level based on their knowledge level, for the different concepts related to the experiments.

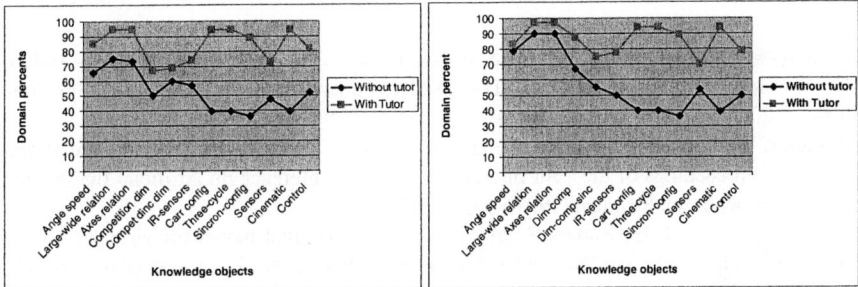

Fig. 8. Results after performing experiments 1, 2, 3, and 4 (left graph for novice students, right graph for intermediate students)

For the control group the average of number of repetitions of experiment 2 was 9, but only 50% of the learners increase the categorization level. As shown in figure 8, students with intelligent support improved their knowledge level of the targeted knowledge objects.

7 Conclusions and Future Work

We have developed an intelligent tutoring system coupled to a virtual laboratory, which constitute a semi–open learning environment. It provides the student with the opportunity to learn through free exploration, but with specific performance criteria that guide the learning process. In virtual laboratories, we considered important aspects of open learning environments, because the student has the liberty to explore different parameters to observe their effects inside the virtual laboratory.

We incorporated a student model based on probabilistic relational model that has several advantages: *flexibility*, it allows to consider different models for each student in a common framework, *adaptability*, by obtaining an initial model of a new learner from similar student models, and *modularity*, it can be easily extended to include more students, and more experiments and others domains.

The intelligent tutoring system keeps track of the students' knowledge at different levels of granularity, combining the performance and exploration behavior in several experiments, in order to decide the best pedagogical actions. We have evaluated the system with an initial group of students. The results show that the students who explore the semi-open virtual environment with the help of the tutor have a better performance, and students with intelligent support improved significantly their knowledge level of the targeted knowledge objects.

We are currently extending our evaluation of the tutor with more experiments and validating the best pedagogical actions of the tutor. In the future we plan to integrate an affective behavior model to the intelligent tutoring system in order to provide students with a suitable response from a pedagogical and affective point of view.

References

1. Bunt A. and Conati C. "Probabilistic StudentModelling to Improve Exploratory Behaviour". Journal of User Modeling and User-Adapted Interaction, (2003) vol 13 (3), pp. 269-309.
2. Friedman N., Getoor L., Koller D., and A. Pfeffer. "Learning Probabilistic Relational Models", Proceedings of the 16th International Joint Conference on Artificial Intelligence (IJCAI), Stockholm, Sweden, (1999), 1300-1307
3. Noguez J. , Sucar L.E., Ramos F. "A probabilistic relational model for virtual laboratories". In U. Hoppe, F. Verdejo, and J. Kay, editors, International Conference on Artificial Intelligence in Education, Vol. 11. Sydney Australia. 2003. IOS Press. Pp. 533-534.
4. Noguez J. , Sucar L.E. "A Probabilistic Relational Student Model for Virtual Laboratories". To be published in Encuentro Internacional de Ciencias de la Computación. 26-30 de septiembre. Puebla, México. 2005.
5. Pearl J. "Probabilistic Reasoning in Intelligent Systems". Morgan Kauffman. San Mateo California. 1988.
6. Richard L., Gourderes G., "An agent-Operated Simulation-Base Training System – Presentation of the CMOS Project", A. I., In S.P. Lajoie and M. Vivet. Artificial Intelligence in Education, IO Press (1999) 343-351.
7. Russel S., Norvig G. "Artificial Intelligence". Ed. Prentice Hall. 1996. Pp.513-519.
8. Self J., "The Role of Student Models in Learning Environments". Lancaster University, Technical Report No. 194 (1994).
9. Shute V. Glaser R. "A Large Scale Evaluation of an Intelligent Discovery World". Smithtown. Interactive Learning Environments 1. (1990). 55-77.
10. Sucar L.E., Noguez J. "Project oriented learning for basic robotics using virtual laboratories and intelligent tutors". To be published in 35th ASEE/IEEE Frontiers in Education Conference. October 19-22, (2005),Indianapolis, IN. USA.

Author Index

Abraham, Ajith   623, 673
Accary-Barbier, Tiphaine   51
Aguilar M, Sheyla   1164
Aguirre, Eugenio   337
Aguirre, José Luis   98, 254, 297
Akbar, Yusaf H.   721
Alencastre-Miranda, Moises   990
Allende, Héctor   702
Almanza-Ojeda, Dora Luz   379
Alvares, Luis Otávio   287
Álvarez, Raziel   359
Alvarez-Gallegos, Jaime   1093
Andrade, Leila C.V.   1113
Arámbula Cosío, Fernando   910
Arroyo-Figueroa, Gustavo   1175
Avina-Cervantes, Gabriel   379
Ayala, Gerardo   109
Ayala-Ramirez, Victor   379, 1001

Baldisserotto, Carolina   939
Baldisserotto, Julio   939
Barnden, John A.   900
Barrón, Ricardo   318
Batyrshin, Ildar   514
Bisbal, Empar   806
Bittencourt, Guilherme   142
Blansché, Alexandre   682
Bock, Peter   369
Bolshakova, Elena I.   790
Bolshakov, Igor A.   790
Bonev, Boyan   770
Brena, Ramón F.   98, 297, 970
Brisaboa, Nieves   80
Buccella, Agustina   80

Cai, Yunze   435
Calabretto, Sylvie   51
Camacho, J. Horacio   524
Cantú, Francisco   275
Cantú Ortiz, Francisco J.   583
Caro, Paz   483
Castro, Carlos   162
Ceballos, Rafael   1082
Cechich, Alejandra   80

Cervantes-Casillas, Griselda P.   1103
Chávez, Edgar   405
Che, Jianguo   1145
Chesñevar, Carlos Iván   98
Choi, Ho-Jin   1042
Coello Coello, Carlos A.   603, 652
Corona-Castuera, Jorge   347, 1052, 1062
Cortés, Ulises   928
Cruz, Adriano J.O.   1113
Cruz Sánchez, Vianey Guadalupe   11
Cruz Villar, Carlos Alberto   1093
Cui, Jie   328

de Oliveira, Adriano Lorena Inácio   939
de Weerdt, Mathijs   264
Delmas, Patrice   307
Del Valle, Carmelo   1082
Devy, Michel   1001
Diaz, Raul   369
Dikovsky, Alexander   741
Domínguez, Jesús   297
Domínguez-López, Jorge Axel   1022, 1032
Dong, Hongbin   593
Duenas, Alejandra   234

Emmert-Streib, Frank   415
Engin, Seref Naci   504
Eroglu, Emre   1155
Espinosa, Jose   61

Feng, Boqin   204
Feng, Xiaoyi   328
Fernández, Luis Marcelo   297
Ferreira, Emília B.   1113
Fidalgo, Raúl   443
Figueroa, Christian   162
Figueroa, Karina   405
Fitzgerald, John A.   843

Galicia-Haro, Sofía N.   780
Gançarski, Pierre   682
García-Gamboa, Ariel   494
Garcia-Silvente, Miguel   337
Gargouri, Yassine   90

Garrido, Leonardo   254, 297
Garrido, Rubén   1134
Garza Castañon, Luis E.   583, 1164
Gasca, Rafael M.   1082
Gelbukh, Alexander   623, 673, 780, 833
Gimel'farb, Georgy   307
Goddard, John   800
Gómez, Carlos   483
Gómez-Soriano, José Manuel   816
Gonzalez, Antonio   337
González B., Juan Javier   833
González-Mendoza, Miguel   494
Grosan, Crina   623, 673
Gu, Mingyang   544
Guan, Tao   204
Guedea-Elizalde, Federico   1073, 1164
Guo, Jun   854
Guo, Xiuping   663
Guo, Yang   175
Gutiérrez, Agustin   41

Hadid, Abdenour   328
Hallé, Sylvain   425
Han, Jiuqiang   1012
Han, Sang Yong   623, 673
Hao, Hongwei   565
Hao, Jin-Kao   613
He, Jun   593
He, Yong   574, 712
Heinemann, Bernhard   21
Heinze, Mikael   224
Hernández, Yasmín   1175
Hernández Aguirre, Arturo   641
Hernández-Gress, Neil   494
Hou, Wei   593
Huang, Bing Quan   843
Huang, Houkuan   396, 534, 593
Huang, Min   574
Huang, Pingmu   854
Hutchinson, Seth   990

Ibarra-Orozco, Rodolfo   494
Inui, Nobuo   473

Jiang, Jixiang   152

Kang, Dazhou   152
Kaynak, Okyay   1124, 1155
Kechadi, Tahar   843
Ko, In-Young   1042

Kong, Jun   918
Korczak, Jerzy J.   682
Kozareva, Zornitsa   770
Kri, Fernanda   483
Kuri-Morales, Angel F.   880
Kurnaz, Sefer   1155
Kuvulmaz, Janset   504

Larsen, Henrik Legind   224
Lee, Hwayoun   1042
Leboeuf Pasquier, Jérôme   959
Lefebvre, Bernard   90
Li, Bing   761
Li, Huaqing   454
Li, Qunxia   854
Li, Ruifan   565
Li, SiKun   175
Li, Tun   175
Li, Yanhui   152
Li, Yuangui   435
Liang, Ying-Hong   752
Lieberman, Henry   61
Lima, Cabral   1113
Liu, Bingquan   761
Liu, Gang   854
Liu, Jiang   307
Liu, Pengfei   1012
Lodhi, Huma   890
López-Juárez, Ismael   347, 1052, 1062
Loreto, Gerardo   1134
Lu, Jianjiang   152
Lu, Yinghua   918
Łukaszewicz, Witold   31

MacKinney-Romero, René   800
Madalińska-Bugaj, Ewa   31
Malkoc, Umit   1155
Manhães, Laci Mary B.   1113
Marchi, Jerusa   142
Marin-Hernandez, Antonio   1001
Marrufo, Gilberto   1022
Martinez, Emmanuel   970
Martínez-Alfaro, Horacio   692, 1103
Mata-Hernández, Josafat M.   1073
Meneses, Rafael   162
Meunier, Jean-Guy   90
Mezura-Montes, Efrén   652
Millán, Erik   359
Modgil, Sanjay   928
Monfroy, Eric   162

Monroy, Raul 990
Montes de Oca, Marco Antonia 254
Montes Rendón, Azucena 11
Montes-y-Gómez, Manuel 816
Montoyo, Andres 770
Mora-Vargas, Jaime 494
Morales, Rafael 443
Morales-Luna, Guillermo 132
Morales-Menéndez, Rubén 275, 583, 1073, 1164
Moratori, Patrick B. 1113
Moreno, Lidia 806
Moreno, Sebastián 702
Morris, John 307
Motta, Enrico 70
Muggleton, Stephen 890
Muñoz-Gómez, Lourdes 990
Muñoz-Salinas, Rafael 337
Muñoz Zavala, Angel E. 641
Muppirala, Teja 990
Murrieta-Cid, Rafael 990

Nagy, Miklos 70
Navarro, Gonzalo 405
Nie, Zhenli 386
Nikolenko, Sergey I. 214
Noguez, Julieta 1175, 1185
Nolazco-Flores, Juan Arturo 863
Noriega, B.V. Pablo 275
Núñez, Marlon 443

Ordaz-Hernández, Keny 1062
Ortega, Joaquín Perez 11
Ortiz, Magdalena 109
Ortiz-Arroyo, Daniel 224
Ortiz-Posadas, Martha R. 880
Osorio, Maria A. 980
Osorio, Mauricio 109
Osorio, Roman 347

Pavón, Juan 244
Pazos Rangel, Rodolfo A. 833
Pedro, Márcia V. 1113
Peña, Alejandro 41
Peña-Cabrera, Mario 347, 1052, 1062
Peng, Tao 824
Pérez Espinosa, Humberto 870
Pérez O., Joaquín 833
Perrussel, Laurent 142
Petrovic, Dobrila 234

Petrovic, Sanja 234
Pietikäinen, Matti 328
Pinto, Hugo da Silva Corrêa 287
Plikynas, Darius 721
Pogrebnyak, Oleksiy 731
Portilla Flores, Edgar Alfredo 1093
Pozo, Sergio 1082

Qi, Feihu 454

Ramírez, Ricardo 583
Reyes Galaviz, Orion Fausto 949
Reyes García, Carlos Alberto 870, 949
Reyes Salgado, Gerardo 11
Reyes Sierra, Margarita 603
Rios-Cabrera, Reyes 347, 1052, 1062
Robles P., Armando 275
Rodríguez, Ciro A. 1164
Rodriguez-Henriquez, Francisco 224
Rodríguez M., Myriam J. 833
Rodriguez-Tello, Eduardo 613
Rosso, Paolo 816

Saavedra, Carolina 702
Sáez, Pablo 119
Salas, Rodrigo 702
Salhi, Abdellah 195, 524
Sánchez, Abraham 980
Sanchez, Antonio 369
Sanchez Fernandez, Luis Pastor 731
Sanchez-Yanez, Raul E. 379
Sanchis-Arnal, Emilio 816
Sansores, Candelaria 244
Sarmiento, Alejandro 990
Segura, Enrique Carlos 1
Shao, Chao 396, 534
Shen, Haifeng 854
Sheremetov, Leonid 514
Shi, Wenqi 900
Shinano, Yuuji 473
Shiu, Simon Chi Keung 554
Sidorov, Grigori 833
Sossa, Humberto 41, 318
Suárez, Armando 806
Sucar, L. Enrique 1175, 1185
Sun, Caihong 554
Sun, Zengqi 1145
Swain, Ricardo 990
Swain-Oropeza, Ricardo 359

Tavernier-Deloya, Juan Manuel 185
Terashima-Marín, Hugo 185, 692
Tolchinsky, Pancho 928
Tomás, David 806
Topalov, Andon Venelinov 1124
Torres-Jimenez, Jose 613
Tu, Xuyan 565
Tulupyev, Alexander L. 214

Usanmaz, Serkan 504

van der Krogt, Roman 264
Valenzuela-Rendón, Manuel 185, 692
Vázquez Rodríguez, José Antonio 195
Vargas-Vera, Maria 70
Vázquez, Roberto Antonio 318
Vergara Villegas, Osslan Osiris 11
Vicedo, José Luis 806
Villa Diharce, Enrique R. 641
Villaseñor-Pineda, Luis 816

Wang, Cong 565
Wang, Guoli 435
Wang, Jianzhong 918
Wang, Rujing 633
Wang, Shaoyu 454
Wang, Xiaolong 761
Wang, Xizhao 554

Whitty, Robin 1
Wu, Fangfang 462
Wu, Zhiming 663

Xiang, Liguo 712
Xiao, Jinghui 761
Xu, Baowen 152

Yanez Marquez, Cornelio 731
Yang, Genke 663
Yu, Changjie 1145
Yu, Hailong 824

Zeng, Zhenbing 386
Zhang, Jingdan 918
Zhang, Qingfu 524
Zhang, Weidong 435
Zhang, Wenyin 386
Zhang, Xiaoming 633
Zhang, Yun 712
Zhao, Tie-Jun 752
Zhao, Yinliang 462
Zhou, Yanjun 918
Zhu, Dan 175
Zhu, Danjun 204
Zhu, Jihong 1145
Zuo, Wanli 824

Lecture Notes in Artificial Intelligence (LNAI)

Vol. 3789: A. Gelbukh, Á. de Albornoz, H. Terashima-Marín (Eds.), MICAI 2005: Advances in Artificial Intelligence. XXVI, 1198 pages. 2005.

Vol. 3735: A. Hoffmann, H. Motoda, T. Scheffer (Eds.), Discovery Science. XVI, 400 pages. 2005.

Vol. 3734: S. Jain, H.U. Simon, E. Tomita (Eds.), Algorithmic Learning Theory. XII, 490 pages. 2005.

Vol. 3721: A. Jorge, L. Torgo, P.B. Brazdil, R. Camacho, J. Gama (Eds.), Knowledge Discovery in Databases: PKDD 2005. XXIII, 719 pages. 2005.

Vol. 3720: J. Gama, R. Camacho, P.B. Brazdil, A. Jorge, L. Torgo (Eds.), Machine Learning: ECML 2005. XXIII, 769 pages. 2005.

Vol. 3717: B. Gramlich (Ed.), Frontiers of Combining Systems. X, 321 pages. 2005.

Vol. 3702: B. Beckert (Ed.), Automated Reasoning with Analytic Tableaux and Related Methods. XIII, 343 pages. 2005.

Vol. 3698: U. Furbach (Ed.), KI 2005: Advances in Artificial Intelligence. XIII, 409 pages. 2005.

Vol. 3690: M. Pěchouček, P. Petta, L.Z. Varga (Eds.), Multi-Agent Systems and Applications IV. XVII, 667 pages. 2005.

Vol. 3684: R. Khosla, R.J. Howlett, L.C. Jain (Eds.), Knowledge-Based Intelligent Information and Engineering Systems, Part IV. LXXIX, 933 pages. 2005.

Vol. 3683: R. Khosla, R.J. Howlett, L.C. Jain (Eds.), Knowledge-Based Intelligent Information and Engineering Systems, Part III. LXXX, 1397 pages. 2005.

Vol. 3682: R. Khosla, R.J. Howlett, L.C. Jain (Eds.), Knowledge-Based Intelligent Information and Engineering Systems, Part II. LXXIX, 1371 pages. 2005.

Vol. 3681: R. Khosla, R.J. Howlett, L.C. Jain (Eds.), Knowledge-Based Intelligent Information and Engineering Systems, Part I. LXXX, 1319 pages. 2005.

Vol. 3673: S. Bandini, S. Manzoni (Eds.), AI*IA 2005: Advances in Artificial Intelligence. XIV, 614 pages. 2005.

Vol. 3662: C. Baral, G. Greco, N. Leone, G. Terracina (Eds.), Logic Programming and Nonmonotonic Reasoning. XIII, 454 pages. 2005.

Vol. 3661: T. Panayiotopoulos, J. Gratch, R.S. Aylett, D. Ballin, P. Olivier, T. Rist (Eds.), Intelligent Virtual Agents. XIII, 506 pages. 2005.

Vol. 3658: V. Matoušek, P. Mautner, T. Pavelka (Eds.), Text, Speech and Dialogue. XV, 460 pages. 2005.

Vol. 3651: R. Dale, K.-F. Wong, J. Su, O.Y. Kwong (Eds.), Natural Language Processing – IJCNLP 2005. XXI, 1031 pages. 2005.

Vol. 3642: D. Ślęzak, J. Yao, J.F. Peters, W. Ziarko, X. Hu (Eds.), Rough Sets, Fuzzy Sets, Data Mining, and Granular Computing, Part II. XXIII, 738 pages. 2005.

Vol. 3641: D. Ślęzak, G. Wang, M. Szczuka, I. Düntsch, Y. Yao (Eds.), Rough Sets, Fuzzy Sets, Data Mining, and Granular Computing, Part I. XXIV, 742 pages. 2005.

Vol. 3635: J. Winkler, M. Niranjan, N. Lawrence (Eds.), Deterministic and Statistical Methods in Machine Learning. VIII, 341 pages. 2005.

Vol. 3632: R. Nieuwenhuis (Ed.), Automated Deduction – CADE-20. XIII, 459 pages. 2005.

Vol. 3630: M.S. Capcarrère, A.A. Freitas, P.J. Bentley, C.G. Johnson, J. Timmis (Eds.), Advances in Artificial Life. XIX, 949 pages. 2005.

Vol. 3626: B. Ganter, G. Stumme, R. Wille (Eds.), Formal Concept Analysis. X, 349 pages. 2005.

Vol. 3625: S. Kramer, B. Pfahringer (Eds.), Inductive Logic Programming. XIII, 427 pages. 2005.

Vol. 3620: H. Muñoz-Ávila, F. Ricci (Eds.), Case-Based Reasoning Research and Development. XV, 654 pages. 2005.

Vol. 3614: L. Wang, Y. Jin (Eds.), Fuzzy Systems and Knowledge Discovery, Part II. XLI, 1314 pages. 2005.

Vol. 3613: L. Wang, Y. Jin (Eds.), Fuzzy Systems and Knowledge Discovery, Part I. XLI, 1334 pages. 2005.

Vol. 3607: J.-D. Zucker, L. Saitta (Eds.), Abstraction, Reformulation and Approximation. XII, 376 pages. 2005.

Vol. 3601: G. Moro, S. Bergamaschi, K. Aberer (Eds.), Agents and Peer-to-Peer Computing. XII, 245 pages. 2005.

Vol. 3596: F. Dau, M.-L. Mugnier, G. Stumme (Eds.), Conceptual Structures: Common Semantics for Sharing Knowledge. XI, 467 pages. 2005.

Vol. 3593: V. Mařík, R. W. Brennan, M. Pěchouček (Eds.), Holonic and Multi-Agent Systems for Manufacturing. XI, 269 pages. 2005.

Vol. 3587: P. Perner, A. Imiya (Eds.), Machine Learning and Data Mining in Pattern Recognition. XVII, 695 pages. 2005.

Vol. 3584: X. Li, S. Wang, Z.Y. Dong (Eds.), Advanced Data Mining and Applications. XIX, 835 pages. 2005.

Vol. 3581: S. Miksch, J. Hunter, E.T. Keravnou (Eds.), Artificial Intelligence in Medicine. XVII, 547 pages. 2005.

Vol. 3577: R. Falcone, S. Barber, J. Sabater-Mir, M.P. Singh (Eds.), Trusting Agents for Trusting Electronic Societies. VIII, 235 pages. 2005.

Vol. 3575: S. Wermter, G. Palm, M. Elshaw (Eds.), Biomimetic Neural Learning for Intelligent Robots. IX, 383 pages. 2005.

Vol. 3571: L. Godo (Ed.), Symbolic and Quantitative Approaches to Reasoning with Uncertainty. XVI, 1028 pages. 2005.

Vol. 3559: P. Auer, R. Meir (Eds.), Learning Theory. XI, 692 pages. 2005.

Vol. 3558: V. Torra, Y. Narukawa, S. Miyamoto (Eds.), Modeling Decisions for Artificial Intelligence. XII, 470 pages. 2005.

Vol. 3554: A.K. Dey, B. Kokinov, D.B. Leake, R. Turner (Eds.), Modeling and Using Context. XIV, 572 pages. 2005.

Vol. 3550: T. Eymann, F. Klügl, W. Lamersdorf, M. Klusch, M.N. Huhns (Eds.), Multiagent System Technologies. XI, 246 pages. 2005.

Vol. 3539: K. Morik, J.-F. Boulicaut, A. Siebes (Eds.), Local Pattern Detection. XI, 233 pages. 2005.

Vol. 3538: L. Ardissono, P. Brna, A. Mitrović (Eds.), User Modeling 2005. XVI, 533 pages. 2005.

Vol. 3533: M. Ali, F. Esposito (Eds.), Innovations in Applied Artificial Intelligence. XX, 858 pages. 2005.

Vol. 3528: P.S. Szczepaniak, J. Kacprzyk, A. Niewiadomski (Eds.), Advances in Web Intelligence. XVII, 513 pages. 2005.

Vol. 3518: T.-B. Ho, D. Cheung, H. Liu (Eds.), Advances in Knowledge Discovery and Data Mining. XXI, 864 pages. 2005.

Vol. 3508: P. Bresciani, P. Giorgini, B. Henderson-Sellers, G. Low, M. Winikoff (Eds.), Agent-Oriented Information Systems II. X, 227 pages. 2005.

Vol. 3505: V. Gorodetsky, J. Liu, V.A. Skormin (Eds.), Autonomous Intelligent Systems: Agents and Data Mining. XIII, 303 pages. 2005.

Vol. 3501: B. Kégl, G. Lapalme (Eds.), Advances in Artificial Intelligence. XV, 458 pages. 2005.

Vol. 3492: P. Blache, E.P. Stabler, J.V. Busquets, R. Moot (Eds.), Logical Aspects of Computational Linguistics. X, 363 pages. 2005.

Vol. 3490: L. Bolc, Z. Michalewicz, T. Nishida (Eds.), Intelligent Media Technology for Communicative Intelligence. X, 259 pages. 2005.

Vol. 3488: M.-S. Hacid, N.V. Murray, Z.W. Raś, S. Tsumoto (Eds.), Foundations of Intelligent Systems. XIII, 700 pages. 2005.

Vol. 3487: J.A. Leite, P. Torroni (Eds.), Computational Logic in Multi-Agent Systems. XII, 281 pages. 2005.

Vol. 3476: J.A. Leite, A. Omicini, P. Torroni, P. Yolum (Eds.), Declarative Agent Languages and Technologies II. XII, 289 pages. 2005.

Vol. 3464: S.A. Brueckner, G.D.M. Serugendo, A. Karageorgos, R. Nagpal (Eds.), Engineering Self-Organising Systems. XIII, 299 pages. 2005.

Vol. 3452: F. Baader, A. Voronkov (Eds.), Logic for Programming, Artificial Intelligence, and Reasoning. XI, 562 pages. 2005.

Vol. 3451: M.-P. Gleizes, A. Omicini, F. Zambonelli (Eds.), Engineering Societies in the Agents World V. XIII, 349 pages. 2005.

Vol. 3446: T. Ishida, L. Gasser, H. Nakashima (Eds.), Massively Multi-Agent Systems I. XI, 349 pages. 2005.

Vol. 3445: G. Chollet, A. Esposito, M. Faundez-Zanuy, M. Marinaro (Eds.), Nonlinear Speech Modeling and Applications. XIII, 433 pages. 2005.

Vol. 3438: H. Christiansen, P.R. Skadhauge, J. Villadsen (Eds.), Constraint Solving and Language Processing. VIII, 205 pages. 2005.

Vol. 3430: S. Tsumoto, T. Yamaguchi, M. Numao, H. Motoda (Eds.), Active Mining. XII, 349 pages. 2005.

Vol. 3419: B. Faltings, A. Petcu, F. Fages, F. Rossi (Eds.), Recent Advances in Constraints. X, 217 pages. 2005.

Vol. 3416: M.H. Böhlen, J. Gamper, W. Polasek, M.A. Wimmer (Eds.), E-Government: Towards Electronic Democracy. XIII, 311 pages. 2005.

Vol. 3415: P. Davidsson, B. Logan, K. Takadama (Eds.), Multi-Agent and Multi-Agent-Based Simulation. X, 265 pages. 2005.

Vol. 3403: B. Ganter, R. Godin (Eds.), Formal Concept Analysis. XI, 419 pages. 2005.

Vol. 3398: D.-K. Baik (Ed.), Systems Modeling and Simulation: Theory and Applications. XIV, 733 pages. 2005.

Vol. 3397: T.G. Kim (Ed.), Artificial Intelligence and Simulation. XV, 711 pages. 2005.

Vol. 3396: R.M. van Eijk, M.-P. Huget, F.P. M. Dignum (Eds.), Agent Communication. X, 261 pages. 2005.

Vol. 3394: D. Kudenko, D. Kazakov, E. Alonso (Eds.), Adaptive Agents and Multi-Agent Systems II. VIII, 313 pages. 2005.

Vol. 3392: D. Seipel, M. Hanus, U. Geske, O. Bartenstein (Eds.), Applications of Declarative Programming and Knowledge Management. X, 309 pages. 2005.

Vol. 3374: D. Weyns, H. V.D. Parunak, F. Michel (Eds.), Environments for Multi-Agent Systems. X, 279 pages. 2005.

Vol. 3371: M.W. Barley, N. Kasabov (Eds.), Intelligent Agents and Multi-Agent Systems. X, 329 pages. 2005.

Vol. 3369: R.V. Benjamins, P. Casanovas, J. Breuker, A. Gangemi (Eds.), Law and the Semantic Web. XII, 249 pages. 2005.

Vol. 3366: I. Rahwan, P. Moraitis, C. Reed (Eds.), Argumentation in Multi-Agent Systems. XII, 263 pages. 2005.

Vol. 3359: G. Grieser, Y. Tanaka (Eds.), Intuitive Human Interfaces for Organizing and Accessing Intellectual Assets. XIV, 257 pages. 2005.

Vol. 3346: R.H. Bordini, M. Dastani, J. Dix, A.E.F. Seghrouchni (Eds.), Programming Multi-Agent Systems. XIV, 249 pages. 2005.

Vol. 3345: Y. Cai (Ed.), Ambient Intelligence for Scientific Discovery. XII, 311 pages. 2005.

Vol. 3343: C. Freksa, M. Knauff, B. Krieg-Brückner, B. Nebel, T. Barkowsky (Eds.), Spatial Cognition IV. XIII, 519 pages. 2005.

Vol. 3339: G.I. Webb, X. Yu (Eds.), AI 2004: Advances in Artificial Intelligence. XXII, 1272 pages. 2004.

Vol. 3336: D. Karagiannis, U. Reimer (Eds.), Practical Aspects of Knowledge Management. X, 523 pages. 2004.

Vol. 3327: Y. Shi, W. Xu, Z. Chen (Eds.), Data Mining and Knowledge Management. XIII, 263 pages. 2005.